זוה״ר כעצם השמים לטוהר

# ספר הזוהר

על התורה מאיש אלהים קדוש הוא נורא
מאד התנא ר׳ שמעון בן יוחאי ז״ל עם
חדושים רבים׳ והמה׳ סתרי תורה׳
ומדרש הנעלם׳ ותוספתא על קצת
פרשיות׳ והוספנו חדושים על זולתינו
גם על ספר בראשית כל חבור הרעיא
מהימנא׳ וחדושי הבהיר׳ ומדרש רות
מדרש חזית׳ ומאמר תא חזי׳ והיכלו׳
ומורה מקום מהפסוקי׳׳ ובסוף הספר
תמצא לוח מפסוקי הפתיחות׳ ושאר
כל הפסוקים הנדרשים והנכפלים
בהזוהר׳ נדפס עם רב העיון׳

## בקרימונה

קרית מלך רב׳ אדוננו המלך פיליפו
יר״ה אמן׳ שנת כי לא יט״ש
יי׳ את עמו׳ ונסתיים
שנת השי״ך׳

כרסיון סוויקא״ריאו וסאינקוויסי״טור
ייכראלו בכדלאס בסוף ספער

# ספר הזהר

*The* ספר הזהר

# ZOHAR

*Pritzker Edition*

VOLUME TEN

*Translation and Commentary by*

*Nathan Wolski*

DANIEL C. MATT, GENERAL EDITOR

STANFORD UNIVERSITY PRESS

STANFORD, CALIFORNIA

2016

*The translation and publication of the* Zohar *is made possible through the thoughtful and generous support of the Pritzker Family Philanthropic Fund.*

Stanford University Press
Stanford, California



For further information, including the Aramaic text of the *Zohar*, please visit www.sup.org/zohar

Library of Congress Cataloging-in-Publication Data is available from the Library of Congress at http://Iccn.loc.gov/2003014884

ISBN 978-0-8047-8804-5 (vol. 10)

Printed in the United States of America on acid-free, archival-quality paper.

Designed by Rob Ehle
Typeset by El Ot Pre Press & Computing Ltd., Tel Aviv, in 10.5/14 Minion.

# *Academic Committee for the Translation of the* Zohar

# *Contents*

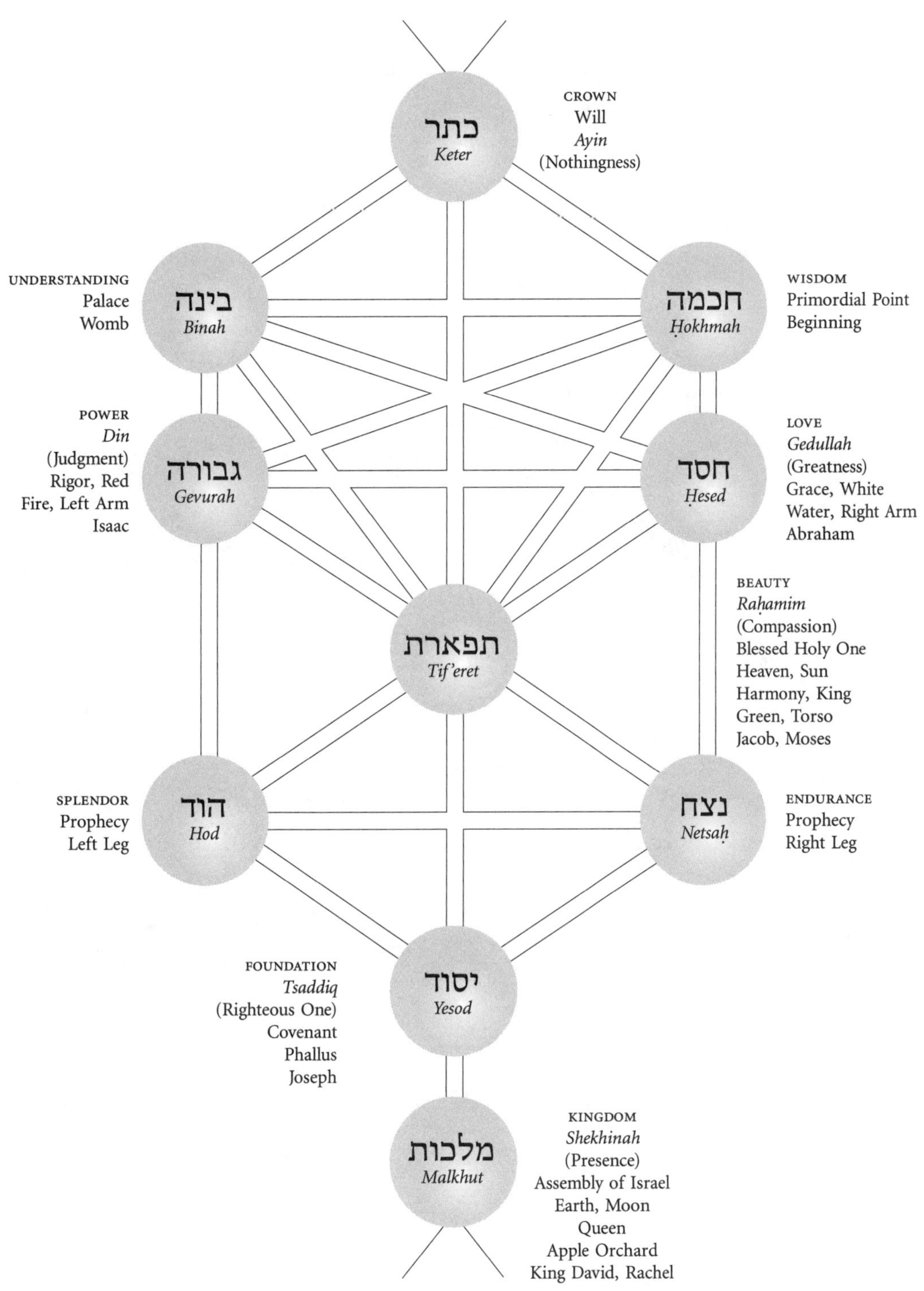

כתר
Keter
CROWN
Will
Ayin
(Nothingness)
בינה
Binah
UNDERSTANDING
Palace
Womb
חכמה
Ḥokhmah
WISDOM
Primordial Point
Beginning
גבורה
Gevurah
POWER
Din
(Judgment)
Rigor, Red
Fire, Left Arm
Isaac
חסד
Ḥesed
LOVE
Gedullah
(Greatness)
Grace, White
Water, Right Arm
Abraham
תפארת
Tif'eret
BEAUTY
Raḥamim
(Compassion)
Blessed Holy One
Heaven, Sun
Harmony, King
Green, Torso
Jacob, Moses
הוד
Hod
SPLENDOR
Prophecy
Left Leg
נצח
Netsaḥ
ENDURANCE
Prophecy
Right Leg
יסוד
Yesod
FOUNDATION
Tsaddiq
(Righteous One)
Covenant
Phallus
Joseph
מלכות
Malkhut
KINGDOM
Shekhinah
(Presence)
Assembly of Israel
Earth, Moon
Queen
Apple Orchard
King David, Rachel

*The Ten Sefirot*

# *Preface*

*Midrash ha-Ne'lam*—"the Concealed Midrash," or perhaps better, "the Midrash of the Concealed"—is recognized by all *Zohar* scholars as the earliest layer of the Zoharic literary corpus. *Midrash ha-Ne'lam* thus stands at the very origin of the Zoharic enterprise and presents the first fruits of the Zoharic world.

*Midrash ha-Ne'lam* on the Torah differs greatly from the main body of the *Zohar*. Sefirotic symbolism is virtually absent from the work (except for parts of *parashat Shemot*), as is the grand epic narrative featuring the Companions gathered around Rabbi Shim'on son of Yoḥai. In their place, one finds philosophical allegory and proto-kabbalistic midrash, as well as homilies and narratives featuring a much larger number of rabbis, including elaborate stories about the Masters of Mishnah—the forerunner to the Zoharic fellowship. Though *Midrash ha-Ne'lam* is in some ways stylistically "undeveloped" in comparison to the main body of the *Zohar*, readers will have no difficulty in sensing the same daring exegetical spirit, the same "Zoharic eye," running through its pages. Indeed, *Midrash ha-Ne'lam* might be regarded as the portrait of the artist as a young man—be that artist Moses de León, or the *Zohar* as a whole—revealing the first stirrings of genius, the original literary breakthrough that lent the *Zohar* proper its distinctive landscape, tone, and rhythm.

Where the *Zohar* proper is concerned with theosophy, i.e., knowledge of the mysteries of the inner workings of divinity and its emanations, lavishly articulated through rich symbolism, *Midrash ha-Ne'lam* presents inter alia allegorical readings of the Torah and more conventional Neoplatonic philosophical teachings. Through the story of the patriarchs, these allegorical readings tell the grand story of the soul's descent from the world above (Abraham signifying the soul and Sarah the body), its sojourns and adventures on earth (in particular battling Lot, the evil impulse), its peregrinations after death (Melchizedek, king of Salem signifying Michael the prince of Jerusalem Above; the King of Sodom signifying the prince of Hell), culminating in the resurrection (Isaac and Rebekah signifying the soul in the resurrected body) and the purification of the evil impulse in the next world (as Lot the accursed is replaced by Laban, the refined impulse.) *Midrash ha-Ne'lam* marks one of the high points, if not *the* high point, of medieval Jewish philosophical allegory.

Philosophical allegory, however, is only one element of *Midrash ha-Ne'lam*. The other is midrash, at times seemingly similar in spirit to classical rabbinic midrash, yet invariably infused with proto-kabbalistic themes. Creation, cosmology, the angelic realm, the origin and nature of the soul, and, of course, the drama of the people of Israel and their ritual and historical life all lie at the center of *Midrash ha-Ne'lam's* concerns. And even if this proto-kabbalistic midrash does not contain the same mythic and erotic element found in the *Zohar* proper, some of the *Zohar*'s most important and characteristic innovations are first found here: the nocturnal delight in the Garden of Eden, as well as the Companions' penchant for "walking on the way" and their concomitant quest to pursue the deeper meaning of Torah.

Significantly, these two aspects, the allegorical-philosophical and the proto-kabbalistic, align with another interesting feature of *Midrash ha-Ne'lam*: its bilingualism. Unlike the main body of the *Zohar*, which is written entirely in Aramaic, *Midrash ha-Ne'lam* combines Hebrew and Aramaic. Sometimes entire sections appear in one language, while on other occasions the language shifts mid-sentence. Interestingly, this linguistic fault-line corresponds, in the main, with the two chief modes of *Midrash ha-Ne'lam*, and so we find that the philosophical allegorical layer of the text is composed in Hebrew, and the proto-kabbalistic midrashic layer in Aramaic. Unfortunately, this crucial element of the texture of *Midrash ha-Ne'lam* is lost in translation, though I have noted significant fault-lines in the notes.



How are we to make sense of this arrangement? Is *Midrash ha-Ne'lam* a unified work? Or might the two languages point to two different compositions brought together by a later editor? And if two different compositions, which is earlier? Or might we assume a single author, who wrote one work in his youth, perhaps the philosophical layer, and appended and interlaced the proto-kabbalistic layer later in his life? Even more intriguing, can we imagine a single author moving between languages as he moved between genres and modes of discourse? Whatever the case (and part of the charm of reading *Midrash ha-Ne'lam* is that we simply do not know), the composition as a whole is best approached as a polyphonic work combing different genres, at times in what appears to be a consciously dialogical fashion.

The difference in style and content between *Midrash ha-N'elam* and the main body of the *Zohar* has led many scholars to wonder whether these two works could possibly have been written by the same author. In contrast to Gershom Scholem, who understood *Midrash ha-Ne'lam* to be the work of a younger Moses de León, some scholars have recently argued for a much earlier date for parts of the composition. While the question of the work's authorship thus remains open to some degree, it is noteworthy that the influence of Maimonides (in particular *Hilkhot Yesodei ha-Torah*, compiled in 1180) and Naḥmanides'

*Commentary on the Torah* (completed circa 1268) is present throughout both the Hebrew and Aramaic layers of the work. A thirteenth-century provenance thus seems secure. Parallels with Moses de León's early and late Hebrew works are also found throughout.

As noted, in contrast to the main body of the *Zohar* and its highly elaborate epic of the Companions headed by Rabbi Shim'on son of Yoḥai, *Midrash ha-Ne'lam* has a much more diverse cast. Alongside Rabbi Shim'on, who appears only on occasion as the leader of the group, we find Rabban Yoḥanan son of Zakkai, Rabbi Eli'ezer son of Hyrcanus, Rabbi El'azar son of Arakh, Rabbi Akiva, as well as countless other *tannaim* and *amora'im*. Though *Midrash ha-Ne'lam* contains sophisticated narratives, in many parts it proceeds as a more conventional midrash, with numerous rabbis presenting short teachings and interpretations.

One distinctive feature of *Midrash ha-Ne'lam* is that its stories often lack a definite end, as narratives blur into related homilies. In addition, the speaker's identity is sometimes unclear. The characters often quote one another and in many passages, teachings are presented anonymously, outside a narrative frame. The resulting confusion, a bane to the translator, is part of the work's texture.



*Midrash ha-Ne'lam* on the Torah spans the first half of the book of Genesis (*Be-reshit, Noaḥ, Lekh Lekha, Va-Yera, Ḥayyei Sarah, Toledot, Va-Yetse*), the Torah portion *Shemot* from the book of Exodus, as well as a brief passage on the Torah portion *Ki Tetse* from Deuteronomy.[1] In standard printed editions, *Midrash ha-Ne'lam's* commentary to *Va-Yera, Ḥayyei Sarah,* and *Toledot* appears alongside the main body of the *Zohar* on Genesis, whereas *Be-reshit, Noaḥ, Lekh Lekha,* and *Va-Yetse* appear in *Zohar Ḥadash*—a misnomer, as the volume comprises some of the earliest Zoharic material.[2] *Midrash ha-Ne'lam* on *Shemot* is embedded within the *Zohar's* commentary to this portion. Three pericopes, which are extant only in manuscripts that were edited and published in the twentieth century (two short and one extensive, all translated here as addenda), complete the *Midrash ha-Ne'lam* on the Torah in our possession. Perhaps more fragments will one day surface.

*Midrash ha-Ne'lam* did not receive the same attention at the hands of later kabbalists as did the *Zohar* proper, perhaps on account of its divergence from

1. *Zohar Ḥadash* contains material under the heading *Midrash ha-Ne'lam* to *parashat Be-Shallaḥ* (*ZḤ* 30b–31a) though as noted by Ronit Meroz, "R. Yosef Angelet u-Khtavav ha-'Zohariyyim,'" 319–20, this passage appears to belong to Joseph Angelet. Likewise, the material appearing under the title *Midrash ha-Ne'lam* to *parashat Aḥarei Mot* (*ZḤ* 46d–48a) displays much greater affinity with *Midrash ha-Ne'lam* on the book of Ruth. It will appear in volume 11.

2. *Zohar Ḥadash,* literally "New Zohar," was first printed in Salonika in 1597. It was so called because it contained material omitted from the first printed editions of the *Zohar* (Mantua 1558–60 and Cremona 1558).

standard kabbalistic theosophy. Nevertheless, *Midrash ha-Ne'lam* generated a canonical and creative interpretative elaboration in the years immediately following its composition. I am referring of course to the *Zohar* itself, which in so many respects drew from and reworked homilies and narratives found in *Midrash ha-Ne'lam* that we cannot but consider the latter "the primal light," or "first foundation."[3]

I am grateful to Dr. Jonatan Benarroch for combing the manuscripts of the *Zohar*, preparing lists of variants. This precious material has enabled me to establish a critical text, upon which this translation is based. The critical text of this volume is available on the website of Stanford University Press. Rabbi Jonathan Matt has kindly and meticulously edited a user-friendly version of this text.[4] I also wish to acknowledge the Australian Centre for Jewish Civilisation, Monash University, for their support. Finally, I extend my gratitude to Rabbi Yehiel Poupko for his guidance, and to Daniel Matt, without whom this work would not have been possible. I thank both of them for the opportunity to have contributed to this monumental project.



I dedicate this work to my parents.

Jerusalem, 5773 (2013)

N.W.

3. On *Midrash ha-Ne'lam* on the Torah, see Scholem, *Major Trends*, 181–86; Tishby, *Wisdom of the Zohar*, 1:2, 12; Belkin, "Ha-Midrash Ha-Ne'lam u-Mqorotav ba-Midrashim ha-Aleksandroniyyim ha-Qedumim"; Werblowsky, "Philo and the Zohar"; Meroz, "Zoharic Narratives and Their Adaptations"; idem, "The Middle Eastern Origins of the Kabbalah"; idem, "Va-Ani Lo Hayiti Sham?"; idem, "The Story in the Zohar about the Grieving Dead"; Asulin, "Midrash ha-Ne'lam li-Vreshit"; Oron, "Midrash ha-Ne'lam: Muqdam u-Me'uḥar"; Wolski, "Metatron and the Mysteries of the Night in Midrash ha-Ne'lam."

4. The site is www.sup.org/zohar. On the various online versions of the critical text, click on "Aramaic Overview."

# MIDRASH HA-NE'LAM

פרשת בראשית

# *Parashat Be-Reshit*

"IN THE BEGINNING" (GENESIS 1:1–6:8)

We have learned: By ten utterances was the world created.[1]

Rabbi Ḥiyya and Rabbi Natan say, "By a single utterance was it created. Which is it? As is written: *By the word of YHVH the heavens were made* (Psalms 33:6)."[2]

Rabbi Abba said, "As is written: *For He spoke and it was, He commanded and it endured* (ibid. 33:9)—one utterance only."[3]

1. **By ten utterances...** According to M *Avot* 5:1, "The world was created through ten utterances." See BT *Rosh ha-Shanah* 32a and *Megillah* 21b: "The ten utterances by which the world was created. What are these? The expressions *And [God] said* in the first chapter of Genesis. —But there are only nine!— The words *In the beginning* are also an utterance, since it is written: *By the word of YHVH the heavens were made* (Psalms 33:6)." See also *Pirqei de-Rabbi Eli'ezer* 3; *Zohar* 1:15a, 16b, 30a; 2:14b (*MhN*).

2. **By a single utterance...** As the verse from Psalms indicates, a single utterance was sufficient to create the heavens. See *Zohar* 1:117a (*MhN*).

Cf. *Pirqei de-Rabbi Eli'ezer* 7: "The blessed Holy One spoke one word, and the heavens were created as the residence of His Throne of Glory, as is said: *By the word of YHVH the heavens were made* (Psalms 33:6)." Cf. John 1:1–3: "In the beginning was the word.... Through him all things were made."

The syntax of this passage is not entirely clear. The question "Which is it?" may be part of Rabbi Ḥiyya and Rabbi Natan's statement, in which case they are asking: "Which verse teaches this idea?" This locution, however, is unusual, as one would expect the expression "How do we know?" that usually precedes a proof-text. Alternatively, the question "Which is it?" is being posed by the "anonymous narrator" of the passage, who in effect is asking "Was the world created by ten utterances or by one?" This question is then followed by two different proofs for creation by one utterance. This reading is supported by Rabbi El'azar's response below, "Neither this nor that!" Namely, the world was created by neither ten utterances nor one.

3. **one utterance only** Rabbi Abba also advocates creation by one utterance, though he offers a different textual proof. See *Alfa Beita de-Rabbi Aqiva*, Version 2 (*Battei Midrashot*, 2:412): "The entire world was created by the utterance of the blessed Holy One, as is said: *For He spoke and it was* (Psalms 33:9)." Cf. ibid., Version 1 (*Battei Midrashot*, 2:391).

Rabbi El'azar said, "Neither this nor that! Rather, by a single letter was the world created—without speech."[4]

As it has been taught: Rabbi Eli'ezer said, "The blessed Holy One took one letter from His Name, and with that letter it was created."[5]

This accords with what Rabbi El'azar said: "What is the significance of the verse *Who is* כמכה (*khamokhah*), *like You, among the* אלים (*elim*), *gods, O YHVH* (Exodus 15:11)? That He is able to create the world."[6]

Now this implies that by ה (*he*) the world was created, with one letter—literally! How then shall we establish *For He spoke and it was*... (Psalms 33:9) and *By the word of YHVH the heavens were made* (ibid., 6)?[7]

Well, Rabbi El'azar said, "To be manifest in the world: for although created, it was not revealed—and every single creation had to be revealed, bringing forth its actions and powers fittingly."[8]

Rabbi El'azar said, "The entire world and all its generations were created at a single moment, in a single hour, on a single day, as is written: *These are the gen-*



4. **by a single letter...** The letter ה (*he*), which represents the (unspoken) sound of mere exhalation. See BT *Menaḥot* 29b: "*These are the generations of heaven and earth* בהבראם (*be-hibbare'am*), *when they were created* (Genesis 2:4). Do not read בהבראם (*be-hibbare'am*), 'when they were created,' but rather בה' בראם (*be-he bera'am*), 'with ה (*he*) He created them.'" See *Bereshit Rabbah* 12:10; JT *Ḥagigah* 2:1, 77c; *Alfa Beita de-Rabbi Aqiva*, Version 1 (*Battei Midrashot*, 2:363); *Zohar* 1:46b, 91b; *ZḤ* 3a, 3d, 17a, 25a, 26a (all *MhN*).

5. **took one letter from His Name...** Namely, the final ה (*he*) from the tetragrammaton, *YHVH*.

The argument about whether the world was created by divine speech or by a letter of the divine name is not merely midrashic quibbling. At stake is the relationship between God and creation: is the world the product of divine speech, or more intrinsically connected to the divine substance?

6. ***Who is* כמכה (*khamokhah*), *like You*, ... *O YHVH*...** In this verse, the word כמכה (*khamokhah*), *like You*, is twice spelled with an additional ה (*he*), i.e., כמכה rather than the more usual כמך. The *Zohar* reads this curious spelling as suggesting that through the power of ה (*he*), God is able to create the world. See *ZḤ* 3a, 3d, 17c (all *MhN*).

7. **How then shall we establish...** If the world was in fact created by one letter, what is the significance of the verses that speak of creation through speech?

8. **To be manifest in the world...** The world was created through the letter ה (*he*) but made manifest through divine speech. Perhaps Rabbi El'azar intends that through the letter ה (*he*) the world was created *in potentia*, or in idea, and made actual through speech.

Cf. *Bereshit Rabbah* 12:4: "Rabbi Yehudah said, 'The heavens and the earth were finished in their own time, and all their array in their own time.' Rabbi Neḥemiah said to him, 'Yet look at what is written: *These are the generations of heaven and earth when they were created* (Genesis 2:4), teaching that on the very day they were created they brought forth their generations!' Rabbi Yehudah replied, 'Yet surely it is written: *And there was evening and there was morning, one day... a second day... a third day... a fourth day... a fifth day... a sixth day*?' Rabbi Neḥemiah said, 'They were like those who gather figs, when each appears in its own time.' Rabbi Berekhiah said in support of Rabbi Neḥe-

*erations of heaven and earth when they were created on the day that* YHVH *God made earth and heaven* (Genesis 2:4)—on that very day, in that very hour, at that very moment!"[9]

It has been taught: Rabbi Abba said in the name of Rabbi Yoḥanan, "Before the blessed Holy One created the world, He and His Name were one. It arose in His mind to create the world, and He created first a thousand worlds, as is said: *the thousand are yours, Solomon* (Song of Songs 8:12). Afterward He created other worlds—to show that all is as naught before Him."[10]

This corresponds with what Rabbi Ḥiyya said: "Why is א (*alef*) first among the letters? Because at first He created אלף (*elef*), a thousand, worlds preceding the other worlds; after that, ב (*bet*)—בנין (*binyan*), the edifice of, heaven and earth."[11]

Rav Huna said, "At first the Throne of Glory, of which is written אלף אלפין (*elef alfin*), *Thousands upon thousands, served Him* (Daniel 7:10); and afterward the other angels and the earth, constituting בית (*beit*), the house of, the world; after that, ג (*gimel*)—גן עדן (*Gan Eden*), the Garden of Eden, which is גמול



miah, '*The earth brought forth* (ibid. 1:12), implying something that was already stored within her.'" Cf. *Tanḥuma* (Buber), *Bereshit* 1–2; Rashi on Genesis 1:14, 24; Maimonides, *Guide of the Perplexed* 2:30.

9. **on that very day, in that very hour...** According to the account in Genesis 1, creation spanned six days, while according to the account in Genesis 2, creation took place *on the day*, i.e., during one day. Here, creation is instantaneous. See below, *ZḤ* 13d (*MhN*), page 113; 16d (*MhN*), page 163.

The simple sense of *on the day* in Genesis 2:4 is "when" and does not connote a specific period of time.

10. **He and His Name were one...** See *Pirqei de-Rabbi Eli'ezer* 3: "Rabbi Eli'ezer son of Hyrcanus [said], '... Before the world was created, there existed only the blessed Holy One and His great name. The thought of creating the world arose in His mind. He traced the world, but it did not endure.'" See *Zohar* 1:15b.

On the motif of creating (and destroying) other worlds prior to this world, see *Bereshit Rabbah* 3:7: "*And there was evening* (Genesis 1:8). Rabbi Yehudah son of Rabbi Simon said, 'It is not written *Let there be evening,* but rather *and there was evening.* Hence we know that a time-order existed before this.' Rabbi Abbahu said, 'This teaches that the blessed Holy One kept creating worlds and destroying them until He created this one and declared, 'This one pleases Me; those did not please Me.'"

The theme of previous worlds that did not endure appears in the *Idrot* (*Zohar* 3:128a [*IR*], 292b [*IZ*]) and inspired Isaac Luria's theory of "the breaking of the vessels."

On the verse from the Song of Songs, see BT *Shevu'ot* 35b: "Every שלמה (*Shelomoh*), *Solomon,* mentioned in the Song of Songs is sacred—the Song to Him who possesses שלום (*shalom*), peace—except this... *the thousand are yours, Solomon* (8:12)." According to the *Zohar,* however, even this *Solomon* refers to God.

11. **Why is א (alef) first...** According to Rabbi Ḥiyya, the order of the Hebrew alphabet corresponds to the order of creation: א (alef), the first letter, signifies the אלף (*elef*), "thousand," worlds preceding this one; ב (*bet*), the second letter, signifies the בנין (*binyan*), "edifice" or "building," of heaven and earth. Cf. *Bereshit Rabbah* 1:10; *Zohar* 1:3b.

(*gemul*), the reward for, the righteous; and after that ד (*dalet*)—the human being comprised of four winds."[12]

Rabbi Yitsḥak said in the name of Rabbi Zrika, "Green seeping streaks of chaos were surrounding the Abyss, and the Abyss was ascending and descending. One letter expanded along its three radii upon the Abyss; and the Abyss was subdued, as is written: *The wind of God hovering* [*over the face of the waters*] (Genesis 1:2)."[13]

Rabbi El'azar said, "This is not implied from there but from here, as is written: *The waters saw You, O God, the waters saw You—they trembled; even the abyss shuddered* (Psalms 77:17)."

As we have learned: A thousand worlds preceded the creation of the world. His radiant glory expanded, and He created worlds and destroyed them, until it arose in will before Him to create this world.[14] At that time, two letters from His name expanded; He established them enduringly. Two other letters were engraved above and below, one within the other.[15] He engraved one, it became



12. **At first the Throne of Glory...** Rav Huna also understands the order of the alphabet to correspond to the order of creation, though he offers an alternate symbolism. In his view, *alef* signifies the *elef*, "thousands," of celestial servants ministering before the divine throne; *bet* signifies the *beit*, "house," of the world; ג (*gimel*), the third letter, signifies both גן (*gan*), "the Garden of," Eden, and גמול (*gemul*), "the reward for," the righteous; and finally ד (*dalet*), the fourth letter, signifies the human being, who is comprised of the four "winds" or directions, namely north, south, east, and west.

According to *Bereshit Rabbah* 1:4, six things preceded the creation of the world, among them the Throne of Glory. See also BT *Pesaḥim* 54a; *Pirqei de-Rabbi Eli'ezer* 3; and below at note 99. According to rabbinic tradition, the dust of Adam's body was gathered from the four directions of the world. See *Targum Yerushalmi*, Genesis 2:7; *Tanḥuma, Pequdei* 3; *Pirqei de-Rabbi Eli'ezer* 11; BT *Sanhedrin* 38a–b.

13. **seeping streaks of chaos...** A conjectural rendering of קלטופין (*qaltufin*), a Zoharic neologism. Cf. קולטוי (*qultoi*) [*Zohar* 1:30a] and קילטא (*qilta*) [*Zohar* 1:33b], rendered by Matt as "seepage." The verbal root קלט (*qlt*) means "to absorb, receive." *Qaltufin* may also derive from the root קטף (*qtf*), "resin, sap, cluster." See Luria, *Va-Ye'esof David*, s.v. *qitpoi*, *qitpin*, *qilta*; *Bei'ur ha-Millim ha-Zarot*, 189, 191. Cf. *Sullam* and *Matoq mi-Devash*: "forces of judgment, green lines." My rendering presumes an allusion to BT *Ḥagigah* 12a: "*Tohu*, Chaos—a green line that encompasses the entire world, out of which darkness proceeds, as is said: *He made darkness His hiding-place round about Him* (Psalms 18:12)."

The letter ה (*he*) from the divine name יהוה (*YHVH*) expands along its three linear strokes, thus placating the תהום (*tehom*), "abyss," which is seemingly conflated here with the תהו (*tohu*), "chaos," of Genesis 1:2. On the wind of God hovering over the waters and the transformation of the chaos (abyss), see *Zohar* 1:16a.

14. **He created worlds and destroyed them...** See above, note 10.

15. **two letters from His name expanded...Two other letters...** Presumably referring to the two letter pairs in the tetragrammaton: first י (*yod*) and ה (*he*); and then ו (*vav*) and ה (*he*).

three. He engraved another and it became two, until they amounted to ten. These ten divided, becoming thirty-two—they are the thirty-two paths of wisdom. These divided by their engravings into ten, becoming forty-two.[16] From here on, whoever contemplates must contemplate with a trembling heart—concealing, not opening. Of this is written *I am YHVH, that is My Name. I will not yield My glory to another, nor My praise to carved images* (Isaiah 42:8), and similarly: *You shall not make for yourself a carved image or any form* (Exodus 20:4).[17]

Rabbi El'azar said, "The Abyss was set in four pedestals sunken below on a single stone—the pillar upon which the world stands. As is written: [*Do you know*] *on what were its pedestals sunk, or who laid its cornerstone?* (Job 38:6)."[18]

Rabbi Zeira said, "This is the stone from which the world was founded, and upon which the world and the Holy of Holies rests; it is the omphalos of the world. From it emerged the stones sunk in the Abyss, from which water issues."[19]

16. **ten . . . thirty-two . . . forty-two** Through engraving and dividing, the four letters of the divine name expand into more diverse potencies: ten, thirty-two, and forty-two. The precise process through which the decade is accomplished is unclear. Perhaps each pair of letters becomes three and two, so there are two fives.

According to *Sefer Yetsirah* 1:1–2, God created the world by means of "thirty-two wondrous paths of wisdom," namely the twenty-two letters of the Hebrew alphabet and the ten *sefirot* or ciphers.

The forty-two-letter name is mentioned in the name of Rav, though not recorded, in BT *Qiddushin* 71a. According to one later view, it consists of the first forty-two letters of the Torah from the ב (*bet*) of בראשית (*Be-reshit*) through the ב of בהו (*bohu*), "void." See *Tosafot, Ḥagigah* 11b, s.v. *ein dorshin*; Trachtenberg, *Jewish Magic and Superstition*, 94–95. See *Zohar* 1:30a: "In forty-two letters the world was engraved and endured, all of them crowning the holy name." Cf. Maimonides, *Guide of the Perplexed* 1:62.

17. ***carved image or any form*** Improper speculation and disclosure of secrets is considered by the *Zohar* a form of idolatry. Cf. the opening of the *Idra Rabba, Zohar* 3:127b–128a (*IR*), which cites Deuteronomy 27:15 (*Cursed be the one who makes a carved or molten image*...).

For sefirotic readings of this passage, see *Sullam* and *Matoq mi-Devash.*

18. **pillar upon which the world stands...** See BT *Ḥagigah* 12b: "Rabbi Yose said, 'Woe to the creatures, for they see, but do not know what they see; they stand, but do not know on what they stand.'... The Sages say that [the world] rests on twelve pillars.... Some say seven pillars.... Rabbi El'azar son of Shammu'a says, '[The earth stands] upon a single pillar named Righteous, as is said: *The righteous one is the foundation of the world* (Proverbs 10:25).'"

19. **stone from which the world was founded...** According to midrashic tradition, the world was created from the Foundation Stone located in the Holy of Holies in the Temple in Jerusalem. See M *Yoma* 5:2; *Tosefta Yoma* 2:14; BT *Yoma* 54b; JT *Yoma* 5:2, 42c; *Vayiqra Rabbah* 20:4; *Pesiqta d-Rav Kahana* 26:4; *Tanḥuma Qedoshim* 10; *Pirqei de-Rabbi Eli'ezer* 35. See *Zohar* 1:71b, 78a, 186a, 231a; *ZḤ* 28a (*MhN*); Lieberman, *Tosefta ki-Fshutah*, 4:772–73.

On the stones sunk in the abyss, see BT *Ḥagigah* 12a: "בהו (*bohu*), 'Void'—the slimy stones sunk in the abyss, from which water issues, as is said: *He will stretch over it a line*

Rabbi Aḥa son of Ya'akov said, "By three letters is the Abyss submerged and divided into three segments—they are the pillars of the earth. Once every three hundred years they loosen from their place, as is said: *Who shakes the earth from her place, and her pillars tremble* (Job 9:6)."[20] [3a]

Rabbi Shim'on taught, "The earth rests on seven pillars, as is said: *she has hewn her seven pillars* (Proverbs 9:1). They are suspended upon the waters—and corresponding to them, King David (peace be upon him) uttered seven voices, as is written: *The voice of YHVH is upon the waters* (Psalms 29:3)."[21]

Everything depends upon seven: the pillars of heaven are seven; firmaments—seven; the planets—seven; seven degrees; seven nations above; seven nations below; seven days of creation; seven lands; seven seas; seven rivers; and the seventh a Sabbath to *YHVH*, a day entirely Sabbath.[22]

We have learned there: Rabbi Yehudah son of Ila'i says, "His seven unfurled royal cloaks were engraved by thirty-five thousand segments. He spread out
8 among them a single measure of the world, until He stretched it in four directions—establishing it on its support, as is written: *I, YHVH, made everything, stretched out the heavens alone, spread out the earth, who was with me?* (Isaiah 44:24)."[23]

*of chaos and plummet-stones of void* (Isaiah 34:11)." See *Zohar* 1:16a.

20. **By three letters...** Apparently the three letters י ה ו (*yod, he, vav*) that comprise the divine name *YHVH*.

See BT *Sukkah* 53a–b, in the name of Rabbi Yoḥanan: "When David dug the hollows [beneath the site of the Temple], the abyss arose and threatened to drown the world.... [David] inscribed the [divine] name on a shard and cast it into the abyss, and it subsided...." On the pillars and the verse from Job, see BT *Ḥagigah* 12b.

21. **seven pillars... seven voices...** In Psalms 29, the phrase "the voice of *YHVH*" appears seven times. On the seven pillars, see BT *Ḥagigah* 12b; *Zohar* 1:82a–b, 186a, 231a.

22. **Everything depends upon seven...** According to Resh Lakish in BT *Ḥagigah* 12b, there are seven firmaments. On the seven planets, see *Pirqei de-Rabbi Eli'ezer* 6.

Numerous texts from the rabbinic corpus extol the number seven. See *Pirqei de-Rabbi Eli'ezer* 18: 'The blessed Holy One created seven firmaments... seven lands... seven deserts... seven seas... seven aeons.... The seventh aeon is entirely Sabbath...." In M *Tamid* 7:4, the Messianic era is described as "a day that is entirely Sabbath." The expression "Sabbath to *YHVH*" derives from Leviticus 25:2, 4, describing the sabbatical year; see also Exodus 20:10; Deuteronomy 5:14. On the seven firmaments and seven earths, see below, *ZḤ* 12a (*MhN*), pp. 90–91 and nn. 298, 299. See also *Avot de-Rabbi Natan* A, 37; *Bemidbar Rabbah* 3:8; *Vayiqra Rabbah* 29:11; *Sefer Yetsirah* 4.

"Seven degrees" apparently refers to the seven degrees of the righteous in the Garden of Eden. See *Sifrei*, Deuteronomy 10; *Midrash Tanna'im*, Deuteronomy, 1:10; JT *Ḥagigah* 2:1, 77a; *Vayiqra Rabbah* 30:2; *Pesiqta de-Rav Kahana* 27:2; *Midrash Tehillim* 11:6, 16:12; [Moses de León?], *Seder Gan Eden*, 133, 135. The expression "seven nations above; seven nations below" apparently refers to the seventy heavenly princes of the nations and the seventy nations of the world.

23. **His... royal cloaks...** This renders גלוסמוי (*glusmoi*), perhaps derived from

Rabbi Shim'on said, "What is the meaning of the verse *I summon* אליהם (*aleihem*), *them—they stand together* (Isaiah 48:13)?"

Well, Rabbi Shim'on said, "When it arose in His thought to create the worlds, at that very moment Above and Below were created and all that is in them, as is said: *I summon* אליהם (*aleihem*), *them—they stand together.* Do not read אליהם (*aleihem*), *them,* but rather אלהים (*Elohim*), God—teaching that by ה (*he*) He created them. As is written: *Who is* כמכה (*khamokhah*), *like You, among the* אלים (*elim*), *gods, O YHVH?* (Exodus 15:11). Like the treasure trove brimming with all the needs of the house, and then they know that all that they require is there."[24]

Rabbi Yehudah said, "The blessed Holy One created His world with three things: בספר וספר וסיפור (*be-sefer ve-sefar ve-sippur*), and—corresponding to them—with: חכמה (*Ḥokhmah*), Wisdom; תבונה (*Tevunah*), Understanding; and דעת (*Da'at*), Knowledge. By Wisdom, as is written: *YHVH founded the earth by wisdom* (Proverbs 3:19). By Understanding, as is written: *He establishes the*
*heavens by understanding* (ibid.). By Knowledge, as is written*: By His knowledge* 9
*the depths were split* (ibid., 20)."[25]

גלימא (*glima*), "cloak." (So *Matoq mi-Devash* and *Sullam.*) This entire paragraph is obscure and—given the subject matter—probably deliberately mysterious. Perhaps the *Zohar* intends that the universe is the product of the weaving and embroidering of seven divine garments, or that the world inhabits the space of the divine garments. Cf. *Matoq mi-Devash* and *Sullam* for different interpretations.

24. ***I summon* אליהם (*aleihem*), *them*...** Above and Below were created instantaneously and simultaneously. See BT *Ḥagigah* 12a: "Our Rabbis taught: The school of Shammai says, 'Heaven was created first'... but the school of Hillel says, 'Earth was created first.'... But the sages say, 'Both were created at one and the same time, as is said: *My own hand founded the earth, My right hand spread out the skies. I summon them—they stand together* (Isaiah 48:13).'" See also *Bereshit Rabbah* 1:15; *Pirqei de-Rabbi Eli'ezer* 18; *Zohar* 2:20a (*MhN*).

The verse from Isaiah, though, contains an additional secret about the process of creation: אליהם (*aleihem*), "them," and אלהים (*Elohim*), "God," contain the same letters. Creation required the transformation of אלים (*elim*), "gods, divine powers," into אלהים (*Elohim*) by adding the letter ה (*he*); therefore God summoned *Elohim*. See *ZḤ* 2d, 3d (both *MhN*). On the letter ה (*he*) as the agent of creation see above, note 4.

Rabbi Shim'on is cited as having taught that the letter ה (*he*) is like a treasure trove comprising all that is required for creation. "Treasure trove" renders אסקופא (*isquppa*), which, depending on context, can mean either "yard of a ship" or "threshold." Here *isquppa* refers to the threshold beneath which household valuables were buried. See BT *Berakhot* 18b; Rashi on BT *Mo'ed Qatan* 11a, s.v. *tsinnor*; idem on Joshua 24:26. See *Zohar* 1:46b, 67a; 2:83b; 3:69a: *ZḤ* 88c (*MhN, Rut*); *Bei'ur ha-Millim ha-Zarot*, 173; Scholem, *Major Trends*, 165, 388, n. 47.

25. **בספר וספר וסיפור (*be-sefer ve-sefar ve-sippur*)...** According to *Sefer Yetsirah* 1:1, an ancient work of Jewish mysticism: "*Yah YHVH Tseva'ot* engraved thirty-two wondrous paths of wisdom, creating the universe in three ספרים (*sefarim*), 'ciphers': *sfr*, *sfr*, *sfr*—boundary, language, and number." The meaning of the triple *sfr* remains unclear, though the gist

Rabbi Neḥuniah says, "By Wisdom alone were all the worlds created, as is written: בראשית (*Be-reshit*), *With beginning, God created* (Genesis 1:1)—and *reshit*, beginning, is Wisdom."[26]

This accords with the one who says, "By ה (*he*) He created them"—the three of them comprised therein.[27] [3d]

## Passage[28]

Rav Yehudah said in the name of Rav, "It is written: *YHVH founded the earth by wisdom; He establishes the heavens by understanding* (Proverbs 3:19), and it goes on to say: *By His knowledge the depths were split* (ibid., 20). By these three things

is that God created and determines the universe through word and number. Here the triple *sfr* of *Sefer Yetsirah* is correlated with three divine creative potencies: wisdom, understanding, and knowledge.

On the role of wisdom, understanding, and knowledge in creating the world, see BT *Ḥagigah* 12a: "Rav Zutra son of Tuvyah said in the name of Rav, 'By ten things was the world created: By wisdom and by understanding and by knowledge and by strength and by rebuke and by might, by righteousness and by judgment, by loving-kindness and by compassion.'" See also *Pirqei de-Rabbi Eli'ezer* 3: "Some say by ten utterances was the world created—and in three are these comprised, as is said: *YHVH founded the earth by wisdom; He establishes the heavens by understanding. By His knowledge the depths were split* (Proverbs 3:19–20)." See below, *ZḤ* 3d, 4a; *Zohar* 2:14b (all *MhN*).

26. ***reshit*, beginning, is Wisdom** The identification of ראשית (*reshit*), *beginning*, with wisdom appears widely. See *Targum Yerushalmi* (frag.), Genesis 1:1; Wolfson, *Philo*, 1:242–45, 266–69; *Bereshit Rabbah* 1:1; Azriel of Gerona, *Peirush ha-Aggadot*, 81; Naḥmanides on Genesis 1:1. See *Zohar* 1:2a, 3b, 15a, 16b, 20a, 145a; *ZḤ* 4a, 11c (both *MhN*); Moses de León, *Sheqel ha-Qodesh*, 21–22 (25–26). Cf. *Zohar* 2:20a (*MhN*).

Relying on an alternative meaning of the preposition ב (*be*), the *Zohar* reads the first word of the Torah, בראשית (*be-reshit*), as "with *reshit*," that is, with wisdom.

27. **By ה (*he*) He created them...** The three strokes of the letter ה (*he*) signify the three potencies—wisdom, understanding, and knowledge—comprised together. Presumably, this statement seeking to harmonize the teaching of the creation of the world through three potencies with the earlier statement about the world's having been created through the letter ה (*he*), refers to Rabbi Yehudah's statement and not Rabbi Neḥuniah's, as the latter rejects the view of three potencies. Alternatively, this statement belongs to Rabbi Neḥuniah or is an editorial comment by the anonymous narrator seeking to harmonize his teaching of a single potency with the earlier view, in which case the letter ה (*he*) signifies wisdom—while comprising the other potencies within. Cf. *Matoq mi-Devash*, ad loc.

The remainder of *ZḤ* 3a belongs to the *Matnitin* section of the *Zohar* and will be translated in a different volume.

28. **Passage** The manuscripts and printed editions contain the word פיסקא (*pisqa*), indicating a distinct passage, though the opening statement and theme follow from the preceding. Elsewhere the word פרשה (*parashah*) or פרשתא (*parsheta*), "section," appears, perhaps reflecting an early attempt to order the materials of *MhN* on the Torah. See *ZḤ* 10b, 13a, 14a, 17c, 19c, 28a, end of *parashat Lekh Lekha*, below, page 311 (all *MhN*); *Zohar* 2:20a (*MhN*).

the world was created, and on two of them it stands—on understanding and knowledge. Yet we have learned: three!"[29]

Rabbi Yitsḥak said, "The blessed Holy One removed wisdom above—it is His Name—to convey to His righteous servants, and two remained in the world; they are its existence."[30]

Rabbi Abba said, "All three are hinted in the small mirror, and they are the three movements of the mouth—upper, intermediate, and lower—by which the mouth's movements are conducted."[31]

Rabbi Abba explained, "They are wisdom, understanding, and knowledge."

What does it mean that by these two—namely understanding and knowledge—the world is maintained?[32]

As we have learned: These conduct the world: the heavens were created by understanding, and the deep by knowledge; but wisdom is the name of the Omnipresent—He is called Wisdom. And we have learned: He and Wisdom are one. As Rabbi Yehoshu'a said: "What is the meaning of the verse *I am YHVH—that is My Name* (Isaiah 42:8)? It teaches that He and His Name are one."[33] 11

29. **we have learned: three** What of the third creative potency: wisdom?

30. **removed wisdom above...** Wisdom is the preserve of the righteous alone. On wisdom as the divine name, see below, note 33; see also *ZḤ* 11c (*MhN*), page 83.

31. **hinted in the small mirror...** The human being is a microcosm, and the three creative potencies are reflected in the movements of the mouth. This idea is derived from *Sefer Yetsirah* 2:3: "Twenty-two foundation letters—He engraved them with voice, carved them with breath, He set them in the mouth in five places: אחהע—in the throat; גיכק—in the palate; דטלנת—in the tongue; זסשרצ—in the teeth; בומפ—in the lips." Apparently, Rabbi Abba intends the palate, the throat, and the tongue. On the human as microcosm, see *Tanḥuma, Pequdei* 3; *Avot de-Rabbi Natan* A, 31; *Qohelet Rabbah* on 1:4; *Zohar* 1:90b, 134b, 186b; 2:23b, 75b; *ZḤ* 6d (*MhN*), page 30.

32. **by these two...the world is maintained** Again, what has become of wisdom and its involvement in the world?

Cf. *Shemot Rabbah* 15:22: "Three creations preceded the world—water, wind, and fire. The waters conceived and gave birth to thick darkness; the fire conceived and gave birth to light; the wind conceived and gave birth to wisdom, and with these six things the world is maintained: wind, wisdom, fire, light, darkness, and water."

33. **but wisdom is the name...** Unlike understanding and knowledge, wisdom—which is the name of God and which has been removed above—appears absent from the natural economy.

The characterization of God as Wisdom or Intellect was common in Jewish philosophical literature. Whereas in the Bible (see Proverbs 8) and for the Rabbis (see *Bereshit Rabbah* 1:1) the divine wisdom is external to God and is presented as His confidant by which the world was made, here the equation is total—He and wisdom (His name) are one. Cf. Maimonides, *Mishneh Torah, Hilkhot Yesodei ha-Torah* 2:10: "He is the knower, He is the known, and He is the knowledge itself. All is one."

On the verse from Isaiah, see *Zohar* 2:86a; 2:177b.

Rabbi Abbahu said, "He bequeathed all, but His great Name He did not bestow, nor did He loan it to another, as is written: *I am YHVH*—alone, teaching that He did not bequeath this Name to any creation."[34]

Rabbi Abbahu also said, "Come and see how concerned the blessed Holy One was for the honor of His blessed Name! Know that when the Temple stood, whoever presented an offering and his sacrifice was to this name designated as *Elohim* was liable to death, as is said: *Whoever sacrifices to* אלהים (*Elohim*), *a god, except to YHVH alone shall be put under the ban* (Exodus 22:19)—teaching that one must invoke the unique Name alone. Therefore, so that people would not err, He commanded concerning the sacrifices, saying: *Should a person among you bring forward to YHVH an offering* (Leviticus 1:2); *When you sacrifice a thanksgiving sacrifice to YHVH* (ibid. 22:29); *When you sacrifice a well-being sacrifice to YHVH* (ibid. 19:5); *Should a person bring forward a grain-offering to YHVH* (ibid. 2:1)—all to *YHVH*; *Elohim* is not mentioned!"[35]

Why so?

12 Rabbi Abbahu said, "This name is polysemous; for angels are called *Elohim*, human beings are called *Elohim*, the dignitaries of the generation are called *Elohim*, judges are called *Elohim*—and we cannot determine to which of them he is sacrificing. Rather, one must invoke the unique Name alone."[36]

Rabbi Ḥiyya said, "Come and see: Concerning one who curses the name, it is written: *Should anyone curse* אלהיו (*elohav*), *his God, he shall bear his offense* (Leviticus 24:15). For look, if he cursed this name by itself he does not incur the death penalty nor is he ostracized, for he can claim that he was referring to one of the judges or to the leader of the generation."[37]

34. **His great Name He did not bestow...** Here begins a discourse on the divine names *YHVH* and *Elohim*—the two most common names for God in Scripture. Unlike the name *Elohim*, which can refer to various creations (see below, note 36), the explicit Name *YHVH* refers to God alone.

35. **all to *YHVH*...** See BT *Menaḥot* 110a: "It has been taught: Rabbi Shim'on son of Azzai said, 'Come and see what is written in the chapter of the sacrifices—neither אל (*El*) nor אלהים (*Elohim*) are mentioned, but only *YHVH*, so as not to give sectarians any pretext to rebel.'" Cf. *Sifrei*, Numbers 143. See also Naḥmanides on Leviticus 1:9; *Zohar* 2:108a; 3:5a. Cf. Moses de León, *Sefer ha-Rimmon*, 286–87, which parallels this passage. On the significance of the divine names *Elohim* and *YHVH* in *MhN*, see *ZḤ* 18c–d, 19c.

36. **This name is polysemous...** The word *Elohim* has various meanings in Scripture. See Maimonides, *Guide of the Perplexed* 1:2: "Every Hebrew knew that the term *Elohim* is equivocal, designating the deity, the angels, and the rulers governing the cities." On the polysemous nature of the name *Elohim*, see *Zohar* 1:2a; *ZḤ* 17b (*MhN*); Moses de León, *Sefer ha-Mishqal*, 42–3; *Sefer ha-Rimmon*, 287. On the word *Elohim* as signifying angels, see *Zohar* 1:9b; cf. *Zohar* 1:111b; 3:113a.

See Margaliot, *Millu'im ZḤ*, ad loc.

37. **if he cursed this name by itself...** Because it has multiple significations, one who curses the divine name *Elohim* is not punished. See next note.

Rabbi Abbahu said, "He does not incur the death penalty, but he does incur ostracism on account of a Torah prohibition, as is written: *You shall not curse Elohim* (Exodus 22:27)—in general. However, if he cursed the unique Name, he incurs the death penalty, as is written: *He who reviles the name YHVH shall be doomed to die* (Leviticus 24:16)—teaching that he is not liable to death until he invokes His unique Name."[38]

A certain man consecrated his son, saying, "This child who was born shall be consecrated to *Elohim*!"

Rabbi Ḥiyya heard and placed him under a ban.[39]

He said to him, "Because I dedicated my son to the blessed Holy One I should be placed under a ban?!"

He replied, "Not because of that did I act, but rather because you consecrated him to the name designated *Elohim*, and Torah said: *Whoever sacrifices to* אלהים *(Elohim) shall be put under the ban* (Exodus 22:19)."

He asked, "What should I have said?"

He replied, "'This child who was born shall be consecrated to *YHVH*'—not to 13
another name. From where do we learn this? From Hannah, as is written: *I will dedicate him to YHVH* (1 Samuel 1:11)—she did not say 'to *Elohim*.'"[40]

Rabbi Shalom said, "Look, we have established that the world was created by the name *Elohim*. If so, one can argue similarly—that they were angels, the dignitaries of the generation, or judges!"[41]

38. **if he cursed the unique Name . . .** Cursing the name *YHVH* incurs the death penalty, whereas cursing the name *Elohim* incurs ostracism. The *Zohar* reprises a Talmudic debate. See BT *Shevu'ot* 36a: "Our Rabbis have taught: *Should anyone curse his God, he shall bear his offense* (Leviticus 24:15). What does this come to teach? Is it not already said: *He who reviles the name YHVH shall be doomed to die* (ibid., 16)? One might think he should be liable only for the unique Name; how then do we know to include the other names? Therefore it is said: *Should anyone curse his God*—in all instances; this is the opinion of Rabbi Meir; but the Sages say: for the unique Name, [the penalty is] death; for the other names, there is a warning." See also BT *Sanhedrin* 56a; *Zohar* 3:106b. Cf. Maimonides, *Mishneh Torah, Hilkhot Avodah Zarah* 2:7.

39. **placed him under a ban** On the laws of *niddui* (ostracism) and *ḥerem* (excommunication), see Maimonides, *Mishneh Torah, Hilkhot Talmud Torah* 7:2–5.

40. **not to another name...** Because of its equivocal reference, one may not dedicate a child to the name *Elohim*. See *ZḤ* 19c (*MhN*), page 207.

The full verse in Samuel reads: *She vowed a vow and said, "YHVH of Hosts, if You really will look on Your servant's woe and remember me, and forget not Your servant and give Your servant* זרע אנשים (*zera anashim*), *male seed* [or: *an offspring suitable for dedicating to God's service*], *I will dedicate him to YHVH all the days of his life, and no razor shall touch his head."* Cf. *ZḤ* 11b (*MhN*).

41. **created by the name *Elohim*...** One can argue that the name *Elohim* in Genesis 1:1 does not refer to God.

In the creation account found in Genesis 1, it is *Elohim* (God), not *YHVH*, who is the

Rabbi Abbahu replied, "But the world was created before people appeared, before the judges of the generation or the nobles of the generation appeared. Therefore, there can be no mistake!"

As Rabbi El'azar, the precious and beloved, said: "It is written: *Who is* כמכה (*khamokhah*), *like You, among the* אלים (*elim*), *gods, O YHVH* (Exodus 15:11)—that is able to create the world? Indicating that אלים (*elim*), *gods*, could not create the world, until the blessed Holy One took one letter from His Name—the letter ה (*he*)—and with it the world was created; this letter expanded into אלהים (*Elohim*) and His name *Elohim* was inscribed. Concerning this we have learned: With ה (*he*) He created them."[42]

Rabbi Yose said, "Look, we see that there is no crown or kingdom [4a] aside from His holy Name that He has not lent to another—it is *YHVH*, יוד הא ואו הא (*Yod, He, Vav, He*)!"[43]

As Rabbi Yose said: "In it are comprised Above and Below, heaven and earth and all their array, the Throne of Glory, and the holy living beings. All are as naught before Him, accounted as nothing. He was, He is, He will be. May He be blessed, and may His Name be blessed, forever and ever! Amen."[44]



agent of creation. See *Shemot Rabbah* 30:13: "The blessed Holy One... created the world with justice, as is said: *In the beginning Elohim created* (Genesis 1:1). It does not say *YHVH created*, but *Elohim*." See *ZḤ* 12a (*MhN*), page 90.

42. **and His Name *Elohim* was inscribed...** Following Rabbi Shalom's observation that the world was created with the name *Elohim*, the *Zohar* elaborates how this was so. The letter ה (*he*) from the divine Name יהוה (*YHVH*) is added to אלים (*elim*), "celestial powers," so that the name אלהים (*Elohim*), "God," is attained. This homily appears three times in *MhN Bereshit*, twice in the name of Rabbi El'azar and once in the name of Shim'on. See *ZḤ* 2d, 3a (both *MhN*).

43. **there is no crown or kingdom...** The name *YHVH* alone is sovereign and is not shared with other creations.

In *Guide of the Perplexed* 1:61, Maimonides writes of the name *YHVH*: "This is the name of God (may He be exalted) that has been originated without any derivation, and for this reason it is called the articulated name. This means that this name gives a clear and unequivocal indication of His essence (may He be exalted).... Generally speaking, the greatness of this name and the prohibition against pronouncing it are due to its being indicative of the essence of Him (may He be exalted) in such a way that none of the created things is associated with Him in this indication."

44. **In it are comprised...** The name *YHVH*, the personal and explicit name of God, is said to derive from the Hebrew verb הוה (*hvh*), "to be." It comprises all the existents. It alone is truly existent. Cf. Moses de León, *Sheqel ha-Qodesh*, 86 (109), 100 (127–28); *Sefer ha-Rimmon*, 288.

Commenting on the divine name "I Am That I Am," Maimonides writes in *Guide of the Perplexed* 1:63: "This is a name derived from the verb 'to be' (*hayah*), which signifies existence, for *hayah* indicates the notion 'he was.' And in Hebrew there is no difference between your saying 'he was' and 'he existed.' The whole secret consists in the repetition in a predicative position of the very word indicative of existence.... Accordingly,

Rabbi Yehudah said, "May the Name of the supreme King of Kings—the blessed Holy One—be praised and exalted! For He is the first, and He is the last, and aside from Him there is no God. He created the world through the mystery of three great and magnificent things—knowledge, wisdom, and understanding—as is said: *YHVH founded the earth by wisdom; He establishes the heavens by understanding* (Proverbs 3:19), and it goes on to say: *By His knowledge the depths were split* (ibid., 20).

"Why did the blessed Holy One create the earth—the lowly world—by the mystery of *wisdom*, and the heavens—a more sublime world—by *understanding*, which is a lesser quality than wisdom? We have already learned: When is a person called 'wise in wisdom'? When he is asked about anything and he duly answers and replies, grasping all, then he is called 'wise in wisdom'—which is greater than understanding or knowledge. Therefore, He (may He be praised) ought to have made the heavens by *wisdom*, and the earth, which is lower than them, by *understanding*![45]

"You should know that wisdom is the greatest of them all, and that is why a 15
person is called 'wise'—because he is wise in all the wisdoms. Understanding, however, is lesser than wisdom; and that is why a person is called 'understanding'—that is to say, he can deduce one thing from another, by himself and in his mind, inferring one thing from another. In other words, when he sees the foundation principle, he is able to build upon it. Similarly the one who understands: when he sees a certain thing or an aspect of it, he is able to add to it.[46]

"The blessed Holy One (may His Name be praised) created the heavens by the mystery of *understanding*, for it pertains to בינה (*Binah*), derived from a foundation. In the beginning of all the creations, He created the form of the holy angels—the first of all creations, emanated from the radiance of His majestic light. In their mystery they are called by ten names, and among their names they are called *Elohim*. Therefore Scripture comes to teach: בראשית ברא אלהים (*Be-reshit bara Elohim*), *In the beginning He created Elohim* (Genesis 1:1)—that is to say, He (may His Name be praised) created the form of the angels called

Scripture makes, as it were, a clear statement that the subject is identical with the predicate .... He is existent not through existence ... the existent that is the existent, or the necessarily existent...."

45. **When is a person called 'wise in wisdom'?...** See BT *Shabbat* 114a: "Rabbi Yoḥanan ... said, 'Who is a *talmid ḥakham*, "disciple of the wise"? One who is asked a *halakhah* in any place and can state it.'" Cf. BT *Qiddushin* 49b: "one who can be asked a matter of wisdom in any place and can answer it."

46. **deduce one thing from another...** See BT *Ḥagigah* 14a: "And the *navon*, person of understanding—this means one who understands one thing from another."

Wisdom (the foundation) takes priority over understanding (the elaboration and expansion of the foundation).

*Elohim*, and they are the foundation of all the other creations. From this foundation, the heavens were created afterward through the mystery of understanding. Just as understanding signifies deducing one thing from another, so the heavens were created one thing from another: from the mystery of the light of the angelic form—that is to say, they are בנין (*binyan*), a construction, from a foundation. Therefore: *He establishes the heavens* בתבונה (*bi-tvunah*), *by understanding*.[47]

"The earth, however, came into being from a different foundation—because it is suspended over the waters, and the blessed Holy One established a foundation for it made by wisdom. Therefore it is said: *YHVH founded the earth by wisdom; He establishes the heavens by understanding*—one thing from another. The heavens were created from the same light emanated to *Elohim*, and He fashioned them one thing from another.[48]



47. ***He establishes the heavens* בתבונה (*bi-tvunah*), *by understanding*** The heavens were fashioned from the angelic form termed *Elohim*, itself emanated from the divine being. Because the heavens were built from something else, "understanding" (*Binah* or *Tevunah*, from the same root)—which signifies deriving one thing from another—is the appropriate quality for their creation. See below, *ZḤ* 17b (*MhN*), page 171.

The creation of the angelic form *Elohim* is the first creative act. Reading the opening verse from Genesis hyper-literally, the *Zohar* transforms *Elohim* from the subject to the object: *Elohim*, the form of the angels, is the first creation. Cf. *Zohar* 1:15a. This interpretation is found in Moses de León's earliest known work, *Or Zaru'a*, 259–60, where *Elohim* signifies Metatron, the Active Intellect: "Understand the matter and the precise mystery that the first of all existents was the creation of the form of the intellects; afterward the heavens; and afterward the earth, the lowly world. You will find this matter articulated in the mystery of the verse *Be-reshit bara elohim*.... Here is the complete, precise mystery through the eye of intellect: the beginning of the emanation of all the existents was the form of the intellects termed *Elohim*.... He (may He be blessed) created the form called *Elohim*." Cf. idem, *Mishkan ha-Edut*, 4a.

On the term *Elohim* as signifying one class of angels or intellects, see Maimonides, *Mishneh Torah*, *Hilkhot Yesodei ha-Torah* 2:7–8: "The different names by which the angels are called reflect their rank. Therefore they are called: *Ḥayyot ha-qodesh*...; the *ofanim*; the *er'ellim*; the *ḥashmalim*; the *seraphim*; the *malakhim*; the *elohim*; the sons of *elohim*; the *keruvim*; the *ishim*. All these forms are alive. They recognize and know the Creator with very immense knowledge." See also *Guide of the Perplexed* 2:4.

48. **from a different foundation...** In contrast to the heavens, the earth was created *ex nihilo* and therefore made by wisdom, a higher quality. See below, *ZḤ* 17b (*MhN*).

See Tishby, *Wisdom of the Zohar*, 2:554: "Here we have a definite cosmogonic idea: the spiritual, non-divine forces originated by a process of emanation; and from their light the essence, or perhaps only the form, of the heavens was created—whereas the earth, together with perhaps the matter of the heavens, was created *ex nihilo*."

According to BT *Ḥagigah* 12b, the earth is suspended upon the waters: "Upon what does the earth stand? On the pillars, as is said: *Who shakes the earth from its place, till its pillars quake* (Job 9:6). The pillars upon the waters, as is said: *Who spread the earth above the waters* (Psalms 136:6).'"

"By these three things the Dwelling was made, as is said: *I have filled him with the spirit of God—in wisdom, and in understanding, and in knowledge* (Exodus 31:3). These three are by supernal gift, and He bestows them to whomever He desires, as is said: *For YHVH grants wisdom, knowledge, and understanding by His decree* (Proverbs 2:6)."[49] [4d]

בראשית (*Be-reshit*), *In the beginning, God created* (Genesis 1:1).[50]

Rabbi Abba opened, saying, "*On that day YHVH made a covenant with Abram, saying* (Genesis 15:18). Concerning five things covenant is mentioned. The first is the covenant of circumcision, as is said: *My covenant in your flesh shall be an everlasting covenant* (ibid. 17:13). The second is the covenant of the rainbow, as is said: [*My bow I have set in the clouds*] *to be a sign of the covenant* (ibid. 9:13). The third is the covenant of salt, as is said: *a perpetual covenant of salt* (Numbers 18:19). The fourth is the covenant of retribution, as is said: *These are the words of the covenant* (Deuteronomy 28:69). The fifth is the covenant of priesthood, as is said: *It shall be for him and for his seed after him a covenant of perpetual priesthood* (Numbers 25:13).[51]



49. **By these three things...** See *Pirqei de-Rabbi Eli'ezer* 3: "Some say by ten utterances was the world created—and in three are these comprised, as is said: *YHVH founded the earth by wisdom; He establishes the heavens by understanding. By His knowledge the depths were split* (Proverbs 3:19–20). By these three the Dwelling was made, as is said: *I have filled him with the spirit of God—in wisdom, and in understanding, and in knowledge.* ...With these three attributes will the blessed Holy One give three good gifts to Israel in the future, as is said: *For YHVH will grant wisdom, knowledge, and understanding by His decree* (Proverbs 2:6)." See also *Zohar* 2:221a.

50. **בראשית (*Be-reshit*), *In the beginning...*** From here until folio 6d is a series of homilies on the opening word of the Torah: בראשית (*Be-reshit*), *In the beginning. Tiqqunei ha-Zohar*, a later stratum of the Zoharic corpus, is organized in this way.

51. **Concerning five things...** The contexts of the five verses cited are as follows: (1) *My covenant in your flesh shall be an everlasting covenant* (Genesis 17:13) refers to the Covenant of Circumcision. The earlier verse from Genesis 15:18: *On that day YHVH made a covenant with Abram, saying, "To your offspring I assign this land..."* refers to the Covenant Between the Pieces. (2) [*My bow I have set in the clouds*] *to be a sign of the covenant* (ibid. 9:13). After the Flood, God makes a covenant with the world not to destroy it again. This covenant is marked by the rainbow, the bow now facing away from the earth. (3) *A perpetual covenant of salt* (Numbers 18:19) refers to sacrifices that must be accompanied by salt, as per Leviticus 2:13: *You shall season your offering of meal with salt; you shall not omit from your meal offering the salt of your covenant with God; with all your offerings you must offer salt.* See Rashi and Naḥmanides, ad loc.; *ZḤ* 12c (*MhN*). (4) *These are the words of the covenant that YHVH commanded Moses to conclude with the Israelites in the land of Moab* (Deuteronomy 28:69) concludes a passage that lists the blessings and curses consequent respectively upon covenantal observance or disobedience. (5) *It shall be for him and for his seed after him a covenant of perpetual priesthood, because he was impassioned for his God, making expia-*

"Before these five covenants were given, the only covenant was fire, as is said: *and, look, a smoking brazier with a fiery torch* (Genesis 15:17), and similarly: *On that day YHVH made a covenant with Abram, saying* (ibid., 18). Initially the covenant was of fire! This is בראשית (*Be-reshit*), *In the beginning*: remove אש (*esh*), *fire*, and ברית (*brit*), *covenant*, remains. In other words: ברית אש (*brit esh*), covenant of fire."[52]

Rabbi Yoḥanan said, "The blessed Holy One made a sealed covenant with the world on condition that Abraham would arise and the world endure by his merit, as is said: *These are the generations of heaven and earth* בהבראם (*be-hibbare'am*), *when they were created* (ibid. 2:4)—באברהם (*be-Avraham*), through Abraham; and at the moment that He established the covenant of fire with him, the world stood enduringly. This is the meaning of בראשית (*Be-reshit*), *In the beginning*: ברית אש (*brit esh*), *covenant of fire, God created heaven and earth*—that it would endure by virtue of that covenant of fire.[53]

"Wisdom asks, 'Why did the blessed Holy One bring a flood of water upon
18 the world, rather than something else as His first judgment?'[54]

"Well, the blessed Holy One saw that the world was created through a covenant of fire, and He saw that were He to judge the world with a different punishment, the wicked might be able to endure in the world—by virtue of that covenant of fire when the world had been created. So what did He do? He punished the world with the appropriate substance to extinguish the fire, in order to remove the wicked—who were compared to fire—from the world. As is said: *from fire they emerged, but fire shall consume them* (Ezekiel 15:7), implying that they emerged from the fire at the beginning of the world when it was created.[55]

*tion for the Children of Israel* (Numbers 25:13) refers to the covenant of peace awarded to Phinehas son of Eleazar son of Aaron, as a result of his act of zealotry.

52. **ברית אש (*brit esh*), covenant of fire** The Torah's opening word בראשית (*Be-reshit*), *In the beginning*, is an anagram of ברית אש (*brit esh*), "covenant of fire." Before the other covenants were instituted, the original covenant, established at creation, was of fire. Hence the Covenant Between the Pieces concluded by Abram and God was marked by a fiery torch.

See Baḥya ben Asher on Genesis 1:2; cf. *Tiqqunei ha-Zohar*, *Tiqqun* 22, 23, 28, 37; *ZḤ* 117b (*Tiq*).

53. **on condition that Abraham would arise...** The word *Be-reshit*, *In the beginning*, contains an allusion to the *brit esh*, "covenant of fire," established between God and Abraham. Only though Abraham's *brit esh* is *bereshit*, "creation," placed firmly on its foundation. See below, note 58.

According to Rabbi Yehoshu'a son of Korḥah (*Bereshit Rabbah* 12:9), בהבראם (*be-hibbare'am*), *when they were created*, is an anagram of באברהם (*be-Avraham*), "through Abraham," indicating that the world was created for his sake. See *Zohar* 1:3b, 86b, 91b, 93a, 105b, 128b, 154b, 230b, 247a; 2:31a, 48b, 79a, 220b; 3:117a; *ZḤ* 17a (*MhN*).

54. **Wisdom asks...** An odd locution not found elsewhere in the *Zohar*. Cf. *Zohar* 1:62a.

55. ***from fire they emerged...*** Because of the original covenant of fire at creation,

"At first He said, *I will wipe out the human race I created* (Genesis 6:7)—with water, as is said: *The wicked are like the tossing sea* (Isaiah 57:20). Afterward is said: *from fire they emerged, but fire shall consume them.* The blessed Holy One said, 'Until now they perished in water. From here on: *from fire they emerged, but fire shall consume them.*'[56]

"When they sinned afterward, He judged them by fire, as is said: *And YHVH rained brimstone and fire on Sodom and Gomorrah* (Genesis 19:24). When was the world rendered firm and fragrant? When they stood upon Mount Sinai, and it was entirely covered in smoke, as is said: *and the mountain was ablaze with fire to the heart of heaven* (Deuteronomy 4:11)."[57]

Rabbi Yitshak said, "Torah became a covenant between the Name and the world, analogized to fire, as is said: *Behold, My word is like fire* (Jeremiah 23:29). This is: ברית אש (*brit esh*), *covenant of fire*—בראשית (*Be-reshit*), *In the beginning.*"[58]

only water could remove the wicked from the world. Only the first part of the verse from Ezekiel is interpreted here. The continuation is explained in the next paragraph. Cf. *Shir ha-Shirim Rabbah* on 2:15.

56. **From here on...** Having been tempered with water, they are now vulnerable to fire.

On comparing the wicked to the tossing sea, see *Shir ha-Shirim Rabbah* on 2:16; *Tanḥuma, Vayiqra* 7; *Midrash Tehillim* 2:2; *Zohar* 1:74b, 106b (*MhN*), 171b.

57. **rendered firm and fragrant...** Although the world endured by virtue of Abraham, it is only with the covenant at Mount Sinai that the continued existence of the world is assured.

Cf. BT *Shabbat* 88a: "Resh Lakish said, 'Why is it written: *There was evening and there was morning:* יום הששי (*yom ha-shishi*), *the sixth day* (Genesis 1:31)? Why the extra letter ה (*he*)? This teaches that the blessed Holy One stipulated a condition with the works of Creation, saying to them: 'If Israel accepts the Torah [given at Mount Sinai on the sixth day of the month Sivan], you will endure. If not, I will return you to *chaos and void* (ibid. 1:2).'"

"Firm and fragrant" renders נתבסם (*nitbassem*), "was sweetened" or "was firmly established," given that Rabbi Yoḥanan appears to play upon both senses of the verbal root *bsm*. See *Bereshit Rabbah* 66:2; *Midrash Shemu'el* 26:4; *Zohar* 1:30b, 31a, 34a, 37a, 56a, 73b, 137a; 2:143a, 168a, 227a; 3:18a; *ZḤ* 19b (*MhN*); Scholem, *Major Trends*, 165, 388, n. 44; idem, *Kabbalah*, 228.

58. **Torah became a covenant...** After the revelation at Mount Sinai, the Torah, which is compared to fire, became the ultimate covenant of fire (*brit esh*) underwriting creation (*Be-reshit*).

See *Shemot Rabbah* 47:4: "[God said to Israel], 'Had you not accepted My Torah, I would have returned the world to *chaos and void* (Genesis 1:2), as is said: *Were it not for My covenant with day and night, [I would not have established the laws of heaven and earth]* (Jeremiah 33:25). Why? Because with Torah I created heaven and earth.... If you annul the covenant [of Torah], you cause Me to return the upper and lower realms to *chaos and void*.'" Cf. BT *Shabbat* 33a, 137b; *Zohar* 1:32a, 56a, 66b, 89a, 93b.

On the comparison of Torah to fire, see Deuteronomy 33:2: *From His right hand, a fiery law for them.* See *Mekhilta de-Rashbi*, Exodus 20:1; BT *Berakhot* 22a; *Ta'anit* 4a, 7a; *Midrash Tehillim* 16:7, 29:2. See also BT *Bava Batra* 79a, and Rashbam, ad loc., s.v. *me-ha-esh yatsa'u*; *Zohar* 2:151a.

Rabbi Yoḥanan opened, "*By wisdom a house is built* (Proverbs 24:3). A man must do three worldly things: build a house in which to live; plant a vineyard to support himself; and afterward take a wife, have children, and support them. Not like the way of the fools—who first take a wife, and then plant a vineyard, and afterward build a house!"[59]

As Rabbi Simon said: "Whoever takes for himself a wife without first being able to provide for her, such a person is free of the commandments—like the dead who are called 'free,' as is said: *free among the dead* (Psalms 88:5). Why is he called *free*? Because he is free of the commandments, unable to strive in the service of his Creator, but rather in the service of his wife."[60]

Rabbi Yehudah says, "He is as though he marries an idol!"[61]

As Rabbi Yehudah said: "In the past, the sages and the pious used to take a wife without having adequate means to support them, and they would kill themselves with hunger and thirst, forsaking all the life of this world, engaging in Torah and commandments, serving their Creator. But nowadays—when the world is obsessed with livelihood—one must first establish a house and prepare his sustenance, and afterward take a wife, [5a] so that one will be able to serve



59. **three worldly things...** It is an act of wisdom to first build a house. See BT *Sotah* 44a: "Our Rabbis taught: *who has built, who has planted, who has betrothed* (Deuteronomy 20:5–7). The Torah has taught worldly advice—that a man should build a house, plant a vineyard, and then marry a wife."

See also Maimonides, *Mishneh Torah, Hilkhot De'ot* 5:11: "The way of sensible men is that first, one should establish an occupation by which he can support himself. Then, he should purchase a house to live in, and then marry a wife. As is said: *Is there anyone who has planted a vineyard, but not redeemed it; is there anyone who has built a new house, but not dedicated it; is there anyone who has betrothed a woman, but not taken her [to wife]* (Deuteronomy 20:6, 5, 7). In contrast, a fool begins by marrying a wife. Then, if he can find the means, he purchases a house. Finally, toward the end of his life, he will search about for a trade...." Although Maimonides famously inverted the order in the Torah and in BT *Sotah*, his statement would appear to lie at the heart of the *Zohar*'s formulation. The *Zohar* adopts the order found in the Talmud. Cf. *ZḤ* 59b (*MhN*), where Rabbi Yoḥanan says that a person should trust in God, marry, and have children, i.e., not delay marrying for fear of inadequate livelihood.

On this verse from Proverbs, see *Zohar* 1:15b, 29a–b.

60. **free of the commandments...** Focused on securing his livelihood, he cannot devote himself to Torah and commandments. See BT *Shabbat* 30a: "*The dead cannot praise Yah* (Psalms 115:17).... A person should always engage in Torah and good deeds before he dies, for once he is dead he is released from Torah and good deeds, and the blessed Holy One gets no praise from him. As Rabbi Yoḥanan said, 'What is the meaning of the verse *free among the dead* (Psalms 88:5)? When a person dies, he becomes free of the Torah and good deeds.'"

61. **he marries an idol** According to Rabbi Yehudah, one who marries without the adequate means of support is not only free of the commandments, but also tantamount to being an idolator.

his Creator and engage in Torah. As our Rabbis of blessed memory said: Where there is no meal, there is no Torah!"[62]

Rabbi Yehudah also said, "Only once a man has married a woman is he called A Servant of YHVH, because his heart is free from contemplating transgression and gazing upon women—from following his heart and eyes, as is said: *You shall not stray after your heart and after your eyes*... (Numbers 15:39). Therefore one should strive to establish a house first and [then] settle the home.[63]

"From whom do you learn this? From the blessed Holy One! For first He built
a house and established it, preparing all the sustenance and provisions before
the human being came into the world. How so? First of all He created the
world—the house—and prepared all the sustenance. How? He created the animals and the beasts, the birds and the fish, the plants and trees—the preparation of all the sustenance. After He prepared the house and the sustenance, He
brought forth the human being and created him and his wife, and they engendered children and settled the home.[64] That is why it says: בראשית (Be-reshit), *In*
*the beginning*—בית ראש (bayit rosh), a house first. When you understand the 21
letters you find: בית ראש (bayit rosh), house first. And so Torah begins with
בראשית (Be-reshit), *In the beginning*, implying ב ראשית (bet reshit), a house is the
beginning, and it is all a single matter.[65]

62. **when the world is obsessed with livelihood...** The manuscripts and earliest printed versions of the *Zohar* preserve an alternate reading. Rather than פרנסה (parnasah), "livelihood," some read פרוטה (prutah), "a penny," i.e., the world is desperate for a penny. Either way, the materialism of the times prevents the asceticism of earlier days.

"Where there is no meal, there is no Torah!" derives from M *Avot* 3:17.

63. **because his heart is free...** Only when married and therefore free of lustful thoughts is a man able to devote himself to Torah, commandments, and God. See *ZḤ* 59b (*MhN*).

Cf. BT *Qiddushin* 29b: "Our Rabbis taught: On studying Torah and marrying a woman? He should study Torah and then marry; but if he cannot manage without a wife, he should marry and then study Torah. Rav Yehudah said in the name of Shemu'el, 'The *halakhah* is that he should marry and then study Torah.' Rabbi Yoḥanan said, 'A millstone around his neck—and he will study Torah?!' And they do not disagree: that [rule] is for us, and that [other rule] is for them." (See Rashi and Tosafot, ad loc.)

See also Maimonides, *Mishneh Torah, Hilkhot Talmud Torah* 1:5: "A person should always study Torah and marry afterward. If he marries first, his mind will not be free for study. However, if his natural inclination overcomes him to the extent that his mind is not free, he should marry, and then study Torah."

64. **After He prepared the house...** See BT *Sanhedrin* 38a: "Our Rabbis taught: Adam was created on the eve of Sabbath. Why?... So he could immediately go to the banquet. An analogy: A king of flesh-and-blood built palaces and decorated them, prepared a banquet, and only then brought in the guests." See also *Zohar* 1:34b: "Adam was last of all, fittingly, so as to arrive in a consummate world."

65. **בית ראש (bayit rosh), a house first...** When the letters are rearranged, the Torah's opening word בראשית (Be-reshit), *In the be-*

"Even so, a person must pursue a worldly occupation and make time for Torah—his toil in both these paths—for exertion in both banishes sin. Now, should a person say, 'Look, I am of distinguished ancestry, from an important family; it is not fitting that I should work and demean myself!' Say to him, 'Fool! Your Creator has preceded you, as is said: *In the beginning God created heaven and earth* (Genesis 1:1)—He worked before you came into the world!' How do we know? As is said: [*He rested*] *from all His work that He had made* (ibid. 2:3). Scripture calls it *work*! Similarly: *He ceased on the seventh day from all the work He had done* (ibid., 2)."[66]

As Rabbi Yoḥanan said: "Come and see: Why did the blessed Holy One create the human being the last of all the creations? In order to teach you that on every single day He performed His work, creating the world and its entire array, and on the sixth day, the last of His work, He created humankind. He said to the human being, 'Until now I was engaged in the work. From here on, you will engage in it.' This is *In the beginning God created* (Genesis 1:1)—before humankind
22 came into the world."[67]

Rabbi Yoḥanan also said, "Why was the human being created in the image of God, as is said: *God created the human in His image* (Genesis 1:27)? This may be compared to a king who ruled over a city and built palaces and amenities for the city, and all the city's inhabitants were subject to him. One day he summoned all the people of the city and appointed one of his princes over them. He said,

*ginning,* can be read as *bayit rosh,* "a house first"—the advice proffered by Rabbi Yoḥanan and Rabbi Yehudah and exemplified by God. Additionally, without rearranging the letters, the opening word of the Torah can be divided into *bet* (the second letter, but also symbolizing a house) and *reshit,* beginning. Both derivations point to the same advice; hence it is all a single matter. Cf. *Zohar* 1:15b, 29a–b.

66. **Fool! Your Creator has preceded you...** The *Zohar* finds scriptural support for the value of work through God's work in creating the world. Just as He worked, so should you! Even if you have secured your house, you must still pursue a worldly occupation.

See M *Avot* 2:2: "Rabban Gamliel the son of Rabbi Yehudah ha-Nasi said, 'Excellent is the study of Torah together with a worldly occupation, for toil in both banishes sin. And all Torah study that is not combined with work comes to naught and leads to sin.'" See also M *Avot* 1:10.

In *Mishneh Torah, Hilkhot Talmud Torah* 3:6–11, Maimonides outlines the relationship between work and Torah study. See especially 3:10–11: "Anyone who thinks that he should study Torah without doing work and derive his livelihood from charity—he desecrates the Name, dishonors Torah, extinguishes the light of faith, brings evil upon himself, and forfeits the life of the world to come.... It is of great benefit for a person to derive his livelihood from his own efforts, and it is an attribute of the former pious ones."

67. **From here on, you will engage in it...** Initially, God performed all the work of the world. Following the creation of humanity, however, the task devolves to them. See next note.

'Until now I was concerned with all the needs of the city, building citadels and palaces. From here on, this one shall be like me.' Similarly, 'Look, I have commanded the entire city and everything in it. Just as I ruled over it, building it according to My desire, so you shall build and perform the work of the world. From here on, everything is handed over to you, and all will be under your dominion—in awe of you, just as they were in awe of Me, as is said: *Fear and dread of you shall be upon all the beasts of the earth* (ibid. 9:2).' Therefore: *In the image of God did He make him*; *God created the human in His image* (ibid. 1:27)—to tend to all the world's needs and amenities as He did at first."[68]

*In the beginning.*

It is written: *YHVH created me* ראשית (*reshit*), *at the beginning of, His way, before His works of old* (Proverbs 8:22). This verse applies to the entire Torah, the beginning of God's ways, for Torah was created two thousand years before the creation of the world.[69]

As Rabbi El'azar said: "Seven things were created before the world was
created: Torah, the Garden of Eden, Hell, the Throne of Glory, the Temple, 23
the name of the Messiah, and *teshuvah*."[70]

With Torah He created the world, for Torah is called ראשית (*reshit*), *beginning*, as is said: *YHVH created me* ראשית (*reshit*), *at the beginning of, His way*, and with this beginning—which is Torah—He created the world. This is בראשית (*Be-reshit*), *With beginning, God created* [5d] *heaven and earth* (Genesis 1:1).[71]

68. ***in His image . . .*** The human being is God's regent. Human dominion over the earth, including the capacity and responsibility to tend to all the world's needs, are an expression of the divine image in which humanity was created. See *ZḤ* 17d (*MhN*), page 178. I have been unable to locate a precise rabbinic parallel for this idea.

Genesis 1:27 actually reads: *In the image of God did He create him*. Apparently the author has confused this verse with Genesis 5:1: *In the likeness of God did He make him*.

69. **created two thousand years before . . .** See *Bereshit Rabbah* 8:2: "Rabbi Shim'on son of Lakish said, 'The Torah preceded the creation of the world by two thousand years.'" See also *Vayiqra Rabbah* 19:1; *Pesiqta de-Rav Kahana* 12:24; *Shir ha-Shirim Rabbah* on 5:11; *Tanḥuma, Vayeshev* 4; *Midrash Tehillim* 90:12; *Bahir* 4 (5); *Zohar* 1:2b; 2:49a, 161a; 3:128a (*IR*), 159a.

70. **Seven things were created . . .** See *Bereshit Rabbah* 1:4; BT *Pesaḥim* 54a; *Nedarim* 39b; *Tanḥuma, Naso* 11; *Pirqei de-Rabbi Eli'ezer* 3; *Zohar* 1:113a (*MhN*); 3:34b.

71. **With Torah He created the world . . .** See *Bereshit Rabbah* 1:1: "Rabbi Osha'ya opened, '*I was with Him as* אמון (*amon*), *a nursling* (Proverbs 8:30). . . . אמון (*Amon*)—אומן (*umman*), "an artisan." Torah says, "I was the artistic tool of the blessed Holy One." According to the custom of the world, when a mortal king builds a palace he does not build it by his own skill but rather by the skill of an architect. And the architect does not build it out of his own knowledge, but rather has parchments and tablets [with plans and diagrams] to know how to make the rooms and doors. Similarly, the blessed Holy One gazed into Torah and created the world. The Torah says: בראשית (*Be-reshit*), *In* [*or: with*] *the beginning, God created* (Genesis

Rabbi Yehudah said, "Come and see how great is the difference between Torah and the world! The world was created in six days, and Torah in forty days and forty nights!"[72]

Rabbi Yoḥanan was traveling from Caesarea to Lydda, and Rabbi Ḥiyya son of Abba was walking with him. When they reached a certain field, Rabbi Yoḥanan said, "This used to be mine, but I sold it to attain Torah."

Rabbi Ḥiyya son of Abba wept.

He asked him, "Why are you crying?"

He replied, "Because you haven't left anything for your old age."

He said to him, "Ḥiyya, my son, is what I have done a light matter in your eyes? For I have forfeited something created in six days for something created in forty days, as is said: *He was there with YHVH forty days and forty nights* (Exodus 34:28). And I have acquired magnificent and beautiful things not of the world—and they are: counsel, sound judgment, wisdom, and might, as is said: *Counsel and sound judgment are mine, I have understanding and might* (Proverbs 8:14)."[73]

24 Whenever Rabbi Yoḥanan would engage in Torah, his face shone like the radiance of the sun. One day Rabbi Yose met him. He said to him, "I see your face is shining like the radiance of the sun!"[74]

He replied, "It is only the teaching that illuminates me!"

He proclaimed for him: *His lovers are as the sun rising in its might* (Judges 5:31).

Rabbi Yitsḥak said, "At first the Torah is called תושיה (*tushiyyah*), *sound judgment*, and afterward *might.* Know that at first she is called *tushiyyah* because she מתשת (*matteshet*), enfeebles, a person's strength—for he must battle the evil impulse, pulverizing his entire body in the House of Study until it is accus-

1:1); and *reshit*, beginning, means only Torah, as is said: *YHVH created me at the beginning of His way* (Proverbs 8:22).'"

See M *Avot* 3:14; *Seder Eliyyahu Rabba* 29; *Tanḥuma, Bereshit* 1; *Tanḥuma* (Buber), *Bereshit* 5; *Zohar* 1:5a, 47a, 134a–b; 2:161a–b; 3:35b; Wolfson, *Philo*, 1:242–45, 266–69. See below, note 76.

72. **forty days and forty nights** See Exodus 24:18, 34:28; Deuteronomy 9:9.

73. **magnificent and beautiful things . . .** The *Zohar* paraphrases a story found in *Shemot Rabbah* 47:5 (see also *Vayiqra Rabbah* 30:1; *Pesiqta de-Rav Kahana* 27:1). With some minor modification (Tiberias is replaced with Caesarea and Sepphoris is replaced with Lydda) the story follows the rabbinic source. The moral is clear: the goods of this world do not compare with Torah!

74. **his face: shone . . .** According to Ecclesiastes 8:1, *A person's wisdom lights up his face.* See *Pirqei de-Rabbi Eli'ezer* 2: "Rabbi Eli'ezer was sitting and expounding [matters greater than those revealed to Moses at Sinai] and his face was shining like the light of the sun, and his radiance went forth like the radiance of Moses—and no one knew whether it was day or night." See also *Avot de-Rabbi Natan* B, 13; JT *Pesaḥim* 10:1, 37c, *Shabbat* 8:1, 11a; *Tanḥuma* (Buber), *Ḥuqqat*, add. 1; *Vayiqra Rabbah* 1:1, 21:12; *Qohelet Rabbah* on 1:7. In the *Zohar*, see 1:94b; 2:15a (*MhN*);

tomed to Torah. Once he is accustomed to engage in Torah, then he possesses joy and might, as is said: *I have understanding and might* (Proverbs 8:14), meaning: when a person is accustomed to Torah and wisdom, then he possesses *Tif'eret*, Splendor. What is meant by *might*? Fighting the battles of *YHVH*, as is said: *Therefore it is said in the Book of the Wars of YHVH* (Numbers 21:14)—the war and might should be there![75]

"With Torah the blessed Holy One created His world, as is said: *I was with him as a nursling* (Proverbs 8:30). Do not read אמון (*amon*), *nursling*, but rather אומן (*umman*), *artisan*. This is *Be-reshit*, *In the beginning, God created* (Genesis 1:1)—with *reshit*, *beginning, God created heaven and earth*—namely Torah."[76]

Rabbi Yehudah says, "The world was created solely for awe—which is called *reshit*, *beginning*, as is said: *The awe of YHVH is* ראשית (*reshit*), *the beginning of, knowledge* (Proverbs 1:7). How do we know that the world was created for awe? As is said: *God* עשה (*asah*), *acted, that they be in awe of Him* (Ecclesiastes 3:14)—(*Asah*), He made, the world that they be in awe of Him. For the sake of awe, which is *reshit*, *God created heaven and earth*."[77]



בראשית (*Be-reshit*), *In the beginning.*

Rabbi El'azar opened, "שיר המעלות (*Shir ha-ma'alot*), *A song of degrees. In my distress I cried to YHVH, and He answered me* (Psalms 120:1). The blessed Holy One created songs of desire at the creation of heaven and earth, so as to praise and glorify Him as the Creator of All. The heavens utter song in His presence, as is said: *The heavens declare the*

3:132b (*IR*), 163a; *ZḤ* 20d, 24a (in this volume), 28b (all *MhN*). See Hellner-Eshed, *A River Flows from Eden*, 305–8.

75. **she is called *tushiyyah*...** According to *Pirqei de-Rabbi Eli'ezer* 3, *tushiyyah* is the name of the Torah. See BT *Sanhedrin* 26b: "Rabbi Ḥanin said, "Why is she [Torah] called תושיה (*tushiyyah*)? Because she מתשת (*matteshet*), enfeebles, a person's strength [through constant effort].'" See *ZḤ* 25c (*MhN*). Cf. *Shir ha-Shirim Rabbah* on 5:14; *Qohelet Rabbah* on 1:8; BT *Yoma* 71a. On the weak physical condition of the Companions in the *Zohar*, see *Zohar* 2:61b, 143a, 198b, 225a–b.

In BT *Sukkah* 52b and *Qiddushin* 30b, the School of Rabbi Yishma'el teaches: "If that repulsive wretch [the evil impulse] meets you, drag him to the House of Study." See *ZḤ* 24b (*MhN*).

The *Book of the Wars of YHVH* is a lost ancient work that is quoted by Scripture. According to Rabbi Yitsḥak, the battles of *YHVH* should be in the book, i.e., one should devote one's bravery and might to Torah study. See *Sifrei*, Deuteronomy 321; *Seder Olam Rabbah* 25; JT *Ta'anit* 4:6, 69b; BT *Qiddushin* 30b, Rashi, s.v. *et vahev*; *Eikhah Rabbah* 2:4; *Zohar* 2:56a; *ZḤ* 14a (*MhN*), page 119.

76. **With Torah...** See above, note 71.

77. **solely for awe...** The preposition ב (*bet*) of בראשית (*be-reshit*), which typically means "in" or "with," is construed here in its causal sense: "for the sake of." That is, it was for the sake of *reshit*—which signifies awe—that God created heaven and earth. See BT *Shabbat* 31b, where this teaching is cited in the name of Rav Yehudah. See below, note 120. Cf. *Zohar* 1:11b.

*glory of God* (ibid. 19:2); and the earth utters song, as is said: *Sing to YHVH all the earth* (ibid. 96:1).[78]

"Furthermore, the entire world desires and delights to glorify their Creator, when they gaze upon His wonders in the heavens and on the earth. This is בראשית (*Be-reshit*), *In the beginning*: contemplate the letters and you will see שיר תאב (*shir ta'ev*), *a song of desire*; in other words, for a song of desire, God created heaven and earth—that every person will desire to utter song about His wonders in the heavens and the earth.[79]

"What are those degrees that King David (peace be upon him) used to recite? They are the songs of those degrees comprising the heavens, as is said: *Who constructs His degrees in heaven* (Amos 9:6). David desired them and uttered them, and this is שיר תאב (*shir ta'av*), *he desired song*."[80]



Rabbi El'azar also said, "It is written: *When the morning stars sang together, and all the sons of God shouted for joy* (Job 38:7). Who are the *sons of God*? They are the angels who every night chant song in the presence of the Creator of the Beginning, corresponding to the three watches of the night. In every single watch, each of the companies chants song. In the last watch, at night's end just before morning, all the stars and constellations, and the angels called *sons of God* utter [6a] song, as is said: *When the morning stars sang together*; each company according to its degree, teaching that *height upon height keeps guard* (Ecclesiastes 5:7), for they are arranged by degrees, one above the other. Therefore it is said: *A song of degrees* (Psalms 120:1)—of the degrees of the angels who

78. **songs of desire...** That is, songs that express and arouse desire. See next note.

The continuation of Psalms 19:2–5 presents a stunning image of cosmic song: *The heavens declare the glory of God, the sky proclaims His handiwork. Day to day makes utterance, night to night speaks out, whose sound goes unheard. Their voice carries throughout the earth, their words to the end of the world.*

The term שיר המעלות (*shir ha-ma'alot*) opens numerous psalms. In its simple sense, the word *ma'alot* means "ascents" and refers to a pilgrimage to the Temple in Jerusalem.

79. **This is בראשית (*Be-reshit*), *In the beginning*...** The Torah's opening word, בראשית (*Be-reshit*) is an anagram of שיר תאב (*shir ta'ev*), "song of desire." Additionally, *shir ta'ev* might also be understood as meaning "he desired song." In contemplating God's creation, the human being is moved to praise God with songs of desire—and it is for this reason that God created the world.

On the creation of the world for the sake of song, see *Alfa Beita de-Rabbi Aqiva*, Version 1 (*Battei Midrashot*, 2:343–4).

Cf. Maimonides, *Mishneh Torah, Hilkhot Yesodei ha-Torah* 2:2: "What is the path to love and fear Him? When a person contemplates His wondrous and great deeds and appreciates His infinite wisdom that surpasses all comparison, he will immediately love, praise, and glorify [Him]—yearning with tremendous desire to know the Great Name, as David said: *My soul thirsts for God, the Living God* (Psalms 42:3)."

80. **David desired them...** King David, the traditional author of the Psalms, is the paragon of such praise. David's "song of degrees" is thus the song of the heavenly degrees.

utter song. This is בראשית (*Be-reshit*), *In the beginning*—שיר תאב (*shir ta'ev*), *for a song of desire, God created heaven and earth.*"[81]

Rabbi Ḥizkiyah was walking on the way, and Rabbi Yose son of Ḥalafta was with him. They arose to walk on after midnight. While they were walking, Rabbi Yose said to Rabbi Ḥizkiyah, "What have we done? For look, we have learned: 'A person should always set out by daylight and enter by daylight.'"[82]

He replied, "Rabbi Yose my son, come and hear the arrangement of the sweet melody of the spheres of the living beings extolling song before their God."[83]

As he was inclining his ear, he heard voices of melodious praise—and heard that they were uttering *YHVH abides forever* (Psalms 9:8).

Rabbi Ḥizkiyah asked him, "My son, did you hear something?"

He replied, "Melodious voices. And from the melodious exaltation of the verse I just heard I now know its meaning, as is written: *YHVH abides forever, He has established His throne for judgment* (ibid.). For whenever judgment is executed, the *Shekhinah* of the blessed Holy One—His Throne of Glory—is there arrayed, as implied by what is said: *He has established His throne for judgment.*"[84]



81. **angels who every night chant song...** The celestial realm is a chorus of nocturnal song and praise.

In medieval Jewish philosophical literature, the angels signify the separate intellects or spiritual forms emanating from God. According to Maimonides in *Hilkhot Yesodei ha-Torah* (2:8), they are alive and "recognize and know the Creator with very immense knowledge, each of the forms according to its level." See also 2:5: "each one is below the level of the other—and exists by virtue of its influence, one above the other.... Solomon in his wisdom alluded to this, saying: *height upon height keeps guard* (Ecclesiastes 5:7)."

Already in the Bible, the term בני אלהים (*benei elohim*), literally *the sons of God*, represents celestial beings—the divine retinue. On the watches of the night, see BT *Berakhot* 3a–b; Rashi on BT *Berakhot* 3a, s.v. *i qa-savar*; *Zohar* 1:159a, 189a, 231a–b; 2:18b (*MhN*), 143b, 173a–b, 195b; 3:64b; *ZḤ* 17d (*MhN*), 88a (*MhN, Rut*); Moses de León, *Sefer ha-Rimmon*, 403; idem, *Sheqel ha-Qodesh*, 70–71 (88–89). On the theme of angels constantly reciting song, see BT *Ḥagigah* 12b, 14a; *Ḥullin* 91b. In the pre-kabbalistic Heikhalot corpus, the motif of angelic praise is ubiquitous; see, for example, 3 Enoch 35–40.

82. **Rabbi Ḥizkiyah was walking on the way, and Rabbi Yose...** Part of this story is quoted in Todros Abulafia, *Otsar ha-Kavod, Rosh ha-Shanah* 24b, s.v. *ve-shuv ra'iti be-midrash*. It is one of the earliest citations of the *Zohar*. See Scholem, *Major Trends*, 188.

See BT *Ta'anit* 10b: "Rav Yehudah said in the name of Rav, 'A person should always set out [from a town] by daylight and enter it by daylight.'" See also BT *Pesaḥim* 2a.

83. **sweet melody of the spheres...** The living beings, namely the angels or intellects, correspond to the celestial spheres of medieval Ptolemaic astronomy. The Pythagorean notion of the music of spheres is given a Jewish coloring, as the angels praise God with a variety of psalms. See *Zohar* 1:41b (*Heikh*), 161b (*ST*), 233b (*Tos*); 2:196a, 211a; 3:165a, 209a; [Moses de León?], *Seder Gan Eden*, 132. See also Scholem, "Parashah Ḥadashah," 437–38 on the song of the sun (Addendum 1 in this volume); *ZḤ* 8a (*MhN*); *ZḤ* 76c (*MhN, Rut*) on the stars.

84. **For whenever judgment is executed...** The execution of justice causes

He asked him, "Do you know which watch of ministering angels utters this?"

He replied, "No."

He said to him, "It is the watch of the angels called *Elohim*. As it has been taught: There are ten watches of ministering angels in the firmament, and they are divided among the three watches of the night.[85]

"You should know how [they are arranged]: When Israel complete their prayers at night, those called *Ishim* take up singing after them, uttering song. What song do they chant? *What is a human that You are mindful of him.... You have made him a little less than God, and adorned him with glory and majesty...YHVH our Lord, how majestic is Your name throughout the earth!* (ibid. 8:5–6, 10).[86]

"In the second watch, those called *Malakhim*, *Ḥashmalim*, and *Er'ellim* take up song. What do they chant? *Ascribe to YHVH, O sons of God* (Psalms 29:1).

"At precisely midnight, as the second watch is finishing, which is the hour
when the blessed Holy One actually gazes upon Eden—which He has concealed
28 for the righteous in the time to come—*Ḥayyot ha-Qodesh*, holy living beings,
open; and after them, *Seraphim*, *Ophanim*, and *Keruvim*, uttering: *How abundant is Your goodness that You have hidden away for those in awe of You* (Psalms 31:20); *Exalt Him who rides upon the clouds, Yah is His name* (ibid. 68:5).[87]

"At the beginning of the third watch, those called *Elohim* take up song, uttering, *YHVH abides forever*... (ibid. 9:8).

the indwelling of the *Shekhinah*; His throne is established through judgment. Cf. BT *Berakhot* 6a: "How do we know that if three [judges] are sitting in judgment, the *Shekhinah* is with them? For it is said: *In the midst of the judges He judges* (Psalms 82:1)."

85. **ten watches of ministering angels...** See Maimonides, *Mishneh Torah, Hilkhot Yesodei ha-Torah* 2:7–8 (above, note 47). Cf. *Guide of the Perplexed* 2:4. The *Zohar* here does not follow Maimonides' order. Cf. *Zohar* 2:43a.

See Isaac ibn Sahula, *Peirush Shir ha-Shirim*, 464, where this passage enumerating the watches is cited (with variations). See also Scholem, "Qabbalat Rabbi Yitsḥak ben Shelomoh," 112–16.

86. **When Israel complete their prayers...** Following the evening prayer, the first of the angelic companies begins singing. Human prayer and celestial adoration combine to form a continuous succession of praise. See *ZḤ* 17d–18a (*MhN*).

According to Maimonides (*Hilkhot Yesodei ha-Torah* 2:7, 7:1), the *Ishim* are the lowest angelic rank and closest to the human realm. They are the spiritual form with which a human being comes into contact in prophecy. Interestingly, the verses that they chant are about the exalted status of humankind.

87. **At precisely midnight...** Midnight marks the central moment of the cosmic praise, as God gazes upon Eden.

See Idel, "Qeta Lo Yadu'a," 86 (Addendum 2 in this volume). On midnight, see BT *Berakhot* 3b. Elsewhere in the main body of the *Zohar* and in *Midrash ha-Ne'lam*, the moment of midnight—as God enters the Garden of Eden to delight with the righteous—receives more lavish treatment and is developed into an elaborate mystical practice. See *ZḤ* 13c (*MhN*), 18a (*MhN*); *Zohar* 1:92b.

"When morning appears, the heavens open, uttering, *The heavens declare the glory of God*... (ibid. 19:2). The morning stars chant, *He reckoned the number of stars.... Great is our Lord and full of power* (ibid. 147:4–5). The angels called בני אלהים (*benei elohim*), *sons of God*, open, uttering: *Ascribe to YHVH, O* בני אלים (*benei elim*), *sons of God; ascribe to YHVH glory and strength* (ibid. 29:1)."

While they were walking, they saw the dawn darken—and afterward the light illuminated. Rabbi Ḥizkiyah said to Rabbi Yose, "Come, and I will show you that so is the redemption of Israel! In the era when the sun of redemption will shine upon them, affliction upon affliction and darkness upon darkness will befall them. Trapped within, the light of the blessed Holy One will shine upon them, as is said: *His appearance as sure as the dawn* (Hosea 6:3), and similarly: *For you who revere My name, the sun of victory will rise, with healing in its wings* (Malachi 3:20).[88]

"At that time, wars will be aroused in the world—nation against nation, city against city—and countless new afflictions will come upon Israel, until their faces will be blackened like the bottom of a pot. Afterward, their redemption will be revealed upon them from within the groan of their distress and oppression.[89]



"This is as David said: *For the leader on* אילת השחר (*ayyelet ha-shaḥar*), *the doe of the dawn. My God, my God, why have You abandoned me?* (Psalms 22:1–2). *Ayyelet ha-shaḥar, the doe of the dawn*—he should have said, *the doe of the morning*. Well, this refers to the power and potency of Israel's שחרותא (*shaḥaruta*), darkness, as is said: [*I am*] *a man without* איל (*eyal*), *power* (ibid. 88:5). At that time, in pain, the people of Israel will cry out, saying, *My God, my God, why have You abandoned me*? Afterward, what is written? *You have opened my sackcloth and girded me with joy* (ibid. 30:12)."[90] [6d]

88. **so is the redemption of Israel . . .** The redemption of Israel is compared to the brightening dawn that follows the night of exile. See JT *Berakhot* 1:1, 2c: "Rabbi Ḥiyya the Great and Rabbi Shim'on son of Ḥalafta were walking together in the valley of Arbel at daybreak. They saw אילת השחר (*ayyelet ha-shaḥar*), the doe of the dawn, as daylight broke forth. Rabbi Ḥiyya the Great said to Rabbi Shim'on son of Ḥalafta, 'Master, so is the redemption of Israel. It begins little by little, and as it proceeds it grows greater and greater.'" See also JT *Yoma* 3:2, 40b; BT *Yoma* 29a; *Shir ha-Shirim Rabbah* on 6:10; *Midrash Tehillim* 22:13.

89. **countless new afflictions...** See BT *Sanhedrin* 97a; cf. *Zohar* 2:7b–8b.

On the motif of faces being blackened (*yiqqaderu*) like the bottom of a pot (*qederah*), see BT *Megillah* 11a; *Bereshit Rabbah* 2:4; *Midrash Tehillim* 120:5; *ZḤ* 23c (*MhN*).

90. **אילת השחר (*ayyelet ha-shaḥar*), *the doe of the dawn*...** In the Bible, this term is a metaphor for the dawn; the streaks of morning light are compared to a doe's antlers. It also refers to a musical melody. See BT *Yoma* 29a.

Rabbi Ḥizkiyah asks why David employed this particular formulation. If he was intending to sing about Venus, the morning

Rabbi says, "The שיתין (*shittin*), hollows, were created during the six days of creation. The blessed Holy One ברא שית (*bara shit*), *created the hollow*, and this is בראשית (*Be-reshit*), *In the beginning*—meaning ברא שית (*bara shit*), *He created the hollow*. The ram of Isaac—there is a question whether it was created during the six days of creation. The blessed Holy One ברא שית (*bara shit*)—תיש (*tayish*), *billy goat*, when the letters are rearranged."[91]

בראשית (*Be-reshit*), *In the beginning.*

Praised be the Name of the supreme King of kings, the blessed Holy One, who created the entire world—establishing it by wisdom, understanding, and knowledge! Corresponding to them, He created three worlds: the supernal world, the intermediate world, and the lower world; and He placed in the small lower world the form of all three: the vegetative form, the speaking form, and the intellectual form.[92]



star, he ought to have said "the doe of the morning." The answer turns on an additional meaning of the word *shaḥar*, namely "darkness" or "blackness." In saying *ayyelet ha-shaḥar*, then, David was referring to the power of the darkness of Israel's exile. Cf. *Zohar* 2:10a. In the main body of the *Zohar*, the doe of the dawn becomes a central symbol for *Shekhinah*.

Psalms 30 continues (verse 13): *Oh, let my heart hymn You and be not still, YHVH my God; I will praise You forever*, concisely expressing the desire expressed by *MhN* to unite with the celestial realms in continuous praise of God.

91. **ברא שית (*bara shit*), *created the hollow*...** See BT *Sukkah* 49a: "Rabbah son of Bar Ḥana said in the name of Rabbi Yoḥanan, 'The hollows [under the Temple altar, into which the wine and water of libation flowed] were formed during the six days of Creation.'... It was taught in the school of Rabbi Yishma'el: '*Be-reshit*... Do not read בראשית (*be-reshit*), but rather ברא שית (*bara shit*), He created the hollow.'" See *Zohar* 1:30a, 56a; *ZḤ* 62d–63a (*ShS*); cf. *Zohar* 1:3b. See Baḥya ben Asher on Genesis 1:2 for a close parallel to this passage.

On the ram of Isaac, see M *Avot* 5:6: "Ten things were created on Sabbath eve at twilight:... Some say also... the ram of Abraham our Father." See *Zohar* 1:120b.

Here, as in rabbinic literature, a specific reference to "Rabbi" (without a name following) indicates Rabbi Yehudah ha-Nasi (the Patriarch), who redacted the Mishnah. He was so highly esteemed that he was simply called "Rabbi": the Master.

92. **He created three worlds . . .** This passage is not entirely clear. The order of the worlds and the various forms differs in the manuscripts. The reading here follows P3, M7, V12, and OM1. It seems that the supernal world, indicating the world of the angels (or intelligences), corresponds with wisdom and the intellectual form; the intermediate world, indicating the heavens, corresponds with understanding and the speaking form; and finally the lower world, indicating the earthly realm, corresponds with knowledge and the vegetative form. Cf. Tishby, *Wisdom of the Zohar*, 2:705–6, where he suggests that the speaking form may be the highest degree, though this seems to contradict what follows.

The "small lower world" refers to the human being—the microcosm—who contains and reflects all the worlds. See above, note 31.

This tripartite nature of the soul goes back to Aristotle in *De Anima*. He posited

You should know that the lower world is sustained by the ether—just as you see that the body is sustained by the soul; and the soul is sustained by the ether; and the ether by the Creator (may He be praised).[93]

Know that the Creator (may He be blessed) created the human being; He created him in image and form, arraying him from four distinct substances—from fire, air, water, and earth, as is said: *The earth was chaos and void, with darkness over the face of the abyss, and the wind of God* (Genesis 1:2). These are the four substances previously mentioned. As is said: There is a place among the coastal towns where they call fire תהו (*tohu*), *chaos*—this is the first element; ובהו וחשך (*va-vohu va-ḥoshekh*), *void and darkness*—they are water and earth. How do we know that darkness implies earth? As is said: *its name is covered with darkness* (Ecclesiastes 6:4), and they have explained that this refers to a clod of earth; and רוח (*ruaḥ*), wind, is air itself.[94]



a nested hierarchy of soul functions or activities: the nutritive soul, responsible for growth and nutrition (plants); the sensitive soul, responsible for locomotion and perception (animals); and the rational soul, responsible for intellect (human beings). The human being alone possesses all three degrees. This structure was widely applied in diverse combinations in medieval Jewish philosophical writings. See, for example, Maimonides, *Shemonah Peraqim* 1; Rabbi Samuel ibn Tibbon, *Peirush ha-Millim ha-Zarot*, s.v. *koaḥ medabber, nefesh medabberet*; Naḥmanides on Genesis 2:7; Moses de León, *Sefer ha-Mishqal*, 38; idem, *Mishkan ha-Edut*, 10b.

Although conventionally the tripartite structure as presented by the medievals assumed a vegetative soul, an animal soul, and then a rational or intellectual soul, here the structure is different. Curiously, this passage presents the speaking soul and intellectual soul—usually understood as synonymous—as two distinct levels. The vegetative and animal souls are therefore conflated. The author may have wished to differentiate between the practical and speculative intellect.

*MhN* presents numerous and conflicting accounts of the soul. See *ZḤ* 8d–9a, 10c–11a, 14b, 16a–c, 21c; *Zohar* 1:109a–b; Meroz, "Va-Ani Lo Hayiti Sham?," 170 (Addendum 3 in this volume); Tishby, *Wisdom of the Zohar*, 2:703–12.

93. **sustained by the ether...** See below, note 98.

94. **from four distinct substances . . .** The theory of the four elements was introduced by Empedocles and adopted by Plato, Aristotle, and most of their successors. It dominated Western cosmology until the Renaissance. According to this theory, everything below the sphere of the moon is composed of various combinations of fire, air, water, and earth, all of which interact and are capable of transforming into one another.

See Aristotle, *On Generation and Corruption* 2:1–8; *Sefer Yetsirah* 3:3–4; *Bemidbar Rabbah* 14:12; Maimonides, *Mishneh Torah, Hilkhot Yesodei ha-Torah* 3:10–11; 4:1–6; idem, *Guide of the Perplexed* 1:72, 2:30; *Zohar* 1:5b, 80a (*ST*); 2:13b, 23b; 3:170a. In *MhN*, see *ZḤ* 10a, 13d, 16b; *Zohar* 1:122b. Cf. Naḥmanides on Genesis 1:1. On the biblical derivation of the elements, see Moses de León, *Or Zaru'a*, 267–68. For the expression "a place among the coastal towns," see BT *Rosh ha-Shanah* 26a; *Zohar* 1:137a (*MhN*); Scholem, "Parashah Ḥadashah," 429 (Addendum 1 in this volume).

The verse from Ecclesiastes refers to the body after death.

Indeed, God (may He be praised) created the human being—who is called the lower world, corresponding to the great supernal world—and He placed within him the existence of the soul, animating the entire body, thereby distinguishing him from all the other creatures alongside him below. How is the human being distinguished from the other creatures? By virtue of that soul! Which soul is that? The speaking soul.[95]

Rabbi Yehudah asked Rabbi Dostai, "The soul in the human being that is called 'intellectual,' what kind of soul is it, and what is its place?"[96]

He replied, "Do you not know that the Omnipresent created the human being, and when he grows up and gazes upon the ways of the world and considers its vanities, he acquires that soul by himself? For when he gazes upon and perceives the wonders of the Creator—the creation of the world, the shining of the luminaries evening and morning, and how the entire world is suspended by His power (may He be praised)—he strives by himself to investigate and acquire a holy and pure apprehension. Then he possesses that נפש השכלית (*nefesh ha-sikhlit*), intellectual soul, because he is משכיל (*maskil*), enlightened, to know and investigate wisdom.[97]

"Rabbi Azariah says, 'The abode of the soul is in the heart. It animates the entire body and is placed in the center of the body, illuminating the entire body, just as the sun is in the middle of the sky.' The body is sustained by the soul, the soul by the ether, and the ether by the Creator (may He be praised); and the Creator bears all the worlds by His power, as is said: *I have made; I will carry and I will bear* (Isaiah 46:4)."[98]



95. **The speaking soul** It is the capacity for speech that marks the human being. The term "speaking form" or "speaking soul" goes back to Onqelos, who famously translated the verse *YHVH God fashioned a human . . . and blew into his nostrils the breath of life, and the human became a living being* (Genesis 2:7), as ". . . the human became a speaking spirit." See Rashi and Naḥmanides, ad loc. See *ZḤ* 10d (*MhN*), page 71.

Cf. Judah Alḥarizi, *Sefer ha-Nefesh* (attributed to Galenus), ed. Jellinek, 16.

96. **what kind of soul is it . . .** This and the following two paragraphs appear in Isaac ibn Sahula's *Meshal ha-Qadmoni*, Gate Three, 362–65.

97. **Then he possesses that נפש השכלית (*nefesh ha-sikhlit*), intellectual soul . . .** The intellectual soul is acquired through contemplation, in particular contemplation of Creation and of the very fact of creation (literally the "innovation" of the world). See Maimonides, *Mishneh Torah, Hilkhot Yesodei ha-Torah* 2:2.

The idea that one acquires the intellectual soul is derived from philosophical literature, where human intellect is imagined as passing from a passive or potential state to an active or acquired state during the act of cognition. See, for example, Maimonides, *Guide of the Perplexed* 1:68: "Thus in us, too, the intellectually cognizing subject, the intellect, and the intellectually cognized object are one and the same thing wherever we have an intellect *in actu*. We, however, pass intellectually from potentiality to actuality only from time to time."

98. **abode of the soul is in the heart . . .**

Rabbi Yehudah says, "Why did the blessed Holy One mention the creation of heaven and earth first? Weren't the angels and the Throne of Glory created first?! Well, it was in order that a person not ponder matters concealed from the eye, which He did not divulge at the beginning."[99]

Rabbi says, "It is in order to demonstrate to the human being that he does not possess wisdom, and that it is not fitting to reveal to him mysteries of Torah. As Rabbi Yitsḥak said: 'One does not divulge mysteries of Torah except to one who is wise, learned in Scripture and Mishnah, retains his learning, fears God, and is expert in every matter.' One who is not so, yet inquires about mysteries and concealed matters above—tell him, 'What are you asking? Raise your eyes and see that *In the beginning God created heaven and earth* (Genesis 1:1). Know that the Torah did not divulge any more!"[100]

Now, you might say, "There are no mysteries in the Torah!" You should know that concerning every single word there are heaps and heaps of mysteries, laws, and explanations, as is said: קווצותיו תלתלים (*qevutsotav taltalim*), *his locks are wavy* (Song of Songs 5:11)—on every קוץ וקוץ (*qots va-qots*), jot and tittle, there



See Judah Alḥarizi, *Sefer ha-Nefesh* (attributed to Galenus), ed. Jellinek, 13, 15–16; Moses de León, *Sefer ha-Rimmon*, 407.

According to *Midrash Mishlei* 1:1, the abode of wisdom is in the heart.

See *Vayiqra Rabbah* 4:8: "What prompted David to praise the blessed Holy One with his soul? Well, he said, 'The soul fills the body, and the blessed Holy One fills His world, as is said: *Do not I fill heaven and earth—declares YHVH* (Jeremiah 23:24); let the soul, which fills the body, come and praise the blessed Holy One, who fills all the world. The soul carries the body, and the blessed Holy One carries His world, as is said: *I have made; I will carry and I will bear* (Isaiah 46:4); let the soul, which carries the body, come and praise the blessed Holy One, who carries His world.'" See also Meroz, "Va-Ani Lo Hayiti Sham?" 170, 178 (Addendum 3 in this volume).

99. **Weren't the angels...** Genesis 1:1 opens with the creation of heaven and earth. Why doesn't it begin with the creation of the angels and the Throne of Glory? On the angels and Throne of Glory as the first creations, see *ZḤ* 4a, 7d (both *MhN*), and above at note 12; Cf. *Zohar* 1:146a. On the timing of the creation of the angels in rabbinic literature, see *Bereshit Rabbah* 1:3, 21:9; *Yalqut Shim'oni* 247:34. On the throne, see *Bereshit Rabbah* 1:4; BT *Pesaḥim* 54a; *Pirqei de-Rabbi Eli'ezer* 3.

On the prohibition of pondering concealed matters, see next note.

100. **not fitting to reveal...** Just as the Torah conceals her secrets by not beginning with esoteric matters, divine mysteries must not be divulged to the unworthy. See *ZḤ* 19c (*MhN*), pages 206–8, at nn. 702, 708, 709. Cf. *ZḤ* 12d (*MhN*), page 102.

See M *Ḥagigah* 2:1: "The Account of Creation may not be expounded in the presence of two persons, nor the [Account of the] Chariot in the presence of one person, unless he is a sage who understands on his own. Whoever contemplates four things, it would have been better for him if he had not come into the world: what is above, what is below, what before, what after. Whoever shows no concern for the glory of his Maker, it would have been better for him if he had not come into this world." See also *Bereshit Rabbah* 8:2: "Rabbi El'azar said in the name of Ben

are תלי תלים (*tillei tillim*), mounds and mounds.[101] Just like Rabban Yoḥanan son of Zakkai, who concerning the verse *His wife's name was Mehetabel* (Genesis 36:39) once rendered three hundred legal decisions, but he did not wish to divulge them—except to his students Rabbi El'azar son of Arakh [7a] and Rabbi Eli'ezer son of Hyrcanus, who engaged in the Account of the Chariot with him.[102]

Sira, 'About what is too great for you, do not inquire; what is too hard for you, do not investigate; what is too wondrous for you, know not; of what is hidden from you, do not ask! Contemplate what was permitted to you: you have no business with hidden things.'"

On the identity of Rabbi, see above, note 91.

101. **on every קוץ וקוץ (*qots va-qots*), jot and tittle...** Even though the Torah's secrets should not be revealed, this does not mean that they don't exist. Rather, the Torah is brimming with mysteries.

See BT *Menaḥot* 29b: "Rav Yehudah said in the name of Rav, 'When Moses ascended on high, he found the blessed Holy One engaged in affixing coronets to the letters. Moses said, "Master of the Universe, who stays Your hand?" He replied, "There will arise a man at the end of many generations, Akiva son of Yosef by name, who will expound upon each tittle mounds and mounds of laws."'" See also BT *Shabbat* 89a; *Tanḥuma, Bereshit* 1: "*His locks are wavy, black as a raven* (Song of Songs 5:11). What does it mean קווצותיו תלתלים (*qevutsotav taltalim*), *his locks are wavy*? On every קוץ וקוץ (*qots va-qots*), jot and tittle, תלי תלים (*tillei tillim*), mounds upon mounds, of *halakhot*." See also BT *Eruvin* 21b; *Zohar* 3:79b.

Cf. Origen, *Philocalia* 1:28, *Jeremiah Homily 39*: "Not a single tittle of the sacred Scriptures is without something of the wisdom of God."

102. ***His wife's name was Mehetabel...*** Elsewhere in the *Zohar*, this seemingly insignificant verse is expounded to reveal immense wisdom relating to the demonic realm. The subject of the verse is Hadar, last of the Edomite kings listed in Genesis 36, who are reinterpreted in Kabbalah as demonic archons. See Scholem, *Origins of the Kabbalah*, 296; and on this verse, *Zohar* 3:135b (*IR*), 142a (*IR*), 292a (*IZ*). Here, as in *Zohar* 1:145b, the verse's mystery is not revealed but is merely used to illustrate the existence of supernal mysteries hidden within the Torah's words.

Rabbi Yoḥanan's manifold interpretations of this verse are mentioned in Todros Abulafia, *Otsar ha-Kavod, Pesaḥim* 62b; David ben Judah he-Ḥasid, *Mar'ot ha-Ẓove'ot*, 177. For references to the "three hundred legal decisions" in the realms of impurity, magic, and witchcraft, see *Tosefta Sanhedrin* 11:5; BT *Sanhedrin* 68a, 106b; *Ḥagigah* 15b; *Avot de-Rabbi Natan* A, 25; *Kallah Rabbati* 6:4.

Rabbi El'azar son of Arakh was an outstanding student of Rabban Yoḥanan son of Zakkai, who engaged in speculation on the *merkavah* (the divine chariot). See M *Avot* 2:8; *Tosefta Ḥagigah* 2:1; JT *Ḥagigah* 2:1, 77a; BT *Ḥagigah* 14b; David Luria, *Shem ha-Eḥad Eli'ezer* (preface to *Pirqei de-Rabbi Eli'ezer*), n. 4.

Rabbi Eli'ezer ["the Great"] son of Hyrcanus was also a leading student of Rabban Yoḥanan. See M *Avot* 2:8; *Avot de-Rabbi Natan* A, 6; BT *Sukkah* 28a; BT *Bava Metsi'a* 69a–b; BT *Avodah Zarah* 16b–17a; *Bereshit Rabbah* 42:1; *Bemidbar Rabbah* 19:7; *Tanḥuma, Lekh Lekha* 10; *Pirqei de-Rabbi Eli'ezer* 1; David Luria, *Shem ha-Eḥad Eli'ezer* (preface to *Pirqei de-Rabbi Eli'ezer*).

This paragraph might be construed as the continuation of Rabbi's teaching.

Rabbi said, "Come and see what is written concerning Solomon: *He spoke three thousand proverbs, and his songs numbered one thousand and five* (1 Kings 5:12)—about every single statement [in the Torah] he would provide one thousand and five reasons! Now, if Solomon, who was but the servant of the blessed Holy One, could provide three thousand proverbs and one thousand and five reasons for every single statement, how much more so the blessed Holy One, who reveals *the deep and hidden* (Daniel 2:22), and who bestows wisdom and understanding, as is said: *For YHVH grants wisdom, knowledge, and understanding by His decree* (Proverbs 2:6)?!"[103]

Rabbi Levi said, "It is written: *How great are Your works, O YHVH, how very profound Your thoughts!* (Psalms 92:6). *How great are Your works, O YHVH*—the work of creation, for they are the works of the blessed Holy One. *How very profound Your thoughts*—mysteries of Torah."[104]

Rabbi Eli'ezer the Great says, "It is written: *YHVH gave Solomon wisdom as He promised him* (1 Kings 5:26), teaching that he grasped the fine points of Torah, but he did not fathom her depths. When he sought to fathom her, he said: *I said, 'I will be wise,' but she is beyond me* (Ecclesiastes 7:23)."[105]



Rabbi Dostai asked Rabbi Eli'ezer the Great, saying, "Rabbi, establish for me the mystery of this verse: *A perpetual burnt offering* העשויה (*ha-asuyah*), *instituted, on Mount Sinai as a fragrant odor, a fire offering to YHVH* (Numbers 28:6)."[106]

He said to him, "My son, by your life! It seems to me that you are not yet worthy to grasp it. No one has asked me about this except for Akiva my disciple, and the root of balsam is still in my hand!"[107]

103. **what is written concerning Solomon...** See *Shir ha-Shirim Rabbah* on 1:1: "Rabbi El'azar said, '*He spoke three thousand proverbs*—about every single statement [in the Torah]; *and his songs numbered one thousand and five*—one thousand and five reasons for every single statement.' The Rabbis say, '*He spoke three thousand proverbs*—on every single verse; *and his songs numbered one thousand and five*—one thousand and five reasons for every single proverb.'" See BT *Eruvin* 21b; *Zohar* 1:135a; 2:145a.

The full verse in Daniel reads: *He reveals deep and hidden things, knows what is in the darkness, and light dwells with Him.*

104. ***How very profound Your thoughts...*** The mysteries of Torah are God's thoughts.

105. **but he did not fathom her depths...** See BT *Yoma* 14a; *Zohar* 1:135a.

106. **Rabbi Dostai . . .** Some of the manuscripts read Rav Ḥisda or Rabbi Ḥasdai.

107. **No one has asked me...except for Akiva my disciple...** According to BT *Ḥagigah* 6b, Rabbi El'azar and Rabbi Akiva disagreed about the meaning of the verse. The key word is העשויה (*ha-asuyah*), which can mean either "instituted" or more literally "done," i.e., offered up: "*A perpetual burnt offering* העשויה (*ha-asuyah*), *instituted* [or: *done*], *on Mount Sinai.* Rabbi El'azar said, 'The manner of its offering was enjoined at Sinai, but it was not actually offered up.' Rabbi Akiva said, 'It was offered up and was never discontinued.'"

The *Zohar* appears to have conflated the

Rabbi Akiva heard. He said, "Since the flowers have blossomed, I have eaten the roots!"[108]

He said to him, "Akiva, Akiva, you will be prepared as a fragrant odor to YHVH, and still the sweet savor shall remain."[109]

One day they were walking on the way. He asked him, "How then did you eat the roots as you said?"

He replied, "Rabbi, once you told me the mystery, I fathomed its essence."

He told him how.

He said to him, "You fathomed and ate, but still the sweet savor remains!"[110]

At that time he revealed to him forty mysteries of Torah.

While they were walking they saw a spring of water; they sat there. Rabbi Eli'ezer said to him, "Akiva, come and I will show you a fountain of water, and when the waters issue they are clear and flowing, as is written: *a well of living waters, flowing from Lebanon* (Songs of Songs 4:15)."[111]

Concerning that verse, he revealed to him the speech of ministering angels, the speech of the stars and constellations, knowledge of the windows of the sun in its seasons and times, the speech of palm trees and birds, the speech of spirits, and knowledge of calendric calculations and intercalations.[112]



figure of Rabbi El'azar with Rabbi Eli'ezer the Great, who was Rabbi Akiva's teacher. In BT *Sanhedrin* 68a, while on his deathbed, Rabbi Eli'ezer laments that no one asked him about certain mysterious laws aside from Rabbi Akiva.

In saying "the root of balsam is still in my hand," Rabbi Eli'ezer is suggesting that the deep mystery of the verse remains with him.

108. **I have eaten the roots** Rabbi Akiva boldly claims that he has fathomed the mystery.

109. **you will be prepared as a fragrant odor...** Not only does Rabbi Eli'ezer reject Rabbi Akiva's claim, but also he uses the verse from Numbers to predict his student's untimely death. See BT *Sanhedrin* 68a: "yours shall be crueller than theirs." On Rabbi Akiva's martyrdom, see JT *Berakhot* 9:5, 14b; BT *Berakhot* 61b; BT *Menaḥot* 29b; *Zohar* 1:98b (*MhN*).

"Sweet savor" renders בליעת המתוק (*beli'at ha-matoq*), literally, "the swallowing of the sweet."

110. **still the sweet savor remains** Again, the mystery remains with the teacher.

111. **fountain of water...** In rabbinic literature, Torah is frequently compared to flowing water, and in the *Zohar* springs are the locus of many stories. See *Mekhilta, Vayassa* 1; BT *Bava Qamma* 82a; BT *Horayot* 12a; *Shir ha-Shirim Rabbah* on 1:2.

According to *Pirqei de-Rabbi Eli'ezer* 2, Rabbi Eli'ezer's teachings flow like a bubbling spring: "[Rabbi Yoḥanan] said to him [Rabbi Eli'ezer], 'I will tell you a parable. To what can you be compared? To this fountain, which is bubbling and sending forth its waters, and it is able to effect a discharge more powerful than what it takes in. Similarly, you are able to speak words of Torah in excess of what Moses received at Sinai.'"

On this verse from the Song of Songs, see *ZḤ* 15b (*MhN*), page 140.

112. **the speech of ministering angels...** See BT *Sukkah* 28a: "They said of Rabban Yoḥanan son of Zakkai that he did not leave [unstudied] Scripture, Mishnah, Gemara,

At that moment Rabbi Akiva wept.

He asked, "Why are you crying?"

He replied, "Woe to the generation that will remain orphaned of you!"[113]

He said, "Do not say that, but rather 'Woe to the generation that will be orphaned without a father—with neither guiding sage nor contemplative student!' Days shall arrive when the entire generation will be brazen and barefaced, and Torah will be forgotten, with none to ask and none to inquire, while he who arouses his heart in Torah *will be despised and shunned by men* (Isaiah 53:3). Woe to that generation when it arises!"[114]

He said to him, "That generation endures solely through the breath of children—and only when they are young; because when they are older, Torah is forgotten from among them."[115]

As Rabbi Yehudah said: "What is the meaning of the verse *For this youth I prayed* (1 Samuel 1:27)? She should have said, 'For this son I prayed!' Well, Hannah said, 'May it be Your will that when he grows up, he will devote himself to the service of the Omnipresent, like now when he is a youth.'"[116]



Everyone who merits in his old age to be as in his youth attains the degree of Samuel the Prophet, as is written: *A little robe would his mother make him*

Halakhah, Aggadah; fine points of the Torah, fine points of the Scribes, a fortiori inferences, analogies; calendric computations; *gimatriyyas*; the speech of the ministering angels, the speech of spirits, and the speech of palm-trees; fullers' parables and fox fables; great matters or small matters."

On Rabbi Akiva's knowledge of intercalations, see BT *Berakhot* 63a; *Sanhedrin* 12a.

113. **orphaned of you** See Rabbi Akiva's exclamation at the death of Rabbi Eli'ezer son of Hyrcanus in *Avot de-Rabbi Natan* A, 25: "Woe unto me, my master, because of you! Woe unto me, my teacher, because of you! For you have left the whole generation orphaned!" Cf. BT *Ḥagigah* 3b; *Bemidbar Rabbah* 14:4. See *Zohar* 1:99a (*MhN*); *Zohar* 2:23a, 68a; 3:236a; *ZḤ* 19c (*MhN*).

Some of the manuscripts and printed editions (V12, OM1, Salonika) read: "Woe to the generation that will be thirsty for you!"

114. **Days shall arrive...** See BT *Sotah* 49a–b: "Rabbi Eli'ezer the Great says, 'From the day the Temple was destroyed, the sages began to be like schoolteachers, schoolteachers like synagogue attendants, synagogue attendants like common people, and the common people became more and more debased; and there was no one to ask, none to inquire.... In the footsteps of the Messiah, brazenness will increase....'" See also BT *Sanhedrin* 97a.

See BT *Shabbat* 138b: "Our Rabbis taught: When our Masters entered the vineyard at Yavneh they said, 'The Torah is destined to be forgotten in Israel....' Cf. *Zohar* 3:58a.

115. **breath of children...** See BT *Shabbat* 119b: "Resh Lakish said in the name of Rabbi Yehudah the Patriarch, 'The world endures only for the sake of the breath of children in the house of study.'" See *Zohar* 1:1b, 47a, 146b (*ST*); 2:39a; 3:17b.

116. ***For this youth I prayed...*** The context is the birth of the prophet Samuel. Why did his mother say that she had prayed for a *youth* rather than a *son* (which would have

והעלתה לו (*ve-ha'altah lo*), *and bring it up to him, year after year* (ibid. 2:19). Now, do you really believe it was so? Rather, his righteousness and merit continually grew with him by virtue of his mother's prayer. According to Rabbi Yehudah, it was an actual robe.[117]

Rabbi said, "What is the meaning of the verse *Before a gray head you shall rise;* והדרת פני זקן (*ve-hadarta penei zaqen*), *and you shall show deference to the old* (Leviticus 19:32)?"[118]

Rabbi explained, "Herein is moral guidance for the young. Namely, *Before a gray head you shall rise*—before you become a gray head [7d] and ascend to old age, *you shall rise* to be good; and when you strive to be good in your youth, eventually והדרת פני זקן (*ve-hadarta penei zaqen*), *you will be adorned in old age.* The end of the verse proves that it is referring to this, as indicated by what is written: *you shall fear your God* (ibid.)."[119]

Rabbi Yitsḥak said, "The beginning of the entire world and its formation were
38 solely for the sake of awe, that a person will possess awe of heaven, and awe for
creatures. As is written: בראשית (*Be-reshit*), *In the beginning, God created heaven* (Genesis 1:1)—to be in awe of heaven; *and earth* (ibid.)—to be in awe of the creatures. Additionally, it teaches that the entire world was created solely on account of awe, called ראשית (*reshit*), *beginning*, as is said: ראשית (*Reshit*), *The beginning of, wisdom is awe of YHVH* (Psalms 111:10), and that is why it is written בראשית (*Be-reshit*), *on account of awe*."[120]

been the natural way for a mother to refer to her child)? Cf. *ZḤ* 11b (*MhN*).

117. ***A little robe would his mother make him...*** The proof-text from Samuel suggests that because he remained in his old age as he was when a youth, a little robe continued to suffice. Yet that literal meaning is rejected in favor of a homiletic interpretation suggesting that it was his mother's prayer that raised him (*ve-ha'altah lo*) in righteousness. Rabbi Yehudah, however, upholds the verse's simple sense.

118. **Rabbi...** On his identity, see above, note 91.

119. **והדרת פני זקן (*ve-hadarta penei zaqen*), *you will be adorned in old age...*** In its simple sense, the verse from Leviticus reads: *Before a gray head you shall rise; and show deference to the old.* Reading *ve-hadarta*, *and show deference to*, in another of its meanings (as in Isaiah 63:1)—as *you will be adorned* (that is, treated with esteem)—Rabbi interprets the second clause as the consequence of the first. The end of the verse (*you shall fear your God*) confirms that the verse is conveying moral guidance for the young: when you fear God in your youth, you will be esteemed in your old age.

See BT *Sukkah* 53a: "Our Rabbis have taught:... Happy our youth that has not disgraced our old age." See *Zohar* 3:87b. See also David ben Abraham Maimuni (the grandson of Maimonides), *Midrash David*, 14.

120. **solely on account of awe...** See above, note 77. Awe of creatures is manifested by a concern for their welfare.

*God said, "Let there be light." And there was light* (Genesis 1:3).

Rabbi Ḥiyya opened, "*Light is sown for the righteous, joy for the upright in heart* (Psalms 97:11). The blessed Holy One gazed and foresaw that the world could not endure without the foundation. What is the foundation upon which the world stands? It is the righteous one, as is said: וצדיק יסוד עולם (*ve-tsaddiq yesod olam*), *the righteous one is the foundation of the world* (Proverbs 10:25). This is the first foundation that the blessed Holy One created in His world, for it is called light—as is said: *Light is sown for the righteous* (Psalms 97:11), and similarly as is written: *God saw the light, that it was good* (Genesis 1:4). Here it says כי טוב (*ki tov*), *that it was good*, and later it says *Say of the righteous one* כי טוב (*ki tov*), *that he is good* (Isaiah 3:10)."[121]

Rabbi says, "This light is the light of the angels, created first before the whole world. Now, you might say, 'But look, we see that heaven and earth were created first!' This poses no difficulty. For that which was said above until now merely introduces the story, and this '*Let there be*' is the first; from here began 39
all the creations."[122]

Rabbi Yehudah says, "This is the light of the Throne itself—and from this light all the other creations were created. From it the heavens were created; but the Throne was created previously, as is said: *Throne of Glory, set on high from the first* (Jeremiah 17:12)."[123]

121. ***the righteous one is the foundation of the world...*** See BT *Ḥagigah* 12b: "Rabbi El'azar son of Shammu'a says, '[The world stands] on a single pillar named Righteous One, as is said: *The righteous one is the foundation of the world.*'" In its simple sense, the verse means *a righteous one is an everlasting foundation*. See also BT *Yoma* 38b.

In the main body of the *Zohar*, Righteous One symbolizes the *sefirah Yesod*. Here, its correlate is the primal light.

See BT *Ḥagigah* 12a: "Rabbi El'azar said, 'With the light created by the blessed Holy One on the first day, one could gaze and see from one end of the universe to the other. When the blessed Holy One foresaw the corrupt deeds of the generation of the Flood and the generation of the Dispersion [due to the Tower of Babel], He immediately hid it from them, as is written: *The light of the wicked is withheld* (Job 38:15). For whom did He hide it? For the righteous in the time to come, as is said: *God saw that the light was good*, and *good* can only mean the righteous one, as is said: *Say of the righteous one that he is good* (Isaiah 3:10).'" See also *Shemot Rabbah* 35:1; *Zohar* 1:33a; *ZḤ* 26b (*MhN*).

The name of the rabbi expounding this homily varies in the manuscripts. I have followed the Salonika and Venice printed editions. Alternatives include: Rabbi Bo, Rabbi Abba, Rabbi Yitsḥak, and Rabbi.

122. **merely introduces the story...** The opening verse of the Torah merely introduces the account of creation in a general manner; the first actual creative act is the utterance *Let there be light*, referring to the angelic light. See above, *ZḤ* 4a (*MhN*), page 16. In his earliest known work, *Or Zaru'a*, 261, Moses de León presents a nearly identical interpretation.

123. **the light of the Throne itself...** The light of the angels is also the divine throne. On this throne, see *Bereshit Rabbah*

Rabbi Eli'ezer the Great says, "The light of the angels was created first, as is written: *God saw that the light was good, and God separated the light from the darkness* (Genesis 1:4). Namely, the blessed Holy One established a separation between this light and the darkness—which is this world; and it is the heavens that separate between this world and the light of the angels, separating between the light and the darkness."[124]

Rabban Yoḥanan son of Zakkai says, "The blessed Holy One gave dominion to the angels over the heavens, and the heavens over the earth, but they are all dependent on His Throne (may His Name be praised), teaching *that height above height keeps guard* (Ecclesiastes 5:7)."[125]

*Let there be light.*

Rabbi Alexandrai says, "One who sees the stars in their course is required to make a blessing. What does he bless? 'Blessed is He who arranges the stars in the firmament.' If he sees one star, he does not bless; two, he blesses. When? When night falls, they bless: 'Blessed is He who brings on evenings.'"[126]

40 Rabbi says, "Those small hamlets whose custom is to flee while it is still day—out of fear of animals—bless: 'Who guards His people Israel forever,' and accordingly they established it for every evening prayer."[127]

1:4; *Pirqei de-Rabbi Eli'ezer* 3; *Zohar* 1:113a (*MhN*); *ZḤ* 2d (*MhN*), 15b (*MhN*). In *Or Zaru'a* 271–72, the Throne indicates Metatron, so perhaps Rabbi Yehudah intends to differentiate between Metatron and the other angels.

Cf. Solomon Ibn Gabirol, *Keter Malkhut*, Canto 26: "Who can approach Your dwelling place, in your raising over the sphere of Intellect the Throne of Glory—in which is the abode of mystery and majesty, the secret and foundation [i.e., form and matter], where the mind reaches and yields?"

124. ***God separated the light from the darkness...*** Compared to the angelic light, our world is darkness. The heavens separate the two realms.

125. **angels over the heavens, and the heavens over the earth...** On this fourfold hierarchy outside of the godhead—Throne, angels, heaven, and earth—see *ZḤ* 16c (*MhN*), page 158.

In place of "dependent on His Throne," some manuscripts (O2, P3, M7) read "dependent on His power."

126. **One who sees the stars in their course...** The blessing "who arranges the stars in the firmament" is taken from the opening of the *Ma'ariv* (Evening) prayer, which can be recited when night falls. See Maimonides, *Mishneh Torah, Hilkhot Tefillah*, 3:6; *ZḤ* 17d (*MhN*), page 181. See also Ta-Shma, *Ha-Nigleh she-ba-Nistar*, 118, n. 40.

According to the Talmud (BT *Berakhot* 59b), a different blessing is recited: "Our Rabbis taught: One who sees the sun at its turning point, the moon in its power, the planets in their orbits [or: the stars in their course], and the signs of the zodiac in their orderly progress, should say: Blessed be He who has wrought the work of creation."

127. **out of fear of animals—bless . . .** The blessing "who guards His people Israel forever" is the second blessing recited after the *Shema* in the weekday evening liturgy. It is a prayer for protection from the menacing

Rabbi El'azar son of Rabbi Shim'on was traveling to see Rabbi Yose son of Rabbi Shim'on son of Lekonya, his father-in-law. Near the village, night dusked. He said to Rabbi Yose, who was traveling with him, "Do you see those shining stars?"[128]

He replied, "I do see. It is a comet. I have been gazing at it for a long time, but in all my days I have never been told anything about it."[129]

He said to him, "I have heard two matters. One: that everything the blessed Holy One made among the heavens—the stars and constellations—possesses knowledge and intelligence, and they all perform the mission of the blessed Holy One; and that star to which you referred: do not say, or for a moment think, that it's unique. Rather, there are many—for you can see one on this side and one on the other, and sometimes [8a] all of them at once. I heard from my father that there are seven, and when the time arrives for each of them to utter song, from the immense joy they possess they radiate their splendor—soaring and uttering song. The other matter: that these seven stars do not travel or journey from their place except at the moment that the Master of the Universe summons one of them to illuminate in the place that He desires, as is written: *He calls them each by name* (Isaiah 40:26); and as they soar, they radiate their splendor that travels with them."[130]



forces of the night. See *Zohar* 1:48a; 2:130a, where its recitation is associated with protection from demonic forces. See JT *Berakhot* 1:1, 2a: "[people in] small hamlets who usually leave the roads when there is still some daylight, because they are afraid of wild beasts."

On the identity of "Rabbi," see above, note 91.

128. **Rabbi Yose son of Rabbi Shim'on son of Lekonya...** According to rabbinic tradition, Rabbi El'azar's father-in-law was named Rabbi Shim'on son of Yose son of Lekonya. The *Zohar* consistently switches father and son, transforming Shim'on son of Yose into Yose son of Shim'on. See *Pesiqta de-Rav Kahana* 11:20; JT *Ma'aserot* 3:8, 50d; *Shir ha-Shirim Rabbah* on 4:11; *Devarim Rabbah* 7:11; *Seder ha-Dorot*, s.v. *Shim'on ben Yose ben Lekonya*; *Zohar* 1:5a, 61b; 3:84b, 188a, 193a; *ZḤ* 10d, 14a, 20d, 22c (last four *MhN*).

In BT *Bava Metsi'a* 85a, the name of Rabbi El'azar's brother-in-law is given as Rabbi Shim'on son of Issi (Yose) son of Lekonya, which would make Yose his father-in-law, as in the *Zohar*—but nowhere in rabbinic literature is he named Yose son of Shim'on.

"Dusked" renders the verb רמש (*remash*), an apparently Zoharic coinage based on רמשא (*ramsha*), "evening." See *Zohar* 1:34b; 2:36b, 171a, 173a, 188a, 208a; 3:21a–b, 52a, 113b, 149a–b, 166b; *ZḤ* 25d, 28b (both *MhN*).

129. **comet...** כוכבא דשרביטא (*Kokheva de-sharvita*), "Star of a scepter," echoes the rabbinic term *kokheva de-shaveit*, "a star that flies," a comet. See BT *Berakhot* 58b; *Zohar* 1:223b; 2:171b; 3:233a.

130. **possesses knowledge and intelligence...** According to Maimonides, *Mishneh Torah, Hilkhot Yesodei ha-Torah* 3:9: "All the stars and spheres possess a soul, knowledge, and intellect. They are alive and stand in recognition of the One who spoke and the world was." See also idem, *Guide of the Perplexed* 2:5.

The full verse in Isaiah reads: *Lift your eyes on high and see: Who created these? He who brings forth their array by number and calls them each by name. Because of His great*

When they reached his father-in-law's house, he was not there. When he arrived, he said, "You are here, and I have just come from observing a certain star that was soaring, fulfilling the will of its Master!"

He asked him, "Which one?"

He replied, "A comet. And I saw one of them soaring according to the command of its Master."

They sat there for thirty days.[131]

Afterward, when the light appeared, they rose early to leave, and his father-in-law accompanied him for half a mile. His father-in-law blessed him, saying, "This is the hour when the blessing of the righteous is fulfilled. How do we know? As is written: *God saw the light, that it was good* (Genesis 1:4). Here is written *that it was good*, and there is written *that it was good in the eyes of* YHVH *to bless Israel* (Numbers 24:1)."[132]



He said to him, "Even the blessing of an ordinary person is fulfilled at this hour, for the heavens, stars, and angels utter song. I also heard from my father that an extra blessing is added to him—namely delight—because at that hour the heavens utter: *He is like a groom coming forth from his canopy* (Psalms 19:6). Just as a groom coming forth rejoices, so one who sets forth on a journey at that hour rejoices."[133]

*might and vast power, not one fails to appear.* Cf. *Zohar* 1:2a; 2:171b.

On the song of the sun, see Scholem, "Parashah Ḥadashah," 437–38 (Addendum 1 in this volume); on the song of the stars, *ZḤ* 76c (*MhN, Rut*).

131. **thirty days** See *ZḤ* 15d (*MhN*). Some of the manuscripts read "three days."

132. **accompanied him for half a mile...** According to Rav Sheshet (BT *Sotah* 46b), one should escort his teacher the distance of a parasang. A distinguished teacher, however, is to be escorted for three parasangs. (The Persian parasang equals about 3.5 modern miles.) The term here in the *Zohar* is *mil* (miles) and refers to the Roman mile, slightly shorter than the modern mile. See *Pesiqta de-Rav Kahana* 18:5; *Bereshit Rabbah* 32:10; *Zohar* 1:51a, 87a, 96b, 150b, 217a; 2:164a, 187a; 3:8b; *ZḤ* 15a–b (*MhN*).

On the time of day "when the blessing of the righteous is fulfilled," see *Mekhilta, Beshallaḥ* 5: "*At the morning watch* (Exodus 14:24)—you find that the prayers of the righteous are heeded in the morning."

Throughout the *Zohar*, morning is associated with the divine quality of *ḥesed*, love. See *Zohar* 1:182b, 189a, 203a–b, 247b; 2:21a–b (*MhN*), 63a, 81a; 3:63a, 64b, 204a–b, 233a, 242a.

On the verse from Numbers, see *Zohar* 1:46a.

133. **heavens, stars, and angels utter song...** The appearance of the morning is accompanied by celestial song—in particular, Psalms 19—and it is this concurrence that gives blessings additional potency; see above, *ZḤ* 6a (*MhN*).

The full verse in Psalms reads: "*He is like a groom coming forth from his canopy, rejoicing like a hero running his* ארח (*oraḥ*), *course.*"

In setting forth (*la-derekh*), "on the way," in the morning, one enjoys an additional feeling of delight. On morning as an auspicious time to set out, see *Zohar* 3:22b; *ZḤ* 13b (*MhN*).

*God said, "Let there be light."*

We have learned there: Rabbi Yose said, "What is the meaning of the verse *An oracle of Dumah: One calls to me from Seir, 'Watchman, what of the night? Watchman, what of the night?'* (Isaiah 21:11). This word accords with what Rabbi Yoḥanan said: 'All the exiles in which Israel were exiled from their land were revealed to all. But the fourth exile has never been revealed. Which is the fourth exile? That of Seir, which is Esau, as is written: *Esau settled in Mount Seir* (Genesis 36:8).'"[134]

Rabbi said, "Why was his name *Seir*? On account of the severity and intensity of the heavy yoke they place upon Israel; שעיר (*Seir*) is numerically equivalent to תקף (*toqef*), severity. This exile in which Israel dwells is משא דומה (*massa dumah*), a burden of silence, that is, in secrecy, something undisclosed from heart to mouth, as is said: *For the day of vengeance is in My heart* (Isaiah 63:4)."[135]

Rabbi Yitsḥak opened, "*He buried him in the valley in the land of Moab, opposite Beth Peor* (Deuteronomy 34:6). It is also written: *No one knows his*



134. ***An oracle of Dumah: One calls to me from Seir...*** This obscure oracle is addressed to Dumah, which may be a poetic form of the name Edom, which in turn refers to a biblical-era nation located southeast of Judah and also known as Seir. In rabbinic literature, the names Edom and Seir represent Rome; in medieval literature, they represent Christianity. This biblical passage is understood as conveying Israel's anguished cry from the darkness of exile, and God's response.

See JT *Ta'anit* 1:1, 64a; BT *Sanhedrin* 94a; Rashi and Radak on Isaiah 21:11; *Zohar* 1:144a; 2:38b, 130b–131a; 3:22a.

The passage in Isaiah (21:11–12) reads: משא (*Massa*), *An oracle of, Dumah. One calls to me from Seir: "Watchman, what of the night? Watchman, what of the night?" The watchman said, "Morning came* [or: *is coming*], *and also night. If you would inquire, inquire. Return, come!"*

The noun *massa*, which derives from the verbal root נשא (*ns'*), "to carry, lift, raise," can mean "burden" (that which is carried), or "utterance, pronouncement, oracle" (raising of the voice).

Unlike the first three exiles, whose durations were pre-ordained, the duration of the fourth exile (namely the Roman exile that began in 70 CE and had lasted already more than a millennium in the *Zohar*'s day) has not been revealed. See also *Zohar* 3:6a; *ZḤ* 23c–d (*MhN*), 48a.

Mention of the four exiles may allude to the four kingdoms in Daniel's vision (chapters 7 and 8), which are generally correlated with Babylon, Media, Greece, and Rome. See *Bereshit Rabbah* 2:4; 44:17; *Leqaḥ Tov* on Exodus 3:14; Naḥmanides on Genesis 15:12, 47:28; cf. *Vayiqra Rabbah* 29:2; *Pesiqta de-Rav Kahana* 23:2; *Tanḥuma, Vayetse* 2; *Pirqei de-Rabbi Eli'ezer* 35. Alternatively, the *Zohar* may understand the four exiles as signifying Egypt, Babylon, Greece, and Rome. The Egyptian exile lasted 430 years (or 210, according to the Rabbis), the Babylonian exile 70 years, and the Greek "exile"—although there is no precise traditional figure for its duration (though Daniel 8:14 does mention an enigmatic figure of 2300 days)—came to an end with the Maccabean uprising and establishment of the Hasmonean dynasty.

135. **משא דומה (*massa dumah*), a burden of silence...** Now the word *dumah* is construed as its homonym, meaning "silence." Its duration unrevealed, the exile of Edom is therefore an oracle of silence. It is also a

*burial place to this day* (ibid.). The blessed Holy One said, 'Those who calculate messianic ends are fools! It is something I have never divulged, as is said: *For the day of vengeance is in My heart* (Isaiah 63:4)—undisclosed from heart to mouth, yet they endeavor to calculate end times![136]

"'Come and see! Concerning the burial place of My servant Moses, I have written and indicated three signs to the world's generations: *in the valley*; *in the land of Moab*; *opposite Beth Peor*, yet still they do not know his burial place, as is written: *No one knows his burial place* (Deuteronomy 34:6)! How then can they utter such lies and nonsense before Me about something I have neither divulged nor indicated?!'[137]

"As is written: *An oracle of Dumah: One calls to me because of Seir* (Isaiah 21:11)—this is Israel, who call out to the blessed Holy One because of the heavy yoke of the children of Seir. What do they say? '*Watchman, what of the night?*' (ibid.). Namely, 'Master of the World! You, O YHVH, are the watchman of Israel. We remain in this exile—which is like night. Tell us! What of the night? What shall become of this night? When will You bring us out?'[138]



"Come and see what is written afterward: *The watchman said, 'Morning came, and also night'* (ibid., 12). The blessed Holy One, who is the watchman of Israel,

"burden of silence" as long as the Jewish people bear the yoke of exile.

שעיר (*Seir*) is numerologically equivalent to תקף (*toqef*), "severity"—both have the numerical value of 580.

See BT *Sanhedrin* 99a: "*For the day of vengeance is in My heart, and the year of My redemption is come* (Isaiah 63:4). What is meant by *the day of vengeance is in My heart*? Rabbi Yoḥanan said, 'I have revealed it to My heart, but not to My limbs.'" See also *Midrash Tehillim* 9:2.

On the identity of "Rabbi," see above, note 91.

136. **Those who calculate messianic ends are fools!...** See BT *Sanhedrin* 97b: "Rabbi Shemu'el son of Naḥmani said in the name of Rabbi Yonatan, 'Blasted be the bones of those who calculate end times! For they would say: Since the predetermined time has arrived and yet he [that is, the Messiah] hasn't come, he will never come.'" See Maimonides, *Mishneh Torah, Hilkhot Melakhim* 12:2; *Zohar* 1:118a.

137. **How then can they utter such lies...** Even with numerous indications, Moses' burial place remains unknown. How much more so the messianic end, whose timing has not even been hinted! On Moses' burial place, see BT *Sotah* 13b–14a: "*He buried him in the valley in the land of Moab, opposite Beth Peor* (Deuteronomy 34:6). Rabbi Berekhiah said, 'A sign within a sign—and even so: *No one know his burial place* (ibid.).'" See also *Zohar* 2:89a, 157a–b.

138. ***Watchman, what of the night?*** ... In its biblical context, the identity of the one calling from Seir is not specified. Now the meaning is made apparent: it is Israel calling from the night of exile. On Israel's exile as night, see *Shir ha-Shirim Rabbah* on 3:1; *Zohar* 1:170a; 2:163b.

In its simple sense, the clause from Isaiah reads: *One calls to me from Seir*. Here, the prefixed preposition *mi-*, "from," is being construed not in a locational sense, but as the marker of the situation's cause, i.e., "because of"—as, for example, in Deuteronomy 7:7.

said, '*Morning came*—I have brought and led you out from exile, but you were not worthy to abide in morning. *And also night*—I brought you the night and darkened you in the pit of this exile, which is night. *If you would inquire, inquire* (ibid.)—if you seek to know when the time of your redemption shall be, and when you will return to your land, שובו (*shuvu*), *return, come* (ibid.)—return in *teshuvah* and immediately you will come. As Rabbi Yehudah said: 'The end of exile depends solely on *teshuvah*, as is said: *Today—if you would heed His voice* (Psalms 95:7).'[139] [8d]

"Since the world was created, this sublime hint was intimated in concealed mystery, as is said: *God said, 'Let there be light.' And there was light* (Genesis 1:3); namely let there be רז (*raz*), *mystery*—for *raz* and אור (*or*), *light*, are a single matter. *God saw* (ibid., 4)—this mystery; *that it was good* (ibid.)—to abide in mystery and secrecy, so that it not be revealed to anyone; for should it be revealed, many worthless folk from among our people would meet their ruin.[140]

"And because it was to be in mystery and secrecy, God separated the light from the darkness—His nation (which is the light) from the nations (which are the darkness), as is said: *The wicked are like darkness* (1 Samuel 2:9), and similarly: *they go about in darkness* (Psalms 82:5)."[141]



139. ***'Morning came, and also night'...*** The children of Israel were redeemed from the exile of Babylon and enjoyed the morning of redemption. Unworthy, they were cast yet again into the night of exile, i.e., the Roman exile.

On the relationship between the exile's end and Israel's repentance, see BT *Sanhedrin* 97b: "Rav said, 'All the predestined dates [for redemption] have passed, and the matter [now] depends solely on repentance and good deeds.'" See *Zohar* 1:117b; 2:188b; *ZḤ* 23c (*MhN*).

See also BT *Sanhedrin* 98a: "Rabbi Yehoshu'a son of Levi met Elijah, who was standing by the entrance of Rabbi Shim'on son of Yoḥai's cave. [He asked him], 'When will the Messiah come?' He replied, 'Go and ask him himself!'... He went to him and greeted him, saying, 'Peace upon you, Master and Teacher!' He replied, 'Peace upon you, son of Levi!' He asked him, 'When will the Master come?' He replied, 'Today!' He returned to Elijah, who asked him, 'What did he say to you?'... He replied, 'He lied to me, for he said that he'd come today, but he hasn't!' He [Elijah] answered him, 'This is what he said to you: *Today—if you would heed His voice* (Psalms 95:7).'"

140. **רז (*raz*), *mystery*... and אור (*or*), *light*, are a single matter...** Both words have the numerical value of 207. See also *Zohar* 1:140a (*MhN*). The verse from Genesis, *Let there be light*, is now read as *Let there be a mystery*, i.e., may the messianic end remain concealed. The next verse, *God saw that the light was good*, is also reinterpreted to mean *God saw that the mystery was good*, i.e., that it was fitting that the messianic end not be revealed—for were the distant end time to be revealed, many would meanwhile abandon their faith in despair. See above, note 136.

141. **God separated... His nation (which is the light)...** Because the exile is protracted and its end unknown, God separated the Jews from the other nations, thus ensuring the Jews' continual survival.

*God called the light Day* (Genesis 1:5).

Rabbi said, "This is the day of redemption, as is said: *Lo, a day of YHVH is coming* (Zechariah 14:1)—the day of the End."[142]

Rabbi Yose son of Ḥalafta was sitting in the presence of Rabbi Yitsḥak. He asked him, "Has my master heard something about why the day of the Messiah has been prolonged from this exile?"

He replied, "It has been prolonged solely because of neglect of Torah. For so I have heard from Rav Hamnuna Sava:[143] 'Israel were exiled with three exiles, and they returned by the merit of the three patriarchs. But from the fourth exile they will return by the merit of Moses.'

"Come, and I will show you that Israel were exiled solely because of neglect of Torah, as is said: *YHVH said, 'Because they have forsaken My Torah'* (Jeremiah 9:12). The blessed Holy One said, 'In the first exiles, they returned by the merit of Abraham, Isaac, and Jacob. Now they have sinned with the Torah that I gave to Moses, which is called by his name, as is said: *Remember the Torah of My servant Moses* (Malachi 3:22). When they repent and engage in his Torah, by Moses' merit I shall redeem them.'[144]



"Therefore it is said in the Torah: *Torah did Moses command us* (Deuteronomy 33:4)—to observe her and engage in her. If not: מורשה (*morashah*) *for the assembly of Jacob* (ibid.). מורשה (*Morashah*)—poverty, as is said: *YHVH* מוריש (*morish*), *makes poor, and makes rich* (1 Samuel 2:7), teaching that poverty comes upon the children of Jacob only because they do not engage in the commandments of Torah."[145]

142. **Rabbi . . .** On his identity, see above, note 91.

143. **Rav Hamnuna Sava . . .** Rav Hamnuna the Elder, a Babylonian teacher who lived in the third century. In the main body of the *Zohar*, he attains mythical status, appearing to the Companions at first as a donkey driver. See 1:6a, 240a, 250a; 2:88a, 124a, 136b; 3:87b, 103b, 145b (*IR*).

144. **exiled solely because of neglect of Torah . . .** See JT *Ḥagigah* 1:7, 76c; BT *Nedarim* 81a; *Zohar* 1:185a; 2:58a–b; *ZḤ* 70d (*Shir ha-Shirim*). On return to the land as conditional on Torah study, see *Zohar* 3:270a; cf. *Vayiqra Rabbah* 7:3.

On returning through the merit of the patriarchs, see Leviticus 26:41–42: *I, for My part, will come in encounter against them and bring them into the land of their enemies; and then shall their uncircumcised heart be humbled, and then shall they expiate their guilt. Then I will remember My covenant with Jacob and also My covenant with Isaac and also My covenant with Abraham I will remember, and the land I will remember.*

145. **If not: מורשה (*morashah*) *for the assembly of Jacob* . . .** In its simple sense, the verse in Deuteronomy reads: *Torah did Moses command us, a heritage for the assembly of Jacob.* Construing *morashah* as "poverty" based on the cited verse in Samuel, Rabbi Yitsḥak reads the second clause as a consequence of failure to fulfill the first.

Rabbi Ḥizkiyah said, "I was in the regions of the Arabs and I saw men who used to conceal themselves among cliffs—in caves among the mountains—but every Sabbath eve they would return to their homes.

"I inquired of them, 'What is this that you do?'

"They replied, 'We are hermits, and we engage in Torah every single day. Sometimes we eat only wild herbs.'[146]

"I asked them, 'With what are you nourished at other times?'

"They replied, 'In the desert we find trees sprouting acorns and we eat them. When the teaching illuminates us, in great joy some of us slip away, cook them, and we eat. Such a day is reckoned by us as especially good. When the trees do not sprout, we eat whatever herbs we can find; we cook them and we eat.'[147]

"I said to them, 'May my share be with you in the world that is coming! Happy are you in this world, and it will be well with you in the world to come! Now I know that you will not be ashamed when Moses comes to demand justice for Torah.'[148]

47

146. **hermits . . .** פרישי עלמא (*prishei alma*). The word *prishut* connotes seclusion and asceticism, i.e., people who have withdrawn from or forsaken the world. This is one of two accounts in the *Zohar* extolling the life of hermits. The other is 2:183b–184a, where Rabbi Shim'on encounters *prishei midbara*, hermits of the desert. See also *Zohar* 3:56b, 149b–150a. According to Tishby (*Wisdom of the Zohar*, 3:1331, 1335 n. 16), the author altered the original "Arab ascetics" into Jewish ascetics living among the Arabs.

Jewish sources usually discouraged extreme asceticism. See Maimonides, *Shemonah Peraqim* 4: "The perfect law . . . aims at man's following the path of moderation in accordance with the dictates of nature, eating, drinking, enjoying legitimate sexual intercourse—all in moderation—and living among people in honesty and uprightness, but not dwelling in the wilderness or in the mountains, or clothing oneself in garments of hair and wool, or afflicting the body." But some authors (for example, Baḥya Ibn Paquda, *Ḥovot ha-Levavot, Sha'ar ha-Prishut*) did sympathize with the elect who secluded themselves from society.

According to BT *Ketubbot* 62b, the disciples of the wise must return to their wives every Sabbath eve to fulfill the commandment of conjugal rights.

147. **we eat whatever herbs we can find . . .** The description here is very similar to Baḥya Ibn Paquda's account (*Sha'ar ha-Prishut*, chapter 3) of the most extreme form of ascetics, who abandon civilization for the desert, wastelands, or high mountains—eating whatever they find among the wild herbs and trees.

148. **you will not be ashamed . . .** Because you have not neglected Torah.

On displaying knowledge of Torah so as to avoid shame in the world that is coming, see *Seder Eliyyahu Rabbah* 1; *Midrash Mishlei* 10; *Zohar* 2:123b; 3:144a (*IR*), 196b; *ZḤ* 2c (*SO*), 70d (*ShS*). Cf. *Zohar* 1:4a; 2:134b; 3:205b.

עלמא דאתי (*Alma de-atei*), "the world that is coming," is the Aramaic equivalent of the rabbinic Hebrew העולם הבא (*ha-olam ha-ba*). This term has often been understood as referring to the hereafter and often been translated as "the world to come." From another point of view, however, "the world that is coming" already exists, occupying another dimension. See *Tanḥuma, Vayiqra* 8: "The wise call it *ha-olam ha-ba* not because it does

"I said to them, 'My children, by your life, what new insight did you innovate today?'

"They replied, 'Concerning this verse: *God said, "Let there be light." And there was light* (Genesis 1:3). Rabbi Kruspedai taught, "Great was the additional light, unlike any other, a light without peer. This is the light of the Great Intellect, formed from the light of His resplendent splendor; and this is who resides beyond the curtain."[149]

"'As we have learned: What is the meaning of the verse *He wraps in light as in a garment* (Psalms 104:2)? It teaches that the blessed Holy One made the other angels just like that primordial light, from that very light itself. Now, do you really believe that they are just like him? Rather, just as he is a separate, intelli-



not exist now, but for us today in this world it is still to come." See Maimonides, *Mishneh Torah, Hilkhot Teshuvah* 8:8; and Guttmann, *Philosophies of Judaism*, 37: "'The world to come' does not succeed 'this world' in time, but exists from eternity as a reality outside and above time, to which the soul ascends."

149. **the light of the Great Intellect...** Namely, the Active Intellect of medieval philosophy, which is apparently equated here with Metatron ("who resides beyond the curtain"), the highest angel and first creation. See *ZḤ* 4a, 7d, 16a (all *MhN*); *Zohar* 1:126b, 127b (both *MhN*).

In medieval philosophical literature (for example, Maimonides, *Guide of the Perplexed* 2:4, 6, 11, 36), the Active Intellect was understood as the lowest divine emanation governing the activities of the sub-lunar realm. Comprising the wisdom of divinity, it is the highest level to which human intellect may aspire. See Davidson, *Alfarabi, Avicenna and Averroes on Intellect*, 180–209. The Active Intellect–Metatron equation is found in the writings of numerous thirteenth-century kabbalists, including Jacob ha-Kohen, Abraham Abulafia, Joseph Gikatilla, and Moses de León (see *Or Zaru'a*, 260). Here, as in *Or Zaru'a*, the Great (or Active) Intellect is the first emanant (or creation) outside the godhead. In contrast to other angels who reside "below the curtain," Metatron is above it and closest to God.

Metatron is the chief angel, variously described as the Prince of the World, Prince of the Countenance (or Presence), celestial scribe, and even יהוה קטן (*YHVH Qatan*), "Lesser *YHVH*" (3 Enoch 12:5, based on Exodus 23:21). In Heikhalot literature, Metatron is also identified with Enoch, a biblical personage who ascended to heaven (based on Genesis 5:24). See BT *Sanhedrin* 38b; *Ḥagigah* 15a; *Yevamot* 16b; *Tosafot, Yevamot* 16b, s.v. *pasuq zeh*; Scholem, *Kabbalah*, 377–81; Tishby, *Wisdom of the Zohar*, 2:626–31; Margaliot, *Mal'akhei Elyon*, 73–108. On Metatron in the *Zohar*, see 1:21a, 37b, 95b, 143a, 162a–b; 2:65b–66b, 131a; 3:217a–b; *ZḤ* 42d–43a; 69b (*ShS*). In *MhN* see *Zohar* 1:126a–b; *ZḤ* 4a, 9d–10b, 12b, 24a, 25c–26a, 28a–c; Scholem, "Parashah Ḥadashah," 437 (Addendum 1 in this volume); Wolski, "Metatron and the Mysteries of the Night."

Rabbi Kruspedai's interpretation may be based on the distinctive wording that follows the command *Let there be light*: the text does not say *and it was so*, as with the subsequent creations, but rather *And there was light*.

Regarding the additional light, see *Bereshit Rabbah* 61:4: "Bar Kappara said, 'The addition granted by the blessed Holy One exceeds the principal.'"

Cf. *Zohar* 1:46a, where the divine command *Let there be light* is read as referring to the creation of the angels.

gible entity, so the other angels are separate, intelligible entities—though their apprehension is not like his apprehension.[150]

"'As Rabbi Kruspedai taught: "The apprehension of the angels is a sublime apprehension—not so below them. The second apprehension is the apprehension of the heavens, which attain an apprehension that those below them do not attain. The third apprehension is the apprehension of the lowest rung, whose foundation is dust—the apprehension of human beings—which [9a] all the other creatures do not attain."[151]

"'Corresponding to these three degrees, the human being possesses three forms of souls. The first form is the intellectual soul; the second is the speaking soul; the third is the animal soul that desires desires—it is the soul that commits iniquity.[152]

"'You might say as follows: The first soul is the animal soul, corresponding to the lowest rung we mentioned; the speaking soul corresponds to the heavens, which is an additional degree above the first; the intellectual soul corresponds to the rung of the angels, the highest degree above them all.'"



150. **just as he is a separate, intelligible entity...** Even though the other angels were created from the light of the Great Intellect (or Metatron), they are of a lower rank. Their apprehension of divinity is also inferior.

According to Maimonides, *Mishneh Torah, Hilkhot Yesodei ha-Torah* 2:7–9, the angels (or intellects) are arranged in a hierarchy and are marked by different degrees of intellectual apprehension: "The highest degree ... apprehends and knows more than the form that is below it" (2:8). The terms "separate" and "intelligible" are derived from medieval philosophical literature, where angels were referred to as "separated intelligences" or "separate intellects" because they were understood as pure spiritual forms—totally separate from matter. See Maimonides, *Guide of the Perplexed* 2:4, 6.

On the motif of wrapping in light, see *Pirqei de-Rabbi Eli'ezer* 3: "Whence were the heavens created? From the light of the garment with which the blessed Holy One was robed. He took of this light and stretched it like a garment, and (the heavens) began to extend continually until He said to them, 'It is sufficient!'... Whence do we know that the heavens were created from the light of His garment? As is said: *He wraps in light as in a garment. He spreads out the heavens like a curtain* (Psalms 104:2)." See *Bereshit Rabbah* 3:4 (and Theodor, ad loc.); *Tanḥuma* (Buber), *Vayaqhel* 7; Maimonides, *Guide of the Perplexed* 2:26; *Zohar* 1:15b, 29a, 245a; 2:39b, 164b.

151. **The apprehension of the angels...** On the three tiers—angels, heavens, humans—see Maimonides, *Mishneh Torah, Hilkhot Yesodei ha-Torah* 3:9: "The knowledge of the stars and spheres is less than the knowledge of angels, but greater than that of human beings." See also idem, *Guide of the Perplexed* 3:13.

I have construed this and the following two paragraphs as the continuation of the hermits' report. Alternatively, the story may end earlier (perhaps at "his apprehension," or maybe even earlier in the preceding paragraph at "beyond the curtain"). Such "soft boundaries" are not uncommon in *MhN* narratives, as story flows into associated homily.

152. **three forms of souls...** See above, note 92. Here the vegetative soul is replaced with the animal soul; it is this soul that

*God said, "Let there be a firmament in the midst of the waters, that it may separate from water to water"* (Genesis 1:6).

Rabbi El'azar opened, "*God, you are my God; I will search for You* (Psalms 63:2).[153] Come and see: There is no place in the world devoid of water, because the earth is suspended upon the waters, as is said: *He founded it upon seas, and established it upon rivers* (ibid. 24:2). Now, can you even entertain the notion that the waters—which are beneath the earth, and the earth is the heaviest of all the elements poised above the waters—that the waters ascended above to the sky?"[154]

Rav Ḥisda said to him, "But look at what is written: *the waters above the firmament* (Genesis 1:7)!"[155]

He replied, "This is to be understood only in accordance with its translation—'in the middle of the waters,' for the firmament separates between them. The waters were one, but because the firmament interposed in the middle, they were considered as two. The firmament is spherical and splits the waters of the ocean, separating between the waters. Thus: waters above and waters below."[156]



Rabbi Yehudah said, "The firmaments revolve, sometimes from east to west, and sometimes from west to east. They enter the middle of the sea, separating midway between. This is the meaning of *It separated the waters* (ibid.).[157]

desires worldly things, and that leads a person to sin. The expression "soul that commits iniquity" derives from Leviticus 5:15.

153. ***I will search for You...*** The verse continues: *My soul thirsts for You, my flesh yearns for You, in a parched and weary land with no water.*

154. **can you even entertain the notion...** Apparently, Rabbi El'azar is perplexed by how the waters that lie beneath the heavy earth could have ascended to the sky above. That there are waters above is made clear by a verse in Scripture (see next note), as well as by observing natural phenomena (the rain).

According to the standard medieval scientific view, the elements are arranged in a hierarchy from heaviest to lightest: earth, water, air, and fire. The earth, however, is miraculously poised upon the waters: see *ZḤ* 4a, 12a (both *MhN*).

On Psalms 24:2, see *Zohar* 3:32b.

155. **But look at what is written: *the waters above the firmament*** The verse quoted by Rav Ḥisda suggests that the waters do seem to have ascended—or at the least are higher than the earth.

The full verse reads: *God made the firmament, and it separated the waters below the firmament from the waters above the firmament.*

156. **because the firmament interposed in the middle...** Rabbi El'azar explains that the waters above are higher only because the firmament splits them into higher and lower, not because they ascended on their own. Cf. *Targum Yerushalmi*, Genesis 1:7; *Bereshit Rabbah* 4:2. On the spherical firmament, cf. *Pirqei de-Rabbi Eli'ezer* 3.

The verse from Genesis describing the firmament's location—*in the midst*—is imprecise. The Aramaic translations (Targum) clarify: in the middle. See also *Bereshit Rabbah* 4:3; Naḥmanides on Genesis 1:6. Cf. *Zohar* 1:32b.

157. **The firmaments revolve . . .** The word רקיע (*raqi'a*), "expanse, firmament," was also used to signify the celestial spheres of medieval cosmology. See Maimonides, *Mishneh Torah, Hilkhot Yesodei ha-Torah* 3:2:

"Why is sea water salty? It is because of the firmament's scorching heat. Come and see: A pot resting on the flame—the longer it cooks on the flame, the saltier the dish, on account of the fire's intensity!"[158]

Rabbi Yehudah also said, "Were the firmament to rest between the waters, all the waters would congeal like salt. But it moves and revolves, never resting between the waters."

Rabbi Yitsḥak said, "Come and see: Why doesn't it say *that it was good* on the second day? Because this matter pertains to יחודו (*yiḥudo*), His unity, illustrating that there is no second alongside Him, and that good does not apply to the second. That is why on the first day it says יום אחד (*yom eḥad*), *one day* (Genesis 1:5)."[159]

As Rabbi Yitsḥak taught: "Why doesn't it say 'first' instead of *one*? To show that had it said 'first' then 'second' would necessarily follow, for 'first' is followed by 'second,' whereas *one* is not followed by 'second.'"[160]



"Some of the spheres revolve from the west to the east, and some revolve from the east to the west." See also idem, *Guide of the Perplexed* 1:72.

158. **the firmament's scorching heat...** In line with the established medieval scientific hierarchy—earth, water, air, and fire—the firmament, which lies above the three other foundation elements, must be a fiery substance. Cf. *Bereshit Rabbah* 4:5.

159. **Why doesn't it say *that it was good* on the second day?...** In the biblical account of Creation, the statement *God saw that it was good* (or a variant) is included in the description of each of the six days, except for the second. See *Bereshit Rabbah* 4:6: "Why is *that it was good* not written concerning the second day? Rabbi Yoḥanan said..., 'Because on that day Hell was created....' Rabbi Ḥanina said, 'Because on that day conflict was created: *that it may separate water from water.*'... Rabbi Shemu'el son of Naḥman said, 'Because the work of the water was not completed. Therefore *that it was good* is written twice on the third day: once for the work of the water (Genesis 1:9–10), and once for the work of the [third] day (ibid., 11).'" See BT *Pesaḥim* 54a; *Pirqei de-Rabbi Eli'ezer* 4; *Zohar* 1:18a, 33a, 46a.

See *Bereshit Rabbah* 3:8: "*One day* (Genesis 1:5)—... Rabbi Yudan said, 'The day in which the blessed Holy One was one in His universe.'" See also Rashi on Genesis 1:5: "According to the arrangement of the wording of the passage, it should have written 'the first day,' as is written with respect to the other days: second, third, fourth. Why did it write *one*? Because the blessed Holy One was solitary in His world, for the angels were not created until the second day." Cf. *Bereshit Rabbah* 3:9.

Here, both the absence of *that it was good* on the second day, and the peculiar locution *one day*, are taken to indicate God's uniqueness. See next note.

Some MSS read "Rabbi Yehudah" in place of Rabbi Yitsḥak.

160. **Why doesn't it say 'first' instead of *one*?...** See Naḥmanides on Genesis 1:5: "It could not have said 'the first day' because the second had not yet been made; the first precedes a second in number or degree... whereas *one* does not imply the existence of a second." The *Zohar* expands this idea to suggest that God is not merely the first in a series, who is thus followed by a second. Rather, He is unique, i.e., one.

See also Baḥya ibn Paquda, *Ḥovot ha-*

Rabbi Yehudah said, "But look, it is said: *I, YHVH, am the first* (Isaiah 41:4)!"[161]

He replied, "The continuation of the verse supports the previous explanation. As is written: *and with* אחרנים (*aḥaronim*), *the last ones, I am He* (ibid.). Even though there are אחרים (*aḥerim*), others, after the first, *I am He.* But are there really others after the first? Indeed! His explicit Name is primary and unique; the others are: *alef dalet nun yod* [אדני (*Adonai*)], *Elohim*, *Shaddai*, *El*, *Tseva'ot*—they are epithets for His uniqueness. But He Himself is exalted, as is written: *and with* אחרנים (*aḥaronim*), *the last ones, I am He* (ibid.)."[162]

Rabbi Yose son of Ḥalafta, Rabbi Yehudah son of Pazzi, and Rabbi Yitsḥak were eating at the celebration banquet for Rabbi El'azar son of Rabbi Shim'on. Rabbi Ḥiyya the Great, who was then a child, was sitting there. Rabbi Yose asked Rabbi Shim'on, "Why doesn't it say *that it was good* on the second day?"[163]

He replied, "Because the work of the waters was not complete on the second day; but when it was completed on the third say, it says *that it was good* twice."[164]

They said, "Let us ask this child; for since the Temple was destroyed,
52 prophecy is found in the mouths of children. Perhaps we will find a word in his mouth."[165]

They said to him, "Ḥiyya, my child, tell us why it doesn't say *that it was good* on the second day?"

He replied, "Because good pertains only to One."

*Levavot, Sha'ar ha-Yiḥud,* chapter 8. Cf. idem, *Baqqashah*: "You alone are one. One without fathoming, one without likeness, one without beginning or end.... One—not like one that is the head of all numbers. One—not like one that is the first of all counted." See also Solomon Ibn Gabirol, *Keter Malkhut,* Canto 2.

161. ***I, YHVH, am the first*** In contrast to the preceding, the verse from Isaiah suggests that the epithet "first" is in fact applied to God.

162. **Even though there are אחרים (*aḥerim*), others...** The "others" after the first are additional holy divine names. Even though they are holy names, the explicit name *YHVH* is primary. See BT *Shevu'ot* 35a; Maimonides, *Mishneh Torah, Hilkhot Yesodei ha-Torah* 6:2; idem, *Guide of the Perplexed* 1:61.

163. **celebration banquet for Rabbi El'azar...** Perhaps for his becoming a bar mitsvah (see *ZḤ* 10c–d (*MhN*); see also *Zohar* 3:191b. Alternatively, the banquet may connote his *brit milah* feast, or maybe even his wedding.

On Rabbi Ḥiyya in *MhN,* see *Zohar* 2:14a–15a; *ZḤ* 15d.

164. **the work of the waters was not complete...** See *Bereshit Rabbah* 4:6, quoted above, note 159.

165. **since the Temple was destroyed...** See BT *Bava Batra* 12b in the name of Rabbi Yoḥanan: "Ever since the day the Temple was destroyed, prophecy has been taken from the prophets and given to fools and children." See *Zohar* 2:6b, 170a.

On the motif of the wunderkind, see *Zohar* 1:92b, 148a, 238b; 2:6b, 169b; 3:39a, 162a, 171a, 186a, 204b; *ZḤ* 10b (*MhN*), 14d (*MhN*), 48a, 49a–b, 77d (*MhN, Rut*), 84b–c (*MhN, Rut*).

Rabbi Shim'on came and kissed him. He proclaimed for him: *Behold, I have put My words in your mouth* (Jeremiah 1:9).[166]

They said, "It is a propitious time for him! Let us inquire."

They asked him, "What is the meaning of the verse *His lovers are as the sun rising in its* [9d] *might* (Judges 5:31)? What kind of praise is this for the righteous?"

He replied, "Just as when the sun rises in its might there are some who are gladdened by it and some who are not, so with the righteous: the righteous like them will rejoice, whereas the wicked will not rejoice. Just as there are some for whom [the sun] bestows healing whereas for others it does not, so the righteous will be a healing for the good—and a blow for the wicked."[167]

They asked him, "Ḥiyya, my child, why is the unique Name not mentioned in the Account of Creation?"[168]

He replied, "It is not becoming for the King of Glory to associate His Name with the dead or with any perishable thing, that it will not be said that just as all the creations He created are liable to destruction and decay, so too His Name! He did not mention His unique Name until all the creations liable to destruc- 53
tion and decay were created. Afterward He associated His Name with something abiding eternally, for all time, as is said: *On the day YHVH Elohim made earth and heaven* (Genesis 2:4). Of all the creations He created, only that which abides eternally is mentioned here. It does not say *On the day YHVH Elohim made earth and heaven and humankind and animals and beasts and birds*—which are perishable things—but only something existing eternally—earth and heaven."[169]

They asked him, "What is the meaning of the verse *God fashioned the firmament and separated the waters...* (Genesis 1:7)? What need did the blessed Holy One have to fashion a firmament to separate the waters?"

He replied, "It is already written: *YHVH made everything for a purpose* (Proverbs 16:4). The blessed Holy One did not create anything unnecessarily. He created the firmament; and when it revolves, it revolves solely at set times.

166. ***I have put My words in your mouth*** These words are taken from God's reply to Jeremiah, who according to one reading of Jeremiah 1:6 was a child when called to prophecy. Although verse 9 reads נתתי (*natati*), the MSS read שמתי (*samti*), a locution found elsewhere in the Bible, e.g., Exodus 4:15. Cf. *Zohar* 3:41a.

167. **bestows healing...** Cf. BT *Nedarim* 8b: "*A sun of righteousness with healing* [*in its wings*] (Malachi 3:20)—...the blessed Holy One will draw forth the sun from its sheath: the righteous shall be healed, but the wicked shall be judged and punished thereby."

168. **unique Name not mentioned in the Account of Creation?** In chapter 1 of Genesis, the divine name *YHVH* does not appear, only the generic name *Elohim* (God).

169. **He associated His Name with something abiding eternally...** The explicit name *YHVH* is first mentioned in the Torah at Genesis 2:4, in the second creation account. See *ZḤ* 17a (*MhN*), page 168. Cf. Moses de León, *Or Zaru'a*, 263; idem, *Sefer ha-Rimmon*, 288.

A stream of water flows from the depths, and a stream of water flows from Hell, descending along a channel to the stream of the deep, as is written: *Deep calls to deep at the sound of Your channels* (Psalms 42:8). The firmament interposes between the two of them—and were it not to interpose in between, they [the waters] would slay those who imbibe them. This is the meaning of *It separated the waters that were below the firmament from the waters above the firmament* (Genesis 1:7)."[170]

Come and see! Rabbi Yose said, "This child has spoken with the holy spirit, for so it is indeed! As is written: *Let there be a firmament in the midst of the waters* (ibid. 1:6)—*in the midst*, precisely; in the middle of the waters.[171] When the firmament interposes in the middle, it drives the evil waters flowing from Hell back to their place. Of those waters, only one *log*, in the days of Elisha, has flowed into the world. Of them is said *the water is bad and the land causes bereavement* (2 Kings 2:19)—that is to say, because the waters are bad, the land is bereft of human beings who perish on their account."[172]

54 Rabbi Yehudah said, "The entire verse attests to this interpretation."

As Rabbi Yehudah said: "Of all that the blessed Holy One made, He did not make anything in vain. Since it was revealed before Him that those waters flowing from Hell would mingle with other waters, injuring His creatures, He fashioned the firmament to interpose in the middle of the two of them, separating between them. This is the meaning of *that it may separate from water to water* (Genesis 1:6)—from the bad waters and the good waters. At that precise

170. **A stream of water flows from the depths...** The waters of Hell seek to join the waters of the deep. Were they to mix, the consequences would be calamitous. The firmament revolves; and at precisely the right time, it separates the waters of Hell (below the firmament) from the waters of the deep (above the firmament).

The idea that the waters of Hell are proximate to the waters of the deep is found in *Pirqei de-Rabbi Eli'ezer* 5, though the motif of their commingling is absent: "All the fountains arise from the depths to give water to all creatures. Rabbi Yehoshu'a said, '... one of the depths near Hell bubbles with water and produces water for the delight of human beings.'" See also BT *Shabbat* 39a. See *ZḤ* 15a (*MhN*), page 135.

171. ***in the midst*, precisely ...** The verse's wording *in the midst* is imprecise. The Targum specifies that this means "in the middle."

172. **Of those waters, only one *log*...** A *log* is a small liquid measure, equal to the contents of six eggs. Yet even a small amount of the waters of Hell can be fatal.

The simple sense of 2 Kings 2:19–22 reads: *The men of the town said to Elisha, "Look, the town is a pleasant place to live in, as my lord can see; but the water is bad and the land causes bereavement." He replied, "Bring me a new dish and put salt in it." They brought it to him; he went to the spring and threw salt into it. He said, "Thus says YHVH: I heal this water, no longer shall death and bereavement come from it!" The water has remained wholesome to this day, in accordance with the word spoken by Elisha.*

moment, when the waters flow forth to mingle with the good waters, then the firmament revolves and interposes between them, driving them back."

Come and hear! Rabbi El'azar said, "Those waters that are the life of the world and for the welfare of creatures—what are they called?"

Rabbi Berekhiah said, "The waters above the heavens, which are good waters."[173]

Rabbi Ḥiyya son of Abba was walking on the way. Weary from the intensity of the sun, he thirsted for water. He came upon a desert and found a solitary tree; he sat beneath it. As he raised his eyes, he noticed a spring of water. He delighted to drink some. He drank from the waters, but they were bitter. He said to his servant, "This corresponds with Rabbi El'azar's explanation, for Rabbi El'azar said, 'There is nowhere in the world that does not contain residue from the stream of Hell, except for in the land of Israel. Were the entire world not to drink from the drippings of the land of Israel, they would not be able to drink from them [the waters of the world].'"[174]

Rav Huna said, "The expanse of which is written *God made the expanse* (Genesis 55
1:7) is the known expanse above—over the heads of the living beings—as is written: *An image over the heads of the living being, an expanse like awesome ice* (Ezekiel 1:22)."[175]

173. **The waters above the heavens...** According to *Pirqei de-Rabbi Eli'ezer* 5 there are two kinds of rain. The first originates from the depths and is not a source of blessing, while the second originates from the heavens: "When the blessed Holy One desires to bless the produce of the earth and to give provision to the creatures, He opens the good treasuries in heaven and sends rain upon the earth, namely, the masculine waters. Immediately, the earth becomes fruitful—like a bride who conceives from her first husband and produces offspring of blessing, as is said: *YHVH will open for you His goodly treasure, the heavens* (Deuteronomy 28:12)." See Luria, ad loc.

174. **Were the entire world...** Only in the land of Israel are the waters untainted, and it is only because of those waters that people can drink other water at all.

See BT *Ta'anit* 10a: "The land of Israel drinks water directly from the rain, while the rest of the world drinks of the drippings." See *Zohar* 1:84b, 108b; 2:152b; 3:209b; *ZḤ* 61b (*MhN, ShS*), 81a (*MhN, Rut*); Naḥmanides on Deuteronomy 11:10.

175. **the known expanse above...** The Hebrew term רקיע (*raqi'a*) means "expanse, firmament." In Genesis 1:6–8, the *raqi'a* is the firm vault of heaven dividing the upper waters from the lower waters. In Ezekiel 1, it is the platform upon which the divine throne stands. An equation between those two "expanses" is found in *Pirqei de-Rabbi Eli'ezer* 4: "Which expanse did He create on the second day? Rabbi Eli'ezer says, 'It was the expanse that is above the heads of the four living beings, as is said: *An image over the heads of the living being, an expanse like awesome ice* (Ezekiel 1:22).'"

See BT *Ḥagigah* 13a; Cf. *Zohar* 1:21a, 211a; 2:211a–b; Moses de León, *Peirush ha-Merkavah*, 70.

Rabbi Yitsḥak said, "Concerning these living beings, it is written: *living being*—one. Why then does it say ראשי (*rashei*), *heads of*?"[176]

Rav Huna replied, "There is one great living being ruling over all the other holy living beings. Its radiances are mighty and many, with numerous branches of splendor. Therefore it is written ראשי החיה (*rashei ha-ḥayyah*), *the branches of the living being* (ibid.). This is the *living being* Ezekiel beheld in his prophetic vision. Now, should you think that this refers to the living beings, come and hear what is written: *I gazed on the living beings...* (ibid. 1:15)! He saw this one and he saw the living beings."[177]

This expanse—what is it for?

Rabbi Ḥizkiyah said, "To distinguish between the holy angels beneath that expanse and the holy angels who merited that they be above, as is written: *God fashioned the expanse and separated the waters below the expanse from the waters above the expanse* (Genesis 1:7). *The waters below the expanse*—the angels who are beneath the expanse; *the waters above the expanse*—the angels above."[178]

56 Rabbi Yitsḥak said, "Conclude from this that it is the curtain dividing between."[179]

Rabbi Eli'ezer inquired of Rabban Yoḥanan son of Zakkai. He asked him, "The expanse created on the second day, what is it?"

He replied, "It is a supernal mystery. The blessed Holy One created an archon beneath Him, and chose him—granting him dominion over all the hosts of heaven. Because of this matter, *it was good* is not said of the second day—even though he possesses additional dominion over all in his charge—to show the entire world that there is no goodness, glory, salvation, or grandeur except in the blessed Holy One alone."[180]

176. ***living being*—one...** The חיות (*ḥayyot*), "living beings, creatures," bearing the throne in Ezekiel's vision are sometimes described in the singular (Ezekiel 1:20–22), apparently to emphasize their unity. If singular, why then does the verse employ the plural—"heads"?

177. **There is one great living being...** Apparently Metatron, known elsewhere as the Prince of the Countenance. The plural *ḥayyot* refers to the four living beings, i.e., various angelic forms bearing the throne, whereas the singular *ḥayyah* refers to Metatron. Ezekiel beheld both of them. On Metatron, see above, note 149; see also *ZḤ* 12b (*MhN*). For *rashei* as *branches of*, see Genesis 2:10.

178. **angels... beneath... angels above** Just as the expanse in Genesis separated the lower waters from the upper waters, the expanse in Ezekiel's vision separates the upper and lower angelic realms.

179. **curtain...** Hebrew פרגוד (*pargod*). See BT *Berakhot* 18b; *Ḥagigah* 15a; *Pirqei de-Rabbi Eli'ezer* 4.

180. **created an archon...** Precisely because of this archon's exalted status—and so as not to mislead anyone into thinking that he actually rules the world—*it was good* was not said of the second day. See above, note

Rabban Yoḥanan son of Zakkai said further, "What is the meaning of the verse *I descended to the nut garden to see the verdure of the valley* (Songs of Songs 6:11)? This refers to what Ezekiel beheld in that expanse created on the second day, which the blessed Holy One created, and which He concealed from all His myriads of holy ones. But as for those worlds that the blessed Holy One desires, He concealed them from him. He concealed His majestic glory! From those worlds and above He concealed, hiding them from all. All inquire and respond, 'Where is His glorious majesty? *Blessed be the glory of YHVH from His place!*' (Ezekiel 3:12).[181]

"Come and see what was said: *I descended to the nut garden* (Songs of Songs 6:11)! It is not written *into the nut garden*, but rather *to the nut garden*, like one who descends and approaches the garden but does not enter within. Surely he did not draw near to the nut, but rather to the garden—and certainly he did not gaze upon what is within the nut! So much the more so since he said *to see* (ibid.), and did not say *I saw*! In other words: to the garden that is without,



159. This figure is elsewhere called Metatron, on whom see above, note 149.

According to *ZḤ* 8d (and *Zohar* 1:126b, *MhN*), Metatron was the first creation—alluded to in the verse *Let there be light* (Genesis 1:3). Here, he is described as having been created on the second day, perhaps following the rabbinic idea (*Bereshit Rabbah* 1:3, 3:8; *Pirqei de-Rabbi Eli'ezer* 4) that the angels were created on the second day.

181. ***I descended to the nut garden...*** In the writings of Ḥasidei Ashkenaz, in particular El'azar of Worms, the "nut" symbolizes the *merkavah*, the divine chariot. Descending to the nut garden therefore connotes speculating on the divine throne. See Dan, *Torat ha-Sod*, 208–10; Farber, "Tefisat ha-Merkavah be-Torat ha-Sod be-Me'ah ha-Shelosh-Esreh"; Abrams, *Sexual Symbolism and Merkavah Speculation*. On the nut motif in *MhN*, see *Zohar* 2:15b; *ZḤ* 17c–18a, 83a (*Rut*). See also *Zohar* 1:19b, 44b (*Heikh*); 2:233b, 254b (*Heikh*); Moses de León, *Sefer ha-Mishqal*, 156–8; Liebes, *Peraqim*, s.v. אגוזא (egoza), 20–21, 27.

While Ezekiel beheld the "expanse," namely Metatron (who is so exalted that even the other angels cannot fathom him), he did not see beyond. Alternatively, the "him" from whom the worlds are concealed may refer to Metatron.

The "worlds that the blessed Holy One desires" refers to the inner essence of the divine realm, concealed from all. See *ZḤ* 13b, 18a, 22a (all *MhN*); Scholem, "Parashah Ḥadashah," 445 (Addendum 1 in this volume).

See BT *Ḥagigah* 13a: "Rav Aḥa son of Ya'akov said, 'There is still another expanse [i.e., beyond the seven heavens] above the heads of the living creatures, as is written: *An image over the heads of the living being, an expanse like awesome ice* (Ezekiel 1:22). Until here you have permission to speak; from here on you are not permitted to speak. For so is written in the book of Ben Sira: What is too wondrous for you, do not expound; what is concealed from you, do not inquire. You have no business with hidden matters!'"

See *Pirqei de-Rabbi Eli'ezer* 4: "The living beings stand at the side of the His Throne of Glory, and they do not know the place of His glory. They respond and say in every place where His glory is, '*Blessed be the glory of YHVH from His place*.'" Cf. BT *Ḥagigah* 13b; *Zohar* 1:103a; 3:159a; *ZḤ* 16a (*MhN*). See also the *Musaf Qedushah*.

I approached and descended to see. He didn't say that he saw even the garden that is without!"[182]

Rabban Yoḥanan son of Zakkai said further, "How pained was that man, of whom it is written: *Not so My servant Moses—he is trusted throughout My house* (Numbers 12:7), to behold a certain servant ministering before Him! Yet permission was not granted him, as is written: *Oh, show me Your glory* (Exodus 33:18)."[183]

Rabban Yoḥanan son of Zakkai explained, "He of whom is written *the glory of God* (Psalms 19:2)—Metatron.[184]

"How could Moses request to behold this? Well, Moses [10a] reasoned that since he saw himself go forty days and forty nights without eating or drinking, and was nourished by the speculum above, he thought that he was worthy to request this.[185]

"How did He answer Him? *You cannot see My face* (Exodus 33:20)—this is the Prince of the Countenance. Permission was not granted him until his soul departed, fulfilling what is said: *No human can see Me and live* (ibid.). Permis-



182. **It is not written *into*...** The inner essence of the divine realms remains concealed. Although Ezekiel beheld the divine throne, he did not fathom its innermost nature; he apprehended only the exterior.

In contrast to the main strata of the *Zohar*, *Midrash ha-Ne'lam* often posits an upper limit to the human capacity to behold the divine. See next note. See Asulin, "Midrash ha-Ne'lam li-Vreshit," 228–30.

183. **permission was not granted him...** According to Exodus 33:18–23, Moses requests but is denied a vision of the divine glory. Here, the glory is correlated with Metatron, the first emanant, who is also known as God's face (see below, note 186). Not only can one not fathom God, but also even Metatron cannot be seen directly: "*You will see My back, but My face will not be seen*" (ibid., 20). Cf. Maimonides, *Guide of the Perplexed* 1:54; idem, *Mishneh Torah, Hilkhot Yesodei ha-Torah* 1:9.

184. ***the glory of God*...** Metatron is the divine glory. See *ZḤ* 24a, 26a (both *MhN*); Scholem, "Parashah Ḥadashah," 445 (Addendum 1 in this volume). The full verse from Psalms reads: *The heavens declare the glory of God, and His handiwork the sky proclaims.*

185. **the speculum above...** אספקלריא דלעילא (*ispaqlarya de-l'eila*). *Ispaqlarya* means "glass, mirror, lens." See BT *Yevamot* 49b: "All the prophets gazed through an opaque glass [literally: an *ispaqlarya* that does not shine], while Moses our teacher gazed through translucent glass [literally: an *ispaqlarya* that shines]." See also *Vayiqra Rabbah* 1:14. Cf. 1 Corinthians 13:12: "For now we see though a glass darkly, but then face-to-face." See *Zohar* 1:97b, 122a (both *MhN*); *ZḤ* 13b, 15b, 15d, 16c, 17a, 21a, 24a (all *MhN*).

On Moses' celestial nourishment, see *Shemot Rabbah* 47:5: "*He was there with YHVH forty days and forty nights* (Exodus 34:28). Is it possible for a person to go forty days without food or drink? Rabbi Tanḥuma said in the name of Rabbi El'azar son of Rabbi Avin in the name of Rabbi Meir, 'The proverb runs: When you go into a city, follow its customs. When Moses ascended on high, where there is no eating or drinking, he emulated them....' *He ate no bread* (ibid.)—eating only the bread of the Torah; *and drank no water* (ibid.)—drinking only of the water of the Torah.... Whence did he derive his nourishment? He was nourished by the splendor of *Shekhinah*." See also *Shemot Rabbah* 3:1, 47:7; *Vayiqra Rabbah* 20:10; *Zohar* 1:135b (*MhN*); *ZḤ* 15b (*MhN*).

sion is granted to every soul of the righteous to fathom and apprehend what it cannot in this world."[186]

Our Rabbis have taught: Every single day, the blessed Holy One fashions holy angels; and these are the souls of the righteous, as is written: *He makes spirits His angels, His servants glowing fire* (Psalms 104:4). It does not say *He made*, but rather *He makes*, implying that He does so every day![187]

Rabbi Abbahu said, "Let this not trouble you. For look, there are angels that are created from the Throne of Glory, and they are messengers appointed on a mission of the blessed Holy One. If it is so concerning the other angels that are formed from the Throne of Glory, how much more so concerning the souls of the righteous—who hail from there and who fulfilled the Torah—that the blessed Holy One makes them supernal, holy angels!"[188]

186. ***You cannot see My face*...** The divine face indicates Metatron, שר הפנים (*sar ha-panim*), literally Prince of the Face. Although one cannot behold Metatron in life, in death one can. See *Sifra, Vayiqra, dibbura dindavah* 2:12, 4a: "Rabbi Dosa says, 'Scripture states: *No human can see Me and live.* In their lifetime they do not see, but in their death they do!'" See *Pirqei de-Rabbi Eli'ezer* 34; *Zohar* 1:65b, 79a, 98a (*MhN*), 99a (*ST*), 218b, 226a, 245a; 3:88a, 147a. See *ZḤ* 25d (*MhN*).

187. ***He makes spirits His angels*...** עושה מלאכיו רוחות (*Oseh malakhav ruḥot*), whose simple sense means: *He make the winds His messengers.* Reading *ruḥot* as "spirits" and *malakhav* as "His angels," the *Zohar* finds support for the idea that upon death, the spirits (or souls) of the righteous become angels. Cf. *Tanḥuma, Ḥayyei Sarah* 3; *Pirqei de-Rabbi Eli'ezer* 4; *Zohar* 1:40b (*Heikh*), 81a (*ST*), 101a, 144a; 2:98b, 173a, 229b; 3:126b, 152a; *ZḤ* 81b (*MhN, Rut*). On the souls of the righteous transforming into angels, see *Zohar* 1:100a, 129b; *ZḤ* 19a, 20d–21a (both *MhN*); *TZ, Haqdamah*, 16b.

On angels being made every day, see BT *Ḥagigah* 14a: "Shemu'el said to Rabbi Ḥiyya son of Rav, 'O son of a lion! Come, I will tell you one of those fine words said by your father: Every single day, ministering angels are created from a river of fire, chant a song, then cease to be, as is said: *New every morning, immense is Your faithfulness* (Lamentations 3:23).'" See also Daniel 7:10; *Eikhah Rabbah* 3:8.

188. **created from the Throne of Glory...** Both human souls and angels are created from the Throne of Glory. In BT *Shabbat* 152b, the souls of the righteous are said to be "hidden beneath the Throne of Glory" after death; see also *Avot de-Rabbi Natan* A, 12. According to *MhN*, the soul is created from the substance of the Throne of Glory, which may refer to the *Shekhinah*. See *Zohar* 1:113a, 125b, 126b (all *MhN*); *ZḤ* 10b–d, 20b, 22a, 24a, 26a (all *MhN*). This idea may also derive from the writings of El'azar of Worms, *Sefer Ḥokhmat ha-Nefesh*, 1a, 3d, 4d, 5d. Cf. Solomon Ibn Gabirol, *Keter Malkhut*, Canto 29: "From your radiant glory, you created pure radiance, hewn from rock.... You imbued it with the life of wisdom and called it soul."

The equation of angels and souls is also found in *Keter Malkhut*, Canto 25: "Who can fathom Your thoughts! From the splendor of *Shekhinah*, You made the radiance of soul and spirits on high. They are messengers of Your will, ministers of Your presence."

Rabbi Pinḥas said, "The blessed Holy One comprised four things in the human being—fire, air, water, and earth."[189]

Rabbi Yehudah said, "Look, in Torah they are inverted!"[190]

Rabbi Pinḥas said to him, "Are they even mentioned in Torah?"[191]

He replied, "Indeed, and they are: air, fire, water, and earth. Two of them were hewn from ministers above, and two were hewn from below. How do we know? As is written: *He makes His angels* רוחות (*ruḥot*), *winds* (Psalms 104:4)—רוח (*ruaḥ*), air; *His servants glowing fire* (ibid.)—fire. *He established the earth on its foundations* (ibid., 5)—according to its obvious meaning; *With the deep, You covered it like a garment; over mountains, the waters stood* (ibid., 6)—water. All of them fuse, one with another—air, fire, earth, and water."[192]

Rabbi Pinḥas said, "Even though they are inverted, it does not matter, and Rabbi Yehudah spoke well!"

Rabbi Yehudah also said, "The blessed Holy One comprised them all in the human being. The blessed Holy One said to him, 'I created you supernal and
60 crowned you above all My creatures. I placed in you power from the angels, and power from the servants above, the power of the deep, and the power of the earth. I placed in you a pure intellect hewn from My Throne—yet still you sin before Me!'"[193]

189. **fire, air, water, and earth** See above, *ZḤ* 6d, and note 94.

190. **in Torah they are inverted** The conventional ordering of the four elements follows their weight, with earth—the heaviest of the elements—at the bottom. Rabbi Yehudah notes that the Bible presents them in reverse order.

191. **mentioned in Torah** The theory of the four elements derives from ancient Greece and is not found in the Bible. Medieval commentators "discovered" them in the text of Scripture through creative exegesis.

192. **Two of them... and two...** Air and fire derive from above; water and earth, from below. The biblical derivation of the elements here differs from *ZḤ* 6d.

193. **power from the angels . . . servants... deep... earth...** Namely, air, fire, water, and earth. The "pure intellect" refers to the soul.

Cf. *Bereshit Rabbah* 8:11: "Rabbi Yehoshu'a son of Rabbi Neḥemiah said in the name of Rabbi Ḥanina son of Rabbi Yitsḥak, and the Rabbis said in the name of Rabbi El'azar, 'He created him with four attributes of Above and four attributes of Below. He eats and drinks like an animal; procreates like an animal; excretes like an animal; and dies like an animal. Of Above: He stands upright like the ministering angels; he speaks like the ministering angels; he understands like the ministering angels; and he sees like the ministering angels.'... Rabbi Tifdai said in the name of Rabbi Aḥa, 'The celestial beings were created in the image and likeness and do not procreate, while the terrestrial creatures procreate but were not created in image and likeness. The blessed Holy One said, 'Behold, I will create him [the human] in the image and likeness of celestial beings, while he will procreate like terrestrial beings.' Rabbi Tifdai said in the name of Rabbi Aḥa, 'The blessed Holy One said: If I create him of the celestial elements, he will live and never die; and if I create him of the terres-

Rabbi Yitsḥak said, "The blessed Holy One desired to make the human being supernal above all His creations, that he would be unique in this world—as He is unique above. When he sinned, the blessed Holy One said, '*Here, the human was* כאחד (*ke-eḥad*), *like one, of us* (Genesis 3:22)—I intended to make him כאחד (*ke-eḥad*), *unique*, but now: *now, lest he send forth his hand* (ibid.).'"[194]

Rabbi Yehudah said, "The blessed Holy One fashioned one expanse, and from it the heavens were formed, as is said: *God called the expanse Heavens* (Genesis 1:8)."[195]

Rabbi Yehudah said, "Not only this, but also regarding everything that the blessed Holy One made during the work of creation, He only ever made one instantiation of all, and that entity generated all its operations according to its kind. For example, the heavens—He made one, the most sublime of all; and He made one earth."[196]

Come and hear: Rabbi Yehudah said, "He made one of all, the most sublime
of all, and this is the *expanse like awesome ice* (Ezekiel 1:22), from which the 61
heavens were formed. This is the meaning of what is written: *God called the expanse Heavens* (Genesis 1:8). As for the ארץ (*erets*), earth, which is more sublime than all, this is ארץ ישראל (*erets yisra'el*), the land of Israel, from which the others lands were formed, as is written: *He had not yet made* ארץ וחוצות (*erets ve-ḥutsot*), *land and outsides* (Proverbs 8:26). ארץ (*Erets*), *Land*— ארץ ישראל (*erets yisra'el*), land of Israel; וחוצות (*ve-ḥutsot*), *and outsides*—the other lands outside of the Land. [Similarly,] one human from which the others came into

trial elements, he will die and not live [in a future life]. Therefore I will create him of the upper and of the lower elements: if he sins he will die; while if he does not sin, he will live.'"

194. **I intended to make him כאחד (*ke-eḥad*), *unique*...** See *Bereshit Rabbah* 21:5: "*Here, the human was* כאחד (*ke-eḥad*), *like one, of us*—... Rabbi Yehudah the son of Rabbi Simon interpreted: 'Like the Unique One of the universe, as is written: *Hear, O Israel, YHVH our God, YHVH is one* (Deuteronomy 6:4).'"

In its simple sense, the full verse from Genesis reads: *YHVH God said, "Here, humankind has become like one of us, knowing good and bad; now, lest he send forth his hand and take also from the Tree of Life and eat and live forever!"* Because of Adam's sin, he and his mate are no longer worthy of eating from the Tree of Life and will therefore be banished.

195. **from it the heavens were formed...** According to the account in Genesis 1, the expanse is called *Heavens*. According to Rabbi Yehudah, this means that the heavens were formed from the first expanse. See *ZḤ* 14a (*MhN*), page 117.

See also Maimonides, *Guide of the Perplexed* 2:30; Naḥmanides on Genesis 1:8 (see below, note 198).

196. **one instantiation of all...** All of creation follows the same pattern, namely a supernal prototype or pattern from which the lower entities derive.

being, as is written: *the world's first clumps of clay* (ibid.); and so on, in a like manner."[197]

Rabbi Yitsḥak said, "How do we know? From the verse David uttered: *Praise YHVH from heaven* (Psalms 148:1)—from that one out of which the heavens were made."[198]

Our Rabbis have taught: Once Rabbi Yoḥanan was traveling to see Rabbi Shim'on, and Rabbi Yose was walking with him. Rabbi Yose asked him, "Where are you going?"

He replied, "To see Rabbi Shim'on."

He said, "You are going to see your master of dissension?!"

He replied, "Conclude from this that Rabbi Shim'on dissents for the sake of heaven! Since it is so, the love of my heart [10b] abides with him."[199]



197. **the most sublime of all...** The expanse described in Ezekiel's vision is the supernal expanse from which the heavens derive.

The proof-text from Proverbs, which was spoken by Wisdom, is used to illustrate the same principle for the earth and for humankind. In its simple sense, the verse reads: *He had not yet made earth and fields, nor the world's first clumps of clay.*

See BT *Ta'anit* 10a: "Our Rabbis taught: The land of Israel was created first, and afterward the rest of the world, as is said: *He had not yet made* ארץ וחוצות (*erets ve-ḥutsot*), *land and outsides* (Proverbs 8:26)." The word חוצות (*ḥutsot*) is read by the Talmud and the *Zohar* hyperliterally as "outsides," i.e., locations outside the land of Israel. Cf. BT *Yoma* 54b; see above, *ZḤ* 2d (*MhN*).

198. **How do we know?...** How do we know that the blessed Holy One created one particular expanse/heaven from which the others were formed?

The verse uttered by David reads: *Praise YHVH from heaven, praise Him on the heights,* and the psalm later continues: *Praise Him, heaven of heavens, and the waters above the heavens* (ibid., 4). Apparently Rabbi Yitsḥak understands the psalm as attesting to the existence of an upper heaven, from which the lower heavens were made.

Cf. *Bereshit Rabbah* 12:11: "Rabbi Eli'ezer said, 'All that is in heaven was created out of heaven.'" Cf. also BT *Ḥagigah* 12b: "Rabbi Yehudah said, 'There are two firmaments, as is said: *Look, to your God YHVH belong the heavens, and the heavens beyond the heavens* (Deuteronomy 10:13).

See also Naḥmanides on Genesis 1:8: "The heavens mentioned in the first verse [of Genesis] are the upper heavens, which are not part of the lower spheres but are above the *merkavah* (divine chariot).... These spherical bodies [the firmaments] He also called 'heavens' by the name of the first upper heavens. This is why they are called in this chapter 'the firmament of the heaven'—*God set them in the firmament of the heaven* (Genesis 1:17), in order to explain that they are not the heavens mentioned by that name in the first verse, but merely the firmament called 'heavens.'... The heavens mentioned here in the first verse (Genesis 1:1)... are the ones mentioned in *Praise YHVH from heaven.* (Psalms 148:1)."

199. **Rabbi Shim'on dissents for the sake of heaven!...** See M *Avot* 5:17: "Every conflict that is for the sake of heaven is destined to endure, while every conflict not for the sake of heaven is not destined to endure."

This is the first time in *MhN* that Rabbi Shim'on is presented as a significant personage. He is portrayed here as מארי פלוגתא (*marei plugta*), "a master of dissension," i.e.,

They rose to walk on. It was night. They said, "Let us sit here until light appears and engage in Torah."

They sat down. Rabbi Yoḥanan said, "The firmament created on the second day is the supernal firmament, and it has been taught: It is the curtain that divides between, as is written: *An image over the heads of the living being, a firmament like awesome ice* (Ezekiel 1:22). From this firmament all the other firmaments were made—those that revolve, and those that do not—all of them connected to that firmament. He called it *firmament* and He called it *heavens*, as is written: *God called the firmament Heavens* (Genesis 1:8), because from it they were formed."[200]

While they were sitting, Rabbi Yose's son approached his father. He said to him, "Concerning what Solomon said, ואתה תשמע השמים (*ve-attah tishma ha-shamayim*), *Oh, hear heaven, Your dwelling place* (1 Kings 8:39). It should have said *from heaven*!"[201]

Rabbi Yoḥanan heard. He said to him, "Speak, my child, speak, for the word in your mouth is holy!"[202]



Rabbi Yose said, "He asked about this verse: *Oh, hear heaven, Your dwelling place* (1 Kings 8:39). It should have said *from heaven*!"

Rabbi Yoḥanan said, "The verse is deficient. Like שועת עניים (*shav'at aniyyim*), *cry of the poor*: it should have said *from the poor*; and similarly צעקת ענוים (*tsa'aqat anavim*), *cry of the lowly* (Psalms 9:13), and so in many places."[203]

a troublemaker, akin to the Socratic gadfly. This depiction accords with the classic (pre-Zoharic) presentation of Rabbi Shim'on as an uncompromising figure—such as the anecdote (BT *Shabbat* 33b) in which everything he looked at caught fire.

On the figure of Rabbi Shim'on in the *Zohar*, see Hellner-Eshed, *A River Flows from Eden*, 31–61.

200. **He called it *firmament* and He called it *heavens*...** Although in Genesis 1 the firmament is called *Heavens*, the heavens actually derive from the supernal firmament described in Ezekiel's vision. See below, note 206.

See Maimonides, *Guide of the Perplexed* 2:30: "The words *God called the firmament Heavens* is intended... to make clear that the term is equivocal.... Because of this equivocality of the terms, the true *heavens* are sometimes likewise called *firmament*, just as the true *firmament* is called *heavens*." See also Naḥmanides on Genesis 1:8.

201. **It should have said *from heaven*!** In its simple sense, the verse means *Oh, hear from* [or: *in*] *heaven*. Rabbi Yose's son notes the absence of an explicit locational preposition. Cf. BT *Ḥagigah* 12b.

202. **Speak, my child...** Having overheard the child ask his father a matter of Torah, Rabbi Yoḥanan too wishes to hear the child's question.

The motif of the wunderkind appears throughout the *Zohar*. See *Zohar* 1:92b, 148a, 238b; 2:6b, 169b; 3:39a, 162a, 171a, 186a, 204b; *ZḤ* 9a (*MhN*), 14d (*MhN*), 48a, 49a–b, 77d (*MhN, Rut*), 84b–c (*MhN, Rut*).

203. **The verse is deficient...** Rabbi Yoḥanan suggests that the absence of the word "from" does not pose a problem. It is

He approached his father and said to him, "I have heard something about this."

Rabbi Yoḥanan said to him, "Speak, my child, speak."

He said, "I have heard that when Israel offer their prayers and supplications in their houses of prayer, Metatron—the Prince of the Countenance—gathers all the prayers of Israel and raises them aloft, depositing them in that firmament. When the blessed Holy One desires to call to mind the merits of Israel, He gazes upon that firmament called heaven—where the prayers of Israel abide—and has compassion upon them. As is written: *Oh, hear heaven* (1 Kings 8:39)—heaven, precisely! Similarly David said: *Praise YHVH from heaven* (Psalms 148:1)—for there reside the praises of Israel."[204]

Rabbi Yoḥanan came, kissed him on his head and blessed him, saying, "A pearl was in your hand; a pearl shall you be in your generation!"[205]

Rabbi Yitsḥak said, "Come and see: The blessed Holy One created this firmament; and from it He fashioned heavens, ordained beneath. Firmament above, heavens below. Beneath these, He made another heaven, called 'the firmament of the heavens,' in which are appointed all the luminous lights.[206]



merely a contraction, and the word "from" can be inferred. The child, however, will find a deeper meaning. (The expression *shav'at aniyyim*, "cry of the poor," is from the *Nishmat kol ḥai* prayer recited on Sabbath morning.)

204. **Metatron . . . gathers all the prayers . . .** On Metatron, see above, note 149. On Metatron as the conduit between the upper and lower worlds, see *ZḤ* 24a, 25d–26a, 28b (all *MhN*); Scholem, "Parashah Ḥadashah," 437 (Addendum 1 in this volume).

Cf. *Shemot Rabbah* 21:4: "Rabbi Pinḥas said in the name of Rabbi Me'ir, and Rabbi Yirmeyah said in the name of Rabbi Abba, 'When Israel prays, you do not find them all praying as one, but rather each assembly prays on its own, one after the other. When they have all finished, the angel appointed over prayers gathers all the prayers offered in all the synagogues and weaves them into wreaths, which he places on the head of the blessed Holy One.'" Cf. BT *Ḥagigah* 13b, where it is the angel Sandalphon who binds crowns to his maker, causing each crown to ascend and rest on God's head.

The odd phrasing of the verse from Kings contains a mystery, now revealed by the child. God is implored to hear heaven—and not from or in heaven—for heaven is the supernal depository of the praises of Israel. Just as the heaven referred to in David's call to *Praise YHVH from heaven* signified the upper heaven, so the heaven to which Solomon implores God to pay heed. See *ZḤ* 12b (*MhN*), page 95.

205. **A pearl was in your hand . . .** On possessing pearls of wisdom, see BT *Ḥagigah* 3a; *Zohar* 1:148b; 2:209a; *ZḤ* 14a (*MhN*); Scholem, "Parashah Ḥadashah," 432 (Addendum 1 in this volume). Cf. BT *Berakhot* 17a, *Sanhedrin* 50b, *Zevaḥim* 36b.

206. **Firmament above, heavens below . . .** According to Rabbi Yitsḥak, the heavenly realm has three tiers: the supernal firmament (described in Ezekiel's vision); the heavens; and finally, "the firmament of the heavens." What we perceive as the sky—with planets and stars—is but the lowest tier. See *ZḤ* 14a (*MhN*), page 118; cf. *Zohar* 1:34a, 162b.

See BT *Ḥagigah* 12b: "Resh Lakish said,

"Come and see: Between this firmament called 'the firmament of the heavens' and the firmament spread above the living beings, there are 390 other firmaments—and 7450 component parts, resting on two other luminaries. From these lights the blessed Holy One drew, placing them in this firmament of the heavens, to shine upon the earth."[207]

## Section 4[208]

*God said, "Let the earth bring forth* נפש חיה (*nefesh ḥayyah*), *living beings, according to their kind"* (Genesis 1:24).

Rabbi Bo opened with this verse: "*Not like these is the share of Jacob, for He is the one who forms all* (Jeremiah 10:16). Come and see: When the blessed Holy One created the world, He gazed and foresaw that in the future Israel would rise and receive His Torah. So He hewed from His Throne all the souls destined to be placed within them, and He fashioned above a certain storehouse, where all the souls hewn from His Throne reside, and He called it Body of Souls."[209]

Why is it called Body of Souls?[210]



"There are seven heavens.... The one called רקיע (*raqi'a*), firmament, is that in which the sun, moon, stars, and constellations are set."

207. **390 other firmaments . . .** 390 is the numerical value of שמים (*shamayim*), "heavens."

See BT *Ḥagigah* 13a: "It has been taught: Rabban Yoḥanan son of Zakkai said...'the distance from the earth to the firmament is a journey of five hundred years, and the thickness of the firmament is a journey of five hundred years, and likewise [the distance] between one firmament and the other.'" See also *Bereshit Rabbah* 6:6.

The blessed Holy One drew the light of the sun and moon from the radiance above. See *ZḤ* 14a, 15b–c (both *MhN*). Cf. *Bemidbar Rabbah* 15:9: "Immense is the light of the blessed Holy One! The sun and moon illuminate the world. But from where do they derive their radiance? They snatch from sparks of lights above.... [God says,] 'I made the sun and the moon to shine before you,' as is said: *God set them in the firmament of heaven to shine upon the earth* (Genesis 1:17)."

208. **Section 4** Most of the manuscripts preserve this section heading פרשה ד (*parashah* 4), perhaps reflecting an early attempt to arrange the materials of *MhN* on the Torah. See *ZḤ* 3d, 13a, 14a, 17c, 19c, 28a, end of *parashat Lekh Lekha*, below, page 311 (all *MhN*); *Zohar* 2:20a (*MhN*).

209. **He fashioned above a certain storehouse... Body of Souls** See BT *Yevamot* 62a: "Rabbi Assi said, 'The Son of David will not come until all souls in the body have been depleted.'" "The body" is the heavenly treasure house of unborn souls.

See Rashi, ad loc., and on BT *Avodah Zarah* 5a; *Bahir* 126 (184); *Zohar* 1:28b (*TZ*), 119a; 2:142a, 157a, 161b, 174a, 253a (*Heikh*); 3:152a; *ZḤ* 53c. See Tishby, *Wisdom of the Zohar*, 2:701–2; Liebes, *Peraqim*, 179–80, 226.

On the soul's originating from the divine Throne, see above, note 188.

The full verse in Jeremiah reads: "*Not like these [idols] is the share of Jacob, for He is the one who forms all, and Israel is the tribe of His inheritance; YHVH of Hosts is His name.*" On this verse, see also *Zohar* 2:172a.

210. **Why is it called Body of Souls?** If this is the abode of souls before they enter

Rabbi Bo explained, "Because when all the souls depart this world, the blessed Holy One prepares for them the form of bodies—just as they were in this world—and places them in this storehouse."[211]

This storehouse—where is it?

Rabbi Yoḥanan said in the name of Rabbi Yitsḥak, "In the place where are the treasuries of the dead and the treasuries of good life—it is called *Aravot*. In *Aravot* there are many treasuries, and the treasuries of souls are there."[212]

But look, Rabbi Bo said that there is one storehouse, yet here we have learned "treasuries"![213]

Rabbi Yoḥanan said, "Let this not trouble you. There are two storehouses. The storehouse of souls destined to be placed within human beings, as we have learned: In precisely the same form and image as one will appear in this world, so is one in that form there. It is called Body of Souls because He fashions for them a body, just as they are destined to become [10c]. There is another storehouse corresponding to this one, for those souls that were in this world and fulfilled the Torah, and it is called The Treasuries of Eternal Life. This is as Rabbi Shim'on used to say: 'May so-and-so (who has departed this world) abide in the Treasuries of Eternal Life!'"[214]

Our Rabbis have taught: Every single day, a herald proclaims: "Awaken children of the supernal Holy One, and perform the service of your Lord—who has

the world, what is the relevance of the word "Body"—which would seem to apply to earthly existence?

211. **the blessed Holy One prepares for them the form of bodies...** When they have left this world, the souls are garbed in a garment of light on the pattern of the body. See *ZḤ* 18b (*MhN*), page 187; see below, note 214. The storehouse, according to Rabbi Bo, is thus the abode of the souls before and after earthly existence.

212. ***Aravot*...** See BT *Ḥagigah* 12b: "Resh Lakish said, '[There are] seven [heavens].... The one called *Aravot* is where are righteousness, justice, charity, treasuries of life, treasuries of peace, treasuries of blessings, the souls (*neshamot*) of the righteous, and the spirits and souls (*ruḥot* and *neshamot*) that are to be created in the future, and the dew with which the blessed Holy One will revive the dead.'" See *ZḤ* 21a (*MhN*).

213. **yet here we have learned "treasuries"** In the plural, implying more than one storehouse.

214. **There are two storehouses...** In contrast to Rabbi Bo, Rabbi Yoḥanan says that there are two storehouses: one, where the soul abides in its ethereal body, resembling the physical body it will later inhabit on earth; and another, where the soul resides in its regained ethereal body after death.

On the ethereal body, see Naḥmanides on Genesis 49:33; *Zohar* 1:7a, 38b (*Heikh*), 81a (*ST*), 90b–91a, 115b (*MhN*), 131a, 217b, 219a, 220a, 224a–b, 227a–b, 233b; 2:11a, 13a–b, 96b, 141b, 150a, 156b–157a, 161b; 3:13a–b, 43a–b, 61b, 70b, 104a–b; *ZḤ* 18b (*MhN*), 90b (*MhN, Rut*); Moses de León, *Sefer ha-Rimmon*, 390; [Moses de León?], *Seder Gan Eden*, 133; Scholem, *Shedim, Ruḥot u-Nshamot*, 215–45; idem, *Kabbalah*, 158–59; idem, *On the Mystical Shape of the Godhead*, 251–73;

distinguished you from the other nations and placed within you a holy soul hewn from His Throne of Glory!"[215]

Rabbi Yuda said, "If so, from which site do the souls of the other nations derive?"[216]

He encountered Rabbi El'azar. He said to him, "Come and see what is written: *He blew into his nostrils* נשמת חיים (*nishmat ḥayyim*), *the breath of life* (Genesis 2:7). This is נשמתא קדישא (*nishmeta qaddisha*), the holy soul, hewn from the supernal King's Throne of Glory. What is written about him? *The human became* נפש חיה (*nefesh ḥayyah*), *a creaturely soul* (ibid.)."[217]

Rabbi El'azar explained, "This is the power given to animals, beasts, and fish, created from the earth, as is written: *Let the earth bring forth* נפש חיה (*nefesh ḥayyah*), *a creaturely soul, according to its kind* (Genesis 1:24)."[218]

Tishby, *Wisdom of the Zohar,* 2:770–73. Cf. Rashi on BT *Ḥagigah* 12b, s.v. *ve-ruḥot u-nshamot.*

215. **Every single day, a herald proclaims: "Awaken...** Cf. *Avot* 6:2, in the name of Rabbi Yehoshu'a son of Levi, "Every single day, an echo reverberates from Mount Horeb [Sinai], proclaiming: 'Woe to creatures for the humiliation of Torah!'"

On the language of awakening in the *Zohar,* see Hellner-Eshed, *A River Flows from Eden,* 204–28.

216. **from which site do the souls of the other nations derive?** Israel is distinguished by the holy soul hewn from the divine Throne. What of the other nations? Cf. *Zohar* 1:47a.

217. **נשמתא קדישא (*nishmeta qaddisha*), the holy soul... נפש חיה (*nefesh ḥayyah*), *a creaturely soul*** Genesis 2:7 describes the creation of human beings: *He blew into his nostrils* נשמת חיים (*nishmat ḥayyim*), *the breath of life, and the human became* נפש חיה (*nefesh ḥayyah*), *a living being.* Here, the *nishmat ḥayyim* is distinguished from the *nefesh ḥayyah*: the former signifies the holy soul (*neshamah*) hewn from the divine Throne—and through which one attains knowledge of divinity and life in the world to come; the latter signifies the "creaturely (or animal or vital) soul." See next note.

On the distinction between these two kinds of soul in *MhN,* see *ZḤ* 11c, 16b–c, 17c. See also Tishby, *Wisdom of the Zohar,* 2:708–9. In the main body of the *Zohar,* the term *nefesh ḥayyah* is used differently, signifying the holy soul emanated from the living being, namely the soul derived from *Shekhinah.* See, for example, *Zohar* 1:12b; 3:70b.

According to Rabbi El'azar, while human beings were originally created with the holy soul, through their sin they have forfeited it—and reverted to the creaturely soul. See below.

On the diverse theories of the soul in *MhN,* see Tishby, *Wisdom of the Zohar,* 2:703–12.

Cf. Naḥmanides on Genesis 2:7: "This alludes to the superiority of the soul, its foundation and secret... to inform us that the soul did not come to man from the elements. ... Rather, it was the spirit of the Great God."

218. **This is the power given to animals...** The *nefesh ḥayyah, creaturely soul,* derives from the earth, i.e., the soil, the ground. It is the soul that imparts life to all creatures. It is not associated with spiritual or intellectual activity. Cf. Naḥmanides on Genesis 2:7; See *ZḤ* 11c (*MhN*), page 82.

Rabbi Yitsḥak said, "Torah cries out over the human being saying, 'The blessed Holy One created the human being, and placed within him a holy soul that he might attain life in the world to come. But through his sin, he reverted to that נפש חיה (*nefesh ḥayyah*), creaturely soul, hewn from the earth for animals and beasts!'"

Rabbi Yehudah said, "This is implied from what is written: *The human became* נפש חיה (*nefesh ḥayyah*), *a creaturely soul* (Genesis 2:7). The verse does not say *He made him* [*a creaturely soul*], but rather *The human became*—teaching that he brought this on himself—reverting to that soul hewn from the earth."[219]

Rabbi Yoḥanan said, "The blessed Holy One said, 'Adam, I created you supernal above all My creatures, and I breathed into you נשמת חיים (*nishmat ḥayyim*), *the soul of life*, hewn from My Throne, bestowing life to those who possess it. Yet you reverted to that creaturely soul I created from the earth for animals! By your life! Henceforth, whoever engages in My Torah and observes it, I will



bequeath him that soul hewn from My Throne, bestowing life to those who possess it. As for all those who do not engage in My Torah—their portion will be that creaturely soul they have chosen, that they might be annihilated with it.'"[220]

Rabbi Yitsḥak said, "Come and see what is written: *Who knows if the spirit of the sons of men ascends on high and the spirit of the beast descends below into earth* (Ecclesiastes 3:21)? *The spirit of the sons of men ascends on high*—the holy soul of the righteous. *The spirit of the beast*—the creaturely soul hewn from the earth for beasts, which will be annihilated, and which descends to be obliterated from the world."[221]

Rabbi Ḥiyya said, "If so, do non-Jews not possess a *neshamah* but only that creaturely soul?"[222]

219. ***The human became a creaturely soul...*** This homily appears again at *ZḤ* 17c (*MhN*), page 176.

220. **Henceforth, whoever engages My Torah...** Following the primal sin, the holy soul will no longer be bestowed at birth, but must be earned through Torah study and performance of the commandments. Human beings thus have an option: either abide with the creaturely soul (which will be annihilated), or acquire the soul of life, the *neshamah* (which lives forever).

221. ***Who knows if the spirit of the sons of men ascends on high...*** Whereas the holy soul of the righteous abides eternally, the creaturely soul is obliterated from the world. Cf. *Zohar* 1:54a.

222. **do non-Jews not possess a *neshamah* but only that creaturely soul?** If the holy soul is acquired through Torah study and commandments, what then of the other nations? As Rabbi Yoḥanan makes clear, Jews alone can possess a holy *neshamah*. See also *ZḤ* 10d–11a (*MhN*), pages 72 and 77; *Zohar* 3:25b.

Cf. Judah Halevi, *Kuzari* 1:27–47, 95, 102–11. Cf. *Zohar* 1:47a: "The soul of other nations—whence does it come?" to which

Rabbi Yoḥanan said, "That is correct."

Rabbi El'azar said, "And Israel—who bestows?"

Rabbi Ḥiyya was astonished.[223]

Rabbi El'azar said, "Come and see what we have learned: If one comes to purify himself, he is given assistance. What assistance is he given? It is none other than the holy soul, to be a boost for him. It is bequeathed him to assist him in this world and in the world to come."[224]

Rabbi El'azar said, "Until thirteen years a person's striving is with that creaturely soul. From thirteen years and upward, if he wishes to be righteous, the holy supernal soul—hewn from the King's Throne of Glory—is bequeathed him."[225]

Rabbi Yehudah said, "This accords with the explanation we have learned in the Thirteen Attributes of Mercy, in the Mishnah of Rabbi El'azar."[226]

Rabbi El'azar replies, "From those impure aspects of the left," i.e., from demonic powers stemming from the left side of the *sefirot*. Cf. *Zohar* 1:13a, 20b, 131a.

223. **Rabbi Ḥiyya was astonished** He was astonished by the question, perhaps because the answer ought to be obvious, and perhaps also because the answer is so astonishing—from God Himself. See below.

224. **If one comes to purify himself...** Rabbi El'azar answers his own question. See BT *Shabbat* 104a: "Resh Lakish said, '...If one comes to defile himself, he is provided an opening; if one comes to purify himself, he is given assistance.'"

Cf. BT *Yoma* 39a: "Our Rabbis taught: '*Do not defile yourselves with them, and thus become defiled* (Leviticus 11:43). If one defiles himself slightly, he is defiled greatly; below, he is defiled from above; in this world, he is defiled in the world to come.' Our Rabbis taught: '*Hallow yourselves and you will be holy* (ibid., 44). If one sanctifies himself slightly, he is assisted greatly; below, he is sanctified from above; in this world, he is sanctified in the world to come.'"

See BT *Makkot* 10b: "Rabbah son of Bar Ḥana said in the name of Rav Ḥuna (some say in the name of Rabbi El'azar), 'From the Torah, the Prophets, and the Writings it can be demonstrated that one is led on the path one wishes to take.'" See also *Zohar* 1:62a; *ZḤ* 20d, 24b (both *MhN*).



225. **Until thirteen years...** According to rabbinic tradition, while the evil impulse attempts to seduce a person from the moment of birth, the good impulse enters only at age thirteen. See *Avot de-Rabbi Natan* A, 16; *Qohelet Rabbah* on 4:13; *Midrash Tehillim* 9:5. This rabbinic idea is here correlated with the two types of soul: *nefesh ḥayyah* and *neshamah*.

On the *neshamah* entering at age thirteen, see *Zohar* 1:78a–79b (*ST*); 2:98a; Tishby, *Wisdom of the Zohar*, 2:762. On the significance of the age of thirteen, see *Zohar* 1:179a–b; *ZḤ* 15d (*MhN*), page 148.

226. **Thirteen Attributes of Mercy, in the Mishnah of Rabbi El'azar** One of the many books housed in the real or imaginary Zoharic library. It is not the rabbinic work *The Mishnah of Rabbi Eli'ezer or The Midrash of the Thirty Two Hermeneutic Rules*, ed. Enelow, which does not mention this idea. An apparently similar work known as the Thirteen Attributes of Mercy is referenced in *Zohar* 1:124b, 129b (both *MhN*); see also *ZḤ* 13a (*MhN*). See *Ketem Paz*, 1:22d: "All such books mentioned in the *Zohar*...have been lost in the wanderings of exile.... Nothing is left of them except what is mentioned in the *Zohar*." Here, the thirteen attributes of

Rabbi Shim'on son of Yoḥai invited the Masters of Mishnah to eat at a great feast he prepared for them, and he decorated his entire house with precious adornments. He seated the rabbis on one side and himself on the other, and he was exceedingly joyous.[227]

They said to him, "Why is the joy of our master greater today than other days?"

He replied, "Today the holy, supernal soul is descending—via the four wings of the creatures—upon Rabbi El'azar, my son. At this celebration I will attain consummate joy."[228]

He seated Rabbi El'azar next to himself. He said, "Be seated, my son, be seated, for on this day you are holy—among the share of the holy ones."

Rabbi Shim'on said a certain word and fire surrounded the house. The rabbis went out and saw smoke [10d] ascending from the house the entire day.[229]

Rabbi Yose son of Rabbi Shim'on son of Lekonya arrived. He found the rabbis astonished, standing in the street. He said to them, "What's going on?"[230]



mercy, derived from Exodus 34:6–7, are correlated with the age of thirteen. Perhaps the *Zohar* intends that the story that follows is from this very work.

227. **Masters of Mishnah...** This term, מארי מתניתא (*marei matnita*), occurs throughout *Midrash ha-Ne'lam* in various formulations. It appears to signify a particular (undefined) group of sages possessing esoteric wisdom. In some ways, the Masters of Mishnah are a forerunner to the *Ḥavrayya*, the Companions headed by Rabbi Shim'on, found in the main body of the *Zohar*. Significantly, however, Rabbi Shim'on does not always occupy a privileged position in this group. The Mishnah of which they are masters is not the Mishnah of the rabbinic sage Rabbi Yehudah ha-Nasi, but rather a body of esoteric knowledge often relating to the soul and the structure of the cosmos. See *Zohar* 1:123b (*MhN*, though mistakenly labeled as *Tosefta*); 1:127a–b, 129a–b, 130a, 135a, 138a, 139b; 2:5a, 14a (all *MhN*); *ZḤ* 12c, 13a, 14c, 15b–c, 16a, 59b (all *MhN*); Scholem, "Parashah Ḥadashah," 443, 444 (Addendum 1 in this volume); Meroz, "Va-Ani Lo Hayiti Sham?," 168 (Addendum 3 in this volume). Cf. *Pesiqta de-Rav Kahana* 11:15, 23:12. See also Matt, "Matnita di-Lan," 132–34.

Cf. the term מארי דמתיבתא (*marei de-metivta*), Masters of the Academy, also found in *Midrash ha-Ne'lam*; see Scholem, "Parashah Ḥadashah," 432–33, 443. The expression "exceedingly joyous" echoes BT *Berakhot* 30b–31a.

228. **At this celebration . . .** The bar mitsvah of Rabbi El'azar. See *ZḤ* 9a (*MhN*); *Zohar* 3:191b. The creatures are the bearers of the divine chariot-throne, described in Ezekiel 1. See also Ta-Shma, *Ha-Nigleh sheba-Nistar*, 34–35.

229. **a certain word...** Perhaps a divine name or some other mysterious formula. The *Zohar* does not specify.

230. **Rabbi Yose son of Rabbi Shim'on son of Lekonya...** According to rabbinic tradition, Rabbi El'azar's father-in-law was named Rabbi Shim'on son of Yose son of Lekonya. The *Zohar* consistently switches father and son, transforming Shim'on son of Yose into Yose son of Shim'on. See *Pesiqta de-Rav Kahana* 11:20; JT *Ma'aserot* 3:8, 50d; *Shir ha-Shirim Rabbah* on 4:11; *Devarim Rabbah* 7:11; *Seder ha-Dorot*, s.v. *Shim'on ben Yose ben Lekonya*; *Zohar* 1:5a, 61b; 3:84b, 188a, 193a; *ZḤ* 7d, 14a, 22c (all *MhN*).

In BT *Bava Metsi'a* 85a, the name of Rabbi El'azar's brother-in-law is given as Rabbi Shim'on son of Issi (Yose) son of Lekonya, which would make Yose his father-in-law, as

They replied, "Look at this smoke from the celestial fire! It is because today Rabbi El'azar is being crowned with a holy crown."

The rabbis saw four wings of an eagle descending in fire, surrounding him and Rabbi Shim'on, his father. Rabbi Yose sat there until the fire abated.

He entered in his presence and said, "Crowning and secrecy, most sublime exaltation. May this celebration attain consummation!"[231]

Rabbi Shim'on asked, "What do you mean?"

Rabbi Yose replied, "Look, my daughter for Rabbi El'azar, your son!"

He said, "Certainly."

They summoned the rabbis and he gave him his daughter. They sat there for three days, delving in Torah in his presence, and there was not a single mystery of Mishnah that Rabbi Shim'on didn't teach them. It was said about Rabbi Shim'on that the rainbow was not seen in his days, for he was a sign in the world.[232]

Rabbi Yitsḥak said, "The soul abides enduringly forever. Just as the blessed
Holy One abides, so it abides. However, concerning that creaturely soul, Scrip- 71
ture said: *That soul shall surely be cut off, its iniquity is upon it* (Numbers 15:31)."[233]

Rabbi Yose said, "What prompted Onqelos to translate *The human became* נפש חיה (*nefesh ḥayyah*), *a living being* (Genesis 2:7), as '[The human became] a speaking spirit'? If this refers to the animal soul, why then do they not speak?"[234]

in the *Zohar*—but nowhere in rabbinic literature is he named Yose son of Shim'on.

231. **Crowning and secrecy . . . exaltation . . . consummation!** The Aramaic is melodious and enigmatic: אכתרא וסיתרא גבהותא על כלא האי הילולא להוי שלימתא (*akitra ve-sitra gavhuta al kula, hai hilula lehevei shleimata*). The crowning and secrecy apparently refers to the bestowal of the holy soul upon Rabbi El'azar. Rabbi Yose intends that given the exaltation of the moment, the occasion ought to have an appropriate climax, as explained immediately below.

232. **the rainbow was not seen in his days...** The rainbow is a sign of the divine covenant with the world (see Genesis 9:12–17), but if a fully righteous person is alive, he himself serves as such a sign—so the rainbow is unnecessary. See *Pesiqta de-Rav Kahana* 11:15; *Bereshit Rabbah* 35:2; JT *Berakhot* 9:2, 13d; BT *Ketubbot* 77b; *Zohar* 1:225a; 2:174b; 3:15a, 36a; Scholem, 'Parashah Ḥadashah,' 432, n. 29 (Addendum 1 in this volume); Liebes, *Studies in the Zohar*, 15.

233. **Just as the blessed Holy One abides, so it abides...** The soul, namely, the *neshamah*, is eternal, whereas the creaturely soul perishes. See below, note 244.

Cf. *Vayiqra Rabbah* 4:8: "What reason did David see for praising the blessed Holy One with his soul? He said, '... The soul outlasts the body, and the blessed Holy One outlives the world; let the soul that outlasts the body come and praise the blessed Holy One who outlives His Universe.'"

234. **What prompted Onqelos to translate...** In *Targum Onqelos*, an Aramaic translation of the Torah from antiquity, the term *nefesh ḥayyah*, "living being," is rendered רוח ממללא (*ruaḥ memalela*), "speaking spirit." Following the infusion of the soul of life, the human being attains the capacity for speech. See *Onqelos* to Genesis 2:7.

Rabbi Yitsḥak replied, "Because they were kneaded from coarser clods of earth than human beings; and because they do not raise their heads, nor gaze up at the expanse as humans do. Had they been kneaded from finer dust like human beings, and were they able to raise their heads and gaze up at the expanse, they would speak."

Rabbi Yose said, "Granted kneading and raising their heads, but why gazing up at the expanse?"

He replied, "It is a great help to human beings. Come and see: When Nebuchadnezzar was banished, a beast among the mountains, he found no help until he gazed upon the expanse, as is written: *I, Nebuchadnezzar, raised my eyes to heaven, and my reason returned to me* (Daniel 4:31). Until he contemplated the expanse, his reason was not restored."[235]

Rabbi Kruspedai said, "The non-Jews and the ignorant—who neither believe in the blessed Holy One nor engage in Torah—possess only that creaturely soul that came forth from the earth; therefore they do not have faith. But concerning
72 Israel, who believe in the blessed Holy One and engage in Torah and observe His commandments, the blessed Holy One said, *Not like these is the share of Jacob* (Jeremiah 10:16)—they will not have a creaturely soul. What will they have? *For He is the one who forms all* (ibid.). *All*—His *Shekhinah*. The holy soul is hewn from her, to be the share of Jacob. What is it? Namely, *All*—the soul, since it is hewn from her."[236]

235. **It is a great help to human beings...** On the benefit of gazing up at the expanse, see BT *Berakhot* 34b and Rashi's gloss: "Rabbi Ḥiyya son of Abba said in the name of Rabbi Yoḥanan: 'A person should only pray in a room that has windows, since it says: *Now his windows were open in his upper chamber toward Jerusalem* (Daniel 6:11)." Rashi, ad loc.: "This causes him to attune his heart, for when he looks toward the heavens, his heart submits." Cf. *Midrash Tehillim* 32:1.

On Nebuchadnezzar's banishment, see Daniel chapter 4. Verse 30 reads: *There and then the sentence was carried out upon Nebuchadnezzar. He was driven away from men, he ate grass like cattle, and his body was drenched with the dew of heaven—until his hair grew like eagle's [feathers] and his nails like [the talons] of birds.*

236. ***All*—His *Shekhinah*...** In contrast to the nations—who possess only a creaturely soul—Israel possesses the holy soul, termed here הכל (*ha-kol*), *All*, because it derives from the *Shekhinah*, also termed "All." See *ZḤ* 25a (*MhN*). The second phrase in Jeremiah 10:16 is כי יוצר הכל הוא (*ki yotser ha-kol hu*), *For He is the one who forms of all*, which perhaps is being read as *for the All forms him*, i.e., the soul of Israel derives from the All, the *Shekhinah*.

In *MhN* the soul is understood to derive from the Throne of Glory (see above, note 188), which at times seems to be correlated with the *Shekhinah*. Cf. *Zohar* 1:97a–b (*MhN*).

See Naḥmanides on Genesis 24:1: "The blessed Holy One has an attribute called *Kol*, All, so called because it is the foundation of everything." The use of the term "All" here may also derive from the writings of Abraham Ibn Ezra, who uses *ha-kol* variously to signify the second and third of the Neoplatonic hypostases: the Universal Intellect

Rabbi Yehudah said, "If it is true that non-Jews do not possess faith, look: we see that when they are lame and blind and struck by all kinds of afflictions and illnesses, they visit their idols—and are healed!"[237]

He replied, "So as to cause them to perish in the world to come, as is written: *He makes nations great and destroys them* (Job 12:23). Furthermore, we have learned: *malignant and* נאמנים (*ne'emanim*), *relentless, illnesses* (Deuteronomy 28:59). What is meant by נאמנים (*ne'emanim*)? They act מהימנותא (*meheimenuta*), faithfully, for when the time comes, they depart from that person; and sometimes they are in the proximity of those idols, because they visit their idols when they are sick, and they are healed—and they say that it was the idol that caused this!"[238]

and the Universal Soul. See Ibn Ezra on Genesis 1:26: "The upper soul of man, which does not die, is compared in its being to God.... God is one, and He is the creator of All, and He is the all—though I cannot explain." See also idem on Psalms 22:22: "in separating from the body, she [the soul] is gathered to the All."

Perhaps the author intends to correlate the *Shekhinah* with the Neoplatonic Universal Soul. Cf. Plotinus, *The Enneads* IV.3.2: "the particular soul—this 'part of the All-Soul'—is of one Ideal-Form with it."

On the different souls of Jews and Gentiles, see *ZḤ* 10c (*MhN*) and above, note 222.

237. **they visit their idols—and are healed** See BT *Avodah Zarah* 55a: "[An Israelite named] Zunin said to Rabbi Akiva, 'We both know in our heart that there is no reality in an idol; nevertheless we see people enter [the shrine] crippled and come out cured. Why?' He replied, 'I will give you a parable: To what is the matter like? To a trustworthy man in a city, and all his townsmen used to deposit [their money] in his charge without witnesses. One man, however, came and deposited [his money] in his charge with witnesses; but on one occasion he forgot and made his deposit without witnesses. The wife [of the trustworthy man] said to [her husband], "Come, let us deny it." He answered her, "Because this fool acted in an unworthy manner, shall I destroy my reputation for trustworthiness!" It is similar with afflictions. At the time they are sent upon a man, the oath is imposed upon them, "You shall not come upon him except on such and such a day, nor depart from him except on such and such a day, and at such an hour, and through the medium of so and so, and through such and such a remedy." When the time arrives for them to depart, the man chanced to go to an idolatrous shrine. The afflictions plead, "It is right that we should not leave him and depart; but because this fool acts in an unworthy way shall we break our oath!'" This is similar to what Rabbi Yoḥanan said, 'What is the meaning of the verse: *Malignant and faithful illnesses* (Deuteronomy 28:59)? *Malignant* in their mission and *faithful* to their oath.'"

238. **What is meant by נאמנים (*ne'emanim*)?...** Sometimes illnesses are decreed to last for a certain time, and after "faithfully" fulfilling their role, they depart. While it may appear that the idol healed them, it is merely a coincidence of timing. In this verse, the simple sense of *ne'emanim* is "enduring, lingering, persistent, constant, relentless, chronic." Here, the verse is read hyperliterally, as "faithful." See previous note; *Leqaḥ Tov*, Deuteronomy 28:59; *Zohar* 1:227a–b.

Apparently, Rabbi Yitsḥak is the speaker here.

Rabbi Yoḥanan said, "Once a certain Jew told me that he was afflicted with many illnesses and he could not be healed. He saw how the Arabs used to visit their idols when they were sick and would be healed.[239]

"He said, 'I will go there even though it is forbidden. There is no problem with having a look!'[240]

"He went there, entered among them, and spent the night there with the plagued and diseased people. They all fell asleep but he did not sleep. He saw a certain demon walking among them, with healing objects in his hand, [11a] placing them on everyone whereupon they were healed. He passed by him but he did not place them upon him. He said to him, 'My master, look—I am also sick, place them upon me!'

"He said to him, '*Not like these is the share of Jacob* (Jeremiah 10:16), for they have been handed to me to make them perish in the world to come; but the Children of Jacob are not like these. How so? Because *He is the one who forms all* (ibid.). Just as one who forms destroys and builds, so the blessed Holy One afflicts and heals, destroys and builds.'[241]

"The man left and told me the incident. I said, 'Blessed be the Compassionate One, who sent you there to behold this and hear from his mouth!' And Yose the sorcerer told me something similar."

Rabbi Yitsḥak said in the name of Rabbi Aḥa, "What is the meaning of the verse *The soul of Shaddai gives them understanding* (Job 32:8)? Well, it is the soul that leads a person to recognize his Creator, bringing him into Torah and good



239. **Arabs...** טעיין (*ta'ayan*) Or: Arabian caravaner, derived from the Arabian tribe *Tayyi'*.

240. **There is no problem with having a look!** Or: "merely to see what goes on."

241. ***Not like these is the share of Jacob...*** While it appears that non-Jews are healed at their idolatrous shines, this is only a ruse that they might perish in the next world. Jews, however, can only be healed directly by God. Cf. *ZḤ* 13b (*MhN*).

See *Midrash Aseret ha-Dibberot* (*Beit ha-Midrash*, 1:71): "It once happened that a certain lame Jew heard that there was an idol in a given place, to which all the sick in the world used to come and be healed. So he went to be cured. He entered the shrine with the sick people at midnight; a man came holding in his hand a small cruse filled with oil, and he anointed all the sick and they were cured. When he came to the Jew, he said, 'Are you not a Jew?' He replied, 'Yes.' 'Then what are you doing here?' He replied, '[I came] to be healed.' Thereupon he said to him, 'Know you not that [the idol] itself is a demon who does these things in order to entice people to idolatry, so that he can destroy them from the world?'" See Urbach, *The Sages*, 25.

See *Shemot Rabbah* 16:2: "You have heard the shame of idolatry, now come and hear the praises of the Omnipresent! As is said: *Not like these is the share of Jacob for He is the one who forms all* (Jeremiah 10:16). The blessed Holy One said, 'Since it [an idol] is like a mute stone, and not real, and others have to guard it from being stolen, how can it possibly give life to those who are sick?' It is for this reason that one must not seek a cure from anything that belongs to it."

deeds. Happy are they who enter the path of Torah and the path of the soul, thereby attaining life of the world to come and the rank of the holy ones!"[242]

Rabbi Yitsḥak said in the name of Rabbi Aḥa, "Whoever engages in Torah acquires the *neshamah* by himself. As we have learned: One who comes to purify himself is given assistance. Woe to the wicked who cleave to the power of the earth called 'the creaturely soul'—created from the earth—and because of which they will be annihilated forever and ever!"[243]

Rabbi Dostai asked Rabbi Eli'ezer, saying, "That creaturely soul—what becomes of it in the world to come?"

He replied, "Do not speak thus; but rather ask 'What becomes of it in any event?' Come and hear: Rabbi Bo said, 'What is the meaning of the verse *That soul shall surely be cut off* (Numbers 15:31)? Well, it is like the breath that emerges out of a person's mouth, unable to rise even up to his eyes but immediately disappears. So the creaturely soul is like that breath which is immediately cut off from the mouth and disappears, never seen, as though it never was.'"[244] 75

Rabbi Yose said, "But we have learned: The souls of the wicked are the harmful spirits in the world!"[245]

242. **it is the soul that leads a person to recognize his Creator...** Namely, the *neshamah*. On the verse from Job, cf. Naḥmanides on Genesis 2:7.

243. **acquires the *neshamah* by himself...** Human beings have the choice to acquire the holy soul and thereby attain life in the world to come, or cleave to the creaturely soul, thereby facing annihilation. On the acquired soul/intellect, see above, *ZḤ* 6d (*MhN*), note 97.

244. **the creaturely soul... disappears... as though it never was** Unlike the *neshamah*, which lives forever, the creaturely soul is totally annihilated with the death of the body.

See Maimonides, *Mishneh Torah, Hilkhot Teshuvah* 8:1, 5: "The good that is hidden for the righteous is the life of the world to come. ...Whoever does not merit this life is dead and will not live forever. Rather, he will be cut off in his wickedness and perish as a beast. This is the meaning of the term *karet* in the Torah, as is said: *That soul shall surely be cut off* (Numbers 15:31).... After these souls become separated from bodies in this world, they will not merit the life of the world to come. Rather, even in the world to come they will be cut off.... This refers to the obliteration of the soul.... It is the nullification after which there is no renewal, and the loss that can never be recovered."

In saying "Do not speak thus," Rabbi Eli'ezer is apparently rejecting any association between the creaturely soul and the world to come.

On this passage, see Belkin, "Ha-Midrash ha-Ne'lam u-Mqorotav," 43; Werblowsky, "Philo and the Zohar," 39–40; Finkel, "The Alexandrian Tradition," 94–95.

245. **The souls of the wicked are the harmful spirits in the world!** Rabbi Eli'ezer has just stated that the creaturely soul (the soul of the wicked) is annihilated, yet according to Rabbi Yose, this cannot be—as tradition teaches that these souls are transformed into malevolent forces after death.

The main body of the *Zohar* does indeed support this view, apparently derived from the Pietists of Germany. *Midrash ha-Ne'lam*,

Rabbi Yitsḥak replied, "You have spoken well insofar as they harm their owners, displacing the power of the *neshamah* and the service of their Creator. The only malevolent force that harms a human being is that *nefesh*, insofar as it is obliterated and annihilated with the body."[246]

Rabbi Aḥa said, "We have not learned thus. But rather, that the souls of the wicked become harmful spirits in the world after they have departed the body!"[247]

Rabbi said, "We have learned: The souls of the wicked in the world.... How does the *nefesh* harm the body? All are astounded how those *nefashot* are the malevolent forces in the world, insofar as human beings cleave to them!"[248]

Our Rabbis have taught: Rabbi Yehudah son of Ya'akov said, "I wonder about the people of this generation, whether most of them were conceived fittingly! Come and see: What is the meaning of the verse *Sanctify yourselves and be holy* (Leviticus 11:44)? This teaches that a person must sanctify himself during intercourse."[249]



What is the relevance of sanctity here?

Rabbi Yehudah son of Ya'akov said, "That one not carry on licentiously and impudently, or with lewd intentions like animals, for animals behave solely in this fashion.

however, rejects this view. See next note. See *Zohar* 1:100a; 3:25a, 70a. See also *Zohar* 1:20a (*TZ*), 29a (*TZ*); 2:118a (*RM*); 3:16b (*RM*); *ZḤ* 118c (*Tiq*). See *Sefer Hasidim*, ed. Margaliot, par. 1170; El'azar of Worms, *Sefer Ḥokhmat ha-Nefesh*, 24c; Moses de León, *Mishkan ha-Edut*, 51b. See also Tishby, *Wisdom of the Zohar*, 2:704–5; Liebes, *Studies in the Zohar*, 93–94.

246. **You have spoken well insofar as they harm their owners...** Rabbi Yitsḥak rejects the demonological view. The only harm the (creaturely) soul (the *nefesh*) causes is through combating the power and influence of the holy *neshamah*.

247. **after they have departed the body** Rabbi Aḥa restates and sharpens the objection: it is post-mortem that the souls of the wicked become malevolent forces.

248. **All are astounded how those *nefashot*...** The manuscripts and printed texts differ considerably here. My reading follows V11 and V12, though the reconstruction remains tentative. Once again, the demonological interpretation is rejected. The souls of the wicked are harmful only inasmuch as the wicked cleave to the *nefesh*—forfeiting the *neshamah*, and hence forfeiting eternal life. Cf. Tishby, *Wisdom of the Zohar*, 2:729.

249. **sanctify himself during intercourse** In rabbinic literature, this verse from Leviticus is applied to sanctifying sexual relations. See BT *Shevu'ot* 18b: "Rabbi El'azar said, 'Whoever sanctifies himself during intercourse will have male children.'" See also BT *Niddah* 71a; *Bemidbar Rabbah* 9:7; Moses de León, *Sefer ha-Rimmon*, 93; *Zohar* 1:54a, 90b, 112a (*MhN*), 155a (*ST*), 204a; 2:11b; 3:56a. On sexual holiness, see *Zohar* 1:49b–50a; 2:89a–b; 3:81a–b, 168a; *Iggeret ha-Qodesh*, in *Kitvei Ramban*, 2:333; Tishby, *Wisdom of the Zohar*, 3:1363–64. Cf. *Zohar* 3:80a, where Rabbi El'azar wonders about his generation and its sexual practices.

"For look at what we have learned: Whoever has sex with lewd intentions or in the way we have just mentioned, and is not on guard against the essential matters that we have learned in the Mishnah, then the child that will be born to him will be licentious and impudent, promiscuous and wicked, and will not be reckoned among the seed of truth.[250]

"But whoever has sex to fulfill the commandment, sanctifies himself, and attunes his heart to heaven—he will have virtuous children, righteous and pious, God-fearing and holy, as is written: *Sanctify yourselves—and you will be holy.*"[251]

Rabbi Yehudah said, "Because the non-Jews procreate solely with lewd intentions, impudently and obscenely, they possess only that creaturely soul given to animals, for their conduct is just like animals! However, concerning Israel—who know how to sanctify themselves—it is written: *I planted you as a noble vine, entirely* זרע אמת (*zera emet*), *seed of truth* (Jeremiah 2:21)."[252]

What is meant by אמת (*emet*), *truth*?



250. **the essential matters that we have learned in the Mishnah...**

See BT *Nedarim* 20b: "*And I will remove from you the rebellious ones and the criminals* (Ezekiel 20:38). Rabbi Levi said, 'These are the nine categories [of children conceived through improper sexual behavior]: Children of fright; children of rape; children of despised women; children of excommunication; children of exchange; children of strife; children of drunkenness; children of one whom he has divorced in his heart; children of mixture; children of a brazen woman.'" See Rashi, ad loc.

According to *Derekh Erets Zuta* 10, if one marries a woman with whorish intentions, wicked children will ensue.

Cf. BT *Nedarim* 20a: "Rabbi Yoḥanan son of Dabai said, 'The Ministering Angels told me: Why are there lame children? Because they [their fathers] turn over the tables [i.e., engage in non-conventional sex]. Why are there dumb children? Because they kiss that place [i.e., female genitals]. Why are there deaf children? Because they talk during intercourse. Why are there blind children? Because they look at that place.'"

251. **sanctifies himself and attunes his heart to heaven...** Just as improper sexual behavior engenders morally blemished offspring, sanctified sexual behavior engenders virtuous children. The verse from Leviticus thus contains cause and effect. If you sanctify yourselves during sexual intercourse, then you will have holy children.

252. **they possess only that creaturely soul...** Sanctified sexual behavior affects not only the moral dispositions and character of the child to be born, but also determines the nature of that child's soul. Whereas improper sexual behavior engenders the creaturely soul, sanctified sexual behavior engenders a *seed of truth*, the holy *neshamah*.

On non-Jews' possessing only the creaturely soul, see *ZḤ* 10c (*MhN*), page 68. On the distinction between the creaturely soul and the holy *neshamah*, see *ZḤ* 10c, 16b–c, 17c (all *MhN*).

See *Zohar* 2:89b: "Woe to the inhabitants of the world who conduct themselves like animals"; 3:49b: "If humans distance themselves from Him, acting like animals, where is their holiness, making them holy? Where are the holy souls that they draw from above?" Cf. *Zohar* 3:80a.

Rabbi Aḥa said, "True in all. That he does not fantasize about another woman but is true to his wife."[253]

Rav Huna said, "That he sanctifies himself and attunes himself to heaven, as is said: *Unless YHVH builds the house, its builders labor in vain* (Psalms 127:1). In other words, unless one's intention is directed [11b] to heaven when building the house and producing children, *its builders labor in vain*—for one introduces in that child a labor of vanity. What is this labor of vanity? It is the creaturely soul, which will be annihilated and cut off, like the breath that comes out of the mouth—which is vanity. Since he introduces it in that child, his labor is in vain."[254]

Rabbi Yitsḥak said, "אמת (*emet*), *truth*, is an acronym: אמת (*emet*), *truth*; מארץ (*me-eretz*), *from the earth*; תצמח (*titsmaḥ*), *will spring*. That is: *Truth will spring from the earth* (Psalms 85:12)."[255]

What does this imply?

Rabbi Yitsḥak said, "That at the moment of conception there must be truth
78 and integrity; at the moment when [the embryo] comes into being from the
earth and נתייסד (*nityased*), is formed, and not when it is already well kneaded. This corresponds with what Rav Huna said: 'Any building without יסוד (*yesod*), a foundation, cannot endure.' What is the foundation that a person requires? At the moment of union, as we have just explained."[256]

Rabbi Zeira said, "Once, I was walking in the desert and I came upon a certain Arab who was lugging a load of ten *se'ahs* on his shoulders—even though he was elderly. I said to him, 'Such strength ought to be for plying Torah!'[257]

253. **not fantasize about another woman...** Cf. BT *Nedarim* 20b: "One may not drink out of one goblet and think of another." See *Zohar* 1:155a (*ST*).

254. ***Unless YHVH builds the house, its builders labor in vain...*** Without divine assistance, itself predicated on correct or true intention during sexual intercourse, the resultant offspring will contain only the creaturely soul destined to be annihilated. Hence, the labor is in vain.

Verse 3 in the same psalm reads: *Sons are the provision of YHVH, the fruit of the womb, His reward.*

255. **אמת (*emet*), *truth*, is an acronym...** The first word of the verse is itself an acronym for the first three words of the verse. The significance of truth's springing from the earth is explained below.

256. **at the moment of conception there must be truth and integrity...** At the precise moment of conception, when the embryo is formed from the element of earth, there must be truth, i.e., correct intention. Thus: *truth springs from the earth.* Once the embryo has developed into a fetus and is "well kneaded," correct intention is of no avail.

257. **Arab who was lugging a load of ten *se'ahs*...** Presumably a Jew from Arabia, or from a region inhabited by Arabs.

A *se'ah* is a measure of volume used in biblical and Talmudic times. It is one third of an *ephah*. One *se'ah* equals approximately 13 quarts (12–13 liters). The man is therefore carrying an extremely heavy load.

On the expression "such strength ought to be for plying Torah!" see BT *Bava Metsi'a* 84a, where Rabbi Yoḥanan exclaims to Resh Lakish, "Your strength for Torah!"

"He replied, 'Not for that did my mother and father make me; but for this toil! For I heard from my father that at the moment that he conceived me, his desire was for a strapping son, who would bring in the produce from the field, and he focused on that thought at that moment. And look, I am old. What can I do?'"[258]

Rabbi Yehudah said, "Happy are those whose fathers contemplated noble matters! How do we know? From Bathsheba, Solomon's mother, for the verse attests that she was the perfect mother for Solomon; for he was founded from her—from her conduct, from her contemplation, and from her striving, as is said: *What, my son? And what, son of my womb?...* (Proverbs 31:2).[259]

"Granted that this applies to his mother, but concerning his father, how do we know? As is written: *A song of ascents. Of Solomon. Unless YHVH builds the house, its builders labor in vain* (Psalms 127:1)."[260]

But didn't Solomon utter this song!?[261]



258. **he focused on that thought at that moment...** The father's intentions at the moment of conception determined the man's physical disposition and character illustrating the principle above.

259. ***What, my son? And what, son of my womb?*** The verse continues: *And what, son of my vows?* The proof-text is from a passage that begins: *Words of King Lemuel, an utterance with which his mother admonished him* (31:1). Lemuel is traditionally identified with Solomon. See below.

Bathsheba was thus contemplating noble matters, and hence Solomon was born. See BT *Sanhedrin* 70b: "*What my son? And what, son of my womb? And what, son of my vows.* ...All the women of your father's household used to vow [by] praying 'May I bear a son fit for the throne,' but I vowed, saying, 'May I bear a zealous son, filled with Torah and fit for prophecy.'"

According to Tishby, *Wisdom of the Zohar*, 3:1395, the proof-text may also indicate that at the moment of conception, Bathsheba was contemplating the *Shekhinah*, designated by the term מה (*mah*), what. There may also be an allusion to the fact that the name שלמה (*Shelomoh*), "Solomon," can be read as של מה (*shel mah*), "of what," i.e., deriving from *Shekhinah*.

260. **concerning his father, how do we know...** How do we know that King David likewise contemplated sublime matters when conceiving Solomon? The answer lies in the verse from Psalms, *Unless YHVH builds the house, its builders labor in vain*, cited above to convey the idea that without divine assistance brought about by correct intention at the moment of union, a holy and virtuous child cannot be born.

In its simple sense, the verse reads in full: *A song of ascents. Of Solomon. Unless YHVH builds the house, its builders labor in vain; unless YHVH watches over the city, the watchman guards in vain.*

261. **But didn't Solomon utter this song?** Rabbi Yehudah has just proven King David's holy intentions at the moment of conception by citing Psalms 127:1. Although David is the traditional author of the Psalms, this verse begins "*A song of ascents. Of Solomon*," suggesting that Solomon composed this particular psalm.

See Rashi and Radak on Psalms 127:1. Cf. *Midrash Tehillim* 72:6; *Tosafot, Bava Batra* 15a, s.v. *va-al yedei Shelomoh*. For the view that King Solomon composed this psalm, see *Shir ha-Shirim Rabbah* 1:10 (on 1:1); see also *Zohar* 2:164a, 226a; 3:221a.

Rabbi Yitsḥak said, "Heaven forbid! Rather, David uttered it about Solomon with the holy spirit! When the prophet told David, '*Behold, a son shall be born to you, his name shall be Solomon*' (1 Chronicles 22:9), David said, 'I had a son from Bathsheba but he died. Now another will be born to me—he comes from heaven!'; and so he uttered this song, and through it attuned himself to heaven, as is written: *A song of ascents.* לשלמה (*Li-shlomoh*), *Of Solomon* (Psalms 127:1)—for Solomon's sake.[262]

"He said, '*Unless YHVH builds the house*—if His aid does not complement my consummate attunement; *its builders labor in vain*—in vain shall we labor, as at first when we labored in vain, and it was because of that sin he died. As for me, I must be banished from Jerusalem, and while I am away, *unless YHVH watches over the city* (ibid.)—from everyone, *the watchman guards in vain* (ibid.).'"[263]

Rabbi Pinḥas said, "He left ten concubines to watch the house, and still what happened, happened! Therefore: *the watchman guards in vain* (ibid.)."[264]

Rabbi Yehudah said, "This song was uttered for Solomon. For his sake he
80 recited, attuning himself to heaven; and his mother attuned herself to heaven,
and from them Solomon came forth, of whom is written *Solomon sat upon the throne of YHVH as king* (1 Chronicles 29:23)."[265]

Rabbi Yitsḥak said, "That is why he was called Lemuel. What is the meaning of למואל (*Lemu'el*), Lemuel? It is like למו (*lemo*), *upon, my mouth* (Job 40:4), teaching that both of them concentrated למואל (*lemo el*)—in other words, upon God.[266]

262. **לשלמה (*Li-shlomoh*), *Of Solomon* (Psalms 127:1)—for Solomon's sake** Reading the prefixed preposition *li-*, "of," in another of its senses: to specify the topic of concern.

263. **if His aid does not complement my consummate attunement...** If God does not respond to my sacred intention at the moment of union, a holy child cannot be born. (David is the speaker.)

Because the first child of David and Bathsheba was conceived while Bathsheba was still married to Uriah (and because of the ensuing cover-up and conspiracy to kill Uriah), the child died as a divine punishment. Hence, they labored in vain because *YHVH* did not *build the house.* See 2 Samuel 12:15–23.

On David's being forced to flee Jerusalem, and on the continuation of the verse from Psalms, see next note.

264. **what happened, happened . . .** 2 Samuel 15–16 recounts the story of Absalom's rebellion and cohabitation with David's concubines, thereby fulfilling Nathan's prophesy in 12:11. David is forced to flee Jerusalem, leaving *his ten concubines to watch over the house* (ibid. 15:16). The final insult is recounted in 16:21: *Ahithophel said to Absalom, "Come to bed with your father's concubines whom he left to watch over the house..."* Both verses employ the expression *to watch over the house,* now connected with the verse from Psalms: *unless YHVH watches over the city, the watchman guards in vain.* See also BT *Sanhedrin* 21a.

265. **he attuned himself . . . and his mother attuned herself...** Solomon was able to be king because both his mother and father directed their thoughts to heaven at the moment of conception.

266. **That is why he was called Lemuel...** Proverbs 31:1 reads: *Words of King Lemuel, an utterance with which his mother admonished him.* The term *lemu'el* is found in the Bible

"Hence we have learned: Whoever is attuned to heaven at that moment engenders a virtuous child. How do we know? From Samuel, for whose sake his mother continually attuned herself to heaven, as is written: *I will dedicate him to YHVH* (1 Samuel 1:11), and similarly: *For this lad I prayed* (ibid., 27). In the same way David said, 'If I now have a son he shall be designated למואל (*lemo el*)—given to God.'"[267]

Our Rabbis have taught: Rabbi Yose son of Pazzi said, "I was once walking on the way and I came upon the mountain of Kardu Village. The inhabitants were happy in their share, and I slept there on Sabbath eve and on Saturday night. I saw that my innkeeper wanted to lie with his wife; he stood on one side and prayed and she stood on the other and prayed. I asked them, 'What is your prayer at this moment?'[268]

"They answered, 'Our timing [11c] is to couple every Sabbath, and we offer prayer before the blessed Holy One that we will have a son who will perform His service, a sin-fearing son, a son who will observe His commandments—not straying from Torah to the right or left.'[269]

"I said to them, 'May it be [His] Will that your request be fulfilled, for you have acted for the sake of heaven!'"

Rabbi Yose said, "I will behold the face of *Shekhinah*! For some time later, I happened to be there and I saw the son who was born to them, and he was seven years old. He saw me in the house but did not wish to speak with me. His father said to him, 'Approach him, for he is a great man.'[270]

only in this verse (with an apparent variant vocalization three verses later). Its precise meaning—or even whether it is a name—is uncertain. Rabbi Yitsḥak's explanation apparently derives from Rashi, who quotes the same proof-texts from Job, which reads: *I lay my hand* למו (*lemo*), *to* [or: *on, upon*], *my mouth.* See Rashi on this verse and on BT *Sanhedrin* 70b, s.v. *lemu'el melekh*. See *Zohar* 1:249a.

267. ***For this lad I prayed*...** Cf. *ZḤ* 7a (*MhN*), page 37.

268. **the mountain of Kardu Village...** No such place is known in rabbinic literature or from the geography of Palestine in antiquity. In *Targum Onqelos* (Genesis 8:4), the mountains of Ararat—the resting place of Noah's ark—are called *turei qardu*, the mountains of Kurdistan, and it is from here that the author created Kardu Village. The mountains of Kardu are cited numerous times in the *Zohar*, which implies that they lie near the land of Israel, for the rabbis stumble upon them without journeying far.

See *Zohar* 1:63a; 3:149a; *ZḤ* 49a; Tishby, *Wisdom of the Zohar* 1:116.

269. **Our timing is to couple every Sabbath...** In accordance with the practice of the *talmidei hakhamim*, "disciples of the wise," as established in BT *Ketubbot* 62b: "When is the *onah* [timing of conjugal rights] of the disciples of the wise? Rav Yehudah said in the name of Shemu'el, 'From one Sabbath eve to the next.'" See *Zohar* 1:112a (*MhN*). Offspring conceived on Sabbath eve with the correct intention are particularly virtuous. Cf. *Zohar* 2:89a–b.

270. **I will behold the face of *Shekhinah*!...** See *Mekhilta, Amaleq* (*Yitro*) 1: "Whoever receives the face of [i.e., wel-

"He said, 'I am afraid to converse with him or approach him because I don't know whether he possesses a holy soul or not! For so my teacher taught me this day: It is forbidden to converse with or approach anyone who does not possess a holy soul.'[271]

"He said to him, 'Heaven forbid! He is a great man and a dignitary of the generation.'

"He approached me, and immediately upon speaking with me said, 'I see in you that you possess a new soul for only a short while and that it was not infused within you when you came into the world.'[272]

"I was astounded. I said, 'So it is! For I was a bachelor when I engaged Torah and a soul was bequeathed me.'[273]

"He asked me, 'Do you know about נפש חיה (*nefesh ḥayah*), *the creaturely soul*, that Scripture said was from the earth? Now look, it implies a *living soul*. Why?'[274]



comes] the wise, it is as if he receives the face of *Shekhinah*."

Cf. JT *Eruvin* 5:1, 22b: "Rabbi Shemu'el said in the name of Rabbi Zeira, '... Whoever receives the face of his teacher, it is as if he receives the face of *Shekhinah*.' ... Rabbi Yishma'el taught ... 'One who receives the face of his friend, it is as if he receives the face of *Shekhinah*.'" Cf. Genesis 33:10; *Tanḥuma, Ki Tissa* 27; *Shir ha-Shirim Rabbah* on 2:5.

See *Zohar* 1:9a, 94b, 115b (*MhN*); 2:5a (*MhN*); 3:6b, 148a, 298a; *ZḤ* 25b (*MhN*).

271. **I am afraid to converse with...** Apparently based on BT *Yoma* 9b, which recounts that Resh Lakish was particularly careful with whom he would speak: "But did Resh Lakish converse with Rabbah son of Bar Ḥana? Even with Rabbi El'azar, who was the master of the land of Israel, Resh Lakish did not converse."

In the famous *Yanuqa* narrative in the main body of the *Zohar*, the child of Hamnuna Sava displays similar powers; he is able to sense that Rabbi Yitsḥak and Rabbi Yehudah have not yet recited the *Shema*. See *Zohar* 3:186a.

The motif of the wunderkind appears throughout the *Zohar*. See *Zohar* 1:92b, 148a, 238b; 2:6b, 169b; 3:39a, 162a, 171a, 186a, 204b; *ZḤ* 9a (*MhN*), 14d (*MhN*), 48a, 49a–b, 77d (*MhN, Rut*), 84b–c (*MhN, Rut*).

272. **it was not infused within you when you came into the world** In contrast to Rabbi El'azar, who stated above (at note 225) that the *neshamah* is acquired when one reaches one's thirteenth year, the child appears to suggest that in some cases the *neshamah* is bestowed at birth. Another view is stated explicitly in *ZḤ* 10c (*MhN*; above, page 68) that following the primal sin, the *neshamah* must be earned.

273. **For I was a bachelor...** Rabbi Yose began studying Torah when already an adult and hence attained his holy soul only recently.

See *Zohar* 1:88a–b (*ST*) and *ZḤ* 24a (in this volume), which recount the beginnings of Rabbi Yose son of Pazzi's Torah path. There he is also described as unmarried. Seeking wealth and honor, he comes to learn Torah—and only later learns the value of Torah for its own sake, a theme developed in the child's following homily. Hence his ironic name: Rabbi Yose son of Pazzi—in Hebrew, *paz* means "gold."

274. **Now look, it implies a *living soul*. Why?** The נפש חיה (*nefesh ḥayah*), "creaturely soul," is the lower aspect of the human soul shared with all creatures. In contrast to the *neshamah*—which derives from

"I replied, 'Speak, my son.'

"He said, 'So my teacher taught me: This is the soul that the earth brought forth; it was hewn from the earth. Even so it is alive, moving here and there, the way animals and creeping things and all [creatures] do. But it does not possess insight or wisdom of the worship of the blessed Holy One. It was created solely for animals and creatures to move about with, lacking insight—to be obliterated when it departs, like the breath of the mouth.'[275]

"I said to him, 'My son, who is your teacher?'

"He replied, 'Rabbi Alexandrai.'

"I asked him, 'What did you learn today?'

"He answered me, 'This verse as is written: ראשית (*Reshit*), *The beginning of, wisdom is fear of YHVH, good insight to all who practice them* (Psalms 111:10). So said Rabbi Alexandrai: What is wisdom? It is the name of the blessed Holy One. He is Wisdom![276] He never revealed it to anyone—nor will He reveal it in the future—aside from a fraction to Moses alone. He did not fathom in its entirety, but comprehended what no person had fathomed about that ראשית (*reshit*),  *beginning*, which is wisdom. As is written of Moses: *He saw* ראשית (*reshit*) *for himself* (Deuteronomy 33:21)—this refers to wisdom.[277]

"'Now, you might say, "Look, it is written: *YHVH gave Solomon wisdom* (1 Kings 5:26)!" Come and see: It is not written *YHVH gave* [*Solomon*] *the wisdom*, but rather *wisdom*—he fathomed a part of its truth. The Messiah is also destined to know a part of it, as is written of him: *The spirit of YHVH will alight upon him, a spirit of wisdom and understanding*... (Isaiah 11:2).[278]

---

the Throne of Glory—the *nefesh* derives from the earth (see *ZḤ* 10c, *MhN*). If it is so base, why is it designated by the term חיה (*ḥayyah*), implying that it is alive?

275. **But it does not possess insight...** The creaturely soul has no role in intellectual cognition or spiritual life. It is, rather, the locomotive faculty.

276. **He is Wisdom!** The equation between God and wisdom appears above; see *ZḤ* 3d (*MhN*), page 11. Cf. *Zohar* 2:79b.

277. ***He saw* ראשית (*reshit*) *for himself*...** In its simple sense, the clause in Deuteronomy means: *He selected the prime for himself*, as spoken by Moses about the tribe of Gad. Here, the child applies the verse to Moses himself—and connects the word *reshit*, "beginning," with wisdom.

In rabbinic literature, the verse from Deuteronomy is applied to Moses' burial place in the territory of Gad. See *Sifrei*, Numbers 106; *Tosefta Sotah* 4:8; BT *Sotah* 13b.

The identification of ראשית (*reshit*), "beginning," with wisdom appears widely. See *Targum Yerushalmi* (frag.), Genesis 1:1; Wolfson, *Philo*, 1:242–45, 266–69; *Bereshit Rabbah* 1:1; Azriel of Gerona, *Peirush ha-Aggadot*, 81; Naḥmanides on Genesis 1:1. See *Zohar* 1:2a, 3b, 15a, 16b, 20a, 145a; *ZḤ* 3a, 4d (both *MhN*); Moses de León, *Sheqel ha-Qodesh*, 21–22 (25–26).

278. **It is not written *YHVH gave* [*Solomon*] *the wisdom*, but rather *wisdom*...** If Moses fathomed only a part of the divine wisdom, how can the verse from Kings say that God gave Solomon wisdom, implying that he received more than Moses? As the child deftly notes, the verse from Kings does

"'Wisdom is the beginning of all and precedes all, but *fear of YHVH is good insight* (Psalms 111:10). That is to say, fear abides in [one's] insight and understanding in order to know and investigate the awe of *YHVH*. *To all who practice them* (ibid.)—to one who first practices the commandments in fear, until he accustoms himself to practice out of love.'[279]

"I asked him, 'What is your name?'

"He replied, 'Love.'

"I said to him, 'Sir Love,' and proclaimed for him: *I have loved you with eternal love* (Jeremiah 31:3). And I was privileged to see his son, Rav Adda, and told him about this."[280]

not use the definite article—which would suggest that Solomon received the totality of wisdom—but rather says simply *wisdom*, implying that he too fathomed only a portion.

In a similar vein, the Messiah will only perceive *a spirit of wisdom*, and not wisdom itself.



The clarification regarding Solomon's wisdom is perhaps motivated by the verses in 2 Chronicles 1:7–8, 10–12: *That night God appeared to Solomon and said to him, "Ask, what shall I grant you?" Solomon said to God,... "Grant me wisdom and knowledge...." God said to Solomon, "Because you want this and have not asked for wealth, property, and glory, nor have you asked for the life of your enemy or long life for yourself, but you have asked for wisdom and knowledge—to be able to govern My people, over whom I have made you king—*החכמה והמדע *(ha-ḥokhmah ve-ha-mada), the wisdom and the knowledge, are granted to you...."* The child's homily thus removes any doubt.

On the Messiah and his wisdom, see Maimonides, *Mishneh Torah, Hilkhot Teshuvah* 9:2: "In that era [the Messianic age], wisdom and truth will become abundant... because the king who will arise from David's descendants will be a greater master of wisdom than Solomon—and a great prophet, close to the level of Moses, our teacher."

Cf. Moses de León, *Sheqel ha-Qodesh*, 16–17 (21): "No one can apprehend His truth. ... He made manifest only a fraction of the paths of being. In sum, when the wise *maskil* arouses himself to investigate and know the nature of truth, he may apprehend only a small fraction of the truth of His being."

279. **in fear... out of love** Fear of God is necessary to launch the inquirer on his path into knowledge of the divine wisdom: the awe of *YHVH*. In the main body of the *Zohar*, "awe of *YHVH*" usually signifies *Shekhinah*, the portal to the divine realm—and on occasion, the higher *sefirah Ḥokhmah*, Wisdom. See *Zohar* 1:7b–8a; *ZḤ* 17d (*MhN*), 45c–d; Tishby, *Wisdom of the Zohar*, 3:988–89.

On the distinction between serving God out of fear or out of love, see *Sifrei*, Deuteronomy 32; BT *Sotah* 31a; BT *Yoma* 86b; Baḥya ibn Paquda, *Ḥovot ha-Levavot, Sha'ar Ahavat Ha-Shem*, chapters 1 and 6.

The tenth chapter of Maimonides' *Hilkhot Teshuvah* in the *Mishneh Torah* contains an extensive discussion of this theme. See, for example, 10:1: "It is not fitting to serve God in this manner [i.e., to receive a reward or to avoid punishment]. A person whose service is motivated by these factors is considered one who serves out of fear. He is not on the level of the prophets or of the wise. The only ones who serve God in this manner are common people, women, and minors. They are trained to serve God out of fear until their knowledge increases and they serve out of love." See also ibid. 10:5; idem, *Pereq Ḥeleq*; Tishby, *Wisdom of the Zohar*, 3:974–78, 987–90.

280. **'Sir Love'...** In light of the child's great wisdom, Rabbi Yose bestows upon him the honorific title "sir" (or "master").

Rav Adda son of Ahavah (love) was a Babylonian Amora.

Rabbi Ya'akov son of Idi said, "Adam was wise because he could recognize and perceive all who possessed the creaturely soul and who possessed the holy *neshamah*; when they came before him, he recognized them all. As is written: *whatever Adam called him* (Genesis 2:19)—[נפש חיה (*nefesh ḥayyah*), *creaturely soul* (ibid.)—to whoever does not perceive and recognize the service of his Creator; and *neshamah*]—to whoever perceived and recognized the service of his Creator. So it is until this very day: whoever does not perceive and recognize the service of his Creator, and does not engage in Torah, possesses a creaturely soul and not the *neshamah*."[281]

Rabbi Yehudah said, "Even though beasts, animals, and their kind possess that creaturely soul and they have been permitted to human beings, the blessed Holy One has compassion upon them in their death—that pain not be afflicted upon those possessing the creaturely soul. For there is no one who does not possess the creaturely soul until he turns to worship his Creator, distinguishing himself from other people, in order to engage in Torah and commandments—thereby acquiring the holy *neshamah*.[282]



"That is why a [11d] slaughterer from whose hand has emerged *nevelah* or *terefah*—the first time, he is to be removed; the second time he is to be placed under the ban; the third time, it is proclaimed about him in the market that everything he slaughtered is *terefah*, and he is never appointed as a slaughterer again."[283]

281. **recognize and perceive all who possessed the creaturely soul...** In its simple sense, the verse in Genesis means: *whatever the human called each* נפש חיה (*nefesh ḥayyah*), *living creature, that would be its name.* Focusing on the term *nefesh ḥayyah*, which in *MhN* signifies the lower aspect of the soul, Rabbi Ya'akov creates his new midrash. The phrase in square brackets is not found in the manuscripts or the earliest printed editions. Though an addition, it seems that the MSS and printed editions skipped a line.

The soul-discerning power possessed by Adam is also possessed by the child in the preceding exchange.

On acquiring the *neshamah*, see above, note 97 and at note 243. On recognizing and perceiving, see *Heikhalot Rabbati* 1 in Schäfer, *Synopse zur Hekhalot-Literatur*, §83; [Moses de León?], *Seder Gan Eden*, 134.

282. **pain not be afflicted upon those possessing the creaturely soul...** Because human beings and animals share the creaturely soul, animals must be slaughtered humanely with minimal suffering. The rabbinic term צער בעלי חיים (*tsa'ar ba'alei ḥayyim*), "[unjustified] pain to living beings," includes numerous injunctions regarding the way animals ought to be treated. See BT *Bava Metsi'a* 32b. See also Moses Maimonides, *Guide of the Perplexed* 3:48: "The commandment concerning the slaughtering of animals is necessary.... Now since the necessity to have good food requires that animals be killed, the aim was to kill them in the easiest manner, and it was forbidden to torment them through killing them in a reprehensible manner by piercing the lower part of their throat or by cutting off one of their members...."

The creaturely soul—the lower aspect of the human being—is what first rouses a Jew to seek Torah and God.

See Tishby, *Wisdom of the Zohar*, 2:708.

283. **a slaughterer from whose hand has emerged *nevelah* or *terefah*...** It is in def-

Rabbi Yitsḥak said, "For the first offence, is he not punished aside from this? Look at what we have learned: A slaughterer who does not present a knife to a sage is to be placed under the ban, is to be removed, and it is to be proclaimed that his meat is *terefah*. If this is the case concerning a knife that is not satisfactory, how much more so concerning one from whose hand has emerged *nevelah* or *terefah*, that he is to be placed under the ban and removed, and that it is to be proclaimed that his meat is *terefah*!"[284]

Rabbi Yose said, "I saw Rabbi Yehudah—who had invited Rabbi Yose and Rabbi Ḥaggai. There was a certain slaughterer who was called Rabbi Abba, who slaughtered a chicken, intending to cut two marks. They examined and found that he cut one mark, but the other he did not cut.[285]

"Rabbi Yehudah said to him, 'What was your intention?'

"He replied, 'Two marks.'

"He said, 'But I found only one was cut. Nevertheless, the meat is kosher; and even though intention is not essential in slaughtering, henceforth you shall not be a slaughterer!'[286]



erence to the creaturely soul that the laws pertaining to slaughtering are so strict.

*Nevelah* and *terefah* are terms indicating animals that were not slaughtered in accordance with the laws of ritual slaughtering—and hence cannot be eaten.

The passage here derives from BT *Ḥullin* 18a. See next note.

The procedural order that starts with removal, followed by ban, is found in all the manuscript witnesses. It contradicts both the Talmud passage (below) and the following paragraph.

284. **A slaughterer who does not present a knife to a sage...** See BT *Ḥullin* 18a: "Rav Huna said, 'A slaughterer who does not present a knife to a sage [for examination] is to be placed under the ban.' Rava said, 'He is to be removed [from his vocation], and it is proclaimed that his meat is *terefah*.' There is no disagreement, for the former deals with the case where the knife was found to be satisfactory, whereas the latter deals with the case where it was not found to be satisfactory.... There was a case of a slaughterer who did not present his knife [for examination] to Rava son of Ḥinena. He placed him under the ban, removed him [from his vocation], and proclaimed that his meat was *terefah*."

285. **intending to cut two marks ...** Marks, סימנים (*simanim*), signifying the two organs of the throat that must be cut during slaughtering. See M *Ḥullin* 2:1. See next note.

Presumably Rabbi Yehudah invited the other rabbis to adjudicate the slaughtering with him.

286. **Nevertheless, the meat is kosher...** See Maimonides, *Mishneh Torah, Hilkhot Sheḥitah* 1:9: "Both the trachea and esophagus must be cut. A perfect *sheḥitah* (slaughter) is to totally cut both, whether in a bird or an animal, and this is what the slaughterer should intend to do. If the majority of one of them in the case of a bird, or the majority of two in the case of an animal was cut, the *sheḥitah* is valid." See also Vidal Yom Tov of Tolosa, *Maggid Mishneh*, ad loc.

On the expression "intention is not essential in slaughtering," see BT *Ḥullin* 31a–b, which establishes that with regard to nonsacred slaughter, the lack of intention to slaughter does not invalidate: "*Mishnah*: If a knife fell down and slaughtered [an animal], even though it is slaughtered in the proper way, the slaughtering is invalid.... *Gemara*:

"Rabbi Yose said to him, 'Intention does not refer to this, but rather intention to the blessed Holy One—that one slaughter for the sake of His Name, and not for any other purpose. If he intended two marks yet cut only one, it is permitted after the fact. As we have learned: If a person cut one [mark] in the case of a bird—after the fact it is valid, in the first instance it is prohibited.'"[287]

Rabbi Ya'akov said, "Come and see: Everything that was created with the creaturely soul was permitted by the blessed Holy One to human beings, because they do not possess a *neshamah* to perceive and recognize. If they had a *neshamah*, they would not have been permitted."

Rabbi Abba inquired of Rabbi Ḥiyya. He said to him, "You have said that *neshamah* enters a person only when he contemplates the worship of the blessed Holy One—whereupon he possesses *neshamah*. And you have said that *neshamah* is holy, supremely sublime. If so, what is implied by the verse *All that had* נשמת רוח חיים (*nishmat ruaḥ hayyim*), *the breath of the spirit of life, in its nostrils—of all that was on dry land—died* (Genesis 7:22)? Why did they die? Since they possessed *neshamah*, they should have been saved!"[288]

He could not answer. They went and asked Rabbi El'azar son of Rabbi Shim'on.

He said to them, "Certainly it is so, and this verse helps us. For so did my father say: When the Flood arrived, there was no one for whom the blessed Holy One could act, aside from Noah and his sons. But their merit was sufficient to shield only themselves and their wives; their merit was inadequate to shield the entire generation. As for those who were righteous beforehand, like Enoch and Jared, who possessed holy *neshamah* and deserved that the blessed Holy One should act for their sake, they had died. As the verse says: *All that had the breath of the spirit of life in its nostrils*—referring to those who possessed the holy

Now this is so only because it fell down [by itself], but if one threw it [and it slaughtered an animal], the slaughtering would be valid, even though there was no intention [to slaughter according to ritual]. Who is the *Tanna* that maintains that the intention to slaughter [according to ritual] is not essential? Rava said: It is Rabbi Natan. For Osha'ya, the junior of the companions, taught: If one threw a knife intending to thrust it into a wall and in its flight it slaughtered an animal in the proper way, Rabbi Natan declares the slaughtering valid...."

287. **Intention does not refer to this...** Namely, intention to cut two marks, for intention is not essential at all in *sheḥitah*. Intention, rather, applies to one's motivation and spiritual stance.

On the phrase "after the fact it is valid, in the first instance it is prohibited," see BT *Ḥullin* 27a.

288. **Since they possessed *neshamah*, they should have been saved!** The verse in Genesis describes the annihilation of all living beings during the Flood. Rabbi Abba reads the verse literally and wonders how people with the *nishmat ḥayyim*, "the soul of life"—the holy *neshamah*—could have perished during the Flood. See *Zohar* 1:206a for a direct parallel.

*neshamah*. That you will not think the verse is referring to those who were in the Flood, the verse goes on to say: *all that was on dry land died*—they were no longer alive at that time, in the days of the Flood. Rather, *on dry land they died*—namely they had already departed from the world, and there did not remain in the world a righteous person to shield his generation. Then judgment was executed upon the wicked."[289]

Rabbi Ḥiyya said to Rabbi Abba, "Didn't I tell you that this golden head from the Masters of Mishnah would be able to answer! Happy are you, O Masters of Mishnah! Your share in the world to come is greater than all!"[290]

Rabbi El'azar said further, "What is the meaning of the verse *Praise Him with the blast of the shofar, praise Him with the lute and lyre. Praise Him with timbrel and dance, praise Him with strings and flute* (Psalms 150:3–4)? Does the blessed Holy One require any of this? Rather, David said, 'All your praise with these instruments before the blessed Holy One isn't worth a thing!' Like a person who says to his fellow: Now do this and do that, yet all that you do isn't worth a thing until you do this specific thing. So did David say: *Praise Him with sounding cymbals, praise Him with crashing cymbals* (ibid., 5)—this does not constitute praise. What then is praise? *Let every* neshamah *praise Yah. Hallelujah!* (ibid., 6). The others are not worth anything; only the praise of the *neshamah*! As is written: *Let every* neshamah *praise Yah. Hallelujah!*" [12a]



*God said, "Let the waters be gathered..."* (Genesis 1:9).[291]

Our Rabbis opened with this verse: *Go, gaze upon the works of God, how He has brought* שמות (*shammot*), *desolation, on earth* (Psalms 46:9).[292]

Rabbi El'azar said, "Come and see how human nature differs from the nature of the blessed Holy One! It is the nature of human beings that their deeds

289. **As for those who were righteous... who possessed holy *neshamah*...** Rabbi El'azar answers Rabbi Abba's question, noting that while it is indeed correct that the *neshamah* only enters the righteous, the verse does not refer to the wicked masses who perished in the Flood, but to the righteous few (such as Enoch and Jared), who possessed *neshamah* and had died before the Flood, *on dry land*. See *Zohar* 1:206a.

On Enoch and Jared, see Genesis 5:18–24; *Bereshit Rabbah* 25:1 (and Theodor's note); *Midrash Aggadah*, Genesis 5:18, 24. On removing the righteous in order to execute judgment upon the wicked, see *ZḤ* 12c–d (*MhN*).

290. **golden head...** גולגלתא דדהבא (*gulgalta de-dahava*). See Ecclesiastes 12:6; *Qohelet Rabbah*, ad loc. The expression may also derive from BT *Bava Metsi'a* 85a, where a גולתא דדהבא (*gulta de-dahava*), "golden cloak," is a symbol of the ordination of Rabbi Yose (Rabbi El'azar's son).

On the Masters of Mishnah, see above, note 227.

291. ***Let the waters be gathered...*** The full verse reads: *God said, "Let the waters under heaven be gathered to one place and let the dry land appear!" And it was so.*

292. ***gaze upon the works of God...*** Such a reading is attested in many late medieval biblical manuscripts, as well as the

outlive them, but the blessed Holy One outlives His deeds. As Hannah said: *There is none holy like YHVH, for there is none* בלתך (*biltekha*), *beside You* (1 Samuel 2:2). What is the meaning of *for there is none* בלתך (*biltekha*), *beside You*? Do not read *biltekha*, *beside You*, but rather בלותך (*balotekha*), *who outlives you.*"[293]

So it is written: *Go, gaze upon the works of God*... (Psalms 46:9). Rabbi El'azar said, "King David was astounded by the works the blessed Holy One performs in this world. He said, *Go, gaze upon the works of God.* He should have said, 'Come!' Rather, David said, 'All the inhabitants of the earth in this world—go from one end of the world to the other and you will discover the works of the blessed Holy One; as are His works at one end of the world, so are His works at the other end of the world. He establishes inhabitants in the world. If they are worthy—he settles them, their children, and their children's children until the end of the world. If they are not worthy—He obliterates them from there, and that place and that city are never built again, demonstrating to humanity that that place was the abode of the wicked, and that the blessed Holy One has executed judgment upon it, as is written: *how He has brought desolation on earth* (ibid.).'"[294]



Septuagint (codex Alexandrinus). The Masoretic text reads:... *the works of YHVH*. The Zoharic rabbis are aware of both variants. See *Zohar* 1:58b: "Rabbi Ḥiyya said, '... whether it be one name or another, all is praise.'"

See *Bereshit Rabbah* 84:8; 88:3 (and Theodor, ad loc.); *Tanḥuma, Vayelekh* 1; Radak on Psalms 46:9; *Zohar* 1:60a, 157b (*ST*); 2:5a (*MhN*); *ZḤ* 73a (*ShS*); Moses de León, *Sefer ha-Rimmon*, 288; *Minḥat Shai* on Numbers 23:9; Psalms 46:9; 66:5; Menaḥem Azariah of Fano, *Yonat Elem*, 99; Margaliot, *Sha'arei Zohar, Berakhot* 7b.

Psalms 66:5–6 similarly reads: *Come and see the works of* אלהים (*Elohim*), *God, who is held in awe by men for His acts. He turned the sea into dry land; they crossed the river on foot.* Presumably this motif of turning sea into dry land led the author to interpret Psalms 46, which has no such motif, in connection with the verse from Genesis about the gathering of the waters.

293. **Do not read *biltekha*, *beside You*...** See BT *Berakhot* 10a (and BT *Megillah* 14a): "This is what Hannah said: *There is none holy like YHVH, for there is none beside You.* ... What is the meaning of: *for there is none beside You*? Rabbi Yehudah son of Menasiah said, 'Do not read *there is none biltekha, beside you,* but rather *there is none le-balotekha, to consume You.* For the nature of flesh-and-blood is not like that of the blessed Holy One. It is the nature of flesh-and-blood to be outlived by its works, but the blessed Holy One outlives His works.'"

Whereas the blessed Holy One brings desolation upon the earth, He lives eternally and is never consumed.

294. ***how He has brought desolation on earth*** The desolation wrought by God upon the earth is in fact a sign of His providence, as the wicked are uprooted and their cities destroyed. Perhaps Rabbi Abba is focusing on the word God (*Elohim*) in the verse from Psalms, which according to rabbinic tradition signifies divine justice or judgment, as opposed to divine compassion or mercy, signified by *YHVH*. Hence, the works of *Elohim*—the workings of divine judgment—bring about the consequent punishment of desolation. Cf. *Zohar* 1:58b.

Alternatively: *Go, gaze upon the works of* אלהים (*Elohim*), *God.* Rabbi Pinḥas said, "What prompted David to say *the works of Elohim*, rather than 'the works of *YHVH*'?"

Well, Rabbi Pinḥas said, "Because the entire Work of Creation was founded with the name *Elohim*.[295]

"When the blessed Holy One created the world, the waters were advancing and descending. When He saw the earth below, He thrust it between the waters; it was concealed and congealed between the waters. The blessed Holy One performed a miracle within a miracle! It is the nature and way of the world that water is light and earth is heavy, and that which is heavy sinks below, while that which is light rises above. But the blessed Holy One—to display His miracles and deeds to humanity—cast down and lowered the light below, while the heavy He raised above, over the light, as is written: *To the one who spread the earth above the waters* (Psalms 136:6), that is to say, water (which is light) below, and earth (which is heavy) above.[296]

90 "Furthermore, from between the waters He brought forth and revealed dry land, for it is not the way of the earth to bring forth dry land from between the waters, but rather moisture. When He brought forth the dry land from between the waters, He called it Earth, as is written: *God called the dry land Earth* (Genesis 1:10).[297]

"It has been taught: He called it by seven names: *Erets*, *Adamah*, *Gai*, *Neshiyyah*, *Tsiyyah*, *Arqa*, and *Tevel*. *Tevel* is the greatest of them all, as is written: *He will judge Tevel, the world, with righteousness* (Psalms 9:9). This is the meaning of

295. **founded with the name *Elohim*** In the creation account found in Genesis 1, it is *Elohim* (God), not *YHVH*, who is the agent of creation. See *Shemot Rabbah* 30:13: "The blessed Holy One... created the world with justice, as is said: *In the beginning Elohim created* (Genesis 1:1). It does not say '*YHVH* created,' but '*Elohim*.'" See *ZḤ* 3d (*MhN*), page 13.

David's intent was thus that people contemplate the works of creation.

296. **water (which is light) below, and earth (which is heavy) above** The creation of the earth is miraculous, contradicting the ordinary laws of nature. According to the standard medieval scientific view, the elements are arranged in a hierarchy according to weight. As earth is the heaviest element, it should lie beneath the waters, yet we see the earth resting upon the waters.

See Maimonides, *Mishneh Torah, Hilkhot Yesodei ha-Torah* 4:2: "Water is lighter than earth. Therefore it is found above it."

See Naḥmanides on Genesis 1:9; *ZḤ* 4a, 9a (both *MhN*).

297. **it is not the way of the earth . . .** This is the second miracle. Usually when a dry substance comes into contact with water it becomes moist. Not so with the creation of the earth, where dry land rises from between the waters.

Cf. *Bereshit Rabbah* 5:8: "Why is it called ארץ (*erets*), earth? Because it רצתה (*ratstah*), wanted, to fulfill רצון (*ratson*), the will, of its Master."

what is written: *how He has bestowed* שמות (*shemot*), *names, upon the earth* (Psalms 46:9)."[298]

Rabbi Yehudah said, "The blessed Holy One created seven firmaments, and corresponding to them seven earths. It has been taught: The waters brought forth one veritable earth—from which the seven earths were formed, as we have said."[299]

Rabbi Yose said, "The foundation of all was water. For we find that the essence of all the works of creation derived from water.[300] It has been taught: Initially the waters were dispersed beneath the heavens—until the blessed Holy One rebuked them, and gathered and assembled them *to one place and the dry land appeared* (Genesis 1:9). Afterward they dispersed as at first, and He spread the earth upon them, as is written: *Who spread the earth above the waters, for His love is forever* (Psalms 136:6)."[301]

298. ***how He has bestowed* שמות *(shemot), names, upon the earth*** Rabbinic literature depicts "seven earths," namely seven strata of the earth. The order of these strata varies, but all versions include: *Erets* ("earth"), *Adamah* ("earth, ground"), *Arqa* (Aramaic: "earth"), *Gai* ("valley"), *Tsiyyah* ("dry region"), *Neshiyyah* ("oblivion"), *Tevel* ("firm land, world").

On the levels of the earth, see *Vayiqra Rabbah* 29:11; *Ester Rabbah* 1:12; *Pesiqta de-Rav Kahana* 23:10; *Midrash Tehillim* 9:11; *Avot de-Rabbi Natan* A, 37; B, 43; *Sefer Yetsirah* 4:12; *Shir ha-Shirim Rabbah* on 6:4; *Midrash Mishlei* 8:9; *Seder Rabbah di-Vreshit* 9 (*Battei Midrashot*, 1:24); *Midrash Konen* (*Beit ha-Midrash*, 2:32–33); *Zohar* 1:9b, 39b–40a (*Heikh*), 54b, 157a; 2:30b, 100a; 3:9b–10a; *ZḤ* 8c–9b (*SO*), 87b (*MhN*, *Rut*).

*Tevel*, our world, is distinguished by judgment with "righteousness," a symbol for the *Shekhinah* in the main body of the *Zohar*.

On the word play *shammot*, "desolation," and *shemot*, "names," see BT *Berakhot* 7b.

299. **one veritable earth—from which the seven earths were formed...** The seven earths originate from one perfect archetypal earth. See above, *ZḤ* 10a (*MhN*), page 61.

On the seven firmaments, see BT *Ḥagigah* 12b.

300. **the essence of all the works of creation derived from water** The opening verse of Genesis (1:1) describes the creation of the world, beginning with the watery chaos: *when the earth was wild and waste, darkness over the deep, a wind from God hovering over the face of the waters.* See *ZḤ* 16a (*MhN*), page 153.

See also *Tanḥuma*, *Vayaqhel* 6: "When the blessed Holy One created His world, it was entirely water intermingled with water."

301. **until the blessed Holy One rebuked them...** The motif of a primeval battle against the sea derives from Canaanite mythology; it is preserved in fragments throughout the Hebrew Bible. See, for example, Psalms 74:12–17; Isaiah 51:9–11; Job 38:8–11. The myth is present (in attenuated form) also in certain rabbinic texts.

The *Zohar* here is drawing on *Pirqei de-Rabbi Eli'ezer* 5: "On the third day all the earth was flat like a plain and the waters covered the surface of all the earth. When the word of the Almighty issued forth, *Let the waters be gathered* (Genesis 1:9), the mountains and hills arose from the ends of the earth and they were scattered over the surface of all the earth, and valleys were formed over the inner parts of the earth; and the waters rolled together and gathered into the valleys, as is said: *The gathering place of the waters He called Seas* (ibid., 10). Immediately the waters became proud and they arose

Ulla said, "What is the relevance of love here?"

Rabbi Yose said, "The blessed Holy One acted with great love for His world—for were the earth not above, the whole world would be erased at once!"

Rav Ḥisda said, "Were it not so, human beings would not be able to plant and sow. Now that the earth is above, they plant and sow, and the earth abides enduringly in its power and vitality because of the moisture of the waters beneath the earth. From below: countless rivers, springs, and pools flow forth—invigorating the entire world, causing all to flourish. This is the love that the blessed Holy One rendered His creatures and the entire world." [12b]

Our Rabbis have taught: One day, Rabbi Shim'on was sitting by the portal of the gate of Lydda,[302] and Rabbi Yose, Rabbi Ḥaggai, and Rabbi El'azar his son were there. Rabbi Pinḥas arrived. He said to him, "Look, the Luminary of Mishnah is seated!"[303]



to cover the earth as at first, whereupon the blessed Holy One rebuked them and subdued them and placed them beneath the soles of His feet and measured them with the hollow of His hand—that they should neither decrease nor increase. He made the sand as the boundary of the sea, just like a man makes a fence for his vineyard. When they rise and see the sand before them, they return to their former place, as is said: *Do you not fear Me, says YHVH? Will you not tremble before Me, who set the sand as a boundary to the sea?* (Jeremiah 5:22). Before the waters were gathered together, the depths were created. These are the depths that are beneath the earth; for the earth is spread upon the water like a ship that floats in the midst of the sea—so likewise is the earth spread out over the water, as is said: *Who spread the earth above the waters* (Psalms 136:6)."

See David Luria, ad loc.; BT *Ḥagigah* 12a; BT *Bava Batra* 74b; *Tanḥuma* (Buber), *Ḥuqqat* 1; *Midrash Tehillim* 93:5. On the verse from Psalms, see also BT *Ḥagigah* 12b; Cf. *ZḤ* 76b (*MhN*, *Rut*).

302. **portal of the gate...** בבא דתרעא (*Bava de-tar'a*), a redundancy found only in the *Zohar*, perhaps signaling a deep inner meaning about to unfold. See *Zohar* 1:201b; 2:28a; 3:15a; *ZḤ* 90a (*MhN*, *Rut*). Cf. *Zohar* 2:169b.

303. **Luminary of Mishnah . . .** בוצינא דמתניתא (*Botsina de-matnita*), an epithet for Rabbi Shim'on. In the main body of the *Zohar*, Rabbi Shim'on is described as *botsina qaddisha*, "holy luminary."

On the title Luminary (or Lamp), see 2 Samuel 21:17; *Bereshit Rabbah* 85:4; BT *Ketubbot* 17a, where Rabbi Abbahu is called Lamp of Light; and *Berakhot* 28b where Rabban Yoḥanan son of Zakkai is called Lamp of Israel. On Rabbi Shim'on as Luminary, see *Zohar* 1:3b–4a, 156a, 197b; 3:159a, 171a; *ZḤ* 85d (*MhN*, *Rut*). See also Liebes, *Peraqim*, 139, 151.

Rabbi Pinḥas son of Ya'ir lived in the second century in Palestine and was renowned for his saintliness and ability to work miracles. See BT *Ḥullin* 7a; JT *Demai* 1:3, 22a. In the *Zohar*, he is accorded special status; generally he is in a class by himself among the Companions. See 1:11a; 3:59b–60b, 62a–b, 200b–202a, 203a, 225b, 288a, 296b (*IZ*); *ZḤ* 19a (*MhN*). According to BT *Shabbat* 33b, Rabbi Pinḥas was the son-in-law of Rabbi Shim'on, however the *Zohar* elevates him further by transforming him into Rabbi Shim'on's father-in-law. This new role could

Rabbi Shim'on arose and sat him next to himself.

He said to him, "Why is this day different from other days that you are silent and your mouth is not dripping with the sweetness of the honey of wisdom?"[304]

He replied, "I was contemplating in my heart that which Ezekiel said, as is written: *I heard the sound of their wings like the sound of mighty waters, like the sound of Shaddai* (Ezekiel 1:24). Did he measure mighty waters and measure the voice of *Shaddai*—and conclude that the sound of mighty waters is like the voice of *Shaddai*?"[305]

He said to him, "That is why I was astonished by you, that your lips were not murmuring supernal mysteries."

He said to him, "This is a mystery of the Account of the Holy Chariot. Come and see what we have learned in our Mishnah: Four holy angels travel with the King's Throne of Glory as it journeys. Who are these angels? They that are called 'the holy living being.' These four are more precious and exalted than all the other angels, except for one. Some say that this one is of those four, but it is not so, for so we have found in the Book of Wisdom of King Solomon.[306]



be the result of a simple mistake: confusing חתן (*ḥatan*), "son-in-law" with חותן (*ḥoten*), "father-in-law." However, the switch may also be deliberate, another instance of interchanging father and son.

In noting that he is seated, perhaps Rabbi Pinḥas intends that Rabbi Shim'on has not shown him appropriate respect.

304. **sweetness of the honey of wisdom** Rabbi Pinḥas is the speaker. On the equation of wisdom and honey, see Ezekiel 3:1–3; Psalms 19:10–11; BT *Ḥagigah* 13a. See also *ZḤ* 15d (*MhN*), page 145.

305. ***I heard the sound...*** This verse derives from Ezekiel's vision of the divine throne (or chariot). This vision formed the basis of much Jewish mystical speculation. Ezekiel is describing the sound generated by the movement of the divine throne borne by the living beings.

Rabbi Shim'on is perplexed by the verse, and that is why he is silent. How can it be that Ezekiel compared the sound of the living beings bearing the throne to the sound (or voice) of God Himself (*Shaddai*)?

On this verse, cf. *Zohar* 1:71b.

306. **Book of Wisdom of King Solomon** One of the many volumes housed in the real or imaginary library of the authors of the *Zohar*. For other references to this book, see *Zohar* 1:7b, 13b, 225b; 2:67a, 70a (*RR*), 125a, 139a, 172a, 204b; 3:10b, 65b, 70b, 104a, 151b, 164a, 193b; *ZḤ* 17c (*MhN*). Naḥmanides several times refers to, and quotes from, an Aramaic version of the Apocryphal Wisdom of Solomon. See the introduction to his *Commentary on the Torah*, 5–6; idem, *Kitvei Ramban*, 1:163, 182.

See Matt, *Zohar: The Book of Enlightenment*, 25; and the comment by Shim'on Lavi, *Ketem Paz*, 1:22d, on *Zohar* 1:7a: "All such books mentioned in the *Zohar*... have been lost in the wanderings of exile.... Nothing is left of them except what is mentioned in the *Zohar*. For a catalogue of these books, see Neuhausen, *Sifriyyah shel Ma'lah*.

The four angels are the four living beings described in Ezekiel's vision. Traditionally, they are identified as Michael, Gabriel, Uriel, and Raphael. The angel who is yet "more precious and exalted" is Metatron (on whom see above, note 149). Cf. *ZḤ* 1c (*SO*).

On the expression "our Mishnah," see *Zohar* 1:37b, 55b, 74a, 91b, 93a, 95b, 96a, 124b (*MhN*), 136b (*MhN*), 137a (*MhN*), 139a (*MhN*), 223b; 2:5a (*MhN*), 123b; 3:75b, 78a,

"When these four assemble together on their travels, the sound of their journeys is heard throughout the entire firmament, like the sound of innumerable, supernal angels referred to by *Thousand upon thousands* [*served him*]; *myriads upon myriads* [*attended Him*] (Daniel 7:10); and like the sound of that one minister ministering before the supernal King. The assembly in which they gather is at the time when he comes to infuse them with the glorious bounty of their King."[307]

Rabbi Pinḥas wept, saying, "With the key of the engraved keys that sprays profusely! When they ascend, you were there! If it pleases you, complete the verse."[308]

He said, "*A sound of tumult like the sound of a camp* (Ezekiel 1:24). What is meant by *the sound of a camp*? So have we learned: When they praise the blessed Holy One, the sound of the word they praise in His presence is like the word of the praises of the camp of Israel when they praise Him below.[309]



284b, 285a, 293b (*IZ*); *ZḤ* 15b–c, 16a, 18b, 20a (all *MhN*); Scholem, "Parashah Ḥadashah"; Matt, "Matnita di-Lan."

307. **like the sound of innumerable, supernal angels . . . and like the sound of that one minister . . .** The explanation of the verse from Ezekiel is as follows: The sound of the movement of the divine throne is like the sound of mighty waters (namely the innumerable angels), and like the sound of *Shaddai* (the archon Metatron). Both מטטרון (Metatron) and שדי (*Shaddai*) have the numerical value of 314. Rabbi Shim'on has resolved his own perplexity: Ezekiel was not comparing the sound to God Himself, but to *Shaddai*, namely Metatron.

Metatron links the angelic realm with the divine realms. He is the axis mundi upon which the divine bounty flows. See *ZḤ* 28b–c (*MhN*); cf. Moses de León, *Or Zaru'a*, 259–60, 271–2.

308. **With the key of the engraved keys that sprays profusely . . .** A conjectural rendering of בקלידא דקלדיטין גליפין דאמיד נתוזריטא (*bi-qlida de-qaldditin gelifin de-amid netozrita*), one of the many enigmatic and baffling phrases found throughout the *Zohar*. The manuscript witnesses differ widely here and I have followed the print editions. Apparently, Rabbi Pinḥas' point is that Rabbi Shim'on unlocks supernal mysteries.

"Key" renders קלידא (*qlida*), based on the rabbinic term אקלידא (*aqlida*), which derives from the Greek *kleida*, "key." See *Zohar* 2:5a–b (*MhN*), 14a (*MhN*), 66b, 174a; 3:15b.

The last two words in the phrase דאמיד נתוזריטא (*de-amid netozrita*) are enigmatic and are not attested elsewhere in the *Zohar*. אמיד (*Amid*) connotes wealth, and נתוזריטא (*netozrita*) may derive from the verb נתז (*nataz*), "to fly away, gush, squirt out." See also BT *Bava Qamma* 62a, where *amid* is found on the same page as נטירותא (*netiruta*), "guarding, care," perhaps the inspiration for *netozrita*.

Cf. Edri and *Sullam*, "With the key of depths sealed treasuries are opened"; *Matoq mi-Devash*, "With the key that unlocks engravings, supernal lights are opened." See also Ḥayyim Palagi, *Sefer Ḥayyim u-Mazon*, 16.

The precise force of "When they ascend, you were there!" is not entirely apparent, though presumably Rabbi Pinḥas intends that Rabbi Shim'on has experiential knowledge of the angelic realm. See Asulin, "Midrash ha-Ne'lam li-Vreshit," 234–35.

For a different reading of this phrase, see Freedman, "Astral and Other Neologisms," 143–45.

309. ***like the sound of a camp . . .*** The verse in Ezekiel proceeds to compare the sound of the movement of the living beings

"בעמדם (Be-omdam), *When they stood still, they let down their wings* (ibid.) What is meant by *When they stood still*? It is like *Because* עמדו (amedu), *they ceased, and answered no more* (Job 32:16). For when the camp of Israel do not praise the blessed Holy One below, immediately: *they let down their wings* (Ezekiel 1:24)—the power of that holy assembly wanes, and they do not have strength to offer consummate praise in His presence.[310]

"Further, another verse supports this interpretation, as is written: *There was a voice from above the expanse over their heads*... (ibid. 1:24). *There was a voice*—the voice of Jacob. When they abound in prayer, where does it ascend? Above the expanse over the heads of the living beings—where the prayers of the righteous are deposited.[311]

"When they desist from raising their voice, from prayer and from reading Torah, what is written? *When they stood still* (ibid. 1:24)—that is to say, because of their silence in Torah and prayer, the wings of the living beings *let down* (ibid.), as we have said."[312]

He said to him, "That is why I came—to hear from your mouth the spirit of wisdom, harmony, and supernal peace that have been bestowed upon you."[313]



to the tumult of a camp or army. Rabbi Shim'on explains that the sound of the celestial camp is like the sound of the camp of Israel below. That is to say, there is a direct relationship between the celestial praises above and the earthly praises of Israel below. The reason behind this analogy is explained in the following paragraph.

See Jacob ha-Kohen's *Commentary on the Chariot*, in Farber and Abrams, *The Commentaries to Ezekiel's Chariot*, 128.

310. **when the camp of Israel do not praise...** In the verse from Job, the word *amedu*, literally "stood," is associated with silence: *For they did not speak, because they ceased and answered no more.* The celestial praise of the angels is dependent on the praises lauded by Israel. When Israel is silent below, the angels lose their power and cease their praise above. See Moses de León, *Peirush ha-Merkavah*, 72.

311. ***There was a voice*—the voice of Jacob...** In its simple sense, the clause from Ezekiel reads: *There was* קול (*qol*), *a sound, from above the expanse over their heads.* Here, Rabbi Shim'on construes *qol* as *a voice*, which he connects with "the voice of Jacob," namely the praises of Israel that ascend above. On the expression "voice of Jacob," see Genesis 27:22. On the prayers of the righteous deposited above, see *ZḤ* 10b (*MhN*), page 64.

312. **because of their silence in Torah and prayer...** When the voice of Jacob does not ascend above the expanse over their heads, the living beings let down their wings, i.e., they lose their power and cease their praise.

313. **the spirit of wisdom, harmony, and supernal peace...** רוח חכמתא שוריא ושלמא דלעילא (*Ruaḥ ḥokhmata shurayya u-shlama di-l'eila*).

Rabbi Pinḥas' phrasing derives from Naḥmanides' introduction to his commentary on Genesis, where he cites from the Aramaic translation of the book called *The Great Wisdom of Solomon.* "There is nothing new in the birth of a king or ruler; there is one entrance for all people into the world, and one exit alike. That is why I have prayed and רוחא דחכמתא (*ruḥa de-hokhmata*), the spirit of wisdom, was bestowed upon me.... It is God alone who gives knowledge that contains no falsehood—to know how the world arose, the composition of the constellations,

Rabbi Yehudah said, "יקוו המים (*Yiqqavu ha-mayim*), *Let the waters be gathered* (Genesis 1:9)—like the קו (*qav*), plumb line, that the craftsman lays down to construct a building that it not deviate in any direction, so the blessed Holy One established a line for the waters that they not escape their boundary in any direction, as is written: *And I said, 'Until here you may come, but no farther'* (Job 38:11)."[314]

It has been taught: The blessed Holy One established a boundary for the sea. What is this boundary?

Rabbi Abba said, "It is the sand, as is written: *I made the sand a boundary for the sea* (Jeremiah 5:22). When they [the waters] see the sand, they turn back and do not breach the line the blessed Holy One established for them."[315]

Rabbi Yitsḥak said, "Come and see how profoundly the essence of the world is water! For the heavens derived their name from there: מים (*mayim*), *water*—שמים (*shamayim*), *heavens*. The blessed Holy One added fire to water, creating from them השמים (*ha-shamayim*), the heavens—namely אש (*esh*), fire, and מים
96 (*mayim*), water."[316] [12c]

Rabbi Yudai said, "This cannot be, for the heavens were created from the love that is before the blessed Holy One!"[317]

שוריא ושולמיא (*shurayya u-shulamayya*), the beginning and the end, and middle of the times, the angles of the ends of the constellations...; everything hidden and everything revealed I know." Here, *shurayya u-shulamayya*, meaning "beginning and end," have become *shurayya u-shlama*, apparently meaning "harmony [or: arrangement, order] and peace"—with *shurayya* understood as שורה (*shurah*), "line, row, chain, cord," perhaps conveying the interconnectedness of the angelic and human realms. Like Solomon, Rabbi Shim'on possesses knowledge of the celestial mysteries.

314. **like the קו (*qav*), plumb line...** The equation between יקוו (*yiqqavu*) and קו (*qav*) is found in *Bereshit Rabbah* 5:1: "Rabbi Berekhiah said in the name of Rabbi Abba son of Yama, 'Let a measure be made for the waters, as is said: וקו (*Ve-qav*), *And a line, will be stretched out over Jerusalem* (Zechariah 1:16).'" See also *Zohar* 1:18a.

The verse from Job continues: *Here is where your proud waves halt.*

315. ***I made the sand a boundary for the sea...*** The verse continues: *an everlasting barrier it cannot cross. The waves may roll, but they cannot prevail; they may roar, but they cannot cross it.* See *Pirqei de-Rabbi Eli'ezer* 5; see above, note 301.

316. **מים (*mayim*), *water*—שמים (*shamayim*), *heavens*...** See BT *Ḥagigah* 12a: "What is the meaning of שמים (*shamayim*)? Rabbi Yose son of Ḥanina said, 'ששם מים (*She-sham mayim*), for there is water.'" See also Radak and Naḥmanides on Genesis 1:8.

See *Bereshit Rabbah* 4:7 in the name of Rav: 'The blessed Holy One took אש (*esh*), fire, and מים (*mayim*), water, mixed them with one another—and from them שמים (*shamayim*), heavens, were made." See also *Zohar* 2:164b; 3:137b (*IR*); *ZḤ* 15a (*MhN*).

317. **This cannot be...** According to Rabbi Yudai, the heavens could not possibly have been created from fire, which would imply anger and severity. Rather, they were created out of love.

Rabbi El'azar said, "Rabbi Yitsḥak has spoken well, and it does not contradict what Rabbi Yudai said. For when you comprehend what water signifies, you will fathom the essence of the matter."[318]

When Rabbi Bo arrived, Rabbi Yehudah and Rabbi Ḥiyya entered in his presence. They said to him, "May our master tell us the essence of a certain matter from those supernal mysteries."

He said, "I shall tell you one matter, beneficial for whoever possesses a comprehending heart. The Masters of the Mystery of Mishnah say that whoever desires to comprehend and to contemplate in his heart from the wisdom of the supernal King, should first understand what water signifies. And whoever desires to know the meaning of the congealment of His throne, should contemplate the covenant of salt, as is written: *it is a perpetual covenant of salt* (Numbers 18:19)—from these two he will contemplate holy wisdom on high."[319]

Rabbi Abba said, "Whoever desires to comprehend the nature of the existence of this world, should understand the matter of salt administered by the minister appointed beneath his Master. He must know what it signifies and how it is dissolved in water; [then] he will contemplate wisdom."[320] 97

318. **when you comprehend what water signifies...** Rabbi El'azar states explicitly that the water from which the heavens were created is in fact a symbol. Though he does not reveal the referent, it is clear that water symbolizes love, and therefore fire symbolizes judgment (or severity). Hence both Rabbi Yitsḥak and Rabbi Yudai are correct: the heavens were created out of love (as per Rabbi Yudai) and out of water and fire—the fusion of love and judgment (as per Rabbi Yitsḥak).

In Kabbalah, water and fire are standard symbols for the *sefirot Ḥesed* and *Din*, the right and left sides of divine being, respectively.

"The essence of the matter," עיקרא דמילתא (*iqqara de-milta*), indicates the deeper meaning as opposed to the plain or midrashic sense. See *ZḤ* 15c, 16a, 25d (all *MhN*); Gikatilla, *Sha'arei Orah*, 2a; Moses de Leon, *Sefer ha-Rimmon*, 307.

319. **congealment of His throne... covenant of salt...** The supernal, holy wisdom is encapsulated in the mystery of water and salt. Water symbolizes love; and now we learn that salt symbolizes its opposite, namely judgment (or severity).

The reference to the congealment of His throne is enigmatic—and deliberately so. Apparently Rabbi Bo is indicating two states of the divine throne: one, when its waters are not congealed; and another, signified by salt, when its waters are frozen. (Perhaps because salt crystals resemble ice in their appearance, solidity, and preservative ability.)

Cf. *Zohar* 1:29b on the congealing waters of *Shekhinah*, which are thawed only by *Ḥesed*.

On the Masters of Mishnah, see note 227.

320. **the matter of salt administered by the minister...** Apparently, it is Metatron who is responsible for administering the balance between salt and water, *Din* and *Ḥesed*. This world is poised between these two opposing forces. Importantly, just as water dissolves salt, so the forces of *Ḥesed* dissolve the forces of *Din*.

The dialectic between *Ḥesed* and *Din*, which is so central to kabbalistic thought, has its origin in rabbinic literature. See, for example, *Bereshit Rabbah* 12:15, explaining

Rabbi Yitsḥak said in the name of Rav, "Those soothsayers who set up their occult cups with water and salt—this pertains to light; to flame—to contemplate wisdom."[321]

Alternatively, *God said, "Let the waters under heaven be gathered to one place"* (Genesis 1:9). Rabbi opened, saying, "*More than the sound of many waters, the sea's majestic breakers, majestic on high is YHVH* (Psalms 93:4). *More than the sound of many waters*—when the blessed Holy One commanded the waters to gather in one place, they dashed to and fro, exalting themselves on high."[322]

Rabbi Yitsḥak said, "At that time the waters surged over the earth, which was immersed within them, covering it over. The blessed Holy One said to them, 'Not like this! Rather, gather yourselves together *to one place and let the dry land appear*' (Genesis 1:9), implying that the earth existed previously as dry land without moisture amidst the waters. It is not written *dry land*, but rather *the dry land*.[323]



the appearance of both divine names, *YHVH* and *Elohim* in Genesis 2:4, *On the day YHVH Elohim created heaven and earth*: "This may be compared to a king who had some thin glasses. Said the king, 'If I pour hot water into them, they will burst; if cold, they will contract [and snap].' What then did the king do? He mixed hot and cold water and poured it into them, and so they remained [unbroken]. The blessed Holy One said, 'If I create the world by the quality of compassion, its sins will abound; by the quality of justice, the world will not endure. Rather, I will create it by both the quality of justice and the quality of compassion. Oh, that it may endure!' So, *YHVH Elohim*." See also BT *Berakhot* 7a.

321. **soothsayers who set up their occult cups...** A conjectural rendering of קלודטי דזקפין בלודטיהון (*qeludtei de-zaqfin beludteihon*).

*Qeludtei* may derive from כלדי (*kalddi*), which denotes a "Chaldean" but implies a soothsayer or astrologer—whose occult arts are forbidden. It might also derive from קלודיא (*qalludayya*), a hot drink of wine and water (see *Vayiqra Rabbah* 5:3; *Bemidbar Rabbah* 10:3). Perhaps the symbolism of wine and water suited the author's comments about water and salt.

*Beludteihon* may be derived from בלטיהם (*be-lateihem*) in Exodus 7:22, where it refers to the occult arts practiced by the Egyptian sorcerers. See Rashi, ad loc., and BT *Sanhedrin* 67b. In some manuscripts and printed editions, *beludteihon* appears as כלודטיהון (*keludteihon*). If so, it may derive from קלודיא (*qalludayya*), like *qeludtei*, above.

Rabbi Yitsḥak's point is that the nations of the world also possess knowledge of the two opposing forces that underwrite the world: light, signifying compassion (or love); and flame, signifying justice (or severity).

322. **they dashed to and fro, exalting themselves on high** See above, note 301.

"Rabbi" indicates Rabbi Yehudah ha-Nasi (the Patriarch), who redacted the Mishnah. He was so highly esteemed that he was simply called "Rabbi": the Master.

323. **It is not written *dry land*, but rather *the dry land*** The definite article, *ha-yabbashah*, suggests a previously existent entity.

According to Wald, *The Doctrine of the Divine Name*, 55–56, the symbolism of the previous section continues here, and the primeval surging waters indicate unrestricted

"The waters were advancing, rising and descending, raising their voices to the ends of heaven, until the blessed Holy One rebuked them—dispatching them to the Abyss, the gathering place of the waters; still their voices did not subside, and He called them Seas. When they rise up there, in that place, their power is broken, and they descend—not gushing out, for fear of their Master's power, as is written: *more than the sea's majestic breakers, majestic on high is YHVH* (Psalms 93:4)."[324]

Rabbi Yose said, "If so, what is the meaning of that which is written afterward: *Your testimonies are very faithful, holiness befits Your house* (ibid. 93:5)? What is the connection between this verse and the previous one?"[325]

Rabbi Yitsḥak replied, "David said, 'Master of the World, the testimonies You established through the Work of Creation are the truth that one must attest every day.' As we have learned: Whoever testifies every day concerning the Work of Creation is assured of being a scion of the world to come.[326]

"David said further, 'You are the one who made the entire world, and You made the waters. In their great abundance the waters engulfed the whole world, but You decreed that they assemble, entirely contracted, to one place. So may it be Your will before You that Your *Shekhinah* that fills the entire world be contracted in Your house, for it is more fitting that she abide there, as is written: *holiness befits Your house*; and not for a short while, but rather, *for all time* (ibid.).'"[327]



*Ḥesed*. The waters must be gathered so that the dry land—signifying judgment and more concretely the space occupied by the world—can appear. In the Bible and in the rabbinic tradition, however, the waters are a more chaotic and sinister force.

324. **still their voices did not subside...** Although the waters were dispatched at the beginning of time, it is only through *YHVH's* majestic power that they are held at bay and do not inundate the world.

325. **What is the connection between this verse...** What do God's testimonies and the Temple have to do with God's supremacy over the waters?

326. **testifies every day concerning the Work of Creation...** Acknowledging the fact of creation is of supreme importance and the *sine qua non* of spiritual life.

Cf. Naḥmanides on Genesis 1:1: "this is the root of faith; and he who does not believe in this—and thinks that the world was eternal—denies the essential principle of the religion, and has no Torah at all."

On testifying every day to the works of creation, see *Sefer ha-Rimmon*, 284, where Moses de León uses almost identical language in the name of the sages, though there is no such source in the Talmud or midrashim.

327. **You decreed that they assemble, entirely contracted...** Just as the waters were בצמצום (*be-tsimtsum*), "contracted," to allow the dry land to appear, so David yearns that the *Shekhinah*, the divine presence that fills the world, be contracted into the Temple. Thus the references to God's testimonies and the Temple in Psalms 93:5 are apposite to the theme of water in the preceding verse.

On the contraction of the *Shekhinah* in rabbinic literature, see *Vayiqra Rabbah* 29:4; *Bemidbar Rabbah* 12:8; *Shir ha-Shirim Rabbah* on 3:11; *Tanḥuma*, *Vayaqhel* 7; *Pesiqta de-Rav Kahana* 1:3, 2:10, 23:4.

Alternatively, *God said, "Let the waters under heaven be gathered to one place and let the dry land appear"* (Genesis 1:9). Rabbi Tanḥum opened with this verse, "*The righteous one perishes and no one takes it to heart, devout people are taken away, while no one understands that because of evil the righteous one was taken away* (Isaiah 57:1). We have learned there: When the blessed Holy One examines the world and finds that there are no righteous people, and that many wicked people are flourishing in the world, it is then that He executes judgment upon the world."[328]

Rabbi Tanḥum said, "Like the conduct of the body with the soul, so the blessed Holy One deals with the generation."

Rabbi Yitsḥak asked, "How so?"

He replied, "It follows this pattern: The righteous are [12d] the soul, and the wicked are the body. When the blessed Holy One examines the world, He seizes the soul, while the body is left behind and the flesh decays. What does He seize? He seizes the soul (the righteous), while the body (the wicked) is left behind."[329]



Rabbi Tanḥum said, "As is written: *God said, 'Let the waters be gathered'.* These are the righteous gathered to their eternal rest, which is *one place* designated for them in accordance with their rank. When they are gathered to the world to come, what is written? *Let the dry land appear*—referring to the wicked, without deeds, without anyone to shield and protect them. As is said: *The entire community* ויראו (*va-yir'u*), *saw, that Aaron had expired* (Numbers 20:29). Do not read וַיִּרְאוּ (*va-yir'u*), *saw*, but rather וַיֵּרָאוּ (*va-yera'u*), *they were seen.*"[330]

328. ***because of evil the righteous one was taken away...*** The simple sense of מפני הרעה (*mi-penei ha-ra'ah*), *because of evil*, is apparently "as a result of evil," though it was explained midrashically as anticipatory: "so that he not experience the impending evil." See Rashi and Radak, ad loc. Cf. BT *Bava Qamma* 60a; *Kallah Rabbati* 3:23; 6:4; *Pirqei de-Rabbi Eli'ezer* 17 and David Luria, ad loc.

Rabbi Tanḥum's opening statement would seem to imply that the blessed Holy One executes judgment on the world because there are no righteous people. A more profound explanation follows.

329. **When the blessed Holy One examines the world, He seizes the soul...** When the world is found guilty, the blessed Holy One first removes the righteous (the soul), leaving the wicked (the body) to face judgment.

330. ***Let the waters be gathered... Let the dry land appear...*** The righteous are removed, leaving the wicked to face judgment without anyone to protect them.

See BT *Rosh ha-Shanah* 3a: "*The Canaanite, king of Arad, heard* (Numbers 33:40). What news did he hear? He heard that Aaron had died, and that the clouds of glory had disappeared; he thought that he was free to wage war on Israel, as is written: *The entire community* ויראו (*va-yir'u*), *saw, that Aaron had expired* (Numbers 20:29). Rabbi Abbahu said, 'Do not read *va-yir'u*, *saw*, but rather *va-yera'u*, *they were seen* [because the clouds had now departed and Israel became visible and exposed].'" See also BT *Ta'anit* 9a; *Zohar* 3:103a; *ZḤ* 14d (*MhN*), page 131.

On the expression "one place," cf. *Zohar* 1:18a, where it refers to *Shekhinah*.

Look at what we have learned: Rabbi Yitsḥak said in the name of Rav, though according to others it was Rav Yehudah in the name of Rav, "As long as the righteous abide in the generation, the attribute of judgment cannot prevail upon them, as is written: *He said that He would annihilate them—had not Moses, His chosen one, stood in the breach before Him to turn away His wrath from destroying* (Psalms 106:23). When the blessed Holy One desires to execute judgment upon the wicked, He removes the righteous from among them—then He executes judgment upon the wicked.[331]

"A parable. To what can the matter be compared? To a king who had an orchard. One day he entered his garden and noticed that it was completely overgrown with many thistles. He said, 'I wish to eradicate them from here.' He raised his eyes—and saw beautiful and pleasing roses. He said, 'For the sake of these roses, I will permit all the thistles.' When the roses wafted fragrance, he took them and plucked them from the garden. Once he had plucked them, he said, 'Now is the time to uproot the thistles of the garden, to eradicate them from here.' Similarly with the blessed Holy One: As long as the righteous abide in the generation, judgment is not executed upon the wicked. When the righteous depart from among them, then judgment is executed upon the wicked."[332]

Rabbi Yitsḥak asked Rabbi El'azar while they were traveling in the desert, saying, "I wish to ask a certain question—if it is not a sin."[333]

He replied, "You may inquire of Torah whatever you desire. Ask!"

He said, "Concerning the verse *God saw that it was good* (Genesis 1:10)—were this before the work, it would be fine and well, but since it is said after the work it implies that beforehand He did not know the essence of the work, neither its perfection nor its beauty. When the work was complete, it seems He examined

331. **As long as the righteous abide in the generation...** According to a rabbinic tradition, the righteous are removed to protect their generation. See BT *Shabbat* 33a: "Rabbi Gorion (according to others, Rabbi Yosef son of Rabbi Shema'yah) said, 'When there are righteous ones in the generation, the righteous are seized [killed] for the generation.'"

Here God intentionally removes the righteous individual in order to expose his generation to harsh judgment; without his protective virtue, they are completely vulnerable. Hence: מפני הרעה (*mipenei ha-ra'ah*), *before evil* [literally: *because of evil*], *the righteous one was taken away* (Isaiah 57:1).

See *Bereshit Rabbah* 33:1; *Vayiqra Rabbah* 2:6; *Kallah Rabbati* 6:4; Rashi on BT *Ta'anit* 11a, s.v. *ha-tsaddiq avad*; *Zohar* 1:67b; *ZḤ* 11d, 23a (both *MhN*). See especially *Zohar* 1:180a for a direct parallel.

332. **To a king who had an orchard...** See *Shir ha-Shirim Rabbah* on 2:2. Cf. *ZḤ* 20a (*MhN*), where Rabbi Yehudah presents a similar orchard parable, illustrating how the righteous are plucked in their prime, before they wither and sin. Cf. *Shir ha-Shirim Rabbah* on 6:2.

333. **if it is not a sin** Rabbi Yitsḥak fears that his question is heretical as it casts doubt on divine omniscience.

just how it turned out—and only then declared *that it was good,* as is written: *He saw,* and afterward He said *that it was good.*"[334]

He replied, "It is not a sin, and you are required to ask this. It serves as a warning to human beings. As Rabbi Yehudah said: 'When a person studies the Account of Creation and the works of every single day, let him not inquire concerning that which he has not been commanded, saying, "Why was this work act done in this form, and that one in that form?" Answer him, "You should know why: *God saw that it was good* to make it so; therefore do not ask any more!"'"[335]

"Furthermore, so as to set an example to human beings and teach them the proper path, that even though the work was revealed and known to Him before it was performed, He did not wish to pronounce that it was good until the work had been completed. Similarly, it is not fitting for a person to praise something until it is finished, lest he find in it a deficiency and he be proven false and trapped in his words."[336]

Rabbi Berekhiah said, "So we have seen in numerous places that the blessed Holy One set an example to human beings to which to pay heed even though He had no need for it—for it was perfectly well known to Him; however, in order to set an example for human beings, it was necessary to act in this way.[337]

"Come and see: It is written: *Let Me go down and see whether as the outcry that has come to Me they have dealt destruction* (Genesis 18:21). Was it not perfectly well known to Him that He needed to examine and investigate?"[338]

334. ***He saw,* and afterward He said *that it was good*** The phrase *God saw that it was good* (or a variant) appears repeatedly throughout the account of creation in Genesis 1 and always follows the creative acts, implying that only after the fact God saw how they turned out. Rabbi Yitsḥak is perplexed—surely God knew beforehand!

335. **let him not inquire...** God alone knows the divine will. His word *that it was good* should suffice!

See *Bereshit Rabbah* 8:2 in the name of Ben Sira: "About what is too great for you, do not inquire; what is too hard for you, do not investigate; what is too wondrous for you, know not; of what is hidden from you, do not ask! Contemplate what was permitted to you: you have no business with hidden things."

See also BT *Berakhot* 10a: "What have you to do with the secrets of the Merciful One? You should do what you were commanded—and let the blessed Holy One do what He pleases!"

See also M *Ḥagigah* 2:1: "Whoever speculates about four things, it would have been better for him if he had not come into the world: what is above; what is below; what before; what after."

Cf. *Zohar* 3:159a; *ZḤ* 6d (*MhN*), page 33.

336. **be proven false and trapped...** See BT *Berakhot* 4a: "Teach your tongue to say 'I don't know,' lest you be proven false and trapped [by your words]."

337. **set an example to human beings...** Sometimes Scripture depicts God acting in a way that is seemingly not in keeping with His omniscience. This is not for His benefit, but for ours, as explained in the following paragraph.

338. ***Let Me go down and see...*** The context is the impending destruction of Sodom and Gomorrah.

Well, Rabbi Berekhiah said, "From here a warning to the court that they not rely on their own opinion—but rather must examine, investigate, and scrutinize the matter thoroughly, as is written: *You are to scrutinize, investigate, and inquire well* (Deuteronomy 13:15)—you are not permitted to rely on your own opinion."[339] [13a]

While they were sitting they saw Rabbi Abba arriving. They said, "Look, one of the Masters of Mishnah is coming!"[340]

They approached him and asked this question.

He said, "So have the Masters of Mishnah decreed: Everything the blessed Holy One did, He did by His commands through an intermediary. He commanded the earth 'Do this,' and she did as she was commanded, without deviating. He commanded the waters 'Do this,' and the waters performed their work as they were commanded, without deviating. And similarly to the firmament—following the same pattern.[341]

"When each of them had performed its work as commanded, the blessed Holy One saw that it had acted in the way He commanded, and He praised that specific work, as is written: *God saw that it was good* (Genesis 1:10), that is, *He saw* that particular work, that they performed it as He commanded, and then said *that it was good*, namely that it was good that it had done as commanded. This is the meaning of *God saw that it was good*."[342]

Rabbi Yitsḥak said, "They have all spoken well, but this word is the finest of all!"[343]



339. **a warning to the court...** See Rashi on Genesis 18:21: "This has taught judges not to issue a verdict in capital cases except through seeing." See also idem on Genesis 11:5: "He did not need this, but to teach judges that they should not convict the defendant until they see and understand."

See also *Tanḥuma, Noaḥ* 18: "*YHVH came down to examine* [*the city and the tower that man had built*] (Genesis 11:5). Now did He need to come down and examine? Isn't everything known and revealed before Him, as is said: *He knows what is in the darkness; light dwells with Him* (Daniel 2:22)? Rather, it was to teach people not to finalize judgment—and not to say anything at all—until they see for themselves."

On the verse from Deuteronomy, see BT *Sanhedrin* 40a.

340. **Masters of Mishnah...** On this epithet, see above, note 227.

341. **He did by His commands through an intermediary...** See below, *ZḤ* 16a–b (*MhN*), page 153, where these three intermediaries are referred to as "artisans" and are correlated with the four foundation elements. See also *Zohar* 3:219b (*RM*); Tishby, *Wisdom of the Zohar*, 2:553.

342. **they performed it as He commanded...** Because creation occurred through intermediaries, and because these intermediaries could (theoretically at least) have acted contrary to the divine will, it is only after seeing His will fully executed that God proclaims the work good.

343. **They have all spoken well...** Although Rabbi El'azar and Rabbi Berekhiah provided adequate resolutions to his query, Rabbi Yitsḥak proclaims Rabbi Abba's interpretation the most profound. Whereas the former resolved his question by finding moralistic advice in God's actions, Rabbi Abba's

Rabbi Berekhiah said to Rabbi Yitsḥak, "If that is the case, this word poses more problems than everything that was said! For if so, the verse should have said *God saw all that they had made, and look, it was very good.* Why does it say *all that He had made* (Genesis 1:31)?"[344]

Rabbi Yitsḥak replied, "You raise a good point!"

They walked after Rabbi Abba. They told him this word. He said to them, "It is a good point, but this helps us. It is written: *all that He had made*—in general, and it does not say *all that they had made*—implying the intermediaries He had made, who brought forth all they had been commanded; and look, it was good. Therefore it is written *all that He had made.*"[345]

Rabbi Ḥiyya said, "*God saw all that He had made, and look, it was* [*very*] *good* (Genesis 1:31)—that they abide forever in the precise existence and manner He made them, never altering from this form."[346]



Rav Huna said in the name of Rav, "Upon three the blessed Holy One bestowed names at the Work of Creation. They are: the heavens, the earth, and the waters. The heavens—how do we know? As is written: *God called the expanse Heavens* (Genesis 1:8). The earth—how do we know? As is written: *God called the dry land Earth* (ibid., 10). The waters—how do we know? As is written: *the gathering of waters He called Seas* (ibid.). Why? To perform through them all His work. But that which emerged from them, He granted to Adam to bestow upon them names."[347]

Rabbi Berekhiah said, "Everything that heaven and earth brought forth, Adam bestowed upon them names, as is said: *Adam called names to all the cattle and to the fowl of the heavens and to all the beasts of the field* (Genesis 2:20)."

explanation goes to the very essence of creation, as befits a Master of Mishnah.

344. **the verse should have said . . . *all that they had made* . . .** If the intermediaries were indeed responsible for creation, why then is this not reflected in the verse in Genesis? The verse explicitly states: *all that He had made*, without referring to the intermediaries.

345. **implying the intermediaries He had made . . .** The statement in Genesis, *all that He had made* does not refer to creation, but rather to the intermediaries made by God to perform His work.

346. **never altering from this form** See *ZḤ* 17a (*MhN*), page 166.

Cf. Naḥmanides on Genesis 1:4: "*God saw the light, that it was good*— . . . The order followed in the process of creation is that the bringing forth of things into actual existence is called *amirah* ('saying') . . . and the permanence of things called forth into existence is called *re'iyah* ('seeing'). . . . The purport of the word 'seeing' is thus to indicate that their continued existence is at His will, and if that Will should for a second depart from them, they will turn into naught."

347. **Why? To perform through them all His work . . .** Because heaven, earth, and the waters performed the work of creation, their names were directly bestowed upon them by God Himself.

## Section 5[348]

*God said, "Let the earth sprout vegetation—seed-bearing plants, fruit trees of every kind"* (Genesis 1:11).

Rabbi Yitsḥak opened, "*Awake, north wind! Come, south wind! Blow upon my garden, let its spices flow. Let my beloved come into his garden and eat its luscious fruits* (Song of Songs 4:16)."[349]

Rabbi Abbahu said, "How assiduous must a person be in his actions, scrutinizing them every day! For the blessed Holy One placed within him a pure soul to perceive and recognize his Creator, to contemplate the wonders He performs each day."[350]

It has been taught: Rabbi Yitsḥak said, "Every day four winds blow from the four directions of the world. The east wind blows from the morning until the middle of the day, flowing forth from the Beloved Treasury. As we have learned: There is a treasury above among the gates of the east—named 'Beloved'—and it contains 3075 healing breezes for the world."[351]



348. **Section 5** The printed editions and some manuscripts preserve the section heading פרשתא ה (*parsheta* 5), perhaps reflecting an early attempt to arrange the materials of *MhN* on the Torah. See also *ZḤ* 3d, 10b, 14a, 17c, 19c, 28a, end of *parashat Lekh Lekha*—below, page 311 (all *MhN*); *Zohar* 2:20a (*MhN*).

349. **Rabbi Yitsḥak opened, "*Awake, north wind!*...** In this and the two following sections of *MhN*, the treatment of the creation accounts in Genesis begins with a verse from the Song of Songs. See below, pages 117 and 177. On the relationship between these two works, see *ZḤ* 14d (*MhN*), where the grandson of Rabbi Ḥiyya the Great informs Rabbi Yose: "My father used to teach me verses of the Song of Songs and the portion of *Bereshit*," perhaps implying that the secrets of creation are decoded through the Song of Songs. See Asulin, "Midrash ha-Ne'lam li-Vreshit," 225.

350. **a pure soul...to contemplate the wonders...** See Maimonides, *Mishneh Torah, Hilkhot Yesodei ha-Torah* 2:2: "What is the path to love and fear Him? When a person contemplates His wondrous and great deeds and creations...."

See above, *ZḤ* 6d (*MhN*), page 32.

351. **four winds blow...** On the various winds and their prevailing times, see BT *Gittin* 31b; *Berakhot* 3b; *Yevamot* 72a; *Bava Batra* 25a; *Arukh*, s.v. *kinnor*; Rashi on BT *Berakhot* 3b, s.v. *kinnor*: "Every single day, four winds blow: the first six hours of the day—an easterly wind blows with the sun; the last six hours—a southerly wind; at the beginning of the night—a westerly wind; at midnight—a northerly wind." See also idem on BT *Sanhedrin* 16a, s.v. *kinnor*. See Idel, "Qeta Lo Yadu'a," 80, 84 (see Addendum 2 in this volume).

See also *Mekhilta, Beshallaḥ* 4, which discusses the east wind with which the Egyptians were punished, and which quotes a verse from Hosea (13:15) that may be the source for the *Zohar*'s names of the various storehouses of winds: *For though he flourish among reeds, a blast, a wind of YHVH shall come blowing up from the wilderness; his spring shall be parched, his fountain dried up. That wind shall plunder treasures, every beloved object.*

See also *Zohar* 1:139a (*MhN*); 2:173b.

This corresponds with what we have learned in the Mishnah of Rabbi Eli'ezer: As is written: *morning without clouds* (2 Samuel 23:4). Namely, when it is morning, whoever is beset by afflictions and illness is not seized by clouds.[352]

Correspondingly, Rabban Yoḥanan son of Zakkai said, "In that wind that stirs from the east, an angel is empowered from the morning until the middle of the day—named Michael; he is appointed over the east."[353]

Rabban Yoḥanan son of Zakkai also said, "Michael, about whom is written *Look,* מלאכי (*malakhi*), *My angel, shall go before you* (Exodus 32:34). When you contemplate closely you find: מיכאל (*mikhael*), [13b] מלאכי (*malakhi*). This is what the blessed Holy One said to Moses: *Look, My angel shall go before you*—that is, *Look, Michael shall go before you.*"[354]

It has been taught: When the east wind rouses to flow into the world, whoever is walking on the way and attunes his spirit to this matter—at that hour, all the blessings with which he is blessed are fulfilled, and he will rejoice the entire day.[355]



352. ***morning without clouds...*** In the morning, those suffering from illness enjoy some respite.

See BT *Bava Batra* 16b: "When the day advances, illness lightens." See also BT *Nedarim* 8b: "The motes of the sun's morning rays heal." See also ibid. 40a; *Zohar* 3:22b.

Cf. *Zohar* 1:203b; 2:81a, where clouds symbolize the dark forces of judgment (*Din*) as opposed to the love (*Ḥesed*) that characterizes the morning.

The full verse in Samuel reads: *Like morning's light when the sun rises, morning without clouds; from radiance, from rain—vegetation from earth.*

A work titled *The Mishnah of Rabbi Eli'ezer or The Midrash of the Thirty Two Hermeneutic Rules* is extant (ed. Enelow), though it does not mention the idea put forth here. A work called The Mishnah of Rabbi El'azar (not Eli'ezer) is mentioned above, folio 10c, at note 226.

353. **Michael... appointed over the east** According to *Bemidbar Rabbah* 2:10, four archangels are aligned with the four cardinal points: "Just as the blessed Holy One created the four cardinal directions and four standards [of the tribes] corresponding to them, so also did He set about His throne four angels—Michael, Gabriel, Uriel, and Raphael." According to the *Bemidbar Rabbah* passage, however, Michael is aligned with the south. See also *Pirqei de-Rabbi Eli'ezer* 4.

See Idel, "Qeta Lo Yadu'a," 80 (Addendum 2 in this volume); see also *Zohar* 1:40b (*Heikh*); 2:254a (*Heikh*); 3:118b, 154b–155a.

354. **When you contemplate closely you find...** In Exodus 32, God informs Moses that following the sin of the Golden Calf, an angel (rather than God Himself) will accompany the Israelites. The unnamed angel is identified with Michael, whose name is an anagram for *malakhi*, "my angel."

See *Midrash Aggadah* (Buber) on Exodus 23:20; Ibn Ezra on Exodus 23:20; Naḥmanides on Exodus 33:12.

355. **whoever is walking on the way...** The morning hours are particularly auspicious for setting out on a journey and are accompanied by delight and blessing.

See *Mekhilta, Beshallaḥ* 5: "*At the morning watch* (Exodus 14:24)—you find that the prayers of the righteous are heeded in the morning."

See above, *ZḤ* 8a (*MhN*), page 42.

The west wind blows from the middle of the day until the night, and with it 465 breezes flow forth from the Fountain Treasury—causing plants, trees, and crops to thrive. It has been taught: An angel is empowered from the middle of the day until the night—named Raphael; he is appointed over the west.[356]

Rabbi Yose son of Pazzi said, "If so, there is a difficulty here! For look, we have learned: The angel empowered over healing is called Raphael. Yet you have said that healing comes from the east, over which Michael is appointed!"[357]

Come and hear: Rabban Yoḥanan son of Zakkai said, "The blessed Holy One's conduct toward human beings is entirely in order that they will acknowledge Him—that He afflicts and that He heals; that human beings will not set [their minds] either to an angel or a prince. For this reason He switches the seasons and times, so that they will not say 'Such and such an angel did this for me,' but rather 'all is in His power.' That is why He alternates the winds—so that they will pray before Him and repent, whereupon He commands healing to alight upon him, and the angel empowered over healing acts as commanded according to the will of his Master.[358] 107

"Come and see the compassion of the blessed Holy One! For He does not afflict a person until his deeds are weighed on the scale in the court above, and the one appointed over judgment is Michael! The compassion of the blessed Holy One is such that even though he is deserving of judgment, every day He arouses for him a healing wind, until the person mends his deeds, repenting of them before his Master. Then He sends him healing by the hand of the messenger so appointed."[359]

356. **west wind blows... Raphael...** On the west wind, see above, note 351. See Idel, "Qeta Lo Yadu'a," 80 (Addendum 2 in this volume).

In *Bemidbar Rabbah* 2:10 and in *Zohar* 3:154b–155a, Raphael is aligned with the west.

357. **The angel empowered over healing is called Raphael...** The name רפאל (*Rapha'el*) means "God heals." On Raphael as the angel of healing, see BT *Bava Metsi'a* 86b: "Who were the three men [who appeared to Abraham in Genesis 18:2]? Michael, Gabriel, and Raphael. Michael came to bring the tidings to Sarah [of Isaac's birth]; Raphael, to heal Abraham [after his circumcision]; and Gabriel, to overturn Sodom." See also *Tanḥuma* (Buber), addendum 1 to *Ḥuqqat*; *Zohar* 3:204a.

358. **For this reason He switches the seasons and times...** The inconsistency is deliberate, so that people will not ascribe healing to a particular angel, but to God directly.

Cf. *Eikhah Rabbah* 2:5, where the blessed Holy One employs a similar ruse, switching the names of the angels, so that when invoked they would not respond.

See also JT *Berakhot* 9:1, 13a: "If trouble should befall a person, let him not call out to Michael or Gabriel, but let him cry out to Me and I shall answer him immediately."

By alternating the winds, God ensures that people do not make cardinal error of setting their heart upon an angel or a prince, i.e., ascribing efficacy to the angels rather than God. See Maimonides, *Mishneh Torah, Hilkhot Avodat Kokhavim* 1:1–2; *Zohar* 1:56b.

359. **the one appointed over judgment is Michael...** In rabbinic literature Michael

The south wind blows from the beginning of the night until midnight, and with it 275 breezes flow forth from that Beloved Treasury, invigorating the earth and warming the cold. An angel is empowered over it—named Uriel; he is appointed over the south, in that wind. That wind is difficult for the sick and they are oppressed thereby, though it is beneficial for the world. It has been taught: At that time, the wicked are judged in the fire of Hell. The entire world lies down, dreaming in sleep, and there is no one to pray on their behalf.[360]

The north wind blows from midnight until morning. It has been taught: 300,000 currents and whirlwinds accompany it, and it is the most violent of all for everyone. It is, however, beneficial for the sick—on account of its extreme cold—for the excess heat they possess.[361]

It has been taught: Rabbi Shim'on son of Yoḥai said, "At that moment, the blessed Holy One ventures forth from those innumerable worlds that He desires, coming to delight with the righteous in the Garden of Eden. The voice of a herald proclaims before Him, saying, '*Awake, north wind! Come, south wind!*' (Song of Songs 4:16); namely: awake north wind and rouse to flow through the world, to blow upon the spices of the garden, as is written: *Blow upon my garden, let its spices flow* (ibid.)."[362]



is the chief advocate of Israel (see Daniel 10:13, 12:1; *Shemot Rabbah* 18:5; *Pesiqta Rabbati* 44). In the Kabbalah, he is associated with *Ḥesed*. Placing Michael at the head of the heavenly tribunal is akin to having a caring and loving companion adjudicate one's case.

360. **south wind . . .** The south wind is a warm wind that—while beneficial for vegetation—is difficult for the sick, who require a cooler breeze. Cf. BT *Gittin* 31b, which describes the south wind in menacing terms: "Rabbi Ḥanan son of Rava said in the name of Rav, 'Four winds blow every day and the north wind blows with all of them; for were it not so, the world would not be able to exist for a moment. The south wind is the most violent of all, and were it not that the Son of the Hawk [an angel] keeps it back, it would devastate the whole world.'"

On Uriel appointed over the south, see *Zohar* 3:154b–155a; cf. *Bemidbar Rabbah* 2:10; *Zohar* 2:254a (*Heikh*). On praying for the wicked in Hell, see *ZḤ* 25a–b (*MhN*).

361. **The north wind . . .** See BT *Berakhot* 3b. In BT *Gittin* 31b, the south wind is described as the most violent. The *Zohar* here has switched the winds.

Cf. Idel, "Qeta Lo Yadu'a" 80, 84 (Addendum 2 this volume), where the details of the northern and southern winds differ.

Here ends the formal presentation of the various winds, now followed by a discussion of the significance of midnight, the central concern of this portion of *MhN*.

362. **coming to delight with the righteous in the Garden of Eden . . .** Midnight marks the onset of a great celestial drama, triggered by the north wind, as the blessed Holy One delights with the departed souls of the righteous in the Garden of Eden.

On the *Zohar*'s midnight ritual, see below, note 367. On the verse from the Song of Songs, see Idel, "Qeta Lo Yadu'a," 84 (Addendum 2 in this volume). On the innumerable worlds that He desires, see *ZḤ* 9d, 18a, 22a (all *MhN*); Scholem, "Parashah Ḥadashah," 445 (Addendum 1 in this volume).

As it has been taught: When the north wind blows at midnight, and the blessed Holy One enters, all the spices and all the trees in the Garden of Eden emit their fragrance—singing in His presence, as is written: *Then all the trees of* היער (*ha-ya'ar*), *the forest, will sing before* YHVH (1 Chronicles 16:33).[363]

Rabbi Shim'on said, "This forest is like that of which is said: *I have eaten* יערי (*ya'ari*), *my honeycomb, and my honey* (Song of Songs 5:1). All the righteous delight from the splendor of the speculum above; they are nourished by it—and sing in the presence of their Creator in the Garden of Eden, as is written: *Let my beloved come into his garden and eat* פרי מגדיו (*peri megadav*), *its luscious fruits* (ibid. 4:16)."[364]

Rabbi Menaḥem said, "What is implied by *eat*? Now, could you possibly think that the blessed Holy One eats? This cannot be! Rather, it is like one who says 'Let the master of the house come, so that the guests may eat.' So it is written: *Let my beloved come into his garden* (ibid.); namely when my beloved comes to His garden, those who are waiting for him shall eat. Who is this? פרי מגדיו (*Peri megadav*), *His luscious fruits*—the [13c] righteous, who are the luscious fruits of the blessed Holy One."[365]

363. **trees in the Garden of Eden . . . singing in His presence . . .** See *Pereq Shirah* 2:57, 80; JT *Ḥagigah* 2:1, 77a; BT *Ḥagigah* 14b; *Zohar* 1:7a, 77a, 213b; 3:22b; [Moses de León?], *Seder Gan Eden*, 138.

364. **All the righteous delight from the splendor of the speculum above . . .** Once the blessed Holy One has entered the Garden of Eden, the souls of the departed righteous bathe in His presence.

Song of Songs 5:1 reads in full: *I have come into my garden, my sister, my bride; I have gathered my myrrh and spice; I have eaten my honeycomb and my honey; I have drunk my wine and my milk.*

"Speculum above" renders אספקלריא של מעלה (*ispaqlarya shel ma'alah*). *Ispaqlarya* means "glass, mirror, lens." See BT *Yevamot* 49b: "All the prophets gazed through an opaque glass [literally: an *ispaqlarya* that does not shine], while Moses our teacher gazed through a translucent glass [literally: an *ispaqlarya* that shines]." See also *Vayiqra Rabbah* 1:14; *Zohar* 1:97b, 122a (both *MhN*); *ZḤ* 10a, 15b, 15d, 16c, 17a, 21a, 24a (all *MhN*).

365. **could you possibly think that the blessed Holy One eats . . .** Rabbi Menaḥem (though some manuscripts read: Rabbi Tanḥum) is troubled by the implicit anthropomorphism of the verse from the Song of Songs, when construed as a reference to God's actions. The manuscripts preserve two different questions. Some read "What is implied by *eat*?" while others ask "Who eats?" Either way, the difficulty is the same. The problem is resolved by reinterpreting the final clause of the verse: פרי מגדיו (*pri megadav*), *its* [or: *his*] *luscious fruits.* It is not that God eats, but rather that once He has arrived in the garden, then *His luscious fruits*—the souls of the righteous—eat; i.e., they are nourished by His presence. Cf. *Shir ha-Shirim Rabbah* on 6:2; *Zohar* 2:37b.

Cf. Idel "Qeta Lo Yadu'a," 85 (Addendum 2 in this volume) for a different treatment of the same problem.

On souls as fruit, see *Bahir* 14 (22); Ezra of Gerona, *Peirush le-Shir ha-Shirim*, 489, 504; *Zohar* 1:15b, 19a, 33a, 59b–60a, 82b, 85b, 115a–b; 2:223b; Moses de León, *Sefer ha-Mishqal*, 51; idem, *Sheqel ha-Qodesh*, 56 (69).

Our Rabbis have taught: When the north wind begins to blow, all the heavens and all the firmaments, the holy living beings and the *ophanim*, and the entire host of heaven—all of them tremble and quiver, bursting forth in song and praise to the One who spoke and the world was, until He enters with the righteous in the Garden of Eden. This is at midnight.

Rav Yehudah said in the name of Rav, "Whoever possesses a holy soul hears the voice of the rooster calling at midnight."[366]

For Rav Yehudah said in the name of Rav: "At midnight, when the blessed Holy One enters the Garden of Eden, a spark of fire flashes from between the wheels of the living beings, soaring throughout the world, striking beneath the wings of the rooster. At that moment—in fear—it beats its wings against one another and calls out. This is at midnight.

"Whoever possesses intelligence in his heart, and rouses and rises to engage in Torah, his voice soars and is heard in the Garden of Eden, and the blessed Holy One listens. The righteous ask Him, 'Master of the World, who is this?' He replies, saying, 'It is so-and-so and the holy soul within him is plying Torah. Pay heed, all of you! For this is more pleasing to Me than all the songs and praises uttered above.'[367]



366. **the voice of the rooster...** A rooster's call at midnight is a sign to the righteous elect that they must rise and study Torah.

See *Pereq Shirah* 2:57 (s.v. *tarnegol*): "When the blessed Holy One comes to the righteous in the Garden of Eden, all the trees of the Garden sprinkle spices before Him. Then he [the rooster] praises." See Naḥmanides on Job 38:36; *Zohar* 1:10b, 77b, 92b, 218b; 2:196a; 3:23a–b, 52b, 171b; *ZḤ* 47d (*MhN, Rut?*), 88a (*MhN, Rut*). See Liebes, *Pulḥan ha-Shaḥar*, 168–197.

367. **rouses and rises to engage in Torah...** Based on King David's legendary custom of rising at midnight to study Torah (see below, note 369), the *Zohar* develops an elaborate ritual—the nocturnal delight—whereby kabbalists are expected to rise at midnight and ply Torah until the break of dawn. At midnight, God delights with the souls of the righteous in the Garden of Eden; and those who study Torah here below partake of the celestial joy. In the main body of the *Zohar*, this ritual is understood as adorning the *Shekhinah* in preparation for Her union with the blessed Holy One. This parallels the midnight vigil common among Christian monks from early medieval times. In *Zohar* 3:119a, Rabbi Yehudah alludes to the Christian practice: "I have seen something similar among the nations of the world."

See JT *Berakhot* 1:1, 2d; *Sifra, Beḥuqqotai* 3:3, 111b; *Aggadat Bereshit* 23:5; BT *Sanhedrin* 102a; 2 Enoch 8:3; *Zohar* 1:10b, 72a, 77a–b, 82b, 92a–b, 136b, 178a, 206b–207b, 231b, 242b; 2:26b, 36b, 46a, 130a–b, 136a, 173b, 195b–196a; 3:13a, 21b–22b, 49b, 52b, 67b–68a, 81a, 193a, 260a; [Moses de León?], *Seder Gan Eden*, 138; Scholem, *On the Kabbalah*, 146–50; Hellner-Eshed, *A River Flows from Eden*, 121–45. Cf. Matthew 25:6.

On the *Zohar*'s midnight ritual in *MhN*, see *Zohar* 2:18b (*MhN*); *ZḤ* 6a, 18a (both *MhN*); Scholem, "Parashah Ḥadashah," 445 (Addendum 1 in this volume). On Torah study as more pleasing than the songs of the celestial realm, see *Zohar* 2:46a; *ZḤ* 18a (*MhN*); Scholem, "Parashah Ḥadashah," 437 (Addendum 1 in this volume); cf. BT *Ḥullin* 91b. On engaging in Torah at night, see also

"As is written: *You who dwell* בגנים (*ba-gannim*), *in the gardens* (Song of Songs 8:13). Namely, 'O holy soul, you dwell in that world amidst גנותא (*gnuta*), muck, and mire, yet you engage in Torah! At this moment *companions listen for your voice* (ibid.), for the righteous like you are listening for your voice, which is sweet. Since it is so, *let me hear* (ibid.)—raise your voice in My Torah, and I will bestow upon you a reward of love in the world to come.'"[368]

Rabbi Tanḥum said, "Come and see: David knew this moment. For we have learned: A harp was suspended above David's bed; and when it was midnight, the north wind would stir and blow upon it. Immediately he would rise and invigorate himself in song and praise, as is written: *Awake, my glory! Awake, harp and lyre! I will awaken dawn* (Psalms 57:9)."[369]

Rabbi Zeira said, "How do we know that the north wind blows upon the harp?"

Rabbi Yitsḥak replied, "From here! Here is written *Awake, my glory* (ibid.), and there is written *Awake, north wind!* (Song of Songs 4:16). Just as there it



*Mishnat Rabbi Eli'ezer* 13; Maimonides, *Mishneh Torah, Hilkhot Talmud Torah* 3:13.

368. ***You who dwell* בגנים (*ba-gannim*), *in the gardens*...** The full verse reads: *You who dwell in the gardens, companions listen for your voice; let me hear!* This verse is cited repeatedly in the *Zohar* in the context of the nocturnal vigil, as the Companions below join with the blessed Holy One in the Garden of Eden above. In this case, there is no reference to the scholars below residing in the garden, but rather a midrashic play, celebrating the kabbalists' Torah endeavor despite their dwelling in the garden (*gannim*) amidst the muck (*gnuta*) of this world. Dwelling in the muck and mire may also allude to the soul stuck in the body.

The companions "listening for your voice" refers to the souls of the departed righteous, who—along with the entire celestial realm and the blessed Holy One—listen to the words of Torah from the scholars below.

See BT *Shabbat* 63a: "Rabbi Abba said in the name of Rabbi Shim'on son of Lakish, 'When two disciples of the wise listen to one another in *halakhah*, the blessed Holy One listens to their voice, as is said: *You who dwell in the gardens, companions listen for your voice; let me hear!*'" See *Zohar* 1:77b, 178b, 231b; 2:46a; 3:13a, 22a, 213a; *ZḤ* 47d (*MhN, Rut?*).

On the reward of love, see BT *Ḥagigah* 12b: "Resh Lakish said, 'Whoever engages in Torah at night, the blessed Holy One emanates a thread of love upon him by day, as is said: *By day YHVH directs His love* (Psalms 42:9). Why? Because *at night His song is with me.*' Others say: Resh Lakish said, 'Whoever engages in Torah in this world, which is like night—the blessed Holy One emanates a thread of love upon him in the world to come, which is like day, as is said: *By day YHVH directs His love, at night His song is with me* (ibid.).'" *His song* is construed as the song of Torah.

The "sweet voice" alludes to Song of Songs 2:14: *Let me hear your voice, for your voice is sweet.*

369. **A harp was suspended above David's bed...** See BT *Berakhot* 3b: "Rabbi Shim'on the Ḥasid said, 'There was a harp suspended above [King] David's bed. As soon as midnight arrived, a north wind came and blew upon it, and it played by itself. He immediately arose and engaged in Torah until the break of dawn."

On the verse from Psalms, see *Zohar* 1:82b; 2:27a. See also Psalms 119:62.

refers to the north, so here it refers to the north; and every night, the blessed Holy One and the righteous would listen to him in the Garden of Eden."[370]

Our Rabbis have taught: The blessed Holy One made a Garden of Eden on earth below, and it is aligned corresponding to the Throne of Glory and the awesome curtain. It has been taught: There is a certain place above it—Eden is its name—that no prophet's eye has been empowered to see; neither in a vision nor apparition, as is written: *No eye has seen, O God, but You* (Isaiah 64:3).[371]

Rabbi Shim'on said, "From that Eden above, the garden below is nourished; from there all the trees, all the plants, and all the produce in the garden are invigorated."[372]

Rabbi Shim'on also said, "Three times every day, the supernal Eden above the garden exudes all manner of beautiful aromas, supernal radiancies, pleasures, and delights. From that aroma, delight, and pleasure trickling down upon it, the entire world is nourished."[373]

112 It has been taught: Rabbi Shim'on said, "When the blessed Holy One said, '*Let the earth sprout vegetation*' (Genesis 1:11), immediately the earth sprouted all the produce, verdure, and trees in the Garden of Eden first; afterward she sprouted for the entire world."[374]

370. **From here!...** Rabbi Yitsḥak connects the Talmudic myth about King David to the Song of Songs. For the *Zohar*, the latter contains the deepest mysteries about the nocturnal delight.

371. **Garden of Eden on earth below...** Above the earthly (or lower) Garden of Eden stands a yet more mysterious and wondrous Eden. See BT *Berakhot* 34b; *Zohar* 1:106b, 125a (both *MhN*); *ZḤ* 18a–b, 21a (both *MhN*).

On the earthly and heavenly Gardens of Eden, see Naḥmanides on Genesis 3:22; idem, *Kitvei Ramban*, 2:295–99; *Zohar* 1:7a, 38b (*Heikh*), 81a (*ST*), 106b (*MhN*), 224b; 2:209b–210b, 211b–212a, 231b; 3:13a, 53a, 70b; Moses de León, *Shushan Edut*, 350–51; idem, *Sheqel ha-Qodesh*, 27 (32), 59–62 (73–76); [Moses de León?], *Seder Gan Eden*, 138; Tishby, *Wisdom of the Zohar*, 2:591–94, 749–51.

As the curtain divides between the Holy and the Holy of Holies in the Dwelling (see Exodus 26:33), the awesome curtain divides the mundane and celestial realms. Cf. *Pirqei de-Rabbi Eli'ezer* 4.

See also BT *Berakhot* 34b: "Rabbi Ḥiyya son of Abba said in the name of Rabbi Yoḥanan, 'All the prophets prophesied only concerning the days of the Messiah; but as for the world to come, *No eye has seen, O God, but You* (Isaiah 64:3).'"

372. **From that Eden above, the garden below is nourished...** Rabbi Shim'on clarifies: Eden above, garden below. See *ZḤ* 18a–b (*MhN*), page 184.

373. **the entire world is nourished** The bounty flowing from the supernal Eden sustains the lower garden, which in turn sustains the world. See BT *Ta'anit* 10a: "Rabbi Yehoshu'a son of Levi said, 'The entire world is watered by the residue of the Garden of Eden, as is said: *A river issues from Eden* [*to water the garden*] (Genesis 2:10).'"

See also *Zohar* 1:125a (*MhN*).

374. **in the Garden of Eden first...** See *Pirqei de-Rabbi Eli'ezer* 5: "He opened an entrance to the Garden of Eden, from where He brought forth plants upon the face of all the earth...." See also Luria, ad loc.

Rabbi Yehudah said, "The earth sprouted for the entire world, while the blessed Holy One sprouted for the Garden of Eden, as is written: *YHVH God planted a garden in Eden* מקדם (*mi-qedem*), *at first* (Genesis 2:8)."[375]

Rabbi Shim'on said, "The earth brought forth everything, but the blessed Holy One selected all the choicest among them and planted them in the Garden of Eden.[376] From that which trickles down from Eden, all are nourished, as is written: *The trees of YHVH are sated, cedars of Lebanon that He planted; where the birds build their nest* (Psalms 104:16–17). Who are these *birds*? They are the righteous. For the blessed Holy One fashions them wings like birds, to fly above—with knowledge and insight—raising them aloft to the site concealed for them, [13d] about which is written *No eye has seen, O God, but You...* (Isaiah 64:3)."[377]

Rabbi Yehudah said, "The earth bore vegetation that continued to sprout afterward—plants for the utility of the world, and all the medicinal herbs for the creatures to be healed; the earth bore and sprouted all of them at once."[378]

Rabbi Yehudah son of Shalom said, "On the same day that heaven and earth were created, on that very day they engendered all their generations—nothing was lacking from them, as implied by the verse *These are the generations of heaven and earth* (Genesis 2:4). When were these generations made? *On the day*



375. ***YHVH God planted a garden in Eden* מקדם (*mi-qedem*), *at first*** In its simple sense, the verse reads: *YHVH God planted a garden in Eden* מקדם (*mi-qedem*), *to the east.* Here, Rabbi Yehudah construes *mi-qedem* in its temporal sense as "previously, before, at first" (see Onqelos, ad loc.). Though he agrees with Rabbi Shim'on that the Garden of Eden sprouted before the rest of the world, in his view the plantings of the Garden were planted directly by God.

See *Zohar* 2:150a; *ZḤ* 18b (*MhN*).

376. **planted them in the Garden of Eden** See *Bereshit Rabbah* 15:1: "*YHVH Elohim planted a garden in Eden* (Genesis 2:8).... As is written: *The trees of YHVH are sated, cedars of Lebanon that He planted* (Psalms 104:16). Rabbi Ḥanina said, 'They resembled antennae of grasshoppers, and the blessed Holy One uprooted them, transplanting them in the Garden of Eden.'"

377. **Who are these *birds*? They are the righteous...** See BT *Sanhedrin* 92b: "Should you inquire, 'In those years during which the blessed Holy One will renew His world, as is written, *YHVH alone shall be exalted in that day* (Isaiah 2:11), what will the righteous do?' The blessed Holy One will fashion them wings like eagles, and they will fly above the water, as is written: *Therefore we will not fear, though the earth reel and mountains topple into the sea* (Psalms 46:3). Should you imagine that they will suffer pain, Scripture says: *But they who trust in YHVH shall renew their strength as eagles grow new plumes* (Isaiah 40:31)." See also Psalms 11:1; 84:3–4; *Avot de-Rabbi Natan*, A, addendum 2, 7:3; Idel, "Qeta Lo Yadu'a," 84 (Addendum 2 in this volume).

See Moses de León, *Sefer ha-Rimmon*, 202, where the verse from Psalms is also quoted in connection with the bird (or soul) motif. Cf. *Zohar* 1:34b, 47a; 3:196b.

378. **all the medicinal herbs...** See *Bereshit Rabbah* 10:6: "The son of Sira said, 'God caused drugs to spring forth from the earth; with them the physician heals the wound, and the apothecary compounds his preparations.'"

*YHVH God made earth and heaven* (ibid.). Precisely! All the world's requirements were made on the same day. Afterward, He revealed them, each day in turn, elaborating each and every thing on the day it was revealed."[379]

In a similar vein, Rabbi Yitsḥak said in the name of Rabbi Yoḥanan, "On the same day that the earth was created, on that very day she bore and sprouted all her offspring. They were all concealed beneath her until the blessed Holy One commanded her to bring them forth, as is written: *Let the earth bring forth* (Genesis 1:24). It does not say *Let the earth create*, but rather *Let the earth bring forth*—something concealed within her. She then brought forth each thing in its appropriate natural form, to propagate and seed itself, as is written: *according to its kind* (ibid.)."[380]

Rabbi Yehudah said, "So did the blessed Holy One act with regard to the earth: like a pregnant female, subsequently bringing forth her fetus from within. Similarly the earth: when she was created, she was pregnant with all the elements that had been implanted within her; they brought forth all her generations."[381]



Rabbi Yitsḥak said, "Like the vessels of a mother's uterus filled with a man's sperm containing all the elements, so the earth: on the day she was created, on that very day she was impregnated with all that she engendered, as is written: *In the beginning God created the heavens and the earth* (Genesis 1:1); and immedi-

379. **Afterward, He revealed them, each day in turn...** According to Genesis 1, creation spanned six days, whereas in Genesis 2 creation occurred *on the day*. The *Zohar* resolves the contradiction by noting that all of creation was indeed accomplished on one day, but revealed or made manifest over six days.

See *Bereshit Rabbah* 12:4: "Rabbi Yehudah said, 'The heavens and the earth were finished in their own time, and all their array in their own time.' Rabbi Neḥemiah said to him, 'Yet look at what is written: *These are the generations of heaven and earth when they were created* (Genesis 2:4), teaching that on the very day they were created, they brought forth their generations.' Rabbi Yehudah replied, 'Yet surely it is written *And there was evening and there was morning, one day... a second day... a third day... a fourth day... a fifth day... a sixth day*?' Rabbi Neḥemiah said, 'They were like those who gather figs, when each appears in its own time.' Rabbi Berekhiah said in support of Rabbi Neḥemiah, '*The earth brought forth* (ibid. 1:12), implying something that was already stored within her.'"

See also *Tanḥuma* (Buber), *Bereshit* 1–2; Rashi on Genesis 1:14, 24; Maimonides, *Guide of the Perplexed* 2:30; *ZḤ* 2d, 16d (both *MhN*).

380. ***Let the earth bring forth*—something concealed within her...** Just as on the first day, where creation was complete yet latent, so the earth contained all her offspring within her in a latent state, until commanded by the blessed Holy One to "bring forth."

See *Bereshit Rabbah* 12:4 (previous note); *Zohar* 1:46b, 97a. Cf. BT *Ḥullin* 60a–b.

381. **pregnant with all the elements...** Namely, the four foundational elements. See next paragraph and above, note 94. See Maimonides, *Guide of the Perplexed* 2:30; Naḥmanides on Genesis 1:3 and 1:10; *ZḤ* 16b (*MhN*). Cf. *Pirqei de-Rabbi Eli'ezer* 5; *Zohar* 3:87a.

ately: *The earth was chaos and void, and darkness* [ . . . ] *and wind* (Genesis 1:2)—look, here are the four elements: fire, water, darkness, and wind. These generated all her generations; from these all of them were established; all the generations came into being from these forces."[382]

Rabbi Abba said, "The swamps of the earth are filled with sperm—like a female—from the waters above; she is pregnant with them like a female impregnated by a male."[383]

Rabbi Ḥaggai asked Rabbi Dostai saying, "Look at what is written: *The earth brought forth vegetation, plants yielding seed, fruit trees bearing fruit of each kind* (Genesis 1:12)![384] If the earth brought forth trees and fruits, why is it written afterward *no bush of the field was* טרם *(terem) on earth, and no plant of the field had* טרם (*terem*) *sprouted* (ibid. 2:5)—if the meaning of *terem* follows its translation?"[385]

He replied, "So it is. But at that time they did not possess their powers to engender. Why? Because *YHVH God had not rained upon the earth* (ibid.), and there was no flow to *well up from the earth* (ibid., 6). For had it been so, all their powers would have been primed to generate and germinate. But because of this, the earth did not possess the generative power."[386]



382. **the four elements: fire, water, darkness, and wind . . .** Darkness indicates earth. See above, *ZḤ* 6d, 10a (both *MhN*) and note 94.

383. **like a female—from the waters above . . .** Cf. *Bereshit Rabbah* 13:13: "Rabbi Shim'on son of El'azar said, 'Every single handbreadth [of water] descending from above is met by two handbreadths emitted by the earth. What is the reason? *Deep calls to deep . . .* (Psalms 42:8).' Rabbi Levi said, 'The upper waters are male; the lower, female. The former cry to the latter, "Receive us! You are creatures of the blessed Holy One and we are His messengers." They immediately receive them, as is written: *Let the earth open* (Isaiah 45:8)—like a female opening to a male.'"

384. ***The earth brought forth vegetation . . .*** The *Zohar* here simplifies the verse, which in the Masoretic text reads: *The earth brought forth vegetation, plants yielding seed of each kind, and trees bearing fruit that has its seed within it of each kind.*

385. **If the earth brought forth trees and fruits . . .** Onqelos on Genesis 2:5 renders *terem* as "not yet." See Rashi, ad loc.: "Every instance of the word *terem* in Scripture means 'not yet,' and it does not mean 'before.'"

See BT *Ḥullin* 60b: "Rabbi Assi pointed out a contradiction: It is written: *The earth brought forth vegetation* (Genesis 1:12) [already] on the third day, but it is written: *No bush of the field was yet on earth,* [*and no plant of the field had yet sprouted, for YHVH Elohim had not rained upon earth and there was no human to till the soil*] (Genesis 2:5). This teaches that plants began to grow but stopped as they verged on breaking through the soil—until Adam came and prayed for them; then rain fell and they sprouted. This teaches you that the blessed Holy One yearns for the prayers of the righteous." See also *Zohar* 1:46b, 97a.

386. **the earth did not possess the generative power** Rabbi Dostai resolves the contradiction. While the earth had already brought forth her offspring, they did not yet possess their own generative capacity. See Naḥmanides on Genesis 2:5.

Rabbi Yitsḥak went to visit Rabbi Zeira. He entered his house and found him strolling in the garden.[387]

He opened, saying, "*The sons of Jethro, Moses' father-in-law, went up from the City of Date-Palms* (Judges 1:16). What prompted the sons of Jethro to go up from there? For Rav Yehudah said in the name of Rav: 'Jericho was the equal of all the land of Israel, on account of the abundant delights it possessed.' As Rav Yehudah said in the name of Rav: 'Why was it called יריחו (*Yeriḥo*), *Jericho*? In reference to the ריח (*reiaḥ*), *fragrance*.' The sons of Jethro said, 'We must engage in Torah, and Torah does not require delights. Let us ascend from here to the mountain and engage in Torah!'"[388]

Rabbi Zeira said, "I know what you are implying. It is only because the sons of Jethro did not yet know Torah and required the mountain, whereas I already know Torah and require thirsting clarity to fathom the teaching."[389]

He asked him, "What is the meaning of the verse *The earth brought forth vegetation* (Genesis 1:12)?"

116 He replied, "The earth brought forth all the generations hidden within her without, but they did not possess their powers until the blessed Holy One rained

387. **strolling in the garden** Cf. BT *Ta'anit* 9b: "Rav Daniel son of Kattina had a garden, and every day he would stroll around in it and inspect it. He said, 'This bed needs water, and that one does not'; and rain would fall on those beds that needed water."

388. ***The sons of Jethro...*** The Masoretic text actually begins: *The sons of the Kenite...* (Moses' father-in-law is identified as a Kenite in this verse and in Judges 4:11, but as Jethro in Exodus 3:1; 18:1–12.)

Rabbi Yitsḥak's homily is a thinly veiled criticism of Rabbi Zeira for strolling around in the garden. Just as the sons of the Kenite (Jethro) forsook the luxuries of Jericho (the city of date-palms) to pursue Torah, so Rabbi Zeira should not be engaging in worldly pleasures but focusing entirely on Torah study.

On the sons of Jethro pursuing Torah, see *Mekhilta, Amaleq (Yitro)*, 2; *Mekhilta de Rashbi* on Exodus 18:27; *Tanḥuma, Yitro* 4. On Jericho as the equal of the rest of the land, see *Yalqut Shim'oni, Joshua* 8.

In some rabbinic texts, dates are a symbol of worldly pleasure. See BT *Bekhorot* 18a and *Bava Batra* 107b: "Rabbi Yoḥanan said to Rabbi Ḥiyya son of Abba, 'While you were eating date-berries in Babylon, I was expounding....'" See Rashi, ad loc.; cf. BT *Ketubbot* 104a, Tosafot, s.v. *lo neheneti*; *Seder Eliyyahu Rabbah* 24.

See also *Zohar* 3:59b.

389. **I already know Torah and require thirsting clarity...** Rabbi Zeira responds that while it is true that when one begins to study Torah all worldly distractions should be removed, once Torah has been mastered, earthly pleasures may even facilitate one's learning.

"Thirsting clarity" renders צחותא (*tsaḥuta*), an Aramaic word for thirst but playing on the Hebrew word צחות (*tsaḥut*), "clarity." See BT *Megillah* 28b: "A legal decision requires as much צילותא (*tsiluta*), clarity, as a day of the north wind." See BT *Eruvin* 65a; *Targum* on Song of Songs 6:7; *Zohar* 1:72a; 2:89a; 3:23a, 46a, 207b, 221b, 266b; Scholem, *Major Trends*, 389, n. 49.

upon the earth, whereupon all the generations endured in their consummate power, as is written: *God saw that it was good* (ibid. 1:12)."[390] [14a]

**Section**[391]

*God said, "Let there be lights in the firmament of the heavens... to shine upon the earth"* (Genesis 1:14–15).[392]

We have learned there: Rabbi Yitsḥak son of Ya'akov said, "What is the meaning of the verse *You are entirely beautiful, my darling; there is no blemish in you* (Song of Songs 4:7)? Come and see! When the blessed Holy One created His world, He fashioned it out of the light emanated from above; and He created the heavens from that first firmament that the blessed Holy One prepared and created at first. That firmament generated all the other heavens that were formed thereby."[393]

Rav Yehudah said in the name of Rav, "That firmament generated all the lights from the light it receives from above. When the blessed Holy One created the firmament of the heavens, He took the lights and placed them in the firmament called 'the firmament of the heavens,' for that firmament was formed from the heavens."[394]



390. **generations endured in their consummate power...** See above, at note 386.

391. **Section** Some manuscripts and the printed editions contain this section heading: פרשתא (*parsheta*), perhaps reflecting an early attempt to arrange the materials of *MhN* on the Torah. See also *ZḤ* 3d, 10b, 13a, 17c, 19c, 28a, end of *parashat Lekh Lekha*—below, page 311 (all *MhN*); *Zohar* 2:20a (*MhN*).

392. ***God said, "Let there be lights in the firmament of the heavens...*** The passage from here until the word "Alternatively" on folio 14b is also found (with minor variations) in the *Hashmatot* (additions) to *Zohar* 1:251b–252a.

This verse is also expounded at length in a passage from *MhN* discovered by Scholem in a manuscript and not printed in *ZḤ*. See Scholem, "Parashah Ḥadashah" (Addendum 1 in this volume).

393. **He fashioned it out of the light emanated from above...** This light is the angelic form. See above, *ZḤ* 4a, 7d (both *MhN*).

The first firmament or expanse is the supernal expanse above the heads of the living creatures recounted in Ezekiel 1. That firmament generated all the other heavens (or firmaments). According to *MhN*, the heavenly realm has three tiers: the supernal firmament, the heavens, and finally "the firmament of the heavens." See *ZḤ* 10a–b (*MhN*). Cf. Maimonides, *Guide of the Perplexed* 2:30; Naḥmanides on Genesis 1:8.

The cited verse from the Song of Songs conveys the universe's perfection, though—as will be made apparent below—the cosmic order is marked by a blemish of sorts.

394. **from the light it receives from above...** The generative capacity of the supernal firmament derives from the light above. This uppermost light is then redeployed in the "firmament of the heavens." Cf. Naḥmanides on Genesis 1:14.

Cf. *Bemidbar Rabbah* 15:9: "Immense is the light of the blessed Holy One! The sun and moon illuminate the world. But from where do they derive their radiance? They snatch from sparks of lights above.... Immense is the light above, for only one hundredth of it is given to the created beings, as is said: *He knows what* [*mah*, read as *me'ah*,

Rav Yehudah said in the name of Rav, "The supernal firmament generated the heavens beneath, and the heavens generated this firmament called 'the firmament of the heavens.' The blessed Holy One took the two lights and placed them within, as is written: *God placed them in the firmament of the heavens* (Genesis 1:17)."[395]

Rabbi Yitsḥak said, "The blessed Holy One fashioned two lights and placed them in this firmament to have dominion over the earth, and so that the creatures might benefit from them. When He created them, they both emitted their light equally. The moon said, 'Master of the Universe, You cannot conduct equally with two crowns!' What did the blessed Holy One do? He diminished her. This is the significance of the monthly goat of atonement, of which is said [*a sin offering*] *for YHVH* (Numbers 28:15)."[396]

Rabbi Ya'akov said, "We have learned this in numerous places, but the matter is not settled in my heart."[397]



hundred) *is in the darkness* [*and light dwells with Him*] (Daniel 2:22). 'Therefore' [says God] 'I made the sun and the moon to shine before you,' as is said: *God set them in the firmament of the heavens to shine upon the earth* (Genesis 1:17)." See *ZḤ* 15b (*MhN*).

395. **The blessed Holy One took the two lights and placed them within...** The celestial lights that we perceive—sun, moon (and stars)—are set in the lowest tier, the "firmament of the heavens." Cf. *Zohar* 1:20a, 34a, 162b, 168b.

See BT *Ḥagigah* 12b: "Resh Lakish said, 'There are seven heavens.... The one called רקיע (*raqi'a*), firmament, is that in which the sun, moon, stars, and constellations are set.'" See also *Bereshit Rabbah* 6:6.

396. **You cannot conduct equally with two crowns!...** On the diminution of the moon, see BT *Ḥullin* 60b: "Rabbi Shim'on son of Pazzi pointed out a contradiction. 'It is written: *God made the two great lights* (Genesis 1:16), and it is written: *the greater light... and the lesser light* (ibid.). The moon said before the blessed Holy One, "Master of the Universe! Can two kings possibly wear one crown?" He answered, "Go, and diminish yourself!" She said before Him, "Master of the Universe! Because I have suggested something proper I should make myself smaller?" He replied, "Go and rule by day and night." She said, "But what is the value of this? What good is a lamp at noon?" He replied, "Go. Israel shall reckon by you the days and the years." She said, "But it is impossible to do without the sun for the reckoning of the seasons, as is written: *they shall serve as signs for the set times, the days and the years* (ibid., 14)." "Go. The righteous shall be named after you—as we find: Jacob the Small, Shemu'el the Small, David the Small." Seeing that her mind was uneasy, the blessed Holy One said, "Bring an atonement for Me, for making the moon smaller.'" As was said by Rabbi Shim'on son of Lakish: 'Why is the goat offered on the new moon distinguished by the phrase *to* [or: *for*] *YHVH* (Numbers 28:15)? The blessed Holy One said, "Let this goat be an atonement for My having made the moon smaller."'"

See *Bereshit Rabbah* 6:3; *Pirqei de-Rabbi Eli'ezer* 6, 51; *Zohar* 1:19b–20a, 181a–b; 2:144b, 147b–148a, 219b; *ZḤ* 70d–71a (*ShS*); Moses de León, *Sefer ha-Rimmon*, 189; idem, *Mishkan ha-Edut*, 35b; Scholem, "Parashah Ḥadashah," 429 (Addendum 1 in this volume).

397. **the matter is not settled in my heart** Rabbi Ya'akov senses that there must be more to the legend of the diminution of the moon. Perhaps it encodes a deeper signification.

When Rav Naḥman arrived, they went and asked him about this.

He said, “According to its literal meaning!”

Rabbi Yehudah said to Rabbi Ya'akov, “Do you wish to overstep your Companions' words?”[398]

He was silent.

Rabbi Yose son of Rabbi Shim'on son of Lekonya went to see his son-in-law, Rabbi El'azar son of Rabbi Shim'on. His daughter came out and took hold of his hands to kiss them.[399]

He said to her, “Go and מעטי (*ma'ati*), humble, yourself before your husband—for he is holy.”

Rabbi El'azar heard. He said, “I have now remembered a certain word—a precious pearl uttered about the moon. As we have learned: The blessed Holy One said to the moon, ‘Go and מעטי (*ma'ati*), diminish, yourself,’ for the moon thought that dominion had been bequeathed to her.”[400]

His father-in-law said to him, “I have also heard thus, and so is it arrayed in
my mind, such that I will not overstep the opinion of the Companions.”[401] 119

Rabbi El'azar opened his mouth, saying, “*Happy are you, O Israel! Who is like you, a people saved by YHVH, your protecting shield who is your majestic sword?* (Deuteronomy 33:29). But is the majesty of Israel the sword? Surely not! For look, the sword was bequeathed to Esau, as is written: *You will live by your sword* (Genesis 27:40). Not so for Israel![402]

“Rather, so have I heard from my father: These are the disciples of the wise. For when they hear a word that is not settled in their hearts, they battle with one another like warriors with the sword—seeking to kill one another.[403]

398. **Do you wish to overstep your Companions' words?** Rabbi Yehudah is imploring Rabbi Ya'akov to let the simple meaning suffice and not seek out the mystery.

399. **Rabbi Yose son of Rabbi Shim'on son of Lekonya...** See note 230.

400. **I have now remembered...a precious pearl...** A nearly identical expression appears in Scholem, “Parashah Ḥadashah,” 432 (Addendum 1 in this volume). On possessing pearls of wisdom, see BT *Ḥagigah* 3a; *Zohar* 1:148b; 2:209a; *ZḤ* 10b (*MhN*). Cf. BT *Berakhot* 17a, *Sanhedrin* 50b, *Zevaḥim* 36b.

401. **that I will not overstep the opinion of the Companions** Like Rabbi Yehudah above, Rabbi Yose son of Shim'on son of Lekonya is content with the simple meaning of the legend.

402. **But is the majesty of Israel the sword?...** Unlike Esau (signifying Rome and Christendom), the prowess and renown of Israel is not military might (“the sword”), but Torah study. See *Zohar* 3:192b. On Esau and the sword, see *Mekhilta, Baḥodesh* 5.

403. **they battle with one another like warriors with the sword...** See BT *Shabbat* 63a: “*Gird your sword upon your thigh, O hero, your glory and your majesty* (Psalms 45:4)....Rabbi Yirmeyah said in the name of Rabbi El'azar, ‘When two disciples of the wise sharpen each other in *halakhah*, the blessed Holy One gives them success, as is said: והדרך (*va-hadarkha*), *and your majesty, be successful* (ibid., 5). Do not read והדרך (*va-hadarkha*), your majesty, but rather וחדדך (*ve-ḥiddedekha*), your sharpening.’”

On the motif of Torah study as battle, see also BT *Sanhedrin* 36a; *Ḥullin* 6a; *Qiddushin*

"This word that our Companion uttered is in this vein, and so have we decreed in the mystery of our Mishnah: When the blessed Holy One created the sun and the moon, He decreed upon the sun that it transpose to become the dominion of Esau, and He decreed upon the moon that, in this world, it be the dominion of Jacob. He appointed over them mighty princes until these two nations would appear.[404]

"The prince appointed over the moon for the nation of Jacob requested of the blessed Holy One that dominion be bestowed upon the moon in this world, that is to say, upon the nation of Jacob. The blessed Holy One said, 'What does the nation of Jacob require aside from the world to come, where they will be granted dominion over all the nations? However, in this world, go and diminish yourself; subjugate yourself in exile to attain the world to come.'[405]



30b; *Bemidbar Rabbah* 11:3; *Zohar* 2:56a; 3:59b, 127b (*IR*), 188b; *ZḤ* 5d (*MhN*).

404. **He decreed upon the sun that it transpose...** Rabbi El'azar now begins to explain the deep mystery of the diminution of the moon. This secret is presented as having been "decreed in the mystery of our Mishnah," though what follows is not found in the Mishnah of Rabbi Yehudah ha-Nasi, but is an innovation of the author(s).

Rabbi El'azar establishes two relationships that will inform the rest of his homily: the sun pertains to Esau, and the moon to Jacob. It is not that the sun rules over Esau, and the moon over Jacob, but rather that the character and nature of the sun (that is, dominant) is fitting for Esau; and that of the moon (diminished) for Jacob. That the sun is commanded to "transpose" or "switch over" suggests that the sun, as the greater light, really ought to be the domain of Jacob rather than Esau. The meaning behind this transposition is explained below. See also *ZḤ* 27c (*MhN*); Scholem, "Parashah Ḥadashah," 433, 443 (Addendum 1 in this volume).

On the use of the term "decree" (from the root גזר (*gzr*)) for establishing a teaching, see *Zohar* 1:123a, 124b, 125a (all *MhN*); *ZḤ* 15b, 16a, 18b, 20a (all *MhN*); 62b (*ShS*); Scholem, "Parashah Ḥadashah," 443 (Addendum 1 in this volume); Meroz, "Va-Ani Lo Hayiti Sham?" 168 (Addendum 3 in this volume). On the expression "our Mishnah," see *Zohar* 1:37b, 55b, 74a, 91b, 93a, 95b, 96a, 124b (*MhN*), 137a (*MhN*), 139a (*MhN*), 223b; 2:5a (*MhN*), 123b; 3:75b, 78a, 284b, 285a, 293b (*IZ*); *ZḤ* 12b, 15b–c, 16a, 18b, 20a (all *MhN*); Scholem, "Parashah Ḥadashah"; Matt, "Matnita di-Lan."

405. **subjugate yourself in exile to attain the world to come** The diminution of the moon is an analogue to the diminished state of Israel in this world. Just as the moon is smaller than the sun, so Israel is subjugated to Esau (Rome, Christendom). Importantly, this exilic order is the will of God, and though this world is under the dominion of Esau, the world to come will be under the dominion of Israel. Indeed, subjugation in this world is the way to attain the world to come.

Cf. *Bereshit Rabbah* 84:3: "Rabbi Aḥa said, 'When the righteous... wish to dwell in tranquility in this world, Satan comes and accuses them, saying, "Is it not enough that it [tranquility] is arrayed for them in the world to come, but they also wish to dwell in tranquility in this world too?!" You should know that this is so. Our father Jacob, because he wished to dwell in tranquility in this world, was seized by the troubles he had concerning Joseph.'"

"When the nation of Jacob appeared, they protested before the blessed Holy One that dominion had been seized from them and granted to Esau. The blessed Holy One said [14b] to them, 'Why do you require dominion in this world? For look, I pledge to grant you dominion over all the nations in the world to come. On this account, offer for Me an atonement—that is, over that promise for which I am guarantor. Offer atonement and engage in Torah, and it will be for Me to bestow upon you a good reward; and it will be for Me to grant you dominion over all the nations, for that is why I diminished the moon in this world.'"[406]

Rabbi Yose, his father-in-law, came and kissed him on his head. He summoned his daughter and said to her, "A shooting ray of light and a spark bountifully refracted is by you! Happy are you and happy is your share! Happy is my share in this world that I merited to behold this!"[407]

Rabbi Yoḥanan said, "If Israel are worthy, the blessed Holy One illuminates them and they do not require another lamp, as is written: *YHVH shall be your eternal light* (Isaiah 60:19)."[408]

Rabbi Abbahu said, "Since dominion was switched for them, Israel calculate their calendar according to the moon; according to her, Israel מנהגין (*menahagin*), conduct, their counting. As is written: *You are beautiful* רעיתי (*ra'yati*), *my darling* (Song of Songs 4:1)—מנהיגתי (*manhigati*), my guide; it is derived from [*Give ear*] רעה (*ro'eh*), *O shepherd* [*of Israel*; נהג (*noheg*), *who guides*,] *Joseph like a flock*



406. **offer for Me an atonement...** The New Moon goat offering (see above, note 396, quoting BT *Ḥullin* 60b) is not merely an atonement for God's having made the moon smaller. It also serves as a reminder of the divine pledge that in the time to come, He will restore the original order, such that Jacob will have dominion. See also Scholem, "Parashah Ḥadashah," 431, 436 (Addendum 1 in this volume).

407. **A shooting ray of light and a spark bountifully refracted...** "A shooting ray of light" renders קוזטיפא דנהירותא (*qoztipha de-nehiruta*), a Zoharic neologism. See *Zohar* 2:14a (*MhN*); *ZḤ* 59c (*MhN*). The manuscripts and printed editions contain numerous variants; I have followed V22. See the expression קסטיפא דשמשא (*qastipha de-shimsha*), "ray of the sun" (*Zohar* 3:283b); the Arabic root *qdf*, "to throw"; and the neologism קוספיתא (*quspita*), "hollow of a sling," discussed by Liebes, *Peraqim*, 345–48. See *Zohar* 1:167a; *Bei'ur ha-Millim ha-Zarot*, 189; cf. *Zohar* 1:53b.

The phrase "a spark bountifully refracted" may also be rendered "a spark distinguished in goodness."

Rabbi Yose's point is that Rabbi El'azar radiates wisdom.

408. **If Israel are worthy, the blessed Holy One illuminates them...** The full verse reads: *No longer shall you need the sun for light by day, nor the shining of the moon for radiance, for YHVH shall be your eternal light* (Isaiah 60:19). The following verse reads: *Never again will your sun set, and your moon will not be withdrawn—for YHVH shall be a light to you forever* (ibid., 20). Both verses apply to the eschatological era, though Rabbi Yoḥanan may also be suggesting that even in this world, when Israel does not enjoy dominion, she needs no light save that of the blessed Holy One.

(Psalms 80:2)]; *There is no blemish in you* (Song of Songs 4:7)—you lack neither seasons nor [appointed] times."[409]

Alternatively, *You are beautiful my darling, there is no blemish in you* (Song of Songs 4:1,7). Our Rabbis have taught: At four periods in the year, the world is judged. Rabbi Alexandrai said, "But is a person really judged only at these times? For look at what is written: *You inspect him each morning—and examine him every moment* (Job 7:18)! And Rabbi Yitsḥak said, 'There is not a single moment when the blessed Holy One does not scrutinize the human being and all that he does.' Yet we have learned here: at four periods in the year!"[410]

Rabbi Alexandrai said, "I retract, for the word of Torah applies to a different matter and not to the subject of the word of our Rabbis. The verse says 'inspection and examination,' while our Rabbis say 'judgment'; implying that the blessed Holy One scrutinizes the world every single day, but executes judgment only at these four times, to judge the entire world."

 For the sake of human beings, the blessed Holy One executes judgment in the world through all these judgments:[411]

409. **Israel calculate their calendar according to the moon...** See BT *Sukkah* 29a: "Our Rabbis taught:... 'Israel counts by the moon, idolators by the sun.'"

See also *Bereshit Rabbah* 6:3: "Rabbi Levi said in the name of Rabbi Yose son of Ila'i, 'It is natural that the great should calculate by the great, and the small by the small. Esau calculates by the sun, which is large, and Jacob by the moon, which is small.' Rabbi Naḥman said, 'That is a happy presage. Esau calculates by the sun, which is large: just as the sun rules by day but not by night, so does Esau have a share in this world, but has no share in the world to come. Jacob calculates by the moon, which is small: just as the moon rules by day and by night, so Jacob has a share in this world and in the world to come!'"

On the lunar and solar calendars, see *Mekhilta, Pisḥa* 1; *Tosefta Sukkah* 2:6; *Pesiqta de-Rav Kahana* 5:1, 14; *Zohar* 1:46b, 236b, 239a; 3:220b; Scholem, "Parashah Ḥadashah," 432–33 (Addendum 1 in this volume).

See also *Bereshit Rabbah* 6:1: "*God said, 'Let there be lights'* (Genesis 1:14). Rabbi Yoḥanan opened: *He made the moon to mark the seasons* (Psalms 104:19). Rabbi Yoḥanan said, 'The orb of the sun alone was created to give light. If so, why was the moon created? *For seasons* (ibid.)—in order to sanctify new moons and years." See also *Pesiqta de-Rav Kahana* 5:1.

In the Song of Songs, *ra'yati* means "my beloved," but the verbal root רעה (*r'h*) also means "to shepherd, guide, lead, rule." Rabbi Abbahu connects both meanings.

410. **four periods in the year...** See M *Rosh ha-Shanah* 1:2: "At four periods the world is judged: on *Pesaḥ* for the produce; on *Atseret* [*Shavu'ot*] for the fruits of the tree; on Rosh Hashanah all who come into the world pass before Him in a single file...; and on the Festival [*Sukkot*] they are judged for water." See *Zohar* 1:226b; Moses de León, *Sefer ha-Rimmon*, 140.

On a person's being judged constantly, see *Tosefta Rosh ha-Shanah* 1:13; JT *Rosh ha-Shanah* 1:2, 57a; BT *Rosh ha-Shanah* 16a. See also *Zohar* 2:99b; 3:177a.

411. **through all these judgments** As mentioned in Mishnah *Rosh ha-Shanah*; see previous note.

On *Pesaḥ*—for the produce. What does this imply? Rabbi Yitsḥak said, "For the produce precisely!" As Rabbi Yitsḥak said: "In the previous year the blessed Holy One gave them produce—ample for the world. If people did not tithe, nor give from it to feed the poor, orphans, or widows, then when the new year comes, He judges the entire world concerning the produce of the year that passed."[412]

On *Atseret*, He judges the world—for which sin? For sin pertaining to the fruit of the tree; because they did not wait their foreskin, nor set them aside in the Sabbatical year for the poor and the stranger.[413]

On Rosh Hashanah, He judges the entire world—the bodies of human beings as well as souls, inspecting them and judging them for everything they did throughout the entire year. It has been taught: Even the steps of a human being are reckoned and come under judgment on that day, as is written: [*Surely He sees my ways*] *and counts all my steps* (Job 31:4)?[414]

Rabbi Yose taught: "Three companies enter Judgment: a company of the completely righteous; a company of the completely wicked; and a company of the intermediate. Corresponding to them are three powers in a human being: the power of the holy *neshamah*; the desiring power; and the motive power."[415]



412. **On *Pesaḥ*—for the produce . . .** Passover, which falls in the spring, is when produce begins to ripen. BT *Rosh ha-Shanah* 16a asks which produce is judged: what is already ripening, or the produce of the coming year. The *Zohar* offers a new interpretation: on Passover, the blessed Holy One judges the world on how they have acted with the produce of the preceding year.

413. **On *Atseret*, He judges the world . . .** According to M *Rosh ha-Shanah* 1:2, on the festival of *Shavu'ot*, the world is judged for the fruits of the trees, that is, whether the trees will bring forth an abundance of fruits or whether it will be a lean year. According to the *Zohar*, as with Passover, God judges Israel on how they have acted with fruits, that is, whether they have fulfilled all the requisite commandments pertaining to fruit.

See Leviticus 19:23: *When you enter the land and plant any kind of tree for eating, you are to regard its fruit like a foreskin. For three years it is to be considered foreskinned for you, not to be eaten.*

414. **On Rosh Hashanah, He judges the entire world . . .** See BT *Rosh ha-Shanah* 16a: "All are judged on Rosh Hashanah."

On the judgment of the body and soul, cf. *Mekhilta de-Rashbi*, Exodus 15:1; BT *Sanhedrin* 91a.

415. **Three companies enter Judgment . . .** See BT *Rosh ha-Shanah* 16b in the name of the House of Shammai: "There are three groups at the Day of Judgment: one of the completely righteous, one of the completely wicked, and one of the intermediate."

Cf. ibid: "Rabbi Kruspedai said in the name of Rabbi Yoḥanan, 'Three books are opened on Rosh Hashanah: one for the completely wicked, one for the completely righteous, and one for the intermediate.'"

Here *MhN* presents a different tripartite soul structure to those presented above (*ZḤ* 6d, 8d–9a). The holy soul, *neshamah*, corresponds with the completely righteous, the desiring power with the completely wicked, and the motive power with the intermediate. As in Plato's tripartite scheme—intellect, power, and desire (*Republic*, Book 4)—this division makes a strong connection between

What is the motive power? Rabbi Yehudah said, "The power that makes the body grow and moves it in accordance with all its needs."

Rabbi Yose son of Pazzi says, "Come and see the compassion of the blessed Holy One—even though the court above convenes, standing in judgment to judge the creatures, instructing before the blessed Holy One concerning the innocence and guilt of human beings!"

As Rabbi Yose son of Pazzi taught: "Three companies of ministering angels preside in judgment at Rosh Hashanah. Some plead innocence for good, and some plead guilt for evil. Come and see the compassion of the blessed Holy One—who proffered advice that they might be delivered from judgment!"[416]

For it has been taught: What is the significance of *a commemoration by horn-blast* (Leviticus 23:24)? [14c] We have not found [a teaching about] remembrance by horn-blast, aside from what Rabbi Yose said: "It is written: *When you enter into battle in your land against the foe who assails you, you shall sound a blast with the trumpets—and you will be remembered before YHVH your God, and you will be delivered from your enemies* (Numbers 10:9). It is a remembrance of this blast. The blessed Holy One said, 'Sound before Me this blast, which is a commemoration of that blast. Immediately: *you will be delivered from your*



the various parts of the soul and ethical qualities.

On the three powers or faculties, see *Zohar* 1:109a–b, 137a (both *MhN*); *ZḤ* 21c (*MhN*); Meroz, "Va-Ani Lo Hayiti Sham?" 170 (Addendum 3 in this volume); Tishby, *Wisdom of the Zohar*, 2:706, 691.

Cf. Saadia Gaon, *Sefer Emunot ve-De'ot* 6:3: "When, now, the soul is united with the body, three faculties belonging to it make their appearance. Namely, the power of reasoning, the power of appetition, and that of anger. That is why our language applied to them three distinct terms: *nefesh*, *ruaḥ*, and *neshamah*. By the term *nefesh* it alludes to the soul's possession of an appetitive faculty. . . . By the term *ruaḥ* . . . it alludes to the soul's possession of the power to become bold or angry. . . . By means of the term *neshamah* it refers to the soul's possession of the faculty of cognition." Cf. Maimonides, *Shemonah Peraqim* 1. See also Moses de León, *Mishkan ha-Edut*, 10b.

The term "motive power" does not appear in Jewish philosophical literature and may derive from Naḥmanides, who mentions "the soul of movement" to describe the animal soul. See his *Commentary on the Torah*, Genesis 1:22, 26, 29; 2:7. See also *Zohar* 1:109b, 128b (both *MhN*).

On the diverse theories of the soul in *MhN*, see Tishby, *Wisdom of the Zohar*, 2:703–12.

416. **who proffered advice that they might be delivered from judgment** See BT *Rosh ha-Shanah* 16a: "It has been taught: Rabbi Yehudah said in the name of Rabbi Akiva, '[The blessed Holy One said,] ". . . Recite before Me on Rosh Hashanah [scriptural passages referencing] kingship, remembrance, and the shofar: kingship, so that you may proclaim Me king over you; remembrance, so that your remembrance may rise favorably before Me. Through what means? Through the shofar."' Rabbi Abbahu said, 'Why do we blow on a ram's horn? The blessed Holy One said, "Sound before Me a ram's horn, so that I may remember on your behalf the binding of Isaac the son of Abraham, and account it to you as if you had bound yourselves before Me."'"

*enemies* in the same way.' *From your enemies*—who are they? Those who plead a person's guilt."[417]

As it has been taught: Rabbi Abbahu said in the name of Rabbi Yoḥanan, "There are angels who plead a person's guilt, and there are angels who plead their innocence. Even if one among a thousand pleads in his favor, they withdraw from him, as is written: *If he has an angel over him, an advocate, one among a thousand* [*to vouch for his uprightness*] (Job 33:23). Afterward is written: *Then he is gracious to him and says, 'Deliver him from descending to the Pit...'* (ibid., 24)."[418]

But is there really an angel who speaks against a person's favor? Rabbi Shim'on said, "Heaven forbid that an angel speaks against favor! Rather, there are angels appointed to examine and report on a person's guilt whenever he transgresses, and they report that matter as they were commanded."[419]

In a similar vein: *with all the host of heaven standing* עליו (*alav*), *by Him* (1 Kings 22:19). What is meant by עליו (*alav*), *by Him*? עליו (*Alav*), Over, Ahab,
for they were deliberating over his judgment. *On His right and on His left* 125
(ibid.)—those inclining to the right (to acquittal), and those inclining to the left (to condemnation).[420]

417. ***When you enter into battle in your land against the foe...*** The commandment to blow the shofar on Rosh Hashanah derives from Leviticus 23:24, which reads: *In the seventh month, on the first day of the month, you shall observe complete rest,* זכרון תרועה (*zikhron tru'ah*), *a commemoration* [or: *reminder*] *by horn-blast, a sacred convocation.* Rabbi Yose associates this *reminder by horn-blast* with the verse in Numbers describing the sounding of the horn in the Israelite camp before setting out for war. Like the verse in Leviticus, the verse in Numbers also connects the act of sounding a blast with remembrance before God. Just as Israel had to sound the trumpet when setting out for war, so on Rosh Hashanah, Israel must sound the blast as they set out for war against their heavenly accusers. Cf. *Zohar* 2:196b.

On confounding Satan with the shofar, see BT *Rosh ha-Shanah* 16a–b: "Why do we sound a plain blast and a tremolo blast while sitting and then again while standing? In order to confound Satan." See *Arukh,* s.v. *arev*; Rashi and *Tosafot,* BT *Rosh ha-Shanah* 16b, s.v. *kedei le-arbev*.

418. **Even if one among a thousand pleads in his favor...** See BT *Shabbat* 32a: "These are a person's advocates: repentance and good deeds. And even if nine hundred and ninety-nine argue for his guilt, while one argues in his favor, he is saved, as is said: *If he has an angel over him, an advocate, one among a thousand to vouch for his uprightness, then he is gracious to him and says, 'Deliver him from descending to the Pit...* (Job 33:23–24). Rabbi Eli'ezer son of Rabbi Yose the Galilean says, 'Even if nine hundred and ninety-nine parts of that angel are in his disfavor and one part is in his favor, he is saved, as is said: *an advocate, one among a thousand* (ibid., 23).'" See *Zohar* 1:13a, 174b; 2:32b.

419. **they report that matter...** How can it be that holy and sublime beings incite against human innocence? As Rabbi Shim'on explains, they do not actively advocate guilt, but merely faithfully report what one has done. Cf. *Zohar* 2:32b.

420. ***On His right and on His left...*** From the vision of the prophet Micaiah. In the narrative in Kings, the host of heaven are

Rav Yehudah said in the name of Rav, "Why is the judgment of the body and soul on Rosh Hashanah? Because on that day, Adam was born; on that day, the body was made and the soul infused within; on that day, he was judged—and judgment was ordained for the generations."[421]

On the Festival, they are judged for water—because they scorn the washing of hands, and slight *mikveh* and purification, which all involve water. That is why they are judged for water—concerning the subject of water.[422]

Rabbi Aḥa said, "A person is likewise judged at four intervals: on the very day he contemplates transgression; at the time he performs the deed; on Rosh Hashanah day; and in the world to come."[423]

Rabbi Abbahu said, "At the moment he performs the transgression; when he is ill (as Rabbi Abbahu said, "When a person is ill, he is weighed in judgment"); when he dies and his soul departs; and in the world to come."[424]



standing in attendance on God. According to the *Zohar*, they are standing over Ahab. The word *alav* can mean both "by him" and "over him."

Cf. *Shir ha-Shirim Rabbah* on 1:9: "*With all the host of heaven standing by Him on His right and on His left* (I Kings 22:19). Now is there a left hand above? Is not the whole right hand, as is said: *Your right hand, O YHVH, glorious in power, Your right hand, O YHVH, shatters the foe* (Exodus 15:6)? What then does *on His right and on His left* teach? Rather, those inclining to the right and those inclining to the left, namely, those leaning toward acquittal and those to condemnation."

See also *Tanḥuma, Mishpatim* 15; *Tanḥuma* (Buber), *Shemot* 14; *Tanḥuma* (Buber), *Mishpatim* 6.

421. **Why is the judgment of the body and soul on Rosh Hashanah?...** See *Vayiqra Rabbah* 29:1: "The blessed Holy One said to Adam, 'This will be a sign to your children. Just as you stood in judgment before Me this day and came out with an acquittal, so will your children in the future stand in judgment before Me on this day and will come out from My presence with an acquittal.' When will that be? *In the seventh month, on the first day of the month* (Leviticus 23:24)." See also *Zohar* 1:37a; 3:100b–101a.

On Adam's having been born on Rosh Hashanah, see *Pesiqta de-Rav Kahana* 23:1: "Rabbi Eli'ezer taught, 'The world was created on the twenty-fifth of Elul'.... Consequently Adam was created on Rosh Hashanah." See *Vayiqra Rabbah* 29:1; *Pirqei de-Rabbi Eli'ezer* 8, and David Luria, ad loc., n.1; BT *Rosh ha-Shanah* 10b; Asher ben Yeḥiel, on *Rosh ha-Shanah* 8a; *Ḥiddushei ha-Ran* on *Rosh ha-Shanah* 16a; *Tosefot Yom Tov, Rosh ha-Shanah* 1:2.

422. **On the Festival, they are judged for water...** According to M *Rosh ha-Shanah* 1:2, on the festival of *Sukkot*—which falls at the beginning of the rainy season—the world is judged for water. As with *Pesaḥ* and *Shavu'ot*, the *Zohar* here offers a new reading: Israel are judged according to how they have acted with water, namely, whether they have fulfilled the commandments pertaining to water.

423. **A person is likewise judged at four intervals...** Just as the world is judged at four intervals, so too individuals are judged four times.

See M *Rosh ha-Shanah* 1:2, quoted above, note 410.

424. **When a person is ill, he is weighed in judgment...** See BT *Shabbat* 32a: "Rav Yitsḥak son of Rav Yehudah said, 'Let one always pray for mercy not to fall sick, for if he falls sick he is told: Show your merit

Rabbi Yehudah said, "The faith and joy of the righteous—that when they depart this world brimming with good deeds, and they convene to examine the soul, she is not held back. What do they say to her? *You are entirely beautiful, my darling* (Song of Songs 4:7)."[425]

Rabbi Abbahu said, "The righteous person says this about the soul within him: *You are entirely beautiful,* רעיתי (*ra'yati*), *my darling*—my guide, for I did not corrupt you with evil deeds, as is written: *There is no blemish in you* (ibid.)."[426]

Alternatively, *God said, "Let there be* מארת (*me'orot*), *lights"* (Genesis 1:14). Why is it missing the ו (*vavs*)?[427]

Rabbi Yehoshu'a son of Levi said, "[This is] the prayer of the righteous who have departed this world—that their reward not be delayed in the world to come."[428]

As Rabbi Yehoshu'a son of Levi said: "What is the meaning of the verse *an image like the appearance of a man upon it* מלמעלה (*mi-lmalah*), *above* (Ezekiel 1:26)? This is מעלתן (*ma'alatan*), the degree, of the righteous, למעלה (*le-malah*), ascendant, beyond all degrees."[429]



and be acquitted!'.... Our Rabbis taught: ...when [a person] has a headache, let him imagine that he is put in irons; when he takes to bed, let him imagine that he ascended the scaffold to be punished. For whoever ascends the scaffold to be punished, if he has great advocates he is saved, but if not he is not saved." See also *Zohar* 1:227a; *ZḤ* 18d (*MhN*).

425. ***You are entirely beautiful, my darling*** When the soul is judged before entry to the Garden of Eden, the righteous—beautifully adorned by good deeds and untainted by sin—are allowed to pass.

426. **רעיתי (*ra'yati*), *my darling*—my guide...** In the Song of Songs, *ra'yati* means my beloved, but its verbal root רעה (*r'h*) also means "to shepherd, guide, lead, rule." Rabbi Abbahu connects both meanings. The soul, which is the beloved, is also the guide.

427. **Why is it missing the ו (*vavs*)?** In Genesis 1:14, the word מארת (*me'orot*) is written without vowel letters. See JT *Ta'anit* 4:4, 68b: "On the fourth day [of the week, Wednesday], they would fast for infants, so that diphtheria would not enter their mouths. *God said, 'Let there be* מארת (*me'orot*), *lights'*—spelled מארת (*me'erat*), curse." Here the deficient *vavs* are understood as pointing to a "deficiency" (or "blemish") in the created order—and will be connected to the diminished moon and the subjugation of Israel.

Cf. Proverbs 3:33; See *Pesiqta de-Rav Kahana* 5:1; *Soferim* 17:4; Rashi on Genesis 1:14; *Zohar* 1:1a, 12a, 19b–20a, 33b, 46b, 146a, 166a, 169b; 2:35b, 167b, 205a; *ZḤ* 69b–c (*ShS*), *ZḤ* 15c–d (*MhN*); *Minḥat Shai* on Genesis 1:14; Scholem, "Parashah Ḥadashah," 429 (Addendum 1 in this volume).

428. **prayer of the righteous...** Apparently Rabbi Yehoshu'a intends that the righteous pray that they will shine like the celestial lights in the world to come. Unlike this world, which is characterized by the absent *vavs*, the world to come will not be so. See *ZḤ* 15d (*MhN*), page 149.

429. **This is מעלתן (*ma'alatan*), the degree, of the righteous...** In Ezekiel 1, the culmination of the prophet's vision is his apprehension of the fiery anthropos sitting on top

What is the significance of עליו (*alav*), *upon it*?

Rabbi Yehudah said, "That of which is written *Upon it the appearance of the image of the glory of YHVH. When I beheld it, I flung myself down on my face* (ibid., 28)."[430]

Rabbi Yitsḥak said, "This is Jacob, whose rung is above, as is written: *like the appearance of a man.* How is this implied? Here is written עליו (*alav*), *upon it*, and there is written *God ascended* מעליו (*me-alav*), *from upon him* (Genesis 35:13)."[431]

Rabbi Aḥa son of Ya'akov said, "There is not a single night when the herald does not go forth, proclaiming, 'Ascend, O devout ones; come and bless your Creator!' As is written: *Your devoted ones bless you. The glory of Your kingship they say, and of Your might they speak* (Psalms 145:10–11). Why? *To make known to humankind His mighty acts...* (ibid., 12)."

Our Rabbis have taught: Once, Rabbi Yose was walking on the way. Rabbi

Ḥiyya met him, and they walked on together. They encountered a certain mountain—and the mountain terrified them.[432]

Rabbi Yose said to Rabbi Ḥiyya, "Let us say a word of Torah, and walk on."[433]

Rabbi Ḥiyya said, "Certainly. Concerning that which the wise scholars of Mishnah have said about the sun that shone for Jacob—how long till it is so again?"[434]

of the throne located above the expanse. Apparently, Rabbi Yehoshu'a intends that this corresponds to the situation of the righteous in the world to come: *lights in the expanse of heaven* (Genesis 1:14). Cf. *Matoq mi-Devash* for a different explanation.

430. **Upon it the appearance...** The words *upon it* are not found in the Masoretic text.

431. **Jacob, whose rung is above...** According to rabbinic tradition, the image of Jacob is engraved on the Throne of Glory. In Genesis 28:12, Jacob dreams of *a ladder set on earth, its top reaching the heavens, and behold: angels of God were ascending and descending* בו (*bo*), *on it* [or: *on him*]. *Bereshit Rabbah* 68:12 records a dispute between Rabbi Ḥiyya the Elder and Rabbi Yannai concerning this verse: "One said, 'Ascending and descending the ladder,' while the other said, 'Ascending and descending on Jacob'... whose image is engraved on high."

See Theodor's note, ad loc.; *Bereshit Rabbah* 82:2 ("engraved on My throne"); *Eikhah Rabbah* 2:1; *Targum Yerushalmi*, Genesis 28:12; BT *Ḥullin* 91b; *Pirqei de-Rabbi Eli'ezer* 35; *Zohar* 1:72a, 173b; Scholem, "Parashah Ḥadashah," 431 (Addendum 1 in this volume); Wolfson, *Along the Path*, 1–62.

432. **the mountain terrified them** Cf. *Zohar* 1:230a; 3:149a.

Some manuscripts read Yirmeyah in place of Ḥiyya. Perhaps a copyist made the change to avoid confusion, because later in the story Rabbi Ḥiyya the Great appears.

433. **Let us say a word of Torah, and walk on** On the importance of engaging in Torah while on a journey, see Deuteronomy 6:7; M *Avot* 3:7; BT *Eruvin* 54a; *Ta'anit* 10b; *Zohar* 1:7a, 58b, 69b–70a, 76a, 87a, 115b, 157a, 164a, 230a–b; 2:13a, 95a, 138b, 155b. Cf. M *Avot* 3:2–3, 6.

434. **the sun that shone for Jacob—how long till it is so again?** See BT *Ḥullin* 91b:

Rabbi Yose said, "I shall tell you a word that my father once said: that the sun and great light that shone for Jacob is concealed for the righteous in the time to come; it is not the sun [14d] utilized by the children of Esau.[435]

"It was decreed that the children of Jacob be subjugated beneath him. At that time Jacob was saddened. He said, 'Master of the World, look, my light has been given to Esau!' A heavenly voice issued, saying, '*Do not fear, My servant Jacob*... (Jeremiah 30:10)—your light has been concealed for you and your children!' He said, 'Show me!' At that moment the blessed Holy One revealed that sun—which Jacob saw and no one else—as is written: *The sun rose upon him* (Genesis 32:32)—the same sun that was concealed—*as he passed Penuel* (ibid.)."[436]

"*The sun rose upon him* (Genesis 32:32). Rabbi Akiva said, '... Did the sun rise upon him only? Did it not rise upon the whole world?' Rabbi Yitsḥak said, 'It means that the sun—which had set for his sake—now rose for him. As is written: *Jacob departed from Beer-Sheba and went to Haran* (Genesis 28:10).... When he reached Haran, he said [to himself], "Can I possibly have passed through the place where my fathers prayed without praying too?" As soon as he decided to return [to Bethel], the earth contracted—and immediately *he encountered the place* (ibid., 11). After he prayed, he wished to return [to Haran], but the blessed Holy One said, "This righteous man has come to My habitation, shall he depart without a night's rest?" Thereupon the sun set.'" See also BT *Sanhedrin* 95b.

See also *Bereshit Rabbah* 68:10: "*Because the sun had set* (Genesis 28:11)—Our Rabbis say, 'This teaches that the blessed Holy One caused the orb of the sun to set prematurely in order to speak in privacy with our father Jacob.... When did the blessed Holy One restore to him those two hours by which He had caused [the sun prematurely] to set on his account, upon his departure from his father's house? When he was returning to his father's house, as is written: *The sun rose upon him* (ibid. 32:32). The blessed Holy One said to him, 'You are a sign for your children: as on your departure I caused the sun to set for you and on your return I restored to you [the lost hours of] the sun's orb, so shall your children be— when they go forth [into exile, and]... on their return [to their own land].'"

See also *Targum Yerushalmi* (frag.), Genesis 28:10; *Targum Yerushalmi*, Genesis 28:10, 32:32. Cf. *Bereshit Rabbah* 78:5; Scholem, "Parashah Ḥadashah," 433 (Addendum 1 in this volume).

435. **concealed for the righteous in the time to come...** See BT *Ḥagigah* 12a on the concealed light. "Rabbi El'azar said, 'With the light created by the blessed Holy One on the first day, one could gaze and see from one end of the universe to the other. When the blessed Holy One foresaw the corrupt deeds of the generation of the Flood and the generation of the Dispersion [the generation of the Tower of Babel], He immediately hid it from them, as is written: *The light of the wicked is withheld* (Job 38:15). For whom did He hide it? For the righteous in the time to come." See also *Bereshit Rabbah* 3:6; *Shemot Rabbah* 35:1; *Tanḥuma, Shemini* 9; *Bahir* 97–98 (147); *Zohar* 1:7a, 31b–32a, 45b–46a, 47a; 2:127a, 148b–149a, 220a–b; 3:88a, 173b; *ZḤ* 15b–d (*MhN*); Scholem, "Parashah Ḥadashah," 443 (Addendum 1 in this volume).

436. **the blessed Holy One revealed that sun...** The light that shone upon Jacob as he returned to the land of Israel was not the ordinary sun but in fact a harbinger of the world to come, the light that is concealed for the righteous in the time to come. Cf. *Zohar* 1:21b, 170b, 203b.

The verse in Jeremiah continues: *Be not dismayed, O Israel.... Jacob shall again have*

Rabbi Yose said, "When he prevailed upon the Prince of Esau. *Upon him*—implying not for anyone else. Even though Jacob delighted to behold and even though he had prevailed upon the Prince of Esau, what is written about him? *And he was limping on his hip* (ibid.). Rabbi Aḥa said, 'The light illuminated, but his heart was dark—concerning the fruit of his loins who would be subjugated beneath Esau.'"[437]

While they were walking, they heard the voice of a child in the mountain; he was wandering and weeping. Rabbi Yose said, "Let us approach him, for I am not afraid. For we have learned: To one person he shows himself and causes harm; to two he shows himself but does not cause harm."[438]

They approached him and the child was weeping. When they reached him, Rabbi Yose said, "Children of the Master of the World are we! Of the one whose name is designated one above two; in letters three, inscribed in the mystery of four; two engraved above one; applied to the holy living being."[439]

Why did Rabbi Yose say this? He was afraid lest he be a demon—and they are greatly terrified by the Name of the Master of the World.[440]



*calm and quiet with none to trouble him.* See *Vayiqra Rabbah* 29:2; *Pesiqta de-Rav Kahana* 23:2; *Tanḥuma, Vayetse* 2.

437. **Prince of Esau...** On the night before Jacob was reunited with Esau, a man wrestled with him until the break of dawn (Genesis 32:25). According to midrashic tradition, this man was actually Samael, Esau's heavenly prince. On the Prince of Esau, see *Tanḥuma, Vayishlaḥ* 8; *Bereshit Rabbah* 77:3; *Zohar* 1:146a, 166a, 170a–b, 179b.

Although Jacob defeats his nocturnal adversary, he is wounded in his hip or thigh, interpreted here as a sign that his progeny (i.e., those who emerge from his thigh) will be subjugated to Esau. See *ZḤ* 24a (*MhN*); cf. *Bereshit Rabbah* 77:3; Naḥmanides on Genesis 32:26.

Cf. BT *Ḥullin* 91a: "Rabbi Yehoshu'a son of Levi said, 'Why is it [the sciatic nerve] called גיד הנשה (*gid ha-nasheh*)? Because it נשה (*nashah*), slipped away, from its place and rose up, for so it is said: *Their strength* נשתה (*nashtah*), *has slipped away; they are become as* נשים (*nashim*), *women* (Jeremiah 51:30).'"

438. **To one person he shows himself...** See BT *Berakhot* 43b: "To one person [a demon] shows himself and causes harm; to two, he shows himself but does not cause harm; to three, he does not show himself at all." See also *Zohar* 1:230a.

439. **Of the one whose name is designated one above two...** The meaning of the riddle is not entirely clear, though the referent is clearly the ineffable name of God, יהוה (*YHVH*). The divine name comprises four letters, though the letter ה (*he*) appears twice, hence: mystery of four in letters three. "One above two" may refer to the י (*yod*), the first letter of the divine name, poised above and superior to the other letters. Similarly, "two engraved above one" may refer to the second and third letters, ה (*he*) and ו (*vav*) above the final letter ה (*he*). The "holy living being" may signify Metatron, "whose name is like his Master's" (BT *Sanhedrin* 38b), known also as "*YHVH Qatan*," Lesser *YHVH* (see Schäfer, *Synopse zur Hekhalot-Literatur*, §§15, 73, 76).

See *Matoq mi-Devash* for a sefirotic interpretation, though this seems unlikely.

440. **terrified by the Name of the Master of the World** See BT *Gittin* 68a; *Zohar* 1:48a, 211a.

When the child heard this word, he answered, saying, "I am a Jew. I am the grandson of Rabbi Ḥiyya the Great. My father used to teach me verses of the Song of Songs and the portion of *Bereshit*. My father died and bandits kidnapped me. I just escaped them and fled to this mountain."[441]

Rabbi Yose wept and said, "Woe that the grandson of Rabbi Ḥiyya should wander so!"[442]

He took him by the hand and they walked on.

Rabbi Yose said to him, "Tell me, my son, what you learned with your father."

He replied, "I was engaged in the passage *Let there be lights in the firmament of heaven* (Genesis 1:14)."

He asked him, "What did your father say about this passage?"

The child opened his mouth, saying, "*Well dug by princes, delved by the people's nobles, with scepter, with their staves* (Numbers 21:18). It has been taught: The blessed Holy One bestowed three fine gifts upon Israel, through three
shepherd siblings: Moses, Aaron, and Miriam. By the merit of Moses, the 131
manna descended upon Israel; by the merit of Aaron, the clouds of glory accompanied Israel; by the merit of Miriam, the well traveled with them. Miriam died—the well ceased; Aaron died—the clouds of glory were withdrawn, as is written: *The entire community* ויראו (*va-yir'u*), *saw*, [*that Aaron had expired*] (ibid. 20:29). Do not read וַיִּרְאוּ (*va-yir'u*), *saw*, but rather וַיֵּרָאוּ (*va-yera'u*), *they were seen*. The well ceased—how do we know? As is written: *The people stayed in Kadesh and Miriam died there* (ibid. 20:1), and it is written afterward: *There was no water for the community* (ibid., 2). By the merit of Moses, the three of them were restored.[443]

441. **My father used to teach me verses of the Song of Songs...** The child is no ordinary child but one of the many wunderkinder found throughout the *Zohar*. See *Zohar* 1:92b, 148a, 238b; 2:6b, 169b; 3:39a, 162a, 171a, 186a, 204b; *ZḤ* 9a (*MhN*), 11c (*MhN*), 48a, 49a–b, 77d (*Rut*), 84b–c (*Rut*). See above, note 349.

442. **Rabbi Ḥiyya the Great...** See *Zohar* 2:14a–15a (*MhN*); *ZḤ* 9a, 15d (both *MhN*).

443. **bestowed three fine gifts upon Israel...** See BT *Ta'anit* 9a: "Rabbi Yose son of Rabbi Yehudah says, 'Three fine leaders arose for Israel: Moses, Aaron, and Miriam; and through them, three fine gifts were conferred [upon Israel]: the Well, the Pillar of Cloud, and the Manna. The Well—by the merit of Miriam; the Pillar of Cloud—by the merit of Aaron; the Manna—by the merit of Moses. When Miriam died, the well disappeared, as is said: *Miriam died there* (Numbers 20:1), and immediately afterward is written: *There was no water for the community* (ibid., 2). It returned by the merit of the two. When Aaron died, the clouds of glory disappeared, as is said: *The Canaanite, king of Arad, heard* (ibid. 33:40). What news did he hear? He heard that Aaron had died, and that the clouds of glory had disappeared; he thought that he was free to wage war on Israel. As is written: *The entire community*

"My father used to say that the images of the three of them are engraved in the expanse—that their merit might illuminate upon Israel, as is written: *God placed them in the firmament of heaven to shine upon earth* (Genesis 1:17).[444]

"How do we know that the three of them are engraved in the firmament? For look at what we have learned: Concerning all of them is written *by the mouth of YHVH* (Numbers 33:38; Deuteronomy 34:5), though concerning Miriam it is not written *by the mouth of YHVH*, because it is not the custom of the world. However, my father said: Concerning all of them is written *there*: *Miriam died there* (Numbers 20:1); *Aaron died there* (ibid. 20:28); *Moses died there* (Deuteronomy 34:5). Here is written *there*, and elsewhere is written *there*: *He was there with YHVH* (Exodus 34:28). Just as in that case he was *with YHVH*, so in this case as well *with YHVH*.[445]

"As we have learned: Why did Moses die outside the Land? To teach that through his merit, the dead of the desert would rise. My father said: Moses said before the blessed Holy One, 'Master of the World, I would enter the Land to fulfill your commandments, as is written: *When you come into the land* (Leviticus 23:10); *Now, when you come to the land* (Exodus 12:25)—there inheres



*saw that Aaron had expired* (ibid. 20:29).' Rabbi Abbahu said, 'Do not read *va-yir'u*, *saw*, but rather *va-yera'u*, *they were seen* [because with the disappearance of the clouds of glory, Israel became visible and exposed].' . . . The two [the Well and the Cloud] returned because of the merit of Moses; but when Moses died, all of them disappeared, as is said: *I cut off the three shepherds in one month* (Zechariah 11:8)." See also BT *Rosh ha-Shanah* 3a; *ZḤ* 12d (*MhN*), page 100.

On the various benefits brought by Moses, Aaron, and Miriam, see also *Tosefta Sotah* 11:1–2, 8; *Mekhilta, Vayassa* 5; *Mekhilta de-Rashbi*, Exodus 16:35; *Sifrei*, Deuteronomy 305; *Midrash Tanna'im*, Deuteronomy 34:8; *Seder Olam Rabbah* 9–10; *Vayiqra Rabbah* 27:6; *Bemidbar Rabbah* 1:2, 13:20; *Shir ha-Shirim Rabbah* on 4:5; *Tanḥuma, Bemidbar* 2; *Midrash Mishlei* 14:1; *Zohar* 2:190b; 3:102b–3a, 283b.

The full verse in Numbers reads: *Well dug by princes, delved by the people's nobles, with scepter, with their staves and from the desert* מתנה (*mattanah*), *to* [*or: of*] *Mattanah*. For the midrashic reading "from the desert *mattanah*, a gift," see *Targum Onqelos* and *Targum Yerushalmi*, Numbers 21:18; *Tanḥuma, Ḥuqqat* 21; *Tanḥuma* (Buber), *Ḥuqqat* 48; *Bemidbar Rabbah* 19:26; Rashi and Leqaḥ Tov on Numbers 21:18; *Zohar* 2:113b.

444. **images of the three of them . . .** Cf. Scholem, "Parashah Ḥadashah," 431 (Addendum 1 in this volume).

445. **Concerning all of them is written *by the mouth of YHVH* . . .** See BT *Bava Batra* 17a: "Our Rabbis taught: Over six the Angel of Death had no dominion: Abraham, Isaac, and Jacob; Moses, Aaron, and Miriam. . . . Moses, Aaron, and Miriam—because of them is written [that they died] *by the mouth of the YHVH* (Numbers 33:38; Deuteronomy 34:5). But of Miriam is not written *by the mouth of YHVH*! Rabbi El'azar said, 'Miriam also died by a kiss, as we learn from the use of the word *there* [in connection both with her death] and with that of Moses (Numbers 20:1; Deuteronomy 34:5). Why is it not said of her that [she died] *by the mouth of YHVH*? Because such an expression would be unseemly.'" See also BT *Mo'ed Qatan* 28a; *Zohar* 1:125a.

fulfillment of Your commandments!' He said to him, 'That which you have enjoined completes you! [15a] That which Israel will perform in the Holy Land—your portion will be with them!' As is written: *Therefore I will give him a portion among the great, and he shall divide the spoil with the mighty* (Isaiah 53:12). *Therefore I will give him a portion among the great*—the righteous of Israel; *and he shall divide the spoil with the mighty*—the patriarchs. Why? *Because he poured out his soul unto death* (ibid.).[446]

"As Rabbi Ḥiyya the Elder said: 'We have not found a shepherd who surrendered his soul for his flock like Moses, who said, "*Now, if [only] You would bear their sin! If not, please obliterate me from Your book!* (Exodus 32:32)." What is the

446. **Why did Moses die outside the Land?...** See *Devarim Rabbah* 2:9: "*For you shall not cross this Jordan* (Deuteronomy 3:27). The blessed Holy One said to Moses, 'If you are buried here near those [who died in the wilderness], then by your merit they will enter [the land] with you [at the time of Resurrection].' Rabbi Levi said, 'To what can the matter be compared? To a person who dropped some coins in a dark place; he thought to himself, "If I call out 'Shine a light for me so that I may pick up my coins,' no one will take notice of me." What did he do? He took a gold piece and threw it amongst his coins and began calling out, "Shine a light for me, I had a gold piece and I dropped it here." They brought him a light. What did he do? As soon as he picked up the gold piece he said to them, "I adjure you, wait for me until I have picked up my coins"; and he collected them. Because of the one golden piece, all his coins were collected. Similarly, the blessed Holy One said to Moses, "Should you be buried near those who died in the wilderness, then they will enter the land for your sake, and you will be at their head." As is said: *He chose the prime for himself, for there is the portion of the hidden chieftain, and the heads of the people came* (Deuteronomy 33:21).'" See *Zohar* 1:113b (*MhN*).

On Moses' wishing to enter the Land, see BT *Sotah* 14a: "Rabbi Simlai expounded, 'Why did Moses our teacher yearn to enter the land of Israel? Was it necessary for him to eat of its fruit, to sate himself from its bounty? But this is what Moses said, "Many precepts were commanded to Israel that can be fulfilled only in the land of Israel. I wish to enter the land so that they may all be fulfilled by me." The blessed Holy One said to him, "Since it is only to receive the reward [for obeying the commandments] that you seek [to enter the land], I shall deem it as if you did perform them." As is said: *Therefore I will give him a portion among the great, and he shall divide the spoil with the mighty; because he poured out his soul unto death, and was numbered among sinners, whereas he bore the guilt of the many, and made intercession for sinners* (Isaiah 53:12). *Therefore I will give him a portion among the great*—one might assume that this refers to the [great of] later generations and not former generations, therefore the verse adds: *And he shall divide the spoil with the mighty*—Abraham, Isaac, and Jacob, who were mighty in Torah and the commandments. *Because he poured out his soul unto death*—because he surrendered himself to die, as is said: *If not, please obliterate me [from Your book]* (Exodus 32:32). *And was numbered among sinners*—because he was numbered among those who were condemned to die in the wilderness. *Whereas he bore the guilt of the many*—because he secured atonement for the making of the Golden Calf. *And made intercession for sinners*—because he sought mercy on behalf of the sinners in Israel, that they should return in *teshuvah*.'"

meaning of *please obliterate me*? From this world and the world to come; fulfilling the verse *because he poured out his soul unto death* (Isaiah 53:12).'[447]

"*And was numbered among sinners* (ibid.)—for he was buried with the dead of the desert, who were wicked before the blessed Holy One. *Whereas he bore the guilt of the many* (ibid.)—for he did not budge from there until the blessed Holy One absolved them. *And made intercession for sinners* (ibid.)—for he multiplied his prayer on their behalf. Consequently the three of them are engraved above."[448]

Rabbi Yose came and kissed him and carried him on his shoulders for three miles. He proclaimed for him: *All your children will be taught by YHVH* (Isaiah 54:13).[449]

Rabbi Shim'on taught, "Come and see: The blessed Holy One made the sun solely for the use of humankind. Come and see: The sun travels through 390 places in the inhabited world. It ascends and descends and has known levels and מעלות (*ma'alot*), degrees, corresponding to what is written: *I will cause the shadow of* המעלות (*ha-ma'alot*), *the dial of degrees, which has descended on the dial of Ahaz to recede* [*ten degrees*] (Isaiah 38:8)."[450]



447. **a shepherd who surrendered his soul...** See BT *Berakhot* 32a: "*Moses besought YHVH his God* (Exodus 32:11).... Shemu'el said, 'It is to teach us that he offered to die for them, as is written: *If not, please obliterate me from Your book!*'" See also *Zohar* 1:67b; 3:14b; *ZḤ* 23a (*MhN*).

448. **he did not budge from there...** See BT *Berakhot* 32a: "*Now therefore leave Me alone—that My anger may turn against them—and I will destroy them, and I will make of you a great nation* (Exodus 32:10). Rabbi Abbahu said, 'Were it not explicitly written, it would be impossible to say such a thing: this teaches that Moses took hold of the blessed Holy One—like a man who seizes his fellow by his garment—and said before Him, "Master of the Universe, I will not let You go until You will forgive and absolve them."'"

449. **carried him on his shoulders for three miles...** According to Rav Sheshet (BT *Sotah* 46b), one should escort his teacher the distance of a parasang; a distinguished teacher, for three parasangs. (The Persian parasang equals about 3.5 modern miles.) Here, the term is *mil* (miles) and refers to the Roman mile, slightly shorter than the modern mile. See *Pesiqta de-Rav Kahana* 18:5; *Bereshit Rabbah* 32:10; *Zohar* 1:51a, 87a, 96b, 150b, 217a; 2:164a, 187a; 3:8b; *ZḤ* 15b (*MhN*).

The verse from Isaiah continues: *and great will be the peace of your children.* On this verse, cf. *Zohar* 1:64b, 96b; 2:169b–170a.

450. ***I will cause the shadow of* המעלות (*ha-ma'alot*), *the dial of degrees...*** See BT *Sanhedrin* 96a, which recounts a miracle performed for King Hezekiah similar to the one performed for Jacob: "Rabbi Yoḥanan said, 'The day on which Ahaz died consisted of but two hours [that there would not be enough time to pay him respect], and when Hezekiah fell ill and recovered, the blessed Holy One restored those ten hours, as is written: *I will cause the shadow of the dial of degrees, which has descended with the sun on the dial of Ahaz, to recede ten degrees back-*

Rabbi Yose said, "How does it ascend?"

Rabbi said, "We have already learned from the Masters of the Academy that the world is round like a ball.[451] When it [the sun] ventures from the east, it travels in a circle until it goes down and then evening falls. At that time it travels and descends in a circular way through certain levels, descending and circumnavigating the whole inhabited world. When it descends and is concealed from us, it is night for us, but it illuminates those dwelling beneath us, in accordance with the habitation and spherical nature of the earth.[452]

"Then it continues on and descends, separating the waters beneath the ocean from the waters above. It makes a division in the middle of the waters to prevent the stream of water gushing from Hell from inundating and injuring humankind. Therefore it is called שמשא (*shimsha*), sun, solely because it שמשא (*shammsha*), serves, humankind. That is why it is called *shimsha—shammasha di-meshammesh*, the servant serving, all.[453]

"Rabbi El'azar said, 'If the sun did not dip into the ocean, it would burn and incinerate the entire world.'[454]



*ward. So the sun receded ten degrees, by which degrees it had gone down* (Isaiah 38:8).'"

"390" is the *gimatriyya* (numerical value) of שמים (*shamayim*), "heavens." See *ZḤ* 10b (*MhN*); cf. *Baraita di-Shmu'el ha-Qatan*, 8.

On the movements and levels of the sun, see BT *Berakhot* 32b; *Pesaḥim* 94b; *Eruvin* 56a; *Shemot Rabbah* 15:22; *Pirqei de-Rabbi Eli'ezer* 6; *ZḤ* 15c (*MhN*); Scholem, "Parashah Ḥadashah," 437–39 (Addendum 1 in this volume).

451. **the world is round like a ball** The spherical nature of the earth was taught by Aristotle, Ptolemy, Aquinas, and Dante, and was well known in Western Europe after the twelfth century.

On the world being round "like a ball," see JT *Avodah Zarah* 3:1, 42c; *Bemidbar Rabbah* 13:14, 17; *Zohar* 3:10a; Scholem, "Parashah Ḥadashah," 442 and n. 163; idem, "Ha-Tsitat ha-Rishon"; Isaac ibn Sahula, *Meshal ha-Qadmoni*, Gate Five, 665. Cf. Judah Halevi, *Kuzari* 3:49; Maimonides, *Guide of the Perplexed* 1:31, 73; Naḥmanides on Genesis 1:9; Gershon ben Solomon, *Sha'ar ha-Shamayim* 13:4, 42a. On the epithet "Masters of the Academy," see *Zohar* 1:115b (*MhN*), 123b (*MhN*, this volume); *ZḤ* 25d (*MhN*); Scholem, "Parashah Ḥadashah," 432–33, 443.

452. **When it descends and is concealed from us, it is night for us...** From a medieval perspective (as from a contemporary naïve one), as the sun revolves daily around the globe of the earth and shines on part of it, the opposite side of the earth is in darkness.

"Those dwelling beneath us" refers to inhabitants of the southern hemisphere.

See *Zohar* 3:10a; Scholem, "Parashah Ḥadashah," 441–42 (Addendum 1 in this volume); idem, "Ha-Tsitat ha-Rishon"; Isaac ibn Sahula, *Meshal ha-Qadmoni*, Gate Five, 663–65.

The speaker here is identified simply as Rabbi; on this designation, see above, note 91. Here, the text perhaps intends Rabbi Shim'on.

453. **the stream of water gushing from Hell...** See *ZḤ* 9d (*MhN*), page 54. On the wordplay *shimsha-shammasha*, see also Scholem, "Parashah Ḥadashah," 429; *ZḤ* 15c (*MhN*).

454. **dip into the ocean...** See *Pirqei de-Rabbi Eli'ezer* 51: "Rabbi Yannai said, 'All the hosts of heaven pass away and are renewed

"It ascends from beneath the inhabited world and reaches the level called קרבוסא (*qarbosa*) in Greek. From that level it begins to ascend above, and the sound of its revolutions is heard throughout all the firmaments as it journeys, singing as it goes. No one has ever heard it other than Moses, the faithful servant of the King, and Joshua, who ministered to him.[455]

"When Joshua needed it, and he heard the roaring, melodious sound of the sun, he could not bear it. What is written? *He said in the presence of the Israelites, 'O sun at Gibeon,* דום (*dom*), *be still!'* (Joshua 10:12). What is meant by דום (*dom*)? Cease uttering song; cease your roaring, melodious sound. For he could hear the sound of its journeys as it traveled."[456]



every day. What are the hosts of heaven? The sun, the moon, the stars, and the constellations. Know that it is so. Come and see, for when the sun turns in order to set in the west, it bathes in the waters of the ocean, and extinguishes the flames of the sun, and no light is left, and it has no flame all night long until it comes to the east. When it arrives in the east it washes itself in the river of fire, like a man who kindles his lamp in the midst of the fire. Likewise the sun kindles its lamps and puts on its flames and ascends to give light upon the earth, and it renews every day the Work of Creation.'"

From the context, it appears that Rabbi El'azar is quoted rather than being an independent voice.

455. ***qarbosa*...** There is no such word in Greek with a comparable meaning (Tishby, *Wisdom of the Zohar*, 2:661). According to David Luria in his commentary to *Pirqei de-Rabbi Eli'ezer* 3, *qarbosa* indicates the point on the horizon from where the sun begins to rise. Luria suggests that קרבוסא (*qarbosa*) may in fact be a corruption of the word קרכוסא (*qarkosa*), "hooks," based on the passage in *Pirqei de-Rabbi Eli'ezer* 3: "The קורקוסי (*qorqosei*), hooks, of the heavens are fixed in the waters of the ocean." In Greek, *kurkos* means "ring" or "hook." See Scholem, ad loc. *Qarbosa* appears again in *ZḤ* 15c (*MhN*), where it is described as one of the apertures of the sun, in contrast to *Pirqei de-Rabbi Eli'ezer* 6. See also Liebes, *Pulḥan ha-Shaḥar*, 19, n. 18.

On the sound of the sun, see BT *Yoma* 20b: "Rabbi Levi said, 'Why is the voice of a person not heard by day as it is heard by night? Because of the revolution [literally: wheel] of the sun, which saws in the firmament like a carpenter sawing cedars.'... Our Rabbis taught, 'Were it not for the revolution of the sun, the sound of the tumult of Rome would be heard: and were it not for the sound of the tumult of Rome, the sound of the revolution of the sun would be heard.' Our Rabbis taught, 'There are three voices going from one end of the world to the other: The sound of the revolution of the sun; the sound of the tumult of Rome, and the sound of the soul as it leaves the body.'" See also *Bereshit Rabbah* 6:7.

456. **What is meant by דום (*dom*)?...** In the verse in Joshua, the word *dom* means "be still," though the *Zohar* here opts for a related meaning, "be silent," connecting the famous narrative in Joshua to the theme of the music of the spheres. See *ZḤ* 5d–6a (*MhN*). On the song of the sun, see Scholem, "Parashah Ḥadashah," 437–38 (Addendum 1 in this volume).

See *Qohelet Rabbah* on 3:14: "The blessed Holy One decreed that the heavens should praise Him, as is said: *The heavens declare the glory of God* (Psalms 19:2). Moses stood up and silenced them, as is said: *Give ear, O heavens, let me speak* (Deuteronomy 32:1). Similarly the blessed Holy One decreed that the sun and moon should praise Him, as is said: *From the place the sun rises to where it*

Rabbi Bo said, "The sun makes 640 journeys between day and night—the numerical value of שמש (*shemesh*), sun—circumnavigating the entire world in its orbit. Why is this necessary? To soften and warm the soil, ripening herbs and crops, to make the fruit and trees grow."[457]

Rabbi Yehudah said, "Come and see: Corresponding to the pattern above, the blessed Holy One fashions below. Just as above there is heaven, so below there is heaven."[458]

Why is it called שמים (*shamayim*), heaven?

Rav Huna said, "אש (*esh*), fire, and מים (*mayim*), water."[459]

Rabbi Yitsḥak said, "This is derived from here: *He makes peace in His heights* (Job 25:2). It is not written *among His angels,* but *in His heights*—for they are comprised of fire and water, and He makes peace between them. Correspondingly below: fire and water."[460]

The firmament returns from below, warming the soil from the heat of the fire and the sun—while the blessed Holy One rains down water upon the earth, [15b] cooling the soil, complementing the warmth from below. Both of these regenerate the earth, causing it to flourish. The blessed Holy One created them all for the benefit of human beings.[461]

*sets, YHVH's name is to be praised* (Psalms 113:3)....His disciple Joshua stood up and silenced them, as is said: *O Sun, at Gibeon, be still, O Moon, in the Valley of Aijalon* (Joshua 10:12)." Cf. *Zohar* 1:10a.

457. **ripening herbs and crops...** See Scholem, "Parashah Ḥadashah," 439 (Addendum 1 in this volume).

458. **Corresponding to the pattern above...** The theme of "as above, so below" is a cardinal principle of Kabbalah. See *Zohar* 1:38a (*Heikh*), 57b–58a, 129a, 145b, 156b, 158b, 205b; 2:5a (*MhN*), 15b (*MhN*), 20a (*MhN*), 48b, 82b, 144b, 251a (*Heikh*); 3:45b, 65b; *ZḤ* 19a (*MhN*); Tishby, *Wisdom of the Zohar,* 1:273.

On the similar Hermetic formulation, see *Secretum secretorum,* ed. Robert Steele, *Opera hactenus,* fasc. 5, 262. On the heaven above and the heaven below, see note 460.

459. **אש (*esh*), fire, and מים (*mayim*), water** See *Bereshit Rabbah* 4:7 in the name of Rav: "The blessed Holy One took אש (*esh*), fire and מים (*mayim*), water, mixed them with one another, and from them שמים (*shamayim*), heavens, were made." See also BT *Ḥagigah* 12a; *Zohar* 2:164b; 3:137b (*IR*); *ZḤ* 12b (*MhN*).

460. **Correspondingly below: fire and water** Rabbi Yitsḥak explains Rabbi Yehudah's statement. Either the "heaven above" refers to the actual heavens made out of fire and water, while the "heaven below" refers to the existence of fire and water on earth below; or the "heaven below" refers to the actual heavens made of fire and water, while the "heaven above" signifies the divine realm marked by the balance between fire (*din,* judgment) and water (*ḥesed,* mercy).

The verse in Job refers to God's making peace among the ostensibly incompatible elements of heaven. See *Pesiqta de-Rav Kahana* 1:3; *Shir ha-Shirim Rabbah* on 3:11; *Devarim Rabbah* 5:12; *Tanḥuma, Vayiggash* 6; *Tanḥuma* (Buber), *Bereshit* 13; *Derekh Erets, Pereq ha-Shalom* 9; *Bemidbar Rabbah* 12:8. Cf. *Zohar* 2:147b.

461. **The firmament returns from below...** The *Zohar* here imagines the sun as set within a particular firmament, the rota-

Rabbi Abbahu, Rabbi Ḥiyya, and Rabbi Natan were walking on the way. Rabbi Natan said, "Are you not astounded by those Masters of Mishnah? For the decree of their mouth is like the decree of the holy angels! And I have recalled what they have said: The sun's light is emanated from the splendor of the speculum above and its light is not its own. As implied by what is written: *Let there be* מארת (*me'orot*), *lights* (Genesis 1:14). The verse should have said *Let there be* אורות (*orot*), *lights*. What is the significance of *me'orot*? Rabbi Zeira said, 'מן אורות (*min orot*)—the word is in fact *orot*, lights; the מ (*mem*) functions as an addition; in other words, *min orot*, *from the lights*.'"[462]



tion of which gives the sun its appearance of movement (see below, *ZḤ* 15c, *MhN*, page 143). The firmament itself is also a source of heat.

462. **What is the significance of *me'orot*?...** Genesis 1:14–16 uses the noun *ma'or* (plural, *me'orot*) to describe the celestial lights, rather than the more common אור (*or*) or its plural, אורות (*orot*). Rabbi Natan understands the apparently superfluous initial letter מ (*mem*) as a prefixed contraction of the preposition *min*, "from," thereby conveying the idea that the sun receives its light "from the lights," namely, from the splendor of the speculum above. See Scholem, "Parashah Ḥadashah," 440 (Addendum 1 in this volume).

See *Bereshit Rabbah* 17:5 in the name of Rabbi Avin: "The orb of the sun is the unripe fruit of the supernal light."

Cf. *Bemidbar Rabbah* 15:9: "Immense is the light of the blessed Holy One! The sun and moon illuminate the world. But from where do they derive their radiance? They snatch from sparks of lights above.... Immense is the light above, for only one hundredth of it is given to the created beings, as is said: *He knows what* [*mah*, read as *me'ah*, a hundred) *is in the darkness* [*and light dwells with Him*] (Daniel 2:22). 'Therefore' [says God] 'I made the sun and the moon to shine before you,' as is said: *God set them in the firmament of the heavens to shine upon the earth* (Genesis 1:17)."

"Speculum above" renders אספקלריא דלעילא (*ispaqlarya de-l'eila*). *Ispaqlarya* means "glass, mirror, lens." See BT *Yevamot* 49b: "All the prophets gazed through an opaque glass [literally: an *ispaqlarya* that does not shine], while Moses our teacher gazed through a translucent glass [literally: an *ispaqlarya* that shines]." See also *Vayiqra Rabbah* 1:14. Cf. 1 Corinthians 13:12: "For now we see though a glass darkly, but then face-to-face." In *MhN*, the "speculum above" appears to signify a potency very close to divinity (perhaps *Shekhinah*). See *Zohar* 1:97b, 122a (both *MhN*); *ZḤ* 10a, 13b, 15d, 16c, 17a, 21a, 24a (all *MhN*); Scholem, "Parashah Ḥadashah," 440 (Addendum 1 in this volume).

The term מאריהון דמתניתא (*mareihon de-matnita*), "Masters of Mishnah," occurs throughout *Midrash ha-Ne'lam* in various formulations. It appears to signify a particular (undefined) group of sages possessing esoteric wisdom. In some ways, the Masters of Mishnah are a forerunner to the *Ḥavrayya*, the Companions headed by Rabbi Shim'on, found in the main body of the *Zohar*. Significantly, however, Rabbi Shim'on does not always occupy a privileged position in this group. The Mishnah of which they are masters is not that of Rabbi Yehudah ha-Nasi, but rather a body of esoteric knowledge often relating to the soul and the structure of the cosmos. See *Zohar* 1:127a–b, 129a–b, 130a, 135a, 138a, 139b (all *MhN*); 2:5a, 14a (both *MhN*); *ZḤ* 10c, 12c, 13a, 14c, 16a, 59b (all *MhN*); Scholem, "Parashah Hadashah," 443, 444 (Addendum 1 in this volume); Meroz, "Va-Ani Lo Hayiti Sham?" 168 (Addendum 3 in this volume). See also Matt, "Matnita di-Lan," 132–34. Cf. *Pesiqta de-Rav Kahana*

Rabbi Ḥiyya said, "Do not be surprised by it, for Torah was emanated from supernal wisdom; and the heavens were emanated from the supernal firmament that is above the heads of the living beings. Similarly, when you contemplate with wisdom: all that is above and below was emanated—this from that, and one from another—and the blessed Holy One is above all. From the Throne of Glory they began to emanate, one from another, and the Throne of Glory from Him. All of them are as naught compared to Him, as is written: *All the inhabitants of the earth are considered as nothing, He does as He wishes with the host of heaven* (Daniel 4:32)."[463]

Rabbi Abbahu said, "Let this not trouble you, for—with all due difference—our leader begins at first by teaching Torah to the translator; and the translator to those near him; and those near him to those near them. So we find that when the teaching is completed, all is dependent on the leader. Likewise we find above and in all worlds."[464]

Rabbi Abbahu also said, "Moses was illuminated from the supernal splendor. Joshua was illuminated from Moses, the elders illuminated from Joshua, the prophets illuminated from the elders, the chiefs and the leaders of the people were illuminated from the prophets—all of them, one from another."[465]



11:15, 23:12. Cf. the term מארי דמתיבתא (*marei de-metiva*), Masters of the Academy, also found in *Midrash ha-Ne'lam*; see Scholem, "Parashah Ḥadashah," 432–33, 443.

On the use of the term "decree" (from the root גזר (*gzr*)) for establishing a teaching, see also *Zohar* 1:123a, 124b, 125a (all *MhN*); *ZḤ* 14a, 16a, 18b, 20a (all *MhN*); 62b (*ShS*); Scholem, "Parashah Ḥadashah," 443–4 (also on the motif of holy angels); Meroz, "Va-Ani Lo Hayiti Sham?" 168.

463. **Do not be surprised...** Not only does the sun receive its light from that which is above it, but also in fact the entirety of existence is an interconnected chain of emanation, extending back to the blessed Holy One. Even though the chain has many links, the blessed Holy One is the ultimate reality.

Cf. Plotinus, *The Enneads* V.2.1: "The One is all things and no one of them; the source of all things is not all things; and yet it is in all things in a transcendent sense—all things, so to speak, having run back to it."

"Emanated" renders אתצל (*ittsel*), an aramaization of the medieval Hebrew verb "to emanate." This philosophical term does not appear in the main body of the *Zohar*, which prefers instead "expand, spread, illuminate."

On Torah emanated from supernal wisdom, see *Bereshit Rabbah* 17:5 in the name of Rabbi Avin: "Torah is an unripe fruit of supernal Wisdom." See *Zohar* 1:47b; 2:62a, 85a; 3:81a, 182a, 192b; 2:121b; Moses de León, *Sefer ha-Rimmon*, 106–8, 326–30. On the heavens emanating from the supernal firmament, see *ZḤ* 10a–b, 14a (both *MhN*). On the Throne (which may refer to Metatron) as the beginning point of emanation, see *ZḤ* 7d, 16c (both *MhN*).

464. **our leader begins at first by teaching Torah to the translator...** The chain of emanation can also be likened to the transmission of teachings in the academy. The translator stood next to the presiding teacher and restated his teachings in a loud voice so that all might hear. See Rashi, s.v. *la hava amora*, in BT *Yoma* 20b.

465. **Moses was illuminated from the supernal splendor...** Rabbi Abbahu offers another example. The chain of emanation can also be compared to the transmission of knowledge across the generations, from

While they were walking, they met Rabbi El'azar. They said, "Look, one of the Masters of the Mishnah has arrived!"[466]

They said to him, "Is it true that you have said that the sun's light is illuminated from the splendor of the speculum above?"

He replied, "It is so."

He opened, saying, "*A spring in the garden, a well of living waters, a flowing stream from Lebanon* (Song of Songs 4:15). Scripture calls her a spring, afterward a well, afterward a flowing stream. Here one should contemplate! The spring extends from the well, and the well from the flowing stream, and the flowing stream from Lebanon—to convey that they were all emanated—this from that, and one from another. So it is with the sun. Its light is not its own, but rather one thread of splendor extends, illumining the sun.[467]

"Look at what we have learned in our Mishnah: With the light that the blessed Holy One created at first, one could gaze and see from the beginning of the world to its end. Come and see: The light of the sun is a sixty-thousand-and-seventy-fifth of the light of the speculum of the concealed light. If even at this light of the sun a person cannot gaze, how much more so at that light![468]



master to student. See M *Avot* 1:1: "Moses received Torah from Sinai and transmitted it to Joshua, Joshua to the Elders, the Elders to the Prophets, and the Prophets to the Men of the Great Assembly."

"Illuminated" renders אתצל (*ittsel*), which in addition to "emanate" also connotes "drawing upon, being inspired or infused by." See Numbers 11:17, 25.

466. **Masters of Mishnah...** Some of the manuscripts (and the printed editions) read: "Masters of the Academy."

467. **The spring extends from the well...** Rabbi El'azar demonstrates that the idea of an emanatory chain can also be found in Scripture, in this case the Song of Songs. The flow of emanation is now likened to flowing water, extending from Lebanon—perhaps signifying *lavan*, "whiteness," the purity of the blessed Holy One.

On this verse from the Song of Songs, see *Shir ha-Shirim Rabbah* on 4:15; *Zohar* 1:135b; 3:201b, 266a, 298a. On the sun's being illuminated from a site above, cf. *Zohar* 1:136a.

468. **With the light that the blessed Holy One created at first...** See *Vayiqra Rabbah* 11:7: "Rabbi Yehudah son of Simon said, 'With the light created by the blessed Holy One on the first day, one could gaze and see from one end of the universe to the other. When the blessed Holy One foresaw the corruption of the generation of Enosh and the generation of the Flood, He hid it away from them, as is written: *The light of the wicked is withheld* (Job 38:15). Where did He hide it? In the Garden of Eden, as is said: *Light is sown for the righteous, joy for the upright in heart* (Psalms 97:11).'" See also BT *Ḥagigah* 12a; *Bereshit Rabbah* 3:6; *Shemot Rabbah* 35:1; *Tanḥuma, Shemini* 9; *Bahir* 97–98 (147); *Zohar* 1:7a, 31b–32a, 45b–46a, 47a, 121b (*MhN*); 2:127a, 148b–149a, 220a–b; 3:88a, 173b; *ZḤ* 14d (*MhN*); Scholem, "Parashah Ḥadashah," 443 (Addendum 1 in this volume).

Note the slight change in *Midrash ha-Ne'lam*'s presentation of this myth. Whereas the rabbinic texts note that one could see "from one end of the universe to the other," *MhN* reads "from the beginning of the world to its end," implying a visionary capacity across time. This slight change connects the myth of the concealed light with another

"Yet we have said that a person could see with it from the beginning of the world to the end of the world! Well, so have we decreed in our Mishnah: With that light, a person could know and see—with the radiance of wisdom—all that was and all that will be, from the beginning of the world to the end of the world, and it has been concealed for the righteous in the world to come. What is meant by 'in the world to come'? When the holy soul leaves this world and enters the world to come.[469]

"Come and see: It is written: *He was there with YHVH forty days and forty nights; he ate no bread and drank no water* (Exodus 34:28). How come? Because he delighted in that splendor! And even though he descended from there and that light did not descend with him, they were unable to gaze upon Moses' face, on account of what he had seen previously when he was there; and his face remained radiant like the sun."[470]

midrashic motif about Adam found in *Bereshit Rabbah* 24:2 and BT *Sanhedrin* 38b, which describes how the blessed Holy One showed Adam "every generation with its expounders." See *ZḤ* 16d (*MhN*); Matt, "Matnita di-Lan," 133.

On the expression "our Mishnah," see *Zohar* 1:37b, 55b, 74a, 91b, 93a, 95b, 96a, 124b (*MhN*), 136b (*MhN*), 137a (*MhN*), 139a (*MhN*), 223b; 2:5a (*MhN*), 123b; 3:75b, 78a, 284b, 285a, 293b (*IZ*); *ZḤ* 12b, 14a, 16a, 18b, 20a (all *MhN*); Scholem, "Parashah Ḥadashah"; Matt, "Matnita di-Lan."

On the sun's relative brightness, cf. BT *Ḥullin* 59b–60a: "The emperor said to Rabbi Yehoshu'a son of Ḥananiah, 'I wish to behold your God.'... He went and placed the emperor facing the sun during the summer solstice. He said to him, 'Look at it.' He replied, 'I cannot.' Rabbi Yehoshu'a said, 'If at the sun—which is but one of the ministering servants of the blessed Holy One—you admit you cannot look, how much more so the *Shekhinah*!'" Cf. 3 Enoch 5:4.

469. **With that light, a person could know and see—with the radiance of wisdom...** How can we say that one cannot gaze upon the concealed light, if we also say that at the dawn of time one could use it to see with? The answer is that such seeing was a form of spiritual vision.

Rabbi El'azar then specifies that the concealed light is available to the righteous after death. He defines "the world to come" because in rabbinic literature it is an ambiguous term, sometimes connoting the messianic era, and sometimes life after death. Cf. Maimonides, *Mishneh Torah, Hilkhot Teshuvah* 8:8: "The Sages did not use the expression 'the world to come' with the intention of implying that it does not exist at present, or that the present realm will be destroyed and then that realm will come into being. The matter is not so. Rather [the world to come] exists and is present.... It is called the world to come only because that life comes to a person after life in this world, in which we exist as souls in bodies."

470. **Because he delighted in that splendor!...** When Moses was on Mount Sinai, he had access to the concealed light. Delighting in this light, he had no need for any other nourishment. Moses' face continued to shine because of his encounter with the concealed light.

See *Shemot Rabbah* 47:5: "*He was there with YHVH forty days and forty nights* (Exodus 34:28). Is it possible for a person to go forty days without food or drink? Rabbi Tanḥuma said in the name of Rabbi El'azar son of Rabbi Avin in the name of Rabbi Meir, 'The proverb runs: When you go into a city,

Rabbi El'azar turned to go on his way, and they walked after him to accompany him on his journey for three miles. [15c] They said to Rabbi El'azar, "Happy are you, O Masters of Mishnah, for you were right behind Moses when the Torah was given by him!"[471]

Rabbi Ḥiyya and Rabbi Natan walked on, while Rabbi Abbahu did not wish to part from him; he walked with him on his way.

Rabbi El'azar opened, saying, "*Let there be lights in the firmament of heaven* (Genesis 1:14). Come and hear: The blessed Holy One made eighteen firmaments that travel on their journeys, orbiting the entire world. Each one is delayed the measure bestowed upon it by its Master. When a particular firmament completes its measure, many magnificent events are innovated in the world.[472]

"Now, the fool-hearted imagine in their minds that this is on account of the orbiting of the firmament. But it is not so! For every single day—from morning to evening—the blessed Holy One originates supernal, magnificent, and mighty events. Sometimes, when a particular firmament completes its journey, a decree of the Supernal King transpires in the world, and the fool-hearted imagine that this was on account of that firmament; yet their hearts err in foolishness.[473]



follow its customs. When Moses ascended on high, where there is no eating or drinking, he emulated them. . . .' *He ate no bread* (ibid.)—eating only the bread of the Torah; *and drank no water* (ibid.)—drinking only of the water of the Torah. . . . Whence did he derive his nourishment? He was nourished by the splendor of *Shekhinah*." See also *Shemot Rabbah* 3:1; *Zohar* 1:135b (*MhN*).

See also *Shemot Rabbah* 47:6: "*Moses didn't know that the skin of his face was beaming* (Exodus 34:29). Whence did Moses derive the beams of glory? Our Sages say, 'From the cleft of the rock, as is said: *while My glory passes by* . . .' (ibid. 33:22). . . . Rabbi Yehudah son of Naḥman said in the name of Rabbi Shim'on son of Lakish, 'A little ink was left on the pen with which Moses wrote [the Decalogue]; and when he passed this pen through the hair of his head, the beams of splendor appeared, as is said: *Moses didn't know that the skin of his face was beaming.*'"

Cf. Abraham Ibn Ezra (long commentary) on Exodus 34:29: "*Moses didn't know* [*that the skin of his face was beaming*]—and the reason [was] *since he had spoken with Him*, because the glory appeared on his face, and therefore it was radiant like the radiance of the sky."

471. **accompany him on his journey for three miles . . .** Out of respect; see above, note 449.

The Masters of Mishnah are able to reveal profound insights because their souls were present at the giving of the Torah, just behind Moses. See Matt, "Matnita di-Lan," 132.

472. **eighteen firmaments . . .** These firmaments are the spheres of medieval cosmology. See Maimonides, *Mishneh Torah*, *Hilkhot Yesodei ha-Torah* 3:5: "The total number of spheres surrounding the Earth entirely is eighteen."

473. **Now, the fool-hearted imagine . . .** Even though the revolution of the various spheres coincides with events on earth, they are not the cause. The pseudo-science of astrology is thus rejected in the strongest terms. The *Zohar*'s polemic here is influenced by Solomon Ibn Gabirol's poem *Keter Malkhut*, which also castigates those who ascribe agency to the celestial objects. See Canto 12: "Those who imagine that the sun is their

"The blessed Holy One fashioned the fourth firmament and placed within it this sun—which orbits the entire world according to the seasons and times, for the benefit of the world and to serve human beings. It has been taught in our Mishnah: The sun moves through 340 windows, ascending and descending according to the seasons and times. It rises and begins from the window of the east, from the window called נוגה (*Nogah*), Gleam, traveling in a circular fashion until it reaches the window called קרבוסא (*Qarbosa*). Then it travels six months to the extremity of the north, until it reaches the window of זהרא (*Zahara*), Radiance, traveling six months to complete the year for the benefit of the creatures—for sowing and harvesting. As is written: *So long as the earth endures, seedtime and harvest, cold and heat, summer and winter* [*shall not cease*] (Genesis 8:22)—three in its travels to the extremity of the south, and three when it travels to the extremity of the north; seedtime, cold, and winter in its travels to the extremity of the south, in accordance with the habitation of the earth; harvest, heat, and summer in its travels to the extremity of the north. All is according to habitation of the earth, as we have said.[474]

"In the same way, just as people use the light of this firmament, so all the hosts of heaven use the light of the firmament that is above the heads of the living beings."[475]

Rabbi Abbahu said, "Why is it lacking the *vavs*?"[476]

god will at that time be ashamed of their imaginings for their words will be tested." See also Cantos 11, 13, 14 and 15, which all stress that the tidings brought by the movements of the celestial object are always "by the will of the Creator." On the influence of *Keter Malkhut* on the *Zohar*, see Scholem, "Parashah Ḥadashah," 435 n. 78; Tishby, *Wisdom of the Zohar*, 1:76.

474. **The blessed Holy One fashioned the fourth firmament...** On the location of the sun in the fourth firmament (or sphere), see Solomon Ibn Gabirol, *Keter Malkhut*, Canto 15; Maimonides, *Mishneh Torah*, *Hilkhot Yesodei ha-Torah* 3:1; Scholem, "Parashah Ḥadashah," 435, n. 78.

On the journey of sun to the north and south, see *Pirqei de-Rabbi Eli'ezer* 6; Solomon Ibn Gabirol, *Keter Malkhut*, Canto 16; Scholem, "Parashah Ḥadashah," 440 (Addendum 1 in this volume). On the six seasons, see BT *Bava Metsi'a* 106b; Rashi on Genesis 8:22. On the celestial windows and journeys of the sun, see *Pirqei de-Rabbi Eli'ezer* 6: "In 366 degrees the sun rises and declines; it rises 183 [degrees] in the east, and it declines 183 [degrees] in the west, corresponding to the solar year. [The sun] goes forth 366 windows and enters by the east." Of the names of the various windows, only *Nogah* appears in *Pirqei de-Rabbi Eli'ezer*.

See also *Shemot Rabbah* 15:22: "The blessed Holy One created 365 windows in the firmament: 183 in the east, and 182 in the west." See also JT *Rosh ha-Shanah* 2:6, 58a. *Zohar* 2:172a–b also contains an account of the celestial windows that mentions the windows Gleam and Radiance.

On *Qarbosa*, see above, note 455. Some witnesses read קנבוסא (*qanbosa*), on which see *ZḤ* 16a (*MhN*), page 151.

475. **just as people use the light of this firmament...** As the sun is for us, so is the celestial light above for the heavenly realm.

476. **Why is it lacking the *vavs*?** In Genesis 1:14, the word מארת (*me'orot*) is written

He replied, "It is as we have said previously, because its light is not complete. For its light is only that which it receives from the light above, like a single ray from beyond the wall.[477]

"That is why it is not called complete light. The only light worthy of being called complete is that referred to by *light dwells with Him* (Daniel 2:22). [The light] that was concealed for the righteous is a sixty-thousand-and-seventy-fifth of the light that dwells with the blessed Holy One; and the light of the sun is one sixty-thousand-and-seventy-fifth of the light that was concealed for the righteous in the world to come. Consequently, the light of the sun is not called complete light, nor is it fitting that it be called so.[478]

"Therefore the blessed Holy One said, 'Let it not trouble you that it is written מארת (*me'erat*), *curse*, and that it is not complete—for I did not make it except for that which is written: *to shine upon the earth* (Genesis 1:15), to serve the people of the earth; and let it be enough for you, O people of the earth, that this luminary will serve you.'"[479]

144 Rabbi El'azar said, "If at this small [light] people cannot gaze, how much more so at the light concealed for the righteous!?"

without the usual vowel letters; their absence must be meaningful. See JT *Ta'anit* 4:4, 68b: "On the fourth day [of the week, Wednesday], they would fast for infants, so that diphtheria not enter their mouths. *God said, 'Let there be* מארת (*me'orot*), *lights*'—spelled מארת (*me'erat*), curse."

See Proverbs 3:33; *Pesiqta de-Rav Kahana* 5:1; *Soferim* 17:4; Rashi on Genesis 1:14; *Zohar* 1:1a, 12a, 19b–20a, 33b, 46b, 146a, 166a, 169b; 2:35b, 167b, 205a; *ZḤ* 69b–c (*ShS*), *ZḤ* 14c (*MhN*); *Minḥat Shai* on Genesis 1:14; Scholem, "Parashah Ḥadashah," 429 (Addendum 1 in this volume).

477. **like a single ray from beyond the wall** See Maimonides, *Shemonah Peraqim*, 7; *Zohar* 1:232b (*Tos*); 2:69a–b, 82a, 130b, 213a; 3:174b; *ZḤ* 39d; Scholem, "Parashah Ḥadashah," 436 (Addendum 1 in this volume).

478. **the light of the sun is not called complete light...** Given how deficient is the light of the sun in comparison with the concealed light, and with the ultimate light that dwells with God, it would be inappropriate to designate this light as "complete." Scripture conveys this principle through the deficient spelling of *me'orot*. See Scholem, "Parashah Ḥadashah," 440.

The full verse in Daniel reads: *He reveals deep and hidden things, knows what is in the darkness, and light dwells with Him.*

It is possible that the series of three lights corresponds with the tripartite structure of the heavens: the supernal firmament (the light dwelling with God, perhaps Metatron), the heavens (the concealed light), and finally the firmament of the heavens (the sun). See *ZḤ* 10b, 14a (both *MhN*).

See Wolfson, "The Anonymous Chapters of the Elderly Master of Secrets," 250.

479. **Let it not trouble you that it is written, מארת (*me'erat*), *curse*...** Even though the sun's light is not "complete," humanity is enjoined to be content with it, being ample for their needs. Even though the human plane of existence is deficient, it is not cursed.

There is a play on words here: the sun (*shimsha*) was created to serve (*le-shammasha*) humanity. See *ZḤ* 15a (*MhN*).

Rabbi Abbahu said, "How much more so at the light of the luminary dwelling before the supernal King!?"

He came to kiss Rabbi El'azar's hands. He said, "Now I know that it is truly appropriate that this מארת (*me'orot*), *lights*, be deficient; and it is fitting that it be even more deficient than this!"[480]

He said, "Woe to the world when you will depart from it! For until today I have asked this question—yet did not find the essence of the matter until now! The way on which you set forth will be for me a sign of blessing, in that I encountered you."[481] [15d]

He sat with him for three days and he taught him every doubt and difficulty he had. He taught him sixty insights concerning the chapter of creation. He walked on his way. He found Rabbi Ḥiyya. He said to him, "May it please you, Rabbi Abbahu, that I might taste of the sweetness of the honey that you sucked from the instruction of the supernal holy ones?"[482]

He said to him, "Palm excrement and intoxication of honey do not go together!"[483]



480. **it is fitting that it be even more deficient than this** Even the absent *vavs* do not convey how deficient the sun is in relation to the divine lights.

481. **essence of the matter...** עיקרא דמילתא (*Iqqara de-milta*), which indicates a deeper meaning—as opposed to the simple or midrashic senses. See *ZḤ* 12c, 16a, 25d (all *MhN*); Gikatilla, *Sha'arei Orah*, 2a; Moses de Leon, *Sefer ha-Rimmon*, 307.

482. **that I might taste of the sweetness of the honey...** Unlike Rabbi Abbahu, Rabbi Ḥiyya did not pursue study with Rabbi El'azar.

On the equation of wisdom and honey, see Ezekiel 3:1–3; Psalms 19:10–11; BT *Ḥagigah* 13a; *ZḤ* 12b (*MhN*). On staying with one's master for three (or thirty) days, see *ZḤ* 8a (*MhN*), page 42.

483. **Palm excrement and intoxication of honey do not go together!** A conjectural rendering of חררתא דאפיקותא וסובתא דדובשא לא מיישרי חדא (*hararta de-afiquta ve-sovta de-duvsha la meyyashrei ḥada*). It seems clear that Rabbi Abbahu is castigating Rabbi Ḥiyya for having left Rabbi El'azar and not continuing to learn from him. He is thus not worthy of the honey of wisdom.

חררתא (*ḥararta*) may derive from חרותא (*ḥaruta*), which, according to Rashi in BT *Sukkah* 32a (s.v. *ḥaruta*), signifies "a palm branch that has hardened for two or three years and fronds have come out of it... and have become hard... and become wood. One turns this way and one turns that way." Alternatively, *ḥararta* may derive from חרר (*ḥarar*), "to discharge, excrete," or from חררה (*ḥararah*), which means "cake."

אפיקותא (*afiquta*) may derive from אופתא (*ofata*), which, again according to Rashi in BT *Sukkah* 32a (s.v. *ofata*), signifies "the trunk of the palm tree—which is smooth and no branch comes out of it any direction." Alternatively, if *ḥararta* is derived from *ḥararah* ("cake"), then perhaps *afiquta* derives from אפתא (*afta*), "bread." *Afiquta* may also connote excrement, from the verb stem נפק (*nafaq*), "to go out."

סובתא (*sovta*) may derive from סאובתא (*sa'uvata*), connoting contamination or uncleanness; or from סבא (*sava*), connoting intoxication and satiety. Hence, this statement might also be rendered "Cake-bread and the filth of honey do not go together" or perhaps "The palm branches and the filth of honey do not go together." If the latter, the palm

Nevertheless he taught him. Rabbi Ḥiyya wept, saying, "I hereby swear that until I learn before the Masters of the Supernal Mishnah I will not return here!"[484]

He sat there for twelve years. When he came, they called him Rabbi Ḥiyya the Great.[485]

Rabbi Yitsḥak said, "Light is concealed for the righteous in the time to come—that which was concealed, as is written: *Light is sown for the righteous, joy for the upright in heart* (Psalms 97:11)."[486]

*God said, "Let there be lights..."* (Genesis 1:14).

Rabbi Pinḥas opened with this verse: *O daughters of Zion, come out and gaze upon King Solomon, upon the crown with which his mother crowned him* (Song of Songs 3:11).[487]

Rabbi Pinḥas said, "We have gone over the entire Torah—and have not found that Bathsheba made a crown for Solomon![488] Here one should cite what Rabbi



may signify the righteous. Yehuda Liebes has suggested that סובתא (*sovta*) is a corruption of טובתא (*tovata*), "goodness," and hence the phrase should be rendered "Bits [or: cakes] of excrement and goodness of honey do not go together." This reading is supported by some of the manuscripts.

On this phrase, see Meroz, "Zoharic Narratives," 27 nn. 90, 91, 92. See *Sullam* for a different reading.

484. **Masters of the Supernal Mishnah...** מארייהון דמתניתא עילאה (*Mareihon de-matnita ila'ah*), referring to a Mishnah or teaching that is not the ordinary Mishnah of Rabbi Yehudah ha-Nasi, but one comprising sublime mysteries of creation and of the soul.

485. **He sat there for twelve years...** Cf. BT *Shabbat* 33b–34a, which recounts Rabbi Shim'on and Rabbi El'azar's stay in a cave for thirteen years.

For another account of Rabbi Ḥiyya's initiation, see *Zohar* 2:14a–15a (*MhN*).

486. ***Light is sown for the righteous...*** On Psalms 97:11, see above, note 468.

487. **O daughters of Zion, come out and gaze upon King Solomon...** The verse continues: *on the day of his wedding, on the day of his heart's delight.*

488. **We have gone over the entire Torah—and have not found...** See *Shir ha-Shirim Rabbah* on 3:11: "Rabbi Yoḥanan said, 'Rabbi Shim'on son of Yoḥai asked Rabbi El'azar son of Rabbi Yose, "Perhaps you have heard from your father the meaning of *upon the crown with which his mother crowned him*?" He replied, "Yes." He asked him, "How [did he explain it]?" He replied, "Like a king who had an only daughter whom he loved lavishly, calling her 'my daughter.' He went on loving her until he called her 'my sister.' He went on loving her until he called her 'my mother.' So the blessed Holy One loved Israel lavishly and called them 'My daughter,' as is written: *Listen, O daughter, and consider* (Psalms 45:11). He went on loving them until He called them 'My sister,' as is said: *Open to me, my sister, my love* (Song of Songs 5:2). He went on loving them until He called them 'My mother,' as is said: *Listen to Me, My people; and give ear to Me,* ולאומי (*u-le'ummi*), *O My nation* (Isaiah 51:4)—it is written [or more precisely: if the vowel letter is ignored, it yields] ולאמי (*u-le-'immi*), *and to My mother.*" Rabbi Shim'on son of Yoḥai stood and kissed him on his head, saying, "If I have come just to hear this interpretation from your mouth, it is enough for me!"' Rabbi Ḥanina son of Yitsḥak said, 'We have

Yitsḥak said, 'What is the meaning of *come out and gaze*? It should have been written *come and see*! Why *come out*?' Well, Rabbi Yitsḥak said, 'This verse was uttered concerning the righteous who have departed this world and were buried in the holy land of Israel.' Rabbi El'azar said, 'And whose soul departed there.' In the future, a heavenly voice will arouse over every single tombstone in the cemeteries and say, '*Come out and gaze*! Come out from beneath the putrefied earth, and awaken from your sleep, *O daughters of* ציון (*tsiyyon*), *Zion*!' as is said: *What is this* ציון (*tsiyyun*), *tombstone* [*I see*]? (2 Kings 23:17)."[489]

Rabbi Pinḥas said, "Happy are you, O righteous, to behold the supernal, glorious splendor of the Holy King who possesses all peace! By what right? By virtue of *the crown with which his mother crowned him* (Song of Songs 3:11); because of the crown with which the righteous crowned Him through words of Torah in this world."[490]

gone over the entirety of Scripture, and we have not found that Bathsheba made a crown for her son Solomon, and yet you say *upon the crown with which his mother crowned him*? What it means, however, is that just as a crown is set with precious stones and pearls, so the Tent of Meeting was distinguished by blue and purple and scarlet and fine linen.'" See also *Pesiqta de-Rav Kahana* 1:3.

On this verse from the Song of Songs, see M *Ta'anit* 4:8; *Sifra, Shemini, millu'im*, 15, 44c; *Eikhah Rabbah, Petiḥta* 33; *Pesiqta de-Rav Kahana* 1:3; Naḥmanides on Genesis 24:1; *Zohar* 1:29b, 218a, 246a; 2:22a, 84a, 100b; 3:61b, 77b, 95a, 98a.

489. **Come out from beneath the putrefied earth...** Rabbi Pinḥas reads the verse from the Song as applying to the eschatological era. Reading ציון (*tsiyyon*), *Zion*, as ציון (*tsiyyun*), *tombstone*, Rabbi Pinḥas interprets the verse as referring to the awakening of the righteous, who will merit to gaze upon Solomon—meaning the splendor of God, as explained in the next paragraph.

On the heavenly voice rousing the dead, see *Zohar* 1:118a (*MhN*); 2:199b. On the importance of burial in the land of Israel, see JT *Kil'ayim* 9:4, 32c–d; *Bereshit Rabbah* 96; *Tanḥuma, Vayḥi* 3; *Tanḥuma* (Buber), *Vayḥi* 6; *Zohar* 1:225b–226a; 2:141b; 3:72b.

See BT *Ketubbot* 111a: "Ulla was in the habit of visiting the land of Israel, but he came to his eternal rest outside the land. [When people] came and reported this to Rabbi El'azar, he exclaimed, 'O Ulla, should you die in an unclean land?!' They told him, 'His coffin has arrived.' He replied, 'Receiving a person in his lifetime is not the same as receiving him after his death.'... Rabbi El'azar said, 'The dead outside the Land will not live [i.e., be resurrected], as is said: *I will set* צבי (*tsvi*), *glory, in the land of the living* (Ezekiel 26:20). The land in which is צביוני (*tsivyoni*), My desire—her dead shall live; [lands] where My desire does not abide—their dead shall not live.'"



490. **glorious splendor of the Holy King who possesses all peace...** After rising from their graves, the righteous gaze upon King שלמה (*Shelomoh*), "Solomon," namely the splendor of God—the King who possesses שלמא (*shelama*), "peace."

On the phrase "the King who possesses peace," see *Sifra, Shemini, millu'im*, 15, 44c; *Pesiqta de-Rav Kahana* 1:2, 3; *Shir ha-Shirim Rabbah* on 1:1 and 1:2; *Zohar* 1:5b, 29a, 184a, 226b, 248b; 2:5a (*MhN*), 14a (*MhN*), 127b, 132a–b, 143b–144b; 3:10b, 20a, 60a, 73b; *ZḤ* 22a, 25c (both *MhN*).

According to the simple meaning of the verse, the daughters of Zion gaze בעטרה (*be-atarah*), "upon the crown." Rabbi Pinḥas,

Rabbi Abbahu said in the name of Rabbi Yitsḥak, "אמו (*Immo*), *His mother*—as in אום (*um*), people; in other words, אומו (*ummo*), His people. Who are the people of the blessed Holy One? These are the righteous—who are the people known by Him."[491]

*On the day of his wedding* (ibid.). Whose wedding is this?

Rabbi Pinḥas said, "Of that people, the wedding of that people of His. What is meant by *his wedding*? The day they become fit to perform commandments of Torah—which is the joy of the righteous. When are they rendered fit? Rabbi Yitsḥak said, 'From thirteen years and up, for on that day the righteous are required to celebrate, delighting their heart, like the day one enters the wedding canopy.' By virtue of this merit, in the future the blessed Holy One will rouse them, summoning a herald to pass before them in joy: *O daughters of Zion, come out and gaze.*"[492]

Rabbi Yitsḥak said, "Come and hear: *Let there be lights in the firmament of heaven* (Genesis 1:14). When the blessed Holy One revives the dead, summoning



however, reads the prefixed preposition ב (*bet*) of the word *be-atarah* in its occasional sense as "because of." That is, *by virtue of the crown* of Torah with which the righteous adorned God in this world, they merit to rise and gaze upon Him in the next.

Cf. BT *Ketubbot* 111b: "[*Your dead will live, my corpses will arise. Awake and shout for joy, O dwellers in the dust!*] *For your dew is a dew of lights, and the earth will give birth to spirits of the dead* (Isaiah 26:19). Whoever makes use of the light of Torah, the light of Torah will revive him. Whoever does not make use of the light of Torah, the light of Torah does not revive him."

See also Maimonides, *Mishneh Torah, Hilkhot Teshuvah* 8:2: "In the world to come... the righteous will sit with their crowns on their heads and delight in the splendor of *Shekhinah*.... They will possess the knowledge that they grasped that allowed them to merit the life of the world to come. This will be their crown, like that which was said by Solomon: *With the crown with which his mother crowned him* (Song of Songs 3:11)."

491. **אמו (*Immo*), *His mother* . . . אומו (*ummo*), His people...** The word אום (*um*), "people," is attested in the Bible only in the plural, in the book of Psalms. Cf. *Shir ha-Shirim Rabbah* on 3:11 (quoted above, note 488), which makes a different verbal link using the same "mother–people" motif. See also *Pesiqta de-Rav Kahana* 1:3.

492. **What is meant by *his wedding*?...** If the wedding day mentioned in the verse from the Song of Songs refers to the righteous, what does it signify? According to Rabbi Pinḥas it refers to their becoming a bar mitsvah, the joy of which is compared to a wedding day.

Cf. *Shir ha-Shirim Rabbah* on 3:11: "*On the day of his wedding*—Sinai.... *On the day of his heart's delight*—words of Torah, as is said: *The commandments of YHVH are just, rejoicing the heart* (Psalms 19:9)." See also M *Ta'anit* 4:8.

On the significance of the age thirteen, see *Avot de-Rabbi Natan* A, 16; *Bereshit Rabbah* 53:10; *Qohelet Rabbah* on 4:13; *Midrash Tehillim* 9:5; *Zohar* 1:78a–79b (*ST*), 179a–b; 2:98a; *ZḤ* 10c (*MhN*); Tishby, *Wisdom of the Zohar*, 2:762; Ta-Shma, *Ha-Nigleh she-ba-Nistar*, 34–35.

The "merit" for which the righteous are revived refers to Torah study and the performance of the commandments.

a herald to pass over every single tombstone, at that time the *neshamah* will descend like a luminous spark—radiating the brilliance of the firmament of heaven upon the body awakening from the earth, as is written: *Let there be lights in the firmament of heaven.* Why? *To shine upon the earth* (ibid., 15)—upon the body emerging from the earth."[493]

Rabbi Abbahu said, "This is זהר הרוח (*zohar ha-ruaḥ*), the radiance of the spirit, hovering over the body to revive it, illuminating its darkness, as is written: *Let there be lights in the firmament of heaven.* Why? *To shine upon the earth*—upon that emerging from the earth, as we have said."[494]

Rabbi Yehudah son of Pazzi encountered Rav Naḥman. He asked him, "That spirit with which the blessed Holy One is destined to revive the dead, what is it?"

He replied, "It is the spirit of the speculum above, whereby people will attain true knowledge. How do we know? From what is written: *I will place My spirit in you and you will live* (Ezekiel 37:14). The verse does not say *I will place spirit in you,* but rather *My spirit*—the one emanated from My speculum, and similarly: *I will place My spirit in your midst* (ibid. 36:27). Afterward they will be a manifest sign in the world, as is written: *they will be for signs and for appointed times, for days and years* (Genesis 1:14)."[495] [16a]



493. **the *neshamah* will descend like a luminous spark...** The divine utterance *Let there be lights* is interpreted to signify the revival of the dead—with the *me'orot*, "celestial lights," intimating the brilliance of the soul returning to earth to awaken the body. On the revival of the dead, cf. *Pirqei de-Rabbi Eli'ezer* 34: "Rabbi Yehudah said, '... In the time to come, the blessed Holy One will bring down a dew of revival, reviving the dead... *For your dew is a dew of lights* (Isaiah 26:19)....'" See also *Zohar* 1:116a–b (*MhN*), 130b, 232a; 2:28b.

494. **This is זהר הרוח (*zohar ha-ruaḥ*), the radiance of the spirit...** At the resurrection, the body is infused with the soul's light, now termed "radiance of the spirit."

495. ***My spirit*—the one emanated from My speculum...** At the resurrection, the dead will not merely receive spirit, but will be infused directly by the divine spirit. The context of the first verse cited from Ezekiel is the famous vision of dry bones: *Thus said the Lord YHVH, "I am going to open your graves and lift you out of the graves, O My people, and bring you to the land of Israel. You shall know, O My people, that I am YHVH when I have opened your graves and lifted you out of your graves. I will place My breath* [or: *spirit*] *in you and you will live....*" (Ezekiel 37:12–14). Similarly, Ezekiel 36:26–27 reads: *I will give you a new heart and put a new spirit into you. I will remove the heart of stone from your body and give you a heart of flesh, and I will place My spirit in your midst. Thus I will cause you to follow My laws and faithfully observe My rules.*

On the "speculum above," see above, note 462.

Infused with the divine spirit and possessing perfected knowledge, the resurrected righteous will be signs to the world, just as the luminaries are signs in the firmament.

The idea that the resurrected righteous will attain הדעות הנכונות (*ha-de'ot ha-nekhonot*), "true knowledge," is reminiscent of Maimonides' accounts of the world to come in *Mishneh Torah, Hilkhot Teshuvah* 8:2, and in *Pereq Ḥeleq*. Where for Maimonides attainment of the truth of the blessed Holy One is

*God said, "Let us make a human being in our image"* (Genesis 1:26).[496]

Rabbi Abbahu opened, "*What is a human that You are mindful of him, a human being that You take note of him? You made him little less than God!* (Psalms 8:5–6)."[497]

Rabbi Tanḥum said, "When the blessed Holy One sought to create the human being, He consulted with the angels surrounding His throne. He said to them, 'Let us make a human being.' They replied, 'Master of the Universe, what is the nature of this human being? *What is a human that You are mindful of him?*'"[498]

conditional upon the absence of a body, for *MhN* metaphysical apprehension and corporeality can co-exist. See *Zohar* 1:113b–114a, 126a, 135a–b, 140a (all *MhN*).

496. ***Let us make a human being in our image*** The verse continues: *by our likeness.* This verse is famous for its use of the plural form—seemingly challenging God's unity.



497. ***What is a human that You are mindful of him...*** The preceding verse reads: *When I behold Your heavens, the work of Your fingers, the moon and stars that You set in place....* The Psalmist wonders about the exalted status of the human being when viewed against the backdrop of the celestial realm.

498. **He consulted with the angels surrounding His throne...** See BT *Sanhedrin* 38b: "Rav Yehudah said in the name of Rav, 'When the blessed Holy One sought to create the human being, He [first] created a company of ministering angels and asked them, "Is it your desire that we make the human being in our image?" They responded, "Master of the Universe, what are his deeds?" He replied, "Such and such are his deeds." They exclaimed, "Master of the Universe, *What is a human that You are mindful of him, a human being that You take note of him?* (Psalms 8:5)." He stretched out His little finger among them and burned them. The same thing happened with a second company. The third company said to Him, "Master of the Universe, the former ones who spoke in Your presence—what did they accomplish? The entire world is Yours! Whatever you wish to do in Your world, do it."'... Rabbi Yoḥanan said, 'The blessed Holy One does not do anything without consulting with the *pamalya*, retinue, above, as is said: *This sentence is decreed by the watchers; this verdict is commanded by the holy ones* (Daniel 4:14).'"

See also *Bereshit Rabbah* 8:4: "Rabbi Ḥanina... [said], 'When He came to create Adam He consulted with the ministering angels, saying to them, "*Let us make a human being in our image, by our likeness.*" They said to Him, "This human, what is his nature?" He replied, "Righteous people shall spring from him."... Had He revealed to them that the wicked would spring from him, the attribute of Justice would not have permitted him to be created.'"

See also *Bereshit Rabbah* 8:8: "Rabbi Shemu'el son of Naḥman said in the name of Rabbi Yonatan, '...*Let us make a human being in our image*—[God explained this to Moses as follows:] "If a great man comes to obtain permission [for a proposed action] from one that is less than he, he may say, 'Why should I ask permission from my inferior!' Then they will answer him, 'Learn from your Creator, who created the upper and lower [realms], yet when He came to create the human being He consulted with the ministering angels.'"' Rabbi Levi said, 'There is no taking counsel here, but it may be compared to a king who was strolling at the door of his palace when he saw a clod lying about. He said, "What shall we do with it?" Some answered, "[Use it in building] public baths"; others answered, "private

Rabbi Buta said, "We have gone over the entire Torah—and have not found that the blessed Holy One ever consulted with the angels about anything concerning all that He needed to do. Furthermore, we have found that there is nothing above and below that apprehends the blessed Holy One's mind! When they run to apprehend—immediately they return back from their apprehension, like canary cannabis that flies and returns to its place of origin. So with them, until they return, saying, '*Blessed be the glory of YHVH from His place* (Ezekiel 3:12).'"[499]

Rabbi Buta said further, "We have seen that the blessed Holy One created the primal light, and from this light created His other servants. If He did not consult with the primal light created at first when He wished to bring forth His other hosts, how much more so concerning the *human being who is like unto breath* (Psalms 144:4)?"[500]

Rabbi Yitsḥak said, "Let Rabbi Buta be, for he has set his abode with the Masters of Mishnah!"[501]



baths." The king said, "I will make a statue of it." Who then can hinder him?'"

Cf. *Bereshit Rabbah* 8:3, 8:5, 8:7, where the plural form is explained in diverse ways. Cf. Maimonides, *Guide of the Perplexed* 2:6.

499. **We have gone over the entire Torah...** The classical midrashic solutions fail for lack of evidence. Moreover, the angels are so far removed from God that they could not possibly fathom His thought. Consulting with them is therefore nonsensical.

The angels' limited apprehension of the divine mind is compared to קנבוסא דקונארי (*qanbosa de-qonarei*), rendered here as "canary cannabis," though the term is of uncertain meaning. See Matt, *Zohar: The Book of Enlightenment*, 226. See Ḥayyim Palagi, *Sefer Ḥayyim u-Mazon*, 24: "a spindle of linen that is thrown above and returns to its starting place, like that which is said: Throw a stick into the air, and it will fall back to its place of origin [the ground].... More likely it speaks of a kind of bird that has just started to move [or: hop] about and is emerging from its nest, but can't yet move about [stably] and returns to its nest." Edri, *Sullam*, and *Matoq mi-Devash* understand the phrase as referring to a kind of bird. On the motif of flying and returning to the place of origin, cf. Ezekiel 1:14, where the creatures surrounding the divine throne are described as *darting to and fro.*

This disparaging view of the angels should be contrasted with other passages in *MhN* (8d and 16c), where they are viewed as sitting atop the chain of being—beneath only the blessed Holy One. See Asulin, "Midrash ha-Ne'lam li-Vreshit," 240.

On the limited angelic apprehension, see *Pirqei de-Rabbi Eli'ezer* 4: "The living beings stand at the side of the Throne of His Glory and they do not know the place of His glory. They respond and say in every place where His glory is, '*Blessed be the glory of YHVH from His place.*'" Cf. BT *Ḥagigah* 13b; *Zohar* 1:103a; 3:159a; *ZḤ* 9d (*MhN*). See also the *Musaf Qedushah*.

500. **If He did not consult with the primal light...** The primal light is the first creation, the angelic form, referred to above as the "light of the Great Intellect" (*ZḤ* 8d, *MhN*)—apparently signifying Metatron, the chief angel. See also *Zohar* 1:126b, 127b (both *MhN*).

The preceding verse from Psalms reads: *YHVH, what is a human creature that You should know him, the son of man, that You pay him mind?* (Psalms 144:3).

501. **set his abode with the Masters of**

Rabbi Buta replied, "I have not merited that my abode be with them. But the question was theirs, and I have heard the solution. As Rabbi Bo said: 'Like a king ruling over all who wished to demonstrate that all are comprised within him, and that he is all—and thus referred to himself in the plural. So with the blessed Holy One; in order to demonstrate that the entire world is His, and all is comprised in His hand, He spoke in the plural—demonstrating that He is all.'"[502]

Rabbi Yitsḥak said, "Only if from a voice on high you had heard this, would I say that it is fine, because this solution does not sit well in my heart."[503]

Rabbi Shim'on son of Yoḥai came to Tiberias to purify all the streets of Tiberias.[504] Rabbi Pinḥas, Rabbi Bo, and Rabbi Yitsḥak saw him. They said, "How long must we sit on a single pillar unable to proceed?"[505]

They said, "Look, a Master of Mishnah is here! Let us inquire in his presence."



**Mishnah** It may be that Rabbi Yitsḥak is suggesting that Rabbi Buta's interpretation (rejecting angelic consultation and more generally criticizing the angelic rank) be granted, as he belongs to the group of esoteric masters whose teachings are authoritative. Alternatively, perhaps Rabbi Yitsḥak is being ironic: Oh, that Rabbi Buta—he hangs out with the *marei de-matnitin*, Masters of Mishnah, and they think that angels are nothing! The following pages appear to contain a subtle argument between those who would place human beings (or the human soul) at the head of the chain of being just beneath God, and those who would place angels in this position.

On the term "Masters of Mishnah," see above, note 462.

502. **referred to himself in the plural...** On the majestic plural, see Saadia, *Sefer Emunot ve-De'ot*, 2:6; Abraham Ibn Ezra on Genesis 1:26; Baḥya ben Asher on Genesis 1:26: "It is the manner of kings and dignitaries that the individual speaks in the plural; this is the style of stature and honor."

From Rabbi Buta's reply to Rabbi Yitsḥak, it seems that "membership" of the Masters of Mishnah is not rigid. Apparently, some rabbis are loosely associated with them without formally belonging to this group.

503. **if from a voice on high...** Rabbi Yitsḥak is not satisfied with Rabbi Buta's interpretation. His dissatisfaction is the "trigger" for the story that follows.

504. **to purify all the streets of Tiberias...** According to rabbinic sources, after emerging from thirteen years in a cave, Rabbi Shim'on and his son soaked their sore and sickly bodies in the mineral hot springs of Tiberias. In gratitude for being healed and rejuvenated, Rabbi Shim'on proceeded to purify the city, which was considered impure because it had been built by Herod Antipas on the site of obliterated tombs.

See JT *Shevi'it* 9:1, 38d; *Bereshit Rabbah* 79:6; BT *Shabbat* 33b–34a; *Pesiqta de-Rav Kahana* 11:16; *Qohelet Rabbah* on 10:8. See *Zohar* 2:37a; 3:72b.

505. **How long must we sit on a single pillar...** Namely, how long will we be without a firm foundation, unable to answer heretics about the plural form in the verse from Genesis.

Cf. the opening of the *Idra Rabbah* (*Zohar* 3:127b), where Rabbi Shim'on asks the Companions: "How long will we sit on a one-legged stand?" See Liebes, *Peraqim*, 359–60; idem, *Studies in the Zohar*, 12–19.

Rabbi Abbahu arrived there. They said to him, "If we do not hear about this matter, then look, this verse provides an opening for the heretics!"[506]

He said to him, "May the master tell us the essence of the verse."

He asked him, "Which one?"

He replied, "This one: *Let us make a human being in our image, by our likeness* (Genesis 1:26)."

Rabbi Shim'on said, "It is written: *O deaf ones, listen! O blind ones, look and see!* (Isaiah 42:18). Now, did the Torah really say this to the blind and the deaf?! Rather, *blind ones*—blind in Torah; for though the straight path is before them, they stumble round about like the blind, not comprehending the essence of the matter.[507]

"This verse has been decreed in our Mishnah, and so have we ordained: When the blessed Holy One created the world, the fundamental element of all was water; from water the entire world disseminated. The blessed Holy One made three artisans to perform His handiwork in this world: heaven, earth, and water. Through them everything that exists in this world was created.[508]



506. **this verse provides an opening for the heretics** See *Bereshit Rabbah* 8:8. See also Rashi on Genesis 1:26.

On trinitarian interpretations of this verse—which may be the polemical context for the *Zohar*'s comments—see, for example, Augustine of Hippo, *City of God* 16:6; *On the Trinity* 7:6; 12:6; *Unfinished Literal Commentary on Genesis*, no. 56, 61.

507. ***O deaf ones, listen! O blind ones, look and see!...*** See *Aggadat Bereshit* (Buber) 70:2; *Zohar* 1:224a. Cf. BT *Ḥagigah* 12b: "Rabbi Yose said, 'Woe to creatures—for they see, but do not know what they see; they stand, but do not know on what they stand!'"

See Asulin, "Midrash ha-Ne'lam li-Vreshit," 239. On "essence of the matter," see above, note 481.

508. **three artisans to perform His handiwork...** See *Bereshit Rabbah* 12:5: "Rabbi Neḥemiah of Sikhnin expounded, '*For in six days YHVH made heaven and earth, [the sea, and all that is in them]* (Exodus 20:11): these three things constitute the fundamental elements of the creation of the world. They waited three days and then produced three offspring. According to the House of Hillel, the earth was created on the first day, [then] waited three days—the first, second, and third—and brought forth three offspring: trees, vegetation, and the Garden of Eden. The firmament [heaven] was created on the second day, waited three days—the second, third, and fourth—and brought forth three offspring: the sun, moon, and constellations. The waters were created on the third day, waited three days—the third, fourth, and fifth—and brought forth three offspring: birds, fish, and the Leviathan.'"

See also *ZḤ* 13a (*MhN*), page 103; cf. *Zohar* 3:219b (*RM*).

As is made clear below, these "three artisans" comprise the four foundation elements.

Genesis 1:1–2 suggests that water was the fundamental element of all: *At the beginning of God's creating of the heavens and the earth, when the earth was wild and waste, darkness over the ocean-deep, the spirit of God hovering over the waters.* See above at note 300, *ZḤ* 12a (*MhN*).

"Disseminated" renders אשתיל (*ishetil*), literally "was planted," a play on "from which the world הושתת (*hushtat*), was founded," as found in rabbinic texts about the Foundation

"He summoned these three, each one of them, to produce the creations necessary for the world. He summoned the waters; He said to them, 'You, bring forth the earth beneath you; you, go and assemble in a single place.' The waters did so, as is written: *Let the waters be gathered* (Genesis 1:9). He summoned the earth; He said to her, 'You, bring forth creatures from within you: beasts and animals and the like.' Immediately she did so, as is written: *God said, 'Let the earth bring forth living beings according to their kind'* (ibid., 24). He summoned the heavens; He said to them, 'You, separate between water and water.' They did so, as is written: *God made the expanse* [*and separated the waters*] (ibid., 7).[509] [16b]

"He summoned the earth and said to her, 'Bring forth grasses, vegetation, crops, and trees of the field.' What is written immediately after? *The earth brought forth vegetation, plants yielding seed* (ibid., 12). He likewise summoned the heavens; He said to them, 'Let there be in you lights and luminaries to illuminate the earth,' as is written: *Let there be lights in the expanse of heaven* (ibid., 14). He likewise summoned the waters; He said to them, 'You, bring forth swarms of fish and fowl and the like,' as is written: *Let the waters swarm with a swarm of living beings* [*and let fowl fly above the earth*] (ibid., 20).[510]

"Through these three, all the work of creation was performed, each one in its own way.

"When the sixth day arrived, all of them were ready to create just like the other days. The blessed Holy One said to them, 'None of you can create this creation alone—as was the case with all the other creations until now. Rather, all of you must join in unison and I with you—and we will make the human being, for you are unable to make him by yourselves. Indeed the body will be yours—from the three of you—but the soul will be Mine.'

"Therefore the blessed Holy One summoned them and said to them, '*Let us make a human being* (Genesis 1:26)—Me and you; Me the soul, and you the body.' So it was; for the body came from the three of them, the artisans of the work of creation, while the blessed Holy One bestowed the soul, through which He partnered with them.[511]

Stone (see, for example, BT *Yoma* 54b). See *ZḤ* 28a (*MhN*); Moses de León, *Sheqel ha-Qodesh*, 74–75 (95); *Zohar* 1:72a, 78a, 82a, 231a; 2:48b, 222a; Liebes, *Peraqim*, 372–73.

On the use of the term "decree" to establish a teaching, see note 404. On the expression "our Mishnah," see note 468.

509. **He summoned these three...** Corresponding to the creative acts of days 3, 6, and 2.

510. **He summoned...** Corresponding to the creative acts of days 3, 4, and 5.

511. ***'Let us make a human being*—Me and you...** This homily derives from Naḥmanides on Genesis 1:26, which in turn derives from Radak, ad loc.: "The correct explanation of נעשה (*na'aseh*), *let us make*, is as follows: It has been shown to you that God created something from nothing only on the first day.... *Let us make a human being*—the earth to bring forth the body from its elements (as it did with animals and beasts), as is written: *YHVH God formed the human of the dust from the soil*, and

"'*In our image, by our likeness* (ibid.)—that is to say, befitting us; through the body taken from you, to know you and be similar to you; through that taken from Me, namely the soul, to withdraw from worldly affairs—that his yearning and desire be for sublimely holy matters.[512]

"'Further, *In our image, by our likeness*—the body taken from you will not abide enduringly like you. What is meant by "like you"? Like the creations you engendered, because it is dust like all the other creations. But the holy soul that I have placed within him will exist eternally, for it is incorporeal, similar in its existence to Me.'"[513]

Rabbi Abbahu said, "This is indeed the lucidity of the matter! For we find that these three—heaven, earth, and water—were present at creation."[514]

Rabbi El'azar son of Rabbi Shim'on said, "This is fine, but the earth alone absorbed the power of the three of them, so that the four foundations inhered in her—from the heavens, two; from the waters, one; and one from within herself. She produced the lifeless matter of the human being; and the blessed Holy One, the soul—as is written: *YHVH God formed the human of dust from the soil* 155
*and blew into his nostrils the soul of life* (Genesis 2:7). Look, the two of them—the earth and the blessed Holy One—partnered as one to create him. That is why He said, '*Let us make a human being*' (ibid. 1:26)—the blessed Holy One said to her, 'You make the body, and I the soul.'"[515]

He . . . bestowed the spirit. . . . And He said: *In our image, by our likeness*, as the human will then be similar to both. In the capacity of his body, he will be similar to the earth from which he was taken, and in spirit he will be similar to the higher beings, because it . . . will not die." See *Zohar* 3:238b (*RM*). See Gottlieb, *Meḥqarim*, 540–42; Oron, "Midrash ha-Ne'lam: Muqdam u-Me'uḥar," 134; Asulin, "Midrash ha-Ne'lam li-Vreshit," 238–39.

Cf. *Bereshit Rabbah* 8:3: "*God said, 'Let us make a human being . . .'* With whom did He consult? Rabbi Yehoshu'a son of Levi said, 'He consulted with the works of heaven and earth, like a king who had two advisers without whose knowledge he did nothing whatsoever.'" Cf. *Zohar* 1:34b; 2:55a, 173b.

512. **through the body taken from you, to know you and be similar to you . . .** The duality of the human being means that he is both at home in the world and capable of turning from physical existence to more spiritual pursuits. See *ZḤ* 18b (*MhN*), page 186.

513. ***In our image, by our likeness . . .*** In the image of heaven and earth and divinity, the human being is both finite (i.e., the body dies and decays) and eternal (i.e., the soul, *neshamah* lives forever in the world to come). While heaven and earth are not finite, their offspring are.

On the human being as dust and returning to dust, see Genesis 2:7: *YHVH God formed the human of dust from the soil*; ibid. 3:19: *for dust you are, and to dust you shall return*; and Ecclesiastes 3:20: *All comes from the dust and all returns to the dust*. See *Zohar* 1:170a.

514. **heaven, earth, and water—were present at creation** See *Bereshit Rabbah* 12:5. See above, note 508.

515. **the two of them . . . partnered as one to create him . . .** Rabbi El'azar simplifies Rabbi Shim'on's homily, reducing the agents of human creation to two: the blessed Holy One and the earth. The earth absorbed the

Rabbi Yitsḥak said, "At last, this doubt has been entirely resolved for us!"[516]

Rabbi El'azar said further, "The blessed Holy One always takes part in the creation of human beings in the same way. For look at what we have learned: There are three partners in the creation of a human being: a man, and his wife, and the blessed Holy One!"[517]

Rabbi Yehoshu'a said, "Similarly, heaven, earth, and the blessed Holy One."[518]

Rabbi Shim'on said, "Heaven—corresponding to the man; earth—corresponding to his wife; and the blessed Holy One always partnered with them. That is why it says *Let us make a human being*—employing an expression of partnership. The blessed Holy One, however, is not partnered with any other creature aside from the human being."

Rabbi Yose said, "And the other creatures—who is partnered with them?"

Rabbi Shim'on replied, "The power of the earth, as we have said, namely the creaturely soul. The blessed Holy One, however, partners only with the human being alone."[519]

156 Rabbi Yehudah said, "Woe to the wicked, who do not desire to cleave to the partnership of the blessed Holy One!"

How so?[520]

power of the other artisans—from the heavens, fire and wind; as well as water—so that the four elements were concentrated within her alone. The human being is thus a composite of the earth (with the four elements comprising the body) and of the soul bequeathed from God.

Cf. Maimonides, *Guide of the Perplexed* 2:30: "'Earth' is an equivocal term used in a general and a particular sense. In a general sense, it is applied to all that is beneath the sphere of the moon—I mean the four elements. In a particular sense, it is applied to one element—the last among them, namely earth."

516. **this doubt has been entirely resolved for us** Namely, the use of the plural form in the verse *Let us make a human being.* (Rabbi Yitsḥak had been dissatisfied with Rabbi Buta's earlier solution to the problem.)

517. **There are three partners...** God is directly involved in the creation not only of the first human, but also of all people. See BT *Niddah* 31a: "Our Rabbis taught: There are three partners in [the creation of] a human being: the blessed Holy One, his father, and his mother. His father inseminates the white substance—out of which are formed the child's bones, sinews, nails, the brain in his head, and the white in his eye. His mother inseminates the red substance—out of which is formed the child's skin, flesh, hair, and the black of his eye. The blessed Holy One bestows spirit, breath (*neshamah*), countenance, eyesight, the capacity to hear, the capacity to speak, the capacity to walk, understanding, and discernment." See also BT *Qiddushin* 30b; *Zohar* 2:93a, 3:83a (*Piq*), 219b; *ZḤ* 49a.

518. **Similarly, heaven, earth...** Heaven and earth are the source of the physical elements comprising the body; hence they are continuously involved in the creation of human beings.

519. **The blessed Holy One...partners only...** Only human beings enjoy the intimate association with God through the gift of the soul, *neshamah*. Other creatures possess only the creaturely soul.

520. **How so?** How does a person cleave

Rabbi Yitsḥak said, "To the *neshamah* He bestowed—cleaving instead to the power of the beasts, as is written: *The human does not abide in glory, he is like the beasts that perish* (Psalms 49:13). *Does not abide*—for he did not wish to remain in the glory and splendor of the *neshamah*. But what sin then did he commit? That *he is like the beasts*—in respect of their power, which is quickly destroyed and perishes, [16c] not ascending above."[521]

Rabbi Shim'on son of Pazzi said, "This accords with what Rabbi Ya'akov son of Idi said, 'What is the meaning of the verse *His eye beholds every glorious thing* (Job 28:10)? These are the souls of the righteous, who are glory and splendor forever and ever.'"[522]

Rabbi Abbahu said in the name of Rabbi Yonatan, "Come and see the sublimity of the human being, for the blessed Holy One distinguished him from all the other creations!"

How so?

Rabbi Abbahu explained, "Whatever that the blessed Holy One created, He instructed those workers to do on their own, without joining with them. Concerning the creatures of the earth He said, '*Let the earth bring forth living beings . . .*' (Genesis 1:24); He said to the waters, '*Let the waters swarm*' (ibid., 20); but He did not join with them. But when He created the human being, the blessed Holy One joined with them in his creation and said, '*Let us make a human being*' (ibid., 26). He bestowed upon him: countenance; sight; the sense of smell; the ability to get up, walk, feel, speak, and make. And He gave him dominion over the work of His hands, as is written: *You make him rule over the*



to the partnership of the blessed Holy One? In contrast, how do the wicked behave?

521. ***The human does not abide in glory, He is like the beasts that perish . . .*** Instead of abiding in glory, i.e., cleaving to the *neshamah*, most human beings opt instead to cleave to the *nefesh ḥayah*, "creaturely soul." On the *neshamah* and *nefesh ḥayah* in *MhN*, see *ZḤ* 10c, 11a, 11c, 17c.

Rabbi Yitsḥak reinterprets a rabbinic myth about Adam's not abiding in the Garden of Eden for even one night. Adam's failure, like the wicked after him, was his cleaving to the creaturely soul. See BT *Sanhedrin* 38b: "Rabbi Yoḥanan son of Ḥanina said, 'The day consisted of twelve hours. In the first hour, his [Adam's] dust was gathered; in the second, it was kneaded into a shapeless mass; in the third, his limbs were shaped; in the fourth, a soul was infused into him; in the fifth, he arose and stood on his feet; in the sixth, he gave [the animals their] names; in the seventh, Eve became his mate; in the eighth, they ascended to bed as two and descended as four; in the ninth, he was commanded not to eat of the tree; in the tenth, he sinned; in the eleventh, he was tried; and in the twelfth he was expelled and departed, as is said: *The human does not abide* [literally: *spend the night*] *in glory*.'" See also *Bereshit Rabbah* 11:2, 12:6; *Avot de-Rabbi Natan* A, 1; *Pirqei de-Rabbi Eli'ezer* 19.

522. ***every glorious thing? . . .*** The word יקר (*yaqar*), *glorious* [or: *glory*], refers to the righteous. Cf. *Bemidbar Rabbah* 19:6; *Tanḥuma* (Buber), *Ḥuqqat* 24, where this verse is applied to "Rabbi Akiva and his companions."

*work of Your hands, all things You set under his feet* (Psalms 8:7). When He infused the *neshamah* within him, he rose to his feet and resembled the lower and upper realms. His body resembled the earth, and his *neshamah* the upper worlds—in appearance, majesty, glory, fear, and awe, as is written: *You adorned him with glory and majesty* (ibid. 8:6)."[523]

Rabbi Yonatan said, "The beginning of this verse raises doubts in my heart, as is written: *You made him little less than God* (ibid.)!"[524]

Rabbi Abbahu said, "By virtue of his *neshamah*, which is holy and similar to Him. What then constitutes his deficiency? Because he is corporeal, taken from the earth.[525]

"Now, you might say, 'By virtue of knowledge and wisdom'—but this is impossible, for the human being is far indeed from the supernal realms. As Rabbi El'azar said in the name of Rabbi Tanḥum: 'The angels that are nearest are first to receive the power of the influx of the speculum above; from them, it descends to those that are not so near; and from them it descends to the heavens and all their array; and from them to the human being.'"[526]



Rabbi Yose said, "The Throne of Glory receives first; from it to the supernal angels; and from them to those not as exalted or supernal as they; and from them to the heavens; and from them to the human being."[527]

523. **resembled the lower and upper realms...** Cf. Naḥmanides on Genesis 1:26: "Thus the human being is similar both to the lower and upper beings in appearance and majesty, as is written: *You adorned him with glory and majesty*, meaning that the goal before him is wisdom, knowledge, and skill of deed. In real likeness his body thus compares to the earth, while his soul is similar to the higher beings." Note that in the *Zohar*'s paraphrase of Naḥmanides' commentary, there is no mention of wisdom and knowledge. See below, note 526. See Asulin, "Midrash ha-Ne'lam li-Vreshit," 239.

On being bestowed with a human countenance and various capacities, cf. BT *Niddah* 31a; see above, note 517.

524. ***You made him little less than God*** The verse's formulation seems troubling: Is the human being only a little less than God?! How can one make such a comparison?

Cf. BT *Rosh ha-Shanah* 21b, where Rav and Shemu'el teach: "Fifty gates of understanding were created in the world, all of which were given to Moses except for one, as is said: *You made him little less than God* (Psalms 8:6)."

525. **By virtue of his *neshamah*...** The comparison with God is possible by virtue of the soul. Human beings are *less than God* on account of their corporeality.

526. **Now, you might say, 'By virtue of knowledge and wisdom'...** The comparison with God is only possible because of the soul. In terms of wisdom and knowledge, such a comparison is unfathomable.

In contrast to the attitude of Naḥmanides (see above, note 523) and of most Jewish philosophers, Rabbi Abbahu here rejects the notion that human beings are god-like because of their intellectual faculties. As is clear from Rabbi El'azar's statement, in terms of intellectual apprehension, human beings are at the very bottom of the hierarchy (see also *ZḤ* 8d *MhN*). The *neshamah* alone accounts for humanity's exalted status. See Asulin, "Midrash ha-Ne'lam li-Vreshit," 239.

On the "speculum above," see above, note 462.

527. **The Throne of Glory receives first...**

How then does the human being resemble Him?

Rabbi Abbahu said, "By virtue of the *neshamah* that is holy, never to be annihilated, for it derives from Him—from His power and His might—unlike the body derived from the ground, which will be annihilated and return to dust as it once was."

Rabbi Yitsḥak said in the name of Rav, "Adam and his partner with him were created together, as is written: *male and female He created them* (Genesis 5:2). He removed her from his back, and brought her to the man, as is written: *He took one of his sides* (ibid. 2:21)."[528]

Rabbi Yehoshu'a said, "This was the original Eve. He took her from him; she is 'wounds wreaked upon creatures.' As is written: *He took one of his sides* (ibid. 2:21)—the first one taken from him, because she is a malignant spirit. *And he closed the flesh in its place* (ibid.)—for he raised another in her place."[529]



Rabbi Yose offers a different "chain of being," though the point is the same: human beings are at the bottom.

As noted in the Introduction, in *MhN* the choice of language (Hebrew versus Aramaic) sometimes reflects the argument. This is one such passage. The more conventional philosophical view—which places human beings beneath the angels (i.e., the separate intellects)—is expressed in Hebrew. The competing view—ascribing the human soul to divinity itself—is couched (overwhelmingly) in Aramaic. See Asulin, "Midrash ha-Ne'lam li-Vreshit," 238–40.

528. **Adam and his partner with him were created together...** Namely, conjoined. See *Bereshit Rabbah* 8:1: "Rabbi Yirmeyah son of El'azar said, 'When the blessed Holy One created Adam, He created him androgynous, as is said: *Male and female He created them* (Genesis 5:2).' Rabbi Shemu'el son of Naḥman said, 'When the blessed Holy One created Adam, He created him with two faces. Then He sawed him and gave him two backs, one on this side and one on that.'"

On the androgynous nature of the original human being, see Plato, *Symposium* 189d–191d; BT *Berakhot* 61a, *Eruvin* 18a; *Vayiqra Rabbah* 14:1; *Tanḥuma, Tazri'a* 1; *Tanḥuma* (Buber), *Tazri'a* 2; *Midrash Tehillim* 139:5; *Bahir* 116–17 (172); *Zohar* 1:2b, 13b, 34b–35a, 37b, 47a, 55b, 70b, 165a; 2:55a, 144b, 167b, 176b (*SdTs*), 178b (*SdTs*), 231a–b; 3:5a, 19a, 44b, 292b (*IZ*).

The word צלע (*tsela*) in Genesis 2:21, often construed as "rib," can also mean "side," as in Exodus 26:20. The passage's simple sense tolerates either reading of this word.

See *Bereshit Rabbah* 18:1: "*YHVH Elohim* ויבן (*va-yiven*), *fashioned, the rib* (Genesis 2:22). . . . It was taught in the name of Rabbi Shim'on son of Yoḥai: 'He adorned her like a bride and brought her to him. There are places where they call a braid בניתא (*binyata*).'" See also BT *Berakhot* 61a; *Avot de-Rabbi Natan* A, 4.

529. **original Eve...** See *Alfa Beita de-Ven Sira*, ed. Yassif, 231–34, according to which Lilith was Adam's original wife. Insisting on her equality, Lilith refused to lie beneath Adam and flew away. Here, as throughout the *Zohar*, she is presented as a demonic spirit, seeking to harm human beings.

See *Zohar* 1:34b, 148a–b (*ST*); 2:231b; 3:19a, 76b–77a; Margaliot, *Mal'akhei Elyon*, 235–41; Scholem, *Kabbalah*, 356–61; Tishby, *Wisdom of the Zohar*, 2:464–65.

See also *Bereshit Rabbah* 17:6: "Rabbi Ḥanina son of Rav Adda said, 'From the beginning of the book until here [i.e., the

Rava said, "This one was flesh, while the other was not flesh. What was she? Rabbi Yitsḥak said, 'Slime and dregs of the earth.'"[530]

Rabbi Tanḥum said, "When the blessed Holy One created the human being, He bestowed upon him a radiant visage—illuminating the entire world. As soon as he sinned, what is written about him? *The splendor of his visage has changed* (Ecclesiastes 8:1)."[531]

Rabbi Eli'ezer and Rabbi Akiva were walking on the way. Rabbi Akiva said to him, "Rabbi, tell me, concerning what is written: *Let us make a human being* (Genesis 1:26), why doesn't it immediately say *it was so*, as is the case with all the other days? For whenever the blessed Holy One commanded a particular thing, immediately it says *it was so* (ibid., 7, 9, 11, 15, 24). Here, however, it is not stated. Rather, after He said *Let us make a human being*, it is written: *God created the human being* (ibid., 27). The verse should have said *it was so!*"[532]

He replied, "Akiva, was that the only instance in the Account of Creation? Look at what is written: *God said, 'Let there be an expanse amid the waters'* (ibid., 6), and the verse says only: *God made the expanse* (ibid., 7)! Similarly: *Let there be lights in the expanse of heaven to shine upon the earth* (ibid., 14, 15). The verse should have immediately stated *it was so*, however it is written: *God made* [16d] *the two great lights* (ibid. 1:16).[533]



verse *He took one of his sides* ויסגור (*va-yisgor*), *and He closed, the flesh in its place*], no ס (*samekh*) appears. Once she was created, סטן ["Satan," using a nonbiblical variant spelling], was created with her.'"

"Wounds wreaked upon creatures" renders נזקי דברייתא (*nizqei de-beriyyata*), "injuries inflicted upon human beings" (see *Tosefta Bava Qamma* 1:1; BT *Bava Qamma* 84a). Here the word *nizqei*, "injuries" is associated with רוח מזקת (*ruaḥ mazzeqet*), "malignant spirit." See *Zohar* 1:100a, 201b.

530. **This one was flesh...** The second clause in Genesis 2:21 (*And He closed the flesh in its place*) means that the second Eve was flesh-and-blood—unlike the first Eve, Lilith, who was a malignant spirit.

Apparently Rabbi Yitsḥak intends that the original Eve had to be removed from Adam because she was in fact a "side effect" (pun intended) of the creation of human beings. Cf. *Zohar* 1:148a (*ST*).

531. **As soon as he sinned...** In its simple sense, the verse from Ecclesiastes reads: *A person's wisdom lights up his face;* עז (*oz*), *the boldness* [or: *sternness, harshness*], *of his face is changed.* Here, Rabbi Tanḥum construes עז (*oz*) as "splendor" or "majesty," another sense of the word.

See *Bereshit Rabbah* 12:6: "Our Rabbis say: On Sabbath eve, his luster was withdrawn from him and He banished him from the Garden of Eden, as is written:... *You change his visage and send him away* (Job 14:20)." Cf. BT *Ta'anit* 7b.

532. **why doesn't it immediately say *it was so*...** The creation account in Genesis 1 displays a tight structure, generally marked by a creative utterance followed by the observation that all was performed exactly as commanded. Why doesn't the creation of humanity—the pinnacle of creation—follow this order? Cf. Naḥmanides on Genesis 1:7.

533. **was that the only instance in the Account of Creation...** Rabbi Eli'ezer points out that this structure is not total.

"Now I will tell you. Concerning every entity not possessing the power emanated from above, it is immediately stated *it was so.* For the earth brought them forth with all their works complete, not needing to wait for the supernal power to consummate that work. However, every single entity that the earth brought forth—where the consummate existence of the work did not inhere within her—needed to wait for the arrival of the power from above, engendering the consummate existence of the work.[534]

"So here, concerning the human being. The earth produced what she was able to do, and stood aside until power was conferred from the one able to bestow. That is why it does not immediately say *it was so*—until the blessed Holy One came, imbuing him with the power from above, engendering vital existence."[535]

Rabbi Akiva asked him, "Rabbi, what was the reason the blessed Holy One created the human being specifically on the sixth day?"

He replied, "That there not be an opening for the human to say that he assisted with anything of all that was created."[536]

They walked on. While they were walking Rabbi Eli'ezer rose, lowered his head, and placed his hands over his mouth and wept. Rabbi Akiva asked him, "Rabbi, why are you weeping?"



He replied, "About that which you asked, I have envisioned a vision—and the matter is distressing. O Akiva, Akiva, who will merit [to endure] this prolonged exile? For the person destined to reach *the clouds of heaven* (Daniel 7:13)[537] will

There are other instances where the formula is not followed.

There is an error here in the homily. Rabbi Eli'ezer notes that following the creation of the luminaries in Genesis 1:14, Scripture does not record "it was so." In fact, verse 15 does contain this statement.

534. **Concerning every entity not possessing the power emanated from above...** The various creations can be divided into two categories: those that emerged "fully formed," and those requiring an additional divine boost—the power emanated from above. The former are accompanied by the statement "it was so" as their creation was complete; the latter are accompanied by various other statements, as they required additional divine action for completion—consummate existence.

535. **imbuing him with the power from above...** The human being follows the same pattern. While the earth produced the body, the human being was only complete once infused with the divine breath (the soul).

Rabbinic texts mention Adam as a lifeless mass that is only later infused by divine spirit. See *Bereshit Rabbah* 14:8: "*He blew into his nostrils* [*the soul of life*] (Genesis 2:7). This teaches that He set him up as a lifeless mass reaching from earth to heaven—and then infused a soul into him." See also BT *Sanhedrin* 38a–b; *Avot de-Rabbi Natan* A, 1; *Pirqei de-Rabbi Eli'ezer* 11.

536. **that he assisted with anything of all that was created** See BT *Sanhedrin* 38a: "Our Rabbis taught: Adam was created [last of all beings] on Sabbath eve. Why? Lest the heretics say, "The blessed Holy One had a partner in the work of creation.'" Cf. *Bereshit Rabbah* 1:3.

537. ***the clouds of heaven*** The context is Daniel's nocturnal vision of the Messiah in Daniel 7:13–14: *As I looked on, in the night*

not rise until the sixth day—the sixth millennium—and not before its end without profound repentance, for the dominion of that person is only in the sixth.[538]

"In the seventh, the world will remain fallow and desolate. In the eighth, the world will be renewed as before—and what shall be, shall be! About this is written: *Whoever is left in Zion, who remains in Jerusalem, will be called holy* (Isaiah 4:3). For their sake is said: *May the glory of YHVH endure forever, may YHVH rejoice in His works* (Psalms 104:31)."[539]



*vision, one like a human being came with clouds of heaven. He reached the Ancient of Days and was presented to Him. Dominion, glory, and kingship were given to him. All peoples and nations of every language must serve him. His dominion is an everlasting dominion that shall not pass away, and his kingship, one that shall not be destroyed.* See also BT *Sanhedrin* 98a; *Tanḥuma, Toledot* 14.

538. **will not rise until the sixth day—the sixth millennium...** The Messiah can come anytime between 1240–2240 C.E., though whether he comes sooner rather than later depends entirely upon Israel's behavior.

See BT *Sanhedrin* 97a: "Rav Kattina said, 'The world will exist for six thousand years and for one thousand lie desolate, as is written: *YHVH alone will be exalted on that day* (Isaiah 2:11).'... It has been taught in accordance with Rav Kattina: Just as the seventh year releases one year in seven [by letting the earth lie fallow], so the world releases one millennium in seven [by being fallow and desolate], as is written: *YHVH alone will be exalted on that day*. And it says: *A psalm, a song for the Sabbath day* (Psalms 92:1)—a day that is totally Sabbath [a period of total rest, ceasing, desolation]. And it says: *For a thousand years in Your eyes are like yesterday gone by* (ibid. 90:4)." See also BT *Sanhedrin* 98a on *I, YHVH, will hasten it in its time* (Isaiah 60:22): "Rabbi Yehoshu'a son of Levi pointed out a contradiction. It is written: *in its time*; yet it is written: *I will hasten it*. If they prove worthy, *I will hasten it*; if not, *in its time*."

According to the biblical law of *shemittah*, every seventh year the land is allowed to lie fallow, and at the end of that year all debts are canceled. See Leviticus 25:1–24; Deuteronomy 15:1–3.

According to traditional Jewish chronology, the world was created less than 6000 years ago, at a date corresponding to 3761 B.C.E. Hence, the fifth millennium corresponds to 240/41 C.E.–1239/40 C.E.; the sixth began in 1240/41; and the seventh begins in 2240/41.

See *Zohar* 1:116b–117b; 119a, 127b–128a (*MhN*), 139b–140a (*MhN*); 2:9b–10a; *ZḤ* 28c (*MhN*), 56b–c. Cf. *Zohar* 2:176b (*SdTs*).

539. **In the eighth, the world will be renewed as before...** After one thousand years of complete Sabbath (which can variously mean "rest, ceasing, desolation"), the world will be renewed—though its future nature is totally unknown.

See BT *Sanhedrin* 97b: "Rav Ḥanan son of Taḥlifa sent [word] to Rav Yosef, 'I once met a man who possessed a scroll written in Hebrew in Assyrian characters. I said to him, "Where did you get this?" He replied, "I hired myself as a mercenary in the Roman army, and found it amongst the Roman archives. In it is stated that 4,291 years after the creation, the world will be orphaned. [As to the years following,] some of them will be spent in the war of the great sea monsters, and some in the war of Gog and Magog, and the remaining will be the Messianic era, whilst the blessed Holy One will renew His world only after seven thousand years."'"

On the verses from Psalms and Isaiah, see BT *Sanhedrin* 92a; *Zohar* 1:114a (*MhN*), 119a; 2:10a, 57b.

*These are the generations of heaven*... (Genesis 2:4).[540]

Rabbi Abba said in the name of Rabbi Berekhiah, "After recounting all the generations engendered by heaven and earth, Scriptures comes to clarify, lest you say that all of them were created in six days—this one on this day, and that one on that day. Rather, all the generations that came into being from heaven and earth—when did they come into being? You must know when—*on the day that YHVH God made earth and heaven* (ibid.). Namely, on the very same day precisely, all the generations that came into being from heaven and earth inhered within them, as is written: *on the day that YHVH God made earth and heaven.*"[541]

Rabbi Yeisa said, "Look at what is written: *This is the book of the generations of Adam on the day God created the human being* (Genesis 5:1): if so, on the very same day precisely all the generations came into being!"[542]

540. ***These are the generations of heaven*** The verse continues: *and earth when they were created, on the day that YHVH God made earth and heaven.* The word תולדות (*toledot*), rendered here as "generations," can also mean "offspring, story, account."

541. **on the very same day precisely...** According to the creation account in Genesis 1, creation spanned six days, with God resting on the seventh. According to the second creation account in Genesis 2, creation occurred *on the day*, i.e., in one day. Rabbi Berekhiah has resolved the contradiction: all of creation was indeed accomplished on one day, but revealed (or made manifest) over six days. See above, *ZḤ* 2d (*MhN*), page 4; 13d (*MhN*), page 113.

See also *Bereshit Rabbah* 12:4: "Rabbi Yehudah said, 'The heavens and the earth were finished in their own time, and all their array in their own time.' Rabbi Neḥemiah said to him, 'Yet look at what is written: *These are the generations of heaven and earth when they were created* (Genesis 2:4), teaching that on the very day they were created, they brought forth their generations.' Rabbi Yehudah replied, 'Yet surely it is written: *And there was evening and there was morning, one day... a second day... a third day... a fourth day... a fifth day... a sixth day?*' Rabbi Neḥemiah said, 'They were like those who gather figs, when each appears in its own time.' Rabbi Berekhiah said in support of Rabbi Neḥemiah, '*The earth brought forth* (ibid. 1:12), implying something that was already stored within her.'" See also *Tanḥuma* (Buber), *Bereshit* 1–2; Rashi on Genesis 1:14, 24; Maimonides, *Guide of the Perplexed* 2:30.

On the *generations* [or: *offspring*] *of heaven and earth*, see also *Bereshit Rabbah* 12:7: "All have offspring. Heaven and earth have offspring, as is said: *These are the offspring of the heaven and of the earth.* The mountains have offspring, as is said: *Before the mountains gave birth*... (Psalms 90:2). Rain has offspring, as is said: *Does the rain have a father* (Job 38:28)? Dew has offspring, as is said: *Who begot the dewdrops* (ibid.)?... It was taught: Whatever has offspring dies, decays, [and] is created but cannot create; but what has no offspring neither dies nor decays, [and] creates but is not created. Rabbi Azariah said in the name of Rabbi, 'This was said in reference to the One above.'"

542. **if so, on the very same day precisely...** If concerning heaven and earth the expression *on the day* signifies that all their *generations* (or *offspring*) were created at once, then what of humanity—concerning whom the same expression is employed?

Rabbi Berekhiah said, "It is so; they came into being on the same day! For the blessed Holy One showed him on that very day all his generations, passing their souls in their image before him, saying, 'This is so-and-so, and this is so-and-so; this is the sage of the generation, this is the judge of the generation,' and so on for all the generations and their leaders."[543]

Rabbi Yitsḥak said in the name of Rabbi Ḥiyya, "Why is it written before this subject: *The heavens and the earth were completed, with all their array* (ibid. 2:1), since it said: *God saw all that He had done—and look, it was very good* (ibid. 1:31)? What is the meaning of: את כל (*et kol*), *all, that He had done*? את כל (*Et kol*), *All*—amplifying the meaning to include the angels, who are *very good*. Concerning all the creations it says only *that it was good*, while here *that it was very good*—teaching that the angels were created, and that *very* was uttered about them."[544]

Rabbi Yitsḥak also said, "Scripture added further, saying: ויכלו (*va-ykhullu*), *were completed* (Genesis 2:1)!"[545]



Rabbi Berekhiah said, "It is an expression of longing. *With all their array*—in general, referring to the angels, who are called *the array of heaven*, as is written: *with all the array of heaven standing over Him* (1 Kings 22:19). When He finished the work, longing and yearning were aroused in all who beheld it."[546]

543. **showed him on that very day all his generations...** See BT *Avodah Zarah* 5a: "Did not Resh Lakish say: 'What is the meaning of the verse *This is the book of the generations of Adam...*? Did Adam possess a book? Rather, this teaches that the blessed Holy One showed Adam every generation with its expounders, every generation with its sages, every generation with its leaders.'" See *Seder Olam Rabbah* 30; *Bereshit Rabbah* 24:2; BT *Bava Metsi'a* 85b–86a; *Sanhedrin* 38b; *Tanḥuma, Ki Tissa* 12; *Shemot Rabbah* 40:3; *Zohar* 1:55a, 90b, 227b; 2:70a; *ZḤ* 37b; 67c; Ginzberg, *Legends* 5:117–18, n. 110.

544. **את כל (*Et kol*), *All*—amplifying the meaning to include the angels...** Scripture does not mention the creation of the angels. Their creation is thus "uncovered" through exegesis. See Naḥmanides on Genesis 1:8: "Scripture... did not mention the creation of the angels."

Grammatically, the accusative particle את (*et*) has no ascertainable independent sense, but Naḥum of Gimzo and his disciple Rabbi Akiva taught that when *et* appears in a biblical verse, it amplifies its original meaning. See BT *Pesaḥim* 22b; *Ḥagigah* 12a.

According to this passage, it seems that the angels were created on the sixth day, whereas rabbinic views pointed to either the second or fifth day. See *Bereshit Rabbah* 1:3, 3:8; *Pirqei de-Rabbi Eli'ezer* 4. See Ḥayyim Palagi, *Sefer Ḥayyim u-Mazon*, 25.

Cf. *Bereshit Rabbah* 9:10: "Rabbi Shemu'el son of Yitsḥak said, '*Look, it was very good* (Genesis 1:31) alludes to the angel of life; *and look, it was very good* to the angel of death.'"

On the apparent redundancy of the two verses, see the next note.

545. **Scripture added further...** Scripture had already stated: *God saw all that He had done and look, it was very good* (Genesis 1:31), a fitting conclusion to the creation account. Why add another concluding statement?

546. **an expression of longing...** Construing the verb ויכלו (*va-ykhullu*), *were completed*, as if derived from the verbal root כלה

Rav Naḥman said, "*Were completed*—completed in thought, completed in deed. The blessed Holy One made the Sabbath the paradigm of the world to come, for in the future the blessed Holy One will rest *on the seventh*. What is implied by *on the seventh*? The seventh millennium."[547] [17a]

Rav Naḥman also said, "An additional soul is added to a person on the Sabbath."[548]

Rabbi said, "What is this additional soul?"[549]

He replied, "The holy spirit dwelling upon him, adorning the human being with a holy crown, with the crowns of the angels; it derives from the same spirit destined to dwell upon the righteous in the time to come. Consequently a person is obligated to honor the Sabbath, on account of the holy guest dwelling with him."[550]

(*klh*), "pine, yearn, long." See Psalms 84:3: *My soul longs, even* כלתה (*kaltah*), *pines, for the courts of YHVH*. There is therefore no redundancy, as Genesis 2:1 recounts the longing aroused by the created order.

See *Bemidbar Rabbah* 10:1; *Ba'al ha-Turim* on Genesis 2:2; Kasher, *Torah Shelemah* on Genesis 2:2, note 26, citing *Targum Yerushalmi II*: Ginsburger, *Das Fragmententargum* (Berlin, 1899); (1) *Targum* according to Cod. 110 of the National Library at Paris; (2) variants from Cod. Vat. 440 and Lips. 1; (3) quotations from old writers.

On the array referring to the angels, see Naḥmanides on Genesis 2:1: "The array of heaven... also includes the Separate Intelligences, as is written: *I saw YHVH sitting on His throne with all the array of heaven standing over Him* (1 Kings 22:19).... It is here that He has hinted at the formation of the angels in the Account of Creation."

547. **Sabbath the paradigm of the world to come...** See BT *Berakhot* 57b: "Three [things] reflect the world to come: Sabbath, sunshine, and sexual union." See *Zohar* 1:1b; 48a; 3:95a.

On the blessed Holy One's resting during the seventh millennium, see BT *Sanhedrin* 97a, quoted above, note 538.

See also Naḥmanides on Genesis 2:3: "The seventh day, which is the Sabbath, alludes to the world to come, 'which will be entirely Sabbath and bring rest for life everlasting' (M *Tamid* 7:4)."

On the perfection and completion of creation in deed as in thought, cf. *Zohar* 1:47a; *Targum Onqelos* on Genesis 2:1.

548. **additional soul... on the Sabbath** The image of an additional soul derives from BT *Beitsah* 16a, in the name of Rabbi Shim'on son of Lakish: "On Sabbath eve, the blessed Holy One imparts an additional soul to a human being. When Sabbath departs, it is taken from him, as is said: שבת וינפש (*shavat va-yinnafash*), *He ceased and was refreshed* (Exodus 31:17)—once *shavat*, *it* [the Sabbath] *has ceased*, וי אבדה נפש (*vai avedah nefesh*), 'Woe, the soul is gone!'"

See *Zohar* 1:48a, 81b (*ST*); 2:88b, 98a, 135b, 204a–205b, 256a (*Heikh*); 3:95a, 173a, 288b (*IZ*); Moses de León, *Sefer ha-Mishqal*, 111, 114; Tishby, *Wisdom of the Zohar*, 3:1230–33; Ginsburg, *The Sabbath in the Classical Kabbalah*, 121–36.

549. **Rabbi said...** Presumably indicating Rabbi Yehudah ha-Nasi (the Patriarch), who redacted the Mishnah. He was so highly esteemed that he was called simply "Rabbi": the Master.

Cf. *Matoq mi-Devash*, who construes the speaker as Rabbi Yitsḥak and renders: "He said, 'Rabbi, what is this additional soul?'"

550. **The holy spirit dwelling upon him...** The additional Sabbath soul is of

Rav Naḥman said, "What is this spirit called? It is called 'honored' and it is called 'holy,' as is written: *Call the Sabbath 'delight'* (Isaiah 58:13)—according to its literal meaning; *the holy of YHVH 'honored'* (ibid.)—the additional spirit called *the holy of YHVH*, and called *honored*."[551]

Rabbi Yitsḥak said, "When they had completed all the works, the blessed Holy One blessed them and arrayed them in the world. He commanded every single one that it not alter its form from the manner in which He made it, and that henceforth and forevermore each and every one would generate offspring befitting it, as is written: *that God had created to make* (Genesis 2:3). What is implied by *to make*? To generate and engender everything like itself."[552]

the same substance as—and a foretaste of—the spirit that is destined to alight upon the righteous in the world to come. See Ezekiel 36:26–27, 37:12–14; BT *Berakhot* 57b, in which the Sabbath is said to resemble the world to come and is one-sixtieth of the world to come; *ZḤ* 15d (*MhN*), above at note 494. Cf. *Pirqei de-Rabbi Eli'ezer* 34: "Rabbi Yehudah said, '... In the time to come, the blessed Holy One will bring down a dew of revival, reviving the dead... *For your dew is a dew of lights* (Isaiah 26:19).'"

On the "crowns" of the angels, see BT *Shabbat* 88a: "Rabbi Simlai expounded: 'When Israel said *We will do* before *We will listen* (Exodus 24:7), 600,000 ministering angels came to each and every Israelite, setting two crowns upon him: one for *We will do*, and one for *We will listen*. As soon as Israel sinned [by worshiping the Golden calf], 1,200,000 angels of destruction descended and removed them.'" These crowns are destined to be returned in the post-messianic era.

On honoring the Sabbath, see Maimonides, *Mishneh Torah, Hilkhot Shabbat* 30:1–3: "Four [aspects of observance] are said of the Sabbath, two originating in the Torah, and two originating in the words of the scribes, given exposition by the prophets. In the Torah—Remember and Observe; given exposition by the prophets—Honor and Delight, as is said: *Call the Sabbath a delight, the holy of YHVH honored* (Isaiah 58:13). What is meant by Honor? This refers to our Sages' statement that it is a commandment for a person to wash his face, hands, and feet in hot water on Friday in honor of the Sabbath. He should wrap himself in *tsitsit* and sit with proper respect, waiting to receive the Sabbath as one goes out to greet a king." See also *halakhot* 4–6.

Rav Naḥman explains why the Sabbath is owed this honor: because of the Sabbath guest, the additional soul.

551. ***Call the Sabbath 'delight'... the holy of YHVH 'honored'...*** According to the verse's simple meaning, the Sabbath is "the holy of YHVH." Here, Rav Naḥman reads it as referring to the additional Sabbath spirit.

On the commandment of Sabbath delight, see BT *Shabbat* 118b: "How does one delight [in the Sabbath]? Rav Yehudah son of Rav Shemu'el son of Sheilat said in the name of Rav, 'With a dish of beets, large fish, and heads of garlic." See also Maimonides, *Mishneh Torah, Hilkhot Shabbat* 30:7–10, 14. On the verse from Isaiah, cf. *Zohar* 1:5b; 2:47a.

552. **When they had completed all the works...** When the artisans of creation (heaven, earth, and water) had completed their creative acts throughout the six days of creation, God arrayed them, i.e., He bestowed upon the created order the capacity for continued creation. This continued creative capacity is alluded to in Genesis 2:3: *God blessed the seventh day and hallowed it, because on it He ceased from all the work* אשר ברא אלהים לעשות (*asher bara elohim la'asot*), *that God created to make*. The simple sense of the

Rabbi Yehudah says, "This refers to the body of the demons, for their work was not completed."[553]

Rabbi Yose son of Naḥman said, "As soon as Sabbath entered, all the entities created during the Work of Creation ceased and were at ease, each one according to its nature. As we have learned: The artisans that brought forth their generations on every single day were at ease and rested; they saw that all were consummate, that all their generations abided with them in enduring vitality and actuality, as is written: *These are the generations of heaven and earth when they were created* (ibid. 2:4)."[554]

Rav Naḥman said, "Like a person lauding praise who says, 'These are the things that have no peer!'"[555]

בהבראם (*be-hibbare'am*), *When they were created.* Rabbi Yitsḥak said, "בה׳ בראם (*be-he bera'am*), With ה (*he*) He created them."[556]

Rabbi Yehudah says, '*When they were created*—precisely in their form and consummation!'"

Rav Naḥman said, "Do not read בהבראם (*be-hibbare'am*), *when they were created*, but rather באברהם (*be-Avraham*), through Abraham, who received His



difficult final clause is something like *that by creating God had made.* Here, Rabbi Yitsḥak adopts a more literal reading, in which the final word, the infinitive לעשות (*la'asot*), *to make*, implies continued activity. The created order is thus imbued with the capacity for continuous generation. See next note.

Cf. Abraham Ibn Ezra, ad loc.: "The roots of all the species to which He gave the power *to make* [i.e., to produce] after their own kind."

See above, at note 346.

553. **the body of the demons...** See *Tanḥuma* (Buber), *Bereshit* 17: "It is not written here *that* [*God*] *created and made*, but rather [*that God created*] *to make* (Genesis 2:3)—for the Sabbath came first, with the work not yet completed. Rabbi Benaya said, 'This refers to the demons, for He had created their souls; and as He was creating their bodies, the Sabbath day was hallowed. He left them [as is], and they remained soul without body.'" See also M *Avot* 5:6. See *Bereshit Rabbah* 7:5; 11:9; *Zohar* 1:14a, 47b–48a, 178a; 2:155b; 3:142b (*IR*); Moses de León, *Sefer ha-Rimmon*, 397.

554. **artisans...** Namely, heaven, earth, and water. See *ZḤ* 13a, 16a (both *MhN*); cf. *Zohar* 3:219b (*RM*).

555. **Like a person lauding praise . . .** God is speaking like a craftsman—drawing attention to His work, pointing with praise: Look at these! See *Bereshit Rabbah* 12:1: "Rabbi Yitsḥak son of Marion said, 'It is written: *These are the generations of heaven and earth when they were created.* When their Creator praises them, who may disparage them.... But they are comely and praiseworthy, as is said: *These are the generations of heaven and earth....*'"

556. **With ה (*he*) He created them** See BT *Menaḥot* 29b: "*These are the generations of heaven and earth* בהבראם (*be-hibbare'am*), *when they were created* (Genesis 2:4). Do not read בהבראם (*be-hibbare'am*), when they were created, but rather בה׳ בראם (*be-he bera'am*), with ה (*he*) He created them." See *Bereshit Rabbah* 12:10; JT *Ḥagigah* 2:1, 77c; *Alfa Beita de-Rabbi Aqiva*, Version 1 (*Battei Midrashot*, 2:363); *Zohar* 1:46b, 91b; *ZḤ* 3a, 3d, 17c, 25a, 26a (all *MhN*).

Torah and the covenant He placed within him. Were it not for Abraham—who received the Torah and covenant of the blessed Holy One—heaven and earth would not endure, as is said: *Were it not for My covenant, I would not have established day and night,* [*nor*] *the laws of heaven and earth* (Jeremiah 33:25). Now, do not be surprised by this. For look at what we have learned: It is written: *The high mountains for the gazelles, the crags a shelter for badgers* (Psalms 104:18). If the high mountains were created solely for gazelles, and the crags created solely for badgers, do not be surprised that the world should be created for Abraham, who fulfilled the entire Torah and all he was commanded by the blessed Holy One."[557]

Rabbi Yitsḥak said in the name of Rabbi Yehudah, "With ה (*He*) He created them, as is written: *Because My Name is within it* (Exodus 23:21)."[558]

Rabbi Yitsḥak said further in the name of Rabbi Yehudah, "The name of the blessed Holy One did not unite with any of the creations aside from these, as is written: *on the day that YHVH God made earth and heaven* (Genesis 2:4), as we have said. Neither animals and creatures, nor any creation among those that perish and decay are mentioned; only with those enduring forever did He mention His name."[559]

557. **that the world should be created for Abraham...** According to Rabbi Yehoshu'a son of Korḥah (*Bereshit Rabbah* 12:9), בהבראם (*be-hibbare'am*), *when they were created* (Genesis 2:4) is an anagram of באברהם (*be-Avraham*), "through Abraham," indicating that the world was created for his sake. See *Zohar* 1:3b, 86b, 91b, 93a, 105b, 128b, 154b, 230b; 3:117a, 298a; *ZḤ* 4d (*MhN*).

In its simple sense, the verse from Jeremiah reads: *Were it not for My covenant with day and night, I would not have established the laws of heaven and earth.* Rabbinic midrash rearranged the syntax, as in BT *Shabbat* 137b: "Were it not for the blood of the covenant, heaven and earth would not endure, as is said: *Were it not for My covenant, I would not have established day and night,* [*nor*] *the laws of heaven and earth.*" See also BT *Pesaḥim* 68b, in the name of Rabbi El'azar: "Were it not for Torah, heaven and earth would not endure, as is said: *Were it not for My covenant....*" See *Zohar* 1:32a, 56a, 59b, 66b, 89a, 91b, 93b, 189b.

See also BT *Yoma* 28b: "Abraham our father fulfilled the entire Torah." The *a fortiori* argument about the gazelles and badgers also derives from *Bereshit Rabbah* 12:9. See also the passage from *MhN* at the end of *parashat Lekh Lekha*, below, page 312.

558. ***Because My Name is within it*** That is, the divine name (or at least one letter from the divine name) is within creation. In contrast, in its simple sense, the verse reads: *Because My Name is within him,* referring to the angel sent to lead the Israelites in the desert.

559. **The name of the blessed Holy One did not unite...** In chapter 1 of Genesis, the divine name *YHVH* does not appear, only the general name *Elohim* (God). The explicit name *YHVH* is first mentioned in the Torah at Genesis 2:4, in the second creation account. Rabbi Yehudah here reprises a theme presented earlier, see *ZḤ* 9d (*MhN*), page 53, where the wunderkind Ḥiyya explains that it is not fitting for the explicit name *YHVH* to be associated with corruptible things, but only with that which abides eternally. Cf. Moses de León, *Or Zaru'a*, 263; idem, *Sefer ha-Rimmon*, 288.

Rav Huna said, "The day when the creation of heaven and earth pined for the blessed Holy One. He saw the Sabbath—repose and holiness—and established it for the generations.[560]

"It has been taught: There is not a single Sabbath when the blessed Holy One does not venture to dance with the righteous in the Garden of Eden, and they are nourished by the splendor of the resplendent speculum, as is written: *Before the day breathes* (Song of Songs 4:6)—the Sabbath day; *I will hasten to the mountain of myrrh and to the hill of frankincense* (ibid.)—the world to come."[561]

Rav Huna said, "Do not be surprised by this. If in this world the blessed Holy One bestows a holy spirit upon everyone on the Sabbath through which they are adorned, how much more so that in the world to come He should adorn the righteous on the Sabbath with a crown!"

Come and see: Rav Huna said, "Even the wicked in Hell are crowned on the Sabbath, and are at rest and at ease."[562]

As Rav Huna said: "You cannot find a wicked person among Israel who does not possess good deeds benefiting him in the world to come. When do they benefit him? On the Sabbath—that all might be adorned with the Sabbath crown."



Rabbi Yose said, "But do the wicked who profaned the Sabbath in public gain the [17b] Sabbath crown?"[563]

560. **the day when . . . creation . . . pined . . .** In Genesis 2:4, *the day* refers to the Sabbath.

On the yearning of creation, see above, note 546.

561. **dance with the righteous in the Garden of Eden . . .** This dance occurs every Sabbath. In contrast, in rabbinic texts it is reserved for the messianic era. See BT *Ta'anit* 31a: "Ulla of Biri said in the name of Rabbi El'azar, 'In the future the blessed Holy One will arrange a dance for the righteous. He will sit among them in the Garden of Eden and every single one of them will point with his finger, as is said: *In that day they will say, "This is our God. We trusted in Him and He delivered us. This is* YHVH *in whom we trusted. Let us rejoice and exult in His deliverance!* (Isaiah 25:9).'"" See also *Vayiqra Rabbah* 11:9; *Shir ha-Shirim Rabbah* on 7:1; *Midrash Tehillim* 48:5.

"Resplendent speculum" renders אספקלריא המאירה (*ispaqlarya ha-me'irah*). *Ispaqlarya* means "glass, mirror, lens." See BT *Yevamot* 49b: "All the prophets gazed through an opaque glass [literally: an *ispaqlarya* that does not shine], while Moses our teacher gazed through a translucent glass [literally: an *ispaqlarya* that shines]." See also *Vayiqra Rabbah* 1:14. Cf. 1 Corinthians 13:12: "For now we see though a glass darkly, but then face-to-face." See *Zohar* 1:97b, 122a (both *MhN*); *ZḤ* 10a, 13b, 15b, 15d, 16c, 21a, 24a (all *MhN*).

562. **the wicked in Hell are crowned on the Sabbath . . .** According to *Tanḥuma, Ki Tissa* 33, one of the dwellers of Hell reports: "Whoever does not observe the Sabbath properly in your world comes here and observes it against his will. . . . All week long we are punished, and on the Sabbath we rest." See *Bereshit Rabbah* 11:5; BT *Sanhedrin* 65b; *Zohar* 1:14b, 48a, 197b; 2:31b, 88b, 136a, 150b–151a, 203b, 207a; 3:94b.

563. **the wicked who profaned the Sabbath . . .** Does not justice require that they be punished on the Sabbath?

He replied, "Yes, for look at what we have learned: *On the sixth day, they gathered double bread* (Exodus 16:22)—correspondingly the wicked are judged doubly on the sixth day, so that they might enjoy relief on the Sabbath![564]

"For the Sabbath is called consummate, undiminished. Therefore it does not diminish its bounty and delight, whether for the righteous or the wicked; demonstrating that not in vain did the Torah say *You shall keep the Sabbath* (ibid. 31:14)—and caution about the Sabbath [even] more than the whole Torah. It has been taught: Whoever fulfills the Sabbath is as though he has fulfilled the entire Torah."[565]

Rav Yehudah said in the name of Rav, "The blessed Holy One did not sit upon His Throne of Glory until the Sabbath arrived, whereupon He ascended upon His throne."[566]

Rabbi Yose said to him, "But surely before the world was created He sat—He was, He will be![567]



Rav Yehudah said, "Does this imply upon His actual Throne of Glory? No! Rather, so have we learned: Until the world was created, there was no one to exalt or acknowledge the blessed Holy One. When He created His world, He created the angels, the holy living-beings, the heavens and all their array, and He created the human being. All of them were prepared to praise their Creator and glorify Him. But still there was no exaltation or praise before Him, until the Sabbath entered and all were at ease; and Above and Below burst forth in song and praise—whereupon He sat upon His Throne of Glory. In other words, then there was someone to acknowledge His glory and praise His glory."[568]

Rav Yehudah said, "There is no praise or exaltation before the blessed Holy One like the praise of the Sabbath! Above and Below all praise Him as one.

564. ***On the sixth day, they gathered double bread...*** According to the account in Exodus, when the Israelites gathered manna on every Sabbath eve, they managed to collect a double portion.

565. **Whoever fulfills the Sabbath is as though...** On Sabbath as equivalent to the whole Torah, see JT *Berakhot* 1:4, 3c; JT *Nedarim* 3:9, 38b; *Mishnat Rabbi Eli'ezer* 20; *Devarim Rabbah* 4:4; *Devarim Rabbah* (ed. Lieberman), p. 92; *Tanḥuma, Ki Tissa* 33; *Shemot Rabbah* 25:12; Maimonides, *Mishneh Torah, Hilkhot Shabbat* 30:15; *Zohar* 2:47a, 89a, 92a, 151a; *ZḤ* 45a; Moses de León, *Sefer ha-Rimmon*, 335; idem, *Sefer ha-Mishqal*, 110.

566. **sit upon His Throne of Glory until the Sabbath arrived...** See the Sabbath morning liturgy: "To the God who rested from all works, who on the seventh day ascended and sat on His Throne of Glory."

567. **He was, He will be...** God is eternal and His being enthroned is not dependent on creation or on the Sabbath!

568. **then there was someone to acknowledge His glory...** It is not that God literally sat on His Throne of Glory with the onset of the first Sabbath, but rather that He was enthroned upon the praises of creation, lauding His glory.

On the praises lauded by Above and Below on the Sabbath, cf. *Seder Rabbah di-Vreshit* 15–16 (*Battei Midrashot*, 1:26–7).

Even the Sabbath day itself praises Him, as is written: *A psalm, a song for the Sabbath day* (Psalms 92:1)."[569]

*YHVH God formed [the human]* (Genesis 2:7).

Rabbi Tanḥum opened, "*Thus says God, YHVH, who creates the heavens and stretches them out...* (Isaiah 42:5). When the blessed Holy One created His world, He created them from nothing, bringing them into actuality, imbuing them with substance. Wherever you find בורא (*bore*), *create*, it refers to something He created from nothing and brought into actuality."[570]

Rav Ḥisda asked, "But were the heavens really created from nothing? Weren't they created from the light above?"[571]

Rabbi Tanḥum replied, "It is so—the matter of the heavens came from nothing, but their form from an entity of substance; similarly with the human being.[572]

"Concerning the heavens you will find בריאה (*beri'ah*), *creating*, and afterward עשיה (*asiyyah*), *making*. *Creating—who creates the heavens* (Isaiah 42:5); in other words, from nothing. *Making—who makes the heavens* (Psalms 136:5), from an entity of substance, from the light above."



569. **Even the Sabbath day itself praises Him...** According to *Midrash Tehillim* 92:3, the Sabbath Day herself recited this psalm together with Adam. See also *Pirqei de-Rabbi Eli'ezer* 19; *Zohar* 2:138a; 3:79b, 284b.

570. **בורא (*bore*), *create*... refers to something He created from nothing...** See Naḥmanides on Genesis 1:1: "The blessed Holy One created all things from absolute non-existence. Now, we have no expression in the sacred language for bringing forth something from nothing—other than the word ברא (*bara*)." Cf. Abraham Ibn Ezra on Genesis 1:1; *Bahir* 10 (13).

On the verse from Isaiah, see also *Zohar* 1:205b.

571. **Weren't they created from the light above?** Namely, from the light of the angelic form. If so, how can you say they were created *ex nihilo*?

See *Pirqei de-Rabbi Eli'ezer* 3: "Whence were the heavens created? From the light of the garment with which the blessed Holy One was robed. He took of this light and stretched it like a garment, and (the heavens) began to extend continually—until He said to them, 'It is sufficient!'... Whence do we know that the heavens were created from the light of His garment? As is said: *He wraps in light as in a garment. He spreads out the heavens like a curtain* (Psalms 104:2)." See Maimonides, *Guide of the Perplexed* 2:26; Naḥmanides on Genesis 1:8; Oron, "Midrash ha-Ne'lam: Muqdam u-Me'uḥar," 127.

On the angelic form's light, see *ZḤ* 4a, 7d (both *MhN*); cf. *ZḤ* 10a, 14a (both *MhN*).

572. **but their form from an entity of substance...** This resolves the contradiction: the heavens' matter (literally "body") was indeed created *ex nihilo*, but their form derived from the angelic form above. The human being is similarly constructed: the first human's body was created *ex nihilo*, while the soul derived from the Throne of Glory and God.

Rabbi Tanḥum also said, "*Asiyyah*, *making*, refers to the enhancement of something in terms of its size and stature—compared to how it was before—as is said: *David* ויעש (*va-ya'as*), *enhanced*, [*his*] *name* (2 Samuel 8:13)."[573]

Rabbi Ḥanilai said, "This verse appears only that it might be expounded! וייצר (*Va-yyitser*), *He formed* (Genesis 2:7)—with two *yods*; while all the others you find are with one *yod*. The explanation is that of everything that the blessed Holy one created in His world, only the human being alone was created with the excellence of insight. For He placed within him power from the upper realms to perceive and cognize and to distinguish between good and evil, and he is adorned with glory and majesty, as is said: *You adorned him with glory and majesty* (Psalms 8:6). He rules over all the work of His hands, as is written: *You make him rule over the work of Your hands* (ibid. 8:7). After all this praise, when he remembers that he is dust—and that to dust he shall return—everything seems futile and pointless to him, and he says, 'Woe!' Rabbi Yoḥanan said, 'Divide the word: וי יצר (*vay yitser*): *Woe that YHVH God formed the human being of dust from the soil* (Genesis 2:7), and that he will return to the dust just as he was!'"[574]



Alternatively, *YHVH God* וייצר (*va-yyitser*), *formed, the human being of dust from the soil.* Rabbi Shalom said, "He formed him with two יצרים (*yetsarim*), impulses—the good impulse and the evil impulse—which was not the case with

573. ***Asiyyah*, *making*, refers to the enhancement...** See Naḥmanides on Genesis 1:7: "The word *asiyyah* always means adjusting [or: enhancing] something to its required proportion."

See also Moses de León, *Or Zaru'a*, 269–70; *Zohar* 1:116b, 142b; 3:113a–b.

Cf. *Sifrei*, Deuteronomy 212: "*And she shall shave her head* ועשתה (*ve-asetah*), *and do, her nails* (Deuteronomy 21:12). Rabbi Eli'ezer said, 'She shall cut them.' Rabbi Akiva said, 'She shall let them grow.' See also BT *Yevamot* 48a.

574. **וייצר (*Va-yyitser*), *He formed* (Genesis 2:7)—with two *yods*...** The word describing the formation of the human being in the second creation account is spelled with a double *yod*, וייצר (*va-yyitser*). This anomalous spelling generated rich interpretations at the hands of the Rabbis. See BT *Berakhot* 61a; *Bereshit Rabbah* 14:2–4. Here, the additional *yod* signifies human superiority—the human being sits at the head of the created order marked by his intellectual and moral capacity. Although not stated, perhaps it is understood that the additional *yod* derives from the tetragrammaton.

The unique spelling of the word also encodes the existential situation of the human being: acute awareness of mortality. Although Rabbi Yoḥanan's homily, dividing the word וייצר (*va-yyitser*) into (*vay yitser*), *Woe* [*that YHVH God*] *formed*, is original, the basic components of the homily can be found in BT *Beitsah* 16a: "Woe, the soul is gone!" (see above, note 548), and in BT *Berakhot* 61a: "Rabbi Shim'on son of Pazzi said, 'Woe is me because of (*yotsri*), my Creator, woe is me because of (*yitsri*), my evil impulse!'"

On the sense of הבל (*hevel*), "futility," see Psalms 144:4: *The human is likened unto* hevel, *breath*; *his days are like a passing shadow*; and Ecclesiastes 12:7: *The dust returns to the ground as it was, and the spirit to God who bestowed it. Utter futility, said Kohelet. All is futile!*

the other creatures, with which to test the human being, so that there might be an opening for the righteous, and so that there might not be an opening for the wicked."[575]

Rabbi Abba said, "Why is it written *YHVH* and afterward *Elohim*? The reason is that the name which is His actual name, the fully existent Name, is said about the soul abiding enduringly in the human being. *Elohim*—שם משותף (*shem meshutaf*), the polysemous name, is said of the body, for it involves שותפות (*shutafut*), partnership."[576] [17c]

Rabbi Abbahu said, "The fully existent Name ordains and presides, like driven leaves underfoot; it is not lent to another. Consequently only a single letter from His name is mentioned in the Account of Creation, in accordance with the one who says, 'בה' בראם (*be-he bera'am*), With ה (*he*) He created them.'"[577]



575. **He formed him with two יצרים (*yetsarim*), impulses...** See BT *Berakhot* 61a: "Rav Naḥman son of Rav Ḥisda expounded, 'Why is it written וייצר (*va-yyitser*), [*YHVH Elohim*] *formed*..., spelled with two *yods*? Because the blessed Holy One created two impulses, one good and the other evil.'" See *Bereshit Rabbah* 14:4; *Targum Yerushalmi*, ad loc.; *Zohar* 1:49a; 3:46b.

It is only because human beings also possess an evil impulse that their righteous behavior has value. Conversely, because humans also possess a good impulse, they have no excuse for being wicked.

"Opening" renders פתחון פה (*pitḥon peh*), "opening of the mouth," meaning an opportunity for fault-finding.

On animals not possessing an evil impulse, see *Avot de-Rabbi Natan* A, 16: "For there is no evil impulse in beasts."

576. **Why is it written *YHVH* and afterward *Elohim*?...** Beginning at Genesis 2:4, the combined divine name *YHVH Elohim* is used. This dual name befits the creation of the human being because of the human being's dual nature: the explicit name *YHVH* applies to the soul that abides eternally, while the more general name *Elohim* applies to the body. Furthermore, the name *Elohim*—which, as noted earlier (see *ZḤ* 3d *MhN*), is *shem meshutaf*, a polysemous name applied also to other creations (angels, judges, etc.)—befits the human body because it is the product of the *shutafut*, "partnership," between one's mother, father, and the blessed Holy One. See *ZḤ* 16b (*MhN*), above, at note 517.

On the complete name *YHVH Elohim*, see *Bereshit Rabbah* 13:3; cf. *Zohar* 2:113b.

577. **The fully existent Name ordains and presides...** This paragraph is difficult and mysterious, deliberately so. The fully existent name (*shem ha-qiyyum*)—*YHVH*—is transcendent, ruling over all. Unlike the name *Elohim*, the name *YHVH* is not shared with any other creations. In fact, so transcendent is this divine reality that it is only barely connected with the created order.

While the fully existent name—the explicit name *YHVH*—does not appear in the first creation account (lest it be associated with entities that decay), one letter of this name does appear: the small letter ה (*he*) in בהבראם (*be-hibbare'am*), *when they were created*. Perhaps Rabbi Abbahu also intends that the ה (*he*) is present in the divine name אלהים (*Elohim*).

On the name *YHVH*, whose unique referent is totally transcendent and unsullied by association with the created order, see *ZḤ* 3d (*MhN*), also in the name of Rabbi Abbahu: "He bequeathed all, but His great Name He did not bestow, nor did He loan it to another, as is written: *I am YHVH* (Isaiah 42:8)—alone;

We have learned in the Book of Great Wisdom of Solomon: The detached name; darkened burden; rent garment of the King. Imbued with dominion by the minor seal to rule beneath Him, as is said: *Who is* כמכה (*khamokhah*), *like You, among the* אלים (*elim*), *gods, O YHVH?* (Exodus 15:11).[578]

teaching that He did not bequeath this Name to any creation."

"Driven leaves underfoot" renders טריפין שקיפין דרגלין (*terifin sheqifin de-raglin*). The expression appears to derive from Onqelos' translation of Leviticus 26:36, where עלה נדף (*aleh nidaf*), "a driven leaf," is rendered טרפא דשקיף (*tarfa de-shaqif*). See Rashi, ad loc. Compared to *YHVH*, all else is like a driven leaf.

Cf. Finkel, "The Alexandrian Tradition," 80–81, who renders the opening phrase: "The hypostatic Name manages and effectuates its impact similar to that of the kicks (i.e., strokes = טריפין) of the toes (שקיפין = peaks or extremities) of the extended feet, which themselves, however, are not lent to others." See also Belkin, "Ha-Midrash ha-Ne'lam u-Mqorotav," 29; Werblowsky, "Philo and the Zohar," 35.



On "With ה (*he*) He created them," see above, note 556.

578. **We have learned in the Book of Great Wisdom of Solomon...** Even more difficult and mysterious than the preceding! Apparently this paragraph (which can also be construed as the continuation of Rabbi Abbahu's teaching) is discussing the name *Elohim*, which seems to be a lower hypostasis or appellation of the divine being. The point seems to be that it is invested with authority and power by *YHVH*. According to *ZḤ* 18c, 19c (both *MhN*), the primal sin is to separate the name *Elohim* from the name *YHVH* and worship it alone.

The cited teaching is: שמא דשמיטה מטול שזיפא קרעוי דמלכא קושטיזא דאטיל ביה בחותמא זעירתא למשלטא תחותוי (*Shema di-shmittah matul shezifa qar'oi de-malka qoshtiza de-atil bei be-ḥotama ze'irtta le-mishlata teḥotoi*). See Ḥayyim Palagi, *Sefer Ḥayyim u-Mazon*, 27: "Who is wise enough to understand these, intelligent enough to know the meaning of these matters and what is intended?!"

שמא דשמיטה (*Shema di-shmitta*) may connote "the detached name" or "the withdrawn name," meaning the name *Elohim*—which has been detached from the name *YHVH* (see below, *ZḤ* 18c *MhN*). Alternatively, "the fallow name" (*Elohim*).

שזיפא (*Shezifa*) appears to derive from the biblical verbal root *shzf*, "gaze upon, sunburn," which in rabbinic literature also connotes "blackened, sullied, tarnished." In *Shir ha-Shirim Rabbah* on Song of Songs 1:6, the root is associated with idolatry.

קרעוי דמלכא (*Qar'oi de-malka*) may connote either the rent garment of the King, or alternatively, the grooved imprint of the King. The root קרע (*qr'*) usually means "to tear, rend" as applied to garments. The noun form can also refer to the grooves that a scribe makes by marking the outline of letters.

קושטיזא (*Qoshtiza*) is a Zoharic neologism, perhaps deriving from the Castilian word *castizo*, meaning "pure, genuine, of noble origin." Or perhaps it is related to Aramaic קושטא (*qushta*), "true." Cf. קוזדיטא (*qozdita*), *ZḤ* 18d (*MhN*). Many Zoharic neologisms with the sound *qos*, *qoz*, *qor*, convey the sense of governance and authority.

The "minor seal" may refer to the small letter ה (*he*) in בהבראם (*be-hibbare'am*), *when they were created* (Genesis 2:4). As noted earlier, the name אלהים (*Elohim*) is attained by adding the letter ה (*he*) from יהוה (*YHVH*) to the word אלים (*elim*), "gods, powers." See *ZḤ* 2d, 3a, 3d (all *MhN*).

Cf. Finkel, "The Alexandrian Tradition," 80–82, who renders: "The (ineffable) Name is omitted, for blurred is the grooved imprint of the Exalted King, because He stamped upon him a puny seal of His that warrants (only man's) surrogate rule of His." Accord-

את האדם (*Et ha-adam*), *The human being* (Genesis 2:7)—amplifying the meaning to include all the powers within him.[579]

*Dust from the soil* (ibid.). Rabbi Abbahu said, "Come and see: How can a person abide in this world, since Torah attests that he is dust?"

Rabbi Yitsḥak said, "Dust and not clay! Were he from clay he would abide more enduringly, for look, a building constructed of clay endures, while dust by itself does not endure, as is written: *For dust you are, and to dust shall you return* (ibid. 3:19)—it does not say *for clay you are*!"[580]

Rabbi Ḥanin said, "But look at what is written: *How much less those who dwell in houses of clay, whose foundation is dust?* (Job 4:19)!"[581]

ing to this reading, this passage is about the human being, who—though created in the divine image—is created by *Elohim* with only the puny seal, the letter ה (*he*) (and not the name *YHVH*). See also *Sullam* and *Matoq mi-Devash* for different interpretations.

The Book of King Solomon is one of the many volumes housed in the real or imaginary library of the authors of the *Zohar*. For other references to this book, see *Zohar* 1:7b, 13b, 225b; 2:67a, 70a (*RR*), 125a, 139a, 172a, 204b; 3:10b, 65b, 70b, 104a, 151b, 164a, 193b; *ZḤ* 12b (*MhN*). Naḥmanides several times refers to, and quotes from, an Aramaic version of the Apocryphal *Wisdom of Solomon*. See the introduction to his Commentary on the Torah, 5–6; idem, *Kitvei Ramban*, 1:163, 182; Marx, "An Aramaic Fragment of the Wisdom of Solomon." On the numerous scientific and magical books attributed to King Solomon, see *Old Testament Pseudepigrapha*, 1:956–57.

See Matt, *Zohar: The Book of Enlightenment*, 25; and the comment by Shim'on Lavi, *Ketem Paz*, 1:22d, on *Zohar* 1:7a: "All such books mentioned in the *Zohar*... have been lost in the wanderings of exile.... Nothing is left of them except what is mentioned in the *Zohar*." For a catalogue of these books, see Neuhausen, *Sifriyyah shel Ma'lah*.

579. **to include all the powers within him** Precisely which powers are meant is unclear, though presumably the *Zohar* intends the various dispositions of the soul, which on occasion are termed כחות (*koḥot*), "forces" or "powers." See above, *ZḤ* 14b (*MhN*), page 123: "[there are] three powers in a human being: the power of the holy *neshamah*; the desiring power; and the motive power." See also *Zohar* 1:109a–b, 137a (both *MhN*); Tishby, *Wisdom of the Zohar*, 2:706, 691.



Grammatically, the accusative particle את (*et*) has no ascertainable independent sense, but Naḥum of Gimzo and his disciple Rabbi Akiva taught that when *et* appears in a biblical verse, it amplifies its original meaning. See BT *Pesaḥim* 22b; *Ḥagigah* 12a.

580. **while dust by itself does not endure...** According to *Matoq mi-Devash*, the unstated logic is that the body of the human being ought not to endure—having been fashioned from dust, which does not abide enduringly. It does so only because of the powers of the soul inhering in the body. Once the soul departs, the body decays.

It is possible that Rabbi Yitsḥak is being quoted by Rabbi Abbahu.

581. ***How much less those who dwell in houses of clay...*** The passage continues: *who are crushed like the moth, shattered between daybreak and evening, perishing forever, unnoticed* (Job 4:19–20). The verse cited by Rabbi Ḥanin appears to suggest that human beings are indeed fashioned from clay. See Abraham Ibn Ezra, ad loc.: "The souls of human beings are hewn [from above] *yet dwell in houses of clay*, namely, bodies, *whose foundation is dust*."

Rabbi Abbahu said, "This verse helps us. It was uttered about this world, about that which does not endure. For this verse applies to people whose abode is in this world, whose buildings are from clay. Since the building is from clay and is intended to abide enduringly, what would be a suitable foundation? As is said: *huge blocks of precious stone to lay the foundations of the house* (1 Kings 5:31). But if of clay, and its foundations of dust, it is not a mighty building—and consequently it does not abide enduringly. As is written: *How much less those who dwell in houses of clay, whose foundation is dust?* (Job 4:19)—that it does not endure."[582]

*He blew into his nostrils the breath of life*... (Genesis 2:7). Torah cries out over the human being, "Look what this person did! The blessed Holy One placed within him נשמתא קדישא (*nishmeta qaddisha*), a holy soul, to bestow upon him life in the world to come. But through his sins, he reverted to that creaturely soul—the beastly soul that the earth brought forth for beasts and animals, as is written: *Let the earth bring forth* נפש חיה (*nefesh ḥayyah*), *a creaturely soul, according to its kind* (ibid. 1:24). Who are *its kind*? Beasts, creeping things, and animals of the earth."[583]



Rabbi Ḥiyya said, "Come and see: It does not say *YHVH made him into a creaturely soul* but rather *The human became nefesh ḥayyah, a creaturely soul* (ibid. 2:7). He himself reverted to the beastly power hewn from the soil—forsaking the power of the *neshamah* hewn from above, bestowing life to those possessing her."[584]

Rabbi Tanḥum said, "Let us return to what we began earlier: *Thus says God, YHVH, who creates the heavens and stretches them out* (Isaiah 42:5). He created

582. **For this verse applies to people...** Rabbi Abbahu rejects Rabbi Ḥanin's suggestion that the verse from Job applies to the soul enclosed within houses of clay. The verse, rather, was uttered about human constructions, which if lacking mighty foundations—like the huge blocks of stone in the Temple of Solomon—do not endure, but crumble with time.

583. **he reverted to that creaturely soul...** The *Zohar* here reprises a homily found above, *ZḤ* 10c (*MhN*), page 68.

Genesis 2:7 describes the creation of human beings as follows: "*He blew into his nostrils* נשמת חיים (*nishmat ḥayyim*), *the breath of life, and the human became* נפש חיה (*nefesh ḥayyah*), *a living being.*" Here, the *nishmat ḥayyim*, signifying the holy soul hewn from the divine Throne—and through which one attains knowledge of divinity and life in the world to come—is distinguished from the *nefesh ḥayyah*, usually rendered as "a living being," signifying the "creaturely" (or "animal" or "vital") soul. The *nefesh ḥayyah* derives from the earth, i.e., the soil, the ground. It is the soul that imparts life to all creatures. It is not associated with spiritual or intellectual activity. Cf. Naḥmanides on Genesis 2:7. On the distinction between these two kinds of soul in *MhN*, see *ZḤ* 11a, 11c, 16b–c; Tishby, *Wisdom of the Zohar*, 2:708–9.

According to *MhN*, while human beings were originally created with the holy soul, through their sin, they have forfeited it and reverted to the creaturely soul.

584. **He himself reverted to the beastly power...** See *ZḤ* 10c, 16b–c (both *MhN*).

their matter from nothing—and afterward spread them like a tent, as is written: *He spreads them out like a tent to dwell in* (ibid. 40:22)."[585]

Rav Huna said, "This is derived from here: *Who stretches out the heavens like a canopy* (ibid.)."

*Who spreads out the earth and what emerges from it* (ibid. 42:5). Rabbi Yitsḥak said, "All the forms and powers inhering within her expanded within.[586]

"*Who gives* neshamah *to the people upon her* (ibid.)—once she made the body, I gave the soul *upon her*. What is implied by *upon her*? Upon the body she made."[587]

Rabbi Ḥiyya said, "*Upon her*—to those prevailing upon her powers; to them I have given the *neshamah*.[588]

"*And* רוח (*ruaḥ*), *spirit, to those who walk with her* (ibid.)—to those who become associated with her powers, for they possess only the creaturely soul, called *the spirit of the beast that descends below into earth* (Ecclesiastes 3:21). That is why it says *who gives* neshamah *to the people upon her*: to those who prevail over her—over her powers—they possess a holy *neshamah* hewn from above. But *to those who walk with her*—who become associated with her powers, they 177
possess only *the spirit of the beast that descends below into earth*, as is written: *And* רוח (*ruaḥ*), *spirit, to those who walk with her*."[589]

## Section 7[590]

*YHVH God planted a garden in Eden to the east* (Genesis 2:8).

Rabbi Yose and Rabbi Ḥiyya both say, "It is written: *I descended to the nut garden, to see the verdure of the valley* (Songs of Songs 6:11). [17d] Look how assiduously a person must contemplate and examine his heart every single day, scrutinizing his deeds, examining all his affairs! Let him ponder in his heart that the blessed

585. **He created their matter from nothing—and afterward spread them...** See above, at note 570. The full verse (Isaiah 42:5) reads: *Thus says God, YHVH, who creates the heavens and stretches them out, who spreads out the earth and what emerges from it; who gives* נשמה (*neshamah*), *breath, to the people upon her, and* רוח (*ruaḥ*), *life, to those who walk thereon.*

586. **the forms and powers inhering within her...** Apparently signifying the various elements concentrated in the earth, as primed in order to fashion the human body.

587. **I gave the soul *upon her*...** On the human being as a partnership between the body derived from the earth and the soul bequeathed by God, see *ZḤ* 16b (*MhN*), page 155.

588. ***Upon her*—to those prevailing upon her powers...** The *neshamah*, the higher aspect of the human soul, is bequeathed only to those who prevail over their (lower) earthly dispositions. See next note.

589. ***And* רוח (*ruaḥ*), *spirit, to those who walk with her*** The simple meaning of this phrase is: *and* רוח (*ruaḥ*), *life, to those who walk* בה (*bah*), *thereon*. Here, Rabbi Ḥiyya opts for a hyperliteral reading: those who associate or partner with the earth (i.e., who walk *bah*, "with her") achieve only רוח (*ruaḥ*), "spirit"—that is, the creaturely soul. See *ZḤ* 10c (*MhN*).

590. **Section 7** Some of the printed edi-

Holy One created him, placing within him a supernal soul and rank above His other creations—solely that he contemplate His service, cleaving to Him, not pursuing vanity!"[591]

As Rabbi Yose said in the name of Rabbi Ḥiyya: "When the blessed Holy One created the human being, He raised him aloft before Him in the form in which he would abide. He warned him and said to him, 'I made you for My sake, so you would be ruler and king over all like Me; Me above and you below! Furthermore, I am placing within you a soul to comprehend intelligence and wisdom, unlike the other creatures. Be careful to contemplate My glory! Be careful to perform My commandments! Aside from Me, none will possess glorious dominion like you!'[592]

"How do we know that He cautioned and warned him about this? As is written: *He said to Adam, 'See! Awe of YHVH is wisdom; to shun evil is understanding'* (Job 28:28). Namely, when My awe rests upon you, then you will attain wisdom that is ascendant above all.' When Adam saw that he possessed glorious dominion over all, he forgot the commandments of his Master and did not do what he was commanded."[593]



Rabbi Tanḥum said in the name of Rabbi Ḥanilai, "The blessed Holy One made the human being solely so he would engage in the glory of His Maker, as is written: *Everyone who is called by My Name, whom I created for My glory* (Isaiah 43:7). What is meant by *for My glory*? Striving to know My glory, repenting of his deeds, so I might give him a good share in the world to come."[594]

tions and manuscripts preserve the section heading פרשתא ז (*parsheta* 7), perhaps reflecting an early attempt to order the materials of *MhN* on the Torah. See *ZḤ* 3d, 10b, 13a, 14a, 19c, 28a, end of *parashat Lekh Lekha*—below, page 311 (all *MhN*); *Zohar* 2:20a (*MhN*).

591. **Let him ponder in his heart...** The connection with the verse from Song of Songs is not yet apparent. As will become clearer below at note 612, the *nut garden* (the Garden of Eden) connotes speculation on divine mysteries, and it is precisely for this purpose that the human being was bequeathed a supernal soul. On the verse from the Song of Songs, see *ZḤ* 9d (*MhN*).

592. **Be careful to contemplate My glory!...** The warning is issued to Adam while he is still soul, in his ethereal body.

Cf. BT *Niddah* 30b: "It [the baby] does not emerge from [the womb] until it is made to take an oath:... Be righteous, and do not be wicked; and even if all the world tells you 'You are righteous,' consider yourself wicked. Always know that the blessed Holy One is pure, that His ministers are pure, and that the soul which He gave you is pure; if you preserve it in purity, well and good—but if not, I will take it away from you." See also *Zohar* 1:76b (*ST*), 233b; 2:161b; 3:13b.

On the human being as ruler and king, see Genesis 1:28 (*fill the earth and conquer it, and have dominion*); *Bereshit Rabbah* 21:5; *ZḤ* 5a, 10a (both *MhN*); *Zohar* 1:208a; 2:150a.

593. **when My awe rests upon you...** The simple sense of אדם (*adam*) here is "human being(s)." Rabbi Yose now reads it as referring to Adam. See *Zohar* 1:199a.

On awe as the gateway to wisdom, see *Zohar* 1:7b–8a; *ZḤ* 11c (*MhN*), 45c–d; Tishby, *Wisdom of the Zohar*, 3:988–89.

594. **Striving to know My glory...** In

Rav Yehudah said, "Every single day a heavenly voice issues from above. When? At the moment the sun rises. It proclaims, 'Woe to the creatures who do not behold My glory, who do not contemplate to know and seek out My glory!'"[595]

As we have learned: Rabbi El'azar son of Rabbi Shim'on said, "When the sun inclines its wings to soar by the force of its wheels, they tread with their hooves on the leaves of the trees of the Garden of Eden. All the supernal angels and holy living beings, the King's Throne of Glory, the fragrant spices of the Garden of Eden, and the trees, heaven and earth and all their array, tremble and praise the Master of All. They rise and see the letters of the holy explicit Name engraved upon the sun in its journeys—and laud praise to the Master of Worlds."[596]

its simple sense, the verse from Isaiah refers to people created for God's honor, fame, or praise. Here, Rabbi Tanḥum reads it as: Everyone who has been called by My name and invested with a holy soul was so created only that they might explore My glory, i.e., the mysteries of Torah and divinity. See *Zohar* 2:155a.

595. **Woe to the creatures...** See *Avot* 6:2: "Rabbi Yehoshu'a son of Levi said, 'Every single day an echo resounds from Mount Horeb [Sinai], proclaiming: "Woe to the creatures for the humiliation of Torah!"'"

See also BT *Berakhot* 7a: "It was taught in the name of Rabbi Meir: When the sun begins to shine and all the kings of the East and West put their crowns upon their heads and bow down to the sun, immediately, the blessed Holy One turns angry." See also *Zohar* 1:95b; cf. *Zohar* 2:188a.

596. **When the sun inclines its wings...** The rising sun sparks the celestial praise.

"By the force of its wheel" renders בתקיפותא דגלגלוי (*be-tqifuta de-galgeloi*). Alternatively, "on the circuit of its revolutions," based on Psalms 19:6–7: *He placed in them a tent for the sun, who is like a groom coming forth from the chamber, like a hero eager to run his course. His rising place is at one end of heaven,* ותקופתו (*u-tqufato*), *and his circuit, reaches the other, nothing escapes his heat.*

The striking yet otherwise unattested image of hooves treading upon the leaves of the Garden of Eden may derive from the mythological motif of the sun's being driven by a horse-drawn chariot across the sky. See *Pirqei de-Rabbi Eli'ezer* 6: "The sun rides in a chariot and rises." See also 2 Kings 23:11; *Bemidbar Rabbah* 12:4; Meroz, "Zoharic Narratives," 26, 28.

Alternatively, the word טלפיהון (*talfeihon*), "their hooves," might signify the sun's rays. In rabbinic literature טלפים (*telafim*), "hooves," are often associated with קרנים (*qarnayim*), "horns." The verbal root קרן (*qrn*), however, also means "ray." If this is the case, then the passage should be rendered: "When the sun inclines its wings to soar on the circuit of its revolutions, its rays strike the leaves of the trees of the Garden of Eden."

On the word טלפיהון (*talfeihon*), see also *ZḤ* 24a (*MhN*, in this volume).

According to *Pirqei de-Rabbi Eli'ezer* 6: "Three letters of the Name [apparently: *YHVH*] are inscribed on the heart of the sun." See Scholem, "Parashah Ḥadashah," 440 (Addendum 1 in this volume); Isaac ibn Sahula, *Meshal ha-Qadmoni*, Gate Five, 662. See also *Zohar* 2:188a; *ZḤ* 76c (*MhN*, *Rut*).

On the trees in the Garden of Eden lauding praise, see *Pereq Shirah*, 2:57, 80; JT *Ḥagigah* 2:1, 77a; BT *Ḥagigah* 14b; *Zohar* 1:7a, 77a, 213b; 3:22b; *ZḤ* 13b (*MhN*); [Moses de León?], *Seder Gan Eden*, 138. On the Throne of Glory lauding praise, see Schäfer, *Synopse zur Hekhalot-Literatur* (*Heikhalot Rabbati*),

That voice issues forth, proclaiming, "Woe to the creatures who are not attentive to the glory of Supernal King, like the other creatures who do pay heed, lauding praises to His Name!"[597]

Accordingly, Rabbi El'azar said, "It is forbidden for a person to utter praises of his prayer unaccompanied by the twilight of the sun, as is written: *May they revere You with the sun* (Psalms 72:5)."[598]

Rabbi El'azar said similarly, "The prayer and praise of the night is from the setting of the sun until when the moon appears, as is written: *May they revere You with the sun*—morning prayer; *before the moon* (ibid.)—nighttime prayer."[599]

Rabbi Yehudah said, "This is derived from here: *From the rising of the sun to when it sets, My Name is magnified* (Malachi 1:11). In which place? *Among the nations* (ibid.). Among those of whom is written *a great nation* (Deuteronomy 4:7, 8)."[600]

Why? As we have learned: Rabbi Yehoshu'a said in the name of Rabbi Yoḥanan in the name of Rav, "The blessed Holy One made ministering angels above to



§§99, 161, 162. On the angels, see below, notes 601 and 602.

597. **who are not attentive...** Unlike the celestial and Edenic realms, which respond immediately to the sun's rays, the human realm (righteous notwithstanding) is not attentive; hence the heavenly voice.

598. ***May they revere You with the sun*** The morning prayer, *Shaharit*, cannot be recited while it is still dark. See BT *Berakhot* 29b: "Rabbi Ḥiyya son of Abba said in the name of Rabbi Yoḥanan, 'It is a commandment to pray with דמדומי חמה (*dimdumei ḥamah*), the twilight of the sun.'" See Rashi, ad loc. See also BT *Shabbat* 118b; *Zohar* 1:178a; 2:196a; Scholem, "Parashah Ḥadashah," 430 (Addendum 1 in this volume).

The morning *Amidah* is ideally recited as soon as the first ray of sunlight appears. See BT *Berakhot* 9b: "Devotees used to complete it [the recitation of the *Shema*] with the first ray of the sun, in order to join *ge'ullah* [redemption, the name of the blessing following the *Shema*] to *tefillah* [prayer, the *Amidah*] and consequently pray [the *Amidah*] in the daytime. Rabbi Zeira said, 'What is its verse [its Scriptural support]? *May they revere You with the sun* (Psalms 72:5).'"

In its simple sense, the clause from Psalms means: *May they revere You as long as the sun* [*exists*]. Here, Rabbi El'azar reads literally the preposition עם (*im*), yielding *with the sun*—that is, by daylight.

See M *Berakhot* 1:2; *Tosefta Berakhot* 1:2 (and Lieberman, ad loc.); JT *Berakhot* 1:2, 3a–b; BT *Berakhot* 26a; *Tur, Oraḥ Ḥayyim* 58, 89; *Beit Yosef* and *Shulḥan Arukh, Oraḥ Ḥayyim* 58:1; 89:1,3,8.

599. **The prayer and praise of the night...** The evening Ma'ariv prayer. In its simple sense, the second part of the verse means: *as long as the moon* [*exists*]. Here, Rabbi El'azar reads literally the preposition לפני (*lifnei*), yielding *before the moon.*

600. **This is derived from here...** The verse from Malachi serves as a proof-text. In its simple sense, *From the rising of the sun to when it sets, My Name is magnified among the nations* refers to the nations of the world. The phrase from Deuteronomy modifies the referent, *the nations*, to refer to Israel.

The verses from Deuteronomy read: *Who is a great nation that has gods so close to it as YHVH our God, in all our calling upon Him? Who is a great nation that has laws and rules as perfect as all this Teaching that I set before you this day?*

praise and exalt Him, and they chant song and hymn before Him every single night. Corresponding to them, He made Israel below to praise and exalt Him, to recite song and praise before Him every single day."[601]

It has been taught: The night has three watches. In these three watches, three companies of ministering angels alternate—praising their Creator in every single watch. Corresponding to them are three prayers in the day, when Israel assemble to praise their Creator in every single prayer.[602]

Come and hear: Rabbi Yehoshu'a said in the name of Rabbi Yoḥanan in the name of Rav, "In the morning when the sun rises, it is the time for Israel's prayer and supplication. From six hours until nine hours is the time for the *Minḥah* prayer. From when the sun sets until it is dark is the final prayer."[603]

As Rabbi Yehoshu'a said in the name Rabbi Yoḥanan in the name of Rav: "From when the sun sets until two stars are visible is the time for the final prayer.[604] [18a]

"For so have we learned: From when two stars are visible is the beginning of the first watch, when the first company of ministering angels arrives, waiting for Israel until that hour, whereupon they begin uttering song. All the gates are sealed from praises below, and the gates are opened solely for the ministering angels chanting song."[605]



But did Rabbi Yehoshu'a really say this? For look at what we have learned: Whoever studies by night, the blessed Holy One extends upon him a thread of love by day, as is said: *By day YHVH directs His love* (Psalms 42:9). Why? Because

601. **angels . . . every single night . . . Israel . . . every single day** Israel must begin their prayer and praises with the first light (and not before) because they combine with the angels to form a continuous succession of praise—angels by night, Israel by day. See BT *Ḥagigah* 12b; *Zohar* 2:18b (*MhN*); *ZḤ* 5d–6a (*MhN*).

602. **three watches . . .** See BT *Berakhot* 3a–b; Rashi on BT *Berakhot* 3a, s.v. *i qa-savar*; *Zohar* 1:159a, 189a, 231a–b; 2:18b (*MhN*), 143b, 173a–b, 195b; 3:64b; *ZḤ* 5d–6a (*MhN*), 88a (*MhN, Rut*); Moses de León, *Sefer ha-Rimmon*, 403; idem, *Sheqel ha-Qodesh*, 70–71 (88–89).

The three daily prayers are: *Shaḥarit* (morning prayer), *Minḥah* (afternoon prayer), and *Ma'ariv* (evening prayer).

This paragraph might also be construed as the continuation of Rabbi Yehoshu'a's teaching.

603. **six hours until nine hours . . .** See BT *Berakhot* 26b: "Which is *minḥah gedolah*, "the great afternoon"? From six-and-a-half hours onward [i.e., from 12:30 P.M. until 6 P.M., measuring the daytime as lasting from 6 A.M. to 6 P.M.]. Which is *minḥah qetanah*, "the small afternoon"? From nine-and-a-half hours onward [i.e., from 3:30 P.M. until 6 P.M.]." See Scholem, ad loc.

604. **until two stars are visible . . .** The practice here follows Ashkenazic custom, as noted by Ta-Shma, *Ha-Nigleh she-ba-Nistar*, 28. See above, *ZḤ* 7d (*MhN*), page 40. Cf. Maimonides, *Mishneh Torah, Hilkhot Tefillah* 3:6; *Shulḥan Arukh, Oraḥ Ḥayyim*, 233. See also JT *Berakhot* 1:1, 2b.

605. **waiting for Israel until that hour . . .** The angels wait for Israel to complete the evening prayer, whereupon they begin their celestial praise. See *ZḤ* 6a (*MhN*).

*at night His song is with me* (ibid.). Yet here you have said that all the gates below are sealed![606]

Rabbi Yehoshu'a said, "In that instance, what are they referring to? When one completed all the praises by day. But from midnight on, one engages in Torah. Why? Because at that hour the blessed Holy One ventures from those worlds that He desires, proceeding to delight with the righteous in the Garden of Eden. This accords with what David said: *At midnight I rise to praise You* (ibid. 119:62)."[607]

As we have learned: When the blessed Holy One enters with the righteous in the Garden of Eden, all the gates of heaven above are opened—those beyond

606. **Whoever studies by night...** How can you say that the gates are sealed from praises below—yet also say that the blessed Holy One bestows love upon those studying Torah at night?

See BT *Ḥagigah* 12b: "Resh Lakish said, 'Whoever engages in Torah at night, the blessed Holy One emanates a thread of love upon him by day, as is said: *By day YHVH directs His love* (Psalms 42:9). Why? Because *at night His song is with me*.'" See also BT *Avodah Zarah* 3b; *Mishnat Rabbi Eli'ezer* 13; Maimonides, *Mishneh Torah, Hilkhot Talmud Torah* 3:13; *Zohar* 1:82b, 92a, 178b, 194b, 207b; 2:18b (*MhN*), 46a, 149a; 3:36a, 44b–45a, 65a; Scholem, "Parashah Ḥadashah," 437 (Addendum 1 in this volume); Moses de León, *Sefer ha-Rimmon*, 54.

See Asulin, "Midrash ha-Ne'lam li-Vreshit," 231.

607. **from midnight on, one engages in Torah...** While the gates are sealed from prayer below, they remain open to nocturnal Torah study.

Based on King David's legendary custom of rising at midnight to study Torah (see below), the *Zohar* develops an elaborate ritual—the nocturnal delight—whereby kabbalists are expected to rise at midnight and ply Torah until the break of dawn. At midnight, God delights with the souls of the righteous in the Garden of Eden; and those who study Torah here below partake of the celestial joy. In the main body of the *Zohar*, this ritual is understood as adorning the *Shekhinah* in preparation for Her union with the blessed Holy One. This parallels the midnight vigil common among Christian monks from early medieval times. In *Zohar* 3:119a, Rabbi Yehudah alludes to the Christian practice: "I have seen something similar among the nations of the world."

See JT *Berakhot* 1:1, 2d; *Sifra, Beḥuqqotai* 3:3, 111b; *Aggadat Bereshit* 23:5; BT *Sanhedrin* 102a; 2 Enoch 8:3; *Zohar* 1:10b, 72a, 77a–b, 82b, 92a–b, 136b, 178a, 206b–207b, 231b, 242b; 2:26b, 36b, 46a, 130a–b, 136a, 173b, 195b–196a; 3:13a, 21b–22b, 49b, 52b, 67b–68a, 81a, 193a, 260a; [Moses de León?], *Seder Gan Eden*, 138; Scholem, *On the Kabbalah*, 146–50; Hellner-Eshed, *A River Flows from Eden*, 121–45. Cf. Matthew 25:6.

On the *Zohar*'s midnight ritual in *MhN*, see *Zohar* 2:18b; *ZḤ* 6a, 13c.

See BT *Berakhot* 3b: "Rabbi Osha'ya said in the name of Rabbi Aḥa, 'David said, "Midnight never passed me by in my sleep."' Rabbi Zeira said, 'Till midnight, he used to doze like a horse; from then on, he became mighty like a lion.' Rav Ashi said, 'Till midnight, he engaged in Torah; from then on, in songs and praises.'... But did David know the exact moment of midnight?... Rabbi Shim'on the Ḥasid said, 'There was a harp suspended above [King] David's bed. As soon as midnight arrived, a north wind came and blew upon it, and it played by itself. He immediately arose and engaged in Torah until the break of dawn.'"

On the worlds that He desires, see *ZḤ* 9d, 13b, 22a (all *MhN*); Scholem, "Parashah Ḥadashah," 445 (Addendum 1 in this volume).

the creatures and those beneath them—and it is a propitious time to engage in Torah. Those companies of ministering angels and all the fragrant aromas of the Garden of Eden as well as the righteous all burst forth in song in the presence of He who spoke and the world was, as is written: *Surely the righteous will praise Your Name* (ibid. 140:14). When will the righteous praise Your Name? When *the upright dwell in Your presence* (ibid.)—in the hour when they dwell in His presence in the Garden of Eden.[608]

The third company of ministering angels chants song in His presence until the dawn splits. When the pillar of dawn ascends, Israel are obliged to rise and fortify themselves with song and praise before the blessed Holy One. Why? Because they take up song after the ministering angels, and the blessed Holy One is found with them below, as is written: *Those who seek Me early will find Me* (Proverbs 8:17).[609]

Rabbi Yehudah said, "Only on condition that he not cease once he began, until he prays when the sun rises."[610]

Rabbi Yoḥanan said, "When the blessed Holy One ventures from those worlds that He desires, coming to enter with the righteous in the Garden of Eden, He waits—seeing whether He hears a voice engaging in Torah. For we have learned: That voice is more pleasing before Him than all the songs and praises uttered by the ministering angels above. As is written: *I descended to the nut garden to see* (Songs of Songs 6:11). What is implied by *to see*? Those engaging in Torah."[611] 183

Rabbi Yitsḥak asked, "But is the Garden of Eden really called *the nut garden*?"

Rabbi Yoḥanan replied, "Yes. It is called גנת אגוז (*ginnat egoz*), *the nut garden*, that is to say גנת עדן (*ginnat eden*), the Garden of Eden. Just as the nut is concealed on all sides and is enveloped by numerous husks, similarly Eden is concealed on all sides and is guarded by numerous watches—who are not empowered to see, neither angel, nor *seraph*, nor *ḥashmal*, nor prophetic eye, nor visionary, as is written: *No eye has seen, O God, but You* (Isaiah 64:3)."[612]

608. ***the upright dwell in Your presence...*** On this verse from Psalms, see *Zohar* 1:226b; *ZḤ* 19a (*MhN*).

This and the following paragraph might also be construed as the continuation of Rabbi Yehoshu'a's teaching.

609. ***Those who seek Me early...*** In its simple sense, the verse in Proverbs—spoken there by Wisdom—reads: *I love those who love me;* ומשחרי (*u-mshaḥarai*), *those who seek me, will find me.* Here, the *Zohar* construes *meshaḥarai* as playing upon the unrelated noun שחר (*shaḥar*), "dawn." See *Devarim Rabbah* 8:1; *Zohar* 2:131a, 140a.

610. **on condition that he not cease...** The special intimacy intimated by the verse in Proverbs is conditional on the adept's not sleeping throughout the night and connecting his nocturnal Torah study with his morning prayer.

611. **That voice is more pleasing...** See *Zohar* 2:46a; *ZḤ* 13c (*MhN*); Scholem, "Parashah Ḥadashah," 437 (Addendum 1 in this volume); cf. BT *Ḥullin* 91b.

612. **It is called גנת אגוז (*ginnat egoz*), *the nut garden*...** In the writings of *Ḥasidei Ashkenaz*, in particular El'azar of Worms, the nut symbolizes the *merkavah*, the divine

Rabbi Shim'on said, "I was in the presence of Rabbi Beroka who used to say, 'Then I will attain the degree of the nut garden with the pious of Israel,' but I did not know what it was—until I heard what Rabban Yoḥanan son of Zakkai said: 'The blessed Holy One called the Garden of Eden *the nut garden.* Just as the nut has husk upon husk and its kernel lies within, so Eden has world after world and it is within.'"[613]

Rabbi Shim'on taught, "This garden, whence did the blessed Holy One plant it? He planted it beneath Eden. Now, should you say that they are equal—this is impossible! Rather, the garden is on earth and Eden is above it on high. Whence derive the drippings of the garden? From Eden!"[614]

Rabbi Yehudah asked him, "In accordance with your opinion, why then is it written: *A river issues from Eden to water the garden* (Genesis 2:10)? The verse should have said, 'A river descends from Eden to water the garden,' implying that it descends from above to the garden below!"[615]

Well, Rabbi Shim'on said, "There is Eden above and Eden below; garden above and garden below. The two of them are aligned corresponding to one another; the blessed Holy One planted one beneath the other."[616]



chariot. Descending to the nut garden therefore connotes speculating on the divine throne. Here, the correlate is the Garden of Eden. See Dan, *Torat ha-Sod,* 208–10; Farber, "Tefisat ha-Merkavah be-Torat ha-Sod be-Me'ah ha-Shelosh-Esreh"; Abrams, *Sexual Symbolism and Merkavah Speculation.* On the nut motif in *MhN,* see *Zohar* 2:15b; *ZḤ* 9d, 83a (*Rut*). See also *Zohar* 1:19b, 44b (*Heikh*); 2:233b, 254b (*Heikh*); Moses de León, *Sefer ha-Mishqal,* 156–8; [Moses de León?], *Seder Gan Eden,* 138; Liebes, *Peraqim,* s.v. אגוזא (egoza), 20–21, 27.

On the concealed Eden above, see *ZḤ* 13c (*MhN*). See below, notes 614 and 616. On the verse from Isaiah, see BT *Berakhot* 34b, in the name of Rabbi Yoḥanan: "All the prophets prophesied only concerning the days of the Messiah, but as for the world to come, *No eye has seen, O God, but You,* [*what You will do for one who awaits You*]."

613. **Rabbi Beroka . . .** See *ZḤ* 18c–d (*MhN*).

614. **the garden is on earth and Eden is above . . .** Genesis 2 mentions the Garden of Eden (verse 15) as well as a garden planted in Eden (verse 8). Rabbi Shim'on differentiates between the two terms—the garden is below and Eden is above on high. See BT *Berakhot* 34b; *Zohar* 1:106b (*MhN*), 125a (*MhN*); 2:150a; *ZḤ* 13c, 21a (both *MhN*). Cf. *Bereshit Rabbah* 15:2.

On the earthly and heavenly Gardens of Eden, see Naḥmanides on Genesis 3:22; idem, *Kitvei Ramban,* 2:295–99; *Zohar* 1:7a, 38b (*Heikh*), 81a (*ST*), 106b (*MhN*), 224b; 2:150a, 209b–210b, 211b–212a, 231b; 3:13a, 53a, 70b; Moses de León, *Shushan Edut,* 350–51; idem, *Sheqel ha-Qodesh,* 27 (32), 59–62 (73–76); [Moses de León?], *Seder Gan Eden*; Tishby, *Wisdom of the Zohar,* 2:591–94, 749–51.

615. ***A river issues from Eden . . .*** If Eden is indeed above the garden, why doesn't the verse convey the sense of a downward flow? On the verse from Genesis, see Hellner-Eshed, *A River Flows from Eden,* 229–51.

616. **Eden above and Eden below; garden above and garden below . . .** The river issues (rather than descends) from Eden above to the Garden above, and the river issues (rather than descends) from the Eden below to the Garden below.

Precisely what these terms designate is

Now, did He really [18b] plant it Himself? Yes! As Rabbi Yehudah said: "Since its plantings are not like other plantings, but are superior to other plantings, it was a planting of YHVH, as is said: *a planting of YHVH so He may be glorified* (Isaiah 61:3)—namely for praise, and this is the meaning of *so He may be glorified*; as if to say, 'This is none other than *a planting of YHVH*—and no one else's!'"[617]

Rabbi Ya'akov son of Idi said, "By all counts it was *a planting of YHVH*, for He planted there *every tree lovely to look at* (Genesis 2:9). How did He plant? Well, when the earth produced her trees and fruits, she first brought them forth in the Garden of Eden, and afterward throughout the entire world. The blessed Holy One selected that place—and arrayed them to abide there forever. He tends it, graciously watering it from the bounty flowing from Eden above, as is written: *The trees of YHVH are sated, the cedars of Lebanon that He planted* (Psalms 104:16). *The trees of YHVH are sated*—the trees in the Garden of Eden."[618]

unclear, though perhaps Rabbi Shim'on intends that there is a domain above termed the Garden of Eden (where the river of emanation flows from Eden to the Garden), and there is another domain below, the earthly Garden of Eden (where the river flows in the same way). These four terms thus correlate with his earlier terminology: Eden above with the heavenly Garden of Eden above; and garden below with the earthly Garden of Eden. Cf. *Sullam*, who correlates these four domains with the *sefirot*.

On upper and lower Eden, cf. *Zohar* 2:210b; 3:129b (*IR*), 182b.

617. ***a planting of YHVH...*** In context in Isaiah, the verse refers to mourners who—comforted by the prophesy—will be called *oaks of righteousness, a planting of YHVH so He may be glorified*. Here, Rabbi Yehudah construes the phrase as referring to the Garden of Eden.

See also Isaiah 60:21: *Your people, all of them righteous, will inherit the land forever—sprout of My planting, work of My hands so I may be glorified.*

On the superiority of the plantings in the Garden of Eden, see next note.

618. **By all counts...** We have no need to prove that God planted Eden Himself. Genesis states explicitly: *YHVH God caused to spring up from the soil every tree lovely to look at and good to eat.* (Ironically, the preceding verse is even more explicit: *YHVH God planted a garden in Eden.*)



See Naḥmanides on Genesis 2:8: "The purport of the expression *YHVH God planted* is to state that it was the *planting of YHVH*, for before He decreed upon the earth *Let the earth bring forth grass* (Genesis 1:11), He had already decreed that in that place there be a garden, and He further said, 'Here shall be this tree, and here that tree'—like the rows of planters.... He decreed that they grow branches and bear fruit forever... never to die in the ground. These trees were not to need anyone to tend and prune them.... This is also the meaning of *YHVH God planted*—that they were His plantings, the work of His hands, existing forever."

Cf. *Bereshit Rabbah* 15:1: "*YHVH God planted a garden in Eden* (Genesis 2:8).... As is written: *The trees of YHVH are sated, cedars of Lebanon that He planted* (Psalms 104:16). Rabbi Ḥanina said, 'They resembled antennae of grasshoppers, and the blessed Holy One uprooted them, transplanting them in the Garden of Eden.'"

On the Garden of Eden's sprouting first, see *Pirqei de-Rabbi Eli'ezer* 5: "He opened an entrance to the Garden of Eden, from where He brought forth plants upon the face of all the earth...."; see also *ZḤ* 13c (*MhN*), page 112.

Rabbi Ḥaggai asked Rabbi Yehudah, "Saying that the Garden of Eden is on earth—why is it necessary?"[619]

He replied, "For the pleasure of the soul receiving from that Eden above. Now, should you think that it is for all the souls, look at what we have learned: Those not granted permission to ascend above enjoy pleasure and delight in the one below, from that which it receives from above."[620]

Rabbi Yehudah said, "On every single new moon, they ascend to the supernal academy on high, as is written: *From new moon to new moon and from Sabbath to Sabbath* [*all flesh shall come to bow down before Me*] (Isaiah 66:23).[621]

"In this Garden of Eden below did Adam reside. The blessed Holy One placed him there so his abode would be within, as is written: *He placed there the human He had fashioned* (Genesis 2:8)."[622]

Rabbi Ḥiyya and Rabbi Yose were walking on the way. Rabbi Yose said to Rabbi Ḥiyya, "We have learned in our Mishnah: Everything that the blessed Holy One made, whether above or below, yearns assiduously to pursue its kind. The body goes after its kind—to the earth from which it was taken, while the soul's only desire is for the site from which it was taken, for everything that He made yearns after its kind, as is written: *My soul yearns, even pines for the courts of YHVH* (Psalms 84:3)—not for this world like the body."[623]

Rabbi Ḥiyya said to him, "I shall tell you something that is a mystery which people do not know."



619. **why is it necessary?** Isn't the supernal Garden of Eden sufficient?

620. **For the pleasure of the soul . . .** Two degrees of Edenic pleasure await the soul: the earthly Garden of Eden, and Eden above. The latter is superior and the source of the delight of the former. See *ZḤ* 21a (*MhN*).

621. **ascend to the supernal academy on high . . .** That is, the heavenly academy where the souls of the righteous study Torah with God. See BT *Bava Metsi'a* 85b–86a.

On the soul's ascent based on the verse in Isaiah, see *Zohar* 1:115b–116a (*MhN*); 2:156b–157a; 3:144b–145a (*IR*), 159b, 182b; see below, *ZḤ* 18b (*MhN*).

622. **In this Garden of Eden below did Adam reside . . .** See below, *ZḤ* 18c (*MhN*). Cf. *Zohar* 1:38a (*Heikh*).

623. **yearns assiduously to pursue its kind . . .** See BT *Bava Qamma* 92b: "It was taught in the Mishnah: 'Anything attached to something subject to impurity is itself subject to impurity. Anything attached to something that remains pure will itself remain pure.' It was taught in a *baraita* [a Tannaitic teaching not included in the Mishnah]: Rabbi Eli'ezer said, 'Not for nothing did the starling follow the raven, but because it is of its kind.'" See *Bereshit Rabbah* 65:3; *Zohar* 1:20b, 126b, 137b, 167b; 2:141a; Moses de León, *Sefer ha-Mishqal*, 46; idem, *Sefer ha-Rimmon*, 39 (see Wolfson notes, ad loc.). In the Kabbalah, this Talmudic idea receives a Neoplatonic twist: soul pursues divinity.

On the body's affinity to this world and the soul's affinity to the upper world, see above, *ZḤ* 16b (*MhN*), page 155; cf. *Zohar* 2:141a–b; see Tishby, *Wisdom of the Zohar*, 2:683. On the expression "our Mishnah," see above, note 468.

He lowered his head, wept, and laughed. Rabbi Yose was silent.[624] After some time, Rabbi Ḥiyya said to him, "Happy are the righteous! Woe to the wicked! Happy are the righteous—who are called 'living' in the world to come. Now, is it because of the soul that abides enduringly that they are alive? For the body rots in the ground even though he was perfectly righteous; and we have learned: The soul always abides enduringly.[625]

"Rather, so has been decreed: When a righteous person departs this world the blessed Holy One prepares for him another body, pure and good—without the contamination and filth of this body—and inserts the holy soul within. He establishes him enduringly in that body in the Garden of Eden below. It will be for them another world—the world to come.[626]

"Every single new moon, they venture forth and gaze upon the wicked tormented in Hell, as is written: *They will go out and stare at the corpses of the people who rebelled against Me* (Isaiah 66:24). From which place do they go out? Rabbi Abba taught, "From the Garden of Eden below. Why? To gaze upon the wicked." Every single Sabbath and every single new moon, the blessed Holy One raises them aloft to the Academy of the Firmament, as is written: *From new moon to new moon, [and from Sabbath to Sabbath, all flesh shall come to bow down before Me]* (ibid., 23)."[627]



624. **Rabbi Yose was silent** On Rabbi Yose's silence, see BT *Shabbat* 33b, *Nazir* 50a; *Zohar* 2:17b (*MhN*), 36b. Cf. *Zohar* 1:115b; 2:4a, 217b.

625. **Happy are the righteous—who are called 'living'...** In what way are the righteous "alive" in the next world? It cannot be on account of their earthly body, which rots in the earth, nor can it be on account of the soul, for the soul survives eternally in any event. Hence, life and death do not pertain to the soul, but only to the body.

See BT *Berakhot* 18a–b: "Rabbi Ḥiyya said, 'These are the righteous, who even in death are called "living." ... These are the wicked, who even in life are called "dead."'" Cf. *Zohar* 1:132a, 164a, 207b; 2:106b; 3:182b, 287b (*IZ*); *ZḤ* 20b (*MhN*).

626. **another body, pure and good...** It is on account of the ethereal body bequeathed to the righteous that they are considered "living" in the world to come.

On the ethereal body, see Naḥmanides on Genesis 49:33; *Zohar* 1:7a, 38b (*Heikh*), 81a (*ST*), 90b–91a, 115b (*MhN*), 131a, 217b, 219a, 220a, 224a–b, 227a–b, 233b; 2:11a, 13a–b, 96b, 141b, 150a, 156b–157a, 161b; 3:13a–b, 43a–b, 61b, 70b, 104a–b; *ZḤ* 10b (*MhN*), 90b (*MhN, Rut*); Moses de León, *Sefer ha-Rimmon*, 390; [Moses de León?], *Seder Gan Eden*, 133; Scholem, *Shedim, Ruḥot u-Nshamot*, 215–45; idem, *Kabbalah*, 158–59; idem, *On the Mystical Shape of the Godhead*, 251–73; Tishby, *Wisdom of the Zohar*, 2:770–73. Cf. Rashi on BT *Ḥagigah* 12b, s.v. *ve-ruḥot u-nshamot*.

On "the world to come," see *Tanḥuma, Vayiqra* 8: "The wise call it *ha-olam ha-bah*, the world to come, not because it does not exist now, but for us today in this world it is still to come." See also Maimonides, *Mishneh Torah, Hilkhot Teshuvah* 8:8; and Guttmann, *Philosophies of Judaism*, 37: "'The world to come' does not succeed 'this world' in time, but exists from eternity as a reality outside and above time, to which the soul ascends." On the use of the term "decree" to establish a teaching, see above, note 404.

627. **gaze upon the wicked tormented in**

Rabbi Yehoshu'a of Sakhnin said, "Every single night! When morning arrives, He renews their souls for them, as is written: *New every morning, immense is Your faithfulness* (Lamentations 3:23)."[628]

Rabbi Yitsḥak said, "Even for all human beings as well! In this world every night when a person sleeps, he ascends above and is found to possess numerous sins before the blessed Holy One. Through the blessed Holy One's great faithfulness, He restores her [the soul] to the body, renewing her within. Why? *Immense is Your faithfulness*—because Your faithfulness is immense."[629]

Hence, Rabbi Yitsḥak [18c] said, "If one owes money to his companion and his companion offers him a pledge as a surety, it is forbidden him to hold on to it until his companion returns it [the loan] to him, even if the court gives it to him, as is written: *If you should indeed take in pledge your fellow's cloak* (Exodus 22:25)."[630]

Rabbi Yehudah son of Rabbi Simon said, "*He placed there the human He had fashioned* (Genesis 2:8)—in general."[631]



**Hell...** Verse 24 continues: *Their worms shall not die, nor their fire be quenched. They shall be a horror to all flesh.* See BT *Eruvin* 19a; *Zohar* 1:107a (*MhN*); 2:151a.

On Isaiah 66:23 and the ascent to the celestial academy, see above, note 621.

628. **Every single night!...** According to Rabbi Yehoshu'a the souls of the righteous enjoy celestial ascent and renewal (or rebirth) every night, not only on Sabbaths and New Moons. See *Zohar* 1:19a–b; 2:213b–214a. Cf. BT *Ḥagigah* 14a, where the verse is applied to angels who are born daily.

629. **when a person sleeps, he ascends above...** Not only do the righteous ascend nightly, but also the souls of all human beings during sleep. See next note.

630. **offers him a pledge as a surety...** That is, if A owes money to B, and then A offers collateral to B, it is forbidden for B to hold on to it.

The verse in Exodus continues: *before the sun comes down you shall return it to him.*

See *Tanḥuma* (Buber), *Mishpatim* 9, where the biblical law of the returned pledge is connected with the nightly return of the soul: "*If you should indeed take in pledge your fellow's cloak* (Exodus 22:25). The blessed Holy One said, 'How much do you owe Me! You sin before Me, yet I wait for you. Your soul ascends before Me every single night, gives an accounting and is found to be in debt—yet I return it to you even though you are guilty. So you, even though he is in debt to you, *before the sun comes down you shall return it to him* (ibid.).'" See also Rashi on Exodus 22:25; BT *Bava Metsi'a* 31b, 114b.

On the soul's nocturnal ascent and the need to pledge one's soul before going to sleep, see *Zohar* 1:11a, 36b, 83a, 92a, 183a; 3:119a, 120b, 121b; *ZḤ* 89a (*MhN, Rut*); Tishby, *Wisdom of the Zohar*, 2:809–13; see also BT *Berakhot* 5a: "Abbaye said, 'Even a disciple of the wise should recite one verse of compassion [before going to bed], such as: *Into Your hand I entrust my spirit; You redeem me, YHVH, God of truth* (Psalms 31:6).'"

631. **in general** Rabbi Yehudah reads the verse as though it is speaking about all human beings (their souls) and not specifically about Adam.

Rabbi Shim'on said, "*He placed him in the Garden of Eden* לעבדה ולשמרה (*le-ovdah ul-shomrah*), *to cultivate her and tend her* (ibid. 2:15). What kind of cultivation is implied here? It means the cultivation of the soul, consummating her perfections unaccomplished in this world."[632]

Rabbi Yehoshu'a said, "The blessed Holy One placed Adam in the Garden of Eden and gave him His Torah לעבוד בה (*la'avod bah*), to toil in her, and to tend to her commandments, as is written: *the Tree of Life in the midst of the garden* (ibid. 2:9), and: *a Tree of Life to those who grasp her* (Proverbs 3:18). The blessed Holy One said, 'When Adam enjoys pleasure in this garden, he will engage in her and fulfill her.' But because of the עדונין (*idunin*), delights, and pleasures Adam enjoyed there, he did not fulfill His Torah—so that He banished him from there."[633]

Rabbi Abba said in the name of Rabbi Ḥiyya, "It was an actual tree! There were two: one—bestowing life upon the human being; the other—whoever ate of it would know good and evil, knowing the good path by which a person becomes righteous, as well as the evil path by which a person is corrupted. That is why the blessed Holy One commanded him not to eat from it, lest he reject the good and cling to evil.[634]



"Therefore He said: *From every tree of the garden you are free to eat* (Genesis 2:16). This refers to the Tree of Life, from which Adam was supposed to eat. He

632. **cultivation of the soul...** The verse is usually translated: *to cultivate it and tend it*, referring to the Garden. Rabbi Shim'on, however, focuses on the feminine suffixes in *le-ovdah ul-shomrah*, "to cultivate her and tend her," which he interprets as referring to the soul (which is likewise grammatically feminine). In the Garden of Eden, human beings are given the chance to perfect their souls. Cf. *Bereshit Rabbah* 16:5.

633. **to toil in her, and to tend to her commandments...** In contrast to the preceding homily, Rabbi Yehoshu'a reads the verse as applying specifically to Adam.

See *Sifrei*, Deuteronomy 41: "*He placed him in the Garden of Eden* לעבדה ולשמרה (*le-ovdah ul-shomrah*), *to work it and keep it*. ... *To work it*—Torah study; *to keep it*—this refers to the commandments." Cf. *Zohar* 2:165b.

On Torah as the Tree of Life, see *Sifrei*, Deuteronomy 47; BT *Berakhot* 32b.

The word עדן (Eden), when used as a common noun, means "delight." On the relationship between pleasure and delight and Torah study in *MhN*, see above, *ZḤ* 13d (*MhN*), page 116.

634. **whoever ate of it would know good and evil...** Rabbi Abba insists on a more literal reading of the narrative. The tree is not merely a symbol!

Whereas *the Tree of Life* bestows (long) life, *the Tree of Knowledge of Good and Evil* bestows knowledge of good and evil, i.e., how to become good or evil.

Cf. Naḥmanides on Genesis 2:9: "Now it was the fruit of this tree that gave rise to will and desire, that those who ate it should choose a thing or its opposite, for good or for evil. This is why it is called *the Tree of the Knowledge of Good and Evil*."

The manuscripts differ regarding the name of the speaker. I have followed Venice and Margaliot.

sinned only with the Tree of Knowledge of Good and Evil, for he was commanded not to eat from it, as is written: *But as for the Tree of Knowledge of Good and Evil, do not eat from it—for on the day you eat from it, you will surely die* (ibid., 17)."[635]

Hence Rabbi Shim'on said, "A decree was ordained beforehand that Adam should die, since he was taken from the ground. As implied by what is written: *on the day you eat from it* [*you will surely die*] (ibid.)—teaching that had he not sinned, he would have had a long life. As soon as he sinned, the punishment was that his days be shortened—and that he die on that very day. After he repented, the blessed Holy One granted him His day—which is one thousand years."[636]

This proves that the decree that he die was prior. For were it not so, when he repented He should have rescinded the decree![637]

Rabbi Shim'on explained, "He repented and He rescinded the decree ordained for him—*on the day you eat from it* (ibid.); He lengthened his days, granting him His day."[638]

190

Rabbi Beroka said, "He was commanded about the Name—and he sinned with the Name. He was commanded about the Name—the unique Name, as is written: *the Tree of Life*... (Genesis 2:9). He sinned with the Name—the polysemous name, as is written: *the Tree of Knowledge of Good and Evil* (ibid.)."[639]

635. **the Tree of Life...** Even though after his expulsion from the Garden Adam was forbidden to eat from the Tree of Life, originally it had been permitted.

636. **A decree was ordained beforehand...** Adam was created mortal; having been created from the earth, it was a given that he would die. Eating from the forbidden tree did not bring death into the world; it merely shortened his life.

On the view that had Adam not sinned he would have lived forever, see Naḥmanides on Genesis 2:17; *Zohar* 1:60a; 2:55a. On the view that he was always intended to be mortal, see *Zohar* 3:159a–b. On Adam's repentance, see *Bereshit Rabbah* 22:13; BT *Avodah Zarah* 8a; *Pirqei de-Rabbi Eli'ezer* 20; *Zohar* 1:55b, 224a; *ZḤ* 19b (*MhN*), page 205. On Adam's being granted a "day," see *Bereshit Rabbah* 19:8; *Zohar* 1:139b–140a; *ZḤ* 19b (*MhN*). See *Bereshit Rabbah* 8:2: "A day of the blessed Holy One is a thousand years, as is said: *For a thousand years in Your eyes are like yesterday gone* (Psalms 90:4)."

According to Genesis 5:5, Adam lived until the age of 930.

637. **This proves that the decree...** Had God intended that Adam be immortal, when he repented and the punishment was annulled, he should have become immortal once again.

638. ***on the day you eat from it...*** The decree was rescinded insofar as Adam did not die on the very day that he sinned.

639. **He was commanded about the Name...** Here begins a central theological theme of *MhN*: the nature of Adam's sin in the Garden of Eden. The unique name, *YHVH*, is correlated with the Tree of Life (from which Adam was permitted—even commanded—to eat), and the polysemous name, *Elohim*, corresponds to the Tree of Knowledge of Good and Evil (from which he was forbidden to eat). See below, *ZḤ* 19c (*MhN*), pages 206–7.

The divine name *Elohim* is termed "polysemous" because it has various meanings in Scripture. See Maimonides, *Guide of the Per-*

Rabbi Abbahu said, "If concerning one who offers a sacrifice to this name the Torah said: *Whoever sacrifices to Elohim shall be proscribed* (Exodus 22:19), all the more so one who exchanges His unique Name for it!"[640]

How do we know that he sinned with the Name?

Rabbi Beroka said, "As is written: *she took of its fruit and ate* (Genesis 3:6)—the name derived from it, paradigm of the fruit derived from the tree."[641]

Rabbi Abbahu said, "That is why the entire matter was ascribed to those trees of the Garden of Eden."[642]

Rabbi Yitsḥak said, "We see that four of the Companions were punished for this!"[643]

*plexed* 1:2: "The term *Elohim* is equivocal—designating the deity, the angels, and the rulers governing the cities." On its polysemous nature, see *Zohar* 1:2a; *ZḤ* 3d, 17b (both *MhN*); Moses de León, *Sefer ha-Mishqal*, 42–3; idem, *Sefer ha-Rimmon*, 287.

The nature of Adam's sin is explained below.

640. ***Whoever sacrifices to Elohim shall be proscribed...*** On sacrifices being directed exclusively to *YHVH*, see *Sifrei*, Numbers 143; BT *Menaḥot* 110a; Naḥmanides on Leviticus 1:9; *Zohar* 1:247b; 2:108a; 3:5a; *ZḤ* 3d (also in the name of Rabbi Abbahu), 19c (both *MhN*); Moses de León, *Sefer ha-Rimmon*, 287.

641. **paradigm of the fruit derived from the tree** Just as fruit derives its life and vitality from the tree to which it is attached—and withers and dies once it is separated—so the divine name *Elohim* derives its life and vitality only when attached to the Tree, the name *YHVH*. Adam and Eve's sin therefore was that they separated the fruit from the tree; the name *Elohim* from the name *YHVH*; the Tree of Knowledge from the Tree of Life.

In philosophical terms, Adam's sin was that he partook of the derived rather than the essence; the known rather than the unknown.

In the main body of the *Zohar*, Adam's sin was that he partook only of *Shekhinah* (the Tree of Knowledge of Good and Evil), splitting Her off from the other *sefirot* and divorcing Her from Her husband, *Tif'eret* (the Tree of Life). See *Zohar* 1:12b, 35b–36a, 53a–b, 221a–b, 237a; Scholem, *Major Trends*, 231–2, 236, 404–5, n. 105; Tishby, *Wisdom of the Zohar*, 1:373–76. (On the psychological plane, Adam's sin corresponds to the splitting off of consciousness from the unconscious. See Jung, *Collected Works*, 8:157; Neumann, *Origins and History of Consciousness*, 102–27; Jaynes, *Origin of Consciousness*, 299; Scholem, *Major Trends*, 216, 236–37.)

Cf. Maimonides, *Guide of the Perplexed* 1:61: "All the names of God ... derive from actions.... The only exception is one name: namely, *Yod*, *He*, *Vav*, *He*. This is the name of God (may He be exalted) that has been originated without any derivation ... this name gives a clear unequivocal indication of His essence."

642. **That is why the entire matter was ascribed...** The story in Genesis conceals the true nature of their sin. The narrative tells a story about two trees—but this is merely a metaphorical cover for the deeper meaning: separating the fruit (*Elohim*) from the tree (*YHVH*).

643. **four of the Companions were punished for this** That is, they recapitulated Adam's primal sin, separating *Elohim* from *YHVH*, knowledge from life. This appears to allude to a Talmudic tale, in which, however, only three were punished. See BT *Ḥagigah* 14b: "Four entered *pardes*, an orchard, [whence: paradise]: Ben Azzai, Ben Zoma, Aḥer [that is, Elisha son of Avuyah], and Rabbi Akiva.... Ben Azzai glimpsed and died.... Ben Zoma glimpsed and went mad.... Aḥer severed the saplings [apparently: left the fold]. Rabbi Akiva emerged in

Rabbi Yehudah said, "Concerning what Rabbi Beroka said—one must not ponder this portion further. For I have heard something similar from my father and now recall. From here on, conventional interpretation is required!"[644]

*The serpent was slier than any creature of the field* (Genesis 3:1). Rabbi Yose taught, "This is the evil impulse—the serpent that entices human beings. Why is it called *serpent*? Just as the serpent writhes and does not move in a straightforward manner, so the evil impulse leads a person astray—along the evil path, and not along the straight path."[645]

Rabbi Yose taught, "What is the meaning of: *slier than any* חית השדה (*ḥayyat ha-sadeh*), *creature of the field* (ibid.)? It was slier and cleverer than נפש החיה (*nefesh ha-ḥayyah*), the creaturely soul, in the body. It enticed Adam until he was banished from the delight of the Garden of Eden."[646]

We have learned there: Rabbi Yehudah son of Rabbi Simon said, "I have pondered the word that Rabbi Beroka spoke and inquired of him; and I found that he possessed the essence of the קבלה (*qabbalah*), tradition, and that thus was decreed in the first book of the Mishnah of Rabbi El'azar son of Arakh."[647]



peace." See *Tosefta Ḥagigah* 2:3; JT *Ḥagigah* 2:1, 77b; *Shir ha-Shirim Rabbah* on 1:4.

644. **conventional interpretation is required** "Conventional interpretation" renders דרשה (*derashah*), "interpretation, homiletical interpretation," contrasted here with deeper wisdom. Although Rabbi Beroka's interpretation is correct and indeed the final word on the matter, it ought not to be discussed, as it is a supernal secret that should be concealed.

See *ZḤ* 25d (*MhN*), where *derashah* is contrasted with "the essence of the matter." See also Gikatilla, *Sha'arei Orah*, 2a quoting *ZḤ* 25d (*MhN*): "I have not come here for *derashah*, but rather for the essence of the matter." Cf. *Zohar* 2:145a.

This reluctance to reveal secrets appears two more times in this textual unit; below, *ZḤ* 18d, at nn. 652 and 659. See also below, *ZḤ* 19c, page 208, also in the name of Rabbi Yehudah. The dialectical tension between disclosure and concealment receives its quintessential expression in Rabbi Shim'on's comments in the opening of the *Idra Rabba* (*Zohar* 3:127b): "Woe if I reveal! Woe if I do not reveal!"

645. **This is the evil impulse...** See *Zohar* 1:35b, 49b; *ZḤ* 24b (*MhN*). Cf. BT *Bava Batra* 16a: "Resh Lakish said, 'Satan, the evil impulse, and the Angel of Death are one and the same.'" Cf. *Pirqei de-Rabbi Eli'ezer* 13.

See Isaiah 27:1: *In that day,* YHVH *will punish with His great, cruel, mighty sword Leviathan the elusive serpent, Leviathan the writhing serpent....* Cf. *Zohar* 2:35a.

646. **cleverer than נפש החיה (*nefesh ha-ḥayyah*), the creaturely soul...** The evil impulse outwitted the creaturely soul, the lower aspect of the human being, connected to the earth. On the creaturely soul, see above, notes 217, 218.

See *Targum Onqelos*, who renders the word ערום (*arum*), "sly," as חכים (*ḥakim*), "wise, crafty, cunning." See also *Zohar* 1:138a.

647. **I have pondered the word...** Perhaps because Rabbi Beroka's interpretation concerning the nature of Adam's sin pertains to sublime mysteries, it is subject to yet further scrutiny. Not only is it found to be authentic, but also it can be found in a respected book. This book, though, is one of the many books housed in the real or imaginary Zoharic library. See *Ketem Paz*,

Rabbi Shim'on [18d] said, "When the serpent beguiled the woman, what is written? *The woman saw that it was good* (Genesis 3:6). What is indicated by *that it was good*?[648]

"Rabbi El'azar son of Shalom said, 'She agreed in her mind that it was good, as is said: *For YHVH is good* (Psalms 100:5), *Praise YHVH for He is good* (ibid. 107:1). *And a delight to the eyes* (Genesis 3:6)—that it is the delight which Above and Below desire to know and apprehend. Immediately, *she took of its fruit and ate* (ibid.).'"[649]

Rabbi Shim'on said, "She exchanged dominion for service."[650]

Rabbi El'azar said, "As is said: *Do not* תמר (*tamer*), *defy, him* (Exodus 23:21)."[651]

Rabbi Yehudah said, "Didn't I say that one should not ponder this portion further! For look, that which Rabbi Beroka said explains the entire portion! No more is needed, only conventional interpretation!"[652]

Rabbi Yitsḥak said, "What is the significance of *they sewed fig leaves* (Genesis 3:7)? Rav Naḥman translates as follows: they composed false accusations."[653]



1:22d: "All such books mentioned in the *Zohar*... have been lost in the wanderings of exile.... Nothing is left of them except what is mentioned in the *Zohar*."

On El'azar son of Arakh in *MhN*, see *ZḤ* 25c–26a, 27d–28a.

648. ***The woman saw that it was good...*** The full verse reads: *The woman saw that the tree was good for eating and a delight to the eyes, and that the tree was desirable to contemplate. She took of its fruit and ate, and also gave to her husband beside her, and he ate.*

649. **She agreed in her mind that it was good...** Instead of clinging to *YHVH* (about whom one can say "is good"), Eve determined that the Tree of Knowledge (that is, *Elohim*, and perhaps *Shekhinah*) *was good* and worthy of adoration alone, separate from *YHVH*. See *Zohar* 1:36a.

The printed editions and some of the manuscripts allude to *Shekhinah*, reading: "that She is the delight whom Above and Below desire to know and apprehend," rather than the grammatical masculine pronoun, which can refer to "it" or "Him." In *MhN* on the Torah, it is not clear whether the divine hypostasis signified by *Elohim* is gendered, as it is in the other strata of the *Zohar*. I have followed O2 and OM1.

It is not clear whether Rabbi El'azar is being quoted by Rabbi Shim'on or is an independent voice.

650. **She exchanged dominion for service** That is, *YHVH* for *Elohim*. Cf. *Zohar* 1:112b.

651. ***Do not* תמר (*tamer*), *defy, him...*** In BT *Sanhedrin* 38b, this verse is interpreted to mean "Do not תמירני (*tamireni*), exchange Me, with him [Metatron]." Here, the sin is exchanging *YHVH* with *Elohim*. Cf. Moses de León, *Or Zaru'a*, 273.

652. **Didn't I say that one should not ponder...** See above, at note 644. Despite Rabbi Yehudah's earlier warning, the Rabbis continued to expound the secret of Adam's sin.

653. **false accusations** "False accusations" renders תסקופי מילין (*tasquppei millin*), a phrase deriving from *Targum Onqelos*, Deuteronomy 22:14, in rendering עלילות דברים (*alilot devarim*), "false accusations" (of sexual misconduct, made by a husband against his wife). See also *Targum Yonatan*, Judges 14:4, where תוסקפא (*tusqafa*) renders תאנה (*to'anah*), "pretext." See Radak on Judges 14:4; *Zohar* 1:169b, 179b; 2:65a–b; 3:172b, 266b.

In its simple sense, the biblical expression עלה תאנה (*aleh te'enah*) means *fig leaves*. Here, Rav Naḥman implicitly reads those words as akin to עלילה (*alilah*), "false charge," and to

*They heard the sound of YHVH Elohim moving* [or: *walking*] *about in the garden in the breeze of day* (Genesis 3:8).[654] Rabbi Pinḥas said, "Why does the Unfathomable Cosmocrat require the daytime breeze? We have learned: Rabbi El'azar said, 'Cloud within brilliance for this one!' As we have said: To what can a human being be likened in this world? To a bird stumbling about when its goes forth from its nest, not finding anyone to bring it in. So the human being: as soon as the soul departs, once again he does not know or understand—without that body of brilliant light awaiting him to delight in the Garden of Eden."[655]

Rabbi Abba said, "מתהלך (*mithallekh*), *moving about* (Genesis 3:8). The verse should have said מהלך (*mehallekh*), moving. What is indicated by מתהלך (*mithallekh*)?"[656]



*to'anah*, "pretext." This interpretation alludes to the fact that both Adam and Eve are about to blame others for their sin (Genesis 3:12–13).

654. ***They heard the sound of YHVH Elohim...*** The verse continues: *and the man and his wife hid from YHVH Elohim among the trees of the garden.*

655. **Why does the Unfathomable Cosmocrat require the daytime breeze?...** Why is the verse in Genesis so strikingly anthropomorphic—recounting God's stroll through the garden in particular weather?

The verse's expression לרוח היום (*le-ruaḥ ha-yom*), *in the breeze of day*, conveys the manner of God's manifestation to Adam and Eve after their sin. The idea that God appeared to them as "cloud within brilliance"—that is, that He shielded His overwhelming radiance from them—may derive from Naḥmanides' commentary on this verse: "The *Shekhinah* was revealed in the garden approaching them in the wind of the day.... That is, in the garden, like the wind of ordinary days—not a great and strong wind as in the vision of other prophecies—in order that they should not be frightened or terrified."

Apparently, Rabbi Pinḥas intends that due to their sin, Adam and Eve forfeited their holy soul (see *ZḤ* 10c, 17c, *MhN*); hence, even despite God's "moderate" revelation *in the breeze of the day*, they could not withstand His presence. Cf. *Zohar* 1:52b: "Until they sinned, they used to hear a voice from above, perceive supernal wisdom, endure supernal radiance fearlessly. Once they sinned, even a voice below they could neither understand nor withstand." See *Shir ha-Shirim Rabbah* on 3:8.

Later, adorned in their luminous body in the Garden of Eden, human beings can again fathom and withstand the divine.

"The Unfathomable Cosmocrat" renders קוזדיטא דאהירנא (*qozdita da'ahirna*), a Zoharic neologism. (See Ḥayyim Palagi, *Sefer Ḥayyim u-Mazon*, 29: "Who is wise enough to understand this, sufficiently insightful to know what this wants to say!") Cf. קוזדורוטין (*qozdorotin*), rendered by Matt as "quaestors" (*Zohar* 2:56b), which he suggests may derive from קוסדור (*qusdor*), based on Latin *quaestor*, meaning "official, prosecutor, judge." Many Zoharic neologisms with the sound *qos*, *qoz*, or *qor* convey the sense of governance and authority. Cf. *ZḤ* 17c (*MhN*), קושטיזא (*qoshitiza*).

The second term דאהירנא (*da'ahirna*) is entirely baffling. Both O2 and R1 read דנהירנא (*de-nahirna*), and OM1 reads דאנהירא (*deanhira*), in which case the word may connote light—like, e.g., נהורא (*nehora*) and נהיר (*nahir*). Following the principle of *lectio difficilior praeferenda*, I have preserved the more enigmatic reading.

On the stumbling bird motif, see Proverbs 27:8: *Like a bird wandering from its nest is a man who wanders from his place.*

656. **What is indicated by מתהלך (*mith-***

Rabbi Abba said, "Do people think that it was the blessed Holy One? Come and hear: It is written את קול (*et qol*), *the voice* (ibid.), the one about which is written *Elohim answered him with voice* (Exodus 19:19), and similarly *There was a voice from above the expanse over their heads* (Ezekiel 1:25)."[657]

Rav Ḥisda said in the name of Rabbi Yoḥanan, "It is written: *voice!* מתהלך לרוח (*mithallekh le-ruaḥ*), *Moving about in the wind*, as is written: *and as I prophesied, there was a voice, and behold a shaking* (Ezekiel 37:7)."[658]

Rabbi Yoḥai said, "Look, our companion Rabbi Yehudah said that conventional interpretation is required here, yet you are expounding the Account of the Chariot!"[659]

Rabbi Alexandri replied, "It is even greater than the account of the Chariot, for I see that supernal mysteries were revealed here!"[660]

***allekh*)?** The verb describing God's walk through the Garden of Eden uses a form that is rare for this root.

Distinctively, it includes an infixed letter ת (*tav*), which is often a feminine marker. Cf. *Bereshit Rabbah* 19:7: "Rabbi Abba son of Kahana said, 'The verse does not read מהלך (*mehallekh*), "moving," but rather מתהלך (*mithallekh*), "moving about, leaping up." The essence of *Shekhinah* was in the lower realms. As soon as Adam sinned, it withdrew to the first heaven.'" See Naḥmanides on Genesis 3:8; Gikatilla, *Sha'arei Orah*, 15–17; *Zohar* 1:52a, 76a.

657. **Do people think that it was the blessed Holy One?...** The additional *tav* in *mithallekh* appears in order to dispel the notion that God Himself was walking through the garden. The feminine marker proves that it was the *Shekhinah*. Rabbi Abba offers further proofs that the subject of Genesis 3:8 is the *Shekhinah*. The קול (*qol*), *sound* [or: *voice*], of God described in the verse is prefaced by the particle את (*et*), often a marker for the *Shekhinah*. Also, *qol* is associated with the divine voice from Mount Sinai, spoken by *Elohim* to Moses—apparently indicating *Shekhinah* rather than *YHVH* (God Himself). Finally, the *voice* is correlated with the voice above the living creatures in Ezekiel's vision—apparently understood to be the abode of the *Shekhinah*.

658. **Rav Ḥisda said in the name of Rabbi Yoḥanan...** Rav Ḥisda offers two additional proofs. Firstly, Genesis 3:8 states explicitly that it was the *voice of YHVH Elohim* that walked about—the voice and not God Himself. Secondly, the voice moving about in the wind is associated with Ezekiel's famous vision of the bones, where *voice* and רוח (*ruaḥ*), "wind, spirit, breath," also figure together (see Ezekiel 37:1–10). Perhaps Rav Ḥisda intends that what infused the dead bones had derived from *Shekhinah*, hence proving that the term *ruaḥ* in Genesis also applies to *Shekhinah* and not to God Himself.

659. **Rabbi Yoḥai said...** Oddly, it is Rabbi Yoḥai who objects that the Companions appear to have exceeded their bounds. Earlier, Rabbi Shim'on (presumably son of Yoḥai) had engaged in such speculation. In contrast to the main body of the *Zohar*, *MhN* on the Torah is not always consistent in its treatment of distinct characters. Some of the manuscripts read "Yoḥanan" instead of "Yoḥai."

660. **greater than the account of the Chariot...** The secrets concerning Adam's sin pertain to the mysterious unity (and fragmentation) of the godhead. Hence they are even more sublime than the mysteries of the divine chariot. See below, *ZḤ* 19c (*MhN*), page 208, where Rabbi Alexandri appears again, advocating the view that secrets can in fact be revealed among the Companions.

Our Rabbis have taught: When Rabbi Shim'on son of Yoḥai fell ill, Rabbi Pinḥas, Rabbi Ḥiyya, and Rabbi Abbahu entered in his presence.[661]

They said to him, "Will he who is the pillar of the world lie down?!"[662]

He replied, "It is not the court above that is examining my case, for I see that I have not been handed over to the angels and judges above—for I am not like other people. Rather, the blessed Holy One is judging my case—not His court. This is the significance of what David said in his prayer before Him: *Judge me, O God, and plead my cause* (Psalms 43:1); and similarly Solomon said: *to execute judgment for His servant* (1 Kings 8:59)—He alone and not another.[663]

"For look at what we have learned: When a person lies ill, the court above examines his case. Some of them incline to innocence, pointing out the person's merits; while others incline to guilt, pointing out the person's sins—and such a person does not emerge from the case as he would wish.[664]

"However, one who is judged by the Supernal King—ruling over all—is fortunate, and such a person emerges from judgment only well. Why? As we have learned: The attributes of the Supernal King always incline to innocence, and He



661. **When Rabbi Shim'on son of Yoḥai fell ill...** The story that follows was later reworked and served as the frame narrative for the *Idra Zuta*. See *Zohar* 3:287b–296b (*IZ*). Note especially the opening: "The other time I was ill... they extended my life until now." See Liebes, *Studies in the Zohar*, 11–12.

Although Rabbi Shim'on appears throughout *MhN* on the Torah, he is not always depicted as the leader of a particular group. His exalted status here approximates his treatment in the main body of the *Zohar*.

In the *Idra Zuta*, the list of companions present differs: Rabbi Pinḥas is dead and appears from the next world; Rabbi Abbahu is absent, perhaps replaced by Rabbi Abba. In the version of this story printed in *Zohar* 3:309a–b (*Tosafot*), Rabbi Abba, rather than Rabbi Abbahu, is present. As is made clear below, Rabbi El'azar is also present in the *MhN* narrative. On Rabbi Pinḥas, see below, note 670.

662. **Will he who is the pillar of the world lie down?!** Is it possible that he who sustains the world will die? The motif of Rabbi Shim'on as pillar of the world is associated with the verse from Proverbs (10:25): *The righteous is an everlasting foundation*, but frequently read by the Rabbis as: *The righteous is the foundation of the world.*

See BT *Ḥagigah* 12b: "[The world] rests on a single pillar name Righteous, as is said: *Righteous is the foundation of the world* (Proverbs 10:25)." See also BT *Yoma* 38b. On Rabbi Shim'on as "pillar of the world," see *Zohar* 1:4a; 3:127b (*IR*); Liebes, *Studies in the Zohar*, 12–15. Cf. BT *Sukkah* 45b.

663. **the blessed Holy One is judging my case...** The significance of being judged directly by God is about to be explained. On David's asking that God judge him directly, see *Zohar* 3:231a.

664. **When a person lies ill...** See BT *Shabbat* 32a: "Rav Yitsḥak son of Rav Yehudah said, 'Let one always pray for mercy not to fall sick, for if he falls sick he is told: Show your merit and be acquitted!'... Our Rabbis taught:... when [a person] has a headache, let him imagine that he is put in irons; when he takes to bed, let him imagine that he ascended the scaffold to be punished. For whoever ascends the scaffold to be punished—if he has great advocates, he is saved; but if not, he is not saved." See also *Zohar* 1:227a; *ZḤ* 14c (*MhN*).

is entirely the facet of compassion; He has the capacity to absolve sins and iniquities, as is written: *With You there is forgiveness* (Psalms 130:4)—but not with another.[665]

"That is why I have pleaded before Him that He judge my case; that I will enter thirteen portals to the world that is coming, traversed only by the patriarchs. No one will hinder me. What's more—I will not seek their permission!"[666]

Rabbi Shim'on said a word—and they noticed that he was not in his sickbed. They were astonished. None of them was able to speak because of the great terror that had seized them. While they were sitting, aromas of numerous fragrances wafted around them, and each one of them regained his composure, whereupon they saw Rabbi Shim'on—who was uttering words, but they did not see anyone else other than him.[667]

After a while Rabbi Shim'on asked them, "Did you see something?"

Rabbi Pinḥas replied, "No. But we are all astounded that [19a] we did not see you in your sickbed for a long time. And when we did see you, aromas of the fragrances of the Garden of Eden wafted around us; and we heard your voice speaking—but we didn't know who was speaking with you."[668]



He said to them, "And you didn't hear any other words except mine?!"

They replied, "No."

He said to them, "You are not worthy to behold the Countenance of Days!"[669]

665. **one who is judged by the Supernal King...** In contrast to the heavenly tribunal, which judges a person in accordance with his merits and faults, the blessed Holy One always inclines to compassion. See *Bereshit Rabbah* 33:3 in the name of Rabbi Shemu'el: "It is His nature to be compassionate."

On God alone having the capacity to forgive, cf. Exodus 23:21; BT *Sanhedrin* 38b; Moses de León, *Or Zaru'a*, 273.

666. **thirteen portals...** Presumably, these correlate with the thirteen attributes of divine mercy (see Exodus 34:6–7). Cf. *Zohar* 2:128b, which mentions twelve such gates.

Rabbi Shim'on's self-assuredness ("No one will hinder me," "I will not seek their permission") remains characteristic of his personality in the main body of the *Zohar*, and in the reworking of this narrative found in the *Idra Zuta*.

667. **Rabbi Shim'on said a word...** Perhaps he uttered a divine name. He then disappears for a while to another realm. (Similarly, in the *Idra Zuta*, an unseen Rabbi Pinḥas manifests from the next world.)

Fragrant aromas often accompany heightened experiences throughout the *Zohar*. See, for example, *Zohar* 3:144b (*IR*); Hellner-Eshed, *A River Flows from Eden*, 302–4. Not only do they indicate the blurring of the boundaries between this world and the Edenic realm, but also they also serve here to fortify or anchor the overwhelmed companions. See next note.

668. **aromas of the fragrances of the Garden of Eden...** Cf. *Bereshit Rabbah* 65:22 and *Tanḥuma*, *Toledot* 11: "When Jacob entered, he was accompanied by the fragrance of the Garden of Eden."

669. **You are not worthy...** That is, worthy of being privy to celestial secrets, or of witnessing a higher dimension of reality.

The title Countenance of Days derives from Daniel 7:9: *As I watched, thrones were placed, and the Ancient of Days sat—His garment like white snow, the hair of His head like*

He said to them, "I will tell you something. I am surprised that Rabbi Pinḥas didn't see, for just now I saw him in that world, beneath my son Rabbi El'azar. Just now they sent for me from above and showed me the place of the righteous in the world to come, and the only place that pleased me was with Ahijah the Shilonite. I selected my place and left. Three hundred souls of the righteous accompanied me, and above them was Adam—who was sitting next to me, speaking with me. He pleaded that his sin not be revealed to the whole world, beyond what the Torah had recounted—concealed in that tree in the Garden of Eden.[670]

"I told him, 'Look, the Companions have revealed!' He replied, 'That which the Companions have revealed among themselves is fine, but not so to the rest of the world.'

"Why? Because the blessed Holy One is concerned for His glory and does not wish to publicize his sin beyond mentioning that tree from which he ate.[671]



*clean fleece, His throne flames of fire, its wheels blazing fire.*

In BT *Pesaḥim* 119a, secrets of Torah are referred to as "things hidden by the Ancient of Days." See *Bereshit Rabbah* 35:2; *Zohar* 1:83a, 89b (*ST*), 130a, 188a; 3:132b (*IR*), 201a; *ZḤ* 25c (*MhN*).

670. **I will tell you something...** When Rabbi Shim'on was uttering words, apparently alone, he was in fact speaking with Adam—who pleaded that the true nature of his sin must not be revealed, and that the outer (metaphorical) narrative of the tree should suffice. See next note.

Surely Rabbi Pinḥas—whose place in the next world is so exalted—should have been worthy to witness Rabbi Shim'on's conversation with Adam! Hence the surprise that he did not see it.

Rabbi Pinḥas son of Ya'ir lived in the second century in Palestine and was renowned for his saintliness and ability to work miracles. See BT *Ḥullin* 7a; JT *Demai* 1:3, 22a. In the *Zohar,* he is accorded special status and generally he is in a class by himself among the Companions. See 1:11a; 3:59b–60b, 62a–b, 200b–202a, 203a, 225b, 288a, 296b (*IZ*); *ZḤ* 12b (*MhN*). According to BT *Shabbat* 33b, Rabbi Pinḥas was the son-in-law of Rabbi Shim'on, however the *Zohar* elevates him further by transforming him into Rabbi Shim'on's father-in-law. This new role could be the result of a simple mistake: confusing חתן (*ḥatan*), "son-in-law" with חותן (*ḥoten*), "father-in-law." However, the switch may also be deliberate, another instance of interchanging father and son.

Ahijah was the prophet who revealed to Jeroboam that Solomon's kingdom would be divided; see 1 Kings 11:29–39. According to rabbinic tradition, he was a master of the secrets of Torah (BT *Sanhedrin* 102a; *Midrash Tehillim* 5:8) and the teacher of Elijah (JT *Eruvin* 5:1, 22b). Rabbi Shim'on associates himself with Ahijah in *Bereshit Rabbah* 35:2; see also *Zohar* 1:4b; 3:287b (*IZ*).

Cf. *Midrash Tehillim* 149:5 on the righteous delighting in their heavenly resting place.

671. **the blessed Holy One is concerned for His glory...** Widespread knowledge of the true nature of Adam's sin would injure the divine glory by revealing the fragility of divine being—namely that *Elohim* can be split from *YHVH*. See Scholem, *Major Trends,* 232: "the subject [was] extremely dangerous, as it touched the great question, where and

"The blessed Holy One revealed it to me through the Holy Spirit, and to the Companions—that they will discuss it among themselves—but not among the novices of the Companions, or those who will yet come to the world; for it is a subject that not all people comprehend and in which they err, not because of the sin that he sinned, but because of the glory of the supernal Name, with which people are not careful. It is written: *This is My Name* לעלם (*le'alem*), *to conceal* (Exodus 3:15)—for they will come to ask what they ought not.[672]

"This accords with what is written: *Lest they break through to YHVH to see* ונפל ממנו רב (*ve-nafal mi-mennu rav*), *and many of them fall* (Exodus 19:21). What is *ve-nafal mi-mennu rav*, *and many of them fall*? So have we decreed: That companion who teaches the Holy Name to anyone—he falls and is seized in that sin more than them, as is written: *ve-nafal mi-mennu rav*, *the teacher falls more than them*—the *rav*, teacher, falls and is seized by that iniquity."[673]

Rabbi El'azar his son approached him. He asked him, "Father, what am I there?"[674]

He replied, "Happy is your share, my son! For a long time you will not be buried next to me, but I have selected my place and yours in that world. Happy 199

how the unity of God's life has been disturbed and whence comes the breach that is now manifest in the whole universe."

Cf. *Bereshit Rabbah* 15:7.

672. **they will discuss it among themselves...** The secret must remain within the closed circle of initiates; those outside the circle cannot handle this awesome truth.

In its simple sense, the clause from Exodus reads: *This is My Name forever.* The word לעלם (*le-olam*), *forever*, is written without the usual vowel-letter *vav*, which means that it looks like לעלם (*le'alem*), *to conceal.* The Rabbis construed this as suggesting that God's Name must be kept secret. See BT *Pesaḥim* 50a: "Rava considered lecturing [on the divine Name *YHVH*] at the session. A certain old man said to him, 'It is written: לעלם (*le'alem*), *to be concealed.*'" See also BT *Qiddushin* 71a. Here, the need for concealment is applied to the knowledge of the sundering of *Elohim* from *YHVH*.

673. **who teaches the Holy Name to anyone...** In its simple sense, the verse from Exodus refers to the boundary established around Mount Sinai that must not be breached during revelation. Here, teaching the secret of Adam's sin and the fissure within divinity is equated with teaching the divine name. Both breach the boundary.

The word רב (*rav*), "many," is construed as "the teacher" or "the great one." Cf. *Berakhot* 62b; *Zohar* 2:53a.

On rabbinic injunctions against teaching the holy Name, see BT *Qiddushin* 71a: "Rabbah son of Bar Ḥana said in the name of Rabbi Yoḥanan, 'The name of four letters—the sages convey it to their disciples once every seven years'.... The Rabbis taught: At first the name of twelve letters was transmitted to everyone. When the licentious became rife, it was transmitted to the modest [or: discreet], among the priests.... Rav Yehudah said in the name of Rav, 'The forty-two-letter name is transmitted only to one who is modest, humble, middle-aged, free from anger, sober, and not insistent on retaliating.'"

674. **what am I there** In the world to come. See *ZḤ* 20d (*MhN*), where Rabbi El'azar asks a similar question of his father.

are the righteous, destined to praise the Master of the Universe like the angels ministering in His presence! As is written: *Surely the righteous will acclaim your Name, the upright will dwell in Your presence* (Psalms 140:14)."[675]

Rabbi Bo said in the name of Rav Huna, "When Adam sinned and those decrees were ordained upon him, the blessed Holy One banished him from the delights he enjoyed in Eden, and appointed guardians to the gates of the Garden of Eden. Who are they? The *keruvim*, as is written: *He placed east of the Garden of Eden the cherubim and the flame of the whirling sword* (Genesis 3:24)—in order to guard the way and the opening.[676]

"For then it was decreed that henceforth human beings would not be permitted to enter there, aside from the souls first clarified by the *keruvim*. For if they see that she is worthy to enter, she enters; if not, they thrust her aside and she is burned by that flame and then receives her punishment.[677]

"It has been taught: Corresponding to them there were [*keruvim*] in the Temple when the priest entered within, within. For it has been taught: Rabbi Abba said in the name of Rav Huna, 'Within, within is the paradigm of the Garden of Eden.' When the priest entered there, he entered in soul and not in body—with fear, awe, trembling, quaking, and with innocence and purity—and the *keruvim* would stand guard.[678]



675. **For a long time you will not be buried...** On Rabbi El'azar's delayed burial and his relocation to his father's burial chamber, see BT *Bava Metsi'a* 84b; *Qohelet Rabbah* on 11:2; *Pesiqta de-Rav Kahana* 11:23; *Zohar* 3:71a.

On the souls of the righteous as ministering angels, see *Zohar* 1:100a, 129b; *ZḤ* 10a, 20d–21a (both *MhN*); *TZ, Haqdamah*, 16b. On the verse from Psalms, see *Zohar* 1:226b; *ZḤ* 18a (*MhN*).

676. **those decrees were ordained upon him...** See Genesis 3:17–19: *Cursed be the ground because of you...for from there you were taken; for dust you are, and to dust you shall return.*

The full verse in Genesis reads: *He drove out the human—and placed east of the Garden of Eden the cherubim and the flame of the whirling sword, to guard the way to the Tree of Life.* Cf. *Zohar* 1:53b, 219a, 237a.

677. **henceforth human beings would not be permitted...** Not only Adam is prohibited from entering the Garden of Eden following his sin and expulsion, but also every human being; entry is now reserved for purified souls alone.

"Clarified" renders צרופות (*tserufot*), whose range of meaning includes "refined, purified, tried, tested." It also connotes being passed through fire. Hence: souls are tested and purified by passing through the angelic flame at the entrance to the garden. See *Zohar* 1:219a; *ZḤ* 19d, 21a (both *MhN*). On the burning of the soul, cf. BT *Shabbat* 113b.

678. **he entered in soul and not in body...** Given that only (righteous) souls can enter the Garden of Eden, and that the Temple was a microcosm of the Garden of Eden, it logically follows that when the high priest entered the Holy of Holies ("within, within") to perform the Yom Kippur service, he had to shed his corporeality. This may suggest a state of ecstasy.

See *Vayiqra Rabbah* 21:12: "*No person shall be in the Tent of Meeting* (Leviticus 16:17).

"If the priest was worthy, he entered in peace and emerged in peace. If he was not worthy, a flame shot forth from between the *keruvim* and he was burned within—patterned on those *keruvim* stationed at the gates of the Garden of Eden."[679]

Rabbi Yehudah said, "Happy is the one who merits to pass them in peace!"

Rabbi Peraḥyah said, "There is nothing in the world that does not have its counterpart."[680] [19b]

"The serpent that deceived Eve is an instance of a verbal correspondence."[681]

Rabbi Yeisa said, "How so?"

He replied, "As implied by its translation: נחש (*naḥash*)—חיויא (*ḥivya*). חויא (*Ḥivya*), Serpent, is masculine; while חוה (*Ḥavvah*), *Eve*, is feminine: a verbal correspondence! Just like נחש נחשת (*neḥash neḥoshet*), *a serpent of bronze* (Numbers 21:9), is a verbal correspondence."[682]



...Rabbi Abbahu said, 'Was the high priest not a person? The explanation follows what Rabbi Simon said: "When the Holy Spirit rested upon Pinḥas, his face flamed like torches about him. Hence is written: *For the priest's lips should keep knowledge*... [*for he is the angel* (literally: *messenger*) *of YHVH of hosts*] (Malachi 2:7)."'" That is, when the high priest entered the Holy of Holies, he transformed into an angel—and hence there was no person in the Tent of Meeting.

On the *keruvim* in the Dwelling and the Temple, see Exodus 25:18–22; 37:7–9; 1 Kings 6:23–30; 2 Chronicles 3:10–13. On the *keruvim* in the Temple as corresponding to the *keruvim* of the Garden of Eden, see *ZḤ* 21a (*MhN*). On the high priest in the Holy of Holies, see *Zohar* 3:67a, 102a; *ZḤ* 21a (*MhN*). On the potential death of the high priest in the Holy of Holies, see Leviticus 16:2; M *Yoma* 5:1; Maimonides, ad loc., s.v. *she-lo lahav'it*; Israel Lipschutz, *Tif'eret Yisra'el*, ad loc., par. 22; Cf. M *Yoma* 7:4; BT *Yoma* 19b.

See also Belkin, "Ha-Midrash ha-Ne'lam u-Mqorotav," 79–82; Werblowsky, "Philo and the Zohar," 128–9; Scholem, *Major Trends*, 378, n. 9; Tishby, *Wisdom of the Zohar*, 3:888.

679. **entered in peace and emerged in peace...** This phrase derives from a Talmudic account of four rabbis who engaged in mystical contemplation of the divine realm. Only Rabbi Akiva "entered in peace and emerged in peace." See JT *Ḥagigah* 2:1, 77b; *Shir ha-Shirim Rabbah* on 1:4 (cf. *Tosefta Ḥagigah* 2:4; BT *Ḥagigah* 14b).

680. **its counterpart** That is, in the celestial realms. The correspondence between the Holy of Holies and the (celestial) Garden of Eden illustrates this principle.

The theme of "as above, so below" is a cardinal principle of Kabbalah. See *Zohar* 1:38a (*Heikh*), 57b–58a, 129a, 145b, 156b, 158b, 205b; 2:5a (*MhN*), 15b (*MhN*), 20a (*MhN*), 48b, 82b, 144b, 251a (*Heikh*); 3:45b, 65b; *ZḤ* 15a (*MhN*); Tishby, *Wisdom of the Zohar*, 1:273. On the similar Hermetic formulation, see *Secretum secretorum*, ed. Robert Steele, *Opera hactenus*, fasc. 5, 262.

681. **verbal correspondence** דבר נופל על הלשון (*Davar nofel al ha-lashon*), literally "something falling onto the tongue," a rabbinic idiom for a play on words. See next note.

It seems that Rabbi Peraḥyah is speaking here.

682. **נחש (*naḥash*)—חיויא (*ḥivya*)...** The Aramaic translations of the Torah render נחש (*naḥash*), serpent, as *ḥivya*, which is close to

Rabbi Yeisa said, "But look at what is written: *The human named his wife* חוה (*Ḥavvah*), *Eve, for she was the mother of all* חי (*ḥai*), *living* (Genesis 3:20)!"[683]

Rabbi Peraḥyah replied, "He named her in reference to the future. He should have named her חיה (*Ḥayyah*), referring to חי (*ḥai*), the living, but she was named חוה (*Ḥavvah*), *Eve*, in reference to the future—for חיויא (*ḥivya*), the serpent, was about to seduce חוה (*Ḥavvah*), Eve."[684]

*He will strike you at the head* (Genesis 3:15).[685]

Rabbi Yehudah said, "So is the way of the serpent: the human being strikes it solely at the head, whereas the serpent bites the human being solely at the heel."

Rabbi Yitsḥak son of Rabbi Yose said, "What will the one who says that it was the evil impulse say about this verse?"[686]

Rabbi Yose replied, "It teaches that this serpent can be killed only by the head. Who is the head? The head of the academy. Furthermore, this serpent kills a human being solely when he performs sins with contempt—trampling on them with the heel—as is written: *the iniquity of my heels encompassing me* (Psalms 49:6)."[687]

the Hebrew *Ḥavvah*, "Eve." This correspondence is noted in *Bereshit Rabbah* 20:11; 22:2.

On the serpent of bronze (Numbers 21:8–9), see *Bereshit Rabbah* 31:8: "[Moses] reasoned, '. . . I will make it of *neḥoshet*, bronze, since this word corresponds to the other,' as is said: *Moses made* neḥash neḥoshet, *a serpent of bronze*: this proves that the Torah was given in Hebrew." Cf. JT *Rosh ha-Shanah* 3:9, 59a.

683. **But look at what is written . . .** Rabbi Yose queries Rabbi Peraḥyah's explanation of Eve's name, for the Torah explicitly offers a different etymology.

684. **He should have named her חיה (*Ḥayyah*) . . .** Had the Torah wished solely to convey that Eve's name derives from life, she would have been called *Ḥayyah* and not *Ḥavvah*. While the Torah's etymology is not wrong—for technically, *vav* and *yod* can be interchanged—nonetheless we must account for why *vav* was used and not *yod*. The answer is that the name *Ḥavvah* alludes to *ḥivya*, "serpent."

See Rashi on Genesis 3:20 explaining the name *Ḥavvah*: "It alludes to the expression חיה (*ḥayyah*), 'living,' for she gives life to her children, just as you say *What* הוה (*hoveh*), *is there, for man* (Ecclesiastes 2:22)—with the word *hoveh* as a form of היה (*hayah*), 'is.'" See also *Bereshit Rabbah* 20:11; *Zohar* 2:137a.

According to the simple sense of the Torah narrative, Eve was not named until after her encounter with the serpent.

685. ***He will strike you at the head* . . .** This verse is spoken by God to the serpent after Adam and Eve's sin. The full verse reads: *Enmity will I set between you and the woman, between your seed and hers. He will strike you at the head, and you will strike him at the heel.*

686. **What will the one who says that it was the evil impulse say . . .** What is the meaning of this curse if the serpent is understood metaphorically as the evil impulse? See *ZḤ* 18c, note 645, and 24b (both *MhN*).

687. **It teaches that this serpent . . .** If the serpent is the evil impulse, then the meaning of the curse *He will strike you at the head*, or more literally *He will strike*

Rabbi Yitsḥak said, "This is derived from here: *Woe unto them who haul iniquity with* חבלי השוא (*ḥevlei ha-shav*), *flimsy cords, and sin as with cart ropes* (Isaiah 5:18)—that is, he performs transgressions and tramples on them with the heel, for he considers them as nothing, like חבלי השוא (*ḥevlei ha-shav*), *cords of nothingness*, spun by a spider. Afterward they are *as with cart ropes*—strong and firm, until they are all entwined and kill the human being. Similarly He says: *and you will strike him at the heel* (Genesis 3:15)—through that iniquity of the heel, the evil impulse kills the human being."[688]

Rabbi Yitsḥak said, "Come and see: As they were corrupted, so were they judged—at first the serpent, afterward the woman, and afterward the man, as is written: *To Adam He said, 'Because you listened to the voice of your wife'* (ibid. 3:17)."[689]

Rabbi Ya'akov son of Idi said, "If the human being sinned, how did the ground sin?"[690]

Well, Rabbi Ya'akov son of Idi said, "When the world was created, heaven and earth were witnesses—teaching that the blessed Holy One appointed them



*you—head*, is that the "head" will strike you. That is, the head of the academy—and more generally, the rabbinic leadership—can defeat the evil impulse ("you"), presumably by leading and exhorting the public to a life of Torah and commandments.

Conversely, and following the metaphor, the serpent striking at the heel refers to the "minor" sins one performs—seemingly insignificant misdeeds or peccadilloes—that are trampled by the heel, i.e., treated with disdain. According to the rabbinic reading of Psalms 49:6, such "minor" offenses constitute *the iniquity of my heels*, i.e., sins that are often trampled underfoot as being too trivial to justify altering one's course; yet these very sins threaten to eventually encompass the careless person on the Day of Judgment. See BT *Avodah Zarah* 18a; *Tanḥuma, Eqev* 1; *Zohar* 1:198b.

688. **This is derived from here...** Here is a different proof-text to support the same point.

See BT *Sukkah* 52a: "Rabbi Assi said, 'The evil impulse at first resembles the thread of a spider, but ultimately it resembles cart ropes, as is said: *Woe unto them who haul iniquity with flimsy cords, and sin as with cart ropes.*'" At first one may assume that minor offenses are insignificant (flimsy, nothing) and hence trample on them, but before long they begin to dominate. Cf. *Bereshit Rabbah* 22:6; See *Zohar* 1:5a, 57a, 199a.

689. **As they were corrupted, so were they judged...** According to the narrative in Genesis (3:14–19), God first sentences the serpent, then Eve, and finally Adam—corresponding to the order in which they sinned: the serpent seduced Eve, who in turn seduced Adam.

See also *Bereshit Rabbah* 20:3: "Rabbi Ḥiyya taught, 'In subjecting to degradation, we commence with the smallest, as is said: *YHVH God said to the serpent* (Genesis 3:14); *To the woman He said, "I will greatly multiply your birth pangs"* (ibid., 16); *To Adam He said, "Because you listened to the voice of your wife"* (ibid., 17). This teaches that first the serpent was cursed, afterward Eve was cursed, and afterward Adam was cursed.'" See also BT *Berakhot* 61a, *Ta'anit* 15b.

690. **how did the ground sin** As part of Adam's punishment, the ground is cursed: *Cursed be the ground for your sake* (Genesis

witnesses to everything the human being would do, so he would not say, 'Who can see me?' Those witnesses publicize his sins, as is written: *Heaven will expose his sin, and earth will rise up against him* (Job 20:27).[691]

"It has been taught: On the very day that Adam transgressed, the heavens darkened their light; but the earth didn't know what to do. Whereupon the blessed Holy One came and cursed her for withholding her testimony—so that she would no longer bestow her power for sowing and harvesting, as at first. She abided in her curses until Abraham appeared, whereby the world was rendered fragrantly firm."[692]

Rav Naḥman said, "Until Noah appeared—as is written: *This one will provide us relief, from our work and from the painful toil of our hands* (Genesis 5:29). That is why she was called by his name, as is written: *man of the earth* (ibid. 9:20)—for she was liberated from her curse because of him."[693]

Rav Naḥman son of Yitsḥak said, "When Adam was banished from the Garden of Eden, he thought that he would die immediately. He began weeping and beseeching and returning in *teshuvah*, until the blessed Holy One accepted him in *teshuvah* and extended his days—fulfilling His word, as is written: *on the*



3:17). What did it do to deserve this punishment? See below, note 692.

Cf. *Bereshit Rabbah* 5:9: "It was taught in the name of Rabbi Natan: 'Three were brought to justice and four were convicted: Adam, Eve, and the serpent were brought to justice; and the earth was cursed along with them, as is said: *Cursed is the ground* (Genesis 3:17).'"

691. ***Heaven will expose his sin...*** On the verse from Job, cf. *Zohar* 2:56a, 85b; 3:23b, 101a, 285a.

692. **cursed her for withholding her testimony...** Whereas the heavens fulfilled their mandate, seeking to warn the human being before he sinned, the earth was silent. See *Pirqei de-Rabbi Eli'ezer* 14: "If Adam sinned, what was the sin of the earth that it should be cursed? Because it did not speak out against the deed—therefore it was cursed." See Luria, ad loc. See also *Targum Yerushalmi*, Genesis 3:17.

As the earth's punishment, it can no longer produce food effortlessly (see Genesis 3:17–19). Precisely how Abraham later undid this curse is unclear. Perhaps it is because with the advent of Abraham in Genesis 12, a series of blessings appears, in contrast to the curses of Genesis 3.

"Fragrantly firm" renders נתבסם (*nitbassem*), "was sweetened" or "was firmly established." The verbal root *bsm* conveys both senses. See *Bereshit Rabbah* 66:2; *Midrash Shemu'el* 26:4; *Zohar* 1:30b, 31a, 34a, 37a, 56a, 73b, 137a; 2:143a, 168a, 227a; 3:18a; *ZḤ* 4d (*MhN*); Scholem, *Major Trends*, 165, 388, n. 44; idem, *Kabbalah*, 228.

693. **Until Noah appeared...** It was not Abraham but rather Noah who undid the earth's primal curse.

The full verse reads: *He* [*Lamech*] *called his name* נח (*Noaḥ*), *Noah, as to say, "This one* ינחמנו (*yenaḥamenu*), *will provide us relief, from our work and from the painful toil of our hands, from the soil that* YHVH *has cursed.*

See *Tanḥuma, Bereshit* 11: "How did he [Lamech] know to say, '*This one will provide us relief from our work...*?' Was he a prophet? Rabbi Shim'on son of Yehotsadak said, 'They had been taught that when the blessed Holy One said to Adam, *Cursed be the soil because of you; by painful toil will you eat of it all the day you eat from it [you will surely die]* (Genesis 2:17), granting him His day—which is one thousand years; demonstrating to the entire world that the blessed Holy One is compassionate and gracious, receiving penitents in *teshuvah*, desiring only that they will live, as is written: *Return and live... Why should you die, O house of Israel* (Ezekiel 18:31–32)."[694]

Rabbi Yitsḥak said, "Happy are the children whose father tells them thus! Woe to the children who do not hear from Him!"[695]

Rav Yehudah said in the name of Rav, "We do not find compassion like the compassion of the blessed Holy One! In every instance, you find that when Israel sinned and they returned to Him, He extended His hand and received them—absolving them immediately, as is written: *Who is a God like You, who forgives iniquity and passes over transgression?* (Micah 7:18)."[696] [19c]

*days of your life* (Genesis 3:17), Adam had asked, "Master of the World, for how long?" He replied, "Until a human is born circumcised." When Noah was born circumcised, Lamech immediately knew and said, "Indeed, *this one will provide us relief...!*"'" Cf. *Bereshit Rabbah* 36:3; *Zohar* 1:38a, 58b, 62b, 70b; 2:168a; 3:15a; *ZḤ* 22c (*MhN*).

694. **He began weeping and beseeching and returning in *teshuvah*...** On Adam's repentance, see *Bereshit Rabbah* 22:13; BT *Avodah Zarah* 8a; *Pirqei de-Rabbi Eli'ezer* 20; *Zohar* 1:55b; 224a; *ZḤ* 18c (*MhN*).

On Adam's being granted "a day," see *Bereshit Rabbah* 19:8; *Zohar* 1:139b–140a; *ZḤ* 18c (*MhN*). See also *Bereshit Rabbah* 8:2: "A day of the blessed Holy One is a thousand years, as is said: *For a thousand years in Your eyes are like yesterday gone* (Psalms 90:4)."

According to Genesis 5:5, Adam lived until the age of 930.

The full verses from Ezekiel read: *Cast away all the transgressions by which you have offended, and get yourselves a new heart and a new spirit, for why should you die, O house of Israel. For it is not My desire that anyone shall die, declares the Lord YHVH. Return and live!*

695. **Woe to the children who do not hear from Him!** The ever-present possibility to return in *teshuvah* is a great boon—for nearly everyone. Cf. the story of Elisha son of Avuyah ("Aḥer") in BT *Ḥagigah* 15a, in which a heavenly voice proclaimed: "*Return, rebellious children* (Jeremiah 3:22)—except Aḥer!" See *ZḤ* 22b (*MhN*).

696. **like the compassion of the blessed Holy One...** The possibility of being accepted in penitence is a historical (or cosmic) law, in keeping with God's merciful nature.

The complete passage from Micah (7:18–19) reads: *Who is a God like You, who bears* [or: *raises, lifts*] *iniquity and passes over transgression; who has not maintained His wrath forever against the remnant of His own people, because He loves mercy. He will again have compassion on us; He will cover up our iniquities—You will hurl all their sins into the depths of the sea.*

Cf. *Midrash Tehillim* 30:4: "Rabbi El'azar said, 'If the scale is evenly balanced—sins on this side, merits on that—what does the blessed Holy One do? He tips it toward love, as is said: *Love is Yours, O YHVH* (Psalms 62:13).' Rabbi Yose son of Rabbi Ḥanina said, 'What does the blessed Holy One do? He snatches one bond of debt from the sins, and instantly the merits tip the scales, as is said: *He lifts iniquity and passes over transgression* (Micah 7:18).'" See also *Pesiqta de-Rav Kahana* 25:2; BT *Rosh ha-Shanah* 17a.

## SECTION 8[697]

*The man knew Eve his wife* (Genesis 4:1).[698]

Rabbi Yehoshu'a son of Levi said, "We should assiduously contemplate this section, and all the more so this verse uttered by Eve: *I have created a male* את יהוה (et YHVH), *along with* YHVH (ibid.)."[699]

Rabbi Yitsḥak said, "I understand it according to its simple meaning. As we have learned: Rav Yehudah said in the name of Rav, 'This refers to one to whom a son has been born—when he begins to talk, it is incumbent upon him to teach him verses of Torah, which [arouse] awe before YHVH, so that when he grows he will recall those scriptures, to be in awe before his Master.'"[700]

Rabbi Akiva was sitting in the presence of Rabbi Eli'ezer. He said to him, "What is the meaning of this section—and this verse that says: *She bore Cain, saying, 'I have created a male* את יהוה (et YHVH), *along with* YHVH' (ibid.)?"[701]

He replied, "Akiva, Akiva, I shall tell you. The day that Rabbi Beroka and the other Companions revealed that sin that Adam committed—though it ought



697. **Section 8** The printed editions and some of the manuscripts preserve the section heading פרשה ח (*parashah* 8), perhaps reflecting an early attempt to order the materials of *MhN* on the Torah. See *ZḤ* 3d, 10b, 13a, 14a, 17c, 28a, end of *parashat Lekh Lekha*—below, page 311 (all *MhN*); *Zohar* 2:20a (*MhN*).

698. **The man knew Eve his wife** The verse continues: *and she conceived and bore* קין (*Qayin*), *Cain, saying,* "קניתי (*Qaniti*), *I have created, a male along with* YHVH."

The passage here, extending until 19d ("in appearance and beauty"), is found in an anonymous kabbalistic work apparently associated with the Zoharic circle, as published by Wolfson, "The Anonymous Chapters of the Elderly Master of Secrets," 215–19.

699. **We should assiduously contemplate this section...** In particular, Eve's formulation *et YHVH* to denote "with God." The homilies that follow explore numerous meanings of this phrase.

Cf. *Bereshit Rabbah* 22:2, citing Rabbi Akiva on *et YHVH*: "Previously, Adam was created from the ground, and Eve was created from Adam, but henceforth *in our image, after our likeness* (Genesis 1:26): neither man without woman, nor woman without man, nor both of them without the *Shekhinah*"; *Pirqei de-Rabbi Eli'ezer* 21; Rashi, ad loc.: "*Et YHVH*—like 'with YHVH.' When He created me and my husband, He created us by Himself; but in this case we are partners with Him"; Naḥmanides, ad loc.

700. **I understand it according to its simple meaning...** Rabbi Yitsḥak understands *et YHVH* to mean "devoted to God," or "wholly with God." His interpretation is according to the "simple meaning" insofar as he does not venture into the domain of supernal secrets that will soon follow. Eve's naming announcement thus means: "I hereby engage an agent-and-successor in the service of YHVH." Any such designee must be properly trained in order to fulfill his role of serving "his Master." See Naḥmanides on Genesis 4:1: "This son will be for me an acquisition for YHVH—for when we shall die, he will exist in our stead to worship his Creator."

See BT *Sukkah* 42a: "If he is able to speak, his father must teach him Torah and the reading of the *Shema*...." See also Maimonides, *Mishneh Torah, Hilkhot Talmud Torah* 1:6.

701. **Rabbi Akiva was sitting in the presence of Rabbi Eli'ezer...** Rabbi Eli'ezer son of Hyrcanus [Rabbi Eli'ezer the Great] was Rabbi Akiva's teacher. See *Zohar* 1:97b, 98b–99a; *ZḤ* 7a (all *MhN*).

not have been to those who do not fathom the deep and the hidden—on that day that it was revealed, all was divulged from this verse.[702]

"He was commanded about the Name; and he sinned with the Name. He was commanded about the Name—the unique Name, as is written: *the Tree of Life*... (Genesis 2:9). He sinned with the Name—the polysemous name, as is written: *the Tree of Knowledge of Good and Evil* (ibid.).[703]

"Eve was first in this, as is written: *she took of its fruit* (Genesis 3:6). After they sinned and comprehended their iniquity concerning what they had transgressed, they were aggrieved about what they had sinned—she the more so, for she was first in transgression, transgressing against His great Name. As soon as a son was born to her, she perceived the matter and said: '*I have created a male* את יהוה (*et YHVH*), *along with YHVH*' (Genesis 4:1)—the unique Name; that is why she did not mention the polysemous Name."[704]

Rabbi Akiva said, "This explanation accords with what Rabbi Abbahu said, '*Whoever sacrifices to Elohim shall be proscribed* (Exodus 22:19).'"[705]

Rabbi Eli'ezer said, "Eve repented, confessing the sin she transgressed, saying, 207
'This one will not be like us, bestowing honor upon another aside from Him! Rather, this one will be את יהוה (*et YHVH*), *to YHVH*, precisely—not to another!'"[706]

Rabbi Yitsḥak said, "Rabbi Akiva spoke well that the matter accords with what Rabbi Abbahu said. Consequently Eve said, 'את יהוה (*et YHVH*), *to YHVH*' (Genesis 4:1)—and not another name. Similarly Hannah said, '*I will dedicate him to YHVH all the days of his life*' (1 Samuel 1:11)—not to another name. Concerning this Torah said: *For you shall not bow down to another god, for YHVH, Jealous One is His Name, a jealous god is He* (Exodus 34:14)."[707]

702. **The day that Rabbi Beroka and the other Companions revealed...** See *ZḤ* 18c (*MhN*).

"The deep and the hidden" derives from Daniel 2:22: *He reveals deep and hidden things, knows what is in the darkness, and light dwells with Him.*

703. **He was commanded about the Name...** Because the secret meaning of *et YHVH* in Eve's declaration turns upon Rabbi Beroka's teaching, Rabbi Eli'ezer begins by restating it. See *ZḤ* 18c (*MhN*); see above, notes 639 and 641.

704. **she perceived the matter...** Having sinned previously by choosing *Elohim*, the polysemous name, rather than *YHVH*, the unique Name, Eve—now aware of her sin—is careful to make amends. She invokes *YHVH* (and not *Elohim*) at the birth of her son.

705. **This explanation accords with what Rabbi Abbahu said...** See above, *ZḤ* 18c (*MhN*), note 640; see also *ZḤ* 3d (*MhN*).

706. **this one will be את יהוה (*et YHVH*), *to YHVH*, precisely...** Rather than *along with YHVH*, the phrase *et YHVH* actually means *for YHVH* (or *to YHVH*). The child will not recapitulate the sin of the parents, exchanging *Elohim* for *YHVH*.

707. **Similarly Hannah said, '*I will dedicate him to YHVH*...** In dedicating her son, the prophet Samuel, to God Hannah was also careful to invoke *YHVH* and not *Elohim*. See above, *ZḤ* 3d (*MhN*), page 13.

In its simple sense, the verse from Exodus

Rabbi Yehudah said, "For how long will the Companions amble among the supernal mysteries of the King?"[708]

Rabbi Alexandrai said, "We have learned: Secrets of Torah are divulged to the disciples who are worthy—like us and the Companions like us!"[709]

*She continued bearing: his brother, Abel* (Genesis 4:2).[710]

Rabbi Eli'ezer asked Rabbi Akiva, "What have you heard about this?"

He replied, "That is why I sit before you."

He said to him, "Close your mouth, open your ears, and listen! This intimates a hint about that minor Name emanated from the Holy Name that you and



refers to the cardinal sin of serving another god—whether an idol or another nation's god. Here, it is applied to the sin of serving the name *Elohim* alone.

708. **For how long will the Companions amble...** Despite Rabbi Yehudah's earlier protestations, the Companions have again delved into the realm of secrets, returning to Rabbi Beroka's interpretation of Adam's sin. See above, *ZḤ* 18c–d (*MhN*).

On ambling, cf. *Zohar* 1:60b; Hellner-Eshed, *A River Flows from Eden*, 133–35.

709. **Secrets of Torah are divulged to the disciples who are worthy...** Unlike Rabbi Yehudah, Rabbi Alexandrai advocates the disclosure of secrets to an appropriate audience. See above, *ZḤ* 18d (*MhN*), page 193. See also *ZḤ* 28a (*MhN*).

See M *Ḥagigah* 2:1: "The Account of Creation may not be expounded in the presence of two persons, nor the [Account of the] Chariot in the presence of one person, unless he is a sage who understands on his own. Whoever contemplates four things, it would have been better for him if he had not come into the world: what is above, what is below, what before, what after. Whoever shows no concern for the glory of his Maker, it would have been better for him if he had not come into this world."

On criteria for determining whether secrets of Torah can be disclosed, see *ZḤ* 6d (*MhN*), page 33.

710. ***She continued bearing: his brother, Abel*** The Hebrew syntax is instructive and may serve as the basis for the enigmatic homily that follows: ותסף ללדת את אחיו את הבל (*va-tosef laledet et aḥiv et Havel*). When a direct object is followed by an appositive, biblical Hebrew sometimes unites the two nouns—but at other times it separates them. One example of keeping them together appears conspicuously in the preceding verse (4:1): את חוה אשתו (*et Ḥavvah ishto*), *Eve, his wife.* Thus, in the present verse we would reasonably expect to find a parallel construction: *et Havel aḥiv*, *Abel, his brother.* Yet the text reads *et aḥiv et Havel*. That is, it has split apart the apposition—the two designations for the same referent. Moreover, it has reversed the order of those designations—giving priority to the generic-relational term rather than the unique identifier. This construction might be seen as symbolically akin to splitting apart the divine names *YHVH* and *Elohim*, while emphasizing the generic-relational name at the expense of the unique name. (My thanks to David E. S. Stein for this subtle insight.)

The word *Hevel* (Abel), when used as a common noun, means "vanity, futility, absurd, breath, vapor."

See Rashi on Genesis 4:1; Naḥmanides (Genesis 4:1): "The secret received by tradition concerning Abel is very profound," though he does not elaborate.

I know. Many people sin with this name. It is a hint of faith for one who contemplates wisdom."[711]

Rabbi Eli'ezer said further, "Akiva, the hint that Abel was slain intimates faith in the precious, supernal name of the King, as is written: *YHVH alone will be exalted* (Isaiah 2:11)."[712]

Rabbi Akiva said, "Woe to the world when you depart from it! Now I contemplate great wisdom!"[713]

He replied, "That is why I told you to close your mouth, for I see that you and I are sufficient for the world!"[714]

Rabbi Yehudah said, "Cain became a tiller of the soil and Abel a herder of sheep. This one brought a sacrifice and that one brought a sacrifice."[715]

Rabbi Yehudah said, "Cain approached haughtily and Abel humbly, as is written: *The sacrifices of God are a broken spirit* (Psalms 51:19). What is written? *YHVH gazed upon Abel and his offering with favor, but upon Cain and his offering He gazed not* (Genesis 4:4)."[716] 209

711. **This intimates a hint about that minor Name...** The name *Elohim*, which derives from the ultimate Name—*YHVH*. Just as the verse prioritizes the relational over the unique, *his brother* over *Abel*, so people sin by prioritizing *Elohim* over *YHVH*. See *ZḤ* 18c–d (*MhN*).

712. **the hint that Abel was slain...** Apparently, Abel (*Hevel*)—whose name means "vanity" or "futility"—signifies *Elohim*, perhaps also *Shekhinah*.

It seems that the murder of Abel intimates the fragility of *Elohim*, who can be torn asunder from *YHVH*. The verse from Isaiah points to the superiority of *YHVH*. For alternative interpretations, cf. *Sullam*, *Matoq mi-Devash*. See below, *ZḤ* 19d (*MhN*), page 214.

713. **Woe to the world when you depart from it!...** See Rabbi Akiva's exclamation at the death of Rabbi Eli'ezer son of Hyrcanus in *Avot de-Rabbi Natan* A, 25: "Woe unto me, my master, because of you! Woe unto me, my teacher, because of you! For you have left the whole generation orphaned!" See also BT *Sanhedrin* 68a; *Zohar* 1:99a (*MhN*); 2:68a; 3:236a; *ZḤ* 7a (*MhN*).

714. **you and I are sufficient for the world** See BT *Shabbat* 33b, where these words are spoken by Rabbi Shim'on son of Yoḥai to his son Rabbi El'azar.

715. **Cain became a tiller of the soil...** See Genesis 4:2–5: *Abel became a herder of sheep while Cain was a tiller of the soil. It happened in the course of time that Cain brought an offering to YHVH from the fruit of the soil, and as for Abel he too brought—from the firstlings of his flock, from their fat portions. YHVH gazed upon Abel and his offering with favor, but upon Cain and his offering He gazed not and Cain was very incensed and his face fell.*

716. **Cain approached haughtily and Abel humbly...** God's differential response to the brothers' offerings turns upon their respective attitudes. For a sacrifice to be honest communication, it requires humility.

Scripture does not explain the rejection of Cain's offering and acceptance of Abel's offering—save for mentioning the fact that Abel brought from the choice firstlings, implying a more precious gift. The Rabbis added their own explanations; see *Bereshit Rabbah* 22:5; *Tanḥuma*, *Bereshit* 9; *Pirqei de-Rabbi Eli'ezer*, 21.

The verse from Psalms continues: *God*,

Rabbi Yehudah said, "Why did his face fall? Because his offering was not accepted."[717]

It has been taught: Rabbi Yehudah said, "That day was Rosh Hashanah—the day that judgment of all souls [19d] passes before the Omnipresent. He said to him, '*Why are you upset... if you do right, is there not* שאת (*se'et*)?' (ibid. 4:6–7)."[718]

Rabbi Yehudah explained, "In other words, if you do right, you will attain superiority and greatness over your brother.[719]

"*But if you do not do right, sin crouches at the opening* (ibid., 7)—namely at those openings of the Garden of Eden that the souls traverse, *sin crouches*. The sin you will perform lies there in waiting; there you will receive your punishment.[720]

"*Its desire is toward you* (ibid.)—that is to say, if you mend your deeds and that sin craves for you to perform transgressions, *you will rule over it* (ibid.)—it will not be able to incite you."[721]



*You will not despise a contrite and broken heart.*

Cf. *Zohar* 1:54a–b; 2:34a, 181b.

717. **Why did his face fall?...** See Genesis 4:5: *Cain was very incensed and his face fell.* See *Zohar* 1:36b.

718. **That day was Rosh Hashanah...** In its simple sense, the narrative in Genesis states that these offerings were made מקץ ימים (*mi-qets yamim*), *in the course of time.* Here, that phrase is read as *at the end of a year*, i.e., at the turning of the year. (On *yamim* as *a year*, see Judges 17:10; 21:19; 1 Samuel 1:21; 2 Samuel 14:26; cf. Genesis 18:11.) On the timing of the offerings, see *Bereshit Rabbah* 22:4; cf. *Targum Yerushalmi* on Genesis 4:3; *Pirqei de-Rabbi Eli'ezer* 21. See also *Zohar* 3:231a.

See M *Rosh ha-Shanah* 1:2: "On Rosh Hashanah, all the inhabitants of the world pass before Him in single file."

Genesis 4:6–7 read in full: *YHVH said to Cain, "Why are you upset, and why is your face fallen? If you do right, is there not se'et? But if you do not do right, sin crouches at the opening. Its desire is toward you, yet you can rule over it."* The word שאת (*se'et*) is difficult. The verbal root נשא (*ns'*) has a range of meanings, including "lift, remove, forgive." See *Onqelos*, ad loc.; *Bereshit Rabbah* 22:6; Rashi and Naḥmanides on Genesis 4:7; *Zohar* 1:36b, 54b; Kasher, *Torah Shelemah*, Genesis 4:7, n. 68.

719. **you will attain superiority and greatness over your brother...** If you mend your ways, your rightful superiority as the firstborn will be reinstated. See Naḥmanides on Genesis 4:7.

720. ***sin crouches at the opening...*** The referent of *the opening* (or *the entrance*) is not apparent from the narrative. Here, the sin lies waiting by the flame of the whirling sword stationed at the entrance to the Garden of Eden.

Cf. Rashi, ad loc.: "At the entrance of your grave, your sin is preserved." See also Ibn Ezra, ad loc. Cf. *Onqelos*, *Targum Yerushalmi*, and *Targum Yerushalmi* (frag.), ad loc.

On the openings of the Garden of Eden traversed by the soul, see *ZḤ* 19a; 20d–21a (both *MhN*).

721. ***Its desire is toward you...*** See Rashi, ad loc.: "This is the evil impulse. It constantly longs and desires to trip you up." See also *Sifrei*, Deuteronomy 45; BT *Qiddushin* 30b; Naḥmanides on Genesis 4:7.

It has been taught: Rabbi Yose said, "I saw Rabbi Akiva—who asked Rabbi Eli'ezer about this matter. He said to him, 'Akiva, raise your eyes on high and sit next to me; for all is explained through what I have said.'[722]

"He raised his eyes and afterward he lowered his head. He said, 'Look, I have enacted the posture of the serpent, yet I do not know!'[723]

"Rabbi Eli'ezer approached him and whispered to him. Rabbi Akiva approached, kissed his hands, wept, and said, 'All is as you said at first! Those who raise are exalted; those who lower are debased; for the blessed Holy One cannot abide associates.'"[724]

Rabbi Shim'on said, "Eve said that she created *a male* את יהוה (et YHVH), *to YHVH* (Genesis 4:1)—the unique Name. But he corrupted his deeds, not wishing to maintain the upright path, as is written: *Cain went out from the presence of YHVH* (ibid., 16)—departing from that principle his mother proclaimed. Consequently, what is written? *He dwelled in the land of* נוד *Nod* (ibid.)—נד (*nad*),



722. **I saw Rabbi Akiva—who asked Rabbi Eli'ezer about this matter...** Presumably Rabbi Akiva asked his teacher about the phrases *is there not se'et?* or *sin crouches at the opening.* Apparently Rabbi Eli'ezer intends that the deeper meaning of the verse is connected with his previous remarks about the name YHVH and Elohim, and Rabbi Beroka's exposition of Adam's sin. Rabbi Eli'ezer is encouraging Rabbi Akiva to discover the mystery for himself.

723. **I have enacted the posture of the serpent...** Following his teacher's advice, Rabbi Akiva seeks to fathom the verse. His serpentine body movements serve to concentrate his mind. The posture of the serpent may also be relevant here as Rabbi Akiva is seeking to fathom the mystery of the sin crouching at the opening—identified with the evil impulse, in turn identified with the serpent.

Cf. BT *Berakhot* 12a–b, where prostration during prayer is compared to a serpent: "When Rav Sheshet bowed [during prayer] he used to bend like a reed [i.e., quickly and at once]; and when he raised himself, he used to raise himself like a serpent [i.e., slowly, first raising the head]." See also BT *Berakhot* 49a.

724. **whispered to him ...** Although Rabbi Eli'ezer reveals the mystery of the verse to his student, we are left in the dark.

Rabbi Akiva's statement, "Those who raise are exalted; those who lower are debased" is not entirely clear. Perhaps he is paraphrasing the rabbinic dictum in the name of Resh Lakish: "If one comes to defile himself, he is provided an opening; if one comes to purify himself, he is assisted" (BT *Shabbat* 104a).

Alternatively, the phrase might be construed as referring to the superiority of YHVH over Elohim, and rendered "the high [namely: YHVH] are exalted, the lowly [namely: Elohim] are lowered."

For different explanations, see *Sullam, Matoq mi-Devash.*

The intolerable "associates" (or "partners") apparently refer to one's elevating Elohim to the rank of YHVH. Cf. BT *Sanhedrin* 38a, 63a.

Cf. the Islamic sin of *shirk*, "idolatry," derived from the root "to share," but understood as attributing a partner to Allah. See, for example, Qur'an 4:116: "Indeed, Allah does not forgive association with Him. ... And he who associates others with Allah has certainly gone far astray."

wandering, the earth. He too repented when he acknowledged his sin, and he accepted his punishment. As we have learned: Whoever confesses his sins and is ashamed of them is immediately absolved of all his transgressions, as is written: *whoever confesses and renounces them finds mercy* (Proverbs 28:13)."[725]

Rabbi Ḥiyya said, "This is derived from here: *and confesses his sin* (Leviticus 5:5), and it is said: *it shall be forgiven him* (ibid., 10)."[726]

Rabbi Yeisa said, "There is nothing in the world that stands in the way of repentance. It was decreed upon Cain: *wavering and wandering will you be on earth* (Genesis 4:12). When he repented, half was voided, as is written: *He dwelled in the land of Nod* [or: *Wandering*] (ibid., 16)—wavering is not mentioned."[727]

Our Rabbis have taught: Concerning everything the blessed Holy One absolves, but He does not absolve concerning the glory of His Name.

Is it really true that He does not absolve? For look, Manasseh, king of Judah, exchanged the glory of the Omnipresent for idol-vanities!

"Manasseh was different—because he personally knew that it was vanity, and did not take the essence to heart." These are the words of Rabbi Yehudah. Rabbi Shim'on says, "There is nothing at all in the world that stands in the way of repentance."[728]

725. **departing from that principle his mother proclaimed...** Despite Eve's best intentions in devoting Cain *to YHVH* (see above, *ZḤ* 19c, notes 704 and 706), Cain recapitulated his parents' sin, for he was unable to hold fast to the unique name YHVH exclusively.

On Cain's repentance, see below, note 727.

See BT *Berakhot* 12b: "Rava son of Ḥinena the elder said in the name of Rav, 'Whoever commits a sin and is ashamed of it, all his sins are forgiven him.'"

726. **This is derived from here...** Here is a different proof-text to illustrate that one who confesses is forgiven.

Rabbi Ḥiyya misquotes the verse slightly, citing והתודה על חטאתו (*ve-hitvaddah al ḥatato*) instead of והתודה אשר חטא עליה (*ve-hitvaddah asher ḥata aleiyah*), *and confesses how he has sinned thereby*. See Maimonides, *Mishneh Torah, Hilkhot Teshuvah* 1:1.

727. **nothing in the world that stands in the way of repentance...** See JT *Pe'ah* 1:1, 16b: "Nothing withstands any master of repentance." See Maimonides, *Mishneh Torah, Hilkhot Teshuvah* 3:14; *Zohar* 1:62a; 2:106a; 3:78b, 122b; Tishby, *Wisdom of the Zohar*, 3:1504.

On Cain's punishment and repentance, see *Vayiqra Rabbah* 10:5: "Rabbi Yehudah says, 'Repentance effects half [atonement], but prayer effects a complete [atonement]....' Whence is derived the view of Rabbi Yehudah son of Rabbi that repentance effects only half? From the case of Cain, against whom a decree was issued. When he repented, half of the decree was withheld. How do we know that Cain repented? As is said: *Cain said to YHVH, 'My iniquity is too great to be forgiven'* (Genesis 4:13). And how do we know that half the sentence was withheld? As is written: *Cain went out from the presence of YHVH, and dwelt in the land of Nod* [i.e., Wandering], *east of Eden* (ibid., 16). It is not written *wavering and wandering* [as initially decreed (ibid., 12)], but rather *the land of Nod* (Wandering), *east of Eden*." See also BT *Sanhedrin* 37b; *Zohar* 1:54b (*Tos*).

728. **Concerning everything the blessed Holy One absolves...** See *Vayiqra Rab-*

Rabbi Yitsḥak said, "Why is it written *And the sister of Tubal-Cain was* נעמה (*Na'amah*), *Na'amah* (Genesis 4:22)?"[729]

Well, Rabbi Yitsḥak said, "She was a righteous woman and נעימה (*ne'imah*), pleasing, in her deeds."[730]

Rabbi Abbahu said, "The simple sense of Scripture indicates that she was learned in metal-working, like her brother Tubal-Cain, as implied by what is written: *he was the progenitor of every implement of bronze and iron—and the sister of Tubal-Cain, Na'amah* (ibid.). He invented this craft and his sister with him, as is written: *and the sister of Tubal-Cain, Na'amah*—she was skilled like him. The 'and' of 'and the sister' joins the preceding statement."[731]

Rabbi Bo said, "She was the mother of demons; she bore them. For look, the mother of Ashmedai, king of the demons, is named Na'amah."[732]

*bah* 22:6: "We find that the blessed Holy One showed indulgence toward idolatry—but did not show indulgence concerning desecration of the Name."

If, as the Rabbis say, God does not absolve sins pertaining to the desecration of the Name, how is it that King Manasseh was forgiven? According to Rabbi Yehudah, it was because Manasseh did not really believe in the other gods whom he publicly worshipped. But according to Rabbi Shim'on, even if Manasseh did believe in those deities, this would not matter—as nothing stands in the way of repentance.

On Manasseh, see 2 Kings 21:1–10. Manasseh built pagan shrines and altars and placed a sculpture of Asherah in the Temple: *He bowed down to all the host of heaven and worshipped them* (v. 3). The account of his reign in 2 Chronicles 33 adds an episode on his repentance following his exile to Babylon. See verses 12–13: *In his distress, he entreated YHVH his God and humbled himself greatly before the God of his fathers. He prayed to Him and He granted his prayer, heard his plea, and returned him to Jerusalem to his kingdom. Then Manasseh knew that YHVH alone was God.* See also verses 15–17. See BT *Sanhedrin* 102b–103a; *Pirqei de-Rabbi Eli'ezer* 43; *Zohar* 1:39a (*Heikh*); *ZḤ* 23c (*MhN*).

729. **Why is it written *And the sister of Tubal-Cain*...** Na'amah, whose name means "lovely" or "pleasant," was the great-great-great-great-granddaughter of Cain. Although her brother was famous for inventing metal tools, Rabbi Yitsḥak wonders why the Torah bothers mentioning her at all. See *Zohar* 1:55a.

730. **She was a righteous woman . . .** Rabbi Yitsḥak answers his own query. Na'amah is singled out for special mention because she was righteous. See *Bereshit Rabbah* 23:3 in the name of Rabbi Abba son of Kahana: "Why was she called Na'amah? Because her deeds were *ne'imim*, pleasing." Furthermore, according to Rabbi Abba son of Kahana, Na'amah was the wife of Noah—whom Genesis calls *righteous* (6:9).

731. **learned in metal-working, like her brother Tubal-Cain...** Na'amah, like her famous brother Tubal-Cain, co-invented metal working, and hence she was worthy of being mentioned in the Torah. This conclusion comes from logically connecting the verse's last clause—which begins with a conjunction—with its primary clause.

In its simple sense, the verse reads: *As for Zillah, she bore Tubal-Cain, who forged every implement of bronze and iron. And the sister of Tubal-Cain was Na'amah.* The *Zohar* misquotes the verse slightly, apparently influenced by the two verses that precede it.

732. **She was the mother of demons...** On Na'amah as mother of demons, see Naḥ-

Rabbi Yitsḥak said in the name of Rabbi Yoḥanan, "She was so called on account of her beauty. From her emerged those of whom is written *that they were attractive* (ibid. 6:2)—in appearance and beauty."[733]

Rabbi Yose said, "Why is it said of Seth *he engendered in his likeness, according to his image* (ibid. 5:3), but of Cain and Abel it is not said?"[734]

Rabbi Ḥiyya replied, "Cain and Abel existed solely to manifest a supernal hint and a precious mystery—and did not arise that the world be populated through them. Seth, however, came to the world solely so it would unfurl through him; therefore it said *in his likeness, according to his image*."[735]



manides on Genesis 4:22; *Zohar* 1:9b, 19b, 55a; 3:76b–77a; Tishby, *Wisdom of the Zohar*, 2:531.

Cf. *Bereshit Rabbah* 23:3: "The Rabbis said, ... 'Why was she called Na'amah? Because she would מנעמת (*man'emet*), sing, to the timbrel in honor of idolatry.'"

On Ashmedai, see BT *Gittin* 68a–b; Ginzberg, *Legends*, 4:165–72; *Zohar* 2:128a; 3:19a, 43a, 77a.

733. **She was so called on account of her beauty...** Na'amah also means "lovely," alluding to her status as ancestor of the beautiful women described in Genesis 6:1–2: *When humankind began to increase on the face of the earth and daughters were born to them, the sons of God saw that the daughters of humankind were attractive, and they took themselves wives, whomever they chose.*

According to rabbinic tradition, the fallen angels were attracted to her beauty. See *Tanḥuma* (Buber), *Ḥuqqat*, add. 1; *Midrash Aggadah* and *Midrash ha-Gadol*, Genesis 4:22.

Most of the diverse views expressed here about Na'amah are found in Nahmanides' commentary to Genesis 4:22.

734. **Why is it said of Seth *he engendered in his likeness*...** See Genesis 5:1–3: *This is the book of the lineage of Adam: On the day God created the human, in the image of God He fashioned him. Male and female He created them, and He blessed them—and called their name Humankind on the day they were created. Adam lived a hundred and thirty years, and he engendered in his likeness, by his image—and called his name Seth.* Cf. Genesis 4:25.

Of all Adam and Eve's children, only with Seth is the *image* and *likeness* mentioned. In fact, Adam's name is not associated at all with Cain or Abel. See BT *Eruvin* 18b; *Pirqei de-Rabbi Eli'ezer* 22; Maimonides, *Guide of the Perplexed* 1:7; *Zohar* 1:36b, 55a; 2:167b–168a, 231b; 3:77a, 143b (*IR*); *ZḤ* 8c–9b (*SO*).

Rabbi Yose's question and the remaining discussion in *parashat Be-Reshit* are absent from all the manuscripts I consulted. It appears first in the Venice edition. Both OM1 and V22 fill the lacuna with Naḥmanides' commentary on the Torah.

735. **Cain and Abel existed solely to manifest a supernal hint...** Apparently, because Cain and Abel came to the world only to demonstrate the superiority and exaltation of *YHVH* over *Elohim* (see above, at note 710; see also at note 704), rather than coming to the world to engender children, there was no need for them to be in Adam's (and thus God's) likeness.

Cf. Naḥmanides on Genesis 5:3.

On Seth as the ancestor of subsequent humanity, see *Bemidbar Rabbah* 14:12: "*He named him* שת (*Shet*), *Seth* (Genesis 5:3), because from him the world הושתת (*hushtat*), was founded." See also *Aggadat Bereshit*, intro 37; *Pirqei de-Rabbi Eli'ezer* 22; *Zohar* 1:36b, 38a, 56a; 3:77a; Liebes, *Peraqim*, 373; Stroumsa, *Another Seed*, 74–76.

It has been taught: Enoch son of Jared was righteous, but he decided to be wicked. The blessed Holy One seized him before his time, dealing kindly with him, so He might grant him a good reward in the world to come.[736]

Rabbi Abbahu said, "We have learned: *For God has heard the voice of the boy there where he is* (Genesis 21:17). Some say [20a] *there where he is* implies that at that time, he was righteous; and that is why the blessed Holy One heard his voice.[737]

"But we have not decreed so in the Mishnah. For Rabbi Yehudah said in the name of Rabbi Yitsḥak, 'Why was Ishmael banished from Abraham's house?

736. **Enoch son of Jared was righteous, but...** Enoch's life and death are recounted enigmatically in Genesis 5:24: *Enoch walked with God; then he was no more—for God took him.*

See *Bereshit Rabbah* 25:1: "Rabbi Aivu said, 'Enoch was a hypocrite: sometimes righteous, sometimes wicked. The blessed Holy One said, "While he is righteous I will remove him."'" See Theodor's note, ad loc.; Wisdom of Solomon 4:10–11.

See also Rashi on Genesis 5:24: "He was a righteous man, but light in his mind, so that he might regress to behaving wickedly. Therefore the blessed Holy One acted quickly and removed him—and put him to death before his time. This is why Scripture deviated regarding his death by writing: *then he was no more* in the world to complete his years; *for God took him*—before his time."

The *Zohar* here derives from Rashi's wording. Rashi writes: קל בדעתו לשוב להרשיע (*qal be-da'ato lashuv leharshi'a*), whereas here it reads: קבל על עצמו להרשיע (*qibbel al atsmo laharshi'a*).

On Enoch, see *Zohar* 1:56b; 2:10b. On removing the righteous or innocent while they are still pure, see BT *Ḥagigah* 5a; *Shir ha-Shirim Rabbah* on 6:2; *Qohelet Rabbah* on 7:15; *Zohar* 1:56b, 118b; 2:10b, 96a–b; *ZḤ* 36b (*RR*); Meroz, "Va-Ani Lo Hayiti Sham?," 169 (Addendum 3 in this volume). Cf. M *Sanhedrin* 8:5; *Sifrei*, Deuteronomy 218.

737. ***there where he is* implies that at that time, he was righteous...** Ishmael is in a situation similar to Enoch: God has foreknowledge that his future actions will be wicked. Yet clearly God does not judge Ishmael—let alone shorten his life—based on that consideration. This instance casts doubt on the claim that God had removed Enoch in order to prevent his becoming wicked.

The context of the verse from Genesis is the expulsion of Hagar and Ishmael from Abraham's house. Wandering in the desert and on the verge of death, God hears the child's cry. The full verse reads: *God heard the cry of the boy; and an angel of God called to Hagar from heaven and said to her, "What troubles you, Hagar? Fear not, for God has heard the cry of the boy there where he is."*

That Ishmael (that is, his descendants) would be wicked in the future can be derived from Genesis 16:12, Isaiah 21:13–15, and Psalms 83:6–7. Consequently, God's intervention to save Ishmael in Genesis 21 can be explained only by assuming that at that time he was still righteous. See *Bereshit Rabbah* 53:14: "*There where he is*—Rabbi Simon said, 'The ministering angels hastened to indict him [Ishmael], exclaiming before Him, "Master of the World! Will You bring up a well for he who will one day slay Your children with thirst?" He asked them, "What is he now? Righteous or wicked?" They replied, "Righteous." He said to them, "I judge a person only as he is at the moment."'" See also BT *Rosh ha-Shanah* 16b: "Rabbi Yitsḥak said, 'A person is judged only according to his actions up to that moment, as is said: *For God has heard the voice of the boy there where he is.*" See also *Zohar* 1:121b.

And what did Sarah see that she said: *Cast out this maidservant and her son* (ibid., 10)? Well, here is written: *Sarah saw the son of Hagar the Egyptian, whom she had borne to Abraham,* מצחק (*metsaḥeq*), *playing* (ibid., 9). Rabbi Yitsḥak said, מצחק (*metsaḥeq*), *playing,* refers solely to idolatry. Here is written מצחק (*metsaḥeq*), *playing,* and there is written *They rose* לצחק (*letsaḥeq*), *to play* (Exodus 32:6). Just as there it refers to idolatry, so here idolatry; and at that time, he was wicked!'[738]

"If so, how then shall we establish *there where he is* (Genesis 21:17)? The explanation derives from what we have decreed in our Mishnah. Rabbi Yehudah said, 'The Higher Court does not judge a person until he is twenty years old, and the Lower Court from thirteen years and higher.' At that time Ishmael was not yet twenty years old—and therefore he wasn't judged; for even though he was culpable, on account of his days he wasn't found guilty. This is the meaning of what is written: *there where he is*—according to the days he was there."[739]

Rabbi Yishma'el said, "But we have seen a child not yet twenty, who was
216 good, learned in Torah and Mishnah—yet has died! What removed him from

738. **But we have not decreed so...** The situations of Enoch and Ishmael are not parallel, because Ishmael was not innocent. Rather, he was an idolator.

See *Bereshit Rabbah* 53:11: "Rabbi Yishma-'el [in parallel sources: Rabbi Akiva] taught, 'This expression of צחוק (*tseḥoq*), "playing, revelry" refers solely to idolatry, as is said: *They rose* לצחק (*le-tsaḥeq*), *to revel* (Exodus 32:6). This teaches that Sarah saw Ishmael building idolatrous altars, catching locusts, and sacrificing them.'"

See Theodor's note, ad loc.; *Sifrei*, Deuteronomy 31; *Tosefta Sotah* 6:6; *Shemot Rabbah* 1:1; *Zohar* 1:118b. Cf. *Bereshit Rabbah* 63:10.

Perhaps to amplify the wordplay, *MhN* substitutes Rabbi Yitsḥak for Rabbi Yishma-'el from the rabbinic source text. See Matt, "Matnita di-Lan," 133–34.

The Mishnah referred to by Rabbi Abbahu is not the Mishnah of Rabbi Yehudah ha-Nasi but a collection of (usually esoteric) teachings possessed by the Companions alone. See above, note 468.

On the use of the term "decree" to establish a teaching, see above, note 404.

The rejection of the tradition of Ishmael's innocence may derive from the fact that by the *Zohar*'s day, Ishmael had come to symbolize Islam.

739. **even though he was culpable...he wasn't found guilty...** God heeded Ishmael's cry not because he was innocent, but owing to a legal technicality: Ishmael was not old enough to be punished. See *Zohar* 1:118b, which is similar to this passage.

See *Midrash Tanna'im*, Deuteronomy 24:16: "The Higher Court punishes only from twenty years and higher, while the Lower Court from thirteen years and one day."

See Numbers 14:29 (where the Israelite men over twenty years old—aside from the tribe of Levi—are condemned to die in the desert); M *Niddah* 5:6; BT *Shabbat* 89b; *Tanḥuma, Qoraḥ* 3; *Bahir* 135 (195); *Zohar* 1:118b; 2:98a, 113a–b, 186b, 248b (*Heikh*); 3:293b (*IZ*); *ZḤ* 43d.

According to rabbinic tradition, Ishmael was a teenager at this time. See *Bereshit Rabbah* 53:13 (and Theodor's note); *Shemot Rabbah* 1:1; *Tanḥuma, Shemot* 1; Naḥmanides on Genesis 21:9; Baḥya ben Asher on Genesis 21:18.

the world? Now, should you say it is on account of his father's sins—he is 'from thirteen and higher'! Should you say on account of his own sins—he is not yet twenty years old!"[740]

Rabbi Yehudah said, "A parable. To what can the matter be compared? To a king who had an orchard. One day, he entered to stroll in that orchard—and noticed young roses flowering within, their fragrance wafting before him, unlike any other in the world. The king said, 'If so now when they are young, how much more so when they are fully grown!' Sometime later he entered that same orchard, expecting to find those same roses—which had emitted fragrance at first when they were fresh and beautiful and had wafted [aroma]—now fully grown and beautiful in which to delight. When he examined them, he found them withered, lacking fragrance. He grew angry and said, 'Had I plucked them before—when they were fresh and beautiful, wafting fragrance—I could have delighted in them. Now, in what shall I delight? Look, they are withered!' The following year, the king entered the orchard and found young roses wafting fragrance. The king said, 'Pluck them now; I will delight in them before they wither as they did previously!'



"Similarly, the blessed Holy One sees young people wafting fragrance. All is revealed before Him and He sees that in the future they will become wicked, worthless as withered straw. He extends them kindness to delight in them in the Garden of Eden; and now, while they are still good, He removes them from this world, granting them a good reward in the world to come. As is written: *I am my beloved's and my beloved is mine, he grazes among the roses* (Song of Songs 6:3)—who conducts His world in accordance with the roses."[741]

740. **What removed him from the world?...** We know from experience that righteous children between the ages of thirteen and twenty are not immune from death. Rabbi Yishma'el wants to know how this can be explained. The parable that follows seeks to solve the perennial question of theodicy.

Though not culpable for his own sins, a child under the age of thirteen can be punished for his father's sins. See *Rut Zuta* 1:5: "Rabbi Ḥiyya son of Abba said, 'Until the age of thirteen, a son is punished for his father's sins; from then on, each person dies for his own sin." See Deuteronomy 24:16; 2 Kings 14:6. See *Zohar* 1:118b.

741. **conducts His world in accordance with the roses** Just as the rose emits fragrance when young but later withers, so the blessed Holy One delights in the aroma of the righteous—and plucks them before they can putrefy.

Rabbi Yehudah's parable answers several questions at once: why children between the ages of thirteen and twenty die; why Enoch was taken; and—more generally—why the righteous die before their time.

The verb רעה (*ra'ah*), "to graze," also means "to shepherd, guide," whence "conducts."

The parable's imagery is derived in part from *Shir ha-Shirim Rabbah* on the previous verse from the Song of Songs (6:2): "*My love has gone down to his garden, to the beds of spices,* [*to graze in the gardens and gather roses*]. Rabbi Yose son of Rabbi Ḥanina said, '... *My love*—this refers to the blessed Holy

Rabbi Abbahu said, "I can support what Rabbi Yehudah said. For look, we have seen that the blessed Holy One acted in the same manner toward Jeroboam son of Nebat; for when he was a youth, he was righteous and good. As we have learned: What is the meaning of *the two of them were alone in the field* (1 Kings 11:29)? It teaches that at that time, they were more righteous and worthy than the whole of Israel.[742]

One; *His garden* refers to the world; *to the beds of spices*—these are Israel; *to graze in the gardens*—these are synagogues and houses of study; *and gather roses*—to take away the righteous in Israel.'... Rabbi Ḥiyya son of Abba and his disciples, or, as some say, Rabbi Akiva and his disciples, or, as others say, Rabbi Yehoshu'a and his disciples used to sit and study under a certain fig-tree. Every single day, the tree's owner used to rise early and gather his figs. They said, 'Let us go to another place, lest he be suspecting us [of stealing].' What did they do? They went and sat in another place. The owner of the tree got up the next day, but he did not find them. He went and looked for them until he found them. He said to them, 'Sirs, you had enabled me to perform a good deed—and now you are preventing me?' They said to him, 'Heaven forbid!' [He asked], 'Why then have you left your [former] place and gone somewhere else?' They answered, 'Lest you suspect us.' He said to them, 'Heaven forbid! But I will tell you why I rise early to gather the fruit of my fig-tree. It is because when the sun shines on the figs, they breed worms.' Immediately they returned to their former place. On that day, they found that he had not gathered. They took some [of the fruit], and when they opened them, they found worms inside. They said, 'The owner of the fig-tree was quite right! As he knows the right time for his figs and gathers them, so the blessed Holy One knows when it is the right time to remove the righteous; and He does remove them.'" See also *Bereshit Rabbah* 62:2; JT *Berakhot* 2:7, 5b–c.



Cf. BT *Ḥagigah* 5a: "When Rabbi Yoḥanan came to the [following] verse, he wept: *He puts no trust in His holy ones* (Job 15:15). If He does not put His trust in His holy ones, in whom will He put His trust? One day, he was going on a journey and saw a man gathering figs. He was leaving those that were ripe—and was taking those that were unripe. He asked him, 'Are not those [the ripe figs] better?' He replied, 'I need those for a journey: these will keep, but the others will not keep.' He [Rabbi Yoḥanan] said, 'This is the meaning of the verse: *He puts no trust in His holy ones.*'"

Cf. *ZḤ* 12d (*MhN*), where the *Zohar* employs a different orchard parable illustrating how God removes the righteous so that judgment can be executed upon the wicked.

See *Zohar* 2:20a–b (*MhN*) for a different interpretation of how God conducts the world in accordance with roses.

742. **Jeroboam son of Nebat...** Jeroboam was the first king of the northern kingdom of Israel. Though bearing the ignominy of having built two golden calves (see next note), both the Bible and the Talmud recount his origins favorably.

See 1 Kings 11:29–31: *During that time, Jeroboam went out of Jerusalem and the prophet Ahijah of Shiloh met him on the way. He had put on a new robe, and the two of them were alone in the field. Ahijah took hold of the new robe he was wearing—and tore it into twelve pieces. He said to Jeroboam, "Take ten pieces; for thus said* YHVH*, God of Israel: I am about to tear the kingdom out of Solomon's hands, and I will give you ten tribes."*

See BT *Sanhedrin* 102a: "*He had put on a new robe, and the two of them were alone in the field.* What is the significance of *a new robe*? Rav Naḥman said, 'As a new robe: just as a new robe has no defect, so Jeroboam's learning was without defect. Alternatively: *a*

"Rabbi Berekhiah said, 'The blessed Holy One said to the retinue above, "The aroma of Jeroboam is wafting before Me. I wish to remove him from the world now, while he is still fragrant." They replied, "Master of the World, You are a true judge! If now he is thus, how much more so when he grows up?" The blessed Holy One said to them, "It is revealed and known before Me that he will do evil in My sight." They replied, "Master of the World, while it may be revealed before You—is it revealed before us and the rest of the world?" The blessed Holy left him alone. What is written? *The king took counsel and he made two golden calves* (ibid. 12:28). He sinned and led astray. At that time, the blessed Holy One said to them, "Didn't I tell you that I wanted to remove him from the world before this?! What a pity I acted this way!"'[743]

"Abijah his son arose; and while he was young, he did what was good. What was the good that he did? Rabbi Yose said in the [20b] name of Rabbi Ḥanina, 'The pilgrims would ascend with his help, without his father's knowledge.' The blessed Holy One saw that he was good and removed him from the world before his days, in order to deal kindly with him—to bequeath him the world to come—before his fragrance putrefied. Such is the kindness that the blessed Holy One administers His creatures.[744] 219

"Similarly Enoch: while he was still righteous and the entire generation wicked, the blessed Holy One saw that if He left him alone, he would learn

*new robe*—they innovated new teachings, such as no ear had ever heard before.' What is the significance of *and the two of them were alone in the field*? Rav Yehudah said in the name of Rav, 'All other scholars were as the grasses of the field before them.' Others say that all the reasons of the Torah were as manifest to them as a field."

743. **I wish to remove him from the world now, while he is still fragrant...** Applying the principle of the roses, and knowing that the sin he will commit later in his life will be especially grievous, the blessed Holy One seeks to remove Jeroboam from the world while he is still righteous. However, fearing that His actions will appear unjust—as only He alone knows the future degradation of Jeroboam—God leaves him alone. See *ZḤ* 47d–48a.

Jeroboam's great sin is the construction of the two golden calves in Bethel and Dan, to dissuade his subjects from making pilgrimage to Jerusalem—and thus returning to the Davidic king, Rehoboam. See 1 Kings 12:25–33; BT *Sanhedrin* 101b–102a; *Rosh ha-Shanah* 17a. See also M *Avot* 5:18.

It is not clear whether Rabbi Berekhiah is an independent voice or is being quoted by Rabbi Abbahu. I have opted for the latter.

744. **Abijah his son arose; and while he was young...** See the account of Abijah's illness and premature death in 1 Kings 14, in which the prophet Ahijah says of him: *he alone of Jeroboam's family shall be brought to burial, for in him alone of the House of Jeroboam has been found some devotion* [literally: *a good thing*] *to YHVH, the God of Israel* (verse 13).

BT *Mo'ed Qatan* 28b asks what precisely the *good thing* was that earned him this honor: "Rabbi Zeira and Rabbi Ḥanina son of Papa [differed]: one said that he left his post and went on a pilgrimage [to Jerusalem]; the other said that he removed the military guards that his father Jeroboam had posted on the roads to prevent Israel from going on a pilgrimage [to Jerusalem]." Cf. *ZḤ* 56b.

from their deeds; and so He removed him from the world before his time—before his aroma putrefied. As is written: *He was no more, for God took him* (Genesis 5:24)—that is to say, *he was no more* in this world to fulfill his days; *for God took him* before his time, dealing kindly with him, bequeathing him the life of the world to come."[745]

*The sons of God saw the daughters of humankind* (Genesis 6:2).[746]

Who are these *sons of* אלהים (*Elohim*), *God*? Rabbi Yirmeyah said, "The dignitaries of the generation, whose fathers had been the dignitaries of the generation—but they did not restrain them."[747]

Rabbi Ḥanina said to Rav Huna, "Concerning what is said: *sons of Elohim*—it is because they were created from this name, as is written: *Elohim created the human* (ibid. 1:27)."[748]



745. **Similarly Enoch... before his aroma putrefied...** Following the same pattern of the roses, Enoch is taken before he is corrupted. See above, note 736.

746. ***The sons of God saw the daughters of humankind*** The context of this verse is the enigmatic mythological fragment found in Genesis 6:1–4: *When humankind began to increase on the face of the earth and daughters were born to them, the sons of God saw that the daughters of humankind were beautiful; and they took themselves wives—whomever they chose. YHVH said, "My spirit shall not abide in the human forever, for he too is flesh. Let his days be a hundred and twenty years." The Nephilim were on earth in those days—and afterward as well—when the sons of God came in to the daughters of humankind, who bore them children. These are the heroes of old, men of renown* [literally: *name*].

The myth behind this fragment in Genesis appears in postbiblical sources that describe angels who rebelled against God and descended to earth, where they were attracted by human women. See Isaiah 14:12; 1 Enoch 6–8; Jubilees 5; *Targum Yerushalmi*, Genesis 6:2, 4; BT *Yoma* 67b; *Aggadat Bereshit*, intro, 39; *Midrash Avkir*, 7 (cited in *Yalqut Shim'oni*, Genesis, 44); *Pirqei de-Rabbi Eli'ezer* 22; *Zohar* 1:23a (*TZ*), 37a, 37a (*Tos*), 55a, 58a, 62b, 117b–118a (*MhN*), 126a; 3:208a–b, 212a–b; *ZḤ* 21c (*MhN*), 81a–b (*MhN, Rut*); Ginzberg, *Legends*, 5:153–56, n. 57.

747. **Who are these *sons of* אלהים (*Elohim*), *God*?...** Although in its biblical context the Hebrew בני האלהים (*benei ha-elohim*), *sons of God*, implies some kind of celestial beings, there is a long tradition of reading the word *elohim* here as signifying "the mighty, judges, nobles," as some interpreters perceive in Exodus 21:6; 22:7–8, 22:27; Judges 5:8; 1 Samuel 2:25; and Psalms 138:1. Both *Targum Onqelos* and *Targum Yerushalmi*, ad loc., render *benei ha-elohim* as בני רברביא (*benei ravrevaya*), *sons of the mighty*.

See *Bereshit Rabbah* 26:5: "Rabbi Shim'on son of Yoḥai called them *the sons of judges*. Rabbi Shim'on son of Yoḥai cursed all who called them *the sons of God*. Rabbi Shim'on son of Yoḥai taught, 'If demoralization does not proceed from the leaders, it is not real demoralization. When the priests steal their gods, by what can one swear or to what can one sacrifice?'" See also Rashi on Genesis 6:2: "the sons of the princes and judges."

See Naḥmanides on Genesis 6:2: "Scripture relates that the judges whose duty it was to administer justice—their children committed open violence, without anyone preventing them."

See *ZḤ* 21c (*MhN*).

748. **because they were created from this name...** As in the preceding statement, Rabbi Ḥanina also "demythologizes" the verse. The *sons of Elohim* are none other than human beings (not celestials)—and are so

[*One day the sons of Elohim* . . . (Job 1:6).][749] Rabbi Shim'on son of Lakish said, "Satan, the evil impulse, and the Angel of Death are one and the same."[750]

Rabbi Yehudah said, "That day was Rosh Hashanah—the day when everyone must return to the right path. Thus you find: It is the way of the evil impulse to provoke solely when a person wishes to return to the right path."[751]

It has been taught: An old man in the house is a good omen for the house; a righteous person in the generation is good for the world. As we have learned: The blessed Holy One casts fear of the judge and ruler upon human beings. As long as the fear of the judge is upon the generation, it is apparent that he is righteous and they are righteous. If his fear is withdrawn from human beings—he is wicked, and they more so than him.[752]

Scripture comes to teach: הנפלים (*Ha-nefilim*), *The fallen beings, were on earth* (Genesis 6:4). These are Adam and his wife, for they are the ones who fell to

called merely because *Elohim* had created them.

Cf. Naḥmanides on Genesis 6:4: "The correct explanation appears to me to be that Adam and his wife are called *benei ha-elohim* because they were God's handiwork and He was their father; they had no father besides Him." See also Moses de León, *Or Zaru'a*, 262.

749. ***One day the sons of Elohim* . . .** The verse continues: *came to stand before YHVH, and Satan also came among them*. This verse is not found in the Venice edition but was added, presumably because later editors sensed a lacuna in the text.

On the sons of *Elohim*, see also Job 38:7; Psalms 29:1.

The following brief statements on the book of Job are not integral to the main homily. Presumably, the discussion about the *sons of Elohim* in Genesis 6 generated this association.

750. **Satan, the evil impulse, and the Angel of Death . . .** See BT *Bava Batra* 16a.

751. **That day was Rosh Hashanah . . .** According to rabbinic tradition, the day on which the heavenly powers assembled was Rosh Hashanah, the fateful Day of Judgment. See *Targum Yonatan* on the verse; *Midrash Iyyov* 1:6 (*Battei Midrashot*, 2:158); Rashi and Ibn Ezra on the verse; *Zohar* 2:32b; 3:231a.

The evil impulse is at its most potent precisely when a human being seeks to return, whether on Rosh Hashanah or any other day.

752. **An old man in the house is a good omen for the house . . .** Cf. BT *Arakhin* 19a: "An old man in the house is a burden in the house, an old woman in the house is a treasure in the house!" See Rashi on Leviticus 27:7; see also *Sippurei ben Sira*, ed. Yassif, 274; Meroz, "Va-Ani Lo Hayiti Sham?," 166–67, n. 17 (Addendum 3 in this volume, which parallels this section). The *Zohar* has transformed the popular saying, perhaps conflating it with the rabbinic idea that a righteous person is a sign (of the covenant) in the world. See *Pesiqta de-Rav Kahana* 11:15; *ZḤ* 10d (*MhN*).

On fear of the ruler, cf. BT *Rosh ha-Shanah* 17a: "Those who *spread their terror in the land of the living* (Ezekiel 32:23): Rav Ḥisda said, 'This is a communal leader who casts excessive fear upon the community for purposes other than the sake of heaven.'" See also Maimonides, *Mishneh Torah, Hilkhot Teshuvah* 3:13. Although casting excessive fear is a sin, an appropriate amount of fear toward the ruler is in order. In fact, the presence of fear is a sign of the ruler's righteousness. Conversely, the absence of such fear is a sign that the ruler has sinned. On the role of leaders and their responsibility, see *Zohar* 2:36b, 47a; 3:114a, 135a (*IR*).

earth without a father and mother. Why were they called *fallen beings*? For they fell from the rank they possessed. In other words—fallen from how they were previously; fallen because they were banished from the Garden of Eden and did not return there.[753]

That is why the Torah reiterates: these ones *were on earth*—their fear was upon all the creatures; they were still alive, but they did not prevent the people of the generation from performing transgressions. Who are the ones who performed transgressions? The dignitaries of the generation: *the men of renown* (ibid.)—the greatest in the generation.[754]

Rabbi Pinḥas said, "Hence the interpretation of the verse: As is written: *The fallen beings were on earth* בימים ההם (*ba-yamim ha-hem*), *in those days* (ibid.). להם (*La-hem*), It was incumbent upon them, to have restraint and restrain themselves from transgressions—for their sake. But they did not hold back, and in front of their very eyes they came *into the daughters of humankind* whorishly, *and they bore them children* (ibid.). Who were those *fallen beings* extant in the generation? Those *mighty men* (ibid.), without peer in the generation; *the men of name* (ibid.)—the known name that the blessed Holy One called them, as is written: *He called their name* אדם (*Adam*), *Human* (ibid. 5:2)."[755]



753. **These are Adam and his wife...** Although in the Genesis narrative *nefilim* apparently refers to fallen celestial beings, the *Zohar* continues its demythologization, reading it as a reference to Adam and Eve. Cf. *Bereshit Rabbah* 26:7; *Pirqei de-Rabbi Eli'ezer* 22; Naḥmanides on Genesis 6:4. See Meroz, "Va-Ani Lo Hayiti Sham?," 167 (Addendum 3 in this volume).

In the later strata of the *Zohar*, the *nefilim* usually refer to the fallen angels Uzza and Azael. See *Zohar* 1:37a, 37a (*Tos*), 58a; 3:144a (*IR*); *ZḤ* 81a–b (*MhN, Rut*).

On Adam and Eve's fallen status, cf. BT *Ḥagigah* 12a; *Sanhedrin* 38b; *Bereshit Rabbah* 12:6.

754. **they were still alive...** Adam and Eve were still alive when the dignitaries of that generation sinned. The *Zohar* intends either that they ought to have prevented the sin but did not, or that following their own sin in the Garden of Eden—and consequently having lost face in the eyes of their fellow human beings (see above, at note 752)—they were ineffective as leaders and could do nothing to prevent the mighty from doing as they pleased.

On the *nefilim* inspiring fear, see Naḥmanides on Genesis 6:4: "The masters of language say that they were so called because a person's heart falls from fear of them."

See Meroz, "Va-Ani Lo Hayiti Sham?," 167 (Addendum 3 in this volume).

755. **It was incumbent upon them...** As leaders, Adam and Eve ought to have set an example for succeeding generations. Instead they were forced to witness the sexual violence perpetrated on their own offspring!

Here the *nefilim* (i.e., Adam and Eve) correspond with the *mighty men*, corresponding in turn with אנשי השם (*anshei ha-shem*), *the men of name*—that is, the name *Human* that God had bestowed. (In contrast, in the previous paragraph, *anshei ha-shem* are the ones who committed the sin.) In its simple sense, *anshei ha-shem*) means *men of renown*.

On Adam and Eve as *mighty men* without peer, cf. Naḥmanides on Genesis 6:4.

See Meroz, "Va-Ani Lo Hayiti Sham?," 167 (Addendum 3 in this volume).

# פרשת נח

# *Parashat Noaḥ*

"NOAH" (GENESIS 6:9–11:32)

Rabbi opened with this verse: "*The watchmen patrolling the city found me; they beat me, they bruised me. They stripped me of my shawl, the watchmen of the walls* (Song of Songs 5:7). How beloved is the soul, bestowed from beneath the Throne of Glory—from a holy site, from the lands of the living—as is said: *I will walk before YHVH in the lands of the living* (Psalms 116:9)![1]

"Why did David call it ארצות (*artsot*), *the lands of, the living*? Are there lands on high? Rabbi Yitsḥak said, 'This does not refer to actual lands, and David did not have lands in mind. Rather, it is an expression of ריצוי (*ritsui*), desire, as is said: ארצה (*ertseh*), *I will desire, you* (Ezekiel 20:41).' In other words, David said *I will walk before YHVH* in the site desired unceasingly by the righteous—who are called 'living'—whose desire [20d] and yearning is to go there. From a pure site the soul descends, illuminating the dim body so as to guide it along the straight path to perform the service and will of its Creator—to reach the morrow and take its reward."[2]

1. **How beloved is the soul...** In BT *Shabbat* 152b, the souls of the righteous are said to be "hidden beneath the Throne of Glory" after death; see also *Avot de-Rabbi Natan* A, 12. According to *MhN*, the soul is created from the substance of the Throne of Glory, which may refer to the *Shekhinah*. See *Zohar* 1:113a, 125b, 126b (all *MhN*); *ZḤ* 10a–d, 22a, 24a, 26a (all *MhN*). This idea may also derive from the writings of El'azar of Worms, *Sefer Ḥokhmat ha-Nefesh*, 1a, 3d, 4d, 5d. Cf. Solomon Ibn Gabirol, *Keter Malkhut*, Canto 29: "From your radiant glory, you created pure radiance, hewn from rock.... You imbued it with the life of wisdom—and called it soul."

Cf. *Zohar* 1:5a, 219b, where the referent "lands of the living" refers to *Shekhinah*.

"Rabbi" indicates Rabbi Yehudah ha-Nasi (the Patriarch), who redacted the Mishnah. He was so esteemed that he was called simply "Rabbi": the Master.

The significance of the verse from the Song of Songs is made clear below, pages 230–31.

2. **the site desired unceasingly by the righteous...** The expression *lands of the living* signifies the celestial realm that awaits

Rabbi Yehudah said, "It would be better for us had we never come into the world, and not have to give an account to the Bookkeeper!"[3]

Afterward he said, "I recant!"

Come and see what is written concerning the human being: *It is not good for the human to be alone. I will make him a fitting helper* (Genesis 2:18). Rabbi said, "This refers to the soul—a helper by his side—to lead him along the paths of his Maker. As we have learned: If one comes to purify himself, he is given assistance."[4]

Our Rabbis have taught: When a person follows the paths of his Maker, many assist him: his soul assists him; the ministering angels assist him; the *Shekhinah* of the Omnipresent assists him. All of them proclaim before him, saying, *When you walk, your stride will be unconstricted; if you run, you will not stumble* (Proverbs 4:12).

Rabbi Natan says, "The souls of the righteous assist him."[5]



the soul after death: the place that the righteous, who are called "living," desire (reading *artsot*, *lands*, as *ertseh*, *desire*).

See *Avot de-Rabbi Natan* A, 34: "The Garden of Eden was called Living, as is said: *I will walk before YHVH in the lands of the living* (Psalms 116:9)."

On the righteous as "living," see BT *Berakhot* 18a–b: "Rabbi Ḥiyya said, 'These are the righteous, who even in death are called "living."... These are the wicked, who even in life are called "dead."'" Cf. *Zohar* 1:132a, 164a, 207b; 2:106b; 3:182b, 287b (*IZ*); *ZḤ* 18b (*MhN*). On the soul illuminating the body, see *Zohar* 1:113a (*MhN*). On reaching the morrow and taking reward, see Rashi on Deuteronomy 7:11.

3. **had we never come into the world...** See BT *Eruvin* 13b: "Our Rabbis taught: For two-and-a-half years, the House of Shammai and the House of Hillel disputed. One said: It would have been better for humanity not to have been created than to have been created. The other said: It is better for humanity to have been created than not to have been created. They took a vote and decided: It would have been better for humanity not to have been created than to have been created; but now that he has been created, let him investigate his deeds. Others say, let him examine his future actions." See *Tosafot*, s.v. *noaḥ lo le-adam*.

Perhaps Rabbi Yehudah intends that in light of the soul's celestial origins and the fact that it must be judged in this world, it would have been better had it remained in the upper realms and hence not need to give an account. See Moses Cordovero, *Or Yaqar* vol. 14, *Shelaḥ*, 28: "It would have been better if from the outset he would abide in that world and not come into this world... and not sin and not depart from it. For it emerges, that his coming and going are in vain... and he has gained nothing other than sin."

See also M *Avot* 3:16.

4. ***a fitting helper...*** In Genesis, the *fitting helper* refers (ultimately) to Eve. Here, to the soul. See below, *ZḤ* 21c (*MhN*), page 234.

See BT *Shabbat* 104a: "Resh Lakish said, '... If one comes to defile himself, he is provided an opening; if one comes to purify himself, he is given assistance.'" See also BT *Yoma* 38b–39a; *ZḤ* 10c, 24b (both *MhN*).

5. **The souls of the righteous assist him** As illustrated by the following story.

Rabbi El'azar and Rabbi Yose his father-in-law were traveling from Usha to Lydda. Rabbi Yose said to Rabbi El'azar, "Did you happen to hear from your father the meaning of the verse *Jacob went on his way, and angels of God encountered him* (Genesis 32:2)?"[6]

He replied, "So have I heard from my father: They were the angels that accompanied him previously from the land of Israel."[7]

He said to him, "Who are they?"

He replied, "I do not know."

He said to him, "That befits you, O righteous ones! The word of your mouth is like a royal crown upon the King's head!"[8]

While they were walking, they reached the cave of Lydda. They heard a certain voice saying, "Two fawns of the doe fulfilled my pleasurable desire before me; they were the holy camp that Jacob encountered before him."[9]



6. **Rabbi El'azar and Rabbi Yose his father-in-law were traveling...** The story that follows appears again with some variations in *Zohar* 3:55b, under the heading *Tosefta*.

For a detailed analysis, see Liebes, "Terein Urzilin de-Ayyalta," 148–59.

According to rabbinic tradition, Rabbi El'azar's father-in-law was named Rabbi Shim'on son of Yose son of Lekonya. The *Zohar* consistently switches father and son, transforming Shim'on son of Yose into Yose son of Shim'on. See *Pesiqta de-Rav Kahana* 11:20; JT *Ma'aserot* 3:8, 50d; *Shir ha-Shirim Rabbah* on 4:11; *Devarim Rabbah* 7:11; *Seder ha-Dorot*, s.v. *Shim'on ben Yose ben Lekonya*; *Zohar* 1:5a, 61b; 3:84b, 188a, 193a; *ZḤ* 7d, 10d, 14a, 22c (all *MhN*).

In BT *Bava Metsi'a* 85a, the name of Rabbi El'azar's brother-in-law is given as Rabbi Shim'on son of Issi (Yose) son of Lekonya, which would make Yose his father-in-law, as in the *Zohar*—but nowhere in rabbinic literature is he named Yose son of Shim'on.

On journeying from Usha to Lydda, see *Zohar* 2:5a (*MhN*), 36b, 45b; 3:122a, 240a. On the verse from Genesis, see *Zohar* 1:165b–166a; 3:298a.

7. **angels that accompanied him previously...** When Jacob departed from Laban and began his journey back to the land of Israel, he was met by angels (Genesis 32:1–3). Earlier, when he had set out for Haran, he beheld angels in a dream (Genesis 28:12). According to Rabbi Shim'on, they were the same angels—bookending, as it were, his stay outside of the land of Israel. See *Aggadat Bereshit* (Buber) 55:1; *Tanḥuma*, *Vayishlaḥ* 3.

8. **That befits you, O righteous ones...** Rabbi Yose may be praising his son-in-law for not commenting on that which he does not know, in which case his secondary statement explains his praise: given the potency of words of Torah, one must convey only authentic traditions (see, e.g., *Zohar* 1:5a). Alternatively, he is being ironic, chastising him for his incomplete knowledge (see Liebes, "Terein Urzilin de-Ayyalta," 148, n. 324).

See BT *Berakhot* 27b, in the name of Rabbi Eli'ezer: "One who says something that he has not heard from his teacher causes *Shekhinah* to depart from Israel."

On the motif of words of Torah settling on the head of God, see *Zohar* 1:4b. See also BT *Ḥagigah* 13b.

9. **Two fawns of the doe...** The identity of the voice emerging from the cave is not stated. As becomes clearer below, it may be the voice of Rabbi Shim'on—or perhaps the voice of *Shekhinah*. According to Yehuda

Rabbi El'azar was excited but pained in his soul. He said, "Master of the World! Is its nature thus?! It would have been better had we not heard! We heard—but do not understand!"[10]

A miracle happened for him—and he heard that voice say, "They were Abraham and Isaac."[11]

He fell on his face—and saw the image of his father. He said to him, "Father, I asked and was answered that it was Abraham and Isaac who manifested to Jacob when he was saved from Laban!"[12]

He said to him, "Take out your note and heed the voice of your old man, for a mouth speaking grandly it was! And not only in this instance, but also for every righteous person: the souls of the righteous manifest before them to save them; they are supernal, holy angels.[13]



Liebes, "Terein Urzilin de-Ayyalta," 152, yet another possibility is that the voice in the cave belongs to Rav Hamnuna Sava.

The enigmatic statement derives from Song of Songs 4:5 (see also 7:4): *Your breasts are like two fawns, twins of a gazelle, grazing in a field of lilies.* Though the identity of the doe is readily apparent, i.e., *Shekhinah*, the identity of the two fawns is not yet revealed.

The mysterious voice emerges from the cave of Lydda. According to rabbinic tradition, a cave figured prominently in the lives of Rabbi El'azar and his father, Rabbi Shim'on: the Romans sought to execute Rabbi Shim'on for criticizing the government, so he hid from the authorities in a cave together with his son for thirteen years.

See *Bereshit Rabbah* 79:6; JT *Shevi'it* 9:1, 38d; BT *Shabbat* 33b–34a, *Sanhedrin* 98a; *Pesiqta de-Rav Kahana* 11:16; *Qohelet Rabbah* on 10:8; *Midrash Tehillim* 17:13; *Zohar* 1:11a–b, 216b; *ZḤ* 59c–60a; Meroz "Va-Ani Lo Hayiti Sham?," 168 (Addendum 3 in this volume).

On a cave near Lydda, see the story in *Pesiqta de-Rav Kahana* 18:5; *Pesiqta Rabbati* 32; *Zohar* 1:244b; 2:42b; Scholem, "She'elot be-Viqqoret ha-Zohar," 51–52; *Nitsotsei Zohar*, n.1 in *TZ* 1a. On the tradition that the *Zohar* was composed in the cave in which Rabbi Shim'on was hiding, see Tishby, *Wisdom of the Zohar*, 1:13; Huss, "Hofa'ato shel 'Sefer ha-Zohar'," 528.

10. **We heard—but do not understand!** Rabbi El'azar is frustrated by the voice, which conceals as much as it reveals.

11. **They were Abraham and Isaac** The two fawns of the doe signify Abraham and Isaac, and they are the angels who appeared to Jacob on his return to the land of Israel. The meaning of the mysterious statement: "Two fawns of the doe fulfilled my pleasurable desire before me" thus appears to be: When Abraham and Isaac greeted Jacob, *Shekhinah* joined with them, granting her pleasure. See Liebes, "Terein Urzilin de-Ayyalta," 153.

12. **He fell on his face—and saw the image of his father...** Rabbi El'azar performs a prostration (an intentional mystical technique) and sees his father, Rabbi Shim'on son of Yoḥai (cf. *Zohar* 1:4a; *ZḤ* 25c (*MhN*)). It thus seems that this story takes place after Rabbi Shim'on's death, and that the cave of Lydda (and not the cave near Meron, as per *Zohar* 3:296b) is the site of his burial. See Liebes, "Terein Urzilin de-Ayyalta," 151, n. 355.

Rabbi El'azar is still perplexed by the voice: how is it possible that Abraham and Isaac were the angels who visited Jacob? After all, Isaac was still alive when this happened!

13. **Take out your note...** That is, take out the note on which you wrote down what the voice had said—and now add what I tell you. Alternatively, accept the words you

"Come and see: Isaac was still alive at this time; but when he had been bound upon the altar, his holy soul had been taken to his Master's Throne of Glory, whereupon his eyes had been sealed from seeing. This is the significance of what is written: [*Had not...*] *the Fear of Isaac been with me* (Genesis 31:42)."[14]

He asked him, "What am I there?"[15]

heard that fell to you like a message from the sky. The text reads פוק פיקתך וסב סיבתך (*puq piqatakh ve-sav sivatakh*). The version of the story in *Zohar* 3:55b reads פוק פתקך (*puq pitkakh*). See Liebes, "Terein Urzilin de-Ayyalta," 149, n. 336.

In any case, Rabbi Shim'on clarifies and extends the voice's statement: the souls of the righteous manifest as angels assisting the righteous on earth. See *Zohar* 1:7a on Hamnuna Sava: "virtuous ones of that world come to them."

The phrase "a mouth speaking grandly" derives from Daniel's dream-vision (7:8, 20); cf. *Zohar* 2:178b (*SdTs*). Either Rabbi Shim'on is saying this about the *Shekhinah*, the source of the voice, or alternatively about himself. Another possibility is that Rabbi Shim'on identifies himself with the *Shekhinah*.

On the souls of the righteous as ministering angels, see *Zohar* 1:100a, 129b; *ZḤ* 10a, 19a, 21a (all *MhN*); *TZ, Haqdamah*, 16b.

14. **his holy soul had been taken to his Master's Throne of Glory...** Isaac—who was still alive when Jacob returned to the land of Israel—nonetheless could have appeared to him as a soul transformed into an angel, given that his soul had departed decades earlier, when his father Abraham had bound him upon the altar.

See *Pirqei de-Rabbi Eli'ezer* 31: "Rabbi Yehudah said, 'When the blade touched his neck, the soul of Isaac fled and departed. When he heard His voice from between the two *keruvim*, saying, *Lay not your hand upon the lad* (Genesis 22:12), his soul returned to his body....'" See also *Zohar* 1:60a (*Tos*).

See also *Bereshit Rabbah* 65:10: "[*When Isaac was old*] *and his eyes had become too dim to see* (Genesis 27:1)... as a result of that spectacle; for when our father Abraham bound his son upon the altar, the ministering angels wept, as is written: *Behold, the Erelim cried outside; angels of peace weep bitterly* (Isaiah 33:7). Tears dropped from their eyes into his, and left their mark upon them; and so when he became old, his eyes dimmed.... Another interpretation... When our father Abraham bound his son on the altar, he raised his eyes heavenward and gazed upon the *Shekhinah*. The blessed Holy One said, 'If I slay him now, I will make Abraham, My friend, suffer; therefore I rather decree that his eyes should be dimmed.'"



Note that the *Zohar* combines both midrashim: Isaac loses his sight because his soul departed.

On "Fear of Isaac," see Rashi on Genesis 31:42: "He did not want to say 'God of Isaac' because the blessed Holy One does not associate His name with the righteous during their lifetime. Even though [God] said to [Jacob] when he was departing Beersheba: *I am YHVH, the God of Abraham your father and the God of Isaac* (Genesis 28:13) this was because Isaac's eyes were dim—and he could therefore be regarded as dead. Jacob, however, feared to say so and instead said, 'Fear [of Isaac.']" See *Tanḥuma, Toledot* 7, in the name of Rabbi Shim'on son of Yoḥai: "The blessed Holy One does not associate His name with the righteous during their lifetime"; see also Naḥmanides on Genesis 31:42.

Apparently Rabbi Shim'on intends that Isaac's liminal status—alive yet soulless, as indicated by his dim eyes—enabled Jacob to swear by his name. Jacob's oath thus proves that Isaac's soul was already on high.

The version of this story in *Zohar* 3:55b (*Tos*) ends here.

15. **What am I there?** Namely, how is the next world? What kind of existence do we

He replied, "You and I are supernal angels, delighting with King David, the messiah."[16]

He arose. As he was rising, his father-in-law noticed that his face was radiant like the sun. His father-in-law asked him, "Did you hear some new word, or were you contemplating the glorious radiance of the splendor of Moses?"[17]

He replied, "No. But happy are the righteous—for supernal, holy camps protect them, as is said: *For He will command His angels, to guard you in all your ways* (Psalms 91:11)."[18]

Rabbi Yehudah said, "The blessed Holy One fashioned Jerusalem Above corresponding to Jerusalem below, and He swore that He would not enter therein until Israel enters Jerusalem below, as is said: *The Holy One is in your midst, and I will not enter the city* (Hosea 11:9).[19]

"Seven companies of ministering angels guard it round about; at every single opening are companies of ministering angels. They are the openings called



have? See *ZḤ* 19a (*MhN*), where Rabbi El'azar asks a similar question of his father.

16. **You and I are supernal angels...** See *ZḤ* 19a, 25c (both *MhN*). See also *Zohar* 1:4b.

17. **his face was radiant like the sun...** According to Ecclesiastes 8:1: *A person's wisdom lights up his face.* See *Pirqei de-Rabbi Eli'ezer* 2: "Rabbi Eli'ezer was sitting and expounding [matters greater than those revealed to Moses at Sinai], and his face was shining like the light of the sun, and his radiance went forth like the radiance of Moses; and no one knew whether it was day or night." See also *Avot de-Rabbi Natan* B, 13; JT *Pesaḥim* 10:1, 37c, *Shabbat* 8:1, 11a; *Tanḥuma* (Buber), *Ḥuqqat*, add. 1; *Vayiqra Rabbah* 1:1, 21:12; *Qohelet Rabbah* on 1:7. In the *Zohar*, see 1:94b; 2:15a (*MhN*); 3:132b (*IR*); *ZḤ* 5d, 28b (both *MhN*). See Hellner-Eshed, *A River Flows from Eden*, 305–8.

On the expression "Did you hear some new word," see JT *Shabbat* 8:1, 11a.

Cf. *Shir ha-Shirim Rabbah* on 1:10.

18. ***For He will command His angels...*** Rabbi El'azar does not divulge what he has seen and heard.

On the verse from Psalms, see *Zohar* 1:165b–166a; cf. *Zohar* 1:12b.

This story provides a neat illustration of Zoharic literary art, with narrative and homily reinforcing one another. Just as Jacob is met by angels (his father and grandfather), so Rabbi El'azar encounters his deceased father, transformed into an angel.

19. **Jerusalem Above corresponding to Jerusalem below...** See *Tanḥuma, Pequdei* 1: "There is a Jerusalem above aligned with Jerusalem below. Out of His love for the one below, He fashioned another above.... He has sworn that His presence will not enter the heavenly Jerusalem until the earthly Jerusalem is rebuilt."

The verse in Hosea is apparently understood to mean that until God (the Holy One), or holiness, is present once again in Jerusalem (in your midst), He will not enter the heavenly Jerusalem (the city). See BT *Ta'anit* 5a, and Rashi, ad loc.

See also Revelation 21:2; *Targum Yonatan*, Psalms 122:3; *Zohar* 1:1b, 80b (*ST*), 122a (*MhN*), 128b, 183b, 231a; 2:51a; 3:15b, 68b, 147b; *ZḤ* 24b, 25a, 25d, 26b, 28c–d (all *MhN*).

Numerous elements of the following unit appear in Aramaic (the unit here is in Hebrew) in the Zoharic stratum known as *Sitrei Torah*. See *Zohar* 1:80b–81b (*ST*). Presumably the version in *MhN* is earlier and was reworked in *ST*.

*righteousness* (Psalms 118:19)—and they are the openings arrayed for the souls of the righteous to enter therein. King David (peace upon him) yearned for them, as is said: *Open for me the gates of righteousness, I would enter them and acclaim Yah. This is the gate to* YHVH*; the righteous shall enter through it* (Psalms 118:19–20). Above them ministering angels stand guard by the gates of the city, as is said: *Upon your walls, O Jerusalem* (Isaiah 62:6)—Jerusalem Above; *I have set watchmen* (ibid.)—ministering angels.[20] [21a]

"It has been taught: There are seven openings for the souls of the righteous through which to assume their rightful rung; at every single opening there are watchmen.

"The first opening: the soul enters through the Cave of Machpelah—which is adjacent to the Garden of Eden—over which Adam keeps watch. If she is worthy, he proclaims, saying, 'Make room!' 'May your coming be in peace!' whereupon she goes forth from the first opening.[21]

"The second opening is at the gates of the Garden of Eden, where she encounters *the cherubim and the flame of the whirling sword* (Genesis 3:24). If she is worthy, she enters in peace. If not, there she receives her punishment, and is judged by the flame of the *keruvim*. Corresponding to them were the *keruvim* in the Temple, when the priest entered on Yom Kippur. If he was worthy, he entered in peace. If he was not worthy, a flame would shoot forth from between



20. **Seven companies of ministering angels...** The motifs of seven openings to the celestial realm and seven companies of ministering angels derive from a fusion of sources: the seven heavens of the Talmud, the seven palaces of Heikhalot literature, and the seven companies of the righteous. See *Sifrei*, Deuteronomy 10; *Midrash Tannaim*, Deuteronomy, 1:10; JT *Ḥagigah* 2:1, 77a; *Vayiqra Rabbah* 30:2; *Midrash Tehillim* 11:6, 16:12; [Moses de León?], *Seder Gan Eden*, 133, 135.

See *Pesiqta de-Rav Kahana*, 27:2: "*In Your presence is* שבע (*sova*), *fullness, of joy* (Psalms 16:11). Do not read שֹׂבַע (*sova*), fullness, but שֶׁבַע (*sheva*), seven—seven joys; seven companies of righteous, destined to receive the presence of the *Shekhinah*."

On the seven heavens, see BT *Ḥagigah* 12b: "Resh Lakish said, '[There are] seven [heavens]: *Vilon*, *Raqia*, *Sheḥaqim*, *Zevul*, *Ma'on*, *Makhon*, *Aravot*.'" On the verse from Isaiah and the angels guarding celestial Jerusalem, see *Zohar* 1:80b–81a (*ST*); 2:89b, 212a. On the guards of Jerusalem, cf. JT *Ta'anit* 4:4, 68b.

21. **the soul enters through the Cave of Machpelah...** The Cave of Machpelah is first mentioned in Genesis 23, when Abraham purchases it as a burial site for Sarah. Eventually all the matriarchs (except for Rachel) and patriarchs were buried there. According to rabbinic tradition, Adam and Eve were buried in this cave as well. Based on this tradition, the *Zohar* teaches that the Cave of Machpelah leads to the Garden of Eden.

See *Bereshit Rabbah* 58:8; BT *Eruvin* 53a; *Pirqei de-Rabbi Eli'ezer* 20, 36; *Midrash ha-Gadol*, Genesis 23:9; *Zohar* 1:38b (*Heikh*), 57b, 81a (*ST*), 127a–128b, 219a, 248b; 2:151b; 3:164a; *ZḤ* 79d (*MhN*, *Rut*).

On the greeting of the soul and the expression "make room," see BT *Berakhot* 18b; *Ketubbot* 77b, 104a; *Zohar* 1:123b (*MhN*); 3:213a.

the two *keruvim*, and he was burned within and died. They were aligned corresponding to those at the gate of the Garden of Eden, to clarify souls.[22]

"If the soul is worthy, she is given a registration-token to enter, and she enters the earthly Garden of Eden. [There stands] a single column of cloud and glow commingled with smoke round about, as is said: *YHVH will create over the whole foundation of Mount Zion and over her assemblies a cloud by day and smoke with a glow [of flaming fire]* (Isaiah 4:5). It is firmly planted, from below to above—to the gates of heaven. If she is worthy of ascending on high, she ascends by that column; if she is not worthy of [ascending] any farther, she remains there, delighting in the bounty from above. As Rabbi Yose said: 'I saw the Garden of Eden, and it is aligned corresponding to the curtain of awesome ice above.' She enjoys the splendor of *Shekhinah*—but is not nourished by it.[23]

"If she is worthy of ascending, she ascends by that column, until she reaches the third opening, corresponding to the firmament called *Zevul*. She reaches Jerusalem, which is located within; there preside the watchmen. If she is worthy, they open the openings for her; and she enters.[24]



"If she is not worthy, they lock the gates, thrust her aside, and seize her registration from her. The soul says: *The watchmen patrolling the city found me* (Song of Songs 5:7)—the ministering angels watching the celestial Temple and Jerusalem; *they stripped me of my shawl* (ibid.)—her registration-token; *the*

22. **she encounters *the cherubim and the flame of the whirling sword*...** The full verse in Genesis reads: *He drove out the human and placed east of the Garden of Eden the cherubim and the flame of the whirling sword, to guard the way to the Tree of Life.*

On the cherubim in the Dwelling and Temple, see Exodus 25:18–22; 37:7–9; 1 Kings 6:23–30; 2 Chronicles 3:10–13.

"To clarify" renders לצרף (*le-tsaref*), whose range of meaning includes: "to refine, purify, test, try." It also connotes being passed through fire. Hence: souls are tested and purified by passing through the angelic flame at the entrance to the garden. See *Zohar* 1:219a; *ZḤ* 19a, 19d (both *MhN*). On the burning of the soul, cf. BT *Shabbat* 113b.

23. **she ascends by that column...** A column reaches from the earthly Garden and extends to the higher reaches of the heavenly realm.

See *Zohar* 1:39a–b (*Heikh*), 81a (*ST*), 219a; 2:130b, 184b, 210a, 211a; 3:185b; Moses de León, *Mishkan ha-Edut*, 64a–b; [Moses de León?], *Seder Gan Eden*, 132–35, 139–40; Idel, *Ascensions on High*, 101–42, esp. 108–9. Cf. *Midrash Konen* (*Beit ha-Midrash*, 2:28).

On the difference between delighting in and being nourished by the *Shekhinah*, see *Zohar* 1:135b (*MhN*). See also *ZḤ* 18b (*MhN*). On the Garden of Eden as aligned with the "curtain of awesome ice," see *ZḤ* 13c (*MhN*). See also [Moses de León?], *Seder Gan Eden*, 138. See Ezekiel 1:22. On signs or tokens to pass through the various levels of the celestial realm, see *Zohar* 1:81b (*ST*), 123b (*MhN*, this volume); 3:162a (*Rav Metivta*).

24. **She reaches Jerusalem...** According to BT *Ḥagigah* 12b, celestial Jerusalem is located in the fourth heaven: "*Zevul*—in which Jerusalem, the Temple, and the Altar are built; and Michael, the great prince, stands and offers thereon an offering."

*watchmen of the walls* (ibid.)—as is said: *Upon your walls, O Jerusalem, I have set watchmen* (Isaiah 62:6).[25]

"If she is worthy of ascending, she enters there through those gates and praises the blessed Holy One in the celestial Temple; and Michael, the great prince, offers her as an offering."[26]

(Rabbi Yitsḥak said to Rabbi Ḥiyya, "What kind of קרבן (*qorban*), offering, is this? Is it like any other offering?"[27]

Rabbi Ḥiyya said, "The הקרבה (*haqravah*), offering, referred to here is like a person presenting a gift before the king."[28]

"Michael accompanies her to the fourth, fifth, and sixth openings. He says before the blessed Holy One, 'Master of the World! Happy are Your children, the children of those who love you: Abraham, Isaac, and Jacob! Happy are the noble righteous who merit this!'

"Eventually, they reach the seventh gate—*Aravot*—where the treasuries of good life are found, as well as all the souls of the righteous; all of them are there. They are transformed into ministering angels, laud praise before the blessed Holy One, and are nourished by the splendor of the resplendent speculum. There abides המנוחה (*ha-menuḥah*), the serenity, הנחלה (*ha-naḥalah*), the inheritance, and הנח (*ha-noaḥ*), the comfort, of the life of the world to come—which *no eye has seen, O God, but You* (Isaiah 64:3).[29]



25. ***The watchmen patrolling the city found me...*** Only now is the significance of the verse quoted by Rabbi at the beginning of the *parashah* made apparent. The watchmen of the city from the Song of Songs are in fact the ministering angels guarding celestial Jerusalem; and the shawl taken from the young woman in the Song is the soul's token of admission to the upper reaches of the heavenly realm. See *Zohar* 1:81b (*ST*), 123b (*MhN*). On not being able to pass the gates of celestial Jerusalem, see also *ZḤ* 25d (*MhN*).

26. **Michael, the great prince, offers her as an offering** On the heavenly altar. See above, note 24; and BT *Menaḥot* 110a. See *Tosafot Menaḥot* 110a, s.v. *u-mikha'el sar ha-gadol*, which notes that according to some passages, these offerings are comprised of the souls of the righteous. See *Bemidbar Rabbah* 12:12; [Moses de León?], *Seder Gan Eden*, 137; *Zohar* 1:80a, 81a (both *ST*); 2:247a (*Heikh*); *ZḤ* 24b, 25a (both *MhN*).

27. **Is it like any other offering?** Surely the soul is not consumed on the altar—as is the case with other offerings!

The brief exchange between Rabbi Yitsḥak and Rabbi Ḥiyya appears to interrupt Rabbi Yehudah's homily, hence the parentheses.

28. **presenting a gift...** The soul is not consumed but is presented as a gift to God. The verbal root קרב (*qrv*)—the basis of the words קרבן (*qorban*), "offering," and מקריב (*maqriv*), "to sacrifice, offer"—means "close, near, to draw near." Michael thus brings the soul near to God; he offers her as a gift. See Ḥayyim Palagi, *Sefer Ḥayyim u-Mazon*, 32.

29. **they reach the seventh gate—*Aravot*...** The seventh heaven is the ultimate destination of the soul. Here, it is transformed into an angel—and enjoys the bliss of the world to come.

The three terms used to describe the world to come—המנוחה (*ha-menuḥah*), "the serenity"; הנחלה (*ha-naḥalah*), "the inheri-

"This is the meaning of *These are the offspring of Noah. Noah was a righteous man* (Genesis 6:9). Who is deserving of abiding in such delight, serenity, and tranquility? *A righteous, blameless man* (ibid.)."[30]

Rav Pappi said, "This מנוחה (*menuḥah*), serenity, above is the meaning of נח (*Noaḥ*), *Noah, walked with God* (ibid.)—above, not below."[31]

*These are the offspring of Noah* (Genesis 6:9).

Rabbi Alexandrai opened, "*There shall be no alien god among you, and you shall not bow to a foreign god* (Psalms 81:10). *There shall be no alien god within you*—the evil impulse; *and you shall not bow to a foreign god*—do not have intercourse with an Aramean woman."[32]



tance"; and הנח (*ha-noaḥ*), "the comfort"—each play on the name נח (*noaḥ*), "Noah."

See BT *Ḥagigah* 12b: "*Aravot*—in which are righteousness, justice, charity, treasuries of life, treasuries of peace, treasuries of blessings, the souls (*neshamot*) of the righteous, and the spirits (*ruḥot*) and souls (*neshamot*) that are to be created in the future, and the dew with which the blessed Holy One will revive the dead." See *ZḤ* 10b (*MhN*).

See BT *Berakhot* 17a: "A pearl in the mouth of Rav: 'In the world to come, there is no eating or drinking or procreation or business or jealousy or hatred or competition; rather, the righteous sit with their crowns on their heads, basking in the radiance of *Shekhinah*.'"

See BT *Berakhot* 34b: "Rabbi Ḥiyya son of Abba said in the name of Rabbi Yoḥanan, 'All the prophets prophesied only concerning the days of the Messiah, but as for the world that is coming, *No eye has seen, O God, but You* (Isaiah 64:3).'"

"Resplendent speculum" renders אספקלריא המאירה (*ispaqlarya ha-me'irah*). *Ispaqlarya* means "glass, mirror, lens." See BT *Yevamot* 49b: "All the prophets gazed through an opaque glass [literally: an *ispaqlarya* that does not shine], while Moses our teacher gazed through a translucent glass [literally: an *ispaqlarya* that shines]." See also *Vayiqra Rabbah* 1:14. Cf. 1 Corinthians 13:12: "For now we see though a glass darkly, but then face-to-face." In the main strata of the *Zohar*, the *ispaqlarya* that does not shine symbolizes *Shekhinah* and the *ispaqlarya* that shines symbolizes *Tif'eret*. See *Zohar* 1:97b, 122a (both *MhN*); *ZḤ* 10a, 13b, 15b, 15d, 16c, 17a, 24a (all *MhN*).

On Michael's accompanying the soul, see *Zohar* 1:125b (*MhN*); *ZḤ* 25a (*MhN*). On being transformed into ministering angels, see above, note 13.

30. ***These are the offspring of Noah...*** Finally, we see how this unit is connected with the Torah portion of Noah. The delight and tranquility of the world to come are the "offspring" of Noah, i.e., the consequence of being a righteous and blameless person.

31. **serenity, above . . .** The verse describing Noah's virtue is in fact not about his behavior on earth below, but about the serenity awaiting the righteous in the world to come above.

Cf. Rashi and Naḥmanides on Genesis 6:9.

32. ***There shall be no alien god among you...*** The verse in Psalms, which is usually understood to mean *There shall be no alien god* בך (*vekha*), *among you*, is read here hyperliterally: *There shall be no alien god vekha*, *within you.*

On the hyperliteral reading of the verse in Psalms as referring to the evil impulse, see JT *Nedarim* 9:1, 41b; BT *Shabbat* 105b; *Zohar* 2:182a; 3:106a–b.

In the *Zohar*, the prohibition against bowing down to another god includes a warning not to lie down with a foreign woman. See

Rabbi El'azar says, "*There shall be no alien god within you*—do not be נח (*noaḥ*), easily, angered. For whoever is angry is as though he worships idols."[33]

As Rabbi Akiva said: "Such is the way of the evil impulse: Today it tells you 'do such-and-such,' and tomorrow it tells you 'worship idols'; and one goes and worships!"[34]

He used to say, "The anger of the disciples of the wise is the greatest of all! In which instances? In the case of actions against the blessed Holy One, as the Torah said: *No wisdom, no prudence, and no counsel can prevail against YHVH* (Proverbs 21:30). But in other instances, he is forbidden from getting angry. As for the teacher toward the student—it is permitted in order that one respect and fear him; and toward the rest of the people—it is permitted in order that his awe be upon them for the sake of heaven. Other people, however, are forbidden, for their anger is not for the fear of heaven."[35]

Rabbi Shim'on said, "The temperament of the righteous person—difficult to anger and נח (*noaḥ*), easily, appeased; this is the greatest temperament of all. Scripture comes to teach: *These are the offspring of Noah* (Genesis 6:9)—נח (*noaḥ*), at ease, in his mind; נח (*noaḥ*), calm, in his speech; נח (*noaḥ*), pleasant, in his manner. Who acts like this? *A righteous person* (ibid.). When he dies, they say of him, 'Where is the humble one? Where is the pious one? *He was perfect in*



*Zohar* 1:131b, 189b; 2:3b, 61a, 87b, 90a, 243a; 3:13b; *ZḤ* 78c (*MhN, Rut*); Moses de León, *Sefer ha-Rimmon*, 212–13; idem, *Sheqel ha-Qodesh*, 51 (63).

33. **whoever is angry is as though he worships idols** On the relation between anger and idolatry, see *Avot de-Rabbi Natan* A, 3; BT *Shabbat* 105b; Maimonides, *Commentary on the Mishnah, Avot* 2:9; idem, *Mishneh Torah, Hilkhot De'ot* 2:3; *Zohar* 1:27b (*TZ*); 2:182a–b; 3:179a (*RM*), 234b (*RM*); *TZ* 56, 89b; [Moses de León?], *Orḥot Ḥayyim*, 33; Tishby, *Wisdom of the Zohar*, 3:1333–34.

34. **Such is the way of the evil impulse...** On the gradual dominating influence of the evil impulse, see *Avot de-Rabbi Natan* A, 3; BT *Shabbat* 105b.

35. **The anger of the disciples of the wise...** The speaker is Rabbi Akiva. Either he intends that the anger of the sages is more important than everything else as it leads others to the right path and generates awe of Torah; or perhaps he has in mind the saying from Ecclesiastes 1:18: *For as wisdom grows, vexation* [or: *anger*] *grows.*

Apparently the verse from Proverbs is being read as follows: When the wicked act against *YHVH*, do not allow wisdom, prudence or counsel to prevent you from getting angry with them.

On the anger of the sages, see *Zohar* 2:182b; cf. *Zohar* 1:184a. On prohibition against and dire consequences of getting angry, see BT *Berakhot* 29b; *Nedarim* 22b, *Ta'anit* 4a. On instilling fear in one's students and fearing one's teacher, see M *Avot* 4:12; BT *Ketubbot* 103b; BT *Shabbat* 30b; BT *Pesaḥim* 22b; Maimonides, *Mishneh Torah, Hilkhot Talmud Torah* 4:5: "If it appears to the teacher that they [students] are not applying themselves to the words of Torah and are lax about them, and therefore, do not understand, he is obligated to display anger toward them and shame them with his words, to sharpen their powers of concentration. In this context our Sages said, 'Cast fear into the students.'"; idem, *Hilkhot De'ot* 5:1.

*his generation* (ibid.). What will he merit? *Noah walked with God* (ibid.)—beyond all degrees.'"[36] [21c]

*Noah engendered three sons* (Genesis 6:10).[37]

Rabbi Kruspedai taught, "These are the three הנהגות (*hanhagot*), dispositions, in a human being: the disposition of the soul, to be a helper for him in the service of his Creator—it is called Shem; the disposition of desire and the evil impulse, המנהיג (*ha-manhig*), goading, and מחמם (*meḥamem*), riling, the body to sin—it is called Ham; and the disposition of the good impulse, המנהיג (*ha-manhig*), guiding, a person to all that is good, וליפות (*u-lyapot*), to beautify, his deeds through Torah and fear of God—it is called *Yephet*. This disposition guides a person, leading him to the way of life."[38]

Who inhibits and vanquishes him? *The earth was corrupt before God* (Genesis 6:11)—the lifeless clump, vanquishing and corrupting all. About this, Solomon said in his wisdom: *One who would corrupt his soul* הוא יעשנה (*hu ya'asennah*),



36. **The temperament of the righteous person...** See M *Avot* 5:11: "There are four types of temperament: easily angered and easily appeased—his gain is canceled by his loss; difficult to anger and difficult to appease—his loss is canceled by his gain; difficult to anger and easily appeased—he is pious; easily angered and difficult to appease—he is wicked."

See also Maimonides, *Mishneh Torah, Hilkhot De'ot* 5:1, 7, 8.

On the expression, "Where is the humble one? Where is the pious one?," see BT *Berakhot* 6b.

37. ***Noah engendered three sons*** The verse continues: *Shem, Ham, and Japheth.*

38. **three הנהגות (*hanhagot*), dispositions, in a human being...** Rabbi Kruspedai presents a different soul (psychic) structure to those presented above (*ZḤ* 6d, 8d–9a, 10c–11a, 16a–c). Intellect and the comprehension of Torah and divinity are absent in this scheme, which appears entirely concerned with ethical/religious behavior. See Tishby, *Wisdom of the Zohar*, 2:706.

The three dispositions are each named after one of Noah's sons: soul (*neshamah*), perhaps designating the aspect of the soul that first rouses a person to good action, is termed Shem ("name"), either because it leads one to attain a good name or because it leads one to the service of the divine name; desire and the evil impulse, termed Ham (who dishonored his father) because it heats (*meḥamem*) the body with passion, leading it to sin; and the good impulse, termed *Yephet* (Japheth), because through it one's deeds become beautiful (*yapheh*).

On the three dispositions (or powers), see *Zohar* 1:109a (*MhN*); *ZḤ* 14b (*MhN*); Meroz, "Va-Ani Lo Hayiti Sham?," 170 (Addendum 3 in this volume); Tishby, *Wisdom of the Zohar*, 2:705–07; cf. *Zohar* 1:62a. On the soul as helper, see above, *ZḤ* 20d (*MhN*), page 224.

Cf. BT *Rosh ha-Shanah* 16b: "Rabbi Kruspedai said in the name of Rabbi Yoḥanan, 'Three books are opened on Rosh Hashanah: one for the completely wicked, one for the completely righteous, and one for the intermediate.'" Cf. Saadia Gaon, *Sefer Emunot ve-De'ot* 6:3; Maimonides, *Shemonah Peraqim* 1.

On the diverse theories of the soul in *MhN*, see Tishby, *Wisdom of the Zohar*, 2:703–12.

*does so* (Proverbs 6:32). What is meant by הוא יעשנה (*hu ya'asennah*)? Rabbi Kruspedai said, "The lifeless clump יעשנה (*ya'asennah*), *makes her*, corrupt!"[39]

Alternatively, *These are the offspring of Noah* (Genesis 6:9). What is written before this subject? וינחם יהוה (*Va-yinnaḥem YHVH*), *YHVH was sorry, that He had made humankind on earth, and His heart was saddened* (ibid., 6).[40]

Rabbi Eli'ezer says, "Come and see how human nature differs from the nature of the blessed Holy One! It is the nature of a human being that he does what he does—and afterward expresses regret and is saddened. Might the same be true for the blessed Holy One?![41]

"Come and hear. As is written: *See, I have set before you today life and good, and death and evil* (Deuteronomy 30:15), and He cautioned the human being and said: *Choose life, so that you may live* (ibid., 19). If he follows the evil path, by his own iniquity he will die, as is said: *His own iniquities will ensnare the wicked* (Proverbs 5:22). So is written: *YHVH saw that human evil was immense* (Genesis 6:5). The blessed Holy One said, 'I see that they are all guilty. If they perish in their wickedness, then look, My world will be laid waste!' As soon as He saw Noah and his sons who were righteous, and realized that a remnant would remain in the world, He was comforted and rejoiced."[42]

39. **Who inhibits and vanquishes him?...** What prevents human beings from realizing the potential of the soul and of the good impulse? The body, the earthly aspect of the human being.

In its simple sense, the phrase in Proverbs reads: [*He who commits adultery is devoid of sense*], משחית נפשו הוא יעשנה (*mashḥit nafsho hu ya'asennah*), *he who would destroy himself does so*. Here, the *Zohar* reads the phrase as: *mashḥit nafsho*, *he who would corrupt his soul* (i.e., defeat his soul's power): *hu ya'asennah*, *it* [*the body*] *makes her* [*the soul*] [*corrupt*].

Cf. *Zohar* 3:45a.

40. ***YHVH was sorry...*** The word *va-yinnaḥem* can be construed as: "changed His mind, retracted, renounced, relented, repented, regretted, was sorry."

The previous verse reads: *YHVH saw that human evil on earth was immense, and every thought desired by their mind was nothing but evil all day.*

41. **Might the same be true for the blessed Holy One?!** It is the way of human beings to regret their past (bad or failed) actions. Is it possible to posit such regret vis-à-vis the blessed Holy One?

42. **He was comforted and rejoiced** Rabbi Eli'ezer explains that the word *va-yinnaḥem* does not in fact mean that God was sorry or regretful, but rather that he was comforted or consoled—another meaning associated with the verbal root נחם (*nḥm*). Having granted humanity free choice, and having seen their wickedness, God laments their impending destruction. However, God is comforted by Noah and his sons, through whom the continuity of the world is assured.

On the word *va-yinnaḥem*, see *Bereshit Rabbah* 27:4; *Tanḥuma* (Buber), *Noaḥ* 4; BT *Sanhedrin* 108a; *Zohar* 1:57a; Meroz, "Va-Ani Lo Hayiti Sham?," 171 (Addendum 3 in this volume).

Rabbi Eli'ezer said, "This וינחם (*va-yinnaḥem*) is an expression of comfort. Similarly, every *va-yinnaḥem* in the Torah is an expression of comfort. He sees the evil and He sees the good—and takes comfort in the good."[43]

Rabbi Akiva said to him, "According to your view, what is the meaning then of *and His heart was saddened* (Genesis 6:6)?"[44]

He replied, "Come and see the quality of the compassion of the blessed Holy One! For even though he was comforted, He was saddened by the loss of the wicked; for even though they were wicked, He derived no pleasure from their death, and there was no rejoicing in His presence."[45]

Rabbi Yehudah said, "What is the meaning of the verse: *Noah found favor in the eyes of YHVH* (Genesis 6:8)? His name was the cause! נח (*Noaḥ*), Noah, is the reverse of חן (*ḥen*), favor.[46]

"Why did the verse open with his offspring first? In order to demonstrate to the world that just as he was righteous, so they were righteous and deserving that the world be populated through them.[47]



"How do we know? Come and see: As soon as they entered the ark, they perceived the pain of the world and were saddened, and they refrained from

43. **every *va-yinnaḥem* in the Torah...** The meaning of *va-yinnaḥem* is always "was comforted" and never "regretted, relented." It is God's nature, rather, to incline to mercy—to be comforted by the good that is evident. Because God's deeds are perfect, God has no regrets. See Meroz, "Va-Ani Lo Hayiti Sham?," 171 (Addendum 3 in this volume).

44. ***and His heart was saddened...*** If, as you say, the word *va-yinnaḥem* from Genesis 6:6 should be understood as "was comforted" and not "regretted" or "was sorry," how do you explain what follows: *and His heart was saddened*? Surely regret and sadness go together, rather than comfort and sadness!

Cf. *Bereshit Rabbah* 27:4.

45. **He was saddened by the loss of the wicked...** For God's not delighting in the death of the wicked, see Ezekiel 18:23: *Is it my desire that a wicked person shall die?—says the Lord YHVH*. See BT *Sanhedrin* 39b: "The blessed Holy One does not rejoice in the downfall of the wicked"; see also BT *Megillah* 10b; *Tanḥuma, Balak* 8; *Midrash Aggadah* (Buber), *Bemidbar*, 22; *Pesiqta Zutarta, Eikhah* 3. See *ZḤ* 22a–b (*MhN*); Scholem, "Parashah Ḥadashah," 439 (Addendum 1 in this volume).

For a close parallel to this passage, see *Zohar* 1:57a; see also Tishby, *Wisdom of the Zohar*, 3:1419.

Here Rabbi Eli'ezer employs a rare Hebrew idiom, לקח עצבון (*laqaḥ itzavon*), "took sadness," i.e., was saddened, perhaps influenced by an Iberian dialect. See Meroz, "Va-Ani Lo Hayiti Sham?," 164, 171 (Addendum 3 in this volume).

46. **His name was the cause! . . .** On names determining destiny, see BT *Berakhot* 7b. On the wordplay between *Noaḥ* and *ḥen*, see *Kallah Rabbati* 2:7; *Zohar* 1:58b.

47. **Why did the verse open with his offspring first?...** Genesis 6:18 reads in part: *and you shall enter the ark, you and your sons and your wife and your sons' wives with you.* Why does the Torah mention Noah's sons before mentioning his own wife? The question is underscored by the different order later in the narrative: *you and your wife, your sons and your sons' wives* (ibid. 8:16). For the rabbinic sources that address this issue, see the next note.

cohabitation. Even when they emerged they did likewise, until the blessed Holy One saw their deeds and said, 'I did not create My world to be a wasteland! Cohabit and procreate! Couple with your wives and be fruitful and multiply.' At that hour He blessed them, as is said: *God blessed Noah and his sons*... (Genesis 9:1)."[48]

*These are* תולדות *(toledot), the generations of, Noah* (Genesis 6:9).[49]

Rabbi Pinhas opened, "*The sons of God saw the daughters of humankind, that they were beautiful* (ibid. 6:2). Who are these *sons of God*? The children of the dignitaries of the generation. Scripture teaches that they [the daughters of humankind] were of beautiful appearance. Here is written *that they were beautiful* (ibid.), and there is written *very beautiful appearance* (ibid. 24:16). They used to walk around naked and the men used to walk around naked; they would see one another's nakedness and fornicate with each other. Why then were they called *sons of God*? Because they were heroes, the sons of giants."[50]



48. **they refrained from cohabitation...** The righteousness of not only Noah but also his sons is evinced by their refusal, while on the ark, to cohabit with their wives. This is hinted at by the different order in which the parties are listed upon entering the ark, versus upon their disembarking. See the previous note.

Compare *Bereshit Rabbah* 31:12: "Rabbi Yehudah son of Simon and Rabbi Hanin in the name of Rabbi Shemu'el son of Rabbi Yitshak said, 'When Noah entered the ark, cohabitation was forbidden him, as is written: *and you shall enter the ark, you and your sons* (Genesis 6:18)—apart; *your wife and your sons' wives* (ibid.)—apart. As soon as he went out, He permitted it [cohabitation] to him, as is written: *Come out of the ark, you and your wife, your sons and your sons' wives* (ibid. 8:16).'"

See also *Bereshit Rabbah* 34:7; BT *Sanhedrin* 108b; *Pirqei de-Rabbi Eli'ezer* 23 and Luria, ad loc.; Rashi on Genesis 6:18, 7:7, 8:16. See also *ZH* 22b (*MhN*), page 249.

The verse from Genesis continues: *and said to them, "Be fruitful and multiply and fill the earth."*

49. ***These are* תולדות *(toledot), the generations of, Noah*** The word *toledot* can mean "offspring, line, generations, account, story." The account of the sons of God and the daughters of humankind (see next note) took place in the time of Noah—and sets the scene for the Flood.

50. ***The sons of God saw the daughters of humankind...*** The context of this verse is the enigmatic mythological fragment found in Genesis 6:1–4: *When humankind began to increase on the face of the earth and daughters were born to them, the sons of God saw that the daughters of humankind were beautiful; and they took themselves wives—whomever they chose. YHVH said, "My spirit shall not abide in the human forever, for he too is flesh. Let his days be a hundred and twenty years." The Nephilim were on earth in those days—and afterward as well—when the sons of God came in to the daughters of humankind, who bore them children. These are the heroes of old, men of renown* [literally: *name*].

The myth behind this fragment in Genesis appears in postbiblical sources that describe angels who rebelled against God and descended to earth, where they were attracted by human women. See Isaiah 14:12; 1 Enoch 6–8; Jubilees 5; *Targum Yerushalmi*, Genesis 6:2, 4; BT *Yoma* 67b; *Aggadat Bereshit*, intro, 39; *Midrash Avkir*, 7 (cited in *Yalqut Shim-*

Rabbi Yehoshu'a son of Levi said, "Once I happened upon the mountain of the rock of Etam, where I found two people on either side of the rock who seemed to have two mouths, one above the other. They were speaking with one another, 'Come let us dispatch him from the world!'[51]

"The chief minion of Agrat daughter of Maḥalat appeared—Joseph the demon. He said to them, 'Surely this is the great and eminent Rabbi of the generation, by whose decree I was dispatched from the settled regions of the earth! This is the one about whom they proclaim in the firmament!'[52]

*'oni*, Genesis, 44); *Pirqei de-Rabbi Eli'ezer* 22; *Zohar* 1:23a (*TZ*), 37a, 37a (*Tos*), 55a, 58a, 62b, 117b–118a (*MhN*), 126a; 3:208a–b, 212a–b; *ZḤ* 20b (*MhN*), 81a–b (*MhN, Rut*); Ginzberg, *Legends*, 5:153–56, n. 57.

Although in its biblical context בני האלהים (*benei ha-elohim*), *sons of God*, implies some kind of celestial beings, there is a long tradition of reading the word *elohim* here as signifying "the mighty, judges, nobles," as some interpreters perceive in Exodus 21:6; 22:7–8, 22:27; Judges 5:8; 1 Samuel 2:25; and Psalms 138:1. Both *Targum Onqelos* and *Targum Yerushalmi*, ad loc., render *benei ha-elohim* as בני רברביא (*benei ravrevaya*), *sons of the mighty*.

238

See *Bereshit Rabbah* 26:5: "Rabbi Shim'on son of Yoḥai called them *the sons of judges*. Rabbi Shim'on son of Yoḥai cursed all who called them *the sons of God*." See also Rashi and Naḥmanides on Genesis 6:2.

On the nakedness and fornication of the "sons of God" and "daughters of humankind," see *Pirqei de-Rabbi Eli'ezer* 22: "Rabbi said, 'The angels who fell from their holy place in heaven saw the daughters of Cain walking about naked, with their eyes painted like harlots; and they want astray after them, and took wives from amongst them, as is said: *The sons of God saw the daughters of humankind,* [*that they were beautiful, and they took themselves wives—whomever they chose*] (Genesis 6:2).'" See also *Targum Yerushalmi* on Genesis 6:2; *Bereshit Rabbah* 26:7.

Note that although the *Zohar* here has relied on the account in *Pirqei de-Rabbi Eli'ezer*, the "sons of God" have been demythologized, now referring to the dignitaries of the generation and not angels. On the reference to *the sons of God* as ענקים (*anaqim*), "giants," see Numbers 13:33 in light of Genesis 6:4; below, note 53; Meroz, "Va-Ani Lo Hayiti Sham?," 169 (Addendum 3 in this volume).

51. **mountain of the rock of Etam . . .** "The cave of the rock of Etam" appears in Judges 15:8, 11 as Samson's hideout.

The Talmud also mentions the spring of Etam, located southeast of Bethlehem from where water was transported to the Temple (see BT *Yoma* 31a, *Zevaḥim* 54b). Though Rabbi Yehoshu'a son of Levi is referring to the rock of Etam, the motif of purifying waters appears below.

52. **Agrat daughter of Maḥalat...** Maḥalat was the daughter of Ishmael and wife of Esau (Genesis 28:9). According to rabbinic tradition, her daughter Agrat rules over myriads of demonic powers. See BT *Pesaḥim* 112b: "One should not go out alone at night, neither on the eve of Wednesday nor of Sabbath, for Agrat daughter of Maḥalat along with 180,000 angels of destruction emerge, each independently empowered. Originally they were active all day. On one occasion she met Rabbi Ḥanina son of Dosa. She said to him, 'Had they not decreed concerning you in Heaven, "Take heed of Ḥanina and his learning," I would have put you in danger.' He said to her, 'If I am of account in Heaven, I order you never to pass through settled regions.' She said to him, 'I beg you, leave me a little room.' So he left her Sabbath and Wednesday nights."

See *Bemidbar Rabbah* 12:3; *Zohar* 1:55a; 3:113b–114a; Baḥya ben Asher on Genesis 4:22.

On Joseph the demon, see BT *Eruvin* 43a; *Pesaḥim* 110a; *Zohar* 3:253a (*RM*). In the Tal-

"While we were walking, I found the mother of those [21d] people. She said to her little daughter, 'They are tiny grasshoppers, whose strength is in their mouths. Bring them to me. We will make of them a gourmet dish for your brother.'[53]

"Before she arrived, a miracle befell us and a mighty river appeared before her. I heard her say, 'Mommy, mommy, the yummy snack I was hoping for has gone!' and we fled from them and were saved."[54]

Rabbi Yehoshu'a son of Levi also said, "In the days of the generation of the Flood, the blessed Holy One made the stalks of wheat like the trunks of the cedars of Lebanon. They did not sow or reap, but rather the wind would blow, shedding the wheat below whereupon they would gather them. So it was every single year. When they sinned, He said, '*So long as the earth endures, seedtime and harvest, cold and heat, summer and winter, day and night shall not cease* (Genesis 8:22).'"[55]



mud, it is not clear whether Joseph the demon is a person expert in demonology, or a demon who taught the sages about demons. Here, he is clearly demonic. On the abode of demons, see *Zohar* 1:14b, 126a, 169b, 178b; 2:157a, 184a, 236b–237; 3:63b. On demons in the *Zohar*, see Tishby, *Wisdom of the Zohar*, 2:529–32.

53. **tiny grasshoppers, whose strength is in their mouths...** "Grasshoppers" alludes to Numbers 13:32–33, where the scouts return with the following report: *The land through which we passed to scout is a land that consumes those who dwell in it, and all the people we saw in it are men of huge measure. There did we see the Nephilim, sons of the giant from the Nephilim, and we were in our own eyes like grasshoppers, and so were we in their eyes.* The strange people encountered by Rabbi Yehoshu'a are the very Nephilim (giants) first mentioned in Genesis 6:4.

"Whose strength is in their mouths" refers to words of prayer and study. See *Tanḥuma, Beshallaḥ* 9: "*Do not fear, O worm Jacob*! (Isaiah 41:14). Why is Israel compared to a worm? Just as a worm strikes the cedars only with its mouth—though soft, it strikes the hard—so Israel possess only prayer, for the idolatrous nations are compared to cedars." See *Mekhilta, Beshallaḥ* 2; *Zohar* 1:178a.

On the rabbis' lack of physical strength, see BT *Sanhedrin* 26b; BT *Yoma* 71a; *Shir ha-Shirim Rabbah* on 5:14; *Qohelet Rabbah* on 1:8; *ZḤ* 5d, 14a, 25c (all *MhN*). On the weak physical condition of the Companions in the *Zohar*, see *Zohar* 2:61b, 143a, 198b, 225a–b.

54. **a mighty river appeared...** According to various sources, water deters demons. See *Sefer Ḥasidim* (ed. Margaliot), par. 1144; *Zohar* 3:45a; Trachtenberg, *Jewish Magic and Superstition*, 159. Cf. BT *Sanhedrin* 67b; *Zohar* 2:82b.

55. **When they sinned...** The divine promise to maintain the natural order after the Flood is also a punishment, as the rhythm of seasons necessitates sowing and reaping rather than the effortless gathering beforehand.

Cf. *Bereshit Rabbah* 34:11: "Rabbi Yitsḥak said, 'What caused them to rebel against Me? Was it not because they sowed without having to reap?' For Rabbi Yitsḥak said, 'They used to sow once in forty years, and they traveled from one end of the world to the other in no time at all, cutting down the cedars of Lebanon in their course, making no more of the lions and leopards than of the vermin in their skin. How is this to be understood? They enjoyed the pleasant climate [now usual] between *Pesaḥ* and *Shavu-*

Rabbi Yehoshu'a son of Levi also said, "The decree of punishment for the generation of the Flood was not sealed until they stretched out their hands to rob, as is said: *and the earth was filled with violence* (ibid. 6:11).[56]

"In the days of the generation of the Flood, procreation was rife. As soon as a woman gave birth, they could walk and they would send them forth like their sheep, as is said: *They send forth their young like sheep; and their children dance* (Job 21:11). Following all this, what is written of them? *They said to God, 'Leave us alone! We have no desire to know Your ways'* (ibid., 14)—until He decreed their sentence and removed them from the world."[57]

Our Rabbis have taught: Noah warned them beforehand, but they paid him no heed. He lingered in constructing the ark that they might see and repent, but they mocked him—until the deep inundated them. For the waters welled forth



*'ot* [year-round].'" See also *Tanḥuma, Bereshit* 12.

According to one opinion in *Bereshit Rabbah* 15:7, the Tree of Knowledge of Good and Evil was wheat, and it "grew lofty like the cedars of the Lebanon."

56. **The decree of punishment...** See BT *Sanhedrin* 108a: "Rabbi Yoḥanan said, 'Come and see how great is the power of robbery! For the generation of the Flood violated everything, yet their decree of punishment was sealed only when they stretched out their hands to rob, as is written: *For the earth is filled with violence because of them; here, I am about to destroy them along with the earth* (Genesis 6:13).'" See also *Bereshit Rabbah* 31:4; *Tanḥuma, Noaḥ* 4; *Zohar* 1:66b; Meroz, "Va-Ani Lo Hayiti Sham?," 169 (Addendum 3 in this volume).

57. ***They said to God, 'Leave us alone!...*** In numerous rabbinic sources, the verse *They send forth their young like sheep; and their children dance* is used to illustrate the high fertility rate of the generation of the Flood: they gave birth like animals, engendering offspring who could move about on their own immediately after birth, like lambs. See *Bereshit Rabbah* 36:1; *Vayiqra Rabbah* 5:1; *Pirqei de-Rabbi Eli'ezer* 22.

In BT *Sanhedrin* 108a, the same verse is used in a larger homily (drawing on additional verses from the same chapter in Job), explaining why the generation of the Flood rebelled: because they had it too good!

"Our Rabbis taught: The generation of the Flood grew arrogant solely because of the bounty the blessed Holy One bestowed upon them. What is written about them? *Their houses are safe from fear, neither is the rod of God upon them* (Job 21:9); and it is written: *Their bull breeds and does not fail; their cow calves and never miscarries* (ibid., 10); and it is written: *They send forth their young like sheep; and their children dance* (ibid., 11); and it is written: *They sing to the music of timbrel and lute, and revel to the tune of the pipe* (ibid., 12). ...This is what caused them to say *to God, 'Leave us alone! We have no desire to know Your ways. What is Shaddai that we should serve Him? What will we gain by praying to Him?'* (ibid., 14). They said, 'Do we need Him for anything but the drop of rain? We have rivers and springs to supply our wants.' The blessed Holy One said, 'By that very bounty I bestowed upon them they provoke Me, and by that I will punish them, as is written: *As for Me, I am about to bring the Flood—waters upon the earth* (Genesis 6:17).'"

On Job 21:14, see also *Zohar* 1:62a; *ZḤ* 23a (*MhN*).

boiling like fire, as well as the waters from above; and they were blotted out from the world.[58]

Rabbi Yitsḥak said, "What is the meaning of the verse *YHVH sat enthroned at the Flood* (Psalms 29:10)? Did David really need to say such a thing? The whole world knows that He is the first and the last, then and before!"[59]

Well, Rabbi Yitsḥak said, "Come and see: In all cases you find that *Elohim* designates the attribute of judgment; and *YHVH*, the attribute of compassion. Now, even though it was the attribute of judgment, compassion was included—for were it not so, the world would have been destroyed. On account of that attribute of compassion, the world was resettled.[60]

"Similarly, you find this remedy accompanying every judgment He executes. Hence: *YHVH rained upon Sodom* (Genesis 19:24)—a remnant remained; *YHVH sent a plague* (Exodus 32:35)—a remnant remained; and so in all cases."[61]

58. **He lingered in constructing the ark...** See *Tanḥuma*, Noah 5: "Rav Huna said in the name of Rabbi Yose, 'The blessed Holy One warned the generation of the Flood for 120 years, so that they might perform *teshuvah*. Since they did not perform *teshuvah*, He said to him [Noah], *Make yourself an ark of gopher wood* (Genesis 6:14). Noah rose and performed *teshuvah*; and he planted cedars. They said to him, "What are these cedars for?" He replied, "The blessed Holy One intends on bringing a Flood upon the world and He told me to make an ark that I will be saved; my family and I." They laughed at him and ridiculed his words. He watered the cedars and they grew. They said to him, "What are you doing?" and he answered as before and they ridiculed him. Eventually he cut them down and sawed them and they asked him, "What are you doing?" and he told them as before and warned them. Since they did not perform *teshuvah*, immediately He brought the Flood upon them, as is said: *all existence was blotted out* (ibid., 7:23)." See also *Bereshit Rabbah* 30:7; BT *Sanhedrin* 108b; *Pirqei de-Rabbi Eli'ezer* 23; Rashi on Genesis 6:14.

On the boiling waters of the Flood, see *Targum Yerushalmi*, Genesis 7:10; BT *Sanhedrin* 108b; *Pirqei de-Rabbi Eli'ezer* 22; *Yalqut Shim'oni*, Job, 906; *Zohar* 1:62a, 66a. On the waters from above and below, see Genesis 7:11: *All the springs of the great deep burst forth, and the sluices of heaven opened.* See also *Pirqei de-Rabbi Eli'ezer* 23: "Rabbi Tsadok said, '... The waters of the Flood came down upon the earth—namely, the male waters; and they rose from the depths—namely, the female waters. Joining one another, they prevailed to destroy the world.'"

59. ***YHVH* sat enthroned at the Flood...** The verse continues: *YHVH sits enthroned forever.* If God is eternally enthroned, why specify that He was enthroned at the Flood?

60. ***Elohim* designates... judgment; and *YHVH*... compassion...** According to rabbinic tradition, the name *YHVH* connotes compassion, while *Elohim* connotes judgment. See *Sifrei*, Deuteronomy 26; *Bereshit Rabbah* 12:15; 33:3; *Shemot Rabbah* 3:6; *Zohar* 1:173b; 3:269b; Naḥmanides on Deuteronomy 3:24.

On the attribute of compassion prevailing during the Flood, see *Zohar* 1:56b, 64b; 2:187a, 227b; Meroz, "Va-Ani Lo Hayiti Sham?," 171 (Addendum 3 in this volume). Cf. Rashi on Genesis 8:1.

61. **you find this remedy accompanying every judgment...** Namely, judgment ameliorated by compassion; hence the divine name *YHVH*—rather than *Elohim*, the agent

Rabbi Yehudah said, "The generation of the Flood was exceedingly wise, for they knew what was about to happen. But their knowledge went to their heads! They said, 'If the blessed Holy One brings a flood, well, we are of high stature—and will cruise above the waters—and be saved! If He brings up the waters from the deep, well, we will set our feet on the font of the waters—so the waters won't be able to flow out—and we will be saved!'[62]

"When the Flood arrived, the blessed Holy One boiled the waters of the deep; and when they placed their feet on the font of the waters, their skin peeled off and they fell. Waters from above surged along with the waters of the deep, and they rolled and descended, dissolved by the boiling of the deep, to Babylon."[63]

*They came to Noah into the ark* (Genesis 7:15).

Rabbi Yoḥanan opened, "*Happy is the one You choose and draw near to dwell in Your courts!* (Psalms 65:5). Come and see how scrupulous a person must be, scrutinizing himself and his deeds every single day! How so? When he rises in the morning, let him say: 'May it be Your will before You, O *YHVH* my God and the God of my fathers,



of judgment/justice. See *Zohar* 1:64b; 2:227b; Meroz, "Va-Ani Lo Hayiti Sham?," 171 (Addendum 3 in this volume).

According to the account in Genesis 19, Lot and his children survived Sodom. Immediately following the verse from Exodus, which explains this plague as being a punishment for the golden calf, the Torah focuses on the populace that survived the plague.

62. **The generation of the Flood was exceedingly wise...** On their plan to escape the Flood, see *Pirqei de-Rabbi Eli'ezer* 22: "[The giants of the generation of the Flood] said, 'If He brings the waters of the Flood upon us, behold, we are of high stature—and the waters will not reach our necks. If He brings up the waters of the depths against us, behold, the soles of our feet can dam up the depths.' What did they do? They spread the soles of their feet and dammed up all the depths. What did the blessed Holy One do? He boiled the waters of the depths, which seethed their flesh and peeled off their skin.'" See also *Zohar* 1:62a.

On the wisdom of the generation of the Flood, see *Zohar* 1:56b.

63. **the blessed Holy One boiled the waters...** On the boiling waters of the Flood, and on the waters from above and below, see above, notes 58 and 62.

On rolling away to Babylon, see Rashi on Genesis 6:17: "[It is called מבול (*mabul*), flood,] because it בלה (*bilah*), decayed, everything; because it בלבל (*bilbel*), confused, everything; because it הוביל (*hovil*), transported, everything from the high to the low... for it caused all things to float away and brought them to Babylon, which is deep. This is why Babylon is called שנער (*Shin'ar*), because all the dead [variant reading: waters] of the Flood שננערו (*she-nin'aru*) were emptied out, to there."

See also *Qohelet Rabbah* on 12:7: "Rabbi Yoḥanan said, '*Who said* לצולה (*la-tsulah*), *to the deep, "Be dry!"* (Isaiah 44:27)—*tsulah* refers to Babylon. Why is it called *Tsulah*? Because the dead of the generation of the Flood צללו (*tsalelu*), sank, there....' Rabbi Shim'on son of Lakish said, 'It is written: *They found a plain in the land of Shinar* (Genesis 11:2). Why is it called שנער (*Shin'ar*)? Because the dead of the generation of the Flood שננערו (*she-nin'aru*), were emptied out, there.'"

that my heart will be steadfast and devoted, so that I will not forget You'; when he stretches out his legs to walk, let him examine the steps of his feet, so that they will not deviate to evil; if en route to perform a commandment—let him run, as is said: *They shall follow YHVH, roaring like a lion* (Hosea 11:10). Even on the Sabbath it is a commandment to run! When the day has completely passed, he must scrutinize himself and what he has done that day; and should the need arise, immediately perform *teshuvah* before going to sleep."[64]

Our Rabbis have taught: What is the meaning of the verse: *Solomon had a vineyard in Baal-hamon. He gave the vineyard to keepers; and each would obtain for its fruit a thousand pieces of silver* (Song of Songs 8:11)?[65]

Rabbi Yehudah said, "לשלמה (*Li-Shelomoh*), *Solomon, had a vineyard*—the King who possesses שלום (*shalom*), peace; *in Baal-hamon*—these are the angels of peace; *He gave the vineyard to keepers* [22a]—these are the keepers of the guard on earth; *each would obtain for its fruit a thousand* כסף (*kasef*), *pieces of silver*—the thousand delights for which the soul כוספת (*kosefet*), pines."[66]



64. ***Happy is the one You choose and draw near to dwell in Your courts!...*** The significance of the verse from Psalms, and its connection with the verse from Genesis, are made clear below. See *ZḤ* 22a (*MhN*), page 246, at notes 75–77. On Psalms 65:5, cf. *Zohar* 1:94b, 129a–b; 2:79b.

On running to perform a commandment, see BT *Berakhot* 6b: "Abbaye said, '... [For] one going [to the Synagogue], it is a pious deed to run, as is said: *Let us run to know YHVH* (Hosea 6:3).' Rabbi Zeira said, 'At first when I saw the sages running to the lecture on a Sabbath day, I thought: the sages are desecrating the Sabbath. But since I heard what Rabbi Tanḥum said in the name of Rabbi Yehoshu'a son of Levi, "A person should always run, even on a Sabbath, [to listen] to a word of *halakhah*, as is said: *They shall follow YHVH, roaring like a lion* (Hosea 11:10)," I also run.'" See also *Zohar* 1:160a, 223a; 3:379b; cf. M *Avot* 4:2. On blessings recited upon waking and before going to sleep, see BT *Berakhot* 60b. On readying one's feet to walk, and on contemplating one's sins before going to sleep, see *Zohar* 1:191a; 3:178a.

65. ***Solomon had a vineyard in Baal-hamon...*** The following verse reads: *My own vineyard is before me; the thousand are yours, Solomon, and two hundred for those who guard its fruit.* According to the probable simple sense, Solomon entrusted his vineyard to keepers, who tended and guarded it. Each keeper would sell the fruit of the plot in his charge and obtain a thousand (or twelve hundred) pieces of silver for it, of which he would retain two hundred for his labor and give the rest to the king. In the second verse, the speaker contrasts *my vineyard*—representing his beloved maiden—with the lucrative royal vineyard. Solomon must share his vineyard with others, whereas the young lover has his vineyard all to himself. Cf. the reference to Solomon's one thousand wives and concubines in 1 Kings 11:3.

66. **Rabbi Yehudah said...** We should read the verse as follows: *Solomon*, namely God, *had a vineyard in Baal-hamon*, namely the Garden of Eden—which is populated by המון (*hamon*), "a multitude," of angels. The vineyard is the preserve of the *keepers*, namely Israel, who keep the Torah; there, souls enjoy *a thousand pieces of silver*, namely, a thousand delights. Cf. *Shir ha-Shirim Rabbah* on Song of Songs 8:11.

On the phrase "the King who possesses peace," see *Sifra, Shemini, millu'im*, 15, 44c;

Alternatively, *Solomon had a vineyard*—this refers to the Torah; *in Baal-hamon*—from heaven; *He gave the vineyard to keepers*—Israel, who are the keepers of her guard; *each would obtain for its fruit a thousand pieces of silver*—as reward for her.[67]

Rabbi Yose and Rabbi Ḥiyya were walking on the way. Rabbi Ḥiyya said, "Tell us some of those sublime matters that your father used to say about the delights of the soul."[68]

He said to him, "Let's get out of here, for these Cappadocians are lacking good deeds!"[69]

He replied, "If so, it behooves us to ply Torah, and we will be saved from them!"[70]

He said to him, "Our Rabbis did not instruct thus with regard to a place of danger!"[71]



*Mekhilta, Pisḥa* 14; *Pesiqta de-Rav Kahana* 1:2, 3; *Shir ha-Shirim Rabbah* on 1:1 and 1:2; *Zohar* 1:5b, 29a, 184a, 226b, 248b; 2:5a (*MhN*), 14a (*MhN*), 127b, 132a–b, 143b–144b; 3:10b, 20a, 60a, 73b; *ZḤ* 15d, 25c (both *MhN*).

67. **this refers to the Torah...** The vineyard, signifying Torah, originally belonged to Solomon, namely God (see previous paragraph), and it resided in Baal-hamon, among the multitude of angels in heaven. It has been handed over to the keepers, namely Israel, who are rewarded for their observance.

On Torah as vineyard, cf. the rabbinic expression "vineyard of Yavneh," signifying the seat of Torah scholarship after the destruction of Jerusalem in 70 C.E.

68. **sublime matters...** The expression derives from the Talmud and appears often throughout the *Zohar*. See BT *Ḥagigah* 14a; *Ta'anit* 20b; *Zohar* 1:49b, 87a, 96b, 197b; 2:31a; 3:148a, 209b, 231a; *ZḤ* 76c (*MhN, Rut*); Scholem, "Parashah Ḥadashah," 439 (Addendum 1 in this volume).

This brief story appears (with minor variations) in Isaac ibn Sahula, *Peirush Shir ha-Shirim*, 487. See also Scholem, "Qabbalat Rabbi Yitsḥak ben Shelomoh," 112–116.

69. **Cappadocians...** Cappadocia is a province in Asia Minor, though apparently the author(s) of the *Zohar* imagined (or pretended) that Cappadocia was a Galilean village near Sepphoris, based on the phrase "Cappadocians of Sepphoris" in JT *Shevi'it* 9:5, 39a.

In *Zohar* 2:38b, Rav Ḥisda leaves his original residence among the Cappadocians—where "times were stressful for him and sickness pursued him"—for Sepphoris, whereupon he attained "many riches, much Torah." As in the passage here, the Cappadocians are presented as wicked folk lacking good deeds.

On Cappadocia in the *Zohar*, see Scholem, "She'elot be-Viqqoret ha-Zohar," 40–46 (and the appended note by S. Klein, 56); idem, *Major Trends*, 169; idem, *Kabbalah*, 222; Tishby, *Wisdom of the Zohar*, 1:63–64; *Zohar* 1:69b, 132a, 138a (*MhN*), 160a, 223a, 243b; 2:80b, 86a; 3:35a, 75b, 221b.

70. **it behooves us to ply Torah...** On the apotropaic value of studying Torah on the way, see BT *Ta'anit* 10b: "Rabbi Ilai son of Berekhiah said, 'Two disciples of the wise who are walking on the way with no words of Torah between them deserve to be burned.'" See also *Zohar* 1:230b; 3:149a.

71. **a place of danger!** See BT *Qiddushin* 39b: "Wherever injury is likely, we do not rely on a miracle." See also BT *Shabbat* 32a, *Pesaḥim* 8b; *Zohar* 1:112b, 209a, 230b.

As they left and continued on the way, Rabbi Yose said, "I shall tell you a word, concealed among my father's hidden riches in his treasury. This is it: It is written: *Solomon had a vineyard....* This vineyard is the holy soul, planted above, beneath the Throne of Glory; *Solomon*—the King who possesses all peace; *in Baal-hamon*—the Throne of Glory presiding over all the hosts of heaven and earth; the master of all the hosts. It bestowed this soul. To whom? *To keepers*—those who keep His commandments.[72]

"The blessed Holy One has countless worlds on high above all the hosts of heaven, and twelve hundred other worlds that He enters within, to delight with the righteous in the Garden of Eden. *Each would obtain for its fruit a thousand* כסף (*kasef*), *pieces of silver*—the thousand worlds that the blessed Holy One כסיף (*kesif*), desires."[73]

Rabbi Yitsḥak said, "I can support Rabbi Yose's word. As follows, from what is written afterward: *My own vineyard is before me; the thousand are yours, Solomon, and two hundred for those who guard its fruit* (ibid. 8:12). The Throne of Glory proclaims, saying, 'Master of the Universe, that soul was taken from me—she is *before me. The thousand are yours, Solomon*—those thousand worlds belong to You; they are not fitting for another. *Two hundred for those who guard its fruit*—this refers to Eden, containing two hundred worlds of pleasure and delight for the souls of the righteous.'"[74]



72. **the holy soul, planted above, beneath the Throne of Glory...** In BT *Shabbat* 152b, the souls of the righteous are said to be "hidden beneath the Throne of Glory" after death; see also *Avot de-Rabbi Natan* A, 12. According to *MhN*, the soul is created from the substance of the Throne of Glory, which may allude to the *Shekhinah*. See *Zohar* 1:113a, 125b, 126b (all *MhN*); *ZḤ* 10a–d, 20b, 24a, 26a (all *MhN*).

*Baal-hamon* designates the Throne of Glory because it literally means "the master of multitudes," i.e., the master of all the heavenly hosts. On the Throne presiding over all, see *ZḤ* 7d, 15b, 16c (all *MhN*).

73. **The blessed Holy One has countless worlds on high...** On the worlds He desires, see *ZḤ* 9d, 13b, 18a (all *MhN*); Scholem, "Parashah Ḥadashah," 445 (Addendum 1 in this volume).

The significance of the twelve hundred worlds is explained in the following paragraph. On entering within those worlds and delighting with the righteous, see below, note 75.

74. ***The thousand are yours, Solomon...*** See BT *Shevu'ot* 35b: "Every שלמה (*Shelomoh*), Solomon, mentioned in Song of Songs is holy [i.e., it signifies God, the One who possesses שלום (*shalom*), peace'],... except for this one: *My own vineyard is before me; the thousand are yours, Solomon*—Solomon himself [will have *the thousand*]—*and two hundred to those who guard its fruit* (Song of Songs 8:12), namely, the sages." In other words, whereas throughout the rest of Song of Songs the name *Solomon* refers to God, in this verse (spoken by God) the name refers to the human king. God is saying: "From *my vineyard* [namely Israel], *Solomon* shall have *one thousand* men out of every twelve hundred [as soldiers or workers], while *two hundred* will *guard its fruit* [that is, study Torah]." According to Rabbi Yitsḥak, how-

As we have learned: Rabbi said, "Every single night, the blessed Holy One enters all those worlds, while at midnight He enters the two hundred worlds of the Garden of Eden to delight with the righteous, as is said: *new as well as old, my love, I have stored away for you* (ibid. 7:14). When David (peace be upon him) contemplated the rank of the righteous, his heart pined. He said, 'Master of the Universe! *Happy is the one You choose and draw near to dwell in Your courts!* (Psalms 65:5).'[75]

Rabbi Abbahu said, "Come and see how attentive a person must be, since the divine soul is in his nostrils, to purify himself of his iniquities, scrutinize his deeds, and not sin before His Maker—so that his rank might be with the other righteous, when he ascends to behold the countenance of *YHVH*, with no one to hold him back![76]

"From whom do you learn this? From the ark! Come and see what is written: *They came to Noah into the ark* (Genesis 7:15)—without permission. As Rabbi Yitsḥak said: 'All the birds, beasts, and animals that had not sinned came—and the ark received them; but those that had sinned—the ark repelled them without.' If so with the ark—which is but dry wood—how much more so the openings of heaven, the keepers of the guard, and the Throne of Glory, who possess real power, so that they can receive those who have not sinned, and repel those who have!?"[77]



ever, even this "Solomon" is holy, and the twelve hundred worlds are divided into two groups: a thousand worlds reserved exclusively for God, and two hundred worlds as reward for the souls of the righteous.

On the righteous possessing two hundred worlds of delight, and on Song of Songs 8:12, see *Zohar* 1:97b, 124b (both *MhN*). For a different interpretation in *MhN* of the same verse, see *ZḤ* 2d; cf. *Zohar* 2:227a.

75. **at midnight He enters... to delight with the righteous...** On the midnight encounter between God and the souls of the righteous, see above, *ZḤ* 13b–c (*MhN*) and notes. See also *Zohar* 2:18b (*MhN*); *ZḤ* 6a, 18a (both *MhN*).

*New as well as old* indicates the two hundred and one thousand worlds, respectively. Cf. *Zohar* 1:243a, where Song of Songs 7:14 is also used in the context of a nocturnal delight. Cf. *Zohar* 1:134b (*MhN*).

*Your courts* signifies the Edenic worlds enjoyed by the righteous. Cf. *Zohar* 1:94b, 129b.

"Rabbi" indicates Rabbi Yehudah ha-Nasi (the Patriarch), who redacted the Mishnah. He was so esteemed that he was called simply "Rabbi": the Master.

76. **when he ascends to behold the countenance of *YHVH*...** When the righteous ascend to the Garden of Eden, they are not repelled by the ministering angels. See *ZḤ* 21a (*MhN*).

77. **the ark repelled them...** See BT *Sanhedrin* 108b: "*Of every clean animal you shall take seven pairs, each with its mate* (Genesis 7:2).... Rabbi Shemu'el son of Naḥmani said in the name of Rabbi Yonatan, 'It means of those that did not sin [i.e., breeding across species].' How did he [Noah] know? Rav Ḥisda said, 'He led them in front of the ark; those that the ark accepted had certainly not sinned; whilst those that it rejected had certainly sinned.' Rabbi Abbahu said, '[He took only] those that came of their own accord.'"

On the animals entering the ark without

Rabbi Ḥiyya said, "Noah was of the little of faith, for he didn't believe that the Flood would really come; he did not he enter the ark until the waters forced him, as is said: *Noah entered... because of the waters of the Flood* (ibid. 7:7)."[78]

Rabbi Yitsḥak said, "Come and see: When the blessed Holy One brought down the waters, initially He brought them down compassionately, in order to demonstrate to the world that should they repent, He would accept them. As implied by what is written at first: *The rain was* (ibid. 7:12)—whereas afterward it says *The Flood was* (ibid., 17)—that if they were to repent, they would become rains of blessing. They did not repent—and hence there was a Flood!"[79]

Rabbi Yitsḥak also said, "The blessed Holy One swore an oath that He does not desire the death of the wicked, as is said: *As I live—declares YHVH Elohim* [22b]—*I do not desire the death of the wicked, but that the wicked turn from his way* וחיה (*ve-ḥayah*), *and live* (Ezekiel 33:11)—in two worlds, this world and the world to come."[80]

Rabbi Yitsḥak also said, "Happy are the children to whom is said thus: *Return and live!* (Ezekiel 18:32), *for why should you die, O House of Israel?* (ibid. 33:11); *turn back, turn back* (ibid.)—for He does not desire the death of the wicked, [but only] that they return in *teshuvah*, in order that they might live."[81] 

Alternatively, Rabbi Yoḥanan opened, "*The eyes of the wicked will fail; escape is lost to them, their hope* מפח נפש (*mapaḥ nafesh*), *an expiring breath* (Job 11:20). This can be compared to a king and a gang of bandits who were pillaging in the mountains. The king heard and sent his troops after them, who caught them and placed them in a high tower. There were some prudent men among them who said, 'We know בנפשתנא (*be-nafshatana*), in our hearts, that we have done evil things and that we cannot be saved.' What did they do? They dug a hole in the tower, went out, and fled to the mountains. There was a dullard among

permission, i.e., on their accord, see also *Pirqei de-Rabbi Eli'ezer* 23.

78. **Noah was of the little of faith...** See *Bereshit Rabbah* 32:6: "*Noah entered, with his sons,* [*his wife and his sons' wives, into the ark because of the waters of the Flood*]. Rabbi Yoḥanan said, 'He was lacking in faith: if the waters had not reached his ankles, he would not have entered the ark.'" See *Midrash Aggadah* (Buber), *Bereshit* 7; *Zohar* 1:68b, 69a.

79. **initially He brought them down compassionately...** Namely, gently. See Rashi on Genesis 7:12. Cf. *Bereshit Rabbah* 31:12.

80. **in two worlds...** The final two letters of the word וחיה (*ve-ḥayah*), *and live*, allude to the two worlds since, according to rabbinic tradition, this world was created by the letter ה (*he*) and the world to come by the letter י (*yod*).

See *Bereshit Rabbah* 12:10; JT *Ḥagigah* 2:1, 77c; BT *Menaḥot* 29b; *Alfa Beita de-Rabbi Aqiva*, Version 1 (*Battei Midrashot*, 2:363); *Zohar* 1:140a, 141b; 2:22b.

81. **He does not desire the death of the wicked...** See *ZḤ* 19b, 21c (both *MhN*).

Ezekiel 18:32 reads in full: *For it is not My desire that anyone shall die, declares the Lord YHVH. Return and live!*

them; he saw the hole—but did not wish to flee and escape. The following day, the king came to inspect the tower and the bandits. He saw the hole they made and that they had fled and escaped. He said to the one remaining, 'Fool! Your companions fled through this hole and escaped my judgment, what more can I do to them?! But as for you—who saw the hole with your own eyes but did not want to be saved—your eyes shall be gouged, and afterward you will be hanged on a tree!'[82]

"So, the bandits are the wicked who walk about in darkness. The wicked who are prudent—what do they do? They say, 'We have sinned against the King. How can we escape His judgment? Rather, let us open a path of *teshuvah*, beseech mercy, escape, and be saved. This is what they did. As for the dullards—what do they do? They see the path of *teshuvah* open before them, which the others opened and through which they escaped heavenly judgment, but they do not wish to be saved. The blessed Holy One says to them, 'Fools! Your brothers fled and escaped through that path of *teshuvah* they opened; what more can I do to them?! But as for you, your eyes beheld the hole—the path of *teshuvah* open before you—yet you did not wish to enter within to escape and be saved!' What is written about them? *The eyes of the wicked will fail*—for they saw an open path; *escape is lost to them*—for they did not wish to escape and be saved; *their hope* מפח נפש (*mapaḥ nafesh*), *an expiring soul*—in the world to come.



"Similarly with the generation of the Flood: They saw Noah making the ark and forewarning them every day; they saw him enter the ark, but they did not wish to repent. The blessed Holy One said, '*The eyes of the wicked will fail, escape is lost to them*—because they did not wish to repent and escape My judgment; *their hope an expiring soul*—for they will not rise at the Day of Judgment, as is said: *The shades tremble beneath the waters and their denizens* (ibid. 26:5).'"[83]

82. **a king and a gang of bandits...** The *Zohar* reworks an older rabbinic parable. See *Qohelet Rabbah* on Ecclesiastes 7:15: "So long as a person lives, the blessed Holy One looks to him to repent; when he is dead, His hope perishes, as is said: *When a wicked man dies, hope shall perish* (Proverbs 11:7). It may be likened to a gang of bandits shut up in a prison. One of them made an opening and they all escaped. One remained behind and did not escape. When the governor arrived he began striking him with a stick. He said, 'Ill-starred and hapless wretch! There was an opening before you—and you did not escape!' Similarly in the time to come, the blessed Holy One says to the wicked, 'Repentance was before you—but you did not repent,' therefore: *The eyes of the wicked will fail* (Job 11:20)."

The parable and its explanation are found in Moses de León, Commentary on the Ten *Sefirot*, 350a–b.

83. **Similarly with the generation of the Flood...** Just as the wicked who did not perform *teshuvah* are annihilated in the world to come—*their hope an expiring breath* [literally: *soul*], so the generation of the Flood who spurned *teshuvah* and ignored Noah's warnings.

According to M *Sanhedrin* 10:3, "the gen-

*Noah, man of the earth, was the first [to plant a vineyard]* (Genesis 9:20).[84]

Rabbi Yose said, "Why was he called *man of the earth*? Because the earth was settled through him; in other words—master of the earth."[85]

Our Rabbis say: *Man of the soil*—because on his account the earth abided in her power and nature, as is said: *This one will provide us relief from our labor and from the painful toil of our hands caused by the soil that YHVH cursed* (ibid. 5:29). Know that as soon as Adam sinned, the soil was cursed, as is said: *Cursed be the soil because of you* (ibid. 3:17); and she abided in her curses until Noah arose and annulled the curse."[86]

As it has been taught: Rabbi Ḥiyya the Great said, "In the hour when the blessed Holy One said to Noah, *Go out of the ark* (Genesis 8:16), he said before Him, 'Master of the Universe! Whither should I come out? Shall I come out to an earth that has been cursed?! Because she was cursed her inhabitants were destroyed; all of them were cursed and dwindled.' The blessed Holy One replied, 'Not so for you! Rather, pullulate across the earth and multiply upon her. The others were destroyed upon her, but as for you—be fruitful and multiply and abound upon her.' Even so his heart was not at ease, and so he offered up offerings, as is said: *he offered ascent-offerings on the altar* (ibid. 8:20)—the altar upon which Adam sacrificed. The blessed Holy One said to him, 'Here is what



eration of the Flood has no share in the world to come, nor will they stand at the [last] Judgment." Cf. *Avot de-Rabbi Natan* A, 32. See *Tosefta Sanhedrin* 13:6; BT *Sanhedrin* 108a; *Zohar* 1:66a, 68b–69a, 108a; 3:308b (*Tosafot*); Ginzberg, *Legends*, 5:184, n. 44.

On the generation of the Flood's failure to repent, see above, *ZḤ* 21d (*MhN*), page 240. On Job 26:5, cf. *Bereshit Rabbah* 31:12.

84. ***man of the earth...*** איש האדמה (*Ish ha-adamah*), which could also be translated as *man of the soil* or *a tiller of the soil.*

85. **master of the earth** See Rashi on Genesis 9:20; cf. Naḥmanides, ad loc. See also *Bereshit Rabbah* 36:3: "*man of the earth*... because he filled the face of the earth."

86. **until Noah arose and annulled the curse** See *Tanḥuma, Bereshit* 11: "How did he [Lamech] know to say, '*This one will provide us relief from our labor*...?' Was he a prophet? Rabbi Shim'on son of Yehotsadak said, 'They had been taught that when the blessed Holy One said to Adam, *Cursed be the soil because of you; by painful toil will you eat of it all the days of your life* (Genesis 3:17), Adam had asked, "Master of the World, for how long?" He replied, "Until a human is born circumcised." When Noah was born circumcised, Lamech immediately knew and said, "Indeed, *this one will provide us relief*...!" What is meant by: *from our labor and from the painful toil of our hands*? Before Noah was born, people did not reap what they sowed. If they sowed wheat, they reaped thorns and thistles. Once Noah was born, the world became arable once again. They reaped what they sowed, sowing wheat and reaping wheat, sowing barley and reaping barley. Furthermore, until Noah was born, they worked by hand.... Once Noah was born, he invented plows, scythes, spades, and all kinds of tools.'" Cf. *Bereshit Rabbah* 36:3.

On Noah's overturning the curse of the earth and as *man of the earth*, see *Zohar* 1:38a, 58b, 62b, 70b; 2:168a; 3:15a; *ZḤ* 19b (*MhN*).

you have requested: *I will never again curse the earth because of humankind* (ibid., 21),' whereupon his heart was at ease. [22c] That is why he was called *man of the earth*, because he gave his heart and soul for her, to extract her from the curse. Some say, because he engaged in the business of the soil."[87]

*He planted a vineyard* (Genesis 9:20).

He found a banished vine, banished from the Garden of Eden. On the very day he planted it, it flourished, as is said: *On the day of your planting, you make it grow* (Isaiah 17:11).[88]

Rabbi says, "The vine was banished from the Garden of Eden, along with its grapes. He squeezed them, drank from the wine, and exposed himself."[89]

Rabbi Avun opened: "*YHVH spoke to Aaron, saying, 'Wine and beer, do not drink, you and your sons with you, when you enter the Tent of Meeting, lest you die—a perpetual statute throughout your generations'* (Leviticus 10:8–9)."



87. **Shall I come out to an earth that has been cursed?!...** See *Bereshit Rabbah* 34:6 (Theodor-Albeck): "*Go out of the ark* (Genesis 8:16).... [Noah] was reluctant to go out, saying, 'Am I to go out and beget children for a curse?' until the blessed Holy One swore to him that He would not bring another Flood upon the world, as is said: *For this is to Me like the waters of Noah; as I have sworn that the waters of Noah should no more go over [the earth]* (Isaiah 54:9): be fruitful and multiply!"

On Noah offering offerings on Adam's altar, see *Bereshit Rabbah* 34:9: "*Noah built an altar to YHVH... and offered ascent-offerings on the altar.* Rabbi Eli'ezer son of Ya'akov said, 'On the great altar in Jerusalem, where Adam sacrificed.'" According to BT *Avodah Zarah* 8a: "On the day Adam was created when the sun set, he said, 'Woe is me! Because I have sinned, the world is turning dark and will now revert to chaos and void. This is the death decreed against me from Heaven!' He sat up all night fasting and weeping, and Eve wept facing him. As soon as dawn broke, he said, 'This is the normal course of the world!' He rose and offered up an ox." See *Targum Yerushalmi*, Genesis 8:20; *Zohar* 1:69b–70a, 258a (*hashmatot*).

According to one view found in *ZḤ* 19b (*MhN*), it was through Abraham's merit (not Noah's) that the earth was liberated from her curse. Hence Rabbi Ḥiyya's final statement—Noah merely worked the soil.

88. **He found a banished vine...** See *Pirqei de-Rabbi Eli'ezer* 23: "Noah found a vine that had been banished from the Garden of Eden along with its clusters. He took of its fruit and ate—and desired them in his heart. He planted a vineyard with it. That same day, its fruits flourished, as is said: *On the day of your planting you make it grow, and on the morning you sow, you see it bud* (Isaiah 17:11). He drank of its wine and was exposed in the tent." See also Luria, ad loc.

See 3 Baruch 4:8–17; Origen, *Selecta*, Genesis 9:20–21; *Targum Yerushalmi*, Genesis 9:20; *Tanḥuma* (Buber), *Noaḥ* 20; *Zohar* 1:73a, 140b. Cf. *Zohar* 1:35b.

89. **He squeezed them, drank from the wine, and exposed himself** See Genesis 9:21: *He drank of the wine and became drunk and exposed himself in the tent.*

As in *Pirqei de-Rabbi Eli'ezer* (see previous note), the *Zohar* here connects Noah's sin with Adam's. According to one opinion in *Bereshit Rabbah* 15:7 and BT *Sanhedrin* 70a, Adam ate from a vine.

"Rabbi" indicates Rabbi Yehudah ha-Nasi (the Patriarch), who redacted the Mishnah. He was so esteemed that he was called simply "Rabbi": the Master.

As Rabbi Avun said: "There is nothing in the whole world that causes a person's heart to become proud like wine. This was the cause of Nadab and Abihu's punishment, because they ate and drank and their hearts grew proud. This is the meaning of the *strange fire that He had not enjoined upon them* (ibid., 1).[90]

"This had been decreed against them previously, and the attribute of justice arrived to send forth a hand against them, as is said: *Yet against the nobles of Israel, He did not send forth His hand* (Exodus 24:11); even though their sentence—to send forth a hand against them—had been decreed. Why were they punished? Because *they beheld God, and they ate and drank* (ibid.)—they entered when they ate and drank; and at that moment their punishment was decreed.[91]



90. **the cause of Nadab and Abihu's punishment...** See Leviticus 10:1–2: *The sons of Aaron, Nadab and Abihu, each took his firepan and put fire in it and placed incense on it, and offered before YHVH strange fire that He had not enjoined upon them. Fire came forth from before YHVH and consumed them, and they died before YHVH.*

The account in Leviticus is sparse in detail, and the exact nature of their sin is not stated. According to rabbinic tradition, however, they died because they entered the Tent of Meeting drunk. Cf. *Vayiqra Rabbah* 12:1: "As Rabbi Shim'on taught, 'The sons of Aaron died only because they entered the Tent of Meeting drunk with wine.' Rabbi Pinḥas said in the name of Rabbi Levi, 'This may be compared to a king who had a faithful attendant. He found him standing at tavern entrances, severed his head in silence, and appointed another attendant in his place. We would not know why he put the first to death, except for his commanding the second, saying, "You must not enter the doorway of taverns" whence we know that for this reason he had put the first to death. Thus: *Fire came forth from before YHVH and consumed them*, but we would not know why they died, except for His commanding Aaron: *Wine and beer, do not drink*.'"

See also *Targum Yerushalmi*, Leviticus 10:9; *Vayiqra Rabbah* 12:5; 20:9; *Ester Rabbah* 5:1; *Pesiqta de-Rav Kahana* 26:9; *Tanḥuma*, *Shemini* 11, *Aḥarei Mot* 6; *Tanḥuma* (Buber), *Aḥarei Mot* 7; *Zohar* 1:73b, 192a; 3:34a, 39a; Moses de León, *Sheqel ha-Qodesh*, 36–37 (43–44).

On the connection between pride and haughtiness of spirit and idolatry, see BT *Sotah* 4b: "Rabbi Yoḥanan said in the name of Rabbi Shim'on son of Yoḥai, 'Whoever possesses haughtiness of spirit is as though he worships idols, as is written...: *every haughty heart is an abomination to YHVH* (Proverbs 16:5).'" See also BT *Sotah* 5a. On wine's making the heart proud, see Isaiah 28:1, 3.

91. **This had been decreed against them previously...** Although they had been guilty already at Mount Sinai, they were not punished there, but rather later when *they offered strange fire before YHVH* in the Dwelling.

The context (Exodus 24:10–11) reads: *They saw the God of Israel, and beneath His feet was like a fashioning of sapphire pavement and like the essence of heaven for purity. Yet against the nobles of the Children of Israel He did not send forth His hand; they beheld God, and they ate and drank.* In the simple sense of both verses, the last two clauses describe the actions of everyone present—Moses, Aaron, Nadab, Abihu, and the seventy elders (mentioned in the preceding verse)—who held a communion feast to conclude the covenant. Here, Rabbi Avun construes those clauses as refer-

"Afterward, seeing that He did not send forth a hand the first time, they did so again; and a flame shot forth from between the two *keruvim*, and they were burned. For so were they aligned, corresponding to the *keruvim* in the Garden of Eden.[92]

"After they died, He commanded Aaron and the priests who would succeed him to abstain from wine when they enter the Tent of Meeting—lest they enter and their hearts be found to be proud and haughty."[93]

Rabbi said, "There are two things that do not go together: wine and the service of heaven. As we have learned there: One who is tipsy must not pray; and similarly, one who is drunk must not pray—and if he did pray, his prayer is an abomination."[94]



ring only to Nadab and Abihu, Aaron's two eldest sons. Their eating and drinking signifies the casualness with which they dared to gaze upon God.

See *Pesiqta de-Rav Kahana* 26:9: "*Yet against the nobles of the Children of Israel He did not send forth His hand*.... Rabbi Pinḥas said, 'From here it may be inferred that they deserved to have a hand sent forth against them.' Rabbi Hosha'yah said, 'Did they take loaves with them up to Sinai, that it is written: *They beheld God and they ate and drank*? Rather this teaches that they feasted their eyes on *Shekhinah*, like a person looking at his friend while eating and drinking.'... Rabbi Tanḥum said, 'This teaches that they acted brazenly, standing up and feasting their eyes on *Shekhinah*.'... At Mount Sinai they [namely Nadab and Abihu] received their death sentence. This may be compared to a king who was marrying off his daughter, when something blameworthy was discovered among the representatives of the groom's family. The king said, 'If I slay them now, I will confound my daughter's joy. Later my own joyous celebration will arrive, and it is better [to punish them] during my own joy and not during my daughter's joy.' Similarly the blessed Holy One said, 'If I slay Nadab and Abihu now, I will confound the joy of Torah. Later, My own joyous celebration [the erection of the Dwelling] will arrive; it is better [to punish them] during My own joy and not during the joy of Torah.'"

See *Targum Yerushalmi*, Exodus 24:11; *Vayiqra Rabbah* 20:10; *Tanḥuma, Aḥarei Mot* 6, *Beha'alotekha* 16; *Tanḥuma* (Buber), *Aḥarei Mot* 7–8, 13, *Beha'alotekha* 27; *Shemot Rabbah* 3:1; *Bemidbar Rabbah* 2:25; 15:24; *Midrash ha-Gadol*, Exodus 24:11; Rashi on Exodus 24:10–11; *Zohar* 2:126a; 3:37b. Cf. Moses de León, *Sheqel ha-Qodesh*, 37 (44).

92. **corresponding to the *keruvim* in the Garden of Eden...** See *ZḤ* 19a, 21a (both *MhN*).

93. **After they died, He commanded Aaron and the priests...** See *Sifra, Aḥarei Mot* 1:3, 89b: "*YHVH said to Moses, 'Tell your brother Aaron that he is not to come at any time* (Leviticus 16:2).... Rabbi El'azar son of Azariah says, 'A parable: It may be likened to a sick man going to a doctor. He says to him: Do not drink anything cold and do not lie on damp ground. Another patient came and he said to him: Do not drink anything cold and do not lie on damp ground—so that you should not die as so-and-so did. This certainly convinced him more than anything else. That is why it says: *After the death of the two sons of Aaron... YHVH said to Moses, Tell your brother Aaron that he is not to come at any time* (ibid., 1–2).'" See Rashi and Naḥmanides on Leviticus 16:1.

94. **one who is drunk must not pray...** See BT *Eruvin* 64a: "Rabbah son of Rav

Rabbi Yose said, "One who is drunk and prays is as though he worships idols. How do we know? From Hannah. It is written: *Eli thought she was drunk* (1 Samuel 1:13), to which she replied and said, *Do not take your maidservant for a worthless woman* (ibid., 16)." Rabbi Yose continued, "Here is written *worthless woman*, and there is written *worthless men have come out* (Deuteronomy 13:14). Just as the latter indicates idolatry, so here idolatry!"[95]

Rabbi Yitsḥak said, "The only people termed 'holy' are those who abstain from wine, as is written: *All the days of his setting apart for YHVH, he shall be holy* (Numbers 6:5–6)."[96]

Rabbi Yitsḥak also said, "There is no wine worthy of the name 'fine wine' like the wine of the land of Israel. And the finest of all is the wine of the Upper Galilee, for one cannot imbibe even half a *log*!"[97]

Rabbi El'azar son of Rabbi Shim'on went to see his father-in-law, Rabbi Yose son of Rabbi Shim'on son of Lekonya. He was served a tender three-year-old calf, and he opened for him a cask of wine. His father-in-law mixed and he drank; he mixed [again] and he drank.[98] 253

He said to him, "Perhaps you have heard from your father how many to one cup?"[99]

Huna said, 'One who is tipsy must not pray; but if he did pray, his prayer is regarded as a proper one. One who is drunk must not pray; and if he did pray, his prayer is an abomination.' What is meant by tipsy and drunk?... Tipsy—one who is able to speak in the presence of a king; drunk—one who is unable to speak in the presence of a king."

On a drunkard's being forbidden to pray, see also JT *Berakhot* 4:1, 7a; *Terumot* 1:6, 40d; BT *Berakhot* 31a–b; *Zohar* 2:153b; Moses de León, *Sheqel ha-Qodesh*, 37 (44). On the identity of Rabbi, see above, note 89.

95. **One who is drunk and prays is as though he worships idols...** See BT *Berakhot* 31b.

In Deuteronomy 13:14, the worthless men invite the inhabitants of their town to worship other gods.

96. **abstain from wine...** Rabbi Yitsḥak misquotes and conflates two verses. On the Nazirite's abstention from wine, see Numbers 6:1–4.

97. **the finest of all is the wine of the Upper Galilee...** See BT *Megillah* 6a; *Nazir* 31b; *Ketubbot* 112a. According to BT *Eruvin* 64b, even a quarter of a *log* of Italian wine causes intoxication. A *log* can denote a small bottle, or the volume of six eggs.

98. **Rabbi El'azar son of Rabbi Shim'on went to see his father-in-law...** According to rabbinic tradition, Rabbi El'azar's father-in-law was named Rabbi Shim'on son of Yose son of Lekonya. The *Zohar* consistently switches father and son, transforming Shim'on son of Yose into Yose son of Shim'on. See *Pesiqta de-Rav Kahana* 11:20; JT *Ma'aserot* 3:8, 50d; *Shir ha-Shirim Rabbah* on 4:11; *Devarim Rabbah* 7:11; *Seder ha-Dorot*, s.v. *Shim'on ben Yose ben Lekonya*; *Zohar* 1:5a, 61b; 3:84b, 188a, 193a; *ZḤ* 7d, 10d, 14a, 20d (all *MhN*).

This brief narrative is found with minor variations in JT *Ma'aserot* 3:8, 50d.

99. **how many to one cup?** Seeing that you quaff with gusto, I must ask: in how many gulps should one consume a cup of wine?

He replied, "Whatever size it is: one of hot [wine], one of cold! But the Rabbis did not take into account the size of your cup—which is tiny; your wine—which is outstanding; or my belly—which is huge!"[100]

Rabbi Yehudah said, "When Noah came out of the ark—descending from the beasts, and creeping and swarming things—he was confused in his mind. Even though he drank only a little wine, he got drunk and exposed himself."[101]

Rabbi Yehudah also said, "Canaan came and castrated him. He awoke from his wine and found himself emasculated. As is written: *Noah awoke from his wine and knew what his youngest son had done to him* (Genesis 9:24). The verse does not say *what he had seen*, but rather *what he had done to him*—that he had castrated him! That is why he cursed him, as is said: *He said, 'Cursed be Canaan, the lowliest slave shall he be to his brothers'* (ibid., 25)."[102]

Rabbi opened, "*YHVH smelled the pleasing aroma and said,... 'Never again will I curse the earth because of humankind'* (Genesis 8:21). When Noah came out of the ark, he opened his eyes and saw [22d] the whole world completely destroyed. He began weeping for the world. He said, 'Master of the World, if You destroyed Your world because of human sin or because of fools, why did You create it? One or the other You should do! Either do not create the human being, or do not destroy the world!' He offered up offerings, arose, and prayed before Him—and the aroma ascended before the blessed Holy One and was sweet."[103]



100. **one of hot [wine], one of cold . . .** The text may be faulty. According to the version of the narrative found in JT *Ma'aserot,* Rabbi El'azar responds: "As it is [i.e., not mixed], one [gulp]; of cold, two; of hot, three."

Rabbi El'azar's final retort appears (with minor variation) in JT *Ma'aserot* 3:8; and in BT *Pesaḥim* 86b, where the protagonists are Rabbi Yishma'el son of Rabbi Yose and Rabbi Shim'on son of Rabbi Yose son of Lekonya.

On the correct etiquette, see also BT *Pesaḥim* 86b in the name of Rav Huna son of Rav Natan: "One who drinks his cup in one gulp is a glutton; in two, shows good breeding; in three, is of the arrogant."

101. **he was confused in his mind . . .** Surely Noah wasn't a glutton and knew how much he could drink without getting drunk. His confused state of mind explains his error in judgment. Cf. *Bereshit Rabbah* 36:4.

102. **Canaan came and castrated him...** The castration is not mentioned in Scripture but derives from rabbinic tradition (BT *Sanhedrin* 70a, in the name of Rav). Genesis 9:22 merely states: *Ham, the father of Canaan, saw his father's nakedness.* Rabbi Yehudah here switches the actor—Canaan, who ultimately receives the curse, is in fact the perpetrator as well (see *Pirqei de-Rabbi Eli'ezer* 23; cf. *Bereshit Rabbah* 36:7; *Tanḥuma, Bereshit* 15). See also Rashi on Genesis 9:22; Naḥmanides on Genesis 9:18; *Zohar* 1:73b.

103. **the aroma ascended before the blessed Holy One and was sweet** Noah's bold statement is in fact pleasing to God. See below, *ZḤ* 23a (*MhN*), pages 259–60.

Cf. *Midrash Tehillim* 2:2: "Rabbi Yitsḥak said, 'One person says to another, 'Why are you doing that?' and the other gets angry. But the righteous say to the blessed Holy One, 'Why?' and He does not get angry; they

Rabbi continued, "Three aromas ascended before Him: the aroma of his offering; the aroma of his prayer; and the aroma of his deeds. No aroma in the world was as pleasing to Him as that aroma. Therefore He commanded, saying, 'ריח ניחחי (*rei'aḥ niḥoḥi*), *My pleasing aroma, take care to offer Me at its appointed time* (Numbers 28:2). That is, take care to offer Me the aroma that Noah offered up to Me—the aroma of offering, prayer, and right action.'"[104]

Rabbi Aivu said, "Noah was wise and could understand the chatter and chirps of the creatures and their significations. When he was in the ark, he said, 'I know that there is none so clever among the birds as the raven, through which I might ascertain a sign in the world.' Immediately: *He sent out the raven* (Genesis 8:7)."[105]

Rabbi Ḥiyya said, "How could he do this? For Rabbi Bo said, 'It is forbidden to gaze upon those who augur through fowl of the sky.' And surely this is in the category of *You shall not augur or interpret omens* (Leviticus 19:26)—encompassing any form of divination in the world."[106]

Well, Rabbi Ḥiyya said, "Noah was extremely distressed by the destruction of the world. He said, 'Master of the World! I thought that You were compassionate—but You did not have compassion upon Your world! Your compassion turned into cruelty! You did not have compassion upon Your children! May this one who does not have compassion upon its children, and who turns cruelly against them, go forth.' That is why he sent out the raven—intimating an intimation."[107]

are not punished. Why not? Because they have sought good not for themselves but for Israel." Cf. *Bereshit Rabbah* 33:3; *Vayiqra Rabbah* 7:4.

"Rabbi" indicates Rabbi Yehudah ha-Nasi (the Patriarch), who redacted the Mishnah. He was so esteemed that he was called simply "Rabbi": the Master.

104. **ריח ניחחי (*reiaḥ niḥoḥi*), *My pleasing aroma*...** So beloved was Noah's offering, that future offerings offered by Israel are associated with his name—for ניחוח (*niḥoaḥ*), *pleasing*, echoes נח (*Noaḥ*), *Noah*—and are to be offered in the same spirit. Cf. *Zohar* 1:70a.

On Numbers 28:2, cf. *Zohar* 1:164a–b.

105. **understand the chatter and chirps of the creatures...** See *Yad Ramah* on BT *Sanhedrin* 108b.

106. **It is forbidden to... augur through fowl of the sky...** See BT *Sanhedrin* 65b–66a, where the raven's call is specifically mentioned. See Maimonides, *Mishneh Torah, Hilkhot Avodat Kokhavim* 11:4: "It is forbidden to augur as idolators do, as is said: *You shall not augur* (Leviticus 19:26). What is meant by one who augurs?... those who hear the chirping of a bird and say: This will happen (or: this will not happen); it is beneficial to do this (or: it is detrimental to do this)." See also *Zohar* 1:126b; cf. *Zohar* 3:204b.

107. **May this one who does not have compassion upon its children...** On the so-called cruelty of the raven, see *Tanḥuma, Eqev* 2: "How do we know that the raven is cruel to its children? As is said: *Who provides food for the raven, when his young cry out to God and wander about without food?* (Job 38:41). Our sages of blessed memory said that when the raven has children, the male

Rabbi Yose said, "But is it not written concerning him: *a righteous person, he was blameless* (Genesis 6:9)? How could he cast aspersions Above?"

Rabbi Ḥiyya replied, "He spoke out of his great distress. For we have learned: How do we know that we do not judge a person on account of his distress? As is said: *Job speaks without knowledge, his words lack understanding* (Job 34:35). Even though he cast aspersions Above, his judgment is not as an intentional transgressor, but as someone *without knowledge*, on account of his distress.[108]

"The raven did not wish to go on its mission, because it was designated for a different mission—to sustain Elijah, as is said: *The ravens brought him bread and meat* (1 Kings 17:6). It did not wish to carry out its mission *until the drying of the waters from upon the earth* (Genesis 8:7)—which was by Elijah's command. As soon as Noah realized that he did not act appropriately, he sent out the dove."[109]

Rabbi Bo said, "He intimated two matters thereby. One, as is written: כיונה פותה אין לב (*ke-yonah fotah ein lev*), *like a foolish dove with no mind* (Hosea 7:11)—



says to the female that another bird came upon her; he despises them and abandons them." Similarly, according to BT *Ketubbot* 49b, Psalms 147:9—which praises God for giving the beasts their food (*to the raven's brood what they cry for*)—proves that the raven does not care for its young. See also BT *Eruvin* 22a; *Vayiqra Rabbah* 19:1.

108. **He spoke out of his great distress...** According to BT *Bava Batra* 16b, even though Job criticized and challenged the blessed Holy One, he is to be judged lightly—in accordance with Rava's dictum: "A person is not held responsible [for what he says] when in distress." See also *ZḤ* 75c–d (*MhN, Rut*). Hence, even though Noah cast aspersions Above, he is still considered righteous and blameless.

109. **The raven did not wish to go on its mission...** The raven is taken back because it was designated for a later mission in the days of Elijah.

According to the account in Genesis 8, Noah first sends out a raven and then a dove. No reason is given for the switch.

See *Bereshit Rabbah* 33:5: "*He sent out the raven... it went to* ושוב (*ve-shov*), *and fro*, [*until the drying of the waters from upon the earth*] (Genesis 8:7). Rabbi Yudan said in the name of Rabbi Yudah son of Rabbi Simon, 'It began משיבו תשובות (*meshivo tshuvot*), arguing with him. It said to him, "Of all the animals, beasts, and birds here, you send me!" He [Noah] replied, "What need does the world have of you? Neither for food, nor for sacrifice!"' Rabbi Berekhiah said in the name of Rabbi Abba son of Kahana, 'The blessed Holy One said to him [Noah], "Take it back, for the world will need it in the future." He asked him, "When?" He replied, '*Until* יבשת (*yevoshet*), *the drying, of the waters from upon the earth.* In the future a righteous man will rise and dry up the world and I will cause him to have need of it." As is written: *The ravens brought him bread and meat every morning and every evening* (1 Kings 17:6).'" See Rashi on Genesis 8:7.

On Elijah and the ravens, see 1 Kings 17:1–4: *Elijah the Tishbite, an inhabitant of Gilead, said to Ahab, "As YHVH lives, the God of Israel whom I serve, there will be no dew or rain except at my bidding." The word of YHVH came to him, "Leave this place... and go into hiding by the Wadi Cherith... You will drink from the wadi and I have commanded the ravens to feed you there."*

This interpretation may be alluding to the fact that the word יבשת (*yevoshet*), *the drying of*, in Genesis 8:7 is an anagram for התשבי (*ha-tishby*), "the Tishbite."

that is, because of my great distress, אין לבי עמי (*ein libbi immi*), my mind was not clear, ונפתה (*ve-niftah*), and was fooled. The other: Noah said, 'Among all the birds, there is none who can endure death without protest like the dove.' That is why Israel were compared to a dove. Noah said, 'Similarly it befits us to endure death without protest.' Therefore: *He sent out the dove* (Genesis 8:8)."[110]

Rabbi Yoḥanan son of Nuri said, "The blessed Holy One took Shem son of Noah, and set him aside as Priest Most High to minister to Him; He ensconced His *Shekhinah* with him and called him Melchizedek, Priest Most High, king of Salem. His brother Japheth used to learn Torah from him in his house of study, until Abraham arrived and learned Torah in Shem's house of study, whereupon the blessed Holy One became occupied with Abraham and all the others were forgotten. Abraham came and prayed before the blessed Holy One that He would permanently ensconce His *Shekhinah* in the house of Shem; and He consented, as is said: *You are a priest forever. By my word,* מלכי צדק (*malki tsedeq*), *my righteous king* (Psalms 110:4)."[111]



110. **Israel were compared to a dove...** See BT *Berakhot* 53b: "The Assembly of Israel are compared to a dove, as is written: *The wings of the dove are inlaid with silver, and her pinions with precious gold* (Psalms 68:14). Just as the dove is saved only by her wings, so Israel are saved only by the commandments." See also BT *Sanhedrin* 95a; *Gittin* 45a; *ZḤ* 48b; below, page 268.

See *Shir ha-Shirim Rabbah* on Song of Songs 1:15: *Your eyes are doves*: "Just as the dove extends her neck for slaughter, so do Israel, as is said: *For Your sake are we killed all day long* (Psalms 44:23)." See also *Tanḥuma, Tetsavveh* 5.

See also BT *Shabbat* 130a: "It has been taught: Rabbi Shim'on son of El'azar said, 'Every commandment for which Israel submitted themselves to death at the time of the royal decree, for example, idolatry and circumcision, is still possessed firmly by them. Whereas every commandment for which Israel did not submit themselves to death at the time of the royal decree, for example, *tefillin*, is still weak in their hands.' As Rabbi Yannai said, '*Tefillin* require a pure body, like Elisha the man of wings.... Why is he called "Elisha the man of wings"? Because the wicked State [Rome] once proclaimed a decree against Israel that whoever donned *tefillin* should have his brains pierced through; yet Elisha donned *tefillin* and went out into the streets. A quaestor saw him: he fled before him, and he gave chase. When he reached him, he [Elisha] removed them from his head and held them in his hand. He said to him, 'What is that in your hand?' He replied, 'The wings of a dove.' He stretched out his hand and the wings of a dove were found therein. Hence he is called "Elisha the man of wings." And why did he tell him "the wings of a dove"—rather than those of other birds? Because the Assembly of Israel is likened to a dove, as is said: *The wings of the dove are inlaid with silver, and her pinions with precious gold* (Psalms 68:14). Just as a dove is protected by its wings, so Israel is protected by the commandments.'" See also BT *Shabbat* 49a.

111. **The blessed Holy One took Shem son of Noah...** See BT *Nedarim* 32b: "Rabbi Zekhariah said on Rabbi Yishma'el's authority, 'The blessed Holy One intended to bring forth the priesthood from Shem, as is

Rabbi Yoḥanan said, "Surely Japheth was the eldest! Why then did Shem receive the priesthood? Because he was always engaged in Torah, forsaking the ways of the world. From whence did he have Torah? Well, Adam knew the Torah and he transmitted it to his son Seth; afterward it reached Enoch, until it reached Shem—who was constantly engaged in it."[112]

Rabbi Yose said to him, "If the Torah was in Shem's study house, why did the blessed Holy One need to instruct the sons of Noah about the seven commandments with which they were enjoined? For look, they were already written in the Torah before!"[113] [23a]

said: *he* [Melchizedek] *was a priest of God Most High* (Genesis 14:18). But since he gave precedence to the blessing of Abraham over the blessing of the Omnipresent, He brought it forth from Abraham, as is said: *He* [Melchizedek] *blessed him, saying, "Blessed be Abram of God Most High, creator of heaven and earth, and blessed be God Most High"* (ibid., 19–20). Abraham said to him, "Is the blessing of a servant to be given precedence over the blessing of his master?" Immediately it [the priesthood] was given to Abraham, as is said: *YHVH said to my lord, "Sit at my right hand, while I make your enemies your footstool"* (Psalms 110:1), after which is written: *YHVH has sworn, and will not relent, "You are a priest forever,* על דברתי מלכי צדק (*al divrati malki tsedeq*), *by My word My righteous king* (ibid., 4)—על דיבורו של מלכי צדק (*al dibburo shel malki tsedeq*)—because of the words of Melchizedek. As is written: *He was a priest of God Most High*—he was a priest, but not his seed.'" See also *Vayiqra Rabbah* 25:6.



Cf. M *Avot* 5:2: "There were ten generations from Noah until Abraham.... Abraham came and received the reward for all of them."

On Shem as Melchizedek, see also *Targum Yerushalmi*, Genesis 14:18; *Targum Yerushalmi* (frag.), Genesis 14:18; *Pirqei de-Rabbi Eli'ezer* 8.

It seems that *MhN* prefers the view that Abraham received what had always been the patrimony of the elect. According to this passage, he learned the Torah from Shem. Although rabbinic sources do mention Shem's house of study (e.g., *Bereshit Rabbah* 56:11, 63:6; BT *Makkot* 23b), traditionally Abraham is presented as having discovered God by himself. See Maimonides, *Mishneh Torah, Hilkhot Avodat Kokhavim* 1:3 (based on *Bereshit Rabbah* 61:1): "He had no teacher, nor was there anyone to inform him." See also *Bereshit Rabbah* 95:3; cf. *Bereshit Rabbah* 43:6, which asserts that Melchizedek taught Abraham various aspects of Torah. See also *Sefer ha-Yashar, Noaḥ*, 20.

On Psalms 110:4, cf. *Zohar* 1:87a.

112. **Why then did Shem receive the priesthood?...** Cf. *Bemidbar Rabbah* 4:8: "When Adam died, he transmitted them [his priestly garments] to Seth. Seth transmitted them to Methuselah. When Methuselah died, he transmitted them to Noah.... Noah died and transmitted them to Shem. But was Shem a firstborn? Surely Japheth was the firstborn!... Why then did he transmit them on to Shem? Because Noah foresaw that the line of the patriarchs would issue from him."

On Japheth as the elder son, see *Bereshit Rabbah* 37:7; Rashi on Genesis 10:21; Naḥmanides on Genesis 6:10. On Adam's knowing the Torah, see *Zohar* 1:199a; Moses de León, *Sefer ha-Rimmon*, 353. Cf. *Bereshit Rabbah* 24:5; *Qohelet Rabbah* on 3:11. On transmission from Adam to Seth to Enoch to Noah to Shem, cf. *Pirqei de-Rabbi Eli'ezer* 8; Judah Halevi, *Kuzari* 1:95.

113. **the seven commandments...** See BT *Sanhedrin* 56a: "Our Rabbis taught: The

Well, Rabbi Yitsḥak said, "When the Flood came upon the world and they entered the ark, owing to their great distress it was forgotten by Shem, until the blessed Holy One came and renewed for them those seven commandments."[114]

Rabbi Yose said, "Heaven forbid! The Torah was not forgotten by him. Rather, the blessed Holy One said, 'If I tell them that they must keep the entirety of My Torah, they will cast off every yoke, like the others who said *We have no desire to know Your ways* (Job 21:14). Rather, I will give them a few matters, and they will keep them, until the one who will keep all arrives—Abraham, as is said: *Because Abraham has listened to My voice and has kept My charge, My commandments, My statutes, and My teachings* (Genesis 26:5)—as soon as he learned Torah from Shem, he took upon himself to keep the Torah in its entirety. That is why the blessed Holy One selected seven items from the Torah in order that they might keep them."[115]

Our Rabbis have taught: How did the blessed Holy One answer Noah when he came out of the ark and saw the world destroyed, whereupon he began weeping for it, saying, "Master of the World! You are called Compassionate! You should have shown compassion for Your creatures!"? The blessed Holy one replied, "Foolish shepherd! Now you say this—but not when I spoke to you tenderly, as is written: *for you alone have I found righteous before Me in this generation* (Genesis 7:1); *As for Me, I am about to bring the Flood, waters upon the earth, to destroy all flesh* (ibid. 6:17); *Make yourself an ark of gopher wood* (ibid., 14)! I lingered with you and belabored you with all this, so that you might seek



sons of Noah were commanded seven commandments: Courts of justice, [not to commit] blaspheming the divine name, idolatry, sexual immorality, bloodshed, robbery, and eating a limb from a living animal." Traditionally, these basic laws of morality apply to all humankind, whereas Israel received 613 commandments. See *Zohar* 1:71b.

According to BT *Sanhedrin* 56b, these commandments are intimated in Genesis 2:16: *YHVH God commanded the human, saying, "Of every tree of the garden you may surely eat."* Thus, Shem had knowledge of these commandments through possession of the Torah and through tradition from the first human being. See also *Bereshit Rabbah* 16:6.

114. **it was forgotten by Shem . . .** On forgetting Torah, cf. BT *Temurah* 16a on laws forgotten during the period of mourning for Moses.

115. **the one who will keep all arrives . . .** The Torah was not forgotten by Noah, and the chain of transmission from Adam to Abraham remained intact. The seven commandments were thus not renewed for Noah, but commanded to the postdiluvians on account of their weakness—they could not handle all 613!

On Abraham's observing the entirety of Torah (even before it was given at Mount Sinai), see *Bereshit Rabbah* 64:4, 95:3; BT *Yoma* 28b, *Qiddushin* 92a; Rashi and Naḥmanides on Genesis 26:5; *Zohar* 3:13b. On Job 21:14 and its connection with the generation of the Flood, see BT *Sanhedrin* 108a; *Zohar* 1:62a; *ZḤ* 21d (*MhN*), page 240.

compassion for the world. But as soon as you heard that you would be saved in the ark, the evil of the world did not touch your heart; you built the ark and saved yourself! Now that the world has been destroyed, you open your mouth—muttering questions and pleas before Me!" As soon as Noah realized this, he presented sacrifices and offerings, as is written: [*Noah built an altar to YHVH*], *and took of every pure animal and of every pure bird, and offered ascent-offerings on the altar* (ibid. 8:20).[116]

Rabbi Yoḥanan said, "Come and see the difference between Noah and the righteous heroes that arose for Israel afterward! Noah did not shield his generation—and did not pray for them like Abraham. For as soon as the blessed Holy One said to Abraham, '*The outcry of Sodom and Gomorrah is so great*' (ibid. 18:20), immediately: *Abraham came forward and said* (ibid., 23). He countered the blessed Holy One with more and more words until he implored that should just ten righteous people be found there, He would grant atonement to the entire generation for their sake. Abraham thought that there were [ten] in the city, counting Lot and his wife, his daughters and sons-in-law; that is why he beseeched no further.[117]



"Moses arrived and shielded the entire generation. As soon as the blessed Holy One said, 'Moses, Israel has sinned, *quickly they have turned from the way*' (Exodus 32:8), what is written of him? ויחל משה (*Va-yeḥal Moshe*), *Moses implored* (ibid., 11). What is meant by *implored*? This teaches that he prayed until he was seized by חלחלה (*ḥalḥalah*), trembling."[118]

116. **Foolish shepherd! Now you say this...** On Noah's failure to intercede, see *Devarim Rabbah* 11:3 (see below, note 118); *Zohar* 1:67b, 68a, 106a; 3:14b–15a.

Noah is called "foolish shepherd," in contrast to Moses, the faithful shepherd.

On Moses' intercession, see below, note 118. On the righteous seeking compassion for the world and for Israel, see BT *Berakhot* 32a; *Shemot Rabbah* 42:9; *Devarim Rabbah* 3:15; *Zohar* 3:14b–15a. On Noah's offering a sacrifice after the flood, cf. *Zohar* 1:69b–70a; *ZḤ* 22d (*MhN*), page 254.

A nearly identical passage (extending to the passage discussing Gideon son of Joash) is found under the title *Sitrei Torah* in *Zohar* 1:254b (*hashmatot*).

117. **Noah did not shield his generation ...like Abraham...** When God informed Abraham of His intention to destroy Sodom and Gomorrah, Abraham pleaded (and bargained at length) with God that the cities be spared. See Genesis 18:17–33. In contrast, Noah's silence is deafening. See *Zohar* 1:106a. See also *Zohar* 1:104b (*MhN*).

On the ten righteous people, see *Bereshit Rabbah* 49:13: "*He said, 'Let not my Lord be angry... what if ten should be found there?'* (Genesis 18:32). Why ten? So that there might be an assembly [of righteous men to pray] on behalf of all of them. Alternatively: Why ten? Because at the generation of the Flood eight [righteous people] remained, but the world was not given a reprieve for their sake. Alternatively: Why ten? Because he thought that there were ten there: Lot, his wife, his four daughters and four sons-in-law." See also Rashi on Genesis 18:32; Naḥmanides on Genesis 18:24; *Zohar* 1:67b.

118. **Moses arrived and shielded the entire generation...** Following the sin of the Golden Calf, God resolves to annihilate the

Our Rabbis say, "Moses did not leave the blessed Holy One until he pledged his life for them—from this world and from the world to come—as is written: *And now if only You would forgive their sin! If not, erase me from Your book that You have written* (ibid. 32:32)."[119]

Rabbi Yose said, "This is derived from here: *He said that He would annihilate them—had not Moses, His chosen one, stood in the breach before Him* (Psalms 106:23)."[120]

So all the righteous shielded their generations and did not allow the attribute of Judgment to have dominion over them. And Noah? The blessed Holy One lingered with him, speaking many words to him, that perhaps he might seek compassion for them. But he just built the ark—and the whole world was destroyed![121]

Children of Israel. Moses intercedes and the nation is spared. See Exodus 32:10–14.

See BT *Berakhot* 32a: "*Va-yeḥal Moshe, Moses implored,* YHVH (Exodus 32:11)—Rabbi El'azar said, 'This teaches that Moses stood in prayer before the blessed Holy One until החלהו (*heḥelahu*), he wearied Him.' . . . Rava said in the name of Rabbi Yitsḥak, 'This teaches that he caused the Attribute of Compassion to החלה (*heḥelah*), rest, upon them.' . . . Rabbi Eli'ezer the Great says, 'This teaches that Moses stood in prayer before the blessed Holy One until he was seized by אחילו (*aḥilu*).' What is *aḥilu*? Rabbi El'azar said, 'A fire in the bones.' What is a fire in the bones? Abbaye said, 'A kind of fever.'"

On the contrast between Noah and Moses, see *Devarim Rabbah* 11:3: "Noah said to Moses: 'I am greater than you because I was delivered from the generation of the Flood.' Moses replied, 'I am far superior to you; you saved yourself, but you had no strength to deliver your generation; but I saved both myself and my generation when they were condemned to destruction at the time of the [Golden] Calf.' How do we know? As is said: *YHVH relented of the evil He planned to bring upon His people* (Exodus 32:14). To what can the matter be compared? To two ships in the ocean with two captains. One saved himself but not his ship, while the other saved both himself and his ship. Who was praised? Surely the one who saved both himself and his ship. Similarly, Noah saved himself only, whereas Moses saved himself and his generation." See also *Zohar* 1:67b, 106a; 3:14b–15a.

119. **Moses did not leave the blessed Holy One...** See BT *Berakhot* 32a: "*Now therefore leave Me alone that My anger may turn against them, and I will destroy them, and I will make of you a great nation* (Exodus 32:10). Rabbi Abbahu said, 'Were it not explicitly written, it would be impossible to say such a thing: this teaches that Moses took hold of the blessed Holy One—like a man who seizes his fellow by his garment—and said before Him, "Master of the Universe, I will not let You go until You will forgive and absolve them."' . . . Shemu'el said, '. . . He offered to die for them, as is written: *If not, erase me from Your book* [i.e., the Book of Life].'" See also Rashi on Exodus 32:32; *Zohar* 1:67b, 106a; 3:14b; *ZḤ* 15a (*MhN*).

120. ***had not Moses . . . stood in the breach...*** See *Targum Yonatan*, ad loc.; *Zohar* 1:180a; *ZḤ* 12d (*MhN*).

121. **So all the righteous shielded their generations...** Noah's failure to intercede becomes clear when he is compared with Abraham and Moses.

According to *Zohar* 3:15a, he is implicated in the destruction—and that is why Isaiah calls the Flood "the waters of Noah" (Isaiah 54:9).

Cf. *Bereshit Rabbah* 33:3: "Rabbi Shemu'el son of Naḥman said, 'Woe to the wicked,

Rabbi Eli'ezer and Rabbi Yehoshu'a were sitting by the outskirts of Tiberias. Rabbi Yehoshu'a said, "Rabbi, what was Noah thinking by not beseeching compassion for his generation?"[122]

He replied, "He didn't think to himself that even he would be saved! This can be compared to one who finds a cluster of unripe grapes among sour grapes—were they among ripe grapes, they wouldn't be worth anything. As implied by what is written: *for you alone have I found righteous before Me in this generation* (Genesis 7:1). He should have said *righteous before Me*; what is the significance of *in this generation*? Namely, relative to the generation! That is why he did not beseech compassion. He said to himself, 'Would that I could beseech compassion for myself and be saved; and all the more so for [23b] others!'"[123]

Afterward, Rabbi Eli'ezer said, "Nevertheless, he ought to have implored compassion for the world before the blessed Holy One, for whoever speaks kindly of His children pleases Him. How do we know? From Gideon son of Joash, who was neither a righteous person nor the son of a righteous person; and yet because he spoke well of Israel, what is written about him? *YHVH said to him, 'Go with this strength of yours and deliver Israel from the Midianites'* (Judges 6:14). What is the meaning of *this strength of yours*? This kindness you spoke



who turn the divine attribute of Compassion into the attribute of Judgment.... Happy are the righteous, who turn the divine attribute of Judgment into the attribute of Compassion.'"

122. **by the outskirts of Tiberias ...** "Outskirts" renders פלכי (*pilkhei*). In the Talmud, its singular form פלך (*pelekh*) means "district, region," as opposed to the city. According to Scholem, however, *pilkhei* is a corruption of פילי (*pilei*), gates, in which case the two rabbis are sitting by the gates of Tiberias (cf. *Bereshit Rabbah* 96:5; *Tanḥuma, Shofetim* 10; *Zohar* 1:57b, 217a). See BT *Makkot* 7a, where gates and the word *pelekh* are associated.

See Scholem, "Parashah Ḥadashah," 431 (Addendum 1 in this volume); Meroz, "Va-Ani Lo Hayiti Sham?," 165 (Addendum 3 in this volume).

123. **relative to the generation ...** Although termed "righteous," Noah's righteousness was only relative to the corrupt generation in which he lived.

See *Bereshit Rabbah* 30:9: "[*Noah was a righteous man, blameless*] *in his generations* (Genesis 6:9). Rabbi Yehudah and Rabbi Neḥemiah. Rabbi Yehudah said, 'In his generations he was righteous, but if he had lived in the generations of Moses or Samuel, he would not have been righteous.... This can be compared to a person who had a wine cellar. He opened one barrel and found it vinegar; [he opened] a second—the same; the third, however, he found turning sour. They said to him, "It is turning." He replied, "Is there any better here?" They said, "No." Similarly, *in his generations* he was a righteous man....' Rabbi Neḥemiah said, 'If he was righteous *in his generations* [despite the corrupt environment], all the more so if he had lived in the generations of Moses or Samuel. He might be compared to a tightly closed phial of perfume lying in a graveyard, which nevertheless gave forth a fragrant odor; how much more, then, if it were outside the graveyard!'"

See also BT *Sanhedrin* 108a; *Tanḥuma, Noaḥ* 5; *Zohar* 1:60a (*Tos*), 67a, 68a.

about My children. May you have great strength to deliver them from the hands of the Midianites!"[124]

Rabbi Eli'ezer said further, "Even if one is the most righteous person in the entire world, should one speak evil or slanderously of Israel before the blessed Holy One, his punishment is most severe of all. For we have not found in any generation a more noble and righteous person than Elijah, and yet because he spoke slanderously of Israel, as is written: *for the Children of Israel have forsaken Your covenant, torn down Your altars and have put Your prophets to the sword* (1 Kings 19:14), he was greatly befouled before Him at that time.[125]

"Come and see what is written about him: *He found beside his head a cake baked on hot coals* (ibid., 6). What is the significance of *hot coals*? The blessed Holy One said, 'Whosoever speaks slanderously of My children deserves to eat in this manner!'"[126]

124. **From Gideon son of Joash...** See *Tanḥuma, Shofetim* 4, where Gideon is presented as advocating the merits of Israel: "In his days Israel were in distress. The blessed Holy One sought someone who could advocate their favor; but He could not find anyone, because the generation was poor in commandments and deeds. As soon as favor was found with Gideon—who advocated their favor—immediately the angel was revealed to him, as is said: *An angel of YHVH came and said to him, 'Go with this strength of yours'* (based on Judges 6:11, 14)—with the strength of the favor you taught concerning My children.'"

Rabbi Eli'ezer slightly misquotes the verse from Judges.

125. **because he spoke slanderously...** Numerous rabbinic texts criticize Elijah's zeal and his uncompromising accusations against Israel. See *Mekhilta, Pisḥa* 1; *Shir ha-Shirim Rabbah* on Song of Songs 1:6 (see next note); *Seder Eliyyahu Zuta* 8 (see below, note 128); see also *Zohar* 1:93a, 209b. Cf. *Pirqei de-Rabbi Eli'ezer* 29.

126. **What is the significance of *hot coals*?...** Rabbi Eli'ezer slightly misquotes the verse.

Cf. *Shir ha-Shirim Rabbah* on 1:6: "Because [Isaiah] said: *I dwell among a people of unclean lips* (Isaiah 6:5), the blessed Holy One said to him, 'Isaiah, of yourself you are free to say *Because I am a man of unclean lips* (ibid.)—this can pass; but may you say *I dwell among a people of unclean lips*?' Come and see what is written there: *Then one of the seraphim flew to me, with* רצפה (*ritspah*), *a glowing coal, in his hand* (ibid., 6). Rabbi Shemu'el said, 'The word *ritspah* means רוץ פה (*rots peh*), break the mouth—break the mouth of whoever spoke slanderously of My children.' Similarly it is written of Elijah, as is said: *He said, 'I have been very zealous for YHVH, the God of Hosts; for the children of Israel have forsaken Your covenant'* (I Kings 19:14). The blessed Holy One said to him, 'Is it My covenant or your covenant?' [Elijah then said], *They have torn down Your altars* (ibid.). He said to him, 'Are they My altars or your altars?' [Elijah then said], *And have put Your prophets to the sword* (ibid.). He said to him, 'They are My prophets; what concern is it of yours?'... Come and see what is written there: *He looked about and there beside his head was a cake baked on* רצפים (*retsafim*), *hot coals* (ibid., 6). What is meant by *retsafim*? Rabbi Shemu'el son of Naḥman said, 'רוץ פה (*rots peh*), break the mouth—break the mouths of all who spoke slanderously of My children.'... Rabbi Abbahu and Resh Lakish were once on the point of entering the city of Caesarea. Rabbi Abbahu said to Resh Lakish,

Rabbi Eli'ezer said, "What is the meaning of the verse [*He arose and ate and drank,*] *and with the strength from that meal, he walked forty days and forty nights until the Mountain of God at Horeb* (ibid., 8)? Could he really walk that far from the strength gained by eating a cake baked on hot coals?"

Well, Rabbi Eli'ezer said, "The blessed Holy One cast a deep slumber upon Elijah, and He showed him the case of Moses—who sat in His presence forty days and forty nights—and how while he was there, Israel worshipped the calf. Even though he went forty days and forty nights without eating bread or drinking water, he did not budge until the blessed Holy One absolved them![127]

"He said to Elijah, 'This is what you should have done! What's more, you should have realized that they are My children—My beloved children who accepted My Torah at Mount Horeb.' This is the meaning of the verse *and with the strength from that meal he walked forty days and forty nights*—he saw the case of Moses, who lingered with Him forty days and forty nights; and the case of Israel, who accepted the Torah at Mount Horeb—this is the meaning of what is written: *until the Mountain of God at Horeb.*"[128]



Rabbi Yitsḥak said, "Elijah didn't depart from there until he swore before the blessed Holy One that he would always advocate the merits of Israel; whenever someone performs a meritorious act, he is the first to say before the blessed

'Why should we go into a city of cursing and blaspheming?' Resh Lakish dismounted from his ass and scraped up some sand and put it in his [Rabbi Abbahu's] mouth. He said to him, 'Why do you do this?' He replied, 'The blessed Holy One is not pleased with one who slanders Israel.'"

127. **The blessed Holy One cast a deep slumber . . .** The rare noun דורמיטא (*dormita*) appears as a variant reading in *Bereshit Rabbah* 17:5 as one type of תרדמה (*tardemah*), "deep sleep." See the apparatus in Theodor's edition; *Yedei Moshe* and *Ḥiddushei ha-Radal*, ad loc.; *Arukh ha-Shalem*, s.v. *marmata*; *Zohar* 1:207b; 3:142b (*IR*). Cf. Latin *dormio*, "to sleep"; *dormito*, "to be sleepy."

On Moses' going forty days and nights without food or water, see Exodus 24:18; 34:28. On his imploring God, see above, notes 118–19.

128. **This is what you should have done! . . .** See *Seder Eliyyahu Zuta* 8: "The blessed Holy One asked Elijah, '*Why are you here, Elijah?*' (1 Kings 19:9). He should have responded before Him, saying, 'Master of the World! They are Your children, the children of those who have been tested by You, the children of Abraham, Isaac, and Jacob, who have done Your will in the world.' But he did not do this. Instead he said before Him, '*I have been very zealous for YHVH, the God of hosts,* [*for the Children of Israel have forsaken Your covenant, torn down Your altars and have put Your prophets to the sword; and I alone am left*] (1 Kings 19:10).' The blessed Holy One began to utter words of consolation [to placate Elijah].... For three hours, the blessed Holy One waited for Elijah [to entreat mercy for Israel]. But Elijah persisted in the words he had uttered previously: *I have been very zealous for YHVH the God of hosts* (1 Kings 19:14). At that moment the holy spirit said to Elijah, '*Go, return on the way to the wilderness of Damascus . . . and anoint Jehu the son of Nimshi as king of Israel, and anoint Elisha son of Shaphat of Abel-mehola* [*to succeed you as prophet*] (1 Kings 19:15–16). For what you have in mind for Me to do, I cannot do!'"

Holy One, 'So and so just did such and such!' He does not budge until that person's merit is recorded, as is written: *and it was written in a book of remembrance in His presence* (Malachi 3:16)."[129]

Rabbi Yehudah son of Pazzi said, "What was Noah's punishment? That he emerged from the ark lame. He lay down and was disgraced; his son shamed him and did what he did!"[130]

Rabbi El'azar said, "Come and see how assiduously a person must walk the straight path! Come and see: Because Jacob seized the blessings from Esau dishonestly, know that permission has not been granted to any nation in the world to subjugate Israel, aside from the nation of Esau."[131]

Rabbi Pinḥas opened [the verses] as referring to the Assembly of Israel in relation to the blessed Holy One: *He sent out the raven* (Genesis 8:7).[132]

129. **he would always advocate the merits of Israel...** See *Vayiqra Rabbah* 34:8: "Rabbi Kohen and Rabbi Yehoshu'a son of Rabbi Simon said in the name of Rabbi Levi, 'In former times, if a person would perform a good deed, the prophet used to record it. Nowadays, if a person performs a good deed who records it? Elijah and the King Messiah—the blessed Holy One signing beside them—as is written: *Then those who revere YHVH spoke one with another; YHVH listened and heard, and a book of remembrance was written in His presence...* (Malachi 3:16).'" See also BT *Qiddushin* 70a; *Rut Rabbah* 5:6; *Seder Olam Rabbah* 17. See also *Pirqei de-Rabbi Eli'ezer* 15 and Luria, ad loc.

The Masoretic text reads: ויכתב ספר זכרון (*va-yikkatev sefer zikkaron*), *and a book of remembrance was written*, whereas Rabbi Yitsḥak cites: ויכתב בספר זכרון (*va-yikkatev be-sefer zikkaron*), *and it was written in a book of remembrance.* See *Zohar* 1:200b, 243a; Minḥat Shai on the verse.

130. **What was Noah's punishment?...** That is, for not interceding.

On Noah's becoming lame, see *Tanḥuma, Noaḥ* 9: "Rabbi Yoḥanan said in the name of Rabbi Eli'ezer son of Rabbi Yose the Galilean, 'Once, Noah delayed feeding the lion, so the lion bit him; and he came out limping, as is said: אך (*Akh*), *Only, Noah remained* (Genesis 7:23)—*akh*, for he was not intact.'" The word *akh* implies a limitation or diminution. See also *Bereshit Rabbah* 30:6; *Zohar* 1:69a.

That Noah's son Ham is said to have done "what he did" implies that it was unspeakably horrific. Presumably this alludes to something like what Rabbi Yehudah had disclosed earlier: Noah's castration. Cf. above, page 254 and note 102.

131. **aside from the nation of Esau** The later subjugation of Israel by Esau's descendants is due to Jacob's deceptions (as told in Genesis 27 and 25:27–34).

Esau's descendants usually signify Rome in rabbinic literature; in medieval literature, Christendom. On the subjugation of Israel at the hand of Esau in *MhN*, see *ZḤ* 8a, 14a–b, 27c; Scholem, "Parashah Ḥadashah," 433, 443 (Addendum 1 in this volume).

This passage seems to have been dislocated from its original location, as it is not connected with the preceding or following homilies. The next page (in the printed edition) does discuss this theme, however. See *ZḤ* 23d (*MhN*), page 272.

132. **the Assembly of Israel in relation to the blessed Holy One...** Eventually Rabbi Pinḥas will interpret the verse from Genesis describing the dove's flight from the ark as encoding the historical relationship between

As Rabbi Pinḥas said: "It is written: *David said* [*to all the courtiers who were with him in Jerusalem*], *'Rise and let us flee—or none of us will escape from Absalom'* (2 Samuel 15:14). Even though he fled, what is written about him? *A psalm of David, when he fled from his son Absalom* (Psalms 3:1). Even though he was fleeing and was banished from his kingdom, he did not refrain from uttering song before the blessed Holy One and pleading before Him. *He sent out the raven*—this is David, who called out unceasingly like the raven.[133]

"Alternatively, *the raven*—for he hailed from Judah—who is called עורב (*orev*), raven, as is said: *I myself* אערבנו (*e'ervennu*), *will be his pledge* (Genesis 43:9). עורב (*Orev*), Raven—spelled ערב (*orev*), lacking the *vav*."[134]

Rabbi Pinḥas said, "Why was he called raven? Because he used to roam about the mountains like a raven, corresponding with what he said to Saul: *as he would chase a partridge in the mountains* (1 Samuel 26:20). He said to him, 'You have made me as one who calls out in the mountains.' Here is written קורא (*qore*), *a partridge*, and there is written *to the raven's young who* יקראו (*yiqra'u*),
266 *call out* (Psalms 147:9)."[135] [23c]

Rabbi Pinḥas also said, "Come and see the difference between the kings of Judah and the kings of Israel! The blessed Holy One sent David out and banished him from his kingdom, and immediately he returned in *teshuvah* before the blessed Holy One. Now, do not be surprised by this, for even Manasseh king of Judah, who was wicked, immediately returned in *teshuvah* before the blessed Holy One; he seized the art of his ancestors, and returned to his kingdom.[136]

the people of Israel and God. He begins, however, with some homilies about King David (the raven), focusing on *teshuvah*, the theme of his major homily. The full verse reads: *He sent out the raven, and it went forth to and fro, until the waters had dried up from the earth.*

133. ***He sent out the raven*—this is David...** According to Rabbi Pinḥas, the raven sent out by Noah signifies David who was banished from his kingdom. Just as the raven calls out without ceasing, David continued uttering song despite fleeing. See BT *Berakhot* 7b; *Zohar* 1:151b.

134. ***the raven*—for he hailed from Judah...** The spelling of the word הערב (*haorev*), *the raven*, in the Genesis narrative also points to the raven's identification as David. The word's deficient spelling, lacking the *vav*, alludes to David's ancestor Judah, who ערב (*arav*), pledged, to his father, Jacob, that he would return Benjamin safely or else be culpable forever. See also Genesis 44:32.

135. **as one who calls out in the mountains...** קורא (*Qore*), "partridge," is a homonym for "one who calls out." The verb form is applied to David in 1 Samuel 26:14. Although according to verse 20, David likens himself to a partridge, the verse from Psalms associates its homonym with the raven.

136. **even Manasseh king of Judah... returned in *teshuvah*...** According to 2 Kings 21:1–16, Manasseh is the paragon of unfaithfulness to God. He built pagan shrines and altars and placed a sculpture of Asherah in the Temple. The account of his reign in 2 Chronicles 33 adds an episode on his repentance following his exile to Babylon. See verses 12–13: *In his distress, he entreated* YHVH *his God and humbled himself greatly before*

"This is what Scripture comes to teach: *He sent out the raven* (Genesis 8:7)—David, who would call out ceaselessly like the raven. The blessed Holy One sent him out from his kingdom, and took him out of his home. What is written about him? *It went forth* יצוא ושוב (yatso va-shov), *going out and returning* (ibid.). As is written: *David was going up the Slope of Olives, [going up weeping,] his head covered* (2 Samuel 15:30)—he was יוצא ושב (yotse ve-shav), going out and returning, in *teshuvah*, confessing his sins and seeking compassion for them; he knew that it was his sins that caused him to be sent from his kingdom and banished."[137]

"Every single thing brought about by sin in his kingdom or in Israel, he attributed to himself, and he knew that he was the cause. *Until the drying of the waters* (Genesis 8:7)—when he was informed that it was not on his account, but rather *on account of Saul and on account of the house of bloodguilt [because he put the Gibeonites to death]* (2 Samuel 21:1).[138]

"Come and see what is written: *There was a famine in the days of David three years, year after year, and David sought out the presence of YHVH* (ibid.)—because he thought that he was the cause! The blessed Holy One said to him, 'This is not on your account, but on Saul's.' *Until the drying of the waters* (Genesis 8:7)—he attributed everything to himself and immediately returned in *teshuvah*. But then he didn't need to return in *teshuvah* because the matter did not arise because of him. This is the meaning of the verse *He went forth, going out and*



*the God of his fathers. He prayed to Him; and He granted his prayer, heard his plea, and returned him to Jerusalem to his kingdom. Then Manasseh knew that YHVH alone was God.* On Manasseh's repentance, see BT *Sanhedrin* 102b–103a; *Pirqei de-Rabbi Eli'ezer* 43; *Zohar* 1:39a (*Heikh*); *ZḤ* 19d (*MhN*).

On the expression "art of his ancestors," see *Mekhilta, Beshallaḥ* 2; BT *Arakhin* 16b; Rashi and Naḥmanides on Exodus 14:10. On David's repentance (for the sin of killing Uriah, Bathsheba's husband) see next paragraph. See also 2 Samuel 12:13.

Jeroboam was the first king of the northern kingdom of Israel. On the contrast between his failure to repent and David's repentance, see BT *Sanhedrin* 102a: "*After this thing* [or: *word*], *Jeroboam did not turn back from his evil way* (1 Kings 13:33). What is meant by *after*? [That is, after what?] Rabbi Abba said, 'After the blessed Holy One had seized Jeroboam by his garment and urged him, "Repent! Then Me, you, and the son of Jesse [i.e., David] will stroll in the Garden of Eden." He replied, "And who shall be at the head?" [The blessed Holy One replied,] "The son of Jesse shall be at the head." [He replied,] "If so, I do not desire it."'"

137. ***It went forth* יצוא ושוב (yatso va-shov), *going out and returning*...** David is the raven. In its simple sense, the phrase describing the raven's flight (yatso ve-shov) means "to and fro." Here, it alludes to David's departure from Jerusalem—as he fled Absalom—while acknowledging his sin.

On 2 Samuel 15:30, see *Bemidbar Rabbah* 3:2; *Zohar* 2:107b.

138. **he attributed to himself...** See BT *Yevamot* 78b; *Bemidbar Rabbah* 8:4. See next note.

*returning as far as the drying of the waters*—because then the matter was not dependent on him."[139]

Rabbi Pinḥas said, "The blessed Holy One wished to test Israel, so He sent them to Babylon, as is said: *He sent out the dove from himself* (ibid., 8)—the Assembly of Israel. Look at what is written about her: *But the dove found no resting place for the sole of her foot* (ibid., 9)—because the king of Babylon burdened her yoke with famine and thirst, and by slaying countless righteous saints! And because of the weight of her yoke, ותשב (*va-tashov*), *she returned, to him into the ark* (ibid.)—she returned בתשובה (*bi-tshuvah*), in *teshuvah*, and He received her.[140]

"The Assembly of Israel sinned as at first, and He exiled her once again, as is said: *once again he sent out the dove from the ark* (ibid., 10)—to another exile, [the exile] of Greece. As Rabbi Yehudah said: 'The exile of Greece darkened the faces of Israel like the bottom of the pot!'[141]

"Owing to her great pain and distress, what is written of her? *The dove came back to him toward* ערב (*erev*), *evening* (ibid., 11). What is the significance of



139. ***Until the drying of the waters . . .*** Again, the raven's flight alludes to David's repentance. He sought to repent even for the drying of the waters, which were not on his account. As the verse from Samuel implies, David thought that he was the cause of the famine, and hence he sought out God. In the continuation of the verse, God tells David the true cause of the famine: *on account of Saul and on account of the house of bloodguilt, because he put the Gibeonites to death.* According to BT *Yevamot* 78b and *Bemidbar Rabbah* 8:4, the reason for the famine is *on account of Saul*, namely, that he did not receive a proper burial; *and on account of the house of bloodguilt*, interpreted as referring to Saul's massacre of the priests of Nob, as recounted in 1 Samuel 22.

140. **The blessed Holy One wished to test Israel...** On the dove symbolizing the Assembly of Israel, see above, *ZḤ* 22d (*MhN*), page 257. See *ZḤ* 48a.

According to various biblical reckonings, the Babylonian exile lasted seventy years (Jeremiah 25:12; 29:10; Zechariah 1:12; Daniel 9:2). It began in 597 B.C.E. with the appointment of a puppet king and the deportation of the upper echelons of society (2 Kings 24:10–14).

See BT *Sanhedrin* 97b: "Rav said, 'All the predestined dates [for redemption] have passed, and the matter [now] depends solely on repentance and good deeds.'... Rabbi Eli'ezer says, 'If Israel perform *teshuvah*, they will be redeemed; if not, they will not be redeemed.' Rabbi Yehoshu'a said to him, 'If they do not perform *teshuvah*, will they not be redeemed?! Rather, the blessed Holy One will set up a king over them, whose decrees shall be as cruel as Haman's, whereby Israel shall perform *teshuvah*, and thus bring them back to the good [path].'" Cf. *Bereshit Rabbah* 33:6.

141. **The exile of Greece...** Though not technically an exile—as the people remained in their land—the harsh decrees promulgated by the Seleucids in the second century B.C.E. are reckoned by the *Zohar* as another exile. It came to an end with the Hasmonean victory and rededication of the Temple.

On the Greek exile as darkening the faces of Israel, see *Bereshit Rabbah* 2:4; *Pirqei de-Rabbi Eli'ezer* 28. See also *ZḤ* 6a (*MhN*).

*toward evening*? Because the time of relief did not illuminate them as it had at first. The righteous were slain, the day darkened, and the sun אעריב (*a'ariv*), grew dim, for them—and they could not endure because of the great duress that was upon them, as is said: *Woe to us, for the day is fading, shadows of evening spread!* (Jeremiah 6:4). *For the day is fading*—the righteous who illuminate the world like the sun; *shadows of evening spread*—for they remained *like gleanings of the vintage* (Micah 7:1). This is the significance of *toward evening*; and not as when the righteous illuminate them like the sun.[142]

"*Look, a plucked olive leaf was in her bill* (Genesis 8:11). Had the blessed Holy One not aroused the spirit of the priests who kindled lamps with olive oil, then the remnant of Judah would have disappeared from the world. Each time, she returned in *teshuvah* and was received."[143]

Rabbi Pinḥas said, "Aside from the fourth exile, for she has not yet returned. All depends on *teshuvah*!"[144]

Rabbi Pinḥas also said, "You cannot find a single instance where the blessed Holy One did not suspend the sentence of the Assembly of Israel by seven sabbaticals and seven jubilees, perchance she return in *teshuvah*, as is written: *He waited still another seven days* (ibid., 12)—aside from the former.[145]



142. **What is the significance of *toward evening*?...** Throughout the Greek "exile," the people suffered greatly; they were on the verge of total darkness and annihilation. The righteous dwindled and were of insufficient degree to illuminate the people.

Cf. BT *Ta'anit* 29a: "On the seventh [of Av], the heathens [the Babylonians] entered the Temple, ate there, and desecrated it throughout the seventh and eighth. Toward dusk on the ninth, they set fire to it, and it continued burning all that day, as is said: *Woe to us, for the day is fading—shadows of evening spread!*"

On Jeremiah 6:4, see Scholem, "Parashah Ḥadashah," 443 (Addendum 1 in this volume); cf. *Zohar* 1:132b, 230a; 2:21b (*MhN*); 3:75a, 270a; Moses de León, *Sefer ha-Rimmon*, 67.

See Micah 7:1: *Woe is me! I am become like leavings of summer harvest, like gleanings of the vintage. There is not a cluster to eat, not a ripe fig I could desire.* The following verse reads: *The pious are vanished from the land, none upright are left among men....*

Cf. *ZḤ* 21b.

143. **the priests who kindled lamps with olive oil...** Namely, the Hasmoneans, who rededicated the Temple following their defeat of the Greeks, as commemorated in the Festival of Hanukkah. See BT *Shabbat* 21b.

144. **Aside from the fourth exile . . .** Namely, the ongoing exile of Edom (Rome) beginning in 70 CE. The four exiles are: Egypt, Babylon, Greece and Rome, or alternatively: Babylon, Persia, Greece and Rome. See *ZḤ* 8a (*MhN*). See also *ZḤ* 48a.

On *teshuvah* as a prerequisite for redemption, see JT *Ta'anit* 1:1, 63d; BT *Sanhedrin* 97b; *Pirqei de-Rabbi Eli'ezer* 43; *Tanḥuma, Beḥuqqotai* 3; *Zohar* 1:117b; 2:188b; *ZḤ* 8a (*MhN*).

145. **suspend the sentence...by seven sabbaticals and seven jubilees...** In the Genesis narrative (8:8–12), Noah sends forth the dove three times, the latter two after waiting a period of seven days. According to Rabbi Pinḥas, these two intervals of seven signify seven jubilees and seven sabbaticals, i.e., the three hundred and ninety-nine years

"*He sent out the dove* (ibid.)—in the exile of Edom; *but she returned to him again no more* (ibid.)—for until today, she has not returned in *teshuvah*, nor aroused her spirit."[146]

As Rabbi Pinḥas said: "Had she returned in *teshuvah*, she would have remained in exile for only one day!"[147]

Rabbi Eli'ezer said, "In all the exiles suffered by the Assembly of Israel, the blessed Holy One established for her a time and termination; she always aroused to *teshuvah*. The last exile, however, has no termination or fixed time—all depends on *teshuvah*! [23d] As is said: *You shall return to YHVH your God and heed His voice* (Deuteronomy 30:2); and it is written: *If your banished lie at the ends of heaven, from there YHVH your God will gather you in, and from there He will take you* (ibid., 4)."[148]

Rabbi Akiva said to him, "If so, how can it be that they will all arouse to *teshuvah* as one? How can they who are at the end of heaven and they who are at the end of the earth join in unison to perform *teshuvah*?"[149]



that God waited before executing judgment upon Israel. According to tradition, the First Temple stood for four hundred and ten years, and the Second Temple for four hundred and twenty years. Cf. *Bereshit Rabbah* 33:6; Rashi on Genesis 8:8.

146. **the exile of Edom...** In rabbinic literature, Edom signifies Rome; in medieval times, Edom often signifies Christendom. The Roman exile began in 70 CE and by the *Zohar*'s day, had extended for more than one thousand years.

147. **for only one day** Had Israel performed *teshuvah*, the exile of Edom would have lasted one thousand years, comprising one divine day. See *Bereshit Rabbah* 8:2: "A day of the blessed Holy One is a thousand years, as is said: *For a thousand years in Your eyes are like yesterday gone* (Psalms 90:4)."

See *Eikhah Rabbah* 1:40: "*When YHVH afflicted me on the day of His fierce anger* (Lamentations 1:12). Rabbi Aḥa said, 'One day did the anger of the blessed Holy One burn fiercely, and had Israel performed *teshuvah* they would have cooled it.'" See also *Tanḥuma* (Buber), *Toledot* 4; *Pirqei de-Rabbi Eli'ezer* 28; *Zohar* 1:116b; 2:17a (*MhN*), 227b; 3:270a; *ZḤ* 28c (*MhN*); cf. *Bereshit Rabbah* 63:13; 68:13.

148. **The last exile, however, has no termination or fixed time...** Unlike the first three exiles—whose durations were preordained—the duration of the last exile (the Roman exile) has not been revealed. As the order of the verses in Deuteronomy makes clear, return to the land is dependent on returning (*teshuvah*) to God.

According to tradition, the Egyptian exile lasted 430 years (or 210, according to the Rabbis); the Babylonian exile, 70 years; and the Greek "exile"—although there is no precise traditional figure for its duration (though Daniel 8:14 does mention an enigmatic figure of 2300 days)—came to an end with the establishment of the Hasmonean dynasty. See *Zohar* 3:6a; *ZḤ* 8a (*MhN*). See also Naḥmanides on Genesis 47:28. Cf. *Bereshit Rabbah* 2:4; *Pirqei de-Rabbi Eli'ezer* 35.

149. **how can it be that they will all arouse...** Given the dispersal of the exiles, to the uttermost east and west of the earth, how will they perform *teshuvah* as one, to effect the redemption and return to the land?

Rabbi Eli'ezer replied, "By your life! If the heads of the community return [in *teshuvah*], or even one congregation, by their merit all the exiles will be gathered in. For the blessed Holy One constantly looks forward to when they will return, that He might bestow goodness upon them, as is written: *Truly YHVH is waiting to show you grace; truly He will arise to pardon you* (Isaiah 30:18)—constantly waiting for when they will do *teshuvah*."[150]

Rabbi Yose said, "This corresponds with what Rabbi Pinḥas said, 'As is written: *but she returned to him again no more* (Genesis 8:12).' The verse does not say *He did not return to her again*, but rather she did *not return to him again*. Hence, He is poised and waiting for when she will return."[151]

One day, Rabbi was sitting contemplating this matter, as is written: *When you are in distress and all these things befall you in distant days,* ושבת (*ve-shavta*), *and you shall return, to YHVH your God and heed his voice* (Deuteronomy 4:30). He said, "Concerning what Moses said will be at the end of days—all these troubles have already come, yet תשובה (*teshuvah*), repentance, has not yet been effectuated!"[152]



150. **If the heads of the community return...** The leaders of the community or even just one congregation can hasten redemption for the whole people.

The Aramaic is potent, stressing the verbal root כנש (*kanash*), "gather, congregate," and the connection between community, congregation, and ingathering: דאי יחזרון בתשובה רישי כנישתא או חדא כנישתא בזכותם יתכנש כל גלותא (*de-i yaḥzerun bi-tshuvah reishei kenishta o ḥada kenishta, bi-zkhutam yitkenash kol galuta*). See Scholem, *Major Trends*, 250; Tishby, *Wisdom of the Zohar*, 3:1506.

Cf. BT *Yoma* 86b: "Rabbi Yonatan said, 'Great is *teshuvah*—for it brings near the redemption, as is said: *A redeemer will come to Zion, and to those who turn from transgression in Jacob* (Isaiah 59:20). Why will a redeemer *come to Zion*? Because of שבי (*shavei*), *those who turn from, transgression in Jacob*.' ...It has been taught: Rabbi Meir used to say, 'Great is *teshuvah*—for on account of יחיד (*yaḥid*), an individual, who performs *teshuvah*, the whole world is forgiven, as is said: *I will heal their backsliding. I will love them freely, for My anger has turned away from him* (Hosea 14:5). It does not say *from them*, but *from him*.'" See also BT *Ta'anit* 10b on the term *yaḥid*: "one who is worthy to be appointed as leader of the community." Cf. *Seder Eliyyahu Zuta* 14.

On the blessed Holy One anticipating the redemption, see BT *Sanhedrin* 97b.

151. ***but she returned to him again no more...*** The final statement about the dove in the Genesis narrative also points to the dynamics of the future redemption. It is not (heaven forfend) that God has abandoned the Assembly of Israel, never to return to her; rather, she has not returned to Him. See *Zohar* 3:6a.

152. **all these troubles have already come...** Rabbi wonders why only the first part of the verse has been fulfilled.

"Rabbi" indicates Rabbi Yehudah ha-Nasi (the Patriarch), who redacted the Mishnah. He was so esteemed that he was called simply "Rabbi": the Master.

While he was sitting, Elijah (may his memory be a blessing) appeared. He said to him, "Rabbi, with what are you occupied?"[153]

He replied, "With how the Torah said that when troubles befall Israel at the end of days, immediately they will do *teshuvah*, as is written: *in distant days, and you shall return.* But they have not yet returned in *teshuvah*!"

He said to him, "By your life, Rabbi! The blessed Holy One was occupied with this matter this very day. Michael, their supreme guardian, arrived—and inquired when his beloved children would come out from beneath the exile of Edom. He said, 'You wrote in Your Torah that [it will be] when they endure these punishments for what they have done. What is written? *For YHVH your God is a compassionate God* (ibid., 31).'[154]

"He replied, 'Let Samael, the guardian of Edom, come; and argue with him in My presence.' Michael came and pleaded the case as before. Samael said, 'Master of the World! You are the one who said that the Assembly of Israel would be under the dominion of Edom until they will be worthy before You. But look, all of them are guilty until this very day!'[155]



153. **Elijah...** According to the Bible (2 Kings 2:11), the prophet Elijah did not die a normal death but was carried off to heaven in a chariot of fire. He became associated with the Messianic age (Malachi 3:23–24). In rabbinic tradition, he is described as "still existing" (BT *Bava Batra* 121b), and as revealing divine secrets to righteous humans (BT *Bava Metsi'a* 59b).

In Kabbalah, mystical experiences are known as revelations of Elijah. See Scholem, *On the Kabbalah*, 19–21; *Zohar* 1:1b, 151a; 3:221a, 231a, 241b; *ZḤ* 59d, 62c, 63d, 70d, 73c (last four *ShS*). In *MhN*, see *Zohar* 1:100b; *ZḤ* 25b.

154. **Michael, their supreme guardian...** Invoking God's compassion, Michael argues that Israel ought to be redeemed at once, for it has already endured all the sufferings of exile.

On Michael as the chief advocate for Israel, see Daniel 10:13; 12:1; *Shemot Rabbah* 18:5; *Pesiqta Rabbati* 44. In the Kabbalah, he is associated with *ḥesed*, compassion (see *Zohar* 2:139a, 254a (*Heikh*)); in *MhN*, see *Zohar* 2:15a; *ZḤ* 13a–b, 21a, 25d.

155. **Let Samael, the guardian of Edom...** Just as Michael is the celestial guardian of Israel, Samael is the celestial guardian of Esau, who stands for Edom—the nation descended from him. See *Tanḥuma, Vayishlaḥ* 8; *Bereshit Rabbah* 77:3; *Zohar* 1:146a, 166a, 170a–b, 179b; 3:199b; *ZḤ* 14d (*MhN*).

On Michael and Samael arguing before God, see *Shemot Rabbah* 18:5: "Rabbi Neḥemiah said, 'Come and see the love of the blessed Holy One for Israel! For the blessed Holy One made the ministering angels... the guardians of Israel. Who are they? Michael and Gabriel.... Just as the blessed Holy acted [i.e., saved Israel] through Michael and Gabriel in this world, so in the time to come, will He act through them, as is said: *Saviors shall come up on Mount Zion to judge the Mount of Esau* (Obadiah 1:21)—Michael and Gabriel.' Our holy Rabbi says, 'This refers to Michael alone, as is said: *At that time, the great prince Michael—who stands for the children of your people—will rise* (Daniel 12:1), because it is he who advocates Israel's requirements and pleads for them, as is said: *Then the angel of YHVH exclaimed, saying, "O YHVH of hosts, how long will You not have compassion on Jerusalem"* (Zechariah 1:12)....'

"At that moment, the blessed Holy One rebuked him for having spoken slanderously about His children—and he fled three thousand miles. He said to Michael, 'Michael, you ought to have looked at the beginning of the verse, as is written: *and you shall return to YHVH your God and heed his voice*; and afterward: *For YHVH your God is a compassionate God.*'[156]

"Michael said, 'Master of the World! You ought to have shown them compassion! You are compassionate; so are You styled!' He replied, 'I swore an oath on the day the sentence was decreed before Me—"until they return." But if the Assembly of Israel opens *teshuvah* like the eye of a needle, I will open for them immense gates.'"[157]

Rabbi Yehudah said, "Come and see what is written about Jacob: *Jacob was left alone; and a man wrestled with him until the rising of dawn* (Genesis 32:25). At that time, authority was bestowed upon all the hosts of heaven, to the princes empowered over kingdoms—these allocated to preside over those—and authority and dominion was bestowed upon the prince of Edom to rule over the nations.[158]



Rabbi Yose said, 'To what may Michael and Samael be compared? To an intercessor and an accuser before a tribunal.... So Michael and Samael stand before the *Shekhinah*; Satan accuses, while Michael argues Israel's virtues....'"

On Israel under the dominion of Edom, see below, note 162.

156. **Michael, you ought to have looked at the beginning of the verse...** Even though he is rebuked for his slander (see above, *ZḤ* 23b), Samael's argument wins out. Michael ignored the fine print! God's compassion and the end of the exile are consequent upon *teshuvah*, upon the people's returning to God; and the sufferings of exile are insufficient to bring about the redemption. Cf. Naḥmanides on Deuteronomy 32:40.

157. **You ought to have shown them compassion!...** Even without *teshuvah*, the people should be redeemed. Although God's compassion cannot extend this far, and *teshuvah* must be performed, God's compassion is nevertheless apparent through his magnification of the penitent's repentance.

On opening *teshuvah* like the eye of a needle, see *Pesiqta de-Rav Kahana* 5:6: "*Open to me* (Songs of Songs 5:2). Rabbi Yeisa said, 'The blessed Holy One said, "Open an opening for Me like the eye of a needle, and I shall open an opening for you [so wide] that camps [of soldiers] and siege engines could enter it."'" See also *Shir ha-Shirim Rabbah* on Song of Songs 5:2; *Zohar* 3:95a.

158. ***Jacob was left alone; and a man wrestled with him...*** The prince of Edom (Esau), signifying Rome (and later, Christendom), has dominion over all.

According to midrashic tradition, the *man* whom Jacob encountered on the night before he was reunited with Esau was actually Samael, Esau's heavenly prince. See *Tanḥuma, Vayishlaḥ* 8; *Bereshit Rabbah* 77:3; *Zohar* 1:146a, 166a, 170a–171b, 179b; 2:163b; *ZḤ* 14d (*MhN*). Cf. *Zohar* 1:35b

According to rabbinic tradition, the seventy nations of the world are each governed by seventy angels or heavenly princes appointed by God. See Daniel 10:13, 20–21; Septuagint, Deuteronomy 32:8–9; Jubilees 15:31–32; *Targum Yerushalmi*, Genesis 11:8, Deuteronomy 32:8–9; *Tanḥuma, Re'eh* 8; *Le-*

"What is written at that moment? *Jacob was left alone*—because he did not yet have Benjamin and did not possess a celestial guardian; *and a man wrestled with him*—Samael, the chief of Edom, who desired that Jacob be placed under the subjugation of Edom. By virtue of Jacob's great merit, however, he was not handed over to him."[159]

Rabbi Yehudah said, "At that moment, all the hosts of heaven assembled, wishing to argue with Samael on Jacob's behalf. The blessed Holy One said, 'Jacob does not need any of you; his merit shall contend with him!' Immediately: *a man wrestled with him*—he contended with him."[160] [24a]

Rabbi Yehudah said, "Come and see what is written about him: *He saw that he could not prevail against him* (ibid., 26)—for his merit was great, and he could not make his case that Jacob be subjugated beneath Edom. Immediately: *he touched the socket of his thigh* (ibid.)—his children, the offspring of his thigh.[161]

"At that moment, Jacob weakened and was unable to contend with him, as is written: *the socket of Jacob's thigh was wrenched as he wrestled with him* (ibid.)—as he contended with him; and authority was given to Samael to subjugate the children of Jacob under the hand of Edom whenever they transgress the Torah."[162]



*qaḥ Tov*, Genesis 9:19; *Pirqei de-Rabbi Eli'ezer* 24; *Zohar* 1:46b, 61a, 108b, 113a (*MhN*), 149b, 177a; 2:5b (*MhN*), 14b (*MhN*), 17a (*MhN*), 96a, 126b, 209a–b; 3:8a, 298b; *ZḤ* 24c, 28c (both *MhN*); Ginzberg, *Legends*, 5:204–5, n. 91.

159. **because he did not yet...possess a celestial guardian...** Apparently, because Benjamin had not yet been born, and the twelve tribes had not yet attained completion, Jacob did not yet possess a celestial guardian, i.e., Michael, to advocate his cause. Hence, he was left alone. According to *ZḤ* 25d (*MhN*), Michael was appointed to his role as chief advocate (or guardian) of Israel when the Temple was constructed. Cf. *Zohar* 1:158a–b, 165b.

All the manuscripts and early printed editions read בנין (*banin*), "children," and not בנימין (*Binyamin*), "Benjamin." Yet it is difficult to support that reading, given that Jacob did in fact have children at this point in the narrative. Only Benjamin was yet to be born.

160. **his merit shall contend with him...** On Jacob's merit besting the prince of Esau, see *Bereshit Rabbah* 77:3.

161. **his children, the offspring of his thigh** Although unable to defeat Jacob, Samael injures Jacob's thigh: as a sign that his progeny (i.e., those who emerge from his thigh) will later be subjugated to Edom.

See *ZḤ* 14d (*MhN*); cf. *Bereshit Rabbah* 77:3; Naḥmanides on Genesis 32:26; *Zohar* 1:21b; 2:111b.

162. **authority was given to Samael to subjugate the children of Jacob...** See *ZḤ* 8a, 14a–d, 27c (all *MhN*); Scholem, "Parashah Ḥadashah," 433, 443 (Addendum 1 in this volume).

# פרשת לך לך

# *Parashat Lekh Lekha*

"GO YOU FORTH!" (GENESIS 12:1–17:27)

*Go you forth!* (Genesis 12:1).[1]

Rabbi Yehudah opened: *The blossoms have appeared on the earth, the time of singing has arrived; the voice of the turtledove is heard in our land* (Song of Songs 2:12).[2]

Rabbi Yehudah said, "Come and see how vigorously a person must array his deeds before his Creator, and engage in His Torah day and night; for the sublimity of Torah transcends all degree!"[3]

As Rabbi Yehudah said: "Torah possesses two superlative boons—life and wealth, as is written: *Length of days in her right hand; in her left, riches and honor* (Proverbs 3:16)."[4]

Rav Pappa said, "These are three!"[5]

Rabbi Yehudah replied, "*Honor* is included within *riches*, for whoever possesses wealth possesses honor. How does a person merit all this? By virtue of Torah!"

When Rav Kahana went up there, he attained much Torah until his face shone like the sun. When he arrived, they would come before him to merit

1. ***Go you forth!*** The verse continues: *from your land, from your birthplace, from your father's house, to the land I will show you!*

2. ***time of singing...*** עת הזמיר (*Et ha-zamir*). *Zamir* can mean either singing or pruning.

See *Zohar* 1:1a–b, 97a.

The significance of the verse becomes apparent below, at note 21.

3. **engage in His Torah day and night...** See Joshua 1:8: *Let not this book of Torah depart from your mouth; meditate on it day and night, so that you may be careful to do according to all that is written in it. For then you will make your way prosperous, and then you will succeed.*

4. **Torah possesses two superlative boons...** The feminine figure in the verse from Proverbs is Wisdom, which in rabbinic literature is equated with Torah. According to the rabbinic reading of this verse, one who studies Torah for its own sake receives the ultimate reward of length of days in the world to come, whereas one who studies Torah for ulterior motives finds reward in this world.

See *Avot* 6:7; *Sifrei*, Deuteronomy 48; *Bereshit Rabbah* 59:2; BT *Shabbat* 63a; *Zohar* 1:184b–185a, 190a; 2:171b.

5. **These are three!** Rabbi Yehudah mentioned two boons, yet the verse describes three: length of days, riches, and honor.

Torah; and whenever a person came before him, he would say to him, "What do you desire: wealth and honor, or length of days in the world to come?"[6]

One day, a certain person from his neighborhood came before him. He said to him, "Rabbi, I desire to attain Torah that I might possess wealth."[7]

He said to him as follows: "My son, I pledge by the Torah that if it is wealth that you desire, it shall be yours until you will tire from saying 'Enough!'

He sat and studied Torah.

He said to him, "What is your name?"

He replied, "Yose."

He said to his students, "Call him Yosef, Possessor of Wealth and Honor."

When he would enter the house of study, they would rise before him; and he would teach Torah.[8]

After some days, he asked him, "Where is the wealth?"[9]

He said, "Conclude from this that he does not act for the sake of heaven!"[10]



6. **When Rav Kahana went up there . . .** The narrative here (extending until "Rabbi Yehudah said") is not found in the printed editions. It is, however, found here in nearly all the manuscripts. According to the Venice edition, the narrative found in *Zohar* 1:88a–b (*ST*) belongs here. Though the narrative from *ST* and the narrative here are variants of one another, none of the manuscripts I consulted contained the version from *ST*. As Ronit Meroz has noted, the narrative from *ST* belongs to *MhN*.

On this narrative and its parallel in *ST*, see Meroz, "Zoharic Narratives," 17–34, 50–54. See also *Zohar* 1:189b–190a, which shares numerous motifs with this story.

The idiomatic phrase "went up there" is borrowed from the Babylonian Talmud, where it means "went to the land of Israel." Interestingly, this locution implies that "here" is Babylon—somewhat anomalous for the *Zohar*, whose plot transpires almost entirely in the land of Israel. See *Zohar* 1:190a; 2:174b; 3:72b; *ZḤ* 81c (*MhN*, *Rut*); Scholem, "Parashah Ḥadashah," 442 (Addendum 1 in this volume).

On Rav Kahana's migration to the land of Israel, see BT *Bava Qamma* 117a–b. On the shining face, see Ecclesiastes 8:1: *A person's wisdom lights up his face*. See *Pirqei de-Rabbi Eli'ezer* 2: "Rabbi Eli'ezer was sitting and expounding [matters greater than those revealed to Moses at Sinai], and his face was shining like the light of the sun, and his radiance went forth like the radiance of Moses; and no one knew whether it was day or night." See also *Avot de-Rabbi Natan* B, 13; JT *Pesaḥim* 10:1, 37c, *Shabbat* 8:1, 11a; *Tanḥuma* (Buber), *Ḥuqqat*, add. 1; *Vayiqra Rabbah* 1:1, 21:12; *Qohelet Rabbah* on 1:7. In the *Zohar*, see 1:94b, 2:15a (*MhN*); 3:132b (*IR*), 163a; *ZḤ* 5d, 20d, 28b (all *MhN*). See Hellner-Eshed, *A River Flows from Eden*, 305–8.

7. **I desire to attain Torah that I might possess wealth** Rav Kahana's neighbor does not realize that the choice is actually a test. He naively believes that the two options are equally legitimate offers.

8. **they would rise before him . . .** Yose has attained honor as promised by the verse from Proverbs.

9. **Where is the wealth?** What of the other reward he was promised?

10. **he does not act for the sake of heaven** Rav Kahana is disappointed to discover that his student has not progressed spiritually and is still motivated by material reward.

See BT *Pesaḥim* 50b in the name of Rav: "A person should always engage in Torah and *mitsvot* even if not for their own sake, because by doing them not for their own sake, he eventually does them for their own

Rav Kahana bent down and heard a voice saying, "Leave that man alone, and do not punish him, for he will be a great man."[11]

He said to him, "Sit, my son, sit; for great wealth will be yours."

While they were sitting, a person arrived, carrying a precious golden vessel. As he displayed it, light descended upon the house. He said, "Rabbi, I desire to possess my share in the compensation of Torah."[12]

He said to him, "What are your deeds?"

He replied, "My father left me much gold and silver; and whenever I sit at the table, I set upon it thirteen similarly precious vessels. I have not merited a son to toil in Torah—through whom I might obtain the world to come—so I have come to find someone who desires silver and gold, that he will labor in Torah, and that my merit will be reckoned as though I had engaged in Torah."[13]

He said to him, "Look, Rabbi Yose Possessor of Wealth can toil in Torah on your behalf!"[14]

He gave him the precious golden vessel.

Rav Kahana applied to him the verse *Gold and glass cannot equal her, nor can she be exchanged for objects of* פז (*phaz*), *pure gold* (Job 28:17).[15] 

He sat and plied Torah for the sake of that wealth, until he knew *Sifra* and *Sifrei* and *Tosafot* and *Aggadot*, and they called him Rabbi Yose son of Pazzi.[16]

sake." See also *Avot* 6:1; BT *Berakhot* 17a, *Sukkah* 49b, *Ta'anit* 7a, *Sanhedrin* 99b.

11. **Rav Kahana bent down...** Apparently, he communed with the souls of the departed righteous, who inform him of Yose's future greatness. See *Zohar* 3:169a (*Rav Metivta*); *ZḤ* 84b–c (*MhN, Rut*).

In the version of the narrative preserved in *ST*, Rabbi Abba (who takes the place of Rav Kahana) enters a chamber where he hears a similar voice.

12. **I desire to possess my share in the compensation of Torah** אגר (*Agar*) means "wages, payment, reward, compensation." Though it appears that the wealthy man too seeks material benefit for Torah study, the reward he has in mind is very different.

13. **I have not merited a son to toil...** As is now clear, the reward sought by the wealthy man is not material or of this world; he seeks spiritual reward—the world to come. Childless, the ignorant wealthy man has no way of meriting the world to come without employing others to study on his behalf.

On one's son's Torah study as a gate to the world to come, see *ZḤ* 49b; *ZḤ* 84c, 89b (both *MhN, Rut*).

14. **toil in Torah on your behalf** The two contrasting personalities are brought together: the poor scholar seeking wealth, and the wealthy ignoramus seeking the world to come.

15. ***Gold and glass cannot equal her...*** Rav Kahana deploys the verse—which speaks of Wisdom—ironically: Yose and the wealthy man have indeed exchanged gold for Torah, while Yose is still motivated by his desire for gold and riches.

On the verse from Job, see BT *Ḥagigah* 15a; *Zohar* 3:40b.

16. **until he knew *Sifra* and *Sifrei* . . .** Even though his intentions were flawed he still acquired much knowledge.

Throughout the narrative, Rabbi Yose is known by different names, reflecting his spiritual and intellectual progress: Yose; Yosef Possessor of Wealth and Honor; Rabbi Yose Possessor of Wealth; and ultimately Rabbi Yose son of Pazzi. "Pazzi" is here con-

After he became wise, he looked closely at Torah and realized that his deeds were shameful—because he had abandoned the life of the world to come for the sake of gold and silver.

He said, "Conclude from this that the slender scorpion, too, needs to grow up in order to improve its sting!"[17]

He came before Rav Kahana weeping. He said, "Have you heard? The voices flow out of me like water! I do not desire the left on account of the right! Of the left hand is written *riches and honor*; while of her right *length of days* (Proverbs 3:16)."[18]

His teacher arranged for that man to give his wealth to orphans and widows; and that his compensation be through those engaging in Torah.[19]

Rabbi Yose returned all the gold and silver and the precious golden vessel he gave him; and until this very day, the name "son of Pazzi" has not departed from him and his children.[20]



nected with his now abandoned desire for gold (*paz*).

On Yose son of Pazzi, see *ZḤ* 11b–c (*MhN*).

17. **the slender scorpion, too, needs to grow...** Rav Kahana's statement, which expresses his joy at his pupil's spiritual maturation, is an enigmatic epigram. Because it seems corrupted and nearly impossible to decipher, I have followed Meroz's rendition ("Zoharic Narratives," 26). The Aramaic reads: דטלפיהון דטלפין כד עקרבייא דקיקייא עד לאו רברבייא לאו אורח ארעא (*de-talfeihon de-talfin, kad aqravaya deqiqaya, ad lav ravravaya lav oraḥ ar'a*). Leaving aside the first two words, a literal rendition of the remainder of the epigram reads: when the scorpion is young, until it is big, [it does] not [know?] the way of the world. The first word טלפיהון (*talfeihon*) literally means "their hooves" and appears again in another enigmatic saying in *MhN* (see *ZḤ* 17d). It may be that here the *Zohar* intends צלפיהון (*tsalfeihon*), a word deriving from the root צלף (*tslf*), "strike or whip."

In M *Avot* 2:10, the sages are described as possessing a scorpion's sting.

18. **I do not desire the left on account of the right!...** The material rewards pale in comparison to the spiritual rewards: length of days in the world to come.

Rabbi Yose's opening statement אי שמעיא שמעין (*i shama'ya sham'in*) seems garbled. My rendering "Have you heard?" is conjectural. Alternatively, "If any listeners are listening."

19. **that his compensation be through those engaging in Torah** Apparently, he will not just receive reward for Rabbi Yose's Torah study, but for the Torah studied by all of Rav Kahana's students.

On the wealthy man's giving away his wealth, see next note.

20. **the name "son of Pazzi" has not departed...** This story serves an etiological function, as Rabbi Yose son of Pazzi becomes the eponymous ancestor who gives a family of distinguished scholars its name. This family included sages such as Rabbi Yehudah son of Simon, his son, Rabbi Shim'on, and his son's son, Rabbi Yehudah.

In returning the riches he received, Rabbi Yose's spiritual development is complete. As in the beginning of the story he is poor—but now spiritually rich.

On the polemical social context of this story, see Baer, *A History of the Jews in Christian Spain*, vol. 1, 261–66, esp. p. 265.

Rabbi Yehudah said, "Come and see: There is no night in which Metatron, the Prince of the Countenance, does not grasp all the souls of the disciples of the wise who engage in Torah for its own sake, displaying them before the blessed Holy One. The ministering angels wait and desist from reciting song, until the souls of the righteous assemble with them; and they sing together to God Most High. As is said: *The blossoms have appeared on the earth* (Song of Songs 2:12)—those who engage in Torah for its own sake; *the time of singing has arrived* (ibid.)—then is the time to sing to their Creator together; *the voice of the turtledove is heard in our land* (ibid.)—Metatron, who comes to assemble the souls of the righteous, to sing to their Creator every single night, as is said: *Let the pious exalt* בכבוד (*be-khavod*), *in glory, let them sing upon their beds* (Psalms 149:5)."[21]



21. **There is no night in which Metatron, the Prince of the Countenance...** In this world, while asleep, the souls of the righteous enjoy celestial ascent, with Metatron serving as their guide. See *ZḤ* 25d–26a, 28b (both *MhN*).

Metatron is the chief angel, variously described as the Prince of the World, Prince of the Countenance (or Presence), celestial scribe, and even יהוה קטן (*YHVH Qatan*), "Lesser *YHVH*" (3 Enoch 12:5, based on Exodus 23:21). In Heikhalot literature, Metatron is also identified with Enoch, who ascended to heaven. See BT *Sanhedrin* 38b; *Ḥagigah* 15a; *Yevamot* 16b; *Tosafot, Yevamot* 16b, s.v. *pasuq zeh*; Scholem, *Kabbalah*, 377–81; Tishby, *Wisdom of the Zohar*, 2:626–31; Margaliot, *Mal'akhei Elyon*, 73–108.

On Metatron in the *Zohar*, see 1:21a, 37b, 95b, 143a, 162a–b; 2:65b–66b, 131a; 3:217a–b; *ZḤ* 42d–43a; 69b (*ShS*). In *MhN* see *Zohar* 1:126a–b, 127a–128b; *ZḤ* 4a, 8d, 9d–10a, 10b, 12b, 25d–26a, 28a–c. On Metatron as the conduit between the upper and lower worlds, see *ZḤ* 10b, 25d–26a, 28b (all *MhN*); Scholem, "Parashah Ḥadashah," 437, 445 (Addendum 1 in this volume).

This homily appears, nearly verbatim, in Jacob ha-Kohen's *Sefer ha-Orah*, MS JTS 1869, 23a–b (in Abrams, *The Book of Illumination*, 371): "Know, my brother, that every single night, the souls of human beings ascend before the Throne of Glory. They begin to recite all manner of songs before the blessed Holy One. The angels are unable to recite until all the souls are assembled. Now, should you ask 'Who assembles them?' know that it is Metatron, the Prince of the Countenance who assembles them. This is what King Solomon, peace be upon him, alluded to in the book Song of Songs when he said: *The blossoms have appeared on the earth... the voice of the turtledove is heard in our land* (Song of Songs 2:12). This is the mystery of the verse *The blossoms have appeared*—the souls of the righteous; *the time of singing has arrived*—the hour has come to offer praise and adoration before the blessed Holy One and to recite before Him all manner of song; *the voice of the turtledove is heard in our land*—the voice of Metatron, the Prince of the Countenance, who assembles the souls of the righteous."

See also Isaac ibn Sahula, *Peirush Shir ha-Shirim*, 433, where this homily is cited; Scholem, "Qabbalat Rabbi Yitsḥak ben Shelomoh," 112–16; *Bemidbar Rabbah* 12:12; Nathan ben Yeḥiel of Rome, *Arukh*, s.v. *metator*.

Note that Psalms 149:5 reads ירננו (*yerannenu*), *let them sing*, from the verbal root רנן (*rnn*), "singing, song." Perhaps the *Zohar* implicitly associates this root with Metatron. Cf. El'azar of Worms, MS Paris-BN 850, fols. 83a–b (cited in Wolfson, *Through A Speculum*, 258), where a Metatron–*ron* connection

What is meant by בכבוד (*be-khavod*), *with glory*? Rabbi Yehudah said, "This is Metatron."[22]

Rabbi Ya'akov son of Idi said, "All the souls of the righteous have been hewn from beneath the Throne of Glory, to conduct the body like a father guiding a son. For without the soul, the body could not conduct itself—nor be aware to realize the will of its Creator. As Rabbi Abbahu said: 'The soul guides and trains the human being, initiating him into every straight path.'[23]

"When the blessed Holy One sends her forth to the body from the site of holiness, He blesses her with seven blessings, as is written: *YHVH said to* אברם (*Avram*), *Abram* (Genesis 12:1)—the soul, who is אב (*av*), *a father*, to teach the body; and רם (*ram*), *exalted*, above him, for she has come from an exalted and lofty site. What does He say to her? *Go you forth, from your land, from your birthplace, from your father's house* (ibid.)—from your abode, from your place, and from your bliss."[24]

280 *From your father's house*. Rabbi Ya'akov said, "This is the resplendent speculum. *To the land that I will show you* (ibid.)—namely to such-and-such a body, a holy body, an upright body. Even so, *I will bless those who bless you* (ibid., 3)—those who treat you correctly and virtuously, those who bless Me because of

is noted. See also Wolski, "Metatron and the Mysteries of the Night."

On studying Torah for its own sake, see *Avot* 6:1; BT *Pesaḥim* 50b, *Sukkah* 49b, *Ta'anit* 7a, *Sanhedrin* 99b. On angels singing throughout the night, see BT *Ḥagigah* 12b; *ZḤ* 5d–6a, 17d (*MhN*). On Psalms 149:5, cf. BT *Berakhot* 5a.

22. **בכבוד (*be-khavod*), *with glory* . . .** Reading the prefixed preposition ב (*bet*) of בכבוד (*be-khavod*) in its occasional sense as "with," rather than "in." That is, the souls sing with Metatron, identified as the divine glory. See *ZḤ* 9d, 26a (both *MhN*); Scholem, "Parashah Ḥadashah," 445 (Addendum 1 in this volume).

23. **hewn from beneath the Throne of Glory...** In BT *Shabbat* 152b, the souls of the righteous are said to be "hidden beneath the Throne of Glory" after death; see also *Avot de-Rabbi Natan* A, 12. According to *MhN*, the soul (i.e., the *neshamah*, the highest level of soul, the spiritual essence of the human being) is created from the substance of the Throne of Glory, which may refer to the *Shekhinah*. See *Zohar* 1:113a, 125b, 126b (all *MhN*); *ZḤ* 10a–d, 20b, 22a, 26a (all *MhN*).

On the soul leading one to recognize God, see *ZḤ* 11a (*MhN*).

24. **When the blessed Holy One sends her...** Abram's journey to the land is an allegory of the soul's descent from the celestial realm to this world. This passage is closely paralleled in *Zohar* 1:76b–77a (*ST*) and *ZḤ* 75c (*MhN, Rut*).

The seven blessings are pronounced in Genesis 12:2–3; see *Zohar* 1:78a (*ST*). Traditionally, a different set of seven blessings are recited at a Jewish marriage ceremony.

Cf. Rashi on Genesis 12:1: "*Go you forth*—להנאתך (*le-hana'atkha*), for your pleasure." Note the *Zohar*'s inversion—Abram's journey is מהנאתך (*me-hana'atkha*), "from your pleasure (or bliss)."

On the soul's descent in rabbinic literature, see *Tanḥuma, Pequdei* 3. On Genesis 12:1, cf. *Zohar* 1:77b–78a; 2:32a; 3:17a, 157a; *ZḤ* 71b (*ShS*).

you, saying, 'As long as the soul is within me, I shall acknowledge You, YHVH my God.' ומקללך (U-mqalelekha), *Whoever curses you, I will curse* (ibid.)—those who curse you, ומקלקלים (u-mqalqelim), corrupting, [24b] their deeds and paths.[25]

"*Abram went forth as YHVH had directed him* (ibid., 4). Once she was blessed with these seven blessings, what is written? *Abram went forth*—the soul, which is אב (av), *a father*, to the body, and רם (ram), *exalted*, from the highest site. *As YHVH had directed him*—to enter that body she had been commanded, to guide and instruct."

Rabbi Ya'akov said, "Look at what is written about her once she came to enter the body: *Lot went with him* (ibid.)—the Deviser of Evil, destined to enter along with the soul as soon as a human is born! How do we know that the Deviser of Evil is called thus? As is said: *The devisings of the human heart are evil from youth* (ibid. 8:21). This is Lot, who was cursed in the world. And this corresponds with what Rabbi Yitsḥak said: 'The serpent who seduced Eve was the Deviser of Evil.' We have seen that he was cursed, as is said: *Cursed are you above all animals* (ibid. 3:14). Therefore he is called לוט (lut), cursed. When the soul enters the body, immediately: *Lot went with him* (ibid. 12:4)—for he is destined to enter with him, to mislead the human being, to challenge the soul."[26]



25. ***From your father's house...*** Even though the soul is far from her divine source, she is not abandoned.

"Resplendent speculum" renders אספקלריא המאירה (ispaqlarya ha-me'irah). *Ispaqlarya* means glass, mirror, or lens. See BT *Yevamot* 49b: "All the prophets gazed through an opaque glass [literally: an *ispaqlarya* that does not shine], while Moses our teacher gazed through a translucent glass [literally: an *ispaqlarya* that shines]." See also *Vayiqra Rabbah* 1:14. Cf. 1 Corinthians 13:12: "For now we see though a glass darkly, but then face-to-face." In the main strata of the *Zohar*, "the *ispaqlarya* that does not shine" symbolizes *Shekhinah* and "the *ispaqlarya* that shines" symbolizes *Tif'eret*, the female and male aspects of divinity. The soul is often described as the fruit of their union. Here, the speculum that shines appears to signify the divine realm or a potency very close to divinity, perhaps *Shekhinah*. In *MhN*, see *Zohar* 1:97b, 122a; *ZḤ* 10a, 13b, 15b, 15d, 16c, 17a, 21a.

The blessing is from the closing lines of the *Elohai Neshamah* prayer, recited upon awakening. See BT *Berakhot* 60b: "When he wakes he says: 'My God, the soul You placed within me is pure. You fashioned it within me, You breathed it into me, and You preserve it within me; and eventually You will take it from me, and restore it to me in the time to come. As long as the soul is within me, I shall acknowledge You, YHVH my God—the God of my ancestors, Master of all worlds, Lord of all souls. Blessed are You, O YHVH, who restores souls to dead corpses."

26. ***Lot went with him*—the Deviser of Evil...** In Aramaic, the verb *lut* means "to curse" and hence Lot is associated with the cursed serpent, itself identified with יצר הרע (yetser ha-ra), "the evil impulse (or inclination)." The root יצר (ytsr) means "to fashion, devise."

On the evil impulse entering at birth, see *Avot de-Rabbi Natan* A, 16; *Qohelet Rabbah* on 4:13; *Midrash Tehillim* 9:5. On Lot as the evil impulse, see also *Zohar* 1:78a, 79a (both *ST*), 109a–110b, 128b, 137a–138a (all three *MhN*); *ZḤ* 24d (*MhN*). On the serpent as the evil impulse, see *Zohar* 1:35b (in the name

Rabbi Ya'akov son of Rav Idi said, "Concerning what we have said, how do we know that it is an allegory for the soul? From what is written afterward: *Abram took Sarai his wife* (ibid., 5)—the body; *and Lot his brother's son* (ibid.)—the Deviser of Evil, which is his brother's son, associated and connected with the body; *and all the possessions they had accumulated* (ibid.)—their deeds; *and they set out for the land of Canaan* (ibid.)—all of them fixated upon the vanities of the world, pursuing their designs and avarice.[27]

"*Abram passed through the land as far as the site of Shechem* (ibid., 6). Every place that this one desires, the soul follows. *The Canaanite was then in the land* (ibid.)—desire, clinging to the body.[28]

"When the blessed Holy One requites their deeds, withdrawing the soul from the body, the soul wishes to ascend on high. Look at what is written about her: *He went on his journeys from the Negev as far as Bethel* (ibid. 13:3)—wishing to return *to the place where* אהלה (*oholoh*), *his tent, had been at the beginning* (ibid.)!"[29]



of Rabbi Yitsḥak), 49b; *ZḤ* 18c (*MhN*). Cf. BT *Bava Batra* 16a: "Resh Lakish said, 'Satan, the evil impulse, and the Angel of Death are one and the same.'" Cf. *Pirqei de-Rabbi Eli'ezer* 13. On Genesis 8:21, see BT *Sukkah* 52a; *Qiddushin* 30b.

See also *ZḤ* 58d: "All the limbs of the body are in torment, caught between the soul and the Deviser of Evil."

27. **an allegory for the soul...** The following verse extends the allegory (literally parable): *Abram took Sarai his wife, and Lot his brother's son, and all the possessions they had accumulated... and they set out for the land of Canaan.* Read allegorically: the soul took the body and the evil inclination and all the deeds they had performed and set out for the land of avarice.

On Sarai (or Sarah) as the body, see *Zohar* 1:124b (*MhN*): "the body to the soul is as a woman to the male." See also *Zohar* 1:79a (*ST*), 113b, 115a, 122b (all three *MhN*).

Cf. Aristotle, *Generation of Animals* 2:4: "While the body is from the female, it is the soul that is from the male, for the soul is the substance of a particular body."

The body is the soul's brother. As the evil inclination is associated with the body, it is considered to be the son of the body, hence the soul's brother's son.

In Hebrew, the word כנען (Canaan) also means "merchant, trader." Here, it is associated with greed and materialism. See, for example, Isaiah 23:8; Ezekiel 16:29, 17:4; Hosea 12:8; Zechariah 14:21; Proverbs 31:24; Job 40:30.

In the *Zohar*'s day, allegorical interpretations of Scripture—reading Abraham as form and Sarah as matter—were subject to harsh critique. See Abba Mari, *Minḥat Qena'ot*, 316, 345–6, 412.

28. ***The Canaanite was then in the land*—desire, clinging to the body** Although the soul is superior, housed within the body (*the land*) it is victim to both the body's desires and the evil impulse's wiles. On the Canaanite signifying desire, see previous note. Cf. *Zohar* 1:80a (*ST*).

29. ***He went on his journeys from the Negev as far as Bethel...*** The Abram narrative recounts not only the story of the soul's descent, but also its ascent back to the divine realm upon death (*the place where his tent had been at the beginning*). The Negev, i.e., the desert, signifies this world—dry and barren in comparison with the celestial realm, Bethel, the house of God.

On Genesis 13:3, cf. *Zohar* 1:83b–84a.

Rabbi Ya'akov said, "אהלה (*Oholoh*)—spelled with ה (*he*)! Then she is poised *between Bethel and Ai* (ibid.)—between ascending on high and descending below.[30]

"If she is worthy, she ascends *to the site of the altar he had made there at first* (ibid., 4)—the site where Michael, the great prince, offers up the souls of the righteous. *There Abram called out the name of YHVH* (ibid.)—the soul offers praise and thanksgiving in Jerusalem Above, that she merited that degree. If she is not worthy, what is written? *Abram journeyed, continually journeying toward the Negev* (ibid. 12:9)—she is thrust aside and journeys on, until she has traversed the entire world and received her punishment."[31]

Rabbi Yehudah said, "Come and see what the righteous do! If one comes to purify himself, even though the Deviser of Evil comes to challenge him, his soul assists him, as is said: *Abram said to Lot* (ibid. 13:8)—the soul says to the Deviser of Evil, *Let there be no strife between you and me* (ibid.).[32]

"What does this righteous person do? He goes to the house of study, studies Scripture and Mishnah, and challenges the Deviser of Evil. He says to him, '*Is not all the land before you? Please, separate yourself from me!* (ibid., 9)—there are many in the world upon whom you can [prevail], since they have corrupted their deeds. *If to the left, then I to the right* (ibid.)—if you seek to drive me to the left, I to the right: I will go to the right side, so that my feet not stray to the right



30. **אהלה (*Oholoh*)—spelled with ה (*he*)...** The allegory is even more perfect. Normally, the masculine pronominal suffix would be represented by the letter *vav*. Here, however, it is indicated by the letter ה (*he*), which is normally a feminine marker. Construed as such, it implies *her tent*, i.e., the soul's tent—or perhaps even the tent of *Shekhinah*, the source of the soul. See *Bereshit Rabbah* 39:15; *Zohar* 1:73a, 80a (*ST*), 83a, 84a; *Minḥat Shai* on Genesis 12:8.

Before final judgment, the soul lies between עי (Ai)—which is a place name, though the common noun עי (*ai*) also denotes destruction and ruin (see, for example, Psalms 79:1)—and Bethel, signifying the celestial realm. See *Zohar* 1:80a (*ST*).

31. **where Michael, the great prince, offers...** According to BT *Ḥagigah* 12b and BT *Menaḥot* 110a, Michael offers sacrifices on the heavenly altar. See *Tosafot Menaḥot* 110a, s.v. *u-mikha'el sar ha-gadol*, which notes that according to some passages, these offerings are comprised of the souls of the righteous. See *Bemidbar Rabbah* 12:12; [Moses de León?], *Seder Gan Eden*, 137; *Zohar* 1:80a–b, 81a (both *ST*); *ZḤ* 21a, 25a (both *MhN*).

On Jerusalem Above, see *ZḤ* 20d–21a (*MhN*) and p. 228, n. 19. On the soul's roaming the world as punishment, see *Zohar* 1:106b, 123a (both *MhN*). See also BT *Shabbat* 152b.

32. **If one comes to purify himself...** See BT *Shabbat* 104a: "Resh Lakish said, '... If one comes to defile himself, he is provided an opening; if one comes to purify himself, he is assisted.'" See also BT *Yoma* 39a; *ZḤ* 10c, 20d (both *MhN*).

On the strife between Abram (the soul) and Lot (the deviser of evil), see *Zohar* 1:80b (*ST*).

or left. *If to the right, then I to left* (ibid.)—even though I might consider your advice sound, I will do the opposite of your will and desire!'"[33] [24c]

Rabbi Aivu said, "What does the Deviser of Evil do at that moment, when he discovers that his advice has not been heeded? What is written about him? *Lot chose for himself the whole plain of the Jordan* (ibid., 11)—the wicked, who would not challenge him. Accordingly *they parted from one another* (ibid.). What is written then about the soul? *Abram was very heavily laden* (ibid. 13:2)—with all good and upright deeds, with Torah and commandments."[34]

*Abram heard that his kinsman had been captured* (Genesis 14:14).[35]

Rabbi Tanḥum opened: *I rose to open for my beloved... but my beloved had slipped away; my soul departed as he spoke* (Song of Songs 5:5–6).

Rabbi Tanḥum said, "Come and see how assiduously a person must purify himself from his sins while the paths of *teshuvah* are still open before him, before the path is sealed, as is said: *Seek YHVH while He may be found; call upon him while He is near* (Isaiah 55:6)."[36]



Now, can you possibly conceive that there are times when He is near and times when He is far?! How did Rabbi Tanḥum say this, for the verse says: *YHVH is near to all who call Him, to all who call Him in truth* (Psalms 145:18)?![37]

He said, "This verse supports him, as implied by what is written: *to all who call Him in truth*! Even so, what is written? *He performs the will of those in awe of Him* (ibid., 19)."[38]

33. **He goes to the house of study...** See BT *Sukkah* 52b and *Qiddushin* 30b: "The School of Rabbi Yishma'el teaches: 'If the repulsive wretch [the evil impulse] meets you, drag him to the house of study.'" See *ZḤ* 5d (*MhN*).

34. ***the whole plain of the Jordan...*** The location of Sodom and Gomorrah. Perhaps the *Zohar* is associating ירדן (*yarden*), "Jordan," with the root ירד (*yrd*), "to descend," i.e., those who descend to evil. See *ZḤ* 24d (*MhN*), below, at note 53.

35. ***Abram heard that his kinsman had been captured*** Abram is the soul; and his kinsman (Lot) is the evil impulse. Lot's capture is an allegory for the judgment of the evil impulse—and consequently of the soul that it has lured into sin. See below, *ZḤ* 24d (*MhN*), page 289.

Some manuscripts contain the word פרשה (*parashat*), "section," before the opening verse. O2 reads: פרשה יא (*parashat* 11). See below, note 126.

36. **while the paths of *teshuvah* are still open...** Although the verse from Isaiah is frequently expounded as referring to engaging in *teshuvah* during the Ten Days of Repentance from Rosh ha-Shanah through Yom Kippur (see BT *Rosh ha-Shanah* 18a; *Yevamot* 49b, 105a), here the meaning is widened. One must perform *teshuvah* before it is too late, i.e., when repentance is still possible, as explained below.

37. **Now, can you possibly conceive...** How can Rabbi Tanḥum say that there are times when God is far? As the verse from Psalms suggests, *YHVH is near... to all who call Him in truth.*

38. **This verse supports him...** The proof-text used to challenge Rabbi Tan-

This may be compared to a king who was seated, before whom a person arrived and shouted in his presence. The king listened to everything he said—but did not reply. He shouted but the king just listened and remained silent. The man departed. The servants said before the king, "Our Master, why didn't you respond to that pauper at all?" He replied, "I heard everything he said; I listened to him. But he is sinful before me, and it is not seemly to perform his request. For he and his companions had been cautioned numerous times in my name not to be wicked, and to appear before me so I might treat them kindly. But they did not heed me. Now I will not heed them!"[39]

So is the blessed Holy One: *YHVH is near to all who call Him, to all who call Him in truth* (ibid., 18)—He hears them. But of the one who performs His will is written *He performs the will of those in awe of Him, He hears their cry and delivers them* (ibid., 19).[40]

Rabbi Ḥelbo said in the name of Rav Huna, "From whom do you learn this? From Moses our teacher, peace be upon him. As is written: *How then will it be known that I have found favor in Your eyes, I and Your people?* (Exodus 33:16). Moses said, 'Master of the World! We do not require an angel, neither a seraph nor a princely power. For how then will we differ from the nations? They have a princely power, and we have a princely power! Rather: *May we be distinguished, I and Your people, [from every people that is on the face of the earth]. How then will it be known that I have found favor in Your eyes? Is it not by Your going with us?* (ibid.)—You and not a princely power.'"[41]



ḥum's claim in fact supports the view that there are times when God is far—His proximity is conditional on calling Him *in truth.* Furthermore, even though God is near to all who call in truth, as the following verse from Psalms suggests (and as demonstrated in the following parable), He only heeds *those in awe of Him.*

The speaker is not identified.

39. **This may be compared to a king...** The pauper in the parable is now calling out in truth. Yet because he was not in awe of the king previously, his will is not performed.

40. **So is the blessed Holy One...** Calling in truth grants one an audience with God, whereas awe (constantly performing the divine will) leads to one's own request/will being fulfilled.

41. **From whom do you learn this?...** From whom do we learn that the blessed Holy One fulfills the request of those in awe of Him and that He is near and compassionate?

Following the sin of the Golden Calf, God informs Moses that He will not accompany the Children of Israel on their journey. Instead He will send an angel. See Exodus 33:1–3, 12–16; see also Exodus 23:20–22. Moses protests and God rescinds. The Children of Israel are lead by *YHVH* and not an intermediary.

See *Shemot Rabbah* 32:3: "When were they entrusted to a messenger? When they worshipped idols. How do we know? The blessed Holy One said to Moses: '*Go, lead the people... [My angel shall go before you...*'] (Exodus 32:34). Moses replied, '*If Your presence does not go, do not take us up from here*' (ibid. 33:15). Moses said further, 'Master of the World! What will be the difference between us and the idolators? We have prophets, they

Rabbi Yehudah said, "What was Moses thinking in not accepting the angel? Well, Moses reasoned, 'I know these Israelites—that they are sinful and stiff-necked. If they are handed over to an angel, especially to one who is the attribute of judgment, no remnant and vestige of Israel will remain!'"[42]

As Rabbi Yehudah said: "In every instance, YHVH signifies the attribute of compassion. Moses said, 'Master of the World! You said that I have found favor in Your eyes. *Now, if I have found favor in Your eyes, may* YHVH *go in our midst* (Exodus 34:9)—the attribute of compassion.' He asked him, 'Why?' He replied, '*Because it is a stiff-necked people; so forgive* (ibid.). Israel are stubborn and troublesome. As soon as they sin, the angel will be empowered to execute judgment—though not to administer forgiveness and absolution. But You are compassionate and gracious! The capacity and power reside with You; Your compassion is immense! *Forgive our iniquity and our sin, and make us Your inheritance* (ibid.), which an angel is not authorized to do.'"[43]



have prophets; we have a princely power, they have a princely power!' Rabbi Levi said, '...during Moses' lifetime, Israel was not handed over to any princely power....'"

On Moses refusing the angel, see also *Midrash Tanna'im*, Deuteronomy 33:29; *Bereshit Rabbah* 97:3; BT *Sanhedrin* 38b; *Tanḥuma, Mishpatim* 18; *Shemot Rabbah* 32:8; *Midrash Tehillim* 90:9; *Aggadat Bereshit* 32; *Zohar* 2:124b–125a. On the celestial governance of nations, see Daniel 10:13, 20–21; Septuagint, Deuteronomy 32:8–9; Jubilees 15:31–32. According to rabbinic tradition, the seventy nations of the world are governed by seventy angels or heavenly princes appointed by God; see *Targum Yerushalmi*, Genesis 11:8, Deuteronomy 32:8–9; *Tanḥuma, Re'eh* 8; *Leqaḥ Tov*, Genesis 9:19; *Pirqei de-Rabbi Eli'ezer* 24. See *Zohar* 1:46b, 61a, 108b, 113a (*MhN*), 149b, 177a; 2:5b (*MhN*), 14b (*MhN*), 17a (*MhN*), 96a, 126b, 209a–b; 3:8a, 298b; *ZḤ* 23d, 28c (both *MhN*); Ginzberg, *Legends*, 5:204–5, n. 91.

42. **one who is the attribute of judgment...** See Exodus 23:20–21: *I am sending an angel before You.... Watch yourself with him and heed his voice; do not rebel against him, for he will not pardon your transgression—for My name is within him.* According to *Shemot Rabbah* 32:4, this angel is "the attribute of judgment.'" See next note.

The text actually reads: 'no remnant and vestige of the haters of Israel will remain,' a classic Jewish euphemism so as to avoid ascribing catastrophe to Israel.

43. **In every instance, YHVH signifies the attribute of compassion...** Moses refuses the angel because he wants YHVH (symbolizing the attribute of compassion) to be with them, and not the angel (the attribute of judgment).

The Masoretic text in fact reads: *If I have found favor in Your eyes, my Lord, may my Lord go in our midst.*

See Naḥmanides on Exodus 34:6; *Zohar* 2:125a. See also *Targum Onqelos* and *Targum Yerushalmi* on Exodus 34:9.

On the name YHVH as conveying compassion, see *Sifrei*, Deuteronomy 26; *Bereshit Rabbah* 12:15; 33:3; *Shemot Rabbah* 3:6; Naḥmanides on Deuteronomy 3:24; *Zohar* 1:173b; 3:269b.

See also *Shemot Rabbah* 32:4: "*For he will not pardon your transgression* (Exodus 23:21). He is not like Me, of whom is written *who forgives iniquity and passes over transgression* (Micah 7:18); rather he will not pardon your transgression." See also *Tanḥuma, Mishpa-*

Rabbi Simon said, "[Come and see] the blessed Holy One's compassion toward the Assembly of Israel! As is written: *Open to me* (Song of Songs 5:2)—an opening of *teshuvah*, that you might attain all the good in the world; שראשי (*she-roshi*), *for my head, is drenched with dew* (ibid.)—ראש (*rosh*), beginning, of the world; קווצותי (*qvutsotai*), *my locks, with the drops of night* (ibid.)—קצה (*qatse*), *edge*, of the world; in other words—from the beginning of the world to its end, I have filled all good for you. But the Assembly of Israel did not open at that time. What is written afterward, when He pressed her? *I rose to open for my beloved... but my beloved had slipped away; my soul departed as he spoke* (Song of Songs 5:5–6)."[44]

Alternatively, *I rose to open for my beloved*—this is the soul in the possession of the body; as long as [24d] the soul is in the body, they do not seek to arouse paths of *teshuvah*.[45]

Rabbi Pinḥas said, "When the soul wishes to leave the body, she regrets not returning in *teshuvah* before departing the body, when the body is left behind like an unwanted vessel."[46]



Rabbi Pinḥas also said, "All seven days his soul mourns him, saying, *I rose to open for my beloved.* Know that superior *teshuvah* is while the soul is in the body, when the body abides in its vitality; not at a time when it is incapacitated."[47]

*tim* 18; *Aggadat Bereshit* 32; Rashi on Exodus 23:21, 34:9; Naḥmanides on Exodus 23:21, 33:14, 34:9.

44. ***Open to me*... an opening of *teshuvah*...** Having demonstrated that *YHVH* is indeed close and capable of forgiving, the discussion returns to its central theme—repentance before it is too late.

Even though the rewards of *teshuvah* are so abundant, people fail to return until pressed, i.e., afflicted with illness and travail and their approaching death. The significance of Song of Songs 5:5–6 is now apparent. One must open for the beloved before it is too late and he slips away, i.e., before the possibility for repentance disappears.

See *Shir ha-Shirim Rabbah* on Song of Songs 5:2: "*Open to me*—Rabbi Yeisa said, 'The blessed Holy One said to Israel, "My children, open to me an opening of *teshuvah* as the eye of a needle, and I will open for you openings through which wagons and carriages can pass."'" See also *Pesiqta de-Rav Kahana* 5:6; *Zohar* 3:95a.

45. **this is the soul...** The speaker in the Song of Songs is the soul, lamenting her failure to open to her beloved, i.e., to open in *teshuvah* to God before He slipped away—that is, before she leaves the body and the gates of repentance are closed. It is human nature to turn in *teshuvah* only as the soul is leaving, i.e., as death approaches, not before.

46. **like an unwanted vessel** The expression derives from Hosea 8:8, where it is applied to Israel among the nations. Without the soul to animate it, the body has no value and is a discarded, useless shell.

47. **his soul mourns...** For seven days, the soul mourns its having turned in *teshuvah* too late. Now dead, the beloved has already slipped away.

See BT *Shabbat* 152a: "Rav Ḥisda said, 'A person's soul mourns for him all seven [days], as is said: *and his soul mourns for him* (Job 14:22).'" See also JT *Mo'ed Qatan* 3:5, 82b; *Bereshit Rabbah* 100:7; *Vayiqra Rabbah* 18:1; *Tanḥuma*, *Miqqets* 4; *Zohar* 1:122b

As Rabbi Pinḥas said: "A parable. To what can the matter be compared? To a person standing by his table who was ravenous and desperate to eat. While he was eating, a beggar stood at the door. He asked for food—but he didn't even alter his gaze. The beggar left disconsolate. Sometime later, he was served yet more to eat but his belly was stuffed full. When he realized he couldn't eat any more he said, 'Give it to that beggar.' A wise person standing by him said to him, 'Fool! While you were able to eat, you didn't give to him. Now that you don't have the capacity to eat any more, you give to the beggar!'

"So is the human being in this world: He pursues his vain pleasures, ravenous to consume and acquire mammon. The beggar—the good impulse—appears and implores him to return in *teshuvah*, but he does not alter his gaze, because he is so ravenous to acquire wealth. After some time, he is seized by a neck iron. When he realizes that he is not able to acquire any more, he says, 'I will return in *teshuvah*. Perhaps I will be granted some time; perhaps not.' The blessed Holy One says to him, 'Fool! Now that you are not able anymore! Were you able, you would not have returned!' While in this state, his soul departs him."[48]



(*MhN*), 218b–219a, 226a; 2:142a; *ZḤ* 75c, 83a, 83d–84a (all three *MhN, Rut*); Moses de León, *Sefer ha-Rimmon*, 396–7.

Although repentance is always accepted, it is most noble when one is still in good health, before the onset of illness and old age. See BT *Avodah Zarah* 19a: "*Happy is the man who fears YHVH* (Psalms 112:1). Does it mean happy is the 'man' and not the woman? Rabbi Amram said in the name of Rav, '[It means] Happy is he who performs *teshuvah* whilst he is still a man.'"

See *Vayiqra Rabbah* 18:1; BT *Shabbat* 151b; *Qohelet Rabbah* and Rashi on Ecclesiastes 12:1; *Zohar* 3:13b, 87b; cf. *Zohar* 2:47a.

48. **So is the human being in this world...** Human beings turn in *teshuvah* only out of self-interest, when they are on their deathbeds. Like the glutton in the parable, were they able to consume more, they would pay the beggar (the good impulse) no heed. Such *teshuvah* is inferior. Not only does the parable illustrate the principle of turning in *teshuvah* while one is still vital, but also the concluding line ("while in this state his soul departs") elaborates the passage cited from the Song of Songs—נפשי יצאה בדברו (*nafshi yats'ah be-dabbero*), construed as *my soul departed as he spoke*: the soul departs while being castigated for not having turned sooner and with purer motive. In its simple sense, this clause means *I was faint because of what he said.*

On the beggar (literally poor man) as the good impulse, see BT *Nedarim* 32b on Ecclesiastes 9:14–15: *There was a little city with few people in it; and to it came a great king, who surrounded it and built mighty siege works against it. Present in the city was a poor wise man who delivered the city with his wisdom, but nobody remembered that wise man.* "Rami son of Abba said, 'What is the meaning of the verse *There was a little city.... A little city*—the body; *with few people in it*—the limbs; *and to it came a great king who besieged it*—the evil impulse; *and built mighty siege works against it*—to sin; *present in the city was a poor wise man*—the good impulse; *who delivered the city with his wisdom*—*teshuvah* and good deeds; *but nobody remembered that wise man*—for when the evil impulse prevails, none remembers the good impulse.'" See also *Qohelet Rabbah* on Ecclesiastes 9:15 and on 4:13.

The parable of the ravenous man and the beggar was adapted and incorporated into

Rabbi Zrika said, "Elisha son of Avuyah was the greatest among the Companions, but he was not permitted to return in *teshuvah*. For that voice issued forth; and when he was dying, it proclaimed, 'Let all roads and paths above and below be sealed to that man—that he not reach the world to come!'"[49]

Rabbi Yehoshu'a son of Levi said, "Why do we need all this? *Remember your Creator* [*in the days of your youth,*] *before the days of sorrow come* (Ecclesiastes 12:1)."[50]

*Abram heard that his kinsman had been captured* (Genesis 14:14).[51]

Rabbi Abba opened the verse as referring to the evil impulse, as stated above. "Look at what we have learned: Once the evil impulse departs from the body of the righteous, where does it go? To the abode of the wicked, that they will not challenge him.[52]

"How is this implied? As is written: *Lot dwelled in the cities of the plain, pitching his tent as far as Sodom. The people of Sodom were wicked and sinful against YHVH* (ibid. 13:12–13)—to an abode of wicked sinners, there did he establish his tent to dwell. What does the evil impulse do? He sins with them and leads them astray, until he is captured and seized for his iniquities.[53]



Isaac ibn Sahula's *Meshal ha-Qadmoni*, Gate Three, 402–7. See also Loewe's comments, 746–7. The parable is also found in a slightly different form in Moses de León's *Sefer ha-Mishqal*, 79. See Tishby, *Wisdom of the Zohar*, 1:108 n. 84.

On being confined to the sickbed as being "seized by a neck-iron," see *Zohar* 2:61a; 3:53a, 126a–b. Cf. BT *Shabbat* 32a.

49. **Elisha son of Avuyah...** Known as Aḥer ("the other"), he was one of four sages who entered the *pardes* (orchard). He was later punished for his heresy and prevented from returning in *teshuvah*. See BT *Ḥagigah* 15a: "A heavenly voice issued forth and proclaimed, '*Return rebellious children* (Jeremiah 3:22)—except Aḥer.'" See also JT *Ḥagigah* 2:1, 77b; Isaac ibn Sahula, *Meshal ha-Qadmoni*, 406–7; *Zohar* 2:254b (*Heikh*).

50. **Why do we need all this?** Why turn to the story of Elisha or the parable above to illustrate this point? The verse from Ecclesiastes is explicit! According to the rabbinic reading, the verse implies that one should turn back to God before old age. See *Vayiqra Rabbah* 18:1; BT *Shabbat* 151b; *Qohelet Rabbah* and Rashi, ad loc.; *Zohar* 3:13b, 87b.

51. ***Abram heard that his kinsman had been captured*** In the course of the battle of the kings (recounted in Genesis 14), Lot is captured. Abram launches an attack by night and rescues him. See verses 14–16: *Abram heard that his kinsman had been captured. He marshaled his retainers, natives of his household, numbering three hundred and eighteen, and he pursued as far as Dan. He deployed against them by night, he and his servants, and he struck them pursuing them as far as Hobah, which is north of Damascus. He recovered all the possessions—and also brought back his kinsman Lot and his possessions, and the women and the rest of the people.* See *Zohar* 1:80b (*ST*) for a close parallel to *MhN*'s treatment.

52. **referring to the evil impulse...** Vanquished by the righteous, the evil impulse leaves their body—seeking easier prey.

On Lot as the evil impulse, see *ZḤ* 24b (*MhN*) and note 26 above. See also *Zohar* 1:78a, 79a, 80b (all *ST*); 109a–110b, 128b (both *MhN*).

53. **until he is captured and seized for his**

"As for the soul of the righteous—what does he do? *Abram heard*—the soul; *that his kinsman had been captured*—the evil impulse. *He marshaled* חניכיו (*ḥanikhav*), *his retainers, natives of his household* (ibid.)—the righteous המחונכים (*ha-meḥunnakhim*), initiated, into the commandments and the good path. As Rabbi Abbahu said: 'As soon as the righteous person sees that the wicked person has been forsaken and seized for his iniquities, he goes to take hold of him, perchance he might restore him to the right way; he draws him close and teaches him, as is written: *he pursued as far as Dan* (ibid.)—to the root of דינו (*dino*), his judgment, pursuing him to save him from the judgment of Hell.'[54]

"So is the way of the righteous: to pursue the wicked, in order to restore them to the right way. What is written about them? *He deployed against them by night...* (ibid., 15)—the soul of the righteous, who plead and entreat them, so that they will not continue along the path of their wickedness; *he and his servants, and he struck them* (ibid.)—the soul and the righteous pursue them, rebuking and admonishing them.[55]



"*Pursuing them as far as Hobah* (ibid.)—they inform them of their evil, pursuing them until they reveal to them their evil and wickedness so that they will be ashamed of their deeds. This is the meaning of *pursuing them as far as* חובה (*ḥovah*), *guilt.* So does the soul do—informing them of their wicked path. This is the significance of *as far as Hobah*— [25a] how they incline to the left and not the right."[56]

What is written afterward? *He recovered all the possessions and also Lot* (ibid., 16).

**iniquities** Having enticed the wicked to sin, the evil impulse (Lot, Abram's kinsman) is captured, meaning that the wicked person is seized and faces heavenly judgment.

On Lot choosing the cities of the plain and Sodom, see *Zohar* 1:106b; *ZḤ* 24c (both *MhN*).

54. **pursuing him to save him...** Abram's pursuit of Lot is an allegory for the soul's and the righteous person's attempts to rescue the wicked. The righteous do not abandon the wicked but actively seek to save them from their impending doom.

See Rashi on Genesis 14:14 (Reggio di Calabria and Alkabetz editions): "חניכיו (*ḥanikhav*), *his retainers*—for he initiated them into the commandments."

55. **rebuking and admonishing them** In their efforts to save the wicked, the righteous must admonish and rebuke, i.e., deploying by night and striking.

On the role of rebuke and the responsibility of the righteous for the wicked, see Tishby, *Wisdom of the Zohar,* 3:1424–25; Hecker, "The Face of Shame: The Sight and Site of Rebuke."

56. ***Pursuing them as far as Hobah...*** Reading Hobah, a place name, as חובה (*ḥovah*), "guilt." The righteous lay bare their guilt before them.

See *Tanḥuma, Lekh Lekha* 13: "We have checked all the places and have not found any place called Hobah! This teaches you that Dan was called חובה (*ḥovah*), guilt, at the outset—on account of the calf that one day would stand there." See also Rashi on Genesis 14:15.

Rabbi Abbahu said, "They return in *teshuvah* against their will, as is written: *and also brought back his kinsman Lot and his possessions* (ibid.); even the evil impulse returns in *teshuvah* against his will."[57]

Rabbi Abbahu also said, "Come and see how great is the reward of the person who leads others to return in *teshuvah*! How do we know? From what is written afterward: *Melchizedek, king of Salem* (ibid., 18)."[58]

Rabbi Ḥiyya the Great taught, "In the hour when the soul of the righteous person—who turns others to *teshuvah*—departs from the body, Michael, the great prince, who offers the souls of the righteous before his Creator, goes forth and is first to greet the soul of that righteous person, as is said: *Melchizedek* (ibid.)—Michael, head of the guardians of the gates of צדק (*tsedeq*), righteousness; *king of Salem* (ibid.)—Jerusalem Above; *brought out bread and wine* (ibid.)—for he advances and goes forth to meet him, saying, 'May you enter in peace.'"[59]

Rabbi Ḥiyya said, "Hence we have learned: Whoever advances and goes forth to meet someone coming from a journey, offering him greetings, Scripture



57. **the evil impulse returns in *teshuvah*...** See *Zohar* 1:80b (*ST*).

58. **From what is written afterward: *Melchizedek*...** Following his victory, Abram is greeted by the king of Sodom and by Melchizedek, the king of Salem. Genesis 14:18–20 reads: *Melchizedek king of Salem brought out bread and wine. He was priest of God Most High. He blessed him, saying, "Blessed be Abram of God Most High, Possessor of Heaven and Earth. Blessed be God Most High, who has delivered your foes into your hand. He gave him a tenth of everything."*

See next paragraph and next note.

59. **Michael, the great prince...** Melchizedek is Michael, prince of celestial Jerusalem. The first four letters of Melchizedek מלכיצדק are also found in Michael—מיכאל.

According to BT *Ḥagigah* 12b and BT *Menaḥot* 110a, Michael offers sacrifices on the heavenly altar. See *Tosafot Menaḥot* 110a, s.v. *u-mikha'el sar ha-gadol*, which notes that according to some passages, these offerings are comprised of the souls of the righteous. See *Bemidbar Rabbah* 12:12; [Moses de León?], *Seder Gan Eden*, 137; *Zohar* 1:80a, 81a (both *ST*); *ZḤ* 21a, 24b (both *MhN*).

On being greeted by ministering angels, see BT *Ketubbot* 104a: "Rabbi Ḥiyya son of Gamda said in the name of Rabbi Yose son of Sha'ul, 'In the hour when the righteous person departs from the world, the ministering angels say before the blessed Holy One, "Master of the World! The righteous person so-and-so is coming." He says to them, "Let the righteous come [from their resting places], and go forth to meet him." They say to him [the departed righteous], "*Let him enter into peace; let them rest on their couches* [*he who walks uprightly*] (Isaiah 57:2).'" Rabbi El'azar said, 'When a righteous person departs from the world three companies of ministering angels go forth to meet him. One says to him, *Enter into peace*; the other says, *He who walks uprightly*, while the other says, *Let him enter into peace; let them rest on their couches.*'" See also *Zohar* 1:125b (*MhN*); *ZḤ* 21a (*MhN*). On the gates of *tsedek*, "righteousness," signifying the opening to the celestial realm, see *ZḤ* 20d (*MhN*). On Jerusalem Above, see *ZḤ* 20d–21a (*MhN*) and p. 228, n. 19.

See M *Avot* 4:15: "Rabbi Matyah son of Ḥarash said, 'Be the first to greet every person.'"

accounts it to him as though he gives him food and drink. How do we know? From this verse, as is written: *because they did not greet you with food and water* (Deuteronomy 23:5). Now, were Israel in need of food and water? Didn't the manna—which was better and finer than all the food in the world—descend for them? Well, since they didn't come to extend them greetings, Scripture accounts it to them as though they withheld their sustenance. Whoever extends greetings to his fellow and goes forth to meet him on the way, Scripture accounts it to him as though he gives him food and drink."[60]

Rabbi Ḥiyya the Great also said, "Michael and the ministering angels who guard the gates of righteousness go forth to meet him and extend him greetings."[61]

*He was priest of God Most High* (Genesis 14:18). As Rav Yosef taught: "Just as there is a high priest below, so Michael—the great prince—is priest above; he greets and blesses the soul first, and afterward blesses the blessed Holy One. Were the verse not written, it would be impossible to conceive of it, as is said: *he blessed him, saying, 'Blessed be Abram of God Most High, Possessor of Heaven*

*and Earth* (ibid., 19)—happy are you that you attained this!' Afterward: '*Blessed be God Most High who has delivered your foes into your hand* (ibid., 20)—the wicked whom you vindicated through *teshuvah*, and whose souls you made.'"[62]

*He gave him a tenth of everything* (ibid.). Rabbi Yitsḥak said, "In this verse we don't know who gave a tenth to whom! Well, the blessed Holy One gives him a

60. **because they did not greet you with food and water...** As with Melchizedek, food and water signifies greeting and meeting. The passage reads: *No Ammonite or Moabite shall come into the assembly of YHVH... because they did not greet you with bread and water on the way when you came out of Egypt* (Deuteronomy 23:4–5).

61. **angels...go forth to meet him...** That is, to meet the soul of the departed righteous person. See BT *Ketubbot* 104a; note 59 above.

62. **blesses the soul first, and afterward ...the blessed Holy One...** So beloved and esteemed is the soul that it is blessed before God is!

On the order of Melchizedek's blessings, see BT *Nedarim* 32b; *ZḤ* 22d (*MhN*) and p. 257, n. 111.

In leading the wicked to *teshuvah*, Abram is considered to have "made" their souls. This idea derives from the midrashic interpretation of Genesis 12:5: *and the souls they had made in Haran.* According to the simple sense of this verse, נפש (*nefesh*), *souls,* means *persons,* and עשו (*asu*), "made," means *acquired,* referring to the slaves that Abraham and Sarah had acquired. However, the Midrash offers a radically different reading. See *Bereshit Rabbah* 39:14: "*And the souls they had made in Haran.* Rabbi El'azar said in the name of Rabbi Yose son of Zimra, 'If all the nations assembled to create a single mosquito, they could not cast a soul into it, yet you say: *and the souls they had made*?! Rather, these are converts. Then the verse should read: [*and the souls*] *they had converted.* Why *they had made*? To teach you that whoever draws a Gentile near is as though he created him.'" See *Sifrei*, Deuteronomy 32; BT *Sanhedrin* 99b; *Shir ha-Shirim Rabbah* on 1:3; *Tanḥuma, Lekh Lekha* 12; *Avot de-Rabbi Natan* A, 12; B, 26; *Zohar* 1:130a (*MhN*); 2:128b.

On Michael as high priest, see *Zohar* 2:159a (standard editions), 229a, 231a.

tenth. He takes a single letter from beneath the Throne of Glory and bestows it as a crown upon the soul, which is Abram. Which is this single letter? ה (*He*), through which the world was created, to be bound in the bundle of life and consummate in his perfections, as is written: *No longer will your name be called Abram; your name will be Abraham* (ibid. 17:5)—this is the tenth that the blessed Holy One gave him."[63]

Rabbi Yehudah said, "This is the *Shekhinah* of the Omnipresent. For look at what we have learned: Rabbi Berekhiah said, 'What is meaning of the verse *YHVH blessed Abraham with everything* (ibid. 24:1)? That He ensconced His *Shekhinah* with him.'"[64]

Rav Ḥisda said, "The blessed Holy One does not execute justice upon the wicked in the world to come before conferring with the souls of the righteous, as is said: *By the soul of God they perish* (Job 4:9). When they perish, they perish solely on account of the soul's judgment of the wicked."[65]



63. ***He gave him a tenth of everything...*** The subject of this verse's verb is not stated and so its referent is ambiguous. Did Abram give to Melchizedek, or did Melchizedek give to Abram? According to Rabbi Yitsḥak, Melchizedek—signifying Michael—gives Abram a tenth of כל (*kol*), *everything*, whose numerical value is fifty. Hence Melchizedek gives Abram the letter ה (*he*), whose numerical value is five. The bestowal of the letter ה (*he*) is marked in the Torah with Abram's name change from אברם (*Avram*) to אברהם (*Avraham*), Abraham. The additional ה (*he*), the final letter in the Tetragrammaton, thus marks the soul's perfection and passage into the bundle of life, the *Shekhinah*/world to come (see 1 Samuel 25:29; BT *Shabbat* 152b). See *Zohar* 1:123a (*MhN*), 126a (*MhN*); *ZḤ* 26a (*MhN*); cf. *Zohar* 1:87a; see Kasher, *Torah Shelemah*, Genesis 14:20, n. 133.

On being crowned by God, see BT *Megillah* 15b: "Rabbi El'azar said in the name of Rabbi Ḥanina, 'In the future, the blessed Holy One will be a crown upon the head of every righteous person, as is said: *On that day YHVH of hosts shall become a crown of beauty [and a diadem of glory for the remnant of His people]* (Isaiah 28:5).'"

See also BT *Menaḥot* 29b: "Why does the letter ה (*he*) have a coronet? The blessed Holy One said, 'If he repents I will set a crown upon him.'"

On the world's being created through the letter ה (*he*), see BT *Menaḥot* 29b: "*These are the generations of heaven and earth* בהבראם (*be-hibbare'am*), *when they were created* (Genesis 2:4). Do not read בהבראם (*be-hibbare'am*), when they were created, but rather בה' בראם (*be-he bera'am*), with ה (*he*) He created them." See *Bereshit Rabbah* 12:10; JT *Ḥagigah* 2:1, 77c; *Alfa Beita de-Rabbi Aqiva*, Version 1 (*Battei Midrashot*, 2:363); *Zohar* 1:46b, 91b; *ZḤ* 3a, 3d, 17a, 26a (all *MhN*).

64. **This is the *Shekhinah*...** According to a rabbinic interpretation, the phrase *YHVH blessed Abraham* בכל (*ba-kol*), *with everything*, alludes to Abraham's being blessed with a daughter, whose name was *ba-kol*, "with everything." In Kabbalah, this daughter is identified with the divine daughter, *Shekhinah*. See BT *Bava Batra* 16b; *Bahir* 52 (78); Naḥmanides on Genesis 24:1; *Zohar* 1:219a; 2:36a; *ZḤ* 10d (*MhN*). Cf. *Zohar* 1:17a, 130b; 2:157a.

65. **before conferring with the souls of the righteous...** In the Garden of Eden.

Cf. *Tanḥuma* (Buber), *Vayera* 6: "Even when the blessed Holy One grew angry over Sodom because of their wicked deeds and sought to overturn Sodom, He did not seal

It has been taught: ערסיאל (*Arsi'el*), the prince of Hell, confronts the souls of the righteous, so that they will not pray for the wicked before the blessed Holy One, and so that they will hand them over to his dominion—to bring them down to the Pit of Destruction, as is written: *The king of Sodom said to Abram, "Give me the soul"* (Genesis 14:21). *King of Sodom*—the prince of Hell presiding over the wicked.[66]

What does he say to the *neshamah*, which is Abram? "Give me the *nefesh* that sins," as is said: *The nefesh that sins, she shall die* (Ezekiel 18:4). In other words, "Give me the *nefesh* [25b] that craves sins, that she might be judged according to her wickedness, and not spared through your supplications. *But the property take for yourself* (Genesis 14:21)—those who with their *nefashot*, souls, returned in *teshuvah* from their wicked path, *take for yourself* and save them from the judgment of Hell."[67]



Rabbi Yehudah said, "At that time, what does the *neshamah* say? *Abram said to the king of Sodom, 'I raise my hand to YHVH, God Most High* (ibid., 22)—in oath, that I will neither pray for nor take those wicked ones before whom I used to proclaim in that world, whom I admonished to return in *teshuvah*, and to whom I elucidated all the judgments of Hell, but who did not listen to me. *If I should take from anything that is yours* (ibid., 23)—they are yours and are in your dominion.'"[68]

their decree of punishment before conferring with Abraham, as is said: *And YHVH said, 'Shall I hide from Abraham [what I am about to do?']* (Genesis 18:17)." See also *Tanḥuma, Vayera* 5. In line with the *Zohar*'s allegorical reading, the motif of conferring with Abraham has been replaced with conferring with the souls of the righteous.

The simple sense of the verse from Job is: *By a blast of God they perish.*

See *Zohar* 1:104b (*MhN*) also in the name of Rav Ḥisda.

66. ***King of Sodom*—the prince of Hell...** According to the narrative in Genesis, following his encounter with Melchizedek, Abram meets the King of Sodom, who suggests they divide the spoils of war: *The king of Sodom said to Abram, "Give me* הנפש (*ha-nefesh*), *the persons* [i.e., the former prisoners], *but the property take for yourself."* In the *Zohar*'s allegorical reading, *ha-nefesh* is read hyperliterally, referring to the soul of the wicked whom the Prince of Hell seeks to seize for his own.

When speaking of the wicked, the *Zohar* uses the term *nefesh*, signifying the lowest aspect of the soul. When speaking of the righteous, it uses the term *neshamah*—the highest, most sublime aspect of the soul.

The name *Arsi'el* appears to derive from ערס (*eres*), whose meanings include "bier, catafalque, bed." See BT *Sanhedrin* 109b on the "bed of Sodom." See also Naphtali ben Ya'akov Elḥanan Bacharach, *Emeq ha-Melekh* 14:134. Usually, it is *Dumah*, the angel in charge of the souls of the dead, who oversees Hell. See BT *Berakhot* 18b, *Shabbat* 152b, *Sanhedrin* 94a; *Zohar* 1:8a–b, 62b, 94a, 102a (*MhN*), 124a (*MhN*), 130b, 218b, 237b; 2:18a (*MhN*), 150b.

67. ***But the property take for yourself...*** See above, *ZḤ* 24b (*MhN*), page 282, where property (possessions) is understood as signifying good deeds.

68. **what does the *neshamah* say...** In the continuation of the narrative in Genesis (14:22–24), Abram rejects the King of Sodom's offer—he will not take anything be-

As Rabbi Yehoshu'a son of Levi said: "Once I was gazing, and I found myself by the gate of Hell. I heard the sound of the wicked being tormented in Hell—with the excruciating punishments with which the wicked are judged in the world to come. They said, 'Our verdict is executed! We heard but did not incline our ears! Woe to us! We did not heed the words of the righteous!'[69]

"I wept. I heard a voice saying, 'Son of Levi, son of Levi, ascend your ascent and seal your mouth! You are not permitted, for of you and your companions is written *You will trample the wicked, for they will be ashes under the soles of your feet* (Malachi 3:21).'"[70]

Rabbi Yehoshu'a son of Levi also said, "Hell has seven habitations where the wicked are judged in the time to come; and Hell has seven entrances corresponding to the seven entrances through which the soul of the righteous passes. Corresponding to them there are seven entrances through which the *nefesh* of the wicked passes. They are: *Ofel*, *Tsalmavet*, *Sha'arei Mavet*, *Be'er Shaḥat*, *Tit ha-Yaven*, *Sheol*, and *Avadon*—they are punished there for twelve months."[71]



longing to the king of Sodom: *Abram said to the king of Sodom, "I raise my hand to YHVH, God Most High, Possessor of Heaven and Earth; if from a thread to a sandal strap, if I should take from anything that is yours, lest you say, 'It is I who made Abram rich!' Nothing for me, only what the lads have eaten; and the share of the men who went with me—Aner, Eshkol, and Mamre—they shall take their share."*

69. **I found myself by the gate of Hell...** Cf. *Massekhet Geihinnom* (*Beit ha-Midrash*, 1:148); *Ma'aseh de-Rabbi Yehoshu'a ben Levi* (*Beit ha-Midrash*, 2:50).

On the phrase "I was gazing," see Daniel 7:2.

The lament uttered by the denizens of Hell is quite lyrical: פותקנא סייפנא, שמענא ולא אריכנא אודננא, ווי לן מילתא דצדיקיא לא עבדנא (*putqana seyafana, shem'ana ve-la arikhna udnana, vai lan milta de-tsaddiqaya la avadna*).

70. **ascend your ascent and seal your mouth...** Just as Abram swears to the King of Sodom not to pray for the wicked, Yehoshu'a son of Levi is forbidden from praying for the souls of the wicked in Hell. He is thus ordered to return (ascend) to his terrestrial domain.

On the verse from Malachi, see BT *Rosh ha-Shanah* 17a: "Transgressors of Israel who sin with their body, and transgressors of the Gentiles who sin with their body, descend to Hell and are punished there for twelve months. After twelve months, their body is consumed; their soul, burned; and the wind scatters them under the soles of the feet of the righteous, as is said: *You will trample the wicked, for they will be ashes under the soles of your feet.*" See also *Tosefta Sanhedrin* 13:4; *Seder Olam Rabbah* 3.

71. **Hell has seven habitations...** On the seven entrances to Hell, see *Pirqei de-Rabbi Eli'ezer* 53; *Zohar* 1:237b; 2:150b; 3:285b. On its seven habitations (or divisions), see BT *Sotah* 10b; *Midrash Tehillim* 11:6; *Zohar* 1:40a (*Heikh*), 62b, 237b; 2:150b; 263a–68b (*Heikh*); 3:178a, 285b–286a; *Massekhet Geihinnom* (*Beit ha-Midrash*, 1:149); Ginzberg, *Legends*, 5:20, n. 56. For a list of seven names for Hell, see BT *Eruvin* 19a.

On the seven entrances to the Garden of Eden, see *ZḤ* 20d–21a (*MhN*).

Roughly translated, the names of Hell are (in order): Darkness; Deep Gloom [or: Shadow of Death]; Gates of Death; Pit of Destruction; Miry Clay; Underworld; Ruin.

As Rabbi Shim'on said: "The sentence of the wicked in Hell lasts twelve months. There they squeal *teshuvah*, and the souls of the righteous entreat the blessed Holy One; and they are raised up from Sheol—the sixth habitation, as is said: *brings down to Sheol and raises up* (1 Samuel 2:6). But whoever enters the seventh habitation—*Avadon*—does not rise again. As it has been taught: Rabbi Yehudah said, 'Even though one has entered Sheol, he may rise through *teshuvah*, as is said: *From the belly of Sheol I cried out, You heard my voice* (Jonah 2:3).'"[72]

Alternatively, *I raise my hand to YHVH, God Most High... if from a thread...* (Genesis 14:22–23). Rabbi El'azar said, "Those befitting you, who are completely wicked, who never returned in *teshuvah*, I swear that I will never take them."[73]

*Nothing for me, only what the lads have eaten* (ibid., 24). Rabbi Tanḥum said, "Come and see how beloved is the Torah before the blessed Holy One! For on account of her, a person attains life of the world to come; and whoever teaches Torah to others—more so than the rest! Come and see what is written here: *if I should take from anything that is yours* (ibid., 23)—those evildoers befitting you. *Nothing for me, only what the lads have eaten* (ibid., 24)—aside from those who teach Torah to others and little children, whose reward is double.[74]



72. **The sentence of the wicked in Hell lasts twelve months...** See M *Eduyyot* 2:10; BT *Rosh ha-Shanah* 17a; *Seder Olam Rabbah* 3; *Zohar* 1:68b, 106b (*MhN*), 130b.

On rising from Hell, see BT *Rosh ha-Shanah* 16b–17a in the name of the House of Shammai: "There are three groups at the Day of Judgment: one of the completely righteous, one of the completely wicked, and one of the intermediate. The completely righteous are written and sealed immediately for life; the completely wicked are written and sealed immediately for Hell...; the intermediate go down to Hell and squeal [on account of their punishment] and rise. Of them Hannah said: *YHVH deals death and grants life, brings down to Sheol and raises up* (1 Samuel 2:6)." See *Zohar* 2:150a; 3:178a; *ZḤ* 33d, 69a (*ShS*). On rising from Sheol through *teshuvah* and the pleas of the souls of the righteous, see *Zohar* 2:150b; 3:220b.

In the Bible, Sheol—the underworld, the abode of the dead—is sometimes paired poetically with Avadon, "destruction, ruin," which may refer to a distinct area of the underworld reserved for the wicked. See Proverbs 15:11; Job 26:6. Cf. Revelation 9:11, where Avadon is the name of the angel of the bottomless pit. See *Zohar* 1:62b; 3:54b, 178a, 285b–286a.

Cf. Dante, *Inferno* 3: "Abandon hope, all you who enter here."

73. ***if from a thread...*** Rabbi El'azar compares the wicked to a *thread* and *sandal strap*, i.e., lowly, worthless and dispensable. For the simple sense of the biblical passage, see above, note 68.

74. ***only what the lads have eaten...*** Those who have nourished others—and especially the young—with Torah are spared the judgments of Hell. Cf. BT *Bava Metsi'a* 85a: "Whoever teaches Torah to the child of an ignoramus, even if the blessed Holy One makes a decree, He annuls it for his sake, as is written: *If you produce what is noble out of the worthless, you shall be as My mouth* (Jeremiah 15:19)."

Cf. *Bava Batra* 8b: "*The enlightened will shine like the radiance of the sky* (Daniel 12:3)—this refers to the teachers of children."

On the importance of teaching Torah to children, see BT *Shabbat* 119b: "Resh Lakish said in the name of Rabbi Yehudah the Patriarch, 'The world endures only for the sake

"As Rabbi Yitsḥak said: 'One who teaches Torah to little children—his abode is with *Shekhinah*.'[75]

"And this is as Rabbi Shim'on said—when he would go to see the kids at school and would say, 'I am going to behold the face of *Shekhinah*!'[76]

"He says, '*Only what the lads have eaten* (ibid., 24)—aside from those who taught Torah to the young; *and the share of the men who went with me* (ibid.)—in that world. Know that I will hold onto them and will not hand them over to you, even though they deserve to be punished.'[77]

"So vigorously must the soul of the righteous [plead] with the king of Sodom—the prince of Hell, who rules over the wicked. He says to him further, 'I will not hold on to these ones by myself. Rather, *Aner, Eshkol, and Mamre* (ibid.)—who are the patriarchs—*shall take their share* (ibid.).'"[78]

Rabbi El'azar son of Rabbi Shim'on encountered Elijah in the form of a certain old man, and a small child was with him. He was traversing a raging river, to cross to the other side.[79]

He said to him, "Old man, old man, hoist this child upon my shoulder and you upon the other [25c]; and I will carry you across the ford."



He said, "Are you not a master of the generation? You will not be able to carry us."[80]

He replied, "Old man, old man, if I take hold of you and him with both of my hands, I can hurl you to the other side in half a word."[81]

of the breath of children in the house of study.'" See also BT *Bava Metsi'a* 85a–b; *Bava Batra* 21a; *Ta'anit* 24a; Maimonides, *Mishneh Torah, Hilkhot Talmud Torah* 2:1–2.

75. **his abode is with *Shekhinah*** According to BT *Avodah Zarah* 3b, God Himself teaches little children. See also *Zohar* 2:169b: "When . . . children are studying Torah, *Shekhinah* comes and gives them strength and power to study it."

76. **the face of *Shekhinah*** Cf. *Kallah Rabbati* 2:9: "The young welcome the face of *Shekhinah*."

77. **He says . . .** Namely, Abram, the soul.

78. ***Aner, Eshkol, and Mamre* . . .** Abram's allies in his battle against the kings. See Genesis 14:13. They too will save souls from Hell. They are described here as "patriarchs," paralleling Abraham, Isaac, and Jacob.

79. **Elijah in the form of a certain old man . . .** According to the Bible (2 Kings 2:11), the prophet Elijah did not die a normal death but was carried off to heaven in a chariot of fire. He became associated with the Messianic age (Malachi 3:23–24). In rabbinic tradition, he is described as "still existing" (BT *Bava Batra* 121b) and as revealing divine secrets to righteous humans (BT *Bava Metsi'a* 59b).

In Kabbalah, mystical experiences are known as "revelations of Elijah." See Scholem, *On the Kabbalah*, 19–21; *Zohar* 1:1b, 151a; 3:221a, 231a, 241b; *ZḤ* 59d, 62c (*ShS*), 63d (*ShS*), 70d (*ShS*), 73c (*ShS*). In *MhN*, see *Zohar* 1:100b; *ZḤ* 23d.

On Elijah as an old man, see *Tosafot* on BT *Ḥullin* 6a, s.v. *ashkaḥei ha-hu sava*.

80. **Are you not a master of the generation? . . .** Distinguished rabbis are not renowned for their physical strength. See note 82.

81. **hurl you to the other side in half a word** In the time it takes to say a half a word; with ease, in a flash.

He said to him, "Do you toil in Torah?"

He replied, "Yes."

He said to him, "Is she not called תושיה (*tushiyyah*), שמתשת (*she-matteshet*), because she enfeebles, a person's strength?"[82]

He replied, "Is she not called healing and refreshment, as is said: *She will be a healing for your flesh, refreshment for your bones* (Proverbs 3:8)? I too have imbibed deeply from Torah, like one imbibing a healing brew, and my strength has been steeled."[83]

He carried them across.

He said to him, "Old man, old man, who is this child with you?"

He replied, "I am teaching him Torah."

He said to him, "Old man, old man, my power is great in this world and in the world to come. By virtue of this child, I will not permit the angel of Hell to touch you. By force of my power there, I will escort you into the world to come."

298 He said to him, "Rabbi, Rabbi, your power is indeed mighty in the world to come, like one of the servants of the blessed Holy One ministering in His presence."[84]

As he was looking at him, he disappeared. He said, "Conclude from this that he was Elijah." He was happy with the deeds he performed for him.

From that day on, whenever he saw the image of his father, he would say to him, "Father, father, tell that old man, 'There has been much lip-laziness in Torah!'"[85]

82. **Is she not called תושיה (*tushiyyah*)...** According to *Pirqei de-Rabbi Eli'ezer* 3, *tushiyyah* (meaning "sound judgment, prudence," see Proverbs 8:14) is another name for the Torah. See BT *Sanhedrin* 26b: "Rabbi Ḥanan said, "Why is she [Torah] called תושיה (*tushiyyah*)? Because she מתשת (*matteshet*), enfeebles, a person's strength [through constant study].'" See *ZḤ* 5d (*MhN*). Cf. *Shir ha-Shirim Rabbah* on 5:14; *Qohelet Rabbah* on 1:8; BT *Yoma* 71a. See also BT *Bava Metsi'a* 84a.

On the weak physical condition of the Companions in the *Zohar*, see *Zohar* 2:61b, 143a, 198b, 225a–b.

83. **Is she not called healing and refreshment...** On Proverbs 3:8, see *Avot* 6:7 BT *Eruvin* 54a; *Ta'anit* 7a; *Zohar* 3:80b, 160b; *ZḤ* 77d (*MhN, Rut*).

84. **like one of the servants... ministering in His presence** See *ZḤ* 19a, 20d (both *MhN*), where El'azar is again compared to the ministering angels.

85. **whenever he saw the image of his father...** The departed Rabbi Shim'on son of Yoḥai. Presumably, Rabbi El'azar evokes such visions through specific mystical techniques. See *ZḤ* 20d (*MhN*).

El'azar instructs his father to inform Elijah that he has been negligent in his studies, and hence his strength has weakened. Perhaps Elijah can help him.

"Lip-laziness" renders שפמין (*shefamin*), based on BT *Shabbat* 129b: "Rav Yosef said, 'When we were at Rav Huna's academy, on a day that the scholars were weary [i.e., lazy and didn't study] they would say, "Today is יומא דשפמי (*yoma di-shfamei*), a day of lips"

He said to him, "Tell him, 'Old man of the ancients, old man of destiny'—and immediately your strength will be steeled."[86]

*After these things, the word of YHVH came to Abram*... (Genesis 15:1).[87]

Rabbi Azariah opened with this verse, "*Draw me after you; let us run* (Song of Songs 1:4)."[88]

Rabbi Yitsḥak said, "Whoever recites the *Shema* upon his bed fittingly—his soul ascends, soaring through the Land of Life."[89]

Rabbi Bo said, "What is meant by 'fittingly'? Come and listen: There are sixty known letters in the nighttime *Shema*, through which one must focus to know

[i.e., a day without profit, of no value—like animal lips], but I did not know what they meant.'" See Rashi and *Tosafot*, ad loc.

86. **your strength will be steeled** Rabbi Shim'on conveys a talismanic mantra from the celestial realm, the recitation of which will restore Rabbi El'azar's capacity for Torah study.

"Old man of the ancients, old man of destiny" renders סבא דקדמאי סבא דפותקא (*sava de-qadmai sava de-potqa*), though the meaning of the mantra is not entirely clear. The phrase might also be rendered "Old man of the ancients, old man of the ballot." See *Tanḥuma*, *Beha'alotekha* 12 and *Bemidbar Rabbah* 15:19, where פתק (*peteq*), "ballot" and זקן (*zaqen*), "elder" are juxtaposed. There the context is the emanation of the divine spirit upon the seventy elders as recorded in Numbers 11:24–26. Perhaps the mantra serves to evoke the same divine spirit, through which El'azar's capacity to study will be restored.

The expression may also derive from BT *Qiddushin* 33a: "Issi son of Yehudah says, '*Before a gray head you shall rise* (Leviticus 19:32), implying any gray head.'... Rabbi Yoḥanan used to rise before סבי דארמאי (*savei de-aramai*), the heathen aged, saying, 'How many הרפתקי (*harpatqei*), troubles and wonders, have passed over these!'" See Rashi, ad loc.

The manuscripts differ widely here, and the phrasing is not entirely clear. I have followed the Venice edition.

87. ***After these things...*** The full verse reads: *After these things, the word of YHVH came to Abram in a vision, saying, "Fear not, Abram, I am a shield to you; your reward is very great."* The connection between this verse from Genesis and what follows is made apparent below. See notes 112, 113.

On this section in *MhN*, see Wolski, "Metatron and the Mysteries of the Night."

88. ***Draw me after you; let us run...*** The significance of this verse is not explicated here (see below, note 109). It lies at the crescendo of rabbinic Judaism's most famous mystical ascent: the four who entered the *pardes* (orchard). See *Tosefta Ḥagigah* 2:3–4.

89. **Whoever recites the *Shema* upon his bed...** The nighttime *Shema* is recited immediately before going to sleep. It consists of the first paragraph of the regular *Shema*, i.e., Deuteronomy 6:4–9. According to Rabbi Yitsḥak, one who recites it with correct intention attains a mystical ascent during sleep and enjoys contact with the Land of Life, the *Shekhinah*.

See BT *Berakhot* 5a: "Rabbi Yitsḥak said, 'Whoever recites the *Shema* upon his bed, it is as though he holds a double-edged sword in his hand [to protect him from malignant forces], as is said: *Exaltations of God in their throat, and a double-edged sword in their hand* (Psalms 149:6).' How is this implied? Mar Zutra (and some say, Rav Ashi) say, '[This is implied] from the preceding verse, as is written: *Let the pious exalt in glory; let them sing upon their beds* (ibid., 5), after those surrounding the Throne of Glory, totaling sixty, as is written: *Sixty warriors surrounding her, of the warriors of Israel* (ibid. 3:7)."[90]

Our Rabbis have taught: Once, Rabbi Dostai went to see Rabbi El'azar son of Arakh and he encountered Rabbi Ḥaggai. He said to him, "May my master tell me: the way that is arrayed before him, to whom is he going?"[91]

He replied, "To behold the Countenance of Days."[92]

which is written *Exaltations of God in their throat, and a double-edged sword in their hand.*' Rabbi Yitsḥak also said, 'Whoever recites the *Shema* upon his bed, malignant forces keep away from him, as is said: ובני רשף (*u-vnei reshef*), *as the sparks, fly upward* (Job 5:7)... and *reshef* implies only malignant forces....'"

90. **sixty known letters . . .** Precisely what these sixty letters signify is unclear. See Margaliot's comments in *ZḤ* 123c–124b (*millu'im*); Ta-Shma, *Ha-Nigleh she-ba-Nistar*, 40–41. According to *Matoq mi-Devash*, these sixty letters are dispersed among the first paragraph of the *Shema*, and though they are unknown to us, they are known to the angels.



The "letters" may in fact represent words. From the beginning of the *Shema* until the end of the first paragraph there are forty-eight words. If one adds the response ברוך שם כבוד מלכותו לעולם ועד (*barukh shem kevod malkhuto le-olam va-ed*), *blessed be the name of His glorious kingdom forever and ever*, there are fifty-four. Perhaps the number sixty is attained by assuming that this response is uttered twice. The fact that the following narrative focuses on attaining a vision of the *kavod*, "glory," supports this view.

See also *Bemidbar Rabbah* 11:3, *Shir ha-Shirim Rabbah* on 3:7, and *Tanḥuma*, *Naso* 9, which interpret the *sixty warriors* as referring to the sixty letters in the priestly blessing (Numbers 6:24–26). In the nighttime liturgy accompanying the bedtime recital of the *Shema*, Song of Songs 3:7–8 is recited and followed immediately by the priestly blessing.

According to Rabbi Bo, the correct recitation of the nighttime *Shema* involves connecting its sixty letters (words) with the sixty angels (or powers) surrounding the Throne of Glory.

On the angels surrounding the throne, see *ZḤ* 68c (*ShS*); cf. *Targum Yerushalmi* on Genesis 11:7–8; Deuteronomy 32:8; *Pirqei de-Rabbi Eliezer* 24; *Zohar* 3:231a. On the *Shema*, see *Zohar* 2:133b–134b, 139b; *ZḤ* 48a, 56d–58d (*QhM*), 90c (*MhN, Rut*); Tishby, *Wisdom of the Zohar*, 3:971–73.

The full verse from the Song of Songs reads: *Behold the bed of Solomon. Sixty warriors surrounding her, of the warriors of Israel.* See below, note 94.

91. **Our Rabbis have taught...** With the beginning of this narrative, the text switches from Hebrew to Aramaic. See below, note 112. See Asulin, "Midrash ha-Ne'lam li-Vreshit," 233.

El'azar son of Arakh was a student of Rabbi Yoḥanan son of Zakkai and a mystical adept. See JT *Ḥagigah* 2:1, 77a; BT *Ḥagigah* 14b. See below, *ZḤ* 27d–28a (*MhN*), which shares numerous features with this narrative.

See also *Zohar* 1:89a–90a (*ST*), which shares the narrative frame of this section with some variation.

The opening of this story (extending until "You are more worthy than I to go and behold the Countenance of Days!") is cited in Isaac ibn Sahula, *Peirush Shir ha-Shirim*, 439–40. See also Scholem, "Qabbalat Rabbi Yitsḥak ben Shelomoh," 112–16.

92. **Countenance of Days** This title derives from Daniel 7:9: *As I watched, thrones were placed, and the Ancient of Days sat; His garment like white snow, the hair of His head like clean fleece, His throne flames of fire, its wheels blazing fire.*

In BT *Pesaḥim* 119a, secrets of Torah are referred to as "things hidden by the Ancient

He asked him, "Who is that?"

He replied, "The one before whom the supernal princes of the blessed King descend."[93]

He asked him, "Does it please my master that I will go with him on the way?"

He replied, "If you will be able to grasp the reasoning of what you will hear, come. If not, be on your way—so that you will not be punished."

He said to him, "Let my master be not concerned about this, for I have heard a word of supernal mystery, and have contemplated it and grasped the reasoning."

He said to him, "What is it?"

He replied, "I have heard the mystery of this verse: *Behold the bed* שלשלמה (*she-li-shelomoh*), *of Solomon* (ibid. 3:7). This is the Throne of Glory of the King who possesses all שלמא (*shelama*), peace. *Sixty warriors surrounding her*—these are the sixty princes, supernal holy ministers, ministering before the Throne of Glory of the supernal King; *of the warriors of Israel*—for they are appointed under the authority of the holy prince, Michael, guardian of Israel. Since they are beneath him, they are all guardian-princes of Israel, as is written: *of the warriors of Israel*."[94]



Rabbi Dostai said to him, "You are more worthy than I to go and behold the Countenance of Days!"

They walked on. When they reached him and he saw them, he said to his servant, "Go and tell them, 'A throne with three supports, lacking one—what is it?'"[95]

of Days." See *Bereshit Rabbah* 35:2; *Zohar* 1:83a, 89b (*ST*), 130a, 188a; 3:132b (*IR*), 201a; *ZḤ* 19a (*MhN*).

Though one might expect such a lofty epithet to signify God, here the referent is Rabbi El'azar son of Arakh, presumably because he is the repository of supernal secrets.

93. **before whom the supernal princes of the blessed King descend** As is made clear below, see at note 108.

94. **I have heard the mystery...** In the *Zohar*, the *bed of Solomon* is frequently correlated with *Shekhinah* or the Throne of Glory. See *Zohar* 1:37a, 226b; 2:5a (*MhN*), 51a, 66b; 3:60a, 269b; Moses de León, *Sefer ha-Rimmon*, 370; idem, *Sheqel ha-Qodesh*, 62–64 (78–79).

On the epithet "the King who possesses peace," see *Sifra, Shemini, millu'im*, 15, 44c; *Pesiqta de-Rav Kahana* 1:2, 3; *Shir ha-Shirim Rabbah* on 1:1 and 1:2; *Zohar* 1:5b, 29a, 184a, 226b, 248b; 2:5a (*MhN*), 14a (*MhN*), 127b, 132a–b, 143b–144b; 3:10b, 20a, 60a, 73b; *ZḤ* 15d, 22a (both *MhN*); *ZḤ* 60d (*ShS, MhN*).

In rabbinic literature, Michael is the chief advocate of Israel. See Daniel 10:13, 12:1; *Shemot Rabbah* 18:5; *Pesiqta Rabbati* 44. In *MhN*, see *ZḤ* 13a–b, 21a, 23d, 24a.

95. **A throne with three supports...** El'azar poses a riddle (through an intermediary) for his would-be guests. Only if they are worthy will he admit them.

In the rabbinic narratives about El'azar son of Arakh and Yoḥanan son of Zakkai, it is El'azar who must prove his worth to his teacher before the mysteries of the divine chariot are divulged to him. See JT *Ḥagigah* 2:1, 77a, and BT *Hagigah* 14b.

See *ZḤ* 27d–28a (*MhN*) for another story involving El'azar son of Arakh and his servant.

Rabbi Dostai heard, pondered the matter within himself, and said to the servant, "Go and tell the master that not for nothing did David say *The stone the builders rejected has become the cornerstone* (Psalms 118:22). This is King David, who is the fourth."[96]

The servant went and told him this word. He said, [25d] "A fine word has been spoken. Nevertheless, go and ask him, 'Where did they reject David—such that he said *The stone the builders rejected*?'"

He said to Rabbi Ḥaggai, "Have you heard something about this?"

He replied, "I have heard three matters, one of which is conventional interpretation."[97]

He said to him, "I have not come here for conventional interpretation! For I have already heard the incident of Jesse and his sons. But, if you have heard the essence of the word, speak."[98]

He said, "The essence of the word comprises two matters that I have heard. One is that which my father said: On the day that the Temple was built, the



blessed Holy One performed great kindness to King David. For after that sin befell him, even though the blessed Holy One absolved him, when he departed this world the supernal angels did not allow him to pass through the gates of Jerusalem Above, and he sat outside. On the day that the Temple was built, the blessed Holy One summoned Michael, the holy prince, and appointed him and the sixty supernal holy-beings to be guardians for Israel; they are the ones surrounding His Throne of Glory. He charged Michael to escort David the Messiah through the gates of Jerusalem Above, to array him with the Patriarchs—a supernal, holy chariot—as is written: *over all the goodness that* YHVH *had shown to his servant David and His people Israel* (1 Kings 8:66).[99]

96. **This is King David, who is the fourth** Rabbinic tradition applies this verse from Psalms to David, youngest of Jesse's sons, relegated to tending the flock. See 1 Samuel 16:11; BT *Pesaḥim* 119a; *Midrash Shemu'el* 19:7. Here, Rabbi Dostai employs the verse to answer Rabbi El'azar's riddle. The missing leg of the throne is King David.

On Psalms 118:22 and David as the fourth leg of the throne, see *Zohar* 1:20a, 20b, 72a, 89b (*ST*), 99a, 197b, 246b, 248b. See also below, note 99.

97. **conventional interpretation** This renders דרשה (*derashah*), "interpretation, homiletical interpretation," contrasted here with deeper wisdom: "the essence of the matter (or word)." See *ZḤ* 18c (*MhN*); cf. *Zohar* 2:145a.

98. **I have not come here for...** See Joseph Gikatilla, *Sha'arei Orah*, 2a, who cites this passage as "I have not come here for *derashah*, but rather for the essence of the matter." See also *Zohar* 1:213a. On the "essence of the matter," see *ZḤ* 12c, 15c (both *MhN*); Moses de León, *Sefer ha-Rimmon*, 307.

99. **to array him with the Patriarchs—a supernal, holy chariot...** When the Temple was built, the divine chariot was made complete, as David joined with the Patriarchs (Abraham, Isaac, and Jacob).

See *Bereshit Rabbah* 47:6: "Resh Lakish

"The other matter is regarding what is written about Judah his ancestor, whose brothers rejected him, as is written: *Judah went down from his brothers* (Genesis 38:1)—for they removed him from his greatness. But of all the sons of Jacob, it did not please the blessed Holy One to bestow the dominion of eternal kingship on any except Judah, as is written: *The scepter shall not depart from Judah* (Genesis 49:10)—he alone, and not the other sons of Jacob. This is the word my father said.[100]

"I heard further: What prompted the blessed Holy One to bestow rulership on Judah among all his brothers? Well, the blessed Holy One looked upon His great Name that was inscribed in the name of Judah; and because of this, made him rule over all. His rule shall not be withdrawn."[101]

Rabbi Dostai came and kissed him on his head.

Rabbi El'azar heard and went out toward them. He said, "You are masters of the supernal academy! Bring me half and whole—and you will see and live what



said, 'The patriarchs themselves constitute the [divine] chariot.'"

On David joining with the patriarchs to complete the throne (or chariot), see *Zohar* 1:60b, 99a, 154b, 197b, 248b; 2:53a, 144a; 3:262b; Moses de León, *Shushan Edut*, 342; idem, *Sefer ha-Rimmon*, 239–40. Cf. Azriel of Gerona, *Peirush ha-Aggadot*, 57. On the relation between David and the patriarchs, see BT *Pesaḥim* 117b; *Mo'ed Qatan* 16b; *Sanhedrin* 107a; *Midrash Tehillim* 18:8, 25; Moses de León, *Sheqel ha-Qodesh* 45 (54); Jacob ben Sheshet, *Ha-emunah ve-ha-Bittaḥon*, 396; Baḥya ben Asher on Genesis 32:10; Ginzberg, *Legends*, 6:265, n. 94.

See also BT *Shabbat* 30a: "David said before the blessed Holy One, 'Master of the World, absolve me of that transgression [i.e., with Bathsheba].' He said to him, 'You are absolved.' He said to Him, 'Give me a sign while I am alive.' He answered him, 'While you are alive I will not show you; but in your son Solomon's life, I will show you.' When Solomon built the Temple, he sought to bring the Ark of the Covenant into the Holy of Holies; but the gates cleaved to one another. Solomon recited twenty-four songs but was not answered.... When he said '*O YHVH God, do not turn away the face of Your anointed. Remember Your kindness to Your servant David* (2 Chronicles 6:42),' he was answered immediately."

100. ***Judah went down from his brothers...*** According to rabbinic tradition, Judah ruled over his brothers; but following the sale of Joseph he was deposed, i.e., he *went down*. See *Tanḥuma* (Buber), *Vayeshev* 12; *Shemot Rabbah* 42:3; Rashi on Genesis 38:1; *Zohar* 1:186a.

Though rejected by his brothers, he was nevertheless favored by God to be the progenitor of the monarchy and the tribe of kingship. Hence, like his descendant David, Judah was rejected but then became the cornerstone.

101. **His great Name that was inscribed in the name of Judah...** The name יהודה (*Yehudah*), Judah, contains all four letters—in order—of the divine name, יהוה (*YHVH*).

Cf. BT *Sotah* 10b, in the name of Rabbi Shim'on the Pious: "Judah, who sanctified the heavenly Name in public [when he publically confessed his sin with Tamar], merited that the whole of his name should be called after the Name of the blessed Holy One." See also *Zohar* 1:237a; 2:104a.

has never been [revealed], as is written: *for no human can see Me and live* (Exodus 33:20). But you will live!"[102]

They sat in his presence. He was silent, and they were silent. He entered into a chamber and heard a voice saying, "Tell them whatever they desire, for they are worthy."[103]

Before he descended, night dusked. They ate. While they were eating, he was silent, and they were silent. After they ate, they arose to lie down. He said to them, "If one of you has heard a word, tell me."[104]

Rabbi Dostai opened, saying, "We shall grasp the reasoning, but what is good to know, you will tell us."

He said to them, "Have you heard the word that Rabbi Yitsḥak said: 'Whoever recites the *Shema* upon his bed fittingly—his soul ascends, soaring through the Land of Life, as is written: *Sixty warriors surrounding her, of the warriors of Israel* (Song of Songs 3:7)?'"

They replied, "Let our master say."



He said to them, "In the recitation of the *Shema*, there are sixty letters until *and in your gates* (Deuteronomy 6:9); and on every single letter there is a precious mystery of holy kingship, of the supernal ruler. The worship of a human being before Him [should be such] until he draws his mind near to the Throne of Glory of holy kingship; because at that time, the Prince of the Countenance, whose name is like his Master's, takes them from his mouth—for every night he goes forth to raise the souls of the righteous—and deposits them on high before the precious altar above. Sixty angels surrounding the Throne of Glory receive them, each one a single letter, and they sing with them the entire night. This is the meaning of the verse *The priest shall take the basket from your hand and set it*

102. **Bring me half and whole; and you will see and live...** Having solved his riddle, Rabbi El'azar goes out to meet them—and promises them an experience beyond the limits of ordinary human cognition. What even Moses could not see, they will!

"Bring me half and whole" apparently refers to the rabbis' solution of the riddle, first solved in part—and now clarified completely. Cf. *Sullam* and *Matoq mi-Devash* for different readings.

See *ZḤ* 9d–10a (*MhN*), where the verse from Exodus is interpreted as signifying Moses' denied vision of Metatron, the glory of God.

On the epithet "masters of the supernal academy," cf. *Zohar* 1:115b (*MhN*), 123b (*Tos*); *ZḤ* 15a (*MhN*); Scholem, "Parashah Ḥadashah," 432–33, 443 (Addendum 1 in this volume).

103. **He entered into a chamber...** See *ZḤ* 27d (*MhN*). Cf. *Zohar* 1:88b (*ST*). See also Liebes, *Peraqim*, s.v. *idra*, 93–94, 100. See below, at note 111, where the supernal chambers signify the destination of the soul's ascent.

104. **They ate...** On the significance of meals, see Hecker, *Mystical Bodies, Mystical Meals*, 116–41.

"Dusked" renders the verb רמש (*remash*), an apparently Zoharic coinage based on רמשא (*ramsha*), "evening." See *Zohar* 1:34b; 2:36b, 171a, 173a, 188a, 208a; 3:21a–b, 52a, 113b, 149a–b, 166b; *ZḤ* 7d, 28b (both *MhN*).

*down before the altar of YHVH your God* (ibid. 26:4). *The priest shall take*—Metatron; הטנא (*ha-tene*), *the basket*—the sixty letters of the nighttime recitation of the *Shema*."[105]

He taught them. Their souls departed from them, and they saw what they saw—and awoke. They said to one another, "Let us not sit here [26a]; we are not worthy of this! He who is a supernal angel can abide this glory."[106]

What were they thinking? They saw that the angels were thrusting them aside and they were saddened, until they saw what they saw; and Rabbi El'azar's soul brought them through and they were saved.[107]

They saw the High Priest coming to receive the teaching of Rabbi El'azar, saying "Holy Rabbi, ascend, ascend!"[108]

He said to him, "*Draw me after you; let us run* (Song of Songs 1:4)."[109]

105. **In the recitation of the *Shema*...** Amplifying Rabbi Yitsḥak's tradition, Rabbi El'azar teaches that following the correct recitation of the *Shema* (focusing on the Throne of Glory), Metatron appears to raise the letters on high to the awaiting angels. On the sixty letters (words) of the *Shema* and the sixty angels, see above, note 90.

The phrase "a precious mystery of holy kingship" might also be rendered: "a mystery of the glory of holy kingship."

On Metatron as the intermediary between the lower and upper worlds, see *ZḤ* 24a (*MhN*) and note 21. Metatron's name is "like his Master's" in that like the divine name Shaddai, it has the numerical value of 314. See BT *Sanhedrin* 38b; Rashi on Exodus 23:21. On Metatron as high priest, cf. *Zohar* 2:159a (standard editions). See also *Bemidbar Rabbah* 12:12.

The numerical value of *tene*, "basket," is sixty.

106. **Their souls departed from them...** Having learned the technique and performed it, they enjoy mystical ascent (presumably) during their sleep.

On the expression, "saw what they saw," see Scholem, *Kabbalah*, 228.

"Supernal angel" refers to El'azar son of Arakh.

107. **the angels were thrusting them aside...** Just as in Rabbi Ḥaggai's homily—where the angels prevented David from entering Jerusalem Above—here the angels prevent the souls of Rabbi Dostai and Rabbi Ḥaggai from completing their ascent.

The hostility of the angels toward human beings and human mystical ascent is a common motif both in rabbinic literature (see, for example, BT *Shabbat* 88b–89a; *Pesiqta Rabbati* 20:4) and in the Heikhalot corpus (see Schäfer, *The Hidden and Manifest God*, 36–39).

While in the celestial realm and existing as soul only, Rabbi El'azar is still able to assist the neophytes.

108. **High Priest coming to receive...** Metatron. See *ZḤ* 28b (*MhN*).

109. ***Draw me after you; let us run...*** This verse was cited at the beginning of this section, though its connection with the recitation of the *Shema* was not apparent. Only now is Rabbi Azariah's statement made clear: The verse from the Song of Songs is part of the dialogue between the soul and Metatron, as the soul responds to Metatron's invitation to ascend on high.

Note that the verse begins in the singular (*draw me*) and switches to the plural (*let us*). Rabbi El'azar seeks to follow Metatron while accompanied by Rabbi Dostai and Rabbi Ḥaggai (*let us run*).

On Song of Songs 1:4, cf. *Zohar* 3:59a; *ZḤ* 65b, 66d–67b, 68b (all *ShS*).

He said to him, "Who are those with you?"

He replied, "They are the dignitaries of the generation."

He said to him, "I do not have permission, for the blessed Holy One told me to receive your countenance, and I will enter in His presence, as is written: *The king has brought me to his chambers* (ibid.). By your life, O holy one, all the hosts of heaven *delight and rejoice in you* (ibid.)."[110]

Rabbi Yitsḥak said, "So does Metatron, the Prince of the Countenance, for all the righteous—when he raises their soul on high. He says, 'Ascend, ascend,' and the soul replies, '*Draw me after you; let us run. The king has brought me to his chambers*—since it is His will that I ascend to supernal chambers, *let us delight and rejoice with you* (ibid.),' as is written: *Let the pious exalt with glory* (Psalms 149:5)—this is Metatron."[111]

Rabbi Yitsḥak said, "In the hour when the soul of the righteous ascends before the blessed Holy One, He makes him a promise and blesses him, as is written: *After these things the word of YHVH came to Abram in a vision, saying, 'Fear not, Abram, I am a shield to you; your reward is very great'* (Genesis 15:1). *To Abram*—the soul; *in a vision*—when he lies upon his bed. What does he say to him? *Fear not, Abram, I am a shield to you; your reward is very great.*"[112]

Alternatively, *in a vision*, as is said: *The vision of the glory of YHVH as a consuming fire on the top of the mountain* (Exodus 24:17)—this is Metatron, who leads him to his Creator.[113]



110. **I do not have permission...** Metatron refuses to raise Rabbi Dostai and Rabbi Ḥaggai. Though we are not told why, apparently they are unworthy.

Note that the continuation of the verse from the Song of Songs employs the second-person singular (*delight and rejoice* בך [*bakh*], *in you*), thereby supporting Metatron's refusal to raise El'azar's students.

Seeing that they were being refused entry into the celestial realm, Rabbi Dostai and Rabbi Ḥaggai sought to depart. Rabbi El'azar, however, brought them through, i.e., helped them complete their ascent.

111. ***The king has brought me to his chambers...*** Once again, the verse from the Song of Songs encodes the dialogue between Metatron and the soul seeking ascent. In this case, though, the entirety of the verse is spoken by the soul, and the soul delights *with you*, namely Metatron—the agent of her ascent.

On Metatron as glory, see above, *ZḤ* 9d (*MhN*); 24a (*MhN*), pages 279–80.

See Isaac ibn Sahula, *Peirush Shir ha-Shirim*, 413, where this paragraph is cited.

112. ***After these things...*** The *Zohar* here returns to its allegorical reading of the Abraham narrative. Significantly, the text switches back to Hebrew. The divine promise to shield Abram signifies God's protection of the soul from the hostile angels who would thwart her ascent.

113. **Metatron, who leads him to his Creator** Abram's vision corresponds with the vision of the glory, i.e., Metatron.

On Metatron as guide, see *Arukh*, s.v. *metator*; Naḥmanides on Exodus 12:12.

Alternatively, Rabbi Tanḥum said, "What is written before this topic? *Only what the lads have eaten* (Genesis 14:24). Afterward is written *After these things, the word of YHVH came to Abram* (ibid. 15:1)—at the time when the soul sits, nourished and garbed by the light above."[114]

As Rabbi Tanḥum said: "The garment of the soul in the world to come is a radiant light from beyond the Throne of Glory, as is said: *Light is sown for the righteous; joy, for the upright in heart* (Psalms 97:11); and similarly: *YHVH shall be for you an everlasting light* (Isaiah 60:19)—not an angel and not the Throne of Glory! David also said: *YHVH is my light and my salvation—whom should I fear?* (Psalms 27:1)."[115]

114. **when the soul sits, nourished and garbed by the light above** In the previous section, the verse *After these things the word of YHVH came to Abram* במחזה (*be-maḥazeh*), *in a vision*, was expounded to signify the nocturnal vision attained by the soul following the correct recitation of the *Shema* prayer. Rabbi Tanḥum, however, connects the verse with the preceding theme: the reward of the righteous in the world to come. See above, *ZḤ* 25b (*MhN*), page 296.

On the soul sitting and being nourished by the supernal light, cf. BT *Berakhot* 17a: "A pearl in the mouth of Rav: In the world to come, there is no eating or drinking or procreation or business or jealousy or hatred or competition; rather, the righteous sit with their crowns on their heads, basking in the radiance of *Shekhinah* as is said: ויחזו (*Va-yeḥezu*), *They beheld, God; and they ate and drank* (Exodus 24:11)." See also Maimonides, *Mishneh Torah, Hilkhot Teshuvah* 8:2; *Zohar* 1:113b (*MhN*).

This and the following paragraph are cited in Isaac ibn Sahula, *Peirush Shir ha-Shirim*, 444. See also Scholem, "Qabbalat Rabbi Yitsḥak ben Shelomoh," 112–16.

115. **The garment of the soul...** In the world to come, the soul of the righteous—upon being divested of the body—is garbed in a sublime supernal light. The light is from God Himself! By virtue of this garment, the soul is able to enter and experience higher dimensions. The soul's garment is associated with the ethereal body.

On the soul's garment, see *Zohar* 1:66a, 82b, 224a–b, 226b, 233b; 2:98b, 150a, 210a, 229b, 231a, 247a (*Heikh*); 3:69a, 92a–b, 101a, 174b–175a, 214a; Moses de León, *Sefer ha-Rimmon*, 404; idem, *Sefer ha-Mishqal*, 56; Gruenwald, *Apocalyptic and Merkavah Mysticism*, 61; Scholem, *Shedim Ruḥot u-Nshamot*, 215–45; idem, *On the Mystical Shape of the Godhead*, 264–65; Nakamura Hajime, in *Encyclopedia of Religion*, ed. Eliade, 2:458.

On the ethereal body, see Naḥmanides on Genesis 49:33; *Zohar* 1:7a, 38b (*Heikh*), 81a (*ST*), 90b–91a, 115b (*MhN*), 131a, 217b, 219a, 220a, 224a–b, 227a–b, 233b; 2:11a, 13a–b, 96b, 141b, 150a, 156b–157a, 161b; 3:13a–b, 43a–b, 61b, 70b, 88b, 104a–b, 159b, 169b; *ZḤ* 10b–c, 18b (both *MhN*), 90b (*MhN, Rut*); Moses de León, *Sefer ha-Rimmon*, 390; [Moses de León?], *Seder Gan Eden*, 133; Scholem, *Kabbalah*, 158–59; idem, *On the Mystical Shape of the Godhead*, 251–73; Tishby, *Wisdom of the Zohar*, 2:770–73. Cf. Rashi on BT *Ḥagigah* 12b, s.v. *ve-ruḥot u-nshamot*.

On Psalms 97:11, see *Vayiqra Rabbah* 11:7: "Rabbi Yehudah son of Simon said, 'With the light created by the blessed Holy One on the first day, one could gaze and see from one end of the universe to the other. When the blessed Holy One foresaw the corruption of the generation of Enosh and the generation of the Flood, He hid it away from them, as is written: *The light of the wicked is withheld* (Job 38:15). Where did He hide it? In the

This accords with what Rabbi Yehudah said: "The soul of the righteous absorbed from the light of the Throne of Glory and entered this world. If she is worthy and ascends above, is it not fitting that she accrues more light than what she received at first to enter this world?"[116]

From whom does she receive this light? Rabbi Yehudah said, "Were the verse not written, it would be impossible to conceive of it, as is written: *Fear not, Abram, I am a shield to you* (Genesis 15:1)—no other. Why? Because *your reward is very great* (ibid.)."[117]

Alternatively, *your reward is very great.* You have a reward greater than what you had at first. She is garbed from that light; and the blessed Holy One takes a single letter from His Name and sets it upon her head, as we have learned: In the world to come, the blessed Holy One is destined to be a crown upon the head of all the righteous. Which one? The letter ה (*he*), through which He created heaven and earth.[118] This is the significance of the verse *No longer will your name be called Abram; your name will be Abraham* (ibid. 17:5)—so that the soul will be complete with consummate perfection and the ultimate good, as is writ-



Garden of Eden, as is said: *Light is sown for the righteous; joy, for the upright in heart* (Psalms 97:11).'" See also *Shemot Rabbah* 35:1; *Tanḥuma, Shemini* 9; *Zohar* 1:32a, 45b; 2:148b, 220b; *ZḤ* 15d (*MhN*).

The verse uttered by David concludes *whom should I fear?* This correlates with what God says in Abram's vision: *Fear not, Abram.*

116. **is it not fitting that she accrues more light...** Surely there must be a purpose and benefit to descent into this world. Why should the soul descend from the celestial realm if, after her departure, she will not gain anything?

On the soul's hailing from the Throne of Glory, see BT *Shabbat* 152b; *Avot de-Rabbi Natan* A, 12; *Zohar* 1:113a, 125b, 126b (all *MhN*); *ZḤ* 10a–d, 20b, 22a, 24a (all *MhN*). On the soul absorbing from the Throne before descending to the world, see *Zohar* 2:13a.

117. **From whom does she receive this light?...** The garment of light that garbs the soul is sublime and transcendent: a *shield* that hails directly from God Himself.

118. **the blessed Holy One takes a single letter from His Name...** See above, *ZḤ* 25a (*MhN*), page 293.

On being crowned by God, see BT *Megillah* 15b: "Rabbi El'azar said in the name of Rabbi Ḥanina, 'In the future, the blessed Holy One will be a crown upon the head of every righteous person, as is said: *On that day YHVH of hosts shall become a crown of beauty* [*and a diadem of glory for the remnant of His people*] (Isaiah 28:5).'"

See also BT *Menaḥot* 29b: "Why does the letter ה (*he*) have a coronet? The blessed Holy One said, 'If he repents, I will set a crown upon him.'"

On the world's being created through the letter ה (*he*), see BT *Menaḥot* 29b: "*These are the generations of heaven and earth* בהבראם (*be-hibbare'am*), *when they were created* (Genesis 2:4). Do not read בהבראם (*be-hibbare'am*), when they were created, but rather בה' בראם (*be-he bera'am*), with ה (*he*) He created them." See *Bereshit Rabbah* 12:10; JT *Ḥagigah* 2:1, 77c; *Alfa Beita de-Rabbi Aqiva*, Version 1 (*Battei Midrashot*, 2:363); *Zohar* 1:46b, 91b; *ZḤ* 3a, 3d, 17a (all *MhN*).

ten: *No eye has seen, O God, but You, what You will do for the one who awaits You* (Isaiah 64:3).[119]

Rabbi Yehudah son of Pazzi had a certain tenant-laborer who used to torment him. Rabbi Zeira and Rabbi Abba came before him. They said to him, "How is the master dealing with his tenant?"[120]

He replied, "When a thief steals, the Lord of the Sun radiates radiance upon him!"[121]

They said to him, "Let the master pay no heed to his actions."[122]

He replied, "What can I do, since he torments me?"

119. **the soul will be complete with consummate perfection...** Marked by the additional letter ה (*he*) in Abraham's name: from אברם (*Avram*), "Abram" to אברהם (*Avraham*), "Abraham." Hence the soul is greater than it was at first. See above, *ZḤ* 25a (*MhN*), page 293.

On the verse from Isaiah, see BT *Berakhot* 34b: "Rabbi Ḥiyya son of Abba said in the name of Rabbi Yoḥanan, 'All the prophets prophesied only concerning the days of the Messiah, but as for the world to come, *No eye has seen, O God, but You* (Isaiah 64:3).'"

Cf. Moses de León, *Sefer ha-Mishqal*, 47: "... before descending to this world, the soul is imperfect; she is lacking something. By descending to this world, she is perfected in every dimension" (transl. Matt, *Essential Kabbalah*, 148).

120. **tenant-laborer...** A farmer who worked the rabbi's land and received in return a portion of the produce.

See BT *Berakhot* 5b: "Once, four hundred jars of wine belonging to Rav Huna turned sour. Rav Yehudah, the brother of Rav Sala the Pious, and the other scholars (some say: Rav Adda the son of Ahavah and the other scholars) went in to visit him and said to him, 'Let the master examine his actions.' He said to them, 'Am I suspect in your eyes?' They replied, 'Is the blessed Holy One suspect of enacting judgment without justice?' He said to them, 'If somebody has heard of anything against me, let him speak out.' They replied, 'We have heard that the master does not give his tenant his [share of] vine shoots.' He replied, 'Does he leave me any? He steals them all!' They said to him, 'This accords with what the proverb says: If you steal from a thief, you also have a taste of it!' He said to them, 'I pledge myself to give it to him [in the future].' Some say that the vinegar became wine again; others that the vinegar went up so high that it was sold for the same price as wine."

This story appears (with variations and omissions) in Isaac ibn Sahula, *Peirush Shir ha-Shirim*, 453–54. See also Scholem, "Qabbalat Rabbi Yitsḥak ben Shelomoh," 112–16.

121. **the Lord of the Sun radiates radiance...** Even though he is a thief, the sun still shines upon him. Apparently, Rabbi Yehudah is lamenting the fact that even though his tenant is stealing from him, he has not been punished from above, and seemingly God is still smiling upon him. Perhaps he also intends: Given that he is stealing from me, should I be yet more generous with him? Cf. Exodus 22:2.

122. **Let the master pay no heed to his actions** In the Talmudic account, the scholars tell Rav Huna to examine his actions, i.e., perhaps he is the cause of his own suffering. In the Zoharic reworking, the rabbis tell Rabbi Yehudah to ignore the thief's actions, i.e., to turn a blind eye and not focus on the apparent injustice. Alternatively, the rabbis' statement might be construed as a question: Should not the master examine his actions?

They said to him, [26b] "Let the master separate from him, and you will enjoy respite."

While they were sitting they said to him, "Not for this did we come to you. Rather, may the master tell us: the tribes—the sons of Jacob—what are they in the world to come?"

He replied, "The blessed Holy One raised them to the Academy of the Firmament, and for every soul of the righteous that ascends, they testify about his deeds. As is written: *Jerusalem built up* (Psalms 122:3)—Jerusalem Above; *there tribes ascend, the tribes of Yah, a testimony to Israel* (ibid., 4)—in order to offer testimony on behalf of each and every righteous person from Israel. Why? That they will all praise and bless His Name, as is written: *testimony to Israel, to praise the name of YHVH* (ibid.). Each and every one recognizes its own and boasts, saying, 'Master of the World, look at what I have left on earth!' This is the meaning of *to praise the name of YHVH*.[123]



"This corresponds with what we have learned: Every righteous person has a habitation in accordance with his honor, and in accordance with what he deserves. Whoever hails from Reuben, his habitation is with the righteous from Reuben; and so for each and every tribe. Whoever is a convert, converted from the nations of the world, his habitation is with the converts. The tribes stand poised as witnesses for every righteous person, as is written: *There tribes ascend, the tribes of Yah, a testimony to Israel, to praise the name of YHVH*."[124]

Rabbi Yehudah said, "In the world to come, the soul of the righteous fathoms and comprehends what a ministering angel does not fathom and comprehend, as is written: *Say of the righteous one* כי טוב (*ki tov*), *that he is good* (Isaiah 3:10). What is meant by כי טוב (*ki tov*)? טוב (*Tov*), *Better*, than the ministering angels;

123. **raised them to the Academy of the Firmament...** In its simple sense, Psalms 122:3–4 reads: *Jerusalem built up, a city bounded together, where tribes ascend* [i.e., make pilgrimage], *the tribes of Yah.* עדות לישראל (*Edut le-yisra'el*), *An ordinance it is for Israel, to praise the name of YHVH*. Here, the verses convey the tribes' status in the celestial realm, i.e., Jerusalem Above, where they provide עדות (*edut*), *testimony*, for the righteous and give thanks for the holy seed they have left behind on earth [i.e., *praise the name of YHVH*]. Perhaps this final clause is being read as follows: *to praise the name* [of the righteous person to] *YHVH*.

On Psalms 122:3 and Jerusalem Above, see BT *Ta'anit* 5a; *Tanḥuma, Pequdei* 1; *ZḤ* 20d (*MhN*). On the twelve tribes above, cf. *Zohar* 1:158a, 183b, 231b, 242a; 3:78a, 118b.

124. **a habitation in accordance with his honor...** See BT *Shabbat* 152a in the name of Rabbi Yitsḥak: "Every righteous person is given a habitation in accordance with his honor. This may be compared to a king who enters a town together with his servants. When they enter, they all enter though one gate; when they spend the night, each is given a habitation in accordance with his honor." See also *Tanḥuma, Emor* 6; *Vayiqra Rabbah* 27:1; *Zohar* 3:196b; *ZḤ* 34a–b, 49b, 75c (*Rut*). Cf. [Moses de León?], *Seder Gan Eden*.

and it is written: *Light is sown for the righteous; joy, for the upright in heart* (Psalms 97:11)."[125]

## Section 12[126]

Alternatively, *When Abram was ninety-nine years old, YHVH appeared to Abram...* (Genesis 17:1).[127]

Rabbi Yitsḥak opened, "*Like an apple tree among the trees of the forest, so is my beloved among the young men. In his shade I delighted to sit, and his fruit is sweet to my mouth* (Song of Songs 2:3)."

Rabbi Yitsḥak said, "Abraham was three years old when he recognized his Creator, as is said: עקב (eqev), *because, Abraham listened to My voice* (Genesis 26:5). עקב (*Eqev*)—one hundred and seventy-two years. The days of his life spanned one hundred and seventy-five. Hence: עקב (eqev), *one hundred and seventy-two, Abraham listened to My voice,* while for three he did not listen to Him."[128]



125. **the soul of the righteous fathoms...** See BT *Sanhedrin* 92b–93a: "Rabbi Yoḥanan said, 'The righteous are greater than the ministering angels, as is said: *He answered and said, "But I see four men walking about unbound and unharmed in the fire; and the fourth looks like a divine being"* (Daniel 3:25) [i.e., the people are mentioned before the angel].'"

See also *Zohar* 1:127b, 140a (both *MhN*). Cf. JT *Shabbat* 6:9, 8d; *Tanḥuma, Balaq* 14; *Tanḥuma* (Buber), *Balaq* 23; *Tanḥuma, Va-yishlaḥ* 2.

On the apprehension of the righteous in the world to come, cf. [Moses de León?], *Seder Gan Eden*, 137. On the verse from Psalms, see above, note 115. In BT *Ḥagigah* 12a, the verse from Isaiah is connected with the same myth of the concealed light: "Rabbi El'azar said, 'With the light created by the blessed Holy One on the first day, one could gaze and see from one end of the universe to the other. When the blessed Holy One foresaw the corrupt deeds of the generation of the Flood and the generation of the Dispersion [the generation of the Tower of Babel], He immediately hid it from them, as is written: *The light of the wicked is withheld* (Job 38:15). For whom did He hide it? For the righteous in the time to come, as is said: *God saw that the light was good*—and good means only the righteous one, as is said: *Say of the righteous one that he is good* (Isaiah 3:10).'"

Following this passage, the printed editions and a few manuscripts contain a passage that appears in *Zohar* 3:52a. The passage does not seem to belong here and is not found in some manuscripts. Hence I have omitted it.

126. **Section 12** The following passage—extending until the end of *parashat Lekh Lekha*—is not found in the printed editions or in some manuscripts. It is, however, found in three reliable witnesses: OM1, V1, and V22.

Two of the manuscripts contain the section heading פרשת יב (*parashat* 12), perhaps reflecting an early attempt to arrange the materials of *MhN* on the Torah. See *ZḤ* 3d, 10b, 13a, 14a, 17c, 19c, 28a (all *MhN*); *Zohar* 2:20a (*MhN*).

127. ***YHVH appeared to Abram...*** The verse continues: *and said to him, "I am El Shaddai. Walk in My ways and be blameless."*

128. **three years old when he recognized his Creator...** עקב (*Eqev*) has the numeri-

Rabbi Yitsḥak also said, "The entire world was created solely for Abraham's sake, as is said: *These are the generations of heaven and earth* בהבראם (*be-hibbare'am*), *when they were created* (ibid. 2:4)—באברהם (*be-avraham*), *through Abraham.* Now, do not be surprised by this. Come and see what is written: *The high mountains for the gazelles, the crags a shelter for badgers* (Psalms 104:18). The blessed Holy One created the high mountains solely to be a shelter for badgers. If He created the high mountains solely for the gazelles, and the crags for badgers, do not be surprised that the world should be created for Abraham!"[129]

Rabbi Yehudah said, "At the moment that Abraham was born, the blessed Holy One called heaven and earth and said to them, 'Until today you were not worthy of enduring, on account of the wicked. But henceforth you will abide forever and ever, as is said: *I call them—they endure together* (Isaiah 48:13). Here is written *I call*; and there is written *I called him* (ibid. 51:2). Here is written יחדו (*yaḥdav*), *together*; and there is written אחד (*eḥad*), *one* (ibid.). Why was he called *one*? For until that day—from Noah to Abraham—there was no one who believed in the blessed Holy One aside from him; all of them were idolators. Abraham arrived and became *one.* Why wasn't he called 'first'? Rabbi Aḥa said, 'Just as the blessed Holy One is *one* [as in Deuteronomy 6:4] and there is no second alongside Him, so Abraham was *one*, with no second in his generation.'"[130]



cal value of one hundred and seventy-two. See BT *Nedarim* 32a; *Bereshit Rabbah* 64:4, 95:3; *Tanḥuma, Lekh Lekha* 13; Maimonides, *Mishneh Torah, Hilkhot Avodat Kokhavim* 1:3; *Zohar* 3:302a (*Tosafot*).

The verse from Genesis continues: *and kept My charge, My commandments, My statutes, and My teachings.*

129. **world was created solely for Abraham's sake...** Although not stated explicitly, Abraham, who is unique, is the *apple tree* among the *trees of the forest*—as he alone recognized God.

According to Rabbi Yehoshu'a son of Korḥah (*Bereshit Rabbah* 12:9), בהבראם (*be-hibbare'am*), *when they were created* (Genesis 2:4) is an anagram of באברהם (*be-Avraham*), "through Abraham," indicating that the world was created for his sake. See *Zohar* 1:3b, 86b, 91b, 93a, 105b, 128b, 154b, 230b; 3:117a, 298a; *ZḤ* 4d, 17a (both *MhN*).

The *a fortiori* argument about the gazelles and badgers likewise derives from *Bereshit Rabbah* 12:9; it appears again in *ZḤ* 17a (*MhN*).

130. **At the moment that Abraham was born...** The advent of Abraham justifies the continued existence of heaven and earth. On the world's enduring through the merit of Abraham, cf. BT *Shabbat* 137b: "Were it not for the blood of the covenant [circumcision], heaven and earth would not endure, as is said: *Were it not for My covenant, I would not have established day and night,* [*nor*] *the laws of heaven and earth* (Jeremiah 33:25)." See also *ZḤ* 17a (*MhN*).

Isaiah 48:13 reads: *My own hand founded the earth; My right hand spread out the heavens. I call them—they stand* [or: *endure*] *together.* See *ZḤ* 3a (*MhN*).

Abraham is called *one* because, like God, he is unique. In its simple sense, Isaiah 51:2 reads: *Look back to Abraham your father, and to Sarah who brought you forth. For he was*

Rabbi Yoḥanan said, "When Abraham was created, the blessed Holy One wished to demonstrate and make manifest his nature to the world, so He tested him—so that there would not be a pretext for all the inhabitants of the world to say, 'He is a righteous person only because the blessed Holy One has not tested him. Were He to test him, he would be like all other people who sin and do not withstand the trial!' In fact, the blessed Holy One said, 'It is revealed before Me that Abraham will withstand all the trials with which I will test him, but [nevertheless I will test him] so that there will not be a pretext for the inhabitants of the world [to say] that I did not test him and that is why he was righteous.' Therefore He tested him—and he withstood them all."[131]

Rabbi Yitsḥak said, "*Like an apple tree among the trees of the forest* (Song of Songs 2:3)—this refers to Isaac, who was established in the covenant of the blessed Holy One, as is written: *But My covenant I will establish with Isaac* (Genesis 17:21). Prior to being born, he was sanctified in his mother's womb before the blessed Holy One, and his name 'Isaac' was bestowed."[132]



*only one when I called him, but I blessed him and made him many.*

See *Tanḥuma* (Buber), *Noaḥ* 24; *Qohelet Rabbah* on Ecclesiastes 4:8; see also *Bemidbar Rabbah* 2:14; *Zohar* 1:85b.

On God's being *one* (as opposed to 'the first'), see *ZḤ* 9a (*MhN*) and p. 51, nn. 159, 160.

See Naḥmanides on Genesis 1:5: "The first precedes a second in number or degree... whereas 'one' does not imply the existence of a second." See also M *Avot* 5:2: "There were ten generations from Noah until Abraham, to show us how great was His long-suffering, for all the generations continually angered Him—until Abraham came and received the reward for all of them."

131. **to demonstrate and make manifest his nature...** See *Tanḥuma*, *Lekh Lekha* 3: "Rabbi Avin said, 'This can be compared to a flask of spikenard oil hidden in the cemetery, so no one knew of its fragrance. What did they do? They took it and carried it from place to place, until its fragrance became known throughout the world. So Abraham resided among the idolators—until the blessed Holy One said to him, "*Go you forth from your land* (Genesis 12:1) and I will make your nature known throughout the world."'" See also *Bereshit Rabbah* 39:2; *Shir ha-Shirim Rabbah* on 1:3; *Zohar* 1:85a.

According to rabbinic tradition, Abraham withstood ten trials—and hence like Job, his true devotion was established. See M *Avot* 5:3: "With ten trials was our father Abraham tested... and he withstood them all, to show us how great was the love of our father Abraham...." See also *Avot de-Rabbi Natan* A, 33.

Cf. *Bereshit Rabbah* 51:1: "*It came to pass after these things, God* נסה (*nissah*), *tested, Abraham* (Genesis 22:1). It is written: *You have given* נס (*nes*), *a banner, to those in awe of You,* להתנוסס (*le-hitnoses*), *to be unfurled...* (Psalms 60:6)—trial upon trial, elevation above elevation, to test them in the world, to elevate them in the world like a ship's banner. Why to such an extent? *Because of truth. Selah* (ibid.)—so that the attribute of Justice would be verified in the world." As the midrash goes on to say, the case of Abraham proves that God does not reward or punish arbitrarily. The patriarch was rewarded for his extreme devotion in being willing to sacrifice his son.

See *Zohar* 1:106b (*MhN*).

132. ***Like an apple tree...*** Isaac is the *apple tree* compared to Ishmael—who is as

Rabbi said, "How do we know? From this verse! אקים (*Aqim*), *I will establish*—it is an acronym: א (*alef*), אשר (*asher*), who; ק (*qof*), קידש (*qiddesh*), sanctified; י (*yod*), ידיד (*yedid*), the beloved one; מ (*mem*), מבטן (*mi-beten*), from the womb—this is Isaac."[133]

As Rabbi Yoḥanan said: "What is the meaning of the verse *Who would have said to Abraham: Sarah will suckle children* (Genesis 21:7)? At that feast that Abraham prepared for all the dignitaries of the generation, everyone brought their children—and Sarah suckled them all, so that they would believe. When they picked up Isaac, he would not suck from their breasts, all of them seeming to him as an ape compared to a human. This is the meaning of the verse *Like an apple tree among the trees of the forest, so is my beloved among the young men* (Song of Songs 2:3) of the nations of the world."[134]

*In his shade I delighted and I sat* (ibid.). Rabbi Yitsḥak said, "Since it said *I delighted*, what is the significance of *I sat*? This refers to Mount Moriah, where he was bound. *And his fruit is sweet to my mouth* (ibid.)—this refers to Jacob, who is the fruit. As we have learned: The tree signifies Abraham, about whom is



*the trees of the forest.* Following the covenant of circumcision (Genesis 17:1–14), God informs Abraham that Sarah will have a son. In disbelief, Abraham pleads with God that Ishmael should be the heir to the covenant, to which God responds by telling Abraham that not only will Sarah surely have a son, but also he is to be called Isaac—and the covenant will continue through him alone (see Genesis 17:15–21). See Rashi on Genesis 17:19.

133. **אקים (*Aqim*), *I will establish*—it is an acronym...** Rabbi proves that Isaac was sanctified in the womb by interpreting the word אקים (*aqim*), *I will establish*, as an acronym: אשר קידש ידיד מבטן (*asher qiddesh yedid mi-beten*), "who sanctified the beloved one from the womb."

According to BT *Shabbat* 137b, the blessing over circumcision includes this phrase, which Rashi interprets as a reference to Isaac. See *Zohar* 1:96a; 3:39b; *ZḤ* 64a (*ShS*). The acronym is found in *Ba'al ha-Turim* on Genesis 17:21.

"Rabbi" indicates Rabbi Yehudah ha-Nasi (the Patriarch), who redacted the Mishnah. He was so highly esteemed that he was simply called "Rabbi": the Master.

134. ***Sarah will suckle children...*** See *Bereshit Rabbah* 53:9; *Pesiqta de-Rav Kahana* 22:1; *Pirqei de-Rabbi Eli'ezer* 52; and BT *Bava Metsi'a* 87a: "She [Sarah] said, *Who would have said to Abraham: Sarah will suckle children?* How many children did Sarah suckle? Rabbi Levi said, 'On the day that Abraham weaned his son Isaac, he held a great feast. All the nations of the world mocked him, saying, "Have you seen that old man and woman, who brought a foundling from off the streets, and now claim him as their son! Furthermore, they hold a great feast to establish their claim!" What did Abraham our father do? He invited all the dignitaries of the generation, and Sarah our mother invited their wives. Each one brought her baby with her, but not her wet nurse, and a miracle happened to Sarah our mother: her breasts opened like two fountains and she suckled them all.'" See also *Zohar* 1:10b–11a.

On the expression "as an ape compared to a human," see *Tanḥuma, Lekh Lekha* 5: "all women compared with Sarah are like an ape compared with a human"; BT *Bava Batra* 58a; cf. *Zohar* 3:268b, 284b.

written *recline under the tree* (Genesis 18:4); the shade signifies Isaac; and the fruit signifies Jacob—after whom Israel were named, and from whom emerged the twelve tribes, called *seed of truth* (Jeremiah 2:21): the fruit!"[135]

Alternatively, *Like an apple tree among the trees of the forest*—this refers to circumcision bestowed upon Abraham. As Rabbi said, "What was Abraham like when he was circumcised among the uncircumcised nations? To an apple tree standing among the trees of the forest that are suitable only for burning."

*In his shade I delighted and I sat*—this refers to Abraham. And this corresponds with what Rabbi Tanḥum said: "When the blessed Holy One commanded Abraham about circumcision, he was saddened. He said to him, 'Abraham, *at eight days old every male among you shall be circumcised* (Genesis 17:12). By your life! You will preside over all the babies that will be circumcised at eight, as testimony that they received My covenant, and that they will not be consigned to Hell.' Elijah presides on one side, on the chair of the covenant, and Abraham above him, as is written: *In his shade I delighted and I sat*—namely in the shade of Abraham. *And his fruit is sweet to my mouth*—concerning what we say: to bring him into the covenant of Abraham our father."[136] [1:97a]



135. ***In his shade I delighted and I sat...*** The entire verse from the Song of Songs alludes to the patriarchs: Abraham is the tree, Isaac the shade, and Jacob the fruit. Cf. *Zohar* 1:85a.

136. **Elijah presides on one side, on the chair of the covenant...** In response to his excessive zeal (see 1 Kings 19:10–14), Elijah was made to witness Israel's fidelity to the covenant for all eternity. At a ritual circumcision, a special chair is placed at the right of the *sandaq* ("godfather"), and the *mohel* (circumciser) declares: "This is the chair of Elijah, may his memory be a blessing."

See *Pirqei de-Rabbi Eli'ezer* 29: "[The blessed Holy One said to him,] 'By your life! Israel will not enact the covenant of circumcision until you see it with your own eyes!' Hence the sages ordained that a seat of honor be arranged [at every circumcision] for the Angel of the Covenant [namely, Elijah; see Malachi 3:1]." See also *Halakhot Gedolot* (according to *Shibbolei ha-Leqet* 376:6); *Sefer Ḥasidim*, ed. Wistinetzki, par. 585; *Zohar* 1:13a, 93a, 209b; 2:190a; *Shulḥan Arukh, Yoreh De'ah* 265:11; Ginzberg, *Legends*, 6:338, n. 103.

The final phrase derives from the blessing uttered by the father during his son's circumcision: "Blessed are You, *YHVH*, our God, King of the Universe, who has sanctified us with His commandments and has commanded us to bring him into the covenant of Abraham our father."

# פרשת וירא

# *Parashat Va-Yera*

"HE APPEARED" (GENESIS 18:1–22:24)

Our Rabbis opened with this verse: *As for scent, your oils are fragrant; your name is oil poured...* (Song of Songs 1:3).[1]

Our Rabbis have taught: When the soul of the human being ascends to the firmament, abiding in that supernal radiance that we have mentioned, the blessed Holy One pays her a visit.

Come and hear: Rabbi Shim'on son of Yoḥai said, "As soon as each soul of the righteous abides in the site of the glorious *Shekhinah*, dwelling fittingly, the blessed Holy One summons the patriarchs and says to them, 'Go and visit so-and-so the righteous, who is arriving—and extend him peace in My name.' They reply, 'Master of the World! It is not fitting for a father to go to see the son. It is fitting for the son to search and seek and see his father!'[2]

"He summons Jacob and says to him, 'You who endured the sorrow of children, go and receive the teaching of so-and-so the righteous who is arriving here, and I will go with you.' As is written: *who search out your countenance, Jacob. Selah* (Psalms 24:6). The verse does not say *who searches out,* but rather *who search out.*"[3]

1. ***your name is oil poured...*** The verse continues: *Therefore maidens love you.* The significance of the verse is apparent below. See note 12.

On this verse, cf. *Zohar* 3:58b–59a.

2. **extend him peace in My name...** Cf. BT *Ketubbot* 104a: "Rabbi Ḥiyya son of Gamda said in the name of Rabbi Yose son of Sha'ul, 'In the hour when the righteous person departs from the world, the ministering angels say before the blessed Holy One, "Master of the World! The righteous person so-and-so is coming." He says to them, "Let the righteous come [from their resting places], and go forth to meet him." They say to him [the newly departed righteous], "*Let him enter into peace; let them rest on their couches* [*he who walks uprightly*] (Isaiah 57:2).'" Rabbi El'azar said, 'When a righteous person departs from the world, three companies of ministering angels go forth to meet him. One says to him, *Enter into peace*; the other says, *He who walks uprightly,* while the other says, *Let him enter into peace; let them rest on their couches.*'"

3. **You who endured the sorrow of chil-**

Rabbi Ḥiyya said, "This is implied by the beginning of the verse, as is written: *This is the generation of His seekers....*"[4]

Rabbi Ya'akov said in the name of Rabbi Ḥiyya, 'Jacob our father himself is the throne; and similarly it has been taught in the School of Elijah: Jacob our father is a throne in his own right, as is written: *I will remember My covenant with Jacob* (Leviticus 26:42). The blessed Holy One established a covenant with Jacob alone, exceeding all the patriarchs, [97b] to become a Throne of Glory, aside from the first."[5]

**dren...** God turns to Jacob alone to deign to venture forth to greet the departed righteous, who enter the celestial realm with the teachings they learned in this world. See BT *Shabbat* 89b, where God turns to Jacob—who experienced "the sorrow of raising children"—in the hope that he would implore mercy on behalf of the children of Israel.

Psalms 24:6 reads: *This is the generation* [or: *circle*] *of His seekers; who search out Your countenance* [or: *presence,*] *Jacob. Selah.* The verse's rather awkward syntax might lead one to think that it is Jacob who searches out the divine presence, for how can Jacob be the object of the seekers' search? As Rabbi Shim'on notes, however, the clause *who search out Your countenance* is inflected in the plural, leaving no doubt that Jacob is the object of the search rather than its agent. (According to Radak, "Jacob" stands for God.) Here, the clause signifies the souls of the righteous arriving in the celestial realm, who search out Jacob's countenance, as he welcomes them.

4. ***This is the generation of His seekers...*** According to Rabbi Ḥiyya, the beginning of the verse already proves that the verse applies to the souls of the righteous—*the generation of His seekers.*

5. **Jacob our father himself is the throne...** Although the patriarchs together constitute the divine throne, Jacob is a throne in his own right. See *Zohar* 1:173b.

On the patriarchs as the throne, see *Bereshit Rabbah* 82:6: "Rabbi Shim'on son of Lakish said, 'The patriarchs themselves constitute the [divine] chariot.'"

See also *Bereshit Rabbah* 47:6; Naḥmanides on Genesis 17:22; 35:13; Azriel of Gerona, *Peirush ha-Aggadot,* 57; *Zohar* 1:60b, 99a, 150a, 154b, 248b; 2:144a; 3:38a, 99a; *ZḤ* 25d (*MhN*).

According to rabbinic tradition, Jacob's image is engraved on the throne. See *Bereshit Rabbah* 68:12; 82:2; *Eikhah Rabbah* 2:2; *Targum Yerushalmi* and *Targum Yerushalmi* (frag.), Genesis 28:12; BT *Ḥullin* 91b (and Rashi, ad loc., s.v. *bidyoqno*); *Pirqei de-Rabbi Eli'ezer* 35; *Zohar* 1:72a; *ZḤ* 14c (*MhN*); Scholem, "Parashah Ḥadashah," 431 (Addendum 1 in this volume); Wolfson, *Along the Path,* 1–62.

The verse from Leviticus demonstrates Jacob's special status, as of him alone the word אף (*af*), "also," is not used. The full verse reads: *I will remember My covenant with Jacob, and also My covenant with Isaac, and also My covenant with Abraham I will remember; and I will remember the land.* See *Vayiqra Rabbah* 36:5: "Why is the expression *also* used in connection with Abraham and Isaac but not in connection with Jacob? Because his bed was perfect before Him. From Abraham sprang Ishmael and all the sons of Keturah; from Isaac sprang Esau and all the chiefs of Edom; but Jacob's bed was perfect, all his sons being righteous."

On Jacob's special status among the patriarchs, see also *Bereshit Rabbah* 76:1: "Rabbi Pinḥas said in the name of Rabbi Re'uven, '... The chosen of the patriarchs is Jacob, as is said: *For Yah has chosen Jacob for Himself* (Psalms 135:4).'"

Rabbi Eli'ezer was sitting and toiling in Torah; Rabbi Akiva came to him. He said to him, "In what is my master engaged?"

He replied, "In this verse as is written: *a throne of honor He bequeaths them* (1 Samuel 2:8). What is meant by *a throne of honor he bequeaths them*? This is Jacob our father, for He transformed him—by himself—into a Throne of Glory, to receive the teaching of the souls of the righteous.[6]

"Every new moon, the blessed Holy One ventures forth with him; and when the soul beholds the glorious speculum—her Master's *Shekhinah*—she offers blessings and bows down before Him, as is written: *Bless YHVH, O my soul* (Psalms 104:1)."[7]

Rabbi Akiva said, "The soul utters this entire passage of praise before the blessed Holy One."

Rabbi Akiva said, "The blessed Holy One stands poised above him, and the soul opens, saying, '*YHVH, my God, You are very great*... (ibid.)'—[declaiming] the entire chapter until the end, as is said: *Let sinners vanish*... (ibid., 35)."



Rabbi Akiva said further, "Not only this, but she praises Him for the body left behind in this world, saying, '*Bless YHVH, O my soul and all my innermost parts*... (ibid. 103:1).'"[8]

The blessed Holy one ventures forth [with Jacob]. How do we know this? From this verse, as is written: *YHVH appeared to him* באלוני ממרא (*be-elonei mamre*), *by the oaks of Mamre* (Genesis 18:1)—this is Jacob. Why Mamre? Because he inherits two hundred worlds from Eden; and because he is the throne.[9]

6. ***a throne of honor He bequeaths them*...** In the verse from Samuel, the term כסא כבוד (*kisse khavod*) signifies a throne of honor. According to Rabbi Eli'ezer it is a Throne of Glory. The Hebrew noun *kavod* conveys both meanings: "honor" and "glory."

The full verse reads: *He raises the poor from the dust, from the dungheaps the wretched He lifts; to seat among princes, a throne of honor He bequeaths them.*

7. **the blessed Holy One ventures forth with him...** Once a month, the blessed Holy One—together with Jacob—visits the soul in the celestial realm. The soul responds by reciting Psalms 104, known by its opening words *Barekhi Nafshi*, "Bless [*YHVH*], O my soul."

This psalm is traditionally recited at the beginning of each new month. See Jacob ben Asher, *Arba'ah Turim, Oraḥ Ḥayyim, Hilkhot Rosh Ḥodesh*, 423: "It is the custom in Spain." See also BT *Berakhot* 10a; *Vayiqra Rabbah* 4:7.

On "speculum," see above, p. 281, n. 25.

8. **she praises Him for the body left behind in this world...** The soul offers praise not only in response to her own exaltation, but also for the body (which is destined to be revived), as indicated by *all my innermost parts.*

See verses 3–5 of the psalm: *Who forgives all your wrongs, heals all your diseases, redeems your life from the Pit, crowns you with love and mercy, sates you with good while you live—so that your youth will be renewed like the eagle's.*

9. **Why Mamre?...** Jacob and God's celestial visit to the soul is alluded to by the

Rabbi Yitsḥak explained, "The numerical value of ממרא (*mamre*), Mamre, is two hundred and eighty-one: two hundred from Eden, as is written: *two hundred for those who guard its fruit* (Song of Songs 8:12); and eighty-one equaling כסא (*kisse*), throne. Consequently the verse says *YHVH appeared to him* באלוני ממרא (*be-elonei mamre*), *with the oaks of Mamre*, and that is why he is called Mamre."[10]

Rabbi Yehudah said, "What is the meaning of באלוני (*be-elonei*), *by the oaks*? It means to convey 'his potency,' as is written: *the Mighty One of Jacob* (Genesis 49:24). *As he was sitting at the opening of the tent* (ibid. 18:1)—as is written: *YHVH, who can abide in Your tent...* (Psalms 15:1). [98a] *In the heat of the day* (Genesis 18:1)—as is written: *For you, in awe of My name, the sun of righteousness will rise, with healing in its wings* (Malachi 3:20)."[11]

Rabban Yoḥanan son of Zakkai said, "At that time, the blessed Holy One ventures forth; and because the patriarchs—Abraham and Isaac—hear that the blessed Holy One is going toward him [the soul], they ask Jacob if they can go with them and extend him peace; and they stand over him, as is written: *He raised his eyes and saw: here, three men standing over him* (Genesis 18:2). The *three men* standing—these are the patriarchs Abraham, Isaac, and Jacob standing over him, contemplating the good deeds that he has performed. *When he saw, he ran from the opening of the tent to meet them and bowed to the earth* (ibid.)—



verse *YHVH appeared to him by the oaks of Mamre.* Precisely how Mamre connotes Jacob is explained in the following paragraph.

10. **The numerical value...** Jacob is called Mamre based on the following numerology. Jacob inherits the 200 Edenic worlds alluded to in the Song of Songs; and he is the כסא (*kisse*), "throne," equaling 81. In sum, he is 281, which is the numerical value of "Mamre."

Additionally, the preposition ב (*bet*) that is prefixed to באלוני ממרא (*be-elonei mamre*), *by the oaks of Mamre*, is read here as "with." Hence the verse from Genesis is understood as follows: *YHVH appeared to him* (i.e., the soul) *with... Mamre* (i.e., Jacob).

On the two hundred Edenic worlds, see *Zohar* 1:124b (*MhN*); *ZḤ* 22a (*MhN*).

11. **What is the meaning of... *by the oaks?*...** Having explained that *Mamre* means Jacob, Rabbi Yehudah now explains how the phrase *by the oaks* also applies to Jacob. *Oaks* signify might (as in the English expression "mighty as an oak"). The phrase *oaks of Mamre* thus corresponds with the phrase in Genesis, *Mighty One of Jacob.* Hence: *YHVH appeared to him* [the soul] *by the oaks* [with the potency or might] *of Mamre* [Jacob].

Rabbi Yehudah interprets the continuation of the verse from Genesis: *as he was sitting at the opening of the tent in the heat of the day.* The *opening of the tent* is the entrance to the celestial realm, as indicated by the verse from Psalms, where *Your tent* signifies the upper world—and perhaps also *Shekhinah*. The verse from Psalms continues: *who can dwell on Your holy mountain?* As for *the heat of the day*, it signifies the illumination of the soul (by *the sun of righteousness*) in the celestial realm.

On the phrase in Genesis 49:24, see *Targum Yerushalmi*, *Targum Yerushalmi* (frag.) and *Targum Onqelos*. On the verse from Malachi, see BT *Avodah Zarah* 3b–4a.

because he sees the glorious *Shekhinah* with them. This is the significance of the verse *Therefore maidens love you* (Song of Songs 1:3)—these are the patriarchs."[12]

Alternatively, *YHVH appeared to him by the oaks of Mamre* (Genesis 18:1). Our Rabbis opened this verse as referring to the time of a person's departure. For it has been taught: Rabbi Yehudah said, "The time of a person's departure is the day of great judgment, for the soul is separated from the body. A person does not depart the world until he sees the *Shekhinah*, as is written: *No human can see Me and live* (Exodus 33:20). Three ministering angels accompany the *Shekhinah* to receive the soul of the righteous, as is written: *YHVH appeared to him* . . . ; *in the heat of day*—the day of judgment, burning like a furnace to separate the soul from the body. *He raised his eyes and saw: here, three men standing over him*—inspecting his deeds, what he has done; and he acknowledges them with his mouth. As soon as the soul sees this, she leaves the body to the opening of the throat—and remains there until she confesses everything that the body did with her in this world. Then the soul of the righteous rejoices in her deeds and rejoices concerning her pledge. As it has been taught: Rabbi Yitsḥak said, 'The soul of the righteous yearns for when she will leave this world—which is vanity—in order to delight in the world to come.'"[13]



12. ***Therefore maidens love you*** . . . Only now do we learn the significance of the *Zohar* commentary's opening verse (*As for scent, your oils are fragrant; your name is oil poured. Therefore maidens love you*). The *maidens* are the patriarchs who love and lavish the soul, on account of her good deeds (her *fragrant oils*) and of her good name (*your name is oil poured*).

See *Matoq mi-Devash* for a sefirotic interpretation.

See *Vayiqra Rabbah* 3:7: "Oil connotes only Torah and good deeds." See also BT *Avodah Zarah* 35b: "Rav Naḥman the son of Rav Ḥisda expounded, 'What is the meaning of the verse *As for scent, your oils are fragrant?* To what may a disciple of the wise be compared? To a flask of poliatum [fragrant oil]. When opened, its fragrance is diffused; but if covered up, its fragrance does not diffuse. Moreover, matters that are concealed from him become revealed to him, as is said: עלמות (*alamot*), *maidens, love you*—read it as עלומות (*alumot*), hidden matters. What's more, even the Angel of Death loves him, as is said: עלמות (*alamot*), *maidens, love you*—read it as על מות (*al mot*), [the one appointed] over death. Still more, he inherits two worlds—one, this world; and the other, the world to come, as is said: עלמות (*alamot*)—read it as עולמות (*olamot*), worlds."

See also the various interpretations of Song of Songs 1:3 in *Shir ha-Shirim Rabbah*, ad loc.

On the three men as the three patriarchs, see *Zohar* 1:98b–99a.

13. **time of a person's departure** . . . The verse from Genesis signifies the actual moment of death, when the soul is granted a vision of the divine. (Previously, this verse was expounded as referring to the soul's arrival in the celestial realm.) The soul had been bestowed by God as a pledge or deposit, to be returned unsullied upon death.

Traditionally, the day of judgment comes at the end of days, but in the *Zohar* it transpires for each human being on the day of death. See *Zohar* 1:201b, 218b, 227a; 3:88a.

On seeing *Shekhinah* at death, see *Sifra, Vayiqra, dibbura di-ndavah* 2:12, 4a: "Rabbi

Our Rabbis have taught: When Rabbi Eli'ezer the Great fell ill, that day was Sabbath eve. He sat his son Hyrcanus at his right and revealed to him profundities and mysteries; but he was unable to receive his words, because he thought that his mind was deranged. As soon as he realized that his father's mind was clear, he received from him one hundred and eighty-nine supernal secrets.[14]

Dosa says, 'Scripture states: *No human can see Me and live* (Exodus 33:20). In their lifetime they do not see, but in their death they do!'" See *Sifrei*, Numbers 103; *Sifrei*, Deuteronomy 357; *Pirqei de-Rabbi Eli'ezer* 34; *Tanḥuma, Ḥuqqat* 16; *Tanḥuma* (Buber), *Ḥuqqat* 39; *Midrash Tehillim* 22:32; 103:3; *Bemidbar Rabbah* 14:22; 19:18; *Zohar* 1:65b, 79a, 99a (*ST*), 218b, 226a, 245a; 3:88a, 126b, 147a; *ZḤ* 10a, 25d (both *MhN*); Moses de León, *Sefer ha-Rimmon*, 392–93; idem, *Mishkan ha-Edut*, 45a–b.

On the three angels (or companies of angels), see BT *Ketubbot* 104a, note 2 above; *Sifrei Zuta* 6:26; *Beit ha-Midrash*, 5:48–49; *Ḥibbut ha-Qever*, ed. Higger, 257–58; *Zohar* 1:79a; 2:199a; 3:88a. On heat as signifying the fiery day of judgment, see Malachi 3:19: *See, a day is coming for YHVH, burning like a furnace.* See *Bereshit Rabbah* 48:8. On the judgment of body and soul together immediately before death, see *Zohar* 1:65b, 79a, 130b, 201b; 3:53a; Moses de León, *Sefer ha-Rimmon*, 393. Cf. the parable concerning the joint responsibility of body and soul after death in *Mekhilta de-Rashbi*, Exodus 15:1; *Va-yiqra Rabbah* 4:5; BT *Sanhedrin* 91a–b. See *Zohar* 2:199b; 3:126b; *ZḤ* 83d (*MhN, Rut*). On the soul's being poised at the opening of the throat (the opening of the tent), cf. BT *Berakhot* 8a, *ke-fiturei be-fi veset*; *Mo'ed Qatan* 28b–29a; *Tanḥuma* (Buber), *Miqqets*, 15.

Rabbi Yehudah continues his homily below, page 324. Meanwhile, a story intervenes.

14. **When Rabbi Eli'ezer the Great fell ill...** The *Zohar* retells and expands the Talmudic story of his death. See BT *Sanhedrin* 68a: "When Rabbi Eli'ezer fell ill, Rabbi Akiva and his companions went to visit him. He was seated in his canopied four-poster, while they sat in his salon. That day was Sabbath eve, and his son Hyrcanus went in to him to remove his *tefillin*. His father rebuked him, and he departed in disgrace. He said to the companions, 'It seems to me that my father's mind is deranged.' He [R. Eli'ezer] said to them, 'His mind and his mother's mind are deranged: how can one neglect a prohibition that is punishable by death [for he thought that they had not yet kindled the Sabbath lamps and set the meal onto the fire], and turn his attention to something that is merely forbidden as a *shevut* [a lesser rabbinic prohibition (see Rashi, ad loc.)]?' Seeing that his mind was clear, the Sages entered—and sat down at a distance of four cubits [because he was under the ban (see BT *Bava Metsi'a* 59b)]. He said to them, 'Why have you come?' They replied, 'To study Torah.' He said to them, 'Why did you not come before now?' They replied, 'We did not have time.' He said to them, 'I will be surprised if they will die a natural death.' Rabbi Akiva said to him, 'How will mine be?' He replied, 'Yours will be crueler than theirs!' He placed his two arms over his heart and said, 'Woe to you, two arms of mine—that have been like two Torah scrolls wrapped up! Much Torah have I learned, and much Torah have I taught. Much Torah have I learned, yet I have not even carried away from my teachers as much as a dog lapping from the sea. Much Torah have I taught, but my disciples have not carried away from me but as much as a painting stick from its tube. Moreover, I have studied three hundred laws on the subject of a *bright shiny spot* [on skin (Leviticus 13:2)]; yet no one has ever asked me about them. Moreover, I have studied three hundred (or, as others state, three thousand) laws about the planting of cucumbers [by magic]; and no one has ever asked

When he reached the marble stones mingled with supernal water, Rabbi Eli'ezer wept and ceased speaking. He said, "Stand there, my son."[15]

He said to him, "Why, father?"

He replied, "I see that my spirit will pass from the world."[16]

He said to him, "Go and tell your mother to remove my *tefillin* to a lofty site; and that after I depart the world and come here to see them, she shall not weep, for they are near to the higher, not the lower realms; but the human mind perceives nothing of [98b] them."[17]

As they were sitting, the sages of the generation entered to visit him. He cursed them for not coming to minister to him. As we have learned: Greater is the ministry of her than the study of her. Meanwhile, Rabbi Akiva arrived. He said to him, "Akiva, Akiva, why didn't you come to tend to me? For the time to be purified has arrived."[18]

He replied, "Rabbi, I did not have the time."

He was furious. He said, "I will be surprised if you should die a natural death!" He cursed him that his death should be the cruelest of all.[19]



me about them, except Akiva son of Yosef.' . . . They [his visitors] asked him, 'What is the law of a ball, a shoemaker's last, an amulet, a leather bag containing pearls, and a small weight?' He replied, 'They can become impure; and if impure, they are restored just as they are.' Then they asked him, 'What of a shoe that is on the last?' He replied, 'It is pure'; and his soul departed in purity. . . . At the conclusion of the Sabbath, Rabbi Akiva met his bier being carried from Caesarea to Lydda. He beat his flesh until his blood flowed down upon the earth."

See also *Avot de-Rabbi Natan* A, 25; [Moses de León?], *Orḥot Ḥayyim*, 1.

15. **the marble stones mingled with supernal water . . .** See BT *Ḥagigah* 14b: "Four entered the *pardes* [the 'orchard' of mystical speculation]. . . . Rabbi Akiva said to them, 'When you reach the stone of pure marble, do not say: "Water, water."'"

16. **my spirit will pass . . .** Following the reading in V9: דרוחי תחלף instead of the difficult דאוחית חלף. Another possibility noted in *Or ha-Levanah*, though not supported by the manuscript witnesses, is דאור יתחלף (*de-or yithalef*), "that light is passing."

17. **Go and tell your mother . . .** The meaning of this paragraph is not entirely clear. In the account in BT *Sanhedrin*, Eli'ezer's son Hyrcanus wanted to remove his *tefillin*. Here, they become a symbol apparently for the Torah and mysteries that Eli'ezer contemplated during his life. He intends to visit them from the world to come. See *Matoq mi-Devash*.

18. **Greater is the ministry of her than the study of her . . .** Serving and attending to a sage is more important than Torah study. See BT *Berakhot* 7b: "Rabbi Yoḥanan said in the name of Rabbi Shim'on son of Yoḥai, 'Greater is the ministry of the Torah than the study thereof. As is said: *Here is Elisha the son of Shaphat, who poured water on the hands of Elijah* (2 Kings 3:11). It does not say *who learned*, but *who poured water*, teaching that greater is the ministry of her than the study of her.'"

The "time to be purified" may refer to the last rites or to death itself.

19. **his death should be the cruelest of all** On Rabbi Akiva's death, see JT *Berakhot* 9:5, 14b; BT *Berakhot* 61b.

Rabbi Akiva wept and said to him, "Rabbi, teach me Torah!"

Rabbi Eli'ezer opened his mouth about the Account of the Chariot. Fire came and enveloped the two of them.[20]

The sages said, "Conclude from this that we are not fitting or worthy for this."

They went to the outside door and sat there.

What happened, happened; and the fire abated, and he taught three hundred legal decisions concerning the bright spot, and he taught him mysteries of the interpretations of the verses from the Song of Songs. Rabbi Akiva's eyes streamed tears; and the fire returned as at first. When he reached the verse *Sustain me with raisin cakes, refresh me with apples for I am faint with love* (Song of Songs 2:5), Rabbi Akiva could not bear it. He raised his voice—weeping and groaning—and could not speak for fear of the *Shekhinah*, who was there. He taught him all the profundities and supernal secrets contained in the Song of Songs; and he made him swear an oath not to wield a single verse from it, lest the blessed Holy One destroy the world on its account—for it is not His wish that the creatures should employ it, [99a] owing to the great holiness it possesses. Afterward Rabbi Akiva departed; he was groaning, his eyes streaming tears, saying, "Woe my master, woe my master—that the world will remain orphaned of you!"[21]



All the other sages came in to him. They inquired of him and he answered them. Time was pressing for Rabbi Eli'ezer. He stretched out his two arms and placed them on his heart. He opened, saying, "O world, the upper world has

20. **the Account of the Chariot...** Esoteric lore deriving from the first chapter of Ezekiel. In rabbinic texts, the study of the Account of the Chariot is often accompanied by celestial fire. See, for example, BT *Ḥagigah* 14b.

21. **What happened, happened...** On this expression, see Scholem, *Kabbalah*, 228.

On the three hundred legal decisions, see BT *Sanhedrin* 68a; *Avot de-Rabbi Natan* A, 25; *Kallah Rabbati* 6:4; *Zohar* 1:145b; 3:50b; *ZḤ* 6d–7a (*MhN*).

Some of the manuscripts read: He taught him 216 (ריו) interpretations of the verses from the Song of Songs.

On Song of Songs 2:5, see *Shir ha-Shirim Rabbah* on the verse: "*Sustain me* באשישות (*be-ashishot*), *with raisin cakes*—with two אשות (*ishshot*), fires: the fire above and the fire below...." See also *Pesiqta de-Rav Kahana* 12:3; *Zohar* 3:40a. On the sanctity of the Song of Songs, see M *Yadayim* 3:5, in the name of Rabbi Akiva: "The whole world is not worth the day on which the Song of Songs was given to Israel—for all the Writings [the third division of the Bible] are holy, and the Song of Songs is Holy of Holies." See also *Zohar* 2:18b (*MhN*); 143b–144a. On Rabbi Akiva's lament, see *Avot de-Rabbi Natan* A, 25: "Woe unto me, my master, because of you! Woe unto me, my teacher, because of you! For you have left the whole generation orphaned!" See also *Zohar* 2:23b, 68a; *ZḤ* 7a, 19c (both *MhN*).

In rabbinic Hebrew, "creatures" refers either to human beings or specifically to Jews.

turned, to draw in and conceal all light and luminosity from the lower realm! Woe to you two arms of mine! Woe to you two *Torot*—which this day will be forgotten from the world!"[22] (As Rabbi Yitsḥak said, "All of Rabbi Eli'ezer's days, the teaching shone from his mouth as on the day it was given at Mount Sinai.")[23]

He said, "I have fathomed Torah, grasped wisdom, and rendered service. Were all the inhabitants of the world scribes, they would not suffice to record it! My disciples carried away from my wisdom only as a dab of paint in the eye, and I from my teachers as one who drinks from the sea."[24]

(This was only to accord more esteem to his teachers than himself.)[25]

They were asking him about the levir's sandal, whereupon his soul departed, saying, "Pure." Rabbi Akiva was not there.[26]

When the Sabbath departed, Rabbi Akiva discovered that he had died. He tore his clothes and cut all his flesh, and blood poured down over his face; he was screaming and weeping. He went outside and said, "O heavens, O heavens, tell the sun and the moon that the light that shone more brilliantly than them has now darkened!" [99b]



Rabbi Yehudah said, "When the soul of the righteous person wishes to depart, she rejoices; and the righteous person is sure in his death that he will receive his reward, as is written: *He saw and ran to meet them* (Genesis 18:2)—to greet

22. **conceal all light and luminosity from the lower realm...** With Eli'ezer's death celestial mysteries return above. The two *Torot*, signified by his two arms, are the written and old Torah.

Cf. the death of Rabbi Shim'on son of Yoḥai, *Zohar* 1:217a.

23. **as on the day it was given at Mount Sinai** See *Pirqei de-Rabbi Eli'ezer* 2: "Rabbi Eli'ezer was sitting and expounding [matters greater than those revealed to Moses at Sinai] and his face was shining like the light of the sun, and his radiance went forth like the radiance of Moses; and no one knew whether it was day or night." See also *Avot de-Rabbi Natan* B, 13; *Shir ha-Shirim Rabbah* on Song of Songs 1:3: "Rabbi Eli'ezer's house of study was shaped like an arena; and there was in it a stone that was reserved for him to sit on. Once Rabbi Yehoshu'a came in and began kissing the stone and saying, 'This stone is like Mount Sinai; and he who sat on it is like the Ark of the Covenant.'"

24. **Were all the inhabitants of the world scribes...** See *Avot de-Rabbi Natan* A, 25: "For if all the seas were ink and all the reeds pens and all men scribes, they could not write down all the Scripture and Mishnah I have studied, nor what I learned serving under the sages in the academy."

See also *Shir ha-Shirim Rabbah* on Song of Songs 1:3.

25. **to accord more esteem to his teachers...** His teachers' knowledge is compared to the sea while his own he compares to the eye.

26. **They were asking him about the levir's sandal...** As mentioned in Deuteronomy 25:5–10. See *ZḤ* 59a–c (*MhN*), where the rite of levirate marriage is expounded as alluding to the transmigration of souls—a fitting topic for the moment of death. In contrast, in the account in *Sanhedrin* and in *Avot de-Rabbi Natan*, the sages ask Rabbi Eli'ezer about the purity of the shoe on a shoemaker's last.

them in joy. From which place? *From the opening of the tent* (ibid.), as we have said. *And he bowed to the earth* (ibid.)—to the *Shekhinah*."[27]

Rabbi Yoḥanan opened, "*Before the day breathes and the shadows flee, turn away, my love: be like a gazelle or a young stag* (Song of Songs 2:17)."

Rabbi Shim'on son of Pazzi said, "This constitutes a warning to a human being while he is still in this world—that it is like the twinkling of an eye. Come and see what is written: *Even if he lived a thousand years twice over...* (Ecclesiastes 6:6)—on the day of death, all that was appears to him as but a single day."[28]

Rabbi Shim'on said, "A person's soul warns him, saying, *Before the day breathes*—and it will seem to you as the twinkling of an eye while you are still in this world; *and the shadows flee*—as is written: *For our days upon earth are a shadow* (Job 8:9), I implore you: *turn away, my love: be like a gazelle.* Just as the gazelle is swift of foot, so you should be swift like the gazelle or young stag to perform the will of your Creator, that you will inherit the world to come: *the mountains of spices* (Song of Songs 8:14)—and called *the mountain of YHVH* (Isaiah 2:3), the mountain of delight, *the good mountain* (Deuteronomy 3:25)."[29]



27. **When the soul of the righteous person wishes to depart...** Previously, Rabbi Yehudah interpreted the narrative of the *three men* who came to visit Abraham as an allegory for the three angels who accompany the *Shekhinah* to greet the soul when one dies (see above, *Zohar* 1:98a (*MhN*) at note 13). He now extends his homily: certain that he will receive his reward, Abraham (the soul) runs to greet them.

The *opening of the tent* signifies the opening of the throat, the soul's last abode before departing the body. See above, note 13.

The full verse from Genesis reads: *He raised his eyes and saw: here, three men standing over him. He saw—and ran to meet them from the opening of the tent, and he bowed to the ground* [or: *earth*].

Cf. *Bereshit Rabbah* 48:9; BT *Shevu'ot* 35b.

28. **this world—that it is like the twinkling of an eye...** Rabbi Shim'on expounds the verse from the Song of Songs cited by Rabbi Yoḥanan. The first part of the verse may refer to the end of night, just before the break of dawn, when darkness flees. Alternatively, the "fleeing shadows" indicate the late afternoon, when shadows lengthen. Here, the latter meaning pertains, with the end of daylight symbolizing the end of one's life on earth.

See *Zohar* 3:13b, 43a.

29. **I implore you: *turn away, my love*...** Rabbi Shim'on extends the warning, now issued by the soul. Before it is too late, *turn away*, i.e., turn to God, turn in repentance.

On the verse in Job, see *Bereshit Rabbah* 96:2; *Zohar* 1:217b; 3:43b; Moses de León, *Sefer ha-Rimmon*, 390; cf. Naḥmanides on Numbers 14:9.

See M *Avot* 5:20: "Yehudah son of Tema said, 'Be bold as the leopard, light as the eagle, swift as the gazelle, and mighty as the lion to perform the will of your Father in heaven.'"

Similar to the verse with which Rabbi Yoḥanan opened this discussion is the closing verse of Song of Songs: *Hurry, my love, like a gazelle or a young stag, to the mountains of spices* (8:14). Its being the book's final verse perhaps prompts its construal as pointing beyond death.

On the various metaphors for the world to come, cf. Maimonides, *Mishneh Torah, Hilkhot Teshuvah* 8:4.

Rabbi Ḥiyya said in the name of Rav, "If we are to contemplate this passage, then let us contemplate with wisdom! If the subject is the soul, then the end doesn't fit the beginning, or the beginning the end! [100a] If the subject is the departure of the human being from the world, well, then we must invalidate the entire portion. Whether we establish the passage this way or that way, what is the significance of *Let a little water be fetched and bathe your feet*... (Genesis 18:4); *let me fetch a morsel of bread*... (ibid., 5); *Abraham hurried to the tent to Sarah [and he said, 'Quickly, three seahs of choice flour. Knead and make cakes!']* (ibid., 6); *Abraham ran to the herd [and fetched a tender and goodly calf]* (ibid., 7); *He took curds and milk*... (ibid., 8)?"[30]

When Rav Dimi arrived, he said, "Were it not for the intimation of sacrifices intimated here, the soul would have found no use for the body. The sacrifices were annulled, but the Torah was not annulled. Let the one who cannot engage in sacrifices engage in Torah, and he will benefit even more!"[31]



As Rabbi Yoḥanan said: "When the blessed Holy One elaborated the sacrifices, Moses said, 'Master of the World! Granted for the time when Israel will be in their land. But once they are exiled from their land, what will they do?' He replied, 'Moses, let them engage in Torah and I will absolve them for her sake, more so than for all the sacrifices in the world, as is said: זאת התורה (*Zot ha-torah*), *This is the teaching, for the burnt offering, for the meal offering*... (Leviticus 7:37)—namely זאת התורה (*zot ha-torah*), this Torah, is for the sake of the burnt offering, for the sake of the meal offering, for the sake of the sin offering, for the sake of the guilt offering.'"[32]

30. **Whether we establish the passage this way or that way...** Thus far the *Zohar* has expounded the opening verses of *Va-Yera* as referring to the soul's arrival in the celestial realm, or to the moment of death (see above, *Zohar* 1:97b–98a (*MhN*)). Rabbi Ḥiyya wonders how the verses that follow fit with either of these interpretations. That is, how do water, bread, flour, a calf, and milk—these physical, material entities—accord with either (spiritual) interpretation?

See also BT *Kareitot* 17b.

31. **Were it not for the intimation of sacrifices...** The seemingly incongruous verses can be reconciled with the preceding interpretations, as they allude to the sacrifices. All of the items mentioned were classically offered in various sacrifices and offerings. (Here, חלב [*ḥalav*], "milk," is perhaps being read as *ḥelev*, "fat.") Apparently, Rav Dimi is suggesting that the sacrifices justify the body as they provide a means for atonement, thereby enabling the righteous upon death to attain his vision of the divine and to enter the celestial realm. Additionally, as stated in the following paragraphs, recitation of the sacrifices itself averts death.

See *Matoq mi-Devash*.

The expression "When Rav Dimi arrived" appears frequently throughout the Babylonian Talmud. Apparently he served as the bearer of traditions from the land of Israel to the academy in Pumbedita, Babylon.

32. **this Torah, is for the sake of the burnt offering...** Following the Jews' exile from the land, priests no longer offer sacrifices in

Rabbi Kruspedai said, "Whoever recites with his mouth in synagogues and houses of study the passages of sacrifices and offerings—focusing intently upon them—a sealed covenant applies that those angels who recall his sin to do him harm can do him only good. What proves this? This portion proves it! Since it said *here, three men standing over him* (Genesis 18:2). What is meant by *over him*? To consider his judgment. As soon as [100b] the soul of the righteous person sees this, what is written? *Abraham hurried to the tent*... (ibid., 6). What is *to the tent*? To the house of study. What does he say? *Quickly, three seahs*—the passages of sacrifices. The soul focuses intently upon them, as is written: *Abraham ran to the herd*, whereupon they are appeased and can do him no harm."[33]

Rabbi Pinḥas said, "From this verse, as is written: *look, the plague had begun among the people!* (Numbers 17:12); and it is written: *Moses said to Aaron, 'Take the fire-pan...'* (ibid., 11); and it is written: *and the plague was halted* (ibid., 13). Here is written *quickly* (ibid., 11), and there is written *Quickly, three seahs* (Genesis 18:6). Just as in that case it was a sacrifice in order to be saved, so in this case a sacrifice to be saved."[34]



Rabbi Pinḥas said, "Once I was walking on the way and I encountered Elijah. I said to him, 'May my master tell me a word of benefit for the creatures.' He

the Jerusalem Temple. Yet Israel can still win atonement by studying Torah in lieu of the sacrifices.

On Torah as equivalent to (or outweighing) sacrifices, see BT *Menaḥot* 110a (also based on Leviticus 7:37); *Ta'anit* 27b; *Megillah* 31b; *Zohar* 1:191a–b; 3:32a, 35a, 80b, 159a, 164a.

33. **Whoever recites... the passages of sacrifices...** According to the narrative in Genesis, after the three *men* agreed to dine with Abraham, *Abraham hurried to the tent to Sarah and said, "Quickly, three seahs of choice flour. Knead and make cakes!"* (Genesis 18:6). Rabbi Kruspedai interprets the three *men* as three accusing angels—who can be appeased by reciting the sacrifices, alluded to by the *three seahs of flour* (see, for example, BT *Menaḥot* 76b).

The passages on daily sacrifices are recited daily as part of the morning prayers. They include: Exodus 30:17–21; Leviticus 6:1–6; Numbers 28:1–8. (Similarly on Sabbaths and holy days, regarding the special offerings for those occasions.)

On *over him* as signifying angels deliberating over one's judgment, cf. *ZḤ* 14c (*MhN*).

34. **so in this case a sacrifice to be saved** Rabbi Pinḥas supports Rabbi Kruspedai's interpretation of the apotropaic role of the recitation of the sacrifices (*quickly, three seahs*) by drawing an analogy with the incense offered by Aaron to avert the plague in the wilderness.

Following the death of the rebel Korah and his followers, the Israelites murmur against Moses and Aaron, and God sends a plague against the people. Moses commands Aaron to offer incense, and the plague ceases: *Moses said to Aaron, "Take the fire-pan and place fire upon it from the altar and put in incense and carry it quickly to the community and atone for them, for the fury has gone out from before YHVH, the plague has begun!" Aaron took as Moses had spoken and he ran into the midst of the congregation, and, look, the plague had begun among the people! He put in incense and atoned for the people. He stood between the dead and the living, and the plague was halted* (Numbers 17:11–13).

said to me, 'The blessed Holy One has decreed a covenant (and all those angels in charge of recalling the sins of human beings entered in His presence) that whenever a person recites the sacrifices commanded by Moses—setting his heart and aspiration upon them—all of them will recall him for good.[35]

"'Furthermore, whenever a plague befalls human beings, a covenant has been decreed—and a proclamation has been issued through all the legions of heaven—that if His children on earth enter synagogues and houses of study and proclaim with heartfelt and soulful devotion the passages of the aromatic incense that Israel once performed, then the plague will be abolished from among them.'"[36]

Rabbi Yitsḥak said, "Come and see what is written: *Moses said to Aaron, 'Take the fire-pan and place fire upon it from the altar and put in incense'* (Numbers 17:11). Aaron said to him, 'Why?' He replied, '*For the fury has gone out from before YHVH . . .*' (ibid.). What is written? *He ran to* [101a] *the midst of the congregation and look, the plague had begun among the people!* (ibid., 12). And it is written: *He stood between the dead and the living, and the plague was halted* (ibid., 13)—the angel of destruction could not prevail and the plague was thwarted."[37]



Rabbi Aḥa traveled to Clod Village; he arrived at his inn. All the town's residents spoke in hushed tones about him, saying, "A great man has arrived here. Let us go to him."[38]

35. **Rabbi Pinḥas . . . encountered Elijah . . .** According to the Bible (2 Kings 2:11), the prophet Elijah did not die a normal death but was carried off to heaven in a chariot of fire. He became associated with the Messianic age (Malachi 3:23–24) and in rabbinic tradition is described as "still existing" (BT *Bava Batra* 121b) and revealing divine secrets to righteous humans (BT *Bava Metsi'a* 59b, *Ketubbot* 61a).

In Kabbalah, mystical experiences are known as revelations of Elijah. See Scholem, *On the Kabbalah*, 19–21; *Zohar* 1:1b, 151a; 3:221a, 231a, 241b; *ZḤ* 59d, 62c, 63d, 70d, 73c (last four *ShS*). In *MhN*, see *ZḤ* 23d, 25b.

On "creatures," see above, note 21.

36. **aromatic incense . . .** On the power of incense to banish evil forces, see *Targum* on Song of Songs 4:6; *Zohar* 1:230a; 2:218b–219a; 3:151b; Moses de León, *Sefer ha-Rimmon*, 87.

The passages on incense (also recited as part of the morning service) include Exodus 30:34–36, 7–8; BT *Kareitot* 6a; JT *Yoma* 4:5, 41d.

37. **the angel of destruction could not prevail . . .** Aaron's offering of incense to avert the plague (see above, note 34) is the paradigm of incense's power to thwart evil. According to BT *Shabbat* 89a (in the name of Rabbi Yehoshu'a son of Levi), the Angel of Death himself transmitted the secret of incense to Moses.

See *Zohar* 1:230a; 2:218b–219a; 3:33b.

38. **Clod Village . . .** כפר טרשא (*Kefar Tarsha*). The word *tarsha* means "stony, nonarable ground; clod; crag." Judging from *Zohar* 1:92b, it was understood to be located in the Galilee.

On the inn, see *Zohar* 1:72a.

They went to him. They said to him, "Is the master's heart anguished by the destruction?"[39]

He said to them, "What do you mean?"

They said to him, "For seven days, a plague has been hovering over the town. Each day it grows stronger and does not desist."

He said to them, "Let us go to the synagogue and implore mercy from the blessed Holy One."

While they were walking, [some people] arrived and said, "So-and-so and so-and-so have died, and so-and-so and so-and-so are about to die."

Rabbi Aḥa said to them, "Now is not the time to stand by—the hour is pressing! Rather, set aside forty of the most righteous people, in four groups of ten, and I with you; ten for one corner of the town, ten for another corner of the town, and so on for the four corners of the town; and recite with soulful devotion the passages of the aromatic incense that the blessed Holy One gave Moses, accompanied by the passages of the sacrifices."[40]



They did so three times—and passed through all four directions of the town, reciting accordingly. Afterward, he said to them, "Let us go to those verging on death. Set aside [other righteous people] for their houses and let them recite in a similar fashion. When you finish, recite these verses loudly three times: *Moses said to Aaron, 'Take the fire-pan and place fire upon it...'* (Numbers 17:11) [101b]; *Aaron took...* (ibid., 12); *He stood between the dead...* (ibid., 13)."

They did so and the plague ceased.

They heard a voice saying, "Secret striker, primal striker, wait on high; the judgment of heaven does not hover here, for they know how to nullify it."[41]

Rabbi Aḥa's heart was faint. He fell asleep. He heard that they were telling him, "Just as you accomplished that, accomplish this! Go and tell them to return in *teshuvah*, for they are wicked before Me."[42]

39. **Is the master's heart anguished...** Referring politely to Rabbi Aḥa in the third person, in deference to him as a rabbi. Their question could also be rendered: "Can the master take to heart the destruction?" That is, will the master do something about it?

40. **Now is not the time to stand by...** Realizing the gravity of the situation, Rabbi Aḥa determines that mere prayer will not suffice. Only incense can save the town! Hence, he organizes a protective shield of righteous people, whose recitation of the passages on incense will protect the residents.

41. **Secret striker, primal striker, wait on high...** סתרא סתרא קמייתא אוחילו לעילא (*Sitra sitra qammayta oḥilu le-'eila*). The phrase is obscure, though the sense is: agents of destruction, remain above; you do not have permission to descend. Cf. *Derekh Emet*; *Nitsotsei Orot*; *Sullam*, ad loc.

42. **Just as you accomplished that, accomplish this!...** Exhausted from his efforts to save the town, Rabbi Aḥa falls asleep. He has averted the plague this time. However, for the residents to be safe on an ongoing basis, they must return to God.

He arose and returned them in complete *teshuvah*, and they accepted upon themselves never to desist from Torah; and they changed the name of the city to Mata Meḥasya.[43]

Rabbi Yehudah said, "It is not enough for the righteous that they nullify the decree, but afterward they are blessed! Know that it is so, for as soon as the soul says to the body, *Quickly, three seahs*... (Genesis 18:6) and so on, and the judgment is canceled, what is written? *He said, 'I will surely return to you when life is due'* (ibid., 10)—a blessing! As soon as the angels see that this one has taken counsel to heart, what do they do? They proceed to the wicked to consider their judgment, to administer justice, as is written: *The men arose from there and gazed toward Sodom* (ibid., 16)—to the lair of the wicked, to execute justice."[44]

As Rabbi Yehudah said: "So is the way of the righteous person: As soon as he realizes that they are contemplating his judgment, he does not delay in repenting and praying and offering his fat and his blood unto his Rock—until the masters of judgment withdraw from him. For as soon as it said *He raised his eyes* [102a] *and saw: here, three men standing over him* (ibid., 2), what is written of the soul? *Abraham hurried to the tent, to Sarah* (ibid., 6)—hastily, quickly, without any delay. Immediately the soul hurries to the body to restore it to the right path, seeking how it might be atoned, until the masters of judgment withdraw from him."[45]



Rabbi Eli'ezer says, "What is the significance of the verse *Abraham and Sarah were old, advanced in days. The way of women had ceased for Sarah* (ibid., 11)? Well, when the soul abides in its rung, and the body remains on earth for many years, *advanced in days*—many years and days, and has ceased to be active in the way of all other people, it is told about the revival of the body. What does it [the body] say? *'After I have withered, am I to have rejuvenation?* (ibid., 12)—

43. **Mata Meḥasya** "Town of Compassion," because God showed them compassion.

Meḥasya was a suburb of Sura on the Euphrates and the site of a rabbinic academy. See BT *Ketubbot* 4a; *Zohar* 1:72a; and *Zohar* 1:94b, which alludes to the city's deliverance and the inhabitants' conversion to constant Torah study. See also BT *Horayot* 12a in the name of Rabbi Mesharsheya: "Better to sit on the dunghills of Mata Meḥasya than in the palaces of Pumbedita."

Note the story's moral symmetry: At first, the plague would not "desist"; in the end, the townspeople commit themselves never to "desist" from Torah.

44. **It is not enough for the righteous...** Following the recitation of the sacrifices (as alluded to by: *Quickly, three seahs*, see above, notes 33, 34), the righteous person is delivered from judgment. What's more, he receives an additional blessing as indicated by the announcement to Sarah.

45. **offering his fat and his blood...** By fasting.

after I have withered in the dust for many years, am I to have rejuvenation and invigoration? *My husband is old* (ibid.)—many years have passed since he left me and attended to me!' The blessed Holy One says, '*Is anything too wondrous for YHVH? At the set time I will return to you*' (ibid., 14). What is meant by *at the set time*? 'That which is known by Me to revive the dead.'"[46]

*Sarah will have a son* (ibid.). Rabbi Yehudah said, "This teaches that it will be renewed like a son of three years."

Rabbi Yehudah son of Rabbi Simon said, "When the soul is nourished by the supernal splendor, the blessed Holy One says to the angel called Dumah, 'Go and inform the body belonging to so-and-so that I will one day revive him at the set time when I will revive the righteous in the time to come.' He replies, '*After I have withered, am I to have rejuvenation?* (ibid., 12)—after I have withered in the dust and dwelt in the earth, my flesh consumed by maggots and a clod of earth, shall I have invigoration?' The blessed Holy One says to the soul, as is written: *YHVH said to Abraham*... (ibid., 13), '*Is anything too wondrous for YHVH? At the set time I will return to you when life is due* (ibid., 14). *At the set time* known by Me to revive the righteous, *I will return to you* that body which is [102b] holy, renewed as at first, to be holy angels. That day is designated before Me for rejoicing in them,' as is written: *May the glory of YHVH endure forever; may YHVH rejoice in His works!* (Psalms 104:31)."[47] [104b]



46. ***Abraham and Sarah were old...*** The announcement that Sarah will have a son (see Genesis 18:9–15) is an allegory for the resurrection of the body. Sarah (the body) expresses disbelief that her elderly husband (the soul, who has been separated from her for so long, dwelling above in the celestial realm) will attend to her again.

On Sarah's exclamation (*am I to have rejuvenation?*), see *Bereshit Rabbah* 48:17; BT *Bava Metsi'a* 87a. On the resurrection of the body, see below, *Zohar* 1:115b–116a (*MhN*).

47. **When the soul is nourished by the supernal splendor...** דומה (*Dumah*), literally "silence," is a name for the netherworld in the Bible. See Psalms 94:17: *Were not YHVH a help to me, my soul would have nearly dwelled in dumah*. In rabbinic literature, Dumah is the angel in charge of souls of the dead (BT *Berakhot* 18b, *Shabbat* 152b, *Ḥagigah* 5a, *Sanhedrin* 94a; *Tanḥuma, Ki Tissa* 33). See *Zohar* 1:8a–b; 62b, 94a, 121a (*Tos*), 124a (*MhN*), 130b, 218b, 237b; 2:18a (*MhN*), 150b.

See Job 7:5: *My flesh is covered with maggots and clods of earth.*

The verse from Psalms is quoted in an eschatological context in *Vayiqra Rabbah* 20:2; *Tanḥuma, Aḥarei Mot* 2; *Tanḥuma* (Buber), *Aḥarei Mot* 3; *Midrash Tehillim* 75:2; *Zohar* 1:114a (*MhN*), 115a (*MhN*), 116a (*MhN*), 119a, 135a (*MhN*), 182a; 2:57b, 259a (*Heikh*); 3:16a.

On the righteous as angels, cf. Maimonides, *Mishneh Torah, Hilkhot Teshuvah* 8:2: "In the world to come, there is no body or physical form, only the souls of the righteous alone, without a body, like the ministering angels." For the *Zohar*, following the resurrection, human beings will simultaneously possess a body and be like the angels. Cf. *Zohar* 1:100a, 129b; *ZḤ* 10a, 19a, 20d, 21a (all *MhN*).

*And YHVH said, "Shall I hide from Abraham . . ."* (Genesis 18:17).

What is written before this? *The men arose from there and gazed toward Sodom* (ibid., 16)—to execute judgment upon the wicked. What is written after? *Shall I hide from Abraham.*[48]

It has been taught: Rav Ḥisda said, "The blessed Holy One does not execute judgment upon the wicked before conferring with the souls of the righteous, as is written: *By the soul of God they perish* (Job 4:9); and similarly: *Shall I hide from Abraham.* The blessed Holy One said, 'Can I execute judgment upon the wicked before conferring with the souls of the righteous?' He informs them, 'The wicked have sinned before Me, I will execute judgment upon them,' as is written: *YHVH said, 'How great is the outcry of Sodom and Gomorrah!'* (Genesis 18:20)."[49]

Rabbi Abbahu said, "The soul remains in her place, terrified to draw near and say anything at all in His presence, until the blessed Holy One instructs Metatron שיגישנה (*she-yaggishennah*), to present her, before Him to say whatever
332
she pleases, as is written: ויגש אברהם (*va-yiggash Avraham*), *Abraham approached, and said, 'Will you really sweep away the innocent along with the guilty? Far be it from You! . . .'* (ibid., 23, 25).[50]

48. ***Shall I hide from Abraham . . .*** The impending judgment of the wicked in Sodom connotes the judgment of the wicked in the hereafter. Abraham signifies the soul. (See next note.)

Verse 17 continues: *what I am about to do? For Abraham will surely be a great and mighty nation, and all the nations of the earth will be blessed through him.* In the verse's simple sense, God determines to share His plan to destroy Sodom with his covenant partner, Abraham.

Some manuscripts contain the section heading פרשת יב (*parashat* 12). See p. 311, n. 126.

49. **before conferring with the souls of the righteous . . .** In the Garden of Eden.

Cf. *Tanḥuma* (Buber), *Vayera* 6: "Even when the blessed Holy One grew angry over Sodom because of their wicked deeds and sought to overturn Sodom, He did not seal their decree of punishment before conferring with Abraham, as is said: *And YHVH said, 'Shall I hide from Abraham* [*what I am about to do?*'] (Genesis 18:17)." See also *Tanḥuma, Vayera* 5; cf. *Bereshit Rabbah* 49:2. In line with the *Zohar*'s allegorical reading, the motif of conferring with Abraham has been replaced by conferring with the souls of the righteous.

In its simple sense, the verse from Job means *By a blast of God they perish.*

See *ZḤ* 25a (*MhN*), also in the name of Rav Ḥisda.

50. **until the blessed Holy One instructs Metatron . . .** Metatron serves as the intermediary between the soul and God.

Metatron is the chief angel, variously described as the Prince of the World, Prince of the Countenance (or Presence), celestial scribe, and even יהוה קטן (*YHVH Qatan*), "Lesser *YHVH*" (3 Enoch 12:5, based on Exodus 23:21). In Heikhalot literature, Metatron is identified with Enoch (great-grandfather of Noah), who ascended to heaven without dying (see Genesis 5:24). See BT *Sanhedrin* 38b; *Ḥagigah* 15a; *Yevamot* 16b; *Tosafot, Yevamot* 16b, s.v. *pasuq zeh*; Scholem, *Kabbalah*, 377–81; Tishby, *Wisdom of the Zohar*, 2:626–31; Margaliot, *Mal'akhei Elyon*, 73–108.

On Metatron in the *Zohar*, see 1:21a, 37b, 95b, 143a, 162a–b; 2:65b–66b, 131a; 3:217a–b; *ZḤ* 42d–43a; 69b (*ShS*).

In *MhN*, see *Zohar* 1:126a–b; *ZḤ* 4a, 8d,

"*Perhaps there are fifty righteous people . . .* (ibid., 24)—the soul opens, saying, 'Master of the World! Perhaps they have engaged in the fifty portions of the Torah; and even if they have not engaged for its own sake, they have earned a reward in the world to come and should not be consigned to Hell.' What is written after? *YHVH said, 'If I find within Sodom fifty righteous people . . .'* (ibid., 26)."[51]

But there are more portions![52]

Well, Rabbi Abbahu said, "There are five books in the Torah, and each one comprises the Ten Commandments—the ten utterances through which the world was created; reckon ten for each, totaling fifty.[53]

"The soul opens again, saying, 'Master of the World! Even if they have not engaged in Torah, perhaps they have received their punishment for what they sinned in a court of law and have been pardoned, as is said: *Forty is he to be struck, no more* (Deuteronomy 25:3); their shame before them sufficing to affect atonement—so that they should not be consigned to Hell.' What is written after? *I will not do it for the sake of the forty* (Genesis 18:29).[54]



9d–10a, 10b, 12b, 24a, 25d–26a, 28a–c; Scholem, "Parashah Ḥadashah," 437 (Addendum 1 in this volume).

51. ***Perhaps there are fifty righteous people . . .*** Here begins an allegorical reading of Abraham's bargain with God (see Genesis 18:24–32). Each of the various numbers alludes to a virtue that, if possessed by the condemned, would make them worthy of avoiding Hell.

Genesis 18:26 concludes: *I will forgive the whole place for their sake.*

On studying Torah for its own sake, see *Avot* 6:1; BT *Pesaḥim* 50b, *Sukkah* 49b, *Ta'anit* 7a, *Sanhedrin* 99b.

In mentioning "the fifty portions of the Torah," the *Zohar* ignores here the triennial cycle of reading the Torah—which had been practiced in the land of Israel and in Egypt as late as 1170 C.E.—and follows the Babylonian practice (of an annual reading cycle), which held sway in medieval Spain. See Ta-Shma, *Ha-Nigleh she-ba-Nistar,* 108, n. 11.

52. **But there are more portions** Namely, more than fifty. Since the early Middle Ages, there have actually been fifty-four Torah portions in the annual reading cycle, but the last one is read on *Shemini Atseret*, leaving fifty-three for Sabbath reading. Furthermore, in most years there are not as many Sabbaths as the number of Torah portions, and on Sabbaths that coincide with festivals other sections of Torah are read, so two Torah portions are sometimes joined together. See *Nitsotsei Zohar,* ad loc.; *Zohar* 2:206b and *Nitsotsei Orot,* ad loc.; Elbogen, *Jewish Liturgy,* 134–35.

53. **each one comprises the Ten Commandments . . .** The Ten Commandments are found in Exodus and again in Deuteronomy. Nevertheless, according to Rabbi Abbahu they are implied in all the other books as well.

According to M *Avot* 5:1, "The world was created through ten utterances." Only nine explicit commands appear in Genesis 1, but the decade is made complete by counting the phrase *In the beginning.* See BT *Rosh ha-Shanah* 32a, *Megillah* 21b; *Pirqei de-Rabbi Eli'ezer* 3; *Zohar* 1:15a, 16b, 30a; 2:14b (*MhN*); *ZḤ* 2d (*MhN*).

54. ***Forty is he to be struck, no more . . .*** Referring to the forty stripes administered by the court for certain types of crimes.

Genesis 18:29 reads: *And he spoke to him still again and he said, "Perhaps there will be*

"She opens again, saying, '*Perhaps twenty will be found there* (Genesis 18:31)—perhaps they will raise children to the study of Torah, and they should be rewarded for the Ten Commandments, twice every day.' As Rabbi Yitsḥak said: 'Whoever [105a] rears his child to the study of Torah, taking him to and from his teacher, morning and evening, Scripture accounts it to him as though he fulfills the Torah twice each day.' What is written? *I will not destroy for the sake of the twenty* (ibid.).[55]

"She opens again, saying, *Perhaps ten will be found there* (ibid., 32). She says, 'Master of the World! Perhaps they were of those ten found in the synagogue, for look at what we have learned: Whoever is reckoned among the first ten in the synagogue receives a reward equal to all those who come after him.' What is written? *He said, 'I will not destroy for the sake of the ten'* (ibid.).[56]

"All this must the soul of the righteous say on behalf of the wicked. Since they are found to possess nothing, what is written? *YHVH left when He had finished speaking to Abraham; and Abraham returned to his place* (ibid., 33). What is *to his place*? To the place of his particular rung."[57]



Rabbi said, "It is incumbent on a person to pray for the wicked, that they might return to the right path and not be consigned to Hell, as is written: *And I, when they were ill, my dress was sackcloth...* (Psalms 35:13)."[58]

*found forty." And He said, "I will not do it for the sake of the forty."*

The printed editions at this point proceed to expound Abraham's plea: *Perhaps thirty are there* (Genesis 18:30), connecting the number thirty with the thirty-two paths of wisdom: "the twenty-two letters and the ten *sefirot*, which are sometimes comprised in eight." This passage is not found in any of the manuscript witnesses, which proceed immediately from the number forty to twenty. See Meroz, "Merkevet Yeḥezqel," 595–96. *Zohar* 1:255a (*hashmatot*) contains some different interpretations for the various numbers, as well as an additional homily on the number forty-five. None of these interpretations is in the manuscripts at this location.

55. **perhaps they will raise children to the study of Torah...** According to BT *Shabbat* 127a and *Pesaḥim* 113a, one who raises his child to Torah study is rewarded in the world to come.

The Ten Commandments are the essence of Torah, and hence one is rewarded for them twice each day: for morning "drop off" and afternoon "pick-up."

56. **the first ten in the synagogue...** See BT *Berakhot* 47b: "Rabbi Yehoshu'a son of Levi said, 'A person should always rise early to go to the synagogue, so that he will have the merit of being counted in the first ten; since even if a hundred come after him, he receives the reward of them all.' Would you imagine 'the reward of them all'? Say rather: He is given a reward equal to that of them all."

See *Zohar* 1:255a (*MhN, hashmatot*); 2:86a, 250a (*Heikh*); 3:126a; Moses de León, *Sefer ha Rimmon*, 36.

57. **Since they are found to possess nothing...** Of the virtues alluded to in Abraham's bargaining. Following his attempted defense of the wicked, Abraham, signifying the soul of the righteous, returns to his celestial abode.

See *Bereshit Rabbah* 49:14; *Zohar* 1:255a (*MhN, hashmatot*).

58. **to pray for the wicked...** The verse

Rabbi also said, "It is forbidden for a person to pray that the wicked be removed from the world, for had the blessed Holy One dispatched Terah from the world when he was an idolator, Abraham our father would not have come to the world, and the tribes of Israel would never have been, nor King David or the Messiah, and the Torah would not have been given, and all the righteous and the pious and the prophets would never have been in the world!"[59]

Rabbi Yehudah said, "As soon as the blessed Holy One sees that the wicked do not possess anything of all those matters, what is written? *The two angels went to Sodom*... (Genesis 19:1)."[60]

[106a] Rabbi opened with this verse: *These are the nations that YHVH left, so that He might test Israel thereby* (Judges 3:1).

Rabbi said, "I was gazing upon that world—and there is no rank like those [106b] who rule over their passion, as is said: *a testimony, He ordained it for Joseph*... (Psalms 81:6)."[61]

Rav Yehudah said, "Why did Joseph merit that rank and royalty? Because he conquered his impulse. As we have learned: Whoever conquers his impulse—the kingdom of heaven rests upon him."[62]



from Psalms continues: *I afflicted myself with fasting; may my own prayer come back to my bosom.* Here, the sense is as follows: When the wicked were ill (sick with sin and facing judgment), I prayed and fasted for them.

See BT *Berakhot* 10a: "There were some criminals in the neighborhood of Rabbi Meir who caused him much strife. Rabbi Meir prayed that they should die. His wife Beruriah said to him, 'How do you justify such a prayer? Is it because it is written יתמו חטאים (*yittammu ḥatta'im*), *Let sinners cease* [*from the earth*] (Psalms 104:35)? Is it written חוטאים (*ḥot'im*), *sinners*? It is written חטאים (*ḥatta'im*), sins! Further, look at the end of the verse: *and let the wicked be no more.* When sins will cease, the wicked will be no more! Rather, pray that they should repent—and then the wicked will be no more.' He prayed for them, and they repented."

See also BT *Sotah* 14a.

"Rabbi" signifies Rabbi Yehudah ha-Nasi (the patriarch), who lived in the second-third centuries and redacted the Mishnah. He was so highly esteemed that he was called "Rabbi," the Master.

59. **the righteous and the pious and the prophets would never have been...** On taking into consideration the future righteous offspring of the wicked, cf. *Targum Yerushalmi* and *Targum Yerushalmi* (frag.) on Exodus 2:12; BT *Bava Qamma* 38b; *Shemot Rabbah* 1:29; *Vayiqra Rabbah* 32:4; see *Zohar* 1:118a (*MhN*); 140a.

60. ***The two angels went to Sodom*...** To execute judgment upon the wicked in Hell.

61. ***He ordained it for Joseph*** The verse in Psalms 81 includes the divine name יה (*Yah*) within Joseph's expanded name יהוסף (*Yehosef*), "testifying" to his virtue (by withstanding the sexual advances of Potiphar's wife, see Genesis 39). On the divine element within *Yehosef*, see *Vayiqra Rabbah* 23:10; BT *Sotah* 10b, 36b; *Mishnat Rabbi Eli'ezer* 17, pp. 321–22; *Midrash Tehillim* 81:7; *Bemidbar Rabbah* 14:5; *Zohar* 2:221b; 3:14a, 213b.

On the phrase "I was gazing," see Daniel 7:2.

62. **Why did Joseph merit that rank and royalty?...** In the earthly domain, he became grand vizier of Egypt; in the spiritual

As Rabbi Aḥa said: "The blessed Holy One created the evil impulse solely so that He might test human beings thereby."[63]

Now, does the blessed Holy really want to test human beings? Yes, as Rabbi Aḥa said: "How do we know? From what is written: *Should there arise in your midst a prophet ... and the sign and the portent ... for YHVH your God will be testing ...* (Deuteronomy 13:2–4). And why is a test required, for surely all of a person's deeds are revealed before Him?! Well, so as not to provide a pretext for human beings. Look at what is written: *Lot was sitting in the gate of Sodom* (Genesis 19:1)—he was sitting to test the creatures!"[64]

Rabbi Yitsḥak said, "What is the meaning of the verse *The wicked are like the tossing sea ...* (Isaiah 57:20)? Even during the wicked person's hour of judgment, he is impudent and abides in his wickedness. Look at what is written: *They had not yet lain down ...* (Genesis 19:4)!"[65]

domain, he acquired the divine name within



his own.

See *Zohar* 1:93b, 197a.

See M *Avot* 4:1: "Ben Zoma said, '... Who is mighty? He who conquers his impulse.'"

63. **created the evil impulse ... test human beings ...** Cf. *Zohar* 2:163a.

64. **so as not to provide a pretext for human beings ...** God does not test people because He needs to learn the outcome, but rather to demonstrate His just providence.

See *Bereshit Rabbah* 51:1: "*It came to pass after these things, God* נסה (*nissah*), *tested, Abraham* (Genesis 22:1). It is written: *You have given* נס (*nes*), *a banner, to those in awe of You,* להתנוסס (*le-hitnoses*), *to be unfurled* ... (Psalms 60:6)—trial upon trial, elevation above elevation, to test them in the world, to elevate them in the world like a ship's banner. Why to such an extent? *Because of truth. Selah* (ibid.)—so that the attribute of Justice would be verified in the world." As the midrash goes on to say, the case of Abraham proves that God does not reward or punish arbitrarily. The patriarch was rewarded for his extreme devotion in being willing to sacrifice his son.

See also the end of *parashat Lekh Lekha* (*MhN*) in this volume, page 313.

The verses from Deuteronomy read: *Should there arise in your midst a prophet or a dreamer of dreams and give you a sign or a portent, and the sign and the portent that he speaks to you come about—saying, "Let us go after other gods that you do not know and worship them"—you shall not heed the words of that prophet or of that dreamer of dreams; for YHVH your God will be testing you, to know whether you love YHVH your God with all your heart and with all your soul.*

Lot signifies the evil impulse. See below, at note 70.

On "creatures," see above, note 21.

65. **Even during the wicked person's hour of judgment ...** In its simple sense, the verse from Genesis refers to the visiting messengers and the members of Lot's house. Here, Rabbi Yitsḥak reads it as speaking about the people of Sodom, i.e., the wicked, who—before they lie down in the grave—maintain their wicked ways.

The verse from Genesis continues: *and the men of the city, the men of Sodom, surrounded the house—from lads to elders, every last man of them.*

The verse from Isaiah continues: *that cannot be still, whose waters churn up mire and mud.*

See BT *Eruvin* 19a in the name of Rabbi Shim'on son of Lakish: "Even at the entrance of Hell the wicked do not repent, as is said: *They will go out and stare at the corpses of the people who transgress against Me ...* (Isaiah 66:24). It does not say *who trans-*

Rabbi Yitsḥak said, "Just as the blessed Holy One created a Garden of Eden on earth, so He created Hell on earth; and just as He created a Garden of Eden above, so He created Hell above. A Garden of Eden on earth, as is written: *YHVH God planted a garden in Eden, to the east* (Genesis 2:8); Hell on earth, as is written: *A land whose light is darkness...* (Job 10:22). A Garden of Eden above, as is written: *The soul of my lord will be bound in the bundle of life with YHVH your God* (1 Samuel 25:29); and similarly: *and the spirit will return to God who gave it* (Ecclesiastes 12:7); Hell above, as is written: *The soul of your enemies He will sling from the hollow of a sling* (1 Samuel 25:29).[66]

"A Garden of Eden below, as we have said. A Garden of Eden above—for the souls of the completely righteous, to be nourished by the great light above. Hell below—for the wicked, who did not accept the covenant of circumcision, who did not believe in the blessed Holy One and His law, and who did not observe the Sabbath; these are of the nations of the world, who are judged by fire, as is said: *from fire they departed, but fire shall consume them...* (Ezekiel 15:7), and it is written: *They will go out and stare at the corpses of the people...* (Isaiah 66:24). Hell above—for the apostates of Israel, who transgressed the commandments of Torah and did not return in *teshuvah*; they are thrust without until they receive their punishment, roaming and rounding the whole world, as is said: *All around the wicked roam* (Psalms 12:9); they are judged there for twelve months. Afterward their abode is with those who received their punishment at their death, [107a] every single one in accordance with the place that is fitting.[67]



*gressed,* but *who transgress,* implying that they go on transgressing forever."

On the wicked as *like the tossing sea,* see *Shir ha-Shirim Rabbah* on 2:16; *Tanḥuma, Vayiqra* 7; *Midrash Tehillim* 2:2; *Zohar* 1:74b, 171b; *ZḤ* 4d (*MhN*).

66. **Just as the blessed Holy One created...** On the earthly and heavenly Gardens of Eden, see Naḥmanides on Genesis 3:22; idem, *Kitvei Ramban,* 2:295–99; *Zohar* 1:7a, 38b (*Heikh*), 81a (*ST*), 224b; 2:150a, 209b–210b, 211b–212a, 231b; 3:13a, 53a, 70b; *ZḤ* 13c, 18a–b (both *MhN*); Moses de León, *Shushan Edut,* 350–51; idem, *Sheqel ha-Qodesh,* 27 (32), 59–62 (73–76); [Moses de León?], *Seder Gan Eden*; Tishby, *Wisdom of the Zohar,* 2:591–94, 749–51.

On the two Hells, see *Zohar* 2:150b; Moses de León, *Shushan Edut,* 351–53; idem, *Sefer ha-Rimmon,* 374; idem, *Sefer ha-Mishqal,* 63; idem, *Sheqel ha-Qodesh,* 59–60 (73–74); idem, *Mishkan ha-Edut,* 49b–50a.

See BT *Shabbat* 152b: "Rabbi Eli'ezer said, 'The souls of the righteous are treasured away under the Throne of Glory, as is said: *The soul of my lord will be bound in the bundle of life.* Those of the wicked are continually muzzled, while one angel stands at one end of the world, and another stands at the other end; and they sling their souls [the souls of the wicked] to each other, as is said: *The soul of your enemies He will sling as from the hollow of a sling.*'"

On the verse from Samuel, see Radak. The full verse (recording Abigail's blessing to David) reads: *If a person rises to pursue you, to seek your life, the soul of my lord will be bound in the bundle of life with YHVH your God, and the soul of your enemies He will sling from the hollow of a sling.*

67. **A Garden of Eden below...** The earthly Garden of Eden is where Adam and

"The wicked from the nations of the world are judged unceasingly in the fire of Hell and do not ascend again, as is said: *their fire shall not be quenched* (Isaiah 66:24)—the judgment of the wicked in Hell, as is written: *YHVH rained brimstone and fire on Sodom and Gomorrah*... (Genesis 19:24). They do not ascend again and will not rise for the Day of Judgment, as is said: *which YHVH overturned in His anger and His fury* (Deuteronomy 29:22). *In his anger*—in this world; *and His fury*—in the world to come."[68]

Rabbi Yitsḥak said, "It follows this pattern: There is a Garden of Eden below and a Garden of Eden above; there is a Hell below and a Hell above."

Rabbi Ya'akov said, "The wicked who corrupted their covenant of circumcision, desecrated the Sabbath in public, profaned the holidays, and who denied



Eve lived; the Garden of Eden above is the destination of the completely righteous. Hell below is for the wicked of the nations; and Hell above for the wicked of the Jews. Hell above corresponds with the hollow of a sling—the wicked of Israel being forced to roam the world until they are purified of their sins and able to enter the Garden of Eden.

On being thrust without and wandering the world as punishment (often associated with the sling motif from BT *Shabbat* 152a), see *Zohar* 1:123a (*MhN*), 217b; 2:59a, 99b, 142b; 3:185b–186a, 213b; Moses de León, *Shushan Edut*, 351–53 (and n. 171, where Scholem cites de León's likely source in Jacob ha-Kohen's *Sefer ha-Orah*); idem, *Sefer ha-Rimmon*, 373, 399; idem, *Sefer ha-Mishqal*, 67–68; Liebes, *Peraqim*, 345–48.

On the righteous nourished by the light above, see *Zohar* 1:113b, 135b (both *MhN*); *ZḤ* 26a (*MhN*). Cf. BT *Berakhot* 17a: "A pearl in the mouth of Rav: In the world to come, there is no eating or drinking or procreation or business or jealousy or hatred or competition; rather, the righteous sit with their crowns on their heads, basking in the radiance of *Shekhinah*, as is said: *They beheld God and they ate and drank* (Exodus 24:11)." See also Maimonides, *Mishneh Torah*, *Hilkhot Teshuvah* 8:2.

On Ezekiel 15:7, see *ZḤ* 4d (*MhN*). In its simple sense, the verse means *from fire they escaped* [or: *emerged*], *but fire shall consume them.* Perhaps Rabbi Yitsḥak intends that "the nations of the world" departed from the fire of Torah (see Deuteronomy 33:2), i.e., they did not accept the Torah.

The verse from Isaiah continues: *who transgress against Me; for their worm will not die, nor their fire be quenched: they shall be a horror to all flesh.* See BT *Eruvin* 19a (above, note 65).

On the sentence of the wicked in Hell as lasting twelve months, see M *Eduyyot* 2:10; BT *Rosh ha-Shanah* 17a; *Seder Olam Rabbah* 3; *Zohar* 1:68b, 130b; *ZḤ* 25b (*MhN*). On Psalms 12:9, cf. *Vayiqra Rabbah* 32:1.

68. **judged unceasingly in the fire of Hell...** In Hell below, the wicked of the nations are punished for all time. Unlike the wicked of Israel, they neither ascend to the Garden of Eden nor rise at the resurrection.

Cf. M *Sanhedrin* 10:3: "The people of Sodom have no share in the world to come, as is written: *Now the people of Sodom were wicked and sinners before YHVH exceedingly* (Genesis 13:13). *Wicked* in this world, *and sinners* in the world to come; yet they will stand at the [last] judgment. Rabbi Neḥemiah said, 'Neither [the generation of the Flood nor the people of Sodom] will stand at the [last] judgment, as is written: *therefore the wicked shall not stand in the judgment, nor sinners in the assembly of the righteous* (Psalms 1:5). *Therefore the wicked shall not stand in judgment*—the generation of the Flood; *nor sinners in the assembly of the righteous*—the people of Sodom.'" See *Zohar* 1:108a.

the Torah and the resurrection of the dead and their like, descend to Hell below. They are judged there and do not ascend again; but they will rise for the Day of Judgment, and they will rise for the Resurrection. Of them is said *Many of those who sleep in the dust of earth will awake [—these to everlasting life, those to shame and everlasting horror]* (Daniel 12:2); and of them is said *they shall be* דראון (*dera'on*), *a horror, to all flesh* (Isaiah 66:24). What is דראון (*dera'on*)? די ראון (*Dai ra'on*), Enough seeing—for all will say 'Enough!' when they see them. But of the righteous of Israel is said: *Your people, all of them righteous, [will inherit the land forever]* (ibid. 60:21)."[69] [109a]

*Lot went up from Zoar...* (Genesis 19:30).[70]

Rabbi Abbahu said, "Come and see what is written about the evil impulse! You should know that he will never be eliminated from humankind, until that time of which is written *I will remove the heart of stone...* (Ezekiel 36:26). For even though he sees people being judged in Hell, he returns to human beings time and again, as is written: *Lot went up* מצוער (*mi-tso'ar*), *from Zoar*—מצערה (*mi-tsa'arah*), from the suffering, of Hell; ascending from there to entice human beings."[71]



Rabbi Yehudah said, "There are three dispositions in a human being: the disposition of intellect and wisdom—this is [109b] the power of הנשמה הקדושה

69. **The wicked who corrupted...** Although the wicked of Israel generally go to Hell above, those who have committed particularly serious offenses descend to Hell below. They do not ascend to the Garden of Eden, but they do rise at the last judgment—only to endure yet more suffering.

See M *Sanhedrin* 10:1: "All of Israel have a share in the world to come, as is said: *Your people, all of them righteous, will inherit the land forever—sprout of My planting, work of My hands, that I may be glorified.* These do not have a share in the world to come: one who says that the resurrection of the dead is not from the Torah...." See also BT *Sanhedrin* 99a.

On the midrashic reading of *dera'on*, see *Targum Yonatan* on the verse; *Zohar* 2:151a. On Daniel 12:2, see *Zohar* 1:130a (*MhN*).

70. ***Lot went up from Zoar...*** The verse continues: *and settled in the mountains, his two daughters together with him, for he was afraid to dwell in Zoar; and he dwelt in a certain cave, he and his two daughters.*

According to the allegorical method of *MhN*, Lot signifies the evil impulse. See *ZḤ* 24b, 24d (both *MhN*). See also *Zohar* 1:78a, 79a (both *ST*), 255a (*hashmatot*).

71. **he will never be eliminated from humankind...** On the eventual abolition of the evil impulse, see BT *Sukkah* 52a; *Shemot Rabbah* 41:7; *Tanḥuma* (Buber), *Bereshit* 40, *Qedoshim* 15; Naḥmanides on Deuteronomy 30:6; *Zohar* 1:128b, 137a–138a (both *MhN*).

On the evil impulse witnessing the torments of Hell, see below, at note 77.

The full verse from Ezekiel reads: *I will give you a new heart and put a new spirit into you; I will remove the heart of stone from your flesh and give you a heart of flesh.*

See also Isaiah 25:7: *He will destroy on this mount* פני הלוט (*pnei ha-lot*), *the shroud,* הלוט (*ha-lot*), *that is drawn, over the faces of all the peoples, and the covering that is spread over all the nations.*

(*ha-neshamah ha-qedoshah*), the holy soul; the disposition of desire, which desires all evil desires—this is the desiring power; and the disposition that governs man and strengthens the body—it is called נפש (*nefesh*), the soul, of the body. Rav Dimi said, 'This is the strengthening power.'"[72]

Rabbi Yehudah said, "Come and see: The evil impulse only ever dominates these two powers we have mentioned. It is the desiring soul that constantly seeks out the evil impulse, as implied by what is written: *The elder said to the younger, 'Our father is old'* (Genesis 19:31). The desiring soul arouses the other, and she lures her—along with the body—to cleave to the evil impulse. She says, '*Come, let us give our father wine to drink, and let us lie with him* (ibid., 32)—what have we in the world to come?; let us go and follow the evil impulse and the craving for the delights of this world!' What do they do? Both of them determined to cleave to him. What is written? *They gave their father wine to drink* (ibid., 33)—they gorged themselves to arouse the evil impulse with food and drink.[73]



"*The elder came and lay with her father* (ibid.). When a person lies on his bed at night, it is the desiring soul that arouses the evil impulse and muses upon him. He [the evil impulse] clings to every kind of evil imagining, until she is impregnated by him—until he inserts into the person's heart that evil thought,

72. **three dispositions in a human being...** The *Zohar* here presents another tripartite model of the soul. See *ZḤ* 14b, 21c (both *MhN*); cf. *ZḤ* 6d, 8d–9a (both *MhN*); Meroz, "Va-Ani Lo Hayiti Sham?," 170 (Addendum 3 in this volume).

The third and lowest tier of the soul, the soul of the body, or the strengthening power, is responsible for maintaining bodily functions. See *Zohar* 1:128b; *ZḤ* 14b (both *MhN*). In its original philosophical sense, the term "strengthening power" refers to the second part of the digestive function and is usually translated as "retentive faculty" (Tishby, *Wisdom of the Zohar*, 2:707). See Maimonides, *Shemonah Peraqim* 1; idem, *Guide of the Perplexed* 1:72.

On the diverse theories of the soul in *MhN*, see Tishby, *Wisdom of the Zohar*, 2:703–12.

73. **The evil impulse only ever dominates these two powers...** Namely, the desiring and strengthening power. The holy soul is immune to wiles of the evil impulse.

The *Zohar* presents an allegorical reading of the account of Lot and his two daughters: the elder signifies the desiring power; and the younger, the power of the body. Their father, Lot, is the evil impulse. See also *Zohar* 1:111a (*ST*); 1:137a (*MhN*). Cf. Philo, *On the Posterity of Cain and His Exile*, 175; see Belkin, "Ha-Midrash ha-Ne'lam u-Mqorotav," 75–77.

The elder daughter (desire) plays the leading role, luring the younger daughter (the power of the body) to unite with their father (the evil impulse).

As is explained below (see note 82), "old" also alludes to the evil impulse.

On the connections between wine and food, and the evil impulse and sin, see BT *Berakhot* 32a; *Yoma* 74b–75a; *Ḥullin* 4b; *Zohar* 1:202a; 2:154b.

According to *Bemidbar Rabbah* 10:8, wine impairs דעת (*da'at*), "understanding, reasoning."

which cleaves to him. It is still yet only in his heart, not ripe for the evil to be enacted, until that desire arouses the power of the body—as at first—to cleave to the evil impulse. Then the evil is consummated, as is written: *The two daughters of Lot conceived* [110a] *by their father* (ibid., 36)."[74]

Rabbi Yitsḥak said, "The evil inclination is seduced only by food and drink; and it is through the delight in wine that it prevails upon a person. What is written of the righteous? *The righteous eats to satisfy his soul* (Proverbs 13:25), but never gets drunk. As Rabbi Yehudah said: 'To one inflamed by the rabbis who gets drunk, we apply the verse *a gold ring in the snout of a pig* (ibid. 11:22); and what's more, he desecrates the Name of Heaven!' What is the way of the wicked? *Look, rejoicing and merriment, killing of cattle and slaughtering of sheep, eating of meat and drinking of wine* (Isaiah 22:13). Of them Scripture says: *Woe to those who rise early in the morning to chase after liquor*... (ibid. 5:11)—to arouse the evil impulse, for the evil impulse is aroused solely through wine, as is written: *They gave their father wine to drink* (Genesis 19:33)."[75]



Rabbi Abbahu said, "What is the meaning of the verse *he was unaware of her lying down or her rising* (ibid., 35)? Namely, the evil impulse never gives her a second thought: what will become of her in *her lying down*—in this world, *or her rising*—in the world to come. Rather, he arouses together with the bodily power to serve his desire in this world."[76]

As Rabbi Abbahu said: "When the wicked enter Hell, the evil impulse is ushered in to gaze upon them, as is written: *Lot arrived* צערה (*tso'arah*), *at Zoar* (ibid., 23)—לצערה (*le-tsa'arah*), to the suffering, of Hell. But he goes out from

74. **When a person lies on his bed at night...** Sinful thoughts impregnate the desiring power, as the evil impulse embeds these thoughts in a person's heart. Yet only when the soul of the body is also aroused can the evil thought and desire be translated into action.

On sinful thoughts at night, see Moses de León, *Sefer ha-Rimmon*, 263; *Zohar* 3:11a; Scholem, "Parashah Ḥadashah," 437 (Addendum 1 in this volume). On the consummation of thought through action, see *Zohar* 3:6a.

75. **one inflamed by the rabbis...** צורבא מרבנן (*Tsurba me-rabbanan*), perhaps "scorched by the rabbis." This expression refers to a scholar. See BT *Ta'anit* 4a; and M *Avot* 2:10: "Rabbi Eli'ezer says, '...Warm yourself by the fire of the wise—and beware their glowing coals, so that you'll not be burned. For their bite is the bite of a fox; their sting, the sting of a scorpion; their hiss, the hiss of a serpent; and all their words like coals of fire.'" See also *Zohar* 1:63b.

See Maimonides, *Mishneh Torah, Hilkhot De'ot* 5:3: "When a sage drinks wine, he drinks only enough to soften the food in his stomach. Whoever becomes drunk is a sinner, is shameful, and will lose his wisdom. If he becomes drunk before the common people, he desecrates the name [of God]."

On Proverbs 11:22, cf. *Avot* 6:2.

Isaiah 22:13 continues: *Eat and drink, for tomorrow we die!*

76. **the evil impulse never gives her...** He is unconcerned with the soul's suffering at the time of death or her punishment in Hell. Cf. BT *Avodah Zarah* 5a.

there to test the creatures, as we have said, as is written: *Lot went up* מצוער (*mi-tso'ar*), *from Zoar* (ibid., 30)—מצערה (*mi-tsa'arah*), from the suffering, of Hell."[77]

*He settled in the mountains* (ibid.). Rabbi Yitsḥak said, "The significance of *in the mountains*: it teaches that he set his abode in a mountainous area—a body that is dry like a mountain, devoid of goodness. *His two daughters together with him* (ibid.)—the two powers we mentioned. *For* [110b] *he was afraid to dwell in Zoar* (ibid.)—when he beholds the suffering of Hell inflicted upon the wicked and considers that he will be judged there, fear and trembling descend upon him. As soon as he realizes that he is not being judged there, he ventures forth to lure human beings after him."[78]

Whenever Rav Huna would preach to caution people, he would say to them, "My children, be on guard against the emissary of Hell! Who is that? The evil impulse—Hell's emissary."

Rabbi Abba said, "What is the meaning of the verse *The leech has two daughters, 'Give, Give'* (Proverbs 30:15)? These are the two daughters of Lot we have mentioned, the desiring soul and the soul associated with the body, constantly pursuing the evil impulse."[79]

Rabbi Yehoshu'a said, "It is written here concerning Lot: *For he was afraid to dwell in Zoar* (Genesis 19:30), and it is written there: *The leech* (Proverbs 30:15). ירא (*Yare*), *He was afraid*, has the numerical value of עלוקה (*aluqah*), leech."[80]

Rabbi Yitsḥak said, "If he was afraid, why did he proceed to lead the creatures astray?"

He replied, "So is the way of all who do wrong: when he considers the harm, he is afraid for a moment; but immediately returns to his wickedness and fears nothing. Similarly the evil impulse—when he sees the judgment of the wicked, he is afraid; but as soon as he ventures out, he fears nothing."[81]

77. **the evil impulse is ushered in to gaze upon them...** Perhaps seeing their suffering and fearing his own, he will cease his seduction. See next paragraph. On "creatures," see above, note 21.

78. ***he was afraid to dwell in Zoar...*** Although afraid of his own pending judgment, the evil impulse's fear is fleeting—and he soon resumes his craft of seduction. See below, note 81.

The two powers refer to the desiring soul and the soul of the body.

79. ***The leech has two daughters, 'Give, Give'...*** This saying from Proverbs is apparently a retort to someone who constantly begs favors, or perhaps a warning that a greedy parent engenders greedy children. In rabbinic literature it is associated with Hell. See BT *Avodah Zarah* 17a; *Shemot Rabbah* 7:4; *Midrash Mishlei* (Buber) 17:1, 30:15; see also *Zohar* 1:111a (*ST*).

80. **numerical value . . .** Each word equals 211. The *leech* is thus identified with Lot (the evil impulse), who *was afraid.*

81. **when he considers the harm, he is afraid for a moment...** The wicked are not impeded by the consideration of their punishment.

See *Shemot Rabbah* 12:7: "*When Pharaoh saw that the rain and the hail and the thunder*

Rabbi Abba said in the name of Rabbi Yoḥanan, "What is the meaning of the verse *The elder said to the younger, 'Our father is old'* (Genesis 19:31)? What is meant by *our father is old*? This is the evil impulse, who is called 'old,' as is said: *an old and foolish king* (Ecclesiastes 4:13)—*old* because he was born along with the human being."[82]

As we have learned: Rabbi Yehudah said in the name of Rabbi Yosef, "The desiring soul says to the other, '*Our father is old.* Let us go after him and cleave [111a] to him like all the other wicked people in the world. *There is no man on earth to consort with us* (Genesis 19:31)—there is no righteous man on earth, and there is no man who rules over his impulse. There are many wicked people on earth; we are not the only wicked people. Let us act *like the way of all the earth* (ibid.)—wickedly, for until this day, so is *the way of all the earth. Come, let us give our father wine to drink* (ibid., 32)—let us delight in this world. Let us eat and drink and be saturated with wine and cleave to our father—to the evil impulse—*and let us lie with him* (ibid.).' The holy spirit cries out, saying, '*These also stagger from wine and stumble from beer* (Isaiah 28:7).'"[83]



Rabbi Yehudah said, "Come and see what is written: *They gave their father wine to drink* (Genesis 19:33). It is the way of the wicked to stray after wine, to indulge the evil impulse and arouse him. Merry in his drunkenness, he lays upon his bed; immediately: *the elder arose and lay with her father* (ibid.)—she lies poised with him, desiring and musing upon every wicked imagining. The evil impulse unites with her and cleaves to her, and gives no thought to what will become of her at *her lying down or her rising* (ibid., 35)—*her lying down* in this world, *or her rising* in the time to come; *her lying down* in the world to come, when she gives an account and reckoning, *or her rising* to the Day of Judgment, as is written: *Many of those who sleep in the dust of earth will awake* [*some to everlasting life, some to shame and everlasting horror*] (Daniel 12:2). Concerning any of these matters, the evil impulse gives her no thought! Rather, he cleaves to her and she to him, and afterward she arouses the other. Once the potent imagining clings to the evil impulse, the other arrives and cleaves to him.

*had ceased, he continued to offend* (Exodus 9:34). So it is with the wicked: as long as they are in trouble, they humble themselves; but as soon as the trouble passes, they return to their perversity." See also *Shemot Rabbah* 10:6; *Tanḥuma, Va'era* 17.

The speaker is not identified.

82. **This is the evil impulse, who is called 'old'...** In contrast to the good impulse, which one acquires at age thirteen, the evil impulse accompanies a person from birth; hence, relative to the good impulse it is "old." See *ZḤ* 24b (*MhN*).

The verse from Ecclesiastes reads: *Better a poor and wise child than an old and foolish king who no longer knows how to heed warning.* On the identity of *an old and foolish king*, see *Avot de-Rabbi Natan* B, 16; *Qohelet Rabbah* on 4:13; *Midrash Tehillim* 9:5; *Zohar* 1:179a–b; 2:33b.

83. **The desiring soul says to the other...** This and the following two paragraphs re-

"*They gave* [111b] *their father wine to drink* (Genesis 19:33)—likewise to arouse the evil impulse, and likewise she cleaves to him. Then is consummation of wickedness to be enacted, and the two of them are impregnated by the evil impulse, as is written: *The two daughters of Lot conceived by their father* (ibid., 36)—until their deeds are carried out; this one bears her wickedness, and that one bears her wickedness. So is the way of the wicked with regard to the evil impulse, until he kills the person—leading him to Hell, ushering him in. Afterward, he ascends from there to seduce [other] people in the same way. But whoever recognizes him is saved from him and does not join with him."

Rabbi Yitsḥak said, "A parable. To what can the matter be compared? To a gang of bandits who were laying ambush on the roads to steal and murder. They designate one from among them—skilled in seduction and silver tongued. What does he do? He goes in advance to meet them, presenting himself as their servant, until the fools believe him, trusting in his love and delighting in him, whereupon he leads them with his smooth-talk along the road where the bandits wait. As soon as he arrives there with them, after handing them over to the bandits to steal their money and murder them, he is the first to kill them. They cry out, saying, 'Woe, woe that we listened to this one and to his silver tongue!' After they have killed these ones, he ascends from there and ventures forth to lure [other] people as before. As for the prudent, what do they do? When they see this one going forth to meet them and seduce them, they recognize that he is stalking their soul. They challenge him and kill him and take another road. Alternatively, they separate from him and turn down another road.[84]

"So is the evil impulse. He ventures forth from a gang of bandits, ascending from Hell to meet human beings and seduce them with his smooth sweet-talk, as is written: *Lot went up from Zoar and settled in the mountains...* (Genesis 19:30)—like bandits setting ambush. What does he do? He passes before them, and the foolish believe him and in his love—through which he entices them. He serves them as a servant, giving them beautiful and forbidden women, and people to harm—casting off from them the yoke of Torah and the yoke of the Kingdom of Heaven. The foolish [112a] see this and trust in his love, until he goes with them; and he leads them along the road where the bandits wait—along the road to Hell, where there is no way to turn right or left. As soon as he arrives there with them, he is the first to kill them—and he transforms into the Angel of Death. He ushers them into Hell and angels of destruction lower them



prise themes presented at the beginning of this section. See notes 73–76. The "other" refers to the younger daughter, signifying the power of the body.

84. **To a gang of bandits . . .** A similar (yet fragmentary) parable is found in *Zohar* 1:111a (*ST*).

down. They cry out, saying, 'Woe, woe that we listened to this one!' but to no avail. Afterward he ascends from there, venturing forth to lure [other] human beings. When the prudent see him, they recognize him—and overcome him until they rule over him; they turn from that road, taking another, to be saved from him."[85]

When Rav Yosef went down to Babylon he saw unmarried men enter and emerge from among beautiful women without sinning. He said, "Do these not fear the evil impulse?"[86]

They said to him, "We do not hail from foul gluhwein; from the sanctification of a saint were we hewn!"[87]

As Rav Yehudah said in the name of Rav, "A person must sanctify himself during intercourse and he will engender holy and virtuous children who do not fear the evil impulse, as is said: *Sanctify yourselves and you will be holy* (Leviticus 11:44)."[88]

Rabbi Abba said, "What is the meaning of the verse *Sanctify My Sabbaths* (Ezekiel 20:20)? Well, the time for intercourse for the disciples of the wise is from Sabbath to Sabbath, and he cautioned them—since sexual relations are a commandment, *sanctify*! That is to say, sanctify yourselves on My Sabbaths through the commandment of sexual relations."[89]



85. **he transforms into the Angel of Death...** See BT *Bava Batra* 16a: "Resh Lakish said, 'Satan, the evil impulse, and the Angel of Death are one and the same.'"

86. **enter and emerge...** That is, go to and fro. The expression recalls the famous description of four rabbis who "entered the orchard," and engaged in mystical contemplation of the divine realm. Only Rabbi Akiva "entered in peace and emerged in peace." See JT *Ḥagigah* 2:1, 77b; *Shir ha-Shirim Rabbah* on 1:4 (and cf. *Tosefta Ḥagigah* 2:4; BT *Ḥagigah* 14b).

87. **We do not hail from foul gluhwein...** "Gluhwein" renders קונדיטון (*qonditon*), "spiced wine." Because they were conceived in holiness—not in revelry and drunkenness—these bachelors do not fear the evil impulse. As opposed to mulled (spiced) wine, which is made by mixing numerous ingredients, the bachelors' origins are entirely pure, without the intermixture of lewd thoughts and improper sexual behavior.

The "sanctification of a saint" (or "the sanctification of the holy") is explained in the following paragraph.

88. ***Sanctify yourselves...*** In rabbinic literature, this verse from Leviticus is applied to sanctifying sexual relations. See BT *Shevu'ot* 18b: "Rabbi El'azar said, 'Whoever sanctifies himself during intercourse will have male children.'" See also BT *Niddah* 71a; *Bemidbar Rabbah* 9:7; Moses de León, *Sefer ha-Rimmon*, 93; *Zohar* 1:54a, 90b, 155a (*ST*), 204a; 2:11b; 3:56a; *ZḤ* 11a (*MhN*). On sexual holiness, see *Zohar* 1:49b–50a; 2:89a–b; 3:81a–b, 168a; *Iggeret ha-Qodesh*, in *Kitvei Ramban*, 2:333; Tishby, *Wisdom of the Zohar*, 3:1363–64.

89. **the time for intercourse for the disciples of the wise...** The Mishnah (*Ketubbot* 5:6) discusses how often husbands of various professions are required to fulfill the commandment of עונה (*onah*), "conjugal rights," i.e., to satisfy their wives sexually. The Talmud (BT *Ketubbot* 62b) adds: "When

Rav Yehudah said in the name of Rav, "Whoever enters a town and sees beautiful women should lower his eyes and say as follows, 'Look! From the noble have I surely been hewn! Potent stumbler, begone, begone! My father is a saint of Sabbath!' Why so? Because the heat of the journey is prevalent and the evil impulse might dominate him."[90] [113a]

*YHVH attended to Sarah as He had said* (Genesis 21:1).[91]

Rabbi Yoḥanan opened with this verse, "*Your head upon you is like Carmel; the locks of your head are like purple: a king is held captive in the tresses* (Song of Songs 7:6). The blessed Holy One made rulers above, and beneath them rulers below. When the blessed Holy One bestows preeminence upon the princes above, the kings below seize supremacy. He bestowed preeminence upon the prince of Babylon—wicked Nebuchadnezzar seized supremacy, of whom is written *you are the head of gold* (Daniel 2:38); the entire world was subject to him, and his son and his son's son. This is the meaning of what is written: *Your head upon you is like Carmel*—this is Nebuchadnezzar, as is written: *beneath it the wild animals found shelter* (Daniel 4:9). *The locks of your head are like purple*—this is Belshazzar, who proclaimed and said *shall be clothed in purple* (Daniel 5:7). *A king is held captive in the tresses*—this is Evil-merodach, who was held captive until his father Nebuchadnezzar died, whereupon he ruled in his stead."[92]



is the *onah* of the disciples of the wise? [i.e., What is the proper interval between two successive times of fulfilling this commandment?] Rav Yehudah said in the name of Shemu'el, 'From one Sabbath eve to the next.'"

See *Zohar* 1:14a–b, 50a; 2:63b, 89a–b, 136a–b, 204b–205a; 3:49b, 78a, 81a, 82a; *ZḤ* 11c (*MhN*); Tishby, *Wisdom of the Zohar*, 3:1232–33; Wolfson, 'Eunuchs Who Keep the Sabbath.'

90. **Potent stumbler, begone, begone!...** The incantation is mysterious, deliberately so: סך ספאן איגזר איגזרנא קרדיטא תקיל פוק פוק דאבוי קדישא דשבתא הוא (*sakh safa'n igzar igzarna qardita taqil puq puq de-avoi qaddisha de-shabbta hu*). My rendering follows *Derekh Emet*. The "potent stumbler" is the evil impulse. Some manuscripts read קרדינא (*qardina*) in place of קרדיטא (*qardita*); both variants are Zoharic neologisms. On *qardina*, cf. קרדינותא (*qardinuta*), "hard, impenetrable, powerful" (see *Zohar* 1:15a).

See BT *Avodah Zarah* 20a: "A man should not gaze at a beautiful woman even if she is unmarried, nor at a married woman even if she is ugly." See also BT *Nedarim* 20a, in the name of Rabbi Aḥa son of Rabbi Yoshiah: "Whoever gazes at women eventually comes to sin." Cf. BT *Berakhot* 24a; *Eruvin* 18b; *Yevamot* 63b; *Ḥullin* 37b.

See *Zohar* 3:19a for another incantation, in this case directed against Lilith. See also *Zohar* 3:84a.

91. ***YHVH* attended to Sarah . . .** The verse continues: *and YHVH did for Sarah as He had spoken*. The following verse reads: *Sarah conceived and bore a son to Abraham in his old age, at the set time that God had spoken to him.*

Some manuscripts contain the section heading פרשת יג (*parashat* 13). See p. 311, n. 126.

92. **bestows preeminence upon the princes above...** The heavenly prince of

Rabbi Yehudah said, "What is the purpose of this allusion in the Song of Songs?"[93]

Well, Rabbi Yehudah said, "Seven things were created before the world was created. They are [ . . . ] the Throne of Glory, as is said: *Your throne stands firm from of old, from forever You are* (Psalms 93:2), and it is written: *O throne of glory set on high* מראשון (*me-rishon*), *from the first* (Jeremiah 17:12)—for it was ראש (*rosh*), at the head, preceding all. The blessed Holy One drew the pure soul from the Throne of Glory to illuminate the body, as is written: *Your head upon you is like Carmel*—this is the Throne of Glory, at the head of all. *The locks of your head are like purple*—this is the soul, which is drawn from it; *a king is held captive in the tresses*—this is the body. Alternatively, *a king is held captive in the tresses*—this is the body held captive in the grave and decomposed in the dust, of which nothing remains aside from a spoonful of decayed matter from which

Babylon was empowered, and consequently Babylon ascended to dominance.

See *Zohar* 2:6a, 7a, 10a, 16b (*MhN*), 46b. Conversely, according to rabbinic literature, first a nation's heavenly prince is punished or cast down, and consequently his nation on earth. See *Mekhilta, Shirta* 2; *Shemot Rabbah* 21:5; *Shir ha-Shirim Rabbah* on 8:14; *Tanḥuma,* Bo 4, *Mishpatim* 18; *Zohar* 2:18a–b (*MhN*).

According to rabbinic tradition, the seventy nations of the world are each governed by an angel or heavenly prince appointed by God. See Daniel 10:13, 20; Septuagint, Deuteronomy 32:8–9; Jubilees 15:31–32; *Targum Yerushalmi,* Genesis 11:8, Deuteronomy 32:8–9; *Tanḥuma, Re'eh* 8; *Leqaḥ Tov,* Genesis 9:19; *Pirqei de-Rabbi Eli'ezer* 24; *Zohar* 1:46b, 61a, 84b, 108b, 149b; 2:5b (*MhN*), 14b (*MhN*), 17a (*MhN*), 33a, 151b, 209a–b; 3:298b; *ZḤ* 23d, 24c, 28c (all *MhN*); Ginzberg, *Legends,* 5:204–5, n. 91. In midrashic literature these angels are described as ascending and descending Jacob's ladder. See *Vayiqra Rabbah* 29:2; *Pesiqta de-Rav Kahana* 23:2; *Tanḥuma, Vayetse* 2; *Pirqei de-Rabbi Eli'ezer* 35.

Daniel 2:37–38 reads: *You, O king—king of kings, to whom the God of Heaven has given kingdom, power, might, and glory; into whose hands He has given men, wild beasts, and the fowl of heaven, wherever they may dwell; and to whom He has given dominion over them all—you are the head of gold.*

According to Daniel 4, Nebuchadnezzar dreams of a mighty tree reaching to heaven, beneath which all the creatures of the earth find shelter. Daniel informs him that the tree symbolizes the king's dominion.

According to Daniel 5, following the appearance of mysterious writing on a wall, *the king* [Belshazzar] *addressed the wise men of Babylon, "Whoever can read this writing and tell me its meaning shall be clothed in purple. . . ."*

The Bible does not state that Evil-merodach was imprisoned; rather, he released the Judahite King Jehoiachin from prison (2 Kings 25:27–30; Jeremiah 52:31–34). According to rabbinic sources, however, his father Nebuchadnezzar had incarcerated him for fear that he would seize the throne. See *Avot de-Rabbi Natan* B, 17; *Vayiqra Rabbah* 18:2; *Tanḥuma, Tazri'a* 8; *Tanḥuma* (Buber), *Tazri'a* 10.

On Song of Songs 7:6, see *Vayiqra Rabbah* 31:4; *Shir ha-Shirim Rabbah* on 7:6; *Tanḥuma, Tetsavveh* 6.

93. **What is the purpose of this allusion...** Surely the verses of the Song of Songs have more profound matters to disclose, and not merely historical details!

the whole body will be rebuilt. When the blessed Holy One attends to the body He will instruct the earth to disgorge it without, as is written: *And earth will bring forth shades* (Isaiah 26:19)."[94]

Rabbi Yoḥanan said, "The dead of the Land are the first to live, as is written: *Your dead will live* (ibid.)—the dead of the Land. *My corpses will arise* (ibid.)—those outside the Land. *Awake and shout for joy* [113b], *O dwellers of the dust* (ibid.)—these are the dead of the desert."[95]

As Rabbi Yoḥanan said: "Why did Moses die outside the Land? To demonstrate to all who come into the world that just as the blessed Holy One is destined to revive Moses, so is He destined to revive his generation who accepted the Torah, of whom is said *I remember the devotion of your youth, your love as a bride—how you followed Me in the wilderness, in a land not sown* (Jeremiah 2:2).[96]



94. ***Your head upon you is like Carmel...*** As Rabbi Yehudah himself points out, the verse from the Song encapsulates the human condition: the soul (the locks) drawn from the Throne of Glory (the head) is now housed in a body (captive in the tresses).

See BT *Pesahim* 54a: "Seven things were created before the world was created: Torah, *Teshuvah*, the Garden of Eden, Hell, the Throne of Glory, the Temple, and the name of the Messiah." See also *Bereshit Rabbah* 1:4; BT *Nedarim* 39b; *Tanḥuma, Naso* 11; *Pirqei de-Rabbi Eli'ezer* 3; *Zohar* 3:34b; *ZḤ* 5a (*MhN*). According to Rabbi Yehudah, the Throne of Glory was created first (see *ZḤ* 2d, 7d, 15b (all *MhN*)). Rabbi Yehudah doesn't list the other creations, hence the ellipsis points.

In BT *Shabbat* 152b the souls of the righteous are said to be "hidden beneath the Throne of Glory" after death; see also *Avot de-Rabbi Natan* A, 12. According to *MhN*, the soul (i.e., the *neshamah*, the highest level of soul, the spiritual essence of the human being) is created from the substance of the Throne of Glory. See *Zohar* 1:125b, 126b (both *MhN*); *ZḤ* 10a–d, 20b, 22a, 24a, 26a (all *MhN*).

On the spoonful of decayed matter from which the body will be rebuilt, see *Pirqei de-Rabbi Eli'ezer* 34: "Rabbi Shim'on says, 'All bodies crumble into the dust of the earth until nothing remains except a spoonful of decayed matter. This mingles with the dust like leaven mixed with dough. In the time to come... it resurrects the entire body.'" See *Bereshit Rabbah* 28:3; *Vayiqra Rabbah* 18:1; *Zohar* 1:69a, 116a (*MhN*), 126a (*MhN*), 137a (*MhN*); 2:28b; 3:222a, 270b; Moses de León, *Sefer ha-Rimmon*, 271; idem, *Sefer ha-Mishqal*, 87.

On the earth disgorging bodies and the verse from Isaiah, see *Pirqei de-Rabbi Eli'ezer* 34; *Zohar* 1:128b (*MhN*), 182a; 2:199b.

95. **The dead of the Land are the first to live...** At the resurrection. See BT *Ketubbot* 111a: "Rabbi Abba son of Memel objected, '*Your dead will live; my corpses will arise!* Doesn't *Your dead will live* refer to the dead of the land of Israel, and *my corpses will arise* to the dead outside the Land?'"

See *Bereshit Rabbah* 74:1; JT *Kil'ayim* 9:4, 32c; *Tanḥuma, Vayḥi* 3; *Zohar* 1:131a, 140a (*MhN*), 181b; 2:151b; Moses de León, *Sefer ha-Mishqal*, 89–90.

96. **Why did Moses die outside the Land?...** See *Devarim Rabbah* 2:9; *Tanḥuma, Ḥuqqat* 10; *Tanḥuma* (Buber), *Ḥuqqat* 32; *Bemidbar Rabbah* 19:13; *Zohar* 2:157a; *ZḤ* 14d (*MhN*).

On the revival of the generation of the desert, see *Zohar* 3:168b. Cf. BT *Sanhedrin* 108a, 110b.

"Alternatively, *Awake and shout for joy, O dwellers of the dust* (Isaiah 26:19)—these are the patriarchs. As for the dead outside the Land, their body will be rebuilt; and they will roll under the earth until the land of Israel. There will they receive their soul—not outside the Land, as is written: *Therefore, prophesy and say to them, 'I am going to open your graves and lift you out of the graves, O My people, and bring you to the land of Israel'* (Ezekiel 37:12). What is written afterward? *I will put My spirit into you, and you shall live* (ibid., 14)."[97]

Rabbi Pinḥas said, "The soul is drawn from the Throne of Glory, which is the head, as said: *Your head upon you is like Carmel* (Song of Songs 7:6); *the locks of your head are like purple* (ibid.)—this is the soul, the locks of the head; *a king is held captive in the tresses* (ibid.)—the body, held captive in the grave. Body—Sarah—King. The blessed Holy One will attend to it at the set time He mentioned, as is written: *YHVH attended to Sarah as He had said* (Genesis 21:1)—attending to the body at the known time during which He will attend to the righteous."[98]

Rabbi Pinḥas said, "The blessed Holy One will one day beautify the bodies of the righteous in the time to come like the beauty of Adam when he entered the Garden of Eden, as is said: *YHVH will guide you always... You will be like a well-watered garden* (Isaiah 58:11)."[99] 

Rabbi Levi said, "As long as the soul abides in her rung, she is nourished by the light above, garbed within. When she enters the body in the time to come, she will enter with that very same light. Then the body will shine like the radiance of the sky, as is written: *The enlightened will shine like the radiance of the sky* (Daniel 12:3), and human beings will attain perfect knowledge, as is said: *The earth will be filled with knowledge of YHVH* (Isaiah 11:9). How do we know this? From what is written: *YHVH will guide you always; He will satisfy your soul with*

97. **roll under the earth until the land of Israel...** See BT *Ketubbot* 111a: "Rabbi Yirmeyah son of Abba said in the name of Rabbi Yoḥanan, 'Whoever walks four cubits in the land of Israel is assured membership in the world to come.' Now... aren't the righteous outside the Land going to be revived? Rabbi Il'a replied, 'By rolling [underground to the land of Israel].' Rabbi Abba Sala the Great objected, 'Rolling will be painful to the righteous.' Abbaye replied, 'Tunnels will be made for them underground.'"

See *Zohar* 1:69a, 128b (*MhN*), 131a; see below, at note 105.

On the dwellers of the dust signifying the patriarchs, see *Avot de-Rabbi Natan* A, 12; cf. *Zohar* 2:151b; Moses de León, *Sefer ha-Mishqal*, 90.

98. **Body—Sarah—King...** The body is designated here as "king," though usually in *MhN* it is signified by Sarah. Rabbi Pinḥas directs the interpretation of the verse from the Song of Songs about the body and soul, back to the biblical narrative in Genesis.

99. **like the beauty of Adam...** On Adam's beauty, see *Vayiqra Rabbah* 20:2; BT *Bava Batra* 58a; *Pesiqta de-Rav Kahana* 4:4; 12:1; *Zohar* 1:121b (*MhN*), 142b.

*radiancies* (Isaiah 58:11)—this is the light [114a] above; *and invigorate your bones* (ibid.)—this is the attending of the body; *You will be like a well-watered garden, like a spring whose waters do not fail*—this is knowledge of the Creator (may He be blessed). Then the creatures will know that the soul entering within them is נשמת החיים (*nishmat ha-ḥayyim*), the soul of life, the soul of delights, which has received delights from on high, pleasuring the body. All will be astounded at her, saying, *How beautiful and how pleasing you are, O Love, among the delights* (Song of Songs 7:7)—this is the soul in the time to come."[100]

Rabbi Yehudah said, "Come and see that it is so, from what is written: *a king is held captive in the tresses* (ibid., 6), and it is written afterward: *How beautiful and how pleasing you are* (ibid., 7)."[101]

Rabbi Yehudah also said, "At that time, the blessed Holy One is destined to bring joy upon His world and rejoice in His creatures, as is said: *YHVH will rejoice in His works* (Psalms 104:31). Then laughter will prevail in the world—which is not so now, as is written: *Then will our mouths fill with laughter...* (ibid. 126:2). This is the meaning of what is written: *Sarah said, 'Laughter has God made me'* (Genesis 21:6)—for then human beings are destined to recite song, for it will be a time of laughter."[102]

100. **When she enters the body in the time to come...** Resurrection of the body does not entail a "fall" from the exalted status of the soul in the celestial realm. The revived body is illuminated by the very same light the soul enjoyed on high. Indeed, it is only in this condition of perfected corporeality that the human being attains perfect knowledge.

This view should be contrasted with medieval Jewish philosophy, where the ultimate good does not involve the body at all (see, e.g., Maimonides, *Pereq Ḥeleq*; idem, *Mishneh Torah, Hilkhot Teshuvah* 8:2).

On the soul as garbed and nourished by the light above, see *ZḤ* 26a (*MhN*); cf. BT *Berakhot* 17a. On the soul's return to the perfected body, see *Zohar* 1:126a (*MhN*).

"*He will satisfy your soul with radiancies*"— The clause in its simple sense means *He will satisfy your* נפש (*nefesh*), *thirst, in parched regions.* Here, *nefesh* is read according to one of its later meanings as "soul," while the rare word בצחצחות (*be-tsaḥtsaḥot*), *in parched regions,* is understood as "with radiancies," based on the root צחח (*tsḥḥ*), "to gleam." See *Zohar* 1:141a, 224b; 2:97a, 142b, 210b; see also *Vayiqra Rabbah* 34:15.

On the use of the verse from Daniel to describe the revived body, see *Zohar* 1:116a, 130a (both *MhN*). On Isaiah 11:9, see *Zohar* 1:125b, 130a, 140a (all *MhN*); 2:68a; 3:23a. On the attainment of perfect knowledge, see *Zohar* 1:126a, 135a–b, 140a (all *MhN*); *ZḤ* 15d (*MhN*).

101. ***How beautiful and how pleasing you are*** Rabbi Yehudah extends the allegorical reading of the Song of Songs. Where verse 6 (the captive king) refers to the body in the grave, the very next verse refers to the soul of delights destined to pleasure the body in the post-resurrection world.

102. **Then laughter will prevail in the world—which is not so now...** See BT *Berakhot* 31a, in the name of Rabbi Shim'on son of Yoḥai: "It is forbidden for a person to fill his mouth with laughter in this world, as is said: *Then will our mouth fill with laughter and our tongue with glad song* (Psalms 126:2). When? At the time when *they will say among*

Rabbi Abba said, "Since the day the world was created, there has been no joy like the day on which the blessed Holy One will rejoice with His creatures. The righteous remaining in Jerusalem will never again return to their dust, as is written: *Whoever is left in Zion, who remains in Jerusalem, will be called holy* (Isaiah 4:3)—whoever remains in Zion and Jerusalem, precisely!"[103]

Rabbi Aḥa said, "If so, they are few! But rather, all who remain in the holy land of Israel are treated like Jerusalem and Zion in every way, teaching that the whole land of Israel is comprised within Jerusalem, as implied by what is written: *When you enter the land* (Leviticus 19:23)—entirely comprised."[104]

Rabbi Yehudah son of El'azar inquired of Rabbi Ḥizkiyah. He said to him, "Concerning the dead destined to be revived by the blessed Holy One—why doesn't He bestow their souls there, in the place where they were buried, that they might come alive to the land of Israel?"[105]



*the nations: 'Great things has YHVH done with these'* (ibid., 3)." See *Zohar* 1:127a (*MhN*).

On Psalms 104:31, see *Vayiqra Rabbah* 20:2: "The blessed Holy One, so to speak, did not enjoy happiness in His world. The verse does not say YHVH *rejoiced* in His works, but *will rejoice*: in the time to come, the blessed Holy One will rejoice in the works of the righteous." See also *Tanḥuma, Aḥarei Mot* 2; *Tanḥuma* (Buber), *Aḥarei Mot* 3; *Midrash Tehillim* 75:2; *Zohar* 1:102b (*MhN*), 115a (*MhN*), 116a (*MhN*), 119a, 135a (*MhN*), 182a; 2:57b, 259a (*Heikh*); 3:16a.

103. **never again return to their dust...** See BT *Sanhedrin* 92a: "It has been taught in the school of Elijah: The righteous—whom the blessed Holy One will one day resurrect—will not revert to their dust, as is said: *Whoever is left in Zion, who remains in Jerusalem, will be called holy: all who are inscribed for life in Jerusalem.* Just as the Holy One endures forever, so shall they endure forever." See below, *Zohar* 1:116b (*MhN*), page 358.

104. **If so, they are few...** If only those remaining in Jerusalem and Zion will not revert to dust again, then this does not amount to very many people! Rabbi Aḥa resolves his own difficulty by noting that whatever applies to Jerusalem, in fact applies to the entire land—which is comprised and rooted within Jerusalem.

According to *Zohar* 1:128b, the entire land of Israel is enfolded within Jerusalem.

The context of the proof-text from Leviticus reads: *When you enter the land and plant any fruit-bearing tree, you shall leave its fruit uncircumcised. Three years it shall be uncircumcised to you. It shall not be eaten. In the fourth year all its fruit shall be holy, a jubilation before* YHVH (vv. 23–24). Apparently Rabbi Aḥa intends that just as fruits from throughout the land are designated holy and taken to Jerusalem in the fourth year, so the righteous throughout the land are considered holy and treated as though they were in Jerusalem.

See *Avot de-Rabbi Natan* A, 26: "He who is buried in the land of Israel is as though he were buried under the altar [in the Temple in Jerusalem], for the whole land of Israel is fit to be the site of the altar." See also *Pesiqta Rabbati* 1: "In the future, Jerusalem will be like the land of Israel."

105. **why doesn't He bestow their souls there...** Namely, outside the land of Israel. What need is there to bring them through tunnels to the land of Israel first?

He replied, "The blessed Holy One swore to rebuild Jerusalem and that she would never be destroyed again. As Rabbi Yirmeyah said: 'The blessed Holy One is destined to renew His world, to rebuild Jerusalem and lower her down fully built from on high, an indestructible edifice. He swore that the Assembly of Israel would not be exiled again, and He swore that the edifice of Jerusalem would not be destroyed, as is said: [114b] *Never more shall you be called Forsaken; never more shall your land be called Desolate* (Isaiah 62:4). And wherever you find 'Never, never,' an oath is implied, as is written: *the waters shall never again become a flood, and never again shall all flesh be cut off by the waters of a flood* (Genesis 9:15, 11), and it is written: *As I swore that the waters of Noah* (Isaiah 54:9). Hence: 'Never, never' constitutes an oath, and from the negative you derive the affirmative. In the future, the blessed Holy One will establish His world enduringly—so that the Assembly of Israel will not be exiled, and the edifice of the Temple will not be destroyed.' Consequently they receive their soul only in a place of eternal endurance, so that the soul might abide in the body eternally.
352 That is the significance of the verse *Whoever is left in Zion, who remains in Jerusalem, will be called holy. . . .*"[106]

Rabbi Ḥizkiyah said, "From here: He is holy, Jerusalem is holy, whoever remains in her is holy! He is holy, as is written: *holy YHVH of Hosts* (ibid. 6:3) and similarly: *the Holy One is in your midst* (Hosea 11:9); Jerusalem is holy, as is written: *going from the holy site* (Ecclesiastes 8:10); whoever remains in her is holy, as is written: *Whoever is left in Zion, who remains in Jerusalem, will be called holy.* Just as the first holy abides eternally, so the other holies abide eternally."[107]

Rabbi Yitsḥak said, "What is the meaning of the verse *There shall yet be old men and women in the gates of Jerusalem, each with staff in hand because of their great*

106. **receive their soul only in a place of eternal endurance...** To ensure the eternity of the body and soul after the resurrection, the soul herself must be bequeathed in a place of eternal endurance (rebuilt Jerusalem). That is why the bodies of the dead outside the land must first come to the land of Israel.

On the future descent from on high of the divinely built Jerusalem, see 1 Enoch 90:28–29; *Tanḥuma, Noaḥ* 11, *Pequdei* 1; *Nistarot Rabbi Shim'on ben Yoḥai* (*Beit ha-Midrash,* 3:80); Rashi on BT *Sukkah* 41a, s.v. *i nami*; *Tosafot* on BT *Shevu'ot* 15b, s.v. *ein binyan*; *Zohar* 1:183b; 3:221a. On deriving an affirmative oath from a double negative formulation, see BT *Nedarim* 11a–b; *Shevu'ot* 36a (citing the verses about the Flood); *Zohar* 3:215a.

The *Zohar* conflates two verses from Genesis 9. Genesis 9:11 reads: *I will maintain My covenant with you: never again shall all flesh be cut off by the waters of a flood, and never again shall there be a flood.*

Isaiah 54:9 continues: *would never again cover the earth.*

It is not entirely clear where the Rabbi Yirmeyah quote ends.

107. **From here: He is holy...** The eter-

*age* (Zechariah 8:4)? What's so good about walking like that, as is written: *each with staff in hand*?!"[108]

Well, Rabbi Yitsḥak said, "In the time to come, the righteous are destined to revive the dead as did the prophet Elisha, as is written: *take my staff in your hand and go* (2 Kings 4:29), and similarly: *place my staff on the face of the boy* (ibid.). The blessed Holy One said to him, 'Something that the righteous are destined to do in the time to come, you wish to do now?!' What is written? *He placed the staff on the boy's face, but there was no sound or response* (ibid., 31). But in the time to come, the righteous will fulfill this pledge, as is written: *each with staff in hand*—with which to revive the dead of the converts who converted from the nations of the world, of whom is written *He who dies at a hundred years shall be reckoned a youth; and he who fails to reach* [115a] *a hundred shall be reckoned accursed* (Isaiah 65:20)."[109]

Rabbi Yitsḥak said, "The end of the verse proves this, as is written: *because of their great age* (Zechariah 8:4)."[110]



Alternatively, *Sarah said, "Laughter has God made me"* (Genesis 21:6). It is written: *Rejoice with Jerusalem and be glad for her, all you who love her! Rejoice with her in joy, all you who mourn over her* (Isaiah 66:10).[111]

Rabbi Yehudah said, "Since the day the world was created, there has been no joy before the blessed Holy One like that joy He will one day rejoice with the righteous in the time to come, when everyone will point with their finger, say-

nal endurance of the soul and the resurrected body can be derived from the following verses. See BT *Sanhedrin* 92a; above, note 103.

108. **What's so good about walking like that...** Will people need walking sticks in the time to come? This is hardly a fitting messianic promise.

The verse from Zechariah reads *squares*, not *gates*.

109. **righteous are destined to revive the dead...** See BT *Pesaḥim* 68a; *Zohar* 1:135a (*MhN*). According to *Pesaḥim*, the verse from Isaiah refers to the heathens, who will be resurrected in the time to come—but will not live eternally as will the Jews. Rather, they will live for a long time and then die. The *Zohar* has switched converts for heathens.

According to the narrative in Kings, Elisha sends Gehazi with his staff in hand to revive a boy (the child of the Shunammite). Gehazi, however, does not succeed, and it is only upon Elisha's arrival that the boy is brought back to life. See *Pirqei de-Rabbi Eli'ezer* 33 and Luria (additions) note 10.

110. **The end of the verse proves this...** The final phrase in the verse from Zechariah supports the previous interpretation: *each with staff in hand because of their great age*, i.e., because of the great age of the converts. Apparently Rabbi Yitsḥak intends that the righteous will resurrect the converts, who—though resurrected initially—will die; hence they will require additional resurrection.

111. ***Sarah said, "Laughter has God made me"...*** Sarah signifies the body. The צחוק (*tseḥoq*), "laughter," upon engendering יצחק (*Yitsḥaq*), "Isaac," alludes to the great joy of the time to come, as will be explained below.

ing, *'Look, this is our God; we waited for Him and He saved us! This is YHVH, for whom we have waited; let us rejoice and exult in His salvation* (ibid. 25:9)' and it is written: *Sing to YHVH, for He has done gloriously. Let this be known in all the world!* (ibid. 12:5)."[112]

Rabbi Yoḥanan said, "We have not found anyone who explicated this matter like king David, who said: *When You hide Your face, they are terrified*... (Psalms 104:29), from which is derived that the blessed Holy One does not bring harm upon a person; but rather, when He does not watch over him, he expires on his own account, as is written: *When You hide Your face, they are terrified; You withdraw their spirit, they perish* [*and to the dust they return*] (ibid.). *Send forth Your spirit, they are created*... (ibid., 30), and afterward: *May the glory of YHVH endure forever; may YHVH rejoice in His works!* (ibid., 31). Then laughter will prevail in the world, as is written: *Then will our mouths fill with laughter, and our tongues with glad song* (ibid. 126:2). This is the significance of the verse *Sarah said, 'Laughter has God made me'* (Genesis 21:6)—to rejoice in His salvation."[113]



Rabbi Ḥiyya said, "Come and see: As long as the body resides in this world, it lacks perfection. After it has been righteous, having pursued paths of יושר (*yosher*), righteousness, and died ביושרו (*be-yoshro*), in its integrity, it is called שרה (*Sarah*), Sarah, in its perfection. Upon reaching the resurrection of the dead, it is שרה (*Sarah*), Sarah, so that it might not be said that the blessed Holy One revived another. After it lives and rejoices with the *Shekhinah*, and the blessed Holy One removes sorrow and sadness from the world—as is written: *He will swallow up death forever; YHVH Elohim will wipe away tears from all faces*... (Isaiah 25:8)—then it is called יצחק (*Yitsḥaq*), Isaac, on account of השחוק (*ha-seḥoq*), the laughter, and joy that will be for the righteous in the time to come."[114]

112. **when everyone will point with their finger...** See BT *Ta'anit* 31a: "Ulla Bira'ah said in the name of Rabbi El'azar, 'The blessed Holy One will one day hold a dance for the righteous, and He will sit in their midst in the Garden of Eden—and everyone will point with their finger, as is said: *In that day they shall say: Look, this is our God; we waited for Him and He saved us! This is YHVH, for whom we have waited; let us rejoice and exult in His salvation*.'" See *Tanḥuma* (Buber), *Tsav* 16; *Zohar* 1:135a (*MhN*).

113. **We have not found anyone...** According to Rabbi Yoḥanan, the three verses from Psalm 104 artfully present the story of death, resurrection, and the great joy of the time to come. Sarah's laughter signifies the joy of the resurrected body. See above, *Zohar* 1:114a (and note 102), 127a (both *MhN*).

On God's not bringing harm, cf. *Devarim Rabbah* 4:3: "*See, I* [*set before you today blessing and curse*] (Deuteronomy 11:26). Rabbi El'azar said, 'Since the blessed Holy One uttered this on Sinai, it has been laid down that *it is not at the word of the Most High that evil and good transpire* (Lamentations 3:38); rather, evil comes on its own account to those who do evil....'"

114. **Upon reaching the resurrection of the dead, it is שרה (*Sarah*)...** At death, the

When Rabbi Yehudah arrived at the site of Kefar Ḥanan, all the townsfolk sent him a gift.[115]

Rabbi Abba came to him and said, "When is my master leaving?"

He replied, "I shall repay what the townsfolk [115b] gave me, and then I shall leave."

He said to him, "Let my master not think twice about that gift. It was offered for Torah, and they won't take anything from you."

He asked him, "Will they not receive words of Torah?"

He replied, "Yes."

All the townsfolk arrived. Rabbi Yehudah asked him, "Are they all Masters of the Academy?"[116]

He said to him, "If there is anyone who is not worthy to sit here, let him rise and go."[117]

Rabbi Abba arose and designated ten of them to receive from him. He said to them, "Sit with this great man; tomorrow we shall sit with him and receive."

They left. The ten who remained with him sat down, but he didn't say a word. They said to him, "If it pleases our master, we would receive the face of *Shekhinah*."[118]



He said to them, "But Rabbi Abba is not here!"

They sent for him and he came.

body of the righteous person is known as Sarah, meaning "royal or noble lady." (The root שרר (*srr*) conveys "authority, power, greatness.") The resurrected body is also called Sarah (to establish its identity with the original body), but ultimately it is known as Isaac, in reference the laughter of the time to come. Sarah's bearing Isaac is thus an allegory for the renewed body.

On the resurrection of the person's original body, see *Bereshit Rabbah* 95:1; BT *Pesaḥim* 68a, *Sanhedrin* 91b; *Qohelet Rabbah* on 1:4; *Tanḥuma, Vayiggash* 8; *Zohar* 1:126a (*MhN*), 127a (*MhN*), 130b, 181b; 2:28b; Moses de León, *Sefer ha-Mishqal*, 87–89.

115. **Kefar Ḥanan...** See *Zohar* 1:87b, 206b; 2:5a (*MhN*), 157a.

116. **Are they all Masters of the Academy?** On this epithet, see *Zohar* 1:123b (*MhN*, this volume); *ZḤ* 15a, 25d (both *MhN*); Scholem, "Parashah Ḥadashah," 432–33, 443 (Addendum 1 in this volume). Cf. the term "Masters of Mishnah" (see p. 138, n. 462). See also *Zohar* 3:162a (*Rav Metivta*).

Some of the manuscripts read "Rabbi Abba" in place of Rabbi Yehudah, in which case the phrase should be rendered: Rabbi Abba said to him, "They are all Masters of the Academy."

117. **He said to him . . .** Presumably, Rabbi Yehudah is speaking.

118. **we would receive the face of *Shekhinah*...** Namely, we are ready to hear your Torah teaching.

See *Mekhilta, Amaleq* (*Yitro*) 1: "Whoever receives the face of [i.e., welcomes] the wise, it is as if he receives the face of *Shekhinah*." See JT *Eruvin* 5:1, 22b; *Bereshit Rabbah* 63:6; *Shir ha-Shirim Rabbah* on 2:5; *Tanḥuma, Ki Tissa* 27; *Zohar* 1:9a, 94b; 2:5a (*MhN*), 20a (*MhN*), 50a, 94b, 198a; 3:6b, 148a, 298a; *ZḤ* 11c, 25b (both *MhN*); Cf. Genesis 33:10.

He opened, saying, "*YHVH attended to Sarah as He had spoken* (Genesis 21:1). Why the different expression here? The verse should have said *YHVH remembered Sarah*, as is said: *God remembered Rachel* (ibid. 30:22)—for 'attending' applies only to something [promised] previously. Well, it was [promised] previously, as is written: *I will surely return to you [at this very season—and, look, your wife Sarah shall have a son]* (ibid. 18:10), and it was about that matter that it says He now *attended*, as implied by what is written: *as He had spoken*. Had it not said *as He had spoken*, then it would have said 'remembering,' but He attended to that word He had spoken: *In due time I will return to you* (Genesis 18:14)."[119]

Afterward, he said as follows, "The righteous person who is worthy of ascending to the supernal glory has his image engraved in the Throne of Glory; and so for every righteous person—his image is above, as it was below—as a guarantee for the holy soul.[120]

"As Rabbi Yoḥanan said: 'What is the meaning of the verse *Sun [and] moon stand still on high* (Habakkuk 3:11)? That the body and soul—abiding in the supernal holy chamber above—shine, just like the image that existed on earth.'



That image is nourished by the delight of the soul and is destined to garb itself within that bone remaining in the earth, when the earth will excise and disgorge its muck without. This is what is referred to as 'holy.'[121]

"When that image abides above, every new moon it comes [116a] to prostrate before the blessed Holy King, as is written: *From new moon to new moon* (Isaiah 66:23); and He informs it, saying, '*In due time I will return to you* (Genesis 18:14)—

119. **'attending' applies only...** The significance of first promising and then attending is explained below.

See *Zohar* 1:115a, 159b–160a; cf. Naḥmanides on Genesis 21:1.

120. **his image is above, as it was below...** The image is an ethereal body resembling the form of the physical body. It clothes the soul and accompanies a person before descending to this world, while in the world, and again in the celestial realm after death. Here the image serves as a guarantee that body and soul will be reunited upon the body's resurrection.

On the ethereal body, see Naḥmanides on Genesis 49:33; *Zohar* 1:7a, 38b (*Heikh*), 81a (*ST*), 90b–91a, 131a, 217b, 219a, 220a, 224a–b, 227a–b, 233b; 2:11a, 13a–b, 96b, 141b, 150a, 156b–157a, 161b; 3:13a–b, 43a–b, 61b, 70b, 104a–b; *ZḤ* 10b–c (*MhN*), 18b (*MhN*), 90b (*MhN, Rut*); Moses de León, *Sefer ha-Rimmon*, 390; [Moses de León?], *Seder Gan Eden*, 133; Scholem, *Shedim, Ruḥot u-Nshamot*, 215–45; idem, *Kabbalah*, 158–59; idem, *On the Mystical Shape of the Godhead*, 251–73; Tishby, *Wisdom of the Zohar*, 2:770–73. Cf. Rashi on BT *Ḥagigah* 12b, s.v. *ve-ruhot u-nshamot*.

121. **the body and soul...shine...** The sun signifies the soul, and the moon the body—commensurate with the image, which is a garment or "flesh" for the soul.

On the miraculous bone from which the body will be rebuilt, see *Bereshit Rabbah* 28:3; *Vayiqra Rabbah* 18:1; *Zohar* 1:69a, 126a (*MhN*), 137a (*MhN*); 2:28b; 3:222a, 270b; Moses de León, *Sefer ha-Rimmon*, 271; idem, *Sefer ha-Mishqal*, 87–88. Cf. *Pirqei de-Rabbi Eli'ezer* 34; *Zohar* 1:113a, 116a (both *MhN*).

at that time when I am destined to revive the dead, when she will be attended to at that time as promised.' This is the meaning of what is written: *YHVH attended to Sarah as He had spoken* (Genesis 21:1). This is the day when the blessed Holy One shall rejoice in His works, as is written: *YHVH will rejoice in His works* (Psalms 104:31)."[122]

Rabbi Abba said to him, "May the master speak to us of the [weekly] portion."[123]

Afterward he said, "It befits you to open this portion."

He opened, saying, "*It came to pass after these things that God tested Abraham. ... He said, 'Take your son, your only one, whom you love...'* (Genesis 22:1–2). Here one must contemplate! The craftsman who extracts silver from the source of the earth, what does he do? At first he inserts it within a raging fire until the slime of the earth is completely removed, leaving silver—though not unadulterated silver. What does he do afterward? He inserts it in fire—as at first—and extracts the dross, as is said: *Remove the dross from the silver...* (Proverbs 25:4). Then it is pure silver without intermingling.[124]



"Similarly the blessed Holy One inserts the body beneath the ground until it is entirely decomposed and all the foul slime departs, leaving the decayed matter from which the body is rebuilt; but still that body is not unadulterated. After that Great Day of which is written *There will be one day—known to YHVH—neither day nor night* (Zechariah 14:7), all of them are concealed beneath the earth as at first, out of fear and because of the power of the blessed Holy One, as is written: *They will enter hollows in the ground and clefts of the rocks from fear of YHVH and the glory of His majesty [when He rises to terrify the earth]* (Isaiah 2:19, 7:19). Their souls depart them and the decayed matter is consumed, leaving the

122. **When that image abides above...** In the biblical narrative, God first promises Sarah that she will have a son and then attends to her; and she bears a son. Similarly, God first promises the image it will be reunited with the body—and then in the time to come resurrects the body. See above, *Zohar* 1:102a (*MhN*), pages 330-31.

The verse from Isaiah continues: *and from Sabbath to Sabbath, all flesh shall come to bow down before Me.* On this verse, see *Zohar* 2:156b–157a; 3:70b, 144b–145a (*IR*), 159b, 182b; *ZḤ* 18b (*MhN*); Moses de León, *Sheqel ha-Qodesh*, 30 (36).

On the verse from Psalms, see above, note 102.

123. **May the master speak to us ...** Rabbi Abba's request is not entirely clear. Perhaps he is asking how the complete saga of resurrection is encoded in the continuation of the narrative of the weekly portion. Indeed, some of the manuscripts read: May the Master speak to us of the entire portion.

124. ***Take your son, your only one...*** Rabbi Yehudah proceeds to explain the mysteries of resurrection through the story of the binding of Isaac. It should be recalled that following the allegory established above Isaac signifies the resurrected body.

The verse from Proverbs continues: *and a vessel emerges for the refiner.*

body that is rebuilt there—entirely luminous, like the light of the sun and the radiance of the sky, as is written: *The enlightened will shine like the radiance of the sky*... (Daniel 12:3). Then the silver is pure, the body is pure—without other intermingling.[125]

"As Rabbi Ya'akov said [116b]: 'The blessed Holy One will draw down a luminous body from on high, as is written: *For* טלך (*tallekha*), *your dew, is a dew of lights* (Isaiah 26:19), and similarly: *YHVH is going* מטלטלך (*metaltelkha*), *to cast your dew* (ibid. 22:17).' Then they will be called 'holy ones of the Most High,' as is written: [*Whoever is left in Zion, who remains in Jerusalem,*] *will be called holy* (Isaiah 4:3). This is what is referred to as 'the final resurrection of the dead'; this is the final trial; and no more will they taste death, as is written: *By My own self I swear, declares YHVH, that because you have done this thing* [*and have not held back your son, your only one,*] *I will greatly bless you* (Genesis 22:16–17). At that time, the righteous pray that they will not face this ordeal again.[126]



125. **Similarly the blessed Holy One...** Just as the craftsman inserts his raw material into the fire twice to obtain a pure final product, so the resurrection of the body occurs in two phases: The first resurrected body is not yet pure; it is still marked by the dross of corporeality. In order that the body should become entirely pure it dies again. Following the second resurrection, the body is entirely transformed and transfigured. This second phase is alluded to in Scripture through the binding of Isaac. See *Or ha-Ḥammah, Bereshit*, 97a.

On the decayed matter, see *Pirqei de-Rabbi Eli'ezer* 34, cited above, note 94. See *Zohar* 1:113a (*MhN*). On the foul slime, cf. BT *Shabbat* 145b–146a: "Rav Yosef taught, '...When the serpent copulated with Eve, he injected her with slime. Israel who stood at Sinai—their slime ceased. Star-worshipers who did not stand at Mount Sinai—their slime did not cease.'" Although *MhN* does not mention this myth of the serpentine slime, it nonetheless presumes that all human bodies are somehow tainted by a primal corporeality. See also *Zohar* 3:162b (*Rav Metivta*).

Zechariah 14:7 continues: *and in the evening, there will be light.*

On the verse from Daniel, see *Zohar* 1:113b, 130a (both *MhN*).

126. **draw down a luminous body from on high...** Literally, the phrase from Isaiah 22:17 means *YHVH is going to hurl you*, though Rabbi Ya'akov reads מטלטלך (*metaltelkha*), "hurl you," as מטל טלך (*metil tallekha*), "cast your dew," or *me-tal tallekha*, "from the dew [above] your dew." The dew of lights revives and illuminates the body.

See *Pirqei de-Rabbi Eli'ezer* 34: "Rabbi Yehudah said, '...In the time to come, the blessed Holy One will bring down a dew of revival, reviving the dead... *For your dew is a dew of lights....*' Rabbi Tanḥum said, 'From where does it descend? From the head of the blessed Holy One. In the time to come, He will shake the hair of His head and bring down a dew of revival, reviving the dead, as is said: *I was asleep, but my heart was awake... For my head is drenched with dew* (Song of Songs 5:2).'"

See JT *Berakhot* 5:2, 9b; BT *Shabbat* 88b; *Zohar* 1:118a (*MhN*), 130b–131a, 232a; 2:28b; 3:128b (*IR*), 135b (*IR*); Moses de León, *Sefer ha-Mishqal*, 88–89.

On Isaiah 4:3, see *Zohar* 1:114a, 114b (both *MhN*) and note 103 above.

The phrase 'holy ones of the Most High' derives from Daniel 7:18.

"What is written? *Abraham raised his eyes and saw: here, a ram caught behind in the thicket by its horns* (ibid., 13). These are the wicked of the other nations who are called 'rams,' as is said: *the rams of Nebaioth shall serve your needs* (Isaiah 60:7), which we translate as 'the chiefs of Nebaioth.' *Caught behind in the thicket by its horns* (Genesis 22:13), as is said: *All the horns of the wicked I will hack off* (Psalms 75:11). *Abraham went and took the ram and offered it up as a burnt offering in place of his son* (Genesis 22:13)—for they are poised to undergo all manner of horrific ordeals. But the righteous shall remain for the world to come—like supernal holy angels to unify His name, and hence it is written: *On that day, YHVH will be one and His Name one* (Zechariah 14:9)."[127]

He said to them, "From here on, open the gate!"[128]

The following day, all the townsfolk entered before him. They said to him, "May our master tell us words of Torah pertaining to the portion we are reading on Sabbath: *YHVH attended to Sarah* (Genesis 21:1)."

He arose between the pillars, opened, and said, "*YHVH attended to Sarah. . . .*[129]



Three keys lie in the hand of the blessed Holy One and He has not handed them over—neither to an angel nor a seraph: the key of childbirth, of rain, and of resurrection. Elijah came and seized two of them—of rain and of resurrection.[130]

127. ***Abraham raised his eyes and saw: here, a ram...*** Following Isaac's reprieve, Abraham sees a ram caught in the thicket by its horns, which he offers as a burnt offering instead of his son. The ram signifies the wicked, who are destined to be annihilated from the world.

Isaiah 60:7 continues: *they shall be welcome offerings on My altar.* The extant Aramaic translation of this verse reads דכרי (*dikrei*), "men, the male of the flock," rather than רברבי (*ravravei*), "chiefs, nobles, officials, prominent men." According to Genesis 25:13, Nebaioth was Ishmael's first-born son. (See also 28:9, 36:3).

On the verse from Zechariah, see *Zohar* 1:139b (*MhN*).

128. **open the gate** At the beginning of this narrative, Rabbi Yehudah had asked Rabbi Abba to ensure that only the worthy be present at his discourse. (See at note 116.) Apparently he is now suggesting that all who wish to learn may do so. Perhaps having completed his discourse on the second resurrection, he intends to pursue less esoteric themes.

129. **He arose between the pillars . . .** This narrative lacks a clear ending. The homilies that follow this sentence do not seem to be part of the story. Such "soft edges" are not uncommon in the narratives of *MhN* as they have reached us.

130. **Three keys...** See BT *Ta'anit* 2a–b: "Rabbi Yoḥanan said, 'Three keys lie in the hand of the blessed Holy One and have not been handed over to any messenger; namely, the key of rain, the key of childbirth, and the key of resurrection. . . .'" See also *Bereshit Rabbah* 73:4; *Zohar* 1:102b.

On Elijah's possessing the two aforementioned keys, see 1 Kings 17:1: *Elijah . . . said to Ahab, "As YHVH lives, there will be no dew or rain these years except by my word"*; and verse 22: *YHVH heard Elijah's plea. The child's life returned to his body and he revived.* See BT *Sanhedrin* 113a and next note.

Rabbi Yoḥanan said, "Elijah was handed only one!"

As Rabbi Yoḥanan said: "When Elijah pleaded to revive the son of the woman of Zarephath, the blessed Holy One said to him, 'It is not fitting for you to hold two keys in your hand. Rather, give Me the key of rain; and [the key] of resurrection shall remain with you.' He replied, 'Master of the World. [Let it be] so.' This is the significance of what is written: *Go, appear before Ahab, and I will send rain* (1 Kings 18:1). He did not say *send rain*, but *I will send*."[131]

But look, Elisha possessed [117a] them![132]

Indeed! To fulfill the double portion of Elijah's spirit. But the blessed Holy One has not handed over the three of them to a messenger.[133]

As Rabbi Simon said: "Come and see the power of the blessed Holy One! Simultaneously He revives the dead, *casts down to Sheol and raises up* (1 Samuel 2:6), causes the luminaries to shine, sends the rain, *makes the grass grow* (Psalms 104:14), ripens crops, attends to the barren, bestows provision, helps the poor, supports the fallen, *straightens the bent* (Psalms 146:8), *deposes kings and installs kings* (Daniel 2:21)—all at once, at the same time, in a single moment, something that a messenger can never do."[134]



It has been taught: Rabbi Yehudah said, "Everything that the blessed Holy One does, He need do only through speech. For as soon as He says—from the

131. **It is not fitting for you to hold two keys...** See BT *Sanhedrin* 113a: "*After a while, the son of the woman of the house fell sick [and his illness grew worse until he had no breath left in him]* (1 Kings 17:17). Elijah prayed that the key of resurrection might be given him, but he was answered, 'Three keys have not been handed over to a messenger: of childbirth, of rain, and of resurrection. Shall it be said: Two are in the hands of the disciple, and one in the hand of the Master?! Bring this one and take the other.' As is written: *Go, appear before Ahab; and I will send rain.*"

On Elijah and the woman of Zarephath, see 1 Kings 17:7–24.

132. **Elisha possessed them** Two keys, namely of childbirth and of resurrection. See 2 Kings 4:16: *Elisha said, "At this season next year, you shall be embracing a son"*; and 2 Kings 4:32–37 on his revival of the Shunammite's son.

133. **To fulfill the double portion of Elijah's spirit...** See 2 Kings 2:9: *As they were crossing [the Jordan], Elijah said to Elisha, "Ask what I can do for you before I am taken from you?" Elisha answered, "May a double portion of your spirit be upon me."*

See BT *Sanhedrin* 47a: "For Rabbi Aḥa son of Ḥanina said, 'How do we know that a wicked person may not be buried beside a righteous one? As is said: *Once a man was being buried, when the people caught sight of such a band* [of marauding Moabites]*; so they threw the corpse into Elisha's grave and made off. When the* [dead] *man came in contact with Elisha's bones, he came to life and stood upon his feet* (2 Kings 13:21).' Rav Pappa said to him, 'Perhaps that was only to fulfill [the request]: *May a double portion of your spirit be upon me* [i.e., whereas Elijah revived one person, Elisha revived two people: the son of the Shunammite, and now here].'" See also *Zohar* 1:191b.

134. **all at once...** God's "multi-tasking" demonstrates His possession of the keys.

Cf. *Shemot Rabbah* 5:14; *Bereshit Rabbah* 77:1.

place of His holiness—'Let it be so,' immediately it is done. Come and see His potent might, as is written: *By the word of YHVH the heavens were made* (Psalms 33:6)!"[135]

As Rabbi Yehudah said: "What is the significance of the verse *I will pass through the land of Egypt on this night* (Exodus 12:12)? I and not an angel. *I will render judgment, I, YHVH* (ibid.)—not a messenger; *I YHVH*—I am He, and no other. If so, this is a great honor for the Egyptians; for one who is captured by a king cannot be compared to one who is captured by a commoner! What's more, you cannot find a nation as contaminated by every impurity as the Egyptians, of whom is written *whose flesh is the flesh of donkeys, and whose emission is the emission of stallions* (Ezekiel 23:20)—for they are suspected of sodomy; and they hail from Ham, who did what he did to his father, who then cursed him and his son, Canaan. Did the blessed Holy One lack for an angel or messenger to dispatch to wreak vengeance upon Egypt—as He did with Asshur [Assyria] the son of Shem, as is written: *The sons of Shem: Elam and Asshur* (Genesis 10:22)? Shem was priest to God Most High and was blessed by his father, as is written: *Blessed be YHVH, the God of Shem; unto them shall Canaan be a slave* (ibid. 9:26), and Shem attained eminence and blessings over his brothers; and of him is written *An angel of YHVH went out and struck down the Assyrian camp* (2 Kings 19:35; Isaiah 37:36)—enacted by a messenger. How much more so for the Egyptians who are more contaminated and filthy than any nation! Yet He said: 'I—and not an angel'!"[136]



135. **He need do only through speech...** See, for example, the creation account in Genesis 1.

See *Bereshit Rabbah* 44:22: "Rav Huna and Rabbi Dostai said in the name of Rabbi Shemu'el son of Naḥman, 'The mere speech of the blessed Holy One is action....'" See also *Aggadat Bereshit* (Buber) 23:4.

On the verse from Psalms, see *ZḤ* 2d (*MhN*).

136. **I and not an angel...** God's capacity to act through speech is demonstrated by the mode of His retribution against Egypt, as explained in the following paragraph. In constructing his homily, Rabbi Yehudah wonders why God sent a messenger to strike Assyria (descended from the blessed Shem) but not to strike Egypt (descended from the cursed Ham). Surely the more cursed deserved the same treatment! How is the Egyptians' "personal treatment" to be explained? Furthermore, if the Egyptians are so contaminated, how could God go there Himself to enact retribution?

The full verse in Exodus reads: *I will pass through the land of Egypt on this night and strike down every firstborn in the land of Egypt, both human and beast, and upon all the gods of Egypt I will render judgment, I, YHVH.*

According to a midrashic reading in the Passover Haggadah, "*I will pass through the land of Egypt*—I and not an angel. *And I will strike down every firstborn*—I and not a seraph. *And upon all the gods of Egypt I will render judgment, I, YHVH*—I am He, and no other." See *Mekhilta*, *Pisḥa* 7, 13; *Midrash Tanna'im*, Deuteronomy 26:8; JT *Sanhedrin*, 2:1, 20a; Naḥmanides on Exodus 12:12; *Zohar* 1:101b; 2:7a, 36b–37a.

See BT *Shabbat* 108a, in the name of

Well, Rabbi Yehudah said, "From here we learn of the potent might of the blessed Holy One and of His exaltedness, transcending all. The blessed Holy One said, 'This nation of Egypt is contaminated, this nation is filthy. It is not fitting to dispatch either an angel or a seraph—a holy entity—among the cursedly and filthily wicked. Rather, I [117b] will do what neither angel nor seraph nor messenger can, for as soon as I say from the place of My holiness "Let it be so," immediately it is done—which an angel cannot do.' That is why He said: 'I and not an angel.' That is: I can do this—but not an angel; for until the angel gets there, he is unable to act. As for the blessed Holy One, from the place of His holiness He says, 'Let it be so' and immediately whatever He wishes to do is done. That is why this vengeance was not wrought by an angel or messenger—on account of Egypt's disgrace, and to demonstrate the greatness of the Omnipresent, who did not wish that any holy entity would enter among them. Accordingly, it was said: 'I—and not an angel': I can do this, but not an angel."[137]



In a similar vein, Rabbi Yehudah said, "What is meant by the verse *YHVH spoke to the fish, and it spewed Jonah onto dry land* (Jonah 2:11)? If so, what is the difference between the fish and Moses our teacher?! Further, there are countless righteous and pious people from Israel with whom the blessed Holy did not speak, yet He deigned to speak with a fish, something that neither perceives nor comprehends!"[138]

Well, Rabbi Yehudah said, "As soon as Jonah's prayer ascended before the blessed Holy One, from the place of His holiness He spoke, in order that the fish would spew Jonah onto dry land. The ל (*lamed*), *to*, of לדג (*la-dag*), *to the fish*, is like 'in order that.' Namely, *YHVH* spoke in order that the fish would spew Jonah

Rabbi Yehoshu'a the Grits Dealer: "Two men who were condemned to death by the state, one being executed by the king and the other by the executioner. Who stands higher? Surely you must say: he who was slain by the king!"

In the verse from Ezekiel, the word בשר (*basar*), *flesh*, is a euphemism for "penis." See Leviticus 15:2; Ezekiel 16:26; *Zohar* 1:173a, 222b; 2:192b; 3:14b.

On Ham, see Genesis 9:22: *Ham, the father of Canaan, saw his father's* [i.e., Noah's] *nakedness.* According to rabbinic tradition (BT *Sanhedrin* 70a), Ham either castrated or lay with his father. Canaan, Ham's son, was cursed for his father's sin (see Genesis 9:25–26). See also *ZḤ* 22c (*MhN*). According to Genesis 10:6, Egypt descended from Ham. On Egypt's disgrace, see *Zohar* 2:17a (*MhN*).

According to rabbinic tradition, Shem is identified with the high priest Melchizedek. See BT *Nedarim* 32b; *Sukkah* 52b; *Bemidbar Rabbah* 4:8; *ZḤ* 22d (*MhN*).

137. **we learn of the potent might...** God's direct action against the Egyptians confirms His capacity to act through speech, and the Egyptian's disgrace. Whereas no celestial messenger could withstand their impurity, God can act from a distance.

Cf. *Avot de-Rabbi Natan* A, 27 and *Bemidbar Rabbah* 8:3, where God's personal retribution (as opposed to the angel) is viewed as a mark of respect to Pharaoh, and the angel's retribution as a mark of disdain to Sennacherib (king of Assyria).

138. ***YHVH* *spoke to the fish*...** On God's speaking to the fish, see *Bereshit Rabbah* 20:3; BT *Bekhorot* 8a.

onto dry land. From the place of His holiness, the blessed Holy One said 'Let it be so,' and immediately it was done—something a messenger cannot do."[139]

It has been taught: Rabbi Shim'on said, "The key of childbirth is in the hand of the blessed Holy One; and while she [the mother] is sitting on the birthing stool, the blessed Holy One scrutinizes the unborn child. If he is worthy of emerging into the world, He opens the doors of her womb and he emerges; if not, He closes her doors and both of them die."[140]

If so, then no wicked person would ever come forth into the world![141]

Well, so have we learned: On account of three transgressions do women die in childbirth: because they are not meticulous regarding menstrual purity, the dough offering, and the kindling of the [Sabbath] lights.[142]

Rabbi Shim'on said, "Look, Rabbi Yitsḥak said, 'Why does a woman מפלת (*mappelet*), miscarry, the fruit of her womb?' Well, Rabbi Yitsḥak said, '[The blessed Holy One] determines that the fetus is not worthy of coming forth into the world, so He kills it in advance in its mother's uterus, as is said: הנפלים (*Hanefilim*), *The fallen beings, were on earth in those days* (Genesis 6:4)—spelled נפלים (*nefalim*), miscarriages, without the first י (*yod*). Why? Because *afterward the sons of God came in to the daughters of humankind* (ibid.); when they will be bigger, *they will come in to the daughters of humankind, who will bear them children* (ibid.) whorishly, and bastards will abound [118a] in the world. *These are the mighty ones of old, men of name* (ibid.)—for there is none as mighty, roughshod, and ruthless as the bastard; *men of the name*—for all will recognize him to call him by a certain name: "bastard"; for as soon as they see his deeds, how he is roughshod and ruthless and mighty, all will call him by that name.'"[143]



139. **As soon as Jonah's prayer ascended...** See Jonah 2:2–10.

140. **the blessed Holy One scrutinizes the unborn child...** See Meroz, "Va-Ani Lo Hayiti Sham?," 169 (Addendum 3 in this volume).

Cf. *ZḤ* 19d–20b (*MhN*) on God's removing the innocent from the world before they sin. See also *Zohar* 2:96a–b, where this idea is applied to babies.

According to Rabbi Shim'on's formulation, if the unborn child is unworthy, both he and the mother die. See note 142 below.

On the key of childbirth, see above, notes 130, 131.

141. **no wicked person would ever come forth...** Empirical reality would seem to contradict Rabbi Shim'on's claim. After all, there are wicked people in the world! How is it then that some wicked people manage to get born? See below, note 144.

142. **On account of three transgressions...** See M *Shabbat* 2:6 (BT *Shabbat* 31b).

Perhaps this teaching is cited to explain Rabbi Shim'on's statement that both mother and child die. Apparently, the mother dies if she is guilty of one of these sins.

143. **Why does a woman מפלת (*mappelet*), miscarry...** Seeing that the as-yet-unborn child will one day act immorally with women, engendering bastards in the world, God determines to abort the fetus.

The context of the proof-text is the enigmatic mythological fragment found in Genesis 6:1–4: *When humankind began to increase on the face of the earth and daughters were born to them, the sons of God saw that the*

Now, concerning what Rabbi Shim'on said—that the blessed Holy One scrutinizes the unborn child—you cannot find a wicked person in the world, of those who come forth into the world, whom the blessed Holy One does not scrutinize to see if he will leave behind a worthy, righteous, and upright son, or whether he will save a Jew from death, or whether he will perform some other good deed. It is on that account that the blessed Holy One brings him forth into the world.[144]

In Rabbi Yose's day, there were bandits who used to pillage in the mountains—together with bandits from the nations of the world. Whenever they found and caught someone to murder, they would ask, "What is your name?" If he was a Jew, they would accompany him and lead him out of the mountains; but if he was any other person, they would kill him. Rabbi Yose said, "Nevertheless these are worthy of entering the world to come."[145]



*daughters of humankind were beautiful; and they took themselves wives, whomever they chose. YHVH said, "My spirit shall not abide in the human forever, for he too is flesh. Let his days be a hundred and twenty years." The Nephilim were on earth in those days—and afterward as well—when the sons of God came in to the daughters of humankind, who bore them children. These are the heroes of old, men of renown* [literally: *of the name*]. The myth behind this fragment in Genesis appears in postbiblical sources that describe angels who rebelled against God and descended from heaven to earth, where they were attracted by human women. See Isaiah 14:12; 1 Enoch 6–8; Jubilees 5; *Targum Yerushalmi*, Genesis 6:2, 4; BT *Yoma* 67b; *Aggadat Bereshit*, intro, 39; *Midrash Avkir*, 7 (cited in *Yalqut Shim'oni*, Genesis, 44); *Pirqei de-Rabbi Eli'ezer* 22; *Zohar* 1:23a (*TZ*), 37a, 37a (*Tos*), 55a, 58a, 62b, 126a; 3:208a–b, 212a–b; *ZḤ* 20b (*MhN*), 21c (*MhN*), *ZḤ* 81a–b (*MhN*, *Rut*); Ginzberg, *Legends*, 5:153–56, n. 57.

See *Bereshit Rabbah* 26:7: "נפלים (*Nefilim*)—שהפילו (*she-hippilu*), for they hurled, the world down, ושנפלו (*ve-she-nafelu*), and because they fell, from the world, and filled the world with נפלים (*nefalim*), abortions [or: miscarriages], through their immorality."

Although in its Genesis context בני האלהים (*benei ha-elohim*), "sons of God," implies some kind of celestial beings, there is a long tradition of reading the word *elohim* there as signifying "the mighty, judges, nobles," as in Exodus 21:6; 22:7–8, 22:27; Judges 5:8; 1 Samuel 2:25; and Psalms 138:1. Both *Targum Onqelos* and *Targum Yerushalmi* render *benei ha-elohim* in Genesis 6:2 as בני רברביא (*bnei ravrevaya*), "sons of the mighty." See also *Bereshit Rabbah* 26:5.

See Meroz, "Va-Ani Lo Hayiti Sham?," 169, 175 for a direct parallel to this passage (Addendum 3 in this volume).

"Bastard" renders ממזר (*mamzer*), "misbegotten," more precisely the offspring of an adulterous or incestuous union (not a child born out of wedlock). See *Kallah* 1:16; JT *Qiddushin* 4:14, 66b.

144. **concerning what Rabbi Shim'on said...** That is, that only the worthy emerge. Yet the wicked likewise emerge successfully on account of their future righteous progeny or their future righteous deeds.

See *Targum Yerushalmi* and *Targum Yerushalmi* (frag.) on Exodus 2:12; BT *Bava Qamma* 38b; *Vayiqra Rabbah* 32:4; *Zohar* 1:56b, 105a (*MhN*), 140a, 227a.

145. **bandits who used to pillage in the mountains...** On these Jewish bandits, see *Zohar* 2:10b.

Our Rabbis have taught: These three things come to the world solely though voices: the voice of childbirth, as is written: *in pain shall you bear children* (Genesis 3:16), and similarly: *God heard her* (ibid. 30:23); the voice of the rains, as is written: *the voice of YHVH is over the waters* (Psalms 29:3), and similarly: *for there is a sound* [or: *voice*] *of heavy rain* (1 Kings 18:41); the voice of the resurrection of the dead, as is written: *a voice calls out in the desert* (Isaiah 40:3).[146]

What is the purpose of this voice in the desert?

Well, Rabbi Zrika said, "These are the voices to arouse the dead of the desert, and from here we derive that this is the case for the whole world."[147]

Rabbi Yoḥanan said, "Look at what we have learned: When a person enters the grave, he enters with voices; when they arise at the resurrection of the dead, does it not stand to reason that they should arise with great voices?!"[148]

Rabbi Ya'akov said, "A divine voice is destined to burst forth in the graveyards, saying, *Awake and shout for joy, O dwellers in the dust* (Isaiah 26:19); and they are destined to live by the dew of the great light above, as is written: *For your dew is a dew of lights, and earth will bring forth shades* (ibid.). Amen, may it be Your will!"[149] [121a]



146. **three things come to the world solely though voices...** On various voices, see BT *Yoma* 20b–21a; *Bereshit Rabbah* 6:7; *Vayiqra Rabbah* 27:7; *Pirqei de-Rabbi Eli'ezer* 34; *Zohar* 3:168b.

Genesis 30:23 speaks of Rachel and continues: *and opened her womb.*

In its simple sense, Isaiah 40:3 reads: *A voice calls out: In the desert clear a road for YHVH! Level in the wilderness a highway for our God!*

147. **voices to arouse the dead of the desert...** Namely, the wilderness generation. See *Zohar* 1:113b (*MhN*); 3:168b. Cf. BT *Sanhedrin* 108a, 110b.

148. **enters the grave, he enters with voices...** See BT *Berakhot* 15b (and *Sanhedrin* 92a): "Rabbi Tavi said in the name of Rabbi Yoshiah, 'What is the meaning of the verse *Three things are insatiable... Sheol* [i.e., the grave] *and the barren womb* (Proverbs 30:15–16)? What does the grave have to do with the womb? Well, it is to teach you: just as the womb takes in and gives forth, so the grave takes in and gives forth. And have we not here an inference from minor to major? If the womb, which takes in silently, gives forth with great voices [i.e., the sounds of childbirth], does it not stand to reason that the grave, which takes in with great voices [i.e., weeping], should give forth with great voices?'"

149. **the dew of the great light above...** See *Pirqei de-Rabbi Eli'ezer* 34: "Rabbi Yehudah said, '... In the time to come, the blessed Holy One will bring down a dew of revival, reviving the dead... *For your dew is a dew of lights....*' Rabbi Tanḥum said, 'From where does it descend? From the head of the blessed Holy One.'"

See JT *Berakhot* 5:2, 9b; BT *Shabbat* 88b; *Zohar* 1:116b (*MhN*), 130b–131a, 232a; 2:28b; 3:128b (*IR*), 135b (*IR*); Moses de León, *Sefer ha-Mishqal*, 88–89.

On the voice in the graveyard, see *Zohar* 2:199b; *ZḤ* 15d (*MhN*). See also *Tanḥuma, Emor* 7.

# פרשת חיי שרה

# *Parashat Ḥayyei Sarah*

"SARAH'S LIFE" (GENESIS 23:1–25:18)

Our Rabbis opened with this verse: *Come, my beloved, let us go out into the fields, let us lodge in the villages* (Song of Songs 7:12). Our Rabbis have taught: One who sets out on a journey must recite three prayers: the obligatory prayer of each day; a prayer for the journey upon which he is embarking; and a prayer that he will return safely to his home. He may even recite these three together, as we have learned: All of a person's supplications may be included in "who hears prayer."[1]

Rabbi Yehudah said, "All of a person's deeds—good and bad—are inscribed in a book, and one day he will give an account for all of them."[2]

As we have learned: Rav Yehudah said in the name of Rav, "What is the meaning of the verse *Your eyes saw my formless mass; in Your book they were all inscribed* (Psalms 139:16)? Those things done by the formless mass, which pays no heed to the world to come: Your eyes saw all of them, for You have scrutinized them. *In Your book they were all inscribed*—to give an account and reckoning in the world to come. Therefore, let a person always offer his prayer in advance, and it will benefit him."[3]

1. **included in "who hears prayer"** "Who hears prayer" is the name of the sixteenth prayer in the *Amidah*. One is permitted to insert private requests before proceeding to the following prayer. See BT *Berakhot* 31a; JT *Berakhot* 4:4, 8b; JT *Ta'anit* 1:1, 63d; Moses de León, *Sefer ha-Rimmon*, 82.

On the prayer for a journey, see BT *Berakhot* 29b.

2. **inscribed in a book...** See M *Avot* 2:1 in the name of Rabbi: "Consider three things and you will not stray into sin: Know what is above you—a seeing eye, a listening ear, and all your deeds are written in a book."

3. ***Your eyes saw my formless mass*** **...** The verse from Psalms reads in full: *Your eyes saw my formless mass; in Your book they were all inscribed, days were formed—not one of them exists.*

The simple sense of the word גלמי (*golmi*) is "my embryo" or "my formless mass." Here, the sense is the body, as opposed to the soul.

On Psalms 139:16, see *Bereshit Rabbah* 24:2; BT *Sanhedrin* 38a; *Zohar* 1:91a, 224a, 233b.

Rabbi Yitsḥak said, "A person does not perform transgressions unless he is a formless mass and not a person—namely he who does not consider his holy soul; rather all his deeds are like a beast, unaware, unknowing."[4]

Rabbi Bo said, "Now, is David designated 'a formless mass,' since he uttered this verse?!"[5]

Rabbi Yitsḥak replied, "Adam uttered it. He said: [121b] *Your eyes saw my formless mass*—before You infused a soul within me, Your eyes saw to fashion from my image people resembling me. *In Your book they were all inscribed.* Who are they? *Days* יצרו (*yutstsaru*), *were formed* (ibid.)—like my צורה (*tsurah*), form. *Not one of them exists* (ibid.)—for not one of them remains."[6]

Rabbi Bo said, "Why so?"

He replied, "Come and see: All those who resembled him, even slightly, did not die a natural death. All of them were struck by that very matter."[7]

Come and see: Rabbi Yehudah said, "Adam's image and beauty was like the radiance of the supernal firmament above the other firmaments, like that light concealed by the blessed Holy One for the righteous in the world to come. All of those who possessed even an intimation of Adam's image were struck through it and died.[8]



4. **A person does not perform transgressions...** See BT *Sotah* 3a: "Resh Lakish said, 'A person does not commit a transgression unless a spirit of folly enters into him.'"

"Formless mass" thus connotes a cognitive-spiritual state.

5. **Now, is David designated 'a formless mass'...** The first verse of the psalm attributes the composition to David. Is David to be compared to the unknowing beasts?

6. **Adam uttered it...** According to BT *Sanhedrin* 38b and *Vayiqra Rabbah* 29:1, *golem* describes Adam's body when it still lacked a soul. Hence, Rabbi Yitsḥak places the verse in Adam's (not David's) mouth.

On the people fashioned from Adam's image, see next note.

7. **those who resembled him...** See *Pirqei de-Rabbi Eli'ezer* 53: "Six people resembled the first man [Adam] and they were all slain: Samson in his strength, and he was slain in his strength; Saul in his stature, and he was slain in his stature; Asahel in his swiftness, and he was slain in his swiftness; Josiah in his nostrils, and he was slain in his nostrils; Zedekiah in his eyes, and he was blinded in his eyes; Absalom in his hair, and he was slain in his hair."

See also BT *Sotah* 10a: "Our Rabbis have taught: Five were created reflecting a supernal pattern, and all of them were struck through them [i.e., the superior features that distinguished them]: Samson in his strength, Saul in his neck, Absalom in his hair, Zedekiah in his eyes, and Asa in his feet. Samson [was struck] in his strength, as is written: *his strength slipped away from him* (Judges 16:19); Saul [was struck] in his neck, as is written: *Saul took his sword and fell upon it* (1 Samuel 31:4); Absalom [was struck] in his hair, as we shall explain below [see 2 Samuel 18:9–15]. Zedekiah [was struck] in his eyes, as is written: *Zedekiah's eyes were put out* (2 Kings 25:7); Asa [was struck] in his feet, as is written: *But in the time of his old age, he was diseased in his feet* (1 Kings 15:23)."

8. **Adam's image and beauty . . .** On Adam's beauty, see *Vayiqra Rabbah* 20:2: "Resh Lakish said in the name of Rabbi Shim'on son of Menasya, 'The apple [round

"For so are the ways of the blessed Holy One: He bestows wealth upon a person. To what end? To sustain the poor and fulfill His commandments. If he did not do so but becomes conceited by that wealth—with that is he struck, as is written: *wealth hoarded by its owner to his misfortune* (Ecclesiastes 5:12). He grants him children. To what end? To teach them the ways of the blessed Holy One, to observe His commandments, as is said of Abraham: *For I have known him, so that he will instruct his children and his household after him: they will keep the way of YHVH, to do righteousness...* (Genesis 18:19). If he did not do so but is conceited because of them—with them is he struck, as is written: *He has no offspring or progeny among his people...* (Job 18:19). Similarly, in this fashion, when the blessed Holy One bestowed upon them of Adam's celestial and superior beauty (To what end? That they would observe His commandments and perform His will.), they did not act accordingly, but became conceited therein and thereby were they struck, with that beauty."[9]

Rav Yehudah said, "When the blessed Holy One created Adam, he was an unformed mass—until He infused soul within him. He summoned the angel in charge of human images and said to him, 'Look closely and fashion from this image six human beings.' This is the meaning of what is written: *he engendered in his likeness, according to his image, and named him* שת *(Shet), Seth* (Genesis 5:3)—namely שיתא (*shitta*), six."[10]

Rabbi Yitsḥak said, "From precisely the same dust from which Adam was created, the blessed Holy One drew to create these six; and he called him שת (*Shet*), *Seth*—שיתא (*shitta*), six. This is the significance of what is written: [122a] *he engendered in his likeness, according to his image*—from the same dough from

fleshy part] of Adam's heel outshone the globe of the sun. How much more so the brightness of his face!'" See also BT *Bava Batra* 58a; *Pesiqta de-Rav Kahana* 4:4; 12:1; *Zohar* 1:113b (*MhN*), 142b. Cf. BT *Ḥagigah* 12a.

On the concealed light, see BT *Ḥagigah* 12a: "Rabbi El'azar said, 'With the light created by the blessed Holy One on the first day, once could gaze and see from one end of the universe to the other. When the blessed Holy One foresaw the corrupt deeds of the generation of the Flood and the generation of the Dispersion [the generation of the Tower of Babel], He immediately hid it from them, as is written: *The light of the wicked is withheld* (Job 38:15). For whom did He hide it? For the righteous in the time to come." See also *Bereshit Rabbah* 3:6; *Shemot Rabbah* 35:1; *Vayiqra Rabbah* 11:7; *Tanḥuma, Shemini* 9.

9. **For so are the ways of the blessed Holy One...** As with the people resembling Adam who misused their gifts and were struck through that very gift, so is the case with wealth and children.

On Ecclesiastes 5:12, see *Shemot Rabbah* 31:3; *Zohar* 2:65a. On Genesis 18:19, see *Zohar* 1:188a.

10. **unformed mass—until He infused soul...** See BT *Sanhedrin* 38b and *Vayiqra Rabbah* 29:1.

On the six people who resembled Adam, see above, note 7. On the angel in charge of human images, see *Zohar* 2:129a; *ZḤ* 82d (*MhN, Rut*).

which his unformed mass was created. Therefore it says *Your eyes saw my formless mass* (Psalms 139:16)—You looked closely upon it to fashion those resembling him. *In Your book they were all inscribed* (ibid.). Who are they? All those who did not guard what the blessed Holy One bestowed upon them; they were driven from the world, and judged with that judgment."

We have learned there: Rav Yehudah said in the name of Rav, "We find that the night consists of three watches, and in every single one, the blessed Holy One has special interest in the human being—when his soul departs from him and he remains in that unformed mass sleeping in bed, and his soul ascends every night before the blessed Holy One."[11]

Rabbi Yitsḥak said, "If she is worthy, they delight with her. If not, they thrust her aside."[12]

Rav Yehudah said in the name of Rav, "What is the meaning of the verse *I adjure you, O daughters of Jerusalem! If you find my beloved, what will you tell him? That I am faint with love* (Song of Songs 5:8)?"

Rabbi Pinḥas said in the name of Rabbi Yehudah, "*I adjure you, O daughters of Jerusalem!* The soul says to those souls worthy of entering Jerusalem Above, who are called 'daughters of Jerusalem' because they are worthy of entering therein; therefore the soul says to them: *I adjure you, O daughters of Jerusalem! If you find my beloved*—the blessed Holy One."[13]



Rav said, "This is the splendor of the speculum above. *What will you tell him? That I am faint with love*—to luxuriate in His splendor and shelter in His shade."[14]

11. **his soul ascends every night...** See *Midrash Tehillim* 11:6; *Pirqei de-Rabbi Eli'ezer* 34; *Bereshit Rabbah* 14:9; *Zohar* 1:83a, 92a, 121b, 130a, 183a, 200a; 2:195b; 3:67a, 121b; in *MhN*, see *ZḤ* 18b, 25c–26a, 28b; Ginzberg, *Legends*, 5:74–75, n. 18; Tishby, *Wisdom of the Zohar*, 2:809–12.

On the three watches of the night, see BT *Berakhot* 3a–b; Rashi on BT *Berakhot* 3a, s.v. *i qa-savar*; *Zohar* 1:159a, 189a, 231a–b; 2:18b (*MhN*), 143b, 173a–b, 195b; 3:64b; *ZḤ* 5d–6a, 17d (both *MhN*), 88a (*MhN, Rut*).

12. **they thrust her aside** The unworthy are rejected by the angels. See *Zohar* 2:195b; *ZḤ* 26a (*MhN*), 88a (*MhN, Rut*).

13. ***daughters of Jerusalem*...** As the soul ascends into the celestial realm—either while the body sleeps or after death—she encounters the souls already dwelling there (*daughters of Jerusalem*). See *Zohar* 1:125b (*MhN*), page 381; 242a.

On Jerusalem Above, see BT *Ta'anit* 5a; *Tanḥuma, Pequdei*, 1; *ZḤ* 20d, 24b, 25a, 25d, 26b, 28c–d (all *MhN*).

14. **speculum above...** אספקלריאה של מעלה (*Ispaqlarya shel ma'alah*). *Ispaqlarya* means glass, mirror, or lens. See BT *Yevamot* 49b: "All the prophets gazed through an opaque glass [literally: an *ispaqlarya* that does not shine], while Moses our teacher gazed through a translucent glass [literally: an *ispaqlarya* that shines]." See also *Vayiqra Rabbah* 1:14; cf. 1 Corinthians 13:12: "For now we see though a glass darkly, but then face-to-face." In *MhN*, the "speculum above" appears to signify a potency very close to divinity

Rav Huna said, "*That I am faint with love*—the desire and longing with which I pined in the world after vanities; therefore I am faint."[15]

Rabbi Yehudah said, "This is the love with which the soul loves the body, for as soon as the termination of the body is complete—those days decreed for it, as is said: *Sarah's life was* (Genesis 23:1)—what is written? *Abraham rose from before his dead*... (ibid., 3)."[16]

Rav Yehudah said in the name of Rav, "What is the significance of what is written in the preceding verse: *Sarah died in Kiriath-arba—that is Hebron, in the land of Canaan* (ibid., 2)?"

Rabbi Yitsḥak said in the name of Rabbi Yoḥanan, "The blessed Holy One [122b] created the human being, and He inserted within him four substances that are divided in the body."[17]

Rabbi Yehudah said, "That are combined in the body."

Rabbi Yitsḥak said, "That are divided in the body; for when a person departs this world they divide and separate—each one to its element."

370 Rabbi Yehudah said, "That are combined in the body during his life, as implied by the verse *Sarah died*—this is the body; בקרית ארבע (*be-qiryat arba*), *in city of four*—these are the four elements; *that is* חברון (*Ḥevron*), *Hebron*—which were מחוברים (*meḥubbarim*), combined, in the body during his life; *in the land of Canaan*—in this world, in which a person roams about a little while."[18]

(perhaps *Shekhinah*). See *Zohar* 1:97b, 122a (both *MhN*); *ZḤ* 10a, 13b, 15b, 15d, 16c, 17a, 21a, 24a (all *MhN*).

15. ***That I am faint with love...*** Apparently meaning that because the soul desired worldly things, she is now faint, i.e., she must receive her punishment and undergo purification. Hence, she is faint because of her love for this world.

16. **the love with which the soul loves the body...** According to Rabbi Yehudah the phrase "*I am faint with love*" refers to the love of the soul (Abraham) for the body (Sarah) after the body has died. As is explained in the following section (see notes 23 and 25), the verse *Abraham rose from before his dead* is interpreted as signifying the soul's effort to ensure the body's resurrection, thereby demonstrating her love for the body.

17. **four substances...** The theory of the four elements was introduced by Empedocles and adopted by Plato, Aristotle, and most of their successors. It dominated Western cosmology until the Renaissance. According to this theory, everything below the sphere of the moon is composed of fire, air, water, and earth—all of which interact and are capable of transforming into one another.

See Aristotle, *On Generation and Corruption* 2:1–8; *Sefer Yetsirah* 3:3–4; *Bemidbar Rabbah* 14:12; Maimonides, *Mishneh Torah, Hilkhot Yesodei ha-Torah* 3:10–11; 4:1–6; idem, *Guide of the Perplexed* 1:72, 2:30; *Zohar* 1:5b, 80a (*ST*); 2:13b, 23b; 3:170a. In *MhN* see *ZḤ* 6d, 10a, 13d, 16b. Cf. Naḥmanides on Genesis 1:1.

18. ***in the land of Canaan*... in which a person roams about a little while** Reading סוחר (*soḥer*) in place of בוחר (*boḥer*), "chooses." See *Matoq mi-Devash*. The printed editions and the manuscripts all read בוחר (*boḥer*), "chooses"; though if so, it is difficult to make sense of the interpretation offered: "*in the land of Canaan*—in this world, which a person chooses for a little while."

In Hebrew, the word כנען (Canaan) also means סוחר (*soḥer*), "merchant, trader," i.e., one who roams about selling his wares. See,

*Abraham came to mourn for Sarah and to weep over her* (Genesis 23:2). This corresponds to what we have learned: All seven days, a person's soul visits the body and mourns for it, as is written: *Surely his flesh feels pain for him, and his soul mourns for him* (Job 14:22). Accordingly: *Abraham came to mourn for Sarah and to weep over her. Abraham came*—the soul; *to mourn for Sarah*—the body.[19]

Rabbi Yitsḥak said, "At the time when the soul is worthy and ascends to the site of her rung, the body lies in peace, resting on its couch, as is written: *Let him enter into peace; let them rest on their couches*—הולך נכחה (*holekh nekhoḥoh*), *he who walks uprightly!* (Isaiah 57:2)."[20]

What is meant by הולך נכחה (*holekh nekhoḥoh*), *he goes uprightly*?

Rabbi Yitsḥak said, "The soul goes נכחה (*nekhoḥoh*)—to the Edenic site concealed for her."

How is this implied?

Rabbi Yehudah said, "From this: נכחה (*nekhoḥoh*) is written with ה (*he*)! But when she is not worthy and deserves to receive [123a] her punishment, she wanders and roams about, visiting the body and the grave every day."[21]



for example, Isaiah 23:8; Ezekiel 16:29, 17:4; Hosea 12:8; Zechariah 14:21; Proverbs 31:24; Job 40:30. See also *ZḤ* 24b (*MhN*).

19. **All seven days, a person's soul visits the body...** See BT *Shabbat* 152a: "Rav Ḥisda said, 'A person's soul mourns for him all seven [days], as is said: *and his soul mourns for him* (Job 14:22).'" See also JT *Mo'ed Qatan* 3:5, 82b; *Bereshit Rabbah* 100:7; *Vayiqra Rabbah* 18:1; *Tanḥuma, Miqqets* 4; *Zohar* 1:218b–219a, 226a; 2:142a; *ZḤ* 24d (*MhN*), 75c, 83a, 83d–84a (all three *MhN, Rut*); Moses de León, *Sefer ha-Rimmon*, 396–7.

20. ***Let him enter into peace...*** On the verse from Isaiah, see *Midrash Tanna'im*, Deuteronomy 34:5; *Sifrei Zuta* 6:26; JT *Sotah* 1:9, 17c; BT *Shabbat* 152b, *Ketubbot* 104a; *Avot de-Rabbi Natan* B, 25; *Devarim Rabbah* 11:10; *Zohar* 2:199a.

On the *Zohar*'s spelling of נכחה (*nekhoḥoh*), see next note.

21. **נכחה (*nekhoḥoh*) is written with ה (*he*)...** Actually, in Tiberian Masoretic manuscripts, נכחה (*nekhoḥoh*) is written נכחו (*nekhoḥo*)—with a *vav*. See Minḥat Shai, ad loc.

Rabbi Yehudah reads the word as though it is written נכח ה (*nokhaḥ he*), in the presence of ה (*he*), i.e., in the presence of *Shekhinah*.

For other instances of a difference between the Masoretic spelling or wording and the *Zohar*'s reading, see *Zohar* 1:32a–b, 58b, 83b, 84a, 93b, 106b, 151a; 2:3b, 5b (*MhN*), 40a, 41b (*Piq*), 82a, 83a, 124b, 176b (*SdTs*), 182b, 246b (*Heikh*); 3:6a, 30a–b, 34a, 40b, 42b, 57b, 68a, 74b–75a, 76b, 80b, 86a–b, 129a (*IR*), 184a, 202b, 203b, 207a; *Minḥat Shai*, passim; Emden, *Mitpaḥat Sefarim*, 27–34, 73–74; Rosenfeld, *Mishpaḥat Soferim*. On this phenomenon, see *Zohar* 3:254a (*RM*); Tishby, *Wisdom of the Zohar*, 1:55–56; Ta-Shma, *Ha-Nigleh she-ba-Nistar*, 50, 131–32, n. 125; Abrams, *Kabbalistic Manuscripts and Textual Theory*, 389–90.

On the same phenomenon in rabbinic literature, see also Rashi on BT *Zevaḥim* 118b, s.v. *ve-lo*; *Tosafot, Shabbat* 55b, s.v. *ma'aviram*; *Niddah* 33a, s.v. *ve-ha-nissa*; *Sha'arei Teshuvah* (*Teshuvot ha-Ge'onim*), 39; Malachi ben Jacob ha-Kohen, *Yad Mal'akhi* 1:283; Aptowitzer, *Das Schriftwort in der Rabbinischen Literatur*; Kasher, *Torah Shelemah*, 23:113; Maori, "Rabbinic Midrash as Evidence for Textual Variants in the Hebrew Bible"; Rosenthal, "Al Derekh Tippulam shel Ḥazal be-Ḥillufei Nussaḥ ba-Miqra."

Rabbi Yose said, "The robust femur—dangling hither and thither—returns and visits its place. Similarly the soul deserving of punishment roams in the world—without, tending her place for twelve months among the graveyards and throughout the world."[22]

Rabbi Yehudah said, "Come and see what is written: *Abraham rose from before his dead*... (Genesis 23:3)"[23]

Rabbi Abba son of Shalom said, "But look at what we have learned: When the soul abides in supernal perfection, ה (*he*) is added to her; and she is called אברהם (*Avraham*), Abraham—in supernal perfection. Yet here you say that when she is not so worthy, it is written: *Abraham rose*! You have relegated one who sits upon the throne to descent among the inferior and lowly![24]

"Rather, so do I decree: *Abraham rose from before his dead.* As Rabbi Zrika said in the name of Rav Kahana, 'When the soul is worthy of ascending to her Edenic site, she first protects the holy body from which she is departing, and afterward ascends to the site of her rung.' As is written: *Abraham rose from before his dead*—the body; *and spoke to* בני חת (*benei Ḥet*), *the Hittites* (ibid.)—the other bodies of the righteous, who are חתים (*ḥattim*), terrified, and stunned in the world for fear of their Master; חתים (*ḥattim*), terrified, because they are *dwellers in the dust* (Isaiah 26:19)."[25]



22. **The robust femur...** קוליתא דקרדינותא (*qulita de-qardinuta*). The *Zohar* is apparently describing how a dislocated femur seeks to reattach itself to the body (see *Derekh Emet*). So too the soul wandering outside the garden of Eden. Cf. *Dammeseq Eli'ezer* (cited in *Nitsotsei Zohar*, ad loc.), who derives קוליתא from קלניתא (*qlanita*), some kind of bird, as found in BT *Bava Batra* 20a and *Ḥullin* 102b. Cf. Mopsik, "Un solide ballon."

See BT *Shabbat* 152b–153a: "For all twelve months [after death], one's body endures—and his soul ascends and descends; after twelve months, the body ceases to exist—and the soul ascends and never again descends." See *Zohar* 1:81a (*ST*), 225a; 2:199b.

23. ***Abraham rose from before his dead...*** That is, the soul (*Abraham*) separated from the body (*his dead*).

24. **You have relegated one who sits upon the throne...** Rabbi Abba is perplexed by the previous interpretations about the soul's postmortem proximity to the body. How can that which is sublime and deserving of residence in the celestial realm (even if only after receiving her punishment) be associated with a rotting corpse (the inferior and lowly)?!

On the soul's perfection being marked by the additional letter ה (*he*), the last letter of the Tetragrammaton, and signified by Abram's name change to Abraham, see *Zohar* 1:126a (*MhN*), page 383; *ZḤ* 25a, 26a (both *MhN*).

25. **she first protects the holy body...** Rabbi Abba resolves his own query. Before ascending on high, the soul does indeed associate with dead bodies, but for a noble purpose, as explained below.

It is not clear where the Rabbi Zrika quote should end.

On *benei Ḥet*, see *Zohar* 1:139b (*MhN*). On the use of the term "decree"—from the root גזר (*gzr*)—for establishing a teaching, see *Zohar* 1:124b, 125a (both *MhN*); *ZḤ* 14a, 15b, 16a, 18b, 20a (all *MhN*); 62b (*ShS*); Scholem, "Parashah Ḥadashah," 443–44 (Addendum 1

What need has she of them?[26]

Rabbi Yehudah said, "All are inscribed in the count; [the soul speaks with them] that the body be in the count with them. What does he say to them? In a respectful and conciliatory manner, [123b] '*I am a sojourner and settler among you; [give me possession of a burial site among you, so I may bury my dead out of my sight]* (Genesis 23:4)—that this body will be in a single count with you, in a single nexus.'"[27]

Rabbi said, "Look at what is written: *The Hittites replied to Abraham...* (ibid., 5)—similarly, in a respectful and conciliatory manner, as is written: *Listen to us, my lord! You are a prince of God among us* (ibid., 6)."[28]

What is the significance of *You are a prince of God*?

Rabbi Pinḥas said, "Before the righteous person departs the world, a heavenly voice rings forth every day among the righteous in the Garden of Eden: Prepare a place for so-and-so who is coming here! Consequently they say: From God on high *you are a prince of God among us. In the choicest of our burial sites* (ibid.)—count him among the choicest of the righteous, in the company of the righteous elect; insert him in the tally with us; none of us will prevent the count, for all of us rejoice in him and extend him greetings."[29]



Rabbi Yose son of [124a] Pazzi said, "Come and see: After the soul entreats them and they inform her [that she is welcome], she entreats the angel appointed over them. As we have learned: An angel is appointed over graveyards—named Dumah—and every day he proclaims among them concerning the righteous who are destined to enter in their midst. Immediately she entreats him to lodge the body in tranquility, safety, rest, and delight, as is written: *He spoke to Ephron* (ibid., 13)."[30]

in this volume); Meroz, "Va-Ani Lo Hayiti Sham?," 168 (Addendum 3 in this volume).

26. **What need has she of them?** What does the soul want or need from the bodies of the righteous?

27. **All are inscribed in the count...** The bodies of the righteous—which are destined to be resurrected—have been inscribed in a register. The soul (Abraham) pleads on behalf of its own body that it too will be counted among them.

28. **Rabbi...** That is, Rabbi Yehudah ha-Nasi (the Patriarch), who redacted the Mishnah. He was so esteemed that he was called simply "Rabbi": the Master.

29. **a heavenly voice rings forth...** On the proclamation prior to death, see *Zohar* 1:217b, 218b, 219b. Cf. BT *Berakhot* 18b; *Ketubbot* 77b.

The bodies of the righteous are addressing Dumah, as explained below.

30. **named Dumah . . .** דומה (*Dumah*), literally "silence," is a biblical name for the netherworld. See Psalms 94:17: *Were not YHVH a help to me, my soul would have nearly dwelled in dumah*. In rabbinic literature, Dumah is the angel in charge of the souls of the dead (BT *Berakhot* 18b, *Shabbat* 152b, *Ḥagigah* 5a, *Sanhedrin* 94a; *Tanḥuma, Ki Tissa,* 33). See *Zohar* 1:8a–b, 62b, 94a, 102a (*MhN*), 121a (*Tos*), 130b, 218b, 237b; 2:18a (*MhN*), 150b.

On Ephron signifying Dumah, see next paragraph.

Rabbi Yeisa said, "This is the angel called Dumah. Why is he known as עפרון (*Efron*), Ephron? Because he is appointed over שוכני עפר (*shokhenei afar*), the dwellers in dust. It has been taught: All the registers of the righteous and the companies of pious who dwell in the dust are in his care; one day he will bring them out by tally."[31]

It has been taught: Rabbi El'azar said, "In the time to come, when the blessed Holy One will ordain to revive the dead, He will summon the angel in charge of graveyards—named Dumah—and will demand from him a count of all the righteous and pious dead, as well as the righteous converts who were slain for His Name. He will bring them forth by tally just as he received them by tally, as is written: *The one who brings forth their array by number... not one is missing* (Isaiah 40:26)."[32]

It has been taught: Rabbi Shemu'el son of Rabbi Ya'akov said, "נפשות (*Nefashot*), The souls, of the wicked are placed in the charge of that angel whose name is Dumah, to escort them into Hell—where they are judged. Once they are handed over to his charge they do not return again until they enter Hell. This was what David feared when he performed that sin, as is said: *Were not YHVH a help to me, my soul would soon have dwelt with Dumah* (Psalms 94:17)."[33]



Rabbi Yeisa said, "The soul entreats him to admit that body with the other bodies of the righteous in their tally, as is written: *He spoke to Ephron* (Genesis 23:13)."

Rabbi Tanḥum said, "The angel addresses him first! Look at what is written before: *Ephron was sitting among* בני חת (*benei ḥet*), *the Hittites* (ibid., 10)—שחתו (*she-ḥattu*), who were in dread, of dwelling in the dust; he addresses him first to admit that body into the tally of the righteous, as is written: *and Ephron the Hittite answered Abraham in the hearing of the Hittites, all who entered the gate of his town, saying* (ibid.)."

What is meant by *all who entered the gate of his town*?

Rav Naḥman said, "Those [124b] inscribed in his account book."

31. **All the registers of the righteous...** See *Zohar* 1:121a (*Tos*); 127b (*MhN*), page 388.

32. **He will bring them forth by tally...** Cf. BT *Berakhot* 58b: "Our Rabbis have taught: On seeing Israelite graves, one should say, 'Blessed is He who fashioned you in judgment, who nourished you in judgment, who maintained you in judgment, who gathered you in judgment, and who will one day raise you up in judgment.' Mar the son of Ravina concluded thus in the name of Rav Naḥman: 'And who knows the number of all of you; and He will one day revive you and establish you. Blessed is He who revives the dead.'"

On Isaiah 40:26, see *Zohar* 1:131a.

33. **This was what David feared when he performed that sin...** With Bathsheba. See *Zohar* 1:8b, 94a.

On the souls of the wicked handed over to Dumah, see *Zohar* 1:130b; cf. *Zohar* 2:18a (*MhN*).

As Rav Naḥman said: "So has it been decreed: By the account administered by Dumah they enter the graveyards; and by the account-note he will one day bring them out. He is in charge of the denizens of dust."[34]

What is the meaning of *The field I grant you and the cave that is in it* (ibid., 11)?[35]

Rabbi Yose said, "A deposit of serenity and great tranquility."[36]

Rabbi Shalom son of Minyomi said, "You cannot find a single righteous person among those who engage in Torah who does not possess two hundred worlds and desirables on account of Torah, as is written: *and two hundred for those who guard its fruit* (Song of Songs 8:12); and two hundred for surrendering themselves daily, as though they were slain for the sanctification of His Name—like this verse, as is written: *You shall love YHVH your God with all your heart and with all your soul* (Deuteronomy 6:5). It has been taught: Whoever attunes his heart to this verse in order to surrender his soul for the sanctification of His Name, Scripture accords it to him as though he is slain every day for His sake, as is written: *For Your sake we are killed all day long* (Psalms 44:23)."[37]

Rav Naḥman said, "Whoever surrenders his soul through this verse inherits four hundred worlds in the world to come."[38]



Rav Yosef said, "But we have learned 'two hundred'!"

Rav Naḥman replied, "Two hundred for Torah and two hundred for surrendering his soul every day for the sanctification of His Name, as we have said."

[123b][39] Rabbi Yose son of Rabbi Yehudah went to see Rabbi Ḥiyya the Great. He said to him, "May my master tell, if he has heard, how the Masters of Mishnah expounded this passage in reference to the soul."[40]

34. **by the account-note he will one day bring them out...** See BT *Berakhot* 58b (above, note 32) also in the name of Rav Naḥman.

35. ***The field I grant you...*** Spoken by Ephron to Abraham. The verse continues: *I grant it to you in the presence of my people. I grant it to you. Bury your dead.*

36. **A deposit of serenity...** Dumah provides *the field,* i.e., the grave, as a safe resting place for the body until the resurrection.

37. ***two hundred for those who guard its fruit...*** On the two hundred worlds inherited by the righteous as reward for Torah study, see *Zohar* 1:97b (*MhN*); *ZḤ* 22a (*MhN*). See also BT *Shevu'ot* 35b.

On surrendering one's soul and the recitation of the *Shema* prayer, see M *Berakhot* 9:5: "*With all your soul*—even if He plucks your soul." See also *Tosefta Berakhot* 6:7; *Sifrei,* Deuteronomy 32; *Midrash Tanna'im,* Deuteronomy 6:5; BT *Berakhot* 54a, 61b.

On Psalms 44:23, see *Zohar* 2:198a–b.

38. **four hundred worlds...** Cf. *Zohar* 3:128b (*IR*), 288a (*IZ*).

39. **[123b]** In standard editions, this section—extending until the word *book* from Daniel 12:1—is printed under the heading *Tosefta* on the previous folio page. As noted by numerous scholars, the passage is clearly *MhN* and is included as such at this location in all the manuscript witnesses in which the passage is found. Cf. the *Tosefta* at *Zohar* 1:121a. See Asulin, "Midrash ha-Ne'lam li-Vreshit," 236–37.

40. **Masters of Mishnah...** מארי מתניתא (*marei matnita*). This term appears in numerous passages (in various formulations)

He said, "Happy is the share of the righteous in the world that is coming! For Torah is in their hearts like a mighty spring of water. And by dint of the abundant water: even when blocked, the springs flow forth—gushing in all directions. Come and hear, Rabbi Yose, you are beloved! I will tell you about this passage. A person's body is never admitted to the tally of the righteous by Dumah until the soul displays her registration-token, given her by the cherubs in the Garden of Eden."[41]

Rabbi Yose said, "I have heard that when the soul enters there, she proceeds to ascend to her site on high—not descending below—but that before she ascends and enters, she is appointed protector of the body by Dumah; and she shows him that it deserves to receive a reward of four hundred worlds."

Rabbi Ḥiyya said, "Rabbi El'azar said that Dumah knows beforehand, because they issue a proclamation about her in the Garden of Eden. But I have heard as follows: When she is given the registration, she returns to the body to have it admitted to the list of the righteous by Dumah. This is the meaning of the verse *If you would but hear me! Let me pay* כסף (kesef), *the price, of the field; take it from me* [*and let me bury my dead there*] (Genesis 23:13). What is meant by כסף (*kesef*), *the price, of the field*? This is כסופא (*kissufa*), the desire, for the four hundred worlds it is bequeathed to inherit."[42]

When Rav Yosef heard this passage from the Masters of the Academy, he would weep. He said, "Can one who is dust and vanity attain this?! Who will be worthy? Who will rise? As is written: *Who may ascend the mountain of YHVH? Who may stand in His holy place?* (Psalms 24:3)."[43]

throughout *Midrash ha-Ne'lam* and appears to signify a group (though never formally defined) of sages possessing esoteric wisdom. In some ways, the Masters of Mishnah are a forerunner to the *Ḥavrayya*, the Companions headed by Rabbi Shim'on, found in the main body of the *Zohar*. Significantly, however, Rabbi Shim'on does not always occupy a privileged position in this group. The Mishnah of which they are masters is not the Mishnah of the rabbinic sage Rabbi Yehudah ha-Nasi, but rather a body of esoteric knowledge often relating to the soul and the structure of the cosmos. See *Zohar* 1:127a–b, 129a–b, 130a, 135a, 138a, 139b; 2:5a, 14a (all *MhN*); *ZḤ* 10c, 12c, 13a, 14c, 15b–c, 16a, 59b (all *MhN*); Scholem, "Parashah Ḥadashah," 443, 444 (Addendum 1 in this volume); Meroz, "Va-Ani Lo Hayiti Sham?," 168 (Addendum 3 in this volume). Cf. *Pesiqta de-Rav Kahana* 11:15, 23:12; See also Matt, "Matnita di-Lan," 132–34.

41. **her registration-token, given her by the cherubs...** See *Zohar* 1:81b (*ST*); *ZḤ* 21a (*MhN*). Cf. *Zohar* 3:162a (*Rav Metivta*).

42. **כסף (*kesef*), *the price* . . . כסופא (*kissufa*), the desire...** The verse from Genesis is spoken by Abraham to Ephron. According to Rabbi Ḥiyya, it signifies the soul's entreaty to Dumah. The *kesef* Abraham seeks to pay refers to the desire (*kissufa*) for the four hundred worlds the body is worthy of meriting in the world to come.

Cf. *Zohar* 2:97b; *ZḤ* 22a (*MhN*).

On the proclamation, see above, at note 29.

43. **Masters of the Academy...** On this epithet, see *Zohar* 1:115b (*MhN*); *ZḤ* 15a, 25d (both *MhN*); Scholem, "Parashah Ḥada-

Rabbi Abba said, "Come and see: Why is it written *Abraham heeded Ephron* (Genesis 23:16)? What does this mean? To display the soul's worthiness, that she is consummate in her perfection, as is written: *and Abraham weighed out for Ephron* הכסף (*ha-kesef*), *the silver* (Genesis 23:16)—the immense כסופא (*kissufa*), desire, for those worlds and desirables; *four hundred* שקל כסף (*shekel kesef*), *silver shekels* (ibid.)—four hundred worlds, delights, and כסופין (*kissufin*), desirables."[44]

עובר לסוחר (*Over la-soḥer*), *Passing to traverse* (ibid.). Rav Naḥman said, "שיעבור (*She-ya'avor*), Passing through, all the gates of heaven and Jerusalem Above with no one to hold her back. Come and see what is written: *Then Abraham buried his wife Sarah* (ibid., 19)—reckoned with the other righteous, in their company, in the list in Dumah's charge."[45]

Rabbi Yitsḥak said, "So have I learned: All those inscribed in Dumah's list and designated by him will rise on the day when He is destined to revive the denizens of dust. Woe to the wicked not inscribed by him in his list, for they will perish eternally in Hell! Of this is said: *At that time your people will be rescued—all who are found inscribed in the book* (Daniel 12:1)."[46] [124b]



*Abraham was old, coming into days...* (Genesis 24:1).[47]

Our Mishnah: Rabbi El'azar said, "In any event it is so, for this Mishnah is well put, that the soul is made, that of which is written [*I saw the living beings, and*] *behold, one wheel on the ground next to the four-faced creatures* (Ezekiel 1:15), as stated in the first Mishnah."[48]

shah," 432–33, 443 (Addendum 1 in this volume). Some manuscripts read: Masters of Mishnah.

44. ***Abraham heeded Ephron...*** In the narrative in Genesis, once Ephron agrees to allow Abraham to bury his dead in the cave, Abraham insists on paying full price. *Ephron answered Abraham, saying, "Pray, my lord, hear me. Land for four hundred silver shekels between me and you, what does it come to? Go bury your dead." Abraham heeded Ephron* [i.e., he accepted his terms] *and Abraham weighed out for Ephron the silver... four hundred silver shekels...* (Genesis 23:14–16). Here, agreeing to Ephron's terms means that the soul must prove its worth.

On the four hundred worlds, see *Zohar* 3:128b (*IR*).

45. **עובר לסוחר (*Over la-soḥer*), *Passing to traverse...*** This phrase is usually rendered *at the merchants' tried weight.* The root סחר (*sḥr*), "to trade," originally meant "to roam, traverse."

On Jerusalem Above, see note 13.

It is possible that this paragraph should be construed as the continuation of Rabbi Abba's teaching, in which case he is quoting Rav Naḥman.

46. ***all who are found inscribed in the book...*** On this verse, see *Zohar* 1:139b (*MhN*).

47. ***coming into days...*** The verse continues: *and YHVH blessed Abraham with everything.* The idiom בא בימים (*ba ba-yamim*)—normally understood as "advanced in days, advanced in years"—is interpreted below literally. See *Zohar* 1:103a, 129a–b, 142a, 224a; 3:170b.

48. **Our Mishnah . . .** The *Zohar* often cites teachings from a secret, mystical Mish-

Rabbi Abba said to him, "May the master tell us of that Mishnah?"

He replied, "So has it been expounded in The Thirteen Attributes of Mercy, in its portion. But here, we should say:"[49]

He opened, saying, "*One is my dove, my perfect one, only one of her mother...* (Song of Songs 6:9)."[50]

Rabbi El'azar said, "Why is it that here in the Song of Songs we employ the feminine, but there in the Torah the masculine?"[51]

Well, Rabbi El'azar said, "Here in the Torah vis-à-vis the body, it is designated by the masculine, because the body to the soul is as a woman to the male. [125a] But the soul in relation to Above is like the female to the male. Each one inherits its degree."[52]

We have learned there: Every day, four times an hour, Eden trickles down upon the Garden, and from those drops a mighty river emerges, dividing into four heads; it trickles forty-eight drops every day. From there the trees of the Garden are sated, as is written: *The trees of YHVH are sated* (Psalms 104:16).[53]



nah known only to its circle. See *Zohar* 1:37b, 55b, 74a, 91b, 93a, 95b, 96a, 136b (*MhN*), 137a (*MhN*), 139a (*MhN*), 223b; 2:5a (*MhN*), 123b; 3:75b, 78a, 284b, 285a, 293b (*IZ*); *ZḤ* 12b, 15b–c, 16a, 18b, 20a (all *MhN*); Scholem, "Parashah Ḥadashah"; Matt, "Matnita di-Lan." This is to be distinguished from the *Matnitin* of the *Zohar*, on which see Scholem, *Kabbalah*, 216.

Unfortunately, the sense of Rabbi El'azar's statement is not apparent and there seems to be a lacuna in the text. See *Matoq mi-Devash* and *Sullam* for various explanations.

On the verse from Ezekiel, see BT *Ḥagigah* 13b.

49. **The Thirteen Attributes of Mercy...** Alas, Rabbi El'azar does not explain the verse or the Mishnah.

A work entitled "The Thirteen Attributes of Mercy in the Mishnah of Rabbi El'azar" is referenced in *ZḤ* 10c (*MhN*); see also *Zohar* 1:129b (*MhN*), page 398. This work would appear to be one of the many books housed in the real or imaginary Zoharic library. See *Ketem Paz*, 1:22d: "All such books mentioned in the *Zohar*... have been lost in the wanderings of exile.... Nothing is left of them except what is mentioned in the *Zohar*."

Once again, there seems to be a lacuna in the text. One would expect that following "we should say," Rabbi El'azar would continue his homily. Oddly, the next sentence begins with "He opened, saying," interrupting his own words.

50. ***One is my dove...*** The verse continues: *the delight of her who bore her. Daughters see her and call her happy; queens and concubines and praise her.* As is made clear below, the verse is expounded as referring to the soul.

51. **in the Song of Songs we employ the feminine...** Why does the Song of Songs use the feminine to speak of the soul, whereas in the Torah the soul is designated by Abraham, the masculine?

52. **like the female to the male...** The masculine signifies the higher bestowing principle; and the feminine, the lower receiving agent. Hence, with regard to the body, Abraham signifies the soul; but with regard to the masculine divine, the soul is feminine.

Cf. Aristotle, *Generation of Animals* 2:4: "While the body is from the female, it is the soul that is from the male, for the soul is the substance of a particular body."

See Wolfson, "Woman—The Feminine as Other in Theosophic Kabbalah," 166–204.

53. **Eden trickles down upon the Gar-**

Rabbi Tanḥum said, "From here: *Watering mountains from His lofts* (ibid., 13). What is the loft? Eden."[54]

Where is Eden located?

Rabbi Yehudah said, "Above *Aravot*."[55]

Rabbi Yose says, "In *Aravot*. For look at what we have learned: There reside גנזי (*ginzei*), the treasuries, of good life, blessing, and peace—and the souls of the righteous. The upper גנוז (*ganuz*), concealment, is Eden; below, aligned correspondingly, is the Garden on earth, drawing bounty from it every day."[56]

Rabbi Abbahu said, "Forty-eight prophets arose for Israel; and each one took as his share the juice of one drop from those Edenic drops, numbering forty-eight. Now, if each prophet extracted but one drop and exceeded all others in degree of holy-spirit, how much more so Adam who resided in the Garden and received the drops in their potency?! Moreover, each prophet received but one—whereas Adam received from forty-eight! From here you derive the magnitude of his wisdom."[57]



**den...** Genesis 2 mentions the Garden of Eden (verse 15) as well as a garden planted in Eden (verse 8). The *Zohar* differentiates between the two terms—the garden is below and Eden is above on high. See BT *Berakhot* 34b; *ZḤ* 13c, 18a–b (both *MhN*). Cf. *Bereshit Rabbah* 15:2. In the main strata of the *Zohar*, Eden and the Garden signify the flow of emanation from *Ḥokhmah* to *Malkhut*. Here, even without sefirotic designations, the Edenic flow represents the source of all vitality.

See Genesis 2:10: *A river issues from Eden to water the garden; and from there it divides and becomes four riverheads.*

On the verse from Psalms, see *Bereshit Rabbah* 15:1; cf. *Zohar* 1:162b; 3:58a.

54. ***Watering mountains from His lofts...*** On this verse, see BT *Ta'anit* 9b; *Mishnat Rabbi Eli'ezer* 15.

55. ***Aravot*** The seventh and highest heaven according to BT *Ḥagigah* 12b. See also Maimonides, *Guide of the Perplexed* 1:70.

56. **There reside גנזי (*ginzei*), the treasuries...** See BT *Ḥagigah* 12b: "*Aravot*—in which are righteousness, justice, charity, treasuries of life, treasuries of peace, treasuries of blessings, the souls (*neshamot*) of the righteous, and the spirits and souls (*ruḥot* and *neshamot*) that are to be created in the future, and the dew with which the blessed Holy One will revive the dead."

On the earthly and heavenly Gardens of Eden, see Naḥmanides on Genesis 3:22; idem, *Kitvei Ramban*, 2:295–99; *Zohar* 1:7a, 38b (*Heikh*), 81a (*ST*), 106b (*MhN*), 224b; 2:209b–210b, 211b–212a, 231b; 3:13a, 53a, 70b; Moses de León, *Shushan Edut*, 350–51; idem, *Sheqel ha-Qodesh*, 27 (32), 59–62 (73–76); [Moses de León?], *Seder Gan Eden*, 138; Tishby, *Wisdom of the Zohar*, 2:591–94, 749–51.

57. **Forty-eight prophets arose for Israel...** See BT *Megillah* 14a: "Our Rabbis have taught: Forty-eight prophets and seven prophetesses prophesied to Israel."

See also *Shir ha-Shirim Rabbah* on Song of Songs 4:15: *A spring in the garden, a well of living waters, a flowing stream from Lebanon*: "Rabbi Yoḥanan said, '*Well* is written in the Torah forty-eight times, corresponding to the forty-eight qualities through which Torah is acquired [see *Avot* 6:5]....'"

According to *Bereshit Rabbah* 44:6 and *Shir ha-Shirim Rabbah* on 3:4, one of the names of prophecy is הטפה (*hatafah*), "preaching." Perhaps Rabbi Abbahu is playing off the proximity of *hatafah* and טיפות (*tipot*), "drops."

Rabbi Bo said in the name of Rav Kahana, "Whence did the prophets obtain those drops? Well, so have we learned: In every single drop emerging from Eden, a spirit of wisdom flows forth with it. Accordingly it has been decreed in our Mishnah: There are waters breeding the wise, and there are waters breeding fools. The waters breeding the wise derived from the drops of Eden."[58]

As Rabbi Yose said: "Waters in which inhere drops from all those four rivers. The first, as is written: *The name of the first Pishon* (Genesis 2:11). What is meant by *The name* האחד (*ha-eḥad*), *of the first, Pishon*? המיוחד (*Ha-meyuḥad*), The most distinguished, of all is Pishon; it falls in the land of Egypt. That is why the wisdom of Egypt exceeded the entire world. But when the decree was ordained that the wisdom of Egypt be lost, the blessed Holy One seized those drops and cast them [125b] in that garden, in that river of the Garden of Eden, as is written: *A river issues from Eden to water the garden* (ibid., 10). This one gave rise to four others; and the first and most distinguished generated from it was Pishon. When those drops—which have not left the garden—were seized, the wisdom of Egypt was lost.[59]



"From the רוח (*ruaḥ*), spirit, that flowed forth from Eden every prophet wrung, as is written: [*They heard the voice of YHVH Elohim*] *moving about in the garden* לרוח (*le-ruaḥ*), *in the breeze, of day* (ibid. 3:8). This river is concealed in the Garden of Eden for the time to come. This is the river that Ezekiel saw in his prophecy. Therefore it is written: *For the earth will be filled with knowledge of YHVH* [*as waters cover the sea*] (Isaiah 11:9), for those waters always breed knowledge in the world."[60]

Our Rabbis have taught: All the souls of the righteous are above, in Eden. Now, if from that which descends from Eden wisdom flourishes in the world, how much more so for those standing within it, basking in its pleasures and delights?

58. **waters breeding the wise...** On the effects of different types of water, see *Bemidbar Rabbah* 20:22; *Midrash Tehillim* 5:1; *Zohar* 2:30b; 3:101a.

On the use of the term "decree," see above, note 25. On the expression "our Mishnah," see above, note 48.

59. **Pishon; it falls in the land of Egypt...** On Pishon identified with the Nile, see Samaritan Targum, *Midrash Aggadah*, Saadia Gaon, Rashi, Ibn Ezra, and Naḥmanides on Genesis 2:11. See *Zohar* 1:81b; 2:10a. Cf. *Zohar* 2:34b, where Pishon is associated with Babylon.

The verse *A river issues from Eden...* appears approximately fifty times in the *Zohar*. See Hellner-Eshed, *A River Flows from Eden*, 229–51.

The Edenic drops that once flowed through Egypt have been restored to their source in the river in the Garden of Eden.

60. **the river that Ezekiel saw...** According to Ezekiel 1:3, the prophet attained his visions of God by the River Kevar. See *Zohar* 1:6b, 85a, 149a–b, where the River Kevar is read as the River of Already [כבר (*kevar*) means "already"], already existing since the day the world was created.

On Isaiah 11:9, see *Zohar* 1:113b, 130a, 140a (all *MhN*); 2:68a; 3:23a.

Rabbi Yitsḥak said, "As soon as the soul merits entry through the gates of Jerusalem Above, Michael, the great prince, welcomes and accompanies her. Bewildered by him, the ministering angels inquire about her: *Who is this rising from the desert?* (Song of Songs 3:6)—who is this rising among the celestials, from a desolate body resembling vapor, as is written: *The human is like unto vapor* (Psalms 144:4)? He replies, saying, *One is she my dove, my perfect one* (Song of Songs 6:9). *One is she*—singular; *only one of her mother* (ibid.)—the Throne of Glory, mother of soul; she births her, for from her was she hewn. *Daughters see her and call her happy* (ibid.)—the other souls in their station above, called Daughters of Jerusalem."[61]

Rabbi Yose said, "Look, we have returned to what we said! These are called Daughters of Jerusalem; the others are called Daughters of Lot. *Daughters see her and call her happy*—the other souls praise her and say, 'May your coming be in peace.' *Queens and concubines* (ibid.); *Queens*—the patriarchs who are queens; *concubines*—righteous converts. All laud and praise her until she ascends above. Then the soul is at her station, [126a] attaining longevity, as is written: *Abraham was old, coming into days* (Genesis 24:1)—entering into length of days in the world to come."[62]

Rabbi Abba Sava rose to his feet and said, "O Rabbi Shim'on son of Yoḥai, may your bones enjoy peace and tranquility, for you have restored the crown to its pristine state! For we have learned in the first Mishnah: Once the soul abides in her perfection, in a supernal site, she does not return to the body; rather, other souls are created from her and emanate from her, but she remains in [that mode of] existence. Until Rabbi Shim'on arrived and expounded, 'If in this world (which is vanity) and in the body (which is a putrid drop) the soul enters within, in the time to come—when all of them will be refined, and the body will be superior in existence and perfection—is it not fitting that the soul enter within, possessing all her perfections and sublimities?!'"[63]

61. ***only one of her mother...*** The soul (i.e., the *neshamah*, the highest level of soul, the spiritual essence of the human being) is created from the substance of the Throne of Glory, which may refer to the *Shekhinah*. See *Zohar* 1:113a, 126b, 128a (all *MhN*); *ZḤ* 10a–d, 20b, 22a, 24a, 26a (all *MhN*).

On the Throne of Glory as mother of soul, cf. BT *Shabbat* 152b, where the souls of the righteous are said to be "hidden beneath the Throne of Glory" after death; see also *Avot de-Rabbi Natan* A, 12. On Michael welcoming the soul, see *ZḤ* 21a, 25a (both *MhN*). See also BT *Ḥagigah* 12b; *Ketubbot* 104a; *Tosafot, Menaḥot* 110a, s.v. *U-mikhael sar ha-gadol*. On daughters of Jerusalem, see *Zohar* 1:122a (*MhN*), page 369.

62. **the others are called Daughters of Lot...** Whereas the daughters of Jerusalem signify the souls of the righteous in the celestial realm, the daughters of Lot signify the base powers of the soul and hence more generally the souls of the wicked. See *Zohar* 1:109b–110b (*MhN*).

On the verse from Genesis, see above, note 47.

63. **you have restored the crown to its pristine state...** Rabbi Shim'on has re-

Rabbi Aḥa said, "In the time to come, the blessed Holy One will establish the very same soul and the very same body enduringly in their existence, though both of them will enjoy consummate existence, consummate knowledge—to attain what they did not in this world."[64]

*Abraham was old, coming into days* (Genesis 24:1). Rabbi Abba said in the name of Rabbi Yoḥanan, "In that world that is *days*; not in this world, which is night."[65]

stored the crown by supplying an argument for resurrection, against those who claimed that after death the soul remains on high never to descend again.

The "first Mishnah" outlines the views of medieval Jewish rationalists who either denied bodily resurrection and/or interpreted rabbinic sayings about the resurrection/world to come in a metaphorical way. (Presumably the *Zohar* has in mind Maimonides and/or his interpreters). Rabbi Shim'on's view accords with Abraham ben David's rejection of Maimonides' position.



See Maimonides, *Mishneh Torah*, *Hilkhot Teshuvah* 8:2: "In the world to come, there is no body or physical form—only the souls of the righteous alone, without a body, like the ministering angels.... Thus the sages of the previous ages declared [BT *Berakhot* 17a]: 'In the world to come, there is neither eating, drinking, or sexual relations. Rather, the righteous will sit with their crowns on their heads and delight in the splendor of *Shekhinah*.' From this statement it is clear that there is no body, for there is no eating or drinking. [Consequently] the statement 'the righteous sit' must be interpreted metaphorically, i.e., the righteous exist there without work or labor. Similarly, the phrase 'their crowns on their heads' [is also a metaphor, implying] that they will possess the knowledge that they grasped that allowed them to merit the life of the world to come. This will be their crown, like that which was said by Solomon: *With the crown with which his mother crowned him* (Song of Songs 3:11).... What is meant by the expression 'delight in the splendor of *Shekhinah*'? That they will fathom and comprehend of the truth of the blessed Holy One, which they cannot grasp while in a dark and lowly body." See also idem, *Pereq Ḥeleq*.

See Abraham ben David's gloss to Maimonides, *Hilkhot Teshuvah* 8:2: "The statements of this individual resemble those who say that the resurrection will not be for the bodies, only for the souls. I swear that our sages of blessed memory did not share this opinion.... The crowns will be literal, according to their plain meaning; not a metaphor!"

Rabbi Shim'on has thus restored the crown to its pristine state literally! See Gottlieb, *Meḥqarim be-Sifrut ha-Qabbalah*, 204–5; Asulin, "Midrash ha-Ne'lam li-Vreshit," 245.

See BT *Yoma* 69b: "Why were they called the Men of the Great Assembly? Because they restored the crown to its pristine state." See also BT *Qiddushin* 66a: "He [Shim'on son of Shetaḥ] restored Torah to her pristine state"; cf. *Zohar* 2:147a.

On the putrid drop, see M *Avot* 3:1.

64. **the very same soul and the very same body...** Not only is bodily resurrection assured, but also one's original body will be resurrected: the individual is preserved in entirety. See *Bereshit Rabbah* 95:1; BT *Pesaḥim* 68a, *Sanhedrin* 91b; *Qohelet Rabbah* on 1:4; *Tanḥuma*, *Vayiggash* 8; *Zohar* 1:115a (*MhN*), 127a (*MhN*), 130b, 181b; 2:28b; Moses de León, *Sefer ha-Mishqal*, 87–89.

On the attainment of perfect knowledge, see *Zohar* 1:113b–114a, 135a–b, 140a; *ZḤ* 15d (all *MhN*).

65. **In that world that is *days*...** Abraham, the soul, entered the world that is *days*, i.e., the timeless world to come. On this world as night and the world to come as day(s), see

Rabbi Ya'akov said, "In those worlds that are *days*; in those pleasures and delights he inherits."[66]

*And YHVH blessed Abraham with everything* (ibid.)—with the tenth the blessed Holy One bestowed upon him from His Name, the letter ה (*he*), through which the world was created.[67]

It has been taught: Rabbi Yoḥanan said, "Metatron, the Prince of the Countenance, who is a youth, the servant of his Master—the Lord ruling over him—is in charge of the soul, to supply her every day from that light, as commanded. He is destined to receive the tally-note in the graveyards from Dumah, and to display it before his Master. He will then leaven that bone underground, to restore the bodies and establish them in perfected corporeality devoid of soul; for the blessed Holy One [126b] will send her forth to her place."[68]

BT *Ḥagigah* 12b: "Resh Lakish said, 'Whoever engages in Torah in this world, which is like night—the blessed Holy One emanates a thread of love upon him in the world to come, which is like day, as is said: *By day YHVH directs His love; at night His song is with me* (Psalms 42:9).'" See also *Bereshit Rabbah* 59:2; *Pirqei de-Rabbi Eli'ezer* 34.

Cf. *Zohar* 1:103a, 129a–b, 142a, 224a; 3:170b.

66. **In those worlds that are *days* . . .** The four hundred supernal worlds inherited by the soul. See *Zohar* 1:123b (*MhN*, this volume), 124b (*MhN*).

67. ***YHVH blessed Abraham with everything*...** The כל (*kol*), *everything*, that Abraham receives is the last letter from the tetragrammaton, the letter ה (*he*), marked by his name change from Abram to Abraham, signifying the soul's perfection. It is "the tenth" as ה (*he*) has the numerical value of five, a tenth of כל (*kol*), *everything*, which has the numerical value of fifty. See *Zohar* 1:123a (*MhN*), page 372; *ZḤ* 25a, 26a (both *MhN*).

According to a rabbinic interpretation, the verse *YHVH blessed Abraham* בכל (*ba-kol*), *with everything*, alludes to Abraham's being blessed with a daughter, whose name was *Ba-kol*, *With Everything*. In Kabbalah, this daughter is identified with the divine daughter, *Shekhinah*. See BT *Bava Batra* 16b; *Bahir* 52 (78); Naḥmanides on Genesis 24:1; *Zohar* 1:219a; 2:36a; *ZḤ* 10d (*MhN*). Cf. *Zohar* 1:17a, 130b; 2:157a.

On the world's being created through the letter ה (*he*), see BT *Menaḥot* 29b: "*These are the generations of heaven and earth* בהבראם (*be-hibbare'am*), *when they were created* (Genesis 2:4). Do not read בהבראם (*be-hibbare'am*), when they were created, but rather בה׳ בראם (*be-he bera'am*), with ה (*he*) He created them." See *Bereshit Rabbah* 12:10; JT *Ḥagigah* 2:1, 77c; *Alfa Beita de-Rabbi Aqiva*, Version 1 (*Battei Midrashot*, 2:363); *Zohar* 1:46b, 91b; *ZḤ* 3a, 3d, 17a (all *MhN*).

68. **Metatron, the Prince of the Countenance, who is a youth...** Metatron receives the register of the righteous, who are destined to be revived from Dumah, and then proceeds to revive the body. The soul, however, is bestowed by God.

Metatron is the chief angel, variously described as the Prince of the World, Prince of the Countenance (or Presence), celestial scribe, and even יהוה קטן (*YHVH Qatan*), "Lesser *YHVH*" (3 Enoch 12:5, based on Exodus 23:21). In Heikhalot literature, Metatron is also identified with Enoch, who ascended to heaven without dying. See BT *Sanhedrin* 38b; *Ḥagigah* 15a; *Yevamot* 16b; *Tosafot, Yevamot* 16b, s.v. *pasuq zeh*; Scholem, *Kabbalah*, 377–81; Tishby, *Wisdom of the Zohar*, 2:626–31; Margaliot, *Mal'akhei Elyon*, 73–108.

Metatron is often described as נער (*na'ar*),

Rabbi Yitsḥak said, "What is written of that time? *Abraham said to his servant, elder of his household* (Genesis 24:2). What is implied by *to his servant*? If we are to contemplate this with wisdom, what is *to his servant*?"[69]

Rabbi Yehudah said, "Let us reflect closely on what we have said: the servant of the Omnipresent, the one nearest His service. Who is that? Metatron, in accordance with what we say—that it is he who is destined to beautify the body in the graveyards. This is the meaning of what is written: *Abraham said to his servant*—Metatron, servant of the Omnipresent; *elder of his household*—first of God's creations; *who ruled over all that was his*—for the blessed Holy One gave him dominion over all His legions."[70]

It has been taught: Rabbi Shim'on said in the name of Rabbi Yose in the name of Rav, "All the legions of that servant draw light from, and delight in, the splendor of the soul. As it has been taught: The light of the soul in the world to come is greater than the light of the throne."[71]



"youth, servant, lad" and עבד (*eved*), "servant, slave." See 3 Enoch 4:10; BT *Yevamot* 16b: "Rabbi Shemu'el son of Naḥmani said in the name of Rabbi Yoḥanan, 'This verse was uttered by the Prince of the World: *I have been a youth, I have also been old* (Psalms 37:25). Who said it? If you suggest it was the blessed Holy One, does old age pertain to Him? So David must have said it. But was he so old? Rather you must conclude that the Prince of the World uttered it.'" See also *Bemidbar Rabbah* 12:12.

On Metatron in the *Zohar*, see 1:21a, 37b, 95b, 124b, 143a, 162a–b, 181b, 223b; 2:65b–66b, 131a, 143a, 164a, 169b; 3:217a–b; *ZḤ* 42d–43a, 69b (*ShS*), 85c (*MhN, Rut*). In *MhN* see *Zohar* 1:127a, 128a; *ZḤ* 4a, 8d, 9d–10a, 10b, 12b, 25d–26a, 28a–c; Scholem, "Parashah Ḥadashah," 437 (Addendum 1 in this volume).

On Dumah and the tally-note, see above, *Zohar* 1:123b–124b (*MhN*). On the expression "leaven that bone," see *Pirqei de-Rabbi Eli'ezer* 34: "Rabbi Shim'on says, 'All bodies crumble into the dust of the earth until nothing remains except a spoonful of decayed matter. This mingles with the dust like leaven mixed with dough. In the time to come... it resurrects the entire body.'" See *Bereshit Rabbah* 28:3; *Vayiqra Rabbah* 18:1; *Zohar* 1:69a, 113a (*MhN*), 116a (*MhN*), 137a (*MhN*); 2:28b; 3:222a, 270b; Moses de León, *Sefer ha-Rimmon*, 271; idem, *Sefer ha-Mishqal*, 87.

See *Zohar* 1:181b for a close parallel on Metatron and the resurrection. See also *Zohar* 1:128b (*MhN*).

69. **If we are to contemplate this with wisdom, what is *to his servant*?** Genesis 24:2–4 reads: *Abraham said to his servant, elder of his household who ruled over all that was his, "Place your hand under my thigh and I will have you swear by* YHVH *the God of heaven and the God of earth that you shall not take a wife for my son from the daughters of the Canaanites among whom I dwell, but [rather] to my land and to my kindred you shall go and get a wife for my son Isaac."*

If we are to pursue the allegory, and Abraham signifies the soul and the passage at hand refers to the resurrection, what is the soul's servant?

70. **servant of the Omnipresent . . .** Reading the possessive pronoun as referring to God rather than Abraham.

On Metatron as the first of God's creations, see Moses de León, *Or Zaru'a*, 259–60; *ZḤ* 4a, 7d, 8d, 16a (all *MhN*). See also *Zohar* 1:149a (*ST*), 181b; 3:215a (*RM*). On Metatron's dominion, see *ZḤ* 9d (*MhN*).

71. **The light of the soul...** Metatron's

But the soul was drawn from the throne?![72]

Well, this in accordance with what is fitting, and that in accordance with what is fitting.[73]

Rav Naḥman said, "Greater than the light of the throne, indeed! As is written: [*Upon the image of a throne*] *an image like the appearance of a human being upon it above* (Ezekiel 1:26). What is meant by עליו (*alav*), *upon it*? על (*al*), Exceeding, its radiance."[74]

When he goes to perform His mission, all his legions and his chariot are nourished by that radiance, as is written that the soul says to him: *Place your hand* (Genesis 24:2)—namely your entourage, *under my thigh* (ibid.). This is the light that flows upon the soul.[75]

Rabbi Yehudah son of Rabbi Shalom said, "So have we received: When this one embarks on the mission of the Omnipresent, the blessed Holy One propels all His legions above by a single letter of His Name."[76]

Rav Huna said, "It is as follows: ירכי (*yerekhi*), *my thigh*, has the numerical value of רם (*ram*), exalted. In other words, the soul says *Put your hand*—your entourage—under the grade of the Exalted and Supreme, ruling over all. Once he [Abraham] has ordered the celestial entourage under His charge, [the soul says] 'I will make you swear a great oath by Him.'"[77]



hosts bask in, and derive power from, the soul's light—for in the world to come, the soul exceeds the throne. See *ZḤ* 26a (*MhN*).

72. **But the soul was drawn from the throne?!** How can the derived exceed the source? On the soul's originating from the divine throne, see above, note 61.

73. **this in accordance... that in accordance...** In this world, the soul hails from the throne and thus lies below it. But after death, the soul of the righteous ascends on high, transcending the grade of the throne. See *Zohar* 1:123a (*MhN*); *ZḤ* 26a (*MhN*).

74. ***an image like the appearance of a human being upon it above...*** Ezekiel's vision of the divine chariot culminates with a vision of a luminescent figure sitting upon a throne, itself resting above the heads of the angelic beings. The superiority of the soul is thereby confirmed. Cf. *Matoq mi-Devash.*

75. **When he goes to perform His mission...** Metatron's legions are propelled by the power of the soul on high. The soul has Metatron place his hand, i.e., his legions through which he acts in the world, under the soul's power, *my thigh.* Cf. *Zohar* 1:181b.

76. **by a single letter of His Name** Apparently the first י (*yod*) of the divine name. Alternatively, the heavenly legions are propelled by the ה (*he*) bestowed upon the soul.

See *Zohar* 1:127b (*MhN*); *ZḤ* 28b–c (*MhN*).

77. **ירכי (*yerekhi*), *my thigh*, has the numerical value of רם (*ram*), exalted...** Both equal 240. Rav Huna offers a different interpretation of Abraham's (the soul's) request that Metatron place his hand under Abraham's thigh. Perhaps because of Metatron's elevated status, and lest there be no confusion between Metatron and the blessed Holy One, the soul seeks to have Metatron place his entourage in God's charge.

The oath is explained below. See note 81.

Rabbi Yitsḥak said, "[*Place your hand under my thigh; and I will have you swear by YHVH*] *the God of heaven and the God of earth* (ibid., 3). Since he said *by YHVH*—who is all—why does it say *God of heaven and the God of earth*?"

Rav Yehudah said, "Because He is the Lord of all. Simultaneously, in a single moment He propels all; all are as naught [127a] compared to Him."[78]

Rabbi Yitsḥak says, "By two letters from His name; to demonstrate that He is all—and there is no other beside Him."[79]

*And I will have you swear by YHVH the God of heaven and the God of earth.* Rav Huna said, "Had I been with the Masters of Mishnah when they revealed this mystery, I would not have separated from them in this manner. For I see great profundities in their utterances; they have disclosed, though not manifestly for just any one! Come and see: The soul adjures this covenantal oath, as is written: *that you shall not take a wife for my son* (ibid.)."[80]



Rabbi Yitsḥak said, "From here is implied: Since you are embarking on this mission *you shall not take a wife for my son*—namely do not take a body for my son—to enter a different body, a foreign body, a body not fitting him. Rather, in the one that is mine precisely, in precisely the one from which I departed, as is written: *But to my land and to my kindred you shall go* (ibid., 4)."[81]

Rabbi Yose said, "What is the significance of *you shall take a wife for my son,* ליצחק (*le-yitsḥaq*), *for Isaac* (ibid.)?"[82]

Rabbi Yitsḥak said, "The same body that suffered with me in that world, which derived no pleasure or delight therein for fear of its owner, that same body precisely you must take, ליצחק (*le-yitsḥaq*), to laugh, with it in that joy of

78. **Because He is the Lord of all...** According to Rav Yehudah, the supplementary "*the God of heaven and the God of earth*" merely indicates God's absolute dominion.

79. **By two letters from His name...** According to Rabbi Yitsḥak, the supplementary epithets in the oath attest to God's propelling the heavenly host by two letters from His name (rather than one): apparently י (*yod*) and ה (he), or perhaps ו (*vav*) and ה (*he*). See *Matoq mi-Devash* and *Sullam.*

80. **I would not have separated from them in this manner...** Namely, without fully grasping their words. The Masters of Mishnah have disclosed the secret of the passage—though in a manner that conceals the secret from those not worthy. The secret pertains to the soul's adjuration of Metatron, as explained in the following paragraph.

On the Masters of Mishnah, see above, note 40.

81. ***you shall not take a wife...*** In the biblical narrative, Abraham adjures his servant: *you shall not take a wife for my son from the daughters of the Canaanites among whom I dwell, but* [*rather*] *to my land and to my kindred you shall go and get a wife for my son Isaac.* In the *Zohar*'s reading, the soul (*Abraham*) adjures Metatron (the *servant*) not to take a foreign body (*a wife... from the... Canaanites*) for the soul (*my son Isaac*). The servant is thus sworn to reunite the soul with its original body (*my land... my kindred*).

See *Zohar* 1:181b.

On the resurrection of the original body, see above, note 64.

82. **What is the significance of...*for Isaac*?** Why for Isaac? If we are speaking

the righteous; ליצחק (*le-yitsḥaq*), to laugh, with it in the joy of the blessed Holy One; ליצחק (*le-yitsḥaq*), to laugh, with it—for now is the time of laughter in the world, as is written: *Then will our mouths fill with laughter*... (Psalms 126:2)."[83]

Rabbi Yehudah son of Yitsḥak said, "Come and hear: One angel does not perform two missions, and it has been taught: An angel only ever performs one mission at a time. It has been taught: Rabbi Abba said, 'A certain angel *with a scribe's kit at his waist* (Ezekiel 9:3) is destined to inscribe each and every one [righteous person] upon his forehead, and afterward the great prince will proceed to restore each one, preparing him to receive his soul, as is written: *He shall send His angel before you; and you shall take a wife [for my son from there]* (Genesis 24:7). What is meant by *before you*? Before your mission.'"[84]

Rabbi El'azar went to see his teacher Rabban Yoḥanan son of Zakkai; that day was *Rosh Ḥodesh*. When he reached him, he said to him, "What does a brimming well, filled and flowing profusely on its own, seek here?"[85]



about taking a body for the soul, it should say for Abraham!

83. **that same body precisely you must take, ליצחק (*le-yitsḥaq*), to laugh...** Abraham, the soul, instructs Metatron to take a body ליצחק (*le-yitsḥaq*), *for Isaac*, meaning to laugh and rejoice. The name יצחק (*yitsḥaq*) derives from the root צחק (*tsḥq*), "laugh."

See BT *Berakhot* 31a, in the name of Rabbi Shim'on son of Yoḥai: "It is forbidden for a person to fill his mouth with laughter in this world, as is said: *Then will our mouth fill with laughter and our tongue with glad song* (Psalms 126:2). When? At the time when *they will say among the nations: 'Great things has YHVH done with these'* (ibid., 3)." See *Zohar* 1:114a, 115a (both *MhN*). See also BT *Pesaḥim* 119b.

84. **An angel only ever performs one mission at a time...** See *Bereshit Rabbah* 50:2.

Before Metatron (the great prince) restores the bodies of the righteous, the angel Gabriel first marks those to be revived.

See Ezekiel 9:3–4: *He* [YHVH] *called to the man dressed in linen with the scribe's kit at his waist, and YHVH said to him, "Pass through the city, through Jerusalem, and put a mark on the foreheads of those who moan and groan over all the abominations beings committed in it."* According to BT *Shabbat* 55a, this angel is Gabriel. On Gabriel's role in the resurrection, see below, *Zohar* 1:128b (*MhN*), page 392.

85. **What does a brimming well ...** Rabbi Yoḥanan wonders what his brilliant disciple could possibly want to learn from him.

"Brimming well" renders בירא דלא צדייא (*beira de-la tsadayya*), literally "a well that is not desolate," as per OM1, V1, V9, and V22. The printed editions read בירא דלסריין (*beira dilsaryyan*). *Dilsaryyan* is difficult and not attested in the manuscripts, though C9 reads דלסדיין (*dilsadyyan*). See *Derekh Emet*; *Sullam*, Edri, *Matoq mi-Devash*, Mopsik.

Rabbi El'azar son of Arakh was an outstanding student of Rabban Yoḥanan son of Zakkai who engaged in speculation on the *merkavah* (the divine chariot). See M *Avot* 2:8; *Tosefta Ḥagigah* 2:1; JT *Ḥagigah* 2:1, 77a; BT *Ḥagigah* 14b; David Luria, *Shem ha-Eḥad Eli'ezer* (preface to *Pirqei de-Rabbi Eli'ezer*), n. 4.

According to *Avot* 2:8, El'azar is described by his teacher as an overflowing spring.

See also *Pirqei de-Rabbi Eli'ezer* 2: "[Rabbi Yoḥanan] said to him [Rabbi Eli'ezer son of Hyrcanus], 'I will tell you a parable. To what

He replied, "A person is obliged [127b] to receive the countenance of his teacher."[86]

He said to him, "That is not what I meant. Rather, I see on your face that a new word is with you, of those profundities you constantly pursue."[87]

He said to him, "I see that primal light whose journeyings are ten; in ten it sallies; by the mystery of ten it governs all; and through letters ten it enacts its enactments.[88]

"It has been taught: Ten notes; ten keys to the graveyard are in his hand; and ten notes he receives in the Garden of Eden to prime the earth for the bodies of the righteous."[89]

He said to him, "El'azar, my son, you have seen more than the holy angel! For the world was created by ten; by ten is it governed; by ten the holy throne;



can you be compared? To this fountain, which is bubbling and sending forth its waters; and it is able to effect a discharge more powerful than what it takes in. Similarly, you are able to speak words of Torah in excess of what Moses received at Sinai.'"

86. **to receive the countenance of his teacher** On the obligation to visit one's teacher on the New Moon, see BT *Sukkah* 27b; *Rosh ha-Shanah* 16b; *Zohar* 3:265b.

87. **I see on your face that a new word is with you...** Rabbi El'azar goes to receive his teacher's countenance, but it is the teacher who reads the student's face. See *Zohar* 1:96b; 3:6a, 157a; *ZḤ* 72a (*ShS*).

88. **I see that primal light...** Were this passage in the main body of the *Zohar*, one would assume that the "primal light" refers to *Ein Sof* and that the decades allude to the ten *sefirot* in which *Ein Sof* is arrayed and through which it governs the world. As a general rule, however, *MhN* on the Torah does not employ this essential aspect of kabbalistic teaching. However, this enigmatic passage is written in Aramaic and seems to "interrupt" the Hebrew text. According to some recent scholarship, even *MhN* on the Torah is comprised of diverse layers—an earlier Hebrew layer and a later Aramaic layer. Thus even though the "late" Aramaic layer does not reflect the main Zoharic theosophy, we cannot dismiss the possibility that it is aware of this theosophy in one way or another. See Scholem's notes, ad loc.: "Here is an allusion to the ten *sefirot* in *Midrash ha-Ne'lam.*"

Assuming the absence of kabbalistic theosophy in this passage, the "primal light" may refer to the original light of creation, and the decades may refer to various potencies through which the world was created. See M *Avot* 5:1; BT *Ḥagigah* 12a; *Sefer Yetsirah* 1.

In light of what follows, it is also possible that the primal light may refer to Metatron (see *ZḤ* 8d, 16a (both *MhN*)), in which case the decades may allude to angelic potencies or even the ten intellects of medieval philosophy. See also *Zohar* 1:181b. On Metatron, see above, note 68.

See *Nitsotsei Orot*, *Sullam*, and *Matoq mi-Devash* for various interpretations.

89. **Ten notes; ten keys...** Corresponding to the various decades above, Metatron possesses ten notes and ten keys with which to revive the dead. The notes contain the names of the righteous, who are fit for resurrection. Apparently, the ten notes from the Garden of Eden contain the names of the souls on high and the bodies to which they belong. See *Zohar* 1:123b–124b, 126a–b (both *MhN*).

by ten the Torah; He by ten; His journeyings by ten; the upper worlds by ten—and One exalted above all (may He be blessed).[90]

"I shall tell you a word. The Masters of Mishnah pondered this. What is the meaning of the verse *The servant took ten camels from his lord's camels and went* (Genesis 24:10)?"[91]

He said to him, "Rabbi, I have attained this verse. But what is the significance of *with all the bounty of his lord in his hand* (ibid.)?"

He replied, "This is the name of his Master, which goes with him to escort him and guide him."[92]

He said, "This is certainly the meaning of *for My name is within him* (Exodus 23:21)."[93]

We have learned: Rabbi Abbahu said, "Come and see: Whoever knows His name clearly, knows that He and His name are one; the blessed Holy One and His name are one, as is written: *YHVH is one [and His name one]* (Zechariah 14:9), namely the name and He are one."[94]

Rabbi Abba said, "One must contemplate this portion: *He had the camels kneel outside the city by the well of water [at evening time]* (Genesis 24:11)."[95]



90. **world was created by ten...** Again, the referents of the various decades are unclear. See above, note 88.

See *Sullam* and *Matoq mi-Devash* for various interpretations of this passage.

On seeing more than the holy angel (which may refer to Metatron), see *Zohar* 1:140a (*MhN*); *ZḤ* 26b (*MhN*).

91. ***The servant took ten camels...*** The verse continues: *with all the bounty of his lord in his hand; and he rose and went to Aram-naharaim, to the city of Nahor.*

The servant is Metatron, and the ten camels presumably correspond to the ten notes and ten keys with which he goes to revive the dead. Cf. *Zohar* 1:181b.

On the epithet "Masters of Mishnah," see above, note 40.

92. **This is the name of his Master...** The bounty carried by the servant is the name of God, perhaps referring to שדי (*Shaddai*) and/or *Shekhinah*. On *Shaddai*, see next note.

On *Shekhinah* as God's name, see *Targum Onqelos* and *Targum Yerushalmi* on Exodus 20:21.

93. ***for My name is within him*** See Exodus 23:20–21: *I am sending an angel before You.... Watch yourself with him and heed his voice; do not rebel against him, for he will not pardon your transgression—for My name is within him.*

According to BT *Sanhedrin* 38b, the angel is Metatron. See also Rashi on Exodus 23:21: "His name is like his Master's—Metatron has the numerical value of Shaddai [314]."

See Moses de León, *Or Zaru'a*, 259–60, 271–73; *Zohar* 1:149a (*ST*); 3:215a, 231a (both *RM*); *ZḤ* 28b (*MhN*).

94. **He and His name are one...** Though we speak of God's name as though it were a separate entity, God and His name are an inseparable unity.

In the main body of the *Zohar*, the verse from Zechariah often implies that *Tif'eret* (known as *YHVH*) and *Shekhinah* (known as *His name*) are one. It can also imply the unity of all the *sefirot* and *Ein Sof*. See *Zohar* 1:29a, 246b; 2:10a, 134a, 161b–162a; 3:7b, 56a, 77b.

95. ***He had the camels kneel...*** Cf. *Zohar* 1:181b.

Rabbi Abba said, "*Outside the city*—the graveyard; *by the well of water*—for it has been taught: The first from the graves are those who traded in Torah. As we have learned: When a person enters the grave, what is he asked? Whether he set aside times for Torah, as is written: *He will be the faithfulness of your times...* (Isaiah 33:6). When he comes forth, is it not fitting to raise them first?!"[96]

Rabbi Abba said, "*At evening time* (Genesis 24:11)—the sixth day, Sabbath eve, the time to raise [128a] the dead. How is this implied? For we have learned: The world will exist for six thousand years. It is the sixth millennium, culmination of all. This is the significance of *at evening time*—time of the culmination of all. *At the time when the water-drawers come out* (ibid.)—the disciples of the wise who draw the waters of Torah; for it is the time to come out and to shake off the dust."[97]

Rabbi Abba also said, "One must know yet more! As we have learned: Those who strive to know their Creator in this world, and whose souls abide perfected in the world to come, [such that they merit] to come forth by virtue of the soul's oath—he [Metatron] goes to find out which body is precisely hers, and to determine its nature. *Here I am: poised by the spring of water* (ibid., 43)—even though he is a disciple of the wise, he inquires after perfection, as is written: *let it be that the young woman who comes out to draw water to whom I say, 'Let me drink a bit of water from your jug'* (ibid.)—'tell me an intimation of what you



96. **The first from the graves...** Scholars who plied the waters of Torah are the first to enjoy the resurrection. See *Zohar* 1:140a (*MhN*), 175b, 182a.

See BT *Sanhedrin* 7a: "Rav Hamnuna said, 'The first matter for which a person is judged [in the world to come] is regarding the study of the Torah, as is said: *The beginning of a quarrel* [or: *judgment*] *is the letting out of water* [i.e., Torah] (Proverbs 17:14).'"

The full verse from Isaiah reads: *He will be the faithfulness of your times, stronghold of salvation, wisdom, and knowledge; the awe of YHVH is his treasure.* In rabbinic tradition, this verse alludes to Torah study. See BT *Shabbat* 31a: "Rava said, 'When a human is led in for judgment, he is asked, "Were you honest in your business dealings, did you set aside times for Torah, did you generate new life, did you await salvation, did you engage in the dialectics of wisdom, did you understand one thing from another?"'" See also *Seder Eliyyahu Rabbah* 15; *Shemot Rabbah* 30:14; *Zohar* 2:223a.

On graveyards being located outside the city, see M *Bava Batra* 2:9.

97. ***At evening time*—the sixth day, Sabbath eve...** As the six days of Creation were followed by Sabbath, so the world will exist for 6000 years, followed by a millennial Sabbath. The sixth millennium itself began shortly before the appearance of the *Zohar* (in the year 1240/41 C.E.) and is pictured as the eve of the cosmic Sabbath.

See BT *Sanhedrin* 97a: Rav Kattina said, 'The world will exist for six thousand years—and for one thousand lie desolate.'" See *Zohar* 1:116b–117a, 119a, 139b–140a (*MhN*), 181b–182a; 2:9b–10a; *ZḤ* 16d (*MhN*), 56b–c.

On the "world to come" as Sabbath, see BT *Berakhot* 57b; *Avodah Zarah* 3a; *Rut Rabbah* 3:3.

have attained of knowledge of Him'; *And she says to me, 'Drink you also'* (ibid., 44)—'you are also a servant like me! I have not confused knowledge of you with knowledge of the Omnipresent (may He be blessed). You must grasp that you are a created being like me.' *'I will also draw for your camels'* (ibid.)—'namely the knowledge I have attained that your entourage has not attained. I know that there is a degree beyond you, and how you were created from the splendor bestowed upon you.' If he speaks [thus], then all these things will be a sign for me, and I will know that she is the wife—the body belonging to the perfect soul that adjured me."[98]

*He had barely finished speaking...* (ibid., 15). Rabbi Yitsḥak said in the name of Rabbi Yehudah, "While testing the body with all these matters, what is written? *Look, Rebekah was coming out* (ibid.)—this is the holy body, which engaged in words of Torah, pounding itself to know and comprehend its Maker."[99]

בת בתואל (*Bat Betu'el*), *Daughter of Bethuel* (ibid., 47). Rav Yehudah said, "בתו של אל (*Bito shel el*), The daughter of God; בן מלכה (*ben Milkah*), *child of Milcah* (ibid., 15)—בן מלכה (*ben malkah*), child of the queen, of the world; *the wife of Nahor, Abraham's brother* (ibid.)—company of the intellect, body cleaving to intellect, brother of soul; *with her jug on her shoulder* —the weight of wisdom upon her."[100]



98. ***And she says to me, 'Drink you also'...*** From the servant's reprise of what he said to God as he stood by the well: *Here I am, poised by the spring of water; let it be that the young woman who comes out to draw water to whom I say, "Let me drink a bit of water from your jug" and she says to me, "Drink you also and I will also draw for your camels"—she is the wife whom YHVH has appointed for my lord's son.* See also Genesis 24:13–14.

The servant's test of Rebekah's character is interpreted here as an allegory for Metatron's test of the body's worthiness to be resurrected. See *Zohar* 1:182a.

Curiously, the body (rather than the soul) must display its knowledge to Metatron. The key element of this knowledge comprises the understanding that Metatron himself (the active face of divinity, perhaps also the Active Intellect) is not God; rather, he is a created being—just like the human being. (See BT *Ḥagigah* 15a, where Aḥer's great sin consists in the divinization of Metatron.)

The soul's oath refers to the soul having adjured Metatron to reunite the soul with her original body. See *Zohar* 1:127a (*MhN*), page 386.

99. ***Rebekah was coming out...*** Rebekah is now the signifier for the holy risen body.

The full verse reads: *He had barely finished speaking when, look, Rebekah was coming out—who was born to Bethuel son of Milcah, the wife of Nahor, Abraham's brother—with her jug on her shoulder.*

100. ***Daughter of Bethuel...*** The genealogical note about Rebekah is transformed into a concise description of the relationship between body and soul. Rebekah, the resurrected body, is born to/designated for Bethuel, *bito shel el*, the daughter of God, namely the soul, which in turn is the child of Milcah, the child of *malkah*, the queen, namely, the *Shekhinah*. The resurrected body is also the wife of נחור (*Naḥor*), read here as נהור (*nahor*), light, signifying the intellect, and finally, Abraham's brother, namely, the

*The servant ran toward her* (ibid., 17)—Metatron; *and said,* [128b] *"Please, let me sip a bit of water from your jug"* (ibid.)—"tell me a hint of the wisdom of the knowledge of your Creator with which you were engaged in the world you departed." Rabbi Abba said, "As we have explained."

Following all this, what is written? *I put the ring on her nose and the bands on her arms* (ibid., 47). Rabbi Abba said, "The bones that had scattered here and there—he binds them and weighs them, one upon the other, as is said: *and invigorate your bones* (Isaiah 58:11)."[101]

Rabbi Abba said, "At that time, the body stands in the land of Israel, and there its soul enters within."[102]

Rabbi Yoḥanan said, "Who leads the body to the land of Israel?"

Rabbi Zeira said, "The blessed Holy One fashions subterranean tunnels and they roll, reaching the land of Israel, as is written: *And earth will bring forth shades* (ibid. 26:19)."[103]

Rabbi Yitsḥak said, "Gabriel leads them to the land of Israel. How do we know? For it is written: *Will you go with this man?* (Genesis 24:58), and it is written there: *The man Gabriel* (Daniel 9:21)."[104]



brother of soul. (Intellect and soul appear to be synonymous; see *Zohar* 1:109a–b; *ZḤ* 10a (both *MhN*)).

On the soul as the child of the *Shekhinah*, cf. *Zohar* 1:125b (*MhN*), page 381, where the Throne of Glory is described as the mother of soul. In the main body of the *Zohar*, the soul is often presented as the offspring of *Tif'eret* and *Shekhinah*, the masculine and feminine grades of divinity.

On Bethuel as *bito shel el*, see *Zohar* 1:137a (*MhN*). On the soul as the daughter of God, cf. *Zohar* 2:96b.

101. ***I put the ring on her nose and the bands on her arms...*** According to the narrative in Genesis 24, the servant adorns Rebekah with jewelry. Read allegorically, having determined that the body is indeed worthy of resurrection, Metatron proceeds to rebuild the body, assessing and then binding the scattered bones in the grave. See *Zohar* 1:126a–b (*MhN*), page 383.

On Isaiah 58:11, see *Zohar* 1:113b–114a (*MhN*), 141a; 2:142b.

102. **there its soul enters within** See *Zohar* 1:69a, 113b (*MhN*), 114a–b (*MhN*), 131a.

103. **subterranean tunnels and they roll...** See BT *Ketubbot* 111a: "Rabbi Yirmeyah son of Abba said in the name of Rabbi Yoḥanan, 'Whoever walks four cubits in the land of Israel is assured membership in the world to come.' Now... aren't the righteous outside the Land going to be revived? Rabbi Il'a replied, 'By rolling [underground to the land of Israel].' Rabbi Abba Sala the Great objected, 'Rolling will be painful to the righteous.' Abbaye replied, 'Tunnels will be made for them underground.'"

See *Zohar* 1:69a, 113b (*MhN*), 131a.

On Isaiah 26:19, see *Pirqei de-Rabbi Eli'ezer* 34; *Zohar* 1:113a (*MhN*), 182a; 2:199b.

104. **Gabriel leads them to the land of Israel...** According to the narrative in Genesis 24, Rebekah's family ask her whether she is willing to go with Abraham's agent to become Isaac's wife. Elsewhere, Daniel uses the same term to describe the angel Gabriel as God's agent. On the grounds that the terminology is the same, the two figures are here considered identical.

See *Zohar* 1:127a (*MhN*), page 387.

Rabbi Yose said, "What is the significance of *Rebekah had a brother named Laban* (Genesis 24:29)?"[105]

Rabbi Yitsḥak said, "The evil impulse is not eliminated from the world; though not present in entirety, a fraction remains. Come and see! Originally, when thrust into this world he was called Lot. In the world to come he will be eliminated from the world, but not entirely; he is called Laban—not as repulsive as at first, but rather like one who was cleansed of his disgrace."[106]

Why is Laban necessary?[107]

Rabbi Shim'on said, "To enable procreation."

As Rabbi Shim'on said: "If there is no evil impulse, there is no procreation."[108]

105. ***Rebekah had a brother named Laban*** If Rebekah signifies the risen holy body, what is signified by her brother Laban?

106. **The evil impulse is not eliminated...** The name Laban (meaning "white") signifies the cleansed evil impulse. In the post-resurrection world, the base quality of the evil impulse will be eliminated, though its purer and refined aspect will remain. Lot (meaning "cursed") becomes pure Laban ("white").

On the abolition of the evil impulse in the post-resurrection world, see BT *Sukkah* 52a; *Shemot Rabbah* 41:7; *Tanḥuma* (Buber), *Bereshit* 40, *Qedoshim* 15; Naḥmanides on Deuteronomy 30:6; *Zohar* 1:109a, 137a–138a (both *MhN*). Cf. *Zohar* 1:124a, 127a, 131a.

See also Isaiah 25:7: *He will destroy on this mount* פני הלוט (*pnei ha-lot*), *the shroud*, הלוט (*ha-lot*), *that is drawn, over the faces of all the peoples, and the covering that is spread over all the nations.*

On Lot as the evil impulse, see *Zohar* 1:78a, 79a (both *ST*); 109a–110b (*MhN*); *ZḤ* 24b, 24d (both *MhN*). On the evil impulse as "repulsive," see BT *Sukkah* 52b.

107. **Why is Laban necessary?** Why is any evil impulse required in the post-resurrection world?

108. **If there is no evil impulse, there is no procreation** In the post-resurrection world there is still procreation. Cf. BT *Berakhot* 17a: "A pearl in the mouth of Rav: 'In the world to come there is no eating or drinking or procreation or business or jealousy or hatred or competition; rather, the righteous sit with their crowns on their heads, basking in the radiance of *Shekhinah*.'" See also *Midrash Tehillim* 146:4; Maimonides, *Mishneh Torah, Hilkhot Teshuvah* 8:2.

On the relationship between the evil impulse and sexual arousal and procreation, see *Bereshit Rabbah* 9:7: "Naḥman said in the name of Rabbi Shemu'el, '*Behold, it was very good*—this is the good impulse; *And behold it was very good* (Genesis 1:31)—this is the evil impulse. Is the evil impulse *very good*? How astonishing! Yet were it not for the evil impulse, no man would ever build a house, marry a woman, or engender children.'"

According to BT *Yoma* 69b, in the days of Ezra and Nehemiah, the leaders of the Israelites prayed that the evil impulse be eliminated. The impulse to commit idolatry was handed over to them, and they cast it into a lead pot with a lead cover, rendering it powerless. They prayed further and the sexual impulse was also handed over to them, but a prophet warned, "'Realize that if you kill him, the world will be destroyed [because the desire to procreate will vanish].' They imprisoned him for three days; and they looked throughout the whole land of Israel for a fresh egg and could not find it. They said, 'What should we do? If we kill him, the world will be destroyed.'... They

Come and hear: Once the body has been built and stands intact, what is written? *They sent off Rebekah their sister and her nurse* (ibid., 59). What is the significance of *and her nurse*? This is the power of movement.[109]

Rabbi Yitsḥak said, "This is the power of the body."

Rabbi Abbahu opened with this verse: *With me from Lebanon, bride; with me from Lebanon come!...* (Song of Songs 4:8).

Rabbi Abbahu said, "After the body has been built intact and is brought to the land of Israel to receive its soul, the soul awaits it and goes forth toward it, as is said: *Isaac went forth to stroll in the field* (Genesis 24:63). This is the meaning of *With me from Lebanon, bride* (Song of Songs 4:8)—this is the soul; *Look down* [129a] *from the peak of Amana* (ibid.)—as is written: *and he raised his eyes and saw; [and look, camels were coming]* (Genesis 24:63)."[110]

Rabbi Yehudah said, "If the soul, then Abraham is suitable, as we have said! But Isaac—what does that signify?"[111]

Rabbi Abbahu said, "The Companions have said that now she is called Isaac on account of the great joy in the world."[112]



Rabbi Abbahu said, "At first Abraham and the body Sarah. Now the soul is Isaac and the body Rebekah."

We have learned in our Mishnah: Rabbi Shim'on said, "For forty years prior the vivification of the body, the soul awaits the body in the land of Israel. In which place? In the site of the Temple."[113]

blinded him and let him go. This helped inasmuch as he no longer entices a person to commit incest."

See *Zohar* 1:49a, 61a, 137b–138a (*MhN*); 3:189a.

109. **power of movement** This term, which does not appear in Jewish philosophical literature, may derive from Naḥmanides, who mentions "the soul of movement" to describe the animal soul. See his *Commentary on the Torah*, Genesis 1:22, 26, 29; 2:7; *Zohar* 1:109b (*MhN*); *ZḤ* 14b (*MhN*); Tishby, *Wisdom of the Zohar*, 2:706.

110. ***Isaac went forth to stroll in the field...*** Isaac, signifying the soul, goes forth to meet the body (Rebekah) coming to the land of Israel. Apparently, the verse from the Song of Songs is being spoken by the *Shekhinah* who is escorting the bride, namely the soul, from Lebanon, the Temple, to meet the body at the border of the land of Israel (the peak of Amana). The camels seen by Isaac signify the body—the mount for the soul.

On the verse from the Song of Songs, see *Zohar* 2:5b (*MhN*). See also *Mekhilta, Pisḥa* 14; *Shir ha-Shirim Rabbah* on 4:8. On souls in the land of Israel, cf. *Pirqei de-Rabbi Eli'ezer* 34: "Rabbi Ḥanina said, 'All the righteous who die outside the Land, their souls are gathered into the Land, as is said: *The soul of my lord will be bound in the bundle of life* (1 Samuel 25:29).'"

111. **If the soul, then Abraham is suitable...** Rabbi Yehudah wonders why Rabbi Abbahu has just designated the soul as Isaac. Throughout *MhN*, Abraham has signified the soul.

112. **Isaac on account of the great joy...** At the resurrection, the soul is known as יצחק (*Yitsḥaq*), Isaac, whose name derives from צחק (*tsaḥaq*), laugh. See *Zohar* 1:127a (*MhN*) and note 83.

113. **forty years prior the vivification...**

Rabbi Abbahu said, "Come and see: *He took Rebekah as his wife, and he loved her. So Isaac was comforted after his mother* (ibid., 67)—he loves that body and is comforted by it; and it is a time for laughter and joy in the world."[114]

Rabbi Yehudah said, "Look, this entire portion has been clarified for us, but I am unable to comprehend the meaning of *Once again, Abraham took a wife, and her name was Keturah* (Genesis 25:1). Reason would suggest that the whole passage is contradictory!"[115]

When Rav Dimi arrived, he said, "I have heard about this passage, but I cannot recall!"[116]

They said, "If the towering supernals were not inclined to disclose, what can we say?"[117]

Rabbi Yehudah arose and said, "In the academy of our companions, the Masters of Mishnah, it is revealed!"[118]

They arose and went—he, Rabbi Yeisa, and Rabbi Ḥiyya. They found Rabbi El'azar son of Rabbi Shim'on revealing supernal mysteries of *tefillin*. They entered in his presence and said, "In what is our master engaged?"[119]



See *Zohar* 1:136b–137a; 139a–140a (both *MhN*).

On the souls waiting in the Temple, see Luria note 32 on *Pirqei de-Rabbi Eli'ezer* 34 (above, note 110). On the expression "our Mishnah," see above, note 48.

114. ***So Isaac was comforted after his mother...*** Isaac (the soul) unites with his wife Rebekah (the risen holy body) and is comforted after his mother, Sarah, his former body.

115. **Reason would suggest that the whole passage is contradictory!** The preceding homilies outlined the resurrection of the body (Rebekah) and its union with the soul (Isaac), thereby concluding the eschatological drama. Furthermore, according to Rabbi Abbahu, following this union the soul is now known as Isaac. Rabbi Yehudah wonders what might be the significance of the passage outlining Abraham's taking another wife and engendering yet more offspring. Hasn't Abraham, signifying the pre-resurrection soul, completed his task?

Extending until the middle of *Zohar* 1:130a at "Rabbi Abba said," the text is in Aramaic.

116. **When Rav Dimi arrived...** The expression "When Rav Dimi arrived" appears frequently throughout the Babylonian Talmud. Apparently he served as the bearer of traditions from the land of Israel to the academy in Pumbedita, Babylon. See *Zohar* 1:100a (*MhN*), where Rav Dimi is able to solve an apparent contradiction.

117. **towering supernals were not inclined to disclose...** In the absence of a tradition explaining the passage, the anonymous sages are dumbstruck. Expressed differently, they opt for exegetical conservatism. See *Derekh Emet.*

118. **In the academy of... the Masters of Mishnah, it is revealed!** Rabbi Yehudah insists not only that the passage's mystery has been revealed, but also that he is going to find out for himself! The Masters of Mishnah (including Rabbi Yehudah) thus represent interpretative freedom and curiosity. Where others are silent and/or fear to tread, the Masters of Mishnah boldly assert themselves. Here then, they approximate the exegetical spirit of the Companions in the main body of the *Zohar*. Cf. *Zohar* 3:79b. See Huss, *Ke-Zohar ha-Raqi'a*, 38–42.

On the Masters of Mishnah, see above, note 40.

119. **Rabbi Yeisa...** Some of the manuscripts read Rabbi Yose.

He replied, "I was explaining the significance of *tefillin*. For happy is the man who dons *tefillin* and fathoms their significance!"[120]

They said, "If it pleases our master, tell us a word."

He said, "I heard from my father that it was out of the blessed Holy One's great love for Israel that He told them to make Him a Dwelling corresponding to the supernal chariot above, so that He would place His abode with them, as is written: *Have them make Me a sanctuary, and I will dwell among them* (Exodus 25:8). I also heard from my father that the significance of *tefillin* is concealed here in this [129b] verse.[121]

"Come and see: Corresponding to the pattern above, the Sanctuary was made with holy chariots; and afterward the blessed Holy One ensconced His abode



120. **happy is the man who dons *tefillin* and fathoms their significance** Before resolving Rabbi Yehudah's query about the verse concerning Abraham and Keturah, Rabbi El'azar reveals the mystical significance of *tefillin*. His homily is not exegetically related to the verses from Genesis and appears to "interrupt" the discussion. Indeed the tone and content of the entire passage is reminiscent of the main body of the *Zohar*.

*Tefillin* ("phylacteries") consist of two black leather boxes containing passages from the Torah (Exodus 13:1–10, 11–16; Deuteronomy 6:4–9; 11:13–21) written on parchment. They are bound by black leather straps on the left arm and on the head, and are worn (typically by men, as opposed to women or children) during weekday morning services. Each of the biblical passages indicates that the Israelites should place a *sign* upon their hand and a *frontlet* (or *reminder*) between their eyes. In the *tefillah* of the hand, all four passages are written on one piece of parchment in the order of their occurrence in the Torah. The *tefillah* of the head, however, is divided into four compartments, and each of the four passages, written on a separate piece of parchment, is inserted in its own compartment.

By wearing *tefillin* one imitates God, who Himself wears *tefillin*, according to Rabbi Avin in BT *Berakhot* 6a. According to Rabbi Ḥiyya son of Avin, the verse inscribed in God's *tefillin* is 1 Chronicles 17:21: *Who is like Your people Israel, a unique nation on earth?*

The commandment of *tefillin* was widely disregarded in France and Spain in the twelfth and thirteenth centuries. The *Zohar*, seeking to reinforce the commitment to this *mitsvah*, emphasizes its mystical significance. In the main body of the *Zohar*, the *tefillin* encode the mysteries of the *sefirot*, with the two *tefillin* (on the head and the arm) symbolizing *Tif'eret* and *Shekhinah*; and by wearing them faithfully, one unites the divine couple.

See *Tosafot*, *Shabbat* 49a, s.v. *ke-elisha ba'al kenafayim*; Isaac the Blind, *Peirush Sefer Yetsirah*, 4; Ezra of Gerona, *Peirush le-Shir ha-Shirim*, 525; Azriel of Gerona, *Peirush ha-Aggadot*, 4; Naḥmanides on Exodus 13:16; Todros Abulafia, *Otsar ha-Kavod*, *Berakhot* 6a; *Zohar* 1:13b–14a, 141a, 147a; 2:43a–b (*Piq*), 162a; 3:81a, 140a (*IR*), 175b, 236b (*RM*), 262a–263a, 264a, 269a–b; Moses de León, *Sefer ha-Rimmon*, 236–39; Baer, *History*, 1:250; Tishby, *Wisdom of the Zohar*, 3:1161–65.

121. **a Dwelling corresponding to the supernal chariot above...** On the correspondence between the Dwelling and the cosmos/upper worlds, see *Tanḥuma*, *Pequdei* 2; BT *Berakhot* 55a; *Bemidbar Rabbah* 4:13; *Midrash Tadshe* 2; Naḥmanides on Exodus 31:2; *Zohar* 2:127a, 129b, 140b, 149a, 162b, 220b–221a, 222b, 231b, 235b, 277a; *ZḤ* 42d; Tishby, *Wisdom of the Zohar*, 3:872–74.

On the verse from Exodus, see *Zohar* 2:126a, 146a, 222a; 3:4b, 283b.

See also *Tanḥuma*, *Pequdei* 6, *Naso* 11, 16; *Bemidbar Rabbah* 13:2.

with them. In this vein, and following this pattern, the Companions, the Masters of Mishnah, have been aroused by the significance of *tefillin*—that such a man might resemble the supernal chariots: lower chariot, upper chariot, to bring down His Kingship and ensconce His abode upon him.[122]

"We have learned: Inhering within are supernal mysteries and their counterparts: three chariots patterned on holy supernal entities; mysteries of the three letters of the holy, supernal names. Three chariots—three letters; four portions ruling over four. Accordingly: mystery of the triple-crowned *shin* and the quadruple-crowned *shin*. Three kings rule the body; *tefillin* upon him, the blessed Holy One above. These are the *tefillin* of the head.[123]



122. **that such a man might resemble the supernal chariots...** Just as celestial correspondence leads to the indwelling of the divine presence in the Dwelling/Sanctuary, so *tefillin* reflect supernal mysteries, and wearing them leads to the indwelling of the divine presence. According to *Zohar* 1:141a: "the blessed Holy One appears in a person who crowns himself in *tefillin*."

The lower and upper chariots correspond to the *tefillin* of the arm and head, respectively.

See *Matoq mi-Devash* for a different (sefirotic) interpretation.

123. **Inhering within are supernal mysteries ...** Rabbi El'azar proceeds to outline the sublime mysteries encoded in *tefillin*, though the referents are not entirely clear. Interpretation is made more difficult in light of the uncertainty of the presence or absence of Zoharic theosophy in this passage.

The number three perhaps refers to the letter ש (*shin*), which adorns the *tefillin* of the head. (The letter *shin* has the numerical value of 300; and the letter itself contains three strokes.) Possibly the three chariots refer to the three letters of the divine name שדי (*Shaddai*), produced by the letter ש (*shin*) on the *tefillin* of the head; the knot of the straps of the *tefillin* of the head which is in the shape of the letter ד (*dalet*); and the knot on the strap of the *tefillin* of the arm, which is in the shape of the letter י (*yod*). (See BT *Shabbat* 62a and Rashi, ad loc.) Yet another possibility is that the three chariots refer to the three letters found in the divine name יהוה (*YHVH*), namely י ה ו (*yod*, *he*, *vav*). The four portions of the *tefillin* correspond to the four letters of the divine name (see *Zohar* 1:13b).

As noted, the *tefillin* of the head are adorned with the letter *shin*, on one side with a regular *shin* (i.e., with three strokes), and on another side with a decorative *shin* possessing four strokes. Together they reflect the four-lettered name and the three chariots. Cf. *Zohar* 3:262b; Moses de León, *Sefer ha-Rimmon*, 239–40. See also *Zohar* 2:162a–b, where the four portions of the *tefillin* are correlated with the three names *YHVH Eloheinu YHVH* from the *Shema*.

The three kings ruling the body refer to the three main organs: brain, heart, and liver (based on Galen). The initial letters of מוחא (*moḥa*), "brain," לבא (*libba*), "heart," and כבדא (*kavda*), "liver," spell מלך (*melekh*), "king." See Simeon ben Tsemaḥ Duran, *Magen Avot* 5:19: "The experts in medicine agree that there are three major organs in the human being, namely המוח והלב והכבד (*ha-moaḥ ve-halev ve-ha-kaved*), the brain, the heart, and the liver; their sign: מלך (*melekh*), king."

On the three organs, see *Zohar* 1:138a (*MhN*); 2:153a; *ZḤ* 80a (*MhN*, *Rut*); Moses de León, *Sefer ha-Rimmon*, 127.

See also BT *Berakhot* 6a: "*All the peoples of the earth shall see that the name of YHVH is proclaimed upon you, and they shall be in awe of you* (Deuteronomy 28:10).... Rabbi Eli'ezer the Great says, 'This refers to the *tefillin* of the head.'"

See *Matoq mi-Devash* and *Sullam* for dif-

"*Tefillin* of the arm: four portions. The heart rides, resembling the lower chariot; and the lower rides. We have learned further: This rides the arm below, and the heart rides, patterned on the one below—guiding all the heavenly legions in its charge. Similarly, the heart rides below, all the limbs of the body in its charge. Above it, four portions upon the brain of the head, but the blessed Holy One rides—for He is supreme ruler, King of all.[124]

"This spirit of wisdom corresponds with the Sanctuary, as is written: *Make one cherub at one edge, and one cherub at the other edge* (Exodus 25:19); and upon them the abode of the King in four letters—two chariots. Accordingly, heart and brain; heart from here and brain from there—and upon them the abode of the blessed Holy One in four and four portions."[125]

Rabbi El'azar said, "Henceforth the mysteries of the crowns of the letters, the passages in their compartments, and their straps—tradition handed down to Moses at Sinai. Their allusions and all their significations have been revealed in the Thirteen Attributes of Mercy."[126]



ferent (sefirotic) interpretations. See also Mopsik.

124. ***Tefillin* of the arm...** As with the *tefillin* of the head, the *tefillin* of the arm also contain four passages corresponding to the four-lettered name. The remainder of the passage is particularly difficult. The *tefillin* of the arm are placed just below the heart, and hence the heart "rides" upon the *tefillin*. This arrangement resembles the lower chariot, perhaps referring to Metatron (or perhaps *Shekhinah*), who is a chariot for the blessed Holy One. Likewise the lower chariot "rides," apparently meaning that it guides the world; and just as the lower chariot rules the heavenly legions, the heart rules the limbs of the body.

The phrase "This rides the arm below, and the heart rides, patterned on the one below" could also be rendered "This chariot of the arm below—the heart rides, patterned on the one below."

Whatever the precise significations, the following image emerges: the blessed Holy One above illuminates the *tefillin* of the head—and in turn, the brain, the heart; and finally the *tefillin* of the arm—and in turn the arm. While adorned in *tefillin*, the human being is perfectly aligned and linked to the divine.

On the positioning of the *tefillin* of the arm opposite the heart, see BT *Menaḥot* 37b; Maimonides, *Mishneh Torah, Hilkhot Tefillin* 4:2.

See *Matoq mi-Devash*, *Sullam*, and Mopsik for different interpretations.

125. ***Make one cherub at one edge, and one cherub at the other edge...*** The ark in the Dwelling and later in the Temple was adorned with two cherubs. The *Shekhinah* rested above and between them (see Exodus 25:18–22). According to Rabbi El'azar, the *tefillin* follow the same pattern: the two *tefillin* (heart and brain, namely arm and head) correspond to the two cherubs, combining to form a chariot for the *Shekhinah*. The four portions of each *tefillah* correspond to the four-lettered divine name resting upon the wearer. See Baḥya ben Asher on Exodus 13:16.

On the verse from Exodus, see *Bemidbar Rabbah* 4:13; *Tanḥuma, Vayaqhel* 7.

126. **tradition handed down to Moses at Sinai...** According to BT *Menaḥot* 35a–b, many of the intricacies of the laws of *tefillin*, which are not found in the Torah, are mandated as "tradition handed down to Moses at

Rabbi Yehudah said, "Had I come here only for this mystery, it would suffice!"[127]

They said to him, "Happy is your share in the world that is coming, for you are not baffled by any mystery!"

"They said to him, "We came [130a] before our master to comprehend the mystery of this verse: *Once again, Abraham took a wife, and her name was Keturah* (Genesis 25:1)."

He replied, "The meaning of this verse is as revealed by our companions, the Masters of Mishnah. When the soul will enter her holy body, these words [will apply] to the wicked—for they will rise and mend their deeds, and he will grant them from his radiant glory that they will know and repent, and be completely worthy. When Solomon saw this, he was greatly astounded and said: *So I saw the wicked buried and coming, going from the holy site* (Ecclesiastes 8:10)—for they will come and live from a holy site.[128]

"We have learned: Rabbi Abba said in the name of Rabbi Yoḥanan, 'It is written: *Can the Cushite change his skin, or the leopard his spots?* (Jeremiah 13:23). Similarly, the wicked who did not merit to repent in this world ולהקטיר



Sinai." See also BT *Shabbat* 28b, 62a; Maimonides, *Mishneh Torah, Hilkhot Tefillin* 1:3.

The "crowns" refer to decorative markings adorning some of the letters in the Torah passages inside the *tefillin*. See Maimonides, *Mishneh Torah, Hilkhot Tefillin* 2:8–9. On the order of the passages in their compartments, see idem, 3:5–6. On the straps, see idem, 3:12–14.

A work entitled "The Thirteen Attributes of Mercy in the Mishnah of Rabbi El'azar" is referenced in *ZḤ* 10c (*MhN*); see also *Zohar* 1:124b (*MhN*), page 378. This work would appear to be one of the many books housed in the real or imaginary Zoharic library. See *Ketem Paz*, 1:22d: "All such books mentioned in the *Zohar*... have been lost in the wanderings of exile.... Nothing is left of them except what is mentioned in the *Zohar*."

127. **Had I come here only for this...** Similar exclamations appear in rabbinic literature and often in the *Zohar*. See BT *Berakhot* 16a, 24b; *Shabbat* 41a; *Pesiqta de-Rav Kahana* 1:3; *Shir ha-Shirim Rabbah* on 3:11; *Qohelet Rabbah* on 6:2; *Qohelet Zuta* 5:17; *Zohar* 1:2a, 148b, 164b, 235b, 240a; 2:99a, 121b–122a, 193b; 3:26a, 121a, 203a.

128. **he will grant them from his radiant glory...** Only now does Rabbi El'azar answer the sages' original query. Abraham, the soul on high, bestows some of his splendor upon the wicked, thereby enabling them to be worthy of resurrection. Hence: *Abraham took a wife* (meaning a body of the wicked), *and her name was* קטורה (*Qeturah*), indicating that her deeds were as beautiful as קטורת (*qetoret*), "incense" (see *Bereshit Rabbah* 61:4; *Tanḥuma, Ḥayyei Sarah* 8; *Pirqei de-Rabbi Eli'ezer* 30; see next note).

On Ecclesiastes 8:10, cf. *Zohar* 1:188a; 3:216a (*RM*); *ZḤ* 59a–b (*MhN*); *TZ* 69, 99b–100a, 111a; Moses de León, *Shushan Edut*, 358; idem, *Sefer ha-Rimmon*, 246 (and Wolfson's note).

On the verse from Genesis, see also *Zohar* 1:187a, where Abraham symbolizes the soul who is reincarnated (*once again*) in a new body (*a wife... Keturah*).

In place of "these words [will apply] to the wicked," V1 and V22 read: "She [the soul] prays for the wicked," though this appears to be an attempt to smooth a difficult text.

(*u-lhaqtir*), and to offer up, good deeds, will never יקטירו (*yaqtiru*), offer up, in the world to come!'[129]

"Look at what is written: *Once again, Abraham took a wife*—seeking to fashion a soul for their bodies, to draw them near in repentance, as is said: *and the souls they had made in Haran* (Genesis 12:5)!"[130]

Rabbi El'azar said, "Come and see what is written: *She bore him Zimran and Jokshan* (ibid. 25:2)—many wicked deeds until they are banished from the world, as is written: *he sent them away from Isaac his son* (ibid., 6). Of them is said *Many of those who sleep in the dust of earth will awake...* (Daniel 12:2), while of the others is said *The enlightened will shine like the radiance of the sky...* (ibid., 3)."[131]



129. ***Can the Cushite change...*** The text reverts to Hebrew, though Rabbi El'azar is still the speaker. Does this language change mark a seam in an earlier and later text? Be that as it may, the tradition presented in the name of Rabbi Abba and Rabbi Yoḥanan challenges the view that the wicked are capable of repentance in the world to come: Once wicked, always wicked.

Note the word play. Abraham's wife is called קטורה (*Qeturah*), here associated with להקטיר (*le-haqtir*), "to offer up."

130. ***the souls they had made in Haran...*** Just as Abraham and Sarah "made" souls in Haran, so Abraham, the soul on high, "makes" souls for bodies, by drawing the wicked to repentance.

According to the simple sense of this verse, נפש (*nefesh*), *souls*, means *persons*, and עשו (*asu*), "made," means *acquired*, referring to the slaves that Abraham and Sarah had acquired. However, the Midrash offers a radically different reading. See *Bereshit Rabbah* 39:14: "*And the souls they had made in Haran.* Rabbi El'azar said in the name of Rabbi Yose son of Zimra, 'If all the nations assembled to create a single mosquito, they could not cast a soul into it, yet you say *and the souls they had made*?! Rather, these are converts. Then the verse should read [*and the souls*] *they had converted*. Why *they had made*? To teach you that whoever draws a Gentile near is as though he created him.'" See *Sifrei*, Deuteronomy 32; BT *Sanhedrin* 99b; *Shir ha-Shirim Rabbah* on 1:3; *Tanḥuma, Lekh Lekha* 12; *Avot de-Rabbi Natan* A, 12; B, 26; *Zohar* 1:78b–79b; 2:128b, 147b, 198a; 3:168a; *ZḤ* 25a (*MhN*).

131. ***She bore him Zimran and Jokshan...*** Among Keturah's offspring to Abraham.

According to *Bereshit Rabbah* 61:5, their names reveal their wicked ways: "זמרן (*Zimran*), for they would מזמרין (*mezammerin*), cut down, the world; יקשן (*Yokshan*), Jokshan, for they מתקשין (*mitqashin*), were cruel, in the world... זמרן (*Zimran*), for they would מזמרין (*mezammerin*), sing, in honor of idols; יקשן (*Yokshan*), Jokshan, for they would מקשין (*maqshin*), beat, the drum in honor of idols." See also *Midrash Tehillim* 92:13.

Perhaps what is intended is that notwithstanding Abraham (the soul's) help, many of the wicked are beyond salvation—and are thus thrust away from Isaac, the soul destined to be reunited with the risen body.

Genesis 25:6 reads: *To the sons of his concubines, Abraham gave gifts while he was still alive; and he sent them away from his son Isaac eastward, to the land of the East.*

Daniel 12:2 continues: *these to everlasting life, those to shame and everlasting horror.* See *Zohar* 1:107a, 111a (both *MhN*).

On Daniel 12:3, see *Zohar* 1:113b, 116a (both *MhN*).

In place of *Zimran and Jokshan*, the manuscripts and the earliest printed editions read *Pildash and Jidlaph* (from Genesis 22:22), though this is clearly a mistake.

Rabbi Yehudah said, "This is the meaning of the entire passage; also indicating that at that time the soul's designation 'Abraham' is abandoned, and in its place she is called Isaac, as we have said, as is written: *After the death of Abraham, God blessed Isaac his son. And Isaac dwelled by the well* לחי ראי (*la-ḥai ro'i*), *Lahai Roi* (Genesis 25:11)—with the knowledge of החי (*ha-ḥai*), the Living Onc, who is the Life of Worlds, to know and comprehend what he did not in this world, as is written: *For the earth will be filled with knowledge of YHVH* (Isaiah 11:9)."[132] [134a]

132. **This is the meaning of the entire passage...** Namely, concerning Abraham's taking another wife. Rabbi Yehudah is satisfied with Rabbi El'azar's resolution of his difficulty. He finds scriptural support from the same passage for the soul's name change from Abraham to Isaac. See *Zohar* 1:129a (*MhN*), page 394.

On Genesis 25:11, see *Zohar* 1:135b. On Isaiah 11:9, see *Zohar* 1:113b, 125b, 140a (all *MhN*); 2:68a; 3:23a.

# פרשת תולדות

# *Parashat Toledot*

"GENERATIONS" (GENESIS 25:19–28:9)

*These are the generations of Isaac, son of Abraham.*
*Abraham engendered Isaac* (Genesis 25:19).

Rabbi Yitsḥak opened, "*The mandrakes give forth fragrance*... (Song of Songs 7:14). Our Rabbis have taught: In the time to come, the blessed Holy One will revive the dead and shake off their dust, that they will not be a construction of dust as they were at first, when they were created from dust—literally, a substance that does not endure, as is written: *YHVH God formed the human being of dust from the soil* (Genesis 2:7). At that [134b] time they will shake off the dust of that construction and abide in a durable edifice, that they will attain enduring existence, as is written: *Shake off the dust, arise, sit enthroned, O Jerusalem!* (Isaiah 52:2)—they will abide enduringly and ascend from beneath the earth and receive their souls in the land of Israel. At that time the blessed Holy One will waft all manner of fragrances of the Garden of Eden upon them, as is written: *The mandrakes give forth fragrance.*"[1]

Rabbi Yitsḥak said, "Do not read הדודאים (*ha-duda'im*), *the mandrakes*, but rather הדודים (*ha-dodim*), the companions—body and soul, who are companions and friends with one another."[2]

Rav Naḥman said, "Mandrakes, precisely! Just as mandrakes engender love in the world, so they engender love in the world. What is implied by *give forth fragrance*? Their good deeds—knowing and recognizing their Creator."[3]

1. ***The mandrakes give forth fragrance*...** The verse continues: *at our doors all delicacies; new as well as old, my love, I have stored away for you.*

On the impermanence of the body of dust, see *ZḤ* 16b (*MhN*). On receiving souls in the land of Israel, see *Zohar* 1:69a, 113b (*MhN*), 114a–b (*MhN*), 128b (*MhN*), 131a. On Song of Songs 7:14, see *Zohar* 1:156b, 242b–243a; *ZḤ* 22a (*MhN*). On Isaiah 52:2, see *Zohar* 2:7a; 3:6b.

2. **הדודים (*ha-dodim*), the companions—body and soul...** In the post-resurrection world, there is no longer any animosity or tension between the earthly body and the heavenly soul. Instead, total harmony reigns. Cf. the parable of the body and soul in BT *Sanhedrin* 91a.

3. **Just as mandrakes engender love in the world...** On mandrakes and love/sexual arousal/fertility, see Genesis 30:14–17; Naḥmanides, ad loc., verse 14. See also *Bereshit*

*At our doors* (Song of Songs 7:14)—these are the openings of heaven, open to draw down souls to corpses; *all delicacies* (ibid.)—the souls; *new as well as old* (ibid.)—those whose souls departed long ago and those whose souls departed recently, who merited by virtue of their good deeds to enter the world to come; all of them are destined to descend at once, to enter the bodies designated for them.

Rabbi Aḥa son of Ya'akov said, "A heavenly voice goes forth and proclaims: *New as well as old, my love, I have stored away for you* (ibid.)—*I have stored* them away in those worlds; *for you*—for your sake, because you are a holy and untainted body."[4]

Alternatively, הדודאים (*ha-duda'im*) *give forth fragrance*—angels of peace; *give forth fragrance*—the souls, fragrance of the world. What is meant by *give forth*? They allow, as is said: *Sihon did not allow Israel* [*to pass through his territory*] (Numbers 21:23). As it has been taught: Rabbi Yehudah said, "Every new month and every Sabbath, three companies of ministering angels go forth to accompany the soul to the site of her rung."[5]



How then shall we establish *at our doors all delicacies*?[6]

Rabbi Yehudah said, "These are the bodies, poised in the openings of the graves to receive their souls. Dumah delivers the tally-note and proclaims, saying, 'Master of the world! *New as well as old*—those buried long ago and those buried recently; all of them *I have stored away for you*, to bring them forth according to the tally.'"[7] [135a]

Rav Yehudah said in the name of Rav, "At that time the blessed Holy One is destined to rejoice with the righteous, to ensconce His *Shekhinah* with them,

*Rabbah* 72:5; JT *Shabbat* 6:2, 8b; BT *Sanhedrin* 99b.

On mandrakes and their fragrance signifying the righteous and their deeds, see BT *Eruvin* 21b; *Shir ha-Shirim Rabbah* on 7:14; *Shir ha-Shirim Zuta* on 7:14.

4. **A heavenly voice...** The celestial voice addresses the body: your soul has been treasured away in the upper worlds.

5. **הדודאים (*ha-duda'im*) *give forth fragrance*—angels of peace...** The angels are called *duda'im*, "mandrakes," because they are the *dodim*, "companions," of the soul—the fragrance of the world, escorting her to and through the celestial realm.

See *Targum Onqelos* and *Targum Yerushalmi* on the verse from Numbers, where נתן (*natan*), "give," is rendered as שבק (*shevaq*), "leave, allow." Hence: *the mandrakes give forth fragrance*—the angels allow the soul. Cf. *Matoq mi-Devash*.

On the three companies of angels, see BT *Ketubbot* 104a; *Zohar* 1:98a (*MhN*). See also *ZḤ* 18b (*MhN*).

6. **How then shall we establish...** Previously, *delicacies* signified the souls poised to descend. If, however, *fragrance* indicates the soul, what then is implied by *delicacies*?

7. **Dumah delivers the tally-note . . .** Dumah, the prince of the dead, has a list of the righteous bodies worthy of resurrection. See *Zohar* 1:121a (*Tos*), 123a–124b, 127b (both *MhN*).

and all will delight in that joy, as is written: *YHVH will rejoice in His works* (Psalms 104:31)."[8]

Rabbi Yehudah said, "At that time the righteous are destined to create worlds and revive the dead."[9]

Rabbi Yose said to him, "But we have learned: *There is nothing new under the sun* (Ecclesiastes 1:9)![10]

Rabbi Yehudah replied, "Come and hear! As long as the wicked are in the world and proliferate, the entire world is not vitally existent. But when the righteous are in the world—then the world will abide vitally, and they will revive the dead, as we have said: *There shall yet be old men and women in the squares of Jerusalem, each with staff in hand because of their great age* (Zechariah 8:4), as written above."[11]



8. ***YHVH will rejoice in His works . . .*** On Psalms 104:31, see *Vayiqra Rabbah* 20:2; *Tanḥuma, Aḥarei Mot* 2; *Tanḥuma* (Buber), *Aḥarei Mot* 3; *Midrash Tehillim* 75:2; *Zohar* 1:102b (*MhN*), 114a (*MhN*), 115a (*MhN*), 116a (*MhN*), 119a, 182a; 2:57b, 259a (*Heikh*); 3:16a.

On the connection between joy and the indwelling of the *Shekhinah*, see BT *Shabbat* 30b.

9. **righteous are destined to . . . revive the dead** See BT *Pesaḥim* 68a; *Zohar* 1:114b (*MhN*).

10. ***There is nothing new under the sun . . .*** Apparently, Rabbi Yose is wondering: if the righteous do not have the power to resurrect the dead in this world, how will they have such power in the post-resurrection world?

See BT *Shabbat* 30b: "Rabban Gamaliel sat and expounded, 'Woman is destined to give birth every day, as is said: *she conceives and bears simultaneously* (Jeremiah 31:8).' A certain disciple scoffed at him, saying, '*There is nothing new under the sun*!' He replied, 'Come, and I will show you its equal in this world.' He went forth and showed him a hen. Once again Rabban Gamaliel sat and expounded, 'Trees are destined to yield fruit every day, as is said: *it shall bring forth boughs and bear fruit* (Ezekiel 17:23). Just as the boughs [grow] every day, so shall there be fruit every day.' A certain disciple scoffed at him, saying, 'But it is written: *There is nothing new under the sun*!' He replied, 'Come, and I will show you its equal in this world.' He went forth and showed him the caper bush. Once again Rabban Gamaliel sat and expounded, 'The land of Israel is destined to bring forth cakes and fine woolen robes, as is said: *There shall be abundant grain in the land* (Psalms 72:16).' A certain disciple scoffed at him, saying, '*There is nothing new under the sun!*' He replied, 'Come, and I will show you their equal in this world.' He went forth and showed him morels and truffles; and for fine woolen robes [he showed him] the bark of a young palm-shoot."

11. **As long as the wicked are in the world . . .** Apparently Rabbi Yehudah intends that the righteous do indeed possess the power of resurrection in this world, but that the proliferation of the wicked hinders this power (cf. BT *Sanhedrin* 65b). In the future, when the wicked are removed and the existence of the world is fully actualized, the righteous will be able to utilize their full capacities. Hence, by reviving the dead the righteous will not contravene the principle *there is nothing new under the sun.* On the verse from Zechariah, see BT *Pesaḥim* 68a; *Zohar* 1:114b (*MhN*).

See also *Tanḥuma, Nitsavim* 4: "You [the righteous] are the existence of this world and the world to come."

At that time, the righteous will attain perfect knowledge. As Rabbi Yose said, "On the day when the blessed Holy One will rejoice in His works, the righteous are destined to know Him in their hearts, and then understanding will abound in their hearts, as though they have beheld Him with the eye, as is written: *In that day they shall say: Look, this is our God...* (Isaiah 25:9). The joy of the soul in the body is greatest of all, for both of them will exist enduringly, knowing and fathoming their Creator, delighting in the splendor of *Shekhinah*. This is the good concealed for the righteous in the time to come, as is written: *These are the generations of* יצחק *(Yitsḥaq), Isaac, son of Abraham* (Genesis 25:19)—these are the generations of the joy והשחוק *(ve-ha-seḥoq)*, and the laughter, that will be in the world at that time. *Son of Abraham*—the soul worthy of this, consummate in her rung. *Abraham engendered Isaac* (ibid.)—the soul engenders this joy and laughter in the world."[12]

Rabbi Yehudah said to Rabbi Ḥiyya, "Concerning what we have learned—that the blessed Holy One will one day make a banquet for the righteous in the time to come—what is this?"[13]



12. **the righteous will attain perfect knowledge...** Post-resurrection, the righteous will enjoy intellectual apprehension and perfection. They will know God so intimately as to be able to point with their finger.

On the verse from Isaiah, see BT *Ta'anit* 31a: "Ulla Bira'ah said in the name of Rabbi El'azar, 'The blessed Holy One will one day hold a dance for the righteous and He will sit in their midst in the Garden of Eden and everyone will point with their finger, as is said: *In that day they shall say: Look, this is our God; we waited for Him and He saved us! This is YHVH, for whom we have waited; let us rejoice and exult in His salvation.*'" See *Tanḥuma* (Buber), *Tsav* 16, *Bemidbar* 20; *Zohar* 1:115a (*MhN*).

On the attainment of perfect knowledge, see *Zohar* 1:113b, 126a, 140a (all *MhN*); *ZḤ* 15d (*MhN*). On delighting in the *Shekhinah*, see BT *Berakhot* 17a: "A pearl in the mouth of Rav: In the world to come, there is no eating or drinking or procreation or business or jealousy or hatred or competition; rather, the righteous sit with their crowns on their heads, delighting in the splendor of *Shekhinah*, as is said: *They beheld God and they ate and drank* (Exodus 24:11)."

The *Zohar*'s account here of intellectual apprehension and perfection is reminiscent of Maimonides (see *Mishneh Torah, Hilkhot Teshuvah*, 8:2; idem, *Pereq Ḥeleq*), though with one important difference. For Maimonides, such apprehension is the patrimony of the soul alone; for the *Zohar* it is for the reunited soul and body after the resurrection.

As throughout *MhN*, Abraham signifies the soul.

13. **a banquet for the righteous in the time to come...** See BT *Bava Batra* 75a: "Rabbah said in the name of Rabbi Yoḥanan, 'In the future the blessed Holy One will one day make a banquet for the righteous from the flesh of Leviathan...'"

See also BT *Bava Batra* 74b in the name of Rav: "Everything that the blessed Holy One created in His world, He created male and female. Even *Leviathan the elusive snake* and *Leviathan the writhing snake* (Isaiah 27:1) He created male and female; and if they mated with another, they would destroy the entire world. What did the blessed Holy One do? He castrated the male and killed the female, salting her for the righteous in the world to come."

See also *Vayiqra Rabbah* 13:3; *Tanḥuma*,

He replied, "Until I went before those holy angels, the Masters of Mishnah, that is what I heard. But when I heard what Rabbi El'azar said, my heart was at ease. For Rabbi El'azar said, 'The banquet of the righteous in the time to come is like that which is written: *They beheld God, and they ate and drank* (Exodus 24:11), and this is as we have learned: they are nourished.' Rabbi El'azar also said [135b], 'In one place we have learned: they delight, but in another place we have learned: they are nourished. What is the difference between this and that? Well, so did my father say: The righteous who were not so worthy delight in that splendor, for they will not attain so much; but the righteous who were worthy are nourished until they attain consummate apprehension. Eating and drinking connotes only this, and this is the significance of the banquet and the eating. How do we know this? From Moses, as is written: *He was there with YHVH forty days and forty nights; he ate no bread and drank no water* (Exodus 34:28). What is the reason that he ate no bread and drank no water? Because he was nourished by a different banquet, from the splendor on high! Likewise the banquet of the righteous in the time to come!'"[14]



*Nitsavim*, 4; *Pesiqta de-Rav Kahana*, Supplement 2:4; *Pirqei de-Rabbi Eli'ezer* 10; cf. M *Avot* 3:16; BT *Pesaḥim* 119b. See Ginzberg, *Legends* 5:43–6.

14. **Until I went before those holy angels...** Only when Rabbi Ḥiyya learns with the Masters of Mishnah does he understand the true significance of the banquet of the righteous. His heart is at ease, as the banquet no longer entails simplistic or fantastic beliefs.

The *Zohar*'s interpretation of the eschatological banquet as nourishment by the *Shekhinah* derives from Maimonides. See *Mishneh Torah, Hilkhot Teshuvah* 8:4: "The Sages referred to this good that is prepared for the righteous with the metaphor [of] the banquet." See also Abraham ben David's gloss, ad loc., and Baḥya ben Asher on Genesis 1:21. See Scholem, *On the Kabbalah and its Symbolism*, 60; Tishby, *Wisdom of the Zohar*, 1:77.

The context in Exodus 24 (9–11) reads: *Moses and Aaron, Nadab and Abihu, and seventy of the elders of Israel ascended. They saw the God of Israel, and beneath His feet was like a fashioning of sapphire pavement and like the essence of heaven for purity. Yet against the nobles of the Children of Israel He did not send forth His hand—they beheld God, and they ate and drank.*

In numerous rabbinic texts, the verse *They beheld God and they ate and drank* (the plain meaning of which implies a covenant meal) is interpreted as signifying nourishment by, or delight in, the *Shekhinah*. See BT *Berakhot* 17a (quoted above, note 12); *Avot de-Rabbi Natan* A, 1. See also *Vayiqra Rabbah* 20:10: "Rabbi Hosha'yah said, 'Did they take provisions up with them to Sinai, that it is written *They beheld God* [*and they ate and drank*]? Rather this teaches that they feasted their eyes on *Shekhinah*, like a person looking at his friend while eating and drinking.' Rabbi Yoḥanan said, 'Actual eating, as is said: *In the light of the king's face is life* (Proverbs 16:15).'" See also *Pesiqta de-Rav Kahana* 26:9; *Bemidbar Rabbah* 2:25; *Tanḥuma, Aḥarei Mot* 6; *Zohar* 1:104a; 2:126a. See also *ZḤ* 22c (*MhN*).

Rabbi El'azar's distinction—between delighting in and being nourished by the *Shekhinah* as two different levels of celestial bliss—derives from the fact that in some rabbinic texts we find the expression "delight in the *Shekhinah*" (for example, BT *Berakhot* 17a), while in others "nourished by the *Shekhinah*" (for example, *Avot de-Rabbi Natan*

Rabbi Yehudah said, "The banquet of the righteous in the time to come is to rejoice in His joy, as is written: [*In YHVH do I glory*]; *let the lowly hear it and rejoice* (Psalms 34:3)."[15]

Rav Huna said, "From here: *Let all who take refuge in You rejoice; let them ever shout for joy* (ibid. 5:12)."[16]

Rabbi Yitsḥak said, "This and that will be in the time to come."[17]

It has been taught: Rabbi Yose said, "The wine preserved in its grapes since the six days of creation—ancient matters not revealed to anyone since the day the world was created, but destined to be revealed to the righteous in the time to come. This is the significance of the drinking and the eating; certainly it is so!"[18]

A, 1). On this distinction, see *ZḤ* 21a (*MhN*). See also *ZḤ* 18b (*MhN*).

On Moses' having been nourished by the *Shekhinah*, see *Shemot Rabbah* 47:5: "*He was there with YHVH forty days and forty nights* (Exodus 34:28). Is it possible for a person to go forty days without food or drink? Rabbi Tanḥuma said in the name of Rabbi El'azar son of Rabbi Avin in the name of Rabbi Meir, 'The proverb runs: When you go into a city, follow its customs. When Moses ascended on high, where there is no eating or drinking, he emulated them....' *He ate no bread* (ibid.)—eating only the bread of the Torah; *and drank no water* (ibid.)—drinking only of the water of the Torah.... Whence did he derive his nourishment? He was nourished by the splendor of *Shekhinah*." See also *Shemot Rabbah* 3:1, 47:7; *Vayiqra Rabbah* 20:10; *ZḤ* 10a, 15b (both *MhN*).

On Rabbi Ḥiyya learning with the Masters of Mishnah, see *ZḤ* 15d (*MhN*); *Zohar* 2:14a–15a (*MhN*).

The term מארי מתניתין (*marei matnitin*), "Masters of Mishnah," appears in numerous passages (in various formulations) throughout *Midrash ha-Ne'lam.* It appears to signify a group (though never formally defined) of sages possessing esoteric wisdom. In some ways, the Masters of Mishnah are a forerunner to the *Ḥavrayya*, the Companions headed by Rabbi Shim'on, found in the main body of the *Zohar.* Significantly, however, Rabbi Shim'on does not always occupy a privileged position in this group. The Mishnah of which they are masters is not the Mishnah of the rabbinic sage Rabbi Yehudah ha-Nasi, but rather a body of esoteric knowledge often relating to the soul and the structure of the cosmos. See *Zohar* 1:123b (*MhN*, though mistakenly labeled as *Tosefta*); 1:127a–b, 129a–b, 130a, 138a, 139b; 2:5a, 14a (all *MhN*); *ZḤ* 10c, 12c, 13a, 14c, 15b–c, 16a, 59b (all *MhN*); Scholem, "Parashah Ḥadashah," 443, 444 (Addendum 1 in this volume); Meroz, "Va-Ani Lo Hayiti Sham?," 168 (Addendum 3 in this volume); Cf. *Pesiqta de-Rav Kahana* 11:15, 23:12. See also Matt, "Matnita di-Lan," 132–34.

15. **The banquet... is to rejoice in His joy...** According to Rabbi Yehudah (and Rav Huna), the essence of the eschatological banquet is joy, not intellectual apprehension.

16. ***Let all who take refuge in You rejoice...*** See *Zohar* 1:193a.

17. **This and that will be...** Namely, in the post-resurrection world the righteous will attain both perfect knowledge and experience great joy.

18. **The wine preserved in its grapes...** See BT *Berakhot* 34b: "What is implied by the verse *No eye has seen*, [*O God, but You, what You will do for one who awaits you*] (Isaiah 64:3)? Rabbi Yehoshu'a son of Levi said, 'The wine preserved in its grapes since the six days of creation.'"

See *Zohar* 1:192a, 238b; 2:147a, 169b; 3:4a, 12b, 39b–40a, 93b; *ZḤ* 28b (*MhN*), 64c (*ShS*).

On the connection between wine and secrets, see BT *Eruvin* 65a in the name of Rabbi Ḥiyya: "יין (*Yayin*), wine, has the

Rabbi Yehudah son of Rabbi Shalom said, "If so, what is the leviathan and what is the bull, as is written: *Surely the mountains yield him food* (Job 40:20)?"[19]

Rabbi Yose said, "But look at what is written: *On that day YHVH will punish—with His fierce, great, mighty sword—Leviathan the elusive snake, Leviathan the writhing snake; He will slay the serpent of the sea* (Isaiah 27:1)! Look, here are three! This merely intimates a hint about the kingdoms."[20]

Rabbi Tanḥum said, "One must not speak against what our Rabbis have said! Certainly it is so!"[21]

Rabbi Yitsḥak said, "I was in the presence of Rabbi Yehoshu'a, and I asked him about this matter. I said: Concerning the banquet of the righteous in the time to come—if it is so, it does not sit well in my heart. For Rabbi El'azar said, 'The banquet of the righteous in the time to come follows this paradigm [136a], as is written: *They beheld God, and they ate and drank* (Exodus 24:11).' Rabbi Yehoshu'a said, 'Rabbi El'azar has spoken well! It is so.'



"Rabbi Yehoshu'a said further, 'Concerning that belief which our Rabbis instructed the masses of the people—that they are invited to the banquet of Leviathan and the bull, to drink fine wine preserved since the world was created—they found a verse and expounded it, as is written: *you will eat your fill of bread* (Leviticus 26:5). As Rabbi Zeira said, "The blessed Holy One enticed Israel with all manner of enticements to restore them to the right path—and this one more than all others, as He said to them: *you will eat your fill of bread.* And as for curses: *you shall eat and not be sated* (ibid., 26), and this was most difficult of all for them. Why? As is written: *If only we had died by the hand of YHVH in the land of Egypt* [*when we sat by the fleshpots, when we ate our fill of bread!*] (Exodus 16:3)." Rabbi Zeira explained, "This teaches that it was for the sake of food

numerical value of seventy; and סוד (*sod*), secret, has the numerical value of seventy: when wine goes in, secrets come out." On the revelation of secrets in the Messianic era, see *Zohar* 3:152a.

19. **If so, what is the leviathan and what is the bull...** The allegorical interpretation of the banquet is not convincing. Scripture explicitly mentions Leviathan and Behemoth—which Rabbi Yehudah here equates with a bull.

The verse in Job describes the domain of the mythical beast Behemoth, who according to BT *Bava Batra* 74b is also on the eschatological menu.

See *Vayiqra Rabbah* 22:10; *Pesiqta de-Rav Kahana* 6:1; *Tanḥuma, Pinḥas* 12; *Pirqei de-Rabbi Eli'ezer* 11.

20. **This merely intimates a hint about the kingdoms** Rabbi Yose also rejects the idea that Leviathan will literally be consumed by the righteous at the banquet. The slaying of these three mythical beasts, rather, alludes to the destruction of the kingdoms at the eschaton.

21. **One must not speak against...** The plain meaning of the Rabbis' statements about the banquet for the righteous should be accepted without question.

Even as the *Zohar* pursues its allegorical reading "overturning" the plain meaning, it also presents a voice rejecting this very move!

that they surrendered their souls to die by His hand. As soon as the blessed Holy One saw their craving, He said to them, 'If you will heed the voice of the commandments *you will eat your fill*' (Leviticus 25:19)—to put their minds at ease." Similarly, our Rabbis saw that the exile was prolonged; they relied upon verses from Torah and said that they are destined to eat and rejoice at a great banquet that the blessed Holy One will one day arrange for them. Consequently the masses of the people endured the exile—on account of that banquet.'"[22]

Rabbi Yoḥanan said, "We should not destroy what all believe, but rather maintain it, for the Torah attests to it! For look, we know what constitutes the faith of the righteous and their yearning! As is written: *Let us delight and rejoice in you* (Song of Songs 1:4)—not through eating; *let us savor your love more than wine* (ibid.). As for that banquet for which they are destined, we shall have a share in which to delight—the joy and the laughter. *These are the generations of* יצחק (*Yitsḥaq*), *Isaac* (Genesis 25:19)—for the righteous יצחקו (*yitsḥaqu*), will laugh, in the time to come. *Abraham engendered Isaac* (ibid.)—the merit of the soul engenders this laughter and joy in the world."[23] [136b]



*Isaac was forty years old* (Genesis 25:20).[24]

Rabbi Abba opened and said in the name of Rabbi Yose, "*O that he would kiss me with the kisses of his mouth*... (Song of Songs 1:2). The world was created in numerous gradations. As we have learned: Rabbi Aḥa son of Ya'akov said, 'Everything that the blessed Holy One created, aside from Himself, was composite.' Now, did Rabbi Aḥa

22. **Concerning that belief which our Rabbis instructed the masses...** Rabbi Yehoshu'a proceeds to explain the Rabbis' motivation for inculcating belief in the eschatological banquet. Just as God promised the people all manner of goods if they observed the commandments, the Rabbis followed the divine paradigm. Basing themselves upon verses in Scripture, they developed the myth of the banquet as reward. Indeed, according to Rabbi Yehoshu'a, it is only by virtue of this belief that the masses were able to stay faithful to the covenant and endure the exile. Cf. *Eikhah Rabbah* 3:7; *Zohar* 2:188b; Moses de León, *Sefer ha-Mishqal*, 94–95.

The *Zohar* here approaches Maimonides' view of the divine ruse. See *Pereq Ḥeleq*: "Therefore in order that the masses stay faithful and do the commandments, it was permitted to tell them that they might hope for a reward, and to warn them against transgression out of fear of punishment." See also idem, *Guide of the Perplexed* 3:32.

The phrase "if you will heed the voice of the commandments" seems to be modeled on Exodus 15:26.

23. **We should not destroy what all believe...** The Masters of Mishnah know that the ultimate good awaiting the righteous does not comprise worldly goods such as meat, fish, and wine, but rather the knowledge and joy of divine revelation. Even so, they must fortify the fantastic beliefs of the masses, for after all, the Torah employs a similar strategy.

24. ***Isaac was forty years old*** The verse continues: *when he took Rebekah as his wife, daughter of Bethuel the Aramean from Paddan Aram, sister of Laban the Aramean.* On this verse, see *Zohar* 1:136b.

really say such a thing (heaven forbid)?! For through this word, conflict will increase in the world! For should you say so, it could be said of the angels—who are created of the actual holy-spirit—that they are composite! Look, then all natures—theirs and ours—are equal!"[25]

Rabbi Abba said, "Through this word, conflict will not increase, for we have learned in our Mishnah: Everything that the blessed Holy One made, He made patterned on body and soul. Now, you might say 'Angels don't have a body'—this is indeed so; but they are unable to perform any action until the holy soul—aid from above—partners with them. In the same manner, everything that He made requires that aid from above it."[26]

Rabbi Yose said, "At the time when the blessed Holy One is destined to revive the dead, all troubles will cease at forty; a covenant has been decreed: *forty is he to be struck, no more* (Deuteronomy 25:3). The end of Israel's wandering in the desert was in the fortieth year. For forty years prior to the resurrection of the body, the soul awaits it in the land of Israel; in the fortieth year the bodies will rise from their dust. On the fortieth the rains stopped, as is written: *The rain was over the earth forty days* (Genesis 7:12), and similarly: *At the end of forty days, Noah opened* (ibid. 8:6). The time of Israel's redemption is in the fortieth year; in the fiftieth, the settling of the world, the jubilee. The restoration [137a] of the soul to the body is in the fortieth year that she waited for it in the land of Israel, as is written: *Isaac was forty years old* (Genesis 25:20)—for he waited for the body;



25. **Everything that the blessed Holy One created ... was composite ...** Namely, comprised of different forces; comprised of body and soul. Rabbi Abba quotes a tradition by Rabbi Aḥa that he then challenges. If everything outside the godhead is composite, then angels and humans are the same!

On the expression "All natures [or: characters] are equal," see JT *Sanhedrin* 10:2, 28c; *Eikhah Rabbah, Petiḥta* 9; *Pesiqta de-Rav Kahana* 24:11; *Rut Rabbah* 5:6; *Midrash Tehillim* 4:5 (and Buber's note); *Zohar* 2:53a; 3:183b; *Arukh ha-Shalem* and *Tosefot he-Arukh ha-Shalem*, 336, s.v. *appayya*.

26. **requires that aid from above it** Even the purely spiritual angels require divine animation; hence they are like a body infused with a soul. Indeed, all of creation follows the same pattern: every grade of being requires animation or life from the grade beyond. Although not stated explicitly, this is the sense of the verse from the Song of Songs: *Let him kiss me*—let him infuse me with the spirit from the grade above. Cf. *Zohar* 1:22b (*TZ*).

The "holy soul" may designate *Shekhinah*, or more generally, the divine power.

On body and soul, see *ZḤ* 16b (*MhN*). On the idea that angels/spirits need assistance, see *Midrash Tehillim* 20:7; *Vayiqra Rabbah* 24:3; *Tanḥuma, Qedoshim* 9.

The *Zohar* often cites teachings from a secret, mystical Mishnah known only to its circle. See *Zohar* 1:37b, 55b, 74a, 91b, 93a, 95b, 96a, 124b (*MhN*), 137a (*MhN*), 139a (*MhN*), 223b; 2:5a (*MhN*), 123b; 3:75b, 78a, 284b, 285a, 293b (*IZ*); *ZḤ* 12b, 15b–c, 16a, 18b, 20a (all *MhN*); Scholem, "Parashah Ḥadashah" (Addendum 1 in this volume); Matt, "Matnita di-Lan." This is to be distinguished from the *Matnitin* of the *Zohar*, on which see Scholem, *Kabbalah*, 216.

*when he took Rebekah* (ibid.)—when she [the soul] was inserted in the body designated for him. At that time, when she is inserted within, their sole desire and yearning is to delight in the splendor of *Shekhinah* and be nourished by her splendor, as is written: *O that he would kiss me with the kisses of his mouth* (Song of Songs 1:2)."[27]

Rabbi Abba said, "*O that he would kiss me*—O that he would sustain me, for their sustenance is solely through delight in, and nourishment from, the splendor on high."[28]

Rabbi Yose said, "The end of the verse proves this, as is written: *for your love is better than wine* (ibid.)."[29]

*Daughter of* בתואל (*Betu'el*), *Bethuel* (Genesis 25:20)—daughter of בתו של אל (*bito shel el*), the daughter of God.[30]

Rav Huna said, "It is not so! I was in the coastal towns, and I heard that they called that spinal bone—the one that remains in the grave of the entire body—בתואל רמאה (*Betu'el Ramma'ah*), Bethuel the deceiver. I inquired about this, and they said that it is like the head of a serpent, which is deceitful; and that this bone is the most deceitful of all the other bones."[31]



27. ***Isaac was forty years old...*** Forty years is the paradigm for national, universal, and eschatological salvation. Following the ingathering of the exiles, forty years of strife will ensue for Israel, followed by the restoration of the soul to the body.

See *Zohar* 1:128a–129a, 135a–b, 139a–b (all *MhN*).

On the jubilee, see Leviticus 25:10: *You shall hallow the fiftieth year and proclaim* דרור (*deror*), *release* [or: *freedom*], *in the land for all of its inhabitants. A jubilee it shall be for you, and you shall go back each man to his holding, and each man to his clan you shall go back.* Precisely what Rabbi Yose intends will happen in this year is unclear.

28. ***O that he would kiss me*—O that he would sustain me...** The kisses (nourishment by the *Shekhinah*) are the very sustenance of the body and soul.

See Genesis 41:40, where the verb נשק (*nashaq*)—either the same root or a homonym of the one for ישקני (*yishaqeni*), *O that he would kiss me*—is used to describe Joseph's authority: *By your mouth all my people* ישק (*yishaq*), *shall be guided.* The context is Joseph's role as provider and sustainer of Egypt.

On delight in and nourishment by the *Shekhinah*, see *Zohar* 1:135a–b (*MhN*).

29. **The end of the verse proves this...** The continuation of the verse confirms that the divine kisses refer to sustenance. Indeed, such divine kisses are the ultimate sustenance, *better than wine.* See *Zohar* 1:136a (*MhN*).

30. ***Daughter of* בתואל (*Betu'el*), *Bethuel...*** Apparently meaning that the resurrected body (*Rebekah*) is the daughter of God's daughter, namely the daughter of *Shekhinah*.

Cf. *Zohar* 1:128a (*MhN*), where "the daughter of God" signifies the soul.

31. **בתואל רמאה (*Betu'el Ramma'ah*), Bethuel the deceiver...** Bethuel does not designate the *Shekhinah*, but rather the spinal bone from which the body is rebuilt at the resurrection. The nature of its deceitfulness is explained in the following paragraph.

According to Rabbi Yehoshu'a son of Ḥananya in the Midrash, God will resurrect humans from the vertebra at the base of the

As it has been taught: Rabbi Shim'on said, "Why does that bone remain in existence longer than all other bones? Because it is רמאה (*ramma'ah*), deceitful, and does not suffer the taste of human food like other bones. Consequently, it is stronger than all other bones and will constitute the essence from which the body is rebuilt. This is the significance of *daughter of Bethuel* הארמי (*ha-arammi*), *the Aramean* (ibid.)."[32]

It has been taught: Rabbi Shim'on said, "It is רמאי (*rammai*), deceitful; always was *rammai*; and is neighbor of the evil impulse, who is *rammai*. This is the significance of *daughter of Bethuel* הארמי (*ha-arammi*), *the Aramean*: the deceitful bone."[33]

מפדן ארם (*Mi-Paddan Aram*), *From Paddan Aram* (ibid.)—from a pair of רמאין (*ramma'in*), deceivers. As we have learned: פדנא דתורי (*padna de-torei*) is a pair [of oxen]. *Sister of Laban* (ibid.)—sister of the evil impulse, *the Aramean*. As we have learned: Originally when he was repulsive with sins in this world he was called Lot; in the time to come, when he will not be repulsive, but rather like one who has bathed and cleansed himself of his filth, he will be called Laban. Even so, the evil impulse is not eliminated from the world.[34]



spinal column, which does not decompose in the grave. See *Bereshit Rabbah* 28:3; *Vayiqra Rabbah* 18:1; *Qohelet Rabbah* on 12:5; *Pirqei de-Rabbi Eli'ezer* 34; *Zohar* 1:69a, 113a (*MhN*), 116a (*MhN*), 126a (*MhN*); 2:28b; 3:222a, 270b; Moses de León, *Sefer ha-Rimmon*, 271; idem, *Sefer ha-Mishqal*, 87.

On the "coastal towns," see BT *Rosh ha-Shanah* 26a; *ZḤ* 6d (*MhN*); Scholem, "Parashah Ḥadashah," 429 (Addendum 1 in this volume).

32. **does not suffer the taste of human food...** The secret of the spinal bone's endurance is that it does not partake of human food. This constitutes its deception as well, as it deceives the other bones of the body who do partake and therefore wither away. Hence: *Rebekah* (the resurrected body) will be generated from *the daughter of Bethuel* (the spinal bone) *the Aramean* (reading Aramean as *rammai*, "deceiver").

On the connection between Aramean and *rammai*, see below, note 34.

33. **always was *rammai*...** Though not stated explicitly, perhaps what is intended is that the spinal bone deceived the snake in the Garden of Eden. By not tasting food, the spinal bone did not taste of the tree of knowledge and therefore was exempt from the decree of death. Just as the snake (the evil impulse) was deceitful, so the spinal bone was deceitful. Hence it is the neighbor of the evil impulse. See *Matoq mi-Devash*.

34. ***From Paddan Aram...*** The resurrected body hails from a pair of deceivers: Bethuel and Laban.

See *Vayiqra Rabbah* 23:1: "*Like a lily among thorns, so is my beloved among maidens* (Song of Songs 2:2). Rabbi Yitsḥak interpreted this verse as applying to Rebekah. '*Isaac was forty years old when he took Rebekah as his wife, daughter of Bethuel the Aramean from Paddan Aram, sister of Laban the Aramean.* Why does Scripture state *sister of Laban* הארמי (*ha-arammi*), the Aramean? Hasn't it already been stated *daughter of Bethuel the Aramean*? And why does Scripture state: *daughter of Bethuel the Aramean*? Isn't it stated *sister of Laban the Aramean*? The reason is that the blessed Holy One said, "Her father was רמאי (*rammai*), a deceiver, and her brother was a deceiver, and the people of her place were

Come and hear! For so have we established in the Mishnah: *The two daughters of Lot* (ibid. 19:36)—the two powers of the body who arouse the evil impulse. Now that he is not so repulsive and is cleansed of his muck [137b], he is called Laban; and these two daughters are not entirely eliminated, as is written: *Laban had two daughters* (ibid. 29:16).[35]

Rabbi Yose said, "It is so. There is written *elder* and *younger* (ibid. 19:30–38), and here is written *bigger* and *smaller* (ibid. 29:16)."[36]

Rabbi Yose said, "But they are not primed to do evil or to arouse the evil impulse as at first, as implied by what is written: *the name of the bigger one was* לאה (*Le'ah*), *Leah* (ibid.)—שלאה (*she-le'ah*), for she was sapped, of her strength and wickedness; *and the name of the smaller was* רחל (*Raḥel*), *Rachel* (ibid.)—lacking the arousing power, as is said: וכרחל (*ukh-raḥel*), *and as a sheep, silent before her shearers* (Isaiah 53:7)."[37]

Rav Huna said, "The evil impulse and his two daughters are transformed from how they were at first. Originally: Lot—accursed, repulsive; now: Laban—מלובן (*melubban*), refined, not repulsively repugnant as at first. Originally: his



deceivers; yet this righteous woman emerged from among them. Among them she was like a lily among thorns."'" See *Bereshit Rabbah* 63:4; *Shir ha-Shirim Rabbah* on 2:2.

On *padna* as pair, see BT *Bava Qamma* 96b and Rashi, ad loc.; see also Rashi on Genesis 25:20.

Even though the resurrected body is described as the sister of the evil impulse, in the post-resurrection world the evil impulse will have a different hue. Laban, meaning "white," signifies the cleansed evil impulse. The base quality of the evil impulse will be eliminated, though its purer and refined aspect will remain. Lot, meaning "cursed," becomes Laban ("white").

On the abolition of the evil impulse, see BT *Sukkah* 52a; *Shemot Rabbah* 41:7; *Tanḥuma* (Buber), *Bereshit* 40, *Qedoshim* 15; Naḥmanides on Deuteronomy 30:6; *Zohar* 1:109a, 128b (both *MhN*). Cf. *Zohar* 1:124a, 127a, 131a.

See also Isaiah 25:7: *He will destroy on this mount* פני הלוט (*pnei ha-lot*), *the shroud,* הלוט (*ha-lot*), *that is drawn, over the faces of all the peoples, and the covering that is spread over all the nations.*

On Lot as the evil impulse, see *Zohar* 1:78a, 79a (both *ST*); 109a–110b (*MhN*); *ZḤ* 24b, 24d (both *MhN*). On the evil impulse as "repulsive," see BT *Sukkah* 52b.

It is possible that Rabbi Shim'on is still the speaker.

35. ***Laban had two daughters...*** Laban's two daughters supply further proof for the existence of the evil impulse in the post-resurrection world. Just as Lot has two daughters—signifying the power of desire and the bodily power, which are jointly responsible for sin in the present world—so Laban, the purified evil impulse, has two daughters. Cf. *Zohar* 1:163a.

On Lot's daughters, see *Zohar* 1:109b–111b (*MhN*).

36. **There is written *elder* and *younger*...** Of Lot's daughters is written *elder* and *younger*, while of Laban's daughters is written *bigger* and *smaller*. The similarity in contrast highlights their affiliation.

37. **But they are not primed...** Even though still extant, the very names of Laban's daughters attest to the diminished capacity of the evil impulse. לאה (*Le'ah*) means "tired, weary," and רחל (*Raḥel*) means "ewe."

two daughters were powerful, each one primed; now: *the name of the bigger one was* לאה (*Le'ah*), *Leah*—לאה (*le'ah*), sapped, lacking power; לאה (*le'ah*), wearied, lacking strength; לאה (*le'ah*), exhausted, from her former deeds; *and* [*the name of*] *the smaller was Rachel*—as we have said, not like they were at first."

Rabbi Aḥa son of Ya'akov said, "Come and see what is written: *Isaac entreated YHVH on behalf of his wife because she was barren* (Genesis 25:21)."

Rabbi Aḥa said, "Why was she barren? Because the evil impulse is not primed in the world; consequently there is no procreation save through prayer. What is written? *YHVH let Himself be entreated, and his wife Rebekah conceived* (ibid.)—when the evil impulse is aroused, there is procreation."[38]

Rabbi Yose said, "If so, then what is the difference between this world and that time? And what's more, the verse says that the blessed Holy One brings this about!"[39]

Rabbi Aḥa said, "So it is. For the blessed Holy One arouses him for that matter—as required for coupling; but not all the time, that he will always be with people as is the case now, when he is constantly present and people sin thereby. Rather, solely for that coupling! That arousal will be an arousal of the



38. **when the evil impulse is aroused, there is procreation** Isaac had to pray that his wife conceive, as in the absence of a fully primed evil impulse there is no procreation.

According to Rabbi Aḥa, in the post-resurrection world there is still procreation. Cf. BT *Berakhot* 17a: "A pearl in the mouth of Rav: 'In the world to come there is no eating or drinking or procreation or business or jealousy or hatred or competition; rather, the righteous sit with their crowns on their heads, basking in the radiance of *Shekhinah*.'" See also *Midrash Tehillim* 146:4; Maimonides, *Mishneh Torah, Hilkhot Teshuvah* 8:2.

On the relationship between the evil impulse and sexual arousal and procreation, see *Bereshit Rabbah* 9:7: "Rabbi Naḥman said in the name of Rabbi Shemu'el, '*Behold, it was very good*—this is the good impulse; *And behold, it was very good* (Genesis 1:31)—this is the evil impulse. Is the evil impulse very good? How astonishing! Yet were it not for the evil impulse, no man would ever build a house, marry a woman, or engender children.'"

According to BT *Yoma* 69b, in the days of Ezra and Nehemiah, the leaders of the Israelites prayed that the evil impulse be eliminated. The impulse to commit idolatry was handed over to them, and they cast it into a lead pot with a lead cover, rendering it powerless. They prayed further, and the sexual impulse was also handed over to them, but a prophet warned, "'Realize that if you kill him, the world will be destroyed [because the desire to procreate will vanish].' They imprisoned him for three days, and looked within the whole land of Israel for a fresh egg and could not find it. They said, 'What should we do? If we kill him, the world will be destroyed.'... They blinded him and let him go. This helped, inasmuch as he no longer entices a person to commit incest."

See *Zohar* 1:49a, 61a, 128b (*MhN*); 3:189a.

On the verse from Genesis, see *Zohar* 1:137a.

39. **what is the difference between this world and that time?...** If in the post-resurrection world there is still procreation aroused by the evil impulse, what then has changed? Moreover, according to Rabbi Aḥa's reading of the verse from Genesis, it seems that it is God Himself who arouses the evil impulse! How can this be?

blessed Holy One! This is the meaning of the verse *I will remove the heart of stone from your flesh and give you a heart of flesh* (Ezekiel 36:26). What is *a heart of flesh*? Rabbi Yehudah said, 'A heart to engender flesh, and not for any other purpose.'"[40] [138a]

Rabbi Yitsḥak son of Rabbi Yose was traveling from Cappadocia to Lydda; Rabbi Yehudah met him. Rabbi Yitsḥak said to him, "Is it true that our Companions, the sages of Mishnah, have been aroused to this matter—that the evil impulse will be forgotten from the world notwithstanding the hour of coupling?"[41]

He said to him, "By your life! The evil impulse is as essential to the world as rainfall is to the world. Were it not for the evil impulse there would be no joy of learning! But it will not be not contemptible as at first, through which to sin thereby, as is written: *In all of My holy mount nothing evil or vile shall be done...* (Isaiah 11:9)."[42]

Rabbi Shim'on said, "This is the heart, where the abode of the evil impulse inheres within."[43]



40. **solely for that coupling...** According to Rabbi Aḥa, it is indeed God who will arouse the evil impulse, but only for the sublime purpose of procreation. Procreation notwithstanding, the evil impulse will be impotent.

On the verse from Ezekiel, see BT *Sukkah* 52a; *Zohar* 1:109a (*MhN*); 3:267b.

41. **from Cappadocia to Lydda...** This improbable journey from eastern Asia Minor to a city in Palestine recurs frequently in the *Zohar* and usually (though not here) includes an encounter with some surprising character. See 1:69b, 132a, 160a, 197b, 223a; 2:31a, 38b, 80b, 86a; 3:35a, 75b, 221b; *ZḤ* 22a (*MhN*).

The itinerary seems to be intentionally fantastic, though perhaps the author(s) imagined that Cappadocia was a Galilean village near Sepphoris, based on the phrase "Cappadocians of Sepphoris" in JT *Shevi'it* 9:5, 39a. According to a dream interpretation in *Bereshit Rabbah* 68:12, Cappadocia is not far at all from Palestine. Cappadocia figures prominently in M *Ketubbot* 13:11 and BT *Ketubbot* 110b, while Cappadocia and Lydda are linked in *Tosefta Yevamot* 4:5 and BT *Yevamot* 25b.

See Scholem, "She'elot be-Viqqoret ha-Zohar," 40–46 (and the appended note by S. Klein), 56; idem, *Major Trends*, 169; idem, *Kabbalah*, 222; Tishby, *Wisdom of the Zohar* 1:63–64.

42. **joy of learning...** Not only is the evil impulse the source of sexual desire, but also intellectual desire.

See BT *Sukkah* 52a: "*The hidden one I will remove from among you* (Joel 2:20). This is the evil impulse, which is hidden and poised in a person's heart.... *For it has performed mightily* (ibid.). Abbaye said, 'Among the Torah scholars more than anyone!'"

See also BT *Bava Batra* 21a, 22a: "The jealousy of scribes increases wisdom."

43. **This is the heart...** The *holy mount* in the verse from Isaiah signifies the human heart. Numerous rabbinic texts describe the heart as the abode of the evil impulse. See previous note. See also for example, M *Berakhot* 9:5: "*You shall love YHVH your God with all your heart, with all your soul, and with all your might* (Deuteronomy 6:5). *With all* לבבך (*levavekha*), *your heart* [spelled with a double *vet*]—with both your impulses: the good impulse and the evil impulse."

Rabbi Eli'ezer says, "A good heart is the foundation of the body and the soul; consequently it is written: *You shall love YHVH your God with all your heart* (Deuteronomy 6:5), for it is the essence of all!"[44]

When Rav Kahana arrived he said, "In the name of the Masters of Mishnah it is said as follows: The two בנייני (*binyanei*), foundations of, the body are the liver and the heart. For Rabbi Shim'on said in the name of Rabbi Yehudah, 'The liver and the heart rule the body through all the facets of its organs. The ruler of the head is the brain, but of the body there are two: the first is the liver; the second, the heart. This corresponds with what is written in the passage: ויתרצצו הבנים (*Va-yitrotsetsu ha-banim*), *The children jostled each other, within her* (Genesis 25:22)—the two בנייני (*binyanei*), foundations, of the body.'"[45]

What is the significance of ויתרצצו (*va-yitrotsetsu*)? Because the evil impulse is absent from the heart.[46]

*They jostled each other*! The verse should say *They were at ease*![47]

Well, Rav Huna said, "ויתרצצו (*Va-yitrotsetsu*)—they were broken! Namely, their power and strength were broken."[48]



44. **the essence of all** See *Zohar* 2:162b; 3:221b.

45. **The liver and the heart rule the body...** According to medieval physiology (based on Galen), the brain, heart, and liver are the three main organs. The liver receives the digested food and transforms it into "nutritive blood," which flows through the veins, nourishing the peripheral organs. Some blood enters the right chamber of the heart, from which it passes through the lungs and the septum to the left chamber. There the blood mixes with pneuma (spirit), producing "vital blood," which reaches the brain (and the rest of the body) via the arteries.

The description of the three organs as "rulers" apparently alludes to the fact that the initial letters of מוחא (*moḥa*), "brain," לבא (*libba*), "heart," and כבדא (*kavda*), "liver," spell מלך (*melekh*), "king." See Simeon ben Tsemaḥ Duran, *Magen Avot* 5:19: "The experts in medicine agree that there are three major organs in the human being, namely המוח והלב והכבד (*ha-moaḥ ve-halev ve-ha-kaved*), the brain, the heart, and the liver; their sign: מלך (*melekh*), king."

On the three organs, see *Zohar* 2:153a; *ZḤ* 80a (*MhN, Rut*); Moses de León, *Sefer ha-Rimmon*, 127. See also *Zohar* 1:129b (*MhN*). On the brain as "king over all the limbs," see BT *Shabbat* 61a. On Galen's theory, see Siegel, *Galen's System of Physiology and Medicine*, 51, 87–91, 104–6, 113–15, 183–90; Jacquart and Thomasset, *Sexuality and Medicine in the Middle Ages*, 48–50.

On the Masters of Mishnah, see above, note 14.

46. **What is the significance of ויתרצצו (*va-yitrotsetsu*)?...** It is unclear whether this statement is still part of Rabbi Shim'on's teaching or an independent voice. Either way, the speaker is suggesting that the verb ויתרצצו (*va-yitrotsetsu*), whose simple meaning is *they jostled each other* or *they struggled*, points to the elimination of the evil impulse from the heart. Precisely how this is so is explained immediately below.

On the elimination (or tempering) of the evil impulse in the post-resurrection body, see above, note 34.

47. **The verse should say...** If the evil impulse is absent, why does the verse say that the liver and heart jostled or struggled?

48. **they were broken...** The verb ויתרצצו (*va-yitrotsetsu*) derives from the root רצץ (*rtsts*), whose basic meaning is "crush."

Rabbi Yehudah said, "What does the body say? '*If so, for what am I here?* (ibid.). Why was I created?' Immediately: *She went to inquire of YHVH* (ibid.)."[49]

*YHVH said to her, "Two* גוים *(goyim), nations, are in your womb, two peoples . . ."* (ibid., 23)—these are the two גאים (*ge'im*), proud ones: liver and heart.[50]

Rabbi Yose said, "The brain and the heart."[51]

Rabbi Yehudah said, "The brain is not included in this, as implied by what is written: *in your womb.* The brain is not in the womb, but in the head!"

*Two peoples [from your loins shall issue; one people shall be mightier than the other], the greater shall serve the lesser* (ibid.). This refers to the liver—which is greater and larger, and ministers to the heart. As Rabbi Yehudah said, "The liver receives the blood, and with it ministers to the heart."[52] [138b]

*The first came out ruddy* (ibid., 25). Rav Kahana said, "The liver is the first, and it is ruddy. Why is it ruddy? Because it swallows the blood first."

Rabbi Eli'ezer says, "Why it is called *the first*? Because it is first to swallow the blood from every kind of food; first in blood, but not in formation. How then shall we establish *the greater shall serve the lesser*? Because it is greater and larger in size than the heart, but it serves the heart."[53]



Rabbi Abba said, "What is the point of this section? It means to demonstrate to the people of the world that even though there will be perfection on earth, the natural way of the world will not change."[54]

Hence the verb is appropriate; it indicates the breaking of the desirous power of the liver and heart. Cf. *Zohar* 1:137b.

49. **Why was I created?** Rabbi Yehudah's point is not entirely clear. Perhaps the body is lamenting its enfeebled status. Alternatively, the body is wondering what its purpose is in the absence of the evil impulse.

50. **two** גאים **(*ge'im*), proud ones . . .** As rulers of the body, the liver and heart are the "proud ones." In fact the verse itself reads: *two* גיים (*ge'im*), an anomalous spelling for גוים (*goyim*), "nations." See *Minḥat Shai*, ad loc.

See *Bereshit Rabbah* 63:7; BT *Avodah Zarah* 11a; *Leqaḥ Tov* on Genesis 25:23.

It is possible that Rabbi Yehudah is the speaker.

51. **The brain and the heart** See *Midrash Mishlei* 1:1: "*But where can wisdom be found?* (Job 28:12). . . . Rabbi Yehoshu'a [alternate reading: Eli'ezer] says, 'In the head.' Rabbi Eli'ezer [alternate reading: Yehoshu'a] says, 'In the heart. . . . Why in the heart? Because all the organs are dependent on the heart.'"

52. ***the greater shall serve the lesser . . .*** That is, the liver—which is larger than the heart—serves the heart. As noted above, the liver transmits the blood to the heart.

In its biblical context, the oracular statement alludes to Esau, the older (and his descendants) serving Jacob, the younger (and his descendants).

53. **first in blood, but not in formation . . .** Although the liver is first to receive the blood, in the fetus the heart is formed before the liver; and although the heart is created first and is therefore arguably *greater* (older), nevertheless on account of their relative size, the liver is referred to as *greater* and the heart as *lesser.*

Some of the manuscripts read "Rabbi El'azar."

54. **What is the point of this section? . . .** Why, in discussing the post-resurrection body, does the Torah bother to mention

Rabbi Yeisa said, "Come and see: It is the liver that hunts provisions *and has a taste for hunted game* (ibid., 28), while the heart is contemplative, *a dweller in tents* (ibid., 27), as is written: *Jacob was boiling a stew* (ibid., 29)—thinking thoughts, grappling with Torah."[55]

*Jacob was boiling a stew.* Rabbi Bo said in the name of Rabbi Aḥa, "The nature of the world never changes. Come and see what is written: ויזד יעקב נזיד (*Va-yazed Ya'akov nazid*), *Jacob was boiling a stew*, as is said: *that* זדו (*zadu*), *they schemed, against them* (Exodus 18:11), which is translated as 'that they thought.' In other words, the heart thinks and ponders Torah, knowledge of its Creator. What is written? *Esau came in from the field exhausted* (Genesis 25:29). The liver, whose nature is to go forth and hunt game for its mouth to swallow—when it cannot find any, it is called 'exhausted.' It says to the heart: Instead of pondering these matters—words of Torah—ponder food and drink to sustain your body, as is written: *Esau said to Jacob, 'Let me gulp down some of this red stuff'* (ibid., 30)—for it is my custom to swallow the blood and transmit it to the other organs. *For I am exhausted* (ibid.)—lacking food and drink. The heart says: Give me the prime and choice of all you swallow; give me your birthright, as is written: *Sell now your birthright to me* (ibid., 31)—offering of desire. While the heart ponders and thinks about food, the liver swallows—for were it not for the heart's musings and cravings for food, the liver and the organs would not be able to swallow. [139a] As Rabbi Yose said, 'So is the way of servants: they do not eat until the master eats.'"[56]



the workings of the liver and heart? Even following the resurrection, people will still eat and drink, and the body will continue to function normally.

See Maimonides, *Mishneh Torah, Hilkhot Melakhim* 12:1: "Do not presume that in the Messianic Age any facet of the world's nature will change or that there will be innovation in the work of creation. Rather the world will pursue its natural course." See also, idem, *Hilkhot Teshuvah* 9:2. See also BT *Avodah Zarah* 54b for the origin of the expression "the world pursues its natural course."

55. **the liver . . . hunts provisions . . . the heart is contemplative . . .** *Esau* "the hunter" signifies the liver, desirous for food, whereas *Jacob* "the scholar" signifies the heart. Even the post-eschatological body is marked by a kind of duality.

On *dweller in tents* as signifying rabbinic scholarship, see *Bereshit Rabbah* 63:10, where *tents* signify Shem and Eber's houses of study.

On boiling stew as thinking thoughts, see next note.

Genesis 25:27–28 reads: *The boys grew up. Esau became a skilled hunter, a man of the field, while Jacob was a mild man, dwelling in tents. Isaac loved Esau because he had a taste for hunted game but Rebekah loved Jacob.*

56. ***Jacob was boiling a stew* . . .** This alludes to the heart's contemplative nature, for the expression ויזד נזיד (*va-yazed nazid*), "to boil a stew," in fact means "to think a thought." This reading is based on Onqelos' rendering of another word from the same verbal root—זדו (*zadu*), *they schemed*—into Aramaic as חשיבו (*ḥashivu*), "they thought." See Scholem, "Parashah Ḥadashah," 434 (Addendum 1 in this volume).

Thus, the liver arouses the heart to desire food. Though luring the heart away from

Rabbi Yose said, "It is written afterward: *Jacob gave Esau bread and lentil stew* (ibid., 34). Just as lentils are round like a wheel and the sphere revolves eternally, never deviating from its path, so the human being at that time: notwithstanding all the goodness, glory, and perfection that will be, the way of the world—to eat and drink—will not alter."[57]

Our Mishnah: We have learned: Four רוחות (*ruḥot*), winds, of the world blow; and one day the blessed Holy One will arouse a single רוח (*ruaḥ*), comprising four *ruḥot*, to establish the body, as is written: *From four ruḥot come, O ruaḥ* (Ezekiel 37:9). It is not written *in four*, but *from four ruḥot* of the world—comprising all four. It has been taught: This *ruaḥ* is the spirit that procreates, the spirit that eats and drinks. For there is no difference between this world and the days of the Messiah, aside from the subjugation to the kingdoms alone; and there is no difference between this world and the resurrection of the dead, aside from purification and apprehension of knowledge.[58]



sublime matters to more earthly and basic considerations, this "seduction" is vital, as it is only when the heart is aroused for food that the other organs can fulfill their nutritive function.

"Offering of desire" renders קונמיתא דתאיבא (*qonmita de-ta'iva*). *Qonmita* is obscure but may derive from קונם (*qonam*), "sacrifice, offering, vow." See *Nitsotsei Orot*; *Matoq mi-Devash*. Whatever the precise sense, once aroused the heart demands the prime for itself.

On servants not eating until the masters eat, see BT *Ketubbot* 61a.

57. **Just as lentils are round like a wheel...** The round shape of the lentil recalls the ever-revolving celestial sphere, which in turn alludes to the idea that the natural order of the world will not change. See above, note 54.

See *Bereshit Rabbah* 63:14: "Just as a lentil is shaped like a wheel, so the world is like a wheel." See also BT *Bava Batra* 16b.

Medieval cosmology imagined the heavens as containing a series of concentric spheres in which are suspended the heavenly bodies. On the continuous revolution of the celestial sphere (presumably the outermost sphere in which all the other spheres are located), see Maimonides, *Mishneh Torah, Hilkhot Yesodei ha-Torah* 1:5; 3:1. See also BT *Shabbat* 151b.

On eating and drinking after the resurrection, cf. BT *Berakhot* 17a: "A pearl in the mouth of Rav: In the world to come, there is no eating or drinking...."

58. ***From four ruḥot come, O ruaḥ...*** The verse from Ezekiel continues: *and breathe into these slain, that they may live.* The context is Ezekiel's vision of the dry bones. The word *ruaḥ* means "breath, wind, spirit, direction." See *Zohar* 1:175b–176a, 235a; 2:13a–b; 3:130b (*IR*).

According to rabbinic tradition, the dust of Adam's body was gathered from the four directions of the world. See *Targum Yerushalmi*, Genesis 2:7; *Tanḥuma, Pequdei* 3; *Pirqei de-Rabbi Eli'ezer* 11; BT *Sanhedrin* 38a–b. Here, the four directions may also symbolize the four elements (fire, air, water, and earth). In the main body of the *Zohar*, the four winds symbolize the sefirotic quartet of Ḥesed, Gevurah, Tif'eret, and Shekhinah, which are symbolized respectively by south, north, east, and west.

On the four winds of the world, see BT *Gittin* 31b; *Bava Batra* 25a; *ZḤ* 13a (*MhN*).

The *Zohar* here follows Maimonides' adoption of Shemu'el's understanding of the Messianic Age (see BT *Berakhot* 34b; *Shabbat* 63a, 151b; *Pesaḥim* 68a; *Sanhedrin* 91b, 99a):

Rav Naḥman said, "And longevity."[59]

Rav Yosef said, "Aren't the days of the Messiah and the resurrection of the dead one and the same?"

He replied, "No! For we have learned: The Sanctuary prior to the ingathering of the exiles; the ingathering of the exiles prior to the resurrection of the dead—the resurrection is the last of all. How do we know? As is written: *YHVH rebuilds Jerusalem; He gathers the banished of Israel. He heals the brokenhearted and binds up their wounds* (Psalms 147:2–3)—this is the resurrection of the dead, a healing for the brokenhearted for their dead. First He rebuilds Jerusalem; afterward He gathers the banished of Israel; last of all—He heals the brokenhearted."[60]

We have learned: The ingathering of the exiles precedes the resurrection of the dead by forty years, as we have said: *Isaac was forty years old* (Genesis 25:20). What is the nature of these forty years? Rav Kahana said in the name of Rabbi Beroka, "From the ingathering of the exiles until the resurrection of the dead, countless troubles and ever-so-many wars will arouse upon Israel. Happy is the one who escapes them, as is written: [139b] *At that time your people will be rescued, all who are found inscribed in the book* (Daniel 12:1)!"[61]



Rabbi Yehudah said, "From here: *Many will be purified and purged and refined* (ibid., 10)."

"there is no difference between this world and the days of the Messiah, aside from the subjugation to the kingdoms alone." See Maimonides, *Mishneh Torah, Hilkhot Melakhim* 12:2; idem, *Pereq Ḥeleq.*

"Purification" apparently signifies the state of the post-resurrection body, purified of all dross. See *Zohar* 1:116a, 126a (both *MhN*).

On post-resurrection procreation, see *Zohar* 1:128b, 137b–138a (both *MhN*). On post-resurrection eating and drinking, see *Zohar* 138b–139a (*MhN*). On the attainment of knowledge, see *Zohar* 1:113b, 126a, 135a–b, 140a; *ZḤ* 15d (all *MhN*). On the expression "our Mishnah," see above, note 26.

59. **And longevity** Presumably meaning indefinitely extended lifetimes.

Cf. Maimonides, *Pereq Ḥeleq*, on the Messianic era: "All human life will be longer, for when worries and troubles are removed, men live longer."

See also Isaiah 65:20: *No more shall there be an infant or graybeard who does not live out his days. He who dies at a hundred years shall be reckoned a youth; and he who fails to reach a hundred shall be reckoned accursed.* See also BT *Pesaḥim* 68a.

60. ***YHVH rebuilds Jerusalem; He gathers the banished of Israel...*** See BT *Berakhot* 49a; JT *Ma'aser Sheni* 5:2, 56a; *Tanḥuma, Noaḥ* 11; *Zohar* 1:134a.

Presumably, Rav Naḥman is the speaker.

61. **precedes... by forty years...** The verse from Genesis continues: *when he took Rebekah as his wife.* It signifies the union of soul and body post-resurrection. See *Zohar* 1:136b–137a (*MhN*), pages 410–11.

See also BT *Sanhedrin* 99a in the name of Rabbi Eli'ezer: "The days of the Messiah will last forty years, as is said: *For forty years I will be angry with the generation* (Psalms 95:10)."

The full verse from Daniel reads: *At that time, the great prince, Michael, will appear. It will be a time of trouble, the like of which has never been seen since the nation came into being. At that time, your people will be rescued, all who are found inscribed in the book.*

On the wars of the messianic age, see BT *Sanhedrin* 97a; Maimonides, *Mishneh Torah, Hilkhot Melakhim* 12:2; *Zohar* 2:7b.

Rabbi Yitsḥak said, "From here: *I will refine them as one refines silver, and test them as one tests gold* (Zechariah 13:9)."[62]

During those days, there shall be days of which it shall be said *I have no delight in them* (Ecclesiastes 12:1). From the onset of the afflictions until the resurrection of the dead there will be forty years.[63]

Rav Huna said, "Come and see: *For the Israelites had traveled in the wilderness for forty years... because they had not heeded the voice of YHVH* (Joshua 5:6)—similarly here."[64]

Rav Yosef said, "All of these have spoken a single word. At the end of forty years, when the troubles will pass and the wicked will be obliterated, the dead—the dwellers in dust—will live. Why so? On account of what is written: [*What do you imagine against YHVH, that He will make an utter end?*] *Affliction will not rise a second time* (Nahum 1:9)—for what they have endured suffices them. Following the resurrection of the dead, the world will be settled securely in its place, as is written: *On that day YHVH will be one and His name one* (Zechariah 14:9)."[65]



Rabbi El'azar son of Arakh was sitting and was greatly distressed. Rabbi Yehoshu'a entered in his presence. He said to him, "Why is the countenance of the radiance of the lamp of the world darkened?"[66]

62. ***I will refine them...*** According to Rabbi Yehudah and Rabbi Yitsḥak, the troubles of the messianic age serve to test and purify the people. See *Zohar* 2:7b.

63. ***I have no delight in them...*** Cf. BT *Shabbat* 151b.

64. **similarly here** The full verse from Joshua reads: *For the Israelites had traveled in the wilderness for forty years, until the entire nation—the men of military age who had left Egypt—had perished; because they had not heeded the voice of YHVH, and YHVH had sworn never to let them see the land that YHVH had sworn to their fathers to assign to us, a land flowing with milk and honey.*

Just as the Israelites wandered for forty years in the desert before entering the Promised Land so that only the worthy would enter, so there will be forty years of trials and tribulations before the resurrection, to test and refine the people.

65. **All of these have spoken a single word...** Namely, forty years of affliction will precede the resurrection in order to purify the people. According to Rav Yosef, this amount of time is sufficient to refine the remaining righteous.

On the verse from Zechariah, see *Zohar* 1:116b (*MhN*).

66. **lamp of the world...** בוצינא דעלמא (*Botsina de-alma*). An honorary epithet for Rabbi El'azar. Compare *Avot de-Rabbi Natan*, A 25, where Rabban Yoḥanan son of Zakkai is called נר העולם (*ner ha-olam*), "light of the world." See also JT *Shabbat* 2:6, 5b; Liebes, *Peraqim*, 143, 156. See also 2 Samuel 21:17; *Bereshit Rabbah* 85:4; BT *Ketubbot* 17a, where Rabbi Abbahu is called "Lamp of Light." In the main body of the *Zohar*, Rabbi Shim'on son of Yoḥai is referred to as *botsina qaddisha*, "holy lamp." On the "darkened" countenance, see *Zohar* 3:6a.

Some of the manuscripts and printed editions omit this statement by Rabbi Yehoshu'a, proceeding immediately to the next paragraph as though it were spoken by Rabbi Yehoshu'a. I have followed O2, which seems to preserve the best reading here.

He replied, "Great fear and trembling have overcome me. For I see what our Companions—the Masters of Mishnah, upon whom the holy spirit settled—have aroused. Concerning what they have aroused, that salvation shall be in the sixth—this is fine and well. But I foresee a greater duration for the denizens of dust: In the sixth millennium, in its four hundred and eighth year, the denizens of dust shall rise enduringly. Accordingly our Companions were aroused by the verse that referred to them as בני חת (*benei Ḥet*), *the Hittites* (Genesis 23:3)—חת (*Ḥet*), for they shall be aroused in חת, the four hundred and eighth, year. This corresponds with the verse בשנת היובל הזאת (*Bi-shnat ha-yovel ha-zot*), *In this year of jubilee, you shall return, each man to his holding* (Leviticus 25:13)—when הזאת (*ha-zot*) shall be complete, which is five thousand four hundred and eight, *you shall return, each man to his holding*—to his soul: his holding and inheritance."[67]

Rabbi Yehoshu'a said further, "Let this not trouble you. For look at what we have learned: There are three groups: of the completely righteous, of the completely wicked, and of the intermediate. [140a] The completely righteous shall rise with the rising of the dead of the land of Israel some years earlier, preceding at first—in the fortieth year of the ingathering of the exiles. As for the latter, all of them at the 408th year of the sixth millennium, as we have said."[68]

67. **But I foresee . . .** Rabbi El'azar is distressed because—unlike the Companions who claimed that the redemption and resurrection would occur in the sixth millennium (sometime between 1240/41 and 2240/41 C.E., though ideally nearer its beginning)—he foresees a longer duration: the resurrection will occur 408 years into the sixth millennium, i.e., in the year 1648 C.E.

Rabbi El'azar derives this date based on the numerical value of the word חת (*Ḥet*) equaling 408, buttressed by the numerical value of the word הזאת (*ha-zot*), "this," equaling 5,408 (if one counts the ה as 5,000—as is sometimes done—rather than the usual 5). According to *Zohar* 1:123a, 124a (both *MhN*), *benei Ḥet*, "the Hittites," designates the bodies of the righteous dead. The passage here is in Aramaic and appears to be interpreting the earlier passages, which are in Hebrew.

On the significance of the sixth millennium, see BT *Sanhedrin* 97a: "Rav Kattina said, 'The world will exist for six thousand years—and for one thousand lie desolate.'" See *Zohar* 1:116b–117a, 119a, 127b–128a (*MhN*), 181b–182a; 2:9b–10a; *ZḤ* 16d (*MhN*), 56b–c.

On the Messianic significance of the year 1648 C.E., see *Zohar* 2:10a; Scholem, *Sabbatai Sevi*, 88–93; Silver, *Messianic Speculation*, 92, 151–92 passim.

See also *ZḤ* 27d–28a (*MhN*) for another story featuring Rabbi El'azar son of Arakh and his grief.

On the epithet "Masters of Mishnah," see above, note 14.

68. **Let this not trouble you . . .** See BT *Rosh ha-Shanah* 16b–17a in the name of the House of Shammai: "There are three groups at the Day of Judgment: one of the completely righteous, one of the completely wicked, and one of the intermediate. The completely righteous are written and sealed immediately for life; the completely wicked are written and sealed immediately for Hell . . . ; the intermediate go down to Hell and squeal [on account of their punishment] and rise."

On the dead of the land of Israel rising first, see *Bereshit Rabbah* 74:1; JT *Kil'ayim*

"Who will merit this duration?! Who will remain steadfast in his faith until that time?! That is why I was distressed."[69]

He said to him, "Rabbi, look at what we have learned: *Let there be* אור (*or*), *light* (Genesis 1:3)—let there be רז (*raz*), mystery!"[70]

He resumed and said, "Through *teshuvah*, all is brought forward."[71]

Rabbi Yehoshu'a said, "Had you not said so, we would have shut the mouths of those who await salvation every day, as is written: *stronghold of salvation* (Isaiah 33:6). What is meant by *salvation*? Those who await salvation every day."[72]

What is Rabbi El'azar's view? As is written: *Many of those who sleep in the dust of earth shall awake* (Daniel 12:2). As implied by what is written: *of those who sleep*—these are the righteous whose revival precedes this.[73]

By how many years shall they precede?

Rabbi Yehudah says, "Two hundred and ten years."[74]

9:4, 32c; BT *Ketubbot* 111a; *Tanḥuma, Vayḥi* 3; *Zohar* 1:113a (*MhN*), 131a, 181b; 2:151b; Moses de León, *Sefer ha-Mishqal*, 89–90.

69. **Who will merit this duration?!...** Rabbi El'azar is speaking. This tone of despair reappears in *Zohar* 1:219b; 2:9a, 188b; 3:112a; *ZḤ* 16d (*MhN*).

70. **let there be רז (*raz*), mystery** Although Rabbi Yehoshu'a apparently accepted Rabbi El'azar's teaching regarding the 408th year, he now rejects Rabbi El'azar's specific calculation of the end. The end-time is and ought to remain concealed.

Both אור (*or*), "light," and רז (*raz*), "mystery," have the numerical value of 207. The verse from Genesis (*Let there be light*) is now read as "Let there be a mystery," i.e., may the messianic end remain concealed. See *ZḤ* 8d (*MhN*).

See also *ZḤ* 8a (*MhN*): "Those who calculate messianic ends are fools!" See also BT *Sanhedrin* 97b; Maimonides, *Mishneh Torah, Hilkhot Melakhim* 12:2; *Zohar* 1:118a.

71. **Through *teshuvah*, all is brought forward** Though an end-time has been set, the redemption and the resurrection can be brought forward by repentance. Perhaps Rabbi El'azar also intends that because *teshuvah* has the power to advance the end, the mystery of the end remains.

On *teshuvah* and redemption, see JT *Ta'anit* 1:1, 63d; BT *Sanhedrin* 97b; *Pirqei de-Rabbi Eli'ezer* 43; *Tanḥuma, Beḥuqqotai* 3; *Zohar* 2:188b–189a; *ZḤ* 8a, 23c–d (both *MhN*).

72. **Had you not said so...** If the end-time is predetermined, what is the sense of awaiting salvation every day? See *Zohar* 2:189a for a similar problematic.

The full verse from Isaiah reads: *He will be the faithfulness of your times—stronghold of salvation, wisdom, and knowledge; the awe of YHVH is his treasure.*

See BT *Shabbat* 31a, citing this verse: "Rava said, 'When a human is led in for judgment, he is asked: "Were you honest in your business dealings? Did you set aside time for Torah? Did you generate new life? Did you await salvation? Did you engage in the dialectics of wisdom? Did you understand one thing from another?"'" See also *Zohar* 1:4a.

73. **What is Rabbi El'azar's view?...** From where does he derive the idea that *teshuvah* brings the redemption and resurrection forward? The verse from Daniel implies that only some will rise (*many of those*, not all), understood as implying that the righteous who repented are the first to be revived; hence repentance brings forward.

See *Zohar* 1:127b (*MhN*).

74. **Two hundred and ten years** This would set the resurrection of the righteous

Rabbi Yitsḥak says, "רדי, Two hundred and fourteen, years, as is written: וירד (*ve-yerd*), *let him rule, from Jacob*... (Numbers 24:19)—by ירד, two hundred and fourteen, years the righteous precede the remainder of humanity."[75]

Rav Naḥman said, "In accordance with the extent [the body] has withered in the dust."[76]

Rabbi Yose said to him, "If so, there will be many resurrections! Rather, all will occur at the same time, as stated in the vision *the oracle was true and a great host* (Daniel 10:1)."[77]

*There was a famine in the land besides the earlier famine that had occurred in the days of Abraham* (Genesis 26:1).

Rabbi Abbahu opened, "*While the king was on his couch, my nard yielded its fragrance* (Song of Songs 1:12). As we have learned: In the time to come the righteous shall experience four eras and four epochs, each different from one another. The first: At that time, wisdom will flourish in the world; and they shall attain an apprehension unattained in this world. As we have learned: Rabbi Pinḥas said, 'The apprehension of the righteous in the time to come exceeds the ministering angels, as is written: [*The earth will be filled with knowledge of* YHVH] *as waters cover the sea* (Isaiah 11:9).' The second: They shall engage....[78] [*ZḤ* 27b]



at 1438 C.E. No reason or textual support is offered for this number, though in light of the following statement by Rabbi Yitsḥak, it is possible that this number derives from the number of years the Israelites were in Egypt, based on the midrashic interpretation of the word רדו (*redu*), *go down*, from Genesis 42:2, whose numerical value is 210. See *Bereshit Rabbah* 91:2; *Pirqei de-Rabbi Eli'ezer* 48.

75. **Two hundred and fourteen...** The numerical value of ירד (*yerd*) is 214. Hence, according to Rabbi Yitsḥak, the righteous will be resurrected in 1434 C.E.

The context of the verse from Numbers is Balaam's eschatological vision.

76. **the extent...withered in the dust** The sooner the body withers and decomposes, the sooner it rises.

77. **all will occur at the same time...** The expression *great host* proves that many will rise, thereby countering Rav Naḥman's view.

78. ***While the king was on his couch...*** The text of this homily is fragmentary and breaks off mid-sentence. The sense of the verse from the Song of Songs and the opening verse from Genesis is thus not apparent.

On the apprehension of the righteous in the time to come, see above, note 12. On the righteous exceeding the ministering angels, see BT *Sanhedrin* 92b–93a: "Rabbi Yoḥanan said, 'The righteous are greater than the ministering angels, as is said: *He answered and said, "But I see four men walking about unbound and unharmed in the fire; and the fourth looks like a divine being"* (Daniel 3:25) [i.e., the people are mentioned before the angel].'" See also *Zohar* 1:127b; *ZḤ* 26b (both *MhN*). Cf. JT *Shabbat* 6:9, 8d; *Tanḥuma, Balaq* 14; *Tanḥuma* (Buber), *Balaq* 23; *Tanḥuma, Vayishlaḥ* 2. On Isaiah 11:9, see *Zohar* 1:113b, 125b, 130a (all three *MhN*); 2:68a; 3:23a.

פרשת ויצא

# Parashat Va-Yetse

"HE LEFT" (GENESIS 28:10–32:3)

*He knows what is in darkness* (Daniel 2:22) even though *light dwells with Him* (ibid.), as is written: *'If one hides in secret places, do I not see him?' declares YHVH* (Jeremiah 23:24).[1]

Did Rabbi Yehudah really say this? For we have said that there is wisdom in the juxtaposition of these verses concerning all that was said. But now the plain meaning of the verses is required—Abraham was, Isaac was, Jacob was![2]

He replied, "Even though they were, I have contemplated to fathom the wisdom of the verses!"

Rabbi Yitsḥak opened, "*A psalm of David. YHVH, who may abide in Your tent? Who may dwell on Your holy mountain? He who walks blamelessly and does justice and speaks the truth in his heart...* (Psalms 15:1–5). What does this imply?"[3]

Rabbi Yehudah son of Rabbi Yose said, "These ten correspond to the Ten Commandments that the children of Jacob were destined to fulfill at that place."[4]

1. ***He knows what is in darkness...*** The opening section of the *Zohar*'s commentary to *parashat Va-Yetse* is fragmentary. The beginning is clearly missing; hence what initially appears is difficult to interpret.

On the verse from Daniel, see *Tanḥuma*, *Tetsavveh* 8; *Tanḥuma* (Buber), *Tetsavveh* 6; *Zohar* 2:100b–101a. On the verse from Jeremiah, see *Zohar* 1:68a.

2. **Did Rabbi Yehudah really say this?...** Alas, the sense of this statement and the subsequent reply is not apparent. It seems, though, that the speaker is rejecting a particular interpretation in favor of the simple or plain sense of Scripture.

3. ***speaks the truth in his heart...*** The psalm continues: *who has no slander upon his tongue, nor does to his fellow man evil, nor bears reproach for his kin; the debased in his eyes is despised, but to fearers of YHVH he accords honor; when he vows to his hurt he does not revoke it. His money he does not give at interest; and he takes no bribe for the innocent. He who does these will never stumble.*

4. **These ten correspond to...** According to Rabbi Yehudah, Psalms 15 lists ten virtues corresponding to the Ten Commandments. See Moses de León, *Sefer ha-Rimmon*, 380–87 for a parallel discussion.

According to Mowinckel, *The Psalms in*

Rabbi Yose said, "But look, they are eleven!"[5]

He replied, "*Who has no slander upon his tongue, nor does to his fellow man evil* is a single matter. For whoever slanders his companion immediately does him evil. If he does not slander with his tongue then he does not do him evil."

Now, who would ever compare these with the Ten Commandments?

Rabbi Yehudah said, "All of the Ten Commandments are implied in them. *He who walks blamelessly*—corresponding to *I am YHVH your God* (Exodus 20:2), teaching that a person should accept upon himself the dread of the yoke of the kingdom of heaven, and that he is not permitted to question what he is unable to grasp. As implied by what is written: *I am YHVH your God*—unqualified. [27c] Here is written *He who walks* תמים (*tamim*), *blamelessly*, and there is written *Be* תמים (*tamim*), *wholehearted, with YHVH your God* (Deuteronomy 18:13). You are not allowed to contemplate what you have not been permitted!"[6]



*Israel's Worship*, 1:179, Psalms 15 enumerates ten virtues and thus belongs to the decalogical tradition.

"That place" indicates Mount Zion in Jerusalem, the site of the Temple.

5. **they are eleven** According to rabbinic tradition, there are eleven virtues enumerated in the psalm. See BT *Makkot* 23b–24a: "Rabbi Simlai expounded, 'Six hundred and thirteen commandments were communicated to Moses at Sinai... David came and reduced them to eleven, as is written: *A psalm of David. YHVH, who may abide in Your tent? Who may dwell on Your holy mountain?* [1] *He who walks blamelessly and* [2] *does justice and* [3] *speaks the truth in his heart.* [4] *Who has no slander upon his tongue* [5] *nor does to his fellow man evil* [6] *nor bears reproach for his kin;* [7] *the debased in his eyes is despised,* [8] *but to fearers of YHVH he accords honor;* [9] *when he vows to his hurt he does not revoke it.* [10] *His money he does not give at interest and* [11] *takes no bribe for the innocent. He who does these will never stumble.*'"

6. ***He who walks* תמים (*tamim*), *blamelessly*...** According to one strand of tradition, the opening statement of the Ten Commandments, *I am YHVH your God*, is in fact a commandment to believe in the existence of divinity and to accept the sovereignty of the Kingdom of Heaven. (See *Mekhilta, Baḥodesh* 5; Maimonides, *Mishneh Torah, Minyan ha-Mitsvot* 1; idem, *Mishneh Torah, Hilkhot Yesodei Torah* 1:6; Naḥmanides on Exodus 20:2.) According to Rabbi Yehudah, this commandment is intimated in the virtue of walking תמים (*tamim*), understood here as the quality of perfect trust in God: "wholeheartedly." This quality includes not questioning what is forbidden.

Cf. BT *Yoma* 67b, which suggests that the verse *I am YHVH your God* (Leviticus 18:4) is employed to anchor laws that one might be tempted to doubt: "*I am YHVH*—I, YHVH, have made it a statute, and you have no permission to question them." See also *Tanḥuma, Mishpatim* 7.

Cf. *Bereshit Rabbah* 8:2: "Rabbi El'azar said in the name of Ben Sira, 'About what is too great for you, do not inquire; what is too hard for you, do not investigate; what is too wondrous for you, know not; of what is hidden from you, do not ask! Contemplate what was permitted to you: you have no business with hidden things.'"

On Deuteronomy 18:13, see BT *Pesaḥim* 113b: "How do we know that one must not consult astrologers? As is said: *Be wholehearted with YHVH your God.*'" See Rashi on this verse: "Walk with him in utter trust in anticipation of Him. Do not explore the future, rather, whatever befalls you, accept with perfect trust. Then you will be with Him as His portion." See also Naḥmanides,

*And does justice* (Psalms 15:2)—corresponding to *You shall have no other gods beside Me; You shall not bow down to them or serve them* (Exodus 20:3, 5). Hence, Rabbi Yehudah said, "Nothing prevails over desecration of the Name. How do we know? From the enticer, as is written: *Let your hand be the first against him to put him to death* (Deuteronomy 13:10). Why? *For he sought to make you stray from YHVH your God* (ibid., 11). If one kills him, he is called 'righteous,' 'zealous,' and 'one who does justice.' This is the meaning of *and does justice* (Psalms 15:2)."[7]

*And speaks the truth in his heart* (ibid.)—corresponding to *You shall not take the name of YHVH your God in vain* (Exodus 20:7).[8]

Rabbi Yehudah said, "They are not in order. But even though they are not in order, it does not matter."[9]

*Who has no slander upon his tongue nor does to his fellow man evil* (Psalms 15:3)—corresponding to *You shall not bear false witness against your fellow* (Exodus 20:13).

*Nor bears reproach for his kin* (Psalms 15:3)—corresponding to one who desecrates Sabbaths publicly.[10]



ad loc.: "That we are to direct our hearts to Him only and believe that He alone does everything. It is He who knows the truth about all future events. . . ."

7. **corresponding to *You shall have no other gods beside Me*...** Idolatry is the most heinous of all sins and is not permitted under any circumstances. One who kills an idolator thus "does justice."

"Desecration of the Name" is understood variously by different commentators. According to Rashi, BT *Yoma* 86a, s.v. *ḥillul ha-shem*, it refers to one who sins and (by doing so) leads others to sin. Here, it is correlated with idolatry and leading others to idolatry.

On the severity of desecration of the Name, cf. BT *Qiddushin* 40a: "We have learned there: No credit is extended for desecration of the Name, whether unwittingly or intentionally. What is meant by 'no credit is extended'? Mar Zutra said, 'They [i.e., Heaven] do not act like a shopkeeper [i.e., who extends credit and accepts deferred payment —Rashi].' Mar the son of Ravina said, 'This is to teach that if it [one's account of sin and merit] is equally balanced, it [the desecration of God's name] tips the scale.'"

See also BT *Yoma* 86a in the name of Rabbi El'azar son of Azariah in the name of Rabbi Yishma'el: "But if he has been guilty of desecration of the Name, then repentance has no power to suspend punishment, nor Yom Kippur to procure atonement, nor suffering to complete it. Rather, all of them together suspend [the punishment]—and death completes it, as is said: *YHVH of hosts revealed Himself in my ears: this iniquity shall never be expiated by you until you die* (Isaiah 22:14)."

See also Maimonides, *Mishneh Torah, Hilkhot Yesodei ha-Torah* 5:1–2.

8. ***And speaks the truth in his heart*...** "Taking God's name in vain," which is classically understood to have numerous meanings, is understood here as swearing falsely, i.e., lying. See BT *Shevu'ot* 21a.

Although the first two correspondences were outlined by Rabbi Yehudah, from here on they appear to be stated anonymously.

9. **They are not in order...** The first three virtues listed in Psalms 15 correspond to the first three of the Ten Commandments. From here on, however, the correspondences do not follow the order of the Ten Commandments.

10. ***Nor bears reproach for his kin* . . .** The biblical wording is cryptic: וחרפה לא נשא על קרבו (*ve-ḥerpah lo nasa al qerovo*), whose simple sense might be construed as

Rabbi Yose says, "Corresponding to *You shall not steal* (Exodus 20:13), as is written: *If the sun rises upon him* (ibid. 22:2)."[11]

נבזה בעיניו נמאס (*Nivzeh be-einav nim'as*), *He is debased in his eyes—despised* (Psalms 15:4)—corresponding to *You shall not murder* (Exodus 20:13). One who is debased in his own eyes does not engage in disputes that he would kill; nor is he killed.[12]

*But to fearers of YHVH he accords honor* (Psalms 15:4)—corresponding to *Honor your father and mother* (Exodus 20:12).

Rabbi Yose said, "A person is obligated to honor his father and mother in all instances, except if they told him to transgress the words of Torah or worship idols, in which case he is not obligated to honor them; therefore: *but to fearers of YHVH he accords honor.*"[13]

*When he vows* להרע (*le-hara*), *to his hurt, he does not revoke it* (Psalms 15:4)—corresponding to *You shall not commit adultery* (Exodus 20:13). For if his impulse seeks to dominate him, let him impose an oath upon his impulse like Boaz, who said: *As YHVH lives! Lie down until morning* (Ruth 3:13).[14]



[*When his kin behave badly,*] *he does not pass over the misdeed in silence because of kinship* (Alter, *The Book of Psalms,* 44). Alternatively, the phrase might be rendered *nor takes up a reproach against his kin.* Yet another possible rendering: *nor bears reproach for his acts toward his kin.* The *Zohar,* however, appears to be reading the phrase as *nor brings reproach upon his kin*—by casting disgrace. Such disgrace is brought about through public desecration of the Sabbath. Hence, the virtue from the psalm corresponds to the fourth commandment: *Remember the Sabbath day to keep it holy* (Exodus 20:8).

On the severity of desecrating the Sabbath publicly, see BT *Eruvin* 69a; *Ḥullin* 5a; *Vayiqra Rabbah* 2:9.

11. **Corresponding to *You shall not steal*...** According to Rabbi Yose, the Psalms phrase—likewise construed as *nor brings reproach upon his kin*—corresponds to the sixth commandment: *You shall not steal.* That is, their disgrace is brought about by stealing—once the thief's identity comes to light.

Exodus 22:2 reads: *If while tunneling, a thief should be found and is struck down and dies, there is no bloodguilt for him. If the sun rises upon him, there is bloodguilt for him.* See Onqelos on Exodus 22:2, who rendered *If the sun rises upon him* as "if the eye of the witnesses fell upon him." See Naḥmanides, ad loc.

Alternatively, if one understands the phrase from Psalms to mean *Nor takes up a reproach against his kin,* perhaps Rabbi Yose has in mind Rashi's interpretation of *if the sun rises upon him*: "This can only be understood as a metaphor: 'If it is clear to you that he is peaceably disposed toward you.' The metaphor is: just as the sun brings peace to the world, so too is it clear to you that he has not come to kill, even if the victim will resist him—as, for example, a father who breaks in to steal his son's money; it is clear that a father has mercy for his son and he [the father] would not kill him [the son]."

12. ***He is debased in his eyes—despised*...** The phrase is usually construed as *the debased in his eyes is despised.*

See Radak on Psalms 15:4.

13. **except if they told him to transgress...** This exception explains why the psalm alludes to *your father and your mother* in more abstract terms as *fearers of YHVH.*

On the exception, see BT *Bava Metsi'a* 32a; Maimonides, *Mishneh Torah, Hilkhot Mamrim* 6:12.

14. ***When he vows* להרע (*le-hara*), *to his***

*His money he does not give at interest* (Psalms 15:5)—this is corresponding to *You shall not steal* (Exodus 20:13). For if he does not lend at interest, certainly he will not go and steal.

*And takes no bribe for the innocent* (Psalms 15:5)—corresponding to *You shall not covet* (Exodus 20:14).[15]

Rabbi Yose son of Kisma said, "Corresponding to these, ten others were said of Jacob, as is written: *He encountered a certain place; and stayed there for the night; because the sun had set; He took of the stones of the place; and put them at his head; and he lay down in that place; He dreamed: Here, a ladder set on earth; its head reaching to heaven; and here, angels of God; ascending and descending on it* (Genesis 28:11–12)—behold, ten!"[16]

Alternatively, *He encountered a certain place* (Genesis 28:11).[17]

Rabbi Bo opened, "*Do not look at me, for I am blackish, because the sun has scorched me. My mother's sons were incensed at me: they made me guardian of the
vineyards; my own vineyard I did not guard* (Song of Songs 1:6). This verse ap- 429
plies to Jacob. For at first, Jacob's domain was the sun; but that domain transposed to Esau and was withdrawn from him. Jacob said, '*Do not look at me, for I am blackish*—for the domain of the moon, which is sometimes black, has been bestowed upon me; *because the sun has scorched me*—for the domain of the sun was withdrawn from me.'[18]

***hurt...*** The verse's simple sense is not entirely clear. Literally, the verse reads: *When he vows* להרע *(le-hara), to do evil, he does not revoke it.* (Perhaps a scribal error is involved, given that three ancient translations—the Septuagint, Syriac, and Peshitta—bear witness to a slightly different Hebrew spelling: *When he vows* לרעהו [*le-re'eihu*], *to his fellow man.*) The difficulty apparently prompts the *Zohar* to read the word in question ungrammatically, as containing not an infinitive but rather a definite noun: *when he vows to 'the evil'*—i.e., to the evil impulse.

See *Rut Rabbah* 6:4: "Rabbi Yose said, 'There were three who were attacked by their impulse but girded themselves against it with an oath: Joseph, David, and Boaz.... How do we know this concerning Boaz? Because it is said: *As YHVH lives! Lie down until morning.*'... Rabbi Yehudah said, 'That whole night his impulse incited him, saying, "You are single, looking for a wife; and she is single, looking for a husband. Go have intercourse with her—and she will be your wife!" He adjured his impulse, saying, "*As YHVH lives*, I will not touch her!" And to the woman he said, "*Lie down until morning.*"'"

See *Sifrei*, Numbers 88; *Vayiqra Rabbah* 23:11; *Zohar* 1:93b.

15. ***And takes no bribe...*** One who does not take bribes is clearly not covetous of others' money.

16. **ten others were said of Jacob...** At last we come to the Torah portion at hand. Yet precisely how these ten phrases articulate with either the Ten Commandments or the ten virtues of Psalms 15 is not explained.

17. ***He encountered a certain place*** The verse continues: *and he stayed there for the night, because the sun had set; he took of the stones of the place and put them at his head, and he lay down in that place.*

On Genesis 28:11, see *Bereshit Rabbah* 68:10; BT *Ḥullin* 91b; *Sanhedrin* 95b.

18. **at first, Jacob's domain was the sun...** The transferal of the sun refers specifically

"*My mother's sons were incensed at me: they made me guardian of the vineyards*—this is Esau, as is written: *Esau seethed with resentment against Jacob* (Genesis 27:41). *They made me guardian of the vineyards*—as is written: *Often, by day scorching heat consumed me, and cold by night* (ibid. 31:40). *My own vineyard I did not guard*—as is written: *when shall I too provide for my household?* (ibid. 30:30)."[19]

*He encountered a certain place* (Genesis 28:11).[20]

Rabbi Yitsḥak said, "Which place did he encounter? The place where the Temple would one day stand; he prayed there."[21]

Rabbi Yehudah says, "The day was still long, and he wanted to keep moving but was unable."[22]



to the calendar (see BT *Sukkah* 29a: "Our Rabbis taught: . . . 'Israel counts by the moon, idolators by the sun'") but more generally to the status of Israel in the world—small, diminished, and under the authority of Esau (signifying Rome and Christendom).

See *ZḤ* 14a–d, 23d–24a (both *MhN*); Scholem, "Parashah Ḥadashah," 433, 443 (Addendum 1 in this volume).

See also *Bereshit Rabbah* 6:3: "Rabbi Levi said in the name of Rabbi Yose son of Ila'i, 'It is natural that the great should calculate by the great, and the small by the small. Esau calculates by the sun, which is large, and Jacob by the moon, which is small.' Rabbi Naḥman said, 'That is a happy presage. Esau calculates by the sun, which is large: just as the sun rules by day but not by night, so does Esau have a share in this world, but has no share in the world to come. Jacob calculates by the moon, which is small: just as the moon rules by day and by night, so Jacob has a share in this world and in the world to come!'"

On the lunisolar and solar calendars, see *Mekhilta, Pisḥa* 1; *Tosefta Sukkah* 2:6; *Pesiqta de-Rav Kahana* 5:1, 14; *Zohar* 1:46b, 236b, 239a; 3:220b; Scholem, "Parashah Ḥadashah," 432–33 (Addendum 1 in this volume). On Jacob as sun, see *Bereshit Rabbah* 68:10; *Zohar* 1:135a, 136a, 146b, 148a, 166a. On the verse from the Song of Songs, cf. *Zohar* 3:45b, 59b; *ZḤ* 69d–70a (*ShS*).

19. ***My mother's sons were incensed at me...*** Jacob's brother Esau is of course his mother's son. Esau's resentment stems from Jacob's deception to obtain the blessing of the firstborn (see Genesis 27).

After fleeing from Esau, Jacob worked for his uncle Laban in Paddan-aram, tending his livestock. Laban cheated Jacob repeatedly, hence his protest: *when shall I too provide for my household?* See Genesis 30 and 31.

20. ***He encountered a certain place*** For the full verse, see above, note 17.

21. **The place where the Temple would one day stand...** On the "place" signifying the site of the future Temple, see *Targum Yerushalmi* on Genesis 28:11; *Bereshit Rabbah* 68:9; BT *Ḥullin* 91b; *Sanhedrin* 95b; Rashi on Genesis 28:11.

On Jacob's prayer, see BT *Berakhot* 26b: "Rabbi Yose son of Rabbi Ḥanina said, 'The patriarchs instituted the prayers.' . . . Abraham instituted the morning prayer . . . Isaac, the afternoon prayer . . . Jacob, the evening prayer, as is said: ויפגע (*va-yifga*) *in a certain place, and he stayed there for the night,* and פגיעה (*pegi'ah*) means only prayer, as is said: *As for you do not pray for this people, do not raise a cry of prayer on their behalf, do not* תפגע (*tifga*), *plead, with Me* (Jeremiah 7:16)." On *pegi'ah* as prayer, see also *Mekhilta, Beshallaḥ* 2; *Bereshit Rabbah* 68:9; BT *Sanhedrin* 95b.

22. **The day was still long...** See *Bereshit Rabbah* 68:10: "*He encountered a certain place*: He wished to pass on, but the world became like a wall before him; *because the*

Rabbi Yose said, "He prayed in that place—and began complaining before his Master that the dominion of the sun had been transferred from him, as is written: וילן (Va-yalen), *and he complained, there* (ibid.), as is said: וילונו העם (Va-yilonu ha-am), *The people grumbled* [*against Moses*] (Exodus 15:24)—an expression of complaint. Why? *Because the sun had set* (Genesis 28:11)—because it had been transferred from him and given to Esau.[23]

"What did Jacob do? He began weeping. Immediately: *He took of the stones of the place and put them at his head* (ibid.)—to distress his soul. In a similar vein: *they took a stone and put it beneath him and he sat upon it* (Exodus 17:12)."[24]

*He took of the stones of the place* (Genesis 28:11). Rabbi Yose said, "It was one stone, [27d] precisely, as implied by *of the stones*, and not *the stones*. As is said: *of the daughters of the Canaanites* (ibid. 24:3)—he mentioned only one, as is written: *that you will not take a wife for my son of the daughters of the Canaanites* (ibid.)—one of them."[25]

*sun had set*—our Rabbis say, 'This teaches that the blessed Holy One caused the orb of the sun to set prematurely, in order to speak in privacy with our father Jacob.'"

See also *Pirqei de-Rabbi Eli'ezer* 35: "Jacob was seventy-seven years old when he left his father's house.... From Beersheba as far as Mount Moriah is a journey of two days, and he arrived there at midday. The blessed Holy One met him, as is said: *He encountered a certain place, and he stayed there for the night, because the sun had set* [reading מקום (maqom), place, as a name of God].... The blessed Holy One said to him, 'Jacob! The bread is in your bag and the well is before you, so that you may eat and drink and sleep in this place.' He said before Him, 'Master of the World! From now the sun has still fifty degrees to set—and I am lying down in this place?!' The sun then set in the west—although not in its proper time. Jacob looked and saw the sun setting in the west, and he stayed there for the night, as is said: *He stayed there for the night, because the sun had set.*"

23. **began complaining before his Master...** The verbal root לין (lyn) means "stayed, lodged," but also "complain, protest, grumble."

On the transferal of the sun, see above, note 18. On Jacob's complaint, see *ZḤ* 14d (*MhN*).

24. **to distress his soul...** Saddened by the ascendancy of Esau (signifying Edom, Rome, Christendom), Jacob weeps and places stones beneath his head as a mark of his own distress, and also to empathize with Israel's future distress. Moses acted similarly during Israel's battle with Amalek in accordance with the principle that when the public is in distress, one should not enjoy comfort but should share in their distress. See *Targum Yerushalmi*, Exodus 17:12; *Mekhilta, Amaleq* (*Beshallaḥ*) 1; *Mekhilta de-Rashbi*, Exodus 17:12; BT *Ta'anit* 11a; *Tanḥuma, Beshallaḥ* 27; *Pesiqta Rabbati* 12; *Zohar* 2:66a.

25. **It was one stone...** The significance of this one stone is explained in the following narrative.

Cf. BT *Ḥullin* 91b: "It is written: *He took of the stones of the place* (Genesis 28:11), but it is also written: *He took the stone* (ibid., 18)! Rabbi Yitsḥak said, 'This teaches that all the stones gathered themselves together into one place; and each one said, "Upon me shall this righteous man rest his head." Then all of them were fused into one.'"

See also *Targum Yerushalmi* and *Targum Yerushalmi* (frag.) on Genesis 28:10; *Bereshit Rabbah* 68:11; *Tanḥuma, Vayetse* 1; *Tanḥuma* (Buber), *Vayetse* 4; *Pirqei de-Rabbi Eli'ezer* 35; *Zohar* 1:147b; 2:229b.

Rabbi Zeira entered in the presence of Rabbi El'azar son of Arakh. He found him seated, his eyes streaming tears; he was muttering something with his lips and was weeping. Rabbi Zeira turned back. He said to his servant, "What's going on that the master is sitting and weeping?"[26]

He replied, "Twice did I enter to approach him, but I was unable."

While they were sitting, they saw him enter his chamber. Before he came down, his voice resounded throughout the house; he was weeping. He heard that he was saying, "O stone, O stone! Sacred stone! Most sublime in the entire world because of the sanctity of your Master! Someday the children of the nations will debase you, and set impure corpses upon you, defiling your holy site; all the impure will approach you. Woe to the world at that time!"[27]

He came down and sat upon his wicker stool. [28a] Rabbi Zeira said to his servant, "Go and ask the master if I may enter his presence."[28]

His servant entered and said, "Rabbi Zeira is here."

He paid him no heed and didn't even raise his eyes. Afterward, he said, "Rabbi Zeira may come in, but you must sit outside."



Rabbi Zeira entered, kneeled down upon his knees, and sat before him. Rabbi El'azar saw and poked him with his feet. He said, "Get up from there and sit as is your custom."

He arose and sat as usual. Rabbi Zeira said, "Regarding my master's weeping—what did he see?"

He replied, "I saw the prime of the entire world enduring great calamity; that

26. **Rabbi El'azar son of Arakh...** On this figure (and his servant), see *ZḤ* 25c–26a (*MhN*).

Note the anachronism here: judging from Talmudic literature, the historical Rabbi El'azar and Rabbi Zeira were separated by numerous generations.

27. **O stone! Sacred stone!...** Rabbi El'azar's lament refers to the fate of the Foundation Stone, located in the Holy of Holies in the Temple (see below, note 29), but now housed in the Dome of the Rock, built in 691 C.E., on top of the Temple site. His prophecy of defilement did not reflect the historical reality in the Middle Ages; corpses of the dead were (and are) not placed in the mosque.

"Impure corpses" renders גולמי מסאבין (*golmei mesa'avin*), though "impure images" is also possible. Again, graven images were (and are) not placed in the mosque.

"All the impure will approach you" renders וכל מסאבין יקרבון בך (*ve-khol mesa'avin yiqrevun bakh*); alternatively, "all defilements will be offered upon you."

See Tishby, *Wisdom of the Zohar*, 1:69–70, 118 n. 377. See also Rabbi Moses Ḥagiz, *Elleh Mas'ei*, 17–18.

On El'azar son of Arakh and his chamber, see *ZḤ* 25d–26a (*MhN*); cf. *Zohar* 1:88b (*ST*). See also Liebes, *Peraqim*, s.v. *idra*, 93–94, 100.

See also *Zohar* 1:139b (*MhN*) for another story featuring Rabbi El'azar and his grief.

28. **his wicker stool...** סולסלניה (*sulsalneih*), a chair whose precise nature is unclear. See *Arukh*, s.v. *sal*, which mentions (among other meanings) טרסקל (*trisqal*), "folding chair" or "three-legged stool." Perhaps a wicker chair is intended, as in סלסלה (*salsillah*).

precious, holy stone from which the world was disseminated. It was upon that stone that Jacob placed his head.[29]

"Now, the stone from which the entire world was sown, and whose top was set in the Great Abyss—how could Jacob move it?! Well, the edge of that stone was sunk in the Great Abyss, and its top ascended, touching the Temple; upon it [stood] the Holy of Holies and the precious and sublime *Shekhinah*, as is written: *From there feeds Stone of Israel* (Genesis 49:24). The holy name of the supernal king was engraved upon it. When Jacob arrived, he pronounced that holy name and removed it from there—and set it in the site where the Holy of Holies was."[30]

29. **holy stone from which the world was disseminated...** The stone upon which Jacob lay was none other than the Foundation Stone. According to midrashic tradition, the world was created from the Foundation Stone located in the Holy of Holies in the Temple in Jerusalem. See M *Yoma* 5:2; *Tosefta Yoma* 2:14; JT *Yoma* 5:2, 42c; BT *Yoma* 54b; *Targum Yerushalmi*, Exodus 28:30; *Targum*, Song of Songs 4:12; *Vayiqra Rabbah* 20:4; *Pesiqta de-Rav Kahana* 26:4; *Tanḥuma*, *Qedoshim* 10; *Pirqei de-Rabbi Eli'ezer* 35; *Midrash Konen* (*Beit ha-Midrash*, 2:24–25); *Zohar* 1:71b–72a, 231a; 2:50a–b (*Mat*), 91b, 152a, 222a; *ZḤ* 2d (*MhN*), 76a–b (*MhN, Rut*); Moses de León, *Sefer ha-Rimmon*, 333; Ginzberg, *Legends*, 5:14–16, n. 39.

The verb אשתיל (*ishetil*), "was planted" (rendered here "disseminated"), is a play on the rabbinic wording (in a number of the sources cited above, with variations): "from which the world הושתת (*hushtat*), was founded." See *Zohar* 1:72a, 78a, 82a, 231a; 2:48b, 222a; *ZḤ* 16a (*MhN*); Moses de León, *Sheqel ha-Qodesh*, 74–75 (95); Liebes, *Peraqim*, 372–73.

"Prime" renders ארכבתא (*arkavta*). See BT *Bava Metsi'a* 103b, where it means the uppermost layer of a clay dam around a field. Perhaps Rabbi El'azar is also playing on the word מרכבה (*merkavah*), "chariot, throne." The Foundation Stone is the throne of the world.

30. **how could Jacob move it...** Employing the divine name, Jacob is able to move the Foundation Stone to the site of the future Temple, and he is also able to place his head upon it. Perhaps Rabbi El'azar intends that Jacob raised the stone upright.

On Jacob's erecting the Foundation Stone, see *Zohar* 1:72a–b, 231a. Cf. *Pirqei de-Rabbi Eli'ezer* 35: "Jacob returned to gather the stones, and he found them all one stone; and he set it up as a pillar in the midst of the place; and oil descended for him from heaven, and he poured it thereon.... What did the blessed Holy One do? He placed His right foot and sank the stone to the bottom of the depths and He made it the keystone of the earth, just like a man who sets a keystone in an arch; therefore it is called the Foundation Stone—for there is the navel of the earth, and from there all the earth unfolded; upon it stands the Sanctuary of God as is said: *This stone that I have set as a pillar shall be a house of God* (Genesis 28:22)." See Luria, ad loc.

The verse in Genesis reads: *From there,* רועה (*ro'eh*), *the Shepherd, Stone of Israel.* But Rabbi El'azar interprets *ro'eh* as a verbal participle meaning "feeding, grazing," and takes the verse to mean that *Shekhinah* (*Stone of Israel*) feeds from, and is nourished by, the Temple and the Foundation Stone. See *Bahir* 133 (193); *Zohar* 1:146b, 231b, 246b; 2:230a.

On the divine name engraved on the Foundation Stone, see *Targum Yerushalmi*, Exodus 28:30; JT *Sanhedrin* 10:2, 29a; BT *Sukkah* 53a–b; *Zohar* 2:91b, 152a; *ZḤ* 76a–b (*MhN, Rut*); Ginzberg, *Legends*, 6:258, n. 70.

"Ascended, touching" renders אתמגוס (*itmagos*), unattested elsewhere in the *Zohar*;

Rabbi Zeira said, "I heard in the name of Rabbi Bo, who said the mystery of this matter, but I cannot remember!"[31]

Rabbi El'azar said, "O Rabbi Zeira, I have pity upon you. Perhaps this was the word you heard; and so is the lucidity of the matter. As is written: *He took of the stones of the place* (Genesis 28:11)—one of the stones of the place. From which place? From the known place, the place of the Abyss, where the stones that grind water for the whole world are, as is written: *Stones grind water* (Job 14:19).[32]

"*This stone* (Genesis 28:22) was the principal of all of them, and it ascended to the place where the Temple was. Jacob was not intent on any of them other than this one, for it intimated to him an intimation—just as all was disseminated from it, similarly all the world disseminated from Jacob.[33]

"At that time, *He took of the stones of the place* (ibid., 11)—for it is the foundation of the entire world; וישם מראשותיו (*va-yasem me-ra'ashotov*), *and he put it at his head* (ibid.)—שם בלבו (*sam be-libbo*), he took to heart, that it is *at his head*—this is the paradigm of that. Immediately: *he lay down in that place* (ibid.)—in other words, his mind was at ease in that place.[34]



"He derived a certain sign. He said, 'This is my paradigm. If this one should attain some eminence, then it is apparent that I will attain eminence.' That is why he set his heart upon it and vowed a vow, as is written: *This stone that I have set up as a pillar [shall be a house of God]* (ibid., 22)—in other words, if this stone that I have set up as a pillar shall be a house of God, then immediately: *of all that You give me, I will set aside a tithe for You* (ibid.)—he vowed the tithe."[35]

perhaps it is derived from the root גוס (*gus*), "touch; come into contact with; meet; become bold; become haughty."

31. **but I cannot remember** According to BT *Bava Metsi'a* 85a, when Rabbi Zeira migrated to the land of Israel, he fasted that he might forget the Babylonian method of learning.

32. **the stones that grind water...** The verse from Job is usually rendered *water wears away stone*. The *Zohar* reads the phrase hyperliterally: אבנים שחקו מים (*avanim shaḥaqu mayim*), *stones grind water*.

On the stones sunk in the abyss, see BT *Ḥagigah* 12a: "בהו (*bohu*), *Void*—the slimy stones sunk in the abyss, from which water issues, as is said: *He will stretch over it a line of chaos, and plummet-stones of void* (Isaiah 34:11)." See *Zohar* 1:16a; *ZḤ* 2d (*MhN*).

33. **intimated to him an intimation...** Of all the stones in the abyss, Jacob was interested only in the Foundation Stone. The entire world is considered to have disseminated from him, as he was the progenitor of all the tribes of Israel, who in turn are considered the telos of the world.

On the stones' alluding to Jacob's progeny and their uniqueness, see *Bereshit Rabbah* 68:11; *Pirqei de-Rabbi Eli'ezer* 35; *Lekaḥ Tov*, Genesis 28:11.

34. **this is the paradigm of that...** Lying on the stone, Jacob realizes—and is comforted by the fact—that it is *at his head*, i.e., that he and it are somehow equal.

35. **He derived a certain sign...** Understanding that he and the stone somehow correspond, Jacob deduces that should it someday attain eminence (i.e., become a house of God, namely, the Temple), then he too will attain eminence—presumably in terms of the fortunes of his offspring, the children of Israel. Hence his vow: if the pillar he has just

Rabbi Zeira said, "This is certainly what I heard!"

He said to him, "For this reason it is called *Stone of Israel* (ibid. 49:24). Namely, it is so named after him, because he set his heart and eyes upon it. The blessed Holy One made it a Permanent House; there was His *Shekhinah*.[36]

"That is why I was weeping. For I saw that one day, the defilements of the nations and corpses of the dead will be placed upon this stone. Who cannot weep?! Woe to the world! Woe for that time! Woe for that generation!"

He wept as at first. He sighed and was silent. Afterward, he resumed and said, "Woe to those who will be present in the world when the King of the world will arouse!"[37]

Rabbi Zeira wept. He said, "The holy angel knows this, and it is fitting that he should weep over it. Happy are you, O righteous, for you are holy in this world and in the world to come!"[38]

## Section 18[39]

*He dreamed: Here, a ladder set on earth, its head reaching to heaven; and here, angels of God, ascending and descending on it* (Genesis 28:12).

Rabbi opened with this verse: *Your neck is like the Tower of David, built in terraces; a thousand bucklers hang upon it, all the shields of the warriors* (Song of Songs 4:4).[40] 

Rabbi said, "All things will expire, but the Torah will not expire; and there is nothing as beloved before the blessed Holy One as the Torah and her students. As we have learned: Whoever engages in Torah every day, secrets of Above will be invigorated for him. The Torah says to

erected becomes a house of God, then he will set aside the tithe. (Usually Jacob's dedication of the pillar as a house of God is understood as referring to what he will do upon God's fulfilling His end of the deal. According to Rabbi El'azar, however, the opening "if" of the vow is carried forward, so that Jacob is saying: if this pillar becomes a house of God, then I will set aside the tithe.)

The context reads: *Jacob made a vow, saying, "If God shall be with me and guard me on this way that I am going and give me bread to eat and clothing to wear, and I return safely to my father's house, then YHVH will be my God, and this stone that I have set up as a pillar shall be a house of God; and of all that You give me, I will set aside a tithe for You"* (Genesis 28:20–22).

36. **For this reason it is called '*Stone of Israel*'...** The Foundation Stone is also known as the Stone of Israel, named after Jacob—who was also called Israel.

The Permanent House is the Temple, in contrast to the portable Dwelling.

37. **Woe to those who will be present...** On account of the retribution that He will exact. Cf. *Zohar* 2:7b.

38. **The holy angel...** On Rabbi El'azar son of Arakh as "angel," see *ZḤ* 26a (*MhN*).

39. **Section 18** Some of the printed editions and manuscripts preserve the section heading, פרשתא יח (*parsheta* 18), perhaps reflecting an early attempt to order the materials of *MhN* on the Torah. Cf. the similar headings in *ZḤ* 3d, 10b, 13a, 14a, 17c, 19c, end of *parashat Lekh Lekha* (above, page 311) (all *MhN*); *Zohar* 2:20a (*MhN*).

40. ***Your neck is like the Tower of Da-***

him: *I will give you to drink of the spiced-wine, of my pomegranate juice* (ibid. 8:2)—this is the wine of [28b] Torah, the wine preserved in its grapes since the six days of creation; the matters that will one day be revealed to the righteous in the time to come."[41]

Rabbi Bo rose to his feet and said, "If so, should it not have said 'the wine preserved in its grapes since Mount Sinai'!? What is meant by 'since the six days of creation'?"[42]

He replied, "These are the profundities of the orders of creation, which have not been revealed to anyone; but one day the righteous will know them. Likewise, those who engage in Torah constantly will know."[43]

It has been taught: Rabbi Yehudah said, "The mysteries of Torah have been bequeathed to the wise, to those who engage in Torah constantly."[44]

Rabbi Yehudah taught, "Whoever engages in Torah to the full—while he sleeps, his soul is raised on high and he is taught of the profundities of Torah; and from her his lips murmur and stir during the day, as is written: *stirring the lips of sleepers* (ibid. 7:10)."[45]



***vid*...** The significance of the verse and its connection with Jacob's ladder is made clear below. See notes 51–54.

On the verse from the Song of Songs, see *Zohar* 1:209b.

"Rabbi" indicates Rabbi Yehudah ha-Nasi (the Patriarch), who redacted the Mishnah. He was so esteemed that he was called simply "Rabbi": the Master.

41. **All things will expire...** See JT *Megillah* 1:5, 70d: "Rabbi Yoḥanan said, 'The Prophets and the Writings will be annulled in the future, but the Five Books of the Torah will not be annulled in the future. What is the scriptural proof? *A great voice that did not cease* (Deuteronomy 5:19).'"

On the wine of Torah, see *Vayiqra Rabbah* 30:1; BT *Avodah Zarah* 35a; *Pesiqta de-Rav Kahana* 11:1; 27:1; *Shir ha-Shirim Rabbah* on 1:4; *Qohelet Rabbah* on 2:3; *Tanḥuma, Vayḥi* 10; *Bemidbar Rabbah* 14:4. On the wine preserved in its grapes since creation, see BT *Berakhot* 34b (in the name of Rabbi Yehoshu'a son of Levi); *Zohar* 1:135b (*MhN*), 192a, 238b; 2:147a, 169b; 3:4a, 12b, 39b–40a, 93b; *ZḤ* 64c (*ShS*). On the connection between wine and secrets, see BT *Eruvin* 65a in the name of Rabbi Ḥiyya: "יין (*Yayin*), has the numerical value of seventy; and סוד (*sod*), secret, has the numerical value of seventy: when wine goes in, secrets come out." On the revelation of secrets in the time to come, see *Zohar* 3:152a.

42. **should it not have said . . . since Mount Sinai...** If the preserved wine refers to secrets of Torah, surely Torah was revealed at Sinai, not creation.

43. **profundities of the orders of creation...** In the expression about "wine preserved in its grapes," the phrase משׁשת ימי בראשית (*mi-sheshet yemei vereshit*) does not mean "since the six days of creation," as is usually understood, but "of the six days of creation," i.e., pertaining to the creation of the cosmos. (The prefixed preposition מן (*min*) can mean "from, since, of.")

44. **mysteries of Torah have been bequeathed to the wise...** Note the progression from secrets destined to be divulged in the future to secrets already possessed by "the wise" (the kabbalists?) in the here and now. That the heroes of *MhN* already have access to such secrets is highlighted in the following narrative. See *ZḤ* 19c (*MhN*).

45. **while he sleeps, his soul is raised on high...** See *Midrash Tehillim* 11:6; *Pirqei*

Rabbi Yitsḥak said, "Whoever engages in Torah for her own sake—when he sleeps at night, his soul ascends and is shown those things destined to transpire in the world."[46]

Rabbi Yose was sitting and engaging in Torah, when Rabbi Abba came to visit him. Rabbi Yose said, "Look, the Master of Tradition has arrived!"[47]

He arose before him. They sat and engaged in Torah. While they were sitting, night dusked. They sat and engaged in her until midnight. Rabbi Abba fell asleep and Rabbi Yose remained seated. He noticed that Rabbi Abba's face had become very red, and that he was smiling. He saw a great light in the house.[48]

Rabbi Yose said, "Conclude from this that *Shekhinah* is here!"

He lowered his eyes and sat there until the blackness of the morning rose, while the light illuminated the house. As he raised his eyes, he saw the morning; and the house darkened. Rabbi Abba awoke, his face shining and his eyes sparkling. Rabbi Yose took hold of him.[49]

Rabbi Abba said, "I know what you seek. By your life! I have seen supernal mysteries. When the Prince of the Countenance took hold of my soul, he raised it to magnificent, supernal chambers; and I beheld the souls of the other righteous who were ascending there. He said to them, 'Happy are you, O righteous! Because of you, I am built within the holy edifice of the glorious Name, to guide the legions of the supernal King.' And I saw my Torah lying there—תלי תלים



*de-Rabbi Eli'ezer* 34; *Bereshit Rabbah* 14:9; *Zohar* 1:92a, 121b, 183a, 200a; 2:195b; 3:67a, 121b; in *MhN*, see *Zohar* 1:122a; *ZḤ* 25c–26a; Scholem, "Parashah Ḥadashah," 445 (Addendum 1 in this volume); Ginzberg, *Legends*, 5:74–75, n. 18; Tishby, *Wisdom of the Zohar*, 2:809–12.

The full verse from the Song of Songs reads: *Your palate is like fine wine—flowing to my beloved smoothly, gliding over* [or: *trickling over; stirring*] *lips of sleepers.*

On stirring the lips of sleepers, see *Shir ha-Shirim Rabbah* on 7:10: "Rabbi Ḥanina son of Papa and Rabbi Simon. One said, 'Like one who drinks קונדיטון (*qonditon*), spiced wine.' The other said, 'Like one who drinks aged wine: even though he has drunk it, the taste and aroma are still in his mouth.'"

See JT *Berakhot* 2:1, 4b; *Sheqalim* 2:4, 47a; *Mo'ed Qatan* 3:7, 83c; *Midrash Shemu'el* 19:4; *Zohar* 2:134b (*Piq*); 3:39a, 96a, 135a (*IR*); *ZḤ* 85c (*MhN, Rut*).

46. **destined to transpire in the world** According to BT *Berakhot* 57b, "A dream is one-sixtieth of prophecy." Cf. *Zohar* 1:83a, 130a, 150b, 183a, 199b–200a; 2:130a, 264a (*Heikh*), 267a (*Heikh*); 3:25a, 156b.

On studying Torah for its own sake, see *Avot* 6:1; BT *Pesaḥim* 50b, *Sukkah* 49b, *Ta'anit* 7a, *Sanhedrin* 99b.

47. **Master of Tradition . . .** מארי דשמעתא (*marei de-shamata*). See *Pesiqta de-Rav Kahana* 11:15, 23:12. Cf. the term "Master of Mishnah," above, p. 407, n. 14.

48. **night dusked . . .** "Dusked" renders the verb רמש (*remash*), an apparently Zoharic coinage based on רמשא (*ramsha*), "evening."

See *Zohar* 1:34b; 2:36b, 171a, 173a, 188a, 208a; 3:21a–b, 52a, 113b, 149a–b, 166b; *ZḤ* 7d, 25d (both *MhN*).

49. **He lowered his eyes . . .** In awe of the *Shekhinah*.

The blackness of the morning refers to the darkness before dawn.

On facial illumination, see p. 24, n. 74.

(*tillei tillim*), mounds and mounds, like a mighty tower—and that is why I am rejoicing in my share, and my eyes are sparkling."[50]

Rabbi Yitsḥak said, "Do not be surprised by Rabbi Abba, for the verse attests to this, as we have learned: The blessed Holy One established this archon beneath Him ותלה (*ve-talah*), and hung, all the other legions upon him, just like the neck upon which the entire body is hung. When the righteous engage in Torah, the blessed Holy One builds Himself, placing His Name within him, to reach all, to supply the world with the bounty of the Omnipresent. When the righteous do not engage in Torah, the blessed Holy One removes His name from within him, and then the world is lacking, and he is not primed. How do we know? As is written: *Like the Tower of David, your neck is built in terraces* (Song of Songs 4:4)—if the righteous proliferate and increase Torah like this tower, immediately: *your neck* בנוי לתלפיות (*banui le-talpiyyot*), *is built in terraces*—he who is the neck of the world is built within a holy edifice, so that all הפיות תלו (*ha-piyyot talu*), mouths languish, and weary to know his providence. This is the meaning of תלפיות (*talpiyyot*), as is said: ותלה ארץ מצרים (*va-telah erets mitsrayim*), *the land of Egypt languished* (Genesis 47:13)."[51]



50. **Prince of the Countenance took hold of my soul...** Raised aloft by Metatron, Rabbi Abba learns that the righteous enable Metatron to act as a conduit, bestowing the divine bounty on those beneath him.

On Metatron's obscure statement, "I am built within the holy edifice of the glorious Name," see next note.

Metatron is the chief angel, variously described as the Prince of the World, Prince of the Countenance (or Presence), celestial scribe, and even יהוה קטן (*YHVH Qatan*), "Lesser *YHVH*" (3 Enoch 12:5, based on Exodus 23:21). In Heikhalot literature, Metatron is also identified with Enoch, who ascended to heaven without dying. See Genesis 5:24; BT *Sanhedrin* 38b; *Ḥagigah* 15a; *Yevamot* 16b; *Tosafot, Yevamot* 16b, s.v. *pasuq zeh*; Scholem, *Kabbalah*, 377–81; Tishby, *Wisdom of the Zohar*, 2:626–31; Margaliot, *Mal'akhei Elyon*, 73–108.

On Metatron in the *Zohar*, see 1:21a, 37b, 95b, 143a, 162a–b; 2:65b–66b, 131a; 3:217a–b; *ZḤ* 42d–43a; 69b (*ShS*). In *MhN* see *Zohar* 1:126a–b; *ZḤ* 4a, 8d, 9d–10a, 10b, 12b, 24a, 25d–26a. On Metatron as the conduit between the upper and lower worlds, see *ZḤ* 10b, 24a, 25d–26a (all *MhN*); Scholem, "Parashah Ḥadashah," 437, 445 (Addendum 1 in this volume); Wolski, "Metatron and the Mysteries of the Night." On "תלי תלים (*tillei tillim*), mounds and mounds," see Song of Songs 4:4: *Like the Tower of David, your neck is built* לתלפיות (*le-talpiyyot*), *in terraces*. See also BT *Menaḥot* 29b; *Tanḥuma, Bereshit* 1.

51. **the blessed Holy One builds Himself, placing His Name within him...** According to Exodus 23:21, the angel charged with leading the Israelites in the desert comprises the name of God: *My Name is within him.* According to BT *Sanhedrin* 38b, that angel is Metatron. See also Rashi on Exodus 23:21: "His name is like his Master's—Metatron has the numerical value of Shaddai [314]." Here, Metatron is the neck of the world, the conduit between God and the other angels and the world. However, Metatron can function as conduit, comprising the name of God and thus bestowing the divine bounty upon the world, only when the righteous engage in

"Then: *a thousand bucklers hang upon him, all* שלטי (*shiltei*), *the shields, of the warriors* (Song of Songs 4:4)—those called *thousands upon thousands* (Daniel 7:10), and all the other [celestial beings] hang upon him; and all השליטין (*ha-shalitin*), the rulers, and all the worlds are filled with the bounty of the Omnipresent."[52]

Rabbi Yehudah said, "As is written: *He dreamed: Here, a ladder set on earth* (Genesis 28:12). Namely, when the righteous do not engage in Torah, *the ladder is set on earth*—he is not aloft. If the righteous are worthy and engage in Torah, *its head reaching to heaven* (ibid.)—then he is raised high, and all goodness is not lacking. Immediately: *and here, angels of God ascending and descending* בו (*bo*), *on it* (ibid.)."[53]

What is meant by בו (*bo*), *on it*?[54]

Rabbi Yehudah said, "On the name of the Omnipresent, as is said: [28c] *Let us exalt and rejoice* בו (*bo*), *in Him* (Psalms 118:24)."

Rabbi Yitsḥak said, "בו (*Bo*), *On him*—on that archon. Why? As is written afterward: *Here! YHVH was standing upon him* (Genesis 28:13)—upon that archon, and that is why they ascend and descend on his account, because of the name of the Omnipresent standing upon him."[55]

Torah. Hence: he who is the neck of the world is built within a holy edifice. See also Moses de León, *Or Zaru'a*, 259–60, 271–73; *Zohar* 1:127b (*MhN*).

On the study of Torah as building the world, see BT *Shabbat* 114a: "What does 'builders' mean? Rabbi Yoḥanan said, 'These are the disciples of the wise, who are engaged all their days in building the world.'" See also BT *Sanhedrin* 99b; *Zohar* 1:4b, 47a. On languishing in the pursuit of knowledge of Metatron, see *ZḤ* 9d–10a (*MhN*).

Cf. BT *Berakhot* 30a; JT *Berakhot* 4:5, 8c; *Shir ha-Shirim Rabbah* on 4:4.

52. ***a thousand bucklers hang upon him...*** This phrase is usually rendered *a thousand bucklers hang upon it*, referring to the Tower of David, though עליו (*alav*), "upon it," can also mean "upon him." Here, the referent is Metatron. Invested with the name of his master, Metatron bestows the divine bounty upon the angelic realm (the "thousands upon thousands" and the "rulers.")

The full verse in Daniel reads: *A river of fire streamed forth before Him, thousands upon thousands served Him; myriads upon myriads attended Him.*

53. ***its head reaching to heaven...*** Metatron's ascent—or lack thereof—depends on the righteous. Only when the ladder is aloft can the upper and lower worlds commune: *angels of God ascending and descending*. Cf. *Zohar* 1:149b.

54. **What is meant by בו (*bo*), *on it*?** The pronominal suffix ו (*vav*) can mean either "it" or "him"; hence בו (*bo*) can mean "on it" (on the ladder) and "on him." If "on him," which "him" is implied?

55. ***On him*—on that archon...** According to Rabbi Yitsḥak, the "him" upon whom the angels ascend and descend is Metatron. The angels ascend and descend upon him only because he is invested with, and connected to, the divine: *YHVH standing upon him*.

On עליו (*alav*), which can mean either "upon it" (the ladder) or "upon him," see *Bereshit Rabbah* 69:3.

Rabbi Tanḥum said, "Why of all the other legions is he called מלך שלם (*melekh shalem*), *king of Salem* (Genesis 14:18)? For none bears the name of the Omnipresent within like this one."[56]

Rabbi Ya'akov said, "Jacob received a hint and an answer regarding his complaint before the blessed Holy One. Namely, if his children will merit to engage in Torah and commandments—then ascent for this one and ascent for his children; if they do not merit to engage in Torah and commandments—then no ascent for this one and no ascent for his children, as is written: *and here, angels of God ascending and descending* בו (*bo*), *on it* (ibid., 28:12). *Angels of God*—the children of Jacob; if they are worthy—*ascending*; if they are not worthy—*descending*. בו (*Bo*)—*because of him*; when he enjoys ascent, so do they."[57]

Rabbi Yitsḥak said, "All the princes of the nations ascend or descend because of this one. When he ascends, the princes of the nations descend. When he descends, they ascend. All depends on the children of Jacob!"[58]

Rabbi Yehudah son of Shalom said, "Good or evil comes to the world solely on account of the children of Jacob!"[59]



56. **Why of all the other legions is he called...** The verse in Genesis refers to Melchizedek, king of Salem and priest of God Most High. According to *ZḤ* 25a (*MhN*), *Melchizedek* refers to the angel Michael, who in turn is often conflated with Metatron. Metatron is worthy of the name מלך שלם (*melekh shalem*), "king of Salem (peace)" or "perfect king," for he bears the divine name within him (see above, note 51)—and is thus able to bestow the divine bounty upon the world.

On Metatron as high priest, cf. *Bemidbar Rabbah* 12:12; *Zohar* 2:159a (standard editions). On Metatron as Michael, see the passage from *Re'uyyot Yeḥezqel*, as quoted in Scholem, *Jewish Gnosticism*, 46.

57. בו **(*bo*)—*because of him*...** Usually translated *on it*. The preposition ב (*be*) basically means "on, in," but it can also correspond to "with, through, on account of, because." The pronominal suffix ו (*vav*) can mean either "it" or "him." Metatron's and Israel's fortunes are directly correlated. Cf. *Zohar* 1:149b.

Jacob's "complaint" regards Israel's subjugation by Esau (Edom). See above, note 23.

58. **princes of the nations ascend or descend...** Not only Israel's destiny is tied to Metatron, but so too that of all the nations—though in this case, inversely. Everything ultimately depends on the children of Jacob, however, because it is their Torah study that determines Metatron's status.

According to rabbinic tradition, the seventy nations of the world are each governed by a particular angel or heavenly prince appointed by God. See Daniel 10:20; Septuagint, Deuteronomy 32:8–9; Jubilees 15:31–32; *Targum Yerushalmi*, Genesis 11:8, Deuteronomy 32:8–9; *Tanḥuma*, *Re'eh* 8; *Leqaḥ Tov*, Genesis 9:19; *Pirqei de-Rabbi Eli'ezer* 24; *Zohar* 1:46b, 61a, 84b, 108b, 113a (*MhN*), 149b; 2:5b (*MhN*), 14b (*MhN*), 17a (*MhN*), 33a, 151b, 209a–b; 3:298b; *ZḤ* 23d, 24c (both *MhN*); Ginzberg, *Legends of the Jews*, 5:204–5, n. 91. In midrashic literature, these angels are described as ascending and descending Jacob's ladder. See *Vayiqra Rabbah* 29:2; *Pesiqta de-Rav Kahana* 23:2; *Tanḥuma*, *Vayetse* 2; *Pirqei de-Rabbi Eli'ezer* 35.

59. **Good or evil comes to the world...** See BT *Yevamot* 63a: "Rabbi El'azar said, 'What is the meaning of the verse *Through you all families of the earth will be blessed* (Genesis 12:3)?... Even the other families

A certain *hegmon* came to Rabbi Abbahu and said, "The entire world should assemble against you as against this locust—to obliterate you from the world in a single instant! For if this nation does not worship its Lord, it is written: *He will shut the heavens so that there will be no rain, and the earth will not yield her fruit* (Deuteronomy 11:17). If she strays, the entire world is destroyed on her account!"[60]

He replied, "But it is you who cause her to stray and not follow the proper path!"[61]

He said to him, "It is your sins that rouse us!"[62]

Rabbi Yehudah said, "The *hegmon* spoke well."

Our Rabbis have taught: *Here, a ladder set on earth* (Genesis 28:12)—this is the Permanent House; *its head reaching to heaven* (ibid.)—as is said: מכון (*makhon*), *dais, of Your throne You made, O YHVH* (Exodus 15:17). Which is *its head*? Zion—where the *Shekhinah*, the *keruvim*, and the Holy of Holies are.[63]

Rabbi Abba said, "סלם (*Sullam*), *A ladder* (Genesis 28:12)—this is סיני (*Sinai*), Sinai, upon which the Torah was given, where the chariots of the blessed Holy One were revealed."[64]



who live on the earth are blessed solely on account of Israel... even the ships that go from Gaul to Spain are blessed solely on account of Israel.'... Rabbi El'azar son of Avina said, 'Punishment comes into the world solely on account of Israel, as is said: *I wiped out nations, their corner towers are desolate; I have made their streets waste* (Zephaniah 3:6): and it is written [after]: *I thought that she [Israel] would fear Me, would learn a lesson* (ibid., 7).'" See also BT *Shabbat* 139a.

60. **A certain *hegmon*... said...** Israel should be destroyed not merely because of their sins but rather because the fate of the world is in their hands.

In rabbinic literature, *hegmon* means a Roman "prefect, governor" (based on the Greek *hegemon*), while in medieval Hebrew it designates a Catholic bishop. See *Zohar* 2:188b.

The verse from Deuteronomy continues: ואבדתם (*ve-avadtem*), *and you will perish, quickly from off the good land that YHVH is giving you.* Note that the *hegmon* uses the same verb לאובדא (*le-ovda*), "to perish, obliterate."

61. **it is you who cause her to stray...** By subjugating and oppressing her.

62. **your sins that rouse us** Because of Israel's sin, the nations have the power to oppress her in the first place.

63. ***its head reaching to heaven*...** Jacob's ladder symbolizes the Temple (the Permanent House). Its head reaches to heaven as it faces the celestial realm.

As in the rabbinic interpretation of the verse from Exodus, there is a play on words: מכון (*makhon*), "dais," and מכוון (*mekhuvan*), "corresponding to, aligned with, directly opposite." The verse from Exodus thus implies that God fashioned an earthly throne perfectly aligned with the throne on high: *mekhuvan, that which is aligned with, Your throne, You made, O YHVH.* See *Mekhilta, Shirta* 10; JT *Berakhot* 4:5, 8c; *Shir ha-Shirim Rabbah* on 3:9; *Tanḥuma, Vayaqhel* 7, *Pequdei* 1–3. See *Zohar* 1:183b.

On the ladder as Temple, see *Sifrei*, Numbers 119; *Bereshit Rabbah* 68:12, 69:7; Naḥmanides on Genesis 28:17.

64. **this is סיני (*Sinai*), Sinai...** Both *sullam* and *Sinai* have the numerical value of

Rabbi Bo said in the name of Rabbi Yoḥanan, "One should contemplate this verse further as before: *Like the Tower of David, your neck is built in terraces* (Song of Songs 4:4). For we have learned: Rabbi Shim'on said in the name of Rabbi Zeira, 'As long as Israel engaged in Torah, the Temple stood, as is written: כמגדל (*ke-migdal*), *Like the Tower, of David, your neck is built*—if מגדלים (*megaddelim*), they elevate, Torah like this tower, *your neck is built.* What is meant by *your neck*? The Temple, as is written: *He fell upon the neck of his brother Benjamin and wept* (Genesis 45:14)—teaching that he wept over the first and second Temples.'"[65]

Rabbi Yitsḥak said, "What is the significance of *Tower*? Well, just as the Tower of David was מגדל חזק (*migdal ḥazaq*), a mighty tower, so those who engage in Torah require בנין חזק (*binyan ḥazaq*), a mighty edifice."[66]

Rabbi Tanḥum said, "מגדל (*Migdal*), *Tower, of David*—just as David was מתגדל (*mitgaddel*), exalted, through Torah more than all his generation, so those who engage in Torah must be exalted through Torah and not neglect her. Just as David would engage in Torah day and night, so must a person engage in



130 (when *sullam* is spelled without a *vav*). The chariots of the blessed Holy One correspond to the angels ascending and descending (see Psalms 68:18). See *Bereshit Rabbah* 68:12; *Zohar* 1:149a (*ST*), 267a (*Hash*).

65. ***your neck is built...*** See *Shir ha-Shirim Rabbah* on Song of Songs 4:4: "*Like the Tower of David, your neck*—this refers to the Temple. Why is it compared to a neck? Because so long as the Temple was built and standing, Israel's neck was stretched out among the nations of the world, but when the Temple was destroyed, then, Israel's neck was bowed, so to speak.... Alternatively, just as the neck lies at the highest part of a person, so the Temple was in the highest part of the world. And just as most ornaments are hung round the neck, so the priests and Levites were attached to the Temple. And just as if the neck is removed a person cannot live, so since the Temple was destroyed there has been no life for Israel."

The verse in Genesis reads: *He fell upon* צוארי (*tsavverei*), *the neck of, his brother Benjamin and wept.* Actually, the word *tsavverei* is in the plural or perhaps the dual (*the necks of*), which stimulated a midrashic interpretation referring to the two Temples built in Jerusalem, which lies in the territory of Benjamin. The first Temple was destroyed by the Babylonians in 586 B.C.E.; the second by the Romans in 70 C.E. See *Bereshit Rabbah* 93:12; BT *Megillah* 16b; *Zohar* 1:171b, 209b.

66. **those who engage in Torah require...** See BT *Berakhot* 32b: "Our Rabbis taught: Four things require חיזוק (*ḥizzuq*), strengthening [i.e., great energy and exertion]: Torah study, good deeds, prayer, and one's worldly occupation. How do we know this of Torah and good deeds? As is said: *Only* חזק (*ḥazaq*), *be strong, and very resolute to observe faithfully all the Torah* (Joshua 1:7)."

See also BT *Pesaḥim* 53b: "Rabbi Yoḥanan said, "Whoever casts profits into the pockets of the disciples of the wise will be privileged to sit in the Heavenly Academy, as is said: *For to be in the shelter of wisdom is to be in the shelter of money* (Ecclesiastes 7:12).'"

See also *Zohar* 1:171a.

On the Zoharic critique of the wealthy and their lack of support for those engaged in the study of Torah, see Baer, *History*, 1:261–77; Tishby, *Wisdom of the Zohar*, 3:1438–47.

Torah day and night; for as long as they are engaged in and exalted through her like the Tower of David, the neck is built as a mighty and grand edifice."[67]

"But if not, *a thousand bucklers*, תלוי (*talui*), *hang, upon it* (Song of Songs 4:4)—these are the thousand years they will be in exile. Whether they will be redeemed or not, the plight תלוי (*talui*), depends—if they are worthy through Torah, they will redeemed after one thousand years; if they are not worthy, *all the shields of the warriors* (ibid.)."[68]

What is meant by *all the shields of the warriors*?

Rabbi Tanḥum explained, "*All the shields of the warriors*—they will be subjugated by them, and afterward they will be redeemed."[69]

Hence Rabbi Bo said, "*Here, a ladder set on earth* (Genesis 28:12)—this is the Permanent House set upon its edifice by virtue of those engaging in Torah on earth. *Its head reaching to heaven* (ibid.)—for the Temple is of higher degree than the whole world. *And here, angels of God ascending and descending on it* (ibid.)—the ministering priests."[70]

Rabbi Eli'ezer says, "Because it is aligned corresponding to Jerusalem Above; and those watching Jerusalem [28d] Above watch Jerusalem Below, as implied by *ascending and descending*."[71]



67. **just as David...** On David studying Torah day and night, see BT *Berakhot* 3b.

On the wordplay among *migdal*, *megaddel*, and *mitgaddel*, cf. *Shir ha-Shirim Rabbah* on Song of Songs 4:4.

68. **But if not, *a thousand bucklers*, תלוי (*talui*), *hang, upon it*...** If Israel engage in Torah, the Temple remains standing and they are not exiled. If they do not engage in Torah, then a thousand years of exile ensue. Whether they will be redeemed after one thousand years or whether the exile will continue *talui*, "depends," on them.

On Israel's exile lasting a thousand years, see *Eikhah Rabbah* 1:40; 2:3; *Pirqei de-Rabbi Eli'ezer* 28; *Zohar* 1:116b; 2:17a (*MhN*), 227b; 3:270a; *ZḤ* 16d, 23c (both *MhN*). Cf. *Bereshit Rabbah* 63:13; *Tanḥuma* (Buber), *Toledot* 4.

See also BT *Sanhedrin* 97b: "Rav said, 'All the predestined dates [for redemption] have passed, and the matter [now] depends solely on repentance and good deeds.'... Rabbi Eli'ezer says, 'If Israel perform *teshuvah*, they will be redeemed; if not, they will not be redeemed.' Rabbi Yehoshu'a said to him, 'If they do not perform *teshuvah*, will they not be redeemed?! Rather, the blessed Holy One will set up a king over them, whose decrees shall be as cruel as Haman's, whereby Israel shall perform *teshuvah*, and thus bring them back to the good [path].'"

See also BT *Sanhedrin* 98a on *I, YHVH, will hasten it in its time* (Isaiah 60:22): "Rabbi Yehoshu'a son of Levi pointed out a contradiction: it is written *in its time*; yet it is written *I will hasten it.* If they prove worthy, *I will hasten it*; if not, *in its time*."

69. ***All the shields of the warriors...*** Namely, the warriors of the nations.

70. ***angels of God*... the ministering priests** See *Sifrei*, Numbers 119; *Bereshit Rabbah* 68:12.

71. **Because it is aligned corresponding to Jerusalem Above...** The reason the angels ascend and descend on the ladder is because the Temple is aligned with Jerusalem Above, and the angels watching Jerusalem Above also watch (guard) Jerusalem Below.

See *Tanḥuma*, *Pequdei* 1: "There is a Jerusalem above aligned with Jerusalem below.

In what way does it possess an additional degree?[72]

Rabbi El'azar said, "As is written: *Behold! YHVH was standing* עליו (*alav*), *over it* (Genesis 28:13), as is said: *Unless YHVH watches over the city, the watchman guards in vain* (Psalms 127:1); corresponding with what is written: *Behold! YHVH was standing over it*—to be watchman over those watchmen."[73]

What is the significance of עליו (*alav*), *over it*?

Rabbi El'azar said, "For protection, as is said: *set your eyes* עליו (*alav*), *upon him* (Jeremiah 39:12); and similarly: *My eyes and My heart shall ever be there* (1 Kings 9:3). In the time to come the blessed Holy One will one day return to Jerusalem, to be a wall protecting her, as is said: *I Myself—declares YHVH—will be a wall of fire around her and will be glory inside her* (Zechariah 2:9)."[74]

*The land upon which you lie* (Genesis 28:13).[75]

Rabbi Yitsḥak said, "This teaches that He rolled up the land of Israel for him."[76]

Rabbi Yehudah said, "It was the Temple, precisely; about this was he given tidings—and upon this was he lying, as is implied by what is written: *he lay down in that place* (ibid. 28:11)."[77]

Out of His love for the one below, He fashioned another above.... He has sworn that His presence will not enter the heavenly Jerusalem until the earthly Jerusalem is rebuilt."

See also, Revelation 21:2; *Targum Yonatan*, Psalms 122:3; BT *Ta'anit* 5a, and Rashi, ad loc.; *Zohar* 1:1b, 80b (*ST*), 122a (*MhN*), 128b, 183b, 231a; 2:51a; 3:15b, 68b, 147b; *ZḤ* 20d, 24b, 25a, 25d, 26b (all *MhN*).

72. **In what way...** How is earthly Jerusalem distinguished?

73. **to be watchman...** Jerusalem is distinguished by a special degree of divine providence and protection: *YHVH stands over it*—over the watchmen (the angels) who guard Jerusalem.

See Rashi on Genesis 28:13: "*standing over him* (Genesis 28:13)—to guard him."

On the meaning of *alav* in the verse, which can mean either "on it" or "on him," see *Bereshit Rabbah* 69:3.

74. **For protection...** The word *alav* suggests protection, as indicated by the proof-text from Jeremiah. The context reads: *King Nebuchadrezzar of Babylon ordered Nebuzaradan, the chief of the guards, concerning Jeremiah, "Take him and set your eyes* עליו (*alav*), *upon him* [i.e., look after him]; *do him no harm, but grant whatever he asks of you*" (Jeremiah 39:11–12). Similarly, the verse from Kings attests to God's watchful gaze over the Temple.

On the verse from Zechariah, see BT *Bava Qamma* 60b; *Shemot Rabbah* 40:4; *Pesiqta de-Rav Kahana* 20:7; *Zohar* 2:108b; 3:68b, 221a.

75. ***The land upon which you lie...*** The verse continues: *I will give to you and your seed.*

76. **He rolled up the land of Israel...** See BT *Ḥullin* 91b: "*The land upon which you lie.* What is so great about that? [The actual area of land occupied by Jacob's body was miniscule.] Rabbi Yitsḥak said, 'This teaches that the blessed Holy One rolled up the whole land of Israel and placed it beneath our father Jacob, so that it would be easily conquered by his descendants.'" See *Bereshit Rabbah* 69:4; *Zohar* 1:72a, 156a; 3:84a.

77. **It was the Temple...** According to Rabbi Yehudah, Jacob was lying on the site of the future Temple. Hence the divine promise *The land upon which you lie I will give to you*

Rabbi Yehudah said, "Of the three patriarchs, none of them received tidings about the Temple other than Jacob, the third of the patriarchs. Corresponding to these, the third built it: Jesse, David, and Solomon—who is the third—built it."[78]

Rabbi Yehudah said, "Jacob, who is the third, received tidings; Solomon, who is the third, built. This one loved women, and that one loved women. This one maintained his integrity, but that one did not maintain his integrity, as is written: *In Solomon's old age, his wives turned away his heart* [*after other gods*] (1 Kings 11:4)."[79]

Rabbi Yose opened, "*Beautiful in loftiness, joy of all the earth, Mount Zion, summit of the north, city of the great king* (Psalms 48:3). יפה נוף (*Yefeh nof*), *Beautiful in loftiness*—this is Jerusalem, which is *sweet to the soul and healing for the bones* (Proverbs 16:24), as is said: נופת (*nofet*), *honey, drips from your lips* (Song of Songs 4:11)."[80]

Rabbi Yehudah said, "All the beauty of the land of Egypt lay in Noph and Tahpanhes. Noph was the most praiseworthy of all, possessing three hundred and ninety-five adornments of beauty, yet Zion exceeded Noph in beauty and majesty."[81]



As Rabbi Yehudah said: "Why was it called ציון (*tsiyyon*), Zion? Just as הציון (*ha-tsiyyun*), the marker, stands as a signpost to be beheld. And [Zion] exceeded Noph in beauty, as is written: יפה נוף (*Yefeh nof*), *more beautiful than Noph* (Psalms 48:3)."[82]

*and your seed* constitutes the tidings of its construction.

The use of the demonstrative ההוא (*hahu*), *that*, to describe the place upon which Jacob lay suggests a well-known place. Cf. Rashi on Genesis 28:11.

On *place* as signifying the Temple, see *Targum Yerushalmi* on Genesis 28:11; *Bereshit Rabbah* 68:9; BT *Ḥullin* 91b; *Sanhedrin* 95b. Cf. *Zohar* 1:236a.

On Jacob's being shown the Temple, see *Sifrei*, Numbers 119; *Bereshit Rabbah* 69:7.

78. **Corresponding to these...** Jacob, who was the third patriarch following Abraham and Isaac, corresponds to Solomon, who was the third in the line of Jesse (see 1 Samuel 16:1; 17:12; Isaiah 11:1, 10).

79. **This one loved women...** Jacob had four wives. See also Genesis 29:18: *Jacob loved Rachel.* As for Solomon, see 1 Kings 11:1–3: *King Solomon loved many foreign women.*

80. ***Beautiful in loftiness, joy of all the earth...*** On Psalms 48:3, see *Zohar* 2:222b.

81. **All the beauty of the land of Egypt lay in Noph...** According to Rabbi Yehudah, the word נוף (*nof*) in the verse alludes to the famed Egyptian city of the same name. Noph (also known as Memphis) is mentioned in Isaiah 19:13; Jeremiah 2:16, 44:1, 46:14, 19; Ezekiel 30:13, 16. As is made clear in the following paragraph, Jerusalem was יפה נוף (*Yefeh nof*), *more beautiful than Noph* (Psalms 48:3).

The significance of the number 395 is unclear. Some of the manuscripts read 305.

82. **Why was it called ציון (*tsiyyon*), Zion?...** Rabbi Yehudah doesn't complete his thought, but he seems to intend: Just as the marker stands to be beheld, so Zion stood to be beheld on account of her beauty. See Jeremiah 4:6.

*Joy of all the earth, Mount Zion, summit of the north*—for whoever beheld her rejoiced. For it has been taught: Rabbi Yose said in the name of Rabbi Ḥiyya, "Never did a person enter Jerusalem and remain sad—fulfilling what is said: *joy of all the earth.*"[83]

Rabbi Yitsḥak said, "As soon as Jacob lay upon her, his mind was at ease, and the *Shekhinah* ascended upon him and spoke with him—which had not happened before."[84]

As Rabbi Yitsḥak said: "Until Jacob stood in that place, the *Shekhinah* had not revealed upon him.

"As soon as Jacob saw this, he understood that the place was the decisive factor. He awoke from his sleep terrified, lest it have been another entity, and he lay down as at first. The blessed Holy One said to him, 'Jacob, it is not so! *I am YHVH, the God of your father Abraham and the God of Isaac* (Genesis 28:13). Furthermore: *the land on which you lie I will give to you and your seed* (ibid.), and I will not reveal Myself to another nation; and revelation of *Shekhinah* upon this land *I will give to you and your seed*—and not to another nation.'"[85]



Rabbi Yose said, "What is the significance of *on which you lie*? Well, just as you lie on it and prophecy is with you, so prophecy will abide with your seed, and not with another nation."

Rabbi Ya'akov opened: *Favor is shown to the wicked; he learns not righteousness* (Isaiah 26:10). It has been taught: Rabbi Ya'akov said, "Woe that the wicked should be shown favor in this world—the seed of Esau the wicked! Why then are they shown favor and compassion? Because the seed of Jacob does not learn righteousness. *In a land of integrity, he acts corruptly* (ibid.)—Jerusalem, which is the land of integrity."[86]

83. ***Joy of all the earth...*** According to rabbinic exegesis, *joy of all the earth* refers to the joyous relief of atonement provided by offering sacrifice in the Temple. See *Vayiqra Rabbah* 1:2; *Shemot Rabbah* 36:1; *Bemidbar Rabbah* 8:1; *Midrash Tehillim* 48:2.

84. **As soon as Jacob lay upon her...** Upon the land, the site of the future Temple. See above, *ZḤ* 28a (*MhN*).

The revelation to Jacob at *that place* (Genesis 28:11) marks the beginning of his communication with God. See Genesis 28:13–15.

85. **the place was the decisive factor...** Jacob senses that the vision he has just beheld (the ladder and angels) was brought about by the special properties of the place. He is fearful, however, that these properties are sinister: דבר אחר (*davar aḥer*), "another entity," perhaps signifying demonic or impure forces at work. God not only assures him of the veracity of his own experience but also alludes to the relationship between the land, the *Shekhinah*, and prophecy (see next paragraph).

Cf. *Mekhilta, Pisḥa* 1: "Until the land of Israel was chosen, all the lands were suitable for divine speech; once the land of Israel was chosen, all other lands were eliminated.... Rabbi El'azar son of Tsadok said, '...*Shekhinah* is not revealed outside the land [of Israel].'" See also *Zohar* 1:85a, 149a.

86. ***Favor is shown to the wicked...*** In its context in Isaiah, the full verse reads: [*But when*] *favor is shown to the wicked, he learns*

What is meant by *he acts corruptly*?

Rabbi Ya'akov said, "The air of the land of Israel makes one wise and evokes prophecy; but the seed of Esau corrupts the air and prophecy! Why? Because the seed of Jacob *ignore the majesty of YHVH* (ibid.), and do not engage in Torah. Consequently, favor is shown to the wicked, and he corrupts the bounty of the land and prophecy."[87]

Rabbi Yehudah son of Rabbi Yehoshu'a said, "*Favor is shown to the wicked*—the nations of the world who possess dominion in this world—because Israel *does not learn righteousness*."[88] [2:4a]

*not righteousness; in a land of integrity he acts corruptly, he ignores* [literally: *does not see*] *the majesty of YHVH*.

Cf. BT *Megillah* 6a (and Rashi, ad loc.): "Rabbi Yitsḥak said, 'What is the meaning of the verse יוחן רשע (*Yuḥan rasha*), *Favor is shown to the wicked*, בל למד צדק (*bal lamad tsedeq*), *he learns not righteousness*? Isaac said in the presence of the blessed Holy One, "Master of the World! יוחן (*Yuḥan*), *Let favor* [or: *mercy*], *be shown* to Esau." He replied, "He is wicked." He said to Him, "בל למד צדק (*bal lamad tsedeq*), *Has he not learned righteousness?*" [perhaps referring to his fulfilling the commandment of honoring his parents]. He replied, "*In a land of integrity he will act corruptly* [i.e., destroy the Temple]." He said, "If so, *let him not behold the majesty of YHVH*."'"

See also *Bereshit Rabbah* 67:5; *Pirqei de-Rabbi Eli'ezer* 39.

87. **seed of Esau corrupts the air and prophecy...** Because the seed of Jacob does not engage in Torah, Esau (signifying Edom, Rome, and Christendom) has dominion in the land of Israel, which in turn tarnishes the land's prophetic capacities.

On the air of the land of Israel as making one wise, see BT *Bava Batra* 158b.

See Rashi, BT *Megillah* 6a, s.v. *be-erets neḥoḥot ye'avvel*: "In the future, he [Edom] will destroy the land of Israel." See also Tishby, *Wisdom of the Zohar*, 1:117, n. 372.

88. **nations of the world who possess dominion...** Rabbi Yehudah expands the scope of the verse. The wicked does not refer to Esau (Edom) alone, but to all the nations who enjoy dominion while Israel endures subjugation.

The manuscript witnesses contain an additional though fragmentary sentence, suggesting that the *parashah*'s commentary as we now have it is incomplete not only in its beginning, but also at its end.

# פרשת שמות

# *Parashat Shemot*

"NAMES" (EXODUS 1:1–6:1)

*These are the names* (Exodus 1:1).[1]

Rabbi El'azar opened, "*A locked garden is my sister, bride; a locked spring, a sealed fountain* (Song of Songs 4:12). *A locked garden*—Assembly of Israel, who is a locked garden."[2]

As Rabbi El'azar said: "Just as a garden must be guarded, cultivated, watered, and pruned, so Assembly of Israel must be cultivated, guarded, watered, and pruned. She is called 'garden' and she is called 'vineyard.' Just as a vineyard must be cultivated, watered, pruned, and excavated, so Israel, as is written: *For the vineyard of YHVH of Hosts is the House of Israel* (Isaiah 5:7), and it is written: *he enclosed it, cleared it of stones*... (ibid., 2)."[3] [4b]

1. ***These are the names*** The verse continues: *of the sons of Israel who came to Egypt with Jacob, each man with his household they came.*

Though incorporated into the *Zohar*'s commentary to *parashat Shemot*, the material found toward the bottom of *Zohar* 2:4a extending toward the bottom of 5b (notwithstanding the *Matnitin*) is part of *MhN*. See Tishby, *Wisdom of the Zohar*, 1:2, 105 n. 8; Scholem, *Kabbalah*, 217.

The witnesses for *MhN Shemot* display great fluidity and variability in terms of language. Some passages appearing in Aramaic in Margaliot's edition, *Or Yaqar*, and the Mantua edition instead appear in Hebrew in the Cremona edition and certain manuscripts. Indeed, passages appearing in Aramaic in the Cremona edition also appear in Hebrew in some manuscripts. Following the manuscripts, in my reconstruction of the text I have replaced Aramaic sentences with Hebrew—in accordance with the accepted scholarly view that the Hebrew recensions represent an older, more original version. See Meroz, "The Middle Eastern Origins," 40–41; Liebes, "Hebrew and Aramaic," 42.

2. **Assembly of Israel...** כנסת ישראל (*Keneset Yisra'el*). In rabbinic Hebrew this phrase normally denotes the people of Israel. The midrash on the Song of Songs describes an allegorical love affair between the maiden (the earthly assembly of Israel) and her lover ("the Holy One, blessed be He"). In the *Zohar*, *Keneset Yisra'el* can refer to the earthly community but also (often primarily) to *Shekhinah*, the divine feminine counterpart of the people, the aspect of God most intimately connected with them.

On Song of Songs 4:12, see *Shir ha-Shirim Rabbah* on 4:12; *Shemot Rabbah* 20:5; *Zohar* 1:32b, 63a.

3. ***he enclosed it, cleared it of stones...*** Isaiah 5:1–2 reads: *Let me sing for my beloved*

Rabbi Shim'on said, "When *Shekhinah* descended to Egypt, a single living being called Israel descended in the form of that elder—forty-two holy attendants with him, each possessing a holy letter from the holy name. All of them descended with Jacob to Egypt, as is written: *These are the names of the sons of Israel who came to Egypt with Jacob* (Exodus 1:1)."[4]

*a song of my lover about his vineyard. My beloved has a vineyard on a fertile slope. He enclosed it, cleared it of stones, and planted it with choice vines; he built a tower inside it and even hewed a winepress in it. He expected it to yield grapes, but it yielded stinking grapes.* In Isaiah's parable, the vineyard symbolizes Israel, who has yielded bad fruit and whose descendants will be punished. See *Tanḥuma, Vayelekh* 2; *Zohar* 1:95b–96b.

On this passage, see Meroz, "The Middle Eastern Origins," 43.

Although not stated, the homily sets the scene for a central concern of *MhN Shemot*—Israel's exile and the exile of *Shekhinah*.

In the printed editions, this brief homily is followed by a passage belonging to the *Matnitin* stratum of the *Zohar*. *MhN* resumes at 2:4b, about a third of the way down the page.

4. **When *Shekhinah* descended to Egypt...** A (semi)divine figure descended to Egypt in the guise of Jacob. Likewise, each of forty-two angelic attendants descended, bearing a letter of the Name of Forty-Two Letters.

On the exile of *Shekhinah*, see BT *Megillah* 29a: "Rabbi Shim'on son of Yoḥai says, 'Come and see how beloved are Israel in the sight of the blessed Holy One! Wherever they went in exile, *Shekhinah* accompanied them. When they were exiled to Egypt, *Shekhinah* was with them.... When they were exiled to Babylon, *Shekhinah* was with them. ...And even when they are destined to be redeemed, *Shekhinah* will be with them.'" See also *Mekhilta, Pisḥa* 14; *Sifrei*, Numbers 84; JT *Ta'anit* 1:1, 64a; *Eikhah Rabbah* 1:54.

On "the single living being [or: creature] called Israel," see *Midrash Konen* (in *Beit ha-Midrash* 2:39, 6:49); Schäfer, *Synopse*, §406; Ginzberg, *Legends*, 5:307, n. 253; Scholem, *Major Trends*, 62. In the main body of the *Zohar*, "Israel the Elder" designates the *sefirah Tif'eret*—the masculine consort of *Shekhinah*—though this seems unlikely here. See *Zohar* 2:4a. In this context, precisely what Rabbi Shim'on intends through this "living being" is unclear—perhaps the form of the *Shekhinah*, or even Metatron. *The sons of Israel* refers to angels deriving from the celestial being "Israel." See *Zohar* 2:2a. Preceding the *Zohar*, "the single creature Israel" motif was utilized in diverse ways by El'azar of Worms and Jacob ha-Kohen from Castile. See the sources cited by Wolfson, *Along the Path*, 14, 23–25. See also Abrams, "Special Angelic Figures," 368–69, 375, 379, 385. See also *Or Yaqar* ad loc.

On Jacob's "form" in the supernal realm (engraved on the Throne of Glory), see *Bereshit Rabbah* 68:12; BT *Ḥullin* 91b; *Pirqei de-Rabbi Eli'ezer* 35. Jacob is known by the epithet "Israel the Elder"; see *Bereshit Rabbah* 68:11; Moses de León, *Sheqel ha-Qodesh*, 42 (51).

The Name of Forty-Two Letters is mentioned in the name of Rav, though not recorded, in BT *Qiddushin* 71a. Ḥai Gaon indicates that it consists of the following seven sets of six letters: אבגיתץ, קרעשטן, נגדיכש, בטרצתג, חקבטנע, יגלפזק, שקוצית—which are also the initial letters of the forty-two words constituting the prayer *Anna be-Khoaḥ* (Please, with the Strength [of Your Right Hand's Greatness]). According to Jacob ben Meir Tam (Rabbenu Tam), this name consists of the first forty-two letters of the Torah, from the ב (*bet*) of בראשית (*Be-reshit*), *In the beginning*, through the ב (*bet*) of בהו (*bohu*), "empty" (or "void") (Genesis 1:2). See Lewin, *Otsar ha-Ge'onim*, 4:2:23 (on *Ḥagigah* 14b);

Rabbi Yitsḥak said, "As implied by what is said: *sons of Israel*, and afterward: *with Jacob*. It does not say *with him*!"[5]

Rabbi Yehudah inquired of Rabbi El'azar son of Rabbi Shim'on. He said to him, "Since you have heard from your father the passage *These are the names* according to the supernal mystery, what is the meaning of *each man with his house they came* (ibid.)?"[6]

He replied, "The word that father used to say: 'They were supernal angels, higher than those beneath them, as is written: *each man with his house they came*.' So did father say: 'All those angels of a higher grade are called "males," while those of a lower grade are called "females."'"[7]

Rabbi Yitsḥak was standing before Rabbi El'azar son of Arakh. He said to him, "Did *Shekhinah* really descend to Egypt with Jacob?"

He replied, "Is it not so?! For it is written: *I Myself will go down with you to Egypt* (Genesis 46:4)."[8]

He said to him, "Come and see: *Shekhinah* descended to Egypt with Jacob,

and six hundred thousand other holy chariots, as is written: *about six hundred thousand on foot* (Exodus 12:37). As we have learned: Six hundred thousand holy chariots descended with Jacob to Egypt, and all of them ascended from there when Israel went forth from Egypt, as is written: *The sons of Israel journeyed from Rameses to Succoth like six hundred thousand on foot*... (ibid.). It does not

*Tosafot*, *Ḥagigah* 11b, s.v. *ein doreshin*; *Zohar* 1:1a, 15b, 30a–b; 2:92b (*Piq*), 130b, 132b, 175b, 234a–b; 3:78a, 172b; *ZḤ* 42a; Cordovero, *Pardes Rimmonim* 21:12–13; Trachtenberg, *Jewish Magic and Superstition*, 94–95; Idel, "Al ha-Peirushim," 161–62, n. 24; 167–68, n. 52. Cf. Maimonides, *Guide of the Perplexed* 1:62. In *Or Yaqar* 1:4a, Cordovero describes how the name *YHVH* can be permuted into the Name of Forty-Two Letters. See *Zohar* 1:9a; 2:260a (*Heikh*).

The opening word of the book of Exodus is ואלה (*Ve-eleh*), *These are*, which has the numerical value of forty-two.

5. **It does not say *with him*** The opening verse of Exodus mentions both of Jacob's names: Israel and Jacob. The verse could have read more simply *These are the names of the sons of Israel who came to Egypt with him*. Rabbi Yitsḥak explains that the use of different names proves that here the "sons of Israel" refers to angels ("sons" of the celestial Israel) who descended together with *Shekhinah* when the patriarch Jacob went down to Egypt. See *Zohar* 2:2b.

6. **what is the meaning of *each man with his house they came*** If *sons of Israel* refers to angelic beings who descended to Egypt, what of the continuation of the verse? Do angels have a house? See *Zohar* 2:4a for a nearly identical question and answer.

7. **while those of a lower grade are called "females"** In rabbinic literature, "house" can refer to a man's wife (See M *Yoma* 1:1; BT *Yevamot* 62b; *Sotah* 44a.) Thus, *each man* refers to the higher (male) angels, who emanate to the lower (female) angels, each of whom constitutes a *house*. See *Zohar* 2:4a: "whoever receives from another is a house."

8. ***I Myself will go down with you to Egypt*** See *Mekhilta*, *Shirta* 3: "When Israel went down to Egypt, *Shekhinah* went down with them, as is said: *I Myself will go down with you*." See *Mekhilta de-Rashbi*, Exodus 3:8;

say *six hundred*, but rather *like six hundred*. Just as these went forth, so those went forth.[9]

"Come and see the mystery of the matter: When these chariots, holy camps, were leaving, Israel saw; and they knew that they were being detained because of them. All of Israel's haste was for their sake, as is written: *they could not tarry* (ibid., 39). It should have said *they did not want to tarry*, but it is written specifically *they could not*. It was abundantly clear that all of them were sons of Israel—heavenly sons of Israel, as is written: *the sons of Israel who came to Egypt with Jacob*. That is why the verse does not say *These are the names of the sons of Israel who came to Egypt with him*, but rather *These are the names of the sons of Israel who came to Egypt with Jacob. Who came to Egypt*—at first. With whom? *With Jacob*."[10]

Rabbi Yehudah said, "An inference from minor to major! If when Jacob was saved from Laban it is written *Jacob went on his way, and angels of God encountered him* (Genesis 32:2), then when he descended to go forth into exile and the blessed Holy One said, *I Myself will go down with you to Egypt* (ibid. 46:4), [5a] is it not fitting that since the patron has descended, His attendants will descend with Him, as is written: *who came to Egypt with Jacob*?"



Rabbi Ya'akov of Kefar Ḥanan said in the name of Rabbi Abba, "Who are these *sons of Israel* mentioned here? Those called *sons of Israel*—literally!"[11]

Rabbi Abba opened, "*Come, gaze upon the works of Elohim, how he has brought* שמות *(shammot), desolation, on earth* (Psalms 46:9). Do not read שַׁמּוֹת *(shammot), desolation*, but שְׁמוֹת *(shemot)*, names. This corresponds with what Rabbi Ḥiyya said: 'Corresponding to heaven, the blessed Holy One fashioned on earth. In heaven there are holy names; on earth there are holy names.'"[12]

15:2; *Shemot Rabbah* 15:16; *Zohar* 1:211a, 222a, 226a; 2:85a. See below, *Zohar* 2:16a–b (*MhN*).

9. ***like six hundred thousand on foot...*** *Shekhinah* is accompanied by six hundred thousand chariots, corresponding to the number of Israelites departing Egypt. Rabbi El'azar construes the words כשש מאות (*keshesh me'ot*), *about six hundred*, as *like six hundred* or *corresponding to six hundred*. *Shekhinah* and her host and the people of Israel reflect one another. The verse from Exodus, which describes the Israelites' departure, is now read as describing the departure of the celestial sons of Israel.

10. **That is why the verse does not say...** See above, note 5. See *Zohar* 2:16a (*MhN*).

11. ***sons of Israel*—literally** Rabbi Abba disagrees with the preceding homilies. The *sons of Israel* referred to in the opening verse of Exodus are not the sons of the celestial Israel, i.e., angelic beings, but the real sons of Israel, i.e., Jacob, the tribes. Cf. *Zohar* 2:17a (*MhN*), below, page 488, also in the name of Rabbi Abba.

Kefar Ḥanan (also called Kefar Ḥanin) is mentioned numerous times in rabbinic literature, almost always as the residence of Rabbi Ya'akov. See *Zohar* 1:87b, 115a (*MhN*), 206b; 2:157a.

12. **Do not read שַׁמּוֹת (*shammot*), *desolation*, but שְׁמוֹת (*shemot*), names...** See BT *Berakhot* 7b; *Zohar* 1:58b; *ZḤ* 12a (*MhN*). Rabbi Abba and Rabbi Ḥiyya's point is that the earthly sons of Israel are a counterpart to

Rabbi Yehudah said, "On the very day that Jacob descended to Egypt, six hundred thousand ministering angels descended with him."

Rabbi Yehudah opened, "*Look, the bed of Solomon! Sixty warriors surrounding* [*her, of the warriors of Israel*] (Song of Songs 3:7). Regal adornments engraved in a key, revolving in its place; adornments of the seventh, engraved in the sixth, as is written: *Sixty warriors surrounding her.* Alternatively, *Look, the bed of Solomon. Look, the bed*—Shekhinah; שלשלמה (*she-li-shlomoh*), *of Solomon*—the King who possesses שלום (*shalom*), peace; *sixty warriors surrounding her*—the six hundred thousand ministering angels of the retinue of Shekhinah, who descended to Egypt with Jacob; *of the warriors of Israel*—Israel above, as is written: *These are the names of the sons of Israel who came to Egypt with Jacob, each man with his household they came* (Exodus 1:1)—they and their customs."[13]



the celestial sons of Israel. Perhaps the names of both possess some theurgic value.

The theme of "as above, so below" is a cardinal principle of Kabbalah. See *Zohar* 1:38a (*Heikh*), 57b–58a, 129a, 145b, 156b, 158b, 205b; 2:15b (*MhN*), 20a (*MhN*), 48b, 82b, 144b, 251a (*Heikh*); 3:45b, 65b; *ZḤ* 15a (*MhN*), 19a (*MhN*); Tishby, *Wisdom of the Zohar*, 1:273. On the similar Hermetic formulation, see *Secretum secretorum*, ed. Robert Steele, *Opera hactenus*, fasc. 5, 262.

The Masoretic text reads: *the works of* YHVH. See Psalms 66:5: *Come see the works of* Elohim. Such a reading is attested in biblical manuscripts as well as the Septuagint (codex Alexandrinus), and the Zoharic rabbis are aware of both variants. See *Zohar* 1:58b: "Rabbi Ḥiyya said, '... whether it be one name or another, all is praise.'"

See *Bereshit Rabbah* 84:8; 88:3 (and Theodor, ad loc.); *Tanḥuma*, *Vayelekh* 1; Radak on Psalms 46:9; *Zohar* 1:60a, 157b (*ST*); *ZḤ* 12a (*MhN*), 73a (*ShS*); Moses de León, *Sefer ha-Rimmon*, 288; *Minḥat Shai* on Numbers 23:9; Psalms 46:9; 66:5; Menaḥem Azariah of Fano, *Yonat Elem*, 99; Margaliot, *Sha'arei Zohar*, *Berakhot* 7b.

13. **Regal adornments engraved in a key...** This paragraph is obscure. Rabbi Yehudah is referring to the angels surrounding Shekhinah.

"Regal adornments" renders קוזמיטין (*qozmitin*), similar to rabbinic loanwords deriving from Greek *kosmion* or *kosmarion*, "adornment." Cf. the basic forms *kosmeo*, "to order, arrange, rule, adorn," and *kosmos*, "order, ornament, ruler, universe."

See JT *Yevamot* 13:2, 13c; *Nedarim* 4:1, 38c; *Bereshit Rabbah* 19:10: "קוזמירין (*qozmirin*) [or: קוזמידין (*qozmidin*)], ornaments [or: jewels]," and Theodor's note; *Pirqei de-Rabbi Eli'ezer* 13: "קוזמין (*qozmin*), ornaments, of the king" (and Luria's note); *Devarim Rabbah* (ed. Lieberman), p. 69: "קוזמירון (*qozmiron*), ornament" (and n. 1, quoting Isaac Arama, *Aqedat Yitsḥaq*, 63, which copies this midrash and reads קוזמיטין [*qozmitin*], which matches the *Zohar*'s spelling). See *Arukh ha-Shalem*, s.v. *qzm*, *qozmarya*.

In the *Zohar*, *qozmitin* can mean "ornaments" or "rulers." See 2:37b, 56b; *ZḤ* 2a (*Matnitin*); Luria, *Va-Ye'esof David*; s.v. *qozmita*; Freedman, "Astral and Other Neologisms," 132–38.

"Key" renders קלדיטא (*qaldita*), based on the rabbinic term אקלידא (*aqlida*), which derives from the Greek *kleida*, "key." See *Zohar* 2:5b (*MhN*), 14a (*MhN*), 66b, 174a; 3:15b; *ZḤ* 12b (*MhN*). See Freedman, "Astral and Other Neologisms," 138–48, where she suggests that the traditional construal as "key" is mistaken, and that the *Zohar* intends some kind of astrological entity, perhaps the Zodiac.

The phrase "adornments of the seventh, engraved in the sixth" is enigmatic. See *ZḤ*

Rabbi Ḥiyya was traveling from Usha to Lydda, riding on a donkey, and Rabbi Yose was with him. Rabbi Ḥiyya dismounted and grabbed Rabbi Yose with his hands. He said to him, "If the people of the world knew of Jacob's great honor at the moment the blessed Holy One said to him, *I Myself will go down with you to Egypt* (Genesis 46:4), they would lick the dust within three parasangs of his grave![14]

"For so do our masters, the dignitaries of the world, the Masters of Mishnah, explain: It is written: *Moses went out to meet his father-in-law* (Exodus 18:7). Aaron saw [that Moses went out], so he went out with him; El'azar, the chieftains, and the elders went out with him; the clan heads, the notables of the assembly, and all of Israel went out with them. So in actuality all of Israel went out to meet Jethro. Who could see Moses going out—and not go out; Aaron and the dignitaries [going out]—and not go out?! Thus it was because of Moses that they all went out. Now, if this was the case for Moses' sake, how much more so for the sake of the blessed Holy One when He said, *I Myself will go down with you to Egypt*!"[15]



2a (*Matnitin*). It is possible that a sefirotic referent is intended, the seventh corresponding with *Shekhinah*, and the sixth with *Tif'eret* or *Yesod*. If this is the case, perhaps the meaning is that the adornments surround *Shekhinah* but have their root in *Tif'eret* or *Yesod*.

See *Derekh Emet*: "The princes are engraved in the key, which is a circle, and they revolve round and round in their places. They are engraved in the sixth, namely six lights are engraved in a circle around the seven *qozmitin*; and from these six, the sixty warriors are illuminated." See also *Soncino*, "Six luminosities form a circle surrounding a seventh luminosity in the center. The six on the circumference sustain the sixty valiant angels surrounding the *bed of Solomon*"; *Or Yaqar*; *Nitsotsei Orot*; *Matoq mi-Devash*; *Sullam* for various interpretations.

On *Shekhinah* as "bed" or *bed of Solomon*, see *Zohar* 1:37a, 225b, 226b, 248b, 250b; 2:30b, 48b, 51a, 133a, 226a; 3:60a, 114a, 118b, 119b, 210b, 269b; *ZḤ* 25c (*MhN*); Moses de León, *Sefer ha-Rimmon*, 370; idem, *Sheqel ha-Qodesh*, 62–64 (78–79). Cf. BT *Shabbat* 55b, where it is said that Jacob kept a bed in his tent for *Shekhinah*. See Rashi on Genesis 49:4. According to the eleventh-century Catholic reformer Peter Damian, Mary is the golden couch upon which God, tired out by the actions of humanity and the angels, lies down to rest. See Patai, *The Hebrew Goddess*, 280. On the phrase "the King who possesses peace," see *Sifra*, *Shemini*, *millu'im*, 15, 44c; *Pesiqta de-Rav Kahana* 1:2, 3; *Shir ha-Shirim Rabbah* on 1:1 and 1:2; *Zohar* 1:5b, 29a, 184a, 226b, 248b; 2:14a (*MhN*), 127b, 132a–b, 143b–144b; 3:10b, 20a, 60a, 73b; *ZḤ* 15d, 22a, 25c (all *MhN*); *ZḤ* 60d (*ShS*, *MhN*). On "Israel above," see above, at notes 4 and 5. Cf. *Matoq mi-Devash*, who reads it as signifying the *sefirah Tif'eret*.

14. **they would lick the dust within three parasangs of his grave** Corresponding to the jurisdiction of the teacher. See BT *Sanhedrin* 5b; see also BT *Sotah* 46b. (The Persian parasang equals about 3.5 miles).

On journeying from Usha to Lydda, see *Zohar* 2:36b, 45b; 3:122a, 240a; *ZḤ* 20d (*MhN*).

15. **Who could see Moses going out—and not go out...** If all went out for Moses, how much more so that the celestial host would accompany *Shekhinah*.

See *Mekhilta*, *Amaleq* (*Yitro*) 1; Rashi on Exodus 18:7.

"Masters of Mishnah" renders מאריהון דמתניתא (*mareihon de-matnita*). This term ap-

While they were traveling, Rabbi Abba met them. Rabbi Yose said, "Look, *Shekhinah* is here, for one of the Masters of Mishnah is with us!"[16]

Rabbi Abba said, "What are you engaged in?"[17]

Rabbi Yose replied, "In this verse, as is written: *I Myself will go down with you to Egypt*...; when Jacob descended to Egypt, as is written: *These are the names of the sons of Israel who came to Egypt* (Exodus 1:1)—teaching that all of them descended with Jacob to Egypt."[18]

Rabbi Abba said to him, "Was that the only instance?"

He opened and said, "*Happening it happened, that the word of YHVH came to Ezekiel the priest, son of Buzi, in the land of the Chaldeans by the River Kevar* (Ezekiel 1:3). There are three difficulties here! One: For we have learned: The *Shekhinah* does not dwell outside the Land. One: That he was not faithful like Moses, of whom is written *Throughout My House he is faithful* (Numbers 12:7), for he revealed and publicized all the King's treasures! One: He appeared to be out of his mind.[19]



pears in numerous passages (in various formulations) throughout *Midrash ha-Ne'lam* and appears to signify a group (though never formally defined) of sages possessing esoteric wisdom. In some ways, the Masters of Mishnah are a forerunner to the *Ḥavrayya*, the Companions headed by Rabbi Shim'on, found in the main body of the *Zohar*. Significantly, however, Rabbi Shim'on does not always occupy a privileged position in this group. The Mishnah of which they are masters is not the Mishnah of the rabbinic sage Rabbi Yehudah ha-Nasi, but rather a body of esoteric knowledge often relating to the soul and the structure of the cosmos. See *Zohar* 1:123b (*MhN*, though mistakenly labeled as *Tosefta*); 1:127a–b, 129a–b, 130a, 135a 138a, 139b (all *MhN*); 2:14a (*MhN*); *ZḤ* 10c, 12c, 13a, 14c, 15b–c, 16a, 59b (all *MhN*). Cf. *Pesiqta de-Rav Kahana* 11:15, 23:12; Scholem, "Parashah Ḥadashah," 443, 444 (Addendum 1 in this volume); Meroz, "Va-Ani Lo Hayiti Sham?," 168 (Addendum 3 in this volume). See also Matt, "Matnita di-Lan," 132–34.

16. **Look, *Shekhinah* is here...** See *Mekhilta, Amaleq* (*Yitro*) 1: "Whoever receives the face of [i.e., welcomes] the wise, it is as if he receives the face of *Shekhinah*."

Cf. JT *Eruvin* 5:1, 22b: "Rabbi Shemu'el said in the name of Rabbi Zeira, '...Whoever receives the face of his teacher, it is as if he receives the face of *Shekhinah*.'...Rabbi Yishma'el taught...'One who receives the face of his friend, it is as if he receives the face of *Shekhinah*.'" Cf. Genesis 33:10; *Tanḥuma, Ki Tissa* 27; *Shir ha-Shirim Rabbah* on 2:5.

See *Zohar* 1:9a, 94b, 115b (*MhN*); 2:20a (*MhN*), 50a, 94b, 198a; 3:6b, 148a, 298a; *ZḤ* 11c, 25b (both *MhN*).

17. **What are you engaged in?** For the sequence "Meanwhile, so-and-so arrived.... He said, 'What are you engaged in?'," see BT *Yevamot* 105b; *Gittin* 31b; *Zohar* 1:207b, 245a.

18. **teaching that all of them descended...** Namely, the celestial beings.

19. ***Happening it happened, that the word of YHVH came to Ezekiel...*** Rabbi Abba points to Ezekiel's prophetic vision in Babylon to illustrate other instances when *Shekhinah* accompanied the people in exile. The unusual phrase, *happening it happened*, implies a unique event.

On *Shekhinah* revealing Herself only in the land of Israel, see *Mekhilta, Pisḥa* 1: "*Shekhinah* is not revealed outside the land [of Israel]...." See also BT *Mo'ed Qatan* 25a; *Pirqei de-Rabbi Eli'ezer* 10. On Moses and the

"But so have we concluded in our Mishnah: Heaven forbid! Ezekiel was a consummate prophet! With the permission of the blessed Holy One he revealed all that he revealed. Had he revealed and publicized twice as much as he disclosed, all would have been necessary! For so have we learned: One who is accustomed to endure suffering and one who is not accustomed to endure suffering, should suffering befall both of them, whose suffering is more absolute? You must surely say: the one who is not accustomed to suffering. Thus, when Israel descended to Egypt, they were accustomed to suffering all their days—and consequently they bore the yoke of exile. However, there was no great suffering for Israel like the exile of Babylon, about which is written *The precious children of Zion, worth their weight in pure gold* (Lamentations 4:2).[20]

"As we have learned: Rabbi Yitsḥak said, '*For the mountains I take up weeping and wailing* (Jeremiah 9:9). What is meant by *for the mountains*? These are the high mountains of the world. Who are the high mountains? You must surely say: *The precious children of Zion*.'[21]

"They were coming with millstones around their necks, their hands bound tightly behind. When they entered Babylon, they thought that they would never be raised, that the blessed Holy One had abandoned them and would never attend to them.[22]



verse from Numbers, see *Zohar* 1:76a, 218a; 2:21b (*MhN*); Moses de León, *Mishkan ha-Edut*, 72a. On faithful as concealing, see *Zohar* 3:128a (*IR*): *He that has a faithful spirit conceals the matter* (Proverbs 11:13). In contrast to Moses, who kept all that He saw to himself, Ezekiel divulged every detail. See BT *Ḥagigah* 13b. On Ezekiel's appearing out of his mind, see BT *Sanhedrin* 39a: "A certain heretic said to Rabbi Abbahu, 'Your God is a jester, for He said to Ezekiel *Lie on your left side* (Ezekiel 4:4) and *lie on your right side* (ibid., 6).'" In the fourth chapter of Ezekiel, God instructs the prophet to perform various bizarre acts that serve as omens for the house of Israel.

See *Zohar* 1:85a, 149a, 222b; 2:2a–b, 82a–b; *ZḤ* 37c; Moses de León, *Peirush ha-Merkavah*, 58–59.

Rabbi Abba's entire homily has a very close parallel in *Zohar* 2:2a–b (in the name of Rabbi Shim'on).

20. **With the permission of the blessed Holy One...** As will become clearer throughout the homily, *Shekhinah*'s appearance outside the land and Ezekiel's "excessive" disclosure were both in order. The stunned people in exile had to be comforted and reassured. See *Zohar* 2:2b.

The verse in Lamentations concludes: *how are they reckoned as earthen jars, work of a potter's hand!* It is employed by Rabbi Abba to describe the pampered Babylonian exiles, unaccustomed to suffering.

On the expression "our Mishnah," see *Zohar* 1:37b, 55b, 74a, 91b, 93a; 95b, 96a, 124b (*MhN*), 136b (*MhN*), 137a (*MhN*), 139a (*MhN*), 223b; 2:123b; 3:75b, 78a, 284b, 285a, 293b (*IZ*); *ZḤ* 12b (*MhN*), 15b–c (*MhN*), 16a (*MhN*), 18b (*MhN*), 20a (*MhN*); Scholem, "Parashah Ḥadashah"; Matt, "Matnita di-Lan."

21. ***For the mountains I take up weeping...*** See *Zohar* 2:2b (standard printed editions). On the verse from Jeremiah, see *Eikhah Rabbah, Petiḥta* 34; *Pesiqta de-Rav Kahana* 13:10; ibid. Supplement 5:2.

22. **millstones around their necks...** On

"It has been taught: Rabbi Shim'on said, 'At that moment, the blessed Holy One summoned His entire household, all the holy chariots, all His retinue, all His ministers and the entire host of heaven. He said to them, "What are you doing here? My beloved children are in exile, in distress, and yet you remain here? Arise! All of you descend to Babylon, and I along with you!" As is written: *Thus says YHVH: For your sake I was sent to Babylon, I will bring down all bars* (Isaiah 43:14).'[23]

"When they descended, the heavens opened and the holy spirit settled upon Ezekiel. He proclaimed to Israel, 'Behold! Your Lord is here, and all the heavenly hosts and chariots that have come to dwell among you!' They did not believe him until he relayed all that he had seen: *And I saw*... *And I saw*.[24]

"Rabbi Shim'on also said, 'At that moment Israel rejoiced with consummate joy in the companionship of their Lord, who was with them. Every one of them possessed a willing heart, with great love, to submit their souls for the holiness of their Lord.'[25]



"This is why Ezekiel revealed all that he revealed—and all was as it should have been. The blessed Holy One never abandoned Israel in exile before ensconcing His abode among them. How much more so with Jacob, who was descending into exile, that the blessed Holy One and His *Shekhinah*, and higher and lower holy beings and chariots all descended with Jacob, as is written: *who came to Egypt with Jacob* (Exodus 1:1)?!"

this image, see Lamentations 5:13; *Eikhah Rabbah, Petiḥta* 24; ibid. 2:6; 5:13; *Zohar* 2:2b, 118b (*RM*); 3:20b.

On the Babylonian exiles' sense of abandonment, see BT *Sanhedrin* 105a.

23. **descend to Babylon, and I along with you...** The verse in Isaiah reads: *Thus says YHVH, your Redeemer, the Holy One of Israel: "For your sake* שלחתי (*shillaḥti*), *I send, to Babylon; I will bring down all bars.* Here, based on a theologically radical midrash, Rabbi Shim'on revocalizes שלחתי (*shillaḥti*), *I send*, as שולחתי (*shullaḥti*), *I was sent*, indicating that God exiled Himself (or *Shekhinah*) along with Israel.

See *Mekhilta, Pisḥa* 14, in the name of Rabbi Akiva: "Wherever Israel went into exile, *Shekhinah*, as it were, went into exile with them. When they were exiled to Egypt, *Shekhinah* went into exile with them... When they were exiled to Babylon, *Shekhinah* went into exile with them, as is said: *For your sake* שולחתי (*shullaḥti*), *I was sent, to Babylon*.... And when in the future they return, *Shekhinah*, as it were, will return with them...."

See *Sifrei*, Numbers 84; JT *Ta'anit* 1:1, 64a; *Eikhah Rabbah* 1:54; BT *Megillah* 29a.

In the verse from Isaiah, the simple sense of *bars* is apparently "prison bars," while here they are taken to refer to components of the heavenly chariots, which descended to Babylon along with camps of angels.

See *Zohar* 2:2b.

24. ***And I saw*** This formula appears three times in Ezekiel's vision (Ezekiel 1:4, 15, 27). Ezekiel's "excessive" disclosure was to reassure the people.

See *Zohar* 2:2b.

This paragraph might also be construed as the continuation of Rabbi Shim'on's teaching.

25. **At that moment Israel rejoiced...** See *Zohar* 2:2b, the passage printed under *Lishshana Aḥarina*.

Rabbi Abbahu opened: *With me from Lebanon, bride; with me from Lebanon come!* (Song of Songs 4:8).[26]

We have learned: Rabbi Yitsḥak said, "Woe to creatures who do not know and do not attend to the worship of their Creator!"[27]

As it has been taught: Rabbi Yitsḥak said, "Every single day an echo reverberates from Mount Horeb, proclaiming, 'Woe to creatures for the worship of their Creator; woe to creatures for the humiliation [5b] of Torah!'"[28]

As Rabbi Yehudah said: "Whoever strives in Torah in this world and acquires good deeds inherits a complete world; whoever does not strive in Torah in this world and does not acquire good deeds inherits neither this nor that!"[29]

Yet we have learned: There are those who inherit their world in accordance with their place and in accordance with what is fitting them.[30]

Rabbi Yitsḥak said, "We have taught so only regarding those who do not possess any good deeds at all!"[31]

Rabbi Yehudah said, "Were human beings to comprehend the love with which the blessed Holy One loves Israel, they would roar like young lions to pursue them. As it has been taught: When Jacob descended to Egypt, the blessed Holy



26. ***With me from Lebanon...*** The full verse reads: *With me from Lebanon, bride; with me from Lebanon come! Descend* [or: *Look down*] *from the peak of Amana, from the peak of Senir and Hermon, from the dens of lions, from the mountains of leopards.* The verse is explained in the following homilies.

27. **Woe to creatures...** See BT *Ḥagigah* 12b: "Rabbi Yose says, 'Woe to creatures—who see, yet know not what they see; who stand, yet know not upon what they stand!'"

28. **Every single day an echo reverberates...** See *Avot* 6:2 in the name of Rabbi Yehoshu'a son of Levi, "Every single day an echo reverberates from Mount Horeb [Sinai], proclaiming: 'Woe to creatures for the humiliation of Torah!'"

29. **inherits a complete world...** Namely, this world and the world to come. Cf. *Avot* 6:1: "Rabbi Meir said, 'Whoever engages in Torah for its own sake, merits many things; moreover, he is deserving of the whole world.'"

See *Or Yaqar, Matoq mi-Devash* for a different explanation.

30. **inherit their world in accordance with their place...** Assuming that this a question posed to Rabbi Yehudah's preceding statement (rather than the continuation of his statement; see *Or Yaqar*), the sense is as follows: Rabbi Yehudah, you have said that one who doesn't engage in Torah or perform good deeds forfeits this world and the world to come entirely. Yet, we have a different tradition, according to which there is an intermediate way: people inherit in accordance with their deeds—some less, some more. Life is not a zero-sum game.

Cf. BT *Shabbat* 152a in the name of Rabbi Yitsḥak: "...every righteous person is given a habitation in accordance with his honor. This may be compared to a king who enters a town together with his servants. When they enter, they all enter though one gate; when they spend the night, each is given a habitation in accordance with his honor." See also *Tanḥuma, Emor* 6; *Vayiqra Rabbah* 27:1; *Zohar* 3:196b; *ZḤ* 26b (*MhN*), 34a–b, 49b, 75c (*MhN, Rut*).

31. **We have taught so only...** Namely, Rabbi Yehudah's teaching only applies to the completely wicked. The intermediate will receive their just deserts.

One summoned His household. He said to them, 'All of you descend to Egypt and I will descend along with you!' *Shekhinah* said, 'Master of the World! Can there be legions without a king?!' He said to her, '*With me from Lebanon, bride.*' מלבנון (*Mi-Lvanon*), *From Lebanon*—from the site of Eden, המלובן (*ha-melubban*), pure white, in every aspect. *Bride*—*Shekhinah*, for she is a bride under a canopy."[32]

This corresponds with what Rabbi Yehudah said: "What is the significance of *It happened on the day* כלת משה (*kallot Mosheh*), *Moses consummated* (Numbers 7:1)? It is spelled כלת (*kallat*), bride—on the day the bride entered the canopy. *Shekhinah* is the bride![33]

"*With me from Lebanon come!* (Song of Songs 4:8)—from the site of the sanctuary above. *Look down* מראש אמנה (*me-rosh amanah*), *from the peak of Amana* (ibid.)—מראשם של בני אמונה (*me-rosham shel benei emunah*), upon the heads of the sons of faith. Who are they? Jacob and his sons. *From the peak of Senir and Hermon* (ibid.)—for one day, they will receive My Torah from Mount Hermon, to protect them in their exile. ממעונות (*Mi-me'onot*), *From the dens, of lions*



32. ***With me from Lebanon, bride* . . .** On this verse, see *Zohar* 2:2b–3a; cf. *Zohar* 1:128b–129a (*MhN*). See also *Mekhilta, Pisha* 14; *Shir ha-Shirim Rabbah* on 4:8; *Tanhuma* (Buber), *Beshallah* 11.

It is possible that the verse is being used to encode a sefirotic referent here. Lebanon and Eden are both symbols for the second *sefirah*, *Ḥokhmah* (see *Zohar* 2:2b–3a). Alternatively, they merely indicate the celestial realm in a general way.

33. **It is spelled כלת (*kallat*), bride . . .** The verse in Numbers reads: *It happened on the day* כלות משה (*kallot Moshe*), *Moses consummated, setting up the Dwelling, that he anointed it and consecrated it and all its furnishings, and the altar and all its furnishings.* Although in the Masoretic text the word כלות (*kallot*) is spelled with a *vav*, it is interpreted midrashically as if it were spelled without the *vav*, so that it can be read כלת (*kallat*), the bride of, implying that Israel is the bride of God. Here, the bride is *Shekhinah*.

See *Pesiqta de-Rav Kahana* 1:1; *Tanhuma, Naso* 20, 26; *Tanhuma* (Buber), *Vayishlah* 28, *Naso* 28; *Pesiqta Rabbati* 5; *Bemidbar Rabbah* 12:8; Rashi on Numbers 7:1; *Zohar* 1:236b; 2:140b; 3:4b, 148a, 226b (*RM*), 254a (*RM*). See *Minhat Shai* on Numbers 7:1.

For other differences between the Masoretic spelling or wording and the *Zohar*'s reading, see *Zohar* 1:32a–b, 58b, 83b, 84a, 93b, 106b, 122b (*MhN*), 151a; 2:3b, 40a, 41b (*Piq*), 82a, 83a, 124b, 176b (*SdTs*), 182b, 246b (*Heikh*); 3:6a, 30a–b, 34a, 40b, 42b, 57b, 68a, 74b–75a, 76b, 80b, 86a–b, 129a (*IR*), 184a, 202b, 203b, 207a; *Minhat Shai*, passim (e.g., on Numbers 7:1); Emden, *Mitpahat Sefarim*, 27–34, 73–74; Rosenfeld, *Mishpahat Soferim*. On this phenomenon, see *Zohar* 3:254a (*RM*); Tishby, *Wisdom of the Zohar*, 1:55–56; Ta-Shma, *Ha-Nigleh she-ba-Nistar*, 50, 131–32, n. 125; Abrams, *Kabbalistic Manuscripts and Textual Theory*, 389–90.

On the same phenomenon in rabbinic literature, see Rashi on BT *Zevahim* 118b, s.v. *ve-lo*; *Tosafot, Shabbat* 55b, s.v. *ma'aviram*; *Niddah* 33a, s.v. *ve-ha-nissa*; *Sha'arei Teshuvah (Teshuvot ha-Ge'onim)*, 39; Malachi ben Jacob ha-Kohen, *Yad Mal'akhi* 1:283; Aptowitzer, *Das Schriftwort in der Rabbinischen Literatur*; Kasher, *Torah Shelemah*, 23:113; Maori, "Rabbinic Midrash as Evidence for Textual Variants in the Hebrew Bible"; Rosenthal, "Al Derekh Tippulam shel Ḥazal be-Ḥillufei Nussah ba-Miqra."

(ibid.)—the nations, likened to lions and leopards, המענים (*ha-me'anim*), who afflict, My children with all manner of oppressive servitude."[34]

Rabbi Abba said, "*With me from Lebanon, bride.* Was she really coming from Lebanon? Was she not rather ascending to Lebanon!"[35]

Rather, Rabbi Abba said, "When *Shekhinah* descended to Egypt, six hundred thousand ministering angels descended with her—the blessed Holy One preceding first, as is written: *Their king passed before them, and YHVH at their head* (Micah 2:13)."[36]

Rabbi Yitsḥak said, "*With me from Lebanon, bride*—*Shekhinah*; *with me from Lebanon come*—from the site of the sanctuary above. *Look down* מראש אמנה (*me-rosh amanah*), *from the peak of Amana*—from the site of the sanctuary below. As Rabbi Ḥiyya said: '*Shekhinah* never budged from the western wall of the sanctuary, as is said: *There he stands behind our wall* (Song of Songs 2:9)—ראש אמנה (*rosh amanah*), beginning of faith, for the entire world.' *From the peak of Senir and Hermon* (ibid. 4:8)—from the site from which Torah emerges into the world. Why? To protect Israel *from the dens of lions*—the nations. Rabbi Yudan said, '*From the dens of lions*—the disciples of the wise who engage in Torah in study dens and synagogues; lions and leopards in Torah.'"[37]



34. ***Look down* מראש אמנה (*me-rosh amanah*), *from the peak of Amana*...** On the play of the homonyms אמנה (*amanah*), "Amana," and אמנה (*amanah*), "faith," see *Tanḥuma* (Buber), *Beshallaḥ* 11; *Shemot Rabbah* 23:5; *Shir ha-Shirim Rabbah* on 4:8; *Zohar* 2:3a.

On Hermon as Sinai, see *Midrash Tehillim* 42:5; *Zohar* 2:3a; *Miqdash Melekh*; *Matoq mi-Devash*. On the sanctuary above, see *Tanḥuma, Pequdei* 1: "There is a Jerusalem above aligned with Jerusalem below. Out of His love for the one below, He fashioned another above.... He has sworn that His presence will not enter the heavenly Jerusalem until the earthly Jerusalem is rebuilt." See BT *Ta'anit* 5a.

See also *Mekhilta, Shirta* 10; JT *Berakhot* 4:5, 8c; *Shir ha-Shirim Rabbah* on 3:9; *Tanḥuma, Mishpatim* 18, *Vayaqhel* 7, *Pequdei* 1–3.

If the verse encodes a sefirotic referent, then the "sanctuary above" signifies *Binah*.

It is not clear who is speaking, though presumably it is still Rabbi Yehudah.

35. **Was she really coming from Lebanon?...** Rabbi Abba does not disagree with the idea that *Shekhinah* descended into exile, but disagrees that the verse from the Song of Songs can be used as a proof-text. If Lebanon signifies the Temple (as is common in rabbinic texts), then surely *Shekhinah* went up to the Temple after the exile. She could not have descended from there as the Temple was not yet built. The verse from the Song of Songs must then apply to the Babylonian exile. In the following paragraph Rabbi Abba supplies a different proof for *Shekhinah*'s descent. See *Matoq mi-Devash.*

See *Mekhilta, Pisḥa* 14; *Shir ha-Shirim Rabbah* on 4:8.

36. ***and YHVH at their head*** See *Bereshit Rabbah* 51:2: "Rabbi El'azar said, 'Wherever it is said *And YHVH*, this implies: He and His Court.'" In Kabbalah, this "court" symbolizes *Shekhinah*. See *Vayiqra Rabbah* 24:2; JT *Berakhot* 9:5, 14b; Rashi on Exodus 12:29.

37. ***Shekhinah* never budged from the western wall...** See *Shemot Rabbah* 2:2: "Rabbi El'azar says, 'The *Shekhinah* did not budge from the Sanctuary, as is said: *My*

Rabbi Ḥizkiyah was sitting in the presence of Rabbi Shim'on. He said to him, "What prompted the Torah to enumerate the sons of Jacob, first totaling twelve and afterward seventy, as is said: *All the souls of the house of Jacob coming to Egypt were seventy* (Genesis 46:27)? Why seventy and no more?"[38]

He replied, "Corresponding to the seventy nations in the world; they were a unique nation equivalent to them all."[39]

He said further, "Come and see: Luminous keys, branches seated heavily, are appointed over the seventy nations, emanating from twelve conjoined engravings revolving on their travels, weighed against the four directions, as is written: *He set the boundaries of peoples according to the number of the Children of Israel* (Deuteronomy 32:8). This accords with what is written: *For I have scattered you like the four winds of heaven* (Zechariah 2:10)—to demonstrate that they exist by virtue of Israel. It does not say *to the four*, but *like the four*. Just as the world cannot endure without the four winds, so the world cannot exist without Israel."[40]



*eyes and My heart shall be there* [*always*] (2 Chronicles 7:16). So it also says: *I cry aloud to YHVH, and He answers me from His holy mountain. Selah* (Psalms 3:5). Even though it was destroyed, it still retained its holiness. Come and see what Cyrus said: *He is the God who is in Jerusalem* (Ezra 1:3), implying that even though it is destroyed, God did not budge from there.' Rabbi Aḥa said, 'The *Shekhinah* will never budge from the Western Wall, as is said: *There, he stands behind our wall* (Song of Songs 2:9), and similarly: *His eyes behold, His gaze probes the sons of man* (Psalms 11:4).'"

See also *Bemidbar Rabbah* 11:2; *Shir ha-Shirim Rabbah* on 2:9; *Midrash Tehillim* 11:4; *Zohar* 2:116a (*RM*).

See above, note 34.

It is not clear whether Rabbi Yudan is a new voice or is being cited by Rabbi Yitsḥak. Either way, in his view, the phrase *from the dens of lions* does not refer to the nations who threaten Israel in exile, but to the abode of *Shekhinah* in exile, among the scholars. Cf. BT *Megillah* 29a.

38. **first totaling twelve and afterward seventy...** Genesis 46:8–27 lists all of Jacob's significant descendants who came to Egypt. The account enumerates the descendants following the order of the twelve tribes. Rabbi Ḥizkiyah is wondering about the significance of the numbers twelve and seventy.

Some of the witnesses read Rabbi Ḥiyya instead of Rabbi Ḥizkiyah.

39. **Corresponding to the seventy nations in the world...** Seventy nations are listed in Genesis 10. See also Deuteronomy 32:8 (cited in the following paragraph.) See *Zohar* 2:6a, 16b (*MhN*), below, page 483. See *Matoq mi-Devash*.

Cf. BT *Sukkah* 55b in the name of Rabbi El'azar: "To what do those seventy bullocks [that were offered during the seven days of *Sukkot*] correspond? To the seventy nations. To what does the single bullock [of the Eighth Day] correspond? To the unique nation."

40. **Luminous keys, branches seated heavily...** The phrasing and precise meaning are not entirely clear. The general sense, however, is that the seventy nations of the world are ruled by heavenly powers that emanate from twelve engravings. Thus, just as Israel is described in terms of twelve tribes that became seventy, so the nations of the world. Indeed, Israel is the source of this arrangement: "they exist by virtue of Israel."

According to rabbinic tradition, the seventy nations of the world are governed by seventy angels or heavenly princes appointed

[14a][41]Alternatively, *These are the names* (Exodus 1:1).

Rabbi Yehudah opened, saying, "*Black am I but beautiful*... (Song of Songs 1:5). *Black am I*—Assembly of Israel, for she is black from exile; *but beautiful*—for she is beautiful from Torah, commandments, and good deeds; *O daughters of Jerusalem* (ibid.)—for by virtue of this they are worthy of inheriting Jerusalem Above; *like the tents of* קדר (Qedar), *Kedar* (ibid.)—even though she is קודרת (*qoderet*), darkened, in exile, in deeds she is *like the curtains* שלמה (*Shelomoh*), *of Solomon* (ibid.), like the curtains of the King who possesses שלום (*shalom*), peace."[42]

by God. See Daniel 10:13, 20–21; Septuagint, Deuteronomy 32:8–9; Jubilees 15:31–32; *Targum Yerushalmi*, Genesis 11:8, Deuteronomy 32:8–9; *Tanḥuma, Re'eh* 8; *Leqaḥ Tov*, Genesis 9:19; *Pirqei de-Rabbi Eli'ezer* 24; *Zohar* 1:46b, 61a, 108b, 113a (*MhN*), 149b, 177a, 195a; 2:14b (*MhN*), 17a (*MhN*), 96a, 126b, 209a–b; 3:8a, 298b; *ZḤ* 23d, 24c, 28c (all *MhN*); Ginzberg, *Legends*, 5:204–5, n. 91.

The twelve conjoined engravings (which correspond to the twelve tribes) may point to some zodiacal image. See Scholem, ad loc., "Bilder des Zodiak?"; Freedman, "Astral and Other Neologisms," 138–42.

The image of "branches" to describe the nations' heavenly princes may derive from *Bahir* 64 (95): "The blessed Holy One has a single Tree containing twelve diagonal borders.... Paralleling these diagonals are twelve officials." See also *Bahir* 67 (98). See also Daniel 4:7–9.

Cf. *Sefer ha-Razim* (ed. Margaliot), 101: "Twelve princes of glory are seated in magnificent thrones, and the appearance of their thrones is like fire; fourfold in the center of the firmament facing the four corners of the world, three to each side.... they are appointed over the twelve months of the year...."

Some of the witnesses read גוברין (*guvrin*), "men," in place of "branches."

For similar imagery, see *Zohar* 2:58b, 62b, 64b. See also *Zohar* 1:199a.

On קלדיטין (*qalditin*), "keys," see above, note 13.

The full verse from Deuteronomy reads: *When the Most High allotted the nations, when He dispersed humankind, He set the boundaries of peoples according to the number of the Children of Israel.*

See BT *Ta'anit* 3b in the name of Rabbi Yehoshu'a son of Levi: "Scripture says: *For I have scattered you like the four winds of heaven, says YHVH*. What did He say to them? Should you say that the blessed Holy One said to Israel as follows: I have scattered you to the four corners of the world, if so, why did He say *like the four* [*winds*]? He should have said *to the four* [*winds*]! Rather, this is what He meant: Just as the world cannot endure without winds, so too the world cannot exist without Israel." See also BT *Avodah Zarah* 10b.

See *Or Yaqar, Matoq mi-Devash* for various interpretations.

41. **[14a]** Though incorporated into the *Zohar*'s commentary to *parashat Shemot*, the material from *Zohar* 2:14a (top) to 22a (top) belongs to *MhN*.

See *Or Yaqar*, 76; *Nitsotsei Zohar* on 2:14a, n. 5; Tishby, *Wisdom of the Zohar*, 1:2, 105, n. 8; Scholem on 2:14a; idem, *Kabbalah*, 217.

42. ***Black am I but beautiful...*** According to the Midrash on Song of Songs, this verse is spoken by the people of Israel to God. Here, "Assembly of Israel" can refer both to the people and to *Shekhinah*, who suffers with them in exile yet is adorned by their devotion to the *mitsvot*.

See *Shir ha-Shirim Rabbah* on 1:5; *Shemot Rabbah* 23:10; 49:2. The full verse in Song of Songs reads: *Black am I but beautiful, O*

Rabbi Ḥiyya the Great traveled to visit the Masters of Mishnah in order to learn from them. He went to Rabbi Shim'on son of Yoḥai and saw a curtain dividing the house. Rabbi Ḥiyya was astonished. He sat down. He said, "I shall listen to a word from his mouth from here."[43]

He heard someone saying, "*Flee my love, be like a gazelle or a young stag* (Song of Songs 8:14). All the yearning yearned by Israel before the blessed Holy One is as Rabbi Shim'on said, 'Israel's desire is for the blessed Holy One not to depart or be distant, but rather that He should flee like a gazelle or a young stag.' How so? Rabbi Shim'on said, 'No animal in the world behaves like the gazelle or the young stag: as it flees, it goes a little way and looks back to the place from which it departed, always turning its head behind. So did Israel say: Master of the World! If we force You to depart from among us, may it be Your will to flee like the gazelle or the young stag, which flees turning its head to the place it left, as is written: *Yet in spite of all this, when they are in the land of their enemies, I will not reject them or spurn them so as to destroy them* (Leviticus 26:44).'"[44]



Rabbi Ḥiyya heard and said, "Alas, supernals are deliberating within the house while I am sitting outside!"[45]

He wept. Rabbi Shim'on heard and said, "Certainly *Shekhinah* is outside! Who will go out?"[46]

*daughters of Jerusalem—like the tents of Kedar, like Solomon's curtains.* See *Zohar* 3:59b.

On Assembly of Israel as a title of *Shekhinah*, see above, note 2. On the exile of *Shekhinah*, see above, note 4. On the phrase "the King who possesses peace," see above, note 13. On Jerusalem Above, see BT *Ta'anit* 5a; *Tanḥuma, Pequdei,* 1; *Zohar* 1:122a (*MhN*); *ZḤ* 20d, 24b, 25a, 25d, 26b, 28c–d (all *MhN*).

43. **Rabbi Ḥiyya the Great traveled...** When he arrives, he is astonished to encounter a curtain of fire, a sure sign that those assembled are engaging in mysteries of Torah. (See, for example, BT *Ḥagigah* 14b; *Shir ha-Shirim Rabbah* on 1:10.)

For a masterful analysis of this story, and its earlier rescension, see Meroz, "Ḥanikhato shel R. Ḥiyya." For a different account of the initiation of Rabbi Ḥiyya, see *ZḤ* 15d (*MhN*). See also Addendum 2, where this story is quoted.

On the special relationship between Rabbi Ḥiyya and Rabbi Shim'on, see *Zohar* 1:4a–b. On the epithet "Masters of Mishnah," see above, note 15.

44. **He heard someone saying...** The speaker is not identified. It may be one of Rabbi Shim'on's students. According to Liebes, "Hebrew and Aramaic," 45, this is a celestial voice. See *Or Yaqar, Nitsotsei Orot, Matoq mi-Devash.* Following the first "Rabbi Shim'on said," the text switches from Aramaic to Hebrew. On the deer (or gazelle) fleeing and returning, or rather turning back, see *Zohar* 2:138b; 3:155a. See Song of Songs 2:9: *My beloved is a gazelle, or a young deer.* Based on this verse, rabbinic sources compare God to a gazelle, and they describe the gazelle (and the Messiah) as appearing and disappearing. See *Targum*, Song of Songs on 8:14; *Pesiqta de-Rav Kahana* 5:8; *Shir ha-Shirim Rabbah* on 2:9, 15; *Rut Rabbah* 5:6; *Pesiqta Rabbati* 15; *Bemidbar Rabbah* 11:2.

45. **Rabbi Ḥiyya heard and said...** The text reverts to Aramaic.

46. ***Shekhinah* is outside...** Perhaps the weeping is the sign that *Shekhinah* is present. According to Meroz (p. 126), Rabbi Ḥiyya signifies the wandering *Shekhinah* who will now join the nine other companions present

Rabbi El'azar his son said, "I will!"

He said, "If I am burned, it will not be with unholy fire. For look, *Shekhinah* is on the other side of us. Let *Shekhinah* enter and the fire be made whole!"[47]

He heard a voice saying, "The pillars have not yet been erected, the gates not arrayed. He is still one of the lesser spices of Eden."[48]

Rabbi El'azar did not go out.

Rabbi Ḥiyya sat down, sighed, and wept. He opened, saying, "*Turn, my love, be like a gazelle or a young stag* (Song of Songs 2:17)."[49]

A gate opened in the curtain but Rabbi Ḥiyya did not enter. Rabbi Shim'on raised his eyes and said, "Conclude from this that permission has been granted for the one outside—yet we are inside!"

Rabbi Shim'on arose. The fire moved from his place to the place of Rabbi Ḥiyya.

Rabbi Shim'on said, "The radiant light of the key is without, while we are here within!"[50]

Rabbi Hiyya's mouth was struck dumb. As soon as he entered within, he lowered his eyes and did not raise his head. Rabbi Shim'on said to Rabbi El'azar his son, "Arise. Pass your hand over his mouth, for he is unaccustomed to this."



Rabbi El'azar arose and passed his hand over Rabbi Ḥiyya's mouth.

Rabbi Ḥiyya opened his mouth, saying, "[The eye] has seen what I have not seen, raised beyond my imagining. It is good to die in the flaming fire of pure gold, in a place where sparks fly in every direction, every single spark ascending

in the house, signifying the nine upper *sefirot*. Rabbi Ḥiyya's arrival thus marks the culmination of the formation of the Companions, headed by Rabbi Shim'on.

On weeping (opening gates,) see BT *Berakhot* 32b; see also Fishbane, "Tears of Disclosure."

47. **If I am burned...** To escort Rabbi Ḥiyya and *Shekhinah* inside, Rabbi El'azar must pass through the curtain of fire. He knows that this holy fire will not harm him.

48. **The pillars have not yet been erected...** Namely, Rabbi Ḥiyya is not yet worthy to enter and partake of the sublime mysteries. See *Or Yaqar, Derekh Emet, Nitsotsei Orot.*

49. ***Turn, my love...*** Rabbi Ḥiyya cites a verse similar to the one he heard from within the house. He applies the verse to himself—lamenting his distance from the supernals within, and therefore from God—and pleads for proximity.

50. **The radiant light of the key . . .** קוזטיפא דנהורא דקלדיטא (*Qoztipha di-nhora de-qaldita*), one of the many neologistic phrases found throughout the *Zohar*. Whatever the precise meaning, Rabbi Shim'on is referring to Rabbi Ḥiyya. See *ZḤ* 14b, 59c (both *MhN*). See the expression קסטיפא דשמשא (*qastipha de-shimsha*), "ray of the sun" (*Zohar* 3:283b); the Arabic root *qdf*, "to throw"; and the neologism קוספיתא (*quspita*), "hollow of a sling," discussed by Liebes, *Peraqim*, 345–48. See *Zohar* 1:53b, 167a; *Bei'ur ha-Millim ha-Zarot*, 189.

On *qaldita*, the basic meaning of which is "key," see above, note 13.

See Freedman, "Astral and Other Neologisms," 147, for a different interpretation. See also Meroz, "Ḥanikhato shel R. Ḥiyya," 145, n. 82.

to three hundred [14b] and seventy chariots, and every chariot dividing into thousands upon thousands and myriads upon myriads, until they reach the Ancient of Days—who sits on the throne; and the throne trembles because of Him, permeating two hundred and sixty worlds, until it reaches the site of the delight of the righteous, until it is heard throughout all the firmaments, and all the higher and lower beings—all of them at once—are astounded and say, 'Is this Rabbi Shim'on son of Yoḥai, who makes all quake? Who can stand before him? This is Rabbi Shim'on son of Yoḥai, who at the moment he opens his mouth to ply Torah, all the thrones and all the chariots, and all those who praise their Master, listen to his voice! None begins and none concludes—all fall silent—until not an accusing mouth is heard in all the firmaments above and below. When Rabbi Shim'on finishes plying Torah, who has seen the songs? Who has beheld the joy of those who praise their Master? Who has seen the voices soaring throughout all the firmaments?! All of them come on account of Rabbi Shim'on; and they bow and prostrate before their Master, wafting fragrant aromas of Eden unto the Ancient of Days—all of this on account of Rabbi Shim'on!'"[51]



51. **Rabbi Ḥiyya opened his mouth...** His dumbness removed, Rabbi Ḥiyya has an ecstatic vision—though it quickly gives way to a celebration of the unique status of Rabbi Shim'on, whose Torah is described in cosmic terms. Here, then, for the first time in *MhN*, the description of Rabbi Shim'on recalls his superlative portrayal in the main body of the *Zohar*. The point of Rabbi Ḥiyya's profuse description is that Rabbi Shim'on's innovations in Torah not only soar heavenward, but also travel through—and impact—the divine being itself. This passage is similar to a well-known text from the *haqdamah* of the *Zohar* (in the name of Rabbi Shim'on), which describes the power of words of Torah in general—and their flight through the celestial realm. Here, however, the focus is on Rabbi Shim'on's words of Torah, which ascend into the heart of divinity. See *Zohar* 1:4b–5a.

Rabbi Ḥiyya's vision follows Rabbi El'azar's passing his hand over Rabbi Ḥiyya's mouth, as a consequence of which he is able to open his mouth and articulate his vision. This gesture recalls the initiation of Jeremiah the prophet, who despite being a youth is transformed into a prophet of Israel after his mouth is touched by the hand of God. See Jeremiah 1:9: *YHVH reached out His hand and touched my mouth and YHVH said to me, "I have put My words in your mouth."* See also Isaiah 6:7; Ezekiel 3:2; Daniel 10:10.

On the phrase "in a place where sparks fly in every direction," cf. BT *Bava Metsi'a* 85b, where Rabbi Ḥiyya's abode in the heavenly academy is described as "a place of sparks of light and torches of fire." Rabbi Ḥiyya's experience is so overwhelming that he assumes he is about to die.

"Ancient of Days" renders עתיק יומין (*attiq yomin*). See Daniel 7:9: *As I watched, thrones were placed, and the Ancient of Days sat—His garment like white snow, the hair of His head like clean fleece, His throne—flames of fire, its wheels blazing fire.* In the *Zohar*, this name designates the primordial *sefirah* of *Keter*. In BT *Pesaḥim* 119a, secrets of Torah are referred to as "things hidden by the Ancient of Days." See the rabbinic blessing in BT *Berakhot* 17a: "May your steps run to hear words of the Ancient of Days."

The number 370 is presumably an allusion to the three higher *sefirot* and seven lower

Rabbi Shim'on opened his mouth, saying, "Six levels descended with Jacob to Egypt, each one comprising ten thousand myriads. Corresponding to them six levels in Israel, and corresponding to them six levels to the throne above, and corresponding to them six levels to the throne below, as is written: *The throne had six steps* (1 Kings 10:19). This is the significance of the verse *I made you into* רבבה (*revavah*), *ten thousand, as the growth of the field*... (Ezekiel 16:7)—look, six! Corresponding to them it is written: *The Children of Israel were fruitful and swarmed and multiplied and grew mighty exceedingly, and the land was filled with them* (Exodus 1:7).[52]

sefirot. See *Zohar* 1:4b; 3:128b (*IR*), 133b (*IR*). The number 260 is derived by multiplying by ten the numerical value of the tetragrammaton, יהוה (*YHVH*), which equals twenty-six. "Delight of the righteous" apparently signifies *Malkhut* (*Shekhinah*). On Rabbi Shim'on's making things quake, see *Zohar* 3:21b, 296b (*IZ*), paraphrasing Isaiah 14:16; Liebes, "Mar'ish ha-Arets."

"None begins and none concludes" describes what happens whenever Rabbi Shim'on begins to study Torah: the celestial realm falls silent. Angels do not commence their song, while those who have already commenced do not conclude, i.e., they wait for Rabbi Shim'on to conclude. "Accusing mouth" renders פטרא (*pitra*), "opening," short for *pitra de-fuma*, modeled after the Hebrew idiom *pithon peh*, literally "opening of the mouth"—an opportunity for fault-finding, or an accusation by the powers above. Cf. *Zohar* 1:89a (*ST*); 2:262a (*Heikh*); 3:296b (*IZ*). When Rabbi Shim'on speaks, all accusing powers fall silent. The "it" that reaches the site of the delight of the righteous is the spark of Rabbi Shim'on's teaching.

On the special status of Rabbi Shim'on, see *Bereshit Rabbah* 35:2; JT *Berakhot* 9:2, 13d; BT *Sukkah* 45b; *Pesiqta de-Rav Kahana* 11:15; *Zohar* 1:218a, 223a; 2:38a, 97b; 3:59b–61b, 71b, 79b, 132b (*IR*), 159a, 206a, 241b, 296b (*IZ*); Liebes, *Studies in the Zohar*, 1–84; Hellner-Eshed, *A River Flows from Eden*, 31–61; Huss, *Ke-Zohar ha-Raqi'a*, 11–42.

52. **Six levels descended with Jacob to Egypt...** Namely, six companies of angels (perhaps corresponding to the six *sefirot* with Jacob in the middle). These six correspond to the six levels in Israel, namely the 600,000 Israelites who left Egypt.

If the "throne below" signifies *Shekhinah* (*Malkhut*), then the throne's six steps represent six palaces beneath *Shekhinah*, or six aspects of *Shekhinah*, or angelic camps surrounding her. If so, the "throne above" signifies *Tif'eret* (comprising the six central *sefirot*). Alternatively, the "throne above" may signify *Shekhinah*, in which case the "throne below" may be the actual Solomonic throne, or perhaps the celestial chambers beneath *Shekhinah*. See *Zohar* 2:85a, 206a 3:47b, 48a; *ZH* 41a. See also *Esther Rabbah* 1:12; *Bemidbar Rabbah* 12:17.

The simple sense of the verse from Ezekiel is *I caused you to grow like the growth of the field, and you increased and grew up and you came to excellent beauty, and your breasts became firm and your hair sprouted.* Its first word, however, is רבבה (*revavah*), which also means "ten thousand." The verse also alludes to the six levels: (1) *and you increased* (2) *and grew up* (3) *and you came* (4) *to excellent beauty* (5) *and your breasts became firm* (6) *and your hair sprouted.*

As in the verse from Ezekiel, six levels are alluded to in the verse from Exodus: (1) *were fruitful* (2) *and swarmed* (3) *and multiplied* (4) *and grew mighty* (5) *exceedingly* (6) *and the land was filled with them.* Cf. *Zohar* 2:16b (*MhN*), below, page 483. According to the midrash, this verse suggests that the Israelite women bore six children at a time. See *Me-*

"Come and see: Each one ascends to ten, becoming sixty—these are the sixty warriors surrounding *Shekhinah*; and these are the sixty myriads that emerged from exile with Israel, and that entered into exile with Jacob."[53]

Rabbi Ḥiyya said to him, "But we have seen seven, ascending to seventy!"[54]

Rabbi Shim'on replied, "[Seventy] is not relevant here. Now, should 'seven' occur to you, look at what is written: *Three cups shaped like almond blossoms in the one shaft* (Exodus 25:33)—the shaft is not counted, as is written: *opposite the front of the lampstand shall the seven lights give light* (Numbers 8:2)!"[55]

While they were sitting, Rabbi El'azar said to Rabbi Shim'on his father, "What did the blessed Holy One have in mind by bringing Israel down to Egypt in exile?"

He said to him, "Are you asking one question or two?"

He replied, "Two. Why exile? And why Egypt?"

He said to him, "They are two, though they turn out to be one."

He said to him, "Stand erect. Through you this word shall be established on high, in your name. Speak, my son. Speak."



He opened, saying, "*Sixty queens are they, and eighty concubines, and damsels without number* (Song of Songs 6:8). *Sixty queens are they*—supernal גבורים (*gibborim*), warriors, from the power of גבורה (*Gevurah*), clinging to the husks of the holy living being of Israel; *and eighty concubines*—empowered over the engravings beneath it, in luminosity, one one-hundredth. *And damsels without number*—as is said: *Is there any number to His troops?* (Job 25:3). Even so, it is

*khilta, Pisḥa,* 12; *Shemot Rabbah* 1:8; *Tanḥuma, Shemot* 5, *Pequdei* 9; *Aggadat Bereshit* (Buber), 5; *Sekhel Tov* on Exodus 1:7.

Rabbi Shim'on's homily is in Hebrew; the remainder of the narrative, in Aramaic.

53. **sixty warriors... sixty myriads...** On the 600,000 angels who descended into exile in Egypt and the sixty warriors surrounding *Shekhinah*, see *Zohar* 2:4b–5a (*MhN*), above, pages 450 and 452.

54. **seven, ascending to seventy** Rabbi Ḥiyya wonders why Rabbi Shim'on has been focusing on the numbers six and sixty. There are seven lower *sefirot*, and the children of Israel totaled seventy—corresponding to the seventy nations. See *Zohar* 2:5b (*MhN*), above, page 460, where Rabbi Shim'on explained the significance of the number seventy to Rabbi Ḥiyya (or Ḥizkiyah).

55. **the shaft is not counted...** Just as the Torah enumerates only six of the lampstand's cups even though there were seven lights, so when reckoning the *sefirot*. Like the central shaft of the lampstand, *Malkhut* (*Shekhinah*) receives and reflects the light of the six *sefirot* above her; thus she is not to be counted. See Rashi on Numbers 8:2. Cf. Tishby, *Wisdom of the Zohar*, 1:133, n. 19. Cf. BT *Menaḥot* 98b.

On not counting the seventh, see *Bemidbar Rabbah* 12:17: "The six wagons correspond to the six heavens. But are there not seven? Rabbi Avin said, 'Where the King resides is crown property.'"

The verse from Exodus continues: *calyx and blossom, and three cups shaped like almond blossoms in the other shaft, calyx and blossom, thus for the six shafts that go out from the lampstand.*

written: *One she is, my dove, my perfect one; one she is to her mother* (Song of Songs 6:9)—holy *Shekhinah*, emerging from the twelve radiancies of the radiance illuminating all; she is called Mother.[56]

"Correspondingly the blessed Holy One acted on earth. He scattered all the peoples in every direction and empowered princes over them, as is written: *for YHVH your God allotted them to all the peoples* (Deuteronomy 4:19). But as His own share, He took the Assembly of Israel, as is written: *For YHVH's share is His people, Jacob His allotted inheritance* (ibid. 32:9); and He called her *One she is, my dove, my perfect one; one she is to her mother* (Song of Songs 6:9)—*Shekhinah* of His glory, which He ensconced among them, singular and designated for her. *Daughters saw her and called her happy* (ibid.), as is said: *Many daughters have done valiantly, and you transcend them all* (Proverbs 31:29). *Queens and concubines praise her* (Song of Songs 6:9)—the princes appointed over the nations.[57]



56. ***Sixty queens are they, and eighty concubines...*** Rabbi El'azar begins his answer by noting the singularity of *Shekhinah* against the countless celestial powers, in particular the heavenly princes of the nations ("supernal warriors") who cling to *Shekhinah* ("the holy living being of Israel"). These heavenly princes derive their power from *Gevurah*, the attribute of harsh judgment, mediated by the husks of *Shekhinah*.

On the heavenly princes of the nations, see above, note 40.

Song of Songs 6:8–9 reads: *Sixty queens are they, and eighty concubines, and damsels without number. One she is, my dove, my perfect one; one she is to her mother, pure she is to the one who bore her. Daughters saw her and called her happy; queens and concubines praise her.* See *Zohar* 1:159a; 2:51a, 227b. Cf. *Tanḥuma, Qedoshim* 12.

The "twelve radiancies" from which *Shekhinah* emerges apparently refer to the twelve boundaries of *Tif'eret*, in turn deriving from *Binah*, the radiance illuminating all. *Binah* is the supernal mother and mother of *Shekhinah*. The twelve radiancies recall the twelve גבולי אלכסון (*gevulei alakhson*), "diagonal borders" (edges of a cube), mentioned in *Sefer Yetsirah* 5:1. See *Bahir* 64 (95); Ezra of Gerona, *Peirush le-Shir ha-Shirim*, 511–12; *Zohar* 1:76b (*ST*), 199a; 2:2a, 58b, 62b, 64b, 66b, 229b; 3:96b, 118b, 134b (*IR*), 148b, 209a; *ZḤ* 2a (*SO*), 55a, 62a (*ShS*), 63d (*ShS*).

For a different reading, see Tishby, *Wisdom of the Zohar*, 1:133 n. 20, and Meroz, "Ḥanikhato shel R. Ḥiyya," 141, 157, n. 100. See also *Or Yaqar, Derekh Emet, Matoq mi-Devash, Sullam* for various interpretations.

"Luminosity" renders חוורא (*ḥivra*), literally, "white, whiteness." The celestial forces beneath pale in comparison to *Shekhinah*.

57. **Correspondingly the blessed Holy One acted on earth...** Just as above there is *Shekhinah* and the other celestial forces, so below there is Israel and the other nations of the world. Whereas the nations are under the aegis of the heavenly princes, the Assembly of Israel is under the aegis of God and *Shekhinah*. Furthermore, just as *Binah* is mother to *Shekhinah*, *Shekhinah* is mother to the Assembly of Israel. See *Zohar* 1:96b, 195a; 2:126b.

The full verse in Deuteronomy 4 reads: *Lest you raise your eyes to the heavens and see the sun and the moon and the stars—all the array of the heavens—and you be led astray and bow down to them and worship them, for YHVH your God allotted them to all the peoples under the heavens.* Here, Rabbi El'azar associates the heavenly bodies with the heavenly princes. See *Zohar* 3:64a.

The hymn to the virtuous woman in Pro-

"Furthermore, mystery of the word: As we have learned: By ten utterances was the world created; but when you contemplate, they are three—by them was the world created: wisdom and understanding and knowledge. The world was created solely for the sake of Israel. When He wished to establish the world enduringly, He fashioned Abraham in the mystery of חכמה (*Ḥokhmah*), wisdom; Isaac in the mystery of תבונה (*tevunah*), understanding; and Jacob in the mystery of דעת (*da'at*), knowledge, as is written: *By knowledge rooms are filled* (Proverbs 24:4). At that moment the entire world was consummated; and when twelve tribes were [15a] born to Jacob, all was consummated, corresponding to the supernal pattern.[58]

"When the blessed Holy One saw the great joy of the lower world—consummated following the model above—He said, 'Perhaps (heaven forbid) they will mingle with the other peoples—leaving a blemish throughout all the worlds!' What did the blessed Holy One do? He made them all wander about—until they descended [to Egypt], setting their abode among a stiff-necked people who regarded them and their laws with contempt, not deigning to marry them or mingle with them, and who considered them as slaves. The men despised them and the women despised them, until all was consummated with holy seed. Meanwhile the guilt of the other peoples was complete, as is written: *for the guilt of the Amorites is not yet complete* (Genesis 15:16). When they emerged, they



verbs 31:1–31 is interpreted in the *Zohar* as applying to *Shekhinah*. See *Zohar* 1:49b, 247a.

58. **mystery of the word...** Though the world was created by ten *sefirot* (the ten utterances), these *sefirot* are divided into three groups (the right, the left, and the center), corresponding to the patriarchs. The twelve tribes complete the celestial structure (elsewhere they are described as the adornment of *Shekhinah*) and complete the construction of the world, which was for Israel's sake.

According to M *Avot* 5:1, "The world was created through ten utterances." Only nine explicit commands appear in Genesis 1, but the decade is made complete by counting the phrase *In the beginning*. See BT *Rosh ha-Shanah* 32a, *Megillah* 21b; *Pirqei de-Rabbi Eli'ezer* 3; *Zohar* 1:15a, 16b, 30a; *ZḤ* 2d (*MhN*). On the reduction to three, see *Pirqei de-Rabbi Eli'ezer* 3: "Some say by ten utterances was the world created—and in three are these comprised, as is said: *YHVH founded the earth by wisdom; He establishes the heavens by understanding. By His knowledge the depths were split* (Proverbs 3:19–20)." See *ZḤ* 3a, 3d, 4a (all *MhN*). See also BT *Ḥagigah* 12a.

Generally in the *Zohar*, Abraham corresponds to *Ḥesed*, Isaac to *Gevurah*, and Jacob to *Tif'eret*. *Ḥesed* and *Gevurah* are rooted in *Ḥokhmah* and *Binah* (or *Tevunah*), respectively. *Da'at* (Knowledge) is a hidden *sefirah* mediating between *Ḥokhmah* and *Binah*, and linking them. It appears on the central line joining *Keter* and *Tif'eret*.

On the verse in Proverbs, see *Zohar* 2:123a; 3:136a (*IR*), 289b (*IZ*), 291a (*IZ*), 296a (*IZ*). The full verse in Proverbs reads: *Through knowledge rooms are filled with all precious and pleasant wealth.* On the twelve tribes corresponding to the supernal pattern, see *Zohar* 1:154b–155a, 157b–158a, 183b, 231b, 240b–241b, 242a; 2:229b; 3:78a, 118b; *ZḤ* 66d (*MhN, Rut*).

emerged holy and righteous, as is written: *tribes of Yah, a testimony to Israel* (Psalms 122:4)."[59]

Rabbi Shim'on came and kissed him on the head. He said, "Resume your position, my son, for the hour is yours!"

Rabbi Shim'on sat down. Rabbi El'azar his son arose and expounded words of wisdom's mysteries. His face shone like the sun, and the words were blessed and soared throughout the firmament. For two days they sat, not eating or drinking, not knowing whether it was day or night. When they emerged, they realized that two days had passed without their having tasted anything at all. About this, Rabbi Shim'on applied the verse *He was there with YHVH forty days and forty nights; he ate no bread* [*and drank no water*] (Exodus 34:28): "If so for us after but a short while, for Moses—regarding whom Scripture attests *He was there with YHVH forty days*—how much more so?!"[60]

When Rabbi Ḥiyya came before Rabbi and told him what had happened, Rabbi was astonished. Rabbi [Shim'on son of] Gamli'el said, "My son, Rabbi Shim'on son of Yoḥai is a lion, and Rabbi El'azar his son is a lion. Rabbi Shim'on is unlike other lions—of him is written *A lion has roared, who can but fear?...* (Amos 3:8). If worlds on high tremble before him, how much more so we?! He is a man who has never decreed a fast for something he requested or



59. **mingle with the other peoples—leaving a blemish...** Rabbi El'azar now answers his own question: why exile and why Egypt. Following the advent of the twelve tribes, the celestial structure was mirrored on earth. The tribes, however, still required time to develop into a people, and they needed to wait until they could inherit the land. This could be accomplished only outside the land of Israel, in Egypt, where they were despised and thus in no danger of intermingling with the people. Had the tribes intermarried (which was more likely in Canaan because of the great esteem in which they were held), not only would the earthly tribes have been forfeit, but also worlds above would have been blemished. Once the people of Canaan had been destroyed (their guilt being complete), the Israelites could return—as there was no longer any danger of intermingling.

The verse from Psalms alludes to the tribes' purity upon emerging from Egypt and their (continued) correspondence to the celestial pattern. See *Zohar* 2:4a, 7a. Cf. *Zohar* 2:229b; 3:78a; *ZḤ* 26b (*MhN*).

On the Israelites' preserving their uniqueness and purity in Egypt, see *Mekhilta, Pisḥa* 5; *Vayiqra Rabbah* 32:5; *Pesiqta de-Rav Kahana* 11:6; *Shir ha-Shirim Rabbah* on 4:12; *Shemot Rabbah* 1:28.

60. **not knowing whether it was day or night...** This ecstatic description echoes the account of Rabbi Eli'ezer: "[When he expounded Torah,] his face shone like the light of the sun, and his radiance beamed forth like the radiance of Moses—and no one knew if it was day or night." See *Avot de-Rabbi Natan* B, 13; *Pirqei de-Rabbi Eli'ezer* 2, and David Luria, ad loc., n. 16; see also *Zohar* 1:94b; 2:105b. Cf. Ibn Ezra on Zechariah 14:7. See also Hellner-Eshed, *A River Flows from Eden*, 300–302.

On words soaring throughout the firmament, see above, page 464.

sought. Rather, he decrees and the blessed Holy One fulfills; the blessed Holy One decrees and he abolishes. As we have learned: What is the meaning of *who rules the awe of God* (2 Samuel 23:3)? The blessed Holy One rules over humanity, but who rules over the blessed Holy One? The righteous one, for He issues a decree—and the righteous one abolishes it!"[61]

We have learned: Rabbi Yehudah said, "There is nothing as beloved before the blessed Holy One as the prayer of the righteous. Yet even though it pleases Him, sometimes He fulfills their request—and sometimes He does not."[62]

Our Rabbis have taught: Once, the world was in need of rain. Rabbi Eli'ezer arrived and decreed forty fasts, yet the rain did not come. He prayed a prayer, yet the rain did not come. Rabbi Akiva arrived, arose, and prayed. He said "He who makes the wind blow"—and the wind blew. He said "He who makes the rain fall"—and the rain fell. Rabbi Eli'ezer's spirit was depressed. Rabbi Akiva took note of his face. Rabbi Akiva stood before the people and said, "I will compose for you a parable, to which the matter can be likened. Rabbi Eli'ezer is like the king's beloved, greatly cherished. Whenever he enters in the presence of



61. **Rabbi Shim'on son of Yoḥai is a lion...** See JT *Shabbat* 10:5, 12c; BT *Bava Metsi'a* 84b; *Pesiqta de-Rav Kahana* 11:24; *Mishnat Rabbi Eli'ezer* 10, p. 190; *Qohelet Rabbah* on 11:2; *Zohar* 1:223a; 3:60a, 79b, 196a; Scholem, "Parashah Ḥadashah," 435 (Addendum 1 in this volume); Yisraeli, *Parshanut ha-Sod ve-Sod ha-Parshanut,* 48, 92–93; Meroz, "Reqimato shel Mitos," 186, n. 78; Huss, *Ke-Zohar ha-Raqi'a,* 140–78; Asulin, "Ha-Pegam ve-Tiqquno," 213.

The full verse in Samuel reads: *The God of Israel has said, to me the Rock of Israel has spoken: He who rules humanity, righteous[ly], who rules [in] the awe of God.* According to a midrashic interpretation, the conclusion of the verse means *The righteous one rules the awe of God.* See BT *Mo'ed Qatan* 16b, where Rabbi Abbahu conveys this sense of the verse and quotes God as saying: "I rule over humanity. Who rules over Me? The righteous one. For I issue a decree, and he abolishes it."

See *Midrash Tanna'im,* Deuteronomy 33:1; *Tanḥuma, Ki Tavo* 1; *Devarim Rabbah* 10:3; *Shemot Rabbah* 15:20; *Zohar* 1:10a, 45b (*Heikh*); 2:262a (*Heikh*); 3:15a, 242a.

"Rabbi" signifies Rabbi Yehudah ha-Nasi (the patriarch), who lived in the second–third centuries and redacted the Mishnah. He was so highly esteemed that he was called "Rabbi": the Master. Rabbi Shim'on son of Gamliel was his father.

62. **nothing as beloved... as the prayer of the righteous...** See *Bereshit Rabbah* 45:4: "Why were the matriarchs barren? Rabbi Levi said in the name of Rabbi Shila of Kefar Tamrata, and Rabbi Ḥelbo said in the name of Rabbi Yoḥanan, 'Because the blessed Holy One yearns for their prayers and supplications, as is said: *My dove in the clefts of the rock* (Song of Songs 2:14). My dove in the clefts, why did I make you barren? In order that [you would ask]: *Let me see your face, let me hear your voice* (ibid.).'" See also *Shir ha-Shirim Rabbah* on 2:14; BT *Yevamot* 64a; *Ḥullin* 60b; *Shemot Rabbah* 21:5; *Tanḥuma, Toledot* 9; *Zohar* 1:167b.

On God sometimes heeding their request and other times not, see *Midrash Ḥaser ve-Yeter,* in *Otsar ha-Midrashim,* ed. Eisenstein, p. 201; *Midrash Ḥaserot va-Yeterot* (*Battei Midrashot,* 2:310).

the king, it pleases him; and he does not wish to grant him his request posthaste—so that he will not leave him, for it pleases him to converse with him. I, however, am like the king's servant who has sought his request before him, whom the king does not wish to enter the gates of the palace, all the more so to converse with him. The king said, 'Grant him his request posthaste, but let him not enter here!' So Rabbi Eli'ezer is the King's beloved, and I the servant. The King desires to converse with him all day, and that he will not leave Him. As for me, the King does not wish that I will enter the gates of the palace."[63]

Rabbi Eli'ezer's spirit was at ease. He said to him, "Akiva, come and I will tell you something I was shown in a dream—this verse: *As for you, do not pray for this people, do not raise a cry of prayer on their behalf, do not plead with Me [for I will not listen to you]* (Jeremiah 7:16). Come and see: He who is adorned in breastpiece and ephod entered within twelve mountains of balsam, and requested of the blessed Holy One to take pity on the world. Until this very moment, it was hanging in the balance."[64]



63. **Once, the world was in need of rain...** The *Zohar* here draws on numerous accounts of fasting in order to bring rain. See JT *Ta'anit* 3:4, 66c-d: "Rabbi Eli'ezer ordained a fast but the rain did not come down. Rabbi Akiva ordained a fast and the rain came down. He arose and said before them, 'I will compose for you a parable to which the matter can be likened: To a king who had two daughters, one impudent and other well mannered. When the impudent [daughter] sought to come before him, he would say, "Give her whatever she wants—and let her be gone!" When the well mannered [daughter] came before him, he would delay and delight to hear her supplication.'" See also BT *Ta'anit* 25b: "It is further related of Rabbi Eli'ezer that he descended before the Ark and recited the twenty-four benedictions [for fast days], but his prayer was not answered. Rabbi Akiva descended after him and exclaimed, 'Our Father, our King, we have no King but You; our Father, our King, for Your sake have mercy upon us'; and rain fell. The rabbis present suspected [Rabbi Eli'ezer, for why was the student answered and not the teacher?]. A heavenly voice rang forth, proclaiming, 'Not because this one is greater than the other, but because he is forbearing while the other is not.'" See also BT *Ta'anit* 24a; *Bava Metsi'a* 85b.

On the motif of the king's servant, see BT *Berakhot* 34b: "On another occasion it happened that Rabbi Ḥanina son of Dosa went to study Torah with Rabbi Yoḥanan son of Zakkai. The son of Rabbi Yoḥanan son of Zakkai fell ill. He said to him, 'Ḥanina my son, implore mercy that he may live.' He put his head between his knees and implored mercy for him and he lived. Rabbi Yoḥanan son of Zakkai said, 'If the son of Zakkai had stuck his head between his knees for the whole day, no notice would have been taken of him.' His wife said to him, 'Is Ḥanina greater than you are?' He replied to her, 'No; but he is like a servant before the king [who can come as he pleases and ask even trifling matters], and I am like a prince before a king [who can only come by invitation and can only ask matters of great import].'"

64. **Akiva, come and I will tell you something...** Rabbi Eli'ezer offers two explanations for why his prayer was not heeded. First, as implied by the verse from Jeremiah, it is not that he was unworthy, but rather that the people were not worthy of being

If so, why was Rabbi Eli'ezer's spirit depressed? On account of people who do not know about this.

Rabbi Eli'ezer said, "The souls of the righteous enter within eighteen supernal mountains of balsam; and every day, forty-nine fragrances ascend [15b] to the site called Eden. Correspondingly: Torah was given in forty-nine impure facets and forty-nine pure facets; forty-nine letters in the names of the tribes; forty-nine days to receive Torah; forty-nine supernal holy beings sit poised every day to receive permission from the shining stones engraved in the breastpiece.[65]

prayed for. Second, Eli'ezer's prayer did in fact initiate a process on high but this process was only brought to completion with Akiva's prayer.

"He who is adorned in breastpiece and ephod" refers to Michael (or Metatron) the celestial priest. See BT *Ḥagigah* 12b; *Menaḥot* 110a; *Bemidbar Rabbah* 12:12; *Tosafot Menaḥot* 110a, s.v. *u-mikhael sar ha-gadol*. See *Zohar* 2:229a–b. In rabbinic literature, Michael is the chief advocate of Israel (see Daniel 10:13, 12:1; *Shemot Rabbah* 18:5; *Pesiqta Rabbati* 44). In the Kabbalah, he is associated with *ḥesed*, "compassion" (see *Zohar* 2:139a, 254a (*Heikh*)); in *MhN*, see *ZḤ* 13a–b, 21a, 23d, 25d.

The ephod was apparently a multicolored apron worn by Aaron the high priest. Its two shoulder straps bore two precious stones, each engraved with the names of six of the twelve tribes. Fastened to the ephod was a breastpiece made of the same multicolored fabric, to which were affixed twelve other gemstones, each engraved with one of the names of the tribes.

According to rabbinic tradition, thirteen rivers of pure balsam await the righteous in the world that is coming. See BT *Ta'anit* 25a; *Bereshit Rabbah* 62:2. In the *Zohar*, the rivers of balsam are the fragrant flow of emanation from *Binah*, who is known as "the world that is coming, constantly coming, never ceasing" (3:290b [*IZ*]); see 1:4b, 7a; 2:127a, 146b; 3:181a. Here, the rivers are mountains, apparently signifying the sefirotic heights—perhaps *Binah*, the source of divine judgment that Michael seeks to sweeten.

On mountains of balsam, see *Zohar* 1:35a; 2:83a–b, 87b, 175b, 200b–201a; 3:67a, 91a, 144b (*IR*). Cf. the reference to *mountains of spices* in Song of Songs 8:14.

For various interpretations of this passage, see *Or Yaqar*, *Derekh Emet*, *Nitsotsei Orot*.

65. **enter within eighteen...** Whereas Michael enters within twelve mountains of balsam, the souls of the righteous enter within eighteen. That number may allude to *Yesod*, often referred to as חי עלמין (*ḥei almin*), "vitality of worlds"—given that חי, *ḥei*, has the numerical value of eighteen. The souls' actions cause fragrances to emanate to "Eden," presumably signifying *Ḥokhmah*.

The "forty-nine fragrances" apparently correspond to the forty-nine gates of *binah* ("understanding"). See the statement attributed to Rav and Shemu'el (BT *Rosh ha-Shanah* 21b, *Nedarim* 38a): "Fifty gates of *binah* (understanding) were created in the world, and all were given to Moses except for one." See Naḥmanides, *Peirush al ha-Torah*, intro, 3–4.

According to rabbinic tradition, every divine utterance of Torah includes "forty-nine facets [literally, faces] of 'pure' and forty-nine facets of 'impure'"—that is, forty-nine ways by which something can be proven impure (and thus forbidden) and forty-nine ways by which the same thing can be proven pure (and thus permitted). See *Massekhet Soferim* 16:5; JT *Sanhedrin* 4:1, 22a; BT *Eruvin* 13b; *Vayiqra Rabbah* 26:2; *Pesiqta de-Rav Kahana* 4:2, 4; *Shir ha-Shirim Rabbah* on 2:4; *Qohelet Rabbah* on 8:1; *Tanḥuma*, *Bemidbar* 10, *Ḥuqqat* 4; *Tanḥuma* (Buber), *Ḥuqqat* 7,

"He who is adorned in the breastpiece sits upon the precious holy throne of four pedestals. They gaze upon the breastpiece: by his word they enter, and by his word they emerge. They raise their eyes and gaze above—and behold a medallion sparkling in 620 directions, the holy supernal name engraved upon it. They tremble and quiver—those bound to the holy right side and to the left. With his hands he takes hold of the pillars of heaven and opens them, as is written: *The heavens shall be unfurled like a scroll* (Isaiah 34:4)."[66]

Rabbi Akiva said to him, "What is the meaning of the verse *I descended to the nut garden* (Song of Songs 6:11)?"[67]

18; *Bemidbar Rabbah* 19:2; *Pesiqta Rabbati* 14, 21; *Midrash Tehillim* 12:4; *Zohar* 2:123a, 139b, 183a; 3:97b (*Piq*).

The enumeration of the tribes in Exodus 1:2–4 contains forty-nine letters. The forty-nine days to receive Torah refers to the *Omer*, the period of time between *Pesaḥ* and *Shavu'ot*, the festival commemorating the giving of the Torah.

The "forty-nine supernal holy beings" apparently signify angels who, like the high priest, await instruction from the flashing stones of the breastpiece—in this case worn by Michael (or Metatron). When consulting the Urim and Thummim (an oracular device whose precise character is unknown), the high priest would pose a question; and certain letters of the names of the tribes, engraved in the twelve stones of the breastpiece, would protrude and shine in combination, indicating the answer. See *Zohar* 2:230a.

For various interpretations, see *Or Yaqar, Sullam, Matoq mi-Devash.*

66. **he takes hold of the pillars of heaven...** Michael (Metatron) administers and activates the operations of the heavens, guiding the angels of the right and left.

The simple sense of the verse in Isaiah is *The heavens shall be rolled up like a scroll,* but Rabbi Eli'ezer is reading the verb ונגולו (*va-nagolu*), "rolled up," as deriving from גלה (*gilah*), "to disclose, reveal, make manifest." See Rashi, ad loc.

The ציץ (*tsits*), *medallion* (or *plate, rosette*), was a gold plate worn on the forehead of the high priest over his turban, bearing the inscription קדש ליהוה (*qodesh la-YHVH*), *Holy to YHVH*. See Exodus 39:30: *They made the medallion of the holy diadem of pure gold, and wrote upon it an inscription of seal engravings: "Holy to YHVH."* On this inscription, see JT *Yoma* 4:1, 41c; *Megillah* 1:8, 71d; BT *Shabbat* 63b, *Sukkah* 5a, *Gittin* 20a–b; *Zohar* 2:217b.

620 is the numerical value of כתר (*Keter*), "Crown."

The "four pedestals" of the throne apparently signify four angelic forces. If Metatron is the high priest, they may correspond to Michael, Gabriel, Raphael, and Uriel. They may also refer to the four columns in which the names of the tribes were arranged on the breastpiece. Cf. *Zohar* 2:13a.

See *Or Yaqar, Matoq mi-Devash, Sullam* for various interpretations.

67. ***I descended to the nut garden*** In the writings of Ḥasidei Ashkenaz, in particular El'azar of Worms, the nut symbolizes the *merkavah*, the divine chariot. Descending to the nut garden therefore connotes speculating on the divine throne. See Dan, *Torat ha-Sod*, 208–10; Farber, "Tefisat ha-Merkavah be-Torat ha-Sod be-Me'ah ha-Shelosh-Esreh"; Abrams, *Sexual Symbolism and Merkavah Speculation.* On the nut motif in *MhN*, see *ZḤ* 9d, 17c–18a (*MhN*), *ZḤ* 83a (*MhN, Rut*). See also *Zohar* 1:19b, 44b (*Heikh*); 2:233b, 254b (*Heikh*); Moses de León, *Sefer ha-Mishqal*, 156–8; Liebes, *Peraqim*, s.v. אגוזא (*egoza*), 20–21, 27. See also Scholem, *Major Trends*, 239; Altmann, *Studies*, 172–79; Pope, *Song of Songs*, 574–79; Ta-Shma, *Ha-Nigleh she-ba-Nistar*, 130, n. 118. The nut also ap-

He replied, "Come and see: The garden emerges from Eden; it is *Shekhinah*. *Nut*—the holy chariot of those four riverheads separating from the garden, just like the nut that has four heads within. Now, concerning what is said: *I descended*—this is as we have learned: So-and-so has descended to the chariot."[68]

Rabbi Akiva said to him, "If so, it should have said *I descended to the nut*! What is the significance of *I descended to the nut garden*?"[69]

He replied, "For this constitutes the praise of the nut. Just as the nut is hidden and concealed from all sides, so the chariot emerging from the garden is concealed from all sides. Just as the four heads in the nut are joined from one perspective yet separate from another, so [the potencies of] the chariot are joined in unity, joy, harmony, and perfection—though each one separates in its own direction over that which it is appointed, as is written: *the one that winds through the whole land of Havilah* (Genesis 2:11); *the one that goes to the east of Asshur* (ibid., 14); and so with all of them."[70]

Rabbi Akiva said, "The filth in the husks of the nut—what does it intimate?"



He replied, "Even though Torah has not disclosed, through this it is revealed. Come and see: Some are bitter, some sweet; they offer an intimation. There are masters of harsh judgment and there are masters of leniency, though we find that all intimations disclosed in Torah allude to judgment. So it was with Jeremiah who was shown concerning judgment, as is written: *I see a branch of* שקד (*shaqed*) (Jeremiah 1:11). What is *shaqed*? שקדים (*Sheqedim*), almonds, literally. Similarly with the swallowing of Korah: *and had borne almonds* (Numbers 17:23).

pears as a cosmic symbol in the Orphic Mysteries. See Eisler, *Weltenmantel und Himmelszelt*, 2:521–25.

68. **The garden emerges from Eden...** *Shekhinah* emerges from Eden, presumably signifying *Ḥokhmah*.

The "nut" signifies the chariot beneath *Shekhinah*, comprised of the four archangels Michael, Gabriel, Raphael, and Uriel. Just as a nut has four chambers, so does the chariot.

See Genesis 2:10: *A river issues from Eden to water the garden, and from there it divides and becomes four stream-heads.* Cf. [Moses de León?], *Seder Gan Eden*, 138.

On "descending to the chariot" as the technical term for one who ascends to the divine throne in the Heikhalot corpus, see Scholem, *Major Trends*, 46–47; idem, *Jewish Gnosticism*, 20, n. 1; Halperin, *The Faces of the Chariot*, 226ff.; Schäfer, *The Hidden and Manifest God*, 2–3, n. 4; Dan, *The Ancient Jewish Mysticism*, 79–80. See, for example, Schäfer, *Synopse zur Hekhalot-Literatur*, §258.

69. **If so, it should have said...** If the nut represents the chariot (and not the garden), why doesn't the verse simply say *I descended to the nut*?

70. **this constitutes the praise of the nut...** The chariot's connection with *Shekhinah* (i.e., that an entity outside the godhead is connected with its source in divinity) constitutes its praise, hence: *I descended to the nut garden.*

The comparison between the nut and the chariot is elaborated further. Just as the four parts of the nut are both joined yet separate, so the potencies of the chariot (the four angels) sometimes function as a single entity and at other times separate to fulfill their specific tasks.

The word itself implies harsh judgment, as is written: וישקד (*Va-yishqod*), *Intent was, YHVH on bringing evil* (Daniel 9:14); and similarly: שקד (*shoqed*), *watchful, am I over My word* (Jeremiah 1:12); and so with all of them."[71]

Rabbi Akiva said to him, "This implies that everything the blessed Holy One made was in order that one learn from it great wisdom, as is written: *YHVH made everything for its* [or: *His*] *purpose* (Proverbs 16:4)."

Rabbi Eli'ezer said, "From here: As is written: [*God saw*] *all that He had made, and look, it was very good* (Genesis 1:31). What is implied by *very*? From which to learn supernal wisdom."[72]

Rabbi Yehudah said, "What is the meaning of the verse *God made one corresponding with the other* (Ecclesiastes 7:14)? Corresponding to the heavens, the blessed Holy One fashioned on earth—everything intimates what is above. For when Rabbi Abba saw a certain tree whose fruit transformed into a bird that flew away, he wept and said, 'If people were to fathom what these intimate, they would tear their clothes down to their navels on account of the wisdom that has been forgotten from them. How much more so regarding other [things] the blessed Holy One made on earth?!'"[73]



As Rabbi Yose said: "The trees from which wisdom is manifest—for example, the carob, the palm, and the pistachio and their like—were all constructed according to a single combination. All those producing fruit (aside from apples)

71. **through this it is revealed...** The mystery of the husk is not revealed vis-à-vis the nut, but through the almond, which alludes to harsh judgment. The almond's very name—*shaqed*—is associated with evil. Cf. *Zohar* 2:233b.

Jeremiah 1:11–12 reads: *The word of YHVH came to me: What do you see, Jeremiah? I replied: I see a branch of an almond tree. YHVH said to me: You have seen right for I am shaqed, watchful, to bring My word to pass* [namely to destroy, overturn, etc. ...].

In Numbers 17, Aaron's staff blossoms with almonds as a sign of the divine favor bestowed upon the tribe of Levi, and as a warning to the other Israelites not to challenge Aaron's authority—as Korah and his assembly had done. As punishment, Korah and his supporters had been swallowed alive by the earth (Numbers 16:31–34).

72. **From which to learn supernal wisdom** On the idea that divine wisdom can be learned from everything in the world, see next note.

73. **Corresponding to the heavens, the blessed Holy One fashioned on earth...** The theme of "as above, so below" is a cardinal principle of Kabbalah. See *Zohar* 1:38a (*Heikh*), 57b–58a, 129a, 145b, 156b, 158b, 205b; 2:5a (*MhN*), 20a (*MhN*), 48b, 82b, 144b, 251a (*Heikh*); 3:45b, 65b; *ZḤ* 15a, 19a (both *MhN*); Tishby, *Wisdom of the Zohar*, 1:273. On the similar Hermetic formulation, see *Secretum secretorum*, ed. Robert Steele, *Opera hactenus*, fasc. 5, 262.

On the fantastic bird-transforming fruit, see *Or Yaqar*, *Derekh Emet*, *Nitsotsei Orot*; cf. *Responsa*, Jacob ben Moses Moellin, 134; *Shulḥan Arukh*, *Yoreh De'ah* 84:15; Zimmels, "Ofot Ha-gdelim ba-Ilan"; Ta-Shma, *Ha-Nigleh she-ba-Nistar*, 125, n. 84.

are of a single mystery, notwithstanding diverging paths. All those that are large and do not produce fruit (aside from willows of the brook—which contain a mystery of their own) suckle from a single font. All those that are small (aside from hyssop) were born from a single mother.[74]

"All the herbs of the earth, over which powerful princes are assigned in heaven—every single one contains its own mystery corresponding to the pattern above. Hence it is written: *Your field you shall not sow with different kinds* (Leviticus 19:19)—for each one enters on its own and emerges on its own. This is the significance of *Do you know the law of heaven? Can you recognize its dominion on earth?* (Job 38:33); and similarly: [16a] *He calls them each by name* (Isaiah 40:26).[75]

"Now, if everything in the world contains its own mystery and the blessed Holy One did not wish to disclose them or confuse them and so He called them by their names, how much more so the sons of Jacob, who constitute the holy tribes, sustenance of the world, as is written: *These are the names of the sons of Israel* (Exodus 1:1)?!"[76]



74. **The trees from which wisdom is manifest...** All fruit-bearing trees (aside from apple trees) pertain to *Tif'eret*, the trunk of the sefirotic tree, though their particular paths of influence differ. Similarly, all large trees that do not bear fruit (aside from willows of the brook) pertain to the demonic other side, which is barren. Finally, all non-fruit-bearing small trees (aside from hyssop) pertain to *Malkhut*.

The apple's three colors—the white of the pulp, the red of the skin, and the green of the leaves—correspond to the colors of *Ḥesed*, *Gevurah*, and *Tif'eret*, respectively. See Ezra of Gerona, *Peirush le-Shir ha-Shirim*, 489; Azriel of Gerona, *Peirush ha-Aggadot*, 36; *Zohar* 1:85a, 142b; 2:122a; 3:74a, 133b (*IR*), 286b–287a.

Willows of the brook (in the form of branches) are one of the four species used in the festival of *Sukkot*. In Kabbalah they symbolize *Netsaḥ* and *Hod*. See *Bahir* 119–20 (177–78); *Zohar* 1:220b; 2:98a, 186b; 3:24b, 193b–194a, 220b; Moses de León, *Sefer ha-Rimmon*, 185.

On hyssop's purifying power and its signifying *Yesod*, see Exodus 12:22; Leviticus 14:4, 6; Numbers 19:6, 18; Psalms 51:9; *Zohar* 1:220a; 2:35b, 41a (*Piq*), 80b; 3:53b.

75. **every single one contains its own mystery...** Even small herbs have their own individual mystery: a celestial prince above. Their mystery is particular to them, each one called by name; hence the prohibition on mixing kinds, lest one confuse the celestial order.

See *Bereshit Rabbah* 10:6: "Rabbi Simon said, 'You cannot find a single blade of grass [below (per Oxford MS 147)] that does not have a constellation in the sky, striking it and telling it: Grow!'" See Maimonides, *Guide of the Perplexed* 2:10; *Zohar* 1:34a; 2:30b, 80b, 171b; 3:86a–b; *ZḤ* 8b (*SO*); Moses de León, *Sefer ha-Rimmon*, 181, 294; idem, *Sefer ha-Mishqal*, 135.

Isaiah 40:26, originally referring to the stars and constellations, reads: *Lift your eyes on high and see: Who created these? The one who brings forth their array by number and calls them each by name; because of His great might and vast power, not one is missing.*

76. **the holy tribes, sustenance of the world...** Even prosaic creations have their individual mystery—and consequently their

Rabbi Yose son of Rabbi Yehudah said, "Had it said אלה שמות (*Eleh shemot*), *These are the names*, this would be the implication. But now that it is written ואלה שמות (*Ve-eleh shemot*), *And these are the names*, it implies that it adds to the preceding. Just as the former were sons of Jacob, so here sons of Jacob."[77]

Rabbi Yehudah said, "Heaven forbid that it should occur to you that when the blessed Holy One said *I Myself will descend with you to Egypt* (Genesis 46:4), *Shekhinah* descended with him at that very moment!"

He said to him, "But it is written: *I Myself will descend with you to Egypt*—literally!"[78]

He replied, "The instant there was descent for His children, *Shekhinah* descended, as is written: *I Myself will descend with you to Egypt; I Myself* אעלך גם עלה (*a'alkha gam aloh*), *will surely bring you up as well* (ibid.)—whenever you attain ascent, I attain ascent, so to speak; whenever you undergo descent, *I Myself will descend with you*, so to speak. As soon as Joseph and all his brothers died and they underwent descent, *Shekhinah* arose and descended with them. Just as these descended, so those descended."[79]



individual names. This is all the more so for the tribes; hence the verse in Exodus proceeds to articulate their individual names.

On the tribes as sustenance of the world, see *Zohar* 1:183b; 2:15a (*MhN*), page 468.

77. **it adds to the preceding...** See *Bereshit Rabbah* 12:3: "Rabbi Abbahu said, 'Wherever it is said *these are*, it invalidates the preceding, whereas *and these are* adds to the preceding.'" See *Bereshit Rabbah* 30:3; *Shemot Rabbah* 1:2; 30:3; *Bemidbar Rabbah* 3:10; *Rut Rabbah* 8:1; *Tanḥuma, Shemot* 2, *Mishpatim* 3; *Zohar* 2:223a.

Apparently, Rabbi Yose's point is that the verse does not merely indicate the tribes' importance. In addition, just as the tribes enumerated first in Genesis 46 (before the onset of the Egyptian exile) were the pure stock of Jacob, so now in the opening chapter of Exodus (after the onset of the exile) they remained the pure stock of Jacob. On the Israelites' preserving their uniqueness and purity, see above, note 59.

The full significance of Rabbi Yose's exegetical insight is made apparent below, page 479.

78. **He said...** Apparently, Rabbi Yose is the speaker.

79. **whenever you attain ascent, I attain ascent...** *Shekhinah* and the people enjoy total interdependence. Consequently *Shekhinah* did not descend into exile until the people began suffering in the Egyptian bondage, many years after the divine promise to Jacob. When they underwent descent, so did *Shekhinah* and her host. This mutuality is neatly conveyed by the emphatic expression אעלך גם עלה (*a'alkha gam aloh*), *I will surely bring you up as well*, which more literally might be construed as *I will bring you up, yes, up again*—understood to convey that "your ascent equals My ascent."

On the exile of *Shekhinah*, see above, note 4.

See *Shemot Rabbah* 1:8: "*Joseph died and all his brothers with him, and all that generation* (Exodus 1:8)—to teach you that as long as one of those who went down to Egypt was still alive, the Egyptians did not subjugate Israel." Cf. *Shemot Rabbah* 1:4: "*Who were coming to Egypt* (Exodus 1:1). Did they come today? Had not already many days passed since they came to Egypt? Rather, as long as Joseph was alive, the burdens of Egypt were not upon them, but as soon as Joseph died, they imposed upon them burdens. Accord-

Rabbi Yehudah said, "What is written before this? *Joseph died, a hundred and ten years old, and he was embalmed and placed in a coffin in Egypt* (Genesis 50:26). At that time the children of Israel descended into exile, and *Shekhinah* and the ministering angels with them, as is written: *And these are the names of the sons of Israel* (Exodus 1:1)—for these were added to the preceding, descending into exile."[80]

He said to him, "If so, was Jacob dead or not?"

He replied, "Dead."

He said to him, "What then is the meaning of *who came to Egypt with Jacob* (ibid.)? If he was still alive it makes sense to say *with Jacob*; but if this was after he died, then *with Jacob* should be omitted!"

He replied, "Come and see: Scripture did not say *who descended to Egypt with Jacob*, for Jacob has not yet undergone descent, but rather *who came*—teaching that they came with Jacob, but then went on their way, until these descended into exile, whereupon those descended with them, as is written: *These are the names*."[81]

Rabbi Dostai said, "Every single day, they came and went, as is written: הבאים (*ha-ba'im*), *who were coming, to Egypt*. It is not written אשר באו (*asher ba'u*), *who came*! This is the meaning of הבאים (*ha-ba'im*), *who were coming, to Egypt*—at first, with Jacob; and afterward, when they underwent descent: *each man with his household* באו (*ba'u*), *they came* (ibid.)."[82]

ingly it is written: *who were coming*, as if they had entered Egypt that very day."

On the verse from Genesis, see above, note 8.

80. **for these were added to the preceding, descending into exile** Following the principle "*and these are* adds to the preceding" (see above, note 77), Rabbi Yehudah construes the opening line of the book of Exodus (*And these are the names of the sons of Israel who came to Egypt*) as alluding to descent by the angels (and perhaps by the tribes' souls, correlated with the twelve angelic camps of *Shekhinah*), in addition to the descent of the tribes.

On *sons of Israel* as angels, see *Zohar* 2:4b–5a (*MhN*).

81. **they came with Jacob, but then went on their way...** If the verse in question (*And these are the names of the sons of Israel...*) refers to the descent of the angels, why does it conclude with *who came to Egypt with Jacob*, which might seem to imply that Jacob was alive and that the angels descended with him? According to Rabbi Yehudah, the verse cannot mean that the angels descended into exile with Jacob and stayed there with him, as Jacob had not yet undergone descent—and therefore it would not be fitting for the angels to be in exile with him. Rather, these angels accompanied him on his journey to Egypt and then returned to their abode—returning to Egypt (to exile) only when the children of Israel underwent descent. Hence: *who came to Egypt with Jacob*—they came at first with Jacob, and now went into exile with his children.

82. **הבאים (*ha-ba'im*), *who were coming*...** In describing the descent of the sons of Israel to Egypt, Exodus 1:1 uses the verbal participle הבאים (*ha-ba'im*), *who were coming*—which suggests continuous or repeated action—instead of the perfect באו (*ba'u*), *came*.

Come and see: The sons of Jacob were all dead at that time; these and those descended![83]

Rabbi Yose and Rabbi El'azar said, "This section contains sublime matters! As we have learned: When the holy chariots and camps descended, the images of all the tribes engraved above came to dwell with them, as is written: *each man with his household they came*; and it is written: *Reuben, Simeon, Levi* (ibid., 2)."

Alternatively, *These are the names of the sons of Israel who came to Egypt with Jacob*.... This passage refers what Rabbi Yose son of Rabbi Yehudah said; and it all transpired![84]

Come and see: Whenever Rabbi El'azar son of Arakh reached this verse, he would weep. As it has been taught: Rabbi El'azar son of Arakh said, "When Israel went into exile, all the souls of the tribes assembled in the cave of Machpelah. They cried out, saying, 'Old man, old man! Oh, the pain of the children! Wearied by the toil of this world! All of your children are harshly enslaved. A foreign people are wreaking upon them the vengeance of the world!' At that moment, the spirit of the old man aroused. He sought permission and descended. The blessed Holy One summoned all His chariots and camps—their King at their head—and all of them descended with Jacob and his tribes. The tribes descended alive with their father; the tribes descended dead with their father, as is written: *These are the names of the sons of Israel who came to Egypt* [*with Jacob*]; and it is written: *Reuben, Simeon, Levi*.... Come and see: They were dead, yet descended; and it is written: *Joseph was in Egypt* (ibid., 5)."[85]



Rabbi Yitsḥak said, "Of this is said *As a father has compassion for his children* (Psalms 103:13)."[86]

The end of the verse, however, employs the perfect tense. According to Rabbi Dostai, this alludes to the activity of the angels, who at first came to Egypt and then left again—only later taking up residence with the Israelites in Egypt once the latter were enslaved.

83. **these and those descended** Namely, *Shekhinah* and her angelic hosts as well as the souls of the tribes, as explained below.

84. **what Rabbi Yose son of Rabbi Yehudah said...** See above, note 77, where Rabbi Yose advocates the principle "*and these are* adds to the preceding." Here the point is that the conjunction *and* points to a double descent: the original descent of the tribes with their father Jacob, and the addition to the preceding, namely the descent after death of Jacob's soul and of the souls of the tribes, to be with their children in exile.

85. **assembled in the cave of Machpelah...** They gathered where the patriarchs are buried, to implore mercy directly from Jacob, the "old man."

On the patriarchs as intercessors, see Schäfer, *Synopse zur Hekhalot-Literatur*, §63; BT *Sotah* 34b. On the dead's pleading for mercy on behalf of the living, cf. BT *Ta'anit* 16a; *Zohar* 1:225a; 2:141b; 3:70b–71b.

On the formula "Whenever Rabbi X reached this verse, he would weep," see BT *Ḥagigah* 4b.

86. ***As a father has compassion for his children...*** This verse is applied to Jacob in *Bereshit Rabbah* 78:8; *Pesiqta de-Rav Ka-*

Rabbi Yehudah son of Shalom was walking on the way, and Rabbi Abba was with him. They entered a certain threshing floor and lodged there. They ate. When they wished to lie down, they lay their heads on a mound of earth—where there was a grave. Before they fell asleep, a voice called out from the grave, saying, "A seed is earthbound. For twelve years [16b] I have not awakened, except now; I have just seen the countenance of my son!"[87]

Rabbi Yehudah said, "Who are you?"

He replied, "I am a Jew and I sit reproached; I do not want to enter on account of my son's sorrow, for a gentile kidnapped him when he was young, and he beats him every day. His sorrow prevents me from entering my site, and I have not awakened in this place until now."[88]

He said to him, "Are you aware of the sorrows of the living?"[89]

He replied, "[By the life of] the denizens of the graves! Were it not for our supplications on behalf of the living, they would not survive for even half a day! Now I have awakened here, for today I was told that presently my son would be coming here, though I know not whether dead or alive."[90]



*hana* 19:3; *Zohar* 1:222a. Here, apparently, it is applied to Joseph whose spirit remained in Egypt after his death, though Rabbi Yitsḥak may in fact be speaking of Jacob, who accompanied his children down to exile.

Although rendered here as *has compassion for*, the verb רחם (*rḥm*) may convey the sense of "undertake the protection of." See Sperling, "Biblical *rḥm* I and *rḥm* II," 156.

87. **a certain threshing floor...** חד אדרא (*Had iddera*). The printed editions read "a certain אתרא (*atra*), place," though all the manuscripts read *iddera*. Some of the manuscripts read הר אדרא (*har iddera*), "mountain of threshing." *Iddera*, literally "threshing floor," has a wide range of meanings in the *Zohar*, including also "assembly, room, chamber." See Liebes, *Peraqim*, 93–107.

According to Meroz, *iddera* here actually derives from the Greek *hedra*, implying a sacred site (or abode of gods, or place of omens) where contact with the dead is possible. According to her reading, the traveling sages do not merely happen upon the dead man's voice, but have deliberately sought out communion with the dead.

The dead man's statement is enigmatic. As will become clearer, the seed going into the ground refers to the man's son—who is in grave danger.

For a detailed analysis of this story, see Meroz, "The Story in the Zohar about the Grieving Dead."

88. **I am a Jew and I sit reproached...** On account of his son's sorrow on earth, this protective yet helpless father does not want to depart for the celestial academy. Alternatively, he cannot enter paradise, as his son is unable to study Torah or pray on his behalf. Cf. BT *Sanhedrin* 104a: "A son exonerates a father, a father does not exonerate a son!" Cf. *Zohar* 1:217b–218a. See also BT *Berakhot* 18b, where Levi is prevented from entering the celestial academy.

89. **Are you aware of the sorrows of the living?** On the dead as knowing the sorrows of the living, see BT *Berakhot* 18a–b; *Zohar* 1:81b (*ST*), 225a; 2:141b; 3:70b.

90. **[By the life of] the denizens of the graves...** שרי קברי (*Sharei* [or: *Sarei*] *qivrei*). Cf. *Derekh Emet* and *Haggahot Maharḥu*, who construe this phrase as "[By the life of] the prince of graves." See also *Nitsotsei Zohar*, who understands the dead man to be seeking "pardon from the graves" for the rabbi's insulting question.

Rabbi Yehudah said to him, "What is your business in that world?"

The grave rumbled and said, "Arise, be gone! For now they are beating my son."

They were stunned and fled from there about half a mile. They sat until the morning shone. They rose to walk on. They saw a person running and fleeing, his shoulders dripping blood. They grabbed him and he told them what had happened. They said to him, "What is your name?"

He replied, "Laḥma son of Levai."

They said, "Was not that dead man Levai son of Laḥma?! We are afraid to speak with him anymore!"[91]

They did not return.

Rabbi Abba said, "Concerning what they said: that the prayers of the dead protect the living—how do we know? As is written: *They went up through the Negeb, and he came as far as Hebron* (Numbers 13:22)."[92]

Rabbi Yehudah said, "Come and see: The blessed Holy One vowed two vows to 481
Jacob. One: that He would descend with him, dwelling with him in exile; and the other: that He would raise him from his grave to behold the joy of the holy company abiding with His children, as is written: *I Myself will descend with you to Egypt* (Genesis 46:4)—I Myself will descend with you into exile; *I Myself will surely raise you up as well* (ibid.)—as is said: *and raise you from your graves, O My people* (Ezekiel 37:12); and it is written: *There tribes ascend*... (Psalms 122:4)."[93]

91. **Levai son of Laḥma...** The dead man's name alludes to a passage in BT *Ta'anit* 16a that discusses the practice of going out to a cemetery on a public fast. According to Rabbi Ḥanina, the purpose of this practice is that "the dead should intercede for mercy on our behalf," whereas according to Rabbi Levi son of Ḥama (in manuscripts his name is Rabbi Levi son of Laḥma), this practice serves a metaphorical function only—to signify "we are as the dead before You." In the *Zohar*'s story, Levai son of Laḥma (corresponding to Rabbi Levi son of Laḥma) is made to concede that the prayers of the dead are in fact essential for the living.

92. ***he came as far as Hebron*** The verse in Numbers switches from a plural verb (*they went up*) to the singular (*he came*). According to the BT *Sotah* 34b, this is because Caleb separated from the other scouts and came alone to Hebron, the burial site of the patriarchs. There he prostrated himself on their graves, begging them to pray that he be delivered from the plan of the other scouts, who conspired to issue a negative report on the land. See also Rashi on Numbers 13:22; *Zohar* 2:31a; 3:158b.

93. **to behold the joy of the holy company...** Namely, the angelic host that descended to Egypt with Jacob and was now departing with the Children of Israel. See *Bereshit Rabbah* 92:2: "Rabbi Pinḥas said in the name of Rabbi Hosha'yah, 'The blessed Holy One took the feet of our father Jacob and stood them by the sea, saying to him, "Behold the miracles I am performing for your children." As is written: *When Israel came forth out of Egypt* (Psalms 114:1)—Israel the elder.'" See also Rashi, BT *Ta'anit* 5b, s.v. *af hu ba-ḥayyim*. Cf. *Bereshit Rabbah* 79:1. See also *Zohar* 1:222a, 226a.

The verse from Psalms describes the

*A new king arose over Egypt*... (Exodus 1:8).

Rabbi Shim'on said, "On that day, authority was granted to the prince of Egypt over all the nations. For it has been taught: Until Joseph died, dominion was not granted to the prince of Egypt over Israel. As soon as Joseph died—*A new king arose over Egypt. Arose*—like one who was low and rose."[94]

Rabbi Yitsḥak opened, "*While the king was on his couch, my nard yielded its fragrance* (Song of Songs 1:12). *While the king*—as is written: *Thus says YHVH, King of Israel* (Isaiah 44:6); and similarly: *He became king in Jeshurun* (Deuteronomy 33:5). *Was on his couch*—between the wings of the cherubim; *my nard yielded its fragrance*—for they caused [Him] to depart from among them.[95]

"Alternatively, *While the king was on his couch*—while the blessed Holy One was giving the Torah to Israel, as is written: *He was there with YHVH forty days and forty nights; he ate no bread*... (Exodus 34:28), while He was writing the Torah for Israel, they abandoned their fine fragrance and said: *These are your gods, O Israel!* (ibid. 32:8).[96]



"Alternatively, *While the king was on his couch*—while the blessed Holy One was descending upon Mount Sinai to give the Torah to Israel, *my nard yielded its fragrance*, as is written: *We will do and we will heed* (Exodus 24:7)."[97]

twelve tribes of Israel making pilgrimage to Jerusalem. *There tribes ascend, the tribes of Yah,* עדות (*edut*), *a statute* [literally: *a testimony*], *for* [or: *to*] *Israel, to praise the name of YHVH*. Here, it describes how like Jacob, the tribes too were raised from their graves to witness the departure from exile.

On the verse from Genesis, see above, note 8.

94. **authority was granted to the prince of Egypt...** On the prince of Egypt, see *Shemot Rabbah* 21:5; *Zohar* 2:6a–b, 7a, 10a, 50a; in *MhN*, see 2:17a, 17b, 18a, 19a, 19b. Cf. *Zohar* 1:113a (*MhN*). On the celestial princes (rulers) of the nations, see above, note 40. On the connection with Joseph's death, see *Shemot Rabbah* 1:4, 8 (above, note 79); *Zohar* 2:16a (*MhN*). Cf. *Zohar* 1:180a.

95. ***While the king was on his couch...*** Precisely how this homily connects with the preceding is not clear. According to Cordovero in *Or Yaqar*, it illustrates that sin causes the *Shekhinah* to depart, and that in Egypt it was the Israelites' sin that caused the *new king* (the hostile celestial prince) to arise. Had they not sinned, *Shekhinah* would have remained between the wings of the cherubim and protected them. (On the Israelites sinning in Egypt, see Ezekiel 20:5–8; *Shemot Rabbah* 6:5; Naḥmanides on Exodus 12:42.) See *Shir ha-Shirim Rabbah* on Song of Songs 1:12. Here the nard yielding fragrance signifies the foul stench of the people's sin.

96. **they abandoned their fine fragrance...** At Sinai they lost their *fragrance* by worshiping the Golden Calf. The clause *my nard* נתן (*natan*), *yielded, its fragrance* now means *my nard natan, gave up* [or: *lost*] *its fragrance*. See BT *Gittin* 36b; *Shir ha-Shirim Rabbah* on 1:12; *Seder Eliyyahu Zuta* 4; *Zohar* 3:61b.

97. ***We will do and we will heed*** At Mount Sinai, Israel demonstrated true faith by declaring נעשה ונשמע (*na'aseh ve-nishma*), *we will do and we will heed* [or: *listen*]—thereby committing themselves to fulfill and enact God's word even before hearing the details. This pure act of devotion was

Rabbi Tanḥum said, "Every single nation has a prince above. When the blessed Holy One grants dominion to one, He lowers another; and when He grants dominion to that prince, his dominion is solely on account of Israel, as is written: *Her adversaries have become the chief* (Lamentations 1:5)."[98]

Rabbi Yitsḥak said, "The people of Israel correspond to all the nations of the world. Just as the other nations are seventy, so Israel are seventy, corresponding to all the nations of the world, as is written: *All the souls of the house of Jacob coming to Egypt were seventy* (Genesis 46:27). Whoever rules over Israel is as though he rules over the whole world."[99]

Rabbi Abba said, "From here: *The Children of Israel were fruitful and swarmed and multiplied and grew mighty very exceedingly, and the land was filled with them* (Exodus 1:7)—look, seven; each level by ten, totaling seventy. What is written afterward? *A new king arose over Egypt.*"[100]

Rav Huna said, "Why were Israel subjugated among all the nations? That the world would be preserved through them, for they correspond to the whole world. It is written: *On that day* YHVH *will be one and His name one* (Zechariah 14:9). Just as He is one, so Israel is one, as is written: *one nation on earth* (2 Samuel 7:23). Just as His name is one and divides into seventy, so Israel is one and divides into seventy."[101]



fragrant to God. See *Shir ha-Shirim Rabbah* on 1:12; *Shir ha-Shirim Zuta* on 1:12; *Seder Eliyyahu Zuta* 4; *Zohar* 2:226b–227a; 3:61b.

On the significance of this declaration, see *Mekhilta, Neziqin* 13; *Mekhilta de-Rashbi*, Exodus 24:7; *Sifrei*, Deuteronomy 320; *Tosefta Bava Qamma* 7:9; *Vayiqra Rabbah* 2:4; BT *Shabbat* 88a; *Shir ha-Shirim Rabbah* on 1:5, 12; 2:1–3; 3:9; 4:9; 5:2; 6:5; *Tanḥuma, Vayishlaḥ* 2, *Vayiqra* 1; *Tanḥuma* (Buber), *Vayishlaḥ* 2.

98. **Every single nation has a prince above...** On the idea that nations (and princes) are empowered only on account of Israel, see *Mekhilta, Beshallaḥ* 1; *Mekhilta de-Rashbi*, Exodus 14:5; BT *Ḥagigah* 13b; *Zohar* 2:6a.

As the verse from Lamentations implies, it is because they are *her adversaries* that they have become *the chief.* See BT *Gittin* 56b; *Sanhedrin* 104b.

On the ascent and descent of the celestial princes, cf. midrashic literature, where they are described as ascending and descending Jacob's ladder. See *Vayiqra Rabbah* 29:2; *Pesiqta de-Rav Kahana* 23:2; *Tanḥuma, Vayetse* 2; *Pirqei de-Rabbi Eli'ezer* 35. See also *Zohar* 2:49a.

99. **Israel correspond to all the nations of the world...** See *Zohar* 2:5b (*MhN*; above, page 460), 6a.

100. **look, seven; each level by ten...** Rabbi Abba proves that Israel are seventy from Exodus 1:7: *The Children of Israel* (1) *were fruitful* (2) *and swarmed* (3) *and multiplied* (4) *and grew mighty* (5) *very* (6) *exceedingly* (7) *and the land was filled with them.* Cf. *Zohar* 2:14b (*MhN*), page 465. See also below at note 136.

As Israel total seventy and correspond to the whole world, the king ruling over them is designated *a new king*, as though he rules over the whole world.

101. **That the world would be preserved through them...** Cf. Judah Halevi, *Kuzari* 2:36: "Israel amidst the nations is like the heart amidst the organs of the body."

Cf. *Or Yaqar* and *Matoq mi-Devash*, who understand דישתאר בהון עלמא (*de-yishte'ar*

Rabbi Yehudah opened, "*At three things the earth trembles* [ . . . ] *at a slave who becomes a king* [ . . . ] *and a slave-girl supplanting her mistress* (Proverbs 30:21–23). *At a slave who becomes a king*—as it has been taught: [17a] There is no people as lowly and contemptible before the blessed Holy One as the Egyptians, and yet He granted them dominion on account of Israel. *And a slave-girl supplanting her mistress*—Hagar who bore Ishmael, who inflicted much harm upon Israel, dominating them and afflicting them with all manner of afflictions, and decreeing upon them numerous forced apostasies. Until this very day, they rule over them and do not allow them to practice their religion. There is no exile as harsh for Israel as the exile of Ishmael!"[102]



*be-hon alma*), rendered here as "that the world would be preserved through them," as "that they would remain in the world," i.e., Israel is subjugated by and among all the nations so that all of them will be culpable—and therefore eliminated at the end of days, leaving Israel alone. See *Zohar* 1:177b.

On seventy names and seventy souls of Jacob, see Naḥmanides and *Ba'al ha-Turim* on Numbers 11:16; *Zohar* 2:123a; 3:34b. On the seventy names of God, see *Targum*, Song of Songs 2:17; *Bemidbar Rabbah* 14:12; Naḥmanides, *Kitvei Ramban*, 1:135; *Zohar* 1:5b; 2:51b, 160b; 3:223b (*RM*), 263a; Idel, "Olam ha-Mal'akhim bi-Dmut Adam," 12–13. For various lists of these names, see *Alfa Beita de Rabbi Akiva* (*Battei Midrashot*, 2:350–51); *Shir ha-Shirim Zuta* 1:1; *Aggadat Shir ha-Shirim*, ed. Schechter, on 1:1, pp. 9–10; *Midrash ha-Gadol*, Genesis 46:8; *Ba'al ha-Turim* on Numbers 11:16.

The verse from Samuel reads: *Who is like Your people Israel,* גוי אחד (*goi eḥad*), *a unique nation* [literally: *one nation*], *on earth?*

Israel "divides into seventy" in that they comprise seventy, and perhaps also in that they are scattered across the seventy regions of the earth.

102. **no exile as harsh for Israel as the exile of Ishmael** The slave-girl is Hagar (mother of Ishmael, signifying Egypt and Islam) and the mistress is Sarah (signifying Israel). Hagar has supplanted Sarah (see Genesis 16) as Moslems dominate the Jews. The slave also signifies Egypt, derived from Ham, whose son Canaan was cursed to be a slave (see Genesis 9:25–26); Ham now rules over the king, Shem, the ancestor of Israel.

The historical background to this passage would seem to be a period when Jews were harshly treated under Islam. By the *Zohar*'s day, however, the Jews of Spain were living under Christian rule. See Meroz, "The Middle Eastern Origins," 48–49, where she dates this passage to the 11th century, connecting it with the rule of the Fatimid dynasty based in Egypt, specifically to the rule of Caliph al Ḥakim (996–1021 C.E.), who initiated religious persecutions in the year 1004 C.E. Cf. *Pirqei de-Rabbi Eli'ezer* 32. See also Tishby, *Wisdom of the Zohar*, 1:70–71. See also BT *Shabbat* 11a and Rabbenu Ḥananel, s.v. *amar rav*; Baḥya ben Asher on Deuteronomy 30:7.

See Maimonides, *The Epistle to Yemen*, "You know, my brethren, that on account of our sins, God has cast us into the midst of this people, the nation of Ishmael, who persecute us severely, and who devise ways to harm us and debase us. . . . No nation has ever done more harm to Israel. None has matched it in debasing and humiliating us." Translation from Mark Cohen, *Under Crescent and Cross*, xvi. See Halkin and Hartman, *Epistles of Maimonides*, 126.

The full verses from Proverbs read: *At three things the earth trembles, and four it cannot bear: at a slave who becomes a king, and a scoundrel sated with food; at a loathsome woman getting married, and a slave-girl supplanting her mistress* (Proverbs 30:21–23).

Rabbi Yehoshu'a was going up to Jerusalem, traveling on the road. He saw an Arab traveling with his son. They came upon a Jew. He said to his son, "This Jew is abhorrent, despised by his Lord. Seize him and spit upon his beard seven times, for he hails from the seed subjugated by seven nations."[103]

His son went and grabbed his beard. Rabbi Yehoshu'a said, "O exalted ones, O exalted ones! I decree that the high descend below!"[104]

Before he had finished [speaking] they were swallowed in their place.

Rabbi Yitsḥak opened, "*Before the day expires and the shadows flee, I will hasten to the mountain of myrrh and to the hill of frankincense* (Song of Songs 4:6). *Before the day expires*—this verse was spoken of Israel's exile, for they will be subjugated in exile until the day of the nations' dominion ends."[105]

As we have learned: Rabbi Yitsḥak said, "The dominion of all the nations together over Israel is one thousand years, and there is no nation that will not subjugate them. This is the equivalent of one day for Him, as is written: *There will be one day that will be known to YHVH* . . . (Zechariah 14:7).[106]

"Alternatively, *Before the day expires*—before that day of the nations expires, *and the shadows flee*—the princes ruling over them, *I will hasten to* הר המור (*har ha-mor*), *the mountain of myrrh* (Song of Songs 4:6). The blessed Holy One said, 'I will hasten to shake out the nations from Jerusalem,' which is הר המור (*har ha-mor*), as is said: בהר מוריה (*be-har moriyyah*), *on Mount Moriah, which is in Jerusalem* (2 Chronicles 3:1). *And to the hill of frankincense* (Song of Songs 4:6)—the



See *Zohar* 2:6a–b. Cf. *Zohar* 1:122a–b, 131b, 204a; 2:60b–61a, 96a–b, 117b–118b (*RM*); 3:69a, 266a, 279b (*RM*); *TZ*, intro.

On the earth's trembling at the slave who becomes king, see below, page 491. On Egypt's disgrace, see *Zohar* 1:117a (*MhN*).

103. **Seize him and spit upon his beard . . .** Cf. *Zohar* 2:188b, where a similar attitude and behavior is attributed to Edom, representing Christendom.

According to O2 and O17, the Arab instructs his son as follows: "Demean him and spit upon his beard seven times, for [though] he hails from exalted seed, I know that they are subjugated by the seven nations."

104. **O exalted ones . . .** Rabbi Yehoshu'a is addressing angels on high, perhaps invoking Abraham, Isaac, and Jacob—the exalted seed from which he hails. His decree is directed specifically against the haughty Arab and his son, but more generally it calls for a reversal of the historical order.

105. ***Before the day expires and the shadows flee . . .*** See *Shir ha-Shirim Rabbah* on 2:17.

106. **The dominion of all the nations together over Israel . . .** On Israel's exile lasting a thousand years, see *Eikhah Rabbah* 1:40; 2:3; *Pirqei de-Rabbi Eli'ezer* 28; *Zohar* 1:116b; 2:227b; 3:270a; *ZḤ* 16d, 23c, 28c (all *MhN*). Cf. *Bereshit Rabbah* 63:13; *Tanḥuma* (Buber), *Toledot* 4.

See Psalms 90:4: *For a thousand years in Your eyes are like yesterday that has passed.* See *Bereshit Rabbah* 8:2; BT *Sanhedrin* 97a.

The full verse in Zechariah reads: *There will be one day—known to YHVH—neither day nor night, and in the evening there will be light.*

Sanctuary in Zion, of which is written *Beautiful in loftiness, joy of all the earth, Mount Zion* (Psalms 48:3)."[107]

Rabbi Yehudah said, "As is said: *to seize the corners of the land, that the wicked be shaken out of it* (Job 38:13)—like someone taking hold of a shawl to shake out the filth."[108]

Rabbi Yose said, "Before that day of the nations ends, the blessed Holy One is destined to be revealed in Jerusalem below to purify her of the nations' filthy idols. As Rabbi Ḥiyya said: 'The dominion of the nations over Israel is but one day precisely, as is said: *He has made me desolate, faint all the day* (Lamentations 1:13)—one day precisely, no more!'"[109]

Rabbi Yose said, "If they are to be subjugated for longer, it is not by decree of the King, but rather because they do not wish to return to Him; and it is written: *It shall be, when all these things come upon you at the end of days, you shall return to YHVH your God...* (Deuteronomy 30:1, 4:30), and it is written: *If your banished lie at the ends of heaven, from there* [*YHVH your God*] *will gather you in...* (ibid. 30:4)."[110]



107. ***the shadows...*** The celestial rulers of the nations. See Naḥmanides on Numbers 14:9; Ezra of Gerona, *Peirush le-Shir ha-Shirim*, in *Kitvei Ramban* 2:492, 495; Brody, *Commentary to the Song of Songs*, 64, 74.

On *mor* and *moriyyah*, see *Bereshit Rabbah* 55:7; *Pesiqta Rabbati* 40; *Zohar* 1:220a; 2:39b. See also *Tanḥuma*, *Vayera* 3.

2 Chronicles 3:1 reads: *Then Solomon began to build the House of YHVH in Jerusalem on Mount Moriah....*

108. **taking hold of a shawl to shake out the filth** The quotation from Job is from God's speech out of the whirlwind (38:12–13): *Have you ever commanded morning, assigned dawn its place, to seize the corners of the earth* [or: *land*], *so that the wicked would be shaken out of it?* The interpretation offered here derives from *Pirqei de-Rabbi Eli'ezer* 34. See *Zohar* 1:181b; 2:10a; 3:72b; Moses de León, *Sefer ha-Mishqal*, 89.

109. **filthy idols...** This renders גלולי (*gillulei*), "idols," traditionally connected with גלל (*galal*), "dung; dung ball." See *Avot de-Rabbi Natan* B, 38; the medieval dictionaries of Jonah ibn Janaḥ and David Kimḥi.

On the verse from Lamentations, see *Zohar* 1:117a. See above, note 106.

110. **If they are to be subjugated for longer...** The decree of subjugation lasts one thousand years. After this time, all depends of *teshuvah*. See *ZḤ* 23c, 28c (both *MhN*), 59a. The verses from Deuteronomy emphasize the need for Israel's repentance: *It shall be, when all these things come upon you, the blessing and the curse that I have set before you, that your heart shall turn back among all the nations to which YHVH your God will make you to stray. You shall turn back to YHVH your God and heed his voice as all that I charge you today, you and your children, with all your heart and with all your being. YHVH your God shall turn back your former state and have mercy upon you; and He shall turn back and gather you in from all the peoples to which YHVH your God has scattered you. If your banished lie at the ends of heaven, from there YHVH your God will gather you in, and from there He will take you* (Deuteronomy 30:1–4). Deuteronomy 4:30 (conflated here with 30:1) reads: *When you are in distress and all these things befall you at the end of days, you shall return to YHVH your God and heed His voice.*

*He said to his people, "Look, the people of the sons of Israel"* (Exodus 1:9).[111]

Rabbi Shim'on said, "Come and see: From every angle, this was the ruling angel empowered over Egypt. So it is; for throughout most of the *parashah* it says only *king of Egypt*—anonymous, namely the prince appointed over the Egyptians; [whereas here:] *Pharaoh, king of Egypt*—pharaoh, literally."[112]

Rabbi Shim'on said, "Accordingly, it is written *He said*; that is to say, he put this matter in their heart, as is said: *Because YHVH said to him, 'Curse David'* (2 Samuel 16:10)—the thought alone; and similarly: *Haman said in his heart* (Esther 6:6); and similarly: *he said in his heart, 'To a hundred year old [will a child be born?']* (Genesis 17:17). So too here, he put the thought in their heart—for he said: *more numerous and mightier than we* (Exodus 1:9). What is meant by ממנו (*mi-mennu*), *than we*? Namely, ממני (*mi-menni*), than me; and they thought to themselves that their power is greater and mightier ממנו (*mi-mennu*), than him—than their prince."[113]

Rabbi Yitsḥak said, "The whole world draws power from their princes, but Israel draws their power from the blessed Holy One! They are called 'The people of *YHVH*,' not the people of the princes."[114]



Rabbi Yehudah said, "Here they are called 'his people,' as is written: *He said to his people* (Exodus 1:9), but there it is written *I have indeed seen the plight of My people in Egypt* (Exodus 3:7)—*My people*, literally! Israel are called 'The peo-

111. ***Look, the people of the sons of Israel*** The king's speech continues (verses 9–10): *is more numerous and vast than we. Come, let us deal shrewdly with them—lest they multiply and then, should war occur, they join our enemies and fight against us and go up from the land.*"

112. **this was the ruling angel empowered over Egypt...** According to Rabbi Shim'on, this verse is spoken by Egypt's heavenly prince.

On "king of Egypt" as signifying the celestial prince, and "Pharaoh, king of Egypt" as signifying the actual flesh-and-blood king, see *Zohar* 2:19b (*MhN*; below, page 506), 50a.

113. ***more numerous and mightier than we...*** The celestial prince of Egypt instilled fear in the hearts of the Egyptians to rouse them into action. The fear implanted is that the Israelites' celestial power is mightier than the Egyptians' celestial power.

Cf. BT *Sotah* 35a: "*But the men who had gone with him said, 'We will not be able [to go up against the people, for it is stronger than we]'* (Numbers 13:31). Rav Ḥanina son of Papa said, 'The explorers uttered a great thing at that moment: *For it is stronger than we.* Do not read ממנו (*mi-mennu*), *than we*, but ממנו (*mi-mennu*), *than him.* Even the master of the house, so to speak, cannot remove his tools from there!'" See also BT *Menaḥot* 53b; *Arakhin* 15a.

The verses from Samuel, Esther, and Genesis prove that the verb אמר (*amar*), literally "said," can denote thinking, intention, or placing a thought in someone's mind. See, e.g., Genesis 20:11; 21:16; 26:9, 28; 31:31; 1 Samuel 20:4; 1 Kings 8:12; *Zohar* 1:234b; 2:25b; 3:17b, 88b, 161a.

114. **but Israel draws their power from the blessed Holy One...** On this idea, see *Zohar* 2:14b (*MhN*) and note 57; see also *Zohar* 1:195a; 2:95b, 126b; 3:64a. Cf. Naḥmanides on Leviticus 18:25.

ple of *YHVH*,' while the other peoples are called the people of their prince, as is written: *For all the peoples will walk each in the name of its god, and we will walk in the name of YHVH our God forever and ever* (Micah 4:5)."[115]

Rabbi Abba said, "That verse should have said *Look, the people of Israel*, or *the sons of Israel*. What is the significance of *the people of the sons* (Exodus 1:9)? It means *the people of the sons of Israel*, precisely—of that Israel above; for they thought that they were the people of 'the sons of Israel,' and not the people of *YHVH*. It is written: *they were stung by the sons of Israel* (ibid. 1:12) and not by [17b] the people of the sons of Israel, but rather *by the sons of Israel*, precisely!"[116]

Rabbi Yoḥanan was standing before Rabbi Yitsḥak. He said, "What prompted Balak to say *Look, the people that came out of Egypt* (Numbers 22:11), rather than *the people of the sons of Israel*?"

Rabbi Yitsḥak replied, "Balak was a grand sorcerer, and so is the way of sorcerers to take hold of that which is beyond doubt; accordingly they never mention the name of a person's father, but only his mother's name—a matter beyond doubt. For so is the way of demons, who scrutinize the matter told to them: if false, they disseminate deceptions; if true, everything they say about what is imminent comes true. All the more so if [the sorcerer requests] to perform some deed!"[117]

Rabbi Aḥa said, "Balak spoke contemptuously: *Look, the people that came out of Egypt*—as if to say, we do not know from where they hail!"

115. ***peoples will walk each in the name of its god*...** See *Zohar* 1:117b.

116. **they thought that they were the people of 'the sons of Israel'...** The peculiar phrase *the people of the sons of Israel* points to the Egyptians' mistaken view of the Israelites, whom they believed to be under the aegis of the celestial sons of Israel, i.e., angelic potencies, rather than of God Himself.

That *sons of Israel* designates celestial potencies is made clear by verse 12, which in its simple sense means *and they came to loathe the sons of Israel*, but the *Zohar* reads it midrashically as ויקוצו (*va-yaqutsu*), *they were stung, by the sons of Israel*, i.e., by the angels who descended to Egypt with the descendants of Jacob. See below, *Zohar* 2:18a (*MhN*) and note 139.

On *sons of Israel* as celestial entities, see *Zohar* 2:4b–5a, 16a (both *MhN*).

117. **Balak was a grand sorcerer...** Balak sought to curse Israel; and thus in turning to demons, he was careful to speak only the truth—lest they not heed his request. Given that a person's father's identity can be uncertain, and because the people coming from Egypt may have included other nations as well, Balak omitted mention of the sons of Israel.

See BT *Shabbat* 66b: "Abbaye said, 'Mother told me, "All incantations that are repeated several times must contain the name of the patient's mother."'" See also BT *Nazir* 49a; *Gittin* 69a–b; *Zohar* 1:84a; *Yalqut ha-Makhiri*, Psalms 118:22, par. 28; Trachtenberg, *Jewish Magic and Superstition*, 115–16, 139–40.

On demons possessing limited foreknowledge, see Naḥmanides on Leviticus 17:7; *Zohar* 1:83a, 130a, 200a; 2:251b (*Heikh*); 3:25a. On Balak as master sorcerer, see *Bemidbar Rabbah* 20:18; *Zohar* 3:112b.

Rabbi Yoḥanan said, "Why are the people of the princes protected, while the people of the blessed Holy One are not?"[118]

Rabbi Yitsḥak replied, "The poor man is not like the wealthy man. The poor man must guard what is his; the wealthy man does not guard what is his! All the more so since Israel hail from a King who loves truth and justice, and the first judgment He renders is on the members of His household, for He wishes them to be protected from sin more than anyone else, as is written: *You alone have I known of all the families of the earth—that is why I call you to account for all your iniquities* (Amos 3:2)."[119]

Rabbi Yose set out on a journey, and Rabbi Aḥa son of Ya'akov was traveling with him. While they were walking, Rabbi Yose fell silent and contemplated worldly matters, whereas Rabbi Aḥa contemplated matters of Torah. While they were walking, Rabbi Yose saw a snake chasing after him. He said to Rabbi Aḥa, "Do you see that snake chasing me?"[120]

Rabbi Aḥa replied, "I don't see it."[121]

Rabbi Yose ran away—and the snake after him. Rabbi Yose fell down and blood dripped and flowed from his nose. He heard them saying, '*You alone have I known of all the families of the earth—that is why I call you to account for all your iniquities.*'[122]



118. **Why are the people of the princes protected...** Why do the nations of the world enjoy protection and serenity, whereas the nation of God appears defenseless and suffers?

119. **The poor man is not like the wealthy man...** Israel's suffering is in fact testament to their exalted status. Whereas the poor man must protect what is his—as thieves do not fear him—so the celestial guardians of the nations must protect their own from other nations seeking to dominate them and their territory. The wealthy man, however, has no such fear—be it because of his abundant wealth or because others are in awe of him—and thus need not protect his own. Thus Israel lie seemingly unprotected as their survival and fidelity to God are assured.

Additionally, as the nation of the God of truth and justice, Israel must act accordingly—and accordingly they are chastised. Their suffering is thus a consequence of their intimacy with God—who chastises them first, so that in the long term they will be protected.

Cf. *Zohar* 3:221b. See below, *Zohar* 2:21b (*MhN*).

On the verse from Amos, see BT *Avodah Zarah* 4a.

120. **Rabbi Yose fell silent and contemplated worldly matters...** On Rabbi Yose contemplating worldly matters, see *Zohar* 2:217b. See also *Zohar* 2:36b; Meroz, "Path of Silence," 323.

Cf. M *Avot* 3:7: "Rabbi Shim'on said, 'One who is walking on the road studying, and interrupts his study and says, "How beautiful is this tree! How beautiful is this field!"—Scripture considers him liable to the death penalty.'"

121. **I don't see it** Rabbi Aḥa does not see the snake because it is no ordinary snake, but a sign of the spiritual peril in which Rabbi Yose finds himself.

122. **He heard them saying...** Rabbi Yose hears a heavenly voice. Precisely because he was sage, an intimate of God, he

Rabbi Yose said, "If so for but a single moment, how much more so for one who forsakes her?!"

He opened, saying, "*For* YHVH *your God has blessed you in all the works of your hands. He has watched over your wanderings [in this great wilderness these forty years]* (Deuteronomy 2:7); *who led you [through the great and terrible wilderness]—fiery serpents and scorpions...* (ibid. 8:15). What is the relevance of fiery serpents here? Well, to exact punishment from Israel whenever they separate from the Tree of Life, as is written: *for it is your life and the length of your days* (ibid. 30:20)."[123]

Rabbi Ḥiyya said, "Come and see: It is written: *He who spares the rod hates his son, but he who loves him disciplines him early* (Proverbs 13:24); and it is written: *I have loved you, said* YHVH (Malachi 1:2); and it is written: *but Esau I have hated* (ibid., 3). What is meant by *I have hated*? As is written: *He who spares the rod hates his son*—that is to say, I have hated them, and that is why I have spared the rod from them. All the more so—and all the more so disciples of the wise, for the blessed Holy One does not wish them to separate from the Tree of Life for even an instant!"[124]



*He said to his people* (Exodus 1:9). He proffered them advice to do them harm.[125]

Rabbi Tanḥum said, "The Egyptians knew from their horoscope that their end was to be struck on account of Israel. That is why their prince preempted to do them harm."[126]

was chastised immediately for merely contemplating worldly matters.

123. ***fiery serpents...*** Just as Rabbi Yose was met by a snake for desisting from Torah, so did the Israelites face serpents during their desert sojourn.

See Proverbs 3:18: *She is a tree of life to those who hold fast to her.* In its simple sense, *she* refers to wisdom; but in rabbinic literature, it refers specifically to Torah. See *Zohar* 3:176a: "Everyone who engages in Torah grasps the Tree of Life"; 3:114a: "We must not separate ourselves from the Tree of Life."

124. ***He who spares the rod hates his son...*** God's harsh correction and discipline is in fact a sign of His love for Israel. Conversely, Esau (signifying medieval Christendom), who is hated, is spared the rod. Israel's suffering is thus a sign of God's loving discipline, whereas Esau's rise to power is evidence that God has forsaken him and offers him no correction.

See *Shemot Rabbah* 1:1; *Tanḥuma, Shemot* 1; *Zohar* 3:114b.

125. ***He said to his people...*** The celestial prince of Egypt. This and the following paragraph appear to have been dislocated from their original location. See above, at note 111.

126. **Egyptians knew from their horoscope...** Cf. *Shemot Rabbah* 1:18; *Tanḥuma, Vayaqhel*, 4. See below, note 140.

Rabbi Yitsḥak came upon a certain mountain and saw a person sleeping beneath a tree. He sat there. While he was sitting he noticed the earth trembling; the tree broke and fell. He saw clefts and cavities in the ground, and the ground rising and falling. The man awoke and shouted toward Rabbi Yitsḥak, saying, "O Jew, O Jew, weep and moan! For at this moment an empowered prince, a supernal ruling power, is being elevated in the firmament, and he is destined to do you much harm. That earthquake was on your account! For whenever the earth quakes, it is because a prince who will do you harm is rising."[127]

Rabbi Yitsḥak was astonished and said, "Surely it is written: *At three things the earth trembles* [ . . . ] *at a slave who becomes a king* (Proverbs 30:21–22)—a prince who was appointed beneath another power, now ruling, granted dominion, all the more so when he rules over Israel!"[128]

Rabbi Ḥama son of Gurya said, "Whenever the blessed Holy One places Israel under the dominion of the nations, He sits, roars, and weeps, as is written: *My soul will weep in secret* (Jeremiah 13:17)."[129]



127. **For whenever the earth quakes . . .** See *Midrash Tehillim* 104:25 in the name of Rabbi Shemu'el son of Naḥmani: "Wherever the term *earthquake* appears in Scripture, it connotes the cessation of a kingship." See also JT *Berakhot* 9:2, 13c.

Cf. BT *Berakhot* 59a: "Rav Kattina was walking on the way; and when he came to the door of the house of a certain necromancer, there was a rumbling of the earth. He said, 'Does the necromancer know what this rumbling is?' He called after him, 'Kattina, Kattina, why should I not know? When the blessed Holy One remembers His children—who are plunged in suffering among the nations of the world—He sheds two tears into the Great Sea, and His voice resounds from one end of the world to the other.' Rav Kattina said, 'The necromancer is a liar and his words are false. If it were as he says, there should be one rumbling after another!' [corresponding with the two tears]. —He did not really mean this, however. There really was one rumbling after another, and the reason why he did not admit it was so that people should not go astray after him." See *Zohar* 2:19a–b (*MhN*), below, page 505.

128. ***At three things the earth trembles . . .*** On the verses from Proverbs, see above, note 102.

129. ***My soul will weep in secret*** See BT *Ḥagigah* 5b: "*If you will not listen, My soul will weep in secret because of the pride* (Jeremiah 13:17)—Rav Shemu'el son of Inya said in the name of Rav, 'The blessed Holy One has a place, and its name is *Secret*.' What is *because of the pride*? Rav Shemu'el son of Yitsḥak said, 'For the pride of Israel that has been taken from them and given to the nations of the world.' Rabbi Shemu'el son of Naḥmani said, 'For the pride of the Kingdom of Heaven.' But is there weeping before [i.e., on the part of] the blessed Holy One? Look, Rabbi Papa has said, 'There is no sadness before the blessed Holy One, as is said: *Splendor and majesty are before Him, power and joy in His place* (1 Chronicles 16:27)'! —There is no contradiction: this refers to the inner chambers; that refers to the outer chambers. —Is there no weeping in the outer chambers? For it is written: *YHVH God of Hosts summoned on that day to weeping and mourning, to tonsuring and girding with sackcloth* (Isaiah 22:12). —The destruction of the Temple is different, for even the angels of peace wept, as is said:

Rabbi Yose said, "*In secret*—precisely, literally!"[130]

Rabbi Yehudah went in to Rabbi El'azar. He found him seated, his hand in his mouth, forlorn. He said to him, "In what [18a] is the master engaged?"

He replied, "As is written: *In the light of the king's face is life* (Proverbs 16:15). If the patron is sad—all the more so if he is roaring and weeping—what do his attendants do? As is written: *Behold, the Erelim cried outside* (Isaiah 33:7). What is meant by *outside*? Their Master within, they without; their Master in the inner chambers, they in the outer chambers. What are the inner chambers? Rabbi Yitsḥak said, 'They are of the ten crowns of the King.'"[131]

"*Angels of peace weep bitterly* (ibid.). Are there angels that are not of peace?!"[132]

He replied, "Yes. Come and see: There are masters of harsh judgment, and there are masters of judgment that is not harsh; there are masters of judgment and compassion, and there are masters of compassion without any judgment at all—these ones are called *angels of peace*. Of those below is written *I clothe the heavens in blackness, and make sackcloth their covering* (ibid. 50:3); and it is written: *All the host of heaven shall be dissolved* (ibid. 34:4)."[133]



*Behold, the Erelim cried outside, angels of peace weep bitterly* (Isaiah 33:7)." Cf. *Eikhah Rabbah, Petiḥta* 24.

See also BT *Berakhot* 3a: "Rabbi Yitsḥak son of Shemu'el said in the name of Rav, 'There are three watches in the night, and in every single one the blessed Holy One sits and roars like a lion, saying, "Woe to the children on account of whose sins I destroyed My house, burned down My Sanctuary, and exiled them among the nations!"'"

130. ***In secret*—precisely, literally!** The interiority of divinity or the divine realm, as explained below.

131. **their Master in the inner chambers, they in the outer chambers...** The dominion of the nations over Israel is reflected in the celestial realm by the weeping of the angels and of God Himself. God's weeping takes place in the inner chambers, correlated with "the ten crowns of the King," apparently signifying the ten *sefirot*. See *Zohar* 2:19b (*MhN*), below, page 505; cf. Meroz, "The Middle Eastern Origins," 42.

On the inner and outer chambers, see BT *Ḥagigah* 5b (above, note 129), 12b–13a; *Zohar* 1:248b; 2:257b–258a; 3:15b; Moses de León, *Shushan Edut*, 337.

*Erelim* renders אראלם (*er'ellam*), a word whose form and meaning are dubious. In the verse in Isaiah, it has sometimes been construed as "their valiant ones, their brave men," referring to the Judeans withstanding Sennacherib's onslaught. See Isaiah 29:1–2; *ABD*, s.v. Ariel. In rabbinic tradition, the word is transformed into אראלים (*er'ellim*), meaning "angels" or a group of angels, while in medieval angelology they constitute one of ten such classes.

See *Bereshit Rabbah* 56:5; *Eikhah Rabbah* 1:23; BT *Ḥagigah* 5b, *Ketubbot* 104a; *Midrash Aggadah*, Exodus 33:22; Maimonides, *Mishneh Torah, Hilkhot Yesodei ha-Torah* 2:7; *Zohar* 1:182a, 210a; 2:2b, 43b, 196a, 250b; *ZḤ* 6a (*MhN*); Ginzberg, *Legends*, 5:23, n. 64; 5:417, n. 117.

On the verse from Proverbs and God's sadness, see Scholem, "Parashah Ḥadashah," 439 (Addendum 1 in this volume.)

132. **Are there angels that are not of peace?!** Rabbi Yehudah is asking Rabbi El'azar about the continuation of the verse from Isaiah, which reads in full: *Behold, the Erelim cried outside, angels of peace weep bitterly.*

133. **There are masters of harsh judgment...** There are indeed angels not of peace, namely angels of judgment. According to Rabbi El'azar, there are four classes of

"If so, how come when all those ruling powers appointed over the other nations see their Master sad, they afflict His children with crushing labor?"

Rabbi El'azar replied, "They are merely executing what they were commanded, performing the will of their Master."[134]

Rabbi Dostai said, "When the children of the blessed Holy One are surrendered unto the ruling powers of the nations, twelve courts assemble and immerse within the Great Abyss. The patron roars continuous roars, and two tears descend into the hollow of the Great Sea, as is written: *Your judgments, the great abyss* (Psalms 36:7). Those above cascade below; those below are split open, and two hundred and forty degrees descend, as is written: *A lion has roared, who can but fear?* (Amos 3:8)."[135]

It has been taught: In the hour when the blessed Holy One surrendered Israel to the prince of Egypt, He decreed upon them seven decrees through which the Egyptians would subjugate them, as is written: *They embittered their lives with harsh labor, with mortar and bricks and every work in the field, all their work that they made them work with crushing labor* (Exodus 1:14). Corresponding to them: *The Children of Israel were fruitful and swarmed and multiplied and grew mighty very exceedingly, and the land was filled with them* (ibid., 7).[136]



angels: (1) angels of pure judgment; (2) angels of soft or lenient judgment; (3) angels of judgment and compassion; (4) angels of pure compassion. Cf. *Or Yaqar*, who omits the second class. The angels of pure compassion are the angels of peace. The verses in Isaiah apply to the lowest class—the angels of pure judgment—clothed in blackness to execute judgment, and who will one day be annihilated.

Some commentators align these angels with the *sefirot*: angels of pure judgment correspond with *Gevurah*; angels of soft judgment, with *Malkhut*; angels of judgment and compassion, with *Tif'eret*; and angels of pure compassion, with either *Ḥesed* or the upper reaches of the sefirotic realm. See *Or Yaqar*; *Haggahot Maharḥu*.

134. **merely executing what they were commanded...** Cf. *Zohar* 2:163a.

135. **two tears descend into the hollow of the Great Sea...** See BT *Berakhot* 59a: "When the blessed Holy One remembers His children—who are plunged in suffering among the nations of the world—He sheds two tears into the Great Sea, and His voice resounds from one end of the world to the other." See *Zohar* 1:4b; 2:9a, 195b; 3:132a (*IR*), 172a–b; [Moses de León?], *Seder Gan Eden*, 133. See *Zohar* 2:19a–b (*MhN*), below, page 505, where the two tears signify two attributes of justice (or judgment) sweetening the sea of wisdom.

Following *Or Yaqar*, twelve courts—signifying twelve angelic potencies—ascend to *Binah*; the blessed Holy One (*Tif'eret*) roars, shedding two tears into *Ḥokhmah*, sweetening the judgment—and causing divine abundance to descend below. See also *Matoq mi-Devash*.

Psalms 36:7 reads: *Your righteousness is like the mighty mountains; Your judgments, the great abyss; human and beast You deliver, O YHVH*. Cf. *Zohar* 3:91a on this verse.

Two hundred and forty degrees may derive from מר (*mar*), *bitterly* (whose numerical value is 240); see Isaiah 33:7: *Behold, the Erelim cried outside, angels of peace weep bitterly*. Cf. *Or Yaqar*.

136. **seven decrees...** (1) *They embittered their lives* (2) *with harsh labor*, (3) *with mortar* (4) *and bricks* (5) *and every work in the field,*

הבה (*Havah*), *Come, let us deal shrewdly with them* (Exodus 1:10).

Rabbi Yose said, "הבה (*Havah*), *Come*, is merely an expression of preparation to execute judgment, as is said: הבה (*Havah*), *Come, let us go down* (Genesis 11:7); הבה תמים (*havah tamim*), *show Thammim* (1 Samuel 14:41)."[137]

Rabbi Yoḥanan said, "All instances of הבה (*havah*), *come*, are an expression of consent and preparation, as in: הבה (*Havah*), *Come, let us build a city* (Genesis 11:4); הבו (*havu*), *give, your word and counsel* (Judges 20:7); הבו (*havu*), *give, to YHVH young rams* (Psalms 29:1)."[138]

Rabbi Yitsḥak said, "*Come, let us deal shrewdly with them*—and be in consent to execute judgment upon them *lest they multiply* (Exodus 1:10); but the holy spirit says, '*So will they multiply, and so will they spread*' (ibid., 12). ויקוצו (*Va-yaqutsu*), *They were stung, by the sons of Israel* (ibid.)—for they were מתעקצי (*mit'aqqetsei*), stung, by the ministering angels, just like קוצי (*qotsei*), thorns, by which a person is stung."[139]



(6) *all their work,* (7) *that they made them work with crushing labor.*

On the good decrees found in Exodus 1:7, see above, note 100.

The good decrees represent the sweetening (amelioration) of the harsh judgment.

137. **an expression of preparation...** See Rashi on Genesis 11:3, 38:16, Exodus 1:10; *Zohar* 1:75a; Tishby, *Wisdom of the Zohar*, 1:78.

Genesis 11:7 describes God's judgment of the builders of the Tower of Babel: *Come, let us go down and baffle their language there so that they will not understand each other's language.*

The Masoretic text of 1 Samuel 14:41 appears garbled: *Saul said to YHVH, the God of Israel, "Show Thammim* [innocence?]." *Jonathan and Saul were indicated by lot, and the troops were cleared.* See Rashi and Radak, ad loc. The Septuagint reads: *Saul said, "YHVH, God of Israel, why have you not responded to Your servant today? If there is guilt in me or in Jonathan my son, O YHVH, God of Israel, show Urim; and if it is in Your people Israel, show Thummim." Jonathan and Saul were indicated by lot, and the troops were cleared.* The verse is describing Saul's attempt to use oracular objects to determine guilt or innocence. Thus, *havah tamim, show Thammim,* also pertains to preparation to execute judgment.

138. **expression of consent and preparation...** The verses cited imply respectively the communal consent and preparation to: build the tower and city of Babel; decide on the punishment for the butchering of the concubine of Gibeah; and prepare a sacrifice.

139. **ויקוצו (*Va-yaqutsu*), *They were stung, by the sons of Israel*...** Exodus 1:12 reads: *As they abused them,* כן ירבה וכן יפרוץ (*ken yirbe ve-khen yifrots*), *so did they multiply and so did they spread,* ויקוצו (*va-yaqutsu*), *and they came to loathe, the sons of Israel.* The *Zohar* here adopts and adapts the interpretation found in BT *Sotah* 11a and *Shemot Rabbah* 1:11: "The verse should have said כן רבו וכן פרצו (*ken rabbu ve-khen paretsu*), so did they multiply and so did they spread! [The biblical Hebrew does in fact convey the past tense, but midrashically can be read as conveying the future tense.] Resh Lakish said, 'The holy spirit announced this to them: So will they multiply and so will they spread!' ויקוצו (*Va-yaqutsu*), *And they came to loathe, the sons of Israel*—teaching that they were like קוצים (*qotsim*), thorns, in their eyes." On *sons of Israel* as angels, see above, note 5, and *Zohar* 2:4b (*MhN*), pages 450–51.

Cf. *Zohar* 3:8a, 42b, 114b.

Rabbi Yudai said in the name of Rabbi Yitsḥak, "What were the Egyptians thinking in preventing Israel from multiplying, and what the prince appointed over them who placed this in their heart? Well, they knew that one day, a son would be born and rise for Israel, destined to execute judgment upon their gods."[140]

As Rabbi Yoḥanan said: "The moment Moses said *and upon all the gods of Egypt I will render judgment* (Exodus 12:12), Dumah, the prince of Egypt, ran away four hundred parasangs. The blessed Holy One said to him, 'A decree has been issued before Me,' as is written: *YHVH will punish the host of the heights on high*... (Isaiah 24:21). At that moment, authority was wrested from him, and Dumah was appointed Prince of Hell, to judge there the souls of the wicked. Rabbi Yehudah says, 'He was appointed over the dead.'"[141]



140. **What were the Egyptians thinking...** On their preventing Israel from reproducing, see *Shemot Rabbah* 1:12: "Pharaoh decreed upon them four decrees. At first, he decreed and commanded the taskmasters to insist upon them making their quota [of bricks]. [Then he commanded] that they should not sleep in their homes, thinking to prevent them from multiplying. He reasoned: By not sleeping in their homes, they will not be able to give birth to children." See also *Qohelet Rabbah* on Ecclesiastes 9:14; *Tanḥuma, Pequdei* 9. See also the Passover Haggadah: "*And saw our persecution* (Deuteronomy 26:7)—this refers to [forced] sexual abstinence."

On the Egyptians knowing about their future judgment, cf. *Shemot Rabbah* 1:18: "*Pharaoh charged his whole people,* [*saying, 'Every boy that is born you shall fling into the Nile, and every girl you shall let live'*] (Exodus 1:22). Rabbi Yose son of Rabbi Ḥanina said, 'He decreed against his own people too. Why did he do this? Because the astrologers told him, "The mother of Israel's redeemer is already pregnant with him, but we do not know whether he is an Israelite or an Egyptian." At that time, Pharaoh assembled all the Egyptians and said to them, "Lend me your children for nine months that I may fling them in the Nile," as is written: *Every boy that is born you shall fling into the Nile.* It is not written *every boy who is an Israelite,* but *every boy*—whether he be Jew or Egyptian. But they would not agree, saying, "An Egyptian boy would not redeem them; he must be a Hebrew." *You shall fling into the Nile.* Why did they decree that they should fling them into the Nile? Because the astrologers foresaw that Israel's savior would be smitten by means of water, and they thought that he would be drowned in the water; but it was not so—it was only on account of the well of water that the decree of death was pronounced upon him, as is said: *Inasmuch as you did not trust Me*... (Numbers 20:12).'" See also *Tanḥuma, Vayaqhel* 4; cf. BT *Sotah* 11a.

141. **authority was wrested from him...** That is, Dumah lost authority over the Israelites and his position as prince of Egypt, although he was promptly reassigned to another task.

דומה (*Dumah*), literally "silence," is a biblical name for the netherworld. See Psalms 94:17: *Were not YHVH a help to me, my soul would have nearly dwelled in dumah.* In rabbinic literature, Dumah is the angel in charge of the souls of the dead (BT *Berakhot* 18b, *Shabbat* 152b, *Ḥagigah* 5a, *Sanhedrin* 94a; *Tanḥuma, Ki Tissa* 33). In the *Zohar,* he retains this role and also oversees Hell. See *Zo-*

Rabbi Ḥanina said, "It is written: *and YHVH executed judgment upon their gods* (Numbers 33:4). Can there be judgment upon a god of silver and gold, wood and stone?!"

Well, Rabbi Yose said, "Those of silver and gold melted on their own, while those of wood decayed."[142]

Rabbi El'azar said, "The god of Egypt was a lamb. The blessed Holy One commanded judgment upon it, to burn it in fire, as is said: *The images of their gods you shall burn in fire* (Deuteronomy 7:25), so that its stench should spread; moreover, *its head with its legs and with its entrails* (Exodus 12:9); moreover, that its bones be cast into the street. This was the most painful of all for the Egyptians, as is written: *judgment.*"[143]

Rabbi Yehudah said, "*Upon their gods*, literally! This means their prince. To fulfill *YHVH will punish the host of the heights on high, and the kings of the earth upon the earth* (Isaiah 24:21). The wise among them knew all of this; all the more so their prince. That is why it is written: *Come, let us deal shrewdly with them* (Exodus 1:10)."



Rabbi Yoḥanan said, "Idolatry was rife in Egypt. The Nile was a god [18b] of theirs, among the totality of their gods. Upon all of them *YHVH executed judgment* (Numbers 33:4)."[144]

*har* 1:8a–b; 62b, 94a, 102a (*MhN*), 121a (*Tos*), 124a (*MhN*), 130b, 218b, 237b; 2:150b.

According to Genesis 25:14, Dumah is also the name of Ishmael's sixth son—and thus a grandson of Hagar the Egyptian.

According to BT *Pesaḥim* 94a and *Ta'anit* 10a, the domain of Egypt is 400 parasangs by 400 parasangs. The Persian parasang is about 3.5 miles.

Cf. *Shemot Rabbah* 21:5, where the prince of Egypt is called *Mitsrayim* (Egypt).

On the heavenly princes being deposed, defeated, or punished by God, see *Mekhilta, Shirta* 2; *Shir ha-Shirim Rabbah* on 8:14; *Devarim Rabbah* 1:22; *Tanḥuma, Bo* 4, *Beshallaḥ* 13, *Mishpatim* 18; *Tanḥuma* (Buber), *Bo* 6, 19; *Shemot Rabbah* 9:9; 21:5; 23:15; *Midrash Tehillim* 82:3; *Zohar* 1:69a, 86a; 2:6b, 29a, 46b, 49a, 54b, 175a, 232b; 3:147a. This notion is often linked with Isaiah 24:21: *YHVH will punish the host of the heights on high and the kings of the earth upon the earth*—implying that God first punishes or defeats the heavenly princes and then deals with their nations. On the dethroning of Egypt's prince, see *Zohar* 2:19a–b (*MhN*), below, page 504.

142. **Those of silver and gold melted...** See *Shemot Rabbah* 15:15.

143. **The god of Egypt was a lamb...** Prior to their departure from Egypt, the Israelites are commanded to slaughter a lamb (see Exodus 12:3–10)—thereby attacking a false god of the Egyptians, who worshipped the lamb. The particular manner of this sacrifice was designed to humiliate the Egyptians.

See Genesis 46:34; Exodus 8:22; *Mekhilta, Pisḥa* 5; *Targum Onqelos*, Exodus 8:22; *Pesiqta de-Rav Kahana* 5:17; *Shemot Rabbah* 11:3; 16:2–3; Ibn Ezra (long) on Exodus 8:22; Maimonides, *Guide of the Perplexed* 3:46; Naḥmanides on Exodus 12:3; *Zohar* 2:39b, 40b, 41b (*Piq*), 237a; 3:250b–251b; Tishby, *Wisdom of the Zohar*, 3:1255.

Exodus 12:9 reads: *Do not eat any of it raw, nor in any way cooked in water, but fire-roasted, its head with its legs and with its entrails.*

144. **The Nile was a god of theirs...** On the deification of the Nile, see *Tanḥuma*,

Rabbi Abba said, "What Rabbi Yoḥanan said is accurate and self-evident, because their gods are struck first, and afterward the nation. Hence, the Nile was struck first, and the wood and the stones, as is written: *There will be blood in all the land of Egypt, and in the wood and in the stones* (Exodus 7:19)—for they were their very gods."[145]

Rabbi Yitsḥak said, "It is written: *the host of the heights on high* (Isaiah 24:21). The Nile was not on high!"

Rabbi Yoḥanan said, "The essence of its water has its counterpart on high."[146]

Rabbi Yitsḥak said, "Their prince was struck first; afterward their other gods."

Rabbi Shim'on son of Rabbi Yose says, "The quintessential striking of the Egyptian nation was only at the sea, as is written: *not even one of them remained* (Exodus 14:28). Prior to this, judgment was executed upon their gods. About this is written *Come, let us deal shrewdly with them—lest they multiply and then, should war occur* (ibid. 1:10)—they had a presentiment about the future, in accordance with what befell them; *they join our enemies* (ibid.)—they had a presentiment about the supernal camps dwelling in their midst; *and fight against us* (ibid.)—they had a presentiment about what is written: *YHVH will fight for you...* (ibid. 14:14); *and go up from the land* (ibid. 1:10)—as is said: *the Children of Israel going out with a high hand* (ibid. 14:8)."[147]



*Va'era* 13; *Tanḥuma* (Buber), *Va'era* 14; *Shemot Rabbah* 9:9; *Zohar* 2:29a.

145. ***and in the wood and in the stones...*** The full verse reads: *YHVH said to Moses, "Say to Aaron, 'Take your staff and stretch out your hand over the waters of Egypt, over their rivers, over their channels, and over their ponds, and over all the gatherings of their waters, so that they might become blood. There will be blood in all the land of Egypt,* ובעצים ובאבנים (*u-va-etsim u-va-avanim*), *and in the trees and in the stones.*'" In its simple sense, the final phrase arguably means *and in the wooden and stone vessels.* Here, Rabbi Abba interprets it as *and in the wooden and stone idols.* See *Shemot Rabbah* 9:11; *Zohar* 2:29a.

146. **counterpart on high** Just as there is Pharaoh below and Egypt's celestial prince on high, so the earthly Nile has its heavenly counterpart.

147. **quintessential striking of the Egyptian nation...** According to Rabbi Shim'on son of Rabbi Yose, the plagues do not constitute the ultimate striking of the Egyptians, which happened only at the sea. It was this ultimate defeat that the prince of Egypt had in mind when he said *Come, let us deal shrewdly....*

Apparently Rabbi Shim'on has in mind the midrash which states that the prince of Egypt was defeated only at the sea. See *Shemot Rabbah* 21:5: "Rabbi El'azar son of Pedat said, 'When Israel departed from Egypt, they raised their eyes and [saw] the Egyptians pursuing after them, as is said:, *Pharaoh drew near* [*and the Israelites raised their eyes and, look, Egypt was advancing toward them and they were very afraid*] (Exodus 14:10). It does not say *were advancing,* but *was advancing* [in the singular]. When Pharaoh and the Egyptians began to pursue them, they raised their eyes heavenward and saw the prince of Egypt hovering in the air. When they saw him they became very afraid, as is said: *and they were very afraid.* What is the meaning of *and, look, Egypt was advancing*

*A man from the house of Levi went and took a daughter of Levi* (Exodus 2:1).[148]

Rabbi El'azar opened, "שיר השירים (*Shir ha-shirim*), *The Song of Songs, which is Solomon's* (Song of Songs 1:1). It has been taught: When the blessed Holy One created His world, it arose in desire before Him; and He created the heavens with His right hand, and the earth with His left. It arose in desire before Him that day and night should rule; and He created the angels empowered by His love during the day, and He created the angels empowered to recite song at night, as is written: *By day YHVH directs His love, in the night His song is with me* (Psalms 42:9)—some on the left, some on the right; some listen to the day-song, and some listen to the night-song—the song of Israel, the holy."[149]

Rabbi Yitshak said, "Those who recite song at night listen to the song of Israel by day, as is written: *companions listen for your voice* (Song of Songs 8:13)."[150]

Rabbi Shim'on said, "A company comprising three companies recites song by night, as is written: *She rises while it is still night and provides food to her household* [*and a portion to her maidens*] (Proverbs 31:15)."[151]



*toward them*? The prince of Egypt was called *Egypt*, for the blessed Holy One does not cast down a nation until He casts down their prince first....' Rabbi Yehoshu'a son of Avin said, '... *Egypt* was the name of Pharaoh's prince, and he was hovering in pursuit after them. Before the blessed Holy One drowned the Egyptians in the sea, He first drowned their prince, as is said: *YHVH shook out Egypt into the sea* (ibid., 27)—the prince of Egypt; afterward: *Pharaoh's chariots and his force He pitched into the sea* (ibid. 15:4).'" See *Zohar* 2:19b (*MhN*), below, page 506.

148. ***took a daughter of Levi*** In marriage. This Levite couple are the future parents of Aaron, Miriam, and Moses.

149. **the heavens with His right hand, and the earth with His left...** Just as heaven and earth respectively signify right and left, *Hesed* (Love) and *Din* (Judgment), so too day and night. The angelic realm also reflects this arrangement: angels of love by day, associated with the right; and angels of song by night, associated with the left.

On God's creating with His right and left hand, see *Pirqei de-Rabbi Eli'ezer* 18; *Zohar* 2:20a (*MhN*), 37a, 85b. On angelic song, see BT *Hagigah* 12b: "*Ma'on* [the fifth heaven or firmament], in which there are companies of ministering angels who recite song by night and are silent by day—for the sake of Israel's glory, as is said: *By day YHVH directs His love, in the night His song is with me.*" See also BT *Hagigah* 14a; *Hullin* 91b; *ZH* 5d–6a, 17d–18a (both *MhN*). Cf. *Zohar* 2:131b.

The connection between the Song of Songs and the *man from the house of Levi* is explained in the ensuing homilies.

150. ***companions listen for your voice*** See BT *Shabbat* 63a: "Rabbi Abba said in the name of Rabbi Shim'on son of Lakish, 'When two disciples of the wise listen to one another in *halakhah*, the blessed Holy One listens to their voice, as is said: *You who dwell in the garden, companions listen for your voice; let me hear!*'" See *Zohar* 1:77b, 178b, 231b; 2:46a; 3:13a, 22a, 213a; *ZH* 13c (*MhN*).

151. **A company comprising three companies...** This section in Proverbs, describing the ideal wife—*the woman of strength* [or: *valor*] (Proverbs 31:10)—is applied to *Shekhinah*, who according to this verse pro-

Rabbi El'azar said, "Ten things were created on the first day, including the attribute of day and the attribute of night. About the attribute of night is written *She rises while it is still night and provides* טרף (*teref*), *prey, to her household*, as is said: *His anger* טרף (*taraf*), *tears* (Job 16:9), and it is written: וטרף (*ve-taraf*), *it tears apart, with none to deliver* (Micah 5:7). וחק (*Ve-ḥoq*), *And a portion, to her maidens* (Proverbs 31:15)—as is said: חק (*ḥoq*), *statute, and law* (Exodus 15:25); חקיו (*ḥuqav*), *His statutes, and laws* (Psalms 147:19); *For it is* חק (*ḥoq*), *a statute, for Israel, a law [for the God of Jacob]* (ibid. 81:5)—hence, the attribute of judgment rules by night."[152]

It has been taught: Those who recite song at night are שרים (*sarim*), princes, over all masters of שיר (*shir*), song. When the living open in song, those above add power—to comprehend and perceive and attain what they had not attained; heaven and earth add power to this song.[153]

Rabbi Neḥemiah said, "Happy is the one who is privileged to comprehend this song! For it has been taught: One who is worthy of this song will comprehend matters of Torah and wisdom, ויאזין ויחקור (*ve-ya'azin ve-yaḥqor*), and



vides sustenance each night to Her angels. Just as the *Shekhinah*—who nourishes them—is comprised of *Ḥesed*, *Din*, and *Raḥamim* (respectively love, judgment, and compassion; or right, left, and center), so the nocturnal angelic company is comprised of three classes.

On three companies (or watches) of angels at night, see also *ZḤ* 5d–6a, 17d–18a (both *MhN*).

152. **the attribute of night...** *Shekhinah* rises in the night. To Her angelic companies She provides טרף (*teref*)—usually understood in this verse as *food*, but here specifically as *prey*, corresponding to the image of a lion in the verse from Micah, who טרף (*taraf*), *tears apart*, its prey, and to God's anger in the verse from Job. Hence the word *teref* indicates the activity of judgment, the chief quality of the night. Drawing on the two meanings for the word חק (*ḥoq*)—"portion" and "statute"—Rabbi El'azar demonstrates that this judgment is not the strict judgment of *Din* (*Gevurah*), but the lenient judgment of *Malkhut*, as indicated by the verses contrasting *statute* and *law*, symbols for *Malkhut* and *Tif'eret* respectively.

On the verse from Proverbs, see *Zohar* 1:107a; 2:60b, 204b; 3:60a, 86b, 90a.

On statute and law as alluding to *Shekhinah* and *Tif'eret*, see *Zohar* 2:40a, 60b.

According to BT *Ḥagigah* 12a (in the name of Rav Yehudah in the name of Rav): "Ten things were created on the first day: heaven and earth, waste and void, light and darkness, wind and water, the attribute of day and the attribute of night." Cf. *Pirqei de-Rabbi Eli'ezer* 3.

153. **שרים (*sarim*), princes, over all masters of שיר (*shir*), song...** Human song is empowered by celestial song. Cf. *Or Yaqar*, who understands the phrase "those above add power" to mean that human singing below empowers the celestial singers.

On the wordplay between *shirim*, "songs," and *sarim*, "princes," see *Zohar* 2:143b. See also *Shir ha-Shirim Rabbah* 1:12 (on 1:2).

This paragraph, extending until "the soul of whoever hears [them] joins and cleaves above" (just before note 159), is cited in Isaac ibn Sahula, *Peirush Shir ha-Shirim*, 408–9. See also Scholem, "Qabbalat Rabbi Yitsḥak ben Shelomoh," 112–16.

will seize and probe, and add power and might concerning what was, and what is destined to be. This is what Solomon was privileged to comprehend!"[154]

As Rabbi Shim'on taught: "David, peace be upon him, comprehended this—and arranged many songs and praises in which he alluded to times to come; he added power and might through the holy spirit. He comprehended matters of Torah and wisdom, and seized and probed and added power and might in the holy tongue.[155]

"Solomon attained even more of this song. He comprehended wisdom, seized and probed and arranged many משלים (*meshalim*), parables, and composed a book of this very song, as is written: *I obtained for myself male and female singers* (Ecclesiastes 2:8)—namely I acquired knowledge of song from those supernal singers, and those beneath them. This is the meaning of שיר השירים (*Shir ha-shirim*), *The Song of Songs*—namely שיר (*shir*), the song, of those שרים (*sharim*), singers, on high; the song comprising all matters of Torah and wisdom, and power and might, concerning what was and what is destined to be—the song that the singers on high sing."[156]



Rabbi El'azar said, "These singers waited silently until Levi was born. But from Levi's birth onward they recited song. Once Moses was born, Aaron anointed,

154. **this song...** The celestial song sung on high, but also the Song of Songs.

See *Shir ha-Shirim Rabbah* 1:8 on 1:1: "*Because Koheleth was a sage, he continued to instruct the people.* ואזן וחקר (*Ve-'izzen ve-ḥiqqer*), *He trained his ears and probed, the soundness of many maxims* (Ecclesiastes 12:9). He listened to the words of Torah; he probed the words of Torah; he made אזנים (*oznayim*), handles, for the words of Torah."

Cf. *Pereq Shirah*, intro: "Whoever engages in *Pereq Shirah* (the Chapter of Song) in this world... merits to learn and to teach, to observe, perform, and fulfill; his studies are established in him, his days are lengthened, and he attains life of the world to come."

155. **David... comprehended this...** By attuning himself to the song on high, David was able to compose the Psalms.

See *Midrash Tehillim* 18:1: "Rabbi Yudan said in the name of Rabbi Yehudah, 'Whatever David said in his book pertains to himself, to all Israel, and to all times.'" See also BT *Pesaḥim* 117a; *Zohar* 1:179a.

156. **Solomon attained even more of this song...** Solomon was also attuned to the celestial song, as a result of which he composed משלי (*Mishlei*), the book of Proverbs, and the Song of Songs.

The male and female singers correspond to higher and lower angelic grades.

On *Shir ha-shirim* as the song sung by heavenly singers, see *Shir ha-Shirim Rabbah* 1:12 (on 1:2); *Zohar* 2:143a–b.

The Song of Songs encompasses the entire Torah. Many of its verses are interpreted allegorically as referring to major biblical events and key moments in the history of Israel—including the patriarchs, the exodus, revelation, the Temple, and the redemption. See *Zohar* 2:144a. See Rabbi Akiva's statement in M *Yadayim* 3:5: "The whole world is not worth the day on which Song of Songs was given to Israel; for all the Writings [the 3rd division of the Bible] are holy, and Song of Songs is holy of holies."

On Solomon's composing the Song of Songs under the inspiration of the holy spirit, see *Tosefta Yadayim* 2:14; *Seder Olam Rabbah* 15; *Shir ha-Shirim Rabbah* 1:6–8 (on 1:1).

and the Levites sanctified, the song was completed; and the singers remained at their watches."[157]

Rabbi El'azar also said, "The moment Levi was born, they opened above, saying: *If only you were like a brother to me, nursing at my mother's breasts!* [19a] *If I found you outside, I would kiss you, yet no one would scorn me* (Song of Songs 8:1). Once the singers below came forth from the tribe of Levi and were sanctified, and all of them assumed their watches—these aligned to these: companions as one, worlds one, one King dwelling upon them—Solomon arrived and composed a book from that song of those singers, and wisdom was concealed within."[158]

Rabbi Yehudah said, "Why were the singers below called לוים (*Levi'im*), Levites? Because נלוים (*nilvim*), they are joined, and attached above as one; and the soul of whoever hears [them] נלוה (*nilvah*), joins, and cleaves above. That is why Leah said *my husband* ילוה (*yillaveh*), *will be joined, to me* (Genesis 29:34)."[159]

Rabbi Tanḥum said, "Because the seed of Levi was joined to *Shekhinah* entirely—with Moses, Aaron, and Miriam, and with all his seed after him; they are the ones *joined to YHVH to minister Him* (Isaiah 56:6)."



Come and see: When the singers on high waited, they did not take up their watches until the three siblings were born: Moses, Aaron, and Miriam. Granted Moses and Aaron—but why Miriam?

157. **the song was completed; and the singers remained at their watches** The Levites recited song in the Dwelling and the Temple; hence only with the birth of the Levites' progenitor did the celestial singers begin to sing. However, even though the celestial song now began, this song was complete only after the Levites were sanctified and began their service (see Numbers 8:5–22). Only then did the celestial singers take up their positions in their heavenly משמרות (*mishmarot*), "watches." See *Zohar* 2:143b.

The term משמרות (*mishmarot*) refers both to the rotating divisions in the Temple and to the three watches of the night. See BT *Berakhot* 3a: "There are *mishmarot*, watches, in heaven, and there are watches on earth"; Rashi on BT *Berakhot* 3a, s.v. *i qa-savar*; *Zohar* 1:159a, 189a, 231a–b; 2:143b, 173a–b, 195b; 3:64b; *ZḤ* 5d–6a, 17d (both *MhN*).

158. **companions as one, worlds one...** The advent of the Levites' song on earth marks the culmination of song, as the singers below and the singes on high are now united. This perfection and harmony reaches it apogee with the construction of the Solomonic Temple enabling Solomon to compose the Song of Songs, again identified with the celestial song. See *Zohar* 2:143a.

In proclaiming the verse from the Song of Songs, the celestial singers wish for Levi that he too will suckle from *Shekhinah* and sing like them. On the second clause in the verse, see *Or Yaqar*.

159. **Why were the singers below called לוים (*Levi'im*), Levites?...** The Levites below are joined to the celestial singers; and when the Levites below sing, the souls of those who hear them are joined with the supernal realms.

Genesis 29:34 reads: *She* [*Leah*] *conceived again and bore a son and she said, "This time my husband will be joined to me, for I have borne him three sons." Therefore he is named Levi.*

Rabbi Yose said, "As is written: *and female singers* (Ecclesiastes 2:8), as is said: *Miriam sung out to them* (Exodus 15:21)."[160]

It has been taught: When Levi was born, the blessed Holy One raised him on high and chose him from all his brothers and set him down upon the earth. He engendered Kohath, and Kohath engendered Amram, and he engendered Aaron and Miriam. He separated from his wife and restored her. At that hour the singers on high stood and sung. The blessed Holy One rebuked them and the song subsided, whereupon He stretched out His right line, extending it to Amram.[161]

Why was he called עמרם (*Amram*), Amram? Because עם רם על כל רמים (*am ram al kol ramim*), a nation exalted beyond all exaltations, came forth from him.[162]

Yet his name was not mentioned! Why wasn't his name mentioned?



160. ***and female singers...*** One can understand why the singers on high waited for Aaron and Moses—who were connected with the cult—but why Miriam? Miriam, however, was the earthly counterpart of the female celestial singers. See above, page 500: *I obtained for myself male and female singers* (Ecclesiastes 2:8). The verse from Exodus recounts Miriam's song at the sea.

161. **When Levi was born...** Apparently, because Moses hailed from the Levites (associated with song and the left side), he required the aspect of the right. Hence God extended His right line to Amram. Precisely why God rebukes the celestial singers is not clear. According to Cordovero in *Or Yaqar*, ad loc., God rebukes them for "premature celebration," i.e., for not realizing that without the Levites below, the song is not yet complete.

See *Pirqei de-Rabbi Eli'ezer* 37: "The angel Michael descended and took Levi and raised him up before the blessed Holy One. He spoke before Him, 'Master of the World! This is Your lot and the portion of Your works.' He stretched forth His right hand and blessed him that the sons of Levi should minister on earth before Him, like the ministering angels in heaven."

See also Rashi on Genesis 29:34 (citing *Devarim Rabbah*); Kasher, *Torah Shelemah*, Genesis 29:34, n. 110. Cf. *Zohar* 2:53b.

On Amram separating from his wife and restoring her (and the angel's song), see BT *Sotah* 12a: "It has been taught: Amram was the dignitary of the generation. When he saw that the wicked Pharaoh had decreed *Every son that is born you shall fling into the Nile* (Exodus 1:22), he said, 'In vain do we labor.' He arose and divorced his wife. All [the Israelites] arose and divorced their wives. His daughter said to him, 'Father, your decree is more severe than Pharaoh's; because Pharaoh decreed only against the males, whereas you have decreed against the males and females. Pharaoh decreed only concerning this world, whereas you [have decreed] concerning this world and the world to come....' He arose and restored his wife; and they all arose and restored their wives.... Rav Yehudah son of Zevina said, 'He acted toward her as though it had been the first marriage; he seated her in a palanquin, Aaron and Miriam danced before her, and the ministering angels proclaimed: *A happy mother of children* (Psalms 113:9).'" See also *Targum Yerushalmi*, Exodus 2:1; *Shemot Rabbah* 1:19.

162. **a nation exalted...came forth from him** Namely, Moses, who was equivalent to the entire nation. See *Mekhilta*, *Shirta* 1, 9; *Tanḥuma*, *Beshallaḥ* 10.

Rabbi Yehudah said in the name of Rabbi Abbahu, "Because he went covertly—secretly returning to his wife, that they would not recognize him, as is written: *A man went* (Exodus 2:1)—it does not say *Amram went*, openly. *And took a daughter of Levi* (ibid.)—she too returned covertly, and her name is not mentioned."[163]

Rabbi Abbahu said, "*A man went*—Gabriel, as is written: *the man Gabriel* (Daniel 9:21), for he went and returned her to Amram."[164]

Rabbi Yehudah said, "It was in fact Amram, yet his name was not mentioned because his going to couple with his wife did not stem from him, but from on high."[165]

Rabbi Yitsḥak said, "The coupling of Aaron and Miriam's parents is not mentioned in the Torah, yet of Moses it is written *and took a daughter of Levi*—teaching that the *Shekhinah* is named after Levi. Amram was not worthy of engendering Moses until he had partaken of *Shekhinah*, whereupon he engendered Moses. This is the significance of *and took a daughter of Levi*. Consequently it is written: [*The woman conceived and bore a son,*] *and she saw that he was good* (Exodus 2:2)."[166]



Rabbi El'azar said, "Amram was worthy of producing a son who was worthy of a mighty voice, as is written: *Elohim answered him with voice* (ibid. 19:19). Amram was worthy of בת קול (*bat qol*), daughter of voice, as is written: *and he took a daughter of Levi*, namely daughter of voice. That is why it is written *He*

163. **Because he went covertly...** Neither Amram nor Jochebed are mentioned by name in the account of Moses' birth. The Torah refers to Amram as *a man* and Jochebed merely as *a daughter of Levi*. This anonymity reflects their covert return to one another, lest the Egyptians discover them.

On the need for such secrecy, see BT *Sotah* 12a; *Shemot Rabbah* 1:20. See also BT *Sukkah* 49b; *Makkot* 24a. Cf. Naḥmanides on Exodus 2:1.

164. ***A man went*—Gabriel...** To ensure that Aaron, Miriam, and Moses would eventually be born, God dispatched an emissary to arrange their parents' marriage. This is established by verbal analogy—the oddly anonymous *man* in the verse in Exodus being identified with *the man Gabriel* in Daniel.

See *Targum Yerushalmi*, Genesis 37:15; *Tanḥuma, Vayeshev* 2; *Pirqei de-Rabbi Eli'ezer* 38; Rashi on Genesis 37:15; *Zohar* 1:184a; 2:11a.

165. **did not stem from him, but from on high...** See *Zohar* 2:11b: "a divine echo descended and told him to couple with her."

166. **until he had partaken of *Shekhinah*...** Just as the Torah did not provide details about Aaron's and Miriam's conceptions, the account here (*and took a daughter of Levi*) does not only describe Amram's union with his wife, but also his union with *Shekhinah*. Cf. *Zohar* 2:11b, where both Amram and Jochebed join their desire with *Shekhinah*.

According to rabbinic sources (BT *Sotah* 12a; *Shemot Rabbah* 1:20), the phrase *she saw that he was good* alludes to the radiance surrounding the infant Moses. See *Zohar* 2:11b: "She saw the radiance of *Shekhinah* shining in him." Thus, having partaken of *Shekhinah* himself, Amram sires a child radiating *Shekhinah*.

*went* (Exodus 2:1)—that is, he went to that grade. It has been taught: When Moses was born, the blessed Holy One designated His name upon him, as is written: *and she saw that he was good*, and it is written: *YHVH is good to all* (Psalms 145:9), and it is written: *Taste and see that YHVH is good* (ibid. 34:9)."[167]

*It happened many years later* (Exodus 2:23).

Rabbi Yehoshu'a of Sakhnin said, "*It happened many years later*—the end of their exile, when Israel was enslaved with every kind of servitude. *Many years later*—for they were 'many' for Israel in Egypt. Since the end of their exile was complete, what is written? *The king of Egypt died* (ibid.). What is the significance? That the prince of Egypt was deposed from his rank and fell from his majesty. And since the king of Egypt—their prince—fell, the blessed Holy One remembered Israel and heard their prayer."[168]

Rabbi Yehudah said, "Come and see that it is so! For as long as their prince was granted dominion over Israel, Israel's cry was not heard. As soon as their prince fell, it is written: *the king of Egypt died*, and immediately: *the Children of Israel groaned from the bondage and cried out, and their plea went up to God* (ibid.)—until that time, their cry was not heeded."



Rabbi El'azar said, "Come and see the compassion of the blessed Holy One! When He has compassion upon Israel, He overturns the attribute of judgment,

167. **Amram was worthy of בת קול (*bat qol*), daughter of voice...** Whereas Amram was worthy of *bat qol*—a divine echo or lower grade of revelation, corresponding with *Shekhinah*—Moses attained the "divine voice," presumably signifying *Tif'eret*.

Cf. *Targum Yerushalmi*, Exodus 2:1; BT *Sotah* 12a; *Bava Batra* 119b–120a; *Shemot Rabbah* 1:19, where Jochebed is referred to as בת ק"ל (*bat q + l*), "daughter of 130," i.e., 130 years old.

On *good* as Moses' name, see BT *Sotah* 12a; *Menahot* 53b; *Bereshit Rabbah* 4:6; *Shemot Rabbah* 1:20; *Pirqei de-Rabbi Eli'ezer* 48. Cf. *Zohar* 2:54a.

On "mighty voice" and "voice" (as *Binah* and *Tif'eret*), see *Zohar* 1:50b; 2:226b.

168. ***The king of Egypt died...*** As the exile nears completion, the celestial prince of Egypt is deposed—thereby allowing the cries of Israel to ascend to God.

On the prince of Egypt, see *Shemot Rabbah* 21:5; *Zohar* 2:6a–b, 7a, 10a, 50a; in *MhN*, see 2:16b, 17a, 17b, 18a, 19b. Cf. *Zohar* 1:113a (*MhN*).

On dying as falling from one's former rank and the loss of power, see *Bereshit Rabbah* 96:3; BT *Avodah Zarah* 5a; *Zohar* 3:135b (*IR*), and below, page 506.

See *Shemot Rabbah* 1:34: "*It happened many years later*. They are called *many* because they were years of distress." See also *Vayiqra Rabbah* 19:5; *Tanhuma*, *Metsora* 6.

Exodus 2:23 reads: *It happened many years later that the king of Egypt died, and the Children of Israel groaned from the bondage and cried out, and their plea from the bondage went up to God.* The following verse reads: *God heard their moaning; and God remembered His covenant with Abraham, with Isaac, and with Jacob. God saw the Children of Israel and God knew.*

brings it low, and has mercy upon them. This corresponds with what we have learned—that the blessed Holy One sheds two tears into the Great Sea."[169]

What are these two tears?

Rabbi Yose said, "The [19b] matter is unclear, for it was told him by a bone necromancer who is a liar and his words are false."[170]

Rabbi El'azar said, "We do not follow the bone necromancer! Lucidity of the word: As we have learned: In the ten crowns of the King there are two tears of the blessed Holy One, two attributes of judgment from which judgment hails, as is said: *These two things have befallen you:* [*wrack and ruin—who can console you?*] (Isaiah 51:19). When the blessed Holy One remembers His children, He sheds them into the Great Sea—the Sea of Wisdom—to sweeten them, transforming the attribute of judgment into the attribute of compassion, and He has mercy upon them."[171]

Rabbi Yehudah said, "Two tears—from which tears derive, from which judgment hails."[172]



169. **the blessed Holy One sheds two tears into the Great Sea** See BT *Berakhot* 59a: "Rav Kattina was walking on the way, and when he came to the door of the house of a certain bone necromancer, there was a rumbling of the earth. He said, 'Does the bone necromancer know what this rumbling is?' He called after him, 'Kattina, Kattina, why should I not know? When the blessed Holy One remembers His children, who are plunged in suffering among the nations of the world, He sheds two tears into the Great Sea, and His voice resounds from one end of the world to the other.' Rav Kattina said, 'The necromancer is a liar and his words are false. If it was as he says, there should be one rumbling after another!' [corresponding with the two tears]. —He did not really mean this, however. There really was one rumbling after another, and the reason why he did not admit it was so that people should not go astray after him." See *Zohar* 2:18a (*MhN*), above, page 493. See also *Zohar* 1:4b; 2:9a, 195b; 3:132a (*IR*), 172a–b; [Moses de León?], *Seder Gan Eden*, 133.

170. **The matter is unclear, for it was told him by a bone necromancer...** In the account in *Berakhot*, Rav Kattina calls the necromancer a liar even though he possesses correct knowledge of the divine and natural realms. The tradition is accepted only after Rav Kattina—and the Rabbis after him—supply their own textual proofs for the very same idea.

"Bone necromancer" renders אובא טמיא (*ova tamya*); see Rashi, *Berakhot* 59a, s.v. *ova tamya*.

171. **Lucidity of the word...** Rabbi El'azar accepts the teaching on the two tears shed by God, not on the necromancer's authority but on that of a kabbalistic interpretation of Scripture.

The two attributes of judgment, which are in the "crowns of the king" (presumably the *sefirot*), apparently correspond to *Netsaḥ* and *Hod*, or *Gevurah* and *Malkhut* (see *Or Yaqar*, ad loc.). Again, following *Or Yaqar*, the tears' descent is in fact an ascent into *Binah* and *Ḥokhmah* (the Sea of Wisdom), where the judgment is sweetened. See *Zohar* 2:18a (*MhN*), above, page 492.

On rejection of the necromancer's authority, see the previous two notes.

172. **Two tears—from which tears derive...** The two tears of judgment bring judgment into the world, causing those whom judgment strikes to shed tears.

Rabbi Yehudah said, "It is written: *and look, Egypt was advancing toward them* (Exodus 14:10), which Rabbi Yose said signifies the prince of Egypt. How then can you say that *the king of Egypt died* signifies the prince of Egypt?!"[173]

Rabbi Yitsḥak said, "This word supports the earlier one! Here is written *and look, Egypt,* and there is written *the king of Egypt*—teaching that now he was not king, for he had been brought down from his greatness. Therefore it is written *and look, Egypt,* and not *the king of Egypt.* And concerning what is said: [*the king of Egypt*] *died*—as is said: *for all the men who sought your life are dead* (ibid. 4:19)."[174]

Rabbi Yitsḥak said in the name of Rabbi Yehoshu'a, "Come and see: All kings of Egypt are called Pharaoh, yet here it merely says *king of Egypt*—anonymous; but wherever it says *Pharaoh*—Pharaoh, literally. Come and see: As long as there is dominion above, there is dominion for the nation below; when dominion is withdrawn above, dominion is withdrawn below."[175]



173. ***and, look, Egypt was advancing toward them...*** According to a midrash, Exodus 14:10 describes the celestial prince of Egypt coming to assist his people in battle at the sea. If so, how can the phrase *the king of Egypt died* in Exodus 2:23 also refer to Egypt's prince? See *Zohar* 2:50a, where a similar problem is raised by Rabbi Yose.

See *Shemot Rabbah* 21:5: "Rabbi El'azar son of Pedat said, 'When Israel departed from Egypt, they raised their eyes and [saw] the Egyptians pursuing after them, as is said: *Pharaoh drew near* [*and the Israelites raised their eyes—and look, Egypt was advancing toward them; and they were very afraid*] (Exodus 14:10). It does not say *were advancing,* but *was advancing* [in the singular]. When Pharaoh and the Egyptians began to pursue them, they raised their eyes heavenward and saw the prince of Egypt hovering in the air. When they saw him they became very afraid, as is said: *and they were very afraid.* What is the meaning of *and look, Egypt was advancing toward them*? The prince of Egypt was called "Egypt," for the blessed Holy One does not cast down a nation until He casts down their prince first....' Rabbi Yehoshu'a son of Avin said, '...Egypt was the name of Pharaoh's prince, and he was hovering in pursuit after them. Before the blessed Holy One drowned the Egyptians in the sea, He first drowned their prince, as is said: *YHVH shook out Egypt into the sea* (ibid., 27)—the prince of Egypt; afterward: *Pharaoh's chariots and his force He pitched into the sea* (ibid. 15:4).'" See also *Shemot Rabbah* 15:15.

174. **teaching that now he was not king...** Egypt's celestial prince is still active at the sea but he is no longer a "king," i.e., he no longer enjoys his full power and former rank; he is therefore considered as dead. Cf. *Zohar* 2:18a (*MhN*), above, page 495, on Dumah's dethronement.

Exodus 4:19 reads: *YHVH said to Moses in Midian, "Go, return to Egypt, for all the men who sought your life are dead."* According to the midrashic reading, these dead men refer to Dathan and Abiram—who were in fact alive, but had lost their wealth and so were considered as dead. See Numbers 16; *Bereshit Rabbah* 71:6; *Shemot Rabbah* 5:4; BT *Avodah Zarah* 5a; *Nedarim* 7b; *Targum Yerushalmi* and Rashi on Exodus 4:19.

175. **All kings of Egypt are called Pharaoh...** On Pharaoh as the generic name for Egypt's kings, see Ibn Ezra and Rashbam on Genesis 41:10.

On the distinction between *Pharaoh* and *king of Egypt,* see *Zohar* 2:17a (*MhN*; above, page 487), 50a.

On the idea that each earthly nation has a

Rabbi Abba said, "It is written: *Behold, a day of YHVH is coming* (Zechariah 14:1). Are the other days not His?!"

Well, Rabbi Abba said, "This teaches that the other days are granted to the princes, but that day will not belong to the princes but to the blessed Holy One, in order to execute judgment upon the nations; for on that day, all the princes will fall from their rank. Of this is written *YHVH alone will be exalted on that day* (Isaiah 2:11)—for on that day, the princes will not be ascendant."[176]

Rabbi Abba said, "When the blessed Holy One executes judgment upon the princes above, what is written? *For My sword shall be drunk in the sky* (ibid. 34:5)."[177]

Does *YHVH* possess a sword?[178]

Rabbi Yitsḥak said, "It is written 'sword': *YHVH has a sword, full of blood* (ibid., 6); and it is written: *with His sword against all flesh* (ibid. 66:16)."[179]

Rabbi Abba said, "The sword is the judgment he wreaks, as is written: *David saw the angel of YHVH standing between heaven and earth, with a drawn sword in*



heavenly prince whose fate determines that of his nation below, see *Mekhilta, Shirta* 2; *Shir ha-Shirim Rabbah* on 8:14; *Devarim Rabbah* 1:22; *Tanḥuma, Bo* 4, *Beshallaḥ* 13, *Mishpatim* 18; *Tanḥuma* (Buber), *Bo* 6, 19; *Shemot Rabbah* 9:9, 21:5, 23:15; *Zohar* 1:69a, 86a, 113a (*MhN*); 2:6b–7a, 18a (*MhN*), 29a, 46b, 49a, 54b, 175a, 232b; 3:8a, 147a.

176. ***YHVH* alone will be exalted on that *day*...** See *Zohar* 1:107b, 219b; 2:232b.

On exile as the "day of the nations," see *Zohar* 2:17a (*MhN*), above, page 485.

177. ***For My sword shall be drunk in the sky*...** The verse continues: *Look, it shall come down upon Edom, upon the people* [or: *nation*] *I have doomed, to wreak judgment.* Isaiah 34 describes God's anger at the nations whom He consigns to slaughter.

See *Mekhilta, Shirta* 2; *Tanḥuma, Beshallaḥ* 13; *Midrash Tehillim* 150:1.

178. **Does *YHVH* possess a sword?** See Maimonides, *Mishneh Torah, Hilkhot Yesodei ha-Torah* 1:9: "If so [that God is incorporeal], what is the meaning of the expressions written in the Torah: *Below His feet* (Exodus 24:10); *Written by the finger of God* (ibid. 31:18); *YHVH's hand* (ibid. 9:3); *YHVH's eyes* (Genesis 38:7); *YHVH's ears* (Numbers 11:1); and the like? All these are in accordance with human thought—which know only of corporeal imagery—because the Torah speaks in the language of human beings. They are only descriptive terms, as is said: *When I hone the flash of My sword* (Deuteronomy 32:41). Now, does He have a sword?! Does He need a sword to kill?! Rather, it is a metaphor; they are all metaphors."

179. **It is written 'sword'...** Apparently Rabbi Yitsḥak understands the scriptural references to the divine sword literally.

Isaiah 34:6 reads: *YHVH has a sword, full of blood, gorged with fat—with the blood of lambs and goats, with the kidney fat of rams. For YHVH has a slaughter in Bozrah, a great butchery in the land of Edom.*

Cf. *Or Yaqar* and *Matoq mi-Devash,* who understand the sword from Isaiah 34 as a reference to *Malkhut* and to the divine judgment wrought upon the heavenly princes; and the sword from Isaiah 66 as alluding to an actual sword and to the ensuing wars on earth. (On *Malkhut* as *sword,* see *Zohar* 1:53b, 66a–b, 237a, 238b, 240b; 2:26a, 28b, 61a, 66a; 3:19b, 30b; Moses de León, *Sefer ha-Rimmon,* 69, 213.)

*his hand* (1 Chronicles 21:16). Was a drawn sword really in the angel's hand? Rather, authority was placed in his hand to execute judgment."[180]

Rabbi Yehoshu'a son of Levi said, "The angel of death told me, 'Were it not for the regard I have for the honor of creatures, I would cut their throats like an animal!'"[181]

Rabbi Abba said, "All instances are on account of the authority granted him to administer the sentence, as is written: *a drawn sword in his hand*—authority is placed in his hand to execute judgment."[182]

If so, what is the meaning of [*YHVH ordered the angel*] *to return his sword to its sheath* (ibid., 27)?

Rabbi Abba said, "Judgment reverts to the Master of Judgment, and authority to the one to whom authority belongs!"[183]

ויאנחו בני ישראל (*Va-ye'aneḥu benei Yisra'el*), *The Children of Israel groaned* (Exodus 2:23). It is not written ויתאנחו (*va-yit'anneḥu*) but rather ויאנחו (*va-ye'aneḥu*); that is to say, they were groaned-for above—for the groaning was above, on their behalf.[184]



Rabbi Berekhiah said, "This was the celestial בני ישראל (*benei Yisra'el*), sons of Israel. Who are these sons of Israel? Those called 'sons of service'—namely those מן העבודה (*min ha-avodah*), of the service, on high. *And their plea went up to God* (ibid.)—for until that hour their plea did not ascend before Him."[185]

Rabbi Yitsḥak said, "When the blessed Holy One executes judgment on the Family Above, how does it work?"[186]

180. **The sword is the judgment he wreaks...** Like Maimonides, Rabbi Abba understands the sword as a metaphor. On the verse from Chronicles (slightly misquoted here), see *Zohar* 1:61a.

181. **The angel of death told me...** See BT *Avodah Zarah* 20b in the name of the father of Shemu'el. This account is cited in support of the idea that the sword mentioned above is indeed real, not a metaphor. Just as the angel of death wields an actual knife, so God possesses a sword.

182. **All instances are on account of the authority granted him...** Whenever a sword is associated with an angel, it is but a metaphor for his authority.

183. **Judgment reverts to the Master of Judgment...** To God, who has granted angels temporary authority. Hence, the metaphor remains—and the literal understanding of the sword is rejected.

184. **they were groaned-for above...** Because the verb *va-ye'aneḥu* is in a conjugation that usually expresses a passive role.

185. **those מן העבודה (*min ha-avodah*), of the service, on high...** It was the celestial sons of Israel—angels *min ha-avodah*, of the service on high—who groaned. Exodus 2:23 reads: *The Children* [or: *sons*] *of Israel groaned* מן העבודה (*min ha-avodah*), *from the bondage, and cried out; and their plea from the bondage went up to God.* In the verse's simple sense, *avodah* means "bondage, labor, work," but Rabbi Berekhiah construes it in its sense of "(religious) service."

186. **executes judgment on the Family Above...** Namely, the celestial princes of the nations. See *ZḤ* 29a.

Rabbi Abba said, "He passes them through the river of fire, strips them of their dominion, and appoints different rulers of other nations."[187]

He said to him, "But it is written: *His ministers flaming fire* (Psalms 104:4)!"[188]

He replied, "There is a fire fiercer than fire—and a fire that repels fire."[189]

Rabbi Yitsḥak said, "There are three matters here: groan, cry, and plea—each one distinct from the other. Groan, as is written: *The Children of Israel groaned* (Exodus 2:23); cry, as is written: *and cried out* (ibid.); plea, as is written: *and their plea went up* (ibid.). Each one is distinct on its own—and Israel uttered them all."[190]

Rabbi Yehudah said, "They uttered cry and plea, but they did not groan, as implied by what is written: ויאנחו (*va-ye'anehu*)—the groaning was above, on their behalf."[191]

How are cry and plea distinguished?

Rabbi Yitsḥak said, "Plea always entails prayer, as is said: *Hear my prayer, O YHVH; give ear to my plea* (Psalms 39:13); *With you, O YHVH, I plead* (ibid. 88:14); *I pleaded with You and You healed me* (ibid. 30:3). Cry refers to someone who cries out yet doesn't say anything." 

Rabbi [20a] Yehudah said, "Therefore, cry is greatest of all, for cry hails from the heart, as is written: *Their heart cried out to YHVH* (Lamentations 2:18). צעקה (*Tse'aqah*) and זעקה (*ze'aqah*) are one and the same, and it is closer to the

187. **He passes them through the river of fire...** The image of the river of fire derives from Daniel 7:10: *A river of fire was flowing and gushing from His presence, a thousand thousands serving Him, a myriad of myriads attending Him.*

On the punishment of angels or heavenly princes in the river of fire, see *Ma'yan Ḥokhmah* (*Beit ha-Midrash*, 1:60); *Pesiqta Rabbati* 20; *Sefer Ḥasidim* (ed. Margaliot), 530; [Moses de León?], *Seder Gan Eden*, 139; *Zohar* 1:43b (*Heikh*), 69a; 2:6b, 49a, 52b, 239b, 252b (*Heikh*).

188. ***His ministers flaming fire...*** If the celestial princes are of fire, how can fire harm them?

On heavenly beings issuing from the fiery stream, see BT *Ḥagigah* 14a: "Shemu'el said to Rabbi Ḥiyya son of Rav, 'O, son of a lion! Come, I will tell you one of those fine words said by your father: Every single day, ministering angels are created from a river of fire, chant a song, then cease to be, as is said: *New every morning, immense is Your faithfulness!* (Lamentations 3:23).'" See also BT *Ḥagigah* 13b; *Bereshit Rabbah* 78:1; *Shemot Rabbah* 15:6.

189. **There is a fire fiercer than fire...** The fire of the river is more potent than the fire of the angels—and hence can affect their punishment.

See BT *Yoma* 21b (describing the fire of *Shekhinah* that consumes the fiery angels); *Tanḥuma*, *Yitro* 16; *Tosafot*, *Ḥagigah* 23a, s.v. *she-ein bo*; *Zohar* 1:18b–19a, 50b, 69a; 2:89b, 226b; 3:25b, 27b, 138a (*IR*), 154b, 294a (*IZ*); Moses de León, *Sefer ha-Mishqal*, 63–65.

190. **There are three matters here: groan, cry, and plea...** Cf. *Zohar* 1:132a–b; *ZḤ* 80a (*MhN*, *Rut*). See also *Sifrei*, Deuteronomy 26; *Devarim Rabbah* 2:1.

191. **the groaning was above...** See above, notes 184 and 185. The angels groaned on their behalf.

blessed Holy One than prayer or groan, as is written: *if he cries out to Me, I will surely hear his cry* (Exodus 22:22)."[192]

Rabbi Berekhiah said, "In the hour when the blessed Holy One said to Samuel *I regret that I made Saul king* (1 Samuel 15:11), what is written? *Samuel was incensed, and he cried out to YHVH all night long* (ibid.)—he set aside all else and took to crying out, for it is closest of all to the blessed Holy One. This is the significance of *Now, look, the cry of the Children of Israel has come to Me* (Exodus 3:9)."

Our Rabbis have taught: One who prays, weeps, and cries out until he can no longer move his lips—this is perfect prayer, for it hails from the heart; it never returns unfulfilled.[193]

Rabbi Yehudah said, "Great is a cry, for it annuls the judgment made on a person's whole life."[194]

Rabbi Yitsḥak said, "Great is a cry, for it rules over the attribute of judgment above."

Rabbi Yose said, "Great is a cry, for it rules over this world and the world to come; by virtue of a cry, one inherits this world and the world to come, as is written: *Then they cried to YHVH in their trouble, and He delivered them from their distresses* (Psalms 107:6)."[195]



## Section 72[196]

*Moses was* רועה (*ro'eh*), *shepherding, the flock of Jethro his father-in-law, priest of Midian* (Exodus 3:1).

Rabbi Shim'on opened, "*My beloved is mine and I am his;* הרועה (*ha-ro'eh*), *he grazes, among the roses* (Song of Songs 2:16)."[197]

Rabbi Shim'on said, "Woe to the creatures who are unaware, who do not know! When it arose in Thought before the blessed Holy One to create His world, all worlds arose in a single thought;

192. **cry is greatest of all...** The wordless cry hailing from the heart is more beloved and effective than prayer.

According to *Or Yaqar* and *Matoq mi-Devash*, prayer is associated with *Malkhut*; a cry is associated with *Binah*, the realm beyond speech.

Exodus 22:23 refers to the cry of the widow and orphan.

Both *tse'aqah* and *ze'aqah* mean "a cry."

193. **never returns unfulfilled** On this phrase, see Isaiah 55:11; BT *Berakhot* 32b; *Kallah Rabbati* 3:1; *Devarim Rabbah* 2:12.

194. **Great is a cry, for it annuls the judgment...** See BT *Rosh ha-Shanah* 18a.

195. **this world and the world to come...** As indicated by *distresses*, plural.

196. **Section 72** Most of the manuscripts contain the unusual section heading פרשת ע"ב (*parashat* 72), perhaps reflecting an early attempt to arrange the materials of *MhN* on the Torah. See *ZḤ* 3d, 10b, 13a, 14a, 17c, 19c, 28a, end of *parashat Lekh Lekha*, above, page 311 (all *MhN*).

197. ***roses...*** In Song of Songs, שושנה (*shoshanah*) probably means *lily* or *lotus*, although here it connotes *rose*.

The verb *ro'eh* can mean "shepherd, guide, conduct, graze, feed."

בשושנים (*Ba-shoshanim*), *Among the roses,*

and with this thought, they were all created, as is written: *With wisdom You have made them all* (Psalms 104:24). With this thought—which is Wisdom—this world and the world above were created. He stretched out His right hand and created the world above; He stretched out His left hand and created this world, as is written: *My own hand founded earth, and My right hand spread out heaven. I summon them—they stand together* (Isaiah 48:13)—all of them were created in a single moment, a single instant.[198]

"He fashioned this world corresponding to the world above; all that is above has its counterpart below; and all that is below has its counterpart in the sea—all is one. In the upper realms, He created the angels; in this world, He created human beings; in the sea, He created Leviathan—as is said: *to join the tent to become one whole* (Exodus 36:18).[199]

"Concerning the human being it is written: *In the image of God He made the human being* (Genesis 9:6), and it is written: *You made him little less than God* (Psalms 8:6). (If human beings are so precious among His works and yet are annihilated by a single drop from the well, how can they come to draw from it?) He chose those on high; and He chose the children of Israel. Those on high He did not call children, whereas those below He called children, as is written: *You are children of* YHVH *your God* (Deuteronomy 14:1). He called them children, and they called Him Father, as is written: *For You are our father* (Isaiah 63:16). It is written: *My beloved is mine and I am his* (Song of Songs 2:16)—He chose me, and I chose Him!"[200]



can also be construed as *with* [or: *through*] *roses.*

198. **with this thought they were all created...** On God's creating the world with wisdom and thought (here presumably signifying the *sefirah Ḥokhmah*), see *Targum Yerushalmi* (frag.), Genesis 1:1; Wolfson, *Philo*, 1:242–45, 266–69; Naḥmanides on Genesis 1:1. See *Zohar* 1:2a, 3b, 15a, 16b, 145a; 2:174a, 175b; 3:42b–43a; Moses de León, *Sheqel ha-Qodesh*, 21–22 (25–26). In *MhN*, see *ZḤ* 3a, 3d, 4a.

On God's creating with His right and left hand (here signifying *Ḥesed* and *Gevurah*), see *Pirqei de-Rabbi Eli'ezer* 18; *Zohar* 1:30a; 2:18b (*MhN*), 37a, 85b. Since the verse in Isaiah mentions both *hand* and *right hand*, by implication the former term denotes the left hand. On this verse, see also BT *Ḥagigah* 12a; *ZḤ* 3a (*MhN*).

See BT *Ḥagigah* 12b: "Rabbi Yose said, 'Woe to the creatures—for they see, but do not know what they see; they stand, but do not know on what they stand!'"

199. **He fashioned this world corresponding to the world above...** A general principle of Kabbalah. See *Zohar* 1:38a (*Heikh*), 57b–58a, 129a, 145b, 156b, 158b, 205b; 2:5a (*MhN*), 15b (*MhN*), 48b, 82b, 144b, 251a (*Heikh*); 3:45b, 65b; *ZḤ* 15a, 19a (both *MhN*); Tishby, *Wisdom of the Zohar*, 1:273.

See BT *Ḥullin* 127a: "Everything existing on land exists in the sea, except for the weasel." See also *Zohar* 1:157b.

In its simple sense, the verse from Exodus describes the unity of the Dwelling; here, it refers to the unity of being. Cf. Solomon Ibn Gabirol, *Keter Malkhut*, Canto 9.

200. **those below He called children...** See M *Avot* 3:14: "He [Rabbi Akiva] used to say, 'Beloved is the human being, for he was created in the image [of God]; still greater

"הרועה (*Ha-ro'eh*), *He grazes, among the roses* (ibid.). He רועה (*ro'eh*), shepherds, the roses, even though the thorns surround them; no other can shepherd the roses like Him.[201]

"Alternatively, הרועה בשושנים (*ha-ro'eh ba-shoshannim*), *He shepherds with roses.* Just as the rose is red and its water white, so the blessed Holy One conducts His world from the attribute of judgment to the attribute of compassion, and it is written: *Be your sins like crimson, they can turn snow-white* (Isaiah 1:18)."[202]

Rabbi Abba was walking on the way, and Rabbi Yitsḥak was with him. While they were walking, they came upon some roses. Rabbi Abba picked one with his hand and walked on. Rabbi Yose met them. He said, "Surely *Shekhinah* is here! And I can see from what is in Rabbi Abba's hands that I will learn great wisdom, for I know that Rabbi Abba picked it solely to demonstrate wisdom."[203]



was this love in that it was made known to him that he was created in the image, as is said: *In the image of God He made the human being* (Genesis 9:6). Beloved are Israel, for they are called children of the Omnipresent; still greater was this love in that it was made known to them that they are called children of the Omnipresent, as is written: *You are children of YHVH your God* (Deuteronomy 14:1).'" See also *Qohelet Rabbah* on 4:8; *Shir ha-Shirim Rabbah* on 2:16. On the verse in Deuteronomy, see *Zohar* 1:82b, 245b; 2:89b; 3:42b.

The sentence in parentheses is in Aramaic, whereas the rest of the homily is in Hebrew. Though found in the manuscripts, it appears to be an interpolation, for it interrupts the homily's flow. The meaning of the sentence is also unclear. See *Or Yaqar, Derekh Emet, Nitsotsei Orot, Sullam,* and *Matoq mi-Devash* for various interpretations.

201. **He רועה (*ro'eh*), shepherds, the roses...** God guides and protects Israel (the roses) from the nations (the thorns).

See *Shir ha-Shirim Rabbah* on Song of Songs 2:2: *Like a rose among thorns, so is my beloved among the maidens.* See *Zohar* 2:189b.

This and the following paragraph might also be construed as presented anonymously, rather than as the continuation of Rabbi Shim'on's homily.

202. **rose is red and its water white...** The red of the rose signifies judgment, and the clear (or white) rose water signifies mercy or compassion. God shepherds (administers) His world in accordance with the principle of roses—from red to white, from judgment to mercy, remitting sin.

On the rose signifying judgment and compassion, see *Zohar* 1:1a; 3:107a.

203. **Surely *Shekhinah* is here!...** Alluding to Rabbi Yose's encounter with Rabbi Abba, and also to the rose in his hand—a symbol of *Shekhinah*.

See *Mekhilta, Amaleq* (*Yitro*) 1: "Whoever receives the face of [i.e., welcomes] the wise, it is as if he receives the face of *Shekhinah*."

Cf. JT *Eruvin* 5:1, 22b: "Rabbi Shemu'el said in the name of Rabbi Zeira, '...Whoever receives the face of his teacher, it is as if he receives the face of *Shekhinah*.'...Rabbi Yishma'el taught...'One who receives the face of his friend, it is as if he receives the face of *Shekhinah*.'" Cf. Genesis 33:10; *Tanḥuma, Ki Tissa* 27; *Shir ha-Shirim Rabbah* on 2:5.

See *Zohar* 1:9a, 94b, 115b (*MhN*); 2:5a (*MhN*), 50a, 94b, 198a; 3:6b, 148a, 298a; *ZḤ* 11c, 25b (both *MhN*).

On *Shekhinah* as a rose, see *Zohar* 1:1a, 137a; 3:37b–38a, 107a, 162a, 233b, 286b.

The narrative about Rabbi Abba and the

Rabbi Abba, "Sit, my son, sit."

They sat down. Rabbi Abba smelled the rose. He said, "Surely the world is sustained only by fragrance, for we see that the soul is sustained only by fragrance—for this reason the myrtle at Sabbath's departure."[204]

"He opened, saying, "*My beloved is mine and I am his;* הרועה בשושנים (*ha-ro'eh ba-shoshannim*), *he shepherds with roses* (Song of Songs 2:16). Who made me *my beloved's and my beloved mine* (ibid. 6:3)? Because He conducts His world with roses. Just as the rose has a fragrance and is red, and when distilled turns white yet its fragrance never departs, so the blessed Holy One conducts His world in this way—for were it not so, the sinner could not endure. Sin is called red, as is said: *Be your sins like crimson, they can turn* [20b] *snow-white* (Isaiah 1:18). He brings his offering to the fire, which is red; sprinkles blood around the altar, which is red; the attribute of judgment is red! The fragrance is distilled and the smoke ascends, entirely white. Then red is transformed into white; the attribute of judgment transformed into the attribute of compassion.[205]



rose appears in a different version in V5 (folios 331–32) and P2 (folio 234) under the title *Matnitin*. The narrative frame is basically the same; the ensuing homily, though related, differs. On the variant text, and on the narrative more generally, see Meroz, "Zoharic Narratives," 38–47, 59–63.

204. **the soul is sustained only by fragrance...** See BT *Berakhot* 43b in the name of Rav, "What is it that gives enjoyment to the soul and not the body? You must say that this is fragrance."

On inhaling the fragrance of spices (or specifically myrtle) as Sabbath departs in order to sustain the soul, which is lamenting the departure of an additional Sabbath soul (see BT *Beitsah* 16a, *ZḤ* 17a (*MhN*)), see Simḥah ben Samuel, *Maḥazor Vitri*, 117; Eleazar of Worms, *Peirushei Siddur ha-Tefillah la-Roqeaḥ*, 2:590–91; Zedekiah Anav, *Shibbolei ha-Leqet*, 130, p. 435; *Tosafot, Beitsah* 33b, s.v. *ki haveinan*; *Zohar* 2:208b–209a; 3:35a–b; Moses de León, *Sefer ha-Rimmon*, 130; Tishby, *Wisdom of the Zohar*, 3:1237; Ginsburg, *The Sabbath in the Classical Kabbalah*, 259–67.

On the myrtle, see also *Zohar* 1:17b; *ZḤ* 64d (*ShS*); Lauterbach, "The Origin and Development of Two Sabbath Ceremonies"; Ta-Shma, *Ha-Nigleh she-ba-Nistar*, 125, n. 84; Hallamish, *Ha-Qabbalah*, 177–78, 323.

On the world's being sustained by fragrance, see *Zohar* 3:35b and Rabbi Yitsḥak's homily below.

205. **red is transformed into white... judgment... into... compassion** God conducts His world like the rose. Just as the rose turns white when heated to distill its fragrant oils, so through sacrifice and repentance a person's sins are turned white. It is by virtue of this divine quality that the human–divine bond remains intact, for the world cannot endure strict divine judgment. The passage from judgment to compassion is reflected in the sacrifice itself—as red (the flesh and blood) becomes white (ashes and smoke), as the fragrant aroma is released.

"Distilled" renders מוצקין (*motseqin*), literally, "to pour out." See *Nitsotsei Zohar* n. 9, ad loc., citing Luria—who suggests that צומקין (*tsomeqin*), "to dry, to heat," is intended. Aside from V16 and N47, all the manuscripts and printed editions read *motseqin*. See Meroz, "Zoharic Narratives," 41.

See *ZḤ* 20a (*MhN*) for a different interpretation of how God conducts the world in accordance with roses.

"Come and see: The attribute of judgment has need of the sacrifice's aroma solely on account of the redness. This corresponds with what Rabbi Yehudah said: 'What is the significance of *and gashed themselves according to their practice [with knives and spears] until the blood streamed over them* (1 Kings 18:28)? Well, they knew that they could not attain what they desired from the attribute of judgment save through redness.'"[206]

Rabbi Yitsḥak said, "Furthermore, red and white are always offered [together], and scent ascends from them both. Just as the rose is red-and-white, so the aroma of the offering; and the offering itself is from red and white. Come and see: from the fragrance of incense, some of whose ingredients are red and some of which are white—for example, לבונה (*levonah*), frankincense, which is לבן (*lavan*), white; and wild myrrh, which is red—the fragrance ascends from the red and the white. Therefore: He conducts His world with roses that are red-and-white, and it is written: *to offer Me fat and blood* (Ezekiel 44:15).[207]



"Correspondingly, a person offers his fat and his blood and gains atonement—one red, one white. Just as the rose that is red-and-white is distilled—turning entirely white solely through fire—so with the offering: the aroma is distilled, turning entirely white solely through fire. And now, one who sits and fasts, offering his fat and his blood, heats up, turning entirely white, solely through fire. As Rabbi Yehudah said: 'By means of his fast, his limbs weaken and fire prevails upon him. At that time he must offer his fat and his blood in that fire, and he is called "an altar of atonement."'"[208]

206. **attribute of judgment save through redness** The verse from Kings describes the ritual behavior of the prophets of Baal in their duel with Elijah. In covering their white skin with red blood they sought to transform white/compassion into red/judgment—the very opposite of the righteous, who turn red into white. Hence the attribute of judgment is aroused by redness.

207. **red and white are always offered...** Rabbi Yitsḥak extends Rabbi Abba's teaching. The red-and-white rose signifies not only the transformation of judgment into compassion, but more generally the necessary harmony between these two polarities for the governance of the world. The sacrifices of the Temple, containing red and white (flesh-and-blood and fat, respectively), reflect—and worked to maintain—this harmony.

On frankincense and myrrh as white and red, respectively, see Tishby, *Wisdom of the Zohar*, 1:80–81, who notes a parallel with Ezra ben Solomon of Gerona, *Peirush le-Shir ha-Shirim*, in *Kitvei Ramban* 2:493; Brody, *Commentary on the Song of Songs*, 67.

On the red-and-white rose, see *Zohar* 1:1a. *Rosa gallica versicolor* (also known as *Rosa mundi*), one of the oldest of the striped roses, has crimson flowers splashed on a white background. The striping varies, and occasionally flowers revert to the solid pink of their parent, *Rosa gallica*. The parent was introduced to Europe in the twelfth or thirteenth century by Crusaders returning from Palestine.

208. **Correspondingly, a person offers his fat and his blood...** As the rose and the offering, which are red and white, are transformed entirely into white by virtue of

"This accords with Rabbi El'azar: When he would sit and fast, he would pray—saying, 'It is revealed and known before You, O *YHVH*, My God and God of my fathers, that I have offered before You my fat and my blood, and I have broiled them in the heat of my body's frailty. May it be Your will before You that the scent ascending from my mouth at this time be like the scent of the offering rising from the altar-fire, and may You look favorably upon me.' So we find that during a fast a person offers fat and blood, fragrance and fire, and he is an altar of atonement. Therefore they instituted prayer in place of sacrifice, provided he is attuned to what we have said."[209]

Rabbi Yitsḥak said, "Henceforth—it is written—*everything that can tolerate fire you shall pass through fire, and it will be clean* (Numbers 31:23)."[210]

Rabbi Yose said, "When the Temple stood, a person offered his offering in this manner and gained atonement. Now, a person's prayer atones for him in place of the offering, in the same way."[211]

Alternatively, *My beloved is mine and I am his;* הרועה (*ha-ro'eh*), *he guides, with roses* (Song of Songs 2:16). Just as thorns are found among roses, so the



fire, so during a fast a person offers his red blood and white fat, the fast's heat (fever) turning him pale. The body then becomes a vehicle for atonement, taking the place of the sacrificial rites. See below.

See Moses de León, *Sefer ha-Rimmon*, 127–28; idem, *Mishkan ha-Edut*, 32a; *Zohar* 2:119b (*RM*); *ZḤ* 80a (*MhN*, *Rut*).

209. **When he would sit and fast, he would pray—saying...** See BT *Berakhot* 17a: "When Rav Sheshet would sit and fast, upon concluding his prayer he would say as follows: Master of Worlds! It is known before You that in the time when the Temple stood, if a man sinned he would bring a sacrifice; and though all that was offered of it was its fat and blood, he gained atonement. Now I have sat in a fast, and my fat and blood have diminished. May it be Your will before You that my fat and blood, which have been diminished, be reckoned as if I had offered them before You on the altar—and look favorably upon me."

On the foul breath of a fast as ascending on high, see *Bereshit Rabbah* 42:1; *Pirqei de-Rabbi Eli'ezer* 1 about Rabbi Eli'ezer.

On prayers in place of sacrifice, see BT *Berakhot* 26b: "Rabbi Yehoshu'a son of Levi said, 'The prayers were instituted corresponding to the daily offerings.'" According to Rabbi Yitsḥak, this substitution is only valid provided the person praying is aware of the intention of turning judgment into compassion.

210. ***everything that can tolerate fire...*** This verse serves as a conclusion to the preceding. Fire cleanses and atones in all cases. See *Or Yaqar*, who includes in this statement the fire of any great effort in the service of God that—like a fast—diminishes a person's fat and blood.

211. **When the Temple stood...** Just as offerings in the Temple were offered comprising red and white, and with the intent of turning red into white (judgment into compassion), prayer now functions in the same way.

See *Bemidbar Rabbah* 18:21: "Israel said, 'When the Temple stood, we used to burn fat and portions of sacrifices—and gain atonement. Now [we can only offer] our own fat and blood and souls! May it be Your will before You that these shall be our atonement.'"

blessed Holy One conducts His world with the righteous and the wicked. Just as with roses—were it not for the thorns, there would be no roses—so were it not for the wicked, there would be no righteous. As Rabbi Yehudah said: "How are the righteous recognized? By means of the wicked; for were it not for the wicked, the righteous could not be discerned."[212]

Alternatively, הרועה בשושנים (*Ha-ro'eh ba-shoshannim*), *He guides with roses*—He conducts His world בשש שנים (*be-shesh shanim*), with six years; and the seventh—*a Sabbath unto YHVH*.[213]

Alternatively, בשושנים (*Ba-shoshannim*), *with roses*—through those ששונים (*she-shonim*), who study, Torah.[214]

*Moses was shepherding the flock of Jethro his father-in-law, priest of Midian* (Exodus 3:1).

Rabbi Yehudah opened, saying, "*A Psalm of David. YHVH is my shepherd, I shall not lack* (Psalms 23:1)—namely *YHVH* my guide. Just as the shepherd guides the flock, leading them to good and fertile pasture, to a

place of flowing streams, smoothing their way in righteousness and justice, so the blessed Holy One, as is written: *In grass meadows He makes me lie down, by quiet waters guides me. He restores my life* (ibid., 2–3)."[215]

Rabbi Yose said, "It is the way of the shepherd to guide his flock in justice, to distance them from theft, to lead them in righteousness—staff in hand—that they will not stray right or left. So the blessed Holy One shepherds Israel, leading them in righteousness every moment—staff in hand—that they will not stray right or left."

Alternatively, *Moses was shepherding* (Exodus 3:1). Rabbi Yose said, "You should know that whenever the shepherd directs his flock wisely, he is ready

212. **were it not for the wicked...** Cf. *Zohar* 2:184a, 187a; 3:47b.

213. **בשש שנים (*be-shesh shanim*), with six years...** See Leviticus 25:3–4: *Six years you shall sow your fields; and six years you shall prune your vineyard and gather in its yield. In the seventh year, there shall be an absolute Sabbath for the land, a Sabbath unto YHVH.*

According to *Or Yaqar*, "six years" refers to the six central *sefirot*, and "the seventh" year to *Malkhut*. More likely, the *Zohar* may be alluding to the rabbinic idea that the world will endure for six thousand years, followed by a cosmic Sabbath. See BT *Sanhedrin* 97a: "Rav Kattina said, 'The world will exist for six thousand years, and for one thousand lie desolate, as is said: *YHVH alone will be exalted on that day* (Isaiah 2:11).'"

In M *Tamid* 7:4, the Messianic era is described as "the day that is entirely Sabbath."

See Tishby, *Wisdom of the Zohar*, 1:80; Ezra ben Solomon of Gerona, *Peirush le-Shir ha-Shirim*, in *Kitvei Ramban* 2:492; Brody, *Commentary on the Song of Songs*, 64.

214. **ששונים (*she-shonim*), who study, Torah...** God nourishes the world by virtue of those who study Torah. On the wordplay of *shoshannim* and *she-shonim*, see BT *Shabbat* 30b; *ZḤ* 47d.

215. ***YHVH is my shepherd...*** See *Zohar* 2:170a.

to accept the yoke of the kingdom of heaven. If the shepherd is a fool, to him is applied the verse *there is more hope for a dullard than him* (Proverbs 26:12)."[216]

Rabbi Yehudah said, "Moses was wise and expert in guiding his flock. Come and see—from David, as is said: *he is tending the flock* (1 Samuel 16:11)—to teach you that David [21a] was very wise and tended his flock duly and lawfully; therefore the blessed Holy One appointed him king over all of Israel."[217]

Why sheep and not cattle?

Rabbi Yehudah said, "Israel are called 'flock,' as is said: *You, My flock, flock of My pasture* (Ezekiel 34:31), and it is written: *as the holy flock, as the flock of Jerusalem* (ibid. 36:38)."

Just as by virtue of the sheep [offered] upon the altar [a person] acquires the life of the world to come, so one who leads Israel duly and lawfully acquires the life of the world to come on their account. Furthermore, regarding one who tends sheep: when sheep give birth, the shepherd carries the lambs in his lap, so that they will not tire or weary, leading them after their mothers, treating them compassionately; so one who leads Israel must guide them compassionately, not cruelly. Accordingly, Moses said: *that You should say to Me 'Bear them in your lap . . .'* (Numbers 11:12). Just as one who tends sheep well saves the sheep from foxes and lions, so one who guides Israel well saves them from the nations,



216. **whenever the shepherd directs his flock wisely...** Shepherding is the paradigm for leadership; thus Israel's leaders were shepherds, where their character was tested. See next note.

217. **Come and see—from David...** According to *Shemot Rabbah* 2:2, both David and Moses were tested as leaders by God through sheep: "*YHVH scrutinizes the righteous* (Psalms 11:5). By what does He scrutinize him? By tending flocks. He tested David through sheep and found him to be a good shepherd, as is said: *He chose David His servant and took him from the sheepfolds* (ibid. 78:70). What is the significance of ממכלאת צאן (*mi-mikhle'ot tson*), *from the sheepfolds*? It is like ויכלא הגשם (*va-yikkale ha-geshem*), *the rain was held back* (Genesis 8:2). Because he used to hold back the bigger sheep from going out before the smaller ones, and he would bring the smaller ones out first so that they should graze upon the tender grass, and afterward he would bring out the old sheep to feed from the ordinary grass, and lastly, he would bring out the young sheep to eat the tougher grass. The blessed Holy One said, 'He who knows how to look after sheep, each in accordance with its needs, shall come and tend My people,' as is written: *He brought him forth from minding the nursing ewes to tend His people Jacob* (Psalms 78:71). Moses too was tested by the blessed Holy One solely through sheep. Our Rabbis said that when Moses our teacher, peace be upon him, was tending the flock of Jethro in the wilderness, a little kid escaped from him. He ran after it, until it reached a shady place. When it reached the shady place, it came upon a pool of water and the kid stopped to drink. When Moses approached it, he said, 'I did not know that you ran away because of thirst; you must be weary.' He placed the kid on his shoulder and walked away. The blessed Holy One said, 'Because you have compassion in leading the flock of flesh and blood, by your life, you will tend My flock Israel.' Hence: *Moses was shepherding the flock.*" See also *Shemot Rabbah* 2:3.

from judgment below and from judgment above, and leads them to the life of the world to come. So was Moses a faithful shepherd, and the blessed Holy One saw that he was worthy to shepherd Israel, in exactly the same way he shepherded the flock—the rams fittingly, and the females fittingly.[218]

Accordingly, it is written: *Moses was shepherding the flock of Jethro his father-in-law* (Exodus 3:1)—not his own. As Rabbi Yose said: "Now, would he who *gave Zipporah his daughter to Moses* (ibid. 2:21) not have given him sheep and cattle?! Wasn't Jethro wealthy?! Nevertheless, Moses did not shepherd his own flock, that it would not be said that it was because his own flock was with him that he tended them well. That is why it is written *the flock of Jethro his father-in-law*, and not his own."

*Priest of Midian* (Exodus 3:1). Rabbi Tanḥum says, "Even though he was an idolator, because he had treated him kindly he tended his flock duly and lawfully—in bountiful, lush, and fertile pasture."[219]

*He drove the flock behind the wilderness* (ibid.). Rabbi Yose says, "From the day that Moses was born, the holy spirit didn't budge from him. He saw through the holy spirit that that wilderness was poised to receive the yoke of the kingdom of heaven upon it. What did he do? He drove the flock *behind the wilderness*."[220]



218. **one who tends sheep...** The *Zohar* (perhaps Rabbi Yehudah) presents more comparisons between the shepherd and leader, culminating in Moses, the Faithful Shepherd.

On the leader's acquiring the world to come based on his leadership of the flock, cf. BT *Sanhedrin* 92a in the name of Rabbi El'azar: "Every leader who leads the community with mildness will be privileged to lead them in the world to come, as is written: *He who loves them will lead them; he will guide them to springs of water* (Isaiah 49:10)."

The full verse from Numbers reads: *Did I conceive all this people, did I give birth to them, that You should say to me, 'Bear them in your lap, as the guardian bears the infant,' to the land that You swore to their fathers.*

On Moses as Faithful Shepherd, see *Mekhilta, Beshallaḥ* 6; *Sifrei Zuta* 27; *Eikhah Rabbah, Petiḥta* 24; *Ester Rabbah* 7:13; *Rut Rabbah, Petiḥta* 5.

On leading the males and females fittingly, see Exodus 19:3: *Thus shall you say to the house of Jacob, and tell to the children* [or: *sons*] *of Israel.* According to the midrashic reading of the verse, Moses employed a gentle speaking tone ("saying") for the women, and a harsher tone ("telling") for the men. See *Mekhilta, Baḥodesh* 2; *Shemot Rabbah* 28:2; *Leqaḥ Tov*, *Sekhel Tov*, and *Midrash Aggadah* on Exodus 19:3; Rashi on Exodus 19:3.

219. **Even though he was an idolator...** Rabbi Tanḥum explains why the Torah restates Jethro's religious affiliation, which had already been noted at Exodus 2:16.

Jethro showed Moses kindness by opening his home to him when he fled Egypt, and by giving him his daughter as wife. See Exodus 2:16–22.

220. **From the day that Moses was born...** According to BT *Sotah* 12a and *Shemot Rabbah* 1:20, radiance surrounded the infant Moses. See *Zohar* 1:120b; 2:11b, 12a, 19a (*MhN*). See also BT *Shabbat* 87a; *Shemot Rabbah* 2:6; Moses Maimonides, *Mishneh Torah, Hilkhot Yesodei ha-Torah* 7:6.

On Moses sensing the holiness of the wilderness, see *Shemot Rabbah* 2:4; *Sekhel Tov* (Buber) 3:1.

Rabbi Yitsḥak said, "*Behind the wilderness*—in no way into the wilderness, for he did not want them to enter within. Rather, he kept them afar, *behind the wilderness. And he came to the mountain of God, to Horeb* (ibid.)—by himself."[221]

Rabbi Yehudah said, "Stone that attracts iron—when it comes into proximity, it leaps toward it. Similarly, Moses and Mount Sinai—when they saw one another, he leaped toward it, as is written: *and came to the mountain of God, to Horeb*."[222]

Rabbi Abba said, "They were designated for one another since the six days of creation. That day, the mountain quaked before Moses; but as soon as it saw that he entered within and leaped toward it, the mountain stood still—teaching that they delighted with one another."

Rabbi Yose said, "Moses knew that that mountain was the mountain of God, as is written: *and came to the mountain of God*. As we have learned: What did Moses see on that mountain? He saw birds flying, wings spread, yet not entering within."

Rabbi Yitsḥak said, "He saw birds flying and soaring away from there, falling at Moses' feet. Immediately he perceived the matter, stationed the flock behind the wilderness, and entered alone."[223]



*The angel of YHVH appeared to him in a flame of fire from within a bush* (Exodus 3:2).

Rabbi Tanḥum said, "It was the hour of *Minḥah*, when the attribute of judgment prevails."[224]

Rabbi Yoḥanan said, "But it is written *By day YHVH directs* חסדו (*ḥasdo*), *His love* (Psalms 42:9)—the attribute of חסד (*ḥesed*), love, is specified, not the attribute of judgment!"[225]

221. ***Behind the wilderness...*** Out of respect for its sanctity. See *Tanḥuma, Shemot* 14. Cf. *Shemot Rabbah* 2:3.

222. **Stone that attracts iron...** Moses was drawn to the holy mountain like metal to a magnet. See *Or Yaqar*, ad loc.: "inevitably, on account of the love of the similar."

223. **falling at Moses' feet...** The first sign is ambiguous: perhaps the birds were frightened of something. The second clarifies that Moses is to enter, for the birds land right at his feet.

On birds serving as a sign, cf. BT *Bava Metsi'a* 86a.

224. ***Minḥah*, when the attribute of judgment prevails** *Minḥah* (literally "offering") is the second of the three daily prayers, recited between the afternoon and evening. According to Kabbalah it is associated with judgment. On this and more generally on the morning's association with love and the evening's with judgment, see *Zohar* 1:132b, 182b, 230a; 2:36b, 63a, 156a; 3:64b; Moses de León, *Sefer ha-Rimmon*, 67, 87.

225. ***By day YHVH directs* חסדו (*ḥasdo*), *His love...*** Rabbi Yoḥanan wonders how *Minḥah* can be associated with judgment, for the verse from Psalms implies that *Ḥesed* prevails throughout the day.

Rabbi Yitsḥak said, "From when the light emerges until it inclines to set is called 'day'—attribute of love. From when it inclines to set is called 'evening'—attribute of judgment. This is the meaning of *God called the light Day* (Genesis 1:5)."[226]

Rabbi Yoḥanan said, "The time of *Minḥah* is from six hours onward."[227]

As it has been taught: Rabbi Yitsḥak says, "What is the significance of the verse *At twilight you shall eat meat, and in the morning you shall have your fill of bread* (Exodus 16:12)? *At twilight*, which is the hour [21b] of judgment, *you shall eat meat*; and it is written: *The meat was still between their teeth* [...] *when YHVH's wrath flared against the people* (Numbers 11:33), for royal judgment prevails at twilight. *And in the morning you shall have your fill of bread*—for that hour is called חסד (*ḥesed*), love, and it is written: *God's* חסד (*ḥesed*), *love, endures all day* (Psalms 52:3); and it is written: *God called the light Day* (Genesis 1:5)—from the morning."[228]



Rabbi Tanḥum said, "This red, that white. Red at twilight, as is written: *At twilight you shall eat meat*; white in the morning, as is written: *and in the morning you shall have your fill of bread.*"[229]

Rabbi Yitsḥak said, "It is written: *and the whole congregation of the community of Israel shall slaughter it at twilight* (Exodus 12:6)—for it is the time for executing judgment."[230]

Rabbi Yehudah said, "We learn from the two daily lamb offerings—one offered corresponding to the attribute of love, the other corresponding to the attribute of judgment."[231]

226. **until it inclines to set . . .** Rabbi Yitsḥak resolves Rabbi Yoḥanan's query. The first half of the day is associated with *Ḥesed*, whereas the afternoon is associated with *Din*, "judgment." See *Zohar* 1:132b.

227. **The time of *Minḥah* . . .** See BT *Berakhot* 26b; *ZḤ* 17d (*MhN*).

228. **royal judgment . . .** דינא דמלכותא (*Dina de-Malkhuta*), "Judgment of the Kingdom," deriving from the saying of Shemu'el (BT *Nedarim* 28a): דינא דמלכותא דינא (*dina de-malkhuta dina*), "the law of the kingdom is the law." See *Zohar* 1:92b, 226b; 3:11b.

The verse from Exodus describes the quail and the manna provided by God for the Israelites in the desert.

On morning as associated with the quality of *ḥesed*, "love," see *Zohar* 1:182b, 203a–b, 247b; 2:63a, 81a; 3:63a, 64b, 204a–b, 233a, 242a; see also *ZḤ* 8a (*MhN*); cf. *Mekhilta*, *Beshallaḥ* 5.

229. **This red, that white . . .** Rabbi Tanḥum elaborates the symbolic pairings: evening/meat/red/judgment, and morning/bread/white/love.

230. ***slaughter it at twilight* . . .** The verse describes the paschal sacrifice offered on the eve of the Israelites' departure from Egypt and the final judgment rendered upon the Egyptians.

231. **from the two daily lamb offerings . . .** The correlation in question—of morning and love, and of afternoon (twilight) and judgment—is also apparent from the daily lamb offerings; the former to arouse love, the latter to assuage judgment.

Rabbi Yehudah also said, "Why is it written *One lamb you shall offer in the morning* [*and the second lamb you shall offer at twilight*] (Numbers 28:4), and not *The first lamb*? Well, את הכבש האחד (*Et ha-keves ha-eḥad*), *One lamb*—מיוחד (*meyuḥad*), unique, corresponding to the attribute of love; for in every instance 'that it was good' is not predicated of the second."[232]

Rabbi Tanḥum said, "Accordingly, Isaac instituted the *Minḥah* prayer corresponding to the attribute of judgment."[233]

Rabbi Yitsḥak said, "From here: *Woe to us, for the day is fading, shadows of evening spread!* (Jeremiah 6:4). *For the day is fading*—the attribute of love; *shadows of evening spread*—the attribute of judgment has already prevailed. Abraham instituted the *Shaḥarit* prayer corresponding to the attribute of love."[234]

Our Rabbis have taught: Why, when Moses entered Mount Sinai, was He revealed to him in a flame of fire—signifying judgment?[235]

Rabbi Ya'akov said, "Then, the hour was decisive."[236]

Rabbi Yose said, "All are rooted in a single stock. It is written: *and he came to the mountain of God, to Horeb* (Exodus 3:1); and it is written: *At Horeb you infu-*



232. **'that it was good' is not predicated of the second** The correlation between the morning and afternoon lambs with love and judgment, respectively, is apparent from the use of the word *eḥad*, "one" (rather than "first"), as well as from the fact that according to rabbinic texts, "the second" is associated with conflict and judgment.

In the biblical account of Creation, the statement *God saw that it was good* (or a variant) is included in the description of each of the six days—except for the second. See *Bereshit Rabbah* 4:6: "Why is 'that it was good' not written concerning the second day? Rabbi Yoḥanan said..., 'Because on that day, Hell was created....' Rabbi Ḥanina said, 'Because on that day, conflict was created: *that it may separate water from water.*' (Genesis 1:6)... Rabbi Shemu'el son of Naḥman said, 'Because the work of the water was not completed. Therefore 'that it was good' is written twice on the third day: once for the work of the water [see Genesis 1:9–10] and once for the work of the [third] day [ibid. 11].'" See BT *Pesaḥim* 54a; *Pirqei de-Rabbi Eli'ezer* 4; *Zohar* 1:18a, 33a, 46a; 2:149b; *ZḤ* 9a (*MhN*).

On the one lamb, see BT *Megillah* 28a; *Yoma* 34b, 70b.

233. **Isaac instituted the *Minḥah* prayer...** Isaac's attribute is judgment—so he appropriately instituted the afternoon prayer, when this attribute prevails. See BT *Berakhot* 26b: "Rabbi Yose son of Rabbi Ḥanina said, 'The patriarchs instituted the prayers.'... Abraham instituted the morning prayer;... Isaac, the afternoon prayer;... Jacob, the evening prayer."

234. ***day is fading, shadows of evening spread...*** The verse from Jeremiah also illustrates the principle that when the light of day begins to fade (i.e., after noon), judgment dominates love. See *Zohar* 1:132b, 230a; 3:64b; Moses de León, *Sefer ha-Rimmon*, 67.

On Abraham (whose attribute is love) as instituting the morning prayer, see previous note.

235. **Why... in a flame of fire—signifying judgment?** God informed Moses that He was about to deliver His people from bondage, so why the symbol of judgment, rather than love?

236. **the hour was decisive** It was *Minḥah* time, the time when judgment prevails.

*riated* YHVH [*and* YHVH *was incensed with you enough to destroy you*] (Deuteronomy 9:8); and it is written: *The angel of* YHVH *appeared to him in a flame of fire from within a bush* (Exodus 3:2)—for they were destined to be like the bush, like that which is written: *thorns cut down that are set on fire* (Isaiah 33:12)."[237]

Rabbi Yehudah said, "From here we have learned of the Omnipresent's compassion for the wicked, as is written: *and look, the bush was blazing in fire* (Exodus 3:2)—to execute judgment upon the wicked; *yet the bush was not consumed* (ibid.)—to bring annihilation upon them. *Blazing in fire*—certainly alluding to the fire of Hell; but, *the bush was not consumed*—that they will be annihilated."[238]

Alternatively, *The angel of* YHVH *appeared to him in a flame of fire.* Why to Moses in a flame of fire, but not to the other prophets?

Rabbi Yehudah said, "Moses was not like other prophets! As we have learned: One who comes close to fire is burned. Moses came close to fire yet was not burned, as is written: *and Moses approached the thick cloud where* Elohim *was*



(ibid. 20:18), and it is written: *The angel of* YHVH *appeared to him in a flame of fire from within a bush.*"[239]

Rabbi Abba said, "One should ponder Moses in light of supernal wisdom. It is written: [*She named him* משה (*Mosheh*), *Moses, saying,*] '*For from the water* משיתהו (*meshitihu*), *I drew him out*' (ibid. 2:10). One who has been drawn from water does not fear fire! As it has been taught: Rabbi Yehudah said, 'From the site that Moses was hewn, no other human was hewn.'"[240]

237. **All are rooted in a single stock...** Horeb, the flame, and the bush all point to the attribute of judgment. At Horeb the people sinned with the golden calf and faced God's judgment: *thorns cut down that are set on fire.*

Cf. *Shemot Rabbah* 2:4, where Horeb is associated with חרב (*ḥerev*), "sword," and חרב (*ḥarov*), "destruction."

238. ***the bush was not consumed...*** Although the flame signifies God's judgment upon the wicked, the fact that the bush was not consumed points to His compassion. God does not seek the wicked's annihilation but their repentance and their souls' purification.

239. **Moses was not like other prophets!...** Unlike the other prophets of Israel, Moses could withstand the fire of *Shekhinah*, the angel of YHVH.

See BT *Yevamot* 49b: "All the prophets gazed through an opaque glass, while Moses our teacher gazed through a translucent glass." See also *Vayiqra Rabbah* 1:14.

See BT *Ketubbot* 111b: "Is it possible to cleave to *Shekhinah*? Is it not written: *For* YHVH *your God is a consuming fire* (Deuteronomy 4:24)?"

On *the angel of* YHVH as a name of *Shekhinah*, see *Zohar* 1:61a, 113a–b, 120b, 166a, 230a; 3:187a. Cf. *Mekhilta, Shirta* 3; *Pirqei de-Rabbi Eli'ezer* 40; *Shemot Rabbah* 2:5; Naḥmanides on Exodus 3:2.

According to Deuteronomy 4:11, the clouds surrounding Mount Sinai are associated with flames: *The mountain was ablaze with flames to the heart of heaven, dark with densest clouds.*

240. **One should ponder Moses in light of supernal wisdom...** In accordance with the mysteries of the *sefirot*. According to Rabbi Abba, the water from which Moses

Rabbi Yoḥanan said, "He was arrayed in ten rungs, as is written: *He is trusted throughout My house* (Numbers 12:7), not just a loyal member of My household! Happy is the share of the human being whose Master testifies about him so!"[241]

Rav Dimi said, "But it is written *Never again did there arise in Israel a prophet like Moses* (Deuteronomy 34:10), about which Rabbi Yehoshu'a son of Levi said, 'In Israel none did arise—but among the nations of the world, one did. Who was that? Balaam.'"[242]

He replied, "Surely you raise a good point!"

He was silent.

When Rabbi Shim'on son of Yoḥai arrived, they asked him about this matter. He opened, saying, "Foul resin mixed with fine balsam? Heaven forbid! Rather, certainly it is as follows: Among the nations of the world one did arise. Who was that? Balaam. Moses' actions on high; Balaam's down low. Moses wielded the holy crown of the supernal King, above; Balaam wielded the lower crowns, unholy, below. In precisely this vein it is written: [*the Israelites*] *slew Balaam son of Be'or, the sorcerer, with the sword* (Joshua 13:22). Should you imagine he was any higher, go and ask his ass!"[243]



was drawn (hence his name) is in fact a symbol of *Ḥesed*, flowing divine love. Hailing from water, he can therefore confront fire—namely *Gevurah*, divine judgment. According to the main body of the *Zohar*, Moses is associated with *Tif'eret*—the harmony of *Ḥesed* and *Gevurah*—which he attained.

Throughout *MhN* on the Torah, the soul is described as hailing from the Throne of Glory, *Shekhinah* (see *Zohar* 1:113a, 125b, 126b; *ZḤ* 10a–d, 20b, 22a, 24a, 26a (all *MhN*)). Moses, however, has a higher source, *Ḥesed*. Cf. *Or Yaqar*, who suggests *Ḥokhmah*. See *Zohar* 1:22a; 2:53b–54a.

241. **arrayed in ten rungs...** Connected to all ten *sefirot*. See *Sifrei*, Numbers, 68: "Happy is the mortal human who is given such a promise: anytime he wanted to, he could converse with Him." See also BT *Berakhot* 32a; cf. *Mekhilta*, *Baḥodesh* 9.

On Numbers 12:7, see *Zohar* 1:76a.

242. **Who was that? Balaam** Balaam was the soothsayer from Aram invited by King Balak of Moab to curse the people of Israel before they entered the land of Israel (see Numbers 22–24). In midrashic literature, he is compared to Moses; and so Rav Dimi wonders how Moses' prophecy is distinguished.

See *Sifrei*, Deuteronomy 357: "*Never again did there arise in Israel a prophet like Moses*—In Israel, none arose; but among the nations of the world, one did! Who is this? Balaam son of Beor." See *Bemidbar Rabbah* 14:20; *Zohar* 1:10a; 3:193b; *ZḤ* 47c. See also *Tanḥuma, Balaq* 1; *Bemidbar Rabbah* 20:1; *Vayiqra Rabbah* 1:13; *Seder Eliyyahu Zuta* 10.

243. **Foul resin mixed with fine balsam?...** Whereas Rabbi Yoḥanan could not answer Rav Dimi's query, Rabbi Shim'on articulates the vast gulf separating Moses and Balaam. Indeed, such is the gulf between them that he is astonished by the very comparison ("Heaven forbid!"). As Balaam is foul resin, Moses is fine balsam: while both are prophets, Moses' prophecy is holy and high, pertaining to the *sefirot*, whereas Balaam's prophecy pertains to sorcery, impurity, and the demonic.

"Foul resin" renders קוטיפא דקרנטי (*qotifa de-qarnetei*). *Qotifa* is a variation on *qetaf*, the resin from the balsam tree. *Qarnetei* is a neologism whose meaning is unknown. Cf. *Zohar* 2:175b and Spanish *carantona*, meaning "ugly, false face." See Matt, *Zohar: The Book*

Rabbi Yose came and kissed his hands. He said, "The coveting in my heart has disappeared, for herein is implied: there is high and low, right and left, compassion and judgment, Israel and the nations of the world. Israel wields high and holy crowns; the nations of the world nethermost crowns, unholy; these on the right, those on the left. In every aspect high prophets and low prophets, holy prophets and unholy prophets differ!"[244]

Rabbi Yehudah said, "As Moses was [22a] distinct from all prophets in holy prophecy on high, so Balaam was distinct from other prophets and sorcerers in unholy prophecy below. From every aspect Moses was high, Balaam low, countless levels separating between them!"[245]

Rabbi Yoḥanan said in the name of Rabbi Yitsḥak, "Moses was worried, thinking, 'Perhaps, heaven forbid, Israel might perish from the harsh bondage!' as is written: *and he saw their burdens* (Exodus 2:11). Therefore: *The angel of YHVH appeared to him in a flame of fire . . . ; and he saw, and look, the bush was blazing in fire . . .* (ibid. 3:2), as if to say, they are enslaved with harsh bondage, but *the bush was not consumed.*"[246] [*ZḤ* 59a]



*of Enlightenment*, 239. For various interpretations, see *Or Yaqar*, *Or ha-Ḥammah*, *Derekh Emet*, *Matoq mi-Devash*; *Bei'ur ha-Millim ha-Zarot*, 191.

Balsam—thirteen rivers of it—awaits the righteous in the world to come (JT *Avodah Zarah* 3:1, 42c; BT *Ta'anit* 25a; *Bereshit Rabbah* 62:2). In the *Zohar*, these rivers are the flow of emanation from *Binah*. Moses, who is arrayed in all the *sefirot*, bathes in them.

See M *Avot* 1:13 "[Hillel] said, 'One who makes [theurgic] use of the crown [i.e., the name YHVH] has no share in the world to come.'"

On Balaam and his ass, see Numbers 22:21–35, recounting how his ass sees the angel of YHVH, yet the great wizard sees nothing; and BT *Sanhedrin* 105a–b, according to which Balaam attained his prophecy by engaging in intercourse with his ass; see also *Zohar* 1:125b; 3:207a; *ZḤ* 47c.

See *Zohar* 1:125b–126a; 2:69a–b; 3:193b–194a, 209b; Moses de León, *Sheqel ha-Qodesh* 14–15 (18); idem, *She'elot u-Tshuvot*, 74–75.

244. **The coveting in my heart has disappeared . . .** חמידא דלבאי נפק לבר (*Ḥamida de-libba'i nefaq le-var*). The Aramaic root *ḥmd* means "to desire, covet." The sentence may mean: "The yearning in my heart [to understand the midrash about Moses and Balaam] has been satisfied." The translation here conveys the role played by Kabbalah in Spain: reassuring the Jews that although the Christians were politically, economically, and socially in power, the Jews remained God's chosen people and were ultimately higher. Rabbi Shim'on's interpretation has just this effect on Rabbi Yose, and he thanks the master for helping him see the true state of affairs. (As the archetype of the non-Jewish prophet, Balaam may stand for Jesus: touted as the successor of Moses, but unmasked here as a black magic sorcerer.) See *Zohar* 3:119a–b; Matt, *Zohar: The Book of Enlightenment*, 240.

245. **Moses was distinct from all prophets in holy prophecy on high . . .** See BT *Yevamot* 49b; *Vayiqra Rabbah* 1:14; Moses Maimonides, *Guide of the Perplexed* 2:36, 45; idem, *Mishneh Torah*, *Hilkhot Yesodei ha-Torah* 7:6; *Zohar* 1:170b–171a. See also *Or Yaqar*, ad loc.

246. **Moses was worried . . .** See *Shemot Rabbah* 2:5.

פרשת כי תצא

# *Parashat Ki Tetse*

"WHEN YOU GO OUT" (DEUTERONOMY 21:10–25:19)

Rabbi Shim'on said,[1] "When the soul hailing from the foundation of the supernal flux sins, fire above prevails upon her, kind for kind; and fire below prevails upon the body. Peace upon all Israel."[2]

Whoever says that "one who departs this world without children comes again to this world" speaks the truth.[3]

1. **Rabbi Shim'on said** *Parashat Ki Tetse* is found in *ZḤ* 59a–c. This brief treatment is extant in only two manuscripts, V5 and P2. Though anomalous in that it presents the doctrine of transmigration (otherwise unattested in *MhN* on the Torah), it nevertheless displays quintessential features of *MhN*: the combination of Hebrew and Aramaic, rabbinic personages found only in *MhN*, and the "Masters of Mishnah."

2. **hailing from the foundation of the supernal flux...** מיסודא דשפעא עילאה (*mi-yesoda di-shif'a illa'ah*) as in V5 and P2. The printed editions read "from the flux of the supernal foundation." Either way, this view is unique in *MhN* on the Torah, where the soul is described as hailing from the Throne of Glory (*Shekhinah*). See above, p. 381, n. 61.

3. **comes again to this world...** Reincarnated, the childless man is given another opportunity to fulfill his procreative task.

On reincarnation in Kabbalah, see *Bahir* 86 (121–22), 104 (155–56), 126–27 (184), 135 (195); Naḥmanides on Genesis 38:8; Deuteronomy 25:6; Job 33:30; *Zohar* 1:48a, 131a, 186b–188a, 239a; 2:75a, 91b, 99b; 3:7a, 88b, 182b; *ZḤ* 89b–90a (*MhN, Rut*); Todros Abulafia, *Otsar ha-Kavod, Yevamot* 62a, p. 25c–d; *Ketubbot* 111a, p. 27c; Scholem, *Major Trends*, 242–43; idem, *Kabbalah*, 344–50; idem, *Origins of the Kabbalah*, 188–94, 237–38 (on the Catharist theory of reincarnation), 456–60; idem, *On the Mystical Shape of the Godhead*, 197–250 (on the Catharists, 199–200); idem, *Shedim, Ruḥot u-Nshamot*, 186–214, 298; Tishby, *Wisdom of the Zohar*, 3:1362–63; Werblowsky, *Joseph Karo*, 234–56; Gottlieb, *Meḥqarim*, 370–96; Liebes, *Peraqim*, 291–327; Elior, "Torat ha-Gilgul be-Sefer Galya Raza"; Oron, "Qavvim le-Torat ha-Nefesh ve-ha-Gilgul," 283–89; Schwartz, "Ha-Biqqoret al Torat Gilgul ha-Neshamot"; Yisraeli, *Parshanut ha-Sod*, 113–29 (on Sava de-Mishpatim, the first extensive kabbalistic discussion of reincarnation).

On the importance of procreation, see below, note 12.

Furthermore: The wicked who soar through the air until their sins are requited, after which they enter a body a second time in order to be refined—if virtuous, he does not enter again, but if not—a third time, as is said: *Truly, God does all these things, two or three times to a man* (Job 33:29). If, heaven forbid, he is not virtuous these three times there is no restoration for him, and this is the significance of [*That soul*] *shall surely be cut off* (Numbers 15:31). That is why a person must be careful with his soul, lest he come another time.[4]

We possess proof from Nadab and Abihu—as we have written—who died half a body, because they did not marry.[5]

Moreover, we possess scriptural support, from the matter *her husband's brother shall come to her* (Deuteronomy 25:5)—that his seed will not be uprooted, and that he will not need to enter a body again.[6]

4. ***Truly, God does all these things, two or three times to a man...*** The following verse reads: *To bring his soul back from the Pit, so that he might bask in the light of life.*



The human being is given three chances to mend his ways. Failing this is total annihilation.

In *ZḤ* 89b (*MhN, Rut*), the verse from Job and more generally the idea of triple reincarnation is restricted to those who failed to procreate. Apparently, this is also the intent here (though a more expansive reading is also possible). The same passage from *Rut* also mentions the wicked flying out of Hell through the world, rejected from the gates of life and returning to this world in another body. Here, the soaring appears to function as a preliminary punishment or purification before the soul is ready to transmigrate.

See *Zohar* 3:178b, 216a, 280b (all *RM*); *TZ* 26, 72a; *TZ* 32, 76b; *TZ* 69, 114b, 117a–b.

5. **We possess proof from Nadab and Abihu...** Nadab and Abihu—who were not married and did not have children—were reincarnated in their younger brother's son, Phinehas. See *Zohar* 2:26b; 3:57b, 61b, 213a–b, 215b, 217a, 237b (*RM*).

On their having been unmarried, see *Vayiqra Rabbah* 20:9; *Pesiqta de-Rav Kahana* 26:9; *Tanḥuma, Aḥarei Mot* 6; *Tanḥuma* (Buber), *Aḥarei Mot* 7, 13; *Zohar* 3:5b, 33b–34a, 37b, 57a–b. Cf. Numbers 3:4; 1 Chronicles 24:2, which state that they had no children.

For the phrase "half a body," see *Zohar* 3:5b, 7b, 57b, 109b (*RM*), 296a (*IZ*); *ZḤ* 43d; Liebes, *Peraqim*, 277–79.

See also BT *Yevamot* 62b–63a: "Rabbi Tanḥum said in the name of Rabbi Ḥanilai, 'Any man who has no wife is without joy, without blessing, without goodness.'... Rabbi El'azar said, 'Any אדם (*adam*), man, who has no wife is not an *adam*, as is said: *Male and female He created them... and He named them* adam (Genesis 5:2).'" See Genesis 1:26–27; *Bereshit Rabbah* 17:2; *Qohelet Rabbah* on 9:9; *Midrash Tehillim* 59:2.

6. ***her husband's brother shall come to her...*** According to the biblical custom of levirate marriage, if a married man dies childless, his brother should marry the widow and then father a child who will be considered the offspring of the deceased. Posthumously providing the dead man with a child prevents his name from being blotted out. In Kabbalah, levirate marriage is understood in terms of reincarnation: not only is the name preserved, but also the deceased husband's soul, transmigrating into the embryo that is generated by the union of his widow and his brother.

On levirate marriage, see Genesis 38; Deuteronomy 25:5–10; Ruth 3–4; Tigay, *Deuteronomy*, 231, 482–83. On the medieval context, see Katz, *Halakhah ve-Qabbalah*, 127–74;

Furthermore, we have learned from Onan, about whom Scripture said *so as not to give seed to his brother* (Genesis 38:9).[7]

Yet another proof: *A son is born to Naomi!* (Ruth 4:17). Was he born to Naomi?! Surely Ruth bore him! Well, this teaches that Obed was in fact Mahlon, who died childless.[8]

This is why you see a righteous person who suffers: perhaps he had come to the world on another occasion, and was not all that virtuous and died in this state—so that now, when he comes into this world, he is afflicted for his sins; hence the suffering of the righteous. Similarly, the prosperity of the wicked: perhaps he had come on another occasion and died childless, and he was virtuous though not completely so—and now he is being compensated from his merits in this world. This is the significance of *For the ways of YHVH are right, the righteous walk in them [while transgressors stumble in them]* (Hosea 14:10).[9]

Grossman, *Pious and Rebellious*, 90–101. The term 'levirate' derives from the Latin *levir*, "husband's brother." The Hebrew term יבום (*yibbum*), "levirate marriage," similarly derives from יבם (*yabbam*), "husband's brother."

On levirate marriage and reincarnation, see Ezra of Gerona, *Peirush le-Shir ha-Shirim*, 537; Naḥmanides on Genesis 38:8; *Zohar* 1:155b (*ST*), 186b–188a; 2:99b; 3:167a, 177a; *ZḤ* 89d–90a (*MhN, Rut*); Moses de León, *Shushan Edut*, 353–60; idem, *Sefer ha-Rimmon*, 240–52; idem, *Sefer ha-Mishqal*, 136–46; idem, *She'elot u-Tshuvot*, 58–59; Katz, *Halakhah ve-Qabbalah*, 62–65; 167–71.

7. **we have learned from Onan...** According to Genesis 38, when Judah's firstborn son Er died, Judah instructed Er's brother Onan to perform the rite of levirate marriage with Er's widow Tamar. Onan, however, failed to fulfill his brotherly duty, and instead *when he would come [to bed] with his brother's wife, he would waste [his semen] on the ground so as not to give seed to his brother.* According to the *Zohar*'s reading, Onan did not wish his brother to be reincarnated in his offspring. See Naḥmanides on Genesis 38:8; Moses, de León, *Sefer ha-Rimmon*, 246; *Zohar* 1:187b.

8. **Obed was in fact Mahlon...** The reincarnation of Mahlon, and hence described as born to Naomi, Mahlon's mother, rather than Ruth, his biological mother.

On Mahlon, see Ruth 1:1–5. On Obed as the reincarnation of Mahlon, see *Zohar* 1:188b; 2:103b. See also Naḥmanides on Genesis 38:8; Moses de León, *Sefer ha-Mishqal*, 138; idem, *Sefer ha-Rimmon*, 245.

I have followed the emended reading found in *Sullam*, Edri, and *Matoq mi-Devash*. The reading found in Salonika, Venice, P2, and V5 seems corrupt.

9. **This is why you see a righteous person who suffers...** On reincarnation as an explanation for the suffering of the righteous and prosperity of the wicked, see *Bahir* 135 (195): "[Rabbi Reḥumai said,] 'Why are there wicked who prosper and righteous who suffer? Because the righteous man was previously wicked in the past and is now being punished. Now, should you say, 'Is a man to be punished for [the sins] of his youth? Has not Rabbi Simon said that one is only punished by the heavenly court from one's twentieth year on?' Say to them: I am not speaking of the [present] life, but of that which was in the past.' His companions said to him, 'How much longer will you conceal your words?' He replied, 'Go and see. This is like a person who has planted a vineyard in his garden to bring forth grapes, but it brought forth wild grapes. He saw that he was not

Concerning what we have said: *When brothers dwell together* (Deuteronomy 25:5). Rabbi Yitsḥak said, "*When brothers* ישבו (*yeshevu*), *dwell*—that they should recognize in their heart that they are brothers, as is said: וישב יהוה (*Va-yeshev YHVH*), *YHVH sits, as king forever* (Psalms 29:10)—just as they recognize that He is King of all."[10]

*And one of them dies and he has no offspring* (Deuteronomy 25:5)—if he had children it would not be necessary.[11]

Rabbi Tanḥum said in the name of Rabbi Yose, "*Her husband's brother shall come to her* (Deuteronomy 25:5)—why is this necessary? So as not to diminish the image comprising all images."[12]



succeeding, so he replanted it, placed a fence around it, repaired the breaches, pruned the wild grapes, and planted it a second time. He saw that he was not succeeding—he again fenced it off, and again replanted it after pruning.' How many times? He said to them, 'Until a thousand generations, as is written: *He commanded a word to a thousand generations* (Psalms 105:8).'"

See also Naḥmanides, "Sha'ar ha-Gemul [The Gate of Reward]," *Writings of the Ramban* (trans. Chavel), 2:517–18: "However, [concerning] this rare problem [of the righteous who suffer] together with the more frequent other problem of seeing an absolute and truly wicked man succeeding in all matters of prosperity, the perplexed person may look forward to the troubles that will finally befall that wicked man. Alternatively, he may consider that [the wicked man's] peace is part of the secret mentioned, which is the mystery of the transmigration of souls."

Cf. BT *Berakhot* 7a. See also Moses de León, *She'elot u-Tshuvot*, 59; idem, *Sefer ha-Rimmon*, 247–8; idem, *Sefer ha-Mishqal*, 145; Tishby, *Wisdom of the Zohar*, 3:1419–22.

Regarding the prosperity of the wicked, had the man who had already come to the world been perfectly righteous, his good works would have been considered for him as children, so that he would not need to be reincarnated, hence the detail "virtuous though not completely so." See *Zohar* 1:187b.

10. ***When brothers dwell together*...** The opening phrase of the law of levirate marriage. According to Rabbi Yitsḥak, "dwelling" means "recognition," i.e., the brothers should recognize that they are brothers and love one another. If they do not, and the remaining brother hates his deceased brother, he should not perform levirate marriage.

11. **if he had children...** The deceased would not need to be reincarnated through the union of his wife and brother.

12. **not to diminish the image comprising all images** Levirate marriage is necessary to enable the reincarnation of the deceased, who did not fulfill his procreative responsibilities—thereby diminishing *Malkhut*, the image comprising all images, the source of souls. Reincarnated in his brother's offspring, the deceased has another opportunity to engender children.

On "diminishing the [divine] image," see *Bereshit Rabbah* 34:14, in the name of El'azar son of Azariah: "Whoever abstains from procreation is as though he diminished the image. Why so? *For in the image of God He made the human being* (Genesis 9:6), after which is written *As for you, be fruitful and multiply, swarm through the earth and increase on it* (ibid., 7)."

See *Tosefta Yevamot* 8:7; BT *Yevamot* 63b; *Mekhilta, Baḥodesh* 8; *Bereshit Rabbah* 17:2; *Zohar* 1:13a, 186b, 264b-265a (*Piq*); 3:7a; *ZḤ* 89b (*MhN, Rut*); Moses de León, *Sefer ha-Mishqal*, 138, 140, 142; idem, *Sefer ha-Rimmon*, 241 (and Wolfson's note), 244; idem, *She'elot u-Tshuvot*, 58. See also Tishby, *Wisdom of the Zohar*, 3:1375, n. 63, noting the

Rabbi Yitsḥak opened, "*There is one and not a second; he has neither son nor brother* (Ecclesiastes 4:8). *There is one*—the person who departs this world lacking any good, for he is one, not meriting to generate a second."[13]

As it has been taught: Rabbi Yitsḥak said, "Whoever departs this world single, without a second, is diminished and eliminated from the image comprising all images."[14]

*Two are better than one* (ibid., 9). How so? Since it is written *For they* [59b] *have a good reward for their labor* (ibid.).[15]

Rabbi Yitsḥak said, "Come and see what is written in the verse *For should they fall, one can raise his companion* (ibid., 10)—in that image. *But pity the one who falls with no second to raise him!* (ibid.)."[16]

Rabbi Yehudah sent a question to Rabbi Abba, "You who stand before the Masters of Mishnah, what is the reason that *her husband's brother shall come to her* (Deuteronomy 25:5) *to establish the name of the dead* (Ruth 4:5, 10), rather than another woman?"[17]



origins of the motif in Rabbi Ezra's Commentary to the Song of Songs (in *Kitvei ha-Ramban* 2:537): "To enter into levirate marriage with one's deceased brother's wife is to show mercy to the dead, to prevent the likeness of the image comprising all images from being destroyed or diminished, and to give him a name forever that shall not be cut off." See Liebes, *Peraqim*, 50–51.

13. ***There is one...*** Unmarried (i.e., one), he does not merit to produce a second, namely an offspring. See *Zohar* 1:187a.

On lacking goodness as connoting unmarried status, see BT *Yevamot* 62b, quoted above, note 5.

14. **Whoever departs this world single...** Whoever diminishes the image comprising all images (*Malkhut*) by not engendering new life is in turn excluded from this realm upon death. See below, at notes 41 and 42.

Cf. BT *Bava Batra* 116a: "Rabbi Yoḥanan said in the name of Rabbi Shim'on son of Yoḥai, 'Whoever does not leave a son to succeed him incurs the full wrath of the blessed Holy One.'" See *Zohar* 1:13a, 48a, 90a, 115a, 186b, 228b; *ZḤ* 89b (*MhN, Rut*).

15. ***For they have a good reward for their labor*** The married couple are rewarded for bringing (or striving to bring) children into the world. See *Zohar* 1:187b. See also *Kallah Rabbati* 2 on children benefiting their parents in the afterlife.

16. ***raise his companion...*** A man who was married yet died childless can be raised back into the image (*Malkhut*) by his brother and wife's engaging in levirate marriage. In contrast, he who dies childless and unmarried has no one to raise him.

17. **Rabbi Yehudah sent a question...** Rabbi Yehudah wonders why the deceased brother can be restored and reincarnated only through union with his wife, rather than any other woman.

"Masters of Mishnah" renders מאריהון דמתניתין (*mareihon de-matnitin*). This term appears in numerous passages (in various formulations) throughout *Midrash ha-Ne'lam* and appears to signify a group (though never formally defined) of sages possessing esoteric wisdom. In some ways, the Masters of Mishnah are a forerunner to the *Ḥavrayya*, the Companions headed by Rabbi Shim'on, found in the main body of the *Zohar*. Significantly, however, Rabbi Shim'on does not

He sent back to him, "*A wild donkey accustomed to the desert, in the desire of her soul, snuffing the wind* (Jeremiah 2:24)."[18]

Rabbi Yehudah became excited and said, "Certainly this is a mystery of wisdom, implied by what is said: שאפה רוח (*sha'afah ruaḥ*), *snuffs the wind*—רוח (*ruaḥ*), spirit, precisely!"[19]

This corresponds with what Rabbi Yose said: "As is written: *So I saw the wicked buried and coming* (Ecclesiastes 8:10)—coming, literally!"[20]

Rabbi Yitsḥak said, "The matter is clarified through what is written: *in her desire* (Jeremiah 2:24)—implying that whether betrothed or married they are efficacious in this matter."[21]



always occupy a privileged position in this group. The Mishnah of which they are masters is not the Mishnah of the rabbinic sage Rabbi Yehudah ha-Nasi, but rather a body of esoteric knowledge often relating to the soul and the structure of the cosmos. See *Zohar* 1:123b (*MhN*, though mistakenly labeled as *Tosefta*); 1:127a–b, 129a–b, 130a, 135a 138a, 139b; 2:5a, 14a (all *MhN*); *ZḤ* 10c, 12c, 13a, 14c, 15b–c, 16a (all *MhN*). Cf. *Pesiqta de-Rav Kahana* 11:15, 23:12; See also Matt, "Matnita di-Lan," 132–34.

18. ***A wild donkey accustomed...*** In context in Jeremiah, the verse refers to Israel's lusting after the *ba'alim* (false gods): *Like a lustful she-camel restlessly running about, a wild donkey accustomed to the desert snuffing the wind in her desire.* Rabbi Abba does not explain how this verse resolves Rabbi Yehudah's query, though Rabbi Yehudah grasps its significance immediately.

19. **רוח (*ruaḥ*), spirit, precisely** The clause *sha'afah ruaḥ* is construed as *draws the spirit.* The verse is then interpreted as follows: *A wild donkey*—the wife of the deceased brother, *accustomed to the desert*—having been married to a man without children, *in the desire of her soul*—when she couples with her brother-in-law in levirate marriage, *draws the spirit*—absorbs the spirit of her deceased husband, which is still associated with the widow. Significantly, there is a *Ketiv*/*Qere* in this verse that involves gender: נפשו (*nafsho*), "his soul" / נפשה (*nafshah*), "her soul." Perhaps then it is due to *the desire of his soul* [i.e., the deceased] for a resolution of his fate that the woman draws the spirit; and perhaps the implication is that her soul and his soul somehow coincide in her body, just as the two words co-exist in this verse. (My thanks to David E. S. Stein for this subtle reading.)

Rabbi Yehudah's query is resolved. During his lifetime, through uniting sexually with his wife, the deceased husband had infused into her some of his spirit, which remained in her even after he died. Consequently he can be restored only through union with her. See *Zohar* 1:155b (*ST*); 2:99b, 104b; 3:177a.

On the verse from Jeremiah and on this theme, see Moses de León, *Sefer ha-Rimmon*, 244; idem, *Sefer ha-Mishqal*, 140; idem, *She'elot u-Tshuvot*, 58. See also *Zohar* 1:213a (considered a later imitation of the *Zohar* and not in this edition).

See also the fragment by Naḥmanides published by Scholem in "Peraqim mi-Toledot Sifrut ha-Qabbalah (8)," 417–18.

20. ***So I saw the wicked buried and coming...*** Coming back, reincarnated through levirate marriage. The verse continues: *going from the holy site.*

On this verse, see *Zohar* 1:130a (*MhN*), 188a; 3:216a (*RM*); *TZ* 69, 99b–100a, 111a; Moses de León, *Shushan Edut*, 358; idem, *Sefer ha-Rimmon*, 246 (and Wolfson's note); idem, *Sefer ha-Mishqal*, 138.

21. **whether betrothed or married...** Rabbi Abba explained (allusively) that the restoration of the deceased brother is effec-

*And it shall be, the firstborn whom she bears shall be established* [*in the name of the dead brother*] (Deuteronomy 25:6). Why the firstborn, and not the second or the third?[22]

Rabbi Yudan said, "The firstborn and first without doubt belongs to the deceased, both their minds [focused] on the dead during the first coupling."[23]

It has been taught: Rabbi Yose said, "*His sister-in-law shall go up to the gate of the elders* (ibid., 7). This matter smacks of impudence!"[24]

Rabbi Yehudah said, "Heaven forbid that it is impudent! Rather, it is to demonstrate the kindness she wishes to perform for the deceased. He did not want to, and therefore she disgraces him in front of everyone.[25]

"How does she disgrace him? As is written: *she shall spit in his face* (ibid., 9)—to be ashamed in front of everyone, *because he will not build his brother's house* (ibid.). The verse states: *she shall spit* [*in his face and speak out*] *and say, "So* [*shall be done to the man who will not build his brother's house*] (ibid.), as is said*: If her father spat in her face, would she not be ashamed?* (Numbers 12:14)."



Rabbi Abbahu said in the name of Rabbi Yoḥanan, "Spittle confirmed by all to be spittle and not water, and not covered in the earth is required."[26]

tive only because the spirit of the deceased is still associated with his wife following their earlier sexual unions. Rabbi Yitsḥak expands the teaching. Levirate marriage "works" even if the woman was only betrothed. Even in the absence of sexual union, betrothal is enough for the spirit of the deceased to be embedded in the woman. As the verse implies, *her desire* is sufficient.

22. **Why the firstborn...** Why should only the firstborn of the levirate union, and no subsequent offspring, be named after the dead?

23. **both their minds...** It is fitting to name the firstborn after the deceased, as he without doubt possesses the deceased's soul.

On the couple's focusing their mind and will to draw the deceased's soul, see the sources cited above in notes 6 and 19.

24. **This matter smacks of impudence!** Rabbi Yose wonders about the seemingly brazen behavior prescribed by the Torah. See Deuteronomy 25:7–10: *If the man does not want to wed his sister-in-law, his sister-in-law shall go up to the gate of the elders and say, "My brother-in-law has refused to establish a name for his brother, a name in Israel. He did not want to carry out a brother-in-law's duty toward me." The elders of the town shall call to him and speak to him, and if he stands and says, "I do not want to wed her," his sister-in-law shall approach him before the eyes of the elders and slip his sandal from his foot and spit in his face and speak out and say, "So shall be done to the man who will not build his brother's house." And his name shall be called in Israel: the House of the Slipped-off Sandal.*

25. **to demonstrate the kindness...** To enable the deceased to be reincarnated. See Moses de León, *Sefer ha-Rimmon* 252–53; idem, *She'elot u-Tshuvot*, 58.

26. **spittle confirmed by all to be spittle...** On the need for the woman's spittle to be seen by the judges, see BT *Yevamot* 39b, 106b; *Sanhedrin* 49b. See also Maimonides, *Mishneh Torah, Hilkhot Yibbum ve-Ḥalitsah* 4:7. See next note.

A certain woman came before Rabbi Shim'on and hurled spit. He noticed that she had just eaten and the spit could not be seen—[the ceremony] was not performed that day. Later, they reconciled and coupled with one another.[27]

How could Rabbi Shim'on do this? For we have learned: If they reconciled prior to her ascending before the judge—fine and well. But once she has slipped off his sandal before the judge—no.[28]

Rabbi Yehudah said, "The case of that woman was different, for they had not yet done anything to one another. Rather, she hurled spit for examination, but it was unsuitable; and afterward they went and coupled with one another."[29]

וחלצה (Ve-ḥaletsah), *She shall slip off, his sandal* (Deuteronomy 25:9), as is said: חלץ (Ḥalats), *He has cast, them off* (Hosea 5:6).[30]

Rabbi Yehudah said in the name of Rabbi Ḥiyya, "It is written: *Come no closer here. Remove your sandals from your feet* (Exodus 3:5). Can a sandal purify or contaminate a place? Well, Rabbi Abba said, 'This teaches that the blessed Holy



One commanded him in a respectful manner to separate from his wife completely. About Moses it is written *Remove your sandals*, while of Joshua it is written *Remove your sandal [from your feet]* (Joshua 5:15)—that he need not separate from his wife completely, but only at designated times. *For the place you are standing on [is holy ground]* (Exodus 3:5)—you have a place of higher degree than other human beings, the grade called "holy." That is why He commanded to separate from his wife by means of the shoe.' So too here this sandal connotes separation from the woman."[31]

27. **noticed that she had just eaten...** According to BT *Yevamot* 106b, certain foods generate the involuntary production of spit. For the ceremony to be valid, the woman must spit of her own free will. See also Maimonides, *Mishneh Torah, Hilkhot Yibbum ve-Ḥalitsah* 4:22, 23.

28. **How could Rabbi Shim'on do this?...** How could he allow their reconciliation? Once the sandal has been removed, levirate marriage is no longer permissible. As spitting follows the removal of the sandal, the couple ought not to have been allowed to reconcile. See BT *Yevamot* 104a–b and Rashi, s.v. *yevamah she-raqeqah*; Maimonides, *Mishneh Torah, Hilkhot Yibbum ve-Ḥalitsah* 4:9,14; *Shulḥan Arukh, Even ha-Ezer, Hilkhot Ḥalitsah* 169:45.

29. **had not yet done anything...** The sandal had not yet been removed. The spit hurled by the woman was not yet part of the ceremony but rather merely to determine its suitability. Hence, the parties could still reconcile.

30. **וחלצה (Ve-ḥaletsah), *She shall slip off*...** Though the simple meaning is to remove his shoe, the *Zohar* will now find a deeper allusion. On the meaning of the verb *ḥalats*, see BT *Yevamot* 102b.

31. ***Remove your sandals from your feet*...** Just as with Moses and Joshua, where removal of the shoe(s) signified separation from a woman, so in the case of the aborted levirate marriage, the slipping off of the sandal connotes the severing of any connection between the woman and her brother-in-law.

Unlike Moses, who was instructed to remove both sandals, Joshua was instructed to

Rabbi Yoḥanan said, "A person should trust in his Creator, take a wife, and engender children—that he will not go childless to the world to come. As we have learned: What is the meaning of *Childless they will die* (Leviticus 20:20)? Whoever does not have children in this world is as though he never was; and he is called childless in this world and in the world to come."[32]

As Rabbi Yoḥanan said: "After a man marries a woman and engenders children, he is called A Servant of *YHVH*; and he inherits this world and the world to come, as is written: *that a blessing may rest upon your house* (Ezekiel 44:30)."[33]

remove only one. Moses was told נעליך (*na'alekha*), *your sandals*, whereas Joshua was told נעלך (*na'alkha*), *your sandal*—in the singular. (In its simple meaning, the latter is construed as a collective term, which nonetheless yields *your sandals*.) The difference implies that Joshua's separation from his wife was not ongoing and permanent, as it was with Moses.

According to rabbinic tradition, as a consequence of Moses' direct encounter with God, he abstained from sexual relations with his wife—and became, as it were, the husband of *Shekhinah*, here signified by "the grade called holy" (see *Zohar* 2:222a; cf. 3:91a, where "holy" signifies *Ḥokhmah*).

On God's command *Remove your sandals from your feet* as implying sexual abstinence, see *Zohar* 2:222a; 3:148a, 180a; *ZḤ* 72d (*ShS*); Kasher, *Torah Shelemah*, Exodus 3:5, n. 94. Cf. 2 Samuel 11:8, 11; *Zohar* 1:8b, 112b. On Moses' celibacy, see *Sifrei*, Numbers 99–100; *Sifrei Zuta* 12:1; *Targum Yerushalmi*, Numbers 12:8; Deuteronomy 5:27–28; BT *Shabbat* 87a (and *Tosafot*, s.v. *ve-attah*), *Yevamot* 62a (and *Tosafot*, s.v. *di-khtiv*); *Avot de-Rabbi Natan* A, 2; B, 2; *Pirqei de-Rabbi Eli'ezer* 46; *Devarim Rabbah* 11:10; *Tanḥuma*, *Tsav* 13; *Shemot Rabbah* 19:3; 46:3; Rashi on Numbers 12:8; Maimonides, *Mishneh Torah*, *Hilkhot Yesodei ha-Torah* 7:6; *Zohar* 1:21b–22a, 152b, 234b; 3:148a, 180a, 261b; *ZḤ* 72d–73a (*ShS*). On Moses as איש האלהים (*ish ha-Elohim*), "the husband of *Shekhinah*," see *Pesiqta de-Rav Kahana*, *nispaḥim*, *Vezot Haberakhah*, 443–44, 448 (variants); *Tanḥuma*, *Vezot Haberakhah* 2 (*Ets Yosef*, ad loc.); *Devarim Rabbah* (ed. Lieberman), p. 129; *Midrash Tehillim* 90:5; *Zohar* 1:6b, 21b–22a, 148a, 152a–b, 192b, 236b, 239a; 2:22b, 131b, 219b–220a, 235b, 283b, 244b (*Heikh*); 3:261b; Moses de León, *Sefer ha-Rimmon*, 25; idem, *Sheqel ha-Qodesh*, 101–2 (129).

32. **A person should trust in his Creator...** And not worry about first securing his livelihood. Cf. *ZḤ* 4d (*MhN*), where Rabbi Yoḥanan says that a man should first build a house, ensure his livelihood, and finally marry. See also BT *Sotah* 44a: "The Torah has taught worldly advice: that a man should build a house, plant a vineyard, and then marry a wife." See also Maimonides, *Mishneh Torah*, *Hilkhot De'ot* 5:11. "The way of sensible men is that first, one should establish an occupation by which he can support himself.... In contrast, a fool begins by marrying a wife. Then, if he can find the means, he purchases a house. Finally, toward the end of his life, he will search about for a trade...."

In its original context, the phrase *childless they will die* describes the punishment for having sexual relations with one's aunt: both nephew and aunt will die childless. Rabbi Yoḥanan rereads the words as an independent formulation: those who sin by remaining childless—they will die. See *Zohar* 1:228b; 2:108b.

33. **A Servant of *YHVH*...** Only when married—and therefore free of lustful thoughts—is a man able to devote himself to Torah, commandments, and God. See *ZḤ* 5a (*MhN*).

Cf. BT *Qiddushin* 29b: "Our Rabbis

A parable. To what can the matter be compared? To a king who gave a deposit to three people. One guarded the deposit; the second lost the deposit completely; the third sullied the deposit and gave of it to another to guard.[34]

After some time, the king arrived to demand his deposit. The one who guarded the deposit—the king praised him and made him [59c] a trusted member of his household. The second, שאבד (*she-ibbed*), who lost, the deposit האבידו

taught: On studying Torah and marrying a woman? He should study Torah and then marry; but if he cannot manage without a wife, he should marry and then study Torah. Rav Yehudah said in the name of Shemu'el, 'The *halakhah* is that he should marry and then study Torah.' Rabbi Yoḥanan said, 'A millstone around his neck—and he will study Torah!' And they do not disagree; that is for us and that is for them." (See Rashi and Tosafot, ad loc.)



See also Maimonides, *Mishneh Torah, Hilkhot Talmud Torah* 1:5: "A person should always study Torah and, afterward, marry. If he marries first, his mind will not be free for study. However, if his natural inclination overcomes him to the extent that his mind is not free, he should marry, and then study Torah."

The parable that follows illustrates how engendering children enables one to attain the world to come.

On the verse from Ezekiel, see BT *Yevamot* 62b.

34. **A parable...** The פקדון (*piqqadon*), "deposit, pledge," is the soul. The third character (neither wholly righteous nor wholly wicked) passes on his pledge to his son.

The *Zohar*'s parable draws upon two earlier and famous parables of the soul—one rabbinic, the other from the earliest kabbalistic text, the *Bahir.* See BT *Shabbat* 152b: "Our Rabbis taught: *The spirit returns to God who gave it* (Ecclesiastes 12:7)—give it back to Him as He gave it to you, in a state of purity. This may be compared to a mortal king who distributed royal robes to his servants. The wise among them folded them up and put them away in a chest, while the fools among them went and worked in them. After some time, the king wanted his garments. The wise returned them clean, while the fools return them soiled. The king was pleased with the wise; but he was angry with the fools. Concerning the wise he said, 'Let the garments be returned to the storehouse, and they return to their homes in peace.' Concerning the fools he said, 'Let the garments be given to the laundry, while they be confined in jail.' Similarly, the blessed Holy One. Concerning the bodies of the righteous He says, *Let them come in peace, they will rest on their couches* (Isaiah 57:2), and concerning their souls He says, *The soul of my lord will be bound in the bundle of life* (1 Samuel 25:29). Concerning the bodies of the wicked He says, *There is no peace for the wicked, says YHVH* (Isaiah 48:22), and concerning their souls He says, *The soul of your enemies He will sling from the hollow of a sling* (1 Samuel 25:29)."

See *Bahir* 86 (122): "A parable: To what can the matter be compared? To a king who had servants, and clad them in garments of silk and embroidery in accordance with his wealth. They went astray, so he cast them out and pushed them away and removed his garments. They went on their way. He took the garments and washed them well, until no stain was left on them, and he kept them with him, ready. He then acquired other servants and clad them in those garments, not knowing whether these servants were good or not. So they partook of garments that had already come into the world, and that others had worn before them.... This is the meaning of *And the dust returns to the earth as it was, and the spirit returns to God who gave it* (Ecclesiastes 12:7)."

See also *Tanḥuma, Shofetim* 12; *ZḤ* 89a–b (*MhN, Rut*).

(*he'evido*), he removed, from the world, commanding that he leave neither name nor remnant. The third, who sullied the deposit and gave of it to another—the king said, "Let this one be, until we see what the other makes of what this one has placed in his care." In the meantime he does not leave the king's house.[35]

If the other is worthy, this one shall go free. If he is not worthy—the king said, "Give this one a punishment for sullying the deposit, and the deposit shall remain his."[36]

Rav Huna said, "Once he has entered, he has entered."[37]

If he sullied the deposit and did not leave it in the care of another to guard, he is removed from the king's house until another arrives and restores what this one sullied. The deposit is removed from this one's care and given to the other who restored it.[38]

Rabbi Ḥiyya said, "It is written: *He blew into his nostrils the breath of life, and the human became a living soul* (Genesis 2:7). Since the verse said נשמת חיים (*nishmat ḥayyim*), *the breath of life*, why *and the human became* לנפש חיה (*le-nefesh ḥayyah*), *a living soul*? Well, it was on this condition that the blessed Holy One bestowed נשמה (*neshamah*), soul, in the human, that he would become לנפש חיה (*le-nefesh ḥayyah*), a birthing soul. In the West, they call a birthing woman חיה (*ḥayyah*).[39]



35. **Let this one be, until we see...** Unlike the parable's first two souls, whose fate is decreed immediately (the former gaining entry into paradise, the second annihilated), the third soul's fate remains in abeyance, dependent on the behavior of his offspring—who now bears the father's soul, in accordance with the principle "a son exonerates a father" (BT *Sanhedrin* 104a). Awaiting his ultimate judgment, the father's soul remains in the king's house, in a waiting room (or holding cell) within the divine realm.

"Trusted member of his household" recalls the description of Moses in Numbers 12:7: *He is trusted throughout My house.* "Neither name nor remnant" derives from 2 Samuel 14:7.

36. **If the other is worthy...** If the son is worthy, the father's soul is set free and admitted into the celestial realm. If, however, the son is not worthy, the father receives his due punishment but is permitted to keep his soul, meaning that there is no need for it to be reincarnated, and that after purification he too enters paradise.

37. **Once he has entered, he has entered** Once within the divine realm, even if only provisionally at first, one remains.

38. **until another arrives...** In the absence of a child to exonerate his soul, the sullied soul must await reincarnation outside the king's house (in Hell?) for another opportunity for restoration. Should the second body succeed in effecting restoration, the soul passes irrevocably to it. Hence the childless man is disadvantaged compared to the man with children, who earn him a place in the world to come.

39. **In the West, they call a birthing woman חיה (*ḥayyah*)** On *ḥayyah* as "birthing woman," see M *Yoma* 8:1; Rashi, BT *Yoma* 73b, s.v. *ve-ha-ḥayyah*; *Bereshit Rabbah* 82:7. See also *Arukh ha-Shalem*, s.v. פע (*pa*).

See Exodus 1:19: *The midwives said to Pharaoh, "For not like the Egyptian women are the Hebrew women, for they are* חיות (*ḥayyot*), *lively. Before the midwife comes to them, they give birth."*

"Furthermore, *Elohim* brought forth kinds after His own kind, namely הנשמה (*ha-neshamah*), the soul. The soul divides and expands in the body—while she in the body. But when she goes forth from the body, she expands even more, attaining what she could not attain while in the body.[40]

"Immediately upon separating from the body she desires to cleave to *Elohim*, but since she did not bring forth a body—his kind—just as *Elohim* brought forth נשמתא (*nishmeta*), soul—His kind—she is not received, and continues שואפת (*sho'efet*), yearning, until she enters another body, to establish seed, and to return and cleave to the pure, clear, and clean body. Whoever does not leave behind children is not attached, as is written: *in her desire* שאפה רוח (*sha'afah ruaḥ*), *she draws the spirit* (Jeremiah 2:24)."[41]

Rabbi Shim'on said, "Whoever does not leave after him stock as root, his soul is eliminated from the image comprising all images, until she cycles and is poured from vessel to vessel, as is said: *and has not been poured from vessel to vessel* (Jeremiah 48:11). What is his restoration? It is written: *his redeemer who is related to him shall come and redeem what his brother sold* (Leviticus 25:25)."[42]



Rabbi Yehudah said, "She cycles until she finds a suitable vessel for restoration. If there is no redeemer, ray of budding brilliance is shattered. Of this is said *He pays back those who hate Him to their face to make them perish* (Deu-

40. ***Elohim* brought forth kinds...** Genesis 2:7 reads: *YHVH Elohim formed the human, dust from the soil, and blew into his nostrils the breath of life; and the human became a living soul.* Rabbi Ḥiyya focuses on the word *Elohim*, which he understands as signifying *Malkhut*, the mother of souls.

In the body, the soul divides into its various parts; it expands by virtue of good deeds and Torah study.

41. **she desires to cleave to *Elohim*...** The soul that did not generate new human life—much as *Elohim* (*Malkhut*) generated all souls on a vastly larger scale—is not able to cleave to the divine after death. She must await reincarnation, generate life, and then cleave to *Malkhut* (the pure, clear, and clean body), who *draws* (absorbs) the spirit after death. See Tishby, *Wisdom of the Zohar*, 3:1362, 1375, n. 72.

On the verse from Jeremiah, see above, note 19.

42. **she cycles and is poured from vessel to vessel...** The soul ("she") of the man who did not engender children is prevented from returning to *Malkhut*; rather, it is reincarnated through the levirate union so as to give the deceased another opportunity to fulfill his procreative responsibility.

"Cycles" renders מתגלגלא (*mitgalgela*). On the root גלגל (*gilgel*), "rolling, revolving, circulation, transmigration, reincarnation," see Scholem, *On the Mystical Shape of the Godhead*, 302–3, n. 23; idem, *Shedim Ruḥot u-Nshamot*, 186–93; Liebes, *Peraqim*, 294–96.

"Vessel" may signify a body (or perhaps more specifically a woman's body) in which the reincarnated soul is to be reborn. On "vessel" as a metaphor for a wife, see BT *Sanhedrin* 22b; *Zohar* 2:99b; 3:167a. See also Moses de León, *Shushan Edut*, 355; idem, *Sefer ha-Rimmon*, 244; idem, *She'elot u-Tshuvot*, 58.

On "the image comprising all images," see above, note 12.

teronomy 7:10); *doing kindness to the thousandth generation for My friends and those who keep My commands* (ibid. 5:10)."[43]

Therefore Rabbi Abba said, "*In the image of Elohim He made the human being* (Genesis 9:6)—just as this name brought forth kinds after its kind, so a human being must bring forth kinds after its kind."[44]

43. **ray of budding brilliance is shattered...** In the absence of a redeemer to perform levirate union, the soul is annihilated.

"Ray of budding brilliance" renders קוזטיפא דבודיטא (*qoztipha de-budita*), a Zoharic neologism of uncertain meaning. Its referent is the mysterious bond of body and soul. See *Zohar* 2:14a (*MhN*); *ZḤ* 14b (*MhN*). See the expression קסטיפא דשמשא (*qastipha de-shimsha*), "ray of the sun" (*Zohar* 3:283b); the Arabic root *qdf*, "to throw"; and the neologism קוספיתא (*quspita*), "hollow of a sling," discussed by Liebes, *Peraqim*, 345–48. See *Zohar* 1:53b, 167a; *Bei'ur ha-Millim ha-Zarot*, 189. As for בודיטא (*budita*), it is not attested elsewhere even in the *Zohar*. Its meaning is unknown. (In the context of reincarnation, might it be an allusion to Buddha?) Cf. *Sullam* and Edri, who suggest that *qoztipha de-budita* means "precious vessel." See also *Matoq mi-Devash*.

44. **just as this name...** The name *Elohim*, signifying *Malkhut*, mother of souls.

# Addendum 1

God said,[1] "*Let there be* מארת (*me'orot*), *lights, in the expanse of heaven*" (Genesis 1:14).

Rabbi Tanḥum said, "The word is deficient, lacking ו *vav*!"[2]

Rabbi Yitsḥak said, "Why is it deficient? Because their lights were not complete, for the moon was lessened."[3]

1. ***God said*** The following pericope is not found in printed editions of the *Zohar.* Extant in only one manuscript, C9 (the earliest known *Zohar* manuscript), it was published by Gershom Scholem in 1945; "Parashah Ḥadashah," 425–46. The passage shares themes and concerns with the parallel passage in *ZḤ* 14a–15d (*MhN*), though there are significant differences as well. This pericope also contains the earliest *Zohar* passage to be quoted outside the *Zohar*, in Isaac ibn Sahula's *Meshal ha-Qadmoni.* See below, note 51.

2. **The word is deficient...** In Genesis 1:14, the word מארת (*me'orot*) is written without the *vavs*, the vowel letters. See Proverbs 3:33; JT *Ta'anit* 4:4, 68b; *Pesiqta de-Rav Kahana* 5:1; *Soferim* 17:4; Rashi on Genesis 1:14; *Zohar* 1:1a, 12a, 19b–20a, 33b, 46b, 146a, 166a, 169b; 2:35b, 167b, 205a; *ZḤ* 69b–c (*ShS*), *ZḤ* 14c, 15c (both *MhN*); *Minḥat Shai* on Genesis 1:14.

3. **for the moon was lessened** The absent *vavs* point to the diminution of the moon. See BT *Ḥullin* 60b: "Rabbi Shim'on son of Pazzi pointed out a contradiction. 'It is written: *God made the two great lights* (Genesis 1:16), and it is written: *the greater light... and the lesser light* (ibid.). The moon said before the blessed Holy One, "Master of the Universe! Can two kings possibly wear one crown? [i.e., How can both of us be *great*?]" He answered, "Go, and diminish yourself!" She said before Him, "Master of the Universe! Because I have suggested something proper I should make myself smaller?" He replied, "Go and rule by [both] day and night." She said, "But what is the value of this? What good is a lamp at noon?" He replied, "Go. Israel shall reckon by you the days and the years." She said, "But it is impossible to do without the sun for the reckoning of the seasons, as is written: *they shall serve as signs for the set times, the days and the years* (ibid., 14)." "Go. The righteous shall be named after you, as we find—Jacob the Small, Shemu'el the Small, David the Small." Seeing that her mind was uneasy [i.e., that she could not be consoled], the blessed Holy One said, "Bring an atonement for Me for making the moon smaller."' As was said by Rabbi Shim'on son of Lakish: 'Why is the goat offered on the new moon distinguished

Rav Yehudah said in the name of Rav, "We have learned in the Baraita of the Aggadta of Shemu'el the Lesser: Why was the moon diminished? Well, when the blessed Holy One created the lights, He created them solely for the utility of the earth, and these are the sun and moon alone. Yet it is written ואת הכוכבים (*ve-et ha-kokhavim*), *and the stars* (ibid., 16), and Scripture said *to shine upon the earth* (ibid., 17)! Well, Shemu'el said, 'The implication of what is written: ואת הכוכבים (*ve-et ha-kokhavim*), *and the stars*, with an additional *vav*—they were created separately; and the blessed Holy One saw that the sun was fitting to shine for human beings. Why is it called שמש (*shemesh*)? Because human beings משתמשין (*mishtamshin*), utilize, it; in other words, שמש (*shemesh*), sun—שמשתמשין בו (*shemishtamshin bo*), which they utilize, and therefore its light is great. The moon, however, which human beings do not customarily utilize, had no need for this.'"[4]

Rabbi Yose said, "מארת (*me'erat*)—one, precisely, and the Torah did not say מאורות (*me'orot*), lights; because it is the way of the whole world that when a great person comes to a city, even though he brings with him many people, only the great person is mentioned. Similarly the sun—because it is greater than all of them, and the moon and the stars are all included in the generality of the sun, Scripture needed only to specify the great one, and that is why it said *me'erat*—one."[5] 

by the phrase *to* [or: *for*] *YHVH* (Numbers 28:15)? The blessed Holy One said, "Let this goat be an atonement for My having made the moon smaller."'"

See also *Bereshit Rabbah* 6:3; *Pirqei de-Rabbi Eli'ezer* 6, 51; *Zohar* 1:19b–20a; 181a–b; 2:144b, 147b–148a, 219b; *ZḤ* 14a (*MhN*), 70d–71a (*ShS*); Moses de León, *Sefer ha-Rimmon*, 189; idem, *Mishkan ha-Edut*, 35b.

4. **Baraita of the Aggadta of Shemu'el the Lesser...** A late rabbinic work known as the *Baraita of Rabbi Shemu'el*, dating from the 7th–10th centuries, deals with astronomy and astrology. The quotation here, however, does not derive from that source; it is "invented"—as is the *Zohar*'s custom. Here the work is attributed to Shemu'el the Lesser, namely Shemu'el ha-Qatan (literally: the Small), who according to BT *Sanhedrin* 11a possessed knowledge of intercalation. In BT *Ḥullin* 60b, he is mentioned in connection with the diminution of the moon, and in JT *Sotah* 9:13, 24b, his name is explained as follows: "Because he belittled himself." See below, note 53.

According to Shemu'el, the moon was lessened because the sun was sufficient to bestow light. Cf. *Bereshit Rabbah* 6:1; *Pesiqta de-Rav Kahana* 5:1.

Even though Genesis 1:17 states of the stars that they too are *to shine upon the earth*, the formulation ואת הכוכבים (*Ve-et ha-kokhavim*), *and the stars*, with an additional *vav*, (and) i.e., seemingly tacked on to the end of verse 16, is interpreted as signifying their secondary status. Cf. *Bereshit Rabbah* 6:4.

On the wordplay *shemesh–mishtamishin*, see *ZḤ* 15a, 15c (both *MhN*). See below, at note 46.

5. **מארת (*me'erat*)—one, precisely ...** According to Rabbi Yose, the missing *vavs* indicate a singular referent: one light, namely the sun—the most important of all the luminaries.

Rabbi opened with this verse: *I am black but beautiful*... (Song of Songs 1:5). "*I am black*—the moon. When she does not bask in the radiance of the sun and is concealed from it—black, light unseen—she advances and says: אל תראוני (*Al tir'uni*), *Do not look at me, for I am blackish* (ibid., 6)—that is, you cannot see, for I am blackish. Why? ששזפתני השמש (*She-shezafatni ha-shemesh*), *Because the sun has made me pitch-black* (ibid.)—withdrawing from me at certain times, darkening my light. As Rabbi Ḥanilai said: 'In the cities by the sea, so do they call a person who is far from his friend; or [regarding] one whose friends hold him distant away from them, they say, "So-and-so שזוף (*shazuf*), is darkened, from us."'"[6] [430]

Rabbi Azariah said, "It is written מארת (*me'orot*) in reference to a curse, illuminating the path of its servants. When the blessed Holy One created the sun, He saw that the inhabitants of the world were destined to make it into a deity, so He made it מארת (*me'erat*), a curse, for them, that they would perish from the world on its account, as is written: *lest you raise your eyes to the heavens and see the sun and the moon [and the stars and all the array of the heavens] and you be led astray and bow down to them and worship them* (Deuteronomy 4:19). What is written afterward? *I have called to witness against you the heavens and the earth [that you shall surely perish]* (ibid., 26). Accordingly, it stands poised to be a curse for its worshippers."[7]



6. ***Do not look at me, for I am blackish*...** The simple sense of the verse is: *Do not look at me for I am blackish, because the sun has scorched* [or: *gazed upon*] *me.* Rabbi transforms this to: *You cannot see me because the sun has darkened me*—that is, it has turned away from me, leaving me unillumined—so *I am blackish.* See *Zohar* 3:45b, 59b; *ZḤ* 69d (*ShS*). See also *ZḤ* 27c (*MhN*).

The root of the verbal form ששזפתני (*she-shezafatni*) is probably שזף (*shzf*), "to look upon, catch sight of" (as in Job 20:9; 28:7). However, Rabbi understands it as based on the noun זפת (*zefet*), "pitch," yielding the meaning *because* [*the sun*] *has made me black as pitch.* On *she-shezafatni* and *zefet*, see Pope, *Song of Songs*, 322.

On the expression "cities by the sea," see BT *Rosh ha-Shanah* 26a; *Zohar* 1:137a; *ZḤ* 6d (both *MhN*).

"So-and-so is darkened from us" is akin to the English idiom "He is dead to me!"

"Rabbi" indicates Rabbi Yehudah ha-Nasi (the Patriarch), who redacted the Mishnah. He was so esteemed that he was called simply "Rabbi": the Master.

After "she advances and says," the manuscript reads "*I am black*—the moon. When...." This seems to be a mistake. I have omitted the latter words, proceeding immediately to the following verse from the Song of Songs.

7. **It is written מארת (*me'orot*) in reference to a curse...** The word *me'orot* is spelled deficiently, enabling the word to be read as *me'erat*, "curse." The sun stands poised to be a curse for the idolators, who in elevating the sun to a god, will be punished and eliminated from the world. On *me'erat* as "curse," see Proverbs 3:33; JT *Ta'anit* 4:4, 68b: "On the fourth day [of the week, Wednesday], they would fast for infants, so that diphtheria not enter their mouths. *God said, 'Let there be* מארת (*me-*

It has been taught: Rabbi Yehudah said, "I have heard that the worshipers of the sun fashion windows on the eastern side of their temples, corresponding to twelve hours, and every single hour that the sun descends through these windows, they all bow down in its direction and pray to it. When the sun does not shine, they say that their god is angry with them, and they weep and pray the whole day."[8]

Rabbi Yitsḥak said, "What is the meaning of *May they revere You with the sun* (Psalms 72:5)? That a person should pray accompanied by the twilight of the sun, and bless the one who created it; demonstrating to [all] who come into the world that there is a God beyond who created it. What blessing does one say? 'Who forms light and creates darkness,' concluding with 'Blessed [are You, *YHVH*,] who fashions the luminaries.'"[9]



*'orot*), *lights*'—spelled מארת (*me'erat*), curse." See also *Soferim* 17:4; Rashi on Genesis 1:14.

Cf. *Bereshit Rabbah* 6:1: "Rabbi Azariah said in the name of Rabbi Ḥanina, 'The orb of the sun alone was created to give light. If so, why was the moon created? Well, this teaches that the blessed Holy One foresaw that the peoples of the world were destined to treat them as divinities. The blessed Holy One said, "If when they are two, opposed to each other, and yet idolators treat them as divinities, how much more would they do so if there were but one!"'" See also *Pesiqta de-Rav Kahana* 5:1. On the worship of the luminaries, see Maimonides, *Mishneh Torah, Hilkhot Avodat Kokhavim*, 1:1–2; 2:1. See also Solomon Ibn Gabirol, *Keter Malkhut*, Canto 12.

8. **worshipers of the sun...** The legendary account here derives in part from Maimonides' discussion of the ritual life of the Sabians. See *Guide of the Perplexed* 3:29: "In conformity with these opinions, the Sabians set up statues for the planets, golden statues for the sun, and silver ones for the moon.... And they built temples, set up the statues in them, and thought that the forces of the planets overflowed toward these statues.... You will find that in their books, about which I will give you information, they mention that under certain circumstances they offer to the sun, their highest deity, seven beetles, seven mice, and seven bats." Among their numerous books, Maimonides mentions "The Book of the Degrees of the Sphere and the Forms Appearing in Each of These Degrees."

See also Chwolson, *Die Ssabier und der Ssabismus*, 2:381, on the Arab writer Dimashqi—who described 48 windows in pagan sun temples.

Compare BT *Berakhot* 7a, in the name of Rabbi Meir: "When the sun begins to shine and all the kings of the East and West put on their crowns and bow down to the sun, immediately the blessed Holy One turns angry." See also M *Sukkah* 5:4; BT *Sukkah* 51b.

See *ZḤ* 76c (*MhN, Rut*), which mentions thirteen windows through which the sun passes.

On sun worship in the *Zohar*, see *Zohar* 1:95b; 2:35a, 188a; Liebes, *Pulḥan ha-Shaḥar*.

9. ***May they revere You with the sun...*** The morning prayer, *Shaḥarit*, cannot be recited while it is still dark but rather with the first light of the sun. See BT *Berakhot* 29b: "Rabbi Eli'ezer says, 'One who makes his prayer a fixed task, [his prayer is not a (genuine) supplication].' What is meant by a fixed task?... Abbaye son of Avin and Rabbi Ḥanina son of Avin both said, 'Whoever does not pray with דמדומי חמה (*dimdumei ḥamah*), the twilight of the sun [i.e., the first and last rays of the sun]. For Rabbi Ḥiyya

Alternatively, *May they revere You with the sun.* Rabbi Yehudah said, "When the sun rises, returning to be renewed every day, it goes and bows to its King, to the One who created the sun—then it is time to pray to the One Who Forms All, and bow down to Him, as is written: *May they revere You with the sun.*"[10]

Rabbi Ya'akov son of Idi said, "The blessed Holy One desired Jacob and his offspring to be *His allotted inheritance* (Deuteronomy 32:9)—to inherit the world to come, which is day, and bequeath it to his sons after him."[11]

As we have learned: Rabbi Yehoshu'a son of Levi said, "Jacob was the choice of all the patriarchs."[12]

Rabbi Yitsḥak said to him, "But is it not written *Abraham, My lover* (Isaiah 41:8)—implying that he was the greatest of them all?!"

Rabbi Yehoshu'a replied, "Come and see: Abraham was proximate to Terah, with no intermediary between them. The blessed Holy One chose him [431] and led him lovingly, to draw him to His service. He called him *My lover*, not wishing to coerce him, but rather drawing him lovingly. Isaac appeared; and
542 there was but one intermediary between him and Terah, as is written: *the Fear*

son of Abba said in the name of Rabbi Yoḥanan, "It is a commandment to pray with the twilight of the sun."' Rabbi Zeira said, 'What is its verse [its Scriptural support]? *May they revere You with the sun, and before the moon generations on end* (Psalms 72:5).'" See Rashi, ad loc. See also BT *Shabbat* 118b; *Zohar* 1:178a; 2:196a; *ZḤ* 17d (*MhN*).

The blessing "Who forms light... fashions the luminaries," is one of the *Shema*'s associated blessings in the morning liturgy. Although the *Shema* may be recited as soon as dawn breaks, devotees wait so as to complete it (together with its blessings) immediately before the sun appears, so that they can join it to the *Amidah* precisely at sunrise. That is, they ideally begin the morning *Amidah* as the first ray of sunlight appears. See BT *Berakhot* 9b: "Devotees used to complete it [the recitation of the *Shema*] with the first ray of the sun, in order to join *ge'ullah* [redemption, the name of the blessing following the *Shema*] to *tefillah* [prayer, the *Amidah*] and consequently pray [the *Amidah*] in the daytime. Rabbi Zeira said, 'What is its verse [its scriptural support]? *May they revere You with the sun* (Psalms 72:5).'"

See M *Berakhot* 1:2; *Tosefta Berakhot* 1:2 (and Lieberman, ad loc.); JT *Berakhot* 1:2, 3a–b; BT *Berakhot* 9b, 26a; *Tur, Oraḥ Ḥayyim* 58, 89; *Beit Yosef* and *Shulḥan Arukh, Oraḥ Ḥayyim* 58:1; 89:1,3,8.

10. ***with the sun*** Israel reveres and bows to God below, as the sun reveres and bows to God above; hence: *with the sun.*

On the sun's bowing to the King of Kings, see *Pirqei de-Rabbi Eli'ezer* 6; on the sun's daily renewal, see *Pirqei de-Rabbi Eli'ezer* 51.

The manuscript reads "bows to מלאכה (*malakhah*), its angel," although מלכה (*malkah*), "its king," seems preferable. See Solomon Ibn Gabirol, *Keter Malkhut*, Canto 15.

11. **to inherit the world to come, which is day...** On the world to come as day, see BT *Ḥagigah* 12b; *Pirqei de-Rabbi Eli'ezer* 34.

The full verse from Deuteronomy reads: *For YHVH's share is His people, Jacob His allotted inheritance.*

12. **choice of all the patriarchs** See *Bereshit Rabbah* 76:1: "Rabbi Pinḥas said in the name of Rabbi Re'uven: '... The chosen of the patriarchs is Jacob, as is said: *For Yah has chosen Jacob for Himself* (Psalms 135:4).'"

*of Isaac* (Genesis 31:42). As soon as Jacob appeared, the blessed Holy One said, 'From here on, consummation of the world!' What is written of him? *You, Jacob, My servant* (Isaiah 41:8; 44:1)."[13]

Rabbi Abbahu said, "When he was born, He fashioned his image in the expanse; and whenever Israel sin and the attribute of judgment is upon them, the blessed Holy One gazes upon his image and has compassion on them, as is written: *God said, 'Let there be lights in the expanse of heaven'* (Genesis 1:14). What is meant by *to shine* (ibid., 15, 17)? *To shine upon the earth* (ibid.), for thus does the blessed Holy One illumine and have compassion upon His creatures. Accordingly, Joseph saw in his dream: *and look, the sun and the moon* (ibid. 37:9)—this is Jacob."[14]

Rabbi Yehudah said, "The verse should have said *God set him in the expanse of the sky.* Why *God set them* (ibid. 1:17), implying two?"[15]

Well, Rabbi Ya'akov said, "The blessed Holy One engraved Jacob by His throne, while wicked Esau He engraved in the lower expanse, to be punished there. When the blessed Holy One wishes to have compassion upon Israel, He gazes upon Jacob's image—and has compassion upon them. And when the



13. **From here on consummation of the world!...** Only with the advent of Jacob, twice removed from Terah the idolator, is the world perfected. Hence, Jacob is the choice of the patriarchs.

Here Jacob's arrival is described as שלימותא דעלמא (*sheleimuta de-alma*), "consummation of the world." Elsewhere in the *Zohar*, he is frequently described as שלימו דאבהן (*sheleimu de-avhan*), "consummation of the patriarchs," and as תשבחתא דאבהן (*tushbeḥata de-avhan*), "glory of the patriarchs." For the former term, see *Zohar* 1:144b, 149b, 171b, 172b, 180a; 2:48b. For the latter term, see *Zohar* 1:119b, 133a, 163b, 207b; 2:23a.

On Jacob's being שלם (*shalem*), "complete," see Genesis 33:18; *Sifra, Beḥuqqotai* 8:7, 112c; *Targum Onqelos*, Genesis 25:27; BT *Shabbat* 33b; *Vayiqra Rabbah* 36:5. On drawing Abraham in love, see Rashi on Isaiah 41:8.

Isaiah 41:8 reads: *You, Israel, My servant; Jacob, whom I have chosen, seed of Abraham My lover.* Isaiah 44:1 reads: *Now listen, Jacob, My servant; Israel whom I have chosen!*

14. **He fashioned his image in the expanse...** According to rabbinic tradition, Jacob's image is engraved on the Throne of Glory. See *Bereshit Rabbah* 68:12; 82:2; *Eikhah Rabbah* 2:2; *Targum Yerushalmi* and *Targum Yerushalmi* (frag.), Genesis 28:12; BT *Ḥullin* 91b (and Rashi, ad loc., s.v. *bidyoqno*); *Pirqei de-Rabbi Eli'ezer* 35; *Zohar* 1:72a, 97a (*MhN*), 168a (mentioning gazing upon the image and feeling compassion); *ZḤ* 14c (*MhN*); Wolfson, *Along the Path*, 1–62.

As Scholem noted, this passage presents an original idea: that the luminary above represents Jacob; see "Parashah Ḥadashah," 431, n. 22.

Cf. *ZḤ* 14d (*MhN*), where Moses, Aaron, and Miriam are engraved on high—and are understood as the luminaries in the expanse.

The verse from Genesis describes Joseph's dream. *Look, I dreamed another dream, and look, the sun and the moon and eleven stars were bowing down to me!* In the dream, Jacob is signified by the sun.

15. **The verse should have said...** If Jacob is the sun in the expanse, and his image engraved on high, why does the verse employ the plural? What else is set on high?

blessed Holy One wishes to annihilate a nation of wicked Edom, He gazes upon the image of Esau—and destroys them. To one, dominion in the world to come; and to the other, dominion in this world, as is written: *to have dominion over day and night* (ibid., 18). *To have dominion over day*—Jacob, who has dominion over day: the world to come, which is day; *and night*—in this world, wicked Esau, who has dominion in this world, which is night."[16]

Rabbi Tanḥum said, "Is wicked Esau really engraved on high?! For it is written: *You are not a God who delights in wickedness; evil cannot abide with You* (Psalms 5:5), and it is written: *and Esau I have hated* (Malachi 1:3). How can he be engraved above?!"

Rabbi Abbahu said, "He is not engraved, but his name is engraved, in order to annihilate his children for their sins, through him."

Our Rabbis have taught: Once, Rabbi Shim'on son of Yoḥai was walking by the outskirts of Tiberias. Rabbi Yose met him [432] and said to him, "You are a Master of the Academy; a sign in the world! Look, we have learned in your name: It is forbidden to gaze upon his countenance. If in this world it is forbidden, how much more so above—and in the world to come?! And yet, Rabbi Ya'akov said that wicked Esau is engraved on high!"[17]



16. **while wicked Esau He engraved in the lower expanse...** This idea too is original to *MhN*; see above, note 14.

On the world to come as day, and this world as night, see BT *Ḥagigah* 12b; *Pirqei de-Rabbi Eli'ezer* 34.

On Jacob and Esau as enjoying dominion respectively in the world to come and in this world, see *Seder Eliyyahu Zuta* 19: "It is said that when Jacob and Esau were in their mother's womb, Jacob said to Esau, 'Esau, my brother, our father has two of us, even as two worlds—this world and the world to come—are before us. In this world, there is eating, drinking, the give-and-take of business, marriage, and the begetting of children. But with regard to all these activities, the world to come is quite different. If you so prefer, take this world—and I will take the world to come.' How do we know that it is so? As is said: *Sell me your birthright* כיום (*kayom*), *like that day* (Genesis 25:31)—as we discussed in the womb [on that day]."

See also *ZḤ* 14a–b (*MhN*); cf. *Zohar* 1:170b.

17. **by the outskirts of Tiberias...** "Outskirts" renders פלכי (*pilkhei*). In the Talmud פלך (*pelekh*) means "district, region," as opposed to the city. (See also Nehemiah 3:9–18). According to Scholem, however, *pilkhei* is a corruption of פילי (*pilei*), "gates," and hence Rabbi Shim'on is walking by the gates of Tiberias (cf. *Bereshit Rabbah* 96:5; *Tanḥuma, Shofetim* 10; *Zohar* 1:57b, 217a.) See Nehemiah 3:14–15 and BT *Makkot* 7a, where gates and the word *pelekh* are associated. The form *pilkhei* appears again in *ZḤ* 23a (*MhN*). See Scholem, "Parashah Ḥadashah," 431, n. 28, and Meroz, "Va-Ani Lo Hayiti Sham?," 165 (Addendum 3 in this volume).

The rainbow is a sign of the divine covenant with the world (see Genesis 9:12–17); but if a fully righteous person is alive, he himself serves as such a sign—and the rainbow is unnecessary. See *Pesiqta de-Rav Kahana* 11:15; *Bereshit Rabbah* 35:2; JT *Berakhot* 9:2, 13d; BT *Ketubbot* 77b; *Zohar* 1:225a; 2:174b; 3:15a, 36a; *ZḤ* 10d (*MhN*); Liebes, *Studies in the Zohar*, 15.

On the epithet "Master of the Academy," see *Zohar* 1:115b (*MhN*), 123b (*Tos*); *ZḤ* 15a,

Rabbi Shim'on opened, saying, "*YHVH saw and He spurned, from the vexation of His sons and His daughters. He said, 'Let Me hide My face from them'* (Deuteronomy 32:19–20). What is meant by *YHVH saw and He spurned*? Well, the blessed Holy One was gazing upon the great honor with which wicked Esau honored his father; and when He contemplated that honor, He grew angry with His children who angered Him; and He wished to remove the image of Jacob from His presence so as not to gaze upon it, as is written: *He said, 'Let Me hide My face from them'*—the image of Jacob."[18]

Rabbi said, "Two reckonings have been transposed in this world; for the sun is Jacob—but the children of Esau reckon the year's count thereby, whereas Jacob and his children reckon the year's count by the moon. In the world to come, the blessed Holy One will remove them from this dominion, as is written: *Then the moon shall be ashamed and the sun shall be abashed* (Isaiah 24:23). Why? *For YHVH of hosts will reign* (ibid.). And it is written: *For you, in awe of My name, the sun of justness will rise, with healing [in its wings]* (Malachi 3:20)—the sun of Jacob."[19]



25d (both *MhN*). See *Pesiqta de-Rav Kahana* 11:15, 23:12. Cf. the term "Masters of Mishnah," on which see below, note 59.

On the prohibition of looking upon Esau's countenance, cf. *Tanḥuma*, *Toledot* 8: "Why did Isaac's eyes dim? Because he gazed upon the image of wicked Esau."

18. **wicked Esau honored his father...** See *Shemot Rabbah* 46:4: "*A son honors his father* (Malachi 1:6)—Esau, who honored his father greatly, going out to the fields, hunting game, bringing it back, cooking it, bringing it to his father, and feeding him every day."

See *Pesiqta Rabbati* 23: "Rabbi Neḥunia said in the name of Rabbi Tanḥum son of Yudan, 'Who delayed the honor of Jacob in this world? The great honor rendered to his father.'"

On Esau's honoring Isaac, see *Sifrei*, Deuteronomy 336; *Bereshit Rabbah* 65:16; 76:2; *Devarim Rabbah* 1:15; *Targum Yerushalmi* and *Ba'al ha-Turim*, Deuteronomy 2:5; *Zohar* 1:146b.

19. **Two reckonings have been transposed...** Even though Jacob is the sun, the historical order is marked by an inversion. Israel's calendar is based on the moon, whose diminution signifies Israel's subjugation in this world, while Esau's (signifying Edom, Rome, Christendom) calendar is based on the sun, whose domination of the sky signifies their dominion in this world. In the world to come, dominion will return to Jacob, and his sun will rise again. See *ZḤ* 14b (*MhN*).

See BT *Sukkah* 29a: "Our Rabbis taught: ...'Israel counts by the moon, idolators by the sun.'"

See also *Bereshit Rabbah* 6:3: "Rabbi Levi said in the name of Rabbi Yose son of Ila'i, 'It is natural that the great should calculate by the great, and the small by the small. Esau calculates by the sun, which is large, and Jacob by the moon, which is small.' Rabbi Naḥman said, 'That is a happy presage. Esau calculates by the sun, which is large: just as the sun rules by day but not by night, so does Esau have a share in this world, but has no share in the world to come. Jacob calculates by the moon, which is small: just as the moon rules by day and by night, so Jacob has a share in this world and in the world to come!'"

On the lunar and solar calendars, see *Mekhilta*, *Pisḥa* 1; *Tosefta Sukkah* 2:6; *Pesiqta de-Rav Kahana* 5:1, 14; *Zohar* 1:46b, 236b, 239a;

Rabbi Yoḥanan said, "By your coming here, I now recall a certain pearl. For Rabbi Ḥiyya said, 'What is the meaning of the verse *For you, in awe of My name, the sun of justness will rise, with healing* [*in its wings*]? That sun of Jacob.'"[20]

Rabbi Yoḥanan said, "*He encountered* [433] *a certain place and stayed there for the night because the sun had set* (Genesis 28:11). What is the significance of *because the sun had set*? Rabbi Yitsḥak said, 'It set for him before its time.' Rabbi Ḥiyya used to say, 'It was not on his account. Rather, it was the sun of Jacob; and as soon as dominion was granted to Esau, the sun—which had been Jacob's domain—was withdrawn, as is written: *because the sun had set*—the power of Jacob's domain weakened and was granted to Esau.'"[21]

Rabbi Yehudah said in the name of Rabbi Yitsḥak, "In days gone by, in Italy of [Edom] there was a royal arena in which were engraved all the engravings of



3:220b. On the sun of Jacob and the verse from Malachi, see *Zohar* 1:203a–b. On Jacob as sun, see *Bereshit Rabbah* 68:10 (below, note 21); *Zohar* 1:135a, 136a, 146b, 148a, 166a.

20. **I now recall a certain pearl...** A nearly identical expression appears in *ZḤ* 14a (*MhN*). On possessing pearls of teaching, see BT *Ḥagigah* 3a; *Zohar* 1:148b; 2:209a; *ZḤ* 10b (*MhN*). Cf. BT *Berakhot* 17a, *Sanhedrin* 50b, *Zevaḥim* 36b.

21. ***because the sun had set...*** According to Rabbi Yoḥanan, this setting sun marks the historical (or cosmic) transposition whereby Esau attains dominion over Jacob. See *ZḤ* 14a, 14c–d, 27c (all *MhN*); see also *ZḤ* 23d–24a (*MhN*). See below, at note 57.

According to the rabbinic interpretation of the verse, as Jacob fled to Haran, the sun set prematurely so that Jacob might stay at the site of the future temple and converse with God. See *Bereshit Rabbah* 68:10: "כי בא השמש (*Ki va ha-shemesh*), *Because the sun had set* (Genesis 28:11). Our Rabbis say, 'This teaches that the blessed Holy One caused the orb of the sun to set prematurely, in order to speak in privacy with our father Jacob. This may be compared to a king's close friend who visited him occasionally. The king said, "Extinguish the lamps, for I desire to speak with my friend in privacy." In the same way the blessed Holy One caused the sun to set prematurely so that he might speak to our father Jacob in privacy.' Rabbi Pinḥas said in the name of Rabbi Ḥanin, 'He [Jacob] heard the voices of the angels saying *Ba ha-shemesh, ba ha-shemesh, the sun is coming, the sun is coming* (ibid.). And so when Joseph related *Behold, the sun and the moon... bowed down to me* (Genesis 37:9), Jacob exclaimed, "Who revealed to him that my name is Sun?"' When did the blessed Holy One restore to him those two hours by which He had caused [the sun prematurely] to set on his account, upon his departure from his father's house? When he was returning to his father's house, as is written: *The sun rose upon him* (ibid. 32:32). The blessed Holy One said to him, 'You are a sign for your children: as on your departure I caused the sun to set for you and on your return I restored to you [the lost hours of] the sun's orb, so shall your children be. When they go forth [into exile]: *She who bore seven is forlorn, utterly disconsolate, her sun has set while it is still day* (Jeremiah 15:9); but on their return [to their own land]: *For you, in awe of My name, the sun of justness will rise, with healing in its wings* (Malachi 3:20).'"

See also *Targum Yerushalmi* (frag.), Genesis 28:10; *Targum Yerushalmi*, Genesis 28:10, 32:32; BT *Ḥullin* 91b.

the world. Above them all, they would engrave the image of Esau and Jacob. And above Jacob's head they would draw the sun, and another drawing of the sun's moving and descending upon the head of Esau, who was basking in its splendor; and a drawing of the moon moving and descending upon the head of Jacob, who was utilizing its splendor—a splendor that does not shine. Above the moon was written 'A Deceiver Falling in his Deceit.'"[22]

Rabbi Bo said, "Was the Glory of the Patriarchs—who is engraved on high upon the Throne of Glory, radiance of the supernal King—really a deceiver?! Look at what we have learned: Rabbi Yitsḥak said in the name of Rabbi Yoḥanan in the name of Rabbi Shim'on, 'It is forbidden to mislead people, even Gentiles.' All the more so since he was his brother! How could he have misled with deception?"[23]

Rabbi Abba rose to his feet and said, "O Adam—first creature fashioned by the blessed Holy One in His image, supernal splendor, to serve in His pres-



22. **In days gone by, in Italy...** The account here, while entirely fantastic, graphically represents the historical (or cosmic) transposition whereby Esau inherits Jacob's sun while Jacob inherits the diminished, lusterless moon.

See BT *Avodah Zarah* 11b: "Rav Yehudah said in the name of Shemu'el, 'They have yet another festival in Rome—once every seventy years. A healthy man is brought and made to ride on a lame man; he is dressed in the attire of Adam, on his head is placed the scalp of Rabbi Ishmael, and on his neck are hung pieces of fine gold to the weight of four *zuzim*; the market places [through which these pass] are paved with onyx stones, and the proclamation is made before him: The reckoning of the ruler is wrong. The brother of our lord, the impostor! Let him who will see it, see it; he who will not see it now, will never see it [for this spectacle occurs once every seventy years]. Of what avail is treason to the traitor, or deceit to the deceiver! And they concluded thus: Woe unto the one when the other will arise.' Rav Ashi said, 'Their own mouth causes them to stumble! Had they said "Our lord's brother the impostor," it would have accorded with their intention, but when they say "The brother of our lord, the impostor," it may be taken to mean that it is their lord himself who is the impostor.'" According to Rashi, ad loc., the "healthy man" symbolizes Esau; he is riding upon Jacob the "lame man" (see Genesis 32:32), thereby signifying Edom's dominion over Israel. Furthermore, the incorrect "reckoning" alludes to Jacob's prophecy regarding the end of days (see Genesis 49:1); and the deception refers to Jacob's trickery in obtaining Isaac's blessing (see Genesis 27).

In the manuscript following the words "in Italy of" there is a blank space. I presume that the missing word is "Edom" or perhaps "Rome."

"Royal arena" renders ריסא דעלמא (*risa de-alma*), literally "arena of the world." However, following Scholem, I have emended the text to ריסא דמלכא (*risa de-malka*), "arena of the king." The opening sentence of this story seems garbled; thus the translation here is tentative. See Scholem, "Parashah Ḥadashah," 433, n. 44.

23. **It is forbidden to mislead people, even Gentiles...** See BT *Ḥullin* 94a in the name of Shemu'el. See also Maimonides, *Mishneh Torah, Hilkhot De'ot* 2:6.

On "Glory of the Patriarchs," see above, note 13. On Jacob engraved on the throne, see above, note 14.

ence—who will uncover the dust from your eyes?! For we have found it written in our secrets that he was the Glory of the Patriarchs and the blessed Holy One glories in him every day. He was of consummate mind, and yet, schoolchildren find him to have been of deceptive mind, that he duped his brother, and consequently his children were subjugated beneath him."[24]

While they were sitting, Rabbi El'azar son of Rabbi Shim'on arrived. They said, "Look, the son of the Master of the Academy has arrived!"

Rabbi said, "It is time to be silent!"

He entered. He said, "In what are the rabbis engaged?"[25]

Rabbi Bo, who was standing on his feet, told him.

Rabbi El'azar said, "Were it not for the fact that [434] *Shekhinah* is here, you would deserve a lashing for suspecting a supremely innocent person such as this! And it is written: *To punish the innocent is surely not right* [*or to flog the great for their uprightness*] (Proverbs 17:26)."[26]



24. **who will uncover the dust from your eyes...** On this exclamation, see *Bereshit Rabbah* 21:7; *Vayiqra Rabbah* 25:2; *Tanḥuma, Shemini* 8. See also M *Sotah* 5:2. The sense of the expression is: If only you were alive to hear what they are saying! Namely, that Jacob deceived his brother Esau and that is why Israel is subjugated to Edom.

On the blessed Holy One's glorying in Jacob every day, see *Heikhalot Rabbati*, Schäfer, *Synopse zur Hekhalot-Literatur*, §164: "Bear witness to them of what testimony you see in Me, of what I do to the face of Jacob your father, which is engraved [unto] Me upon the throne of My glory. For in the hour when you speak before Me 'holy,' I stoop over it, embrace, fondle, and kiss it; and My hands lie upon his arms three times, when you speak before Me 'holy,' as is said: *Holy, holy, holy* [*is YHVH of Hosts*] (Isaiah 6:3)."

See idem, *The Hidden and Manifest God*, 46; Wolfson, *Through A Speculum That Shines*, 101–2.

Rabbi Abba and Rabbi Bo appear to conflate here.

25. **In what are the rabbis engaged?** For the sequence "Meanwhile, so-and-so arrived ... He said, 'What are you engaged in?'" see BT *Yevamot* 105b; *Gittin* 31b; *Zohar* 1:207b, 245a; 2:5a (*MhN*).

26. **Were it not for the fact that *Shekhinah* is here...** *Shekhinah* manifests whenever Torah is being studied. See M *Avot* 3:6: "Rabbi Ḥalafta from Kefar Ḥananya says, 'If ten are sitting engaged in Torah, *Shekhinah* dwells among them ... even five ... even three ... even two ... even one.'" See also M *Avot* 3:2.

Cf. *Mekhilta, Amaleq* (*Yitro*) 1: "Whoever receives the face of [i.e., welcomes] the wise, it is as if he receives the face of *Shekhinah*."

Cf. JT *Eruvin* 5:1, 22b: "Rabbi Shemu'el said in the name of Rabbi Zeira, '... Whoever receives the face of his teacher, it is as if he receives the face of *Shekhinah*.' ... Rabbi Yishma'el taught ... 'One who receives the face of his friend, it is as if he receives the face of *Shekhinah*.'" Cf. Genesis 33:10; *Tanḥuma, Ki Tissa* 27; *Shir ha-Shirim Rabbah* on 2:5.

See *Zohar* 1:9a, 94b, 115b (*MhN*); 2:5a (*MhN*), 20a (*MhN*), 50a, 94b, 198a; 3:6b, 148a, 298a; *ZḤ* 11c, 25b (both *MhN*).

The manuscript reads "דחשבתון (*de-ḥashavtun*), for considering, a supremely innocent person ..."; but following Scholem, I have emended the text to דחשדתון (*de-ḥashadetun*), "for suspecting," based on BT *Shabbat* 97a: "Resh Lakish said, 'Whoever suspects worthy folks is struck on his own

He opened his mouth and said, "תמים (*Tamim*), *Wholehearted, shall you be with YHVH your God* (Deuteronomy 18:13). What is meant by תמים (*tamim*), wholehearted? Like a person who is not concerned with the matters of the world, his heart not racing to inquire, 'What is this and what is that?' Rather, he sets himself as a beast to bear a burden. Look at what we have learned in our Mishnah: One should distance oneself from שור תם (*shor tam*), an innocent ox, fifty cubits [and from שור מועד (*shor mu'ad*), an ox known to be violent—out of sight]. What is meant by תם (*tam*), innocent? One that children can touch yet does not gore. Therefore Torah testified about Jacob, saying: *Jacob was* איש תם (*ish tam*), *an innocent man* (Genesis 25:27). Look, Jacob is called innocent, yet you have made him מועד (*mu'ad*), liable—and believed what wicked Esau said, as is written: *Is that why his name was called* יעקב (*Ya'akov*), *Jacob?* [ויעקבני (*Va-ya'qeveni*), *For he has deceived me, these two times. My birthright he took; and look, now he has taken my blessing!*] (ibid. 27:36).[27]

"Rather, so have I heard from my father: Jacob was exceedingly consummate, and used to study Torah in the academy of Eber. Wicked Esau approached him. He wanted to go out to the field and he went out. He said to him, 'Give me something to eat, and my birthright shall be yours.' But because Jacob was of consummate heart, he paid him no heed. He said, 'What need have I of the



body....'" See BT *Yoma* 19b; Scholem, "Parashah Ḥadashah," 434, n. 55.

27. ***Jacob was* איש תם *(ish tam)*...** Rabbi El'azar begins an extended exoneration of Jacob. He was not a deceiver, as Esau's interpretation of his name suggests, but rather was תם (*tam*), "innocent, consummate"; he was שור תם (*shor tam*), "an innocent ox," and not שור מועד (*shor mu'ad*), "a liable ox."

Genesis 25:27 reads: *The boys grew up. Esau became a skilled hunter, a man of the field, while Jacob was* איש תם (*ish tam*), *a simple man, dwelling in tents.* The word *tam* means "simple, innocent, plain, mild, quiet, sound, wholesome, complete, perfect." *Targum Onqelos*, ad loc., renders it שלים (*shelim*), "complete, perfect, consummate."

On *shor tam* (the innocent ox) and *shor mu'ad* (the ox known to be violent and for which one is liable), see BT *Berakhot* 33a; *Pesaḥim* 112b in the name of Rav Osha'ya: "One should distance oneself from an innocent ox fifty cubits, and from an ox known to be violent—out of sight." On *shor tam* as the one with whom children can play safely, see M *Bava Qamma* 2:4 (BT *Bava Qamma* 23b) in the name of Rabbi Me'ir. On submitting oneself as a beast to bear a burden, see BT *Avodah Zarah* 5b: "It was taught in the school of Elijah: A person should always set himself to words of Torah like an ox to the yoke and a donkey to the burden."

See also Rashi on Deuteronomy 18:13: *Wholehearted shall you be with YHVH your God*—"Walk with him in utter simplicity, in anticipation of Him. Do not explore the future; rather, whatever befalls you accept with perfect simplicity. Then you will be with Him as His portion." On this verse, see also *Zohar* 1:167b.

On the expression "our Mishnah," see *Zohar* 1:37b, 55b, 74a, 91b, 93a, 95b, 96a, 124b (*MhN*), 136b (*MhN*), 137a (*MhN*), 139a (*MhN*), 223b; 2:5a (*MhN*), 123b; 3:75b, 78a, 284b, 285a, 293b (*IZ*); *ZḤ* 12b, 14a, 15b, 16a, 18b, 20a (all *MhN*); Matt, "Matnita di-Lan."

On Jacob as *ish tam*, see *Zohar* 1:146a, 167b, 222a; 2:78b, 79a, 175b; 3:12b, 163b.

birthright?' He went out to the field; and Jacob went to the academy and told Eber what Esau had said to him. Eber said to him, 'You do not realize what you lost this day! Today you have lost three supernal portions because you didn't [...] that you did not take the birthright from your brother; they would befit you more than him, for you study Torah while he goes out to the field to kill people! Prepare him something to eat; and when he approaches you and asks you [for some]—for not for nothing *the belly of the wicked will be empty* (Proverbs 13:25)—offer him the deal of the birthright.' Immediately: ויזד יעקב נזיד (*Va-yazed Ya'akov nazid*), *Jacob cooked up a stew* (Genesis 25:29)—he thought in his heart about what his teacher had told him, as is said: *for in this thing that* זדו (*zadu*), *they schemed, against them* (Exodus 18:11), which is translated as 'that the Egyptians thought.' What is written? *Esau came from the field* (Genesis 25:29). He asked [435] him for some food. Jacob said to him, 'In the ledger ratified by seal.' *Sell* כיום (*ka-yom*), *now* [*your birthright to me*] (ibid., 31). Look, his response points to this, as implied by what is written: כיום (*ka-yom*), *this day*, for he used to offer it to him for sale before. If he used to offer it to him for sale before, what deception is there here?![28]

"Furthermore, he did not seize the blessing through deception. His mother pressed him, but he, with his consummate heart, did not wish to—and he

28. **Jacob went to the academy and told Eber...** The account of Eber's convincing Jacob to obtain the birthright from Esau is not found in rabbinic sources. As in the following paragraph, Rabbi El'azar shifts the blame for Jacob's deception to others: first to Eber (regarding the birthright, see Genesis 25:29–34), and then to Rebekah (regarding the blessing, see Genesis 27).

The first two sentences of the paragraph seem confused. Perhaps one should read: "Jacob was exceedingly consummate and used to study Torah in the academy of Eber, whereas wicked Esau desired to go out to the field. He went out. He approached him and said..."

There appears to be a gap in the text (marked by the ellipsis), given that Eber does not explain the significance of the three supernal portions that Jacob forfeited.

Eber was the great-grandson of Noah's son Shem (Genesis 10:21–24), and a patrilineal ancestor of Abraham. According to rabbinic tradition, both Shem and Eber headed an academy of Torah. On Jacob's studying in the academy of Eber, see *Targum Yerushalmi*, Genesis 25:27; *Bereshit Rabbah* 63:10; *Tanḥuma* (Buber), *Vayishlaḥ* 9.

On Esau's going out to kill, see *Targum Yerushalmi*, Genesis 25:27; *Bereshit Rabbah* 63:12; BT *Bava Batra* 16b; *Tanḥuma*, *Ki-Tetse* 4; *Pesiqta de-Rav Kahana* 3:1; *Pirqei de-Rabbi Eli'ezer* 32; *Zohar* 1:139a. On cooking (*va-yazed*) as "thinking, contemplating, scheming," see *Onqelos* on Exodus 18:11 and *Zohar* 1:138b (*MhN*).

"In the ledger ratified by seal" renders בפקססא דמוחדי גושפנקא (*be-piqsasa de-moḥdhi gushpanqa*), a phrase of uncertain meaning. My rendering follows Scholem, reading בפנקסא (*be-pinqasa*), "in a ledger [or: register]," in place of the difficult *piqsasa*. He suggests an allusion here to the account in *Sefer ha-Yashar*, *Toledot*, 31, which mentions that Jacob recorded the details of the transaction in a book. See Scholem, "Parashah Ḥadashah," 435, n. 70.

For a different (allegorical) treatment in *MhN* of the sale of the birthright, see *Zohar* 1:138b.

lingered with her, saying: *What if my father feels me* (ibid. 27:12), and so on, implying that he didn't want to because he was of consummate heart; but his mother accepted the curse upon herself. And he did not stretch forth his hand to cook those kid-goats, as implied by what is written: *and his mother made a delicacy* (ibid., 14)—she and not him! As for Esau, he did so himself, as is written: *He too made a delicacy* (ibid., 31), but Jacob did not wish to engage in any deception. Come and see what is written: *and the skins of the kids she put [on his hands and on the smooth part of his neck]* (ibid., 16)—she and not him, for he was not a deceiver, and knew nothing of this, because of his consummate heart. His mother prepared the dish. She said to him, 'Take this' but he did not take it until she placed it in his hands, as is written: *She placed the delicacy and the bread she had made in the hand of Jacob her son* (ibid., 17). Moreover, when his father inquired, he did not wish to utter a lie. Rather, he said, '*I am; Esau is your firstborn*' (ibid., 19)—and hence the pause between *I am* and *Esau is your firstborn*—whereas Esau said, *I am your son your firstborn Esau* (ibid., 32). Of Jacob is said *who speaks the truth in his heart* (Psalms 15:2)—what was in his heart he brought forth with his lips, and consequently he gained blessings twice, as is written: *Now blessed he stays!* (Genesis 27:33). These verses of Scripture prove that he was no deceiver!"[29]



Rabbi El'azar said, "Whoever says that Jacob was a deceiver, may his breath expire! Rather, he was of consummate mind, consummate heart, consummate ways; consummate with his Master to fulfill what is written: תמים (*Tamim*), *Wholehearted, shall you be with YHVH your God* (Deuteronomy 18:13)."[30]

Whenever Rabbi El'azar son of Rabbi Shim'on would enter the college, Rabbi's face would turn green. His father used to say to him, "Rabbi El'azar is a lion, son of a lion, whereas you are a lion, son of a fox."[31]

29. **he did not seize the blessing through deception...** In Genesis 27, Rebekah masterminds the scheme for Jacob to obtain the blessing from Isaac. According to Rabbi El'azar, Jacob is passive—his consummate heart preventing him from even uttering a lie.

Genesis 27:12–13 read: "*What if my father feels me and I seem a cheat to him—and bring on myself a curse and not a blessing?*" *His mother said, "Upon me your curse, my son...."*

On Jacob as merely bowing to his mother's will, see *Bereshit Rabbah* 65:15. On his pause so as not to lie, between saying *I am* and *Esau your firstborn*, see *Bereshit Rabbah* 65:18; *Tanḥuma* (Buber), *Toledot* 10; *Midrash Aggadah*, *Leqaḥ Tov*, *Sekhel Tov*, Rashi, and Ibn Ezra on Genesis 27:19; *Zohar* 1:167b; 2:85a; *Minḥat Shai* on Genesis 27:19.

On the verse from Psalms as applied to Jacob, see *Midrash Tehillim* 15:6; *Zohar* 1:161a. On speaking what is in one's heart, see BT *Pesaḥim* 113b; *Bava Metsi'a* 49a; Maimonides, *Mishneh Torah*, *Hilkhot De'ot* 2:6.

30. **of consummate mind, consummate heart, consummate ways...** On Jacob's being "consummate," see above, notes 13 and 27.

31. **a lion, son of a lion...** See JT *Shabbat* 10:5, 12c; *Pesiqta de-Rav Kahana* 11:24; *Qohelet Rabbah* on 11:2 (according to which, Rabbi Yehudah's face darkened). See also BT *Bava Metsi'a* 84b; *Mishnat Rabbi Eli'ezer* 10,

Our Rabbis have taught: The blessed Holy One fashioned the sun and set it in the fourth firmament, raising it above the world by four [436] firmaments. Had He not raised it by four firmaments it would incinerate the entire world, and a person would not be able to walk even a single step without it blinding the light of the eyes because of its intense light. He fashioned the moon and set it in the firmament above us, and even though it is set over this world, and there is nothing separating between, our light is not scorched save as light from beyond the wall—for its light is small.[32]

Rav Yehudah said in the name of Rav, "What is the meaning of the verse *The light of the moon shall be as the light of the sun*... (Isaiah 30:26)? If the blessed Holy One is destined to switch the moon for the nations of the world and the sun for Israel, why will the moon shine? Its light should be darkened! Well, Rabbi Yitsḥak said, '*The light of the moon shall be as the light of the sun*—for those about whom is written *Kings shall tend your children*... (ibid. 49:23). *And the light of the sun shall be sevenfold* (ibid. 30:26)—for Israel.'"[33]



Rabbi El'azar said, "The only [light] to shine for Israel is that which is written: *The sun will no more be your light by day, nor will the radiance of the moon shine on you, for* YHVH *will be your everlasting light* (ibid. 60:19)."[34]

*God said, "Let there be lights in the expanse of heaven* [...] *to shine upon the earth"* (Genesis 1:14–15).

Rabbi opened with this verse: *On my bed at night* (Song of Songs 3:1).[35]

Rabbi Yoḥanan said, "Come and see how careful a person must be with his deeds, examining and scrutinizing his affairs! Come and see: The blessed Holy One established a covenant with David that dominion would never be withdrawn from him, as is written: YHVH

p. 190. See *Zohar* 1:223a; 2:15a (*MhN*); 3:60a, 79b, 196a.

32. **and set it in the fourth firmament...** On the sun's location in the fourth firmament (or sphere), see Solomon Ibn Gabirol, *Keter Malkhut*, Canto 15; Maimonides, *Mishneh Torah, Hilkhot Yesodei ha-Torah* 3:1; *ZḤ* 15c (*MhN*).

On the location of the moon immediately above our world, see Maimonides, *Mishneh Torah, Hilkhot Yesodei ha-Torah* 3:1. On the motif "beyond the wall," see Maimonides, *Shemonah Peraqim* 7; *Zohar* 1:232b (*Tos*); 2:69a–b, 82a, 130b, 213a; 3:174b; *ZḤ* 15c (*MhN*), 39d.

33. ***The light of the moon shall be as the light of the sun...*** In the Messianic era, the sun will revert to Jacob (Israel), and the moon to the nations of the world—the inverse of the current world order.

Isaiah 30:26 reads in full: *The light of the moon shall be as the light of the sun, and the light of the sun shall be sevenfold, as the light of the seven days, when* YHVH *binds up His people's wounds and heals the injuries it has suffered.*

Isaiah 49:23 continues: *their queens shall serve you as nurses. They shall bow to you, face to the ground, and lick the dust of your feet. And you shall know that I am* YHVH*—those who trust in Me shall not be ashamed.*

34. ***YHVH will be your everlasting light*** See *ZḤ* 14b (*MhN*).

35. ***On my bed at night*** The verse con-

*swore to David, a truth He will not renounce: 'Of the fruit of your body I will set upon your throne'* (Psalms 132:11)."

As Rabbi Yoḥanan said in the name of Rabbi Yehudah: "You cannot find anyone in the world who strove to serve the blessed Holy One with all his might and to recite countless songs and praises before Him like David! As we have learned: For how long did David sleep [437] at night? Sixty breaths."[36]

Rabbi Ya'akov said, "Is it not already stated *At midnight* [*I rise to praise You for Your just laws*] (ibid. 119:62), implying that he slept until midnight?"[37]

Well, Rabbi Yoḥanan said in the name of Rabbi Yehudah, "David would sit with the Sanhedrin of Israel a quarter of the night; after they left him, he would engage in Torah, recite the *Shema* as is fitting, and lie upon his bed—and until midnight would sleep only sixty breaths. At midnight he would rise mightily with songs and praises, as is written: *My eyes greet the night watches to meditate* [*on your utterance*] (ibid., 148), his songs more pleasing to the blessed Holy One than the songs of the ministering angels. Were his songs really more pleasing before the blessed Holy One than the night song of [the angels]? Indeed! For we have learned: Whoever engages in Torah at night, the blessed Holy One emanates upon him a thread of love by day, as is written: *By day YHVH directs His love, in the night His song is with me* (ibid. 42:9). Why *by day YHVH directs His love*? Because *in the night His song is with me.*"[38]



tinues: *I sought him whom my soul loves—I sought him, but did not find him.* See below, at note 65, where this verse is expounded.

On the identity of Rabbi, see above, note 6.

36. **Sixty breaths** According to BT *Sukkah* 26b (in the name of Abbaye), David's sleep was like that of a horse, which lasts for sixty breaths. That passage discusses daytime sleep, but see the statement by Rabbi Zeira in BT *Berakhot* 3b: "Rabbi Osha'ya said in the name of Rabbi Aḥa, 'David said, "Midnight never passed me by in my sleep."' Rabbi Zeira said, 'Till midnight he used to doze like a horse; from then on, he became mighty as a lion.' Rav Ashi said, 'Till midnight he engaged in Torah; from then on, in songs and praises.'" See *Zohar* 1:207a.

37. ***At midnight...*** Rabbi Ya'akov wonders about David's nightly schedule. If he dozed like a horse, sleeping only sixty breaths, then he must have awakened well before midnight, yet the verse from Psalms (cited also in BT *Berakhot* 3b) implies otherwise. See *Zohar* 1:206b.

38. **David would sit with the Sanhedrin... a quarter of the night...** See *Zohar* 1:206b: "When evening entered, he would sit with all the princes of his household, discussing words of Torah. Afterward, he slept until midnight, when he awoke and engaged in the worship of his lord with songs and praise."

See BT *Ḥagigah* 12b: "Resh Lakish said, 'Whoever engages in Torah at night, the blessed Holy One emanates a thread of love upon him by day, as is said: *By day YHVH directs His love* (Psalms 42:9). Why? Because *in the night His song is with me* (ibid.).'" See also BT *Avodah Zarah* 3b; *Mishnat Rabbi Eli'ezer* 13; Maimonides, *Mishneh Torah, Hilkhot Talmud Torah* 3:13; *Zohar* 1:82b, 92a, 178b, 194b, 207b; 2:18b (*MhN*), 46a, 149a; 3:36a, 44b–45a, 65a; *ZḤ* 18a (*MhN*); Moses de León, *Sefer ha-Rimmon*, 54.

On human nocturnal song as more pleasing than the songs of the angels, see *Zohar*

Rabbi Aḥa said, “Why is night song more pleasing before the blessed Holy One than day song?”

Rabbi Yitsḥak said, “Because a person can attune his heart at night more than by day.”[39]

This accords with what Rabbi Yose son of Pazzi said, “It is customary for a person who awakens at night to think thoughts and arouse the evil impulse. If he switches his imaginings and thoughts, from as is his custom, and he engages in Torah, is it not fitting that it should remain before him more than during the day?!”[40]

Rav Kahana said in the name of Rav Huna, “Through all those degrees that the sun ascends and descends, it recites song before Him and is not silent. The song of the sun is greater than the hosts of heaven and all the stars.”[41]

Why so?

Rabbi Yose said, “Just as the sun is greater than all the stars and other lumi-
554 naries, so its song is greater than all the stars and luminaries.”

What is the song of the sun?

Come and see: As we have learned: The sun ascends and descends twenty-four degrees, and for every single degree recites song.

What song does it recite?

Rabbi Yitsḥak said, “At the first degree, it recites: *The Torah of YHVH is perfect, restoring the soul* (Psalms 19:8).”[42]

2:46a; *ZḤ* 13c, 18a (both *MhN*); cf. BT *Ḥullin* 91b.

The manuscript reads “Were his songs really more pleasing before the blessed Holy One than the night song of people?” although this seems to be an error. Perhaps “angels” was intended instead of “people.”

Psalms 119:148 is also cited in BT *Berakhot* 3b.

39. **attune his heart at night more than by day** See Maimonides, *Mishneh Torah, Hilkhot Talmud Torah* 3:13: “Even though it is a commandment to study during the day and at night, it is only at night that a person acquires most of his wisdom.... The Sages said: The song of Torah is only at night, as is said: *Arise, sing out at night* (Lamentations 2:19).”

See *Zohar* 3:23a: “Rabbi Yehudah said to Rabbi Yose, ‘I see that thirsting clarity of Torah is greater by night than by day.’”

40. **think thoughts and arouse the evil impulse...** On sinful thoughts at night, see *Zohar* 1:109b (*MhN*); 3:11a; Moses de León, *Sefer ha-Rimmon*, 263.

The phrase “that it should remain before him more than during the day” refers to Torah study, which is more enduring at night.

41. **The song of the sun...** See *ZḤ* 15a (*MhN*); see also *Zohar* 2:196a; cf. BT *Yoma* 20b; *Qohelet Rabbah* on 3:14.

On the song of other luminaries and the music of the spheres, see *ZḤ* 5d–6a, 8a (both *MhN*); *ZḤ* 76c (*MhN, Rut*). On the degrees and levels of the sun, see *Pirqei de-Rabbi Eli'ezer* 6; *ZḤ* 15a, 15c (both *MhN*). See also BT *Pesaḥim* 94b; *Eruvin* 56a; *Shemot Rabbah* 15:22.

42. ***The Torah of YHVH is perfect, restoring the soul*** This verse, as well as the verses recited by the sun for the following five

Why does it begin with this verse?

Rabbi Abba son of Kahana said, "You should know: All the souls within human beings belonging to the righteous in the world are raised by Metatron, the Prince of the Countenance, before the blessed Holy One; and as soon as the sun shines they return to their place in order to engage in Torah—then the sun is at the first level. When the souls return to their place, it begins with this verse to offer praise for the souls [438] returning to their place; and it returns to its place to be renewed."[43]

As Rabbi Yehudah said: "The sun does not shine until the hour when Israel is attuned, and then the sun recites its praise from this verse."

At the second level it praises, reciting: *the decrees of YHVH are enduring, making the fool wise* (ibid.).

At the third level: *The precepts of YHVH are upright, delighting the heart* (ibid., 9).

At the fourth level: *the instruction of YHVH is lucid, giving light to the eyes* (ibid.).



At the fifth level: *The fear of YHVH is pure, abiding forever* (ibid., 10).

At the sixth level: *the judgments of YHVH are true* (ibid.). Then it stands in that level until it is granted permission.[44]

It travels to the seventh level, opens, and recites: *May they revere You with the sun, and before the moon—generations on end* (Psalms 72:5).

degrees, comes from Psalms 19, the first half of which is a celebration of the majestic music of the spheres and the journey of the sun: *The heavens declare the glory of God, the sky proclaims His handiwork. Day to day makes utterance, night to night speaks out. There is no utterance, there are no words, whose sound goes unheard. Their voice carries throughout the earth, their words to the end of the world. He placed in them a tent for the sun, who is like a groom coming forth from the canopy, like a hero, eager to run his course. His rising-place is at one end of heaven, and his circuit reaches the other; nothing escapes his heat* (Psalms 19:2–7).

43. **raised by Metatron...** During the night, when the righteous sleep, Metatron raises their souls on high. The souls return to their bodies at precisely the same time that the sun completes its revolution—hence the verse from Psalms. See *ZḤ* 24a, 25d–26a, 28b (all *MhN*). See below at note 67.

Metatron is the chief angel, variously described as the Prince of the World, Prince of the Countenance (or Presence), celestial scribe, and even יהוה קטן (*YHVH Qatan*), "Lesser *YHVH*" (3 Enoch 12:5, based on Exodus 23:21). In Heikhalot literature, Metatron is identified also with Enoch, who ascended to heaven. See BT *Sanhedrin* 38b; *Ḥagigah* 15a; *Yevamot* 16b; *Tosafot, Yevamot* 16b, s.v. *pasuq zeh*; Scholem, *Kabbalah*, 377–81; Tishby, *Wisdom of the Zohar*, 2:626–31; Margaliot, *Mal'akhei Elyon*, 73–108.

On Metatron in the *Zohar*, see 1:21a, 37b, 95b, 143a, 162a–b; 2:65b–66b, 131a; 3:217a–b; *ZḤ* 42d–43a; 69b (*ShS*). In *MhN*, see *Zohar* 1:126a–b, 127a–128b; *ZḤ* 4a, 8d, 9d–10a, 10b, 12b, 24a, 25d–26a, 28a–c.

44. **until it is granted permission** Presumably the sixth level signifies midday. Before beginning its gradual descent, the sun awaits permission to enter the second half of the daytime sky.

At the eighth level it recites: *May his name be eternal; while the sun lasts, may his name endure* (ibid., 17).

At the ninth level it recites: *For YHVH God is sun and shield...* (ibid. 84:12).

At the tenth level, as the sun descends, it recites: *For you, in awe of My name, the sun of justness will shine...* (Malachi 3:20).

At the eleventh level it recites: *Then the moon shall be ashamed and the sun shall be abashed...* (Isaiah 24:23).

At the twelfth degree it recites: *He made the moon for the fixed seasons; the sun knows when to set. You bring on darkness and it is night* (Psalms 104:19–20).

At the thirteenth degree it recites: *The earth and her fullness are YHVH's, the world and those who dwell in her* (ibid. 24:1).

At the fourteenth degree it recites: *Sing to YHVH a new song, for wonders He has done* (ibid. 98:1).

At the fifteenth degree it recites: *Who would not revere You, O King of the Nations? For it befits You* (Jeremiah 10:7).

556 At the sixteenth degree it recites: *Know today and take to your heart that YHVH is God...* (Deuteronomy 4:39).

At the seventeenth degree it recites: *Yours, YHVH, are greatness, power, beauty, victory, splendor...* (1 Chronicles 29:11).

At the eighteenth degree it recites: *Great is YHVH and highly praised* (Psalms 48:2).

At the nineteenth degree it recites: *There is none like You, O YHVH. You are great and Your name is great in power* (Jeremiah 10:6).

At the twentieth degree it recites: *Ascribe to YHVH the glory of His name* (Psalms 29:2).

At the twenty-first degree it recites: *Glory and majesty are before Him* (ibid. 96:6).

At the twenty-second degree it recites: *Yours are the heavens, Yours, too, the earth; it was You who founded the lights and the sun* (ibid. 89:12, 74:16).[45]

At the twenty-third degree it recites: *My soul yearns, even pines [for the courts of YHVH]* (ibid. 84:3).

At the twenty-fourth degree it recites: *May the glory of YHVH endure forever; may YHVH rejoice in His works!* (ibid. 104:31). [439]

45. ***Yours are the heavens...*** There is a conflation here. Psalms 89:12 reads: *Yours are the heavens, Yours too the earth; the world and its fullness—You founded them.* Psalms 74:16 reads similarly: *Yours is the day, also Yours the night. It was You who founded the lights and the sun.*

Rabbi Yitsḥak son of Rabbi Abba said, "When the sun enters the window of *Bilgah*, it is concealed from human beings, in accordance with the nature of [the earth's] habitation—and then the souls are saddened. It traverses and circles the whole world, until it returns through its known windows and bows before the King, the Creator of the Beginning; it is renewed as at first and stands in its level—the blessed Holy One renewing every day, perpetually, the Work of Creation. The Creator of All arrayed it to benefit the whole world—to make plants grow, to invigorate vegetation, to make flowers bloom, to illuminate the world, to generate seed, to delight souls, and to bring forth produce. The blessed Holy One said, 'I created השמש (*ha-shemesh*), the sun, solely for your benefit. It is your שמש (*shamash*), servant, performing all your needs כשמש המשמש (*ke-shamash ha-meshamesh*), like a servant attending, to the needs of his master, and yet you sin and make it a god! *Let there be* מארת (*me'orot*), *lights* (Genesis 1:14)—a curse on that very worship, for I will take pains to eliminate its worshippers from the world.'"[46]



Our Rabbis have taught: Once, Rav Naḥman son of Rav was traveling from Tiberias to Sepphoris, and Rabbi Yose son of Kisma was traveling with him. They arose to walk when morning arrived. They walked on. While they were walking, Rabbi Yose said to Rav Naḥman, "May the master tell me of those sublime matters that he used to say concerning the light of day."[47]

He said to him, "Come and hear: The blessed Holy One arrayed the light of the sun for the benefit of humankind; and when the sky receives the radiance of the sun, it is time to plead requests before the blessed Holy One—for it is a time of favor before Him. Come and see: When the King sits in joy, all the servants are radiant with joyful faces, but when the King is sad, the servants' faces are darkened and saddened, as is written: *In the light of the king's face is life* (Proverbs 16:15). My father did not ordain a fast on a cloudy day; he used to say, 'The King is sad, should I utter requests before Him?!' Now, can the blessed

46. **When the sun enters the window of *Bilgah*...** See *Pirqei de-Rabbi Eli'ezer* 6; *ZḤ* 15a, 15c (both *MhN*); 76c (*MhN, Rut*).

On the sun's bowing to the King of Kings, see *Pirqei de-Rabbi Eli'ezer* 6; on the daily renewal of the sun, see *Pirqei de-Rabbi Eli'ezer* 51. On the wordplay among *shemesh*, *shamash*, and *meshamesh*, see *ZḤ* 15a, 15c (both *MhN*), and above at note 4. On *me'orot* as *me'erat*, "curse," and the sun being viewed as a deity, see above, note 7.

47. **tell me of those sublime matters...** The expression derives from the Talmud and appears often throughout the *Zohar*. See BT *Ḥagigah* 14a; *Ta'anit* 20b; *Zohar* 1:49b, 87a, 96b, 197b; 2:31a; 3:148a, 209b, 231a; *ZḤ* 22a (*MhN*); 76c (*MhN, Rut*).

On morning as an auspicious time to set off on the way, see *Zohar* 3:22b; *ZḤ* 8a, 13b (both *MhN*).

Rabbi Yose addresses Rav Naḥman in deferential third-person terms ("the master"). Judging from what follows, he is seeking to learn about the teachings of Rav Naḥman's father ("he").

Holy One really be sad? Look at what is written: *Splendor and majesty are before Him, power and joy in His place* (1 Chronicles 16:27)! Well, my father said, 'What sadness is there before Him? Concerning the annihilation of the wicked, who were guilty before Him and are eliminated from the world; such is not a time to make requests. King David was attentive to this [440] and said: *As for me, may my prayer to You, O YHVH, come at a time of favor* (Psalms 69:14)—for he desired a time of favor to make requests, and this is the significance of *May they revere You with the sun* (Psalms 72:5)—when the sun rises, it is apt for a person to make his requests before his Master in joy, and not when the light is darkened.'"[48]

Rabbi Yitsḥak said, "From here: *You have screened Yourself off with a cloud, that no prayer may pass through* (Lamentations 3:44)."[49]

Rabbi Bo and Rabbi Ḥiyya said—though according to others, Rabbi Yoḥanan said in the name of Rabbi Bo—"One who is walking on the way and sees the disk of the sun seeking to shine in the gates should say as follows: O you sun, subordinate to the radiant splendor, inferior to the radiance of the great and luminous speculum! You are for your Master; you are for the praise of your Master who created you; and the One who created you and radiates your radiance will create Israel's healing and will illuminate their light, like that great and glorious luminary He created at first that has darkened before Him. But your light was created to serve us. We must offer praise to the One who sent you to us. Therefore: Blessed [are You, YHVH,] who fashions the luminaries."[50]



48. **When the King sits in joy...** The rising sun points to divine joy—an appropriate time to plead requests.

On divine sadness, see BT *Ḥagigah* 5b: "*If you will not listen, My soul will weep in secret because of the pride* (Jeremiah 13:17).... But is there weeping in the presence [i.e., on the part of] the blessed Holy One? Look, Rabbi Papa has said, 'There is no sadness in the presence of the blessed Holy One, as is said: *Splendor and majesty are before Him, power and joy in His place* (1 Chronicles 16:27).' There is no contradiction: this refers to the inner chambers; that refers to the outer chambers."

See BT *Berakhot* 32b: "Rava did not ordain a fast on a cloudy day, because it says: *You have screened Yourself off with a cloud, that no prayer may pass through* (Lamentations 3:44)."

On the verse from Proverbs and God's sadness, cf. *Zohar* 2:18a (*MhN*). On God's being saddened by the annihilation of the wicked, see BT *Sanhedrin* 39b; *Megillah* 10b; *ZḤ* 21c (*MhN*). On the verse *May they revere You with the sun,* see above, note 9.

It is not clear where Rav Naḥman's father's quote ends.

49. ***You have screened Yourself off with a cloud...*** See BT *Berakhot* 32b (above, note 48).

50. **subordinate to the radiant splendor...** This paragraph is particularly difficult and contains numerous neologisms of uncertain meaning. Nevertheless, the main point is that the visible sun pales in comparison to the radiance of the "speculum" above, which apparently corresponds to the withdrawn sun of Jacob (see above, notes 19 and 21), and the concealed light of creation

Our Rabbis have taught: Rabbi Eli'ezer said, "The letters of the explicit name are engraved upon the sun; and it moves toward the south and circles toward the north. It has been taught: For six months it journeys to the northern extremity to warm the air and the chill, and for six months it journeys to the southern extremity to invigorate grass, crops, vegetation, and trees, as is

(see below). See *ZḤ* 15b–c (*MhN*) for a similar reflection on the sun.

See *Bereshit Rabbah* 17:5 in the name of Rabbi Avin: "The orb of the sun is the unripe fruit of the supernal light."

Cf. *Bemidbar Rabbah* 15:9: "Immense is the light of the blessed Holy One! The sun and moon illuminate the world. But from where do they derive their radiance? They snatch from sparks of lights above..."

"Disk" renders קוטבא (*qutba*), unattested elsewhere in the *Zohar*. As Scholem notes ("Parashah Ḥadashah," 440, n. 137), the meaning of this word is not clear. Cf. קטב (*qetev*), "scourge, pestilence." See Psalms 91:5–6: *You need not fear the terror by night, or the arrow that flies by day, the plague that stalks in the darkness, or the scourge that ravages at noon.* Perhaps the author associated *qetev* with *the arrow that flies by day*—in his mind, the sun. See also BT *Pesaḥim* 111b: "there are two *qetevs*, one before noon and one after noon," and Rashi, s.v. *ve-hadar bekada de-kamka*. Alternatively, *qutba* may be related to קוטב (*qotev*), "pole," as in northern and southern, and thus the *Zohar* intends "the edge of the sun," namely the first glimpse of the rising sun.

"O you sun, subordinate to the radiant splendor, inferior to the radiance of the great and luminous speculum" tentatively renders את שמשא קפונקא מזהירותא מזיוא טפילותא מזיוא דא דאספקלריא רבא קטקרא (*at shimsha qafunqa me-zehiruta me-ziva tefiluta me-ziva da de-ispaqlariya raba qatqara*). See Scholem, "Parashah Ḥadashah," 440, n. 138, on the numerous difficult words in this passage: "The meaning of these words escapes me!" Not only their meaning but also the syntax is obscure. *Qafunqa* and *qatqara* are entirely enigmatic. My rendition ("subordinate" and "luminous" respectively) is based on context alone.

On the concealed light, see BT *Ḥagigah* 12a in the name of Rabbi El'azar: "With the light created by the blessed Holy One on the first day, one could gaze and see from one end of the universe to the other. When the blessed Holy One foresaw the corrupt deeds of the generation of the Flood and the generation of the Dispersion [the generation of the Tower of Babel], He immediately hid it from them, as is written: *The light of the wicked is withheld* (Job 38:15). For whom did He hide it? For the righteous in the time to come." See also *Bereshit Rabbah* 3:6; *Shemot Rabbah* 35:1; *Tanḥuma, Shemini* 9; *Bahir* 97–98 (147); *Zohar* 1:7a, 31b–32a, 45b–46a, 47a; 2:127a, 148b–149a, 220a–b; 3:88a, 173b; *ZḤ* 14c–d, 15b–d (*MhN*).

See *Zohar* 1:131a, 203b, where the concealed light is connected with Malachi 3:20: *For you, in awe of My name, the sun of justness will rise, with healing in its wings.*

"Speculum" renders אספקלריא (*ispaqlarya*), which also means "glass, mirror, lens." See BT *Yevamot* 49b: "All the prophets gazed through an opaque glass [literally: an *ispaqlarya* that does not shine], while Moses our teacher gazed through a translucent glass [literally: an *ispaqlarya* that shines]." See also *Vayiqra Rabbah* 1:14; Cf. 1 Corinthians 13:12: "For now we see though a glass darkly, but then face-to-face." See *Zohar* 1:97b, 122a (both *MhN*); *ZḤ* 10a, 13b, 15b, 15d, 16c, 17a, 21a, 24a (all *MhN*).

The blessing "who fashions the luminaries" precedes the *Shema* in the morning liturgy. See above, at note 9.

written: *Moving toward the north*... (Ecclesiastes 1:6). Thus it emerges that the sun journeys to the four [441] extremities of the world, over and over.”[51]

Rabbi Yitsḥak son of Gurya said, “There are [many] places in the inhabited world; and so it is that when the sun shines in a certain place, it is night somewhere else—and this is in accordance with the circling of the sun.”[52]

Rabbi Yitsḥak said, “I once happened upon those villages of the Easterners and spent the night there. I sat down to eat [as night dusked, but did not manage to eat] before it was light. I said, ‘What is this?’ They said to me, ‘Such is the natural order of this place. What's more, there is a place three miles from us where a person cannot doze for even half as long!’ I ventured forth from there. That day I traveled thirty-one miles and spent the night at another place. I sat down to eat. I said, ‘Let us eat quickly before the light of day shines!’ They said to me, ‘Let us eat and rejoice, for the night is long.’ I asked, ‘How long?’ They replied, ‘A person can doze forty miles.’ I was astounded and said to them, ‘In the other place I did not manage to eat before it was light!’ They said to me, ‘Near us it is now day, in a place above here. We know it to be so.’ When I came to Rabbi Shim'on, he said to me, ‘It is so—in accordance with the journey of the sun.’ He opened for me from the book of the Baraita of Shemu'el the First, deriving from the Book of Adam, and I found this very [442] matter.”[53]



51. **The letters of the explicit name...** This paragraph marks the beginning of the passage cited in Isaac ibn Sahula's *Meshal Ha-Qadmoni*, the earliest known appearance of a *Zohar* passage outside the *Zohar*. (The citation extends until note 54 with some omissions.) See Gate 5, 662–65. See also Scholem, “Ha-Tsitat ha-Rishon”; idem, “Parashah Ḥadashah,” 425, 440, n. 140.

According to *Pirqei de-Rabbi Eli'ezer* 6, “Three letters of the Name [apparently: YHVH] are inscribed on the heart of the sun.” See *Zohar* 2:188a; *ZḤ* 17d (*MhN*), 76c (*MhN, Rut*).

On the journey of sun to the north and south, see *Pirqei de-Rabbi Eli'ezer* 6; Solomon Ibn Gabirol, *Keter Malkhut*, Canto 16—quoted here (without attribution) by the *Zohar*; *ZḤ* 15c (*MhN*). On the influence of *Keter Malkhut* on the *Zohar*, see Scholem, “Parashah Ḥadashah,” 435, n. 78; Tishby, *Wisdom of the Zohar*, 1:76.

In the Masoretic text, the verse from Ecclesiastes actually reads: *Moving toward the south, circling toward the north.*

See also *ZḤ* 13b (*MhN*).

52. **when the sun shines in a certain place, it is night somewhere else...** From a medieval perspective (and from a contemporary naïve one), as the sun revolves daily around the globe of the earth and shines on part of it, the opposite side of the earth is in darkness. See *Zohar* 3:10a; *ZḤ* 15a (*MhN*) and note 54 below. Cf. BT *Pesaḥim* 94b.

According to BT *Ta'anit* 29b, Rabbi Yitsḥak is son of Giyori.

53. **villages of the Easterners...** Oddly, this fantastic story transpires in the east; it ought to have taken place in the far north, where the night can be extremely short.

See *Zohar* 3:10a, citing the Book of Rav Hamnuna Sava: “And there is a place where it is entirely day, and night exists for only a brief time.”

On there being places on earth with hardly any darkness, see Ibn Ezra on Job

Rabbi Yehudah said, "The world is round like a ball; and as the sun journeys, it happens that in one place it is illumining while in another dusking. This my own eyes have seen!"[54]

Our Rabbis have taught: The blessed Holy One will one day bring forth the sun from its sheath and judge the wicked thereby, as is written: *They will go out and stare at the corpses of the people*... (Isaiah 66:24).[55]

When Rav Safra went up there, they did not know who he [443] was. He went to the house of study and found the rabbis engaged in this verse, as is written:

38:23, and Naḥmanides on Job 38:20 (both quoting Saadia Gaon). See also Solomon Ibn Gabirol, *Keter Malkhut*, Canto 16.

The words in brackets are found only in *Meshal ha-Qadmoni*; see Gate Five, 662–63.

Dozing "forty miles" means that one can sleep for the time it takes to walk forty miles.

On the Baraita of Shemu'el, see above, note 4. Presumably, Shemu'el the First is the same as Shemu'el the Lesser (Shemu'el ha-Qatan), cited at the beginning of this passage. Perhaps the designation "the First" intends to distinguish this work from the "real" Baraita of Shemu'el, which does not hail from the Book of Adam.

On the Book of Adam, see BT *Bava Metsi'a* 85b–86a, where Rabbi Yehudah the Prince states that he was once shown the Book of Adam, which contained the genealogy of the entire human race. See Genesis 5:1; *Bereshit Rabbah* 24:1; BT *Sanhedrin* 38b, *Avodah Zarah* 5a. The *Zohar*'s Book of Adam is not to be confused with the book of Adam in the Apocrypha. According to various medieval traditions, the angel Raziel transmitted a magical book to Adam. Later, probably in the seventeenth century, *Sefer Razi'el* (the Book of Raziel) was compiled in its present form, comprising ancient magical, mystical, and cosmological teachings.

See *Zohar* 1:17b, 37a–b, 55a–b, 58b, 72b, 90b, 227b; 2:70a–b, 70a–b (*RR*), 77a, 131a, 143b, 180a, 181a, 197a; 3:10a, 68b; *ZḤ* 16d (*MhN*), 37b; Ginzberg, *Legends*, 5:117–18, n. 110; Liebes, *Peraqim*, 85–87; idem, *Pulḥan ha-Shaḥar*, 66–77. Note the comment by Shim'on Lavi, *Ketem Paz*, 1:22d: "All such books mentioned in the *Zohar*... have been lost in the wanderings of exile.... Nothing is left of them except what is mentioned in the *Zohar*."

54. **The world is round like a ball . . .** The earth's spherical nature was taught by Aristotle, Ptolemy, Aquinas, and Dante. This notion was well known among the educated in Western Europe after the twelfth century.

On the world's being round "like a ball," see JT *Avodah Zarah* 3:1, 42c; *Bemidbar Rabbah* 13:14, 17; *Zohar* 3:10a; *ZḤ* 15a (*MhN*); Scholem, "Parashah Ḥadashah," 442 n. 163; idem, "Ha-Tsitat ha-Rishon"; Isaac ibn Sahula, *Meshal ha-Qadmoni*, Gate Five, 665. Cf. Judah Halevi, *Kuzari* 3:49; Maimonides, *Guide of the Perplexed* 1:31, 73; Naḥmanides on Genesis 1:9; Gershon ben Solomon, *Sha'ar ha-Shamayim* 13:4, 42a.

"Dusking" renders the verb רמיש (*remish*), an apparently Zoharic coinage based on רמשא (*ramsha*), "evening." See *Zohar* 1:34b; 2:36b, 171a, 173a, 188a, 208a; 3:21a–b, 52a, 113b, 149a–b, 166b; *ZḤ* 7d, 25d, 28b (all *MhN*).

55. **bring forth the sun from its sheath...** See *Midrash Tehillim* 19:13: "What does the blessed Holy One do on the Day of Judgment? He brings forth the sun and removes it from its sheath, bringing it to the second firmament—judging the wicked thereby and burning them." See also *Bereshit Rabbah* 6:6; BT *Pesaḥim* 54a.

The verse from Isaiah continues: *who rebelled against Me. Their worms shall not die, nor their fire be quenched; they shall be a horror to all flesh.*

*Never again will your sun set*... (Isaiah 60:20). What is the significance of *Never again will your sun set*? As we have learned: When the House was destroyed and the enemies entered the sanctuary, Rabbi Zadok was there praying his prayer. The sun נערב (*ne'erav*), grew dim, everyone was overcome by ערבוביא (*irbuvya*), confusion, and they killed countless saints, pitying neither children nor fathers, as is written: *Woe to us, for the day is fading,* צללי ערב (*tsilelei arev*), *shadows of evening, spread!* (Jeremiah 6:4).[56]

Rav Safra said, “In our Mishnah we have learned this verse, as is written: *Never again will your sun set.* We have found that it corresponds with what Rabbi Ḥiyya said, ‘What is the meaning of [*He encountered a certain place*] *and stayed there for the night because the sun had set* (Genesis 28:11)? It refers to the sun that was Jacob's. For when dominion was bestowed upon Esau, the sun that had been Jacob's domain was withdrawn and given to Esau, as is written: *because the sun had set.* Until this very day the sun and glorious splendor has been withdrawn from Jacob and bestowed upon Esau! In the time to come, the
562 blessed Holy One is destined to renew his dominion; no other shall receive his domain, as is said: *In the days of those kings, the God of Heaven will establish a kingdom* [*that will never be destroyed, a kingdom that will not be left to another people. It will crush and consume all these kingdoms, and will itself endure forever*] (Daniel 2:44).’”[57]

56. **When Rav Safra went up there . . .** The idiomatic phrase “went up there” is borrowed from the Babylonian Talmud, where it means “went to the land of Israel.” Interestingly, this locution implies that “here” is Babylon—somewhat anomalous for the *Zohar*, whose plot transpires almost entirely in the land of Israel. See *Zohar* 1:190a; 2:174b; 3:72b; *ZḤ* 81c (*MhN, Rut*). See also the additions to *ZḤ* 24a (*MhN*) above, page 275.

On Rav Safra, see *Zohar* 2:168a. On the rabbis not knowing him, see *Zohar* 2:174b (printed in the main body of the *Zohar* but probably belonging to *MhN*), where the same language is used about Rav Huna.

See BT *Ta'anit* 29a: “On the seventh [of Av] the heathens [the Babylonians] entered the Temple, ate there, and desecrated it throughout the seventh and eighth. Toward dusk on the ninth, they set fire to it, and it continued burning all that day, as is said: *Woe to us, for the day is fading, shadows of evening spread*!” See also *Tosefta Ta'anit* 3:10; *Seder Olam Rabbah* 27.

On Jeremiah 6:4, see *ZḤ* 23c (*MhN*); cf. *Zohar* 1:132b, 230a; 2:21b (*MhN*); 3:75a, 270a; Moses de León, *Sefer ha-Rimmon*, 67.

According to BT *Gittin* 56a, Rabbi Zadok prayed forty years for Jerusalem to be saved, though there is no mention of his being in the Temple on the day it was destroyed. Indeed, according to *Eikhah Rabbati* 1, he was not even in Jerusalem then.

The verse from Isaiah continues: *and your moon will not be withdrawn. For YHVH shall be a light to you forever, and your days of mourning shall be ended.*

57. ***because the sun had set*...** Rav Safra connects the verse from Isaiah with the withdrawn sun of Jacob and the dominion of Esau. On this motif and the verse from Genesis, see above, note 21.

On the expression “our Mishnah,” see above, note 27.

Rav Safra said further, "Since I have come here, what is meant by *In the days of those kings*? Who are those kings? Well, so have the Masters of our Academy decreed, and they have heard—those of whom has been said: The kings of the world will one day form an alliance against Israel and decree harsh decrees, conspiring as one. When their designs are ordained and the decree befalls them, then the Master of the World will establish their kingdom and illumine their sun upon them—the one that was withdrawn from them, as is written: *Never again will your sun set.*"[58]

Rabbi Yehudah said, "This hails from the Masters of Mishnah; a word like the word issuing from the mouth of the king!"[59]

They asked him, "What is your name?"

He replied, "In my place they call [444] me Rav Safra."

They said, "It is fitting that the tradition was illuminated for us from the mouth of one who was hidden!"[60]

While he was sitting, the disciples of the rabbis were engaged in what is said: ונגינותי ננגן (*U-nginotai nenaggen*), *we will make music* (Isaiah 38:20). What is the meaning of *neginotai*? [61]



58. **conspiring as one...** See *Zohar* 2:7b. On the verse from Daniel, see *Zohar* 1:145b. On the epithet "Masters of the Academy," see above, note 17. On the use of the term "decree" (from the root גזר [*gzr*]) for establishing a teaching, see *Zohar* 1:123a, 124b, 125a (all *MhN*); *ZḤ* 14a, 15b, 16a, 18b, 20a (all *MhN*); 62b (*ShS*); Meroz, "Va-Ani Lo Hayiti Sham?," 168 (Addendum 3 in this volume).

59. **like the word issuing from the mouth of the king** On the king as the source of the Companions' teachings, see Meroz, "Va-Ani Lo Hayiti Sham?," 168, 191–93. The king may represent the head of the Masters of Mishnah.

The term "Masters of Mishnah" מרייהו דמתניתא (*Mareihu de-Matnita*) appears in numerous passages throughout *Midrash ha-Ne'lam*, in various formulations. It seems to signify a never-formally-defined group of sages who possess esoteric wisdom. In some ways, the Masters of Mishnah are a forerunner to the *Ḥavrayya*, the Companions headed by Rabbi Shim'on, found in the main body of the *Zohar*. Significantly, however, Rabbi Shim'on does not always occupy a privileged position in this group. The Mishnah of which they are masters is not the Mishnah of the rabbinic sage Rabbi Yehudah ha-Nasi, but rather a body of esoteric knowledge often relating to the soul and to the structure of the cosmos. See *Zohar* 1:123b (*MhN*, though mistakenly labeled as *Tosefta*); 1:127a–b, 129a–b, 130a, 135a 138a, 139b; 2:5a, 14a (all *MhN*); *ZḤ* 10c, 12c, 13a, 14c, 15b–c, 16a, 59b (all *MhN*); Meroz, "Va-Ani Lo Hayiti Sham?," 168 (Addendum 3 in this volume).

60. **from the mouth of one who was hidden** The manuscript reads מפיסימיים (*mi-pisimayyim*), either a mistake or a Zoharic neologism of unknown meaning. I have rendered it as if it were מפי סימיים (*mi-pi simayyim*), with *simayyim* deriving from סמי/סמא (*sama/sami*), one of whose meanings is "to be hidden." This conjectural reading fits the context, as Rav Safra was unknown to the rabbis of Israel, and his teaching deals with the reemergence of Jacob's hidden light.

61. **(*U-nginotai nenaggen*), *we will make music*...** The meaning of *neginotai* is un-

Rabbi Yitsḥak said, "It is a kind of ניגון (*niggun*), tune."

The Rabbis said, "Look, one of the scions of Mishnah is here, who decree a word like the decree of the watchers; let him explicate this matter!"[62]

Rav Safra said, "So have the scions of our Mishnah decreed: Rabbi Yehudah said in the name of Rabbi Yoḥanan, 'What is the difference between זמר (*zemer*) and ניגון (*niggun*)? Well, *niggun* refers to the intonation of נגינות (*neginot*), tunes, and the raising of voice to soothe the heart, whether with instruments, voice, or throat.' Rabbi Yoḥanan said, 'There are three things that soothe the heart: instruments, voice, and throat. It is written: "*Now bring me* מנגן (*menaggen*), *a minstrel.*" *And then,* כנגן המנגן (*ke-naggen ha-menaggen*), *as the minstrel played,* [*the hand of YHVH came upon him*] (2 Kings 3:15)—they are three: instruments, voice, and throat; and it is written: *Now bring me* מנגן (*menaggen*), *a minstrel*—this is *niggun*.' *Zemer* refers to the intonation of words unaccompanied by melody. As Rabbi Yehudah said in the name of Rabbi Yoḥanan: 'In all instances מזמור (*mizmor*) is without instruments and without melody—rather, his intent was on the essence of the words, not on the tune and melody. In all instances *mizmor* refers to the chanting of words without melody, as is written: מזמור (*Mizmor*), *A psalm, of David when he fled* [*from his son Absalom*] (Psalms 3:1)—conclude from this that he was not focused on the melody, but on the words. So have the Masters of our Mishnah considered every *mizmor* uttered by David, that he focused on the matters he was imploring and not on the melody.'"[63]



certain. This phrase has been translated variously as *we will sing with stringed instruments*; *my songs we sing*; *we will sing my songs to the stringed instruments*; *we will make our stringed instruments sound*; *we will play my music on stringed instruments.* On *neginotai*, see Psalms 77:7; *Pesiqta de-Rav Kahana* 17:1.

62. **decree of the watchers . . .** See Daniel 4:14: *This sentence by decree of the watchers, this verdict by the order of the holy ones.*

"Scions of Mishnah" renders בני מתניתין (*benei matnitin*).

63. **What is the difference between זמר (*zemer*) and ניגון (*niggun*)? . . .** *Zemer* usually means "song" and *niggun* "melody, tune." A different distinction is offered here: *niggun* involves melody; *zemer* does not.

When the prophet Elisha sought divine inspiration, he asked for a musician to play in order to induce a state of joy. The triple appearance of the root נגן (*ngn*), "to play," in the verse from Kings alludes to the three aspects of *niggun*: voice, throat, and instruments. Cf. *Zohar* 1:216b.

While fleeing his son, surely David would not have composed melodies and played instruments; hence *zemer*, and its cognate *mizmor*, indicate chanting without melody. Cf. BT *Berakhot* 7b: "*A psalm of David, when he fled from his son Absalom.* —*A psalm of David*? The verse should read *A lamentation of David*!"

See BT *Berakhot* 57b: "Three things restore a person's spirits: [beautiful] sounds, sights, and smells."

See Isaac ibn Sahula, *Peirush Shir ha-Shirim,* 408, where Rabbi Yoḥanan's second statement is quoted. See also Scholem, "Qabbalat Rabbi Yitsḥak ben Shelomoh," 112–16.

Rabbi Abba rose and said, "This hails from the Masters of Mishnah! We are not worthy to say [anything at all] about their word, for they are holy angels decreeing a holy word with their mouths!"[64]

Rabbi Yitsḥak said in the name of Rav, "We should return to the word we left: *On my bed at night, I sought him whom my soul loves* (Song of Songs 3:1). For we have learned there: Three times during the night hours, the blessed Holy One ventures forth [445] to delight in the thousand worlds He desires; [and every single night He enters with] the souls of the righteous to delight with them in the two hundred other worlds He has concealed for them. He who knows the sign of every one of these hours, and his heart cleaves to that yearning and love, the blessed Holy One grants his soul a share in this world. But he who does not know, and awakens from his sleep and sets his heart to worldly matters, even though he set his heart to this, they do not listen to him, as is written: *at my watch I stay every night* (Isaiah 21:8). It does not say *at the watch*, but *at my watch*."[65]



64. **holy angels decreeing a holy word...** See *ZḤ* 15b (*MhN*) also about the Masters of Mishnah: "For the decree of their mouth is like the decree of the holy angels." See also *ZḤ* 62b (*ShS*).

The phrase in brackets is not found in the manuscript, which reads שלו (*shelo*), "his," which is clearly a mistake. Perhaps כלום (*kelum*), "nothing, anything" was intended.

65. **Three times during the night hours...** Based on King David's legendary custom of rising at midnight to study Torah (see BT *Berakhot* 3b and above, note 36), the *Zohar* develops an elaborate ritual—the nocturnal delight—whereby kabbalists are expected to rise at midnight and ply Torah until the break of dawn. At midnight, God delights with the souls of the righteous in the Garden of Eden; and those who study Torah below partake of the celestial joy. In the main body of the *Zohar*, this ritual is understood as adorning the *Shekhinah* in preparation for Her union with the blessed Holy One. This parallels the midnight vigil common among Christian monks from early medieval times. In *Zohar* 3:119a, Rabbi Yehudah alludes to the Christian practice: "I have seen something similar among the nations of the world."

See JT *Berakhot* 1:1, 2d; *Sifra, Beḥuqqotai* 3:3, 111b; *Aggadat Bereshit* 23:5; BT *Sanhedrin* 102a; 2 Enoch 8:3; *Zohar* 1:10b, 72a, 77a–b, 82b, 92a–b, 136b, 178a, 206b–207b, 231b, 242b; 2:26b, 36b, 46a, 130a–b, 136a, 173b, 195b–196a; 3:13a, 21b–22b, 49b, 52b, 67b–68a, 81a, 193a, 260a; [Moses de León?], *Seder Gan Eden*, 138; Scholem, *On the Kabbalah*, 146–50; Hellner-Eshed, *A River Flows from Eden*, 121–45. Cf. Matthew 25:6.

On the *Zohar*'s nocturnal ritual in *MhN*, see *Zohar* 2:18b; *ZḤ* 6a, 13c, 18a. On the worlds that the blessed Holy One desires, see *ZḤ* 9d, 13b, 18a, 22a (all *MhN*); on the two hundred worlds for the righteous, see *ZḤ* 22a (*MhN*). On the night's three watches and their signs, see BT *Berakhot* 3a: "In the first watch, a donkey brays; in the second, dogs bark; in the third, a child sucks from its mother's breasts, and a woman converses with her husband." On focusing on worldly matters at night, see M *Avot* 3:4.

The proof-text from Isaiah apparently means that one's nocturnal reward is dependent on one's nocturnal activities, i.e., whether one turned to Torah or worldly matters, hence: *my watch*—the one befitting me.

The "they" who do not listen apparently refers to the departed righteous in the Garden of Eden, who heed the words of Torah recited by the righteous who rise at night, as in *companions listen for your voice* (Song of

Rav Naḥman said, “*On my bed at night, I sought him whom my soul loves* (Song of Songs 3:1)—the holy soul, ascending to pursue the teaching of her Master every night.”[66]

As we have learned: Rabbi Abbahu said, “At the beginning of the night, the soul does not ascend first. When the holy virtuous soul is raised, sixty holy princes surrounding the King's Throne of Glory ascend with her, and they protect her. He of whom is written *the glory of YHVH* goes forth to greet her and she basks in his glorious splendor, as is written: *Let the pious exalt in glory* (Psalms 149:5). If he is more virtuous than his companions, he possesses love to know beyond him; but he is not granted permission until he departs this world—the love of the virtuous soul to know and fathom above. This is the matter of the soul *On my bed*.”[67]

Rabbi Tanḥum said, “At that very watch prepared for me *I sought him whom my soul loves* (Songs of Songs 3:1), He who is *preeminent among ten thousand* (ibid. 5:10). What is written? *I sought him but did not find him* (ibid. 3:1).”[68]



Hence Rabbi Yitsḥak said, “A person's merit is not recognized until he departs this world.”

As we have learned: Rabbi Yehudah said, “Why is it written *the God of Abraham and the Fear of Isaac* (Genesis 31:42)? It should have said *the God of Isaac*!”

Songs 8:13), yet pay no heed to those engaging in worldly matters.

The phrase in brackets is not found in the manuscript, which appears to have skipped a few words and is slightly garbled.

66. **the holy soul, ascending to pursue the teaching...** See *ZḤ* 25c–26a; 28b (both *MhN*) and next note. See also *Midrash Tehillim* 11:6; *Pirqei de-Rabbi Eli'ezer* 34; *Bereshit Rabbah* 14:9; *Zohar* 1:92a, 121b, 122a (*MhN*), 183a, 200a; 2:195b; 3:67a, 121b; *ZḤ* 18b (*MhN*); Ginzberg, *Legends*, 5:74–75, n. 18; Tishby, *Wisdom of the Zohar*, 2:809–12.

In his transcription of this manuscript, Scholem skipped a line, which is reinstated here.

67. ***the glory of YHVH* goes forth to greet her...** Raised above by sixty angels surrounding the Throne of Glory, the soul is greeted by Metatron, the glory of YHVH. See *ZḤ* 24a, 25c–26a, 28b (all *MhN*). The perfected soul seeks to know what is beyond Metatron—that is, to know God Himself. However, such knowledge is unattainable in this world, achieved only in death.

On Metatron, see above, note 43. On him as the divine glory, see *ZḤ* 9d, 24a, 26a (all *MhN*). On seeking to know beyond Metatron, cf. *Zohar* 1:128a (*MhN*). On permission to behold and fathom as being granted after death, see *Sifra, Vayiqra, dibbura di-ndavah* 2:12, 4a: “Rabbi Dosa says, ‘Scripture states: *No human can see Me and live* (Exodus 33:20). In their lifetime they do not see, but in their death they do!’” See *Zohar* 1:98a (*MhN*); *ZḤ* 10a (*MhN*). On Psalms 149:5, cf. BT *Berakhot* 5a.

See Song of Songs 3:7: *Behold the bed of Solomon! Sixty warriors surrounding her of the warriors of Israel.*

68. **He who is *preeminent among ten thousand*...** At night, the soul seeks the blessed Holy One—but does not find Him.

*And the Fear of Isaac.* As Rabbi Yehudah said: "Isaac was still alive; and Scripture specified *and the Fear*—in other words, do not trust in yourself until the day of your death. He departs this world—his merit is complete and his reward complete. Therefore Solomon said [446] in his wisdom: *I praise the dead, who have already died, more than the living* [*who are still alive*] (Ecclesiastes 4:2)."[69]

As Rabbi Yehoshu'a son of Levi said: "The righteous cannot attain their rung during their lifetime. Once they depart—their rung is complete and their praise complete, for then they receive their reward in this world."

Rabbi Yehoshu'a son of Levi also said, "The prayer..."[70]

69. ***Fear of Isaac...*** See Rashi on Genesis 31:42: "He did not want to say 'God of Isaac' because the blessed Holy One does not associate His name with the righteous during their lifetime." See *Tanḥuma, Toledot* 7.

On not trusting oneself until the day of death, see M *Avot* 2:4.

70. **The prayer** The passage ends mid-sentence. See *ZḤ* 14c (*MhN*); BT *Berakhot* 26b.

# Addendum 2

Whoever recites the *Shema* by its letters[1]—Hell is cooled for him, as is written: בפרש שדי (*Be-fares Shaddai*), *When Shaddai scatters, kings, it snows* בצלמון (*be-tsalmon*), *in Zalmon* (Psalms 68:15). Do not read בפרש (*be-fares*), when he scatters, but בפרש (*be-faresh*), when one pronounces distinctly; do not read בצלמון (*be-tsalmon*), *in Zalmon*, but בצלמות (*be-tsalmavet*), in the shadow of death.[2]

Rabbi Ḥiyya traveled to the Masters of Mishnah in order to learn from them. He went to Rabbi Shim'on son of Yoḥai and saw a curtain dividing the house. Rabbi Ḥiyya was astonished... as written in *parashat Shemot*.[3]

They approached him and said: "What is the significance of what we have learned: Whoever recites the *Shema* by its letters—Hell is cooled for him?"

Rabbi Shim'on opened and said, "Until the end of the first watch—these are the words of Rabbi [80] Eli'ezer... until the donkey brays. In the second, dogs bark. It has been taught: Four winds were created in the world: the wind of the eastern corner, the wind of the western corner, the wind of the northern corner, and the wind of the southern corner. For these four winds, the blessed Holy One created four angels who are empowered over them by day and by night. Michael, who hails from the aspect of love and compassion, is empowered over the east wind until the middle of the day. From the middle of the day until the

1. **Whoever recites the *Shema* by its letters** This pericope is not found in printed editions of the *Zohar*. It is preserved in numerous manuscripts and was published by Moshe Idel; see "Qeta Lo Yadu'a," 73–87.

2. **Hell is cooled for him...** See BT *Berakhot* 15b: "Rabbi Ḥama son of Rabbi Ḥanina said, 'Whoever recites the *Shema* and articulates its letters distinctly—Hell is cooled for him, as is said: *When Shaddai scatters kings, its snows in Zalmon* (Psalms 68:15)....'" See Rashi, ad loc., s.v. *be-fares Shaddai*.

See also *Zohar* 1:238b.

3. **Rabbi Ḥiyya traveled to the Masters of Mishnah...** See *Zohar* 2:14a (*MhN*), where this story appears in full. Here, only the opening frame is presented; the narrative disappears as soon as Rabbi Shim'on begins speaking. The reference "as written in *para-*

night, Raphael is empowered with the west wind, likewise hailing from the aspect of love. Of them is written *God's love endures all day* (Psalms 52:3), and similarly *By day YHVH directs His love...* (ibid. 42:9). When night arrives, Gabriel, who hails from the power of judgment, is empowered with the north wind until midnight.[4]

"There are two attributes in the world; and they are called ox and donkey, as is written: *Jacob sent messengers ahead of him... He instructed them, saying... 'With Laban I have sojourned'* (Genesis 32:4–5). What does Jacob's telling Esau *With Laban I have sojourned* come to teach us? Well, the whole world [81] knew that there was no sorcerer in the world like Laban. For he would slay whoever did anything bad to him by the power of his lips, with the power of the five attributes in which he was initiated, as is written: *I have acquired ox and donkey, sheep, and male and female slaves* (ibid., 6). All the demons in the world derive from their power. The attribute of the ox is empowered over the day, and the attribute of the donkey over the night. But because the blessed Holy One's love rules the world by day, this ox is unable to accuse the world. But at night, be-



*shat Shemot*" is rather strange for the *Zohar*, so the narrative frame appears to have been inserted artificially or tentatively.

4. **four winds... four angels... empowered over them...** See *ZḤ* 13a–b (*MhN*) for a similar discussion of the winds, though some of the details differ.

On the various winds and their prevailing times, see BT *Gittin* 31b; *Berakhot* 3b; *Yevamot* 72a; *Bava Batra* 25a; *Arukh*, s.v. *kinnor*; Rashi on BT *Berakhot* 3b, s.v. *kinnor*: "Every single day, four winds blow: the first six hours of the day—an easterly wind blows with the sun; the last six hours—a southerly wind; at the beginning of the night—a westerly wind; at midnight—a northerly wind." See also idem on BT *Sanhedrin* 16a, s.v. *kinnor*.

According to *Bemidbar Rabbah* 2:10, the four angels Michael, Gabriel, Uriel, and Raphael are aligned with the four cardinal points: "Just as the blessed Holy One created the four cardinal directions and four standards [of the tribes] corresponding to them, so also did He set about His throne four angels—Michael, Gabriel, Uriel, and Raphael." See also *Pirqei de-Rabbi Eli'ezer* 4.

In rabbinic literature, Michael is Israel's chief advocate (see Daniel 10:13; *Shemot Rabbah* 18:5; *Pesiqta Rabbati* 44). In the Kabbalah, he is associated with *Ḥesed* (Love or Compassion).

The name רפאל (*Repha'el*) means "God heals." On Raphael as the angel of healing, see BT *Bava Metsi'a* 86b.

Gabriel does not appear in the parallel discussion in *ZḤ* 13a–b (*MhN*). Here his name is associated with *Gevurah* (Judgment and Justice).

The opening statement by Rabbi Shim'on derives from BT *Berakhot* 2a–3a, which discusses the appropriate time for reciting the evening *Shema* and proceeds to discuss the night's three watches. The elided quotation begins with the opening *mishnah* and extends into the *Gemarah*'s discussion. This may be a scribal error, and perhaps what was intended was (part of) the statement by Rabbi Eli'ezer in BT *Berakhot* 3a: "In the first watch, a donkey brays; in the second, dogs bark; in the third, a child sucks from its mother's breasts, and a woman converses with her husband."

On "day" and "night" as love and judgment respectively, see *Zohar* 2:21a–b (*MhN*).

cause the attribute of judgment prevails by night, the donkey has permission to accuse; and when he brays in the first watch, the donkeys hear his voice—and they too bray. At that hour, all the demons hear his voice, and all of them come with this attribute. Of these attributes is written in the Torah *bitter scourge* (Deuteronomy 32:24), and in the Writings *scourge raging at noon* (Psalms 91:6). In the second watch, dogs bark.[5]

“When the blessed Holy One created the human being, He gave him two angels—one of compassion and one of judgment, as is said: *For He will order His angels [to guard you in all your ways]* (ibid., 11). Every single night, those angels raise the soul before the blessed Holy One; and she draws life to the body—and says before the blessed Holy One, ‘Master of the World! The body I have entered has done such-and-such, has spoken thus-and-thus.’ Even the small talk between a man and his friend or his wife is recounted to a person at his hour of death, as is said: *and declares to a human what his conversation was* (Amos 4:13). The angels that ascend with the soul bear witness, [82] as is said: *You are My witnesses, declares YHVH, and I am God* (Isaiah 43:12).[6]



5. **two attributes in the world... ox and donkey...** In Ezekiel's vision of the Chariot-Throne (Ezekiel 1:10), the ox appears on the left, symbolizing *Din* (Judgment). As for the donkey, it represents a demonic power. See *Zohar* 2:6a, 64b; 3:86b.

When Jacob said to Esau *I have acquired ox and donkey*, he was referring to what he learned during his many years of serving Laban, who was a mighty sorcerer.

On Laban's powers of witchcraft, see Genesis 30:27; *Targum Yerushalmi*, Rashi, Ibn Ezra, and *Sekhel Tov*, ad loc.; *Zohar* 1:133b, 139b, 158b, 161a, 164b, 166b, 167a. On the scourge, see BT *Pesaḥim* 111b.

Genesis 32:4–6 reads: *Jacob sent messengers ahead of him to Esau his brother in the land of Seir, the steppe of Edom. He instructed them, saying, “Thus shall you say: ‘To my lord Esau, thus says your servant Jacob: With Laban I have sojourned and I tarried until now. I have acquired ox and donkey, sheep, and male and female slaves, and I send ahead to tell my lord, to find favor in your eyes.’”*

6. **two angels...** On the two accompanying angels, see BT *Shabbat* 119b; *Ta'anit* 11a; *Zohar* 1:12b, 165b; 2:106b; *ZḤ* 47a, 84d (*MhN, Rut*).

On the nocturnal ascent of the soul, see *Bereshit Rabbah* 14:9: “It was said in the name of Rabbi Me'ir: ‘This soul fills the body; and when a person sleeps, she ascends—drawing down life from above.’” See Tishby, *Wisdom of the Zohar*, 2:809–14. On the soul and the angels offering testimony, see BT *Ta'anit* 11a; *Ḥagigah* 16a.

Amos 4:13 reads: *For see, He forms mountains and creates wind, and declares to a human what his conversation was.* The final phrase, *what his conversation was*, מה שחו (*mah seḥo*), is often understood as *what His thought is*. According to a midrashic reading, the phrase implies that all of a person's שיחה (*siḥah*), “conversation,” is recorded and read back to him when he dies. See *Vayiqra Rabbah* 26:7; BT *Ḥagigah* 5b.

In its simple sense, the verse from Isaiah is addressed to the people of Israel; here, it is construed as being addressed to the two angels that accompany each individual human soul.

"When a person dies, the angels raise the soul to a distance of three hundred years, for so have our Rabbis of blessed memory taught: From the earth to the firmament is a distance of five hundred years. They ascend to the heights of heaven and say, 'If the soul possesses merit, she shall ascend.' Before they ascend, they set her in a place with 320 million pathways—some straight, some sinuous—all of them called *snares of death* (Psalms 18:6), *highways of Sheol* (Proverbs 7:27). In every single pathway there is a consuming fire, and they say to one another, 'If you see any soul entering any one of these paths, tell me.'[7]

"There is there a certain path, and in that path a certain attribute like a dog. When the soul enters any one of those pathways, the dog sees her and immediately he barks. When the demons and angels of destruction hear his voice, they know that a soul is there. Immediately they come and seize the soul and sling her, as is written: *The soul of your enemies He will sling from the hollow of a sling* (1 Samuel 25:29), until they cast her into Hell. King David, peace upon him, pleaded before the blessed Holy One to save him from that dog, as is said: *Save my soul from the sword, my only one from the clutches of a dog* (Psalms 22:21). Now, was David, king of Israel, afraid of a single dog?! Rather, of that attribute called 'dog.'[8]



"They said further: The souls of Israel do not [83] enter that place or those pathways, and that dog does them no harm, as is said: *But against any of the Children of Israel, no dog will snarl* (Exodus 11:7).[9]

"They said further: Among those paths there is a certain path called 'the path of life,' as is said: *The path of life leads upward for the enlightened, to avoid the snares of death* (Proverbs 15:24), and it is written: *She does not chart a path of life...* (ibid. 5:6), and similarly: *Whoever heeds discipline [is on] the path of life, but whoever ignores reproof leads astray* (ibid. 10:17), that is, if one does not observe the Torah in this world, he will stray in the pathways we mentioned. They said: In that path called 'the path of life' there is darkness for a distance of three days, as is said: *the ark of the covenant of YHVH journeying before them a three days' march to scout for them a resting place* (Numbers 10:33); from there on, en-

7. **earth to the firmament is a distance of five hundred years...** See BT *Pesaḥim* 94b; *Ḥagigah* 13a; *Midrash Tehillim* 4:3.

8. **in that path a certain attribute like a dog...** Paralleling the Cerberus from Greek mythology. See *ZḤ* 75b (*MhN, Rut*); Idel, "Qeta Lo Yadu'a," 75. See also BT *Bava Qamma* 60b. Cf. *Zohar* 2:65a.

On the verse from Samuel and the souls of the wicked, see BT *Shabbat* 152b.

9. ***no dog will snarl*** The context of the verse in Exodus 11 is the tenth plague—the killing of the Egyptian firstborn—when the Israelites were not menaced even by a dog. The verse reads: *No dog* יחרץ (*yeḥerats*), *will sharpen* [or: *point, whet, move*], *its tongue*—i.e., threaten or snarl. See *Zohar* 2:65a.

Cf. M *Sanhedrin* 10:1: "All of Israel have a share in the world to come...."

tirely light, as is said: *The path of the righteous is like gleaming light, shining ever brighter until full day* (Proverbs 4:18), that is, when he goes forth from the darkness and fire, which extends for a distance of three days; from there on, *shining ever brighter until full day*—until the world to come, which is called ‘daylight.’ All the other pathways, aside from this one—their end and their beginning is consuming fire, darkness, *gloom with no dawn* (Isaiah 8:22). All of them lead to Hell and are called ‘depths of Sheol.’ That place in the path of life that is dark is called ‘the valley of the shadow of death,’ and David, peace upon him, pleaded before the blessed Holy One that He would make that path entirely light. The blessed Holy One said, ‘Do not fear it, for I shall be with you in that place.’ At that moment, he began singing [84] and chanting, as is said: *A psalm of David. YHVH is my shepherd, I shall not want* [...] *Though I walk through the valley of the shadow of death, I fear no evil* [*for You are with me*] (Psalms 23:1, 4). When the souls of the righteous pass through that place, that fire is cooled for them, as our Rabbis of blessed memory said: Whoever recites the *Shema* by its letters—Hell is cooled for him, as is said: *When Shaddai scatters kings*... (Psalms 68:15).[10]



“Gabriel is empowered until the middle of the night—at precisely midnight, when that watch ends. At that hour, the blessed Holy One actually gazes upon Eden, showing the righteous their share that He will one day bequeath them. At that hour, Nuriel rises with the south wind and says, ‘*Awake, north wind! Come, south wind! Blow upon my garden*...’ (Song of Songs 4:16). That is, Nuriel says, ‘*Awake*, Gabriel, with the north wind over which you are empowered; *Come, south wind*—the south wind over which I am empowered. *Blow upon my garden, let its spices flow* (ibid.)—let its aromas, trees, and spices flow, as is written: *The trees of YHVH are sated, the cedars of Lebanon*... (Psalms 104:16)’; and he says, ‘*There birds build their nests*... (ibid., 17)—the souls of the righteous, bound in the bundle of life in the Garden of Eden. *Let my beloved come into his garden* (Song of Songs 4:16)—let the blessed Holy One come into the Garden of Eden, *and eat its luscious fruits* (ibid.).’[11]

10. **a certain path called ‘the path of life’...** Aside from this one, all the pathways are of darkness and fire. The “path of life” alone ends in light—though it too begins in darkness.

On the phrase “their end and their beginning,” תחלתן וסופן (*teḥillatan ve-sofan*), see *Sefer Yetsirah* 1:7: “Ten *sefirot belimah*. Their measure is ten, yet infinite. Their end is embedded in their beginning, their beginning in their end, like a flame joined to a burning coal.” On the world to come as day, see BT *Ḥagigah* 12b; *Pirqei de-Rabbi Eli’ezer* 34. On the cooling of Hell and the *Shema*, see above, note 2. On the verse from Psalms and the motif of the cooling of Hell, see *Midrash Tehillim* 23:7.

Proverbs 15:24 reads: *The path of life leads upward for the enlightened, in order to avoid Sheol below*. On depths of Sheol, see Proverbs 9:18.

11. **the blessed Holy One actually gazes upon Eden...** Midnight marks the onset of the celestial drama as God enters the Garden

"Now, does eating pertain to the blessed Holy One?! [85] Not literal eating; and Solomon did not utter this word with eating in mind. The explanation: A parable. To what can the matter be compared? To a king who has one son who used to sin before his father every day. His father would lash him every single day, yet he would not learn a lesson. He said to him, 'My son, for how long will you not learn a lesson? What should I do with you? I lashed you, yet you did not incline your ear. I threw you in jail, yet you did not learn a lesson. I will banish you from my house, for until now you wore distinguished and beautiful clothes, but henceforth you shall walk naked through the lands. In my house you were sated, but in a foreign house you shall go hungry. In my house you were respected, but in a foreign house you shall be despised.' So said the blessed Holy One to Israel, 'When you were good, you were greatly honored—with *Shekhinah*, prophets, *Sanhedrin*, and kings. Now that you have sinned, I will cast you into the pit of exile. *You will serve there gods that are human handiwork, wood and stone, which cannot see and cannot hear, and cannot eat and cannot smell* (Deuteronomy 4:28).' They possess all these attributes! *Which cannot see*—the blessed Holy One sees, as is said: *Let me go down and see* (Genesis 18:21), and it is written: *God saw the Children of Israel* (Exodus 2:25). But wood and stone: *They have eyes but cannot see, they have ears but cannot hear* (Psalms 115:5–6). The blessed Holy One hears, as is said: *For YHVH hears the needy* (ibid. 69:34), and it is written: *God heard their moaning* (Exodus 2:24). But idols: *They have ears but cannot hear* (Psalms 115:6); *and they do not eat* (Deuteronomy 4:28). How does אכילה (*akhilah*), eating, [86] pertain to the blessed Holy One? For we



of Eden to delight with the souls of the righteous (see note 13 below). The drama is preceded by Nuriel's invitation for the south and north wind to unite. According to *Shir ha-Shirim Rabbah* on 4:16, such a union of winds is reserved for the Messianic era. Here, it occurs nightly.

On the verse from the Songs of Songs, see *ZḤ* 13b (*MhN*); there, Uriel is empowered over the south wind. See also *Zohar* 2:37b, where the luscious fruits, the souls of the righteous, constitute a midnight offering to God. On birdlike souls, see BT *Sanhedrin* 92b; *Avot de Rabbi Natan* A, add. 2, 7:3; *Zohar* 3:196b, 217b; *ZḤ* 13c (*MhN*); Moses de León, *Sefer ha-Rimmon*, 202. On souls as fruit, see *Bahir* 14 (22); Ezra of Gerona, *Peirush le-Shir ha-Shirim*, 489, 504; *Zohar* 1:15b, 19a, 33a, 59b–60a, 82b, 85b, 115a–b; 2:223b; *ZḤ* 13b–c (*MhN*); Moses de León, *Sefer ha-Mishqal*, 51; idem, *Sheqel ha-Qodesh*, 56 (69). On the blessed Holy One's gazing upon Eden, see *ZḤ* 6a (*MhN*).

The expression "bundle of life" derives from 1 Samuel 25:29: *The soul of my lord will be bound in the bundle of life.* See BT *Shabbat* 152b; *Zohar* 1:65b, 224b; 2:11b, 36b, 54a, 59a; 3:24b–25a, 70b, 71b, 92a; Moses de León, *Sefer ha-Rimmon*, 123; idem, *Sheqel ha-Qodesh* 61 (75–76).

Song of Songs 4:16 reads in full: *Awake, north wind! Come, south wind! Blow upon my garden, let its spices flow. Let my beloved come into his garden and eat its luscious fruits.*

Psalms 104:16–17 read: *The trees of YHVH are sated, the cedars of Lebanon that He planted. There birds build their nests; the stork has her home in the junipers.*

have said that the blessed Holy One possesses all these attributes. Look, fire does not go forth from before idols ותאכל (*ve-tokhal*), and consume, their sacrifices—as is written of the blessed Holy One: *Fire came forth from before YHVH and consumed on the altar the burnt offering* (Leviticus 9:24). *And cannot smell* (Deuteronomy 4:28)—of the blessed Holy One is written *YHVH smelled the pleasing aroma* (Genesis 8:21), and repeatedly *a pleasing aroma to YHVH* (Leviticus 1:9, *inter alia*). As for them: *They have noses, but cannot smell* (Psalms 115:6).[12]

“In the hour when the blessed Holy One gazes upon Eden, all the hosts of heaven come with Him—*Er'ellim*, *Keruvim*, *Ophanim*, *Seraphim*—and all of them sing as one, reciting: *How abundant is Your goodness that You have hidden away for those in awe of You. You have wrought for those who shelter in You...* (Psalms 31:20). David knew the hour when the blessed Holy One delights with the righteous in the Garden of Eden—and would rise at midnight, as is written: *At midnight I rise to praise You* (ibid. 119:62). How did David know when it was midnight? Well, David would hang his harp facing the north wind; and when Gabriel would venture forth with the northern wind, it would blow upon it—



and the harp would [87] play by itself. When David heard, he would rise at midnight and join with the hosts of heaven, singing and chanting until the break of dawn. At that time, during the morning watch, he would pray.”[13]

12. **does eating pertain to the blessed Holy One...** Song of Songs 4:16 concludes with an invocation for the beloved to enter his garden and *eat its luscious fruits.* Given that the beloved stands for God, what kind of eating is implied? His consumption of sacrificial offerings.

Compare *ZḤ* 13b–c (*MhN*), which raises the same problem but gives a different solution.

On the verse from the Song of Songs as alluding to sacrifices, see *Seder Olam Rabbah* 7; JT *Megillah* 1:11, 72c; *Bereshit Rabbah* 22:5; *Vayiqra Rabbah* 9:6; *Shir ha-Shirim Rabbah* 1:12 (on 1:2) and on 4:16; *Zohar* 2:37b; 3:11a.

The parable is not connected with the anthropomorphic problem of the verse from the Song of Songs. It merely serves as a preamble to the verse in Deuteronomy describing the idols of wood and stone, which—unlike God—do not eat.

On Psalms 115:5–6, see *Eikhah Rabbah* 1:50.

13. **David knew the hour...** On King David's nocturnal practice, see BT *Berakhot* 3b: “Rabbi Osha'ya said in the name of Rabbi Aḥa, ‘David said, “Midnight never passed me by in my sleep.”’ Rabbi Zeira said, ‘Till midnight he used to doze like a horse; from then on, he became mighty as a lion.’ Rav Ashi said, ‘Till midnight he engaged in Torah; from then on, in songs and praises.’... But did David know the exact moment of midnight?... David had a sign, for... Rabbi Shim'on the Ḥasid said, ‘There was a harp suspended above David's bed. As soon as midnight arrived, a north wind came and blew upon it, and it played by itself. He immediately arose and engaged in Torah until the break of dawn.’”

Based on this legendary custom, the *Zohar* develops an elaborate ritual—the nocturnal delight—whereby kabbalists are expected to rise at midnight and ply Torah until the break of dawn. At midnight, God delights with the souls of the righteous in the Garden of Eden; and those who study Torah below partake of the celestial joy. In the main body of the *Zohar*, this ritual is understood as adorning the *Shekhinah* in preparation for Her union with the blessed Holy One. This parallels the midnight vigil common among Christian monks from early medieval times. In *Zohar* 3:119a, Rabbi Yehudah alludes to the Christian practice: "I have seen something similar among the nations of the world."

See JT *Berakhot* 1:1, 2d; *Sifra, Beḥuqqotai* 3:3, 111b; *Aggadat Bereshit* 23:5; BT *Sanhedrin* 102a; 2 Enoch 8:3; *Zohar* 1:10b, 72a, 77a–b, 82b, 92a–b, 136b, 178a, 206b–207b, 231b, 242b; 2:26b, 36b, 46a, 130a–b, 136a, 173b, 195b–196a; 3:13a, 21b–22b, 49b, 52b, 67b–68a, 81a, 193a, 260a; [Moses de León?], *Seder Gan Eden*, 138; Scholem, *On the Kabbalah*, 146–50; Hellner-Eshed, *A River Flows from Eden*, 121–45. Cf. Matthew 25:6.

On the *Zohar*'s nocturnal ritual in *MhN*, see *Zohar* 2:18b; *ZḤ* 6a, 13c, 18a; Scholem, "Parashah Ḥadashah," 445 (Addendum 1 in this volume). On the blessed Holy One's gazing upon Eden and Psalms 31:20, see *ZḤ* 6a (*MhN*).

# Addendum 3

We have learned:[1] Rabbi Yitsḥak said, "Once, Rabbi Shim'on, Rabbi El'azar his son, and Rabbi Pinḥas were by the outskirts of Tiberias.[2]

"Rabbi Shim'on said, 'I have seen the feet of men, pursuers [166] of adultery, seized by the truculent stingers in the world.'[3]

1. **We have learned** The following short pericope is not found in printed editions of the *Zohar*. It is preserved in one manuscript alone (Ms2, Moscow, Guenzburg 262) and was published by Ronit Meroz. Some of the material found here does, however, appear in *ZḤ* 20b, 21c–d (both *MhN*) and in *Zohar* 1:117b–118a (*MhN*). For a masterful analysis of this entire unit, see Meroz, "Va-Ani Lo Hayiti Sham?," 163–93.

This pericope is particularly noteworthy for its treatment of Rabbi Shim'on son of Yoḥai, portrayed as working outside the main chain of mystical transmission and occupying a relatively lowly rung among the sages. As Meroz has suggested, this unique portrayal of the *Zohar*'s hero may have prompted a rejection of this story, accounting for its absence from other manuscripts and the printed text.

2. **outskirts of Tiberias** "Outskirts" renders פלכי (*pilkhei*). In the Talmud פלך (*pelekh*) means "district, region," as opposed to the city. (See also Nehemiah 3:9–18). According to Scholem, however, *pilkhei* is a corruption of פילי (*pilei*), "gates," and hence Rabbi Shim'on, Rabbi El'azar, and Rabbi Pinḥas are by the gates of Tiberias (cf. *Bereshit Rabbah* 96:5; *Tanḥuma*, *Shofetim* 10; *Zohar* 1:57b, 217a.) See Nehemiah 3:14–15 and BT *Makkot* 7a, where "gates" and the word *pelekh* are associated. The form *pilkhei* appears again in *ZḤ* 23a (*MhN*) and in Scholem, "Parashah Ḥadashah," 431, n. 28 (see Addendum 1 in this volume). See Meroz, "Va-Ani Lo Hayiti Sham?," 165, n. 13.

Rabbi Pinḥas son of Ya'ir lived in the second century in Palestine and was renowned for his saintliness and ability to work miracles. See BT *Ḥullin* 7a; JT *Demai* 1:3, 22a. In the *Zohar*, he is accorded special status and generally he is in a class by himself among the Companions. See 1:11a; 3:59b–60b, 62a–b, 200b–202a, 203a, 225b, 288a, 296b (*IZ*); *ZḤ* 12b, 19a (both *MhN*). According to BT *Shabbat* 33b, Rabbi Pinḥas was the son-in-law of Rabbi Shim'on, however the *Zohar* elevates him further by transforming him into Rabbi Shim'on's father-in-law. This new role could be the result of a simple mistake: confusing חתן (*ḥatan*), "son-in-law," with חותן (*ḥoten*), "father-in-law." However, the switch may also be deliberate, another instance of interchanging father and son.

3. **I have seen the feet of men...** In the manuscript, this sentence is garbled. My ren-

"Rabbi Pinḥas said, 'Those mighty men who were born in the world were called Nephilim.'[4]

"Rabbi Shim'on said, 'I am astounded by the whole generation—how they do not consider or contemplate the wisdom right in front of them!'

"He opened, saying, '*Israel served YHVH during the lifetime of Joshua and the lifetime of the elders who lived on after Joshua* (Joshua 24:31). As we have learned: An old man in the house is a good omen for the house; a righteous person in the generation is good for the world. As we have learned: The blessed Holy One casts fear of the judge and ruler upon the generation. As long as the fear of the judge is upon [167] the generation, it is apparent that he is righteous and they are righteous. If his fear is withdrawn from the generation—he is wicked, and they more so than him.[5]

dering follows Meroz's reconstruction ("Va-Ani Lo Hayiti Sham?," 166, n. 14).

"Truculent stingers" renders טריקין (*triqin*), "menacing forces." The root טרק (*trq*) means "to sting, bite." See *Zohar* 1:62b, 130a, 237b, 243b–244a; 3:52b, 62b, 154b, 181a, 291b (*IZ*).

4. **Nephilim** See Genesis 6:1–4: *When humankind began to increase on the face of the earth and daughters were born to them, the sons of God saw that the daughters of humankind were beautiful, and they took themselves wives, whomever they chose. YHVH said, "My spirit shall not abide in the human forever, for he too is flesh. Let his days be a hundred and twenty years." The Nephilim were on earth in those days—and afterward as well—when the sons of God came in to the daughters of humankind, who bore them children. These are the heroes of old, men of renown.*

The myth behind this fragment in Genesis appears in postbiblical sources describing angels who rebelled against God and descended from heaven to earth, where they were attracted by human women. See Isaiah 14:12; 1 Enoch 6–8; Jubilees 5; *Targum Yerushalmi*, Genesis 6:2, 4; BT *Yoma* 67b; *Aggadat Bereshit*, intro, 39; *Midrash Avkir*, 7 (cited in *Yalqut Shim'oni*, Genesis, 44); *Pirqei de-Rabbi Eli'ezer* 22; *Zohar* 1:23a (*TZ*), 37a, 37a (*Tos*), 55a, 58a, 62b, 117b–118a (*MhN*), 126a; 3:208a–b, 212a–b; *ZḤ* 20b (*MhN*), 21c (*MhN*); 81a–b (*MhN, Rut*); Ginzberg, *Legends*, 5:153–56, n. 57.

5. **An old man in the house is a good omen for the house...** Rabbi Pinḥas is the speaker.

Following the opening verse from Joshua, a nearly identical passage (extending for the next two paragraphs) is found in *ZḤ* 20b (*MhN*). 

Cf. BT *Arakhin* 19a: "An old man in the house is a burden in the house, an old woman in the house is a treasure in the house!" See Rashi on Leviticus 27:7; see also *Sippurei ben Sira*, ed. Yassif, 274. The *Zohar* has transformed the popular saying, perhaps conflating it with the rabbinic idea that a righteous person is a sign (of the covenant) in the world. See *Pesiqta de-Rav Kahana* 11:15; *ZḤ* 10d (*MhN*). According to Meroz, the allusion to the righteous as a sign is pointed, for the passage in *Pesiqta de-Rav Kahana* refers to Rabbi Shim'on. See Meroz, "Va-Ani Lo Hayiti Sham?," 167, n. 17.

On fear of the ruler, cf. BT *Rosh ha-Shanah* 17a: "Those who *spread their terror in the land of the living* (Ezekiel 32:23): Rav Ḥisda said, 'This is a communal leader who casts excessive fear upon the community for purposes other than the sake of heaven.'" See also Maimonides, *Mishneh Torah, Hilkhot Teshuvah* 3:13.

Although casting excessive fear is a sin, an appropriate amount of fear toward the ruler is in order. In fact, the presence of fear is a sign of the ruler's righteousness. Conversely,

"'Scripture comes to say: הנפלים (*Ha-nefilim*), *The fallen beings, were on earth* (Genesis 6:4). These are Adam and his wife, for they are the ones who fell to earth without a father and mother. Furthermore, why were they called *fallen beings*? For they fell from the original rank they possessed. In other words, they had already fallen from how they were previously; fallen, for they did not rise, because they were banished from the Garden of Eden and did not return there. That is why the Torah reiterates: these ones *were on earth*—their fear was upon all the creatures; they were still alive, but they did not prevent the people of the generation from performing transgressions such as these. Who are the ones who performed transgressions? The dignitaries of the generation, the men of renown, as is said: אנשי השם (*anshei ha-shem*), *the men of renown* (ibid.)—the greatest in the generation.'[6]

"Rabbi Yitsḥak said, 'Hence, the meaning of the verse is clear, as is written: *The fallen beings were on earth* בימים ההם (*ba-yamim ha-hem*), *in those days* (ibid.). שהם להם (*She-hem la-hem*), It was incumbent upon them, to restrain
578 themselves from transgressions—for their sake. But they did not hold back, and
in front of their very eyes they came *into the daughters of humankind* whorishly, *and they bore them children* (ibid.). Who were those *fallen beings* extant in the generation? They are *the mighty men* (ibid.), without peer in the whole generation; אנשי השם (*anshei ha-shem*), *the men of name* (ibid.)—the known name that the blessed Holy One called them, as is said: *He called their name* אדם (*Adam*), *Human* (ibid. 5:2). What is the significance of אשר מעולם (*asher me-olam*), *of old* (ibid. 6:4)? That they came into being when He made העולם (*ha-olam*), the world. They were מעולם (*me-olam*), *of old*, and not of that time.'[7]

the absence of such fear is a sign that the ruler has sinned.

On the role of leaders and their responsibility in the *Zohar*, see 2:36b, 47a; 3:114a, 135a (*IR*).

6. **These are Adam and his wife...** Although in the Genesis narrative, the *nefilim* apparently refer to fallen celestial beings, here the *Zohar* reads them as Adam and Eve.

Cf. *Bereshit Rabbah* 26:7; *Pirqei de-Rabbi Eli'ezer* 22; Naḥmanides on Genesis 6:4. In the later strata of the *Zohar*, the *nefilim* usually refer to the fallen angels Uzza and Azael. See *Zohar* 1:37a, 37a (*Tos*), 58a; 3:144a (*IR*); *ZḤ* 81a–b (*MhN*, *Rut*).

Adam and Eve were still alive when the dignitaries of the generation sinned. Either the *Zohar* intends that they ought to have prevented the sin but did not, or that following their own sin in the Garden of Eden—and so having lost the respect of their fellow human beings—they were ineffective as leaders and could do nothing to prevent the mighty from doing as they pleased.

On the *nefilim* as inspiring fear, see Naḥmanides on Genesis 6:4: "The masters of language say that they were so called because a person's heart falls from fear of them." On Adam and Eve's fallen status, cf. BT *Ḥagigah* 12a; *Sanhedrin* 38b; *Bereshit Rabbah* 12:6.

7. **Rabbi Yitsḥak said...** Oddly, Rabbi Yitsḥak seems to be quoting himself (in the third person) while narrating this episode. Apparently he was also present. He explains that as leaders, Adam and Eve ought to have

"Rabbi Yitsḥak said, 'Yet the verse stipulates that he had died!'[8] [168]

"He replied, 'There is no early or late in Torah! And I have heard a matter, decreed from the mouths of the Masters of Mishnah.'[9]

"Rabbi Shim'on said, 'And I was not there?!'[10]

"He replied, 'No, for the master and his son were seated beneath the palm in the desert, amidst their company, when the decree was ordained from the house of the king.'[11]

set an example for succeeding generations. Instead they were forced to witness the sexual violence perpetrated on their own children! According to Rabbi Yitsḥak, the *nefilim* (i.e., Adam and Eve) correspond to the *mighty men*, corresponding in turn with אנשי השם (*anshei ha-shem*), usually rendered *men of renown*, but read here literally as *the men of name*, i.e., the name "Human" bestowed by God. (In the previous paragraph, *the men of renown* are the ones who committed the sin.)

On Adam and Eve as "mighty men" without peer, cf. Naḥmanides on Genesis 6:4.

Cf. *Zohar* 1:37a; 2:179a (*SdTs*).

8. **the verse stipulates that he had died** See Genesis 5:5 preceding the Torah's discussion of the Nephilim: *All the days that Adam lived came to 930 years; then he died.*

There appears to be an inconsistency here. In the preceding paragraph, Rabbi Yitsḥak seemed to have adopted Rabbi Pinḥas' interpretation—in which Adam and Eve were still alive; yet now he wonders how this is possible. In *ZḤ* 20b (*MhN*), the preceding paragraph is spoken by Rabbi Pinḥas, which would make Rabbi Yitsḥak's objection more meaningful.

9. **no early or late in Torah...** On the theme "there is no early or late in Torah," see *Mekhilta, Shirta* 7; *Sifrei*, Numbers 64; JT *Megillah* 1:5, 70d; BT *Pesaḥim* 6b; *Bemidbar Rabbah* 9:18; *Shir ha-Shirim Rabbah* on 1:2; *Tanḥuma, Terumah* 8.

The term "Masters of Mishnah" appears in numerous passages throughout *Midrash ha-Ne'lam*, in various formulations. It seems to signify a never-formally-defined group of sages who possess esoteric wisdom. In some ways, the Masters of Mishnah are a forerunner to the *Ḥavrayya*, the Companions headed by Rabbi Shim'on, found in the main body of the *Zohar*. Significantly, however, Rabbi Shim'on does not always occupy a privileged position in this group. The Mishnah of which they are masters is not the Mishnah of the rabbinic sage Rabbi Yehudah ha-Nasi, but rather a body of esoteric knowledge often relating to the soul and to the structure of the cosmos. See *Zohar* 1:123b (*MhN*, though mistakenly labeled as *Tosefta*); 1:127a–b, 129a–b, 130a, 135a 138a, 139b; 2:5a, 14a (all *MhN*); *ZḤ* 12c, 13a, 14c, 15b–c, 16a, 59b (all *MhN*); Scholem, "Parashah Ḥadashah," 443, 444 (Addendum 1 in this volume). Cf. *Pesiqta de-Rav Kahana* 11:15, 23:12. See also Matt, "Matnita di-Lan," 132–34.



On the use of the term "decree" (from the root גזר [*gzr*]) for establishing a teaching, see *Zohar* 1:123a, 124b, 125a (all *MhN*); *ZḤ* 14a, 15b, 16a, 18b, 20a (all *MhN*); 62b (*ShS*); Scholem, "Parashah Hadashah," 443.

10. **And I was not there?!** Not only does Rabbi Shim'on not head the learned Masters of Mishnah, but also he was not even present when they decreed their teachings.

11. **beneath the palm in the desert...** Not only is Rabbi Shim'on not always present when traditions are decreed, but also he does not even belong (at least not entirely) to the central and authoritative source of tradition: the house of the king. He belongs to a different (secondary) company, situated in the desert.

According to numerous rabbinic sources, Rabbi Shim'on and his son El'azar hid from

“He said to him, ‘Speak!’

“He replied, ‘So was decreed there.’

“He opened, saying, ‘*Your righteousness is like the mighty mountains; Your judgments, the great abyss* (Psalms 36:7). Did King David compare the virtue and beneficence of his Master to mighty mountains?! What virtue do they possess? Rather, so has been decreed: For Rabbi Bo said in the name of Rabbi Yuda, “Like the dark waters of the ocean, made open to all, so the blessed Holy One: His righteousness is open to the whole world like the mountains, which are open to all. *Your judgments, the great abyss*—that is, He deals strictly with His creatures unto the abyss.”’[12] [169]



Roman authorities for thirteen years in a cave, where they were miraculously sustained by a carob tree.

Here Rabbi Shim'on remains in the dark, while Rabbi Pinḥas is the conveyor of the tradition from the house of the king. Contrast BT *Shabbat* 33b: “Originally, when Rabbi Shim'on son of Yoḥai raised an objection, Rabbi Pinḥas son of Ya'ir solved it with twelve solutions. Subsequently, when Rabbi Pinḥas son of Ya'ir objected, Rabbi Shim'on son of Yoḥai solved it with twenty-four solutions.” See also *Bereshit Rabbah* 79:6; *Qohelet Rabbah* on 10:9; JT *Shevi'it* 9:1, 38d; *Pesiqta de-Rav Kahana* 11:16; *Midrash Tehillim* 17:13; *ZḤ* 59c–60a (where the cave is located in the desert); *Zohar* 1:11b, 216b. See also *ZḤ* 20d (*MhN*).

Presumably the king is the head of the Masters of Mishnah. See Scholem, “Parashah Ḥadashah,” 443 (Addendum 1 in this volume). On the significance of the term “king,” see Meroz, “Va-Ani Lo Hayiti Sham?,” 191–93.

Cf. *Zohar* 3:79b, where Rabbi Shim'on is described as a king.

On the desert as the abode of mystical fraternities, see *Zohar* 2:183b–187b.

12. ***Your righteousness . . . Your judgments...*** The waters of the ocean and of the abyss signify compassion and judgment, respectively. Apparently, Rabbi Pinḥas is the speaker.

The *Zohar* is reworking an earlier homily. See *Bereshit Rabbah* 33:1: “*Your righteousness is like* הררי אל (*harerei el*), *the mighty mountains; Your judgments, the great abyss*.... Rabbi Yishma'el and Rabbi Akiva [offered different interpretations]: Rabbi Yishma'el says, ‘To the righteous who accepted the Torah that was given on הררי אל (*harerei el*), the mountains of God, You perform righteousness [i.e., show love] reaching unto the mountains of God; but as for the wicked, who did not accept the Torah that was given on the mountains of God, You deal strictly with them, unto the great abyss [i.e., to the depths of their being].’ Rabbi Akiva says, ‘He deals strictly with both, unto the great abyss....’ Rabbi Yonatan in Rabbi Yoshiah's name transposed the verse, ‘Your righteousness [i.e., compassion] is above Your judgments, just as the mountains of God are above the great abyss. Just as these mountains are endless, so the reward of the righteous is endless. Just as these mountains press back the abyss so that it should not ascend and inundate the world, so do the righteous press back punishment, lest it go forth and burn up the world. Just as the mountains are sown and yield fruit, so do the deeds of the righteous yield fruit.... Just as the abyss is not sown and does not yield fruit, so the deeds of the wicked do not produce fruit, for if they produced fruit they would destroy the world.’” See also *Tanḥuma, Emor* 5; *Tanḥuma* (Buber), *Noaḥ* 8; *Pesiqta de-Rav Kahana* 9:1; *Aggadat Bereshit* (Buber) 4. In some of these rabbinic sources, part of this homily is cited in the name of

"Rabbi Yitsḥak said, '*Your judgments, the great abyss*—for the blessed Holy One scrutinizes a person before he is born and determines if he [is worthy] of emerging into the world. If [not], He kills him in advance and he falls. As we have learned: Why does a woman מפלת (*mappelet*), miscarry, the fruit of her womb? Because the blessed Holy One determines that it is not worthy of coming forth into the world, and that the world will be deficient because of it, and He slays it in advance in its mother's uterus, as is said: הנפלים (*Ha-nefilim*), *The fallen beings, were on earth in those days* (Genesis 6:4).'[13]

"Rabbi Yitsḥak also said, 'It is written: נפלים (*nefalim*), miscarriages, without the first י (*yod*). Why? Because afterward *the sons of God came [into the daughters of humankind]* (ibid.). בני האלהים (*Benei ha-Elohim*), *The sons of God*—in the Aramaic translation: sons of the mighty; that is, when they will be bigger; He scrutinizes them that they will come *into the daughters of humankind, who will bear them offspring* (ibid.) whorishly, and bastards will abound in the world. *These are the mighty ones of old, men of the name* (ibid.)—for there is none as mighty, roughshod, and ruthless as the bastard; *men of the name*—all will recognize him to call him by a certain name: "bastard." For as soon as they see how he is roughshod and ruthless and mighty, all recognize him to call him *men of the name*, namely the particular name.'[14]



"Rabbi Shim'on said, 'All this my companions concealed among themselves—and it has not been revealed to me?! I have a complaint against them, and more so against the holy company in which I was seated!'[15]

Rabbi Shim'on. Here, he is the recipient of the teaching!

"Like the dark waters of the ocean" renders כאמבטי דיוקני קרדיני (*ke-ambatei diyoqnei qardinei*), a phrase of uncertain meaning, apparently garbled. My rendering follows Meroz's reconstruction. See "Va-Ani Lo Hayiti Sham?," 168, n. 22.

13. **the blessed Holy One scrutinizes a person before he is born...** Seeing that the as-yet-unborn child will one day act immorally, God determines to abort the fetus.

See *Zohar* 1:117b–118a (*MhN*) for a close parallel to this and the following paragraph.

Cf. *ZḤ* 19d–20b (*MhN*) on God's removing the innocent from the world before they sin. See also *Zohar* 2:96a–b, where this idea is applied to babies.

14. **נפלים (*nefalim*), miscarriages, without the first י (*yod*)...** See *Bereshit Rabbah* 26:7: "נפלים (*Nefilim*)—שהפילו (*she-hippilu*), for they hurled, the world down, ושנפלו (*ve-she-nafelu*), and because they fell, from the world, and filled the world with נפלים (*nefalim*), abortions [or: miscarriages], through their immorality."

Although in its biblical context the Hebrew בני האלהים (*benei ha-elohim*), *sons of God*, implies some kind of celestial beings, there is a long tradition of reading the word *elohim* here as signifying "the mighty, judges, nobles," as some interpreters perceive in Exodus 21:6; 22:7–8, 22:27; Judges 5:8; 1 Samuel 2:25; and Psalms 138:1. Both *Targum Onqelos* and *Targum Yerushalmi*, ad loc., render *benei ha-elohim* as בני רברביא (*benei ravrevaya*), *sons of the mighty*. See also *Bereshit Rabbah* 26:5 (in the name of Rabbi Shim'on!)

On the bastard, see *Kallah* 1:16; JT *Qiddushin* 4:14, 66b.

15. **All this my companions concealed...** Among the larger group of sages, Rabbi

“Rabbi Yitsḥak said, ‘I am destined to usher you into the world to come, and not by virtue of the generation alone, for we have seen in you that solution of Mishnaic difficulties is plucked off in your mouth like the other saints of Mishnah.’”[16]

Rav Huna said, “The Nephilim are the giants, the great mighty ones, so called after their greatness.”[17]

Rabbi Bo said, “The blessed Holy One saw what they were doing—stretching out their hands to rob—and He wanted to eradicate them from the world. He said, [170] ‘They act thus because I prolong them.’ Immediately: *YHVH said,* רוחי (*Ruḥi*), *My spirit, shall not abide in the human forever, since he too is flesh'* (Genesis 6:3).”[18]

We have learned there: Rabbi Ḥiyya son of Ya'akov said, “Three forces are comprised in the force of a human being—נפש (*nefesh*), soul, רוח (*ruaḥ*), spirit, נשמה (*neshamah*), soul-breath. Soul is associated with the body to perform all



the body's needs, drawing the blood to all its organs. That is why נפש (*nefesh*), soul, is predicated by blood, as is said: *for* נפשו (*nafsho*), *its life, is its blood* (based on Leviticus 17:14), and it is written: *the blood is* הנפש (*ha-nafesh*), *the life* (Deuteronomy 12:23), and similarly: *Just so, for* דמכם לנפשותיכם (*dimkhem le-nafshoteikhem*), *your lifeblood* (Genesis 9:5). רוח (*Ruaḥ*), Spirit, is the air that sustains the body; for without the air the body cannot exist. נשמה (*Neshamah*), Soul-breath, is pure and clear.”[19]

Shim'on is the outsider, protesting that he has not been brought in on the secret. As for his own company, the nature of his complaint against them is not clear.

Rabbi Shim'on's portrayal here is light-years away from the semidivine figure found throughout the *Zohar*'s pages. Elsewhere in the *Zohar*, he appears omniscient—and the idea that he could remain in the dark, unthinkable. See Hellner-Eshed, *A River Flows From Eden*, 31–61.

16. **I am destined to usher you...** By virtue of his Torah knowledge, Rabbi Yitsḥak will escort Rabbi Shim'on into the world to come. Again, Rabbi Shim'on is merely like the other saints of Mishnah—no higher. Indeed, he is subordinate to Rabbi Yitsḥak and Rabbi Pinḥas, and presumably to the king.

Cf. *Zohar* 1:217b–218a, where the tables are turned and Rabbi Shim'on is Rabbi Yitsḥak's guarantor to enter the world to come; see also *Zohar* 3:287b (*IZ*); cf. also *Zohar* 2:61b.

The phrase “plucked off in your mouth” derives from Genesis 8:11: *The dove came back to him at eventide; and look, a plucked off olive leaf was in its bill!*

This apparently marks the end of the story recounted by Rabbi Yitsḥak.

17. **The Nephilim are the giants...** On the Nephilim as giants, see Numbers 13:22, 33; *Bereshit Rabbah* 26:7; *Pirqei de-Rabbi Eli'ezer* 22; Rashi on Genesis 6:4. Cf. *ZḤ* 21c (*MhN*) in standard printed editions.

18. **stretching out their hands to rob...** On robbery as the chief sin of the antediluvians, see BT *Sanhedrin* 108a; *Tanḥuma, Noaḥ* 4; *Zohar* 1:66b; *ZḤ* 21d (*MhN*).

19. **Three forces are comprised in the force of a human being...** *MhN* presents numerous (sometimes conflicting) divisions

It has been taught: Rabbi Aḥa said, "As long as the air receives the body as required, helping it, the body is sustained by it. When the air is removed, the body is not sustained. The blessed Holy One said, 'I shall cause the air to be in conflict with him, and then he will not endure,' as is written: לא ידון רוחי (*lo yadon ruḥi*), *My spirit shall not abide, in the human*... (ibid. 6:3). This ידון (*yadon*), *shall abide*, is like *all the people* נדון (*nadon*), *had been arguing* (2 Samuel 19:10), that is, were reconciled. Thus: לא ידון רוחי (*lo yadon ruḥi*), *My spirit shall not abide, in the human*—the air shall not be reconciled with the human, but in conflict with him; and they shall perish in a little while."[20]

Rabbi Yose said, "The blessed Holy One removed the air from them and they fell."

Rabbi Yitsḥak said, "In a similar vein, David said: *take away their spirit, they perish* (Psalms 104:29), as is said: *He will gather in His spirit and soul-breath* (Job 34:14)."[21]

Rabbi Bo said, "*My spirit shall not abide in the human*—My spirit shall not be reconciled with the human forever. Why? Because he *is flesh*, craving to perform transgressions every day. Rather: *Let his days be a hundred and twenty years* (Genesis 6:3) for their existence." 583

Rabbi Yose said, "It is an allusion to Moses, that his days would be a hundred and twenty years, for בשגם (*be-shaggam*), *since too* (ibid.), has the numerical

of the soul. See *ZḤ* 6d, 8d–9a, 10c–11a (not tripartite), 14b, 16a–c (not tripartite), 21c; *Zohar* 1:109a–b. See Tishby, *Wisdom of the Zohar*, 2:703–12.

Leviticus 17:14 reads: *For the life of all flesh, its blood is its life; and I say to the Israelites: the blood of all flesh you shall not consume, for the life of all flesh is its blood—all who consume it shall be cut off.*

Genesis 9:4–5 read: *But flesh with its life, its blood, you shall not eat. Just so, for your lifeblood, from every beast I will requite it; and from humankind, from every man's brother, I will requite human life.*

On the air (spirit) sustaining the body, see *ZḤ* 6d (*MhN*). See also Judah Alḥarizi, *Sefer ha-Nefesh* (attributed to Galenus), ed. Jellinek, 13; Moses de León, *Sefer ha-Rimmon*, 407. On the soul as pure, cf. the prayer in the morning liturgy "My God, the soul You placed within me is pure," mentioned in BT *Berakhot* 60b.

20. **לא ידון רוחי (*lo yadon ruḥi*), *My spirit shall not abide, in the human*...** In the verse from Samuel, the word *nadon* (a unique conjugation of this verbal root) means "arguing" or perhaps "deliberating." See *Targum Yonatan*, Rashi, and Radak, ad loc. Apparently the *Zohar* is reading *nadon* as implying the agreement or reconciliation that follows an argument. See Meroz, "Va-Ani Lo Hayiti Sham?," 170, n. 36.

On Genesis 6:3, cf. *Zohar* 1:37b, 58a. On the pairing of conflict and reconciliation (in the supernal realm), cf. *Zohar* 1:17a–b.

See Wolfson, "The Anonymous Chapters of the Elderly Master of Secrets," 258, where this passage is cited.

21. ***He will gather in His spirit and soul-breath*** Job 34:14 reads: *If He but intends it, He will gather in His spirit and soul-breath; all flesh would perish together, and the human being return to the dust.*

value of משה (*Moshe*), Moses. The blessed Holy One said, ‘If so for Moses, who is destined to receive My Torah, how much more so for others!’”[22] [171]

וינחם יהוה (*Va-yinnaḥem YHVH*), *YHVH was sorry, that He had made humankind on earth, and His heart was saddened* (ibid., 6). Rabbi Abbahu said in the name of Rabbi Yoḥanan, “Every וינחם (*va-yinnaḥem*) in the Torah is an expression of comfort. The blessed Holy One saw that they were worthy of being annihilated from the world, and He was saddened by their loss. Even though they were wicked, וינחם (*va-yinnaḥem*)—He took comfort in their surviving remnant. In all instances you find the blessed Holy One's attribute of compassion—even though He executed judgment upon them, He left a remnant of them to settle the world, for so is the compassion of the Omnipresent. Similarly: וינחם יהוה (*Va-yinnaḥem YHVH*), *YHVH renounced, the evil [He had intended to bring upon His people]* (Exodus 32:14)—He took comfort in the surviving remnant, so as to settle the world, that they would not be annihilated in their wickedness.[23]

584 “In every judgment in which the world is judged, it is judged solely with the attribute of compassion, that the world not be annihilated. As is written: *YHVH sat enthroned at the Flood* (Psalms 29:10); *YHVH rained upon Sodom*... (Genesis

22. **בשגם (*be-shaggam*)... has the numerical value of משה (*Moshe*), Moses...** Both equal 345.

On *be-shaggam* as signifying Moses (who lived a hundred and twenty years, see Deuteronomy 34:7), see *Bereshit Rabbah* 26:6; BT *Ḥullin* 139b; *Pirqei de-Rabbi Eli'ezer* 32; *Zohar* 1:37b–38a; 2:179a (*SdTs*), 238a.

23. **Every וינחם (*va-yinnaḥem*) in the Torah is an expression of comfort...** In its biblical context, the word *va-yinnaḥem* can be rendered variously as “changed His mind, retracted, renounced, relented, repented, regretted, was sorry.” Here, Rabbi Abbahu in the name of Rabbi Yoḥanan explains that *va-yinnaḥem* does not in fact mean that God was sorry or regretful, but rather that he was comforted or consoled—another meaning of the root נחם (*nḥm*).

On the word *va-yinnaḥem*, see *Bereshit Rabbah* 27:4; *Tanḥuma* (Buber), *Noaḥ* 4; BT *Sanhedrin* 108a; *Zohar* 1:57a. In some places in the Torah (Genesis 24:67, 38:12, 50:21), *va-yinnaḥem* does indeed mean “was comforted, consoled.” In Exodus 32:14, however, the simple meaning is clearly “renounced, relented”: וינחם יהוה על הרעה (*va-yinnaḥem YHVH al ha-ra'ah*), *YHVH renounced the evil, He had intended to bring upon His people* (see also Jeremiah 26:13; Jonah 3:10). According to Rabbi Yoḥanan here, the meaning of *va-yinnaḥem* is always “was comforted” and never “regretted, relented, renounced.”

On God's being saddened by the loss of the wicked, see BT *Sanhedrin* 39b: “The blessed Holy One does not rejoice in the downfall of the wicked”; see also BT *Megillah* 10b; *Tanḥuma, Balak* 8; *Midrash Aggadah* (Buber), *Bemidbar* 22; *Pesiqta Zutarta, Eikhah* 3. See also Scholem, “Parashah Ḥadashah,” 439 (Addendum 1 in this volume).

The *Zohar* here employs a rare idiom, לקח נחמה (*laqaḥ neḥamah*), “took comfort,” perhaps influenced by one of the Iberian dialects. See Meroz, “Va-Ani Lo Hayiti Sham?,” 164, 171. Cf. *ZḤ* 21c (*MhN*): לקח עצבון (*laqaḥ itzavon*), “took sadness.”

For close parallels to this passage, see *Zohar* 1:57a; *ZḤ* 21c (*MhN*); see also Tishby, *Wisdom of the Zohar*, 3:1419.

19:24); *YHVH scattered them from there* (Genesis 11:8); *YHVH sent a plague upon the people* (Exodus 32:35)—demonstrating the Omnipresent's attribute of compassion; when He strikes, He strikes with compassion, not with cruelty."[24]

Rabbi Tanḥum said, "Similarly in the time to come: With compassion He struck, with compassion He will gather in our exile, as is written: *For a little while I forsook you, but with vast compassion I will bring you back* (Isaiah 54:7); and it is said: *With compassion I return to Jerusalem. My house shall be built in her*... (Zechariah 1:16)."

24. **judged solely with the attribute of compassion...** According to rabbinic tradition, the name *YHVH* conveys compassion, while *Elohim* conveys judgment. See *Sifrei*, Deuteronomy 26; *Bereshit Rabbah* 12:15; 33:3; *Shemot Rabbah* 3:6; *Zohar* 1:173b; 3:269b; Naḥmanides on Deuteronomy 3:24.

See *ZḤ* 21d (*MhN*) for a close parallel to this passage. See also *Zohar* 1:56b, 64b; 2:187a, 227b.

Genesis 11:8 refers to the builders of the Tower of Babel.

The plague in question was a punishment for the golden calf.

REFERENCE MATTER

# *Abbreviations*

| | |
|---|---|
| ABD | David Noel Freedman, ed. *Anchor Bible Dictionary* |
| add. | addendum |
| Add. | Additional |
| *Arukh* | Nathan ben Yeḥiel of Rome, *Sefer he-Arukh* |
| *Arukh ha-Shalem* | Nathan ben Yeḥiel of Rome, *Arukh ha-Shalem* |
| *Battei Midrashot* | Shlomo Aharon Wertheimer, ed., *Battei Midrashot* |
| B.C.E. | before the Common Era |
| *Beit ha-Midrash* | Adolph Jellinek, ed., *Beit ha-Midrash* |
| *Bei'ur ha-Millim ha-Zarot* | Boaz Huss, ed. *Bei'ur ha-Millim ha-Zarot she-be-Sefer ha-Zohar* |
| BT | Babylonian Talmud |
| C9 | MS Add. 1023, University Library, Cambridge |
| C.E. | Common Era |
| Cremona | Cremona edition of the Zohar |
| Ct1 | MS F 12 140, Trinity College, Cambridge |
| *Derekh Emet* | *Derekh Emet*, in *Sefer ha-Zohar*, ed. Reuven Margaliot |
| diss. | dissertation |
| ed. | editor (plural, eds.); edition; edited by |
| Edri | Yehuda Edri, trans., *Sefer ha-Zohar* |
| esp. | especially |
| fasc. | fascicle |
| frag. | fragmentary |
| *Haggahot Maharḥu* | Ḥayyim Vital, *Haggahot Maharḥu* |
| *Heikh* | *Heikhalot* |
| intro | introduction |
| *IR* | *Idra Rabba* |
| *IZ* | *Idra Zuta* |
| JT | Jerusalem Talmud |
| L33 | MS Gaster 773, British Library, London |
| M | Mishnah |
| M2 | MS Hebr. 203, Bayerische Staatsbibliothek, Munich |
| M5 | MS Hebr. 20, Bayerische Staatsbibliothek, Munich |
| M7 | MS Hebr. 217, Bayerische Staatsbibliothek, Munich |
| Mantua | Mantua edition of the Zohar |
| *Mat* | *Matnitin* |
| *Matoq mi-Devash* | Daniel Frisch, *Peirush Matoq mi-Devash* |
| *MhN* | *Midrash ha-Ne'lam* |

| | |
|---|---|
| *Miqdash Melekh* | Shalom Buzaglo, *Miqdash Melekh* |
| Mopsik | Charles Mopsik, trans. and ed., *Le Zohar* |
| MS (plural, MSS) | manuscript(s) |
| Ms2 | MS Guenzburg 262, Russian State Library, Moscow |
| n. (plural, nn.) | note(s) |
| N41 | MS 1930, Jewish Theological Seminary, New York |
| N47 | MS 2076, Jewish Theological Seminary, New York |
| n.d. | no date |
| *Nitsotsei Orot* | Ḥayyim Joseph David Azulai, *Nitsotsei Orot* |
| *Nitsotsei Zohar* | Reuven Margaliot, *Nitsotsei Zohar* |
| n.p. | no publisher |
| O2 | MS 1564, Bodleian Library, Oxford |
| O3 | MS 1884, Bodleian Library, Oxford |
| O17 | MS 2514, Bodleian Library, Oxford |
| *Or ha-Ḥammah* | Abraham Azulai, *Or ha-Ḥammah* |
| *Or ha-Levanah* | Abraham Azulai, *Or ha-Levanah* |
| OM1 | MS 77 h 22, Merton College, Oxford |
| *Or Yaqar* | Moses Cordovero, *Or Yaqar* |
| P1 | MS héb. 778, Bibliothèque nationale, Paris |
| P2 | MS héb. 779, Bibliothèque nationale, Paris |
| P3 | MS héb. 780, Bibliothèque nationale, Paris |
| par. | paragraph |
| *Pereq Shirah* | Malachi Beit-Arié, ed., *Pereq Shirah* |
| *Piq* | *Piqqudin* |
| *QhM* | *Qav ha-Middah* |
| R1 | MS 2971, Biblioteca Casanatense, Rome |
| *RM* | *Ra'aya Meheimna* |
| *RR* | *Raza de-Razin* |
| Salonika | Salonika edition of *Zohar Ḥadash* |
| Scholem | Gershom Scholem, *Sefer ha-Zohar shel Gershom Scholem* |
| *SdTs* | *Sifra di-Tsni'uta* |
| *ShS* | *Shir ha-Shirim* |
| *SO* | *Sitrei Otiyyot* |
| Soncino | Harry Sperling et al., trans., *The Zohar* (Soncino Press) |
| *ST* | *Sitrei Torah* |
| *Sullam* | Yehudah Ashlag, *Sefer ha-Zohar . . . im . . . ha-Sullam* |
| *Tiq* | *Tiqqunim* (in *Zohar Ḥadash*) |
| *Tos* | *Tosefta* |
| trans. | translator(s); translated by |
| *TZ* | *Tiqqunei ha-Zohar* |
| V1 | MS ebr. 68, Biblioteca Apostolica, Vatican |
| V5 | MS ebr. 206, Biblioteca Apostolica, Vatican |
| V7 | MS ebr. 208, Biblioteca Apostolica, Vatican |
| V9 | MS ebr. 213, Biblioteca Apostolica, Vatican |
| V11 | MS ebr. 290, Biblioteca Apostolica, Vatican |
| V12 | MS ebr. 428, Biblioteca Apostolica, Vatican |
| V13 | MS ebr. 504, Biblioteca Apostolica, Vatican |
| V16 | MS Neofiti 23, Biblioteca, Apostolica, Vatican |
| V22 | MS ebr. 186, Biblioteca Apostolica, Vatican |
| Venice | Venice edition of *Zohar Ḥadash* |
| *ZḤ* | *Zohar Ḥadash* |

# *Transliteration of Hebrew and Aramaic*

| | | | | | |
|---|---|---|---|---|---|
| א | *alef* | ʾ[1] | ל | *lamed* | *l* |
| בּ | *bet* | *b* | מ | *mem* | *m* |
| ב | *vet* | *v* | נ | *nun* | *n* |
| ג | *gimel* | *g* | ס | *samekh* | *s* |
| ד | *dalet* | *d* | ע | *ayin* | ʾ[2] |
| ה | *he* | *h* | פּ | *pe* | *p* |
| ו | *vav* | *v* | פ | *phe* | *f*[3] |
| ז | *zayin* | *z* | צ | *tsadi* | *ts* |
| ח | *ḥet* | *ḥ* | ק | *qof* | *q* |
| ט | *tet* | *t* | ר | *resh* | *r* |
| י | *yod* | *y, i* | שׁ | *shin* | *sh* |
| כּ | *kaf* | *k* | שׂ | *sin* | *s* |
| כ | *khaf* | *kh* | ת | *tav* | *t* |

The English equivalent letter is doubled when a strong *dagesh* in Hebrew or Aramaic characterizes a verbal conjugation or indicates an assimilated letter, e.g., *dibber, yitten.* However, if the Hebrew letter (in which a *dagesh* appears) is represented by two English letters (such as *sh* or *ts*), then that English equivalent is not doubled, e.g., *va-yishaqehu, matsot.* Further, a single English equivalent letter is not doubled when preceded by a hyphenated prefix, e.g., *ha-sefer, la-melekh, mi-tokh.*

Proper names that appear in roman type do not follow the above schema. Biblical names are rendered according to the *JPS Hebrew-English Tanakh.* Rabbinic names are rendered according to common convention, e.g., Akiva, Resh Lakish. Medieval names are Anglicized, e.g., Moses de León, Joseph Gikatilla. Authors' names in the Bibliography follow library listings or the *Encyclopaedia Judaica.*

1. *Alef* is not transliterated at the beginning or end of a word nor after a hyphenated prefix. Elsewhere it is transliterated only when accompanied by a vowel, e.g., *Shemu'el.*
2. *Ayin* is not transliterated at the beginning of a word, nor after a hyphenated prefix, nor, unless accompanied by a vowel, at the end of a word. Thus, *Shema*, but *Bava Metsi'a.*
3. Occasionally transliterated as *ph* to compare or contrast it to the letter *pe.*

# *Glossary*

***aggadah, aggadta*** "Tale"; the nonlegal contents of the Talmud and Midrash, often based on biblical exegesis. It includes ethical and moral teaching, theological speculation, legends, and folklore.

***Amidah*** "Standing"; the central prayer, recited three times daily.

***amora***, pl. ***amora'im*** "Speaker, interpreter"; a teacher living in the three centuries or so following the compilation of the Mishnah (ca. 200 C.E.) and whose opinions are recorded in subsequent rabbinic literature.

**Assembly of Israel** Hebrew, כנסת ישראל (*Keneset Yisra'el*); in rabbinic literature, a phrase normally denoting the people of Israel. In the *Zohar*, the phrase can refer to the earthly community of Israel but also (often primarily) to *Shekhinah*, the divine feminine counterpart of the people.

***Binah*** "Understanding"; the third *sefirah*; the Divine Mother who gives birth to the seven lower *sefirot*.

**blessed Holy One** Common rabbinic name for God. In the *Zohar* it often designates *Tif'eret*.

***Da'at*** "Knowledge"; sometimes designating the hidden *sefirah* that mediates between *Ḥokhmah* and *Binah*.

***Din*** "Judgment"; a divine attribute balancing *Ḥesed*, "Love"; also called *Gevurah*. In the main body of the *Zohar* it is the fifth *sefirah*; the left arm of the divine body.

**Dwelling** Hebrew, משכן (*mishkan*). The portable sanctuary (or Tabernacle), which according to Exodus was constructed by Moses and the Israelites, and then carried from encampment to encampment as the people journeyed through the Sinai Desert.

***Ein Sof*** "There is no end"; that which is boundless; the Infinite. The ultimate reality of God beyond all specific qualities of the *sefirot*; the God beyond God.

***Elohim*** "God, gods"; a biblical name for God. In the *Zohar* it has various sefirotic associations: *Binah*, *Gevurah*, *Shekhinah*.

***Gevurah*** "Power"; the fifth *sefirah*; also called Din.

***gimatriyya*** Derived from the Greek *geometria* ("measuring the earth"); a method of interpretation based on the numerical value of Hebrew letters.

***halakhah*** "Practice, law," from the root הלך (*hlkh*), "to walk": the way that one should follow.

***Hashmatot*** "Omissions"; additions printed at the end of the first of the three standard Aramaic volumes of the *Zohar*, drawn from the Cremona edition and *Zohar Ḥadash*.

***ḥasid***, pl. ***ḥasidim*** "Pious one," devotee, saint, lover of God.

**Heikhalot** "Palaces, Halls"; descriptions of the heavenly and demonic palaces in *Zohar* 1:38a–45b; 2:244b–268b.

***Ḥesed*** "Loving-kindness, love, grace"; a divine attribute balancing *Din*, "Judgment." In the main body of the *Zohar*, it is the fourth *sefirah*; the right arm of the divine body.

***Hod*** "Splendor"; the eighth *sefirah*; the left leg of the divine body; source of prophecy along with *Netsaḥ*.

***Ḥokhmah*** "Wisdom"; in the main body of the *Zohar*, the second *sefirah*; the primordial point of emanation.

***Idra Rabba*** "The Great Assembly"; a description of the gathering of Rabbi Shim'on and the Companions at the threshing house, where profound mysteries of divine being are expounded. *Zohar* 3:127b–145a.

***Idra Zuta*** "The Small Assembly"; a description of the last gathering of Rabbi Shim'on and the Companions, the master's final teachings, and his ecstatic death. *Zohar* 3:287b–296b.

**Israel** Often, the people of Israel.

**jubilee** The year of release, occurring every fifty years at the end of the cycle of seven sabbatical years. According to Leviticus 25, in the jubilee all land reverts to its original owners and all indentured Israelite slaves are freed.



**Kabbalah** Hebrew, קבלה (*qabbalah*), "receiving, that which is received, tradition"; originally referring to tradition in general (or to post-Mosaic Scripture), but from the thirteenth century onward, specifically to the esoteric teachings of Judaism.

***Keter*** "Crown"; the first *sefirah*; coeternal with *Ein Sof*; also called *Ratson* ("Will") and *Ayin* ("Nothingness").

**Lilith** A demoness who harms babies and seduces men; married to Samael.

***Ma'ariv*** The third of the three daily prayer services, recited in the evening.

***Malkhut*** "Kingdom"; the tenth *sefirah*, ruling the lower worlds; also called *Shekhinah*.

***Matnitin*** "Our Mishnah"; short pieces scattered throughout the *Zohar*, most of which appear as utterances of a heavenly voice urging the Companions to arouse themselves and open their hearts to the mysteries. Some of them contain principles of kabbalistic teaching in a condensed form, constituting a kind of mystical Mishnah, expounded in the main section of the *Zohar*.

**Metatron** One of the supreme powers in the divine realm, often depicted as the chief angel. He is sometimes identified as *sar ha-panim* (Prince of the Countenance), standing face-to-face with God, or as *sar ha-olam* (Prince of the World).

**midrash**, pl. **midrashim** Homiletical or legal interpretation of the Bible.

***Midrash ha-Ne'lam*** "The Concealed Midrash, the Esoteric Midrash"; an early stratum of the *Zohar*. Its language is a mixture of Hebrew and Aramaic. *Midrash ha-Ne'lam* on the Torah pertains to several portions of Genesis, the beginning of Exodus, and several other portions; it is printed partly alongside the main text of the *Zohar* and partly in *Zohar Ḥadash*. *Midrash ha-Ne'lam* on Song of Songs, Ruth, and Lamentations is printed in *Zohar Ḥadash*. The subject matter of *Midrash ha-Ne'lam* is mostly Creation, the soul, and the world to come; its style is often allegorical.

***Minḥah*** "Offering"; second of the three daily prayer services, recited in the afternoon.

**Mishnah** Collection of oral teachings compiled near the beginning of the third century by Rabbi Yehudah ha-Nasi; the earliest codification of Jewish Oral Law; the core of the Talmud.

***mitsvah***, pl. ***mitsvot*** "Commandment"; one of the 613 commandments of the Torah or one of various rabbinic precepts; religious duty; by extension, good deed.

***Musaf*** "Supplement"; the additional Sabbath and festival worship service, usually recited immediately after the morning service.

***nefesh*** "Soul," life force; the basic level of the soul, animating the human being.

***neshamah*** "Breath, soul," soul-breath; the highest level of the soul.

***Netsaḥ*** "Endurance"; the seventh *sefirah*; the right leg of the divine body; source of prophecy along with *Hod*.

**Omer** "Sheaf" of newly harvested barley; the seven-week period of ceremonially counting days during the harvest season between the second day of *Pesaḥ* and the eve of *Shavu'ot*.

***parashah*** "Portion"; portion of the Torah read on a particular Sabbath, named after its opening word (or phrase) or a key word (or phrase) in the opening sentences.

***Pesaḥ*** "Passover"; first of the three annual pilgrimage festivals, celebrated in the middle of the month of Nisan, commemorating the Exodus from Egypt.

**Peshitta** "Simple (translation)"; the Syriac translation of the Bible, probably completed by the third century C.E..

***Piqqudin*** "Commandments"; kabbalistic interpretations of the commandments scattered throughout the *Zohar* (to be distinguished from *Ra'aya Meheimna*).

***Qav ha-Middah*** "The Standard of Measure"; a detailed description of the process of divine emanation, delivered by Rabbi Shim'on. *Zohar Ḥadash* 56d–58d.



***Qedushah*** "Sanctification"; one of several prayers describing and emulating the ongoing sanctification of God by the angels in heaven.

***Ra'aya Meheimna*** "The Faithful Shepherd"; a separate composition on the kabbalistic meaning of the commandments, printed piecemeal in the *Zohar*. Here Moses, the Faithful Shepherd, appears to Rabbi Shim'on and the Companions, revealing secrets.

***Raḥamim*** "Compassion"; the sixth *sefirah*, harmonizing the polar opposites *Ḥesed* and *Din*; also called *Tif'eret*.

***Rav Metivta*** "Head of the Academy"; an account of a visionary journey of Rabbi Shim'on and the Companions to the Garden of Eden, where they hear mysteries concerning the life to come from one of the heads of the heavenly academy. *Zohar* 3:161b–174a.

***Raza de-Razin*** "The Secret of Secrets"; a section of the *Zohar* dealing with physiognomy, metoposcopy, and chiromancy (*Zohar* 2:70a–75a [printed alongside the main text], *Zohar Ḥadash* 35b–37c). A second version is incorporated into the main body of the *Zohar* (2:70a–78a).

**Rosh Hashanah** The Jewish New Year, celebrated on the first two days of the Hebrew month Tishrei.

***ruaḥ*** "Spirit, wind, breath"; in some passages, the second level of soul.

***Rut*** The book of Ruth.

***Sava de-Mishpatim*** "Old Man of [Torah portion] *Mishpatim*"; an account of the Companions' encounter with a donkey-driver who turns out to be a master of wisdom. *Zohar* 2:94b–114a.

***Sefer ha-Zohar*** "The Book of Radiance."

***sefirah***, pl. ***sefirot*** Literally, "counting," number, numerical entity; in Kabbalah, one of the ten aspects of divine personality, nine of which emanate from *Ein Sof* and the first *sefirah*, *Keter*. See the diagram on page ix.

***Shaddai*** An obscure divine name, which may originally have meant "[God of] the mountain." In Kabbalah it often denotes *Shekhinah.*

***Shaḥarit*** The first of the three daily prayer services, recited in the morning.

***Shavu'ot*** "Weeks"; second of the three annual pilgrimage festivals, celebrated seven weeks after the beginning of Passover.

***Shekhinah*** "Presence," divine immanence; the tenth and last *sefirah*; female partner of *Tif'eret*; also called *Malkhut.*

***Shema*** Literally, "hear"; central prayer recited morning and evening, comprising Deuteronomy 6:4–9; 11:13–21; and Numbers 15:37–41. The opening verse is: *Hear O Israel! YHVH our God, YHVH is one!*

***Shir ha-Shirim*** The book of Song of Songs.

***Sifra di-Tsni'uta*** "The Book of Concealment"; an anonymous, highly condensed commentary on the beginning of the Torah, consisting of five short chapters and composed in obscure sentences. Its subject is the mysterious dynamics of divine being. *Zohar* 2:176b–179a.

***Sitrei Otiyyot*** "Secrets of the Letters"; a discourse by Rabbi Shim'on focusing on the letters of the divine name *YHVH* and how they symbolize the process of emanation. *Zohar Ḥadash* 1b–7b.

***Sitrei Torah*** "Secrets of Torah"; interpretations of certain verses of Genesis, printed in separate columns parallel to the main body of the *Zohar* and in *Zohar Ḥadash.* It includes allegorical explanations of the mysteries of the soul.

***Sukkot*** "Booths"; festival of Booths, last of the three annual pilgrimage festivals, celebrated in the middle of the month of Tishrei at the conclusion of the summer harvest.

**Talmud** Each of the two compilations of Jewish law, legend, ethics, and theology comprising the Mishnah and its vast commentary (the Gemara) by rabbis of the third through fifth centuries. The Jerusalem Talmud was compiled ca. 400 C.E.; the Babylonian Talmud, about one hundred years later.

***tanna***, pl. ***tanna'im*** "One who repeats, teacher"; an authority cited in the Mishnah or belonging to the Mishnaic period (first two centuries of the Common Era); an Amoraic scholar whose task was to memorize and recite tannaitic texts.

**Targum** "Translation"; an Aramaic translation of the Torah or the Bible.

**tefillin** "Phylacteries"; two black leather boxes containing passages from the Torah (Exodus 13:1–10, 11–16; Deuteronomy 6:4–9; 11:13–21) written on parchment. They are bound by black leather straps on the left arm and on the head, and are prescribed for men to wear during weekday morning prayer. Each of the biblical passages indicates that the Children of Israel should place a sign upon their hand and a frontlet (or reminder) between their eyes.

***teshuvah*** "Return, turning back to God, repentance."

**tetragrammaton** The four-lettered name of God, *YHVH.*

***Tif'eret*** "Beauty, glory"; the sixth *sefirah,* harmonizing the polar opposites *Ḥesed* and *Din*; male partner of *Shekhinah*; the torso of the divine body; also called *Raḥamim.*

***Tiqqunei ha-Zohar*** "Embellishments on the *Zohar*"; an independent book whose setting is similar to *Ra'aya Meheimna.* It comprises a commentary on the beginning of Genesis, each *tiqqun* opening with a new interpretation of the word בראשית (*be-reshit*), "in the beginning."

***Tiqqunim*** "Embellishments"; additional material in the genre of *Tiqqunei ha-Zohar,* printed in *Zohar Ḥadash* 93c–122b.

**Torah** "Instruction, teaching"; the Five Books of Moses (Genesis through Deuteronomy); by extension, the entire corpus of Jewish religious literature.

***Tosafot*** "Additions"; a collection of comments on the Talmud written between the twelfth and fourteenth centuries in France and Germany, printed in standard editions of the Talmud. Also, a set of Zoharic additions printed at the end of the second and third of the three standard Aramaic volumes of the *Zohar*, drawn from the Cremona edition and from *Zohar Ḥadash*.

***Tosefta*** "Addenda"; in rabbinic literature, a collection of precepts parallel to and contemporary with the Mishnah. In the *Zohar*, a collection similar to *Matnitin*.

**world that is coming** Hebrew, העולם הבא (*ha-olam ha-ba*); Aramaic, עלמא דאתי (*alma de-atei*); often understood as referring to the hereafter and usually translated as "the world to come." From another perspective, however, "the world that is coming" already exists—occupying another, timeless dimension. In Kabbalah this phrase often refers to *Binah*, the continuous source of emanation, who "is constantly coming, never ceasing."

***Yah*** A contracted biblical form of the divine name *YHVH*.

***Yesod*** "Foundation"; the ninth *sefirah*, who channels the flow of emanation to *Shekhinah*; the phallus of the divine body; also called *Tsaddiq*.

***YHVH*** The ineffable name of God, apparently deriving from the root הוה (*hvh*), "to be." In the *Zohar* it often symbolizes *Tif'eret*.

**Yom Kippur** The Day of Atonement, observed on the tenth of the Hebrew month Tishrei.

***zohar*** "Radiance, splendor."

***Zohar Ḥadash*** "New Zohar"; a collection of Zoharic texts not included in the early editions of the *Zohar*. It was first printed in Salonika in 1597. The title is misleading since *Zohar Ḥadash* contains much of *Midrash ha-Ne'lam*, an early stratum of the *Zohar*.

# *Bibliography*

This bibliography includes works cited and utilized by the translator for this volume, except for standard rabbinic texts and most reference works. Readers seeking further resources on the *Zohar* can consult the bibliography in volume 1 of the *Zohar: Pritzker Edition*; *The Library of Gershom Scholem on Jewish Mysticism: Catalogue*, edited by Joseph Dan, Esther Liebes, and Shmuel Reem; and Don Karr, "Notes on the *Zohar* in English."

## 1. Manuscripts of the *Zohar*[1]

Cambridge, University Library, Heb. Add. 1023.
Cambridge, Trinity College, F 12 140.
London, British Library, Gaster 773.
Moscow, Guenzburg Collection, Russian State Library, 262.
Munich, Bayerische Staatsbibliothek, Cod. Hebr. 20, 203, 217.
New York, Jewish Theological Seminary, 1930, 2076.
Oxford, Bodleian Library, 1564, 1884, 2514.
Oxford, Merton College, 77 h 22.
Paris, Bibliothèque nationale, Héb. 778, 779, 780.
Rome, Biblioteca Casanatense, 2971.
Vatican, Biblioteca Apostolica, Ebr. 68, 186, 206, 208, 213, 290, 428, 504; Neofiti 23.

## 2. Editions of the *Zohar*

### A. Zohar on the Torah

*Sefer ha-Zohar*. Cremona: Vincenzo Conti, 1558.
*Sefer ha-Zohar*. 3 vols. Mantua: Meir ben Efraim and Jacob ben Naftali, 1558–60.
*Sefer ha-Zohar*. 3 vols. Lublin: Ẓevi Jaffe, 1623.
*Sefer ha-Zohar*. 3 vols. Sulzbach: Moses Bloch, 1684.
*Sefer ha-Zohar*. 3 vols. Amsterdam: Solomon Proops, 1715.
*Sefer ha-Zohar*. 3 vols. Constantinople: Jonah ben Jacob, 1736.
*Sefer ha-Zohar*. 3 vols. Vilna: Romm, 1882.
*Sefer ha-Zohar*. Edited by Reuven Margaliot. 4th ed. 3 vols. Jerusalem: Mossad Harav Kook, 1964.

1. For a list of eighty-four *Zohar* manuscripts, see Rubin, "Mif'al ha-Zohar," 172–73.

### B. Zohar Ḥadash

*Tappuḥei Zahav*. Thiengen: Joseph ben Naftali, 1559. *Midrash ha-Ne'lam* on Ruth.

*Midrash ha-Ne'lam al Megillat Rut.* Venice: Abraham ben Solomon Alon, 1566. Reprint, Jerusalem: Daniel Abrams.

*Zohar u-Midrash ha-Ne'lam*... Salonika: Joseph Abraham Bat Sheva, 1597.

*Zohar Ḥadash u-Midrash ha-Ne'lam*... Cracow: Isaac ben Aragon, 1603.

*Zohar Ḥadash u-Midrash ha-Ne'lam*... Venice: Gerolamo Bragadini, 1658.

*Zohar Ḥadash.* Edited by Reuven Margaliot. Jerusalem: Mossad Harav Kook, 1953. Reprint, 1978.

### C. Tiqqunei ha-Zohar

*Tiqqunei ha-Zohar.* Mantua: Meir of Padua and Jacob of Gazolo, 1558.

*Tiqqunei ha-Zohar.* Edited by Reuven Margaliot. Jerusalem: Mossad Harav Kook, 1948. Reprint, 1978.

## 3. Translations of the *Zohar*

### A. Hebrew



Ashlag, Yehudah, trans. and ed., completed by Yehudah Ẓevi Brandwein. *Sefer ha-Zohar... im... ha-Sullam.* 22 vols. Jerusalem: Ḥevrah Lehotsa'at Hazohar, 1945–58.

Bar-Lev, Yechiel, trans. and ed. *Sefer ha-Zohar... im Bei'ur Yedid Nefesh.* 14 vols. Petaḥ Tikvah: n.p., 1992–97.

Edri, Yehudah, trans. and ed. *Sefer ha-Zohar... meturgam bi-lshon ha-qodesh.* 10 vols. Jerusalem: Yerid Hasefarim, 1998.

______, trans. and ed. *Sefer Zohar Ḥadash... meturgam bi-lshon ha-qodesh.* 2 vols. Jerusalem: Yerid Hasefarim, 2005.

Frisch, Daniel, trans. and ed. *Sefer ha-Zohar... Peirush Matoq mi-Devash.* 23 vols. Jerusalem: Mekhon Da'at Yosef, 1993–99.

Lachower, Fischel, and Isaiah Tishby, trans. and eds. *Mishnat ha-Zohar.* Vol. 1. 3d ed. Jerusalem: Mosad Bialik, 1971. (An anthology.)

Tishby, Isaiah, trans. and ed. *Mishnat ha-Zohar.* Vol. 2. Jerusalem: Mosad Bialik, 1961. (An anthology.)

Zeitlin, Hillel, trans. and ed. "Haqdamat Sefer ha-Zohar, Meturgemet u-Mvo'eret." *Meẓudah* 1 (1943): 36–82.

### B. English

Berg, Michael, ed. *The Zohar by Rabbi Shimon bar Yochai with the Sulam commentary of Rabbi Yehuda Ashlag.* 23 vols. Tel Aviv: Yeshivat Kol Yehudah, 1999–2003. (The English translation is based on the Hebrew translation by Yehudah Ashlag.)

Berg, Phillip S. *The Essential Zohar: The Source of Kabbalistic Wisdom.* New York: Bell Tower, 2002. (Selections.)

Blumenthal, David R. *Understanding Jewish Mysticism: A Source Reader.* New York: Ktav, 1978. (Selections.)

Brody, Seth, trans. and ed. *Rabbi Ezra ben Solomon of Gerona: Peirush Shir ha-Shirim (Commentary on the Song of Songs) and Other Kabbalistic Commentaries,* 147–206. Kalamazoo: Medieval Institute Publications, 1999. (Translation of Midrash ha-Ne'lam on Lamentations.)

Englander, Lawrence A. trans. and ed., with Herbert W. Basser. *The Mystical Study of Ruth: Midrash ha-Ne'elam of the Zohar to the Book of Ruth.* Atlanta: Scholars Press, 1993.

Giller, Pinchas. *Reading the Zohar: The Sacred Text of the Kabbalah,* 159–73. New York: Oxford University Press, 2001. (Translation of *Sifra di-Tsni'uta.*)

Lachower, Fischel, and Isaiah Tishby, Hebrew trans. and eds. *The Wisdom of the Zohar: An Anthology of Texts.* Translated by David Goldstein. Vols. 1 and 2. London: Littman Library of Jewish Civilization, 1989.

Mathers, Samuel Liddell MacGregor. *Kabbala Denudata: The Kabbalah Unveiled.* London: G. Redway, 1887. Translated from *Kabbala Denudata,* by Christian Knorr von Rosenroth. (Translation of *Sifra di-Tsni'uta, Idra Rabba,* and *Idra Zuta.*)

Matt, Daniel Chanan, trans. and ed. *Zohar: The Book of Enlightenment.* Mahwah, N.J.: Paulist Press, 1983. (An anthology.)

———, trans. and ed. *Zohar: Annotated and Explained.* Woodstock, Vt.: Skylight Paths, 2002. (An anthology.)

Miller, Moshe, trans. and ed. *Zohar: Selections Translated and Annotated by Moshe Miller.* Morristown: Fiftieth Gate Publications, 2000.

Rosenberg, David. *Dreams of Being Eaten Alive: The Literary Core of the Kabbalah.* New York: Harmony Books, 2000. (Selections.)

Rosenberg, Roy A. *The Anatomy of God: The Book of Concealment, The Greater Holy Assembly and The Lesser Holy Assembly of the Zohar, with The Assembly of the Tabernacle.* New York: Ktav, 1973. 

Sassoon, George, trans., and Rodney Dale, ed. *The Kabbalah Decoded: A new translation of the 'Ancient of Days' texts of the Zohar.* London: Duckworth, 1978. (Translation of *Idra Rabba, Idra Zuta, Sifra di-Tsni'uta,* and *Zohar* 2:122b–123b.)

Scholem, Gershom G., ed., with the special assistance of Sherry Abel. *Zohar: The Book of Splendor—Basic Readings from the Kabbalah.* New York: Schocken, 1949. Reprint, 1971. (An anthology.)

Sperling, Harry, Maurice Simon, and Paul P. Levertoff, trans. *The Zohar.* 5 vols. London: Soncino Press, 1931–34.

Tishby, Isaiah, Hebrew trans. and ed. *The Wisdom of the Zohar: An Anthology of Texts.* Translated by David Goldstein. Vol. 3. London: Littman Library of Jewish Civilization, 1989.

Wald, Stephen G. *The Doctrine of the Divine Name: An Introduction to Classical Kabbalistic Theology.* Atlanta: Scholars Press, 1988. (Annotated translation of *Sitrei Otiyyot.*)

Wineman, Aryeh, trans. and ed. *Mystic Tales from the Zohar.* Philadelphia: Jewish Publication Society, 1997. (Selections.)

Wolski, Nathan. *A Journey into the "Zohar": An Introduction to "The Book of Radiance."* Albany: State University of New York Press, 2010. (Selections.)

### *C. French*

Mopsik, Charles, trans. and ed. *Le Zohar.* 4 vols. Lagrasse: Verdier, 1981–96.

———. *Le Zohar: Cantique des Cantiques.* Lagrasse: Verdier, 1999.

———. *Le Zohar: Lamentations.* Lagrasse: Verdier, 2000.

———. *Le Zohar: Le Livre de Ruth.* Lagrasse: Verdier, 1987.

### *D. Latin*

Knorr von Rosenroth, Christian. *Kabbala Denudata.* 4 vols. Sulzbach, 1677–84; Frankfurt am Main, 1684. (Translation of *Sifra di-Tsni'uta, Idra Rabba,* and *Idra Zuta.*)

## 4. Commentaries on the *Zohar*

Ashlag, Yehudah, trans. and ed., completed by Yehudah Ẓevi Brandwein. *Sefer ha-Zohar . . . im . . . ha-Sullam.* 22 vols. Jerusalem: Ḥevrah Lehotsa'at Hazohar, 1945–58.

Azulai, Abraham, ed. *Or ha-Ḥammah.* 4 vols. Peremyshlyany: Zupnik, Knoller, and Wolf, 1896–98. Reprint, 4 vols. in 3, Bene-Berak: Yahadut, 1973.

———. *Or ha-Levanah.* Peremyshlyany: Zupnik and Knoller, 1899. Reprint, Jerusalem: Sha'arei Ziv, n.d.

Azulai, Ḥayyim Joseph David. "Nitsotsei Orot." In *Sefer ha-Zohar,* edited by Reuven Margaliot. 4th ed. 3 vols. Jerusalem: Mossad Harav Kook, 1964.

Bar-Lev, Yechiel, trans. and ed. *Sefer ha-Zohar . . . im Bei'ur Yedid Nefesh.* 14 vols. Petaḥ Tikvah: n.p., 1992–97.

Buzaglo, Shalom. *Miqdash Melekh ha-Shalem.* 5 vols. Jerusalem: Benei Yissakhar, 1995–2000.

Cordovero, Moses. *Or Yaqar.* 21 vols. Jerusalem: Achuzat Israel, 1962–95.

"Derekh Emet." In *Sefer ha-Zohar,* edited by Reuven Margaliot. 4th ed. 3 vols. Jerusalem: Mossad Harav Kook, 1964.

Eichenstein, Ẓevi Hirsch (of Zhidachov). *Ateret Tsevi.* 2 vols. Edited by Ẓevi Elimelekh Panet. Bene-Berak: Mekhon Benei Sheloshim, 2009–2012.

Elijah ben Solomon of Vilna. *Yahel Or.* Vilna: Romm, 1882. Reprint, Jerusalem: n.p., 1972.



Emden, Jacob. *Zohorei Ya'bets.* Edited by Abraham Bick. Jerusalem: Mossad Harav Kook, 1975.

Frisch, Daniel, trans. and ed. *Sefer ha-Zohar . . . Peirush Matoq mi-Devash.* 23 vols. Jerusalem: Mekhon Da'at Yosef, 1993–99.

Galante, Abraham. *Zohorei Ḥammah.* 2 vols. Vol. 1, Munkacs: P. Bleier, 1881. Vol. 2, Peremyshlyany: Zupnik and Knoller, 1882. An abridgment by Abraham Azulai of Galante's unpublished *Yareaḥ Yaqar,* incorporated into Azulai's *Or ha-Ḥammah.*

Horowitz, Ẓevi Hirsch. *Aspaqlaryah ha-Me'irah.* Fürth: Itzik ve-Yatmei Ḥayyim, 1776. Reprint, Jerusalem: Mekhon Sha'arei Ziv, 1983.

Lavi, Shim'on. *Ketem Paz.* 2 vols. Leghorn: Eli'ezer Sedon, 1795. 1 vol. Djerba: Jacob Haddad, 1940. Reprint, 2 vols. Jerusalem: Ahavat Shalom, 1981. The first vol. of the Jerusalem edition is a reprint of the Djerba edition; the second vol. is a reprint of the second vol. of the Leghorn edition.

Loanz, Elijah ben Moses. *Adderet Eliyyahu.* 2 vols. Jerusalem: Mekhon Sha'arei Ziv, 1998.

Luria, David. "Nefesh David." Addendum to *Yahel Or,* by Elijah ben Solomon of Vilna. Vilna: Romm, 1882. Reprint, addendum to *Sefer Kitvei ha-Ga'on R. David Luria (Pirqei de-Rabbi Eli'ezer).* Jerusalem: n.p., 1990.

Margaliot, Reuven. "Nitsotsei Zohar." In *Sefer ha-Zohar,* edited by Reuven Margaliot. 4th ed. 3 vols. Jerusalem: Mossad Harav Kook, 1964.

———. "Nitsotsei Zohar." In *Zohar Ḥadash,* edited by Reuven Margaliot. Jerusalem: Mossad Harav Kook, 1953. Reprint, 1978.

Palagi, Ḥayyim. *Sefer Ḥayyim u-Mazon: Peirush ve-He'arot Nifla'ot le-Sefer ha-Zohar ha-Qadosh.* Izmir, 1868. Reprint, Jerusalem: Yosef ben Yitsḥak haKohen, 2000.

Scholem, Gershom. *Sefer ha-Zohar shel Gershom Shalom* [*Gershom Scholem's Annotated Zohar*]. 6 vols. Jerusalem: Magnes Press, 1992.

Vital, Ḥayyim. "Haggahot Maharḥu." In *Sefer ha-Zohar,* edited by Reuven Margaliot. 4th ed. 3 vols. Jerusalem: Mossad Harav Kook, 1964.

Zacuto, Moses ben Mordecai. *Peirush ha-Remez la-Zohar ha-Qadosh.* Moshav Bitḥah: Kol Bitḥah, 1998.

## 5. Lexicons of the *Zohar*

Baer, Issachar. *Imrei Binah.* Prague: Moshe Katz, 1611.

Huss, Boaz, ed. "Bei'ur ha-Millim ha-Zarot she-be-Sefer ha-Zohar." *Kabbalah* 1 (1996): 167–204.

Isaiah ben Eli'ezer Ḥayyim. *Yesha Yah.* Venice: Giovanni Vendramin, 1637.

Liebes, Yehuda. *Peraqim be-Millon Sefer ha-Zohar.* Jerusalem: Hebrew University, 1982.

Lonzano, Menaḥem ben Judah de. *Sefer ha-Ma'arikh.* Printed with *Sefer he-Arukh* by Nathan ben Yeḥiel of Rome, edited by Shemuel Schlesinger. Tel Aviv: Yetsu Sifrei Kodesh, n.d.

Luria, David. "Va-Ye'esof David." Addendum to *Ma'amar Qadmut Sefer ha-Zohar* by David Luria, 73–82. Warsaw: Meir Yeḥiel Halter, 1887.

Neuhausen, Simon A. *Nirdefei Zohar.* Baltimore: Neuhausen, 1923.

## 6. Other Primary Sources

Abba Mari ben Moses, ed. *Minḥat Qena'ot.* In *Teshuvot ha-Rashba,* ed. H.Z. Dimitrovsky. 2 vols. Jerusalem: Mossad Harav Kook, 1990.

Abulafia, Todros ben Joseph. *Otsar ha-Kavod ha-Shalem.* Warsaw, 1879. Reprint: Jerusalem: Makor, 1970.





*Agadath Shir ha-Shirim.* Edited by Solomon Schechter. Cambridge, England: Deighton Bell and Co., 1896.

*Alfa Beita de-Ven Sira.* Edited by Moritz Steinschneider. Berlin: A. Friedlaender, 1858.

Alḥarizi, Judah. *Sefer ha-Nefesh* (attributed to Galenus). Edited by Adolph Jellinek. Leipzig: C.L. Fritzsche, 1852.

Alter, Robert, trans. and ed. *The Book of Psalms: A Translation with Commentary.* New York: W. W. Norton, 2007.

———, trans. and ed. *The David Story: A Translation with Commentary of 1 and 2 Samuel.* New York: W. W. Norton, 1999.

———, trans. and ed. *The Five Books of Moses: A Translation with Commentary.* New York: W. W. Norton, 2004.

Anav, Ẓedekiah ben Abraham. *Shibbolei ha-Leqet ha-Shalem.* Edited by Solomon Buber. Vilna: Romm, 1886.

———. *Shibbolei ha-Leqet ha-Shalem.* Edited by Samuel K. Mirsky. Jerusalem: Sura, 1966.

Arama, Isaac ben Moses. *Aqedat Yitsḥaq.* Pressburg: Victor Kittseer, 1849.

Azriel ben Menaḥem of Gerona. *Peirush ha-Aggadot le-Rabbi Azri'el.* Edited by Isaiah Tishby. 2d ed. Jerusalem: Magnes Press, 1982.

Baḥya ben Asher. *Bei'ur al ha-Torah.* Edited by Chaim D. Chavel. 3 vols. Jerusalem: Mossad Harav Kook, 1971–72.

Beit-Arié, Malachi, ed. "Pereq Shirah: Mevo'ot u-Mahadurah Biqqortit." 2 vols. Ph.D. diss., Hebrew University, 1966.

Bloch, Ariel, and Chana Bloch, trans. and ed. *The Song of Songs: A New Translation with an Introduction and Commentary.* New York: Random House, 1995.

Braude, William G. and Israel J., trans. and eds. *Pesikta de-Rab Kahana: R. Kahana's Compilation of Discourses for Sabbaths and Festal Days.* Philadelphia: Jewish Publication Society, 1975.

———, trans. and eds. *Tanna Debe Eliyyahu: The Lore of the School of Elijah.* Philadelphia: Jewish Publication Society, 1981.

Charlesworth, James H., ed. *The Old Testament Pseudepigrapha.* 2 vols. Garden City, N.Y.: Doubleday, 1983–85.

Clark, E. G. *Targum Pseudo-Jonathan of the Pentateuch: Text and Concordance.* Hoboken, N.J.: Ktav, 1984.

Cordovero, Moses. *Pardes Rimmonim.* Munkacs: Kahana and Fried, 1906. Reprint, Jerusalem: Mordechai Etyah, 1962.

David ben Abraham Maimuni. *Midrash David.* Translated and edited by Ben-Zion Krynfiss. Jerusalem: n.p., 1944.

David ben Judah he-Ḥasid. *The Book of Mirrors: Sefer Mar'ot ha-Ẓove'ot.* Edited by Daniel Chanan Matt. Chico, Calif.: Scholars Press, 1982.

Eisenstein, Judah D., ed. *Otsar Midrashim.* 2 vols. New York: Eisenstein, 1915.

Eleazar ben Judah of Worms. *Ḥokhmat ha-Nefesh.* Lemberg, 1870. Reprint, Jerusalem: Horeb Press, n.d.

______. *Peirushei Siddur ha-Tefillah la-Roqeaḥ.* Edited by Moshe Hershler and Yehudah Alter Hershler. 2 vols. Jerusalem: Mekhon Harav Hershler, 1994.

Enelow, Hyman G., ed. *The Mishnah of Rabbi Eliezer or the Midrash of Thirty-Two Hermeneutical Rules, Edited From Old Manuscripts.* New York: Bloch Publishing Company, 1933.

Ezra ben Solomon of Gerona [attributed to Naḥmanides]. "Peirush le-Shir ha-Shirim." In *Kitvei Ramban,* edited by Chaim D. Chavel, 2:471–548. Jerusalem: Mossad Harav Kook, 1964.

Fano, Menahem Azariah da. *Yonat Elem.* Amsterdam: Yehudah ben Mordechai and Shmuel bar Moshe ha-Levi, 1648.

Farber-Ginat, Asi and Daniel Abrams, eds. *The Commentaries to Ezekiel's Chariot of R. Elazar of Worms and R. Jacob ben Jacob ha-Kohen.* Los Angeles: Cherub Press, 2004.

Fishbane, Michael. *The JPS Bible Commentary: Haftarot.* Philadelphia: Jewish Publication Society, 2002.

Fox, Everett, trans. and ed. *The Five Books of Moses.* New York: Schocken, 1995.

Fox, Michael V. *Proverbs: A New Translation with Introduction and Commentary.* Anchor Bible, vols. 18A–B. New York: Doubleday, 2000; New Haven: Yale University Press, 2009.

Friedlander, Gerald, trans. and ed. *Pirke de Rabbi Eliezer.* London, 1916. Reprint, New York: Sepher-Hermon Press, 1981.

Friedman, Richard Elliott. *Commentary on the Torah with a New English Translation.* San Francisco: HarperSanFrancisco, 2001.

Gershon ben Solomon of Arles. *Sha'ar ha-Shamayim.* Warsaw: Yitzḥak Goldman, 1876.

Gikatilla, Joseph. *Sha'arei Orah.* Warsaw: Orgelbrand, 1883. Reprint, Jerusalem: Mordechai Etyah, 1960.

Goldin, Judah, trans. *The Fathers According to Rabbi Nathan.* New Haven: Yale University Press, 1955.

Greenberg, Moshe. *Ezekiel 1–20: A New Translation with Introduction and Commentary.* Anchor Bible, vol. 22. Garden City, N.Y.: Doubleday, 1983.

Ḥagiz, Moses. *Elleh Mas'ei.* Altona, 1738.

Halevi, Judah. *Sefer ha-Kuzari.* Translated by Yehudah even Shmuel. Tel Aviv: Dvir, 1972.

"Ḥibbut ha-Qever." In *Massekhet Semaḥot,* edited by Michael Higger, 253–61. New York: Bloch, 1931. Reprint. Jerusalem: Makor, 1970.

Ibn Gabirol, Solomon. *A Crown for the King* [*Keter Malkhut*]. Translated by David R. Slavitt. New York: Oxford University Press, 1998.

———. *The Kingly Crown: Keter Malkhut.* Translated by Bernard Lewis. Notre Dame: University of Notre Dame Press, 2003.
Ibn Pakuda, Baḥya. *Torat Ḥovot ha-Levavot.* Translated into Hebrew by Rabbi Yehudah Ibn Tibbon. Jerusalem: Devar Yerushalayim, 2006.
Ibn Sahula, Isaac ben Solomon. *Meshal ha-Qadmoni.* Tel Aviv: Maḥbarot Lesifrut, 1953.
———. *Meshal ha-Qadmoni: Fables from the Distant Past. A Parallel Hebrew-English Text,* edited and translated by Raphael Loewe. 2 vols. Oxford: The Littman Library of Jewish Civilization, 2004.
———. "Peirush Shir ha-Shirim." Edited by Arthur Green. In *Reshit ha-Mistiqah ha-Yehudit be-Eiropa (Meḥqerei Yerushalayim be-Maḥashevet Yisra'el* 6:3–4 [1987]), edited by Joseph Dan, 393–491.
Ibn Tibbon, Samuel. *Peirush ha-Millim ha-Zarot.* Printed at the end of his translation of Maimonides' *Guide of the Perplexed.*
Isaac the Blind. "Peirush Sefer Yetsirah." Appendix to Gershom Scholem, *Ha-Qabbalah be-Provans,* edited by Rivkah Schatz. Jerusalem: Academon, 1970.
Jacob ben Sheshet. "Ha-Emunah ve-ha-Bittaḥon." In *Kitvei Ramban,* edited by Chaim D. Chavel, 2:339–448. Jerusalem: Mossad Harav Kook, 1964.
Jellinek, Adolph, ed. *Beit ha-Midrash.* 3d ed. 6 vols. in 2. Jerusalem: Wahrmann Books, 1967.
Jonah ben Abraham Gerondi. *Sha'arei Teshuvah.* Bene-Berak: Sifsei Chachamim, 1990.
Joseph ben Shalom Ashkenazi. *Peirush Qabbali li-Vreshit Rabbah.* Edited by Moshe Hallamish. Jerusalem: Magnes Press, 1984.
*JPS Hebrew-English Tanakh.* Philadelphia: Jewish Publication Society, 1999.
Judah ben Samuel he-Ḥasid. *Sefer Ḥasidim.* Edited by Reuven Margaliot. Jerusalem: Mossad Harav Kook, 1957.
———. *Sefer Ḥasidim.* Edited by Jehuda Wistinetzki. Berlin: Itzkowski, 1891. Reprint, Jerusalem: Vagshel, 1998.
Kaplan, Aryeh, trans. and ed. *Sefer Yetzirah: The Book of Creation.* York Beach, Maine: Samuel Weiser, 1990.
Kasher, Menaḥem M. *Ḥumash Torah Shelemah.* 2d ed. 12 vols. Jerusalem: Beth Torah Shelemah, 1992.
Lauterbach, Jacob Z., trans. and ed. *Mekhilta de-Rabbi Ishmael.* 2d ed, 2 vols. Philadelphia: Jewish Publication Society, 2004.
Levine, Baruch A. *The JPS Torah Commentary: Leviticus.* Philadelphia: Jewish Publication Society, 1989.
Lewin, Benjamin M., ed. *Otsar ha-Ge'onim.* 13 vols. Jerusalem: Mossad Harav Kook, 1928–62.
Luria, David. *Ma'amar Qadmut Sefer ha-Zohar.* Warsaw: Meir Yeḥiel Halter, 1887.
Maimonides, Moses. *The Guide of the Perplexed.* Translated by Shlomo Pines. Chicago: University of Chicago Press, 1963.
———. *Mishnah im Peirush Rabbeinu Mosheh ben Maimon.* Translated and edited by Joseph Kafah. 3 vols. Jerusalem: Mossad ha-Rav Kook, 1989.
Malachi ben Jacob ha-Kohen. *Yad Mal'akhi.* Livorno: Moshe Etyas, 1766–67.
Margaliot, Mordechai, ed. *Sefer ha-Razim.* Jerusalem: Yediot Aḥaronot, 1966.
Matt, Daniel C., trans. and ed. *The Essential Kabbalah: The Heart of Jewish Mysticism.* San Francisco: HarperSanFrancisco, 1995.
Milgrom, Jacob. *The JPS Torah Commentary: Numbers.* Philadelphia: Jewish Publication Society, 1990.
———. *Leviticus: A New Translation with Introduction and Commentary.* Anchor Bible, vols. 3–3B. New York: Doubleday, 1991–2000.

Moses ben Shem Tov de León. *The Book of the Pomegranate: Moses de León's Sefer ha-Rimmon.* Edited by Elliot R. Wolfson. Atlanta: Scholars Press, 1988.

______. Commentary on the Ten *Sefirot* (untitled fragment). MS Hebr. 47, Bayerische Staatsbibliothek, Munich.

______. *Mishkan ha-Edut.* MS Or. Quat. 833, Staatsbibliothek, Berlin.

______. *Ha-Nefesh ha-Ḥakhamah.* Basle: Konrad Waldkirch, 1608.

______. "Or Zaru'a." Edited by Alexander Altmann. *Kovez al Yad,* n.s., 9 (1980): 219–93.

[______?]. *Orḥot Ḥayyim (Tsavva'at Rabbi Eli'ezer).* Edited by Gershon Henikh. Warsaw: Meir Halter, 1891. Reprint, Bene-Berak: Agudat Ḥasidei Radzyn, 1990.

______. *Peirush ha-Merkavah.* Edited by Asi-Farber Ginat. Edited for publication by Daniel Abrams. Los Angeles: Cherub Press, 1998.

[______?]. "Seder Gan Eden." In *Beit ha-Midrash,* edited by Adolph Jellinek, 3:131–40, 194–98. Jerusalem: Wahrmann Books, 1967.

______. "Sefer ha-Mishqal: Text and Study." Edited by Jochanan H. A. Wijnhoven. Ph.D. diss., Brandeis University, 1964. Largely supersedes an earlier edition: *Ha-Nefesh ha-Ḥakhamah.* Basle: Konrad Waldkirch, 1608.

______. "Sefer Maskiyyot Kesef." Edited by Jochanan H. A. Wijnhoven. Master's thesis, Brandeis University, 1961.

606 ______. "She'elot u-Tshuvot be-Inyenei Qabbalah." In *Ḥiqrei Qabbalah u-Shluḥoteha,* edited by Isaiah Tishby, 1:36–75. Jerusalem: Magnes Press, 1982.

______. *Sheqel ha-Qodesh.* Edited by A. W. Greenup. London, 1911. Reprint, Jerusalem: n.p., 1969.

______. *Sheqel ha-Qodesh.* Edited by Charles Mopsik. Los Angeles: Cherub Press, 1996. Cited in the Commentary according to both this edition and, in parentheses, Greenup's edition.

______. "Shushan Edut." Edited by Gershom Scholem. *Kovez al Yad,* n.s., 8 (1976): 325–70.

______. "Sod Eser Sefirot Belimah." Edited by Gershom Scholem. *Kovez al Yad,* n.s., 8 (1976): 371–84.

______. "Sod Ḥag ha-Shavu'ot." In *Qovets Sifrei Qabbalah.* Jerusalem, Schocken Library, MS Schocken 14.

______. "Sod Yetsi'at Mitsrayim." Jerusalem, Schocken Library, MS Schocken 14.

Naḥmanides, Moses. *Kitvei Ramban.* Edited by Chaim D. Chavel. 2 vols. Jerusalem: Mossad Harav Kook, 1964.

______. *Writings of the Ramban.* Translated and Annotated by Chaim D. Chavel. 2 vols. Brooklyn: Shilo Publishing House, 1978. Reprint 2009.

Naphtali ben Ya'akov Elḥanan Bacharach. *Emeq Ha-Melekh.* Amsterdam: Immanuel Benvenisti, 1648.

Nelson, W. David., trans. and ed. *Mekhilta de-Rabbi Shimon bar Yoḥai.* Philadelphia: Jewish Publication Society, 2006.

*Pesiqta Rabbati.* Edited by Meir Freedman (Ish-Shalom). Vienna: Yosef Kaizer, 1880.

"Pirqei Rabbi Eli'ezer." Edited by Michael Higger. *Ḥoreb* 8 (1944): 82–119; 9 (1946): 94–166; 10 (1948): 185–294.

*Pirqei Rabbi Eli'ezer.* Commentary by David Luria; edited by Samuel ben Eli'ezer Luria. Warsaw: Bomberg, 1852. Reprint, New York: Om, 1946.

Plotinus. *The Enneads.* Translated by Stephen Mackenna. London: Penguin Books, 1991.

Pope, Marvin H. *Song of Songs: A New Translation with Introduction and Commentary.* Anchor Bible, vol. 7c. Garden City, N.Y.: Doubleday, 1977.

Recanati, Menaḥem. *Peirush al ha-Torah (Levushei Or Yeqarot).* Lemberg: Karl Budweiser, 1880–81. Reprint, Jerusalem: Mordechai Etyah, 1961.

Saadia Gaon. *Sefer Emunot ve-De'ot.* [*The Book of Beliefs and Opinions.*] Translated by Samuel Rosenblatt. New Haven: Yale University Press, 1948.

Sarna, Nahum M. *The JPS Torah Commentary: Exodus.* Philadelphia: Jewish Publication Society, 1991.

———. *The JPS Torah Commentary: Genesis.* Philadelphia: Jewish Publication Society, 1989.

Schäfer, Peter, ed. *Synopse zur Hekhalot-Literatur.* Tübingen: J. C. B. Mohr, 1981.

Scholem, Gerhard, trans. and ed. *Das Buch Bahir.* Leipzig: W. Drugulin, 1923. Reprint, Darmstadt: Wissenschaftliche Buchgesellschaft, 1970.

*Sefer ha-Bahir.* Edited by Daniel Abrams. Los Angeles: Cherub Press, 1994. Cited in the Commentary according to both this edition and, in parentheses, Margaliot's edition.

*Sefer ha-Bahir.* Edited by Reuven Margaliot. Jerusalem: Mossad Harav Kook, 1951. Reprint, 1978.

*Sefer Razi'el ha-Mal'akh.* Amsterdam: Moses M. Coutinho, 1701.

*Sefer ha-Yashar.* Venice: Pietro, Aluise, and Lorenzo Bragad, 1625.

*Sefer Yetsirah.* Jerusalem: Lewin-Epstein, 1965.

*Sha'arei Teshuvah (Teshuvot ha-Ge'onim).* Edited by Wolf Leiter. Pittsburgh: Maimonides Institute, 1946. Reprint, Jerusalem: H. Vagshel, n.d.



Simeon ben Tsemaḥ Duran. *Magen Avot.* Jerusalem: Mekhon Haketav, 2003.

Simḥah ben Samuel of Vitry. *Maḥazor Vitri.* Edited by Shim'on Hurwitz. Nüremberg: J. Bulka, 1923.

Steele, Robert, ed. *Opera hactenus inedita Rogeri Baconi,* Fasc. 5, *Secretum Secretorum.* Oxford: Oxford University Press, 1920.

Tigay, Jeffrey H. *The JPS Torah Commentary: Deuteronomy.* Philadelphia: Jewish Publication Society, 1996.

Wertheimer, Shlomo Aharon, ed. *Battei Midrashot.* 2d ed., revised by Abraham J. Wertheimer. 2 vols. Jerusalem: Ketav Vasepher, 1980.

Yassif, Eli. *Sippurei Ben Sira bi-Ymei ha-Beinayim.* Jerusalem: Magnes Press, 1984.

## 7. Other Secondary Sources

Abrams, Daniel. "The Book of Illumination of R. Jacob ben Jacob HaKohen: A Synoptic Edition From Various Manuscripts." Ph.D diss., New York University, 1993.

———. "The Invention of the Zohar as a Book: On the Assumptions and Expectations of the Kabbalists and Modern Scholars." *Kabbalah* 19 (2009): 7–142.

———. *Kabbalistic Manuscripts and Textual Theory: Methodologies of Textual Scholarship and Editorial Practice in the Study of Jewish Mysticism.* Jerusalem: Magnes Press; Los Angeles: Cherub Press, 2010.

———. *Sexual Symbolism and Merkavah Speculation in Medieval Germany: A Study of the Sod ha-Egoz Texts.* Tübingen: Mohr Siebeck, 1997.

———. "Special Angelic Figures: The Career of the Beasts of the Throne-World in Hekhalot Literature, German Pietism and Early Kabbalistic Literature." *Revue des Etudes Juives* 155, 3–4 (1996): 363–86.

Aptowitzer, Avigdor (Victor). *Das Schriftwort in der rabbinischen Literatur.* 4 vols. Vienna, 1906–15. Reprint in 1 vol., New York: Ktav, 1970.

Assis, Yom Tov. "Sexual Behaviour in Mediaeval Hispano-Jewish Society." In *Jewish History: Essays in Honour of Chimen Abramsky*, edited by Ada Rapoport-Albert and Steven J. Zipperstein, 25–60. London: Peter Halban, 1988.

Asulin, Shifra. "Midrash ha-Ne'lam li-Vreshit." In *Ve-Zot le-Yehudah: Qovetz Ma'amarim ha-Muqdash le-Ḥaverenu Prof. Yehuda Liebes le-Regel Yom Hulladto ha-Shishim ve-Ḥamishah*, edited by Maren R. Niehoff, Ronit Meroz, Jonathan Garb, 222–53. Jerusalem: Mossad Bialik, 2012.

______. "Ha-Pegam ve-Tiqquno: Niddah, Levanah, u-Shekhinah." *Kabbalah* 22 (2010): 193–251.

Altman, Alexander. *Studies in Religious Philosophy and Mysticism*. Ithaca: Cornell University Press, 1969.

Baer, Yitzḥak. *A History of the Jews in Christian Spain*. 2 vols. Translated by Louis Schoffman. Philadelphia: Jewish Publication Society, 1978.

______. *Toledot ha-Yehudim bi-Sfarad ha-Notsrit*. 2 vols. Tel Aviv: Am Oved, 1945.

Belkin, Samuel. "Ha-Midrash ha-Ne'lam u-Mqorotav ba-Midrashim ha-Aleksandroniyyim ha-Qedumim." *Sura* 3 (1957–58): 25–92.

Bronsnick, Naḥum M. "Le-Hora'ato shel ha-Shoresh 'Bsm.'" *Sinai* 63 (1968): 81–85.

Chavel, Chaim D. "Sefer ha-Zohar ke-Maqor Ḥashuv le-Feirush ha-Ramban al ha-Torah." *Sinai* 43 (1958): 337–64.



Chwolson, Daniel. *Die Ssabier und der Ssabismus*. 2 vols. St. Petersburg: Imperial Academy, 1856.

Cohen, Mark R. *Under Crescent and Cross: The Jews in the Middle Ages*. Princeton: Princeton University Press, 1994.

Dan, Joseph. *The Ancient Jewish Mysticism*. Tel Aviv: MOD Books, 1993.

______. ed. *Sefer ha-Zohar ve-Doro* (*Meḥqerei Yerushalayim be-Maḥashevet Yisra'el* 8 [1989]). Jerusalem: Hebrew University, 1989.

______. *Torat ha-Sod shel Ḥasidut Ashkenaz*. Jerusalem: Mossad Bialik, 1968.

Dan, Joseph, Esther Liebes, and Shmuel Reem, eds. *The Library of Gershom Scholem on Jewish Mysticism: Catalogue*. 2 vols., especially 1:174–232. Jerusalem: Jewish National and University Library, 1999.

Davidson, Herbert A. *Alfarabi, Avicenna, and Averroes, on Intellect: Their Cosmologies, Theories of the Active Intellect and Theories of Human Intellect*. Oxford: Oxford University Press, 1992.

Eisler, Robert. *Weltenmantel und Himmelszelt*. Munich: C.H. Beck'sche, 1910.

Elbogen, Ismar. *Jewish Liturgy: A Comprehensive History*. Translated by Raymond P. Scheindlin. Philadelphia: Jewish Publication Society, 1993.

Eliade, Mircea, ed. *The Encyclopedia of Religion*. 16 vols. New York: Macmillan, 1987.

Elior, Rachel. "Torat ha-Gilgul be-Sefer Galya Raza." *Meḥqerei Yerushalayim be-Maḥashevet Yisra'el* 3 (1984): 207–39.

Emden, Jacob. *Mitpaḥat Sefarim*. Edited by Reuben Rappaport. Lemberg: Michal Wolf, 1870. Reprint: Jerusalem: Sifriyat Mekorot, 1970.

*Encyclopaedia Judaica*. 2d rev. ed. 22 volumes. Edited by Fred Skolnik and Michael Berenbaum. Detroit, Mich.: Thomson Gale, 2007.

Farber, Asi. "Tefisat ha-Merkavah be Torat ha-Sod be-Me'ah ha-Shelosh-Esreh: 'Sod ha-Egoz' ve-Toledotav." 2 vols. Ph.D diss., Hebrew University, 1986.

Finkel, Joshua. "The Alexandrian Tradition and the Midrash ha-Ne'elam." In *The Leo Jung Jubilee Volume*, edited by Menahem Kasher, 77–103. New York: Jewish Center, 1962.

Fishbane, Eitan. "Tears of Disclosure: The Role of Weeping in Zoharic Narrative." *Journal of Jewish Thought and Philosophy* 11 (2002): 25–47.

Fishbane, Michael. *Biblical Myth and Rabbinic Mythmaking*. New York: Oxford University Press, 2003.

Freedman, Daphne. "Astral and Other Neologisms in the Zohar." *Kabbalah* 25 (2011): 131–58.

Ginsburg, Elliot K. *The Sabbath in the Classical Kabbalah*. Albany: State University of New York Press, 1989.

Ginsburger, Moses, ed. *Das Fragmententhargum (Thargum jeruschalmi zum Pentateuch)*. Berlin: S. Calvary and Co., 1899.

Ginzberg, Louis. *Legends of the Jews*. 7 vols. Translated by Henrietta Szold and Paul Radin. Philadelphia: Jewish Publication Society, 1909–38.

Gottlieb, Efraim. *Meḥqarim be-Sifrut ha-Qabbalah*. Edited by Joseph Hacker. Tel Aviv: Tel Aviv University, 1976.

Grossman, Avraham. *Pious and Rebellious: Jewish Women in Medieval Europe*. Translated by Jonathan Chipman. Waltham, Mass.: Brandeis University Press, 2004.

Gruenwald, Ithamar. *Apocalyptic and Merkavah Mysticism*. Leiden: E. J. Brill, 1980.

Guttmann, Julius. *Philosophies of Judaism*. Translated by David W. Silverman. New York: Schocken, 1973.

Halkin, Abraham and David Hartman. *Epistles of Maimonides: Crisis and Leadership*. Philadelphia: The Jewish Publication Society, 1985.

Hallamish, Moshe. *Ha-Qabbalah bi-Tfillah ba-Halakhah u-ve-Minhag*. Ramat Gan: Bar-Ilan University, 2000.



Halperin, David J. *The Faces of the Chariot: Early Jewish Responses to Ezekiel's Vision*. Tübingen: Mohr Siebeck, 1988.

Hecker, Joel. "The Face of Shame: The Sight and Site of Rebuke (*Zohar* 3:45b–47a)." *Kabbalah* 23 (2010): 29–67.

———. *Mystical Bodies, Mystical Meals: Eating and Embodiment in Medieval Kabbalah*. Detroit: Wayne State University Press, 2005.

Hellner-Eshed, Melila. *A River Flows from Eden: The Language of Mystical Experience in the Zohar*. Translated by Nathan Wolski. Stanford, Calif.: Stanford University Press, 2009.

———. *Ve-Nahar Yotse me-Eden: Al Sefat ha-Ḥavayah ha-Mistit ba-Zohar*. Tel Aviv: Am Oved, 2005.

Huss, Boaz. "Hofa'ato shel Sefer ha-Zohar." *Tarbiz* 70 (2001): 507–42.

———. *Ke-Zohar ha-Raqi'a: Peraqim be-Hitqabbelut ha-Zohar uv-Havnayat Erko ha-Simli*. Jerusalem: Ben-Zvi Institute, 2007.

Hutter, Manfred. "Lilith." In *Dictionary of Deities and Demons in the Bible*, edited by Karel van der Toorn, Bob Becking, and Pieter W. van der Horst, 520–21. 2nd rev. ed. Leiden: Brill, 1999.

Idel, Moshe. "Al ha-Peirushim shel R. Neḥemiah ben Shelomo ha-Navi le-Shem Mem-bet Otiyyot ve-Sefer ha-Ḥokhmah ha-Meyuḥas le-R. El'azar mi-Vorms." *Kabbalah* 14 (2006): 157–261.

———. *Ascensions on High in Jewish Mysticism: Pillars, Lines, Ladders*. Budapest: Central European University Press, 2005.

———. *Kabbalah: New Perspectives*. New Haven: Yale University Press, 1988.

———. *Kabbalah and Eros*. New Haven: Yale University Press, 2005.

———. "'Livyatan u-Vat Zugo': Mi-Mitos Talmudi le-Mitosim Qabbaliyyim." In *Ha-Mitos ba-Yahadut: Historiyah, Hagut, Sifrut*, edited by Moshe Idel and Ithamar Gruenwald, 145–86. Jerusalem: Merkaz Zalman Shazar, 2004.

———. *The Mystical Experience in Abraham Abulafia*. Translated by Jonathan Chipman. Albany: State University of New York Press, 1988.

______. "Olam ha-Mal'akhim bi-Dmut Adam." *Meḥqerei Yerushalayim be-Maḥashevet Yisra'el* 3 (1984): 1–66.

______. "Qeta lo Yadu'a mi-Midrash ha-Ne'lam." In *Sefer ha-Zohar ve-Doro* (*Meḥqerei Yerushalayim be-Maḥashevet Yisra'el* 8 [1989]), edited by Joseph Dan, 73–87.

Jacquart, Danielle, and Claude Thomasset. *Sexuality and Medicine in the Middle Ages.* Translated by Mathew Adamson. Princeton: Princeton University Press, 1988.

Jastrow, Marcus. *A Dictionary of the Targumim, the Talmud Babli and Yerushalmi, and the Midrashic Literature.* 2 vols. New York: Pardes Publishing House, 1943.

Jaynes, Julian. *The Origin of Consciousness in the Breakdown of the Bicameral Mind.* Boston: Houghton Mifflin, 1976.

Jung, Carl G. *Collected Works.* 21 vols. Edited by Gerhard Adler, Michael Fordham and Herbert Read. Translated by R.F.C. Hull. Princeton: Princeton University Press, 1970–79.

Kaddari, Menaḥem Z. *Diqduq ha-Lashon ha-Aramit shel ha-Zohar.* Jerusalem: Kiryath Sepher, 1971.

Karr, Don. "Notes on the *Zohar* in English." Online: www.digital-brilliance.com/kab/karr.

Katz, Jacob. *Halakhah ve-Qabbalah.* Jerusalem: Magnes Press, 1984.

Kiener, Ronald C. "The Image of Islam in the *Zohar.*" In *Sefer ha-Zohar ve-Doro* (*Meḥqerei Yerushalayim be-Maḥashevet Yisra'el* 8 [1989]), edited by Joseph Dan, 43–65 (English section). Jerusalem: Hebrew University, 1989.



Lauterbach, Jacob Z. "The Origin and Development of Two Sabbath Ceremonies." *Hebrew Union College Annual* 15 (1940): 367–424.

Lieberman, Saul. *Tosefta ki-Fshutah: A Comprehensive Commentary on the Tosefta.* 10 vols. New York: Jewish Theological Seminary of America, 1955–88.

Liebes, Yehuda. *Alilot Elohim: Ha-Mitos ha-Yehudi; Massot u-Meḥqarim.* Jerusalem: Carmel, 2008.

______. "Hebrew and Aramaic as Languages of the Zohar." Translated by Daphne Freedman and Ada Rapaport-Albert. *Aramaic Studies* 4 (2006): 35–52.

______. "Mar'ish ha-Arets: Yeḥiduto shel Rashbi." In *Yahadut: Sugyot, Qeta'im, Panim, Zehuyyot. Sefer Rivqah,* edited by Haviva Pedaya and Ephraim Meir, 337–57. Beer-Sheva: Ben-Gurion University of the Negev Press, 2007.

______. "Ha-Mashiaḥ shel ha-Zohar: Li-Dmuto ha-Meshiḥit shel R. Shim'on bar Yoḥai." In *Ha-Ra'yon ha-Meshiḥi be-Yisra'el,* edited by Shemuel Re'em, 87–236. Jerusalem: Israel Academy of Sciences and Humanities, 1982.

______. *Pulḥan ha-Shaḥar: Yaḥas ha-Zohar la-Avodah Zarah.* Jerusalem: Carmel, 2011.

______. *Studies in Jewish Myth and Jewish Messianism.* Translated by Batya Stein. Albany, N.Y.: State University of New York Press, 1993.

______. *Studies in the Zohar.* Translated by Arnold Schwartz, Stephanie Nakache, and Penina Peli. Albany: State University of New York Press, 1993.

______. "'Terein Urzilin de-Ayyalta': Derashato ha-Sodit shel ha-Ari lifnei Mitato." In *Qabbalat ha-Ari* (*Meḥqerei Yerushalayim be-Maḥashevet Yisra'el* 10 [1992]), edited by Rachel Elior and Yehuda Liebes, 113–69. Jerusalem: Hebrew University, 1992.

______. "Zohar ve-Eros." *Alpayim* 9 (1994): 67–119.

Lobel, Diana. *A Jewish-Sufi Dialogue: Philosophy and Mysticism in Baḥya Ibn Paquda's Duties of the Heart.* Philadelphia: University of Philadelphia Press, 2007.

Maori, Yeshayahu. "Rabbinic Midrash as Evidence for Textual Variants in the Hebrew Bible: History and Practice." In *Modern Scholarship in the Study of Torah: Contributions and Limitations,* edited by Shalom Carmy, 101–29. Northvale, N.J.: Jason Aaronson, 1996.

Margaliot, Reuven. *Mal'akhei Elyon*. Jerusalem: Mossad Harav Kook, 1964.
———. *Sha'arei Zohar*. Jerusalem: Mossad Harav Kook, 1978.
Marx, Alexander. "An Aramaic Fragment of the Wisdom of Solomon." *Journal of Biblical Literature* 40 (1921): 57–69.
Matt, Daniel C. "Matnita di-Lan: Tekhniqah shel Ḥiddush be-Sefer ha-Zohar." In *Sefer ha-Zohar ve-Doro (Meḥqerei Yerushalayim be-Maḥashevet Yisra'el* 8 [1989]), edited by Joseph Dan, 123–45. Jerusalem: Hebrew University, 1989.
———. "'New-Ancient Words': The Aura of Secrecy in the *Zohar.*" In *Gershom Scholem's "Major Trends in Jewish Mysticism": 50 Years After*, edited by Peter Schäfer and Joseph Dan, 181–207. Tübingen: J.C.B. Mohr, 1994.
Meroz, Ronit. "'Va-Ani Lo Hayiti Sham?': Quvlanotav shel Rashbi al pi Sippur Zohari Lo Yadu'a." *Tarbiẓ* 71 (2002): 163–93.
———. "Der Aufbau des Buches Sohar." *PaRDeS: Zeitschrift der Vereinigung für Jüdische Studien* 11 (2005): 16–36. Online Hebrew version: www.tau.ac.il/humanities/kabbalah/files/MerozAufbauHebrew.pdf.
———. "Ḥanikhato shel R. Ḥiyya: Shetei Girsa'ot shel Sippur min ha-Zohar." In *Ma'aseh Sippur: Meḥqarim be-Sifrut ha-Yahadut*, edited by Avidov Lipsker-Albeck and Rella Kushelevsky, vol. 3, 115–63. Ramat Gan: Bar Ilan University Press, 2013.
———, ed. *Ḥiddushei Zohar: Meḥqarim Ḥadashim be-Sifrut ha-Zohar (Te'udah* 21–22 [2007]). Tel Aviv: Tel Aviv Univeristy, 2007.
———. "Merkevet Yeḥezqel: Peirush Zohari Bilti Yadu'a." *Te'udah* 16–17 (2001): 567–616.
———. "The Middle-Eastern Origins of Kabbalah." *The Journal for the Study of Sephardic and Mizrahi Jewry* 1:1 (2007): 39–56. Online: http://sephardic.fiu.edu/journal.
———. "The Path of Silence: An Unknown Story from a Zohar Manuscript." *European Journal of Jewish Studies* 1 (2008): 319–42.
———. "Reqimato shel Mitos: Diyyun bi-Shnei Sippurim ba-Zohar." In *Study and Knowledge in Jewish Thought*, edited by Howard Kreisel, 167–205. Beer-Sheva: Ben-Gurion University of the Negev Press, 2006.
———. "The Story in the Zohar About the Grieving Dead." In *Jewish Lifeworlds and Jewish Thought: Festschrift presented to Karl E. Grozinger on the Occasion of His 70th Birthday*, edited by Nathanael Reimer, 43–54. Wiesbaden: Harrassowitz Verlag, 2012.
———. "R. Yosef Angelet u-Khtavav ha-'Zohariyyim.'" In Meroz, *Ḥiddushei Zohar*, 303–404.
———. "Zoharic Narratives and Their Adaptations." *Hispania Judaica Bulletin* 3 (2000): 3–63.
Mowinckel, Sigmund. *The Psalms in Israel's Worship*. Translated by D.R. Ap-Thomas. 2 vols. Michigan: W.B. Eerdmans Publishing Company, 2004.
Nathan ben Yeḥiel of Rome. *Arukh ha-Shalem*. 9 vols. Edited by Alexander Kohut, with *Tosefot he-Arukh ha-Shalem*, by Samuel Krauss. Vienna, 1878–92, 1937. Reprint, New York: Pardes, 1955.
———. *Sefer he-Arukh*. Edited by Shemuel Schlesinger. Tel Aviv: Yetsu Sifrei Kodesh, n.d.
Neuhausen, Simon A. *Sifriyyah shel Ma'lah*. Berehovo: Samuel Klein, 1937.
Neumann, Erich. *The Origins and History of Consciousness*. Princeton: Princeton University Press, 1970.
Niehoff, Maren R., Ronit Meroz, and Jonathan Garb, eds. *Ve-Zot Li-Yhudah: Qovets Ma'amarim ha-Muqdash la-Ḥaverenu Prof. Yehuda Liebes le-Regel Yom Hulladto ha-Shishim va-Ḥamishah*. Jerusalem: Mossad Bialik, 2012.

Oron, Michal. "Midrash ha-Ne'lam: Muqdam u-Me'uḥar." *Kabbalah* 22 (2010): 109–48.

_____. "Qavvim le-Torat ha-Nefesh ve-ha-Gilgul ba-Qabbalah ba-Me'ah ha-Shelosh Esreh uv-Khitvei R. Todros ha-Levi Abulafiyah." In *Meḥqarim be-Hagut Yehudit*, edited by Sara O. Heller Willensky and Moshe Idel, 277–89. Jerusalem: Magnes Press, 1989.

Oron, Michal, and Amos Goldreich, eds. *Massu'ot: Meḥqarim be-Sifrut ha-Qabbalah... Muqdashim le-Zikhro shel Prof. Efraim Gottlieb Z"l.* Jerusalem: Mossad Bialik, 1994.

Patai, Raphael. *The Hebrew Goddess.* 3d ed. Detroit: Wayne State University Press, 1990.

Pedaya, Haviva. *Ha-Ramban—Hit'allut: Zeman Maḥazori ve-Teqst Qadosh.* Tel Aviv: Am Oved, 2003.

Rosenfeld, Samuel. *Sefer Mishpaḥat Soferim.* Vilna: Romm, 1883.

Rosenthal, "Al Derekh Tippulam shel Ḥazal be-Ḥillufei Nussaḥ ba-Miqra." In *Sefer Yitsḥaq Aryeh Zeligman: Ma'amarim ba-Miqra u-va-Olam ha-Attiq*, edited by Yair Zakovitch and Alexander Rofé, 395–417. Jerusalem: Elhanan Rubenstein, 1983.

Rubin, Zvia. "Mif'al ha-Zohar: Mattarot ve-Hessegim." In *Asuppat Kiryat Sefer (Musaf le-Kherekh* 68), edited by Yehoshua Rosenberg, 167–74. Jerusalem: Jewish National and University Library, 1998.



_____. *Ha-Muva'ot mi-Sefer ha-Zohar be-Feirush al ha-Torah le-R. Menaḥem Recanati.* Jerusalem: Academon, 1992.

Schäfer, Peter. *The Hidden and Manifest God: Some Major Themes in Early Jewish Mysticism.* Albany: State University of New York Press, 1992.

_____. ed. *Konkordanz zur Hekhalot-Literatur.* 2 vols. Tübingen: J.C.B. Mohr, 1986–88.

_____. *Mirror of His Beauty: Feminine Images of God from the Bible to the Early Kabbalah.* Princeton: Princeton University Press, 2002.

Schäfer, Peter, and Joseph Dan, eds. *Gershom Scholem's "Major Trends in Jewish Mysticism": 50 Years After.* Tübingen: J.C.B. Mohr, 1994.

Scholem, Gershom G. *Devarim be-Go.* Edited by Avraham Shapira. 2nd ed. 2 vols. Tel Aviv: Am Oved, 1976.

_____. "Ha-Im Ḥibber R. Mosheh de León et Sefer ha-Zohar?" *Madda'ei ha-Yahadut* 1 (1926): 16–29.

_____. "Iqvotav shel Gevirol be-Qabbalah." In *Me'assef Soferei Erets Yisra'el*, edited by Aaron Kabak and Eliezer Steinman, 160–78. Tel Aviv: Agudat Hasoferim, 1940.

_____. *Jewish Gnosticism, Merkabah Mysticism, and Talmudic Tradition.* New York: Jewish Theological Seminary of America, 1965.

_____. *Kabbalah.* Jerusalem: Keter, 1974.

_____. *Major Trends in Jewish Mysticism.* 3d ed. New York: Schocken, 1967.

_____. *On the Kabbalah and Its Symbolism.* Translated by Ralph Manheim. New York: Schocken, 1969.

_____. *On the Mystical Shape of the Godhead: Basic Concepts in the Kabbalah.* Translated by Joachim Neugroschel, edited by Jonathan Chipman. New York: Schocken, 1991.

_____. *Origins of the Kabbalah.* Edited by R. J. Zwi Werblowsky, translated by Allan Arkush. Philadelphia: Jewish Publication Society; Princeton: Princeton University Press, 1987.

_____. "Parashah Ḥadashah min ha-Midrash ha-Ne'lam she-ba-Zohar." In *Sefer ha-Yovel li-Khvod Levi Ginzberg*, 425–46. New York: American Academy for Jewish Research, 1945.

———. "Peraqim Mi-Toledot Sifrut ha-Qabbalah (8)," *Kiryat Sefer* 6 (1929–30): 385–419.
———. "Qabbalat Rabbi Yitsḥak ben Shelomoh ben Avi Sahula ve-Sefer ha-Zohar." *Kiryat Sefer* 6 (1929–30): 109–18.
———. *Sabbatai Sevi: The Mystical Messiah, 1626–1676.* Translated by R. J. Zwi Werblowsky. Princeton: Princeton University Press, 1973.
———. *Shedim, Ruḥot u-Nshamot: Meḥqarim be-Demonologyah me'et Gershom Shalom.* Edited by Esther Liebes. Jerusalem: Ben-Zvi Institute, 2004.
———. "She'elot be-Viqqoret ha-Zohar mi-tokh Yedi'otav al Erets Yisra'el." *Zion* (Me'assef) 1 (1926): 40–55.
———. "Ha-Tsitat ha-Rishon min ha-Midrash ha-Ne'lam." *Tarbiz* 3 (1932): 181–83.
Schwartz, Dov. "Ha-Biqqoret al Torat Gilgul ha-Neshamot bi-Ymei ha-Beinayim." *Maḥanayim,* n.s., 6 (1994): 104–13.
Siegel, Rudolph E. *Galen's System of Physiology and Medicine.* Basel: S. Karger, 1968.
Silver, Abba H. *A History of Messianic Speculation in Israel.* New York: Macmillan, 1927.
Sokoloff, Michael. *A Dictionary of Jewish Babylonian Aramaic of the Talmudic and Geonic Periods.* Ramat-Gan: Bar Ilan University Press; Baltimore: Johns Hopkins University Press, 2002.
———. *A Dictionary of Jewish Palestinian Aramaic of the Byzantine Period.* Ramat-Gan: Bar Ilan University Press, 1990.



Speiser, Ephraim A. *Genesis.* Anchor Bible, vol. 1, 3d ed. Garden City, N.Y.: Doubleday, 1981.
Sperling, S. David. "Biblical *rḥm* I and *rḥm* II." *JANES* 19 (1989): 149–59.
Stroumsa, Gedaliahu A. G. *Another Seed: Studies in Gnostic Mythology.* Leiden: E. J. Brill, 1984.
Talmage, Frank. "Apples of Gold: The Inner Meaning of Sacred Texts in Medieval Judaism." In *Jewish Spirituality: From the Bible through the Middle Ages,* edited by Arthur Green, 313–55. New York: Crossroad, 1986.
Ta-Shma, Israel M. *Ha-Nigleh she-ba-Nistar.* 2d ed. Tel Aviv: Hakibbutz Hameuchad, 2001.
Tishby, Isaiah. *Ḥiqrei Qabbalah u-Shluḥoteha: Meḥqarim u-Mqorot.* 3 vols. Jerusalem: Magnes Press, 1982–93.
Trachtenberg, Joshua. *Jewish Magic and Superstition: A Study in Folk Religion.* New York: Atheneum, 1974.
Twersky, Isadore. *Introduction to the Code of Maimonides* (Mishneh Torah). New Haven: Yale University Press, 1980.
Urbach, Ephraim E. *The Sages: Their Concepts and Beliefs.* 2d ed. 2 vols. Translated by Israel Abrahams. Jerusalem: Magnes Press, 1979.
Verman, Mark. *The Books of Contemplation: Medieval Jewish Mystical Sources.* Albany: State University of New York Press, 1992.
Werblowsky, R. J. Zwi. *Joseph Karo: Lawyer and Mystic.* London: Oxford University Press, 1962.
———. "Philo and the Zohar." *Journal of Jewish Studies* 10 (1959): 25–44, 113–35.
Wolfson, Elliot R. *Along the Path: Studies in Kabbalistic Myth, Symbolism, and Hermeneutics.* Albany: State University of New York Press, 1995.
———. "The Anonymous Chapters of the Elderly Master of Secrets: New Evidence for the Early Activity of the Zoharic Circle." *Kabbalah* 19 (2009): 143–278.
———. *Circle in the Square: Studies in the Use of Gender in Kabbalistic Symbolism.* Albany: State University of New York Press, 1995.

———. “Eunuchs Who Keep the Sabbath: Becoming Male and the Ascetic Ideal in Thirteenth-Century Jewish Mysticism.” In *Becoming Male in the Middle Ages,* edited by Jeffrey Jerome Cohen and Bonnie Wheeler, 151–85. New York: Garland Publishing, 1997.

———. “Forms of Visionary Ascent as Ecstatic Experience in Zoharic Literature.” In *Gershom Scholem’s “Major Trends in Jewish Mysticism”: 50 Years After,* edited by Peter Schäfer and Joseph Dan, 209–35. Tübingen: J.C.B. Mohr, 1994.

———. “God, the Demiurge and the Intellect: On the Usage of the Word *Kol* in Abraham Ibn Ezra.” *Revue des Etudes Juives,* 149, 1–3 (1990): 77–111.

———. *Language, Eros, Being: Kabbalistic Hermeneutics and Poetic Imagination.* New York: Fordham University Press, 2005.

———. “Left Contained in the Right: A Study in Zoharic Hermeneutics.” *AJS Review* 11 (1986): 27–52.

———. *Luminal Darkness: Imaginal Gleanings from Zoharic Literature.* Oxford: Oneworld, 2007.

———. *Through a Speculum That Shines: Vision and Imagination in Medieval Jewish Mysticism.* Princeton: Princeton University Press, 1994.

———. “Woman—The Feminine as Other in Theosophic Kabbalah: Some Philosophical Observations on the Divine Androgyne.” In *The Other in Jewish Thought and History: Constructions of Jewish Culture and Identity,* edited by Laurence. J. Silberstein and Robert. L. Cohn, 166–204. New York: New York University Press, 1994.



Wolfson, Harry A. *Philo: Foundations of Religious Philosophy in Judaism, Christianity, and Islam.* 2 vols. Cambridge: Harvard University Press, 1947.

Wolski, Nathan. “Don Quixote and Sancho Panza Were Walking on the Way: El Caballero Andante and the Book of Radiance (Sefer ha-Zohar).” *Shofar: An Interdisciplinary Journal of Jewish Studies* 27, 3 (2008): 1–24.

———. *A Journey into the “Zohar”: An Introduction to “The Book of Radiance.”* Albany: State University of New York Press, 2010.

———. “Metatron and the Mysteries of the Night in Midrash ha-Ne’elam: Jacob ha-Kohen’s Sefer ha-Orah and the Transformation of a Motif in the Early Writings of Moses de León.” *Kabbalah* 23 (2010): 69–94.

———. “Narrative, Time and Exegesis: Mystical Poetics in the Zohar.” *Prooftexts* 28 (2008): 101–28.

———. “The Secret of Yiddish: Zoharic Composition in the Poetry of Aaron Zeitlin.” *Kabbalah* 20 (2009): 147–80.

Wolski, Nathan, and Merav Carmeli. “Those Who Know Have Wings: Celestial Journeys with the Masters of the Academy.” *Kabbalah* 16 (2007): 83–114.

Yisraeli, Oded. *Parshanut ha-Sod ve-Sod ha-Parshanut: Megammot Midrashiyyot ve-Hermenoitiyyot be-“Sava-de-Mishpatim” she-ba-Zohar.* Los Angeles: Cherub Press, 2005.

Zimmels, Tsvi Y. “Ofot ha-Gedelim ba-Ilan: Bi’ur Halakhah.” In *Minḥat Bikkurim li-Khvod ha-Rav A Schwartz,* 1–9. Vienna: Menorah, 1926.

# *Index of Sources*

This index includes sources that are quoted (rather than merely cited or alluded to) either in the *Zohar* or in the translator's notes. Biblical passages appear mostly in the text of the *Zohar* itself; other listed works appear almost exclusively in the notes.

## BIBLICAL LITERATURE

### *TANAKH* (HEBREW BIBLE)

RABBINIC LITERATURE: MIDRASH

EARLY JEWISH MYSTICAL LITERATURE



MEDIEVAL JEWISH SOURCES

POSTBIBLICAL CHRISTIAN SOURCES



POSTBIBLICAL ISLAMIC SOURCES



OTHER

# בראשית

בריש הורמנותא דמלכא גליף גלופי בטהירו עלאה בוצינא
דקרדינותא נפיק גו סתים דסתימו מרישא דא"ין סו"ף
קוטרא בגולמא נעיץ בעזקא לא חוור ולא אוכם לא סומק ולא ירוק ולאו גוון כלל כד
מדיד משיח' עביד גוונין לאנהר' לגו בגו בוצינ' נפיק חד נביעו דמניה אצטבעו גוונין
לתתא סתים גו סתימין מרזא דא"ין סו"ף בקע ולא בקע אוירא דליה לא אתידע
כלל עד דמגו דחיקו דבקיעותיה נהיר נקודה חדא סתימאה עלאה בתר ההיא נקודה
לא אתידע כלל ובגין כך אקרי ראשית מאמר קדמאה דכלא׃

והמשכילים יזהירו כזהר הרקיע ומצדיקי הרבים ככוכבים לעולם
ועד׃ זהר סתימ' דסתימין בטש אוירא דילי'
דמטי ולא מטי בהאי נקודה וכדין אתפשט האי ראשית ועביד ליה
יקרא להיכליה לתושבחתא׃ תמן זרע זרעא לאולדא לתועלתא דעלמא ורזא דא זרע
קדש מצבתה׃ זהר דזרע זרע' ליקרי' כהאי זרע' דמשי דארגוון טב דאתחפי
לגו ועביד ליה היכלא דאיהו תושבחתא דיליה ותועלתא דכלא׃
בהאי ראשית ברא ההוא סתימאה דלא אתידע להיכלא דא׃ היכלא דא אקרי אלהים
ורזא דא בראשי' ברא אלהי'׃ זהר דמניה כלהו מאמרו' אתבריאו ברזא דאתפשטותא
דנקודה דזהר סתים דא׃ אי בהאי כתיב ברא לית תווהא דכתיב ויברא אלהים
את האדם בצלמו׃ זהר דא בראשית קדמאה דכלא אדיך שמא
קדיש' גליפ' בסטרוי אלהים גליפא בעיטרא אשר
היכלא טמיר וגניז שרותא דרזא דראשי"ת אש"ר רא"ש דנפיק מראשית׃ וכד